2001

Women in World History

A Biographical Encyclopedia

WOMEN IN WORLD HISTORY

A Biographical Encyclopedia

VOLUME
9
Laa-Lyud

Anne Commire, Editor
Deborah Klezmer, Associate Editor

YORKIN PUBLICATIONS

GALE GROUP

Detroit
New York
San Francisco
London
Boston
Woodbridge, CT

Yorkin Publications

Anne Commire, *Editor*
Deborah Klezmer, *Associate Editor*
Barbara Morgan, *Assistant Editor*

Eileen O'Pasek, Gail Schermer, Patricia Coombs, James Fox,
Catherine Cappelli, Karen Rikkers, *Editorial Assistants*
Karen Walker, *Assistant for Genealogical Charts*

Special acknowledgment is due to Peg Yorkin who made this project possible.

Thanks also to Karin and John Haag, Bob Schermer, and to
the Gale Group staff, in particular Dedria Bryfonski, Linda Hubbard, John Schmittroth, Cynthia Baldwin,
Tracey Rowens, Randy Bassett, Christine O'Bryan, Rebecca Parks, and especially Sharon Malinowski.

The Gale Group

Sharon Malinowski, *Senior Editor*
Rebecca Parks, *Editor*
Linda S. Hubbard, *Managing Editor*

Margaret A. Chamberlain, *Permissions Specialist*
Mary K. Grimes, *Image Cataloger*

Mary Beth Trimper, *Production Director*
Evi Seoud, *Assistant Production Manager*

Cynthia Baldwin, *Product Design Manager*
Tracey Rowens, *Cover and Page Designer*
Michael Logusz, *Graphic Artist*

Barbara Yarrow, *Graphic Services Manager*
Randy Bassett, *Image Database Supervisor*
Robert Duncan, *Imaging Specialist*
Christine O'Bryan, *Graphics Desktop Publisher*
Dan Bono, *Technical Support*

Library of Congress Catalog Card Number 99-24692
A CIP record is available from the British Library

ISBN 0-7876-4068-9
Printed in the United States of America.

Library of Congress Cataloging-in-Publication Data

Women in world history : a biographical encyclopedia / Anne Commire, editor, Deborah Klezmer, associate editor.
        p. cm.
    Includes bibliographical references and index.
    ISBN 0-7876-3736-X (set). — ISBN 0-7876-4064-6 (v. 5). —
    ISBN 0-7876-4065-4 (v. 6) — ISBN 0-7876-4066-2 (v. 7) — ISBN 0-7876-4067-0 (v. 8) — ISBN 0-7876-4068-9 (v. 9)
        1. Women—History Encyclopedias. 2. Women—Biography Encyclopedias.
    I. Commire, Anne. II. Klezmer, Deborah.
        HQ1115.W6 1999   99-24692
        920.72'03—DC21

10 9 8 7 6 5 4 3 2 1

L

La Argentina (c. 1886–1936).
See Mercé, Antonia.

La Balteira (fl. 13th c.).
See Perez, Maria.

Labé, Louise (c. 1523–1566)

French Renaissance poet (considered scandalous by some of her contemporaries), who is remembered for her sonnets celebrating the pain and delight of love. Name variations: Louise Labe; Loise or Louize Labé; Charlin, also seen as Charlieu, de Charlieu, Charliu, Charly, Charlie, Cheylieu, Charrieu; Labé also seen as Labbé, L'Abbé, Labe, Labbyt; La Belle Cordière or La Belle Cordiere (The Beautiful Rope-maker); La Dame au Luth (The Lady with the Lute). Pronunciation: LAH-bay. Born Louise Charlin between 1515 and 1526 in Lyons, France; died in the second half of February 1566 in Lyons; one of four children of Pierre de Charlie also seen as Pierre Charlin (ropemaker or, more probably, rope merchant) and second wife Etiennette Roybert also seen as Etiennette, veuve (widow) Deschamps; was taught embroidery, music, languages (Latin, Italian, Spanish), plus riding and fencing; married Ennemond Perrin, before 1545; no children.

Involved as co-conspirator in an attempted murder trial (1552); was permitted to publish her works (1554); began a love affair with Olivier de Magny (1554); wrote letter to Mademoiselle Clémence de Bourges (1555); saw first publication of her works by

Jean de Tournes (1555); cited by Calvin as an example of a bad woman (1561); wrote testament (1565).

Louise
Labé

In the early 16th century, when Louise Labé was born, Lyons was a vibrant, flourishing city which equaled or even surpassed Paris in certain areas. During the wars with Italy, Lyons was more prosperous than any other French town and was often home to the court. There were two major industries at the heart of the city's boom— silk and printing. Of its 60,000 inhabitants, 6,000 made silk, and the trade itself sponsored four annual two-week fairs which brought in visitors from all over the Continent. Lyons' printers were considered among the best in Europe, and the publishers themselves were often authors. Lyons was also a great banking center. This combination of economic and social prosperity, accompanied by an exchange of ideas as well as money, led to an intellectual excitement which made the municipality a center of learning and literary production. Lyons' affluence attracted a number of foreigners as well. The city became home to

Germans, Dutch, Spaniards, and Italians—especially Florentines. The Florentine population became so strong both economically and politically that Lyons became known as "Florence françoyse" (French Florence).

Italy was the cradle of the Renaissance, but Lyons, through Italian contacts, was also a Renaissance city by the 15th century. After 1515, commercial and cultural connections with Italy multiplied rapidly. The city became the home or at least a frequent stopping place for such French writers as Rabelais, Étienne Dolet, Antoine Héroët, and Jacques Peletier. *Margaret of Angoulême, a politically powerful author, spent a great deal of time in Lyons and cultivated the spread of culture there.

Probably the most liberating aspect of Lyons was the absence of Parliament and the Sorbonne. Those two bodies managed to squash many of the more progressive movements in Paris. Parliament was primarily concerned with maintaining the status quo, and the Sorbonne was quick to see heresy in anything new. Lyons became the center of the progressive part of France—a city of liberty and tolerance relatively untouched by the troubles of the time. This same period saw the growth of the Reform movement which eventually led to the civil wars that started in 1562, but Lyons remained for a long time a city of new ideas and cultural growth. It also had its fair share of literary salons (*See Salonnières*).

The honor which learning will obtain for us will be entirely our own: and it can not be taken from us, not by the slyness of a thief, not by numerous enemies, not by length of time.

—Louise Labé

Held by women in private homes, each literary salon usually had a special day of the week when visitors would gather to hear the latest poetry or other work by one or more of the members. Literary works and movements were discussed, and an author's fortune could be made or broken by the salons. The end result was that women gained a new prominence. Since women held these salons which became the center of a brilliant cultural life, it was they who directed and controlled what happened. They were not only hosts, however. There were numerous women-poets whose names have come down to us but whose works have disappeared.

Lyons was at the head of a feminist movement intent on liberating women both culturally and socially. Louise Labé's letter to her friend

Mme **Clémence de Bourges** was a feminist manifesto, urging women to further their educations.

> Since the time has come, Mademoiselle, that the severe laws of men no longer prevent women from applying themselves to sciences and disciplines, it seems to me that those who have that facility should employ that worthy freedom . . . to study these and to show men the wrong they did us . . . ; and if one of us should reach such a level as to be able to put down her conceptions in writing, she should do it carefully and not disdain fame and make of it an adornment rather than [the] chains, rings, and sumptuous clothes, which we can only really count as ours through the use we make of them. . . . The honor which learning will obtain for us will be entirely our own: and it can not be taken from us, not by the slyness of a thief, not by numerous enemies, not by length of time.

As well as trying to obtain more freedom for women, the literary movement in Lyons encouraged the use of French as a literary medium. Until the 16th century, Latin was considered the only language one could use for serious literature. Even before Joachim Du Bellay wrote his defense of the French language, French was being used in Lyons to write what was considered noble poetry—sonnets and elegies. By writing in French rather than Latin, authors broke with authority. Rebelling against the "tyranny of the past," they were reaffirming their freedom and the autonomy of the individual.

Louise Labé was born Louise Charlin, the daughter of Pierre Charlin and his second wife Etiennette Roybert. Labé's exact date of birth is unknown, but most place it some time between 1515 and 1526. Even her place of birth is uncertain, but it is commonly thought that she was born in a district of Lyons called La Gela, probably located near present-day Morel Square, where her mother had a small property. Her father, a ropemaker (*cordier*), or more likely a rope merchant, was an uneducated man, though comfortably well off. This wealth allowed him to educate his fifth child, Louise, beyond her station in life. It is known that she learned the usual things a French girl of her day was taught, including embroidery, dance, and music. In addition, she had a fine classical education, studying poetry and Latin, Italian, and Spanish. She also excelled in riding, archery, and fencing, fields usually reserved for male members of the family. Beautiful and charming, she soon became known as "La Belle Cordière," the Beautiful Ropemaker.

According to the anonymous author of the work *Louenges,* Labé rejected the advances of an old Roman poet who went off to die in Spain. She then supposedly fell in love with a mysterious warrior who passed through Lyons, about whom nothing is known. Some claim that the object of her infatuation was the future king of France, Henry II, who was on his way to Perpignan in 1542, but there are no records to substantiate this. As well, biographies written after Labé's death report that she dressed as a man and participated in the siege of Perpignan where she was known as "Capitaine Loys," but these stories have also never been confirmed. None of her contemporaries mention her participation in the siege except the author of *Louenges* who describes her prowess there. This allusion may refer not to the actual siege of Perpignan but to a tournament put on by the young people of Lyons to entertain Henry and his troops on their way to the siege. Only one of her contemporaries, Antoine du Verdier, mentions that she was called "Capitaine Loys," probably because of her fencing and riding abilities.

This legend of Labé as a warrior-poet continued for centuries. Sainte-Beuve describes a battalion in the Lyons national guard which, in 1790, was stationed in the street "Belle-Cordière" and which put her name and picture on its flag. She was thus turned into a heroine of liberty, not just for women but for everyone.

Known facts skip from 1542 to April 2, 1551, when Labé bought a house adjacent to that of her husband Ennemond Perrin. Historians speculate that she had married Perrin, a wealthy ropemaker or rope merchant like her father, between 1540 and 1545. Born in 1500, Perrin was much older than Labé, and, after 1551, there are no records bearing his name. "Since she was independently wealthy and felt comfortable in her talents, beauty and manner," writes **Bettina Knapp**, "she felt free and unconstrained in her relationship with her husband. He, in turn, allowed her great independence of spirit and deed, quite unusual for the day." In the 16th century, marriage was often a social arrangement, having nothing to do with love and happiness.

Labé's name appears again in 1552 in the proceedings of a trial held in Geneva. On July 15th, Jean Yvard, who had lived in Lyons, claimed that his wife **Antonia Rosset**, a cousin and neighbor of Labé's, had tried to poison him. Two witnesses gave depositions supporting Yvard. Philibert Serrasin claimed that Yvard's wife was constantly with a certain "Belle Cordière" and that the two of them had plotted the poisoning together. A man named Robinet said that Antonia behaved very badly from a moral standpoint and that it was because of her friendship with her cousin the "Belle Cordière."

The trial was interrupted by Yvard's death the following December 15.

During this, the most well-documented period of Labé's life, she seems to have been at the center of the intellectual and cultural society of Lyons. Her salon was open to poets, scholars, and knights, as well as other women who lived in Lyons or were passing through. Labé sumptuously entertained some of the most famous writers of her time, including Lyonnese poets Maurice Scève, Claude Taillemont, Charles Fontaine, Pontus de Tyard, ❧➤ **Pernette du Guillet**, and **Jeanne Gaillardes**. Writes Knapp:

> The warm hues of tapestried walls, the comfortable furnishings and the ebullient personality of the hostess created congenial gatherings. Tea was usually served along with exquisite confections, after which all present participated actively in conversations about the literary trends of the day. Castigating their contemporaries, the didactic and prosaic rhyme-makers, these Lyonnese poets turned to Petrarch, and to his master, Plato, for inspiration. To the admiration of the assembled, Scève would recite Petrarch's sonnets from memory. Pernette might sing love chants accompanying herself on the lute; Pontus de Tyard would read his latest creations. Books were frequently drawn out of Labé's well-stocked library to substantiate a fine point in Plato's *Symposium*.

On March 13, 1554, Labé was granted a *privilège du Roi*, permission to have her works published, and Jean de Tournes would print them for her the following year.

As Labé herself claims in her second elegy, she had plenty of admirers. She was, after all, a beautiful and educated woman. Her success provoked envy—not only from some men who were resentful of her success as an author but also from some women who were jealous of her beauty, charm, and freedom. In 1554, it is thought that she started a love affair with Olivier de Magny, by then a poet of some repute. While he was traveling to Italy in the entourage of Jean d'Avanson, French envoy to the Holy See, de Magny stopped in Lyons and attended

---

❧➤ **du Guillet, Pernette** (c. 1520–1545)
French poet. Born around 1520 in Lyons; died in 1545.

One of the emancipated women of Lyons, Pernette du Guillet was influenced by poet Maurice Scève, who was in love with her. She died at an early age and left behind several short, noteworthy poems.

Labé's circle. It is thought that they fell in love with each other and with each other's writings; there is a strong similarity between one of his sonnets and one of hers. There are also allusions to Labé and her gardens in Olivier's verses. While de Magny was in Italy, Labé encouraged the attentions of Claude de Rubys, a brilliant young lawyer from Lyons, but looked forward to her "amorous reunion" with de Magny. In 1559, Olivier showed up unexpectedly, learned of Rubys, and furiously penned an odious ode addressed to E. Perrin (Labé's husband); in it, he insults both Perrin and Labé in a scandalous manner. Although it is highly probable that Labé and de Magny's love affair took place, the particulars are lost to history. In the 19th century, Prosper Blanchemain fabricated a story about the lovers, but that is merely a tale of what may have happened and is not based on facts. In any case, the ode shows a definite rupture in any friendship, real or imagined. De Magny was not the only one incensed. The jilted Rubys would later refer to Labé, in his *The History of Lyons*, as Loyse L'Abbé, "one of the most notorious courtesans of her time."

Shortly afterwards, her husband died, and a wealthy widowhood granted her some autonomy. Labé may have found the public gossip and slander too much to deal with, because she withdrew into relative obscurity. In 1561, the Protestant reformer John Calvin spoke of her as a *plebeia meretrix* (vulgar harlot) in his case against the Catholic priest Gabriel de Saconay. Calvin accused Saconay of inviting women who dressed as men, like the "Belle Cordière," to dine with him. Another anonymous piece, the *Chanson Nouvelle*, describes Labé as a woman who bestowed her favors on anybody and everybody.

In addition to Labé's personal concerns, religious tensions were also coming to a head, and the tolerance Lyons' citizens had enjoyed would soon end. The city was occupied in 1562 by the Protestants, whose austere lifestyles inhibited the literary movement. Then, in 1565, the plague struck. Lyons, like Louise, had gone through its golden age. The spirit of the young poets in the early part of the 16th century was lost in the disillusionment evoked by wars and pestilence. A morbid reluctance to rebel or quarrel with the status quo began to grip Lyons as it did the rest of France.

It appears that Labé retired to a semi-private life in her villa at Parcieu, where she probably remained except for intermittent trips to Lyons. She reappears on April 28, 1565, sick in bed at the home of a friend in Lyons, Thomas Fortini, dictating her last will and testament. Whether or not she had the plague, she did recover.

Not much is known about Thomas Fortini and their relationship. He was born in Florence in 1513, and lived in Lyons from 1551 until some time before 1572; he may have left as early as 1569 (his name appears several times in the notary records between 1557 and 1559). It is possible that he took Labé's unpublished poems back to Italy with him, but this is mere speculation since none have come to light. In the last years of her life, he helped Labé organize her affairs and advised her on the acquisition of several properties. After her death, he would be less careful with her wealth. She named him as the executor of her estate—a task which he accomplished quite well—and granted him the usufruct (the right to benefit from her estate) of a large portion of her wealth. The charity which was to inherit the wealth after Fortini's death became concerned about his management of the inheritance, took him to court, and had the usufruct annulled.

Labé's last few years are not well documented. Even the exact date of her death is unknown. It has been placed as late as April 1566, but recent research by Georges Tricou seems to prove that it took place before the second half of February 1566. With her beauty fading, the death of her husband and some friends, and the changing times—civil war was brewing and religious debates were raging—Labé may have withdrawn to spend her last years pleasantly, dividing her time between her place in the country and Lyons. According to her will, she had plenty of money and was on good terms with her brother's family (she left a substantial inheritance to her nephew).

All that has truly come down to us, apart from her works, are a glimpse of her public persona during her glory days, the praises of some, and the slanderous accusations of a religious leader, a few (unrequited) men, and an anonymous complaint. It is the contradictory nature of these documents that make it so difficult to find the true Louise Labé. Some describe her as honest and virtuous while others paint her as an immoral wanton. Neither all good nor all bad, she was probably a free and independent woman who had enough wealth to do as she pleased and was educated enough to realize it. Her poems, which include 24 sonnets, three elegies, and a "Debate Between Folly and Love," show her to be passionate, but even her detractors, who claim she was of easy virtue, report that she entertained only cultured and courteous men.

What is truly important is her distinct and distinguished work, though seemingly influenced by her contemporaries Clément Marot and Maurice Scève. In her verse, we meet an intense being whose love songs have survived over 400 years. "Her full-throated cry," writes Knapp, "is expressed throughout her work on a variety of levels, ranging from the Platonically abstract and idealized perfection to the bitterness of reality. She is constantly confronted and perplexed by the dichotomy between the physical and spiritual world: the interplay of both on her well-being." We meet a feminist who encouraged her fellow women to get an education and to be proud of their accomplishments. Her "lust for life was so powerful," writes Knapp, "her desire for learning so pronounced, that she reflected the very spirit of sixteenth-century France." Louise Labé's work continues to speak to those who love truth and beauty and to those who fight for equality and recognition.

SOURCES:

Berriot, Karine. *Louise Labé: La belle rebelle et le François nouveau.* Paris: Editions du Seuil, 1985.

Bourgeois, Louis. *Louise Labé (1523?–1566) et les poètes lyonnais de son temps.* Lyons: Editions Lyonnaises d'Art et d'Histoire, 1994.

Brée, Germaine. *Women Writers in France.* NJ: Rutgers University Press, 1973.

Cameron, Keith. *Louise Labé: Renaissance Poet and Feminist.* Oxford: Berg Publishers, 1990.

Giudici, Enzo. *Louise Labé—Oeuvres Complètes.* Geneva: Librairie Droz S.A., 1981.

———. *Louise Labé Essai.* Rome: Edizioni dell'Ateneo s.p.a., 1981.

Knapp, Bettina L. "Louise Labé: Renaissance Woman," in *Women and Literature.* Vol. 7, no. 1. Winter 1979.

SUGGESTED READING:

Labé, Louise. *Euvres de Louize Labé lionnoize.* Edited by Jean de Tournes. Lyons: Jean de Tournes, 1555.

———. *Oeuvres de Louise Labé.* Edited by Charles Boy. Paris: A. Lemerre, 1887.

Pedron, François. *Louise Labé: La femme d'amour.* Paris: Fayard, 1984.

Lisa Wolffe,
Assistant Professor, Louisiana Scholars' College,
Northwestern State University, Natchitoches, Louisiana

La Belle Otero (1868–1965).

See Otero, Caroline.

Labille-Guiard, Adelaide

(1749–1803)

French artist who was one of the great pastel portraitists. Name variations: Adélaïde Labille-Guiard. *Born in Paris, France, in 1749; died in 1803; youngest of eight children (three of whom survived infancy) of Claude Edmé Labille (a haberdasher) and Marie Anne (Saint-Martin) Labille; married Louis Nicolas Guiard (a financial clerk), in 1769 (legally separated in 1779); no children.*

Considered by some to be the greatest woman pastel portraitist after *Rosalba Carriera, Adelaide Labille-Guiard overcame numerous obstacles to become one of the most respected artists in Paris during the mid-1780s. A devoted teacher as well as a working artist, she served as both a role model and an advocate for her female students, the most famous of whom was *Gabrielle Capet (1761–1817), one of the most distinguished miniature painters of her day.

Labille-Guiard was born in Paris in 1749, the daughter of a haberdasher and one of eight children, of whom only she and her two older sisters survived to adulthood. Although little is known of her early life, it is believed that she attended a convent where she learned to read and write. Her talent was probably apparent at an early age, as her family saw fit to provide her with formal artistic instruction. Her first teacher was François Elie Vincent (1708–1790), a miniaturist whose shop was located close to her father's haberdashery, and she later studied oil painting with Vincent's older son François Andre (1746–1816). In 1769, Labille-Guiard lost her mother and one of her two surviving sisters and also married Louis Nicolas Guiard, a financial clerk. The union was not happy, and she was legally separated ten years later, although she continued to sign her work "Labille f[emme] Guiard" for the rest of her life.

Labille-Guiard was frequently compared to her younger, more outgoing contemporary, *Elisabeth Vigée-Le Brun (1755–1842), and reportedly the two were intense rivals. Both women were royal artists, although Vigée-Le Brun enjoyed the patronage of *Marie Antoinette while Labille-Guiard was relegated to the title "Peintre des Mesdames." (Neither artist ever obtained the ultimate title "Peintre du Roi.") Both had many of the same patrons and both were accepted into the prestigious Académie Royale on the same day, May 31, 1783. If there was any ill feeling between the women, it was probably fueled by Vigée-Le Brun, who, according to **Germaine Greer**, was the more vain and insecure of the two artists. Vigée-Le Brun also included some cutting remarks about Labille-Guiard in her memoirs *Souvenirs*, although she never mentioned her by name. Labille-Guiard, on the other hand, was so earnest and retiring that any malice on her part seems out of the question. Her portraits, like her

*Adelaide
Labille-Guiard,*
Self-Portrait
with two of her
pupils,
Mesdemoiselles
Capet and
Rosemond,
1785.

personality, are direct and unpretentious, but lack the flair of Vigée-Le Brun's.

At the time of her marriage, Labille-Guiard was already a member of the Académie de Saint-Luc, a less exclusive rival to the Académie Royale, which played a considerable role in fostering female talent until its abolition by royal decree in 1776. From 1769 to 1774, Labille-Guiard was one of a select group of artists to study with Maurice Quenton de la Tour, the great 18th-century master of pastel, and, in

1774, she exhibited a miniature and a pastel at the last exhibition sponsored by the Académie de Saint-Luc before it closed. Her work was not viewed by the public again until 1781, at the Salon de la Correspondence, where she displayed a self-portrait executed in pastels. It is said that when she entered the room where the picture was hung the spectators burst into applause. Greer describes the work as moving beyond the exterior image to reveal the artist's inner character. "Despite the facility of the medium and the characteristic lightness of the effects," writes Greer, "she had rendered even more faithfully than the glimmer of silk and velvet and the froth of lace the impression of an earnest, recollected personality, whose will and courage are overlaid by patience and steadfastness. The depth of the impression made by her steady dark eyes is still remarkable." Labille-Guiard also exhibited several pastels the following year, including a portrait of the sculptor Augustin Pajou at work, which served as yet another example of her ability to capture the inner character of her subject. "Energy flows through the sculptor's strong arm and sensitive fingers," writes Greer in her description of the work, "while the face he turns to the beholder is both masculine and distinguished, kindly and intent."

Labille-Guiard was admitted to the Académie Royale on the strength of her work alone, refusing the advocacy of her friend the Ministre des Arts. She was determined that her fame would be won without assistance and without anyone demanding some part in it. Shortly after her admittance, the Académie Royale voted to limit the number of women members to four, a quota that Labille-Guiard found ludicrous. According to **Ann Sutherland Harris** and **Linda Nochlin**, the artist "circumvented the quota symbolically in her *Self-Portrait* of 1785 (New York, Metropolitan Museum) by including portraits of two of her students, Gabrielle Capet and Mlle **Carreaux de Rosemond**, who thus appeared on the walls of the Salon, a point not lost on the spectators."

A supporter of the French Revolution, Labille-Guiard remained in Paris during that volatile time, although her commissions were limited. In 1793, she became a political victim herself when she was forced to destroy her huge, partly finished painting *The Reception of a Knight of St. Lazare by Monsieur, Grand Master of the Order,* because of its glorification of the monarchy. She had worked on the canvas for two-and-a-half years with hopes that it would secure for her the position of history painter in the Académie. The loss of the work was a personal tragedy from which Labille-Guiard did not recover. One of her last surviving works is an oil painting of *Madame de Genlis, a noted musician, writer, and educator.

One of Labille-Guiard's last victories was her access to an apartment in the Louvre, which she obtained in 1795. Her petitions for space there had previously been denied on the grounds that the presence of her young female pupils would be a distraction to the male artists and students in residence. From 1795 to 1799, the artist's output decreased, and by 1800, with her health in decline, she had all but stopped exhibiting. Adelaide Labille-Guiard died in 1803.

SOURCES:

Greer, Germaine. *The Obstacle Race.* NY: Farrar, Straus and Giroux, 1979.

Harris, Ann Sutherland, and Linda Nochlin. *Women Artists, 1550–1950.* NY: Knopf, 1976.

Barbara Morgan,
Melrose, Massachusetts

Labotsibeni Gwamile laMdluli

(c. 1858–1925)

Ruler in Swaziland, as queen-mother and regent, who transcended the usual powers allowed women in her society, grasped the benefits of Western influence, and helped lay the foundations for her country as a nation state. Name variations: laMvelasi; Mgwamie. Born Labotsibeni laMdluli around 1858, at Luhlekweni homestead in the Hhohho region in northern Swaziland; died on December 5, 1925, at Embekelweni, then the Swazi national capital; daughter of Matsanjana Mdluli and a mother of the Mabuza clan; became chief wife of Prince Mbandzeni in 1875; children: sons Bhunu, Malunge and Lomvazi, and a daughter, Tongotongo.

Death of Mbandzeni (1889); brought to power as queen-mother upon appointment of son Bhunu as royal heir (1890); became regent to her grandson Mona (1899); rallied the Swazi people against land incursions by the British (1906); relinquished rule with Mona's coronation as Sobhuza II (1921).

In her lifetime, Labotsibeni laMdluli was given her middle name of Gwamile, meaning "indomitable one," by her Swazi subjects, a tribute also acknowledged by British colonials, members of the administration then occupying her country. Granted for her ability to protect Swazi sovereignty and culture from colonial encroachment, the recognition was a rare case of the oppressor admitting its admiration for the leader of the oppressed.

During festivities marking Swaziland's contribution to the International Year of Women in 1975, Swazi women recalled the stature of Labotsibeni by referring to her as "Mgwamie," an abbreviated form of her name which both commemorates her role in consolidating Swazi nationhood during turbulent times and personalizes the affection felt for her as one of the greatest queen-mothers or regents in their country's history. In an informal conversation in March 1993, almost 100 years after the era of Labotsibeni's greatest contributions to her nation began, a Swazi princess remarked that the opportunities for economic and political stability in Swaziland during the 1990s lie in creating a modern queen-mother of the same moral stature and political shrewdness.

Swaziland is a landlocked country lying west of the Indian Ocean, encircled by modern South Africa except for a small portion that borders Mozambique. Labotsibeni Gwamile laMdluli was born there around 1858, during the reign of Mswati II who ruled from 1844 to 1865 and is considered the father of the modern Swazi state, from which the country's name is derived.

As a member of the Mdluli clan, Labotsibeni came from a distinguished lineage. Referred to as *emakhandzambili* (those "found ahead"), the Mdluli predated two subsequent waves of Swazi settlement before the arrival of white colonials, and over the last 300 years the clan's two branches have played important roles in the evolution of modern Swaziland. Labotsibeni traced her origins from the northern Mdluli clan, distinguished by its expertise in military intelligence. Its members were often military commanders and regional governors in the pre-colonial era. At the time of Labotsibeni's birth, her father Matsanjana Mdluli was part of a Swazi regiment fighting a Pedi chief named Tsibeni near the present-day town of Barberton, in South Africa. Her name was derived from this conflict, which was part of the ongoing effort by Mswati II to consolidate his reign and the boundaries of his state.

Little is known of Labotsibeni's mother, except that she was of the Mabuza clan. In 1870, as Labotsibeni was entering her teens, the death of her father brought with it the seeds of her rise to power, after her father's brother, Mvelasi Mdluli (*babe mncane*, or "young father"), became her guardian. Brought to the national court at Ludzidzini, where her uncle had a regimental residence, she thus acquired the further name of laMvelasi. Despite a pronounced subordination of women, Swazi society traditionally identifies women by their own family names rather than the family names of the persons they marry, and also through the first names of their fathers. Identification as laMvelasi was thus confirmation of Labotsibeni's adoptive pedigree.

Growing up in the Swazi palace, Labotsibeni acquired "knowledge of court etiquette, insight into the politics of the period and self-assurance," writes historian **Hilda Kuper**. If ancestry destined her for fame, personality was to make her a distinguished ruler. At court, she was an attendant to **Tsandzile**, mother of Mswati II, who would also be known for her immense contribution to the creation of the Swazi nation. Labotsibeni learned much from her. Assertive and brave, the young woman had a shrewd understanding of her social position without being arrogant. According to Kuper, when an *umntfwanenkosi* (prince), a grandson of Tsandzile, once made an amorous approach, Labotsibeni rebuffed him with, "I cannot be courted by a person from a common village." A few years later, however, Labotsibeni judged the same man suitable, after he had become Mbandzeni, the king. In 1875, Labotsibeni became Mbandzeni's chief wife, and afterward gave birth to their three sons—Bhunu, Malunge, and Lomvazi—as well as their daughter **Tongotongo**.

According to the laws of Swazi succession, a king should not be followed by a son who has blood siblings. Labotsibeni's children would thus not have ruled, except for her keen perceptions, early exposure to royal politics, and a capacity to manipulate certain foes into becoming her greatest admirers; otherwise, she would have been allotted the obscurity that was the destiny of most royal wives. Skillfully wielding another Swazi tradition, providing that a king is king by the blood of his father through his mother, she made it a mechanism for her own ends.

On October 7, 1889, Mbandzeni died, prematurely and unexpectedly. Almost a year later, on September 3, 1890, Labotsibeni's oldest son, Bhunu, was designated the future king at the age of 15, and she was proclaimed queen-mother, or *indhlovukati* ("she-elephant"). Although Swazi society is patrilineal, its rule is actually a dual monarchy, under which the incumbent king reigns jointly with his mother. The terms of rule even recognize two national centers, one for the king and another for the queen-mother. (As queen-mother and then regent, Labotsibeni's center was at Embekelweni; since 1903, the Swazi state has had a third capital, which is the seat of the modern cabinet and residence of the prime minister.) In the event of the death of the queen-mother, her role becomes ritual, filled either by one of her sisters or by a senior wife of the king.

Since Swazi rulers ascend to the throne while still quite young, the power and influence of the queen-mother over councilors is considerable. Tradition recognizes her seniority in the fact that her appointment is the justification for the selection of her son as king. She is really the source of kingship, therefore, because of her family and clan. In managing the affairs of the state, age also gives her the advantage of experience with the intricacies of royal power. Noting the break with tradition in the ascent of Bhunu to the throne, Kuper argues that "the consideration that finally turned the choice in Labotsibeni's favor was her outstanding intelligence, ability, character and experience."

But Bhunu's reign was to prove relatively short. In 1899, he died while still in his early 20s, leaving behind six widows, each with a single child, and another wife, **laMavimbela**, who was pregnant. In determining his successor, three of the children were easily disqualified, as they were female. When the elders failed to settle on an heir acceptable to all royal factions from among the other candidates, they deferred to Labotsibeni.

The queen-mother's choice was now her grandson Nkhotfotjeni, also known as Mona (meaning "jealous"), a boy then only about three months old whose mother was **Lomawa Ndwandwe**. The decision was welcomed with great acclaim, retaining Labotsibeni as actual ruler now in the role of regent, which she was to hold until her grandson's coronation, on December 22, 1921, as Sobhuza II. In her two consecutive rules, from 1890 to 1921, Labotsibeni thus became the longest-reigning of all Swazi rulers before her, including its kings.

White colonials were apparently pleased with the choice of Mona. On April 29, 1899, Labotsibeni (then in her early 40s) was described by the *Times of Swaziland*, a white settlers' newspaper:

> She is the real ruler. Despite her years, she is a hale and hearty woman; alert and active, and displays untiring zeal in the government of the Swazi nation. She marches through Zombodze kraal with a royal bearing and appearance; not only the wiseman, the councillors but the king himself is awe stricken. She knows the measure of her son better than anyone and does not relax her hold on the reigns of rule one iota.

Nevertheless, as regent she faced major new challenges that required intricate handling. One was to contain the power struggle that resulted from the minority of the crown prince.

According to another Swazi rule of succession, the child who succeeds the father is usually the youngest son who has no blood brothers or sisters. At the time of Bhunu's death, the choice of Mona had been rushed, partly because of a controversy surrounding the clan status of Bhunu's pregnant wife laMavimbela. Labotsibeni's recommendation of Mona had been based on his mother Lomawa Ndwandwe's background, but after laMavimbela gave birth to her son Makhosikhosi, some considered the new infant's claim to the throne as good as that of the chosen ruler. The anti-Mona factions labeled Labotsibeni as partisan and unable to referee the issue fairly.

In the ensuing conflict, Labotsibeni had the able support of her son Malunge, Bhunu's young brother. She had previously preferred Prince Malunge over Bhunu, but Malunge had refused to take what was his brother's right, and now also resisted his mother's overtures for him to supplant the young Mona. But Malunge's public appearances reminded people of his mother's po-

Labotsibeni Gwamile LaMdluli

litical ambitions and schemes. In the early years of Mona's minority, there was pressure for his mother Lomawa, despite her youth, to replace Labotsibeni as the queen-regent. Regional commanders and governors took advantage of these disputes to increase their own autonomy, especially by defying summons for royal duty. It took shrewd and careful handling by Labotsibeni to establish the view that supporters of Lomawa as regent were actually preparing to exploit the young mother's political inexperience in order to bypass and oust both her and her son. By holding resolutely to this position, Labotsibeni eventually left no doubt as to who held the power behind the throne.

At the turn of the century, however, Labotsibeni found herself blamed for a succession of droughts which afflicted the Swazi population from 1902 to 1907. Since tradition assigned the power to make rain to the queen-mother, the Swazi began to interpret the dry spell as a judgment on Labotsibeni's defiance and defiling of the traditions of succession. In the course of the South African War (1899–1902), the power vacuum that existed during the early years of Mona's minority caused fear that Swaziland's neutrality and independence could not be guaranteed. Preoccupation with the war also reinforced the regional commanders' growing bids for autonomy. In 1904, Labotsibeni had to fine her subjects in order to compel them to attend national ceremonies.

By 1906, however, Allister Miller, the strongest critic of Swazi political and cultural life among the white settlers, conceded that "the Swazi were never more united than they were under the Queen Regent in 1906." The issue that drew the Swazi to rally behind Labotsibeni was the systematic allotment by the British of most of the country's land to white settlers; the Land Partition Proclamation of 1907 left the Swazis in control of only about a third of their country. After the regent organized a deputation to London that failed to reclaim the land, Labotsibeni lamented:

> Were the people also sold? What I think is being done is that my people are being taken away too. What about them? You are tearing my skirt. My people are just like the land that is said to have been sold. Where am I going to live with this people of mine. Have they also been sold?

Following this powerful indictment came an equally strong strategy in the form of a Lifa Fund to which her people contributed money for buying back the land from the colonial government and white settlers. In June 1914, she told the resi-

dent commissioner: "I felt I must lose no time. I told the council all our weapons had failed and now with our own strength we must set out with determination to buy back as much as we can of our dear little Swaziland. They all agreed to assist by voluntary contributions." She also noted: "[W]e are against class legislation because it must necessarily interfere with our natural progress and makes the European the sole judge to determine which course the evolution of our natural history and ideals should take."

The fund was eventually discontinued, then revived in the late 1940s, allowing the repossession by Swaziland of about 60% of the country by the late 1960s. At the time of the fund's origin, Labotsibeni's strong determination to attack the British colonial power had greatly enhanced her popularity among her people.

A traditionalist who was also an outstanding social reformer and an intellectual of unusual commitment, Labotsibeni was alone among the leaders of her country in recognizing the importance of Western education for 20th-century Swaziland. Her convictions had been influenced by an earlier ruler, Somhlolo (Sobhuza I), and a vision he is alleged to have had, in which a white man appeared carrying an *umculu*, a scroll representing the Bible, in one hand and money in the other. Somhlolo's advice to the Swazis had been to accept the book and to reject the money. Taking the Bible to signify both Christianity and Western education, Labotsibeni insisted that Crown Prince Mona acquire a modern education, an idea strongly opposed among the Swazi chiefs and other members of the royalty. But the always pragmatic Labotsibeni encouraged the Swazi to accept education as the path to money, perceiving that the combination was the source of much of the power held by white people.

In preparing her grandson for his role as king, Labotsibeni recognized the importance of literacy for a 20th-century head of state. Over the opposition of the councilors and aristocracy, she arranged for the establishment of a school in the Shiselweni region at Zombodze, where the young Mona completed his early education. When the crown prince was sent to Lovedale, in South Africa, for the higher education not available in Swaziland, Labotsibeni encouraged a small group of Swazis to accompany him "wherever he may be sent for his education so that on his return to Swaziland he may have around him during his term of office men of ability to assist him in furthering the development of his country as well as the welfare of his people."

In December 1920, Labotsibeni was probably in her early 60s when she recalled Mona to Swaziland, appointed Reverend J.J. Xaba as his private tutor, and began preparation for Mona's installation as king. At the time of the prince's coronation in 1921, thanks to Labotsibeni's insight, Swaziland had a monarch who had more formal education than several African heads of state would have at the end of the colonial era in the 1960s. Among the tributes Mona would later pay to his grandmother was a technical college built in her name during the 1970s, with Swazi and German funds, in the Manzini region—the Gwamile Vocational and Commercial Training Institute.

The prolonged regency of Labotsibeni proved to be the most challenging and illustrious phase of her life. From 1899, her political career embraced two broad directions: to train the young and future king and to preside over the institutions of the state while mobilizing the Swazi nation against encroaching colonial forces. From the early 1880s, the status of Swaziland was ambiguous. In 1894, it became a condominium (joint rule) under the Transvaal and British administrations. Following the defeat of the Boers in the South African War of 1899–1902, the British became the sole colonial power over the Swazis in 1903. During this time, Labotsibeni managed to lay a foundation which ensured that indigenous or Swazi institutions of political power and control paralleled those of the British until 1968, when British colonial rule was terminated. At the turn of the century, when most of Africa was surrendering political power to colonial governments, she secured an unprecedented power base for the existing Swazi aristocracy.

Closing the 19th century and opening the 20th century, Labotsibeni transcended the status generally assigned to women in her society to enhance the dynamic prospects for her country. Following her death, on December 5, 1925, the *Times of Swaziland* eulogized its longest reigning regent as "the best known native woman in Southern Africa." H.W. Jones, who served in the Swazi colonial service in the 1950s, observed that "in a strong tradition of influential women in Swazi political affairs Mdluli was arguably the most effective and influential." Many of her contemporaries acknowledged her as a shrewd and clever politician. In 1907, T.R. Coryndon, as resident commissioner with a wide colonial experience in Southern Africa, paid her indirect homage when he described her as a "woman of extraordinary diplomatic ability and strength of character, an experienced and capable opposi-

tion which it [the colonial administration] was for some time incapable of dealing with."

SOURCES:

Bonner, P. *Kings, Commoners and concessionaires: The Evolution and Dissolution of the Nineteenth Century Swazi State*. Cambridge: Cambridge University Press, 1983.

———. "Mswati II, 1826–65," in C. Saunders, ed., *Black Leaders in Southern African History*. London: Heinemann, 1979.

Booth, A. *Swaziland: Tradition and Charge in a Southern African Kingdom*. Bounder: Westview Press, 1993.

Crush, J. *The Struggle for Swazi Labour, 1890–1920*. Kingston: McGill-Queens University Press, 1987.

Hailey, Lord. *Native Administration in the British African Territories. Part V*. London: H.M.S.O., 1955.

Jones, H.M. *Biographical Register of Swaziland*. Durban: University of Natal Press, 1993.

Kuper, H. *An African Aristocracy*. London: International African Institute, 1947.

———. *The Uniform of Colour*. Johannesburg: University of Witwatersrand Press, 1947.

———. *Sobhuza II. Nqwenyama and King of Swaziland*. London: Duckworth, 1978.

Marwick, B. *The Swazi*. Cambridge: Cambridge University Press, 1940.

Matsebula, J.S.M. *A History of Swaziland*. 3rd ed. Cape Town: Longman, 1987.

COLLECTIONS:

Sources in the National Archives of Swaziland, Lobamba.

Ackson M. Kanduza,
Professor of History, University of Swaziland,
Kwaluseni, Swaziland

Labouchere, Henrietta (1841–1910).

See Hodson, Henrietta.

Labouré, Catherine (1806–1875)

French saint. Name variations: *Catherine Laboure.* Born in 1806; died in 1875.

Catherine Labouré, who was born in 1806 and grew up in Yonne, France, spent her life caring for the sick in the environs of Paris. In 1832, *Mary the Virgin appeared to Catherine three times in the chapel of her convent on the Rue du Bac in Paris. Catherine claimed that the Virgin had commanded her to have a medal struck in commemoration of the merciful goodness that the Mother of God extended to the human race. This is the origin of the "Miraculous Medal" of the Roman Catholic faith. Labouré's feast day is on December 31.

Labrina, Joanna (1898–1953).

See Lupescu, Elena for sidebar on Lambrino, Jeanne.

Lacey, Maud (fl. 1230–1250)

Countess of Hertford and Gloucester. Name variations: Maud de Clare. Flourished around 1230 to 1250; married Richard de Clare, 6th earl of Hertford, 2nd earl of Gloucester; children: Gilbert de Clare (1243–1295), 7th earl of Hertford, 3rd earl of Gloucester; *Margaret de Clare (1249–1313).

Lachapelle, Marie (1769–1821)

French obstetrician. Born Marie Louise Dugés in France in 1769; died in 1821; both mother and grandmother were influential midwives; married M Lachapelle (a surgeon), in 1792 (died 1795).

Marie Lachapelle was born Marie Louise Dugés in 1769. Upon the death of her mother, Marie was appointed head of maternity at the oldest hospital in Paris, the Hôtel Dieu, where Jean Louis Baudelocque was teaching obstetrics. Though they shared a mutual respect, the two disagreed on many points. Lachapelle believed in restricted use of instruments; she also reduced his 94 fetus position classifications to 22. Her three-volume *Pratique des accouchements* (1821–25), covering 40,000 cases, was her most important work. Lachapelle, who continued her studies in Heidelberg, would later establish a maternity and children's hospital at Port Royal where she trained many midwives, including *Marie Anne Boivin.

Lacis, Asja (1891–1979)

Latvian stage director, actress and author who played a crucial role in introducing the work of Bertolt Brecht to the Soviet stage, wrote the first history of the theater of the Weimar Republic, and was a major influence on the intellectual evolution of the literary critic Walter Benjamin. Name variations: Anna Lacis; Asja Lazis. Born Anna Ernestovna Lacis in Ligatne, Riga District, Russia, on October 19, 1891; died in Riga, Latvia, on November 21, 1979; married Julij Lacis; married Bernhard Reich; children: (second marriage) daughter, Daga Reich.

Unlike many Communist intellectuals and artists who grew up in comfortable circumstances, Latvian theater personality Asja Lacis came from a proletarian background. She was born in 1891 into a working-class family, with a father who made a precarious living as a harness maker and tailor. He was, however, an unusually progressive man for his background and level of education, and with his encouragement Asja se-cured a scholarship to one of Riga's best gymnasia. Upon graduation, she studied for two years at the noted psychiatrist Vladimir Bekhterev's Institute of Psychoneurology in St. Petersburg. But it was the art of drama that excited her during these years in Russia's history, when the arts flourished in a society moving unwittingly toward the twin devastations of war and revolution. In 1914, Lacis moved to Moscow to begin her studies in various aspects of theater at the Kommisarshevski Institute of Theater Sciences. She was in Moscow in 1917, when the hated tsarist regime was overthrown in March, and when the Bolsheviks led by Vladimir Lenin seized power in Petrograd (later Leningrad, now St. Petersburg) in November.

Believing that their rise to power heralded the dawn of a new epoch in history, Lacis sympathized with the Bolsheviks from the start of their rule. Despite the fact that recognition of her theatrical talent had already put her on course to a major career as an actress and director, she regarded herself as "a good soldier of the revolution" and by the end of 1917 had established an experimental theater for children in the city of Orel. Instead of performing in classic plays in Moscow or Petrograd, Lacis carried out a social experiment based in the local theater. Over the next two years, she worked with a group of young girls and boys who had become homeless in the chaos caused by war and revolution. Many of these youths had become hardened thieves and prostitutes. Although there appeared to be no method of bringing them back into the fold of an ordered society, Lacis believed that street-smart kids could work through their anger and bitterness by acting out on stage the most painful episodes from their past. In addition, she spent this period developing a detailed theory of lower-class children's theater based on what in later years would become known as psychodrama. Crucial to this form of drama-as-therapy was the idea that the children ran the theater themselves rather than depending on the knowledge (and whims) of a dictatorial director, whose control, even if benign and well-meaning, would stifle the children's creative impulses.

Lacis returned in 1920 to her native Latvia, now an independent republic, where she directed an innovative theater studio that was part of the Communist-oriented People's University in Riga. The dominant mood of the hour in Latvia was anti-revolutionary, and Lacis had to contend with police repression and official disapproval of her work. The authorities held her efforts in the theater to be part of a Bolshevik plan to subvert the established social order. Despite the unabated hostility of "official" Latvia, some of Riga's most talented actors and writers were attracted to the experimental stage, which developed innovative constructivist and mass-outdoor forms; these quickly became local revolutionary traditions until they were forbidden in 1928. In the midst of police surveillance, Lacis spread revolutionary messages to her audiences by developing an original form of charades, which were able to fool the mentally sluggish censors who were on hand to monitor performances.

Besides her work in Riga, Lacis spent considerable time in Russia and Germany in the 1920s. She lived in Berlin, quickly becoming the unofficial representative of the experimental theater than flourishing in the Soviet republic. In Berlin, she met and exchanged ideas with Fritz Lang, Alexander Granach, and Bernhard Reich, who became her companion.

On an extended visit to Munich that began in late summer 1923, she met most of the leading theater personalities there, including Caspar Neher, Karl Valentin, and a brilliant young playwright named Bertolt Brecht. Recognizing Lacis' talent, Brecht delegated her to direct the mass scenes in his adaptation of Christopher Marlowe's play *Edward II*. Despite her Latvian accent, Brecht also cast Lacis in the small role of the young Edward, which she performed successfully. In her memoirs, Lacis described how strong an impression Brecht's mastery of all aspects of theater made on her—his simplicity, precision, and patience, as well as his ability to create a collective mentality in the entire ensemble of actors. While working with Brecht in Munich during November 1923, she became an eyewitness to the failed putsch of Adolf Hitler and his violent band of National Socialists.

In June 1924, while vacationing in Capri with her companion Bernhard Reich, Lacis met a brilliant Jewish intellectual from Berlin named Walter Benjamin. Benjamin, who had grown up in an upper-middle-class milieu, was then attempting to learn Hebrew and was seriously considering moving to the Zionist community then being created in Palestine. Asja Lacis, with whom Benjamin quickly fell in love, told Benjamin that his plans were profoundly mistaken and that "the path of a right-thinking progressive person can only lead to Moscow, not to Palestine."

Benjamin dropped his plans and over the next few years would follow Lacis to Riga and then to Moscow. Although she remained attached to Reich and did little to reciprocate Benjamin's passion for her, the two developed a strong intellectual bond. Nonetheless, their one

attempt to live together, for several months in Berlin during the winter of 1928–29, proved a failure. Undeterred, the already married Benjamin began divorce proceedings in the spring of 1929 as part of a strategy to marry Lacis. In turn, Lacis concentrated on turning Benjamin into an orthodox Communist. She persuaded him to immerse himself in the basic works of Karl Marx and other leading revolutionary theorists. She also introduced Benjamin to Brecht, creating the basis for one of the most important intellectual-artistic interactions of the next decade.

After leaving Riga, Lacis returned to Moscow, where for a time her major artistic project was to create a motion-picture theater for children. This was accomplished with the encouragement and support of Lenin's widow, *Nadezhda Krupskaya. In 1928, Lacis accepted an assignment to work in the Soviet trade mission in Berlin, promoting the sale of Soviet films in Germany and the West. After her arrival in the German capital, Walter Benjamin introduced Lacis to eminent film critic Siegfried Kracauer, who then played a key role in introducing innovative Soviet documentaries to Germany. During this period, the always complex relationship between Lacis and Benjamin entered into an even

Asja Lacis

more convoluted phase. By 1931, the peripatetic Lacis had returned to the Soviet Union, where her multiple talents were employed to complete the filming of famed German director Erwin Piscator's version of a novel by *Anna Seghers, *Der Aufstand der Fischer von St. Barbara (The Revolt of the Fishermen of Santa Barbara)*.

In 1934, Lacis directed a Latvian-language version of Friedrich Wolf's play *Baur Baetz* at Moscow's Latvian State Theater. In 1935, she published the results of her experience with the revolutionary theater movement in pre-Hitler Germany in *The Revolutionary Theater in Germany*, a book that has yet to be translated into English. Among Lacis' most important work during these years was her advocacy of the Epic Theater theories of Bertolt Brecht, and it was above all else her publicity on behalf of Brecht's plays that would make them well known in the Soviet Union. Lacis was on hand to greet Brecht on his 1935 visit to Moscow, which was reported in *Pravda*.

In early 1938, at the height of the Great Purges in the Soviet Union, Asja Lacis was arrested. She was sent to a labor camp in Kazakhstan and was not released until 1948. She then returned to Latvia, where she became director of a theater in the city of Valmiera. The theater's audience was comprised mostly of members of nearby collective farms. With limited resources, she slowly built up a theatrical ensemble which became known far beyond the frontiers of the Soviet Latvian Republic for its high level of professionalism. The worst terrors subsided for Soviet artists and intellectuals with the death of Joseph Stalin in 1953, and starting in 1956 a cautious "thaw" became a more systematic attempt to de-Stalinize the nation's intellectual landscape. Lacis greeted her old friend Bertolt Brecht on his 1955 visit to Moscow. On this occasion, Brecht promised to write for her a shorter version of his play *Caucasian Chalk Circle* which would be appropriate for her peasant audiences in Valmiera. Brecht died the next year, however, without having had time to produce the promised revision.

Asja Lacis retired from her directorship of the Valmiera Theater in 1957, but she continued to be active as an author, lecturer, and revered veteran of the proletarian theater movement. Her memoirs appeared in both German and Russian editions, and theater historians rediscovered her important role in mediating between two great stage traditions, that of Brecht's Germany and pre-Stalin Soviet Russia. Her significant place in the life of Walter Benjamin, who had committed suicide while fleeing the Nazis in 1940 and in the 1950s began to be recognized as one of the most influential literary critics of the 20th century, was also historically secure. Above all, Lacis began to be cherished by a new generation as one of the last survivors of a golden age of European theater. Having lived a long and productive life in the shadow of a cruel century, Asja Lacis died in Riga on November 21, 1979.

SOURCES:

Aufricht, Ernst Josef. *Und der Haifisch, der hat Zähne: Aufzeichnungen eines Theaterdirektors.* Berlin: Alexander Verlag, 1998.

Benjamin, Walter. *Moscow Diary.* Edited by Gary Smith. Translated by Richard Sieburth. Cambridge, MA: Harvard University Press, 1986.

———. *Selected Writings, Volume 2: 1927–1934.* Translated by Rodney Livingstone, et al. Edited by Michael W. Jennings, et al. Cambridge, MA: The Belknap Press of Harvard University Press, 1999.

"Bert Brekht v Moskve," in *Pravda* [Moscow]. April 23, 1935.

Diezel, Peter. *Exiltheater in der Sowjetunion, 1932–1937.* Berlin: Henschelverlag Kunst und Gesellschaft, 1978.

Eaton, Katherine. "Brecht's Contacts with the Theater of Meyerhold," in *Comparative Drama.* Vol. 11, no. 1. Spring 1977, pp. 3–21.

Gumbrecht, Hans Ulrich. *In 1926: Living at the Edge of Time.* Cambridge, MA: Harvard University Press, 1997.

Haarmann, Hermann, et al. *Das "Engels" Projekt: Ein antifaschistisches Theater deutscher Emigranten in der UdSSR (1936–1941).* Worms: Georg Heintz, 1975.

Haus, Heinz-Uwe. "In Memoriam Asja Lacis (19.10.1891—21.11.1979)," in *The Brecht Yearbook: Brecht: Women and Politics.* Vol. 12, 1983, pp. 141–147.

Hecht, Werner, ed. *Brecht-Dialog 1968: Politk auf dem Theater. Dokumentation 9. bis 16. Februar 1968.* Berlin: Henschelverlag Kunst und Gesellschaft, 1968.

Kaulen, Heinrich. "Walter Benjamin und Asja Lacis: Eine biographische Konstellation und Ihre Folgen," in *Deutsche Vierteljahrsschrift für Literaturwissenschaft und Geistesgeschichte.* Vol. 69, no. 1. March 1995, pp. 92–122.

Kimele, Dagmara, and Gunta Strautmane. *Asja: Rezisores Annas Laces dekaina dzive.* Riga: Liktenstasti, 1996.

Klatt, Gudrun. "Lacis, Anna Ernestovna (genannt Asja)," in Simone Barck, et al., eds., *Lexikon sozialistischer Literatur: Ihre Geschichte in Deutschland bis 1945.* Stuttgart: Metzler-Verlag, 1994, pp. 278–279.

Lacis, Asja. *Revolutionär im Beruf: Berichte über proletarisches Theater, über Meyerhold, Brecht, Benjamin und Piscator.* Edited by Hildegard Brenner. 2nd ed. Munich: Rogner & Bernhard, 1976.

Miglane, Margarita, et al. *Anna Lacis.* Riga: Liesma, 1973.

Parini, Jay. *Benjamin's Crossing: A Novel.* NY: Henry Holt, 1996.

Pike, David. *German Writers in Soviet Exile, 1933–1945.* Chapel Hill, NC: University of North Carolina Press, 1982.

―――. *Lukács and Brecht*. Chapel Hill, NC: University of North Carolina Press, 1985.

Reich, Bernhard. *Im Wettlauf mit der Zeit: Erinnerungen aus fünf Jahrzehnten deutscher Theatergeschichte*. Berlin: Henschelverlag Kunst und Gesellschaft, 1970.

Scholem, Gershom. *Walter Benjamin: The Story of a Friendship*. Translated by Harry Zohn. Philadelphia, PA: Jewish Publication Society of America, 1981.

Völker, Klaus. "Asja Lacis," in *Theater heute*. Vol. 21, no. 1. January 1980, pp. 1–2.

John Haag,
Associate Professor of History,
University of Georgia, Athens, Georgia

Lackie, Ethel (b. 1907).

See Ederle, Gertrude for sidebar.

Lacock, abbess of (d. after 1280).

See Beatrice of Kent.

Lacombe, Claire (1765–?)

French actress who became a vocal champion of women's rights during the French Revolution only to discover that most men, revolutionary or not, were unwilling to concede the political equality of the sexes. Name variations: Rosa Lacombe. Born in Pamiers in southern France on August 4, 1765; date and place of death unknown, though it was after 1795.

Toured southern provinces as a tragic actress in plays of Corneille and Racine and attained a minor reputation in the theaters of Lyons and Marseilles; came to Paris during the French Revolution (1792), just before her 27th birthday, and took a prominent part in the popular attack on the royal palace, the Tuileries (August 10, 1792), that led to the fall of the French monarchy; organized Women's Republican Revolutionary Society in Paris (spring 1793) to agitate for female political rights, and associated with proto-socialist faction known as the Enragés; *denounced by the Jacobin faction and arrested on orders of the Committee of Public Safety (April 1794); detained in prison until 1795 after which she disappeared from public view.*

Claire Lacombe, although not as well known to history as *Manon Roland and *Germaine de Staël, was a talented and dedicated champion of a woman's right to participate in the political life of the French nation during the era of the French Revolution. Devoid of the wealth of Roland and de Staël, and having no social position, Lacombe could not affect the development of the Revolution from the comfort and security of the salon. Instead, a woman of theatrical experience, she entered the drama of the streets, the world of blood and bad odors. Relentlessly, she argued that as women had risked their lives to make and to save the Revolution to the same degree that their brothers had, women should, therefore, speak with equal voices and with equal votes in the new order. Eventually, her voice was stilled.

Nothing is known about Lacombe's girlhood. She was born in poverty in 1765 and drifted into the itinerant life of an actress in a repertory company. Accounts of her as a young woman suggest that she was quite beautiful with her well-proportioned body, dark hair and eyes, wide mouth, and practiced stage presence. Drawn to drama on the stage and in life, she played the heroine in the elevated plays of Racine and Corneille which were so popular in the late 18th century on the eve of the Revolution. By her early 20s, she was an accomplished performer and had trod the boards in Lyons and Marseilles playhouses. Her object (and that of all actresses of her day) to appear in the great theaters of Paris, eluded her, however. At best, Lacombe was a regional luminary, a prisoner of the mobile and insecure career she had chosen. Without connections or family, she made her way as best she could in the filthy hotels, reeking taverns, and provincial theaters of the Old Regime.

During the 1780s, Claire Lacombe grew into adulthood, and in the same decade her native France ventured into a new age of radical political and social transition. In the wineshops and hotels, in the lobbies and stalls of ancient playhouses, in the halls of distinguished *parlements* and provincial assemblies, the talk was of reform, of change, of a new way of life for all the French. Louis XVI, the king of France, became the subject of ridicule, and his queen, *Marie Antoinette, the object of hatred and vicious slanders. The country, deep in debt and unable to satisfy the conflicting demands of aristocrats, peasants, urban workers, or ambitious men of the professions and the market place, drifted from one crisis to the next. Lacombe learned that the playwright Beaumarchais had staged the subversive *Marriage of Figaro* in Paris and had become the darling of the city. Great events seemed to be at hand, and Lacombe, never one to be far from center stage, did not intend to be a spectator.

In May 1789, an exasperated Louis XVI convened a meeting of representatives of the nation, an Estates General, at Versailles. With royal bankruptcy looming, with one reform after another thwarted by vested interests, the king, good hearted if ineffective, hoped that such an extraordinary consultation might produce a solution to the knotty financial problems of his dynasty. The assembled delegates, however, were not content with discussions of loans and taxes. Inundated by a century of literary enlightenment, inspired by the successful American Revolution, and determined to knock down the doors of privilege and secure for themselves and their posterity the blessings of liberty and the rights of man and citizen, the delegates defied the king and formed the National Constituent Assembly. They would, they vowed, write a new constitution for France that would limit the monarch, create uniform justice and rational administration, and bring into existence a national legislature. The Revolution had begun. But little or nothing was said about the one-half of the population that was female.

> *It is not enough to tell the people that its happiness is imminent; it is necessary that the people should feel its effects.*
>
> **—Claire Lacombe at the bar of the National Convention of Revolutionary France, 1793**

Claire Lacombe yearned to go to Paris, to be in the midst of the stirring events of the time. In October 1789, Parisian market women marched to Versailles to demand that the king and the National Assembly take action to control soaring bread prices. After some violence, in which Marie Antoinette almost lost her life, the royal family and the Assembly were coerced into taking up quarters in Paris under the watchful eyes of the increasingly influential municipal government, the Commune, and the newly organized Sections of the city. These Sections, with their local revolutionary assemblies, pressed for significant economic changes to improve the lot of the poor and to bring about political and social equality. The gentlemen of the National Assembly, on their side, feared the leveling designs of the poorer Sections, and placed restrictions on the suffrage while reserving office in the new regime to men of property. Despite petitions for political equality, and regardless of their prominent role in the march on Versailles and in the overthrow of royal power in Paris in July 1789, women were not included as "active citizens" in the Constitution completed by the National Assembly in 1791.

In June 1791, Louis XVI and his family failed in an effort to escape France in order to resist the Revolution from abroad. Leaders of the Assembly, fearing the growing power of the Commune and the urban masses all over France, resisted suggestions for a republic and accepted Louis' promise to rule as a constitutional monarch under the new Constitution. Soon, a new legislature, the Legislative Assembly, was elected and convened. For many, the Revolution seemed to be over, but not for the inhabitants of the Parisian Sections hard hit by inflation under the newly freed economy. Inevitably, perhaps, the revolutionary press blossomed with sharp criticism of the new "bourgeois" government and with demands for a republic to check the "bloodsuckers" of the market place. Torn by factional strife, especially between the provincial clique known as the Girondins, inspired by Madame Manon Roland outside the Assembly, and the Jacobins, led by popular heroes such as the journalist Jean Paul Marat and the lawyer Maximilien Robespierre, also outside the legislature, the Legislative Assembly stumbled into foreign war in April 1792 with the hostile German states of Prussia and Austria. The French, particularly the Girondins, wished to liberate Europe from the tyranny of kings; the Jacobins, at first opposed to war, leaned toward greater democracy at home and sought to liberate France from the tyranny of money. On all sides, suspicions took root and none more firmly than those regarding the loyalty of the royal family.

Having carefully husbanded her money, Lacombe made her way to Paris in July 1792. She arrived in a city at war, in revolution, and in trouble. Despite joyous celebrations on July 14, in observance of the fall of the royal fortress, the Bastille, three years before, in which Lacombe eagerly joined the throngs in dancing and singing, the citizenry was worried and frightened. The war was going poorly. Prussian forces had defeated ill-prepared and poorly disciplined French armies at the front, and invasion was expected daily. Everywhere, people saw spies, traitors, war speculators, and profiteers. The young actress could hardly avoid being influenced by the talk in the streets; she heard of the oppression of the people, and she felt it. From the beginning, her heart was with the underdog citizens of the Sections.

As soon as she could, Lacombe took a room in a cheap hotel and attended sessions of the Legislative Assembly and the Commune. She also visited the Jacobin Club where orators such as Camille Desmoulins and Jean Paul Marat denounced the Girondins for ineptitude and oppression of the people and Louis XVI for treachery. In this heady atmosphere, Lacombe began to make friends, establish contacts, and attempt to pocket a little money by acting in the numerous patriotic tableaus of the time. She sewed herself a dress in the colors of the tricolor, the red, white, and blue flag of the Revolution, and fell into the inflammatory language of the Sections. Although attending the Jacobins and frequenting the Commune, she felt the helplessness of being female in a world owned by men, even if many of those men stood for liberty and equality. Even so, she gained some attention by being called upon to speak before the Legislative Assembly in late July. Employing her best dramatic style, Lacombe proclaimed that she had no money to give for the salvation of France, but, like many other women, she was ready to lay down her life for the nation.

On August 10, 1792, Lacombe got the opportunity to take direct action on behalf of her ringing affirmation and strong political convictions. A conspiracy formed by a new Revolutionary Commune, the Sections, and the Jacobins exploded into a massive attack on the Tuileries by thousands of armed citizens. Determined to save the Revolution from the foreign foe and from internal counterrevolution, the crowd forced its way past the king's Swiss guards, killing most of them, and pursued the king into the Legislative Assembly. Cowed by the mob, the legislators voted to suspend the monarchy and to place Louis under arrest. Claire Lacombe, apparently everywhere at the same time, was among the leaders of the assault, and she was shot through the arm. The next day, she was proclaimed the Heroine of August Tenth and given a "Civic Crown." The time had come for her to perform her most important role.

Two days after the attack on the Tuileries, Lacombe spoke again to the Legislative Assembly. Offering her "Civic Crown" to the delegates, she praised them for their "courage, wisdom, and patriotism." The actress from the south was now a figure of renown, and her circle of comrades expanded, especially among the radical element known as the *Enragés*.

The *Enragés* were a shifting group of politicians, agitators, intellectuals, and workers whose sympathy was generally with the Jacobins. Unlike the majority of that national faction, however, the Parisian *Enragés* wished to see the Revolution bring about a controlled economy to curb the ballooning power of the moneyed middle classes and to reduce, if not abolish, all social distinctions in the new society. More moderate Jacobins, even the fiery journalist Marat, disliked the *Enragés* and suspected them of being destructive of the Revolution ei-

ther by excessive populist demands or by being secret agents of the counterrevolution. Lacombe, on the other hand, found the *Enragés* much to her taste. She began to associate with Jacques Roux, a former priest, sometimes called the "Red Priest." Others in the group included youthful Jean Varlet, in love with his own voice, ❧▶**Pauline Léon**, a laundress, and, of the most significance to Lacombe, Théophile Leclerc, a 22-year-old journalist who served as a deputy from Lyons in the Legislative Assembly. Théophile and Lacombe agreed on many issues, including her intense belief in political rights for women. Fascinated by accounts of his voyages to the French West Indies and his strong devotion to the people, Lacombe fell in love.

The couple were soon caught up in their romance and their dedication to the Revolution. In late 1792 and early 1793, they and other *Enragés* were constantly involved in discussions, plans, and dreams. They survived and probably approved of the dreadful September Massacres in which more than 2,000 political prisoners were murdered through the "people's justice" of the Revolutionary Commune. Then in the spring, Lacombe, with some assistance from Leclerc and Pauline Léon, organized the first purely women's organization of the Revolution. Called the Women's Republican Revolutionary Society (Société des Révolutionaries Républicaines), it was loosely attached to the Jacobin Club and sometimes met in the club's quarters. Pauline Léon became its first president and Claire Lacombe its initial secretary. From the Society's podium, women of the common people gained the opportunity to voice their grievances and to appeal for

---

❧▶ **Léon, Pauline** (1758–?)

French revolutionary and feminist. Born in Paris, France, in 1758; death date unknown; daughter of a chocolate manufacturer; married (Jean) Théophile Leclerc, in November 1793.

The daughter of a father who was a chocolate manufacturer, Pauline Léon joined with her mother in running his business following his death; she also helped raise her five siblings. In 1791, Léon joined the Jacobin Société des Cordeliers and was chosen to speak at the National Assembly where she sought approval for a women's militia. Along with *Claire Lacombe, Léon was one of the principle founders of the Women's Republican Revolutionary Society (Société des Révolutionaries Républicaines), becoming its president in 1793. In 1794, she was arrested, along with her husband Théophile Leclerc, and detained in Luxembourg prison. At this point, she is lost to history.

---

full political rights. Sheltering under the protection of the powerful Jacobins, Lacombe and her comrades took part in the denunciation of the Girondins, carefully examined questions before the newly convened National Convention, occasionally presented petitions to that body, and armed themselves to patrol the streets against counterrevolutionaries. On May 26, for instance, upon seeing the female Girondin, *Anne-Josèph Théroigne de Méricourt, in the gallery of the Convention, Lacombe attacked the woman with a whip and almost killed her.

By the summer of 1793, the Girondins had been proscribed, and the Jacobins began to turn on one another. Marat denounced the *Enragés* as agents of the counterrevolution shortly before he was murdered by a Girondin sympathizer, *Charlotte Corday, on July 13. Shocked by the murder, the *Enragés,* and the Women's Revolutionary Society, proposed a memorial to Marat in the Commune. When nothing was done, Lacombe, now president of the Society, moved ahead on her own to set up a temporary wooden obelisk in the Place du Carrousel. To many in the Commune, in the Jacobins, and in the Convention, however, the Women's Republican Revolutionary Society was beginning to appear an altogether too independent entity. Most ominously, Maximilien Robespierre, the leader of the Jacobins and a key member of the Convention's dominant Committee of Public Safety, expressed his view that the women were bringing ridicule upon the Revolution. In fact, Robespierre, like most men of the time, regarded any political action by women as unnatural. Moreover, the Committee of Public Safety, launching a frightening official Terror to force the nation to destroy internal and external enemies and to make the sacrifices necessary for victory, would not tolerate any "unofficial" terror or political independence. Claire Lacombe either did not understand this or did not care. She pressed on. She petitioned the Convention to establish price controls on basic commodities.

Among the Jacobins, the Women's Republican Revolutionary Society was frequently the target of fierce denunciations and even more so as the autumn of 1793 approached. Lacombe was almost always blamed for every transgression. She stood fast but was, even so, surely hurt by her lover Leclerc's desertion in favor of Pauline Léon. Then, on September 16, François Chabot, a sometimes friend of limited women's rights, bitterly attacked Lacombe's group in the Jacobins and said that Lacombe had attempted to secure freedom for certain counterrevolutionaries. Lacombe had no chance to deny the

charge, and when her female friends burst into the hall, there were shouts of "Down with the new Corday!" Some called for her arrest. Lacombe and her supporters counterattacked, however, by calling for the arrest of the wives of absent counterrevolutionaries, and for the rehabilitation of prostitutes. Indeed, the Society even succeeded in persuading the Convention to decree that all women must wear the national cockade and influenced the enactment of the Law of the Maximum, which placed price controls on key goods.

It was this very success in securing the Maximum, however, that cost the Society the support of many Parisian women. Market women had been a moving force in the great *journées* or days of the Revolution. The Maximum was detrimental to their narrow profit margins, and they blamed Lacombe and the Women's Revolutionary Society for it. Their resentment increased when Lacombe demanded that the Commune conduct inspections to enforce the law and punish violators severely. For its part, the Commune leadership did not consider the advice of the Women's Society necessary and, in fact, listened sympathetically when market women complained that members of the Women's Society were indecently wearing men's clothing in the streets, forcing all women to wear the cockade and the red bonnet of the Revolution, and carrying loaded pistols. Meanwhile, in the Convention, Claire Lacombe was shouted down and her friend, Jacques Roux, was censured in the Jacobins and arrested by the Committee of Public Safety. When Lacombe offered to draw up an accurate list of traitors for the Convention, the delegates regarded her with disgust.

It is almost certain that Robespierre and the Committee of Public Safety would have struck against Lacombe and the other *Enragés* sooner if they had not been preoccupied with their life-and-death struggle with the Girondins that September. The Jacobin press, however, now turned in earnest against both the *Enragés* and the Women's Republican Revolutionary Society. "Rosa" Lacombe, as some of her friends knew her, struck back by accusing Robespierre of mediocrity and claiming he had arranged Roux's arrest to silence him. She could still shout to the Jacobins as late as early October that she believed in the people and that she would rather die than make deals with "robbers and traitors."

The event that finally broke the Women's Society was the riot that erupted between Claire Lacombe and her supporters and the market women on October 28 in the Saint Innocent's Market.

The members of the Women's Society arrived at the market intending to force the market women to don the revolutionary cockade and the red bonnet. Warned of the march, the market women attacked first and, with sticks, stones, and rotten fruit, beat them mercilessly. When Lacombe's women tried to retreat, they were ambushed and beaten the more. Eventually, Lacombe and her ragged defenders made it to their headquarters at the Church of St. Eustache, but many market women soon arrived as well. After some excited exchanges and wild rumors made the rounds of the sanctuary, another fight ensued. More blood flowed before officials from the Convention could break up the fray. Regardless of the responsibility for the violence, in the Commune, in the Jacobins, in the Sections, and in the Convention, Claire Lacombe and the Women's Republican Revolutionary Society were blamed.

On the 29th and 30th of October, several speakers in the Convention, led by Fabre d'Eglantine, who hated the Maximum, and Amar, a member of the powerful Committee of General Security, denounced the Women's Society. The Convention responded by banning all women's clubs and popular societies. On November 12, Lacombe led her women into the Commune to protest the ban but was received with catcalls and threats. Commune leaders and the Jacobin press resounded with admonitions to the women to be good republicans by staying home and attending to their domestic duties and raising tomorrow's citizens. Without her organization, now legally disbanded, Lacombe had no vehicle to carry on her fight.

In January 1794, Jacques Roux killed himself. Others close to Lacombe were under surveillance, and she knew she was not safe. Having lost heart and disgusted with the Jacobin Terror raging across France, the president of the Women's Revolutionary Republican Society decided to leave Paris and resume her career as an actress. Of course, in one sense, she had never left that profession. Before she could depart for Dunkirk, however, she was caught by surprise and arrested on April 2, 1794.

For 16 months, Lacombe was confined in prison. Her friends, such as were left, tried to obtain her freedom but without success. When the Robespierrists were themselves overthrown in August 1794, Lacombe wrote to the victors speaking of her services to the nation. She was ignored. In these long months, she served many of her fellow prisoners with remembered services. Finally, in the autumn of 1795, the doors of her prison swung open and she was free.

The actress in the red bonnet, with a pistol in one hand and a whip in the other, disappeared into the darkness of time. No one knows her end. Perhaps she became one of those market women who had hated her so much; perhaps she returned to the rambling life of her youth. Intemperate, impulsive, and impolitic, Claire Lacombe damaged her own cause, the cause of women's rights. Yet, it is difficult to see how a woman of the streets could have gained popular support without her stridency. In any event, her defeat was ultimately more than the rejection of Claire Lacombe, of the *Enragés,* and of their crude socialism. It was the rejection of women as a legitimate political force, even in a revolution. Many modern women, even those in revolutions, would understand Claire Lacombe's rage.

SOURCES:

Bridenthal, Renate, and Claudia Koonz, eds. *Becoming Visible: Women in European History.* NY: Houghton Mifflin, 1977, pp. 244–249.

Melzer, Sara E., and Leslie W. Rabine, eds. *Rebel Daughters: Women and the French Revolution.* Oxford University Press, 1992.

Sokolnikova, Galina Osipovna. *Nine Women Drawn From the Epoch of the French Revolution.* Translated by H.C. Stevens. NY: Books for Libraries Press, 1932, reprinted 1969.

SUGGESTED READING:

Richet, Dennis. "*Enragés,*" in *A Critical Dictionary of the French Revolution.* Edited by François Furet and Mona Ozouf. Translated by Arthur Goldhamme. Boston, MA: Harvard University Press, 1989.

C. David Rice,
Chair and Professor at the Department of History,
Central Missouri State University, Warrensburg, Missouri

Lacore, Suzanne (1875–1975)

Rural schoolteacher and socialist militant who was one of the first three women in France to be a member of the Cabinet. Name variations: (pseudonym) Suzon. Pronunciation: soo-ZAHN la-COR. Born Marie Lacore in Glandier (Corrèze), on May 30, 1875; died in Milhac d'Auberoche (Dordogne), on November 6, 1975; daughter of André Lacore (1839–82) and Marie Malaure Lacore (b. 1845); educated at a Catholic boarding school in Bugue (Dordogne) and the Dordogne Normal School for Young Women, in Périgueux; never married.

Certified as a teacher (1894); began teaching at Ajat (1903); converted to socialism and joined the Unified Socialist Party (1906); signed the Chambéry Manifesto (1912); helped found the Groupe des femmes socialistes (1913); published important articles on women and socialism (1913–14); defended socialism against the communists (1920s); retired from teaching (1930); helped found the Comité nationale des femmes socialistes and made a major speech at the Tours party congress (1931); reported on women in agriculture (1935); served as undersecretary of state for child protection (1936–37); served as vice-president of the Superior Council for the Protection of Children (1937–38); opposed the CNFS policy on women in the party (1944–46); inducted into the Legion of Honor (1956); published Enfance d'abord *(1960); promoted to officer in the Legion of Honor (1975).*

Writings: Socialisme et féminisme *(Paris: Éditions de L'Équité, 1914);* La Rôle de l'institutrice *and* Féminisme et l'internationalisme *(Cahors: Éditions de la Fédération féministe du Sud-Ouest, 1919);* Femmes socialistes *(Paris: Éditions de la SFIO, 1932);* La Femme dans l'agriculture *(Paris: Cahiers des "Amis de Jacquou le Croquant," 1938);* L'Émancipation de la femme *(Paris: Éditions de la Perfrac, 1945); editor of* Jules Guesde *(Paris: Éditions Perfrac, 1946);* Espoir et lutte *(Périgueux: Éditions Fanlac, 1951);* Enfance d'abord *(Périgueux: Pierre Fanlac, 1960).*

Prefaces: Marianne Rauze, Féminisme économique *(Paris: Éditions de L'Équité, 1914); Eugène Le Roy,* Nicette et Milou *(Paris: Éditions Christian Seignol, 1938);* Jules Guesde *(introduction de Suzanne Lacore, Paris: Éditions Perfrac, 1946).*

Periodical articles: Le Travailleur du Périgord *(1906–07);* Le Travailleur du Centre *(1908–14);* Le Populaire du Centre *(1908–14);* L'Équité *(1913–14);* Socialisme et lutte de classe *(1914);* Le Combat social *(1925–26);* Le Populaire de Paris *(1927–31);* Le Populaire du Périgord *(1930–32);* La Voix socialiste *(1934–39, 1944–47);* La Tribune des femmes socialistes *(1936–39);* Les Cahiers des "Amis de Jacquou le Croquant" *(1938–39);* Espoir et lutte *(1951);* Le Vétéran socialiste *(1949–63).*

When Suzanne Lacore, a 61-year-old retired provincial schoolteacher, was named undersecretary of state for child protection in Léon Blum's Popular Front government (1936–37), she was virtually unknown to the larger public. She was, however, well respected among the Socialists as a party veteran. Fellow undersecretaries *Cécile Brunschvicg (education) and *Irène Joliot-Curie (scientific research) joined her as the first women to sit in a French Cabinet—an anomaly because, until 1944, women still could not vote.

Save for the year she served in the government, Suzanne Lacore lived in rural southwest central France, where she was born Marie Lacore in the hamlet of Glandier (Corrèze) on May 30, 1875. She was the third child and first girl of the six children (three girls) born to André Lacore and **Marie Malaure Lacore**. André was a carpenter-contractor who moved fairly frequently in the region. He died suddenly in 1882, and in 1886 Marie Lacore married a prosperous landowner-merchant with whom she had three more children. Suzanne thus grew up in a large, comfortable family.

After grade school, she attended a Catholic girls' boarding school at Bugue (Dordogne), where she absorbed a strict, highly principled code and a dislike of Catholicism, both of which marked her for life. Graduating on July 13, 1891, she studied from October 1, 1891, to July 30, 1894, at the teachers college for young women at Périgueux (Dordogne). Life there was highly disciplined, the training broad and impressively deep. On October 1, 1894, she began her career at the village of Thenon (Dordogne) near her family at Ajat; from 1900 to 1903, she was at Fossemagne, near Thenon. She taught in the girls' grade school at Ajat from 1903 until her retirement as headmistress in 1930. Much admired as a teacher, she founded a school fund, cafeteria, library, and courses in health and childcare. She also was active in adult education and public discussions of health, social problems, and related issues. Her teaching, marked by loving individual attention, was much influenced by the methods of *Maria Montessori. Lacore taught only by tutoring, never by lecture.

Meanwhile, to the discomfort of many parents and townspeople, she had joined the Unified Socialists (SFIO) in 1906, beginning a lifelong activity as a party militant. She was converted to socialism when she read the anarchist Sébastien Faure's *La Douleur universelle* (The Universal Sorrow, 1894). Humanity's misery is "man-made," he taught. She herself knew the misery of the peasants intimately. She adopted his rational and idealistic approach but rejected his solution—"the anarchist poison," she called it. Influenced in part by a prominent socialist, Paul Faure, to join the SFIO, Lacore was for years the only female SFIO member in Dordogne—in 1913 women comprised only 1% of the national membership—but she became the secretary of Dordogne's organization and a member of its executive committee. Ideologically, she followed Jules Guesde (1845–1922), the "pope" of orthodox Marxism. Mass revolution—not necessarily violent—would crown the evolution of society toward perfect justice and equality. The root of present evils is capitalism; the masses must be educated to understand this and their own condition. Her socialism was not just a doctrine, but a way of life, a vehicle for the highest values, "a living ideal, not an illusion."

At the same time, Lacore was active in the teachers' society (*amicale*). She thought it was ineffective, however, and pushed it to affiliate with the General Confederation of Labor (CGT). Before 1914, the CGT was much influenced by revolutionary unionism (anarcho-syndicalism), which called for the General Strike as the way to bring down capitalism. To prevent war, it also promoted anti-militarism and anti-patriotism. Lacore signed the Chambéry Manifesto in 1912 calling for teachers to join the CGT. The government reacted by forcing the signers to retract under threat of dismissal. She did so with bitterness but at the same time made known her disapproval of the General Strike and anti-patriotism. She found such doctrines divisive and a waste of time. Instead, socialism should be spread and class war pursued in an organized way on the political stage, which was the Guesdist position.

In January 1913, Lacore helped organize the Socialist Women's Group (GDFS), which sought to attract women to the SFIO and give them more prominence. The GDFS did not achieve much success, but the pages of its review, *L'Équité* (1913–14), debated the relationship of socialism to feminism. Lacore took a leading role in this discussion.

When she joined the party in 1906, she had begun to write (using the pen name "Suzon") for its publications on the local and then regional levels. She addressed herself especially to women, and preferred current events or situations to ideology as subject matter. Paul Faure later praised her "elegant and warm style in which vigor of thought was joined to feminine sensitivity." In June 1913, *L'Équité* printed her essay "Féminisme et socialisme." It set off a six-month debate—*Madeleine Pelletier*, notably, opposed her thesis—and in 1914 Lacore published it in a brochure, *Socialisme et féminisme*, significantly reversing the title. Simply put, she placed socialism before feminism: "The liberation of women remains in our eyes subordinate to the revolutionary solution which will free the working proletariat." The fight, she wrote, is not against "the omnipotence of beards and moustaches" but against capitalism. For her, the current burning feminist issue of women's suffrage was secondary. Besides, the feminist movement was dominated by bourgeois women not opposed to capitalism. If they wished to join the SFIO, fine; but even there the GDFS must not become simply a female auxiliary, isolated and pushing an agenda separate from the party's.

Lacore's *Socialisme et féminisme* for better or worse largely fixed the role and place of women in the socialist movement for the rest of the Third Republic (1870–1940). For the moment, at least, she was the most prominent female theorist in the party. Guesde himself compared her role to *Aline Valette*'s in the preceding generation.

During the First World War (1914–18), Lacore supported the war effort to the end against the swelling pacifist current in the party. After the war, she favored American president Woodrow Wilson's program and rejected affiliation with Lenin's communist movement. She thought the Russian Revolution was an aberration because the Russian proletariat was not ready for the true Revolution, and stoutly defended the Socialists against Communist charges of anti-revolutionary "reformism." She continued to write, now signing her brochures "Suzanne Lacore" while keeping "Suzon" for articles until the 1930s. She also began to speak publicly more often. At conferences (1918–26) of the University Feminist Group of the Southwest, she defended her views on women's issues. She favored full legal and economic emancipation while rejecting "suffragism" and "integral" feminism. She wanted a woman to be fully open to the world, not "shut up in her garden." As for women's role in the home, she remained quite traditional: they should be the guarantors of family equilibrium, especially as protectors and educators of children. She liked to quote Nietzsche's "Woman has an insatiable need to give."

I need you. . . . [Y]ou must above all be there, for your presence signifies many things.
—Léon Blum to Suzanne Lacore, 1936

Women's place in the party continued to concern her. The GDSF had broken up during the war over the pacifist issue. It was revived in 1922 but had little success. Lacore was a principal founder (1931) of its successor, the National Committee of Socialist Women (CNFS), and at the party congress at Tours in May 1931 she delivered an impressive speech against the party's neglect of women. Her performance brought her to the attention of the top party leadership. Her brochure *Femmes socialistes* (1932) generally repeated the ideas of the 1913 brochure. The CNFS, she argued, should not be a device to isolate women in their own organization, but rather should be used to put women's problems before the party and recruit female members. In short, feminism per se, no; a more powerful voice for women, yes.

As time passed, she took a deep interest in two subjects: the development and protection of infants and children, and the problems of women in the agricultural sector. Retired since 1930, she conducted a detailed survey (1931–35) of the latter, reported to the Lille conference (1935) of the CNFS, and in 1938 published a brochure on the subject. Dordogne, as always, was the center of her activity. She organized women's groups, a youth group, and meetings on public issues. She was also active in elections and in early 1936 toured France promoting women's and socialist causes. Her principal themes were world peace, workers' security, and anti-fascism. (Hitler was the tool of capitalist interests, she maintained.) For her, the triumph of the Popular Front coalition of left-wing parties on April 21 and May 3, 1936, was a welcome reward for tireless efforts.

To Lacore's astonishment, Léon Blum (1872–1950), premier-designate, now asked her to be undersecretary of state for child protection, a new office. He wanted to make a gesture to women, a growing political force; the idea of women in the Cabinet did not, in fact, cause great public shock. But he did not want to raise the suffrage issue for now because it threatened to divide the left (which feared women would vote for conservatives) and draw attention from the economic crisis, due to the Great Depression, and the foreign crises caused by Hitler's rise and the Spanish Civil War. Blum had known Lacore from the time he was the *directeur* of *Le Populaire de Paris* and had invited her to write for the paper (1927–31); he also had been impressed by her 1931 speech and her women-in-agriculture report of 1935. Lacore firmly declined his offer. But Blum insisted, "I need you." He assured her she wouldn't be expected to administer, but to stimulate (*animer*): "You must above all *be there*, for your presence signifies many things." Her appointment would be "a continuation of the social and educating work which has marked your life." Bowing under this barrage, she gave in.

The official photograph of the new ministry showed her, barely five feet tall, standing demurely in Blum's shadow, dressed in black with a prim cloche hat and looking rather out of place. Appearances proved deceptive, as the public, to whom she was all but unknown, soon discovered. She plunged into her work with enthusiasm. The idea of a Cabinet office devoted to child protection won universal approval. Due to the Depression, child abuse, abandonment, and juvenile delinquency had come to the fore. During the year the ministry lasted (June 4, 1936–June 21, 1937), Lacore's office issued a stream of directives on many subjects. Her energetic chief, Minister of Health Henri Sellier, facilitated her administration, as did the chief of staff she chose, **Alice Jouenne**, like herself a retired teacher and CNFS member, but a Parisienne of a practical bent. Fortunately, Lacore and Brunschvicg (at Education), whose intelligence Lacore admired, got along well in dealing with overlapping spheres (e.g., children with learning problems) which caused tensions between Sellier and Minister of Education Jean Zay.

Lacore's directives dealt many measures. She wanted to aid mothers tempted to abandon their children; to create child-care centers for foundlings; to provide financial aid for vocational education for abandoned children; to ensure that children on welfare would benefit fully from new social and school laws; to coordinate hygiene services and welfare; to create centers for wet nurses so all infants could receive mother's milk; to build recreational centers, especially in rural areas; to increase oversight of children on welfare and encourage adoptions; to start summer camps for children of the unemployed; to conduct a national survey of handicapped children; to institute formal training stages for social workers; and to form three national commissions, and parallel local bodies, to coordinate services for recreation and for handicapped and abused children. Merely to catalog these projects is to underline how much needed to be done to provide services which in the future would be taken for granted.

Although administration necessarily occupied Lacore to some extent, her most signal contribution was to bring children's issues to the fore. She spoke tirelessly, touring everywhere (even to Algeria) to preach her gospel. She wrote articles, attended conferences, and even spoke at Christmas on national radio. She was strikingly successful in these endeavors and drew almost no criticism. **Suzanne Dudit**, in *Minerva*, wrote that she appeared "timid, self-effacing. But this being arises, speaks, and suddenly light shines. . . . If you haven't heard Suzanne Lacore speak, you don't know what faith is."

Of all this, what bore fruit? In the short run, almost nothing. The commissions made some proposals, and the lot of abandoned children did improve. France in the latter 1930s simply lacked both time and money to cope with its massive problems at home and abroad. When Blum's government fell in June 1937, his successor, Camille Chautemps, chose to discontinue Lacore and her office—not a popular decision. He did, however, create a Superior Council for the Protection of Children (Oct. 27, 1937), to which he named Lacore and Brunschvicg as vice-presidents. Still, the council achieved little before it expired in turn in May 1938. In the long run, however, what was begun in 1936–37 laid the foundations of public awareness of children's problems, which led to legislation after World War II providing France with a vast range of social services. In this evolution, Suzanne Lacore as a *prophète-animatrice* played a worthy—and underappreciated—role. Happily for her, she lived long enough to see most of what she had proposed come to pass.

Lacore returned to her village home in Milhac d'Auberoche. She continued to write, speak, and organize for the party in Dordogne and the CNFS. Reporting for the CNFS at the Socialist Party's congress in Royon (June 1938), she was warmly applauded. She defended the role of women in the home, their "elected domain," and in the party as necessary and equal participants. From then on, she faded from the national scene but remained prominent on the regional level.

Facing up to Hitler's takeover of Austria and Czechoslovakia in 1938, she joined (with Irène Joliot-Curie, *Gabrielle Duchêne, and other notable women) the French Union of Intellectuals for Justice, Liberty, and Peace, which pledged armed resistance. During the war, she encouraged the Resistance and was searched by the Vichy police and the Gestapo. In 1945, she published a collection of articles, *L'Émancipation des femmes,* which went further than her previous writings in insisting on total emancipation (women in France had just received the vote) and in refuting anti-feminist arguments. Yet she never became a feminist in the usual sense, for she insisted that the full liberation of women could come only with the social emancipation of all the workers. Predictably, when the revived CNFS approved a policy of directing propaganda exclusively to women, she opposed this (successfully) in Dordogne and also opposed, again, the setting up of autonomous party sections for women. "Socialism," she wrote, "is a whole . . . . [I]ts ideal [is] accessible to women who grasp the relation of their particular interests to those of the whole mass of workers."

For six months in 1951, Lacore published a monthly review on her own, *Espoir et lutte* (Hope and Struggle), until her money ran out. In it, she wrote on a huge range of subjects, notably in defense of the public schools against the controversial Béranger Law, which gave state aid to Catholic schools. She also focused on child welfare, the subject of her last production *Enfance d'abord* (Infancy First, 1960), when she was 85. The older she grew the more the importance of earliest infancy preoccupied her. As ever, children were her first love. She always carried a pocketful of candy for them on her walks.

Lacore remained true to Marxism. In 1946, she published a collection of Jules Guesde's texts, and in her last articles, in the early 1960s, she defended Marx's analyses. Nevertheless, her socialism had become tempered by the humanistic approach of the great pre-World War I leader Jean Jaurès (1859–1914). It was less rigid, more reformist, and broadened beyond the economic and political spheres to embrace all aspects of human existence. As she wrote in *Le Populaire de Paris* in 1959, "Socialism does not have several faces: it is One, at once realistic and idealistic, reformist and revolutionary, national and international, and above all human."

Suzanne Lacore had been inducted into the Legion of Honor in 1956. In a touching ceremony on her 100th birthday, she was made an officer. Six months later, on November 8, 1975, she died peacefully at home and was buried beside her parents.

Suzanne Lacore is a striking example of a teacher whose dedication to children and her ideals never flagged. When, against all expectations, she was called from retirement in her village to serve them at the highest level, she responded with enthusiasm and acquitted herself nobly. When her time in government ended, she simply returned home—and continued to be their advocate to the end.

SOURCES:

Bard, Christine. *Les Filles de Marianne: Histoire des féminismes 1914–1940.* Paris: Fayard, 1995.

Biographical Dictionary of French Political Leaders since 1870. David S. Bell, Douglas Johnson, and Peter Morris, eds. NY: Simon & Schuster, 1990.

Dictionnaire biographique du mouvement ouvrier français. Jean Maitron, dir. Paris: Éditions Ouvrières, 1964—.

Dictionnaire de biographie française. A. Balteau, M. Baroux, M. Prevost, *et al.,* dirs. Paris: Letouzy & Ané, 1933—.

Dougnac, Bernard. *Suzanne Lacore, Biographie 1875–1975: Le Socialisme femme.* Périgueux: Institut Aquitaine d'études sociales-Éditions Fanlac, 1996.

Reynolds, Sian. "Women and the Popular Front in France: The Case of the Three Women Ministers," in *French History* (Gr. Br.). Vol. 8, 1994, pp. 196–224.

Smith, Paul. *Feminism and the Third Republic.* Oxford: Clarendon Press, 1996.

Sowerwine, Charles. *Sisters or Citizens? Women and Socialism in France since 1876.* Cambridge: Cambridge University Press, 1982.

SUGGESTED READING:

Agulhon, Maurice. *The French Republic, 1879–1992.* Translated by Antonia Nevill. Oxford: Basil Blackwell, 1993.

Jackson, Julian. *The Popular Front in France: Defending Democracy, 1934–38.* Cambridge: Cambridge University Press, 1988.

Margadant, Jo Burr. *Madame le Professeur: Women Educators in the Third Republic.* Princeton, NJ: Princeton University Press, 1990.

Moody, Joseph N. *French Education since Napoleon.* Syracuse, NY: Syracuse University Press, 1978.

Vétéran socialiste. No. 18, March 1960, no. 19, May 1961 (articles on Suzanne Lacore).

Weber, Eugen. *The Hollow Years: France in the 1930s.* NY: W.W. Norton, 1994.

COLLECTIONS:

Paris: Bibliothèque Marguerite Durand; Bibliothèque historique de la Ville de Paris, Fonds Bouglé; Office Universitaire de la Recherche Socialiste.

Suresnes: Service de documentation de la Mairie, Archives Henri Sellier.

David S. Newhall,
Pottinger Distinguished Professor of History, Emeritus, Centre College, author of *Clemenceau: A Life at War* (1991)

Lacoste, Catherine (1945—)

French golfer. Name variations: Mme De Prado. Born in Paris, France, on June 27, 1945; daughter of Simone Thion de la Chaume (a professional golfer) and René Lacoste (the French tennis champion); married in August 1969.

Won the first Women's World Amateur Team championships; won the French Closed championship twice, the French Open three times and the British Amateur, and U.S. Amateur; won the U.S. Women's Open (1967); won the French, British, and U.S. amateur titles (1969).

Catherine Lacoste was born in Paris, France, in 1945 into a family of champions. Her mother **Simone Thion de la Chaume** was a golfer and the first outsider to win the British Amateur. Her father René Lacoste was a tennis champion who won both Wimbledon and U.S. championships. In 1964, when she was only 19 and a member of the French team, Lacoste won the first Women's World Amateur Team golf championship. Between 1966 and 1970, she won the French Closed golf championship twice, the French Open three times and the British Amateur, U.S. Amateur, and U.S. Women's Open.

In 1967, shooting 296, Catherine Lacoste startled the world of golf when she defeated America's finest by two strokes, winning the U.S. Women's Open. Along with **Fay Crocker** of Uruguay and *Chako Higuchi of Japan, Lacoste is the only non-American to have ever won this event, and the first amateur. Lacoste then won the French, British, and U.S. amateur titles all in one year (1969).

Karin Loewen Haag,
Athens, Georgia

Lacy, Alice (1281–1348)

Countess of Lincoln. Born in 1281; died on October 2, 1348; buried at Birling, Kent, England; daughter of Henry Lacy, earl of Lincoln; married Thomas Plantagenet, second earl of Lancaster, about 1311 (divorced 1318).

Lacy, Harriette Deborah (1807–1874)

English actress. Born in London in 1807; died in 1874; daughter of a tradesman named Taylor; married Walter Lacy (1809–1898, an actor), in 1839.

Born in London in 1807, Harriette Lacy made her first stage appearance at Bath in 1827 as Julia in *The Rivals;* she was then cast in leading parts in both comedy and tragedy. Her first London appearance was in 1830, as Nina in Dimond's *Carnival of Naples.* Her Rosalind as well as her Aspatia to William Macready's Melantius in *The Bridal* and her Lady Teazle to Walter Lacy's Charles Surface confirmed her position and popularity. Lacy was the original Helen in *The Hunchback* (1832). She also orginated the role of *Nell Gwynn in Douglas Jerrold's play of that name, and the role of the heroine in his *Housekeeper.* Considered the finest Ophelia of her day, Harriette Lacy retired in 1848.

Ladd, Anna Coleman (1878–1939)

American sculptor and author. Name variations: Mrs. Maynard Ladd. Born Anna Coleman Watts in Philadelphia, Pennsylvania, on July 15, 1878; died in 1939; daughter of John S. Watts and Mary (Peace) Watts; attended Mme Yeatmann's school; studied privately in Paris and Rome with Ferrari and Gallori; married Maynard Ladd (a physician), in 1905; children: Gabriella May Ladd; Vernon Abbott Ladd.

Anna Coleman Ladd was born Anna Coleman Watts in Philadelphia, Pennsylvania, in 1878. Her first special exhibition of 40 bronze sculptures took place in January 1913 at Gorham's in New York. Her bronzes reside in the Boston Museum of Fine Arts, New York City's Cathedral of Saint John the Divine, and the Palazzo Bhorghese in Rome; she also did four war memorials in Massachusetts and portrait busts of *Eleonora Duse, *Ethel Barrymore, Raquel Meller, and *Anna Pavlova. Ladd wrote several novels, including *Hyeronymus Rides* and *The Candid Adventure* (both 1912).

Ladd-Franklin, Christine

(1847–1930)

American logician and psychologist who advocated greater academic opportunities for women. Name variations: Christine Franklin. Born in Windsor, Connecticut, on December 1, 1847; died of pneumonia in New York City on March 5, 1930; daughter of Eliphalet Ladd and Augusta (Niles) Ladd (d. 1860); sister of Henry Ladd and **Jane Augusta Ladd McCordia**; *half-sister of* **Kathanne Ladd** *and George B. Ladd; graduated from the Wesleyan Academy in Wilbraham, Massachusetts; Vassar College, B.A., 1869; studied at Harvard University in 1872; attended Johns Hopkins University, 1878–82, completing requirements for Ph.D. which was not awarded until 1926; married Fabian Franklin (a mathematician and editor), in 1882; children: a son who died in infancy (b. 1883); Margaret Ladd Franklin (b. 1884).*

Taught secondary school; awarded an honorary LL.D., Vassar College (1887); was lecturer in psychology and logic, Columbia University (1910–30).

Selected works: "The Algebra of Logic" in Studies in Logic by Members of the Johns Hopkins University (1883); "The Reduction to Absurdity of the Ordinary Treatment of the Syllogism" in Science; Color and Color Theories (1929).

Christine Ladd-Franklin, who belongs to the tradition of philosopher-scientists, was born in Windsor, Connecticut, in 1847. Her undergraduate work at the newly opened Vassar College was in languages, physics and astronomy. Although her mother's family was prominent in Connecticut as was her father's in New Hampshire, Ladd-Franklin's education was interrupted by lack of funding. She therefore spent a year in New York City (where she had spent most of her childhood) studying languages and music on her own. A generous aunt helped finance the rest of her education, and in the last year of her studies at Vassar she turned her attention to mathematics. She chose this as a related but less restricted subject after her acute interest in physics had been frustrated by the fact that women were not allowed into the labs.

Ladd-Franklin completed the requirements for a Ph.D. at Johns Hopkins University in 1882.

Although her thesis was significant enough to merit publication by the university in 1883, she would not be awarded her degree until 1926 because women were not officially admitted into the Ph.D. program. She had only been allowed to pursue her studies at this level because Prof. J.J. Sylvester, who admired some of her early papers on mathematics, had secured a fellowship for her.

Christine Ladd-Franklin

In 1882, Christine Ladd married Fabian Franklin, a professor of mathematics at Johns Hopkins who would later become editor of the *New York Evening Post*. The couple would have two children, a son who would die in infancy (b. 1883) and **Margaret Ladd Franklin** (b. 1884). From the 1890s, she became interested in theories of color perception, particularly color-blindness. Through her lifetime, Ladd-Franklin published a total of over 100 articles on logic and color vision. She is particularly known for contributing to the development of symbolic logic, a system of using mathematical formulas to express the forms of reasoning and argument. As well, Ladd-Franklin devoted a great deal of effort and money toward helping women achieve graduate education.

SOURCES:

Gren, Judy. "Christine Ladd-Franklin (1847–1930)" in *Women of Mathematics*. Edited by Louise S. Grinstein and Paul J. Campbell. NY: Greenwood Press, 1984.

Kersey, Ethel M. *Women Philosophers: a Bio-critical Source Book*. NY: Greenwood Press, 1989.

Waithe, Mary Ellen, ed. *A History of Women Philosophers*. Boston, MA: Martinus Nijhoff Publications, 1987–95.

Catherine Hundleby,
Ph.D. candidate in Philosophy,
University of Western Ontario, Canada

Ladewig, Marion (1914—)

American bowler who was inducted into the International Bowling Museum Hall of Fame in 1991. Born Marion Van Oosten on October 30, 1914, in Grand Rapids, Michigan; married in 1930 (divorced 1940); children: one daughter, LaVonne.

Won the first National All-Star Match Games open to women (1949); won numerous Women's International Bowling Congress (WIBC) tournaments; was the first woman to win the Bowling Proprietors Association of American Women's All-Star title (1949); won seven more All-Star tournaments (1949–53, 1957, 1959, and 1963); named Woman Bowler of the Year nine times (1950–54, 1957–59, 1963); held World Invitational titles (1957, 1960, 1962–64); was Women's International Bowling Congress All-Events champion (1950 and 1955); helped organize the Professional Women's Bowling Association (PWBA); retired from tournament play (1965); raised professional bowling to new competitive heights and wrote syndicated column on bowling tips.

Marion Ladewig was born Marion Van Oosten in Grand Rapids, Michigan, in 1914. She launched her athletic career on the softball field, playing shortstop on her brother's baseball team before moving to the local women's team. Though married at 16, Ladewig continued to

Marion Ladewig

play softball until William T. Morrissey, Sr., a Grand Rapids bowling proprietor and sponsor of the Fanatorium women's softball team, spotted her. Noting her strong throwing arm, Morrissey became convinced that the 21-year-old Ladewig would make an excellent bowler. After a couple of free games at his bowling alley, she was hooked. Morrissey, who became her coach, insisted she practice daily. In order to help pay expenses, she swept up and emptied ashtrays at Morrissey's Fanatorium Lanes for $2.50 a day.

By 1937, Ladewig had dropped softball to devote herself full-time to bowling. In 1941, she won the Western Michigan Gold Pin Classic. In 1943, she took the prestigious Chicago American event. By the late 1940s, Ladewig won her first National All-Star Match Games tournament. In 1949, the first year the tournament was open to women, Ladewig won the first of her eight titles.

In 1950, Ladewig, whose petite appearance belied her power, began to win the Women's International Bowling Congress (WIBC) national championship tournaments as well, making bowling history in the 1951 championship. She defeated all 63 women as well as all 160 men who were competing for the men's title. On the first day, she bowled an eight-game block of 1,981 pins—255, 279, 247, 227, 247, 224, 255, and 247; her average was 247.6 in the qualifying round.

Marion Ladewig bowled a total of 31 annual WIBC championship tournaments and had the third-best average for women who bowled 30 or more WIBC championship tournaments. In addition, she won the World Invitational crown five times, the National Doubles twice, and the Women's International Bowling Congress All-Events title twice. She was chosen Woman Bowler of the Year nine times by the Bowling Writers Association.

Following her divorce in 1940, Ladewig made bowling her livelihood. In 1950, the Brunswick-Balke-Collender Company hired her. She worked for Brunswick for the next 30 years, traveling over 100,000 miles a year throughout the United States, Europe, North Africa, and Asia, putting on exhibitions, conducting instructional clinics, and making television appearances. In 1960, she helped organized the Professional Women's Bowling Association (PWBA). By this time, Ladewig owned her own bowling center in Grand Rapids.

When she retired from tournament play in 1965 at age 50, with a career average of 190, the trim athlete and grandmother of five had dominated bowling for two decades. At the height of her fame, she made $25,000 a year from bowling, a truly respectable sum for the period. In addition, she wrote a syndicated "tips" column, was a sportswear design consultant, and continued to remain on Brunswick's advisory staff. Marion Ladewig demonstrated that professional bowling could be a lucrative sport for women and raised competitive bowling to new heights as a professional. She was one of five female pros to bowl in the first edition of the National Bowling Hall of Fame tournament and, in 1991, was inducted into the International Bowling Museum Hall of Fame. **Helen Duval**, winner of five BPAA All-Star finals, and **Joyce Deitch**, president of the Women's International Bowling Congress, were inducted in 1993 and 1999, respectively.

SOURCES:

Hollander, Phyllis. *100 Greatest Women in Sports*. NY: Grosset & Dunlap, 1976.

Woolum, Janet. *Outstanding Women Athletes: Who They Are and How They Influenced Sports in America*. Phoenix, AZ: Oryx Press, 1992.

Karin L. Haag,
freelance writer, Athens, Georgia

Ladies of Gregynog, The.

See Davies, Gwendoline and Margaret.

The Ladies of Llangollen

The celebrated women of Llangollen who lived together for 50 years in rural Wales in an age when romantic friendship between women and retirement to the countryside were fashionable. Name variations: Ladies of the Vale.

Eleanor Butler (c. 1738–1829). Name variations: became Lady Eleanor when her brother John recovered the earldom of Ormonde (1791). Born in Cambrai, France, in 1738 or 1739; died in Llangollen, Wales, on June 2, 1829; youngest daughter of Eleanor (Morris) Butler and Walter Butler, de jure earl of Ormonde; educated at the English Benedictine Convent of Our Blessed Lady of Consolation in Cambrai by liberal, well-educated and often aristocratic nuns; continued reading and studying on her own when she returned to live in the family's ancestral castle in Kilkenny, Ireland, in 1768.

Sarah Ponsonby (1755–1831). Born in Ireland in 1755; died in Llangollen, Wales, on December 8, 1831; daughter of Chambre Barbazon Ponsonby and Louise (Lyons) Ponsonby (both of whom died when Sarah was a child); in 1768 adopted by her father's first cousin Lady Betty Fownes and her husband Sir William Fownes, who lived in a mansion at Wood-

stock, near Kilkenny; attended Miss Parke's School for Young Ladies in Kilkenny, 1768–73, where Eleanor Butler acted as Sarah's guardian during the Fownes' frequent absences from Woodstock.

The close friendship between Eleanor and Sarah continued after Sarah left Miss Parke's school (1773); they left Ireland forever (early May 1778), Eleanor to avoid being sent back to the nunnery in Cambrai and Sarah to avoid the unwanted sexual advances of her supposed guardian Sir William; after six weeks of wandering in Wales and England, they settled in rural Llangollen in northern Wales, residing in a cottage they called Plas Newydd (New Place) for the rest of their lives; read and studied the classics as well as contemporary literature in English, French, Italian and Spanish; tended a large garden; took frequent walks around Llangollen; kept up a voluminous correspondence with the greatest minds of their day; frequently entertained their genteel neighbors as well as distinguished persons who went out of their way to visit them in Llangollen, "the vale of friendship"; tourists still stream to Llangollen to visit Plas Newydd.

Selected publications: Butler and Ponsonby kept journals and day books and wrote many letters, some of which were published in The Hamwood Papers of the Ladies of Llangollen and Caroline Hamilton *(ed. by Mrs. G.H. Bell, London: Macmillan, 1930) and in* Life with the Ladies of Llangollen *(comp. and ed. by Elizabeth Mavor, NY: Viking Penguin, 1984).*

The story of Lady Eleanor Butler and the Honorable Sarah Ponsonby, known as the "Ladies of Llangollen," reads like a fairy tale. In 1768, the two Irish women met in Kilkenny, where they both lived, fell in love, eloped in 1778, and, retiring to the pleasant vale of Llangollen in northern Wales, lived happily forever after. "Aha," exclaims a contemporary world obsessed with sexuality, "a pair of lesbians." Such a characterization of their romantic friendship would have shocked and dismayed the ladies, their literary friends, and the many distinguished visitors who, over a period of 50 years, came to Llangollen to visit the learned exiles. These included such leaders as the duke of Wellington, Edmund Burke, and Lord Castlereagh, and such writers and poets as William Wordsworth, *Anna Seward and Sir Walter Scott, to name but a few. For in the 18th and well into the 19th century, when romantic friendship between women flourished, "women of the world knew perfectly well what lesbianism was," writes **Claire Tomalin**, "but regarded it as a dirty little vice of servant girls, boarding schools, and actresses, and did not think of applying it to cultivated women of decent upbringing."

However their relationship has been characterized, for the last 200 years the Ladies of Llangollen have fascinated many men and women, a fascination that continues. One central question is why Butler and Ponsonby were sought out by clerics, diplomats, inventors, reformers, philanthropists, actors, scientists, men and women of letters as well as by many now obscure members of the upper classes. Why have they also continued to interest biographers, travel writers, literary historians, novelists, tourists in Wales, and many other people since their deaths over 165 years ago? To answer these two related questions one must first examine the origins of the two women, their upbringing, and the dilemmas they faced as women in 18th-century society which led them to flee their respective homes. Next, one must study why they settled in northern Wales and how for 50 years they lived their lives in rural Llangollen. For it is how Eleanor Butler and Sarah Ponsonby lived their lives and used their time and talents that helps to explain why they were so celebrated in their day and so interesting to succeeding generations. Lastly, one must return to the issues of romantic friendship vs. lesbianism which have so preoccupied mostly, but not exclusively, women writers since *Colette wrote about the ladies in *Ces Plaisirs* (1932).

Eleanor Butler was born into the Irish aristocracy, but because her parents refused to abjure Catholicism, they spent years in exile in France to avoid religious persecution and economic discrimination. As a result, Butler and her two older sisters were educated in prestigious English convents in France. Eleanor demonstrated a great love of learning from her childhood, a love which was fostered by the English and Irish nuns of the Benedictine convent in Cambrai. She studied with the nuns from 1748 to 1756 and possibly from 1763 to 1768. In the latter year, Butler was back in Kilkenny to attend her only brother John's wedding. Eleanor was 29 at the time and showed no interest in marrying, perhaps because in her class "marriage was a commercial affair that replenished family fortunes and united family names." Some relatives and family friends complained that Butler was too sardonic and too masculine to attract men, but a young girl of 13, Sarah Ponsonby, who became acquainted with Butler while enrolled at Miss Parke's School for Young Ladies in Kilkenny, found Eleanor "uncommonly handsome."

Sarah Ponsonby was three when her mother Louise died, and, at the age of seven, she lost her father. For six years, her stepmother raised her, but when **Lady Staples** died in 1768 Sarah was left orphaned and penniless. Lady **Betty Fownes**, a first cousin of Sarah's father, who was wealthy and whose only daughter was married, adopted the melancholy but bright young orphan. After her arrival at the Fownes' mansion at Woodstock, Sarah was almost immediately placed in Miss Parke's School, as Lady Betty and her husband Sir William Fownes, a member of the Irish Parliament, were frequently away in Dublin.

After Sarah was placed at Miss Parke's School, Lady Betty wrote to her friend, Mrs. **Eleanor Morris Butler**, at the Castle of Kilkenny, asking her to keep a "watchful eye" on Sarah, who was among strangers at the school. Mrs. Butler delegated this task to her daughter Eleanor, and within months Eleanor, who was 16 years older than Sarah, became Sarah's mentor, confidante, and friend. Drawn to each other by their love of books and learning, the friendship continued after Ponsonby left Miss Parke's school in 1773 at the age of 18.

By 1776, the Butlers were alarmed at their daughter's passionate attachment to Sarah and insisted that Eleanor, who was now close to 35, enter the nunnery in France where she had studied in her youth. Meanwhile, Ponsonby, who dearly loved her ailing guardian Lady Betty and did not wish to hurt her in any way, was fending off the unwanted sexual advances of Sir William. Confined to Kilkenny Castle and forbidden to see her friend, Eleanor maintained a secret correspondence with the anguished Sarah between 1776 and early 1778. They were helped by Lady Betty's house maid, **Mary Caryll**.

By early 1778, Ponsonby and Butler had made up their minds: the only way to end their intolerable situation was to flee Ireland. As they made elaborate plans for their escape, they may have recalled what Miss Howe wrote to Miss Clarissa Harlowe in Eleanor and Sarah's favorite novel by Samuel Richardson, *Clarissa*: "How charmingly might you and I live together and despise them all." At the end of March, aided and abetted by their champion, Mary Caryll, and attired in men's clothing, Eleanor and Sarah made for Waterford to take a ship across St. George's Channel to northern Wales. They were intercepted by their respective families and persuaded to return to their homes because Sarah was very ill and feverish after a night spent in a damp barn.

Neither Butler nor Ponsonby could be dissuaded from their plan to leave Ireland and live together, hopefully in England. In late April 1778, the Butlers reluctantly agreed to provide Eleanor with an annual income of £200, far less than she was entitled to. Lady Betty's daughter, **Sarah Tighe**, agreed to provide Sarah with a yearly pension of £80. The two bade farewell to their families, their friends, and their country. Eleanor's unforgiving parents treated her with hatred and hostility while Lady Betty, a remorseful Sir William, and their daughter Sarah Tighe all wept profusely when a sorrowful but determined Ponsonby bid them goodbye. The two Sarahs wrote to each other for the rest of their lives, but within two months of Sarah's departure, first Sir William, and then Lady Betty, passed away.

After landing in northern Wales on May 10, 1778, Butler and Ponsonby traveled there and in Northern England for six weeks, finally settling near the Welsh village of Llangollen, not far from the English border. Sarah kept a journal of their travels, "An Account of a Journey in Wales by Two Fugitive Ladies," which she dedicated to "her most tenderly beloved companion." In the journal, she described Llangollen as "a pretty village on the river Dee . . . in the Beautifullest [sic] Country in the World." With a very small income (for women of their class), they also chose to live in Wales because it was less expensive than England. For example, the lovely cottage they rented and which they named Plas Newydd (New Place) cost them under £23 a year, and this included over two acres of land.

Mary Caryll, who had been Eleanor and Sarah's ally through thick and thin, joined them in Llangollen after the death of Lady Betty. She was loyal, intelligent, strong, fearless, and taller than most men. Mary was a great comfort to the fugitives, especially to Ponsonby, who deeply mourned the deaths of the ever-kind Lady Betty and the remorseful Sir William. It was probably Mary who informed Sarah that as Sir William lay dying he told his daughter Sarah Tighe that "his illness . . . was his own fault that he was punished for."

At Plas Newydd, Butler and Ponsonby immediately began cultivating their garden as well as their minds. It is known how they spent each hour, each day, and each month of every year, for Butler kept journals and day books from 1779 until 1823, when failing vision brought an end to her writing. Outside their pleasant cottage they spent many hours converting their two acres into one of the most celebrated gardens of their time. They, with the help of a full-time gardener, planted wild and cultivated flowers, including nearly 50 varieties of roses and 80 varieties of geraniums. They also grew many kinds of berries, at least six different varieties of fruit trees and laburnum and many other species of trees and shrubs. The most celebrated botanist of their day,

Mr. Sneyde, journeyed from Staffordshire, England, to advise the women on the best ways to preserve their trees and shrubbery. And just about every important book on gardening could be found in their impressive library.

By the late 1790s, Sarah and Eleanor, with the help of hired hands, added farming and dairying to their outdoor activities. Food prices skyrocketed as the war between France and Great Britain, which lasted from 1793 to 1815, intensified, and the ladies rented an additional nine acres to grow potatoes, turnips, wheat, and other comestibles. They had acquired a cow, their beloved Margaret, in the 1780s; ten years later, they had a total of four cows to provide them with milk, butter and cheese. The cows were also valuable for another reason. On July 30, 1801, Ponsonby wrote to her cousin and benefactor, Sarah Tighe, that "our cows are vastly obliging in doing all in their power to increase our heaps of manure." Farming and dairying brought them much-needed income, for they were constantly in debt, as was most of the aristocracy of their time.

Those who have loved longest love best.
—Sarah Ponsonby

The women were also great walkers and hikers, walking at least two hours each day, weather permitting. On October 27, 1785, Butler wrote in her journal that "My Love and I spent from five 'till seven in the shrubbery and in the Field endeavoring to talk and walk away our little Sorrows." Their little sorrows were caused by their mounting debts (e.g., they were usually six months behind in their rent) and by Eleanor's severe migraine headaches. On their daily walks and frequent hikes, they relished the changing seasons, were enraptured by the singing of the birds, gazed at the moon and stars (and read the works of the royal astronomer William Herschel, brother of *Caroline Herschel). They also collected unusual rocks and fossils, a passion they shared with Josiah Wedgwood, the famed potter and reformer. During the summer months, the women spent up to eight hours out of doors each day; only severe snowstorms kept them indoors during the winter.

Indoors and usually from noon until three and from nine to midnight, Ponsonby cross-stitched and made purses and letter cases for friends and family while Butler read aloud. They very much enjoyed the works of such contemporary British writers, playwrights, and poets as Richardson, Sheridan, Sterne, Johnson, Fielding,

Seward, Southey, *Hester Lynch Piozzi, and many others. They were both fluent in French before they settled in Llangollen and read the works of Rousseau, *Marie de Sévigné, *Germaine de Staël, Moliere, Corneille, and Racine, in the original. Once settled at Plas Newydd, the ladies learned first Italian and then Spanish so as to read in the original such classic authors as Dante and Petrarch of Italy and Cervantes of Spain. They always meant to study Latin, but were "too busy" to master that classic tongue.

In addition to works in literature and languages, Butler read aloud from books on astronomy, botany, gardening, geography, and religion while Ponsonby sewed or made drawings and maps. Though they had retired from the world and never visited a city of any size for 50 years, Eleanor and Sarah were keenly interested in and well-informed about events in Great Britain and the rest of Europe. They subscribed to at least one newspaper and several journals, and were kept well-informed about politics and government by the numerous letters they received from friends living in Dublin or Bath or London or Paris. Both women were socially and politically conservative and, being staunch royalists, were saddened by the madness of King George III and the execution of Louis XVI.

Ponsonby and Butler enjoyed receiving letters and hearing about the many revolutions, uprisings and counter-revolutions that occurred between the 1770s and 1820. As a result of their large correspondence, it was not unusual for Sarah, especially, but also Eleanor, to devote up to six hours a day writing letters to close friends, such as Hester Piozzi, famed for her travel works and her association with Samuel Johnson. **Helen Bowdler** and Anna Seward, well-known writers and poets in their day, were also frequent correspondents of the "recluses," as Butler and Ponsonby have been incorrectly dubbed for over 200 years.

There was nothing reclusive about the ladies of Llangollen, for they often invited friends to breakfast or lunch or supper, delighting in conversation but eschewing gossip. One day they entertained over 30 visitors, and it was not unusual for at least 10 persons to call on them on any given day. They gladly accepted invitations from the gentry in a radius of some 12 miles around Llangollen, and enjoyed dinner parties, theatricals, and playing whist and backgammon.

As their fame grew, British and foreign travelers on their way to Ireland via Wales stopped to visit Lady Eleanor (her title after 1791) and the Honorable Miss Sarah, but only distinguished persons who bore letters of recommendation from friends of the women gained admittance to Plas Newydd. Others of merit and high social class were permitted to visit their extraordinary garden and some were given a tour of the house by Mary Caryll, who collected such handsome fees from the visitors that at her death in 1808 she left Sarah and Eleanor her life savings of £500.

Through the efforts of such friends in high places as their fellow Irishmen the duke of Wellington, Viscount Castlereagh, George Canning, and Edmund Burke, the ladies were granted government and other pensions that made it possible for them to extensively renovate the cottage, both inside and out, buy the house (but not until 1819) and pay off many of their debts. They were the recipients of occasional gifts from well-off friends and Ponsonby's relatives. The ladies kept records of every pence that went out, spending over £30 a year on each of the following: books, fine writing paper, postage, clothing and shoes, and the wages of their gardener and their three housemaids. By the mid-1820s, their money worries were over, for the ladies enjoyed an income of about £600 a year, which was considered adequate for women of their class.

With respect to class, Sarah, especially, was on good terms with the "mob-ility" as Eleanor jokingly referred to the lower classes. While Butler discharged gardeners "like cannonballs," both of them enjoyed the respect and loyalty of their household staff and anyone else who was an honest worker. They developed a strong sense of community, sharing the ordinary joys and sorrows of their impoverished neighbors. They were viewed as royalty by the people of Llangollen, and when their chimney caught fire in June 1788 dozens of neighbors came and put out the blaze. The grateful women ordered them "plentiful potations of beer," Butler recorded in her diary. "They drank our Health, wished us long life." Similarly, when one of their cows was calving, all their near neighbors came to help. The cow was delivered of a dead calf, and Ponsonby wrote that "all the village came kindly to inquire about our dear cow."

Butler and Ponsonby were highly respected and admired by every strata of society because they were witty, perceptive, intelligent, compassionate, kindly and gracious. Sarah was invariably sweet-tempered, but when provoked Eleanor could be irritable and arrogant. Their close friend, Anna Seward, remarked to a cleric whom Eleanor had offended that "Lady Eleanor, who when pleased is one of the most gracious of

God's creatures, under a contrary impression is extremely haughty and imperious." Yet this same Lady Eleanor always referred to Sarah in the most endearing terms, loved birds and animals tenderly, and did what she could to alleviate the sufferings of the poor.

On June 2, 1829, a year after the ladies celebrated their 50th year together, Butler, who had been blind for over five years, passed away. The entire village put on their mourning clothes and attended her funeral and interment. The same thing happened when Ponsonby, her grieving companion, passed away 18 months later. Save for the duke of Wellington and the poet William Wordsworth, the ladies of Llangollen had outlived most of their friends and contemporaries. It was Wordsworth who best memorialized them in a sonnet he wrote at Plas Newydd in 1824 which he entitled "To Lady Eleanor and the Honorable Miss Ponsonby, composed in the grounds of Plas-Newydd, Llangollen." The last six lines read:

> Glyn Cafaillgaroch, in the Cambrian tongue,
> In ours the Vale of Friendship, let this spot
> Be nam'd where faithful to a low roof'd Cot
> On Deva's banks, ye have abode so long,
> Sisters in love, a love allowed to climb
> Ev'n on this earth, above the reach of time.

In July 1828, when the Prussian prince Puckler-Muskau met Butler and Ponsonby for the first and only time (his father had visited them many years before), he referred to them as the "two most celebrated virgins in Europe." During the rest of the 19th century, they were considered "Victorian models for ideal love and devotion." But in the 20th century, they have been regarded as the two most celebrated lesbians of their time, not only because they shared the same bed but also because they wore semi-masculine attire (i.e. a riding habit and beaver hats). The French writers *Colette and *Simone de Beauvoir took it for granted that they were lesbians, and the women are included in Paul Russell's *The Gay 100: a ranking of the most influential gay men and lesbians, past and present* (1994). **Mary Gordon**'s 1936 novel about the ladies, *Chase of the Wild Goose*, did *not* suggest that the ladies were sapphists, yet the work was reprinted in 1975 by Arno Press in its series on homosexuality. In more recent works of fiction, Butler and Ponsonby have been depicted as lesbians by **Doris Grumbach** in *The Ladies* (1984) and Morgan Graham in *These Lovers Fled Away* (1988).

On the other hand, **Elizabeth Mavor**, who read every word the ladies wrote in preparing her masterful biography, *The Ladies of Llangollen: A Study in Romantic Friendship* (1971), and who has compiled and edited excerpts from their writing, believes that their relationship was platonic. **Lillian Faderman**, the author of *Surpassing the Love of Men: Romantic Friendship and Love between Women from the Renaissance to the Present* (1981) agrees with Mavor. For Faderman, theirs is the great success story of romantic friendship. While writers of fiction are rooted in their times and can distort the past at will, the biographer and historian try to understand the past on its own terms and by a careful study of the evidence. But whether regarded as lesbians by some or as romantic friends by others, Eleanor Butler and Sarah Ponsonby live on in many hearts, "above the reach of time."

SOURCES:

Bell, Mrs. G.H., ed. *The Hamwood Papers of the Ladies of Llangollen and Caroline Hamilton*. London: Macmillan, 1930.

Bradbrook, M.C. "The Elegant Eccentrics," in *The Modern Language Review*. Vol. XLIV. Cambridge: Cambridge University Press, 1949, pp. 184–198.

Colette. *The Pure and the Impure.* Trans. by Herma Briffault. NY: Farrar, Straus and Giroux, 1966.

Faderman, Lillian. *Surpassing the Love of Men: Romantic Friendship and Love between Women from the Renaissance to the Present.* NY: William Morrow, 1981.

Mavor, Elizabeth. *The Ladies of Llangollen: A Study in Romantic Friendship*. London: Michael Joseph, 1971.

SUGGESTED READING:

Gordon, Mary. *Chase of the Wild Goose*. London: Hogarth Press, 1936.

Mavor, Elizabeth, comp. and cd. *Life with the Ladies of Llangollen*. NY: Viking Penguin, 1984.

Anna Macías,
Professor Emerita of History,
Ohio Wesleyan University, Delaware, Ohio

Ladies of the Vale.
See Ladies of Llangollen.

Lady of the Camellias (1824–1847).
See Plessis, Alphonsine.

Lady of the Mercians (869–918).
See Ethelflaed, Lady of the Mercians.

Lady of Winchester (c. 985–1052).
See Emma of Normandy.

Laelia (fl. 2nd c. BCE)

Roman orator. Name variations: (nickname) "Sapiens" (the Wise). Flourished in the 2nd century BCE; eldest of two daughters of Gaius Laelius (a Roman orator who was a Roman consul in 140 BCE).

Roman writer Quintilian (1st century CE) writes that Laelia was the elder of two daughters of Gaius Laelius, a Roman orator, and that she was nicknamed "Sapiens" (the Wise), since she had inherited the powers of her father. The purity of her Latin was admired by Cicero.

La Farge, Margaret Hockaday
(1907–1992).

See Hockaday, Margaret.

Lafarge, Marie (1816–1852)

French murderer. Born Marie Fortunée Cappelle in Paris, France, in 1816; died in Ussat, France, in 1852; eldest of two daughters of Colonel Cappelle (an artillery officer in Napoleon's army); attended the convent school of Saint-Denis; married Charles Lafarge (an iron manufacturer), in 1839 (died, January 1840); no children.

The central figure in one of France's most notorious murder cases, 24-year-old Marie Lafarge was convicted of slowly poisoning her husband to death with arsenic. A beautiful, cultured woman who played the piano and wrote poetry, Madame Lafarge seemed more a romantic heroine than a cold-blooded murderer, and her trial, which took place during the summer of 1840, was one of the most sensational of the century.

Born Marie Fortunée Cappelle in Paris in 1816, Lafarge was the daughter of an artillery officer who had served in Napoleon's army. On her mother's side, her lineage could be traced to the reigning royal family, her grandmother being the daughter of the king's father Philippe-Egalité and his mistress Comtesse *Stéphanie-Félicité de Genlis. In her memoirs, published after her trial, Marie maintained that her childhood was unhappy, although she may have exaggerating the facts. She claimed that her father wanted a boy and was disappointed with her and that her younger sister, born when Marie was five, was thought to be prettier and more endearing. Marie's father died when she was 12, and her mother, who remarried, died in 1835.

Following her mother's death, Marie was sent to live with her mother's sister, the wife of the secretary-general of the Bank of France. Although she was treated well, she was reduced in status to that of a "poor cousin" and was considered a marriage liability. Hoping to boost her prospects for finding a husband, one of her uncles engaged the services of a matrimonial agency. Within a short time, they found a seem-ingly suitable candidate in Charles Lafarge, a wealthy iron manufacturer with an impeccable pedigree and a sizable estate in the south of France, in Le Glandier. Unknown at the time, however, was the fact that Charles was a widower who had married his former wife for her dowry; he had hoped to finance a new smelting process he had developed. Marie did not much like him, although her feelings mattered little. Following the arranged "chance" meeting with Charles at the opera, she declared him boorish and ugly, but within days her aunt had published the marriage banns, and a few weeks later, in the late summer of 1839, the hapless Marie found herself married and on her way to Le Glandier.

Marie was both terrified by the prospect of intimacy with Charles, whom she still considered a stranger, and disillusioned by what she found at her new home. The estate was in complete disrepair, and she felt that her new in-laws, Charles' mother and sister, were less than welcoming. In addition, the ironworks was bankrupt. On her first night at Le Glandier, Marie, in desperation, locked herself in her bedroom and composed a letter to Charles in which she professed love for another man whom she claimed had followed them from Paris. She threatened to either poison herself with arsenic or to leave immediately for Bordeaux to catch a ship for Smyrna. "Spare me, be the guardian angel of a poor orphan girl, or, if you choose, slay me, and say I have killed myself," she wrote. Later that night, however, Marie was cajoled by her mother-in-law into admitting the ruse and reluctantly decided to give the marriage a chance. Charles agreed to defer his "marital privileges" until he had refurbished the house and reclaimed his business.

Reportedly, things improved between the couple over the next few weeks. Charles kept his word, arranging to begin renovations on the Lafarge mansion and applying for a loan to shore up the ironworks. To further placate his young bride, he provided her with subscriptions to magazines and newspapers, and membership in the local lending library, so that she could pursue her intellectual interests. At great expense, he also had Marie's piano shipped from Paris and procured an Arabian horse for her to ride. Marie, for her part, assumed her position as mistress of the house and began to formulate plans to transform the rustic interiors of Le Glandier into something more elegant. One of her first orders of business, however, was to request a supply of arsenic from the local druggist, to rid the place of rats.

In January 1840, less than a year into the marriage, Charles returned home from a lengthy business trip with an intestinal illness that he claimed had begun in mid-December, soon after he had received a cake sent to him by his wife. He immediately took to his bed but continued to endure attacks of cramps, nausea, and vomiting. Marie devoted herself to her husband's care, providing him with food and drink, and attempting to make him comfortable. His condition deteriorated, however, and friends and relatives began to suspect Marie. One visitor claimed to have seen her stirring a white powder into a drink intended for her husband, although Marie insisted that it was merely gum arabic, which was commonly used at the time for stomach complaints. As Charles' condition worsened, Marie's mother-in-law went so far as to have the remains of a glass of eggnog analyzed by a local druggist, who, indeed, found traces of arsenic. Marie was denied further access to Charles, but it was too late; he died on January 14, 1840, the day following the arsenic test. The family immediately demanded an investigation and, within a short time, Marie was charged with murder and taken off to the Brive jail, where she continued to proclaim her innocence.

In the meantime, Marie's aunt secured the services of the best lawyer in Paris, Alphonse Paillet, who with his associates, Charles Lachaud and Théodore Bac, set out to prepare Lafarge's defense. Almost immediately, the case was complicated by a charge of theft brought against Lafarge by her friend **Marie de Nicolai** (Mme de Léautaud), who had discovered her diamond necklace missing after Marie's visit the previous summer. When a search of Le Glandier produced the necklace, Marie adamantly denied taking it, claiming that de Nicolai was being blackmailed by a former lover and had given her the necklace to pawn for payoff money. When further questioned as to why she still had the necklace, Lafarge claimed that after discovering that the blackmailer was no longer a threat, de Nicolai, in appreciation, had made a gift of the necklace. The case of theft was tried by the correctional tribunal at Brive in July 1840, at which time Lafarge was convicted and sentenced to two years in prison.

As she awaited her murder trial, Marie Lafarge became a *cause célèbre*, capturing the attention of the French citizenry, which was divided into pro- and anti-Marie camps. The prisoner received some 6,000 letters, most of which expressed support. Many came from wealthy gentlemen, offering marriage or, at the very least, financial assistance with her defense. She also received sympathetic notes from young women, who often sent along gifts of books and flowers.

Marie perpetuated her romantic image, answering as many letters as possible, and referring to herself as "the poor slandered one." She also embarked on a romantic correspondence with her lawyer Charles Lachaud, then only 22 years old but destined to become one of France's most highly respected lawyers. Lachaud, according to his biographer, was convinced of his client's innocence and never recovered from her conviction.

Marie Lafarge

Despite the best efforts of her attorneys to defend Lafarge, the prosecution presented the more compelling case, though most of their evidence was circumstantial. They first cited her disastrous marriage, presenting into evidence the letter she wrote to Charles during her first night in the Le Glandier estate, in which she mentioned another lover and her plans to leave Charles or kill herself. They put forth her request to the druggist for arsenic to kill the rats in the house, and the subsequent substitution of bicarbonate of soda for arsenic in the paste prepared for the rats. They introduced the switch of a large arsenic-laced cake for small ones in a Christmas package sent to her husband while he was away on business, and the continued dosing of his food and drink with arsenic powder (kept in a pillbox in her apron pocket), after his return home. They ended their presentation with the conclusive report of the famous chemist Mateo Orfila stating unequivocally that arsenic was present in Charles' body. With this last crushing blow, Marie Lafarge, who had kept her composure during the two-week ordeal, collapsed in tears, knowing that there was no hope for her acquittal.

As a "respectable" female criminal, Lafarge was spared the public pillory and hard labor. She was imprisoned in Montpellier, where, while waiting for her appeal, she wrote two volumes of memoirs. When her appeal failed, she wrote a series of articles that were published after her death under the title *Prison Hours*. The cult that had risen around Marie Lafarge gradually dropped away, and she was left a forgotten woman. In 1851, she was removed to the prison hospital suffering with tuberculosis. Following a plea to Napoleon III from her doctors, she was freed early in 1852 and transported to a spa in Ussat by a loyal great-uncle and his daughter. She died there a few months later, swearing her innocence to the end.

SOURCES:

Hartman, Mary S. *Victorian Murderesses.* NY: Schocken, 1977.

Nash, Jay Robert. *Look for the Woman.* NY: M. Evans, 1981.

Barbara Morgan,
Melrose, Massachusetts

Lafargue, Laura (1845–1911).

See Marx, Jenny for sidebar on Laura Marx.

Lafayette, Adrienne de (1760–1807).

See Lafayette, Marie Adrienne de.

Lafayette, Marie Adrienne de
(1760–1807)

French marquise and wife of the American revolutionary hero, the marquis de Lafayette. Name variations: Adrienne de Noailles; Dame Marie Adrienne de Lafayette; Madame de Lafayette or La Fayette. Born Marie-Adrienne-Françoise de Noailles, in Paris, France, in 1760; died in Paris, France, on December 24, 1807; *second of five daughters of the Duke and Duchess d'Ayen; married Gilbert du Motier (1757–1834), marquis de Lafayette (French aristocrat and major general who fought in the American Revolution and played a prominent role in the French Revolution), on April 11, 1774; children:* Henriette de Lafayette *(who died in infancy);* **Anastasie de Lafayette; Virginie de Lafayette;** George Washington de Lafayette.

Adrienne de Noailles was born in Paris in 1760, the second of five daughters of the Duke and Duchess d'Ayen. Five months past her 14th birthday, she married 16-year-old Gilbert du Motier, Marquis de Lafayette, a wealthy and titled orphan to whom she had been betrothed years earlier. A clause inserted in the marriage contract dictated that the couple would live with Adrienne's parents until they were old enough to have their own home, so the first years of their marriage were spent in the lavish Hôtel de Noailles, where Adrienne had spent her childhood. There, Adrienne gave birth to the couple's four children, one of whom, Henriette, died in infancy. While Adrienne cared for her children, the marquis advanced his military career, which included several periods in America, fighting with the American army in the War of Independence. Returning to a hero's welcome in 1782, the marquis de Lafayette split his brief stay between Adrienne and **Aglaé de Hunolstein,** a somewhat older admirer who had watched his rise as a public figure with growing interest and had become his mistress that spring. Gilbert barely had time for romance, however, or even to settle his family into their own home on the left bank of the Seine, before he left for a third voyage to America, quickly followed by a tour of Germany and Austria.

The middle years of Adrienne's marriage were shaped by the French Revolution, during which time her husband, no longer considered a hero, was forced to flee Paris for his life and spent five years languishing in an Austrian prison. Adrienne, clinging to her deep religious faith, passed the time within her close-knit family, attempting to win freedom for her husband while keeping out of harm's way. In June 1794, during the dark days of the Reign of Terror, she was jailed in Le Pessis in Paris, while her grandmother, mother, and sister were incarcerated at the nearby Luxembourg Palace and later executed by the guillotine. After surviving the squalid conditions of Le Pessis and the grief of losing her loved ones, Adrienne was removed to a prison infirmary in the Rue des Amandiers, where she

Marie
Adrienne
de
Lafayette
(1760–1807)

remained through the brutal winter months. She was finally released in January 1795 and, with most of her family connections scattered, took refuge with a youthful aunt, her mother's half-sister. Reuniting with her children, Adrienne once again set about freeing her husband, using money furnished by the United States.

Adrienne made the long journey to Austria with her two grown daughters, Anastasie and Virginie, her son George having left for America. Upon finally reaching the prison at Olmütz, she was given permission to live with her husband in his cramped and primitive prison barracks. As unpleasant as conditions were, it was the first time that Adrienne could claim her husband's full attention. "There was no career or adventure to beckon him across the seas," wrote **Constance Wright** in her biography *Madame de Lafayette*, "no dangerous duties to the state to call him out at all hours, no mistresses, no friends or henchmen clamoring for their share of his attention. He was hers, and hers alone." Adrienne and her daughters set up housekeeping in the barren two-room suite that would be home for several years.

Largely due to the intervention of Napoleon Bonaparte, the marquis de Lafayette was freed in September 1797, after which the family remained in Austria, not far from Hamburg, before their return to France in 1799. Back in their homeland, they took up residence at La Grange-Bléneau, a château that had been in Adrienne's family for years. Now into her 30th year of marriage, she was finally able to enjoy a life free of politics, as her husband clung to his status as a private citizen, even turning down an offer from Thomas Jefferson to govern the territory of the Louisiana Purchase.

Around 1807, Adrienne suffered a recurrence of an illness, diagnosed simply as "a dissolution of the blood," that had first stricken her at Olmütz, the symptoms of which were fever and the swelling of her arms and legs. The high fevers resulted in periods of mental confusion that would clear as suddenly as they had come. Throughout her final illness, she grew closer to her husband, to whom she expressed her love without restraint. "If you don't think you are loved enough," she told him, "you will have to blame God for my shortcomings, for He made me what I am. What a fate to have been your wife! I have loved you in the Christian sense, in the worldly sense—and passionately."

Madame de Lafayette died on Christmas Eve, 1807. The marquis de Lafayette survived her by 27 years, resuming his military career and lending a hand in the fall of Napoleon and the restoration of the Bourbons. While gaining status once again as a beloved hero, he never forgot the woman who had stood by him in darker times. He walled up her bedroom at La Grange, so visitors could not wander into it uninvited, and left everything in the room as it had been when she was alive. Some say he spent each Christmas Eve there in her company.

SOURCES:

Wright, Constance. *Madame de Lafayette*. NY: Henry Holt, 1959.

Barbara Morgan,
Melrose, Massachusetts

La Fayette, Marie-Madeleine de
(1634–1693)

French writer and memorialist whose prose work was a landmark in the history of the novel. Name variations: Marie-Madeleine Pioche de la Vergne; Madame de La Fayette; Comtesse de La Fayette; Lafayette. Born Marie-Madeleine Pioche de la Vergne in Paris on March 18, 1634; died in Paris on May 25, 1693; eldest daughter of Marc Pioche, sieur de la Vergne, and Isabelle (Péna) Pioche de la Vergne; studied Greek, Latin, and Italian in her youth; married François de Motier, count or comte de La Fayette, in 1655 (died 1683); children: Louis (b. 1658); Renaud-Armand (b. 1659).

Spent early childhood in Paris and French countryside; appointed lady-in-waiting to queen-regent Anne of Austria (1650); developed close friendship with poet Giles Ménage (1652); joined her exiled stepfather in Anjou (1653); lived with her husband and two sons in Auvergne (1655–61); returned to Paris and spent the rest of her life there (1661–1693); befriended Henrietta Anne, wife of Louis XIV's brother (1661); ran her own salon and visited the royal court frequently; published first novel anonymously (1662); formed a close relationship with the Duc de La Rochefoucauld (1660s); suffered health deterioration and died (1693).

Selected publications: La Princesse de Montpensier (1662); Zaide (1670); La Princesse de Clèves (1678); Histoire de Madame Henriette d'Angleterre (1720); La Comtesse de Tende (1724); Memoires de la cour de France (written 1688–89, published 1731). Several of her written works were published posthumously.

In April 1678, all of Paris was discussing the recently published *La Princesse de Clèves*. The novel concerned the plight of a young, unhappily married aristocratic woman, living at the court of King Henry II of France, whose love for a noble caused her great mental anguish and despair. The inclusion of emotional issues and a strong focus on the private lives of the fictional characters was unusual at this time. Nevertheless, the novel provoked much controversy and was an instant success. For several months after its publication, numerous Parisian newspapers published letters from readers who debated the motivation behind the heroine's confession to her husband of her attraction to another man. The author of this work, which is now considered to be a landmark in the history of the novel, remained anonymous, and only her closest friends knew of her literary talents. The life that Madame de La Fayette chose to expose to the world was one of devoted wife and mother rather than that of historical novelist.

Marie-Madeleine Pioche de la Vergne was born on March 18, 1634, in Paris at the Petit Luxembourg palace. Her father Marc Pioche, sieur de la Vergne, was a mathematician and military engineer, while her mother **Isabelle Péna Pioche** came from the minor nobility and was lady-in-waiting to the Duc de Richelieu's niece. Marie-Madeleine's birth was followed by two others, both girls who were later forced to give up much of their lives for their eldest sister. Their parents had strong intellectual interests and entertained several of the most important French writers, philosophers and scholars in their house on the rue de Vaugirard. Her father, however, was often absent from home on military campaigns, and increasingly more so once he became tutor to Richelieu's nephew. The entire Pioche family left Paris when the aristocratic rebellion against the crown, known as the Fronde, broke out in 1648. One year later, Marie-Madeleine's father was dead. At age 15, she was now expected to enter Parisian society and find an eligible husband.

Her mother remarried a year after Marie-Madeleine's father died. The circumstances surrounding Isabelle's marriage proved to be the first and last time that Marie-Madeleine faced public embarrassment. The significance of this event also shaped much of her later personality. When Isabelle Pioche married Renaud-René de Sévigné in December 1650, many people in Paris were surprised. They had thought that he would marry Isabelle's daughter, 16-year-old Marie-Madeleine. The embarrassment of this assumption led her to develop a strong, resourceful and independent character as well as a reluctance to show her emotions publicly. Marie-Madeleine's marriage prospects, however, were the predominant motivations behind her mother's decision to place her two younger sisters in a nunnery, thereby enlarging the eldest daughter's dowry. The search for a husband, as well as her entrance into court society, began in 1650 when Marie-Madeleine obtained a position as lady-in-waiting to the queen-regent, *Anne of Austria.

During her years at court, Marie-Madeleine met and formed two friendships that were to last for the rest of her life. Her stepfather's niece, *Marie de Sévigné, was one of Marie-Madeleine's lifelong friends, as was Giles Ménage, a cleric and poet. During the early years of their friendship, Ménage acted as her unofficial tutor by encouraging her to read widely in both French and Italian. Among his numerous publications were several poems that he dedicated to her.

Marie-Madeleine's enjoyment of court life ended abruptly in 1653, when she was forced to join her stepfather at his country estates. He had been exiled the previous year for his participation in, and loyalty to, the Fronde. Not wanting to spend his exile in solitude, Renaud-René demanded that his wife and stepdaughter accompany him. This move temporarily ruined any prospects Marie-Madeleine had for a good marriage and social career.

Although she missed the excitement of Paris and the intrigues of life at court, Marie-Madeleine was able to endure her enforced exile in the countryside by keeping in close contact with Ménage, who not only provided her with the latest gossip from Paris, but forwarded several books and poems to stimulate her intellectual curiosity. Perhaps in reaction to her enforced exile, or as a result of an increasingly cynical attitude about love and marriage, Marie-Madeleine wrote the following to Ménage in December 1653: "I am so convinced that love is unpleasant that I'm glad that my friends and I are free of it." Her words proved strangely prophetic as within two years she was married to a man whom she did not love. More significantly, the plight of unhappily married upper-class women became a predominant theme in her novels.

In the autumn of 1654, Marie-Madeleine fell seriously ill for the first time in her life. Although the details are vague, it appears that she suffered from a pain in her side and a high fever. In December, she returned to Paris with her mother where it was hoped that a cure could be found. Three months later, on February 15, 1655, Marie-Madeleine married François de Motier, comte de La Fayette, a man 18 years older than she and in poor financial circumstances. The couple had not met before December 1654, François was in danger of losing his estates, and the marriage was concluded in haste. These circumstances have led at least one historian to suggest that Marie-Madeleine may have been pregnant by another man and François agreed to marry her in return for a large down payment. For whatever reasons, Marie-Madeleine Pioche was now Madame de La Fayette and returned with her husband to his estates in Auvergne.

During the early years of her marriage, Madame de La Fayette was relatively happy. She enjoyed running her husband's household and appears to have had a satisfactory relationship with him. She kept up her correspondence with Ménage, who continued to provide her with news from Paris. Madame de La Fayette also gave birth to two sons, Louis in March 1658 and René-Armand in September 1659, to whom she remained devoted. However, her husband's financial troubles, including several lawsuits, occupied much of Madame de La Fayette's time and brought her back to Paris on several occasions between 1656 and 1659. From 1661, her return to Paris became permanent, and she took up residence in her childhood home on the rue de Vaugirard. Her husband returned to his country estates and left his wife to deal with his financial affairs. Although they remained on good terms, they never again lived together as husband and wife. By all accounts, the situation was mutually accepted.

Upon her return to permanent residence in Paris, Madame de La Fayette not only reintroduced herself into court life, but began to embark on a lengthy, albeit anonymous literary career. As a result of her friendship with *Henrietta Anne (daughter of *Henrietta Maria and Charles I of England and now wife of Philip, duke of Orleans, brother of Louis XIV), Madame de La Fayette had free access to court society. She composed the history of their friendship and memoirs of Henrietta Anne sometime between 1665 and 1670, although they were not published until 1720. At court, Madame de La Fayette was a keen observer of the rituals and etiquette that surrounded Louis XIV, known as the Sun King. In addition to running her own salon, she made frequent visits to other salons and used her experiences there to construct an accurate and incisive commentary on French court life.

Madame de La Fayette's first novel, *La Princesse de Montpensier,* was published anonymously in August 1662. That she wished her identity to remain unknown is clear from a letter she wrote to Ménage shortly after the book was released. "Happily, it is not under my name," she wrote. "I beg you, if you hear of it, to act as if you had never seen it, and to deny that it

comes from me if by any chance this were said." Her reasons for remaining anonymous were due neither to modesty nor to vanity. Rather, she knew that the constructs of her society not only discouraged court women from writing but, more important, actively disparaged those women whose work was read in the public domain, outside the confines of the court. These restrictions did not deter Madame de La Fayette's literary ambitions or her social acceptability, but did serve to keep her literary career unknown to most of Parisian society during her lifetime.

Madame de La Fayette's life at court and in salon circles enabled her to form friendships with several well-known French writers. Pierre-Daniel Huet succeeded Ménage as her mentor and friend and her second literary work, *Zaide,* published in 1670, was written jointly with the poet Segrais and François, duc de La Rochefoucauld. After the death of Henrietta Anne in 1670, Madame de La Fayette turned to de la Rochefoucauld for support. From this point on, they maintained a close friendship although the duc was 20 years her senior. It is not known if their relationship was sexual, but they certainly shared common intellectual interests; de la Rochefoucauld remained the most important person in Madame de La Fayette's life.

> Find me another woman with a figure like mine, with a taste for wit like the one you inspired in me, who has done as well for her household.
>
> —Madame de La Fayette

Following Henrietta Anne's death, Madame de La Fayette's access to the royal court declined; she attended fewer social occasions, and her health began to deteriorate. She was not a great beauty, but her wit and intelligence attracted significant scholars, poets, and writers to her salon, including Molière and Racine. Although her dislike of hypocrisy and vanity led her to be critical of others and to voice her opinions openly, she remained kind and loyal to the few people she truly loved. She continuously sought to promote and secure the careers of her sons, and was successful in obtaining several ecclesiastical appointments for Louis and military commands for René-Armand.

Madame de La Fayette's devotion to her family did not interfere with her writing. After the publication of *Zaide,* her publisher extracted a promise from her that she would write another novel. What was to become her greatest work took six years to complete. Set one hundred years before her time in the court of Henry II, *La Princesse de Clèves* tells the story of a beautiful aristocratic woman who married for social and political advancement but not for love. When she falls in love with another man, she confesses to her husband and ultimately chooses to exile herself in a convent rather than compromise her honesty and reputation. This work was one of the first novels to focus on the private and emotional lives of its protagonists. More significantly, it was one of the first works of fiction that looked at the concerns and feelings of women. The novel was a commentary on court society, the place of women, and their use of informal power within that society. *La Princesse de Clèves* revolutionized 17th-century novel writing, and Madame de La Fayette is considered to have invented the psychological novel. Through the use of interior monologues, she broke away from the action-oriented model of earlier prose fiction and replaced it with an intensely intimate portrait of court life. Based upon her personal observations of Louis XIV's court, Madame de La Fayette implied in this novel that the truly virtuous woman could remain so only by living as far away from court as possible.

Despite its new style and use of hitherto-ignored themes, the book was an instant success, although Madame de La Fayette continued to deny that she had played any role in its production. Her personal life suffered a blow when the duc de La Rochefoucauld died in 1680. Although she was devastated by the loss of her closest companion, her strength of character prevailed. Three years later, in 1683, her husband died. She took control of his estates and ensured that her sons were well taken care of. This devotion to her family, as well as her business skills, were well-known to her contemporaries, one of whom remarked: "Never has a person, without leaving her place, done such good business. See how Madame de La Fayette is rich in friends on every side and of every rank: she has a hundred arms, she reaches everywhere. Her children appreciate this and thank her daily for having such a winning nature."

In addition to the duties of family life, Madame de La Fayette continued to write. The majority of the works she composed during the later years of her life were not published until after her death. Thus, the novella she wrote sometime between 1680 and 1688, entitled *La Comtesse de Tende*, was not published until 1724. Similarly, the memoirs she wrote of court life during the years 1688 and 1689, *Memoires de la Cour de France pour les annees 1688 et 1689*, were published in 1731. Finally, the *His-*

toire de Madame Henriette d'Angleterre, which was de La Fayette's homage to her close friend, was only published in 1720.

In the remaining years of her life, Madame de La Fayette suffered from ill health, though her mind remained active. When her long-time friend Giles Ménage died in 1692, her strength began to falter. She withdrew from public life and turned to religion for solace. Her health rapidly deteriorated, and she died, at age 59, on May 25, 1693. The woman who had so changed the face of 17th-century prose fiction was buried in the church at Saint-Sulpice, the same church where she had been baptized and married.

SOURCES:

Haig, Stirling. *Madame de Lafayette*. NY: Twayne, 1970.
Levi, Anthony. "Madame de Lafayette" in *Guide to French Literature: Beginnings to 1789*. London: St. James Press, 1994.
Raitt, Janet. *Madame de Lafayette and "La Princesse de Clèves."* London: George G. Harrap, 1971.

Margaret McIntyre,
Peterborough, Ontario, Canada

La Flesche, Susan (1865–1915)

First Native American woman physician. Name variations: Susan La Flesche Picotte. Born Susan La Flesche on the Omaha Reservation in what is now Nebraska, on June 17, 1865; died in Walthill, Nebraska, on September 18, 1915; daughter of the last recognized Chief of the Omahas, Joseph La Flesche (also called Inshta'maza) of Omaha-French descent, and Mary Gale, also called Hinnuaganun, of Iowa-English descent; sister of Susette La Flesche (1854–1902), Marguerite La Flesche, and Francis La Flesche (1857–1932); attended missionary school, Elizabeth Institute of Young Ladies in Elizabeth, New Jersey, and Hampton Normal and Agriculture Institute; graduated from Women's Medical College of Pennsylvania, 1889; interned as assistant to resident physician at Women's Hospital, Philadelphia, March–August, 1889; married Henry Picotte (a mixed-blood Sioux), in 1894 (died 1905); children: Pierre Picotte; Caryl Picotte.

Attended missionary school (1870–79); student at Elizabeth Institute (1879–84); attended Hampton Normal and Agriculture Institute (1884–86); attended Women's Medical College of Pennsylvania (1886–1889); had tenure as government physician assigned to the Omaha Reservation (1889–93); began public health reform as chair of State Health Committee of Nebraska Women's Clubs, lobbied on behalf of Omaha people for public health legislation at the Nebraska State Legislature, active as a prohibitionist and legislative reformer (1897–1915).

Dedicating themselves to the Omaha people was a way of life for the La Flesche family. Susan La Flesche's parents, Joseph and **Mary Gale La Flesche**, had raised their children to revere the Omaha traditions and to become activists on behalf of the beleaguered midwestern tribes, all of whom were under the constant threat of loss of their tribal lands due to the westward expansion then under way in the United States. When Susan was only ten years old, her eldest sister, *Susette La Flesche** Tibbles, began the first of many fund-raising tours of the eastern U.S. on behalf of the Omaha-Ponca Committee.

That Susan wanted to help her people was no surprise; but to insist on a career in medicine from an early age was another matter. Few women and even fewer Native Americans had the opportunity to become physicians at the end of the 19th century. In an age when few women attended college or put a career before marriage and children, even to dream as La Flesche did was nothing short of extraordinary. One advantage of having older siblings who were nationally recognized activists was the contact it gave her with people willing to help her attain her goal. From 1879 to 1884, she followed in the footsteps of her sister at the Elizabeth Institute of Young Ladies in New Jersey. In 1886, she received notification that she had been granted financial aid to attend medical school.

Upon completion of her internship, La Flesche applied for the job of government physician assigned to the Omaha agency. She was accepted and began her tenure on August 5, 1889. For the next four years, she worked tirelessly, often in horrendous and even dangerous conditions, administering medical care to patients; she treated diseases ranging from potentially deadly influenza to dysentery, cholera, tuberculosis and measles. From October 1891 to the spring of 1892, she saw more than 600 patients. Unable to afford a horse and buggy, she often traveled the distances between patients on foot, sometimes in driving rain, freezing snow, or sub-zero weather. Never robust, she allowed her own health to become irrevocably damaged, and by 1893 she was bedridden. One of the many infections she caught eventually cost her her hearing, and she never fully regained her strength. Much to her disappointment, she was forced to resign her position because of her health in 1894, age 29.

During this time, she married Henry Picotte, a mixed-blood Sioux from the Yankton reservation and the brother of Charles Picotte, the late husband of her activist sister **Marguerite La Flesche** Diddock. La Flesche had always claimed

Susan La Flesche

that married life was not for her, and the marriage took everyone by surprise. Despite her lifelong aversion to alcohol, Henry was a hard-drinking man prone to fist fights. The couple eventually had two children, Pierre and Caryl, but the union remained difficult.

La Flesche, never healthy enough to take up her old position as a traveling physician, now turned to public-health reform. Like most tribes of the plains who had been forced to abandon their nomadic traditions, the Omahas were emotionally ill-prepared for the sedentary ways of white farmers. Government promises of much-needed farm equipment and supplies of grain were most often unkept. The result was a people stripped of their traditions and reduced to abject poverty, unable to cope in the substandard, unsanitary living conditions forced upon them, with disease easily running rampant, and alcohol consumption, always forbidden by tribal elders, making the situation infinitely worse.

Working to educate the tribal people to the causes of infection, La Flesche fought an uphill battle, since little was known at the time about how diseases were transmitted. Though the electron microscope had not yet been invented, doctors knew that such diseases as tuberculosis and influenza could be spread through use of the same drinking cup. La Flesche also campaigned against the house fly, which could aid in the spread of numerous infections, from typhoid to tuberculosis. As a result of her efforts, government agencies urged the installation of screen doors, fly traps and lime pits for outdoor toilets or garbage cans.

It was her campaign against alcohol for which La Flesche probably worked most tirelessly, lobbying the Nebraska state legislature to bar it from all reservations. To her, the "demon rum" was killing the Omaha people both physically and spiritually. Ironically, though her efforts helped to institute a ban in her hometown of Walthill, she could never convince her husband of the dangers of alcohol abuse. In 1905, Henry died as a result of excessive drinking, leaving her with two young sons to support. Eventually, she was well enough to return to a small private medical practice, funded by the Blackbird Hills Presbyterian Church, and held her position there until her death, on September 18, 1915.

SOURCES:

Green, Norma Kidd. *Iron Eye's Family: The Children of Joseph La Flesche.* Lincoln, NE: Johnson, 1969.

Mathes, Valerie Sherer. "Dr. Susan La Flesche Picotte: The Reformer and the Reformers," in *Indian Lives: Essays on Nineteenth and Twentieth Century Native American Leaders.* L.G. Moses and Raymond Wilson, eds. Albuquerque, NM: University of New Mexico Press, 1895, pp. 61–90.

SUGGESTED READING:

La Flesche, Susan. "My Childhood and Womanhood, Salutatory by Susan La Flesche, of the Graduating Class," in *Southern Workman.* July 1886.

COLLECTIONS:

La Flesche Family Papers (LFP), Nebraska State Historical Society, Lincoln, Nebraska.

Deborah Jones,
freelance writer, Studio City, California

La Flesche, Susette (1854–1902)

Native American (Omaha-Iowa) writer and political activist who worked on behalf of her nation. Name variations: Inshtatheamba or Inshtatheumba (means Bright Eyes); Susette LaFlesche; Susette La Flesche Tibbles. Born Inshtatheamba also called Susette La Flesche in 1854, on Omaha tribal lands south of the settlement that became Omaha, Nebraska; died in Bancroft, Nebraska, in May 1902; daughter of Joseph La Flesche, also called Inshta'maza, of Omaha-French descent and the last chief of the Omaha Nation, and Mary Gale, also called Hinnuaganun, of Iowa-English descent; sister of Susan La Flesche (1865–1915), Mar-

guerite La Flesche, and Francis La Flesche (1857–1932); attended missionary school, 1860–69, and Elizabeth Institute of Young Ladies, Elizabeth, New Jersey, 1871–75; married Thomas Tibbles, July 23, 1881; no children.

Began teaching on the Omaha reservation (1877); went on first East Coast lecture and fund-raising tour and was the first woman to speak at Faneuil Hall in Boston (1879); testified before Senate subcommittee and went on second lecture and fund-raising tour (1880); published Nedawi, *first children's story, and helped to petition Congress on behalf of Omaha nation regarding land grants (1883–84); made lecture tour to England (1887–88); moved with husband to Washington, D.C., became a correspondent for* The Non-Conformist, *and published additional children's stories (1893); moved with husband to Lincoln, Nebraska, wrote articles and editorials for* Weekly Independent *(1894–99); illustrated* Oo-mah-ha Ta-wa-tha, *stories of the Omahas, written by* Fannie Reed Griffen, *believed to be the first published illustrations by a Native American.*

Though the "Indian question" was hotly debated throughout the United States in 1879, no one expected the guest speaker at St. Paul's Episcopal Church in Omaha to attract such a large crowd. Among the curious was Thomas Tibbles, a maverick journalist who had recently taken up the Indian cause. In town at the invitation of Bishop Clarkson, head of the Omaha-Ponca Committee, Thomas was doubtful about the cleric's bold, perhaps even foolhardy, move in persuading the English-speaking daughter of the Omaha chief Joseph La Flesche to lecture on behalf of her tribe and its closest allies, the Poncas.

That a woman dared to stand up in the pulpit was radical enough in 1879. This one, moreover, was an Indian, educated or not, and for all his good intentions Tibbles held a typically chauvinistic view toward Native American women. In Tibbles' opinion, the timing of the speech, as well, could not have been worse. With members of the territorial legislature debating laws regarding their Indian "wards," any adverse publicity might push the lawmakers to do exactly what Tibbles feared: expel all native nations from Nebraska.

A hush fell over the waiting audience as the bishop stepped in front of the other ministers gathered on the platform. Bidding the gathering welcome, he voiced his hope that the speaker would be heard with an open heart. To his apparent surprise, the audience then gave a standing ovation to the 25-year-old Omaha woman he introduced as "Miss Bright Eyes." The name was a translation of "Inshtatheamba," her Omaha name, and only half of the name she went by; she was also known as Susette La Flesche—a dual name for the dual identity that was a source of both joy and torment throughout this young woman's life.

Tiny, with huge dark eyes, the speaker accepted the warm welcome in a calm, dignified manner. She gripped the podium for a full minute and silently stared into the sea of white faces, while the people settled more deeply into the church pews. Thomas Tibbles felt his throat go dry, assuming she would not be able to summon the courage to speak. Then came the voice, at first barely audible, but rising as her fear gave way to passion, as Bright Eyes spoke on behalf of the desire of her people to stay in their traditional homelands—as moving and eloquent a speech as any Tibbles had heard. Ever the journalist, he began to take notes; at the end, the audience went wild.

The event was so successful, in fact, that the Omaha-Ponca Committee wanted a change of plans. Their original idea had been to send Thomas Tibbles on a lecture and fund-raising tour around the East, to gain the support of sympathetic whites for the plight of the Indians. With Bright Eyes such an obvious speaking success, why not send her as well? She had been educated in white schools, including a prestigious women's college in the East, and was the ideal person to speak to whites from a native perspective in a way they could understand. In addition, her uncle, the Ponca chief Standing Bear, was set to accompany Tibbles and required an interpreter. The young woman viewed this turn of events with panic. One speech had been terrifying enough. Plans were still under discussion when news came of a bill introduced into the U.S. Congress proposing to put all Indians under control of the Department of the Interior. White resentment and anger against Indians had been growing since the glaring military defeat of George Amstrong Custer by the Sioux three years before. Unless public sympathy for the tribes could be aroused, the Omaha people were at risk of being rounded up and shoved onto alien reservation land.

For generations before the 1854 birth of Susette La Flesche, white traders in North America had been marrying into Native American tribes and raising families according to native custom; her paternal grandfather had been a French fur trapper, and her maternal grandfather an English army surgeon. But by the mid-

1850s, the pressure of white invaders seeking to push the Native Americans off tribal lands was causing such intermarriages to be looked upon with increasing disfavor by most whites and some natives. The personal conflict of this young woman over her mixed heritage was to become inextricably intertwined with the struggle between an ever-more aggressive U.S. government and native nations. On a collision course for nearly 200 years, the once "liberal" attitude of "kill the savage, keep the man" was losing ground to the proponents of a deadlier, more final solution. The blunt view of the U.S. general George Sherman that "the only good Indian I've seen is dead" had become the chilling reality of wholesale slaughter of native women and children, taking place at the hands of the U.S. Cavalry at the very time Susette La Flesche was pleading their case. In the fall of 1879, she set out on the lecture circuit with Thomas Tibbles, Standing Bear, and her younger half-brother, Francis La Flesche, fully aware of the importance of rallying support for their cause. With-

Susette La Flesche

out it, the Omaha and Poncas faced the same fate that had been suffered by the Cherokee nation in 1838, when its survivors were driven from the Carolinas along the infamous "Trail of Tears." Those who did not die on the forced march were confined in Indian Territory, "the land of the heat" that is the modern state of Oklahoma. Now an unsympathetic Republican administration was threatening to crowd her people onto that same occupied land.

To the lecture audiences, La Flesche often spoke lovingly about her childhood among the Omahas, a peaceful tribe who had for 450 years occupied the same homelands, in what became Nebraska, Kansas, and Iowa. By the time of her birth, her people had already ceded part of their lands to the United States, but enough tribal land remained for the buffalo to roam freely. Like most nomadic plains tribes, the Omahas were dependent on the buffalo herds for virtually everything in their daily lives—food, clothing, weapons—and their religious ceremonies revolved around the great beasts. Always introduced as Bright Eyes, she told her enraptured white audiences about the ancient traditions of the buffalo hunt, and vision quests, and the yearning of her people to remain free on their lands.

She did all she could to make the world happier and better.

—Thomas Tibbles

Through La Flesche's eyes, her audience witnessed the horror she grew up with, watching the old ways systematically destroyed. In a mere 25 years, most of the buffalo had been exterminated, as treaty after treaty had been broken; her tribespeople died in smallpox and influenza epidemics brought by the white settlers; those who managed to survive disease faced persecution by intolerant missionaries for their religious beliefs. Again and again, she asked how such injustices could have been inflicted on the Omaha and Ponca nations, when her people had been willing to peacefully coexist with whites.

Years before, her father Joseph La Flesche, the last recognized Omaha chief, had seen what lay ahead for his people. The son of a French fur trader and an Omaha woman, Joseph had been named chief by Big Elk, his adopted Omaha father and long-time head of the tribe, and had become a controversial leader. Understanding that the white invasion was never going to end, he insisted that the Omahas' survival depended upon their learning the ways of the whites. What he failed to recognize was that there were "civilized" whites, many of whom occupied power positions among the Washington capital's elite, with a hidden agenda that involved the total annihilation of the "red savages." Over the protests of his more traditional Omaha brothers, Joseph sent his two eldest children, Susette and Louis La Flesche, to a missionary school. He understood that his children's learning English would enable them to read and interpret future treaties so that the Omahas might never again be cheated. Susette was one of several remarkable siblings, including a sister, *Susan La Flesche Picotte, who would become the first Native American woman physician; Francis La Flesche, an anthropologist, and Marguerite La Flesche Diddock, a reformer.

Susette had been five years old when she was sent away to the white missionaries' boarding school. Her only comfort was the fact that her older brother, Louis, was already there. Boys and girls at the school were segregated, but she could see her brother playing in the adjacent schoolyard. Although she never understood why she and other children were beaten if they dared speak the Omaha language, she was a bright child and liked school. She quickly learned English and developed a passionate love for books that was to last a lifetime.

The narrow-minded attitude of the Christian missionaries toward Omaha religious beliefs was something that remained with La Flesche until the day she died. In her lectures, she often spoke of Louis, who had already been on his first vision quest when he entered the mission and was harshly punished at one point for having participated in a "heathen" ceremony. Bitterly, Louis asked his sister why, if the Biblical Isaiah was deemed a prophet after having a vision, an Omaha who had experienced a vision was deemed heathen? Shortly after this incident, Louis contracted an unexplained illness and died within a few days, leaving his sister devastated. Away from home, and with her remaining siblings still too young for the school, the quiet child became even more reclusive. For years, her only solace was in her studies.

In 1869, when Susette was 15, the "peace policy" of President Ulysses S. Grant was enacted. In the name of maintaining "civilization," all tribal governments were dissolved and all native nations were to be segregated onto reservations, by force if necessary. Because native children were not allowed to leave the reservations, the missionary schools were closed and Susette was sent home. It was a terrible time for the young girl, who found her chieftain father mired in tribal conflicts, and the fate of her people uncertain. As well, she had difficulty discerning her own identity. Was she Inshtatheamba, an Omaha girl who should be looking for a husband, or Susette La Flesche, the young woman with dreams of becoming a teacher?

After three years, her prayers seemed to be answered when La Flesche, now 18, was given the rare opportunity, through a teacher from the missionary school, to attend a private college for young women in the East. Joseph La Flesche, convinced that her education would ultimately benefit the tribe, allowed her to go. For the next four years, she studied at the Elizabeth Institute of Young Ladies in New Jersey, a time she considered wonderful, though it did nothing to ease her conflicted identity. Away at school, she missed her tribe and family; during her vacations, she longed to be back with her white friends at school.

In 1875, La Flesche was 21 when she graduated as a fully qualified teacher. However, the fact that she was also "Indian" made her a "ward of the state." Uniquely skilled to teach at a reservation "day" school, she found that the Omaha Bureau of Indian Affairs (BIA) agent absolutely refused to hire her, even though his refusal was against government policy. When she wrote the BIA commissioner threatening to publicize the failure of the agent to implement the bureau's own policy of giving preference to a qualified Indian over a white employee, her point was recognized. In 1877, she was hired as an assistant teacher, at half the salary paid the white staff.

Nevertheless, La Flesche loved teaching. She would probably have been content to spend the rest of her life occupied with her students and her books, had it not been for the crisis in 1879. With the remaining homelands of the Omahas at risk, her father too ill to fight, her older brother dead, and her other siblings still too young, it fell on her to speak for the tribe to the white people at St. Paul's Episcopal Church, beginning a crusade that was to last for the next nine years.

Criss-crossing the country, La Flesche gave hundreds of speeches, raised money for the Ponca-Omaha Committee, and lobbied before the U.S. Congress at every opportunity. Received as Bright Eyes in some of the most prestigious homes in the East, she eventually included Henry Wadsworth Longfellow, Samuel Clemens (Mark Twain), Ralph Waldo Emerson and *Harriet Beecher Stowe among her patrons. Eventually, her main supporter was Thomas Tibbles, 15 years her senior. A widower with grown children, he was one of the most outspoken

white men of his generation. The two were temperamental opposites, but Tibbles, like Susette's father, was a steadfast fighter on behalf of Native American rights. She was 27 when they were married in July 1881.

The two had been on the road together stumping for fair treatment of natives for two years, and so the marriage changed their lives very little. There was still much to be done, starting with a petition to be sent to Congress, asking the government to irrevocably grant a section of land for the Omahas. The major thrust of their lobbying efforts resulted in the passage of the Dawes Act in 1887. In retrospect, the Dawes Act was far from perfect, but, given the alternatives, it seemed the best course of action at the time. The Act provided for the general allotment of native lands, by which each family head received 160 acres, single persons over 18 and orphans under 18 were given 80 acres, and 40 acres went to single persons under 18. What everyone except diehard traditionalists failed to recognize was that native communities were just that— communities. All possessions, all land, had traditionally been held in common. Dividing up the land, which native belief says cannot be owned, only served to further destroy the culture. Once this land came under state jurisdiction, it also became subject to property taxes, which few natives could afford. By the mid-1920s, most "allotment land" had either been foreclosed upon by the various states for back taxes or had been swindled from the natives by greedy whites.

For La Flesche and Tibbles, however, passage of the Dawes Act meant their efforts had paid off. The couple settled in Washington, D.C., where Tibbles turned his endeavors to the Populist Party and La Flesche started to write, first as a reporter for *The Non-Conformist,* a Washington-based weekly, and later as a writer of short stories based on her childhood. Published in a children's magazine called *Wide Awake,* these works are some of the most realistic descriptions of native life ever to reach print.

After a few years in Washington, La Flesche wanted to return home to her family. In 1894, she and Tibbles moved back to Nebraska, where he took a job as an editor of the *Weekly Independent* and she often worked as a contributing writer. She never became reconciled to her dual identity, as Inshtatheamba—Bright Eyes—to her family but Susette La Flesche, teacher and organizer, to her college chums and the literary community. As Mrs. Thomas Tibbles, reporter, in the growing state of Nebraska, she still felt a part of two worlds and never completely at ease and happy in either one. At age 48, she died after a brief illness at her home in Bancroft, Nebraska, with her husband by her side. On her tombstone, he had both names—Susette La Flesche and Bright Eyes—inscribed, along with the epitaph: "She did all she could to make the world happier and better."

SOURCES:

Bataille, Gretchen M., and Kathleen Sands. *American Indian Women: A Guide to Research.* NY: Garland, 1991.

Green, Norma Kidd. *Iron Eye's Family: The Children of Joseph La Flesche.* Lincoln, NE: Johnson, 1969.

Wilson, Dorothy Clarke. *Bright Eyes: The Story of Susette La Flesche.* NY: McGraw-Hill, 1974.

SUGGESTED READING:

Clark, Jerry C., and Martha Ellen Webb. "Susette and Susan La Flesche: Reformer and Missionary," in *Being and Becoming Indian: Biographical Studies of North American Frontiers.* Edited by James A. Clifton. Chicago, IL: Dorsey Press, 1989, pp. 137–159.

La Flesche, Susette. "The Indian Question," in *Christian Union.* Vol. 21, no. 100. March 10, 1880, pp. 222–223.

COLLECTIONS:

La Flesche Family Papers, Nebraska State Historical Society, Lincoln, Nebraska.

Tibbles Papers (MS 1644), Nebraska State Historical Society.

Deborah Jones,
freelance writer, Studio City, California

La Follette, Belle Case (1859–1931)

American social reformer who was the wife and associate of politician Robert M. La Follette. Name variations: Belle Case; Belle Case LaFollette. Born Belle Case in Summit, Wisconsin, on April 21, 1859; died in Washington, D.C., on August 18, 1931; one of six children (three of whom did not survive infancy) of Anton T. Case and Mary (Nesbit) Case; attended public school in Baraboo, Sauk County, Wisconsin; graduated from the University of Wisconsin, 1879; received law degree from the University of Wisconsin Law School, 1885; married Robert Marion La Follette, Sr. (1855–1925, a congressional representative, senator, and presidential candidate), on December 31, 1881; children: Fola La Follette (b. 1882); Robert Marion La Follette, Jr. (1895–1953, who served as a senator for 22 years); Philip Fox La Follette (b. 1897); Mary La Follette (b. 1899).

Born in a log cabin in Summit, Wisconsin, in 1859, Belle Case was educated in public school in Baraboo, Sauk County, Wisconsin, where her family moved when she was three. She graduated from the classical course at the University of Wisconsin in 1879 and taught school for two years before marrying a college classmate, Robert M. La Follette, a young lawyer. The couple settled in Madison and began a family which eventually grew to include four children. Through her husband, La Follette became interested in law, and in 1883 she entered the University of Wisconsin Law School. She became the first woman to receive a law degree from that institution (1885) and was subsequently admitted to the bar and to the Wisconsin supreme court. Although La Follette never practiced law, she used her expertise to assist her husband during his three terms in the House of Representatives (1885–91). Serving as his secretary and administrative assistant, she played an unusually active role in her husband's public life, prompting him to call her his "wisest and best counsellor."

From 1890, when Robert was defeated in his fourth congressional run, to 1900, when he was elected governor of Wisconsin, the couple lived out of the public eye. During this period, La Follette took up her own political causes, many of which involved suffrage and protective legislation for women and children. It was her opinion that women could improve their lives by participating in the political process, an approach which brought her in contact with other activist women, including ***Jane Addams**, ***Florence Kelley**, ***Julia Clifford Lathrop**, ***Mary Eliza McDowell**, and ***Elizabeth Glendower Evans**. When her husband became governor, La Follette joined him in shaping a series of progressive administrative and legislative reforms which became nationally recognized as the "Wisconsin Idea" or "progressivism."

In 1906, Robert La Follette was elected to the U.S. Senate, and the couple returned to Washington. In 1909, they created *La Follette's Weekly Magazine*, for which Belle edited the "Women and Education Department," writing articles on women's issues and on Washington's political and social life. Possessing a lively literary style, she sought both to report on social trends and to influence them. From 1911 to 1912, she also wrote a column for the North American Press Syndicate.

As a senate wife and official host, La Follette was instrumental in organizing the Congressional Club of Washington, activities of which replaced the traditional round of official calls. She became active in the final push for women's suffrage, giving speeches and working on campaigns in Wisconsin, Nebraska, North Dakota, and Oregon. In 1913, at her husband's behest, she spoke on behalf of women's suffrage before the Senate Committee on Suffrage. As an ally of Jane Addams, La Follette was an ardent proponent of peace and one of the organizers of the Women's International League for Peace and Freedom. In 1921, she helped found the National Council for the Prevention of War and was also a leader in the Women's Committee for World Disarmament.

Belle La Follette was active in her husband's campaign for the presidency in 1924. Robert La Follette, who ran on the third party Progressive ticket with Burton K. Wheeler as his running mate, was defeated by incumbent Calvin Coolidge. Upon her husband's death in 1925, La Follette was encouraged to fill his unexpired term in the Senate (as was not uncommon for widows of serving senators and congressmen) but declined. Instead, at the age of 30, her son Robert La Follette, Jr., made a successful bid to complete his father's unexpired term, becoming the youngest senator since Henry Clay. He would serve 22 years. Although always in the shadow of his father's forceful personality, he was a conscientious legislator and functioned as a transitional figure in the history of modern reform movements, achieving national attention during the Great Depression as one of the first to develop a coherent plan for combating declining purchasing power. He was defeated in 1946 by Joseph R. McCarthy (of Communist witch-hunt fame). Preoccupied by poor health and suffering from anxiety and depression, La Follette, Jr., would commit suicide on February 24, 1953.

Belle La Follette continued to advance the Progressive movement by assuming the associate editorship of *La Follette's Magazine* and by preparing her husband's biography, a project that was ultimately completed by her daughter **Fola La Follette**. Belle died unexpectedly in 1931, following an operation for an intestinal obstruction, and was buried beside her husband in Forest Hills Cemetery in Madison, Wisconsin. In her obituary, *The New York Times* praised her as "the most influential of all American women who had to do with public affairs in this country."

SOURCES:

James, Edward T., ed. *Notable American Women, 1607–1950.* Cambridge, MA: The Belknap Press of Harvard University Press, 1971.

SUGGESTED READING:

Case, Belle, and Fola La Follette. *La Follette.* Macmillan, 1953.

Greenbaum, Fred. *Robert Marion La Follette.* Twayne, 1975.

La Follette, Robert M. *La Follette's Autobiography: A Personal Narrative of Political Experiences.* University of Wisconsin Press, 1911, 1913.

Link, Arthur S. and Richard L. McCormick. *Progressivism.* Harlan Davidson, 1983.

Maney, Patrick. *"Young Bob" La Follette: A Biography of Robert M. La Follette, Jr., 1895–1953.* University of Missouri Press, 1978.

Thelen, David. *The Early Life of Robert M. La Follette, 1855–1884.* Loyola University Press, 1966.

———. *Robert M. La Follette and the Insurgent Spirit.* Little, Brown, 1976.

Unger, Nancy C. "The Righteous Reformer: A Life History of Robert M. La Follette, Sr., 1855–1925." Ph.D. dissertation, University of Southern California, 1985.

Barbara Morgan,
Melrose, Massachusetts

Lafont, Bernadette (1938—)

French actress. Born in Nimes, France, on October 26, 1938; children: Pauline Lafont (d. 1988, an actress).

Selected films: (short) Les Mistons (The Mischief-Makers, *1958);* Le Beau Serge *(1958);* A Double Tour (Leda *or* Web of Passion, *1959);* L'Eau à la Bouche (A Game for Six Lovers, *1960);* Les Bonnes Femmes *(1960);* Les Godelureaux *(1961);* Tire-au-Flanc (The Army Game, *1961);* La Chasse à l'Homme (Male Hunt, *1964);* Compartiment Tueurs (The Sleeping Car Murder, *1965);* Le Voleur (The Thief, *1967);* Lost Generation (Walls, Hun., *1967);* Piège *(1969);* La Fiancée du Pirate (A Very Curious Girl, *1969);* Valparaiso Valparaiso *(1970);* Catch Me a Spy (UK/Fr., *1971);* Une Belle Fille comme moi (Such a Gorgeous Kid Like Me, *1972);* La Maman et la Putain (The Mother and the Whore, *1973);* Tendre Dracula *(1974);* Zig Zig (Zig-Zag, *1975);* Vincent mit l'Ane dans un Pré *(1975);* L'Ordinateur des Pompes funèbres *(1976);* Un Type comme moi ne derrait jamais mourir *(1976);* Le Trouble-Fesses *(1976);* Noroit *(1977);* La Tortue sur le Dos (Like a Turtle on Its Back, *1978);* Violette Nozière (Violette, *1978);* Chaussette surprise *(1978);* Certaines Nouvelles *(1979);* La Gueule de L'autre *(1979);* Il Ladrone (The Thief, It./Fr. *1980);* Retour en Force *(1980);* Le Roi des Cons *(1981);* Cap Canaille *(1983);* La Bête Noire *(1983);* Gwendoline (The Perils of Gwendoline in the Land of the Yik Yak, *1984);* Le Pactole *(1985);* L'Affrontée *(1985);* Inspecteur Lavardin *(1986);* Masques *(1987);* Waiting for the Moon (US, *1987);* Les Saisons du Plaisir (The Seasons of Pleasure, *1988);* Prisonnières *(1988);* L'Air de rien *(1989);* Boom Boom (Sp., *1990).*

Bernadette Lafont was born in Nimes, France, in 1938. Originally a dancer, she began to appear in films in the late 1950s and became associated with the French New Wave, particularly the films of Claude Chabrol who specialized in quirky thrillers. She is still a popular film actress in France and in European co-productions. Her daughter, **Pauline Lafont**, an actress with a promising future, was killed in a fall from a cliff in 1988, at age 26.

Laforet, Carmen (1921—)

Spanish writer whose novels depict the quest for self-fulfillment following the Spanish Civil War. Name variations: Carmen Laforet Diaz. Born in Barcelona, Spain, in 1921; married Manuel González Cerezales, in 1946 (separated 1970); children: Marta Cerezales; Cristina Cerezales; Silvia Cerezales; Manuel Cerezales; Agustín Cerezales.

Born in Barcelona in 1921, Carmen Laforet soon moved to Las Palmas, in the Canary Islands, where her father worked as an architect. The family returned to Spain only in 1939, and Carmen thus missed the great upheaval during the 1930s, when Spain was convulsed by the Second Republic and the horrific Civil War (1936–39). She studied philosophy and law at the University of Barcelona but did not graduate. In 1942, she moved to Madrid, a city still ravaged by the fighting of the war.

Two years later, Laforet published her first novel, *Nada* (*Nothing*), written between January and September of 1944. It won the Nadal Prize and helped move Spanish literature away from baroque prose to simple, direct phrasing and mundane, existentialist themes found in daily life. At the same time, as the title indicates, it spoke to the emptiness, violence, and futility of life in a Spain traumatized by family and civil strife. *Nada* remains her most highly regarded novel and helped establish *tremendismo* as a Spanish literary movement, portraying an exaggerated realism emphasizing both psychological and physical violence.

In early 1946, Laforet married Manuel González Cerezales, a journalist, and gave birth to their first child that November. Marriage and motherhood limited the time and energy she could give to writing, and for three years she wrote almost nothing. When she took up her pen again, Laforet wrote for newspapers and magazines, published short stories, and began work on a new novel.

Later books included *La isla y los demonios* (*The Island and Its Devils*, 1952), *La llamada* (*The Vocation*, 1954), *La mujer nueva* (*The New Woman*, 1955), *La insolación* (*Sunstroke*, 1963),

Mis páginas mejores (1967), and *Paralelo 35* (1967). She converted to Roman Catholicism in 1951, and some of her later works analyzed female religiosity. The story of an adulteress' religious conversion, *La mujer nueva* earned the Menorca Prize and the National Literature Prize.

SOURCES:

Cerezales, Agustín. *Carmen Laforet*. Madrid: Ministerio de Cultura, Dirección General de Promoción del Libro y la Cinematografía, 1982.

Illanes Adaro, Graciela. *La novelística de Carmen Laforet*. Madrid: Gredos, 1971.

Johnson, Roberta. *Carmen Laforet*. Boston: Twayne Publishers, 1981.

Kendall W. Brown,
Professor of History, Brigham Young University, Provo, Utah

LaForge, Margaret Getchell (1841–1880)

American businesswoman who was manager of Macy's during the department store's early years. Born Margaret Getchell on July 16, 1841, on Nantucket Island, Massachusetts; died on January 25, 1880, in New York City; daughter of Barzillai (or Barzilla) Getchell and Phebe Ann (Pinkham) Getchell; married Abiel LaForge (a buyer), on March 27, 1869 (died 1878); children: six.

Born and raised on the island of Nantucket, Massachusetts, Margaret Getchell LaForge finished school at 16 and began a teaching career in her hometown. She moved on to positions in Lansingburgh, New York, and at the Lawrenceville Female Seminary in New Jersey, before leaving the profession to work for her distant relative Rowland Macy, who had recently opened a dry goods store in New York City. (According to one source, LaForge left teaching because she had lost an eye and needed employment that would be less taxing on her vision.)

LaForge began as a cashier, but soon displayed an astounding aptitude for figures and was promoted to bookkeeper. In this position, she was responsible for training the "cash girls," and came to be known as demanding but extremely fair in her dealings. Her expertise apparently extended beyond accounting and management to other aspects of the business, and Macy grew to trust her judgment. LaForge convinced him to distinguish his store from others by using his trademark, a five-pointed star, on the letterhead and on price tags. She spotted new trends and suggested new products such as jewelry, sterling silver, gifts, and clocks, all of which became separate departments in the store. Her home furnishings department, including kitchenware and cleaning supplies, became particularly popular with women shoppers. To lure people into the store, LaForge created interesting window displays, and, when soda fountains became the rage in Europe, she established a marble-and-nickel-plated fountain in the center of the store, routing thirsty shoppers past numerous counters of enticing merchandise. By 1866, Macy had such faith in LaForge that he made her superintendent of his growing enterprise, thus freeing himself for buying trips abroad.

In 1869, Margaret Getchell married Abiel T. LaForge, a new buyer employed by Macy. Abiel had served with Macy's son in the Union Army. The couple set up housekeeping over the store and began a family. In 1871, Macy made Abiel a partner, after which Margaret worked without compensation. Although child rearing forced her to curtail her hours somewhat, she continued in the store part time, often laboring on inventory and accounts at night. (When she was pregnant with her third child, the partners left her in charge while they went to Europe on a three-month buying trip.) Abiel LaForge contracted tuberculosis and died in 1878. Margaret fell ill just two years later and died of a combination of ailments which included heart failure and an inflammation of the ovary.

SOURCES:
Bird, Caroline. *Enterprising Women.* NY: W.W. Norton, 1976.
James, Edward T., ed. *Notable American Women, 1607–1950.* Cambridge, MA: The Belknap Press of Harvard University Press, 1971.

SUGGESTED READING:
Hower, Ralph M. *History of Macy's of N.Y., 1858–1919,* 1943.

Barbara Morgan,
Melrose, Massachusetts

Lagerlöf, Selma (1858–1940)

Swedish author of numerous novels, short stories and tales who was the first woman to receive the Nobel Prize for Literature. Name variations: Selma Lagerlof. Born Selma Ottilia Lovisa Lagerlöf on November 20, 1858, at the modest manor house of Maarbacka in Värmland, a district in central Sweden, west of Stockholm; died at Maarbacka on March 16, 1940; fourth of five children of Erik Gustav Lagerlöf and Lovisa (Wallroth) Lagerlöf; attended the Royal Women's Superior Training College, Stockholm; never married; no children.

Enrolled in a teachers' training college in Stockholm (1881); on graduation, was hired as a teacher in the southern Swedish town of Landscrona, where she started her writing career as well; following the suc-

cess of The Story of Gösta Berling (1891), resigned her post and became a full-time writer; revenues from that novel and subsequent works enabled her to buy back her childhood home, Maarbacka, which had been auctioned off (1889); received an honorary doctorate from the University of Uppsala (1907), followed by the Nobel Prize (1909), first Swede and first woman to be honored thus; purchased the property surrounding Maarbacka that had been in the family for generations and resumed the position of landed gentry; was keynote speaker at the International Congress of Women (1911); accepted into the Swedish Academy (1914), the first and only female member.

Selected works: The Story of Gösta Berling *(1891);* Invisible Links *(1894);* The Miracles of Antichrist *(1897);* The Queens of Kungahalla and Other Sketches *(1897);* The Tale of a Manor *(1899);* Jerusalem *(1901–02);* Herr Arne's Hoard *(1903);* Christ Legends *(1904);* The Wonderful Adventures of Nils *(1906–07);* A Saga about a Saga and Other Tales *(1908);* Liljekrona's Home *(1911);* Thy Soul Shall Bear Witness *(1912);* The Emperor of Portugalia *(1914);* Trolls and Men *(2 vols., 1916, 1921);* The Outcast *(1918);* Zachris Topelius *(1920);* Maarbacka *(1922);* The Ring of the Lövenskolds *(1925–28);* Memories of My Childhood *(1930);* The Diary of

$\mathscr{S}$elma
$\mathscr{L}$agerlöf

Selma Lagerlöf *(1932)*; Autumn *(1933)*; Writings and Re-writings *(1933)*.

"When I was five years old," writes Selma Lagerlöf in the opening of *Christ Legends*, "I experienced a great sorrow, so great I have experienced none greater since." She was referring to the death of her grandmother who, until then, had sat on the corner sofa telling stories from morning to night for the enjoyment of Selma and her siblings. "I remember that when she had told a story," continues Lagerlöf, "she would lay her hand on my head and say, 'And all I have told you is just as true as it is that I can see you and you can see me.'" At her grandmother's death, Lagerlöf felt as if something had been cut out of life. The door to a grand and enchanted world where the children had wandered in and out had been locked, and no one had a key. The young Selma had to wait for an older Selma to find the key to the world of imagination and reclaim its inhabitants, but the latter knew the place to look: Maarbacka, the family estate in the region of Värmland.

Lagerlöf was tied with unseverable bonds to her childhood home, a crucial departure point for her writing, and the seat of the only family she expected to have. At age three and a half, she had suffered a bout of temporary paralysis which left her with a chronic limp. She had to walk with care and early on came to consider herself unfit for the mating dance. She therefore thought it necessary to choose a career other than that of wife and mother. According to her notes written at the time of her 50th birthday, the child Selma knew from the time she was seven that she wanted above all to eventually write novels. She started by writing poems for family occasions, and one of those, a celebratory rhymed speech delivered at the wedding of relatives, brought her to the attention of a guest, author **Eva Fryxell**. Fryxell encouraged the young Värmland girl to submit her best poems for possible publication in a Stockholm paper. Though the poems were returned, Fryxell prevailed on Selma's father to send his daughter to Stockholm to prepare herself for matriculation at the Teachers' College for Women. Lagerlöf graduated three years later and, in her first assignment at the High School for Girls in Landscrona, proved herself a gifted teacher. In one of her students' memoirs, Lagerlöf is described as eagerly open to suggestions and yet full of clear explanations and imaginative expression. A born storyteller, she lectured so engagingly that her pupils forgot they were in school and sighed at the sound of the bell.

Much as she loved to impart the words and knowledge of others, Lagerlöf did not forget that her life's work was to be her own writing. Her opportunity to prove her talents came in the spring of 1890, when the women's publication *Idun* invited submissions for a fiction contest. At her sister's instigation, Selma submitted five chapters of a work in progress. It had already occurred to her, while attending school in Stockholm, that in the oral traditions of Värmland she had material as rich and varied as any that had been available to the Swedish romantic poets she admired. Lagerlöf had started writing the folk tales and sagas handed down by her grandmother and others, but she found it impossible to give them expression in the existing literary conventions of realism and naturalism, as dictated by August Strindberg and Émile Zola. Then, she had happened upon Thomas Carlyle's *Hero and Hero-worship* in her school library and found a literary model she could use. Reading the book, she was convinced that she, too, could write from the heart and, like Carlyle, tell what she knew with passion and enthusiasm. This intellectual discovery had been given emotional impetus by what she thought would be her last visit to Maarbacka, which was to be sold at a public auction. The loss of the place to which she was rooted impressed upon her the necessity of preserving the spirit of Värmland and its inhabitants with words. Thus she had written several chapters when the *Idun* contest was brought to her attention. Those chapters brought her a first prize; then a friend found means to secure her a year's leave of absence from school and a place in which to finish the book. It was published by *Idun* in 1891 as *The Story of Gösta Berling*.

In a later essay about the origin of the novel, Lagerlöf describes her role in its creation as that of a "medium" through whom events taking place in the Värmland countryside were given to the world. They are an odd mixture of tales, she writes, "a formless cloud of adventures, which drifted back and forth like a swarm of stray bees on a summer's day, not knowing where they might find someone who could gather them into a hive."

Lagerlöf's double image of herself as "medium" and "gatherer" is striking, and describes her activities as both woman and artist. At the time of this essay, she had repurchased Maarbacka with money earned from the publication of her books. Thus, her works had been the medium through which she could gather together not only the manor house and outlying buildings but eventually the entire surrounding property. Selma, the industrious gatherer, had reclaimed what her father, the swashbuckling hunter Erik Gustav Lagerlöf, had squandered. Lagerlöf's bi-

Selma Lagerlöf

ographers are in agreement that the loss of Maarbacka, though partly due to difficult economic times, was caused primarily by the extravagance and increasing incompetence of its owner. They describe Erik Lagerlöf as a gentleman farmer with progressive ideas which often failed in exe-

cution. His children—at least initially—adored their brilliant father who loved parties and open houses, songs, dances, pageants, speeches, theatricals and illuminations. He is the central character in Lagerlöf's childhood recollections, the revered father who gradually loses his power as she loses her expectations of that power and learns to recognize and control her own.

This shift in reliance from total dependence on her father, and the paternalistic rule he represented, to confidence in her own ability to provide is demonstrated in Lagerlöf's Nobel Prize acceptance speech which she styled as a conversation with her father in heaven. She has come to ask him, she begins, how she may repay an enormous debt. She shows him concerned at first that she is referring to money, but he regains composure when he understands that she is talking about gratitude towards those who have made her work possible. Her gesture *vis-a-vis* her father honors his position in her life: to him she owes all that makes life worth living, intense joy and unparalleled experience, but grief and barely sustainable loss as well. It fell to her, she implies, to reclaim the home and the land he had lost, which hard work and discipline in the service of the word had accomplished. She had done both of them honor and atoned for whatever guilt she may have experienced at leaving Maarbacka in its declining years.

In *The Story of Gösta Berling,* Lagerlöf pits guilt, responsibility, and loyalty against spontaneity and self-indulgence. The hero Gösta Berling, an unfrocked priest, is young, strong, handsome, and irresistible to women. He lodges with 11 other pensioners at Ekeby, ruled by the strong-willed Margareta Samzelius, the wife of a major, who owns six other estates as well. The action takes place on two consecutive Christmas Eves. On the first, the 12 pensioners are enjoying a drunken revel when the evil ironmaster of a neighboring manor appears dressed as the devil. He tells them that he is going to renew his pact with their benefactor Margareta. Since the pensioners have suspected that Margareta's power is supernatural, they believe the rumor that she holds her power by sacrificing the soul of one pensioner to the devil each year. With that knowledge, Gösta Berling signs his own pact: for one year, the 12 will be in charge of the estate and the foundries, with the understanding that if they do anything "sensible or useful or effeminate," they will forfeit all, including themselves. They win the wager with devastating results: their mistress is driven from her home and left to roam the highways like a common beggar, while the pensioners ruin her estates with wild abandon and dissipation. By the following Christmas Eve, however, Margareta has returned. On her deathbed, she listens to the beats of the great hammer in the smithy, which the pensioners are working as a sign of their repentance and reformation. Gösta pledges a life of work instead of play, a life of service rather than indulgence. The reader, along with the author, may want to subscribe to Gösta's proclaimed work ethic, but Lagerlöf has made a life of adventure and indulgence so engaging that the reader's sympathies are conflicted. Maybe it is possible to have fun and be good simultaneously.

Conceivably, Lagerlöf's attachment to Värmland and her lifelong fascination with religious fanatics spurred her interest in a group of Swedes who left their homeland towards the end of the century to follow a preacher to Jerusalem, there to await the imminent coming of the Lord. Their story is the subject matter of her next major work, the two-volume novel *Jerusalem,* which followed upon a series of travels she undertook with her friend and fellow-writer **Sophie Elkan,** first to Florence, Rome, and Sicily in the winter of 1895–96, and later to Turkish-occupied Palestine (now Israel). Set in the 1890s, *Jerusalem* explores the principles of ethics and religion as models to live by. It features a quiet, tradition-bound world of farmers in the region of Dalarna who find their chief pleasure in working the soil, but whose faith in God nonetheless makes some of them follow a returned Swedish-American emigrant to Jerusalem. The novel centers on the Ingmarssons, a deeply religious family fiercely loyal to the soil. To them, God exists in the daily tasks well done from year to year and generation to generation. Lagerlöf pits their love of land and homesteads against religion on one hand and romantic love on the other. Karin Ingmar sacrifices the farm to obey her inner summons to a religious pilgrimage while her brother renounces his fiancé to become engaged to another in order to keep the estate from passing out of the hands of the Ingmars. That Lagerlöf—and likely the reader—comes down on the side of the farm is evident in the sympathy evoked for the departing pilgrims' children who cry out in vain, "We don't want to go to Jerusalem; we want to go home." The Swedish Academy honored Lagerlöf with a gold medal for this novel, which by critical acclaim established her as the greatest novelist in Sweden.

An invitation to write a geography book for children brought on further contemplations of "home" for Lagerlöf even as it offered another opportunity for her descriptions of nature and her ready play in the land of the supernatural. *The Wonderful Adventures of Nils* introduces a tiny, bewitched child who can ride on the back of a farm goose. When his goose joins a flock of migrating geese, Nils rides the length of Sweden. In the process, he learns of the national character of the Swedish people in reference to the landscapes he observes as he flies above them.

Nils also learns more than geography, coming to recognize the tension between his desire to stay home and his attraction to the adventures afforded by his travels. He also learns, as do all Lagerlöf's favorite characters, the importance of love and community.

In 1908, Lagerlöf set up summertime residency at Maarbacka; she would later reside there permanently. Her literary output during those years reflects her return home, and, in a series of novels and tales, she explored the nature of Värmland and its people. In 1909, she was honored with the Nobel Prize in recognition of "the noble idealism, the wealth of imagination, [and] the soulful quality of her style, which characterize her work."

Lagerlöf's idealism became increasingly grounded in her expectations for women. The central women in her novels are without exception strong and independent. Some are beautiful, but all have moral fortitude and all understand the importance of home. Lagerlöf also demonstrated her respect for women in her support of women's right to vote. In June 1911, she addressed members of the World Congress for Women's Suffrage at the Royal Theater of Stockholm advocating gender equality. Women's sphere is the home, she said, "man's, the State. Man has helped woman build the home, and the result at its best has been successful. Now woman wants to help man change the state into a home for the nation." Most specifically, she urged women to bring their power to bear on eradicating the destructive rule of force, though she realized the power of evil in the heart of humankind against which relief work, publications to raise funds for prisoners in Siberia, and support of the Red Cross were palliatives.

The hint of despair in those words foreshadows the devastating impact on her of the ensuing World War I. Yet, the 1920s and early 1930s revitalized her pen, producing both *The Ring of the Lövenskolds* (which includes three stories, *The General's Ring, Charlotte Lövenskold*, and *Anna Svaerd*) and a three-volume autobiography, *Maarbacka*. This includes *Maarbacka* (vol. 1, 1922), *Ett Barns Memoarer* (vol. 2, 1930), later published as *Memories of My Childhood*, and *Dagbok* (vol. 3, 1932), later published as *The Diary of Selma Lagerlöf*. Her faith in the strength of women had remained unchanged, as her creation of female protagonists like Charlotte Lövenskold and Anna Svaerd (or Sward) shows. Colorful, alive and strong, they stand at the core of the Ring trilogy which explores the dynamics of domesticity. A shrewd and experienced observer, by then in her 70s, Lagerlöf writes a riveting tale of the curse on the house of the Lövenskolds. She demonstrates once again that religious zealots and self-indulgent individuals may deserve one another, but they cannot be contained in the community of women and men which depends for its survival on the individual's love of others.

Lagerlöf spent the last decade of her life giving audience to thousands of visitors who wanted to see the Maarbacka described in her later books. These autobiographies are memories of her past, of her parents, brothers and sisters, servants, and others she had known during her life at Maarbacka, through which she reveals herself indirectly and offers a key to an understanding of her works. They also explain two seemingly contrasting drawings of her, one by Carl Larsson, the Swedish painter of country life (1902), the other by Austrian Oskar Kokoschka (1917). Both show Lagerlöf with the half smile recognizable from photographs, but whereas Larsson draws a smooth face radiating calm authority, Kokoschka sketches a thin-lipped older woman with sharp facial features and deep-set eyes. This is the face of a woman who has fought for the qualities depicted by Carl Larsson, and who has not always been a winner; it denotes a woman who has recognized within herself the powers to create or destroy.

SOURCES IN ENGLISH OR WITH ENGLISH RESUMES:

Berendsohn, Walter A. *Selma Lagerlöf: Her Life and Work*. Port Washington, NJ: Kennikat Press, 1931.

Edstrom, Vivi. *Selma Lagerlöf*. Boston, MA: Twayne's World Author Series, 1984.

Vrieze de, F.S. *Fact and Fiction in the Autobiographical Works of Selma Lagerlöf*. Amsterdam, 1958.

Wivel, Henrik. *Selma Lagerlöf og biografien*. Copenhagen: G.E.C. Gad, 1991.

RELATED MEDIA:

The Story of Gösta Berling (four-hour, silent movie) was made in Sweden in 1924 by Mauritz Stiller, with *Greta Garbo playing the second lead; it was the movie that launched Garbo onto the European scene.

The Tower of Lies was an adaption of *The Emperor of Portugalia*, starring Lon Chaney, Metro-Goldwyn-Mayer, 1925.

Inga Wiehl,
a native of Denmark, teaches English at
Yakima Valley Community College, Yakima, Washington

La Grange, Anna de (1825–1905)

Countess of Stankowitch and a coloratura soprano. Name variations: Lagrange. Born Anna Caroline de Lagrange in Paris, France, on July 24, 1825; died in April 1905; studied with Bordogni and Lamperti; married Count Stankowitch also seen as Stankowich.

A French coloratura with remarkable range, Anna de La Grange was born in Paris in 1825. She made her debut in Varese, Italy, in 1842, and sang with success in all the great cities of Europe and the United States. In 1848, she married the wealthy Russian Count Stankowitch. Upon her retirement, she lived in Paris and taught.

Laguna, Grace Mead Andrus de (1878–1978).

See de Laguna, Grace.

La Hye, Louise (1810–1838)

French composer, organist, pianist, singer, and lecturer. Name variations: (pseudonym) Monsieur Leon Saint-Amans Fils. Born in Charenton, France, on March 8, 1810; died at age 28 in Paris on November 17, 1838; daughter of Charles Louis Rousseau.

One wonders what Louise La Hye might have accomplished had she not died at age 28. The grandniece of Jean-Jacques Rousseau, she studied under her father Charles Louis Rousseau and then under Saint-Amans. At age 11, she entered the Paris Conservatoire to study the organ, piano, and singing. In 1826, La Hye received a second place for organ and in 1828 a first place at the Conservatoire. On the recommendation of Luigi Cherubini, the famous opera composer, La Hye taught composition in 1831. That same year, she played her *Fantasia* at the Sociète des Concerts. Like many women, La Hye often published under a masculine name, in her case Monsieur Leon Saint-Amans Fils, using her teacher's last name. She introduced her dramatic opera *Le songe de la religieuse* at the Hôtel de Ville in 1835. Poor health cut short her composing career and her life three years later.

John Haag,
Athens, Georgia

Laia (fl. c. 100 BCE).

See Iaia.

Laila bint al-Akhyal (fl. 650-660).

See Layla al-Akhyaliyya.

Lainé, Jeanne (c. 1454–?).

See Hachette, Jeanne.

Opposite page

$\mathcal{V}$eronica
$\mathcal{L}$ake

Lais (fl. 425 BCE)

Greek hetaerae. Name variations: Laïs; Lais the Elder. Pronunciation: LAY-is. Born probably in Corinth; flourished around 425 BCE.

Lais was a Greek hetaerae or courtesan, probably a native of Corinth, who lived in the 5th century BCE, during the Peloponnesian war (431–404 BCE). She was noted for her beauty and her vices. Following her death at Corinth, a monument was erected to her of a lioness tearing a ram. The German painter, Hans Holbein the Younger (1498–1543), titled his portrait of a beautiful young girl in elegant dress, *Lais Corinthiaca* (The Corinthian Lais).

Lais (fl. 385 BCE)

Greek hetaerae. Name variations: Laïs; Lais the Younger. Born probably in Hyccara, in Sicily, around 365 BCE.

Lais was born around 365 BCE, probably in Hyccara in Sicily, and brought to Corinth when a child. She sat as a model for the court painter Apelles, who, it is said, induced her to live the life of a hetaerae or courtesan. Stunningly attractive, she became a rival of *Phryne. Lais was reputedly stoned to death in Thessaly by some women whose jealousy she had aroused.

Lais (fl. 1st c. BCE)

Greek midwife and physician. Name variations: Laïs. Flourished in the 1st century BCE.

Lais, who lived around the 1st century BCE, is mentioned by Pliny the Elder in his *Historia Naturalis*. She was a midwife who was often at odds with another midwife **Elephantis** over the administering of drugs. They "do not agree in their statements about abortives, the burning root of cabbage, myrtle, or tamarisk extinguished by menstrual blood," complained Pliny, who continued his litany of their divisiveness; therefore, he noted it was better not to place trust in either of their methods. Lais and **Salpe**, a midwife from Lemnos, came up with a treatment for rabies and intermittent fevers, "using the flux on wool from a black ram enclosed in a silver bracelet."

Laisne, Jeanne (c. 1454–?).

See Hachette, Jeanne.

Lais the Elder.

See Lais (fl. 425 BCE).

Lais the Younger.

See Lais (fl. 385 BCE).

Lajoie, Marie Gérin (1867–1945).

See Gérin-Lajoie, Marie.

Lake, Claude (1841–1896).

    See Blind, Mathilde.

Lake, Leonora Marie (1849–1930).

    See Barry, Leonora M.

Lake, Mother (1849–1930).

    See Barry, Leonora M.

Lake, Veronica (1919–1973)

American actress best known for her sultry hairstyle.
Name variations: Constance Keane. Born Constance
Ockleman on November 14, 1919, in Brooklyn, New
York; died on July 7, 1973, in Burlington, Vermont; at-
tended a convent school in Montreal, Canada; attend-
ed the Bliss Hayden School in Hollywood, California;
married John Detlie (a studio art director), in 1940 (di-
vorced 1943); married Andre DeToth (a film director),
in 1944 (divorced 1952); married Joe McCarthy (a
songwriter), in 1955 (divorced 1959); married Robert
Carlton-Munro (a naval captain), in 1972; children:
(first marriage) Elaine Detlie; William Detlie (who
died in infancy); (second marriage) Andre Anthony
Michael DeToth III (known as Mike); Diana DeToth.

    Filmography, all under the name Veronica Lake ex-
cept as noted: (as Constance Keane) All Women Have
Secrets (1939); (as Constance Keane) Sorority House
(1939); (as Constance Keane) Young as You Feel
(1940); (as Constance Keane) Forty Little Mothers
(1940); I Wanted Wings (1941); Sullivan's Travels
(1942); This Gun for Hire (1942); The Glass Key
(1942); I Married a Witch (1942); (cameo) Star Span-
gled Rhythm (1943); So Proudly We Hail (1943); The
Hour Before Dawn (1944); Bring on the Girls (1945);
Out of This World (1945); (cameo) Duffy's Tavern
(1945); Hold That Blonde (1945); Miss Susie Slagle's
(1946); The Blue Dahlia (1946); Ramrod (1947);
(cameo) Variety Girl (1947); Saigon (1948); The Sainted
Sisters (1948); Isn't It Romantic? (1948); Slattery's Hur-
ricane (1949); Stronghold (1952); Footsteps in the Snow
(Can., 1966); (also co-producer) Flesh Feast (1970).

    In her first major film, *I Wanted Wings*
(1941), Veronica Lake launched a national craze
by wearing her long blonde hair seductively cascading over one eye in what came to be known as
the "peek-a-boo" style. The fad reached problematic proportions, however, when women working
in war plants began getting their long hair caught
in the machinery. Government officials petitioned
Paramount to redo the star's golden tresses.
Lake's film career, it seems, did not outlive her famous hair-do much longer, all but coming to a
halt after her 1948 picture *Saigon*.

The diminutive actress (5'2") was born in Brooklyn, New York, in 1919, the daughter of a seaman who died when she was 12. She grew up in Brooklyn and Miami and attended a Catholic convent school in Montreal. At 18, she moved to Hollywood with her mother and stepfather, who was a commercial artist. Already the veteran of several beauty contests and anxious to break into movies, Lake accompanied a friend to RKO Studios, where she landed a small part in the movie *Sorority House* (1939). Billed as Constance Keane, she also played bits in *All Women Have Secrets* at Paramount and *Forty Little Mothers* (1940) at MGM.

Lake's second major success after *Wings* was *Sullivan's Travels* (1942), with Joel McCrea, in which she turned in a credible comic performance, even with her famous hair tucked under a cap for most of the picture. Paramount then paired her with their new contract player Alan Ladd, who at 5'5" was difficult to cast as a leading man. Her first movie with Ladd, *This Gun for Hire*, was a box-office hit, jump-starting Ladd's career and adding to Lake's popularity. The two co-starred in three subsequent films: *The Glass Key* (1941), *The Blue Dahlia* (1946), and *Saigon* (1948).

In 1942, Lake campaigned for and landed the lead in René Clair's *I Married a Witch*, with Fredric March. The film was another smash hit, although Lake's squabbles with her co-star added to her growing reputation for being difficult on the set. The actress was memorable in her next effort, *So Proudly We Hail* (1943), but the subsequent *Hour Before Dawn* (1944), her first film with short hair, marked the end of the Veronica Lake vogue. Paramount then teamed her in a series of bland comedies with Eddie Bracken (*Bring on the Girls*, *Out of This World*, and *Hold that Blonde*) and co-starred her with Sonny Tufts in *Miss Susie Slagle's*, during which she reportedly was so bored that she began blowing lines. Her only substantial films during the late 1940s were the two she made with Ladd.

In the early 1950s, shortly after Lake and her second husband, Hungarian director Andre DeToth, filed for bankruptcy, Lake disappeared from the Hollywood scene, except for occasional tabloid headlines about public drunkenness. Her private life had been troubled from the time of her 1940 marriage to John Detlie, an art director at MGM with whom she had two children, a daughter Elaine and a son William, who died seven days after his birth. Lake divorced Detlie in 1943 and was subsequently linked with millionaires Aristotle Onassis and Howard Hughes, as well as director Jean Negulesco. Her marriage to DeToth, with whom she had a son Andre and a daughter Diana, was fraught with ego battles and money woes and ended unofficially in 1951, two years after DeToth directed her in *Slattery's Hurricane* (1949).

After her divorce from DeToth in 1953, Lake left Hollywood and settled in New York, where she appeared on television and spent summers doing stock. The children, out of necessity, were shuttled back and forth between their father in California and their mother in New York. In 1955, she married songwriter Joe McCarthy, but the union was stormy and lasted only three years. In the late 1950s, a badly broken ankle halted Lake's stage work and marked a low point in her life. "Days on end crawled by me as I spent them dragging myself from the tiny bedroom to the tiny living room at a snail's pace," she later recalled. "I had no way of knowing whether my ankle was healing properly. But my biggest concern was over the financial plight I once again found myself facing." After eight months in a cast and a stint in a small factory pasting felt flowers on lingerie hangers, Lake moved to the Martha Washington Hotel for Women, where she worked as a bartender to pay her rent. A newspaper reporter found her there in 1960, and the resultant flood of publicity brought her briefly back into public notice. She appeared in an off-Broadway revival of *Best Foot Forward*, for which she received good reviews, and made a few low-budget movies, but a real comeback never materialized. Her memoirs, published in 1969, brought another brief period of notoriety, after which Lake moved to England where she had roles in the short-lived *Madame Chairman* and a revival of *A Streetcar Named Desire*. In 1972, Lake was married a fourth time, to Englishman Robert Carlton-Munro, but the two soon began to feud, and she returned to the United States to try to sort out her life. In 1973, while visiting friends in Burlington, Vermont, she was hospitalized with hepatitis. She died there on July 7, at the age of 53.

Few mourners were present at Lake's funeral, which was held at the Universal Chapel in Hollywood. The only relative in attendance was her son Mike, who, like the rest of her children, had been estranged from his mother for a long time. He later expressed sorrow and some bitterness over her plight. "Her four husbands, her two daughters . . . none of them came," he told reporters. "She died a lonely and forgotten woman."

SOURCES:

Agan, Patrick. *The Decline and Fall of the Love Goddesses.* Los Angeles, CA: Pinnacle, 1979.

Katz, Ephraim. *The Film Encyclopedia*. NY: Harper-Collins, 1994.

Lamparski, Richard. *Whatever Became of . . . ?* 1st and 2nd Series. NY: Crown, 1967.

Barbara Morgan,
Melrose, Massachusetts

Lakshmibai (c. 1835–1858)

Legendary Indian rani (queen) of the principality of Jhansi, revered for her bravery and astute leadership, who is a symbol of sacrifice in India's fight for freedom against the British. Name variations: Rani of Jhansi; Maharani of Jhansi; Maharanee of Jhansi; Rani Lakshmibai; Lakshmi Bai; Laksmi; Manikarnika. Pronunciation: RAH-nee Luck-SHMEE-baa-ee. Born Manikarnika, nicknamed Manu, around 1835 in Varanasi, India; died in 1858 (also cited as 1857) on the battlefield in Gwalior, near Jhansi; daughter of Moropant Tambe (a court advisor) and Bhagirathi; educated by private tutors; studied literature, military strategy, and equestrian training; married Gangadhar Rao, in May 1842 but the marriage was not consummated until 1849 (died 1853); children: infant son (b. 1851, who died at age of three months).

In the vast history of India's independence movement which commenced around 1857, Indian tales and legends have focused on the princes, kings, and other men who resisted the British. There is one woman, however, who has shared this august position: Rani Lakshmibai of Jhansi. Indian women have been perceived by the world, and themselves, as being submissive and lacking in heroism comparable to their male counterparts. Rani Lakshmibai's story not only debunks this myth but also stands as a resounding testimony to the numerous women who, after their own fashion, were involved in this struggle. It is no accident that every Indian who has been to school can recite the Subhadra Kumari Chauhan paean to the rani's heroism.

> Thou art thy own memorial
> Thou has shown the way
> And teacheth thou a lesson—
> Of Freedom and Fight
> Of Honour and Pride
> Bundelas sang of the Rani
> The fighter for Right,
> Honor, Justice and Freedom.
> Chivalrous Bundelas sang
> Chanting songs of Lord Shiva,
> The Rani, the damsel fought for Jhansi,
> Recount her valour, people of India!

However, this respect for Lakshmibai was revived only after the women of free and independent India resurrected her memory as a symbol of both Indian nationalism and a woman's strength and fortitude. Her legend has reached epic proportions, and has given her immortality in Indian culture. After all, a 24-year-old widow gallantly fighting against the British East India Company's soldiers was not the order of the day. Rani Lakshmibai represents a potent ideal for Indian women; she and her story live in the Indian woman's continued struggle for freedom from the stranglehold of patriarchy.

The remarkable legend attached to the rani's bravery has sustained itself in the oral tradition of storytelling, as well as ballads, poems, and the cinema. She stands head and shoulders above the freedom-fighters of the 19th century. Lakshmibai's profile goes beyond the defined categories of women: daughter, wife, mother, and temptress. Her legendary status is goddesslike, a function of the Hindu symbol of female heroism manifested in the goddess Shakti (Durga) who rides a tiger destroying evil and has power equivalent to ten men. It is this idiom of Hindu definition that distinguishes Lakshmibai from female heroes of the West and has made her the greatest of all Asian heroines.

Rani Lakshmibai's account is set against the backdrop of the 19th-century expansion of British colonialism into territories that constitute modern unified India. The British East India Company, formed in 1600, had firmly established itself as a political and commercial presence in Eastern India by 1757. For over a century, the tentacles of the company spread under the auspices of the British Crown, consuming within it vast tracts of land and the independence of numerous principalities-states. Besides the military acquisition of states which was the mode of choice for expanding control, the British introduced another technique, the system of "lapse." Enunciated and implemented by Governor-General James Dalhousie, lapse allowed the British to assume control of states whose rulers died without natural heirs, or who, according to Hindu custom, adopted heirs on their deathbeds. The lapse method was unpopular with Indians, who deeply resented such annexation. By the mid-1850s, bitterness had reached immense proportions. Several other factors fed into this resentment, including loss of independence, fear of forcible conversion to Christianity, and exasperation with the ever-increasing presence of the British and their interference with the social practices of Indian states. By 1857, India was on the brink of insurrection, and it came as the Great Rebellion, also called the First War of Independence. In 1857–58, state after state across the subcontinent revolted against British exploitation. British historians, even now, call it a Sepoy Mutiny (*sepoy* is a bastardization of *sipahi*, the Indian word for soldier). The historical debates over causes, and nomenclatures, of the uprising continue as British and Indian historians perceive this watershed event from, understandably, entirely different lenses. Central to the fight for independence was the bravery and heroism of a young woman in a small state in Northern India, who first challenged and defied the orders of the British governor-general, and then rode in battle at the head of her forces, ultimately dying for the independence that was her birthright.

The Rani, the damsel fought for Jhansi,

Recount her valour, people of India!

—Subhadra Kumari Chauhan

What is known of Lakshmibai's early life is a strange blend of fact and fiction, a result of the legends associated with her. Her parents moved to Varanasi, the most holy of Hindu cities, from Poona in Western India. Lakshmibai was born around 1835, the daughter of Moropant Tambe, a court advisor, and **Bhagirathi**. She was originally named Manikarnika and called Manu until her marriage, when her name was changed to Lakshmi after the Hindu goddess of wealth and victory. Lakshmibai lost her mother at a young age, thus missing the traditional nurturance given to young Indian girls. This eventually turned out to be a blessing, for she instead shared the companionship and upbringing of childhood playmates, young boys like Nana Sahib and Tatya Tope, both of whom would later play a crucial role in the Great Rebellion. She also learned to read and write, then unusual skills for a girl. More exceptional was her training in horsemanship and weaponry, including guns. Her father, for reasons unknown, did not impede this unconventional education. One well-known story of her childhood relates that when Nana Sahib refused to take "a girl" for an elephant ride Lakshmibai angrily remonstrated: "I will show you! One day I will have ten elephants to your one. Remember my words!" (After her marriage to a raja, she would gift Nana Sahib with an elephant as a reminder of the childhood promise.) Her bravery and liveliness was evident from early years.

When she reached puberty, Lakshmibai received a proposal of marriage from the recently widowed Raja Gangadhar Rao of Jhansi. Though he was between 40 and 50, the age difference was inconsequential; it was not unusual for Brahmins to marry young girls to older men. The raja needed a wife who could give him an heir, and Moropant wanted a suitable husband for his daughter. Lakshmibai's wishes were immaterial. She was married in May 1842, but the marriage was not consummated until Lakshmi was 14, in 1849. The wedding was celebrated with cannons booming a salute, spectacular fireworks, and the girl's adoption of a new identity as Rani Lakshmibai of Jhansi. It was customary for women of high castes to change their names upon marriage, ensuring adoption of a new persona. What was not customary was the mettle and spirit displayed by the new rani of Jhansi, who continued to display characteristics of her earlier identity.

Rani Lakshmibai's vitality and versatility could not be contained within the confines of the strict rules and codes of the court. She asked her husband's permission (19th-century women could not openly defy the authority of their spouses) to continue her equestrian and military training; she never got it. So she rounded up her maidservants and fashioned an informal regiment of women soldiers; this remarkable initiative won her the support of the populace and her husband's admiration. Soon, she was pregnant and gave birth to a young son, the heir to the throne of Jhansi, but tragedy befell the royal family when the infant died at the age of three months. Gangadhar's grief knew no bounds, and he fell deathly ill. Before he died in November 1853, he adopted Damodar Rao, a young male relative, as a future heir to the throne. At age 18, Lakshmibai became the ruler of the state of Jhansi. She began rigorous training as a soldier and equestrian; her women's military unit also increased in size and prowess. Several British officers of the time have recorded the rani's remarkable literary and military abilities and strength of character. Evident in their accounts is a grudging respect for this Brahmin woman who wielded the reins of power as "any man is wont to do." Her "extraordinary determination and forcefulness," her "logical mind and potent intellect" soon attracted the attention and reverence of the English and Indians alike. However, no one could have anticipated the methodical and confident manner with which the rani soon began dealing with the East India Company officials. From November 1853 until her death in 1858, the rani became, for the British, the proverbial thorn in the side.

Rani Lakshmibai was offended but not surprised when on February 27, 1854, Lord Dalhousie proclaimed the doctrine of lapse for Jhansi. Given the consistently spirited responses from the rani, later historians recorded that Jhansi was "the worst of Dalhousie's annexations." An astute ruler, Lakshmibai had sent appeals to the governor-general's office in Fort William, Calcutta, from December 1853 asking for recognition of her adopted son as the rightful heir to the throne. Though her initial letters preceded the lapse announcements, they were clearly ignored. She employed well-formulated arguments in these lengthy, legalistic dispatches, not only bringing up precedents of such heirs in other states but also referring to the Hindu tradition of adoption. Most important, a British officer had been present when the raja of Jhansi had adopted Damodar Rao as his heir. Thus, officials of the company became uncomfortable, knowing that their only response involved coercion and intimidation. When Dalhousie announced the proclamation anyway, Lakshmibai, now completely offended and angry, wrote another letter to him: "It is notorious, my Lord, that the more powerful a state . . . the less disposed it is to acknowledge an error or an act of arbitrary character." Her appeals and letters were largely ignored by the British government.

To her credit, Lakshmibai turned persistence into an art form. She refused to be ignored. For eight months, she continued to send letters and appeals to the governor-general's office; for eight months, the officials responded with vacuous explanations. Lord Dalhousie was fast and firm in his resolve that Jhansi was to lapse, and the rani and her husband's heir Damodar be deprived of their status. Then, she forwarded "new and arresting arguments." The rani stated that the dispossession constituted "gross violation and negation of the Treaties of the Government of India . . . and if persisted in they must involve gross violation and negation of British faith and honor." She pointed out to Dalhousie that other states were watching the decision regarding Jhansi "with intense interest," and that it would be myopic of the British if they thought there was no "disquietude among the native Princes." (It was true that other states were closely watching the decision-making process of the East India Company. The response to Jhansi was the litmus test for the future of other principalities—"as Jhansi goes, so shall the rest of India.") The rani was, she wrote, concerned with the loss of her authority and reduction to the status of "subjection, dishonor, and poverty," none of which she was willing to accept without question or contest. Lakshmibai had delivered a blow to the very heart of the British presence in India. She had cleverly, but resolutely, threatened the British with imminent upheaval in the states of

Lakshmibai

upper India. Even so, none of her arguments impressed Dalhousie, and Jhansi lapsed to the British in May 1854.

Lakshmibai did indeed lose her "dignity and honor" through British actions, yet she maintained her dignity with honor through her own addresses. She was removed from the fort, so that it could be occupied by British officials, and given a small pension for retention of her retinue. She accepted this defeat but when the British held her responsible for the state's debts she once again challenged the authority of the British. She wrote appeals to, and sought personal interviews with, the assigned British officials and refused to acknowledge the debts as her personal responsibility. The British officer who had to face her wrath wrote: "My impression was that she was a clever, strong-minded woman, well able to argue and too much for many." Even the enormity of British power and presence could not break Lakshmibai's spirit. The British, particularly insensitive to the rani's self-respect, ordered that British forces police her palace. Irate, she broke with tradition by meeting with the British resident herself and even removed the purdah to speak to him face to face. Though she displayed respect in her relations with the British, in keeping with her station, she never lost sight of the fact that Jhansi was rightfully hers.

The chance for assuming control of Jhansi came in a manner that Rani Lakshmibai could never have imagined. Upper India exploded on May 10, 1857. The Indian soldiers in various British-controlled states rebelled against the oppressive nature of British rule, bringing in their wake massacres of British officials and their families. The Rebellion spread like wild fire and by June had reached the fort of Jhansi. Fearing for their lives, the British turned to the rani for assistance. She could not control the local rebel forces, as they were no longer under her authority, but she did extend her help to the British families by inviting them to her palace. However, the rebels reached the British residences before the families could take her up on her offer. English officers later recorded, and some historians concur, that the rani had prompted the rebellion and was responsible for the massacre because she "harbored grievances against the British, predicated on her hatred of the English race." No doubt Lakshmibai disliked the loss of independence but neither did she condone the actions of the rebel soldiers. Her commitment to respect and honor would not countenance such behavior; her pledge to the military code did not allow for attacking civilians. Another British official present in Jhansi wrote: "Not a paper incriminating the Ranee did I find. . . . The Ranee was not present or any man on her part." Jhansi, like other parts of northern India, fell into utter confusion and chaos.

Pending the arrival of a new set of British officials, Lakshmibai reassumed control of the administration of her state. She realized that this was an opportunity to consolidate her position, so that when the British arrived she could resist, this time militarily, the confiscation of Jhansi. She opened a mint, distributed food and clothing to the destitute, and made sure that peace and calm were restored. She moved easily among her subjects, wearing traditional widow's white. Even in this tenuous condition, Lakshmibai did not behave like an orthodox widow; she did not shave her head, break her bangles, or wear a sari exclusively. She wore a garment that allowed easy movement, so that she could ride effortlessly on her horse. In her clothing and manner, she communicated to her people that the time had come for the people to reevaluate the problems facing Jhansi, particularly those of security and defense. This was certainly no helpless widow; this was an unorthodox Brahmin queen preparing herself and the state to build strong fortifications against the inevitable British onslaught. She enlisted troops, cast cannon, and commenced manufacture of other weapons. She personally trained her women's military unit in equestrian and military skills. By March 1858, she was confident of her military strength. Now she openly challenged British authority: she moved from her palace back to her fort and ordered that the Jhansi flag be flown from the wall. She then issued a proclamation that the military be on alert and, on the appearance of the British, conduct the first strike.

When the British forces attacked, the rani of Jhansi was ready. Wrote one observer: "The Rani charged to attack. Now to the right, now to the left. . . . They many; she alone." In the beginning, her forces managed to resist the British. Lakshmibai, who fought at the head of her troops, suffered no qualms when it came to using her weapons. In battle, her intellect and military acumen were whetted, and her tactical skills rendered severe losses on the British side, pushing them further back each day. But she had limited resources, and they had many. She awaited reinforcements from Tatya Tope, her childhood friend, but they did not appear. The British reinforcements, however, arrived in large numbers. Soon her forces were decimated, and she was left with a handful of soldiers. What she did not have in troops she made up for in spirit and determination. Outside of Gwalior, the proud rani rode out in full battle dress with a meager band of soldiers and clashed with the powerful British Hussars. It was there on June 17, 1858, that she was fatally wounded.

The heroic and majestic rani died, and with her death was born a legend. The British generals were the first to write about the fighting spirit of the rani. Here was a young woman who fought better than any could have imagined, the only Indian queen to ever ride out in battle against the power of the British artillery. The British soon forgot her, but Indians never have. Wrote one: "The brave woman cemented with her blood the cause she espoused." She became the first female hero of India's First War of Independence. Indians, women and men alike, have not forgotten the debt of gratitude they owe her:

> Your image shall be in our minds forever,
> Your legend repeated everywhere
> Your memory fresh in mind eternally
> Your ideals practiced by all for all time to come.

SOURCES:

Lebra-Chapman, Joyce. *The Rani of Jhansi: A Study in Female Heroism in India*. Honolulu: University of Hawaii Press, 1992.

Sen, Chandi Charan. *Rani of Jhansi: A Historical Romance* (in Bengali). Calcutta, India, 1894.

Sinha, Shyam Narain. *Rani Lakshmi Bai of Jhansi*. Allahabad, India: Chugh Publishers, 1980.

Smyth, Sir John. *The Rebellious Rani*. London, Great Britain: Muller, 1966.

Jyoti Grewal,
Assistant Professor of History, Luther College, Decorah, Iowa

Lala (fl. c. 100 BCE).

See Iaia.

Lalande, Amélie Lefrançais de (fl. 1790)

French astronomer. Name variations: Mme Lefrançais de Lalande. Born Marie Jeanne Amélie Harlay; married Michel Jean Jérôme Lefrançais de Lalande (1776–1839, an astronomer); children: Caroline Lefrançais de Lalande (b. 1790); Isaac Lefrançais de Lalande.

French astronomer Amélie Lefrançais de Lalande worked as an assistant to her husband Michel Lefrançais de Lalande and his cousin Joseph Jérôme Lefrançais de Lalande (1772–1807), who served as Michel's mentor. Although it is difficult to separate her contributions from those of her husband and his cousin, Amélie is credited with calculating the astronomical tables for several publications. She is known to have constructed the tables appended to Jérôme's *Abrégé de navigation* (1793), which were designed to assist navigators in calculating time at sea, and to have performed the calculations and reductions included in an astronomical almanac he edited, *Connaissance des temps*.

The names of the Lalande children also reflect the family preoccupation with astronomy. Their daughter Caroline was named after *Caroline Herschel who discovered a comet that first became visible in Paris on the day of Caroline's birth (January 20, 1790), and their son Isaac was named after Sir Isaac Newton.

Barbara Morgan,
Melrose, Massachusetts

Lalla Rookh (fl. 1600s)

Indian princess. Lalla Rookh means Tulip Cheek; flourished in the 1600s; supposed daughter of Aurangzeb (1618–1707), Mughul emperor (r. 1658–1707).

Lalla Rookh was the supposed daughter of Aurangzeb, the last great Mughul emperor of India, who had nine children with his harem of four wives (which included *Udaipuri Bai). As presented in the 1817 poem *Lalla Rookh* by Thomas Moore, Lalla Rookh was betrothed to Aliris, sultan of lesser Bulcharia. On her journey from Delhi to Cashmere, she was entertained by Feramorz, a young Persian poet, with whom she fell in love. Lalla Rookh was delighted when she learned that the young poet was the sultan to whom she was betrothed.

La Loca, Juana (1479–1555).

See Juana la Loca.

La Lupe (1939–1992)

Cuban singer who was one of Latin music's most popular performers in the 1960s. Name variations: Lupe Victoria Yoli. Born Lupe Victoria Yoli in Santiago, Cuba, in 1939; died in the Bronx on February 28, 1992; married twice; children: one son, René Camaño, and one daughter, Rainbow Garcia.

La Lupe, who would be known as the Queen of Latin Soul, was born Lupe Victoria Yoli in Santiago, Cuba, in 1939. Her parents insisted she obtain a teaching degree, although she won many local singing contests and was determined to be in show business. She married a singer in the Los Tropicuba trio who also tried to dissuade her; they were soon divorced, and La Lupe became the leading performer in Havana's nightclubs. But in the aftermath of the 1959 Cuban Revolution, she lost all her property ("Castro took my club, my money, and my car," she told *Look* magazine) and immigrated to the United States in 1962.

La Lupe began singing with Mongo Santamaria, recording a number of hit singles. By the end of the 1960s, she was a celebrity throughout Latin America. When jobs began to dwindle in the 1970s, she moved to Puerto Rico to do concerts and television shows. A string of bad luck, including a further decline in her career and medical expenses incurred by her second husband, bankrupted her. By the 1980s, she was living on welfare. In 1984, she injured her spine and was permanently paralyzed; a fire burned down her house not long after. In 1985, she sang from a wheelchair at a concert given to raise funds to help pay her expenses. After being blessed by an evangelical Christian preacher, La Lupe regained her ability to walk; she began singing Christian music and recorded a series of albums. She was only 53 when she died of cardiac arrest.

SOURCES:

Pareles, Jon. "La Lupe, a Singer, Is Dead at 53; Known as the 'Queen of Latin Soul,'" in *The New York Times Biographical Service*. March 1992, p. 272.

John Haag,
Athens, Georgia

Lama, Giulia (c. 1685–c. 1753)

Italian artist. Born around 1685 in Venice, Italy; died around 1753; possibly the daughter of Agostino Lama (a painter); may have studied with Giovanni Battista Piazzetta (1683–1754); never married; no children.

What little is known about the life and work of Italian artist Giulia Lama has been pieced together from a number of sources: a Venetian guidebook from the year 1733, which mentions three altarpieces by Lama in Venetian churches, two of which survive (*Crucifixion with Saints* in San Vitale and *Madonna in Glory with Two Saints* in Santa Maria Formosa); a self-portrait and another portrait painted by her contemporary, Giovanni Battista Piazzetta; and a letter written by Abbot Luigi Conti in March 1728, in which the artist is mentioned. On the basis of her four identified works alone, scholars eventually attributed to Lama 26 paintings previously assigned to other well-known artists, as well as some 200 drawings, including studies for her altarpieces and some remarkable female and male nudes.

In Lama's self-portrait, dated 1725, the artist appears to be around 40 years of age, suggesting that she was born around 1685, although **Germaine Greer**, in *The Obstacle Race*, points out that the painting is so unflattering and so poorly preserved that it could hardly be a reliable indicator of age. Piazzetta's portrait of the artist is more flattering, showing her deeply engrossed in her work. "It is not the portrait one paints of an admiring pupil," Greer declares, "the character that emerges is as strong as Piazzetta's own. The long, swift strokes of his brush can hardly suffice to convey the self-contained energy of this simple figure caught up in creation." Greer also contends that one need only view Lama's *Crucifixion with Saints*, the altarpiece in Venice's San Vitale Church (now a commercial art gallery) to see that she was no dilettante. "She was a highly trained professional carrying out large original commissions with daring and self-confidence."

Abbot Conti's letter is one of the more interesting sources of information about Lama, revealing her as multitalented. "I have just discovered a woman here," he writes to *Marthe Caylus, "who paints better than *Rosalba [Carriera] when it comes to large compositions." He goes on to describe Lama's work in progress, a large painting of the rape of Europa, "but the bull is still in a wood far from the sea; the companions of Europa crowd round the bull on which the laughing Europa is mounting." Conti further describes Lama as a poet, a trained mathematician who studied with the celebrated Father Maffei, and the inventor of a lace-making machine. Although he finds her "as ugly as she is witty," he adds that "she speaks with grace and polish, so that one easily pardons her face." He also remarks that Lama is persecuted by other painters, a claim that in light of 18th-century sexism comes as no surprise. Male painters may have been willing to lose a lucrative commission to one of their own sex, but losing to a woman was unforgivable. Lastly, Conti writes that Lama lives "a very retired life," which is hardly surprising either, given the prevailing prejudices of the day.

Many of Lama's paintings were initially attributed to Piazzetta, and scholars estimate that she came in contact with him in the early 1720s, although there is no tangible proof that he was her teacher. Piazzetta, who was viewed as one of the more eccentric 18th-century Venetian painters, deviated from the strict Rococo manner with his striking chiaroscuro contrasts and his earthy, dramatic interpretation. Lama, it would seem, moved even further from the norm, into the unacceptable. Greer points to Lama's *Crucifixion* as having "none of the superficial sensual and picturesque charm of Piazzetta. The palette is colder; the lines of the composition saw back and forth between the figure of Christ strung in agony between his arms, electrified by the cold light, and the appalled and terrified observers. The earth heaves beneath them, even the planes in which the figures stand lurch painfully in the viewer's vision as he follows the narrative movement of their gesturing arms." **Ann Sutherland Harris** and **Linda Nochlin** also contend that Lama pushed the boundaries of prevailing taste even further than Piazzetta. By way of example, they cite *The Martyrdom of St. Eurosia*, a work that was first ascribed to Piazzetta but later attributed to Lama. They describe the painting as characteristic Lama, possessing "a dramatic compositional structure and figure types that recall Piazzetta but with more stress on the homeliness of the physiognomies and on the anatomical distortions produced by the shifting chiaroscuro. . . . The severed body pours blood toward us, the splayed hand in the foreground still seems alive, the head is held aloft by the triumphant executioner who watches our reaction."

Giulia Lama is now considered a gifted painter worthy of future study. The need to reconstruct her career from such meager data leads to speculation about the number of other women artists yet to be discovered. Greer suggests that if our heritage is to escape destruction "women by the thousands must begin to sift the archives of their own districts, turn out their own attics, haunt their own salesrooms and the auctions in old houses."

SOURCES:

Greer, Germaine. *The Obstacle Race.* NY: Farrar, Straus, and Giroux, 1979.

Harris, Ann Sutherland, and Linda Nochlin. *Women Artists, 1550–1950.* NY: Alfred A. Knopf, 1976.

Barbara Morgan,
Melrose, Massachusetts

La Mara (1837–1927).

See Lipsius, Marie.

La Marr, Barbara (c. 1896–1926)

American actress and screenwriter. Name variations: also billed as Barbara Deely and Barbara La Marr Deely; Barbara LaMarr. Born Rheatha Watson on July 28, 1896 (also seen as September 3, 1898), in Richmond, Virginia; died on January 30, 1926, in Hollywood, California; married Jack Daugherty.

Selected screenplays: (story only) The Mother of His Children *(1920); (story only)* The Little Gray Mouse *(1920); (story only)* Rose of Nome *(1920); (co-story only)* The Land of Jazz *(1920); (story only)* Flame of Youth *(1920); (story only)* My Husband's Wives *(1924).*

Selected films: The Nut *(1921);* Desperate Trials *(1921);* The Three Musketeers *(as Milady de Winter, 1921);* Cinderella of the Hills *(billed as Barbara La Marr Deely, 1921);* Arabian Love *(1922);* Domestic Relations *(1922);* The Prisoner of Zenda *(as Antoinette de Mauban, 1922);* Trifling Women *(in dual role, 1922);* Quincy Adams Sawyer *(1922);* The Brass Bottle *(1923);* The Hero *(1923);* Poor Men's Wives *(1923);* Souls for Sale *(1923);* St. Elmo *(1923); (cameo)* Mary of the Movies *(1923);* Stranger of the Night *(1923);* The Eternal Struggle *(1923);* The Eternal City *(1924);* Thy Name Is Woman *(1924);* The White Moth *(1924);* Sandra *(1924);* Heart of a Siren *(1925);* The White Monkey *(as Fleur Forsyte, 1925);* The Girl From Montmartre *(1926).*

A former dancer and musical comedy star, Barbara La Marr had a brief career in silent movies before her death from a drug overdose at age 29. Considered one of the great beauties of her day and noted for her "vamp" roles, she rose to screen stardom with her portrayal of Milady de Winter in *The Three Musketeers* (1921), opposite Douglas Fairbanks, Sr. Her other notable films include *The Prisoner of Zenda* (1922) and *The Eternal City* (1924), but her scandal-driven private life drew as much attention as her acting. La Marr also wrote the stories for several screenplays and was billed in her early career as Barbara Deely or Barbara La Marr Deely.

Barbara La Marr

Lamarr, Hedy (1913–2000)

Austrian-born American motion-picture star and inventor of the electronic frequency-hopping technology now used in satellites and cellular phones. Name variations: H.K. Markey; Hedwig Kiesler. Born Hedwig Eva Maria Kiesler in Vienna, Austria, on November 9, 1913; found dead in her home in Orlando, Florida, on January 19, 2000; daughter of Emil Kiesler and Gertrud (Lichtwitz) Kiesler; married Friedrich (Fritz) Mandl (the proprietor of one of Central Europe's leading munitions manufacturing plants, the Hirtenberger Patronen Fabrik); married Gene Markey (a Hollywood writer and producer); married John Loder (a British actor), in 1943 (divorced 1946); married Ted Stauffer (an ex-bandleader); married W. Howard Lee (a Texas oil refiner); married Lewis Boies (a lawyer); children: (second marriage) James Markey (adopted); (third marriage) Denise Hedwig Loder; Anthony John Loder.

Her film Ecstasy, *in which she appeared nude in a swimming scene, created an international scandal (1933); arrived in U.S. (1937); changed her name to Hedy Lamarr and co-starred in* Algiers *(1938); received a patent with composer George Antheil for a radio-controlled torpedo (1942); one of the last survivors from the Golden Age of Hollywood.*

Filmography in U.S., unless otherwise noted: (short) Geld auf der Strasse *(Ger., 1930);* Die Blumenfrau von Lindenau *(Sturm in Wasserglas, Ger.-Aus., 1931);* Wir brauchen kein Geld *(Man braucht kein Geld or We Don't Need Money or His Majesty King Ballyhoo, Ger., 1931);* Die Koffer des Herrn O.F. *(Mr. O.F.'s Suitcases, Ger., 1931);* Extase *(Symphonie der Liebe or Ecstasy, Czech., 1933);* Algiers *(1938);* Lady of the Tropics *(1939);* I Take This Woman *(1940);* Boom Town *(1940);* Comrade X *(1940);* Come Live With Me *(1941);* Ziegfeld Girl *(1941);* H.M. Pulham, Esq. *(1941);* Tortilla Flat *(1942);* Crossroads *(1942);* White Cargo *(1942);* The Heavenly Body *(1944);* The Conspirators *(1944);* Experiment Perilous *(1944);* Her Highness and the Bellboy *(1945);* The Strange Woman *(1946);* Dishonored Lady *(1947);* Let's Live a Little *(1948);* Samson and Delilah *(1949);* A Lady Without a Passport *(1950);* Copper Canyon *(1950);* My Favorite Spy *(1951);* Eterna Femmina *(L'Amante di Paride or Love of Three Queens or The Face That Launched a Thousand Ships, It.-Fr., 1954);* The Story of Mankind *(1957);* The Female Animal *(1958);* Instant Karma *(1990).*

Although internationally famous as a Hollywood femme fatale, Hedy Lamarr was also an inventor whose work with composer George Antheil laid the groundwork for both military communications systems and the mobile telephone systems now in use around the world. She was born Hedwig Kiesler in 1913 in Vienna, the only child in a wealthy assimilated Jewish family, less than a year before the outbreak of World War I. Her father Emil was a bank director and her mother Gertrud was a concert pianist who gave up her career to raise their daughter. Known to friends and family as Hedy, Lamarr attended Vienna's most exclusive private schools but showed little interest in her studies. While enrolled in a finishing school, she signed up for a course in design, an unusual subject to pursue for a pampered daughter of Vienna's upper class. During these years, she showed a rebellious streak when on several occasions she ran away from home (always returning, however, to the comforts of her parents' apartment).

By now a remarkably attractive young woman, Lamarr skipped school one day, going instead to Vienna's version of Hollywood, the Sascha Film Studios. While there, she overheard director Alexis Granowsky discuss the casting of a bit part in his upcoming silent film. Although her audition for the part was "terrible," she was hired nevertheless. Now hooked on an acting career, she persuaded her parents to let her drop out of school to devote herself to mastering the dramatic arts. Lamarr attended the renowned acting school of Max Reinhardt in Berlin, where Reinhardt was so convinced of her potential as an actress that he personally took her on as a pupil.

While still at school, she so impressed the director of the film *Geld auf der Strasse* (Money on the Street), Georg Jacoby, that she was given another bit part. Soon after, Jacoby chose her for a larger role. During this time, she also appeared on stage, rapidly improving her acting skills and advancing to second leads; she was in the first Austrian production of Noel Coward's *Private Lives*. Good reviews resulted in an offer for her first leading role in a film, in *Wir brauchen kein Geld* (We Don't Need Money), in which she performed opposite Heinz Rühmann. *Wir brauchen kein Geld* was not a hit, but the next film in which she starred, *Die Koffer des Herrn O.F.* (Mr. O.F.'s Suitcases), was both a critical and box-office success.

By this time, Lamarr was being thought of in film circles as a potential star, and she took advantage of her growing reputation by accepting an offer in 1932 to appear in a film by the Czech director Gustav Machaty. With a working title of *Symphonie der Liebe* (Symphony of Love), the film's script called for its lead actress to appear nude in two brief scenes. It was explained to her that these would be extreme long shots, and she signed up for the project. When the film was released in 1933 under the title *Extase* (*Ecstasy*), it became a worldwide sensation, not only for the nude scenes (one of which shows Lamarr swimming), but also for several sizzling depictions of love-making. Although the film appears tame by contemporary cinematic standards, in its day it was regarded as outrageously daring. Religious commentators including Pope Pius XI denounced it as a threat to public morality. The film was banned in Nazi Germany, partly because the

newly established Hitler dictatorship claimed to be defending traditional moral values and also because Lamarr, being of Jewish ancestry, was regarded as a particular affront to a new state based on anti-Semitic principles. The film was also banned in the United States, where Puritanism still held sway in theory if not always in practice; it would finally be released to the public only after several court decisions.

While her name (then still Hedy Kiesler) was becoming notorious throughout the world,

Lamarr married one of Austria's richest men, Friedrich (Fritz) Mandl, the proprietor of one of Central Europe's leading munitions manufacturing plants, the Hirtenberger Patronen Fabrik. Ruthless in pursuit of profits, Mandl sold his wares to all comers including fascist dictators Hitler and Mussolini. He regarded his beautiful young wife as a trophy and was enraged by the international sensation caused by her appearance in *Ecstasy*. Determined that his wife's nude and love scenes not be seen in public, Mandl tried to track down and buy all prints of the film. Eventually, after spending a large sum of money, he admitted defeat, and the film went on to become a classic of sorts.

After several years of marriage, Lamarr found herself restless. She thought her husband dull and his often shady business dealings morally offensive. Mandl was obsessively jealous, refusing to let her appear on stage even under the most proper circumstances. Meanwhile, Europe slid toward war and anti-Semitism in both Germany and Austria became ever more aggressive. Lamarr decided to flee Vienna for a freer, safer environment. After several failed attempts to leave her powerful husband, she finally succeeded in 1937, going first to Paris and then London. She managed to bring along her most valuable jewels as well as the bulk of a glamorous wardrobe.

In London, she met a Hollywood talent scout who arranged a meeting with movie mogul Louis B. Mayer. On the lookout for new stars in Europe, Mayer at first rejected Lamarr because of her connection with the scandalous film *Ecstasy*. Changing his mind, he then offered her a sum she regarded as insulting, leading to a firm refusal on her part. Finally, Mayer offered her a financially acceptable seven-year contract with the MGM studio, and she signed. At this point, Mayer insisted that she adopt a new, American-sounding name (her last name, Kiesler, reminded him of a Yiddish term for buttocks). Thus, Hedwig Kiesler became Hedy Lamarr, a name that derived from *Barbara La Marr, a silent-film star Mayer admired. Hedy arrived in New York City in style, having crossed the Atlantic on the elegant French liner *Normandie*. She refused to display her knees for the New York photographers and reporters who met her at the pier, and instructed them to no longer write about her as Hedy Kiesler: "Please," she said, "call me Hedy Lamarr."

Lamarr's debut film project in Hollywood, *A New York Cinderella,* was an attempt to turn the Viennese beauty into an instant American superstar. Directed by Josef von Sternberg and co-starring Spencer Tracy, this film was apparently ill-fated from the start. Mayer's constant interference and Tracy's deepening dissatisfaction finally led to the abandonment of shooting. A chance meeting of Lamarr and the noted French actor Charles Boyer at a party led to Boyer's urging his producer, Walter Wanger, to cast her as his co-star in *Algiers*. This was a remake of a much grittier French film (*Pépé le Moko*), with Lamarr playing the role of a slumming society lady who is the protagonist's fatal passion. *Algiers* was a smash hit, and Hedy Lamarr's disturbing beauty became legendary. Undergraduate males at Columbia University voted her the woman they would most like to be marooned with on a desert island. Women began to wear their hair as Lamarr did, parted down the middle. Although her films would feature escapist, arguably mindless plots, Lamarr was able to create the persona of a distinctly foreign and decadent temptress.

Her next film, *Lady of the Tropics* (1939), was successful with audiences but did not win critical acclaim. Writing in *The New York Times,* Bosley Crowther told his readers, "It is necessary to report that she is essentially one of those museum pieces, like the Mona Lisa, who were more beautiful in repose." Over the next few years, Lamarr appeared in a number of successful films, including *Comrade X* and *Boom Town* (both with Clark Gable), *I Take This Woman, Ziegfeld Girl,* and *Tortilla Flat* (with Spencer Tracy and John Garfield). Even more successful film roles eluded her when she turned down memorable parts that then went to *Gene Tierney (*Laura*) and *Ingrid Bergman (*Casablanca* and *Gaslight*).

In 1940, the glamorous actress became involved in the world of science, technology and warfare. She met the film composer George Antheil at a Hollywood dinner party that year, and the two soon discovered they had much more in common than their careers. Their conversation turned to Lamarr's Austrian past, including the threat of Nazi Germany and the education about weapons she had received during her marriage to Fritz Mandl. Lamarr, who felt guilty about earning so much money in Hollywood while millions of people in Europe and elsewhere suffered in wartime, wanted to make a contribution to the defeat of the Nazis. She talked about another femme fatale, Mata Hari (*Margaretha Zelle), who had been both a seductress and a military expert, although her plans had turned out badly.

Antheil quickly became aware that Lamarr had amassed considerable knowledge about armaments and weapons systems during her years as the wife of a leading arms manufacturer in

Austria. She revealed to him her desire to quit MGM and move to Washington, D.C., to work for the National Inventors' Council, an organization newly established to facilitate inventions useful for national defense. Antheil dissuaded Lamarr from leaving California, arguing that she could do more good boosting the nation's morale by remaining in Hollywood. So Lamarr worked at the Hollywood Canteen, entertaining soldiers, and sold war bonds on nationwide tours (she told a Philadelphia crowd that she was just "a gold digger for Uncle Sam," and on one evening alone sold $7 million in war bonds).

Working intensively with Antheil over a period of several weeks, Lamarr explained her idea. Ships under attack often wasted several torpedoes before they hit a target. Such wastage not only endangered the vessel, but it benefited the enemy and munitions barons like her ex-husband Fritz Mandl. Lamarr proposed to Antheil that they work on a design for a radio-controlled torpedo that could successfully respond to shifting targets, unstable weather conditions, and rising and falling tides. The Germans had successfully circumvented radio-controlled missiles by jamming them; Lamarr wanted to come up with an anti-jamming device. The actress and the composer proved to be an ideal inventing team: Lamarr had both a natural bent for technology and considerable information from her years with Mandl, and Antheil was an artist with a strong interest in modern inventions. In his most famous composition, the controversial *Ballet Mecanique*, Antheil had solved the complex problems of command and control—synchronizing a musical composition performed by 16 player pianos—by use of punched tape.

"A simple radio signal sent to control a torpedo was too easy to block," writes **Elizabeth Weise**. "But what if the signal hopped from frequency to frequency at split-second intervals? Anyone trying to listen in or jam it would hear only random noise . . . but if the sender and the receiver were hopping in synch, the message would come through loud and clear." Basically, the Lamarr-Antheil idea boiled down to this communication process known as "frequency hopping" across 88 radio frequencies that enabled transmitter and receiver to be fully synchronized. In their team effort, it was Lamarr who brought up the idea of radio control of the weapon, while Antheil's contribution was to suggest the specific method of coordination of signals. By December 1940, they had sent a description of their system to the National Inventors' Council in Washington, D.C. In their application for a joint patent for a "Secret Communication System," filed on June 10, 1941, the invention used slotted paper rolls similar to player piano rolls to synchronize the frequency changes in transmitter and receiver (the fact that the idea called for the use of 88 frequencies also links it to musical-technological origins, an obvious reminder of the exact number of keys found on a piano). With some technical assistance from a professor at the California Institute of Technology, the final details of the invention were worked out, and it was specified in the patent application's description that the torpedo could be steered to its target by a high-altitude observation plane. When the patent was granted on August 11, 1942, Hedy Lamarr was listed as "H.K. Markey"—a name she retained although she had already been divorced for two years from her second husband, Hollywood writer and producer Gene Markey.

> *I* was a 15-year-old fussing around with a crystal radio set just trying to get a signal in 1941 and, here she was, intellectually articulating a control mechanism for torpedo guidance systems.
>
> —David Hughes, National Science Foundation

In the bureaucratic chaos of wartime, the Lamarr-Antheil patent gathered dust in a Washington file. Apparently, some Navy people who read the patent papers hastily concluded, after seeing the word "player piano" in the text, that somehow a device as bulky as a player piano would have to be jammed into a torpedo. After two decades, the inventors' patent rights to exclusive use or licensing of the device expired. Neither Lamarr nor Antheil, who died in 1959, would ever earn a cent from their invention. Although shunned by the U.S. Navy, the basic Lamarr-Antheil concept had been a sound one, and in 1957 it was reviewed by engineers at the Sylvania Electronic Systems Division in Buffalo, New York. Using modern electronics rather than piano rolls, Sylvania's engineering staff created a system that emerged as a basic tool for secure military communications. It was installed in time to be utilized on American ships sent to enforce a blockade on Cuba in 1962 during the missile crisis, using mainframe computers to protect U.S. military messages from the Soviets.

The essential principle of the Lamarr-Antheil Communication System remains valid. Microchips and digital signal processing have made the technique ready for a mass market, and, by relying on state-of-the-art spread-spectrum technology, it enables mobile telephone transmitters to serve ever more customers. These networks function in principle on the idea first developed by Lamarr and Antheil. Instead of sending a signal on a single frequency, however, the transmitter sends a signal over hundreds of frequencies in coded form. Since the receiver also recognizes the same code, it accepts only that one signal, thus enabling many cellular phones in the same crowded area to receive signals that do not interact with each other. Technological descendants of their original 1942 patent are also used to speed satellite signals across the globe, and frequency hopping remains at the heart of the $25 billion Milstar defense communication satellite system. Although in the final decades of her life, stories appeared occasionally in the media about Hedy Lamarr's inventive talents, it was not until 1997 that she (and, posthumously, George Antheil) were given official recognition for this important discovery. In that year, she received a prestigious Pioneer Award from the Electronic Frontier Foundation. Her only comment on this occasion was, "It's about time."

In 1943, Lamarr began a three-year marriage to her third husband, British actor John Loder, with whom she had a daughter, **Denise Hedwig Loder**, and a son, Anthony John Loder. She had earlier adopted a son, James Markey, while married to Gene Markey. Lamarr was increasingly frustrated in her film roles. In the 1942 film *White Cargo*, she played a seductress on a plantation in a British African colony. Her line "I am Tondelayo" became perfect foil for comedians including Jack Benny, who created a character on his radio show named Tondelayo Schwartzkopf, an imaginary salesgirl. In one of her best-known roles, as Delilah in Cecil B. De Mille's 1949 Biblical epic *Samson and Delilah* (co-starring Victor Mature), she wore a clinging gown made out of feathers from De Mille's personal collection of prize peacocks.

By the early 1950s, starring roles were getting more difficult for Lamarr to find, and she sometimes turned down important roles she did not care for, including one in De Mille's circus epic, *The Greatest Show on Earth*. After divorcing Loder, she married and divorced ex-bandleader Ted Stauffer, and then married a Texas oil refiner, W. Howard Lee. She persuaded Lee to bankroll an Italian-made epic, *Eterna Femmina*, a film in which she portrayed in fantasy episodes such important historical women as Helen of Troy, the Empress *Josephine, and **Genevieve de Brabant**. A financial disaster, the film turned up on television years later, drastically cut, under a new title, *The Love of Three Queens*. Lamarr's

final appearances on film, in the late 1950s, included her roles in *The Story of Mankind*, in which she shared the spotlight with the Marx Brothers and Ronald Colman, among others. In 1957, she gave a critically well-received performance in *The Female Animal*, playing a drunken film star on the skids. Still beautiful at the end of her movie career, she disappointed her many fans when in years to come it became clear that her Hollywood days were over.

Lamarr had divorced W. Howard Lee by 1960. Soon after, she married Lewis Boies, the lawyer who had represented her during the acrimonious divorce from Lee. Like all of her other marriages, this too soon failed, lasting less than two years. By this time, she was no longer a wealthy woman. Lamarr spent considerable sums of money on legal fees, exhibiting as early as the 1940s a tendency toward litigiousness. (In 1943, she sued Loews and MGM because they had failed to pay her $2,000 a week as specified in her contract. Her employers argued that a wartime executive order issued by Franklin D. Roosevelt limiting all salaries to $25,000 a year tied their hands in the matter. Lamarr persisted and the parties finally settled out of court.) In 1966, she made headlines when she went on trial in Los Angeles on a charge of shoplifting from a local department store. She was found not guilty by the jury, and a suit she initiated against the store was dismissed. (During an interview with syndicated columnist **Sheilah Graham**, Lamarr answered her own rhetorical question: "What happened to me? I made $7 million and yet I was on relief and they gave me all of $48 a week.")

The best known of her lawsuits was that which Lamarr directed against the publisher and ghostwriter of her spicy 1966 autobiography, *Ecstasy and Me: My Life as a Woman*. In her suit, she alleged that both publisher and writer had presented a negative image of her life by having "deliberately written [a book that was] obscene, shocking, scandalous, naughty, wanton, fleshy, sensual, lecherous, lustful and scarlet." The case dragged out for years, and she eventually lost the lawsuit and a great deal of money. She found solace in her children and in a new passion, painting. Some of her canvases were highly regarded and exhibited in New York galleries. In 1991, living modestly on a very tight budget in Florida, Lamarr was once more in lurid headlines when she was accused of shoplifting $21 worth of personal-care items from a drugstore.

Hedy Lamarr had achieved star status without ever appearing in an indisputably immortal motion picture. "To be a star is to own the world and all the people in it," she noted. "After a taste of stardom, everything else is poverty." The extraordinary beauty from Vienna, a gifted inventor and one of the last survivors of a legendary era of Hollywood stars, died in her modest Florida home in January 2000.

SOURCES:

Antheil, George. *Bad Boy of Music*. Hollywood, CA: Samuel French, 1990.

Bawden, Liz-Anne. *The Oxford Companion to Film*. London and NY: Oxford University Press, 1976.

Braun, Hans-Joachim. "Advanced Weaponry of the Stars," in *American Heritage of Invention and Technology*. Vol. 12, no. 4. Spring 1997, pp. 10–16.

"Genius, Not Gender," in *Resource*. Vol. 4, no. 4. April 1997, p. 5.

"Hedy Lamarr," in *The Times* [London]. January 20, 2000, p. 27.

Körte, Peter. *Hedy Lamarr: Die stumme Sirene*. Munich: Belleville-Verlag, 2000.

Lamarr, Hedy. *Ecstasy and Me: My Life as a Woman*. NY: Bartholomew House, 1966.

Madden, David. "Hedy Lamarr: London, Rome, the Movies and Pleasures of the Road after the Bijou," in *Goodlife*. Vol. 1, no. 4. June–July 1985, pp. 12–14.

Marovich, Lisa A. "'Let Her Have Brains Too': Commercial Networks, Public Relations, and the Business of Invention," in *Business and Economic History*. Vol. 27, no. 1. Fall 1998, pp. 140–161.

Mattis, Richard L. "Movie Star Inventor: Hedy Lamarr," in *Cobblestone*. Vol. 15, no. 6. June 1994, pp. 29–31.

Meeks, Fleming. "'I Guess They Just Take and Forget About a Person,'" in *Forbes*. Vol. 145, no. 10. May 14, 1990, pp. 136–138.

Selzer, Sabine E. "Hollywood-Star und Technikerin," in *Die Furche* [Vienna]. No. 23. June 10, 1999, p. 18.

Severo, Richard. "Hedy Lamarr, Sultry Star Who Reigned in Hollywood of '30s and '40s, Dies at 86," in *The New York Times*. January 20, 2000, p. A16.

Siegele, Ludwig. "What's the Frequency, Hedy?," in *World Press Review*. Vol. 44, no. 7. July 1997, pp. 34–35.

"A Siren's Swan Song," in *U.S. News & World Report*. Vol. 128, no. 4. January 31, 2000, p. 14.

Thomson, David. *A Biographical Dictionary of Film*. 3rd ed. NY: Alfred A. Knopf, 1994.

Vare, Ethlie Ann, and Greg Ptacek. *Mothers of Invention: From the Bra to the Bomb—Forgotten Women and their Unforgettable Ideas*. NY: Morrow, 1988.

Weise, Elizabeth. "Hedy Lamarr Was Much More than a Pinup Girl," in *The Day [New London, CT]*. March 10, 1997.

Young, Christopher. *The Films of Hedy Lamarr*. Secaucus, NJ: Citadel Press, 1978.

John Haag,
Associate Professor of History,
University of Georgia, Athens, Georgia

Lamb, Caroline (1785–1828)

English aristocrat, poet and novelist, best known for her tempestuous affair with the poet Lord Byron.

Name variations: Caroline Ponsonby; Lady Melbourne; Lady Caroline Lamb; (nickname) Caro. Born Caroline Ponsonby in England in 1785; died in January 1828 at Brocket Hall, Hertfordshire, England; only daughter of Frederick Ponsonby, 3rd earl of Bessborough, and Lady Henrietta Frances Spencer, countess of Bessborough; married William Lamb (1779–1848), later 2nd Lord Melbourne as well as prime minister (1834, 1835–41), in 1805; children: one son Augustus (1807–1836); daughter (b. 1809, died at birth).

Born into a wealthy and aristocratic English family; spent several years in Europe as a child, absorbing European culture; as a young girl, was a member of the "Devonshire House set," a group of rich and intelligent aristocrats based at the London home of her aunt, the duchess of Devonshire; married William Lamb, the future prime minister of England (1805); embarked on a tempestuous affair, which lasted only a few months but defined the rest of her life, with the young poet Lord Byron, then at the height of his fame and popularity (1812); as well as poetry, wrote three novels of which only the first, Glenarvon, *based on her romance with Byron, was successful; spent the last decade of her life in isolation at her country house because of the scandal provoked by her affair and by the novel; died there at age 42.*

Selected writings: Glenarvon *(London, 1816);* Graham Hamilton *(London, 1822);* Ada Reis *(London, 1823).*

George Gordon, 6th Lord Byron, was the sensation of the 1812 London season; his poem, *Childe Harold*, had appeared in March and had been an instant and spectacular success. Every hostess in England conspired to lure the handsome young aristocrat to her social gatherings. Lady Caroline Lamb had already fallen in love with his poetry. Tired of country life and growing bored with her seven-year marriage, she was determined to meet this dazzling new literary star. Within days of his first appearance in London, she got her wish, but when Byron was brought forward to meet her, Caroline gazed into his face for a moment before turning her back and walking away without a word. That night, she recorded her impressions in her diary: "Bad, mad and dangerous to know."

Caroline Ponsonby was born in England in 1785, the only daughter of Frederick Ponsonby, 3rd earl of Bessborough, and Lady ❧➤ **Henrietta Frances Spencer**, countess of Bessborough. She was brought up as part of the "Devonshire House set," an aristocratic household devoted to pleasure and not at all concerned with conven-

❧
*See sidebar
on page 69*

tional ideas about marital fidelity. The household was directed by Lady Elizabeth Foster (later ❧▶ **Elizabeth Cavendish**), the duke of Devonshire's mistress, and ❧▶ **Georgiana Cavendish**, the duchess of Devonshire, sister of Henrietta Frances Spencer, and aunt to Caroline. Henrietta and Georgiana, extremely close sisters, were renowned for their beauty and intelligence; both read French, Italian, Latin and Greek. Caroline, the only daughter in a family with three sons, "grew up in an atmosphere totally free from restraint, backed by an exceptional artistic and literary erudition," and admired and indulged by her wealthy parents and relatives.

When Caroline was five, Lady Bessborough took her daughter and her younger son to live in Italy; she soon reported that it "is quite surprising to hear how well and fluently she reads and speaks both French and Italian." They were to remain in Italy for almost three years. Caroline kept a pet fox and wandered after the sheep in the hills. In later life, she liked to spin tales of the wildness and neglect of those years, saying that she had lived as "an idle, wandering unruly boy." Her claim that she could not write until she was ten years old was an invention, but it was true that her mother took greater pains to expose Caroline to European art and literature than to instill more traditional skills such as spelling or punctuation. As **Margot Strickland** observes, Caroline's letters throughout her life "ran breathlessly on from subject to subject, devoid of commas or paragraphs."

At age 14, Caroline was confirmed in Westminster Abbey, and it was at about this time that William Lamb first saw her. He was 21, had just finished his studies at Cambridge University, and was about to spend a further two winters studying philosophy in Glasgow. William is said to have remarked that, of all the Devonshire House girls, Caroline was the one for him. First impressions were confirmed when he met her again three years later. The young woman who made her debut into London society at the age of 17 had changed little; with a slender, boyish figure, short curly hair and a voice which, in Devonshire House style, elongated vowels in a rather childlike way, she was nicknamed "the Sprite" and "Ariel." Her sheer energy and intensity proved an immediate attraction for the rather indolent and cynical William Lamb. Learned, but unengaged by his studies, William recognized Caroline's spontaneous, unconventional intelligence and saw what Strickland calls "a creative individuality, whimsical, extravagant, enchanting."

Only the unexpected death of William's older brother in 1805 made marriage a possibility; Caroline's lineage was too aristocratic for her to be permitted to marry the younger son of an only recently titled family which had made its fortune in money lending. Once William became his father's heir, and thus the next in line to the title of Baron Melbourne, Caroline's family was, somewhat reluctantly, ready to accept him as a suitor. Her young cousin Hart, the future duke of Devonshire, was heartbroken; he never married and remained Caroline's close friend for the rest of her life. However, it was clear that the strong-willed Caroline had fallen in love, and Lady Bessborough was hopeful that marriage would serve as a steadying and calming influence on her mercurial, highly strung daughter. "Caroline Ponsonby is to be married tomorrow" recorded Lady Elizabeth Foster in 1805; "she looks prettier than ever I saw her. Sometimes she is very nervous. . . . Wm. Lamb seems quite devoted to her." Moods of tearful uncertainty before her wedding gave way to a major scene during the ceremony itself; Caroline, enraged by the behavior of the officiating bishop, tore her wedding gown and had to be carried, fainting, from the room.

One of the most fashionable young couples in London, the Lambs divided their time between their London apartment in Marlborough House and their country estate, Brocket Hall. After a visit to the newlyweds, Lady Elizabeth Foster reported that Caroline "is the same wild, delicate, odd delightful person" and that Caroline and William "flirt all day." William was calmly determined to take charge of his "dearest love." Strickland suggests that "William's vanity was gratified by his capture of an equally adoring pupil-wife, an enchantingly fey sprite who regarded him as a hero rather than a husband." He set about providing his wife with the formal education she had never received, and the two read history, poetry and theology together. Trying to find some context for the classical history which William was currently teaching her, Caroline wrote to her mother in July 1809: "I should take it as a great favour if you would just write me the principal dates and events, wars, risings etc. from Romulus till the time of Constantine the Great—if you are unwell do not do it."

Caroline had suffered some periods of illness herself; a miscarriage early in the marriage had been followed by the birth of her sickly son Augustus in 1807, and a further pregnancy in 1809 produced a daughter who died within hours. She seemed to recover quickly each time and continued to work hard at her studies, al-

❧ Spencer, Henrietta Frances (1761–1821)

Countess of Bessborough. Name variations: Lady Bessborough; Viscountess Duncannon; Henrietta Frances Ponsonby. Born Henrietta Frances Spencer on June 16, 1761; died on November 1, 1821; daughter of John Spencer, 1st earl Spencer, and **Georgiana (Poyntz) Spencer** *(eldest daughter of Stephen Poyntz); sister of* *Georgiana Cavendish (1757–1806); married Frederick Ponsonby, 3rd earl of Bessborough, on November 27, 1780; children: John Ponsonby, 4th earl of Bessborough; Major-General Sir Frederick Ponsonby;* ***Caroline Lamb** (1785–1828); William Ponsonby, 1st Lord De Mauley.*

❧ Cavendish, Elizabeth (1759–1824)

Duchess of Devonshire. Name variations: Lady Elizabeth Foster; Dearest Bess. Born in 1759; died in 1824; daughter of Rt. Reverend Frederick Augustus, bishop of Derry and 4th earl of Bristol (1730–1803), and **Elizabeth Davers**; *married John Thomas Foster (died 1796); married Edmund Gibbon, in 1787; married William Cavendish, 5th duke of Devonshire, on October 19, 1809; children: (first marriage) Frederick (b. 1777); Augustus (b. 1780, who married* **Albinia Hobart***); (with the duke of Devonshire)* **Caroline St. Jules** *(b. 1785, who married George Lamb); Augustus Clifford (b. 1788, who married* **Elizabeth Townshend***).*

Born in 1759, the daughter of **Elizabeth Davers** and Rt. Reverend Frederick Augustus, bishop of Derry and 4th earl of Bristol, Elizabeth Cavendish married John Thomas Foster, Edmund Gibbon, and then William Cavendish, 5th duke of Devonshire. Elizabeth was a close companion of *****Georgiana Cavendish**. While living in Rome, Elizabeth Cavendish subsidized editions of Horace and Virgil.

SUGGESTED READING:

Calder-Marshall, Arthur. *The Two Duchesses*. NY: Harper and Row, 1978.

❧ Cavendish, Georgiana (1757–1806)

English social patron and duchess of Devonshire. Name variations: Lady Georgiana Spencer. Born Georgiana Spencer in London, England, on June 7, 1757; died on March 30, 1806; eldest daughter of John Spencer, 1st earl Spencer, and **Georgiana (Poyntz) Spencer** *(eldest daughter of Stephen Poyntz); sister of* *****Henrietta Frances Spencer** (1761–1821); married William Cavendish, 5th duke of Devonshire (1748–1811), on June 6, 1774; children:* *****Georgiana Cavendish** (b. 1783, later countess of Carlisle); Harriet Cavendish (1785–1862, later Lady *****Harriet Leveson-Gower***); William Spencer Cavendish (1790, the marquess of Hartington and later 6th duke of Devonshire, known as "Hart"); (with Charles, 2nd earl Grey)* **Eliza Courtney** *(b. 1792 and adopted by 1st earl Grey).*

Married at 16 and soon bored, Georgiana Cavendish took to gambling within a year of her reign as hostess of Devonshire House and came under the spell of Charles James Fox. She campaigned for Fox in the Westminster election of 1784. She also took up with Lady Elizabeth Foster (later *****Elizabeth Cavendish**) "with a school-girl's passion" writes Henry Blyth. Foster, known as "Dearest Bess," was soon a member of the Devonshire household. "When Georgiana fell ill," writes Blyth, "Bess nursed her devotedly whilst she was in bed. In due course she was also invited to attend the Duke when *he* was in bed, but not for the purpose of administering physick. . . . Thus there came into existence a *ménage à trois* which gave everyone satisfaction." A social beauty whose portrait was painted by Joshua Reynolds and Thomas Gainsborough, Georgiana Cavendish was a reigning queen of society. Her friends included Richard Brinsley Sheridan and Dr. Samuel Johnson.

SOURCES:

Blyth, Henry. *Caro, The Fatal Passion: The Life of Caroline Lamb*. NY: Coward-McCann, 1972.

SUGGESTED READING:

Calder-Marshall, Arthur. *The Two Duchesses*. NY: Harper and Row, 1978.

Foreman, Amanda. *Georgiana: Duchess of Devonshire*. NY: Random House, 2000.

though it was clear that her initial enthusiasm was fading; learning Greek under William's direction during the spring of 1808, she observed rather pointedly in a letter to her mother: "I am convinced nothing is worse . . . than finding fault, unless it be for things one can help."

With William increasingly involved in politics, Caroline often found herself left alone at Brocket, nursing her son Augustus through his frequent bouts of sickness. She was a devoted mother, but she was beginning to feel increasingly isolated and even uncertain about William's love for her. She felt the strain of having to "perform" to rouse his attention and wrote: "His indolence renders him insensible to everything. When I ride, play and amuse him he loves me." William's journal records his perspective: "Before I was married, whenever I saw the children and the dogs allowed . . . to be troublesome . . . I used to lay it all to the fault of the master. . . . Since I have married I find that this was a very rash and premature judgement." Despite his undoubted love for Caroline, he seems to have regarded his wife in much the same way as he would a child or a dog. His attempts to divert her original and creative intelligence into academic directions were failing. Caroline feared his "smothering severity" but usually blamed herself for their quarrels and in one contrite letter promised him: "I will be silent of a morning, docile, fearless as a heroine in the last vol. of her troubles." All instinct and feeling while William was cool rationality, Caroline took wild gallops over the Downs to sublimate her energies. William preferred sedate walks.

She became a passionate reader, finding in literature a refuge and a source of welcome stimulation. Once again, her response was instinctive rather than analytical—she disliked reading reviews because such an approach "tends to extinguish natural taste," and she claimed that critics "instead of feeling with enthusiasm the beauties of a play or a poem, pretend to judge by rule and discover the defects." She greatly admired *Mary Wollstonecraft's Vindication of the Rights of Women and, consciously or not, made her own statement of resistance by continuing to dress in boy's clothes and cutting her hair short. She particularly enjoyed dressing up as a page; her friends called her Cherubina.

*I*t is all very well if one dies at the end of a tragic scene, after playing a desperate part: but if one lives, and instead of growing wiser, one remains the same victim of every folly and passion, without the excuse of youth and inexperience, what then?

—Caroline Lamb

In 1810, after five years of an increasingly unsatisfactory marriage, Caroline indulged in a very public affair with Sir Godfrey Webster, hoping to rouse William from his indifference— to no avail. However, both her choice of a man of notoriously shady character and the indiscreet way she conducted herself did serious damage to her reputation. Extramarital liaisons were common among the English aristocracy of the early 19th century, but there were very strict codes about how they should be conducted. Caroline, throwing caution and discretion to the winds, violated those codes, and only her youthful inexperience and elevated position in society saved her from complete social ostracism. After William had finally been stirred enough to remonstrate with her in public, Caroline vowed to reform, but did not keep her promise for long.

William Lamb's biographer, Lord David Cecil, blames Caroline for the growing estrangement between the formerly loving couple: "her character was of a kind to make her an unsatisfactory wife for any man. . . . [W]ith a glint of the unique fire of genius, she possessed in the highest degree its characteristic defect. A devouring egotism vitiated every element in her character. In her eyes she was the unquestioned centre of the universe." Cecil asserts that she was "abnormally selfish, abnormally uncontrolled and abnormally unreliable" and that "life was a drama in which she was cast as heroine; and both her fellow actors and her audience were expected to applaud her every movement." This harsh judgment is undoubtedly colored by the event which marked the rest of Caroline's life, her affair with Lord Byron.

Caroline was 27 at the time. Byron, a young man of 24 with the world at his feet, besieged by female admirers, was immediately intrigued by the young woman who silently turned her back on him at their first meeting in March 1812. Within a very short time, they had become lovers. Already deeply engaged by his poetry, Caroline found herself swept away by Byron's physical appearance. He was every inch the romantic hero; tall, dark, melancholy, and mysterious, with a lame leg that merely added to his attraction. William's biographer asserts that Caroline "who had been frigid, though carelessly amoral, became tragically carnal." Byron certainly awoke Caroline's fiery sexuality, and she confidently forecast: "That beautiful pale face will be my fate."

Byron's most recent biographer, **Phyllis Grosskurth**, suggests that he was already a confirmed bisexual and that Caroline's unconventional and androgynous appearance attracted him. She was certainly far from the type of voluptuous, dark-eyed woman he usually preferred—he was later to remark, "I am haunted by a skeleton"—but, regardless of her appearance, Byron seemed incapable of remaining faithful to any one woman for long. Moreover, despite his efforts to present himself as being similar to his Childe Harold hero, cynical and detached from the trifling preoccupations of the world, he cared obsessively about what would now be called his "public image." He called his association with Caroline a "serio-comedy" but it was not long before its tragic elements came to

Caroline
Lamb

dominate. Byron discovered that the affair brought him into the public eye in a way that he neither sought nor welcomed.

David Cecil asserts that neither Byron nor Caroline was really in love, but, rather, that they presented "the extraordinary spectacle of a love drama, performed in the most flamboyant, romantic manner by two raging egoists, each of whom was in fact wholly absorbed in self." Byron's published correspondence clearly indicates that he vacillated between his inclination to play the romantic hero and his desire for quieter, less public relationships. Cecil is wrong, however, about Caroline. She had clearly found the love of her life and was willing to sacrifice everything, including herself, to keep him.

The white hot period of their affair lasted little more than four months. Almost from the first Byron was uneasy at the intensity of Caroline's adoration; he wrote sometime in April 1812, shortly after the start of their liaison:

> I never knew a woman with greater or more pleasing talents . . . but these are unfortunately coupled with a total want of common conduct. . . . Then your heart—my poor Caro, what a little volcano! that pours *lava* through your veins, & yet I cannot wish it a bit colder. . . . you know I have always thought you the cleverest most agreeable, absurd, amiable, perplexing, dangerous fascinating little being that lives now or ought to have lived 2000 years ago.

Within weeks of their first meeting Byron was counseling caution:

> people talk as if there were no other pair of absurdities in London. . . . Our folly has had the effect of a fault—We must make an effort, this dream this delirium of two months must pass away, . . . a month's absence would make us rational. . . . But it is better that I should leave town than you. . . . Now don't abuse me, or think me altered, it is because I am not, cannot alter, that I shall do this, and cease to make fools talk, friends grieve, and the wise pity.

Since Caroline's correspondence, unlike Byron's, has not been published in its entirety, we are compelled to reconstruct her side of the affair from the fragments which appear in the biographies of her husband and her lover and from the accounts of her desperate, love-obsessed behavior. On July 29, she arrived at Byron's rooms dressed as a boy and tried to persuade him to elope with her. He was far from the restrained and rational being which he tried to present himself as in his letters, and was only dissuaded from going with her by the intervention of his best friend at the last minute. On August 9, no doubt sensing that her lover was already tiring of her, she sent him a letter containing some of her pubic hair along with the passionate assertion: "I will kneel and be torn from your feet before I will give you up."

Byron had found an advisor and confidante in Lady ✍▶ **Elizabeth Melbourne**, William's mother, and wrote to her almost daily when his affair with Caroline was at its height, frequently proclaiming his desire to get free of this demanding entanglement and discussing possible strategies. And yet he would not, could not, sever communication with Caroline. Following a meeting sometime in August 1812, he referred to his tears and agitation "through the *whole* of this most nervous *nervous* affair" and told her that "no other in word or deed shall ever hold the place in my affection which is & shall be most sacred to you, till I am nothing." Byron's letter ended with a postscript which is hardly the work of an unwilling love object: "is there anything on earth or heaven would have made me so happy as to have made you mine long ago? . . . I was and am *yours,* freely & most entirely, to obey, to honour, love—& fly with you when, where, & how you yourself *might & may* determine."

William, roused from his indifference and his preoccupation with politics by the public outrageousness of Caroline's behavior, was persuaded to take his wife off to Ireland. Caroline later recorded that he "cared nothing for my morals, I might flirt and go about with whom I pleased. He was privy to my affair with Lord Byron and laughed at it." The culminating incident occurred on August 12. Caroline, rebuked for her scandalous behavior by her father-in-law, Lord Melbourne, ran away and had to be found and taken home by Byron. "I am apprehensive for her personal safety, for her state of mind," Byron had written to Lady Melbourne. Nor was he alone in his concern; according to her cousin Harriet, "She is worn to the bone, as pale as death and her eyes starting out of her head. She seems in a sad way; alternately in tearing spirits and in tears." Caroline, clinging blindly to her relationship with Byron, had become an object of public ridicule.

In September, relieved that Caroline was safely in Ireland, Byron wrote to Lady Melbourne:

> You will not regret to hear that I wish this to end, & it certainly shall not be renewed on my part.—It is not that I love another but loving at all is quite out of my way; I am tired of being a fool, & when I look back on the waste of time, & the destruction of all my plans last winter by this last romance, I am—what I ought to have been long ago.

Yet he was still hesitant and uncertain, confiding to Lady Melbourne, "I do not at all know how to deal with her, because she is unlike every one else." To ensure that Caroline would not pursue him upon her return, Byron determined to marry during her absence; he wrote once again to Lady Melbourne: "[A]ll I have left is to take some step which will make her hate me effectually, for she must be in extremes." Casting about for a suitable wife, Byron settled upon Caroline's pious country cousin, ✍▶ **Anne Milbanke**. For a time, Lady Melbourne, who was also Anne's aunt, served as the go-between in the newly developing relationship. Anne, however, was not to be rushed, and initially refused Byron's proposal. His letters to Lady Melbourne had a distinct tone of panic as he contemplated Caroline's imminent return to London:

> I am out of all patience with her & hers & come what may will have no explanations, no scenes, no *anything*, & if necessary I will quit London or the country altogether rather than subject myself to the renewal of the last years [*sic*] harass. —The sooner, the stronger—the fuller you state this the better—Good God—am I to be hunted from place to place like a Russian *bear* or *Emperor*?

Her stay in Ireland had clearly not cured Caroline of her passion. She appears to have threatened suicide in her letters to Byron, for he informed Lady Melbourne on November 9:

> C. threatens to revenge herself upon *herself*, by all kinds of perverseness.—this is her concern—all I desire is to have nothing more to do with them—no explanations—no interviews—in short I neither can nor will bear it any longer.

Still unmarried, Byron had by November taken refuge with another mistress, the **Countess of Oxford**, a 40-year-old beauty with a calm temperament, a luxurious country estate and a compliant husband. But Caroline's letters followed him and he complained to his confidante:

> Is everyone to be embroiled by C.?—Is she mad or mischievous only? . . . I must pronounce C. to be the most contradictory, absurd, selfish, & contemptibly wicked of human productions. . . . I could wish to feel towards her as a *friend*—but as she herself says she has resolved since she is "not loved to be *detested*."

Caroline wrote to her former lover and to his new mistress, pleading for mementos: a lock of hair, a picture. Now back in England, she threatened to visit the couple if these were not provided. The cynical Byron sent a lock of Lady Oxford's hair, pretending it was his own. And yet still he could not sever ties completely, and their correspondence continued.

By October, he was adopting a firmer line— "correct yr. vanity which is ridiculous and proverbial, exert your Caprices on your new conquests & leave me in peace, yrs. Byron"—and by December the two had begun to negotiate the return of one another's letters. Caroline was certain that if hers were to be circulated her reputation would be ruined: "She writes menacingly, & at the same time accuses me of *menaces*—what menaces have I used?—poor little weak thing!"

But still the exchanges continued: in mid-December Byron told Lady Melbourne: "Her letters are as usual full of contradictions and *less* truth (if possible) than ever."

Lady Melbourne suggested that William should keep Caroline at Brocket Hall to allow the scandal to blow over and lessen the chance of an embarrassing confrontation between the erstwhile lovers. Byron commented in a letter of December 21, 1812:

> I think your plan with her not so good as yr. general plans are—as long as she is in ye. country & has nothing to do but gallop on the turnpike & scribble absurdities she will be unmanageable.

On this occasion, Byron's instincts were correct; confined to the country, Caroline rode and scribbled and, that winter at Brocket, she dressed a group of young girls in white and had them dance around a bonfire made from presents Byron had sent her, into which she cast copies of his letters while reciting lines she had written for the occasion. He remarked when he learned of it: "I begin to look upon her as actually mad or it would be impossible for me to bear what I have from her already." In addition to forging Byron's signature on a letter to a picture dealer to get possession of his portrait, she dressed her male servants in new livery, their buttons bearing the inscription: "Ne crede Byron"—Do not believe Byron.

Yet still her passion burned. Convinced that Byron was leaving the country with Lady Oxford in May 1813, she requested a final meeting, and the two had a teary reunion. The pathos of the letter which she wrote the next day must have torn at Byron's heart:

Milbanke, Anne. *See Lovelace, Ada Byron, Countess of, for sidebar.*

Melbourne, Elizabeth (d. 1818)

*Viscountess Melbourne. Name variations: Lady Melbourne; Elizabeth Milbanke; Elizabeth Lamb. Born Elizabeth Milbanke; died in the spring of 1818; only daughter of Sir Ralph Milbanke, Bart., of Halnaby, in Yorkshire; married Peniston Lamb, 1st viscount Melbourne; aunt of *Anne Milbanke; children: four sons, including Peniston (1770–1805); (possibly with Lord Egremont) Henry William Lamb, 2nd viscount Melbourne (1779–1848); (possibly with George IV, king of England) George Milbanke (1784–1834); and *Emily Lamb, countess of Cowper.*

Along with her importance in the story of Lord Byron, Lady Elizabeth Melbourne was one of the many mistresses of George IV, king of England.

One only word. You have raised me from despair to the joy we look for in Heaven. Your seeing me has undone me for ever—you are the same, you love me still. I am sure of it—your eyes, your looks, your manners, words say so. Oh God, can you give me up if I am so dear? Take me with you—take me, my master, my friend. Who will fight for you, serve you, in sickness and health, live but for your wishes and die when that can please you—who so faithfully as the one you have made yours bound to your heart of hearts? Yet when you read this you will be gone. You will think of me, perhaps, as one who gave you suffering—trouble. Byron, my days are passed in remembering what I once was to you. I wish that you had never known me or that you had killed me before you went. God bless and preserve my friend and master.

Your Caro.

But Byron did not leave, and the two were soon involved in another public scene. Accounts vary but are agreed that in July 1813 at **Lady Heathcote**'s ball, Caroline attempted to provoke Byron's jealousy by asking him if she were *now* allowed to waltz. He had never liked to see her dancing since his lame leg would not allow him to participate. He is reported as contemptuously telling her she could do as she pleased, at which point she grabbed a knife or broke a glass and used the sharp edge to gash her arms. She was held down before she could do much damage, but there was blood on her dress and the newspapers were soon full of the newest scandal.

The same month, Byron was involved in another scandal that had nothing to do with Caroline. Facing the departure of Lady Oxford for Europe, Byron had asked his half-sister, ✒▶ **Augusta Leigh**, to come to London to live with him. She was four years older than Byron and had three children and an indifferent husband. All the evidence suggests that the two became lovers; their affectionate behavior that summer was the talk of London. By October, Byron was in pursuit of another beauty but at the same time had renewed his correspondence with Anne Milbanke. In April 1814, Augusta's fourth child, **Medora Leigh**, probably fathered by Byron, was born. It was clearly time for Byron to marry.

Rumors about his behavior did not diminish Caroline's devotion; during the summer of 1814, she managed to gain entry to Byron's rooms several times. Once, finding a book lying on the table, she wrote "Remember me!" on the first page. Byron's response was a piece of poetic, self-justifying fury:

Remember thee! Ay, doubt it not;
Thy husband too shall think of thee;

By neither shalt thou be forgot,
Thou *false* to him, thou *fiend* to me.

Caroline later claimed that Byron received her with a tenderness that these lines and his protesting letters to Lady Melbourne conceal, but that he also showed her letters which destroyed her passion for him. The letters, presumably, revealed the true nature of his relationship with Augusta. It is evident, despite her claim to the contrary, however, that they did no lasting harm to Caroline's feelings for Byron.

On January 2, 1815, Byron married Anne Milbanke. Caroline sent what, at first glance, appear to be warmest congratulations:

God bless you—you may be very happy. I love and honour you from my heart as a friend may love—no wrong I hope—as a sister feels—as your Augusta feels for you.

Caroline's reference to Augusta probably implied carnal feelings rather than sisterly affection. That her blessings were less than heartfelt is made clear by her remark to Byron's publisher that the poet would "never be able to pull with a woman who went to church punctually, understood statistics and had a bad figure." Her prediction was accurate, but it was the woman who first refused to "pull" any longer; in January 1816, Anne took her month-old daughter (*see* **Lovelace, Ada Byron, Countess of**) and left Byron, never to return. The marriage had been a complete disaster. With scandal, rumors, and recriminations incessantly circling about him, in September 1816 Byron left England forever.

Caroline had last seen the man who shaped and shattered her life during the summer of 1815, when she paid a social call to the newlyweds with her aunt, Lady Melbourne. Caroline is said to have sat silently throughout the visit, and Byron, when he joined the group, was horrified to see her. By the following summer, she was working furiously, as Byron had predicted, at "scribbling" her first novel *Glenarvon*. The work was written at break-neck speed and published two weeks after Byron left England. An overwrought, romantic tale, the novel told their story of love and betrayal, and its characters were barely disguised versions of Caroline, Byron and her friends and relatives who had failed to understand or support her. The work was a bestseller which ran to several editions and was translated into French and German.

While writing the novel no doubt provided welcome catharsis for Caroline, its publication ruined her. She had taken the final step from which neither her noble birth nor her elfin charm could rescue her; she was shunned by society, excluded from respectable houses, ostracized and ignored. William's family pressed him to obtain a legal separation, fearing that his political career would be irreparably damaged. While he resisted, she spent her time at Brocket, writing, sketching and caring devotedly for her son who, it was now evident, was both mildly retarded and epileptic. She claimed not to mind the social exclusion: "If I did not see how anxious William is about it, for myself I should not care if I retired for ever." In 1819, she published a long gloomy poem, portraying the end of the world, which began "I'm sick of fame—I'm gorged with it."

Caroline's usually robust health began to deteriorate under the strain of her isolation. According to Strickland, she "was often ill, distracting herself with wine and unsavoury company, dulling her senses with laudanum." She wrote a second novel, *Graham Hamilton*, which graphically describes the disturbing effects of the drug laudanum (a solution of opium dissolved in alcohol), then freely available and often taken for trivial ailments such as toothache. Caroline wrote of nightmarish hallucinations: "It was as if my imagination was struck . . . as if material objects vanished, and the perceptions of the mind became too bright and vivid for the understanding to bear." The novel failed, as did her third attempt at fiction, *Ada Reis*. While both were imaginative and competent works, they neither contained any sensational gossip nor a Byronic hero and both appeared anonymously, so that the public could not associate them with the fallen star of aristocratic society.

Caroline was deeply discouraged. Her association with Byron had sparked her ambition to write, and she knew that she had ability. She took refuge in frenetic activity, galloping wildly about her Hertfordshire estate. The aspiring poet and admirer Edward Bulwer-Lytton described her at this time—she was now 40—as "a slight rounded figure [with] a childlike mode of wearing her hair, which was of a pale golden colour, in fine curls." She wrote to another friend, William Godwin, the widowed husband of Mary Wollstonecraft, that "Life, after all that has been said of its brevity, is very, very long." In April 1824, Byron died in Greece, and by 1825 the Lamb family was renewing its efforts to persuade William to obtain a legal separation. The family was, by this time, convinced of Caroline's insanity; it is likely that the news of Byron's death accentuated her lifelong tendency to depression and erratic behavior. She wrote to her cousin Hart: "I feel violently. Is that madness?"

After strenuously disputing the terms of her financial settlement, an indication that she was

Leigh, Augusta (1784–1851)

Influential sister of Lord Byron. Name variations: Augusta Byron; Mrs. George Leigh. Born Augusta Mary Byron in Paris, France, on January 26, 1784; died of cancer on November 27, 1851; daughter of John Byron and Lady Carmarthen (formerly the wife of Francis, Marquis of Carmarthen, and later 5th duke of Leeds); aunt of *Ada Byron, countess of Lovelace; married her cousin Colonel George Leigh, in 1807 (died 1850); children: **Georgiana Augusta Leigh** (b. November 4, 1808); **Augusta Charlotte Leigh** (b. February 9, 1811); George Henry John Leigh (b. June 3, 1812); Elizabeth Medora Leigh (b. April 15, 1814); Frederick George Leigh (b. May 9, 1816); **Amelia Marianne** Leigh (b. November 27, 1817); Henry Francis (b. January 28, 1820).

Augusta Leigh was the product of a scandalous liaison between John Byron, known as Mad John, and **Lady Carmarthen**, who was then married to Francis, marquis of Carmarthen. Divorcing her first husband, Lady Carmarthen was eight months pregnant with Augusta when she married John Byron and fled to Paris. Augusta was born on January 26, 1784, and her mother died in childbirth. John Byron had little use for Augusta, foisting her upbringing off on relatives. But the non-essential Augusta, writes Henry Blyth, would later prove to be the "most important factor in shaping the career of her future half-brother George Gordon Byron."

Lord Byron fell in love with his half-sister, and there was speculation that Augusta's daughter **Medora Leigh** was the product of an incestuous relationship between the two. It did not help that the name Medora came from Byron's poem *The Corsair*.

SOURCES:

Mackay, Charles. *Medora Leigh: A History and Autobiography*. 1869.
Turney, Catherine. *Byron's Daughter*. NY: Scribner, 1972.

not as deranged as the family claimed, Caroline agreed to leave for France. She lived for several months in a rented room in Calais but was desperately homesick for her son, her country life, and her horses. William relented and allowed her to return to Brocket. Caroline was soon restless again, in failing health but still burning with energy and ambition. She was without any creative outlet: "Action was the light of life. I cannot labour. . . . [W]ere I to publish what I write, I should only make enemies"; "shall I fret, fret and die?" She confided to her cousin Hart: "I feel too much to live long" and, with the same premonition of impending death, sent a detailed letter to her son. She gently informed Augustus that she wanted him to have some knowledge of the history of England and of current events, to be able to write a decent hand, "and I should like you to know enough of affairs in general to prevent you being in the hands of Ragamuffins . . . no more . . . for you should not overload yr memory nor strain yr understanding."

She saw little of William. In 1827, he was appointed chief secretary for Ireland—by 1834 he was to become prime minister of England—and, freed by the terms of his separation from Caroline, William resumed his affair with his former mistress. In October 1827, Caroline's doctor sent news to her husband that she was very ill but "with feelings of perfect resignation says she does not mind to die." In January 1828, William wrote to his mistress, **Lady Brandon**, that Caroline was dying, observing with his own share of bitterness that "the only bitter feelings which affect her are those which I knew she would suffer . . . repentance of the course she has run." Her devoted cousin Hart, the duke of Devonshire, spoke more gently, praising the honesty which had played its part in destroying her: "She had a candour."

Caroline's candor allowed her to critically evaluate the romantic obsession which had consumed her life: "Love is what an angel may feel for suffering man . . . but my feelings were the overbearing violence of passion." She wrote of the "tumult, the ardour, the romance, which bewildered my reason" and "clouded my understanding." In her gloomy poem "A New Canto," she had prophesied that her name would be kept "in capitals, like Kean." She might as well have written "like Byron," for whenever his life is examined, hers is inextricably linked to it. Whatever his feelings for her, Caroline's passion for him was the archetypal romantic obsession, self-negating, all-encompassing, and everlasting. Despite the agony it cost her, Caroline's devotion endured; her lover was always "that dear, that angel, that misguided and misguiding Byron, whom I adore, although he left that dreadful legacy on me, my memory."

SOURCES AND SUGGESTED READING:

Cecil, Lord David. *Melbourne*. Westport, CT: Greenwood Press, 1971 (first published in Indianapolis by Bobbs-Merrill, 1954).

Grosskurth, Phyllis. *Byron: The Flawed Angel*. Boston, MA: Houghton Mifflin, 1997.

Marchand, Leslie A. *Byron: A Biography*. Volume I. NY: Alfred A. Knopf, 1957.

———, ed. *"Famous in my time"; Byron's Letters and Journals 1810–1812*. Vol. 2. London: John Murray, 1973.

Strickland, Margot. *The Byron Women*. London: Peter Owen, 1974.

(Dr.) Kathleen Garay,
Acting Director, Women's Studies Programme,
McMaster University, Hamilton, Canada

Melbourne, Elizabeth (d. 1818). See Lamb, Caroline for sidebar.

Lamb, Elizabeth (d. 1818).

See Lamb, Caroline for sidebar on Lady Elizabeth Melbourne.

Lamb, Emily (d. 1869)

Countess of Cowper and Shaftesbury. Name variations: Emily Lamb; Lady Palmerston; Viscountess Palmerston; Emily Cowper. Born Emily Lamb; died in 1869; daughter of Peniston Lamb, 1st viscount Melbourne, and Lady Elizabeth Melbourne (d. 1818); sister of William Lamb, 2nd Lord Melbourne (1777–1848), and George Lamb (1784–1834, a politician and writer); sister-in-law of Caroline Lamb; married Lord Cowper of Althorps, 5th earl of Cowper, on July 20, 1805 (died, June 21, 1837); married Henry John Temple, 3rd Viscount Palmerston (British prime minister), on December 16, 1839 (died 1865); children: (with Cowper) Emily Cowper; Fanny Cowper; Fordwich Cowper.

The lovely and warm-hearted Emily Lamb, youngest daughter and one of six children of Lady **Elizabeth Melbourne** and Preston Lamb, grew up with the Cavendishes and the Ponsonbys in the Devonshire House set, and thus became part of English Whig Society. In July 1805, Emily married the somewhat dull but very wealthy Lord Cowper of Althorps. Her brother William Lamb, 2nd lord Melbourne, was married around the same time to *Caroline (Ponsonby) **Lamb**, and while Emily was devoted to her brother, she had little affection for her tempestuous sister-in-law. In fact, she spent a good deal of time trying to protect her brother from Caroline's excesses, since William seemed reluctant to take any positive action himself. Emily's own husband, by at least one account, was less than attentive, but Emily found distractions in her children and in her friendship with the secretary-at-war, Lord Palmerston, who would later become the liberal prime minister. Called "Cupid" because of his twinkling eyes and jovial manner, Palmerston would become Emily's second husband in 1839, following Lord Cowper's death.

Emily Lamb was one of the foremost political hostesses of her day, and as a member of a political family and the intimate friend and later wife of Lord Palmerston, she was privy to the intrigues of the inner circle of the Whig Party. Her correspondence, the bulk of which was the property of *Edwina Ashley Mountbatten, was edited and published in 1957 by Tresham Lever (*The Letters of Lady Palmerston*) and provides a vivid account of English life and politics from the time of King George IV through the middle years of Queen *Victoria's reign.

SOURCES:

Lever, Tresham. *The Letters of Lady Palmerston.* London: John Murray, 1957.

SUGGESTED READING:

Blyth, Henry. *Caro, The Fatal Passion: The Life of Caroline Lamb.* NY: Coward-McCann, 1972.

Lamb, Félix (1809–1875).

See Héricourt, Jenny Poinsard d'.

Lamb, Martha J.R. (1826–1893)

American historian. Born Martha Joanna Reade Nash at Plainfield, Massachusetts, on August 13, 1826; died in New York City on January 2, 1893; attended schools in Goshen, Easthampton, and Northampton, Massachusetts; married Charles A. Lamb, in September 1852 (possibly divorced 1866).

After her marriage in 1852, Martha Lamb moved to Chicago with her husband. There she became friends with *Jane Hoge and *Mary A. Livermore and helped found the Home for the Friendless and the Half-Orphan Society. Possibly after divorcing her husband, Lamb moved to New York in 1866 where she became popular socially. She was secretary of the first Sanitary Fair and held membership in many learned societies. From 1883 until her death, she edited the *Magazine of American History,* in which she published many of her own essays. Her chief book, *The History of the City of New York* (two volumes, 1877–81), was the result of about 15 years of labor and research and is said to surpass *Mary L. Booth's pioneering history of 1859. Other volumes of note are *The Homes of America* and *Wall Street History.*

Lamb, Mary Anne (1764–1847)

English author who, with her brother, wrote the popular Tales of Shakespeare. *Born in London, England, on December 3, 1764; died at St. John's Wood, London, on May 20, 1847; daughter of John Lamb (a servant and clerk) and Elizabeth (Field) Lamb; sister of Charles Lamb (1775–1834, an author); educated at a day school in Fleet Street, London; children: (with her brother Charles) adopted an orphan girl named* Emma Isola, *daughter of an official at Cambridge University (1823).*

There was a taint of insanity in the impoverished family of Mary Anne Lamb. Of seven sib-

lings, only three survived infancy. Mary Lamb resided with her brother Charles until his death, except when fits of insanity caused her removal to an asylum, which, through the years, increased in frequency. On September 22, 1796, during a manic phase, Mary wounded her senile father John and killed her invalid mother **Elizabeth Field Lamb** by stabbing her in the heart. Declared insane at an inquest, Mary was removed to Hoxton under restraints. The next day, Charles, who had also been briefly confined in an institution for six weeks (1795–96), wrote to his friend Samuel Coleridge:

> My poor dear dearest sister in a fit of insanity has been the death of her own mother. I was at hand only time enough to snatch the knife out of her grasp. She is at present in a mad house, from whence I fear she must be moved to an hospital. . . . My poor father was slightly wounded.

But the following year, Charles, who had to forgo a planned marriage with **Ann Simmons** of Hertfordshire, persuaded the authorities to

Emily Lamb

make his sister his ward, and Mary Anne moved in with him. He wrote Coleridge:

My poor dear dearest sister, the unhappy & unconscious instrument of the Almighty's judgments to our house, is restored to her senses; to a dreadful sense & recollection of what has past, awful to her mind & impressive (as it must be to the end of life) but temper'd with religious resignation, & the reasonings of a sound judgment, which in this early stage knows how to distinguish between a deed committed in a transcient fit of frenzy, & the terrible guilt of a Mother's murther. . . . She has a most affectionate & tender concern for what has happened.

Mary Lamb wrote a few slight poems, but her principal work, the immensely popular *Tales from Shakespeare* (1807), was written in conjunction with her brother. Charles delighted in insisting that her stories were the best of the collection. He wrote the tragedies; she, the comedies. The Lambs also collaborated on poetry for children.

When well, Mary Lamb was remarkably placid and had a sweet disposition; the mutual devotion of brother and sister was beautiful and sometimes pathetic. On Charles Lamb's death in 1834, the East India Company granted Mary the pension to which a widow was entitled, and her brother had also made her comfort secure by his own savings as a clerk. Mary Anne Lamb survived her brother by 13 years and was buried beside him at Edmonton. *Dorothy Parker wrote *The Coast of Illyria*, a play based on the life Mary Lamb.

SUGGESTED READING:

Marrs, Edwin W., Jr. *The Letters of Charles and Mary Anne Lamb: Volume I, Letters of Charles Lamb, 1796–1801.* Ithaca, NY: Cornell University Press, 1975.

Lamballe, Marie Thérèse Louise of Savoy-Carignano, Princesse de (1749–1792)

French royal. Name variations: Marie Thérèse Louise de Savoie-Carignan. Born Marie Thérèse Louise of Savoy-Carignano in Turin on September 8, 1749; died in the massacre at La Force on September 3, 1792; fourth daughter of Louis Victor of Carignano (who died in 1774 and was the great-grandfather of King Charles Albert of Sardinia) and **Christine Henriette of Hesse-Rheinfels-Rothenburg**; *married Louis Alexandre Stanislaus de Bourbon, Prince de Lamballe (son of the duke of Penthièvre, a grandson of Louis XIV's illegitimate son, the count of Toulouse), in 1766 (died 1767).*

In 1766, Marie Thérèse Louise of Savoy-Carignano was married to Louis Alexandre Stanislaus de Bourbon, prince of Lamballe, great-grandson of Louis XIV's misbegotten son, the count of Toulouse. When her husband died the following year, Princesse de Lamballe, a widow at 18, retired with her father-in-law to Rambouillet, where she lived until the marriage of the dauphin and *Marie Antoinette (1770); Lamballe then returned to court.

Charmed by Lamballe's gentle and naive manners, Marie Antoinette singled her out for a companion and confidante. The impetuous dauphiness found in Lamballe a submissive temperament, and the two became fast friends. Lamballe was so close to Marie Antoinette that their relationship was used to fuel damaging gossip. Despite this and the dauphin's opposition, Lamballe was made superintendent of the royal household in 1774, the year the dauphin was crowned Louis XVI.

From 1780 to 1785, possibly because she had been replaced as confidante by *Yolande Martine Gabrielle de Polignac, Lamballe lived outside of court, but when the queen tired of the supposed greed of the Polignacs, she turned again to Lamballe. From 1785 to the French Revolution, Lamballe was Marie Antoinette's closest friend and a pliant instrument. She accompanied the queen to the Tuileries in Paris (October 1789), when a mob of women, angry over rising bread prices, marched on Versailles and demanded that the royal couple come to the city and relieve their plight. There, the queen and king and their children were, in effect, held hostage to the demands of both the National Assembly and the more radical city government. Around them swirled innumerable intrigues and counterplots. The royal family made plans to flee the country and find help at foreign courts. As Lamballe's salon served as a meeting place for the queen and the members of the Assembly whom Marie Antoinette wished to win over, the people believed Lamballe to be the soul of all the intrigues.

Mary Anne Lamb

Opposite page

Marie Thérèse Louise of Savoy-Carignano, Princesse de Lamballe

After visiting England to appeal for help for the royal family and writing her last will and testament on October 1791, Lamballe returned to support the queen and to set an example for other emigres. She was imprisoned in the Temple along with the queen on August 10, 1792. On August 19, Lamballe was transferred to La Force. On September 3, after refusing to take the oath against the monarchy, she was torn to pieces by the mob as she left the courthouse. Her head was placed on a pike and carried before the windows of her longtime friend, Marie Antoinette. Mme de Lamballe was 38.

SUGGESTED READING:

Bertin, George. *Madame de Lamballe*. Paris, 1888.

Dobson, Austin. *Four Frenchwomen*. 1890.

Hardy, B.C. *Princesse de Lamballe*. 1908.

Lescure, Comte de. *La Princesse de Lamballe . . . d'après des documents inédits*. 1864.

Lamber, Juliette (1836–1936).

See Adam, Juliette.

Lambert, Anne Thérèse de Marguenat de Courcelles (1647–1733).

See Salonnières.

Lambert, Juliette (1836–1936).

See Adam, Juliette.

Lambert, Madame de (1647–1733).

See Salonnières.

Lambert, Margaret Bergmann

(1914—)

German track-and-field champion and only Jewish athlete besides Hélène Mayer invited to represent the German team for the 1936 Berlin Olympics, though the Nazis refused to let her participate. Name variations: Gretel Bergmann. Born Margarethe Gretel Bergmann in Laupheim, Germany, in 1914; married Bruno Lambert (a doctor), in 1939; children: two sons.

Margaret Bergmann, known as Gretel, was born in Laupheim, Germany, in 1914. As a young girl, she played soccer and field handball on boys' teams. Since Germany had no collegiate sports system and amateur athletes trained in sports clubs, Bergmann joined Ulm's athletic club in 1930 and began winning events in track and field. Her rise in the German world of sports came to an abrupt halt three years later. Despite her many medals, the UFV club (the Ulm Soccer club) notified her that she was no longer welcome because she was Jewish. In response, she and her Jewish friends formed their own soccer club in Stuttgard,

❧▶ **Csák, Ibolya** (1915—)

Hungarian high jumper. Name variations: Csak. Born in January 1915.

In the 1936 Olympics in Berlin, there was a long, drawn-out duel for the gold medal between Hungary's Ibolya Csák and 16-year-old **Dorothy J. Tyler**. Both had jumped 5'3", but the completion ended in a jump off. Csak took first because she had less failures at that height than Tyler. Had a later rule applied for deciding ties, Tyler would have been the champion.

---

playing on a potato field. Bergmann was the only female on the team. As well, she was about to begin her studies at the University of Berlin but was told she could not attend classes. As discrimination intensified, her parents decided to move to Great Britain, and Bergmann enrolled in the London Polytechnic to study English. Competing for her new school, she won the British high-jump championship in 1934.

By 1933, Nazi discrimination had caused a groundswell of protest in the United States over the upcoming 1936 Olympics in Berlin. Germany had decreed that German-Jewish athletes would be barred from participating, while the U.S. Olympic Committee sought to have all athletes participate. The Americans threatened to boycott the Games which the Nazis hoped to use as a propaganda centerpiece. In 1934, Hitler's government seemed to give in, announcing that 21 Jews, including Gretel Bergmann, would be considered for a place on the German Olympic team. Bergmann had received notification that she was to return to Germany and compete for the Nazis. She was likewise informed that if she refused, members of her extended family, as well as all Jewish athletes, would suffer.

In the days leading up to the Olympics, however, Bergmann was not allowed to compete directly with German athletes as she was barred from joining the German Track and Field Association. But her results were as good or better than her teammates. The Nazis also assigned Doro Ratjen to be her roommate. In 1966, it was revealed that "Doro" was actually Hermann Ratjen. Gretel had strongly suspected Doro was a male, but the Nazis knew that, as a Jew, Bergmann could ill afford to betray the Aryan Ratjen. Ratjen, on the other hand, was unlikely to make advances toward Bergmann during the time they shared living quarters, because he would be severely punished for making advances to a Jewish woman.

In 1935, Bergmann was the only member of her group to meet Olympic standards. On June 30, 1936, she equaled the German women's high-jump record of 5'3". Two weeks later, on July 16, the day after the U.S. Olympic team set sail for Europe, Bergmann was informed that her achievements were inadequate. *Hélène Mayer, a tall blonde fencer, would be the only Jew allowed to participate in the Games. Ironically that summer, the half-Jewish Hungarian ❧▶ Ibolya Csák won the Olympic gold medal in Bergmann's event, with a jump of 5'3".

Bergmann left Germany in 1937, arriving in New York with $10, the only money she was allowed to bring out of the country. She began working, first as a maid, then as a masseuse, and eventually as a physiotherapist, earning $100 a month. Bruno Lambert, her fiancé whom she had met in Germany, arrived in 1938 from Switzerland where he had been studying medicine. They were married in 1939 and lived in Jamaica, New York.

Margaret Bergmann Lambert was still competing. Training at the Park Central Athletic Association, she had won the American high-jump and shot-put championships in 1937 and 1938. The outbreak of war and the Holocaust, however, ended her career. With so many family members still in Germany, she had little desire to continue competing. Her husband joined the U.S. Army, and she moved with him from post to post. In 1980, Margaret Bergmann Lambert was recognized by the Jewish Sports Hall of Fame in Israel, one of the countless gifted individuals whose career was destroyed by the Nazis.

SOURCES:
Slater, Robert. *Great Jews in Sports*. Middle Village, NY: Jonathan David, 1983.

Karin L. Haag,
Athens, Georgia

Lambert-Chambers, Dorothea
(1878–1960).

See Chambers, Dorothea.

Lambertini, Imelda (1320–1333)

Italian religious. Name variations: *Blessed Imelda Lambertini. Born in 1320; died near Bologna in 1333.*

Blessed Imelda Lambertini died at age 13 at the Dominican house of Val di Petra, near Bologna. Her feast day is on May 12.

Lambrino, Jeanne (1898–1953).

See Lupescu, Elena for sidebar on Lambrino, Jeanne.

Lamburn, Richmal Crompton

(1890–1969)

English author and creator of William, the legendary scamp of British children's literature, who was featured in many of her books. Name variations: (pseudonym) Richmal Crompton. Born Richmal Crompton Lamburn on November 15, 1890, in Bury, Lancashire, England; died on January 11, 1969, in Borough Green, Kent, England; second daughter and one of three children of Edward John Sewall Lamburn (a cleric and schoolmaster) and Clara (Crompton) Lamburn; sister of Gwen Lamburn Disher and author Jack Lamburn (also known as Jack Lambourne, John Crompton); attended St. Elphins School; Royal Holloway College, University of London, B.A. (honors), 1914; never married; no children.

Selected works: Just William *(1922);* More William *(1922);* The Innermost Room *(1923);* William Again *(1923);* The Hidden Light *(1924);* William the Fourth *(1924);* Anne Morrison *(1925);* Still William *(1923);* The Wildings *(1925);* David Wilding *(1926);* The House *(1926, republished as* Dead Dwelling, *1926);* Kathleen and I, and, of Course, Veronica *(1926);* William the Conqueror *(1926);* Enter—Patricia *(1927);* Leadon Hill *(1927);* Millicent Dorrington *(1927);* A Monstrous Regiment *(1927);* William the Outlaw *(1927);* William in Trouble *(1927);* Felicity Stands By *(1928);* The Middle Things *(1928);* Mist and Other Stories *(1928);* Roofs Off *(1928);* The Thorn Bush *(1928);* William the Good *(1928);* Abbot's End *(1929);* The Four Graces *(1929);* Ladies First *(1929);* Sugar and Spice and Other Stories *(1929);* William *(1929);* Blue Flames *(1930);* William the Bad *(1930);* William's Happy Days *(1930);* The Silver Birch and Other Stories *(1931);* William's Crowded Hours *(1931);* Marriage of Hermione *(1932);* Portrait of a Family *(1932);* The Odyssey of Euphemia Tracy *(1932);* William the Pirate *(1932);* William the Rebel *(1933);* Chedsy Place *(1934);* The Old Man's Birthday *(1934);* William the Gangster *(1934);* Quartet *(1935);* William the Detective *(1936);* Caroline *(1936);* The First Morning *(1936);* Sweet William *(1936);* There Are Four Seasons *(1937);* William the Showman *(1937);* Journeying Wave *(1938);* William the Dictator *(1938);* Merlin Bay *(1939);* William and the A.R.P. *(1939, republished as* William's Bad Resolution, *1956);* Steffan Green *(1940);* William and the Evacuees *(1940);* Narcissa *(1941);* William Does His Bit *(1941);*

Mrs. Frensham Describes a Circle *(1942);* Weatherley Parade *(1944);* William Carries On *(1945);* William and the Brain Trust *(1945);* Westover *(1946);* The Ridleys *(1947);* Family Roundabout *(1948);* Just William's Luck *(1948);* Jimmy *(1949);* Frost at Morning *(1950);* William the Bold *(1950);* Jimmy Again *(1951);* William and the Tramp *(1952);* Linden Rise *(1952);* The Gypsy's Baby *(1954);* William and the Moon Rocket *(1954);* Four in Exile *(1955);* Matty and Dearingroydes *(1956);* William and the Space Animal *(1956);* William and the Artist's Model *(1956);* Blind Man's Bluff *(1957);* William's Television Show *(1958);* Wise Man's Folly *(1959);* The Inheritor *(1960);* William the Explorer *(1960);* William's Treasure Trove *(1962);* William and the Witch *(1964);* Jimmy the Third *(1965);* William and the Pop Singers *(1965);* William and the Masked Ranger *(1966);* William the Superman *(1968);* William the Lawless *(1970).*

A British schoolteacher who delighted youngsters and adults alike with her lively, 11-year-old anti-establishment hero, "Just William," novelist Richmal Crompton Lamburn had hoped to build her reputation as a writer of serious fiction; she would view the popularity of the William stories as something of a mixed blessing. In fact, Lamburn frequently referred to her literary brainchild as her "Frankenstein monster." "I sometimes say that I must have got rid of all my criminal tendencies in William, and if I hadn't written the William stories I might have ended in jail, but he just sort of kept me to the grindstone," she said shortly before her death. "He takes possession of every story I try to write, even though they are not about William."

Christened Richmal, but known as "Ray" to her friends, Lamburn was born in 1890 and grew up in the old mill town of Bury, Lancashire, England, where she was part of a close-knit Victorian family. Her father Edward, a cleric who had chosen to become a schoolmaster instead of taking a parish, believed strongly in the benefits of education for his daughters as well as his son, and Richmal and her elder sister **Gwen Lamburn (Disher)** became model students. Little brother Jack, who was the inspiration for many of William's adventures, was less disciplined, although he would later pursue a literary career of his own. Edward tested his children on history, geography and literature, and posted a world map in the bathroom for them to study. A sensitive and shy child, Lamburn frequently escaped to the attic, a quiet refuge where she read and composed her first stories and poems. She also edited *The Rainbow,* a magazine with an elite circulation of two subscribers, her brother and her rag doll, Lena.

After attending a local private school, Richmal and Gwen entered St. Elphins, an austere boarding school for daughters of the clergy located in Warrington, and dormed together. The school was relocated to Darley Dale, Derbyshire, following an outbreak of scarlet fever three years later in 1904. Jack, not strongly school-minded, remained a pupil in his father's school and their relationship was volatile. Shedding some of the shyness that had marked her childhood, Lamburn excelled in academics, particularly Latin, and contributed to the school magazine. She also enjoyed amateur theatricals and wrote plays for her schoolmates to perform. After graduating, she won a Founder's Entrance Scholarship to Royal Holloway College in London in 1911. Although remembered as a quiet, modest student, she thrived in the university environment, majoring in classics and enjoying a variety of athletics. She graduated in 1914, "being the best candidate of her year."

Richmal Crompton Lamburn

After college, Lamburn returned to St. Elphins, where she taught classics from 1914 to 1917. Her sister Gwen had married Thomas Disher and moved to London. When their father Edward died in 1915, their mother Clara sold the family home and moved to the Disher house. Missing her family, Lamburn followed in 1917. She bought a home and took a position as classics mistress at Bromley (Kent) High School, a private girls' day school in suburban London, to which she biked daily for the next six years. She loved her job and was popular with her students, who called her "inspiring and enthusiastic," with "laughter and fun . . . essential ingredients of the lessons."

Along with her teaching, Lamburn's writing career flourished. Following World War I, a number of magazines seeking short fiction appeared. Lamburn achieved her first professional publication in *The Girl's Own Paper*. Second jobs were forbidden by the school, so she submitted the story "Thomas" under the name Richmal Crompton. Her moonlighting was shortly discovered, but the Crompton stories were so popular that Lamburn was not censured. "Rice-Mould," which appeared in *Home Magazine* (February 1919), was Lamburn's first story containing the character of William. Almost from their inception, all of the William stories were illustrated by Thomas Henry, a talented artist from Nottinghamshire, whose lively style captured the character perfectly. Although Lamburn kept up a lively correspondence with Henry through the years, she met him only once, at a luncheon in Nottingham in 1958. Following his death in 1962, the William stories were illustrated by Henry Ford.

In the summer of 1923, not long after the publication of two volumes of collected William stories, *Just William* and *More William*, Lamburn was stricken with polio which left her without the use of her right leg. Forced to give up full-time teaching, she concentrated on her writing career. From 1922 to 1969, she produced 38 William titles, which were subsequently adapted into four films, and one radio and two television series. The character of William, described by **Mary Cadogan** as "anarchic, disheveled, obstructionist, opinionated and unbookish to the point of Philistinism," was the direct opposite of his creator, who was a staunch Conservative and a member of the Church of England. The first William stories, written for an adult audience, were Lamburn's best; the later efforts, produced exclusively for children, lost some of their wit and charm. By the 1960s, Lamburn felt "written out" and thus devoted much of her time to helping with the film and television scripts of her William stories. The series was never popular in the United States, because, in the opinion of **Margaret Masson**, America had its own version of William in the character of Penrod Schofield, created by Booth Tarkington. But Lamburn had a different take, believing that American children developed "straight from the cradle to adolescence," thus bypassing the prepubescent period of 11-year-old William Brown. Only two of Lamburn's non-William novels—*Dread Dwelling* (1926) and *The Old Man's Birthday* (1934)—were published in America.

Lamburn also produced some 40 other titles, many of them love stories which she turned out at the rate of one a year, but none had the appeal of the William books. Her early novels, *The Innermost Room* (1923) and *Anne Morrison* (1925), are interesting mainly for their autobiographical content; *Anne Morrison* provides a portrait of her father and an interesting account of Lamburn's school days.

Prevented from biking by the paralysis in her leg, Lamburn bought a car, traveled Europe with friends, kept detailed diaries, and doted on her family. With earnings from her William stories, she built a home on Oakley Road in Bromley Common, and her mother Clara came to live with her. A smoker in a day when few women smoked, Lamburn was diagnosed with breast cancer when she was in her 40s and had a mastectomy at home. She was nursed back to health by her mother, who lived with her until her death from a heart attack in 1939.

With the outbreak of World War II, her sister Gwen, who had divorced in 1935, moved into Lamburn's house at Bromley, bringing along her two daughters Margaret and Richmal Disher. Thereafter, Lamburn was their primary source of financial support. Her sister's son had already joined the war effort, and Lamburn volunteered for the Auxiliary Fire Service. During the war, she had a home built for her sister and nieces; after they moved in 1943, Lamburn lived alone with her dog Ming.

In the 1950s, she moved to a smaller house in Chislehurst, Kent, and continued to write. During her later years, Lamburn was drawn to religious mysticism and developed a belief in reincarnation. The author enjoyed good health until 1960, when she twice broke a leg. The following year, she suffered a heart attack and had several ongoing illnesses but fought hard to return to a full, independent life. After spending an evening with her family, Lamburn died of a second heart attack on January 11, 1969, with a new William story outlined on her desk. Her

niece **Richmal Disher Ashbee**, to whom Lambert was closely attached, completed the story from her aunt's notes, and it appeared in the final William collection, *William the Lawless* (1970).

SOURCES:

Cadogan, Mary. "Richmal Crompton," in *This England*. Winter 1990.

Commire, Anne, ed. *Something about the Author.* Vol. 5. Detroit, MI: Gale Research.

Shattock, Joanne. *The Oxford Guide to British Women Writers.* Oxford and NY: Oxford University Press, 1993.

SUGGESTED READING:

Cadogan, Mary. *Richmal Crompton: The Woman Behind William.* London: Unwin, 1986.

Williams, Kay. *Just Richmal: The Life and Work of Richmal Crompton Lamburn*, 1986.

Barbara Morgan,
Melrose, Massachusetts

laMdluli, Labotsibeni (c. 1858–1925).

See Labotsibeni Gwamile laMdluli.

La Meri (b. 1898)

America's leading authority on ethnic dance. Name variations: Russell Meriwether Hughes. Born Russell Meriwether Hughes in Louisville, Kentucky, in 1898; educated at Texas Woman's University, Denton University, and Columbia University; studied ballet with local teachers in San Antonio, 1913–20, Hawaii, 1917, Barcelona, 1922; studied ballet with Aaron Tomaroff and Ivan Tarasoff; studied modern dance with Michio Ito, 1925; also studied dance in Mexico, South America, Spain, Africa, India, Ceylon, the Philippines, and Japan, 1926–39.

La Meri, the stage name of Russell Meriwether Hughes, made her professional debut with a Texas tour in 1923. She continued to tour throughout the world until the advent of World War II in 1939. Returning to New York, she helped found the School of Natya in May 1940 with *Ruth St. Denis. In two years' time, the school melded with the Ethnologic Dance Center, also founded by La Meri, which offered in its prospectus the study of dance from nations throughout the world; the school continued until 1956. Meanwhile, La Meri toured while creating many ethnic dances, including *El Amor Brujo*, a Bharata Natyam interpretation of *Swan Lake*. Her books include *Principles of the Dance Art* (1933), *Dance as an Art Form* (1933), *Gesture Language of the Hindu* (1941), *Spanish Dancing* (1948), and *The Basic Elements of Dance Competition* (1965). Often a guest lecturer at colleges and universities, La Meri also taught at Jacob's Pillow summer dance school. The New York Public Library dance division contains the La Meri Collection, a wealth of photos and clippings from her extensive career.

La Messine (1836–1936).
See Adam, Juliette.

La Montagne-Beauregard, Blanche (1899–1960)

French-Canadian poet. Name variations: Blanche Lamontagne. Born in 1899; died in 1960.

A regionalist, Blanche La Montagne-Beauregard generally wrote pastorals, dealing affectionately with the simpler ways of early times. Her works include *Visions Gaspésiennes* (1913) and *Ma Gaspésie* (1928).

Lamorlière, Rosalie (fl. 1793–1837)

French servant. Name variations: Lamorliere. Flourished between 1793 and 1837; a native of Breteuil in Picardy, France.

A native of Breteuil in Picardy, Rosalie Lamorlière was an illiterate servant who had served as a chambermaid to **Mme Beaulieu** before taking a job at the Conciergerie, a prison on the banks of the Seine, which was the last stop on the way to the guillotine. During *Marie Antoinette*'s 76-day imprisonment there in 1793, Lamorlière became her servant, and the queen held her in high affection.

Over 40 years later, in 1837, Lamorlière dictated a sympathetic, 17-page account of Marie Antoinette's final days to the Abbot Lafont d'Aussonne. The queen, who was under constant surveillance by hostile guards, was experiencing heavy and irregular menses. On October 16, the day she was to mount the scaffold, "She asked me secretly for some linen," recounted Lamorlière, "and I immediately cut up my chemise and put those strips of cloth under her bolster." As she prepared to dress and change her bloody padding, the queen tried to maintain her dignity, motioning for Lamorlière to stand in front of her, to shield her from the gaze of the guard. But as Marie Antoinette bent down and removed her dress, said Lamorlière, the officer approached and "watched the Queen change. Her Majesty immediately put her shawl back across her shoulders and said to that young man, with great gentleness: 'In the name of decency,

Monsieur, allow me to change my linen without a witness.'" The gendarme replied, curtly, "I cannot consent to that." The queen sighed and finished dressing "with all possible precaution and modesty. . . . She carefully rolled up her poor bloody chemise and concealed it in one of her sleeves. . . ; then she stuffed that linen into a chink she noticed between the old canvas wall covering and the wall."

Lamorlière "basked in the aura of martyred sainthood that surrounded Marie Antoinette decades after her death," writes **Marilyn Yalom**. Said to be beautiful even into her dotage, Lamorlière spent her final days in the Hospice des Incurables, a home for the sick, with the aid of her benefactor, *Marie Therese Charlotte, duchess of Angoulême and daughter of Marie Antoinette, who had provided her an annual pension of 200 francs. Modern historians have profited from the servant woman's oral history. Lamorlière's portrayal of Marie Antoinette's courage and calm in her finals days is in direct contrast to British historian J.M. Thompson's 1943 interpretation of her behavior as one of haughty defiance.

SOURCES:
Yalom, Marilyn. *Blood Sisters: The French Revolution in Women's Memory.* NY: Basic Books, 1993.

La Motte, Jeanne (1756–1791).
See Marie Antoinette for sidebar.

Lamour, Dorothy (1914–1996)

American actress, well known for her "Road" films. Born Mary Leta Dorothy Kaumeyer on December 10, 1914, in New Orleans, Louisiana; died on September 22, 1996, in Los Angeles, California; married Herbie Kaye (an orchestra leader), on May 10, 1935 (divorced 1939); married William Ross Howard II (a businessman), on April 7, 1943 (died 1978); children: two sons, Ridgely and Richard Howard.

Filmography: The Stars Can't Be Wrong (1936); The Jungle Princess (1936); Swing High, Swing Low (1937); High, Wide and Handsome (1937); Last Train from Madrid (1937); The Hurricane (1937); Thrill of a Lifetime (1937); Her Jungle Love (1938); The Big Broadcast of 1938 (1938); Tropic Holiday (1938); Spawn of the North (1938); St. Louis Blues (1939); Man About Town (1939); Disputed Passage (1939); Typhoon (1940); Johnny Apollo (1940); Moon over Burma (1940); Road to Singapore (1940); Chad Hanna (1940); Aloma of the South Seas (1941); Road to Zanzibar (1941); Caught in the Draft (1941); Beyond the Blue Horizon (1942); Road to Morocco (1942); The

Dorothy Lamour

Fleet's In *(1942)*; Star Spangled Rhythm *(1942)*; They Got Me Covered *(1943)*; Dixie *(1943)*; Riding High (Melody Inn, *1943)*; Show Business at War *(1943)*; Rainbow Island *(1944)*; And the Angels Sing *(1944)*; Road to Utopia *(1945)*; Duffy's Tavern *(1945)*; A Medal for Benny *(1945)*; Masquerade in Mexico *(1945)*; My Favorite Brunette *(1947)*; Variety Girl *(1947)*; Road to Rio *(1947)*; Wild Harvest *(1947)*; A Miracle Can Happen (On Our Merry Way, *1948)*; Lulu Bell *(1948)*; The Girl from Manhattan *(1948)*; Slightly French *(1948)*; Manhandled *(1948)*; The Lucky Stiff *(1949)*; Here Comes the Groom *(1951)*; The Greatest

Show on Earth *(1952)*; Road to Bali *(1953)*; Screen Snapshots #205 *(1953)*; The Road to Hong Kong *(1962)*; Donovan's Reef *(1963)*; Pajama Party *(1964)*; The Phynx *(1970)*; Won Ton Ton, the Dog Who Saved Hollywood *(1976)*; Creepshow 2 *(1987)*.

Dorothy Lamour captured the imagination of moviegoers as a sarong-clad beauty in her first major motion picture, *The Jungle Princess* (1936), and was typecast in a string of island theme movies that followed during the 1930s and 1940s. She reached her zenith as the sultry foil to Bob Hope and Bing Crosby in a zany series of "Road" movies. The trademark sarong which made Lamour a success was also a curse. The actress felt that from the beginning of her career her looks dictated the kind of roles she was given. "Nobody has ever wanted to take me seriously or admit I can act," she lamented.

She was born Mary Leta Dorothy Kaumeyer in 1914 in New Orleans, the daughter of a waiter and a waitress. After her parents divorced when she was young, her mother married a man by the name of Lambour. Dorothy would later drop the B to form the stage name Lamour. She began performing as a child and won a number of beauty contests in her teens, culminating in Miss New Orleans of 1931. She then moved to Chicago, where she worked at Marshall Field's as a sales clerk while trying to break into show business. Through a talent competition, she came to the attention of band leader Herbie Kaye, who hired her as a vocalist. While on tour, the two fell in love and were married in 1935.

In New York, Lamour got a job singing at the Stork Club, which later led to a contract with NBC and her own radio show in Los Angeles, "The Dreamer of Songs." She made her film debut in a Vitapoint short, *The Stars Can't Be Wrong* (1936), then successfully tested with Paramount and signed a standard seven-year contract. Hoping to cash in on her exotic looks, the studio featured her opposite Ray Milland in *The Jungle Princess* (1936). Appearing in a tight-fitting sarong with her long dark hair cascading down her back, Lamour was a hit despite the film's implausible story. "The main asset of the picture is the naturalness and unsophisticated charm of Dorothy Lamour," reported *Picturegoer*, "who makes the main character as credible as it is possible for it to be." Lamour also sang "Moonlight and Shadows" in the movie and, in 1937, recorded it for Brunswick Records, along with a trio of songs from her second movie *Swing High, Swing Low* (1937). Lamour sang perhaps her most famous screen song, "The Moon of

Manakoora," in the 1937 South Seas romance *The Hurricane*, which she made while on loan to Goldwyn. That same year, she began a two-year stint as a regular on the NBC radio show "The Chase and Sanborn Hour."

With her screen image in place, Lamour's career soared during the 1940s, and she became one of the studio's most valuable stars. There were, of course, the "Road" pictures with Crosby and Hope, the first of which, *Road to Singapore* (1940), found Lamour wearing her sarong and singing "The Moon and the Willow Tree" and "Too Romantic," both of which would be hit recordings. Combining adventure, slapstick, and show-business satire, the "Road" movies included *The Road to Zanzibar* (1941), *The Road to Morocco* (1942), *The Road to Utopia* (1945), *The Road to Rio* (1947), *The Road to Bali* (1953), and *The Road to Hong Kong* (1962), a later venture in which Lamour had only a guest cameo while the younger **Joan Collins**, at Crosby's insistence, took the role as female foil. During the 1940s, Lamour also teamed with Hope in *Caught in the Draft* (1941) and *They Got Me Covered* (1943), and appeared in a series of high-budget musical comedies, including *The Fleet's In* (1942), *Dixie* (1943), and *Riding High* (1943). She was heard regularly on such radio shows as "Lux Radio Theater," "Mail Call," and "Palmolive Party" and, during the war, participated in numerous war-bond drives. At one event, two of her sarongs fetched $2 million at auction. (One of her original sarongs is now on display at the Smithsonian.)

Lamour's personal life also took an upward turn in the 1940s. Divorced from Herbie Kaye in 1939, she married William Ross Howard of Baltimore in 1943, an event which prompted her to reflect on her career. "I got serious about my acting for the first time, I can't explain it," she said. "I wanted to start all over again on a different basis. Maybe to prove something to somebody." After the war, the couple adopted a son Ridgely (1945), and Lamour gave birth to a second son Richard (1949).

Lamour left Paramount in 1947, but her image followed her, and she had difficulty finding decent roles. She made a few forgettable films but had better luck on the singing front with successful engagements at the Palladium and in Glasgow, Scotland. She also made a successful LP album for Decca, *Favorite Hawaiian Songs*, and starred in her own radio show, "The Dorothy Lamour Show" (1948–49). Her only pictures in the 1950s were *The Greatest Show on Earth* (1952), in which she had an inconsequential role, and *Road to Bali* (1953), which lacked some of the usual fun of the "Road" pictures. In 1953, Lamour announced her retirement to raise her sons, but continued to make television and nightclub appearances and spent a week as **Abby Lane**'s replacement in the Broadway musical *Oh Captain!* In the early 1960s, she marketed a line of beauty products and wrote the book *Road to Beauty*.

Lamour's film career pretty much ended with a cameo in the comedy *Pajama Party* (1964), although she returned sporadically for brief appearances in *The Phynx* (1970), *Won Ton Ton, the Dog Who Saved Hollywood* (1976), and a segment of the horror film *Creepshow II* (1987). Her later years were punctuated with stage performances, including tours in *Hello Dolly!* and *Anything Goes*, as well as television appearances on shows like "The Love Boat," "Hart to Hart," "Remington Steele," and "Murder, She Wrote." Widowed in 1978, Lamour busied herself with her autobiography, *The Other Side of the Road*, which was published in 1980. Dorothy Lamour died at her North Hollywood home in 1996, age 81.

SOURCES:

Katz, Ephraim. *The Film Encyclopedia*. NY: Harper-Collins, 1994.

Parish, James Robert, and Michael R. Pitts. *Hollywood Songsters*. NY: Garland, 1991.

Shipman, David. *The Great Movie Stars: The Golden Years*. Boston, MA: Little, Brown, 1995.

Shooman, Annie. "Dorothy Lamour Travels Last Road," in *The Day* [New London, CT]. September 23, 1996.

SUGGESTED READING:

Lamour, Dorothy. *My Side of the Road*. Englewood Cliffs, NJ: Prentice Hall, 1980.

Barbara Morgan,
Melrose, Massachusetts

Lampkin, Daisy (1883–1965)

African-American civil rights activist and suffragist.
Born Daisy Elizabeth Adams on August 9, 1883, in Washington, D.C.; died on March 10, 1965, in Reading, Pennsylvania; daughter of George S. Adams and Rosa Anne (Proctor) Adams; educated at Reading public schools; married William Lampkin (a restaurateur), on June 18, 1912; no children.

A political activist who for over half a century used her formidable fund-raising skills to advance civil rights for all African-Americans, Daisy Lampkin began her career on the streets of Pittsburgh urging black housewives to organize consumer protest groups. In 1915, she was elected president of the *Lucy Stone Woman Suffrage League (which prior to the 19th Amendment promoted suffrage among black women and later, as the Lucy Stone Civic League, financed scholarships for local black students), a post she would hold for over 40 years and one which quickly led to her involvement with the National Association of Colored Women (NACW). In a typical example of her long-term commitment to organizations which shared her goal of equal rights and integration, Lampkin would serve the NACW over many years as national organizer, as vice-president, and as chair of the executive board.

Lampkin became vice-president of the influential black weekly *Pittsburgh Courier* in 1929, a position she would hold throughout her life in addition to her civic activities. Through her work with the NACW, Lampkin came to know noted educator *Mary McLeod Bethune. In 1935, they founded the National Council of Negro Women, which by coordinating the many African-American women's groups around the country combined the local power of those groups into a single entity with national political clout. Lampkin showed keen dedication to both local and national organizations throughout her career, as can be seen in the positions she held with the Republican Party during this period: chair of the Negro Women's Republican League of Allegheny County, Pennsylvania, vice-chair of the Negro Voters League of Pennsylvania, and chair of the Colored Voters' Division of the Republican National Committee. In either 1928 or 1933 (sources differ), she had been the first African-American woman elected as an alternate delegate-at-large to the Republican National Convention.

Some of Lampkin's most significant contributions were through her work with the National Association for the Advancement of Colored People (NAACP), which had been founded in 1909. She became a member of the organization's Pittsburgh branch in the 1920s and soon joined their executive committee. At the time a fairly inactive branch of the national organization, the Pittsburgh chapter gained force and 2,000 new members as a result of a campaign headed by Lampkin in 1929. This success brought her to the attention of the NAACP's national leaders, and in 1930 Lampkin became a regional field secretary. She was promoted to national field secretary in 1935, traveling throughout America to help organize new chapters of the association, to raise memberships and funds, and to speak about the NAACP's vital need for the support of individuals. She was instrumental in fund-raising for the organization's national anti-lynching campaign in those years, and is also considered responsible for getting Thurgood Marshall (later the renowned U.S. Supreme Court justice) to join their Legal Defense Committee. Among the other prominent African-Americans she worked with were *Nannie Helen Burroughs, Walter White, Roy Wilkins, and *Ella Baker. By the time she resigned her post in 1947, due to poor health and a desire not to travel so much, Lampkin was the NAACP's most successful fund raiser.

A woman of prodigious energy, Lampkin did not slow down much in the subsequent years. Devoted to her local church (for which she also helped to raise funds) and to her husband, William Lampkin, with whom she had shared a successful and mutually supportive marriage since 1912, she nonetheless continued to spend much of her time working for the NAACP. She remained a major organizer of branch campaign drives as the American civil-rights movement gained strength throughout the 1950s and 1960s, instituting a highly productive team method of campaigning that involved local urban churches in membership and fund-raising drives. When she ran the campaign in Pittsburgh in 1962, the chapter membership increased by 4,647. In 1963, she ran a campaign in Camden, New Jersey, increasing membership from 2,705 to 4,078 and raising nearly $11,000. Lampkin was on a similar campaign in Camden in 1964 (the year that saw the passage of the federal Civil Rights Act barring segregation in the public sphere), when she suffered a stroke. She died five months later, on March 10, 1965.

Among the honors Daisy Lampkin received for her unstinting efforts to secure equal rights for African-Americans was an award from the National Council of Negro Women for building the largest membership enrollment in NAACP history (1944), and an honorary membership in the community-oriented Delta Sigma Theta Sorority (1947). She was also given the first *Eleanor Roosevelt-Mary McLeod Bethune World Citizenship Award from the NCNW in December 1964, but was too ill to attend the ceremony. *Lena Horne accepted for her. In 1983, Lampkin became the first black woman in Pennsylvania whose house was designated a historical landmark. Important as they are, these honors pale in comparison to the signal achievements being hard-fought for and finally won in the last decades of her life by the NAACP and the rest of the civil-rights movement, achievements to which she contributed and devoted her life. As she had once said in a speech to a branch of the NAACP, "Living in an integrated society is [a] right; it is not a privilege extended . . . by others."

SOURCES:
Sicherman, Barbara, and Carol Hurd Green. *Notable American Women: The Modern Period.* Cambridge, MA: Belknap Press of Harvard University, 1980.
Smith, Jessie Carney, ed. *Notable Black American Women.* Detroit, MI: Gale Research, 1992.

Karina L. Kerr, M.A.,
Ypsilanti, Michigan

Lanahan, Frances Scott (1921–1986).

See Fitzgerald, Zelda for sidebar on Frances Scott Fitzgerald.

Lancaster, countess of.

See Blanche of Artois (c. 1247–1302).
See Chaworth, Maud (1282–c. 1322).
See Alice de Joinville.

Lancaster, duchess of.

See Blanche of Lancaster (1341–1369).
See Beaumont, Isabel (d. 1368).
See Beaufort, Joan (c. 1379–1440) for sidebar on Swynford, Catherine (c. 1350–1403).
See Beaufort, Joan (c. 1379–1440) for sidebar on Constance of Castile (1354–1394).

Lancaster, Isabel of (d. 1368).

See Beaumont, Isabel.

Lancaster, Nancy (1897–1994)

American-born socialite whose influence led to the rise of the English-country style of interior decorating. Name variations: Nancy Tree. Born Nancy Perkins in Albemarle County, Virginia, in 1897; died in Oxfordshire, England, in 1994; daughter of Lizzie Langhorne and T. Moncure Perkins (a meat-packing executive); niece of Irene Langhorne Gibson (1873–1956) and Nancy Witcher Astor (1879–1964); married Henry Field, grandson of department-store magnate Marshall Field, in 1917 (died 1918); married Ronald Lambert Tree (later a Conservative member of Parliament), in 1920 (divorced 1947); married Claud G. Lancaster (a British politician), in 1947 (divorced); children: (second marriage) Michael and Jeremy.

Although Nancy Lancaster refused to call herself a decorator, her talent for cultivating the beauty of her stately homes and gardens into an appearance of "pleasing decay" gave rise to the popular English-country style of decorating. A mixture of bright colors, sun-faded fabrics, and furniture arranged without regard to historical periods, this studiedly casual and highly influential look stood in marked contrast to the rigid formality prevalent in pre-World War II upper-class British interior design.

Lancaster was born in Albemarle County, Virginia, in 1897, the daughter of **Lizzie Langhorne** and T. Moncure Perkins, a meat-packing executive. The family included two highly distinguished aunts: *****Nancy Witcher Astor**, who would become the first woman elected to the British House of Commons in 1919, and ❧➤ **Irene Langhorne Gibson**, the original "Gibson girl," who through the ubiquitous illustrations of her husband Charles Dana Gibson was the epitome of idealized American womanhood during the Gilded Age. After the deaths of her parents when she was 15, Nancy was raised by Irene Gibson.

With her second husband, Lancaster moved to England in 1926, but her Virginia upbringing remained a constant influence throughout her life. The innovative decorating style she created drew upon her memories of the "romantic disrepair" of the plantations of her beloved Virginia, and gained especial popularity with the British upper classes which, battered by two world wars, were undergoing a transformation not unlike that of the post-Civil War Virginian aristocrats. She is credited with bringing vitality to the staid style of English decorating, and she inspired generations of European and American designers, including Mario Buatta and **Sister Parish**. Lancaster also raised old-fashioned roses and was regarded as a world-class hostess; among her guests were painter John Singer Sargent, fashion and portrait photographer Cecil Beaton, Baron De Meyer, Horst P. Horst, and King George VI and Queen *****Elizabeth Bowes-Lyon** of England. Winston Churchill often took weekend refuge at her 3,000-acre estate in Oxfordshire during the London blitz in World War II.

In 1944, Lancaster became co-owner of the design firm Colefax & Fowler in London, which decorated the homes of elite clients. Still preferring not to call herself a professional, she continued working into the mid-1980s. Nancy Lancaster died in her sleep in 1994, age 96.

SOURCES:

Becker, Robert. *Nancy Lancaster: Her Life, Her World, Her Art.* NY: Alfred A. Knopf, 1996.

"Nancy Lancaster, a Leader in Interior Design, Dies at 96," in *The New York Times Biographical Service.* August 22, 1994.

Rebecca Parks,
Detroit, Michigan

Lancefield, Rebecca Craighill

(1895–1981)

American immunologist and microbiologist who produced a system of classification for streptococci. Born Rebecca Craighill in Fort Wadsworth, Staten Island,

New York, on January 5, 1895; died in March 1981 in Little Neck, Queens, New York; daughter of William Edward Craighill and Mary Wortley Montague (Byram) Craighill; Wellesley College, B.A., 1916; Teachers College at Columbia University (in conjunction with Columbia Medical School), M.A., 1918; Columbia University, Ph.D., 1925; married Donald Elwood Lancefield (a scientist), on May 27, 1918; children: Jane Maddox Lancefield (who married George Leonard Hersey).

The daughter of an Army officer, Rebecca Lancefield was born on Staten Island, New York, and experienced a nomadic childhood following her father's postings. Educated at a number of public and private schools, she entered Wellesley in 1912 to study French and English, but her interest soon shifted to zoology. Upon graduating in 1916, she taught at a boarding school in Burlington, Vermont, saving most of her salary for graduate school. With the additional support of a scholarship for daughters of

◄❧
Gibson, Irene Langhorne. See *Astor, Nancy Witcher* for sidebar.

𝒩ancy
ℒancaster

the military, she was able to enroll at Columbia University with the stipulation that she confine her studies to Teachers College at Columbia. Since they offered no courses in bacteriology or genetics, she matriculated at Teachers College but took courses at the university's medical school. In 1918, she earned her M.A. and married a fellow student, Donald Lancefield.

While her husband studied for his Ph.D., Lancefield worked at the Rockefeller Hospital and taught briefly at the University of Oregon, when he had a position there. In 1922, the couple returned to New York, where Lancefield began her work on streptococci at the Rockefeller Institute and finished her Ph.D. Her doctoral work, which centered on developing a system for classifying an elusive strain of streptococcus, was frustratingly slow, and she did not receive her degree until 1925. Her findings were published in the *Journal of Experimental Medicine.* Continuing to investigate other strains of streptococci, she found that isolated substances from her samples could be used to group the streptococci into five different types. In 1940, after 20 years of work, her findings became the basis of the method of classifying streptococci adopted by the International Congress of Microbiology. By 1943, Lancefield's stature was such that she was elected president of the Society of American Bacteriologists.

Throughout her career, Lancefield continued to further classify different strains of streptococci, often utilizing her past research for new problems. In 1960, for example, she used a dried sample from 1935 to identify a strain of streptococci that was attacking lab mice. Advanced age did not slow down her personal research or her work within the broader scientific community. In 1960, at age 65, she was elected the first woman president of the American Association of Immunologists, and in 1970 she was elected to the National Academy of Science. Rebecca Lancefield died in 1981.

SOURCES:
Bailey, Brooke. *The Remarkable Lives of 100 Women Healers and Scientists.* Holbrook, MA: Bob Adams, 1994.

Barbara Morgan,
Melrose, Massachusetts

Lanchester, Elsa (1902–1986)

British-born actress whose Bride of Frankenstein *has become a cult classic. Born on October 28, 1902, in Lewisham, England; died in December 1986; only daughter and one of two children of Edith Lanchester and James Sullivan (a laborer); attended Mr. Kettle's School, London; married Charles Laughton (an actor), in 1929 (died 1962); no children.*

Selected filmography: One of the Best *(UK, 1927);* The Constant Nymph *(UK, 1928);* Day Dreams *(short, UK, 1929);* Comets *(UK, 1930);* The Love Habit *(UK, 1930);* The Stronger Sex *(UK, 1931);* Potiphar's Wife *(UK, 1931);* The Officers' Mess *(UK, 1931);* The Private Life of Henry VIII *(UK, 1933);* The Bride of Frankenstein *(1935);* Ladies in Retirement *(1941);* Son of Fury *(1942);* Tales of Manhattan *(1942);* Forever and a Day *(1943);* Thumbs Up *(1943);* Lassie Come Home *(1943);* Passport to Adventure *(1944);* The Spiral Staircase *(1946);* The Razor's Edge *(1946);* Northwest Outpost *(1947);* The Bishop's Wife *(1947);* The Big Clock *(1948);* The Secret Garden *(1949);* Come to the Stable *(1949);* The Inspector General *(1949);* Buccaneer's Girl *(1950);* Mystery Street *(1950);* The Petty Girl *(1950);* Frenchie *(1951);* Dreamboat *(1952);* Les Misérables *(1952);* Androcles and the Lion *(1953);* The Girls of Pleasure Island *(1953);* Hell's Half Acre *(1954);* Three-Ring Circus *(1955);* The Glass Slipper *(1955);* Witness for the Prosecution *(1958);* Bell Book and Candle *(1958);* Honeymoon Hotel *(1964);* Mary Poppins *(1964);* Pajama Party *(1964);* That Darn Cat *(1965);* Easy Come, Easy Go *(1967);* Blackbeard's Ghost *(1968);* Rascal *(1969);* Me, Natalie *(1969);* Willard *(1971);* Terror in the Wax Museum *(1973);* Arnold *(1973);* Murder by Death *(1976);* Die Laughing *(1980).*

Those who remember the British-born actress Elsa Lanchester tend to envision her as the macabre bride in the 1935 horror film *The Bride of Frankenstein,* a portrayal that Carlos Clarens referred to as "a delicate suggestion of both the wedding bed and the grave." Lanchester actually played dual roles in the film, also appearing as the author of *Frankenstein,* *Mary Wollstonecraft Shelley,* in the opening scenes. The demure and innocent portrayal of Shelley made her transformation into the female monster even more dramatic. While "The Bride" became Lanchester's trademark role, she played a wide range of character parts on both the stage and screen, sometimes teaming with her husband, actor Charles Laughton. For ten years, Lanchester appeared with a small theater ensemble in Hollywood, performing off-beat songs and comic sketches that she eventually turned into several concert shows.

Elsa Lanchester, distinguished by an elfin face and a mop of frizzy copper-colored hair, was the daughter of **Edith Lanchester** and James Sullivan, a pair of radical socialists who refused to marry, thus placing the burden of illegitimacy on their two children. Edith and James—or Biddy and Shamus, as they called each other—devoted their lives to social causes, and civil disobedience became the norm for Lanchester, as did an itinerant lifestyle. "My parents moved six times to avoid having me vaccinated because my brother Waldo had 'taken' very badly six years before," Lanchester recalled in her autobiography *Elsa Lanchester Herself*. Edith, who held several college degrees, also fought to home school her daughter, so Lanchester's formal education was delayed for a year while the battle waged. She finally ended up as the only girl at her brother's school, which was run by the distinguished socialist, Frederick Kettle.

When Lanchester was around 11, Edith began taking classes with Raymond Duncan, *Isadora Duncan's brother, who offered free courses in weaving, spinning, sandal-making, and dance at a local meeting hall. While Edith stitched shoes, Elsa took dance lessons, studying Duncan's own method, "Greek rhythmic gymnastics." As a result of her excellent progress, she was invited, all expenses paid, to attend Isadora's school for talented children in Paris ("To Teach the World to Dance"). "When I joined the school, Isadora was pregnant and I believe having one of her lawsuits with the dancer *Loïe Fuller," Lanchester recalled. "Swathed in draperies, she did most of her teaching lying on a chaise lounge, covered from head to foot, even her face, with the finest veiling of the palest cream color." Unfortunately, all Lanchester learned from Duncan was, in her words, "to run away from or toward an enemy or to become an autumn leaf . . . or something." When the war threatened, Lanchester went home, and Duncan returned to Russia and "melted into history."

When Kettle closed his school in 1914, Lanchester's formal education came to an end, and she became an assistant to **Rose Benton**, a Raymond Duncan disciple who lectured on his method while Lanchester demonstrated. In addition, she took private students and taught at a school in Chelsea run by **Margaret Morris**, who also had a summer school in the Isle of Wight. Eventually, Lanchester established her own children's theater in Soho, where she produced variety shows and adaptations from popular children's stories. When she was 17, she and a small group of friends opened a late-night club, The Cave of Harmony, which was housed in a tiny firetrap of a building which also served as Lanchester's residence. The small company produced cabaret shows and obscure one-act plays that drew the attention of distinguished actors who were anxious to undertake some Pirandello or Chekhov in their off hours. It was here that Lanchester began performing the obscure out-of-print songs that eventually became her specialty, such as "Please Sell No More Drink to My Father" (written as a serious Temperance song) and "The Ratcatcher's Daughter." She also performed in comedy sketches; one skit, with *Angela Baddeley, featured two charwomen, Mrs. Bricketts and Mrs. Du Bellamy, who chatted impromptu about interesting events or newspaper stories while hanging wash. Over the four years that the theater was in business, it attracted a number of the famous, including H.G. Wells, Aldous Huxley, James Whale and Evelyn Waugh, who said he came especially to hear Lanchester sing "My Yiddisher Boy (With His Yoy, Yoy, Yoy)."

It was a patron of the Cave—producer Nigel Playfair—who gave Lanchester her start on the professional stage, casting her in *The Insect Play*, which also starred Baddeley, John Gielgud, and Claude Rains. Winning rave reviews for her role as The Larva, Lanchester was next cast as the sluttish maid in *The Way of the World*. She gradually worked her way up to larger roles and finally landed a lead in the revue *Riverside Nights*, in which she sang and danced her way through four or five of her odd little songs, much to the delight of the critics.

In 1929, Lanchester married Charles Laughton, a portly and insecure young graduate of the Royal Academy of Dramatic Art, whom she had met two years earlier when they were both cast in the play *Mr. Prohack*. Two years into the marriage, Laughton told his young bride that he was homosexual, a confession that so shocked Lanchester that she became deaf for about a week. "I suppose I shut my ears off, probably as a reaction to the news I hadn't wanted to hear," she theorized. Although Laughton's disclosure drove a wedge between the couple, the marriage endured for over 30 years, largely due to Lanchester's sense of duty, but also because of the couple's shared interests and genuine affection for each other. There were frequent estrangements, however, through which Lanchester was sustained by close outside relationships that came and went over the years. As she explained in her autobiography, she grew to accept Charles' affairs with other men as part of her life with him. "Perhaps it was unkind of me not to show disapproval. My acceptance may have been more cruel, in a way, and made Charles feel even more guilty about it all. He was a moral man—about everyone but himself. Himself he shocked; he horrified himself. . . . It made me very sad that Charles should have to feel so guilty about it; that he seemed to need to be so secretive, all the while still wanting to be found out."

Perhaps the greatest bond in their difficult marriage was the theater, which afforded the couple many opportunities to work together both on stage and in film. One of their earlier joint efforts on the stage was *Payment Deferred,* in which Lanchester played Laughton's daughter. (In the later film version of the play, Lanchester's role went to *Maureen O'Sullivan, who had more box-office appeal.) In September 1931, following a run in London, the play was brought to New York with the cast intact, giving the couple their first glimpse of America. When the play closed, they returned to London, only to turn around and sail back to the United States so Laughton could start the movie *The Devil and the Deep,* which launched his American film career. For some time, Laughton commuted back and forth to London, where he and Lanchester frequently appeared together with the Old Vic. In 1933, the couple made the British film *The Private Life of Henry VIII,* in which Lanchester played Henry's fifth wife ◄❧ **Anne of Cleves** to much acclaim. The film netted Laughton an Academy Award and is considered by some to have been the first great English film distributed in the United States.

❧▶

Anne of Cleves.

See Six Wives of Henry VIII.

One of Lanchester's personal triumphs at the Old Vic was the role of Ariel in *The Tempest,* opposite Laughton as Prospero. She felt it was her most serious and interesting acting experience with her husband, and also the play in which she learned to act rather than perform. Critic Harcourt Williams thought that her highly stylized interpretation took away from the play, but James Agate waxed poetic in his praise. "May I be forgiven for saying that until Miss Elsa Lanchester, the part of Ariel has never been acted?," he began. "She has a radiance that cannot be explained, and by an ingenious unwearying, yet unwearisome movement of the arms suggests kinship with that insect creation which, quivering in the sun, puts to shame the helicopter of human invention." Later, in 1935, Lanchester played perhaps her most controversially received role, Peter Pan, again sharing the stage with Laughton, who was Captain Hook. Lanchester found the character of Peter a bit officious and played him like a little general. In his book *A Life in the Theatre,* Tyrone Guthrie called Laughton's soft-pedaled Hook the hero of the evening. "It was when Peter Pan came on that little children hid their faces in their mothers' skirts and strong men shook with fear," he noted.

As Laughton's American film career became more established, the couple settled in California, where over the years they owned several houses. They would become American citizens in 1950. For ten years, beginning in 1941, Lanchester was associated with the Turnabout Theater, which was founded by Forman Brown, Harry Burnett, and Roddy Brandon, or the Yale Puppeteers as they came to be known. The unusual enterprise was housed in a converted theater outfitted with two stages, one for puppets and one for actors. The productions consisted of an hour-long puppet show, then—turnabout—a live revue. Lanchester joined the theater in its third week and soon became a regular, performing the songs and routines she had done at the Cave. Soon Forman Brown was adding his own original compositions to Lanchester's repertoire, the first of which, about a cleaning woman, went "If You Can't Get in the Corners (You Might as Well Give Up)." Through the years, Brown composed some 60 songs for Lanchester, who found him to be the perfect collaborator.

While working at the Turnabout in the evening, Lanchester had her days free to pursue her film career, which was well under way. She had made her film debut in 1927, in several two-reel comedies devised by H.G. Wells. She also made her first feature film that year, *One of the Best,* followed by *The Constant Nymph* in 1928. In America, Lanchester had a tougher time getting established in film, but she finally found her niche in character roles. She won Oscar nominations for her roles in *Come to the Stable* (1949), in which she also sang the song "Through a Long and Sleepless Night," and *Witness for the Prosecution* (1958), in which she was a nurse to the ailing lawyer, played by Laughton.

Lanchester used much of her material from the Turnabout in night-club performances, and also in her concert show, *Elsa Lanchester's Private Music Hall,* produced by Paul Gregory and musically arranged by Ray Henderson, who became her exclusive accompanist. Lanchester toured colleges and town halls throughout the United States and Canada with the production, covering a total of 22,000 miles by car. Later, in 1961, Laughton directed his wife in another one-woman show, the autobiographical revue *Elsa Lanchester—Herself,* which opened in New York City on February 4, 1961, during a major snowstorm. "If there's anyone who can make you forget about 17.4 inches of snow, it's Elsa Lanchester," read *The New York Times* the next morning. "The program notes that the show has been censored by Charles Laughton," it went on. "But his heart wasn't in it. In fact, if this is

Elsa censored, what is Elsa like uncensored? . . . [E]ven if you have to use dog sleds, skis, or bull-dozers, drop in on Elsa. She won't let you down." The show had a ten-week run in New York, followed by three two-week runs at the Ivar Theater in Hollywood.

While Lanchester's show was still in develop-ment, Laughton suffered a massive infection as a result of gallbladder surgery and was hospitalized for several weeks. He never regained his vitality. Lanchester remembered seeing him off on his last tour in 1961. "Sometimes you have a sudden flash that you're not going to see someone in health ever again, and I had the feeling—that I was a free woman. That's a terrible thing to say, in a way. But, at that moment, that's how I felt."

While on that tour, Laughton fell in the tub and broke his collar-bone. Subsequent surgery to repair the fracture revealed an advanced case of osteosarcoma (bone cancer). Lanchester spent the next year caring for her husband, who endured agonizing pain but did not know until the end that he was dying from cancer. Following his

death in December 1962, Lanchester returned to England, spending time with her aging mother and arranging for the sale of Laughton's extensive art collection. Returning to Hollywood, she re-ceived a few offers for movie roles, but "nothing to turn your grapes sour over," as she put it. She credited a stint on the television series "The John Forsythe Show" with connecting her to life again, and she also had two bonus runs of *Elsa Lanches-ter—Herself*. She finally did accept some of those mediocre film offers, a few of which were remi-niscent (in title only) of *The Bride of Franken-stein*: *Blackbeard's Ghost* (1968), *Terror in the Wax Museum* (1973), and *Murder by Death* (1976). In 1983, the actress completed a second autobiography, *Elsa Lanchester—Herself*, a com-panion to *Charles Laughton and I* (1937), which first appeared as a series in London's *Sunday Ex-press*. "I cannot tie up this ending with a pretty pink bow," she wrote. "Getting older is, to put it mildly, gruesome. And, having unloaded the past, memory is of course more localized now, though it seems to be a loyal machine willing to serve if forced. So time is now up to its tricks with me—

Elsa Lanchester and Boris Karloff in Bride of Frankenstein, *1935.*

the Bitch! It's suddenly always Christmas again. Oh, I forgot, it's *Father* Time!"

SOURCES:
Fowler, Glenn. "Elsa Lanchester, 84, Is Dead; Actress Portrayed Eccentrics," in *The New York Times Biographical Service.* December 1986, pp. 1447–1448.
Katz, Ephraim. *The Film Encyclopedia.* NY: HarperCollins, 1994.
Lanchester, Elsa. *Elsa Lanchester—Herself.* NY: St. Martin's Press, 1983.

Barbara Morgan,
Melrose, Massachusetts

Lanclos, Anne de (1623–1705).

See Lenclos, Ninon de.

Lanclos, Ninon de (1623–1705).

See Lenclos, Ninon de.

Lander, Louisa (1826–1923)

American marble sculptor. Born in Salem, Massachusetts, in 1826; died in Washington, D.C., in 1923.

Born in Salem, Massachusetts, in 1826, Louisa Lander was drawn to sculpting at an early age. Working first in Washington, D.C., she had already received a fair number of commissions when, in 1856, she traveled to Rome to become a student-assistant in the studio of Thomas Crawford. There, she became a member of the American artists' colony then thriving in the city and met novelist Nathaniel Hawthorne, also a native of Salem, who became intrigued while he sat for her during the sculpting of a bust. He subsequently modeled all the independent women artists in his novel *The Marble Faun* on Lander, and probed the sculptor's personality and philosophy during their sittings. In his notebooks, Hawthorne described her as "a young woman, living in almost perfect independence, thousands of miles from her New England home, going fearlessly about these mysterious streets by night as well as by day; and no household ties; nor rule or law but that within her; yet acting with quietness and simplicity, and keeping, after all within a homely line of right."

Despite this "keeping . . . within a homely line of right," at some point during her stay in Rome Lander apparently did, or was thought to have done, something that so scandalized her fellow artists that from then on she was largely ostracized. History does not record the nature of Lander's moral lapse, or whether it was real or imagined, but it was serious enough that a number of the members of the colony conducted a special investigation into the charges against her.

Standing tall in the face of widespread gossip (sculptor John Rogers wrote of her at the time, "She snaps her fingers at all of Rome"), Lander refused to admit defeat, although her commissions had dried up completely. Forced to finance her continuing work, she embarked on a major sculpture of *Virginia Dare, the first English child born in the New World. Although Virginia Dare disappeared before she was four years old, along with the rest of the "Lost Colony" of Roanoke Island, North Carolina, at the end of the 16th century, Lander's work depicts her as she might have appeared had she survived into adulthood. Completed in 1860, the marble sculpture is of an attractive young woman draped in a fishnet, gazing out to sea with a heron at her feet.

For a good portion of its years, the large-scale *Virginia Dare,* like its subject, was plagued with misfortune. The vessel transporting the sculpture from Rome to Boston was shipwrecked off the Spanish coast. For two years the statue remained on the ocean floor before Lander hired a salvage firm to raise it. After she cleaned it and repaired all visible damage, Lander arranged for the sculpture to be displayed in Boston, where the exhibition gallery promptly caught fire. Repaired yet again, *Virginia Dare* was sold to a New York collector; he died before remitting payment. The sculpture was then returned to Lander after the collector's heirs refused to pay for it.

Lander moved to Washington, D.C., her best years behind her, and lived out the remainder of her life in relative obscurity. Failing to persuade the state of North Carolina to buy *Virginia Dare* for display at the World's Columbian Exposition of 1893, she nonetheless bequeathed it to the state after her death in 1923. (Although the bust she sculpted of Hawthorne is now in Salem's Essex Institute, much of the other work she produced has been lost.) Her bequest was housed in the state's Hall of History in Raleigh from 1926 to 1938, at which point it began journeying through a number of state offices, basements, and storage areas. In the early 1950s, *Virginia Dare* was given to the Elizabethan Gardens on Roanoke Island, where it occupies a place of honor close to the spot where the real Virginia Dare is believed to have been born.

SOURCES:
Rubinstein, Charlotte Streifer. *American Women Artists.* Boston, MA: G.K. Hall, 1982.

Don Amerman,
freelance writer, Saylorsburg, Pennsylvania

Landers, Ann (b. 1918).

See Friedman, Esther Pauline and Pauline Esther.

Landes, Bertha Knight (1868–1943)

Mayor of Seattle, Washington (1926), who was the first woman elected to lead a major American city. Born Bertha Ethel Knight in Ware, Massachusetts, on October 19, 1868; died in Ann Arbor, Michigan, on November 29, 1943; youngest of nine children of Charles Sanford Knight (a painter and real estate agent) and Cordelia (Cutter) Knight; attended public and private schools; graduated from Indiana University, Bloomington, Indiana, 1891; married Henry Landes (a college professor), on January 2, 1894; children: Katherine Landes (b. 1896); Kenneth Landes (b. 1899); (adopted) Viola Landes.

The first woman elected mayor of a major American city, Bertha Landes was born in 1868 in Ware, Massachusetts, and raised in neighboring Worcester. She was an 1891 graduate of Indiana University and taught school in Worcester before marrying Henry Landes, a fellow student at Indiana. The couple began married life in Rockland, Maine, where Henry was the high school principal for a year, and in 1895, when he joined the faculty of the University of Washington, they settled in Seattle. The couple had two children of their own, Katherine (b. 1896) and Kenneth (b. 1899), and adopted a daughter, Viola.

Bertha Landes was extremely active in the club movement during World War I and was elected to the Seattle city council in 1922. Reelected to a second term, she rose to become president of the council in 1924. One of her responsibilities in that post was to act as mayor during any absences of the elected mayor, Edwin J. Brown. It was on one of these occasions that Landes, in a dramatic effort to draw attention to illegal gambling and other vices ignored by the police force, fired the chief of police. Although the chief was reinstated upon Brown's return, Landes had made her point. In 1926, she ran a vigorous campaign against Brown and was elected.

During her two-year term, Landes attempted to rescue Seattle from the patronage system that allowed gambling and vice to flourish, but she was only marginally successful and was not elected to a second term. Some historians cite her support of Prohibition as the cause for her defeat, while others believe that she simply did not possess the political skills necessary to justify her causes and maintain her office. **Sandra Haarsager**, an assistant professor of communication at the University of Idaho, suggests that Landes was the victim of gender bias and negative campaigning. Whatever the case, Landes, then 60, did not run again for public office but

remained active on the club front, serving a term as president of both the state's League of Women Voters and the American Federation of Soroptimist Clubs. Landes died in 1943, at age 75.

SOURCES:

Haarsager, Sandra. *Bertha Knight Landes of Seattle: Big-City Mayor.* University of Oklahoma Press, 1994.

James, Edward T., ed. *Notable American Women, 1607–1950.* Cambridge, MA: The Belknap Press of Harvard University Press, 1971.

McHenry, Robert, ed. *Famous American Women.* NY: Dover, 1983.

Publishers Weekly. January 24, 1994.

Read, Phyllis J., and Bernard L. Witlieb. *The Book of Women's Firsts.* NY: Random House, 1992.

Barbara Morgan,
Melrose, Massachusetts

Landeta, Matilde (1913—)

Mexican filmmaker. Born in Mexico City, Mexico, in 1913.

Filmography: (as director) Lola Casanova (1948), La Negra Angustias (1949), Trotacalles (1951), Noturno a Rosario (1991); (as writer) Tribunal para menores (1947), La Negra Augustias (1949).

Born in Mexico City in 1913 and orphaned by age three, Matilde Landeta was reared by her grandmother in San Luis Potosi. Landeta's brother, Eduardo, grew up to be an actor and it was he who introduced Landeta to the film industry in Mexico. Early on, she knew she wanted to be a director, but in Mexico in the early 1930s that door was all but closed to women in the tightly controlled, government-subsidized film industry. Determined to succeed, Landeta took a job as a script supervisor in 1933.

After 12 years and with considerable opposition from the Directors' Association, she was finally allowed to serve as an assistant director. For the next three years, Landeta worked for such filmmakers as Emilio Fernandez, Julio Bracho, and Roberto Gavaldon, all considered to be among Mexico's best. But a career as an assistant director was not what Landeta had in mind. Convinced that her only shot would come as an independent filmmaker, Landeta, with her brother and several colleagues, formed Tecnicos y Actores Cinematograficos Associados (TACMA) in 1947. Landeta had written a screenplay, *Tribunal para menores*, which she intended to direct. However, her colleagues in the association seem to have betrayed her, because they assigned Alfonso Corona Blake to direct the film. Ironically, Landeta was awarded the prestigious Ariel Award for her screenplay (the Mexican equivalent of the Academy Award).

In 1948, Landeta finally directed her first feature, *Lola Casanova*. The film, based on a novel by Francisco Rojas Gonzalez, was enough of a success to allow Landeta to direct her own screenplay adaptation of another Gonzalez novel, *La Negra Augustius*. Considered Landeta's best film, the story, told from a decidedly feminist perspective, explores the tensions between race, class, and gender. Landeta followed with her most controversial film by far. Made in 1951, *Trotacalles (Streetwalkers)*, an attack on the sexual exploitation of women, concerns two women caught in a male-dominated power struggle.

Landeta's work was as powerful as it was critically acclaimed. Unfortunately, her career came to an abrupt halt when she had a confrontation with the director of the National Cinematographic Bank. She was literally barred from working for the Mexican film industry from 1956 through 1962. Though technically allowed to return after that, Landeta's career languished. In the 1980s, she was rediscovered by the next generation of Latin American feminist filmmakers, who exhibited her films at several international festivals. In 1990, Landeta was the subject of a **Patricia Diaz** documentary, *My Filmmaking, My Life*. Matilde Landeta took advantage of her new-found celebrity. In 1991, at age 78, she directed the feature *Nocturna a Rosario*.

SOURCES:

Foster, Gwendolyn. *Women Film Directors: An International Bio-Critical Dictionary*. Westport, CT: Greenwood Press, 1995.

Huaco-Nuzum, Carmen. "Matilde Landeta: An Introduction to the Work of a Pioneer Mexican Filmmaker," in *Screen*. Vol. 28, no. 4, 1987, pp. 96–106.

Kuhn, Annette, and Susannah Radstone, eds. *Women's Companion to International Film*. Berkeley, CA: University of California Press, 1990.

Deborah Jones,
Studio City, California

Landi, Elissa (1904–1948)

Austrian-Italian actress. Born Elizabeth Marie Christine Kuehnelt on December 6, 1904, in Venice, Italy; died of cancer in New York City, in 1948; educated privately in Canada and Italy; married in 1928 (divorced 1936); married a second time, in 1943; children: (second marriage) a daughter (b. 1944).

Selected theater: made London stage debut in Dandy Dick *(Playhouse Theater, 1923); appeared in* Storm *(Ambassadors, 1924),* The Painted Swan *(1925),* Lavender Ladies *(1925), and* The Constant Nymph *(1926); made Broadway debut in* A Farewell to Arms *(1930).*

Selected films: London *(UK, 1926)*; Bolibar *(UK, 1928)*; Underground *(UK, 1928)*; Sin *(Sw., 1928)*; The Inseparables *(UK, 1929)*; Knowing Men *(UK, 1930)*; The Price of Things *(UK, 1930)*; Children of Chance *(UK, 1930)*; Mon Gosse de Père *(The Parisian, Fr., 1930)*; Body and Soul *(1931)*; Always Goodbye *(1931)*; Wicked *(1931)*; The Yellow Ticket *(1931)*; Devil's Lottery *(1932)*; The Woman in Room 13 *(1932)*; A Passport to Hell *(1932)*; The Sign of the Cross *(1932)*; The Warrior's Husband *(1933)*; I Loved You Wednesday *(1933)*; The Masquerader *(1933)*; By Candlelight *(1934)*; Man of Two Worlds *(1934)*; Sisters Under the Skin *(1934)*; The Great Flirtation *(1934)*; The Count of Monte Cristo *(1934)*; Enter Madame *(1935)*; The Amateur Gentleman *(UK, 1936)*; After the Thin Man *(1936)*; Mad Holiday *(1936)*; The Thirteenth Chair *(1937)*; Corregidor *(1943)*.

A descendant of Emperor Francis Joseph of Austria on her mother's side, and the stepdaughter of an Italian noble, Count Carlo Zanardi-Landi, actress Elissa Landi was educated in England and Canada and trained as a dancer. Intent on writing a play, she joined an Oxford repertory company to gain experience, but wound up on stage instead, making her acting debut in *Dandy Dick* (1923). She subsequently appeared in a number of London plays and made her film debut in *London* (1926), with *Dorothy Gish. Her next films, *Bolibar* and *Underground* (both 1928), brought her a degree of stardom in Britain, and she also made films in Sweden and France.

Following her Broadway stage debut in *A Farewell to Arms* (1930), Landi was summoned to Hollywood where she signed to a long-term contract with Fox, who marketed her as the "Empress of Emotion." She starred in a series of films during the 1930s, the most memorable of which were Cecil B. De Mille's *The Sign of the Cross* (1932), with Fredric March, and *The Count of Monte Cristo* (1934). Landi's favorite was *The Yellow Jacket*, a 1931 melodrama in which she starred opposite Laurence Olivier and Lionel Barrymore. Despite her intelligent, ladylike demeanor and ethereal good looks, Landi failed to become a box-office draw. After a B thriller, *The Thirteenth Chair* (1937), she left Hollywood, returning in 1943 for a role in *Corregidor*, an independent film with Otto Kruger. Landi, who was married twice and had a daughter in 1944, also wrote several novels. She died of cancer in 1948.

SOURCES:

Katz, Ephraim. *The Film Encyclopedia*. NY: HarperCollins, 1994.

Shipman, David. *The Great Movie Stars: The Golden Years*. Boston, MA: Little, Brown, 1995.

Barbara Morgan,
Melrose, Massachusetts

Landiras, baroness de (1556–1640).

See Jeanne de Lestonac.

Landiras, Jeanne de (1556–1640).

See Jeanne de Lestonac.

Landis, Carole (1919–1948)

American actress. Born Frances Lillian Mary Ridste on January 1, 1919, in Fairchild, Wisconsin; committed suicide on July 4, 1948; daughter of a railroad switchman; married four times.

Selected filmography: A Star is Born *(1937);* A Day at the Races *(1937);* Four's a Crowd *(1938);* Daredevils of the Red Circle *(serial, 1939);* One Million B.C. *(1940);* Turnabout *(1940);* Road Show *(1941);* Topper Returns *(1941);* Moon Over Miami *(1941);* I Wake Up Screaming *(1941);* Dance Hall *(1941);* Cadet Girl *(1941);* It Happened in Flat Bush *(1942);* My Gal Sal *(1942);* Manila Calling *(1942);* Orchestra Wives *(1942);* Four Jills in a Jeep *(1944);* Secret Command *(1944);* It Shouldn't Happen to a Dog *(1946);* Behind Green Lights *(1946);* A Scandal in Paris *(1946);* Out of the Blue *(1947);* The Brass Monkey *(1948);* Lucky Mascot *(1948);* The Noose *(1948).*

Carole Landis was the daughter of a railroad switchman who abandoned the family when she was three. By age 12, Landis was entering beauty contests; by age 15, she had eloped with a policeman. They separated three weeks later. The following year, the well-built teenager migrated to San Francisco and took a job as a singer-hula dancer. With her arrival in Hollywood, the 18-year-old Landis, with the "best legs in town," appeared with little notice in 17 films. She first caught the audience's attention as the lead cavewoman in *One Million B.C.*

One of the first to entertain the troops during World War II, Landis' health suffered when she contracted amoebic dysentery and malaria. The movie *Four Jills in a Jeep* recounted her experiences overseas, and those of fellow performers *Kay Francis, Mitzi Mayfair, and *Martha Raye. After the war, Landis' career seemed to flatten out. She tried to counter it with a 1945 New York stage appearance in *A Lady Says Yes*. The termination of an affair with the married Rex Harrison, husband of *Lilli Palmer, seemed to be too much. Landis was found dead of an overdose of sleeping pills the night after a farewell dinner with Harrison. She was 29.

Carole Landis

Landon, Letitia Elizabeth (1802–1838)

*English poet and novelist. Name variations: (pen name) better known by her initials L.E.L.; Letitia Elizabeth Maclean. Born Letitia Elizabeth Landon at 25 Hans Place, Chelsea, England, on August 14, 1802; died of poison on October 15, 1838; daughter of John Landon (an army agent) and Catharine Jane (Bishop) Landon; granddaughter of Reverend John Landon (famed for his cause against dissenters); attended a school in Chelsea where she studied under Miss Rowden (a poet and also the teacher of *Mary Russell Mitford and Lady *Caroline Lamb); married George Maclean (governor of the Gold Coast, Africa), in June 1838.*

Letitia Landon's father, an army agent, amassed a large property, which he lost by speculation shortly before his death. About 1815, the

Landons moved to Old Brompton and made the acquaintance of William Jerdan, and Letitia began her contributions to the *Literary Gazette* and to various Christmas annuals under the initial "L," and finally "L.E.L." She then published some volumes of verse, which soon won her literary fame. Landon displayed a rich imagination and an aptitude for language, but her work suffered from haste and sentimentality. The gentle melancholy and romantic sentiment incorporated in her writings, however, suited the taste of the period and brought her a wide class of readers. Though she attended a literary salon and made a pleasure trip to Paris (1834), most of the large sums she earned were used to support her family.

For some time L.E.L. was joint editor of the *Literary Gazette.* Her first volume of poetry appeared under the title *The Fate of Adelaide* (1820) and was followed by other collections of verses, including *The Improvisatrice* (1824), *The Troubadour* (1825), *The Golden Violet* (1827), and *The Venetian Bracelet* (1829). She also wrote several novels, of which the best is said to be *Ethel Churchill* (1837), along with the tragedy *Castruccio Castracani* (1837). Various editions of her *Poetical Works* have been published since her death, one in 1880 with an introductory memoir by W.B. Scott. *The Life and Literary Remains of Letitia Elizabeth Landon,* by Laman Blanchard, appeared in 1841, followed by a second edition in 1855.

Romantically, Landon has been linked with a Dr. Maginn, as well as her friend Jerdan. An engagement to the biographer John Forster, it is said, was broken off through the intervention of scandalmongers. On June 7, 1838, she secretly married George Maclean, governor of the Gold Coast, and set sail for a three-year stay in Africa, arriving on August 16. Friends in England received cheerful letters posted on the first African steamer bound for England, but when the next ship arrived from the "dark continent" it bore the startling revelation that Letitia Landon had been found dead in her room with a bottle of prussic acid in her hand. Speculation, which has added a certain glamour and mystique to Landon's life, hypothesized suicide, foul play by her husband or a lurking mistress, or an accidental overdose for chronic spasms. The mystery has never been solved.

Landon, Margaret (1903–1993)

American author who wrote Anna and the King of Siam. *Born Margaret Dorothea Mortenson on September 7, 1903, in Somers, Wisconsin; died on December 4, 1993, in Alexandria, Virginia; daughter of Annenus Duabus Mortenson and Adelle Johanne (Estburg) Mortenson; Wheaton College, Wheaton, Illinois, B.A., 1925; studied journalism at Northwestern University, 1937–38; married Kenneth Perry Landon (a missionary who became the associate dean of area and language studies at the U.S. Department of State Foreign Service Institute), in 1926; children:* **Margaret Dorothea Landon** *(who married Charles W. Schoenherr);* William Bradley II; **Carol Elizabeth Landon** *(who married Lennart Pearson); Kenneth Perry, Jr.*

Taught English and Latin (1925–26); lived in Siam (1927–37); worked there as principal, Trang Girls' School; published Anna and the King of Siam, *based on the memoirs of Anna Leonowens (1944); published novel* Never Dies the Dream *(1949).*

The daughter of **Adelle Mortenson** and Annenus Mortenson, who worked in the business department of the *Saturday Evening Post,* Margaret Landon was born in Somers, Wisconsin, in 1903. After receiving her B.A. from Wheaton College, Illinois, in 1925, Landon tried her hand at teaching English and Latin at a school in Bear Lake, Wisconsin. She later characterized this as "an agonizing year" and concluded she was not cut out for the teaching profession. However, she soon found herself teaching again after marrying Presbyterian missionary Kenneth Perry Landon, with whom she traveled to Siam (now Thailand) in 1927. After a year in Bangkok studying Siamese ("I never lost my American accent or learned to speak it perfectly," Landon later confessed), the Landons moved to Nakon Sritamarat and, in 1928, moved to Trang. There Landon was principal of the girls' school for five years.

At the home of Dr. Edwin Bruce McDaniel, a friend in Nakon Sritamarat, Landon first encountered the works of *Anna Leonowens, a young English widow employed in the 1860s as governess to the court of Mongkut, the fourth king of the Chakri Dynasty of Siam. Landon, a fellow white woman living in isolation in Siam, was immediately hooked by Leonowens' compelling, exotic memoirs, *The English Governess at the Siamese Court* and *The Romance of the Harem:* "Outside . . . automobiles honked continuously. There was the jingle of horse-drawn gharries and bicycle bells. An occasional elephant padded by in ponderous majesty. But as I read all of this dropped away."

On her return to the States in 1937, Landon was encouraged by her friend **Muriel Fuller** to introduce Leonowens to modern readers by combining and rewriting the two books, omitting the lengthy descriptions of Siam and refining the chronology of events. Landon undertook considerable research in the Library of Congress and the National Archives to augment and verify the events depicted by Leonowens. She was also introduced to **Lizzie Avice Moore**, who, as a young girl in Enniscorthy, Ireland, met Anna Leonowens in 1867, after the latter's sojourn in Siam had ended. Through the Moore family, Landon met Leonowens' granddaughter **Avis Fyshe**, who shared letters, diaries and other family materials with Landon. She began work on the book in the fall of 1939 in Richmond, Indiana, where her husband was teaching. She soon found it impossible to simply piece together Leonowens' existing narratives and decided to make her book a third-person narrative that was "seventy-five percent fact, and twenty-five percent fiction based on fact." In 1944, *Anna and the King of Siam* was published, dedicated by Landon to her late sister, **Evangeline Mortenson Welsh**. An accessible, romantic and sometimes melodramatic account of Leonowens' life in Siam, the book was an instant success.

Despite its popularity as a book, *Anna and the King of Siam* found enduring fame as material for a succession of stage and screen adaptations. It was made into a popular film of the same name in 1946, adapted by Talbot Jennings and *Sally Benson, and starring *Irene Dunne and Rex Harrison. Although the movie won an Academy Award for photography, film critic *Pauline Kael dismissed it as "pitifully unauthentic" but conceded that "the story itself holds considerable interest." It was subsequently adapted into *The King and I*, a Rodgers and Hammerstein musical starring *Gertrude Lawrence and Yul Brynner, which made its Broadway debut in 1951, directed by playwright John van Druten. An instant hit, the musical was released on the big screen in 1956, with Yul Brynner reprising his stage role as the king and English-born actress *Deborah Kerr starring as Anna. Directed by Walter Lang, this sumptuously staged film version was both a popular and critical success. Ted Sennett calls it "the best of the Rodgers and Hammerstein adaptations. . . . [The narrative] forms a solid base that never crumbles under the weight of the pageantry. . . . The score is one of the treasures of the musical theater." The film won Academy Awards for best actor, art direction, costume design and music scoring.

The popular film versions were not popular, however, in Thailand, where Landon's book was seen as a derogatory portrait of King Mongkut, adding spuriously romantic episodes to the already disputed memoirs upon which it was based. Popular opinion in modern-day Thailand maintains that Leonowens' recollections were both false and self-aggrandizing; in a country where criticism of the monarchy remains a punishable crime, screenings of all movie versions of the Anna Leonowens story are banned.

In 1999, another version of the book was released as a movie. *Anna and the King* was positioned as not just another lavish dramatic rendition of the story—this time starring **Jodie Foster** and Hong Kong star Chow Yun-Fat—but as a more historically accurate interpretation of the memoirs than Landon's book. Despite additional research and drastic script rewrites, the film had to be shot in Malaysia when the Thai Film Board refused the producers permission to shoot in Thailand, labeling the story an insult to King Mongkut and reigniting the controversy.

Margaret Landon was not able to repeat the success of *Anna and the King of Siam*. After a bout of rheumatic fever in 1946, she wrote little for a while. Her novel *Never Dies the Dream* was published in 1949, drawing on Landon's mission-teaching experiences in Bangkok and noteworthy mainly for its depiction of Siamese life in the 1930s. She spent a large part of her life working on a history of Southeast Asia during the colonial period, but it was never published. Margaret Landon died in Alexandria, Virginia, in 1993.

Margaret Landon

SOURCES:

Landon, Margaret. *Anna and the King of Siam*. Preface. NY: John Day, 1944.

RELATED MEDIA:

Anna and the King, starring Jodie Foster and Chow Yun-Fat, 20th Century-Fox, 1999.

Anna and the King of Siam, starring Irene Dunne, *Linda Darnell, and Rex Harrison, screenplay by Talbot Jennings and Sally Benson, 20th Century-Fox, 1946.

The King and I, musical starring Gertrude Lawrence and Yul Brynner, written by Richard Rodgers and Oscar Hammerstein II, opened on Broadway at the St. James' Theater, 1951.

The King and I (133 min. film), starring Deborah Kerr, *Rita Moreno, and Yul Brynner, directed by Walter Lang, screenplay by Ernest Lehman, 20th Century-Fox, 1956.

Paula Morris, D.Phil., Brooklyn, New York

Landowska, Wanda (1877–1959)

Polish virtuoso, known as the "High Priestess of the Harpsichord," who became an authority on the music of the 17th and 18th centuries and was responsible for the revival of the harpsichord. Name variations: *Alexandra Landowska.* Pronunciation: *VAHN-da Lan-DOFF-skah. Born in Warsaw, Poland, on July 5, 1877; died in Lakeville, Connecticut, on August 16, 1959; daughter of Marjan Landowski (a lawyer and amateur musician) and Eve Landowska (a linguist); married Henry Lew (a folklorist), in 1900 (died in automobile accident, 1919); children: none; naturalized French citizen.*

Began to play piano (1883); studied at Warsaw Conservatory of Music under Alexander Michalowski and Moritz Moszkowski; sent to Berlin to study composition and counterpoint with Heinrich Urban (1895); eloped to Paris with Henry Lew (1900); first played harpsichord publicly (1903); toured Russia (1909); performed for Count Leo Tolstoy at Yasnaya Polnaya (1909); co-authored book with Henry Lew (1909); presented first Pleyel harpsichord publicly (1912); appointed head of harpsichord class, Berlin (1913); interned in Germany (1914–18); toured United States (1923); made first recording (1923); founded École de Musique Ancienne (1925); commissioned Manuel de Falla to compose a chamber concerto for harpsichord (1926); commissioned Francis Poulenc to compose the Concert Champêtre for Harpsichord (1929); gave first public performance of J.S. Bach's Goldberg Variations (1933); awarded the Grand Prix of the Paris Exposition (1937); fled Paris (1940); lived in the south of France for 18 months; toured Switzerland; arrived New York City (December 7, 1941); lived in New York for six years; moved to Lakeville, Connecticut (1947); devoted herself to teaching, writing and recording.

Compositions: Hebrew Poem for Orchestra; Serenade for Strings; Rhapsodie Orientale for Piano; Choir for Female Voices and Orchestra; Polish Folksongs for Solo Voice and Choir and Orchestra; The Hop; Polish Folksongs for Harpsichord solo; Bourrées d'Auvergne for Harpsichord solo; Liberation Fanfare (arranged for band by Edwin Franco Goldman, 1943).

Discography: J.S. Bach. English Suite in G Minor (Victor, 1923); J.S. Bach. Goldberg Variations (HMV, 1933); The Treasury of Harpsichord Music (RCA, 1946); Landowska Plays for Paderewski (RCA, 1951); The Arts of the Harpsichord (RCA, 1957).

Selected publications: (with husband) La Musique ancienne *(1909).*

A virtuoso or musicologist? A teacher or composer? Wanda Landowska was all of these things and more. She was also an interpreter of music in the broadest sense.

She was born in Warsaw, Poland, in 1877, the daughter of Marjan Landowski, a lawyer and amateur musician, and **Eve Landowska**, a linguist. Music came early to her life. Landowska began to play the piano at the age of four and proved herself to be an exceptional musician for such a tender age. Jan Kleczynski, an early teacher and author of *The Works of Chopin and Their Proper Interpretation*, enthused upon hearing her play for the first time "this child is a genius."

Wanda Landowska's talent was quickly recognized, and she was enrolled in the Warsaw Conservatory of Music. There she studied under Alexander Michalowski, the renowned interpreter of Chopin. Landowska characterized him as both a demanding and inspiring teacher: "He was a marvellous master. He played constantly for his pupils, thus adding great value to his teaching. I often had the feeling that he was playing especially for me because he felt my musicality. I understood him."

The repertoire which Landowska studied at the Warsaw Conservatory was comprised mainly of romantic composers, including Franz Lizst, Carl Tausig and Hans von Bülow. From an early age, however, she developed a passion for the baroque masters and insisted on playing Bach along with the rest of her curriculum. That passion was evident when, at her first public concert, Wanda Landowska played Bach's English Suite in E Minor.

In 1895, Landowska went to Berlin to study counterpoint and composition with Heinrich Urban, who also taught such notables as Paderewski, Rudolph Ganz, and Joseph Hofmann. During her time in the German capital, Landowska developed a passion for vocal music. She knew by heart the part of Zerlina from *Don Giovanni* and also heard Bach's *Christmas Oratorio* for the first time. However, she found instruction in Germany rigid and problematic. She wrote of her Berlin period:

> What did I learn? Nothing, really nothing. I was refractory to rules and laws. As soon as they were imposed on me, I stiffened, terrified. My music was covered with exercises in which I had no interest at all. Counterpoint? Yes, but through the direct channel of Bach. I sang the voices separately with a limitless joy. I punctuated them, and they became lively; they sprang forth. Was my teacher inadequate? Or was I a bad pupil?

In 1900, Wanda Landowska eloped to Paris with Henry Lew, a journalist, actor, and renowned ethnologist of Hebrew folklore. She shared his interest in folklore and, as a child, had spent summers in the Polish countryside, where she heard and sang folk songs and danced mazurkas and polonaises with the peasants. With Lew's help, Landowska energetically threw herself into a study of every aspect of 17th- and 18th-century music and its interpretation. The couple collaborated on a book, *La Musique ancienne,* in 1909.

Paris at the turn of the century embodied a spirit of rebellion against the romanticism of the 19th century. In 1902, Debussy's avant-garde *Pelléas et Mélisande* was first performed. A few years later, Les Ballets Russes of Sergei Diaghilev swept the capital and enthralled the artistic community. As for the music of the past, not only was it relatively obscure, but it was often poorly understood. The attempt of the pianist Louis Diemer to revive 17th- and 18th-century harpsichord music met with failure. Not only was his choice of composers poor, but the harpsichord on which he performed was deficient.

During the same period, a new field of study, musicology, was gaining a firm foothold on French soil. In 1894, Henry Expert published the first volume of works by French masters of the Renaissance. Other works followed by such authors as Alexandre Guilmant, Michel Brenet and Maurice Emmanuel. However, as Wanda Landowska noted, "hardly anyone but the musicologists read these remarkable works. Modestly, the authors went their way, preparing the ground."

By the age of 21, Wanda Landowska was emerging as a celebrated virtuoso and composer. Her compositions included *Rhapsodie Orientale,* as well as numerous lieder. She became a well-known social figure and associated with the elite of the Paris artistic community:

> I had the rare privilege of living in the midst of these eminent scholars and musicians who honoured me with their friendship. I often had the opportunity to discuss musical matters with them. Progressing in my studies, I came to the realization that the keyboard works of the seventeenth and eighteenth centuries ought to be played on the

Wanda Landowska playing for Leo Tolstoy at his home.

instrument for which they had been composed, the harpsichord.

Thus Landowska decided to devote herself to playing 17th- and 18th-century works on the harpsichord. Many of her friends did not share her enthusiasm and attempted to dissuade her from abandoning the piano in favor of this so-called "tin-pan" instrument. Others, however, like medical missionary and Bach scholar Albert Schweitzer, were more encouraging. In his book *Bach, Le Musicien-Poète,* Schweitzer wrote that "anyone who has heard Wanda Landowska play *The Italian Concerto* on harpsichord finds it hard to understand how it could ever again be played on a modern piano."

You play Bach your way and I'll play him his way.

—Wanda Landowska

Like Schweitzer, Landowska was fascinated with baroque instruments. She launched a personal campaign to reconstruct the contemporary harpsichord on the pattern of those she had seen in the Musikhistorischen Museum in Cologne. She discussed the construction of such an instrument with Gustave Lyon, the director of France's well-known Pleyel piano company, and Pleyel's chief engineer, M. Lamy. The completion of the Pleyel harpsichord took several years, and it was not until 1912 that she was able to play it at a Bach festival in Breslau. During the interval, Landowska presented works on an inferior instrument, giving her first public performance in 1903. She undertook concert tours of Germany, Italy, Spain, and Russia and prepared the ground for the reintroduction of the harpsichord to its rightful place in the musical world. During her 1909 tour of Russia, she visited Leo Tolstoy at Yasnaya Polnaya, and he supported her crusade for the revival of 17th- and 18th-century harpsichord music.

In 1913, when she and Henry Lew returned to Berlin, Landowska was appointed head of the harpsichord class at the Hochschule Für Musik, a post specifically created for her. However, the First World War intervened. As Russian subjects, both Landowska and her husband were confined to Germany for the duration of the war as enemy aliens. At war's end, the couple prepared to return to France. On the eve of their departure, however, Henry Lew was killed in an automobile accident. Years later, she said of her husband:

> [H]e was an enlightened dogmatist, although he lacked psychological acumen where isolated human beings were concerned; he despised the magnifying glass and the subjective sense of observation of the bi-

ologist. But the ebbs and flows of the crowds, great movements of collective stupidity, inspired impulses of the public, and their sheeplike reactions in following enthusiastically any order given by a dictator or by publicity—all these had in him an admirable observer and sarcastic critic.

The newly widowed Landowska returned to Paris and devoted herself to concert tours and teaching. She held master classes in Basel, Switzerland, and at the École Normale de Musique in Paris. She lectured at the Sorbonne in 1921, on the occasion of the International Congress on the history of art. She also began to write on the topics of musicology and musical criticism.

In the fall of 1923, Wanda Landowska sailed for the United States, arriving "like a lion tamer," she wrote, "dragging along four large Pleyel harpsichords." On November 20, she made her North American debut as soloist with the Philadelphia Orchestra under Leopold Stokowski. She played three concertos: two by Handel and Bach on the harpsichord and one by Mozart on the piano. She followed this with a tour of the United States and Canada, and made her first recording for Victor records. Over the next few years, Landowska undertook numerous tours of Europe, Africa, Asia, and North America. She went out of her way to commission several works for harpsichord. "She even inspired dyed-in-the-wool modernists to compose for her," commented Pitts Sanborn in *Outlook.* In 1926, she commissioned Manuel de Falla to compose a chamber concerto for harpsichord and, in 1929, Francis Poulenc wrote the *Concert Champêtre* for her.

With such a busy touring schedule, Landowska decided to purchase a home in Saint-Leu-La-Forêt, a few miles outside Paris. In 1925, she founded the École de Musique Ancienne, which attracted students from all over the world. She built a concert hall on the grounds of the school in 1927, and each Sunday afternoon gave concerts which were attended by the artistic community of Paris. A mecca for music lovers, it became a "French Bayreuth."

Landowska had been sporadically studying *The Goldberg Variations* for most of her life. In 1933, she performed them in their entirety at Saint-Leu-La-Forêt. Wrote a Paris reviewer: "When Wanda Landowska reconstructs with her infallible hands and her lucid soul, the edifice that is *The Goldberg Variations,* this moment of ancient music becomes a temple open to all mankind." Now that the battle for the revival of the harpsichord had clearly been won, Landowska devoted herself increasingly to writing on the subject of musicology. Many of her articles were published in the scholarly journal *La Revue Musicale*.

When German troops marched on Paris in 1940, Landowska abandoned her beloved school at Saint-Leu-La-Forêt. Though she was now a naturalized French citizen, her Jewish ancestry undoubtedly influenced her decision to leave. When her school's library was looted by Nazi soldiers, thousands of volumes on music were lost, as well as a precious collection of ancient instruments. After spending 18 months in Banyuls-Sur-Mer in the eastern Pyrenees, and on a concert tour in Switzerland, Wanda Landowska sailed for the United States. She reached New York City on December 7, 1941—the day the Japanese attacked Pearl Harbor. In February 1942, she gave her first performance in Town Hall in New York City. She played *The Goldberg Variations* and received a standing ovation, as well as critical and popular acclaim. "No matter what she plays," wrote Virgil Thomson, "it is one of the richest and grandest experiences available to lovers of tonal art. . . . A performance so complete, so wholly interpreted . . . is rarely to be encountered." After living in New York City for several years, Wanda Landowska relocated to Lakeville, Connecticut, in 1947. Two years later, the Grolier Society asked her to write a short history of the revival of the harpsichord.

To celebrate her 70th birthday, Landowska undertook the ambitious project of recording Bach's entire *Well-Tempered Clavier*. As with *The Goldberg Variations*, she engaged in a detailed study of the composition, which lasted for the next five years. "It is simply a story of my experiences in music as a worker in music, a worker who jots down her impressions, prelude after prelude, fugue after fugue." The last years of Wanda Landowska's life were devoted to teaching, writing and recording. She lived peacefully in Lakeville, attracting students from all over the world, as well as many admirers. A charming woman with a sense of humor, she liked to talk of her years in Saint-Leu-La-Forêt, which she considered the happiest in her life.

For her musical achievements, Wanda Landowska was decorated by both the Polish and the French governments. Her pupils, including *Lucille Wallace, formed the next generation of harpsichord virtuosos. The influence of Wanda Landowska was felt throughout the musical world, which she inspired not only with her performances, but with her writing and recording.

Wanda Landowska devoted herself to the revival and development of the modern harpsichord. Her impact was heavily felt in the area of technique, where she laid particular emphasis on proper fingering. Her playing was characterized by vigor and flamboyance; her character, by simplicity and forthrightness. As an advocate of baroque music and period instruments, she shares credit for the revival and popularity of baroque orchestras. However, in the end, as she herself noted, "Since the beginning of my campaign in favor of the music of the past, I have always compelled myself to focus light on the fact that this so-called 'old music' is a living force, sometimes more modern than modern music itself. Long years of battles were necessary to overcome the profound, and deeply rooted, prejudices against an art which was considered desiccated, naivë and incapable of moving the emotions. The same prejudices prevailed for old instruments. . . . [T]here's no such thing as ancient music—simply music, that of today, yesterday and forever."

SOURCES:

Gavoty, Bernard. *Wanda Landowska*. Geneva: R. Kister, 1957.

Landowska, Wanda. *Landowska on Music*. Ed. by Denise Restout. NY: Stein and Day, 1964.

Rothe, Anne, ed. *Current Biography, 1945*. H.W. Wilson, 1946.

Wigoder, Geoffrey, ed. *Dictionary of Jewish Biography*. NY: Simon and Schuster, 1991.

RELATED MEDIA:

"Landowska: Uncommon Visionary," produced and directed by **Barbara Attie** for Attie Goldwater Pontius Productions, first aired on PBS in July 1999.

Hugh A. Stewart, M.A.,
Guelph, Ontario, Canada

Landriani, Lucrezia (fl. 1450s)

Italian noblewoman. Flourished in the 1450s; married Giampietro Landriani; mistress of Galeazzo Maria Sforza, 5th duke of Milan (r. 1466–1476); children: (with Sforza) Carlo (b. 1461); *Caterina Sforza (c. 1462–1509); Chiara Sforza (b. around 1464); and Alessandro.

Landseer, Jessica (1810–1880)

British landscape painter. Born in 1810; died in 1880; daughter of John Landseer (1769–1852, an engraver); sister of Sir Edwin Landseer (1802–1873, animal and portrait painter) and Charles A. Landseer (1799–1879, genre and historical painter).

Jessica Landseer, the sister of Sir Edwin Landseer, was overshadowed by her brother for whom she kept house for most of her life. A painter, etcher, and miniaturist in her own right, she exhibited at the Royal Academy and the British Institution for many years.

Landsfeld, countess of (1818–1861).

See Montez, Lola.

Lane, Elizabeth (1905—)

English lawyer. Name variations: Dame Elizabeth Lane; Mrs. Justice Lane. Born Elizabeth Culborn in 1905; educated privately and attended Malvern Girls College; married Henry Lane, in 1926; children: one son.

Elizabeth Lane became a barrister at the Inner Temple in 1940, at age 35. She was also a member of the Home Office Committee on Depositions in Criminal Cases. Lane was assistant recorder of Birmingham (1953–61), recorder for Derby (1961–62), and commissioner of the Crown Courts at Manchester and a Circuit Court judge (1962–65). Created a DBE in 1965, she became the first female High Court judge in England, attached to the Family Division (the second was Dame *Rose Heilbron), and was also chair of the Committee on the Abortion Acts (1971–73). The first woman barrister to appear in the House of Lords on a murder case and the first judge to work part-time, Lane remained on the High Court until her retirement in 1979.

SUGGESTED READING:

Lane, Dame Elizabeth. *Hear the Other Side, Audi ad Alteram Partem: The Autobiography of England's First Woman Judge.* Butterworths, 1985.

Lane, Harriet (1830–1903)

First niece who acted as White House host during one of the most difficult periods in American history. Name variations: Harriet Lane Johnston; (nickname) "Hal." Born on May 9, 1830, in Mercersburg, Pennsylvania; died of cancer while summering at Narragansett Pier, Rhode Island, on July 3, 1903; sixth of seven children of Elliott Tole Lane and Jane (Buchanan) Lane (who was the sister of James Buchanan, president of the U.S.); graduated from Academy of Visitation in Georgetown, 1848; married Henry Elliott Johnston (a banker), on January 11, 1866 (died 1884); children: James Buchanan Johnston (1866–1881); Henry Elliott Johnston (1868–1882).

When bachelor president James Buchanan arrived in the White House in 1857, he brought with him a breath of fresh air in the form of his 26-year-old niece, Harriet ("Hal") Lane. Hal, who had accompanied "Nunc" Buchanan to England when he was ambassador to the Court of St. James, charmed Washington, just as she had Queen *Victoria and the British court.

Harriet, the youngest daughter of Buchanan's sister **Jane Buchanan Lane**, was orphaned at the age of ten. Designated as guardian, James Buchanan, who was not known for his love of children, set out to educate and refine his "mischievous romp of a niece." Private school in Virginia, followed by the Academy of Visitation in Georgetown, removed all traces of her roughhouse behavior. By the age of 17, Hal had not only developed into a tall, blonde beauty, but she also possessed enough charm and political savvy to become the hostess of Wheatland, Buchanan's estate in Pennsylvania.

In the White House, Harriet refurbished the neglected interior with American furniture and had a conservatory built to ensure a supply of fresh flowers. She entertained often, with ease and tact. With a growing rift between the North and the South, Harriet became known as the "Democratic Queen," skillfully warding off sectional rivalries with judicious seating arrangements and admonishments about discussing politics. She was immensely popular. All over Washington, women adopted her full skirts and low necklines. Countless baby girls were named "Harriet," and a U.S. steamship was christened the *Harriet Lane.* Even a song, *Listen to the Mocking Bird*, was written in her honor. If beautiful and gracious, she was also unassuming and warm-hearted. She won the title "Great Mother of the Indians" for her work in improving Native American living conditions.

Harriet Lane presided over two important diplomatic events during Buchanan's term. First was a grand reception for the prince of Wales (the future King Edward VII), who was the first member of the royal family to visit the former colonies. It is reported that he stayed overnight, sleeping in Buchanan's room while the president slept on a couch in the hall. It is also rumored that Buchanan—ever protective of his young charge—removed Harriet's pictures from his room, so there would be no talk of impropriety. The second occasion was the arrival of the first Japanese ambassadors ever to visit America. Adhering to their strict sense of protocol, they determined that only Harriet and the Cabinet wives—who greeted them in elegant silk robes—were ladies of sufficient rank to meet them.

Leaving the White House at a time when seven states had seceded and the Civil War was imminent, Harriet and her uncle gratefully retired to Wheatland. In 1866, she married Baltimore banker Henry Elliott Johnston. When Buchanan died three years later, she inherited Wheatland, which she and her husband used as their country home. Two sons were born but died in childhood. Widowed in 1884, Harriet spent the rest of her life in Washington, active in philanthropic work and collecting art. She organized the Choir School of the Cathedral of Saints Peter and Paul in Washington, and founded the Harriet Lane Home for Invalid Children at Johns Hopkins. Upon her death in 1903, half of her art collection went to Johns Hopkins and the remainder to the Smithsonian Institution, where it provided the basis for the National Gallery of Art. Harriet Lane is buried next to her family in Greenmont Cemetery in Baltimore, Maryland.

SOURCES:

Healy, Diana Dixon. *America's First Ladies: Private Lives of the Presidential Wives*. NY: Atheneum, 1988.

Paletta, LuAnn. *The World Almanac of First Ladies*. NY: World Almanac, 1990.

COLLECTIONS:

The Buchanan-Johnston Papers, Library of Congress.

Barbara Morgan,
Melrose, Massachusetts

Lane, Jane (d. 1689)

English heroine. Name variations: Lady Fisher. Died in 1689; daughter of Thomas Lane; sister of Colonel John Lane; married Sir Clement Fisher, baronet of Packington Magna, Warwickshire.

To save Charles II after the battle of Worcester in 1651, Jane Lane helped the king escape his enemies by having him ride with her from Bentley, in Staffordshire, to the house of her cousin, Mrs. Norton, near Bristol, disguised as her manservant. She then fled to France and eventually entered the service of *Mary of Orange (1631–1660). For Lane's act of loyalty, the king rewarded her with a pension at the time of the Restoration and granted her family the following coat of arms: a strawberry horse salient (couped at the flank), bridled, bitted, and garnished, supporting between its feet a royal crown proper. Motto: *Garde le roy* (guard the king).

Lane, Lola (1909–1981)

American actress. Born Dorothy Mullican on May 21, 1909, in Macy, Indiana; died at her home in Santa Barbara, California, on June 22, 1981, after a long illness with inflammation of the arteries; eldest of five daughters of a dentist; older sister of Priscilla Lane (1917–1995), Rosemary Lane (1914–1974), and

Harriet Lane

Leota Lane; married Lew Ayres (an actor); married Alexander Hall (a director); married Henry Dunham; married Roland West (a director); married Robert Hanlon (a lawyer); no children.

Selected filmography: Speakeasy (1929); Fox Movietone Follies of 1929 (1929); The Girl From Havana (1929); Let's Go Places (1930); The Big Fight (1930); Good News (1930); Hell Bound (1931); Public Stenographer (1933); Burn 'Em Up Barnes (1934); Murder on a Honeymoon (1935); Alias Mary Dow (1935); Marked Woman (1937); Hollywood Hotel (1938); Four Daughters (1938); Daughters Courageous (1939); Four Wives (1939); Convicted Woman (1940); Zanzibar (1940); Gangs of Chicago (1940); Girls of the Road (1940); Four Mothers (1941); Mystery Ship (1941); Miss V from Moscow (1942); Why Girls Leave Home (1945); They Made Me a Killer (1946); Deadline at Dawn (1946).

The older sister of *Priscilla and *Rosemary Lane, Lola Lane began playing the piano for silent films at the age of 12. She later joined yet another Lane sister, **Leota**, in New York, where they appeared together in Gus Edwards' vaudeville revue and made their Broadway debut in *Greenwich Village Follies*. Lola then landed a leading role in *War Song* (1928), with George Jessell, which led to a contract at Fox. She played mostly small roles at Fox and on loan until the 1930s, when she joined Warner Bros. and co-starred in the "Four Daughters" series with her sisters. Lola retired from the screen in 1946 and went into real estate. The actress' five husbands included actor Lew Ayres and directors Alexander Hall and Roland West.

SOURCES:

Katz, Ephriam. *The Film Encyclopedia*. NY: HarperCollins, 1994.

Lamparski, Richard. *Whatever Became of . . . ?* 4th Series. NY: Crown.

Lane, Louisa (1820–1897).

See Drew, Louisa Lane.

Lane, Priscilla (1917–1995)

American actress. Name variations: Priscilla Howard. Born Priscilla Mullican on June 12, 1917, in Iowa City, Iowa; died at age 77 on April 4, 1995, in a nursing home in Andover, Massachusetts; one of five daughters of a dentist; younger sister of Lola Lane (1909–1981), Rosemary Lane (1914–1974), and Leota Lane; attended Simpson College, a music conservatory in Des Moines, Iowa; married Oren Haglund (a screenwriter), in 1940 (annulled); married Joseph A. Howard (a pilot turned building contractor), in 1943; children: Larry Howard; Hannah Howard; Judith Howard; James Howard.

Filmography: Varsity Show *(1937);* Love Honor and Behave *(1938);* Men Are Such Fools *(1938);* Cowboy From Brooklyn *(1938);* Four Daughters *(1938);* Brother Rat *(1938);* Yes, My Darling Daughter *(1939);* Daughters Courageous *(1939);* Dust Be My Destiny *(1939);* The Roaring Twenties *(1939);* Four Wives *(1939);* Brother Rat and a Baby *(1940);* Three Cheers for the Irish *(1940);* Ladies Must Live *(1940);* Four Mothers *(1941);* Million Dollar Baby *(1941);* Blues in the Night *(1941);* Saboteur *(1942);* The Meanest Man in the World *(1943);* Arsenic and Old Lace *(1944);* Fun on a Weekend *(1947);* Bodyguard *(1948).*

The youngest of five sisters, three of whom were in films during the 1930s and 1940s, Priscilla Lane was born in Iowa City, Iowa, in 1917 and enjoyed the most successful career among the sisters. A blue-eyed, sweet-looking blonde, Lane began performing as a child with her sister *Rosemary. The two were discovered by Fred Waring and joined his orchestra, The Pennsylvanians, in 1931. After years of touring, the sisters appeared with Waring in the Warner Bros. film *Varsity Show* (1937). Both were signed to long-term contracts and joined older sister *Lola, who was already established in films, in a series of sentimental dramas about a family with four girls, the fourth played by **Gale Page**. The popular films included *Four Daughters* (1938), *Daughters Courageous* (1939), *Four Wives* (1939), and *Four Mothers* (1941). Also notable among Priscilla Lane's films were *Brother Rat* (1938), *The Roaring Twenties* (1939), *Saboteur* (1942), and *Arsenic and Old Lace* (1944). After a three-year absence from the screen, she returned to make *Fun on a Weekend* (1947) and *Bodyguard* (1948).

Married briefly to screenwriter Oren Haglund (the union was said to have been annulled after one day), Lane was married for a second time in 1943 to Joseph A. Howard, a bombardier pilot who later became a successful contractor in Andover, Massachusetts. Lane abandoned her career to raise her four children, immersing herself in school activities and scouting and fiercely protecting her family's privacy. Aside from a brief stint on her own local television show in Boston and a commercial for hosiery, she avoided the spotlight. Priscilla and her husband spent their later years in their former summer home in Derry, New Hampshire, beside their own private bay. The actress died in 1995, at age 77.

SOURCES:

Katz, Ephraim. *The Film Encyclopedia*. NY: HarperCollins, 1994.

Lamparski, Richard. *Whatever Became of . . . ?* 4th Series. NY: Crown.

Obituary. *The Day* [New London, CT]. April 6, 1995.

Barbara Morgan,
Melrose, Massachusetts

Lane, Rose Wilder (1886–1968)

American journalist, fiction writer, and proponent of individualist political philosophy. Pronunciation: Layne. Born Rose Wilder on December 5, 1886, in De Smet, Dakota Territory; died in Danbury, Connecticut, on October 29, 1968; daughter of Almanzo James Wilder (a farmer) and Laura Ingalls Wilder (a farmer and author); high school graduate; married (Claire) Gillette Lane (a journalist and merchant), in 1909 (divorced 1917).

Family moved to Rocky Ridge Farm in Mansfield, Missouri (1894); after schooling, left Mansfield to work at a series of jobs around the country (1904); married Gillette Lane in San Francisco; traveled with him promoting various products; became reporter and feature writer for the San Francisco Bulletin *(1915–18); published first novel* Diverging Roads *(1918); sailed to Europe to write on behalf of the Red Cross (1920); remained overseas until late 1923, traveling in the most remote corners of Europe and parts of the Middle East; published* Peaks of Shala, *a travel book about Albania (1923); returned to live with her parents, helping her mother with article writing while two books of her own were published; lived in Tirana, Albania (1926–28); returned to Rocky Ridge Farm (1928–36); in these years, began helping her mother write the "Little House" books and published many magazine articles and two books of her own; wrote one final work of fiction,* Free Land, *a bestseller (1938), after she left Missouri; settled in Danbury, Connecticut (1938); opposed American entry into World War II; refused a ration card; continued to help her mother with the "Little House" books; wrote her most extensive political treatise,* The Discovery of Freedom *(1943); became public opponent of social security and income tax; edited* National Economic Council Review of Books *(1945–50); became influential among other individualist thinkers (1950s–1960s); traveled to Vietnam for* Woman's Day *magazine (1965).*

Selected publications: The Story of Art Smith *(1915);* Henry Ford's Own Story *(1917);* Diverging Roads *(1918);* The Making of Herbert Hoover *(1920);* Peaks of Shala *(1923);* He Was a Man *(1925);* Hill-Billy *(1926);* Cindy *(1928);* Let the Hurricane Roar *(1933);* Give Me Liberty *(1936);* Free Land *(1938);* The Discovery of Freedom: Man's Struggle Against Authority *(1943);* The Woman's Day Book of American Needlework *(1963).*

In late 1932, a two-part novella by Rose Wilder Lane, a well-known journalist and magazine fiction writer with famous friends on several continents, was published in the *Saturday Evening Post*, a prestigious place for popular fiction. Her work, entitled *Let the Hurricane Roar*, would appear as a book in 1933, and despite the dampening effect of the Depression, would sell relatively well. Earlier that same year, Lane's mother, **Laura Ingalls Wilder*, had published her first book, *Little House in the Big Woods*, a children's story based on the early years of her own childhood in Wisconsin in the early 1870s. It was owing to Lane's contacts in the publishing world and to her role in conceptualizing and polishing the manuscript that an unknown writer like Wilder managed to interest a major publishing company in a book based

simply on one year in the life of a child in a pioneer family.

Eleven years later, in 1943, Wilder published the eighth and final book in what had come to be known fondly as the "Little House" series. Laura Wilder had become a beloved figure in the world of children's literature, and for the first time in her life, owing to her handsome royalty checks, was enjoying economic security. Lane, who secretly had collaborated on this book as she had on the seven others in the series, also published a book that year. By then, she had ceased writing fiction, and her lucrative magazine-article writing career was over. Her new book, *The Discovery of Freedom: Man's Struggle Against Authority,* published by a relatively minor publisher who gave her little publicity, was a political treatise arguing for individual responsibility and rights against the incursions of state and society. Although her political writings would be important in the post-World War II American revival of the type of individualist thinking described as libertarianism, Lane had slipped into obscurity, a fate not uncommon to those whose fame comes primarily from the ephemeral forms of magazine writing, private correspondence, and sparkling conversation, and whose political convictions are at odds with the dominant ideas of the time. She and her mother had already changed places in terms of fame, accomplishment, and financial success.

Years after both their deaths, Wilder's continuing popularity, bolstered by a television series based on her books, camouflages the accomplishments of a daughter who was once more famous than her mother, was a more skilled writer, and had a far more dramatic and interesting life. Ironically, Lane's most significant contributions to American ideas and letters are those for which she is least widely known.

Rose Wilder was born to Laura Ingalls Wilder and Almanzo ("Manly") Wilder on their farm near De Smet, Dakota Territory, in 1886. In Rose's early years one disaster after another, personal and financial, struck her family. By the time she was three, the Wilders had given up the idea of farming in South Dakota. Rose, a precocious child, seems to have perceived the anxiety her parents felt about their situation, which she transformed into a vague but persistent sense of guilt, especially toward her exacting mother.

After a four-year period of flux, the Wilders migrated in 1894 to Mansfield, Missouri, in the Ozark Mountains. There, they put a down payment on a farm that they appropriately called Rocky Ridge and that they developed over a long period of time, often living and working in town to acquire capital to put into the farm. Growing up as a bookish only child to poor parents in a town with well-developed social distinctions made Rose an outsider in Mansfield. She escaped the town's "narrow relentless life," as she would later characterize it, as soon as she could, initially to her aunt's house in Crowley, Louisiana, to finish high school, and then in 1904 to Kansas City to be a telegraph operator, the first of her many adult residences and careers.

Individual liberty is individual responsibility. Whoever makes decisions is responsible for results. . . . The question is whether personal freedom is worth the terrible effort, the never-lifted burden and the risks of individual self-reliance.

—Rose Wilder Lane

In the tradition of her family, Rose Wilder became a pioneer, but of a new sort. Although she perceived early that she was not suited for the conventional life of wife and mother, she did not take the common route, followed by her grandmother and mother before their marriages, of becoming a schoolteacher. Instead, she switched from job to job and place to place, using her wits, doing whatever work would pay best. In the 11 years that followed her departure from Mansfield, she had at least five different types of jobs before she began newspaper writing for the *San Francisco Bulletin*. In 1909, in the midst of this period of trying her wings, she married Gillette Lane, a reporter who found himself drawn increasingly to advertising and promotional work; together, he and Rose pursued commissions with mixed success. By early 1915 when she was offered, through a friend's contacts, the job on the *Bulletin*, their marriage had faltered. From that point, writing would be her career and marriage would be something she no longer believed in, later describing it as "the sugar in the tea, that one doesn't take, preferring a simpler, more direct relationship with tea."

The three and a half years when she was on staff at the newspaper would be among the most stimulating of her life. She progressed at the *Bulletin* from the women's pages to writing serial stories of a somewhat slippery blend of fiction and biography, a few of which were also published as books. This writing and her freelance work for *Sunset* magazine gave her recognition in San Francisco and beyond. Through her job, she became friends with a group of intellectuals, artists, and bohemians in whose company she

honed ideas derived from years of reading, listening, and observation. Lane's first novel, *Diverging Roads* (1918), emerged from the musings induced by the end of her marriage, the role of career in an independent woman's life, and the discussions among her like-minded female friends of the effects of women's freedom on conventional marriage.

In May 1920, she sailed to Europe as a writer on behalf of the Red Cross for the first of several extended periods of residence overseas. This first sojourn, undertaken while Europe was still reeling from the effects of war, revolution, famine, and inflation, marked her as a traveler as intrepid as anyone in her family had been in their migrations across the Great Plains in covered wagons. In addition to the expected sites in Western and Central Europe, she traveled to Albania three times (writing a book, *Peaks of Shala* [1923], about her experiences in that country with which she had fallen in love), to Yugoslavia and Constantinople, to the Transcaucasus Peninsula, to Cairo and Damascus and then across the unmarked desert by car to Baghdad. Along the way, she acquired and lost several lovers and friends, continued writing fiction and biography in addition to her travel articles, contracted a fierce case of malaria, and for the moment, had her fill of the exotic.

Her observations during these years laid the groundwork for a personal philosophy cynical about the inherent cruelty of human beings, skeptical about the well-meaning efforts of ideologically motivated governments that meddled beyond their competence in individuals' lives, such as that in the Soviet Union, and admiring of the practicality and accomplishments of American relief workers whom she found in the remotest corners of Europe and the Near East.

An ephemeral homesickness for Rocky Ridge Farm and a tenacious sense of responsibility toward her parents drew her back to Mansfield in December 1923. Her goals, once the claustrophobia and mindlessness of the life there reasserted themselves, were twofold: to earn and save enough money from her own writing and from the stock market to enable her parents to retire from farming, and to continue the training of her mother, begun in the 1910s, in the writing and marketing of mainstream magazine articles. With Lane's rigorous editing and reworking, her mother was able to sell a few articles to national magazines.

In two years, Lane had moved close enough to her goals by publishing two books, one of them *Hill-Billy*, an Ozarks-based story collection, that she felt justified in leaving her parents'

*Rose
Wilder
Lane*

farm to take up residence in Albania. Her stay there turned out to be just 15 months long, owing both to personal difficulties and to the increasing precariousness of Albanian independence. The end of the Albanian adventure brought her back to Rocky Ridge Farm in early 1928, ostensibly just long enough to arrange for her own and her parents' permanent financial independence so that she could leave Mansfield with a clear conscience. In fact, she remained there for eight momentous years during which the investment company holding her money failed after the 1929 stock-market crash, her creative energies for the kind of popular fiction at which she made most of her living became ever more sporadic, the country underwent a serious economic depression, and her mother wrote an autobiography that she expected Lane to help her polish and sell.

Having no luck in marketing her mother's manuscript, Lane successfully split off part of it to sell as a children's story. She worked closely with her mother on the requested revisions and had the satisfaction of seeing the manuscript accepted and published as *Little House in the Big Woods* to good reviews and sales. Seven more books, most culled from the original autobiography and transformed into forms suitable for children, followed over the next 11 years. Lane had a clearer sense than Wilder of how to shape a book overall and how to weave each volume's theme in and out of the individual incidents and descriptions her mother was so good at writing. It became apparent that what had been originally conceived of as a temporary period of tutelage of the mother by the daughter would be a permanent collaboration, one that neither of them was happy with, but that each required for complex psychological as well as creative reasons. Even after Lane left the farm in 1936, at odds with her mother, she continued working on the "Little House" books.

Nothing that Lane had written under her own name had given her satisfaction on as many levels as her mother was receiving from her books, written with Lane's crucial but unacknowledged help. The obligations to her mother took time and energy away from her own writing and left her feeling depressed and trapped. She was helping her parents achieve financial security, but at a considerable price to herself, as she gradually realized.

Nonetheless, the process of piecing together a narrative of Ingalls family experiences in order to write the "Little House" books in the midst of the Depression and the New Deal helped both women rethink the meaning of their family history in the context of changing conceptions of the role of government. Lane came more and more to believe that lucky circumstance had initially propelled Americans into rejecting the inherent right of authority figures to control or take care of them. This repudiation of authority and acceptance of responsibility for oneself, she decided, had released the energies that Americans were able to give to the settling of a continent and to solving problems in innovative and pragmatic ways, much as her parents and grandparents had managed throughout their lives. The New Deal, she concluded, was a reversion to regressive European models of the infantalizing relationship between government and individual.

Just as she gradually infused the "Little House" books with individualist principles, Lane put her politics and her fiction-writing skills together in her last piece of fiction, her ironically titled 1938 novel, *Free Land,* based loosely on her father's experience as a homesteading farmer. The book, well reviewed, was a bestseller, enabling Lane to buy a house in Connecticut, far away from her parents. After she lost her interest in writing fiction and became more preoccupied with her political views, outlets for her ideas shrank to a few sources with limited readerships. Her fascinating, knowledgeable conversation and witty, learned letters that had once bound friends like writers *Dorothy Thompson and Floyd Dell to her, increasingly were reserved for people who shared her political convictions.

By the 1950s, however, there was evidence that she was not alone in believing the American experiment to have been temporarily derailed by the inheritance of the New Deal, and that she had been influential in convincing others of her perspective. Among other markers of her intellectual impact, the Freedom School in Colorado, founded on individualist principles, named a building after her. Perhaps most significant, she served not only as surrogate grandmother but also as mentor to Roger Lea MacBride who ran in 1976 for U.S. president on behalf of the Libertarian Party, which uses her *Discovery of Freedom* as a handbook.

Although she may have been more hostile to government than many ordinary Americans in the 1960s, certainly Lane's anti-communism was in step with the mood of the country. In 1965, *Woman's Day* magazine, for which she had written for years, asked her to go to Vietnam on assignment. At the age of 78, she spent almost a month in the war-torn country. Her appetite for international travel was not sated by this experience; in the fall of 1968, she was set to leave on an ambitious trip to Europe and the Middle East when she died at home several days before the scheduled departure.

SOURCES:

Fellman, Anita Clair. "Laura Ingalls Wilder and Rose Wilder Lane: The Politics of a Mother-Daughter Relationship," in *Signs: Journal of Women in Culture and Society.* Vol. 15, no. 3. Spring 1990, pp. 535–561.

Holtz, William. *The Ghost in the Little House: A Life of Rose Wilder Lane.* Columbia: University of Missouri Press, 1993.

MacBride, Roger Lea. *Little House on Rocky Ridge.* NY: HarperTrophy, HarperCollins, 1993.

SUGGESTED READING:

Anderson, William. "Laura Ingalls Wilder and Rose Wilder Lane: The Continuing Collaboration," in *South Dakota History.* Vol. 16, no. 2. Summer 1986, pp 89–143.

———. "The Literary Apprenticeship of Laura Ingalls Wilder," in *South Dakota History.* Vol. 13, no. 4. Winter 1983, pp. 285–331.

———. *A Little House Sampler.* NY: Perennial Library, Harper & Row, 1989.

Holtz, William, ed. *Dorothy Thompson and Rose Wilder Lane: Forty Years of Friendship: Letters, 1921–1960.* Columbia: University of Missouri Press, 1991.

———, ed. *Travels with Zenobia: Paris to Albania by Model T Ford: A Journal by Rose Wilder Lane and Helen Dore Boylston.* Columbia: University of Missouri Press, 1983.

COLLECTIONS:

Correspondence, journals, diaries and manuscripts are located largely in the Herbert Hoover Presidential Library in West Branch, Iowa, with valuable additional correspondence to be found in the Fremont Older Collection, Bancroft Library, University of California-Berkeley; the Floyd Dell Papers, Newberry Library, Chicago; and the Hader Papers, University of Oregon Library.

Anita Clair Fellman,
Director of Women's Studies and Associate
Professor of History, Old Dominion University, Norfolk, Virginia

Lane, Rosemary (1914–1974)

American actress. Born Rosemary Mullican on April 4, 1914, in Indianola, Iowa; died from pulmonary obstruction and diabetes in Woodland Hills, California,

From the movie Four Daughters, starring Gale Page, Lola Lane, Priscilla Lane, and Rosemary Lane.

on November 25, 1974; one of five daughters of a dentist; sister of Priscilla Lane (1917–1995), Lola Lane (1909–1981) and Leota Lane; attended Simpson College; married; one daughter.

Selected filmography: Varsity Show (1937); Hollywood Hotel (1938); Gold Diggers in Paris (1938); Four Daughters (1938); Blackwell's Island (1939); The Oklahoma Kid (1939); Daughters Courageous (1939); The Return of Dr. X (1939); Four Wives (1939); An Angel From Texas (1940); The Boys from Syracuse (1940); Ladies Must Live (1940); Always a Bride (1940); Four Mothers (1941); Time Out for Rhythm (1941); Chatterbox (1943); All By Myself (1943); Harvest Melody (1943); Trocadero (1944); Sing Me a Song of Texas (1945).

Aside from the "Four Daughters" series of movies she made with her sisters *Priscilla and *Lola, actress Rosemary Lane had a brief film career. Her greatest solo success was her starring role in the Broadway musical Best Foot Forward (1941). Rosemary retired from films in 1945.

Laney, Lucy Craft (1854–1933)

African-American educator. Born in Macon, Georgia, in April 1854 (in various sources seen as April 11, 12, and 13); died in Augusta, Georgia, on October 23, 1933; seventh of ten children, six girls and four boys, of David Laney (a carpenter and lay minister) and Louisa Laney; graduated from Lewis High School, Macon, Georgia; graduated in the first class of Atlanta University, 1873; took graduate courses at the University of Chicago; never married; no children.

The daughter of former slaves, Lucy Laney was born in 1854, the seventh of ten children of David and **Louisa Laney**. Louisa's father, born a slave in South Carolina, later purchased his freedom and became a carpenter and a lay minister in Macon, Georgia, where he settled in 1836. Louisa's mother had been a slave of the prominent Campbell family of Macon. At 13, Louisa married David Laney, who afterward purchased her freedom, although she continued to work for the Campbell family. Lucy was taught to read and write by her mother and later attended Lewis High School in Macon, a private institution for blacks. Upon graduation, she was selected to become a member of the first class of the newly founded Atlanta University.

After graduating in 1873, Laney spent the next 12 years teaching public school in Savannah, Augusta, Macon, and Milledgeville, Geor-

gia. In 1885, she accepted an invitation from the Presbyterian Board of Missions for Freedmen to begin a private school for black youths in Augusta. Securing a charter from the state in January 1886, she opened her school in a rented room in the basement of Augusta's Christ Presbyterian Church. From an initial enrollment of five students, the school quickly caught on, largely because of its superior curriculum. At a time when educational opportunities for blacks were limited to vocational training or a few poor public schools, Laney's goal was to prepare her students to enter reputable colleges and become qualified teachers. To that end, she set high standards and offered a full liberal arts curriculum. By the end of the second year, enrollment had reached 234, and Laney was forced to solicit aid from the General Assembly of the Presbyterian Church to keep the school going. While the assembly could offer only moral support, funds were obtained from several individual donors, among them **Francina E.H. Haines**, in whose honor Laney eventually named her school the Haines Normal and Industrial Institute. Other donors contributed to the construction of several new buildings, and the school eventually expanded to cover an entire city block. The Presbyterian Board assumed some responsibility for maintenance and salaries but financing remained an ongoing concern, and Laney traveled extensively to plead her cause. By the time of World War I, the school had 900 students and 30 teachers, and had built a reputation as one of the best schools of its kind for blacks in the state. Among the many dedicated educators to work with Laney was *Mary McLeod Bethune, who would begin her teaching career at Haines in the early 1900s.

In the early 1890s, Laney established at Haines the city's first kindergarten and a nurses' training department which evolved into the school of nursing at the University Hospital at Augusta. A Lucy Laney League was organized in New York City in 1900, and held a yearly fundraiser to support the school's kindergarten. By the 1930s, the school had dropped the elementary grades and offered a four-year high school course plus a year of college-level studies. Graduates of Haines expressed their gratitude by sending their own children to the school and by supporting its programs.

Following Laney's death in 1933, the Haines Institute was taken over by her niece **Louisa Laney**, who was succeeded after a year by Reverend Augustus Cummings Griggs. Although the Depression caused the Presbyterian Church to gradually withdraw its support, the school managed to operate until 1949, when it was forced to closed. The buildings were razed, and a modern structure, the Lucy C. Laney High School, was built on the site. Laney, whose portrait hangs in the Georgia State House in Atlanta, is remembered as one of the South's foremost educators.

SOURCES:

Igus, Toyomi, ed. *Great Women in the Struggle*. NJ: Just Us Books, 1991.

James, Edward T., ed. *Notable American Women, 1607–1950*. Cambridge, MA: The Belknap Press of Harvard University Press, 1971.

Smith, Jessie Carney, ed. *Notable Black American Women*. Detroit, MI: Gale Research, 1992.

Barbara Morgan,
Melrose, Massachusetts

Lang, Josephine (1815–1880)

German composer of over 150 songs and many pieces for the piano who became a professional singer at the Munich court in 1836. Name variations: Lang-Köstlin, Lang-Kostlin, or Lang-Koestlin. Born Josephine Carolin Lang in Munich, Germany, on March 14, 1815; died in Tübingen in 1880; her father was a court musician; her mother was an opera singer; taught by her mother and Fräulein Berlinghof; married Christian Reinhold Koestlin or Köstlin (an amateur poet and professor of law at Tübingen University), in 1842 (died 1856); children: six.

One of the most published women composers of the Romantic period, Josephine Lang was born in Munich, Germany, in 1815. Like many composers, she came from a musical family; her mother, an opera singer, taught her to sing. Lang composed her first songs in 1828 and in 1836 became a professional singer at the Munich court. In 1842, she married Christian Reinhold Koestlin and moved to Tübingen where he was a professor of law. The couple had six children, three of whom died in tragic circumstances, as would her husband. Despite these enormous reverses, Lang continued to compose and enjoyed the encouragement of composers Felix Mendelssohn, Robert Schumann, and *Clara Schumann, who was also one of Europe's best-known pianists. Young Felix Mendelssohn was so impressed by Lang that he visited her daily for several months in 1830 and 1831. Although Mendelssohn's sister, *Fanny Mendelssohn-Hensel, was also composing during the 1830s and 1840s, it was Lang's work which received the most public attention. After her husband died in 1856, Lang began teaching voice and piano to support her large family. A progressive composer

who concentrated on piano scores and songs, her reputation was established during her lifetime and she was especially popular in the German-speaking world.

John Haag,
Athens, Georgia

Lucy Craft Laney

Lang, June (1915—)

American actress. Name variations: also acted as June Vlasek. Born Winifred June Vlasek on May 5, 1915, in Minneapolis, Minnesota; married briefly to Vic Orsatti (an agent); married briefly to John Roselli (a mobster); married a businessman named Morgan, in 1944 (divorced 1954); one source claims that Lang also married and divorced British actor Josh Ambler; children: (last marriage) Patricia Morgan.

Selected filmography: (as June Vlasek) Young Sinners *(1931); (as June Vlasek)* Chandu the Magician *(1932); (as June Vlasek)* The Man Who Dared *(1933);* Music in the Air *(1934);* Bonnie Scotland *(1935);* The Country Doctor *(1936);* Captain January *(1936);* The Road to Glory *(1936);* White Hunter *(1936);* Nancy Steele Is Missing *(1937);* Wee Willie Winkie *(1937);* Ali Baba Goes to Town *(1937);* International Settlement *(1938);* Meet the Girls *(1938);* Zenobia *(1939);*

Captain Fury (1939); For Love or Money (1939); Convicted Woman (1940); Redhead (1941); The Deadly Game (1941); City of Silent Men (1942); Footlight Serenade (1942); Flesh and Fantasy (1943); Lighthouse (1947).

A striking blue-eyed blonde, June Lang was a professional dancer before breaking into films as an extra in *Young Sinners* (1931). After several other small movie roles, she was placed under contract at Fox, where she was groomed as a potential star. She was cast in a series of awkward roles, however, and, though she photographed well, never clicked as a screen personality. After she walked out of a shoot in London in 1938, her contract was canceled. Lang went on to a series of unremarkable roles in mostly small pictures, the last of which was *Lighthouse* (1947). After a few commercials and a brief stint as an on-air telephone operator for a Los Angeles talk show, she retired. Lang was married at least three times; her second and very brief union with convicted mobster Johnny Roselli was said to have further damaged her career.

Lang, Margaret Ruthven
(1867–1972)

American composer whose songs were included in the repertoire of leading concert singers of her day. Born Margaret Ruthven Lang in Boston, Massachusetts, on November 27, 1867; died in Boston on May 30, 1972; daughter of Benjamin Johnson Lang (who conducted Boston's Cecilia and Apollo Clubs) and Frances Morse (Burrage) Lang; studied piano and composition with her father; studied violin under Louis Schmidt in Boston and under Drechsler and Abel in Munich; also studied composition with Victor Gluth in Munich; studied orchestration under G.W. Chadwick and E.A. MacDowell; never married.

*Had first works—five songs—included in a Boston recital and reviewed favorably (December 14, 1887); had one of her songs performed in Paris during the World's Exposition (1889) and at the inaugural of the Lincoln Concert Hall in Washington, D.C. (1890); in time, enjoyed the inclusion of her songs in the repertoire of leading concert singers, including *Ernestine Schumann-Heink; was the first American woman composer to have a composition played by a major orchestra when the Boston Symphony Orchestra performed her Dramatic Overture, Opus 12 (1893); had another orchestral composition performed three times the same year at the World's Columbian Exposition in Chicago (1893); ceased composing (1917) but retained a strong interest in music for the rest of her life; in her honor, Boston Symphony Orchestra gave a concert for her 100th birthday (1967).*

It would be easy to emphasize her remarkable longevity as being the greatest single accomplishment of Margaret Ruthven Lang, who remained mentally active and intellectually curious as a centenarian. Her greatest legacy to music lovers and women was of course not the length of her life but what she had achieved. The creative part of Lang's days ended at age 50 in 1917, when she decided for reasons best known to herself to stop composing. But what she had accomplished prior to that year was impressive by almost any standard. Lang's father was a talented if domineering man who acted as his gifted daughter's mentor, deciding which of her compositions were of sufficient quality to be submitted for publication, and which ones were not. Her self-confidence was, however, quite high, because she continued to compose throughout her most productive decade, the 1890s. It was in these years, on April 7, 1813, that one of her orchestral works, the *Dramatic Overture*, became the first composition by a woman to be performed by a major symphony orchestra, when the Boston Symphony under the illustrious German conductor Artur Nikisch gave it its premiere. Other orchestral works by Margaret Lang were performed the same year at the Chicago World's Columbian Exposition, and in 1901 at an all-women's composers concert presented by the Baltimore Symphony. Unfortunately, modern listeners cannot judge the quality of these works because their scores have been lost. What is clear is the fact that Margaret Ruthven Lang was an individual of great talent and spirited temperament and should be remembered as a major figure in the formative years of American women's participation in national cultural life.

John Haag,
Athens, Georgia

Lang-Beck, Ivana (1912–1983)

Yugoslav pianist whose compositions were performed on Yugoslav radio and television as well as throughout Europe and the Soviet Union. Born in Zagreb, Yugoslavia, on November 15, 1912; died in 1983.

Ivana Lang-Beck's composing career unfolded in the former Yugoslavia. She studied at the Music Academy of Zagreb and later became a professor there. From 1940 to 1943, Lang-Beck taught at the teachers' academy in Zagreb and then secured a position teaching piano at the Vatroslav Lisinski Music Academy. Some of her compositions were performed in Salzburg at the Mozarteum, where she also attended lectures by Joseph Marx. As her reputation grew, Lang-Beck's compositions were also performed in Hamburg, Strasbourg, Trieste, and what was then the Soviet Union. She wrote over 50 compositions, many for the piano, and composed a full-length opera and several ballet scores. Lang-Beck's work was also performed on Yugoslav radio and television. Much of the inspiration for her composition came from an intensive study of folk music of Istria, a peninsula in the Adriatic Sea.

John Haag,
Athens, Georgia

Lange, Aloysia (c. 1761–1839)

German soprano who originated several roles in operas written by Mozart. Name variations: Aloysia Weber. Born Maria Aloysia Louise Antonia Weber in Zell or Mannheim, Germany, between 1759 and 1761; died in Salzburg, Austria, on June 8, 1839; daughter of Fridolin Weber (1733–1779, a musician and uncle of Carl Maria von Weber) and Cecilia Weber; studied with Mozart in Mannheim; sister of Constanze Weber Mozart (who married Wolfgang Amadeus Mozart), Josepha Weber Hofer (c. 1758–1819, a soprano), and Sophie Weber (1763–1846, who wrote of Mozart's death and married composer Jakob Haibel); married Joseph Lange (1751–1831, a painter), on October 31, 1780.

Aloysia Lange was born Aloysia Weber into a musical family in 1761. Her sister **Josepha Weber Hofer** was a soprano while another sister, **Sophie Weber**, married the composer Jakob Haibel. Aloysia is best remembered for her close association with Wolfgang Amadeus Mozart, who once fell in love with her. They first met in 1777–78. Though Mozart married another of her sisters, *Constanze Weber (Mozart), he first proposed to Aloysia.

Lange studied with Mozart and Vogler in Mannheim, where the young composer wrote seven concert arias and a role in *Der Schauspieldirektor* for her. In 1788, she went to Munich before moving on to Vienna, where she was engaged for the new National Singspiel. A year later, in 1780, she married Joseph Lange, an actor and painter. In 1782, Lange was made a leading singer of the Italian troupe in Vienna. Disagreements over salary and working conditions ended her position eight months later, and she was transferred to the less prestigious Kärntnertortheater. In 1790, Emperor Leopold II retained her for his

HERR UND MADAME LANGE
Mitglieder des K.K. National
Hoftheaters in Wien.

opera seria. She undertook a concert tour with her sister, Constanze, in 1795. Her voice was pleasing but could be weak. Leopold Mozart, the composer's father, writing to his daughter *Maria Anna Mozart, said of Lange:

> It can scarcely be denied that she sings with the greatest expression: only now I understand why some persons . . . would say that she has a very weak voice, while others said she has a very loud voice. Both are true. The held notes and all expressive notes are astonishingly loud: the tender moments, the passage work and embellishments, and high notes are very delicate, so that for my taste the one contrasts too strongly with the other. In an ordinary room the loud notes assault the ear, while in the theater the delicate passages demand a great attentiveness and stillness on the part of the audience.

Mozart was well aware of Lange's strengths and weaknesses, using light orchestration and many high notes as her upper range was remarkable. Gebler says Lange was "a splendid singer [with] a tone and an expression that goes to the heart [and] and extraordinary upper range."

*Aloysia
and
Joseph
Lange*

SOURCES:
Sadie, Stanley, ed. *New Grove Dictionary of Music and Musicians.* 20 vols. NY: Macmillan, 1980.

John Haag,
Athens, Georgia

Lange, Anne Françoise Elizabeth

(1772–1816)

French actress. Born in Genoa, Italy, on September 17, 1772; died on May 25, 1816; daughter of a musician and an actress at the Comédie Italienne; married the son of a rich Belgian named Simons.

Anne Françoise Elizabeth Lange made her first stage appearance at Tours in 1781 and had a successful début at the Comédie Française in 1788 in *L'Écossaise* and *L'Oracle.* In the fomenting stages of the French Revolution, the theater was rechristened the Théâtre de la Nation (July 21, 1789), because of public criticism led by La-Harpe of "the hauty greediness of this usurping troupe" brought about by too much royal privilege. When a dispute between patriots versus royalists broke out between members of the company, Lange followed patriot François Talma and others in 1792 to help found the Théâtre de la République Rue Richelieu. But Lange returned after a few months to the Comédie Française. Here her talent and beauty gave her an enormous success in François de Neuchâteau's *Paméla,* but the play, deemed counter-revolutionary, brought down the wrath of the Committee of Safety upon the theater, and it was closed on September 3, 1793. With the author and other members of the cast, Lange was arrested and imprisoned. After the 9th Thermidor (July 27, 1794), she rejoined her comrades at the Feydeau, but retired on December 16, 1797, reappearing only for a few performances in 1807. Lange died on May 25, 1816.

Lange, Dorothea (1895–1965)

American documentary photographer, famous for her rural scenes in the Great Depression. Name variations: Dorothea Lange (in professional life); Dorothea Nutzhorn (1895–1925); Dorothea Dixon (1920–1935); Dorothea Taylor (1935–1965). Born Dorothea Margaretta Nutzhorn in Hoboken, New Jersey, on May 15, 1895; died in San Francisco, California, on October 11, 1965; daughter of Joan (Lange) Nutzhorn (a librarian) and Henry Nutzhorn; attended high school in New York City; married Maynard Dixon (an artist), in 1920 (divorced 1935); married Paul Schuster Taylor (b. 1895, an economist), on December 6, 1935; *children: (first marriage) Daniel Dixon (b. 1925); John Dixon (b. 1928).*

Owned a photography studio (1919–35); served as government photographer (1935–45); worked as freelance photographer (1945–64).

Dorothea Lange was one of the premier American photographers of the 20th century. Working exclusively in black and white with large format cameras, she made many of the most enduring pictures of the American countryside during the Great Depression, and of the human damage caused by unemployment, migration, and war.

Lange was born Dorothea Margaretta Nutzhorn in Hoboken, New Jersey, in 1895, the daughter of **Joan Lange Nutzhorn** and Henry Nutzhorn. Her parents were recent immigrants from Germany. When she was seven, Lange contracted polio, then a terrifying disease to which poor children were particularly vulnerable (though it also struck down such well-known adults as Franklin Roosevelt and *Marjorie Lawrence). Although she recovered from the paralysis it caused, Lange had a lifelong limp and a withered right leg. She later told an interviewer: "I was physically disabled, and no one who hasn't lived the life of a semi-cripple knows how much that means. I think it perhaps was the most important thing that happened to me, and formed me, guided me, instructed me, helped me, and humiliated me."

Lange reverted as an adult to her mother's maiden name, partly because her father had abandoned the family when she was 12, after which she, her mother, and her younger brother Henry went to live with her grandmother, who was an autocrat and an alcoholic. Despite living in Hoboken, Lange went to school in Manhattan, crossing on the ferries each morning and evening with her mother, a librarian. On graduation from high school, where she was a loner and often a truant, she declared that she was going to be a photographer, though she had shown little interest in the craft until then and did not own a camera. Nevertheless, she made good on this declaration and found work at a series of photographers' studios, meeting rich people for the first time. She learned how to pose and shoot portraits, how to develop photographs, and even how to handle the business aspects of photography. She also took classes from Clarence White, a prominent art photographer of the day.

In 1918, aged 23, Lange and a friend left home in New Jersey and set off to tour the world. But after crossing the United States, they were

Dorothea Lange

robbed in San Francisco, and Lange was again forced to seek work in photo studios. She had the good luck to meet and befriend *Imogen Cunningham, who was to become one of the pre-eminent photographers of the century. With Cunningham's help, Lange established a studio of her own in San Francisco and was soon prospering as a California society portraitist. She also met a Western landscape painter, Maynard Dixon, and married him in 1920, despite the fact that he was already in his mid-40s. The couple had two sons, Daniel and John, born in 1925 and 1928, and

Dixon's teenage daughter from a former marriage usually lived with them, too. But Lange, who claimed she had little aptitude for motherhood, continued with her work rather than surrender to domestic demands. She accompanied Dixon on sketching trips to the American Southwest in the mid-1920s and made some fine photographic studies of the Hopi and Pueblo Indians of Arizona and New Mexico. Her son Dan recalled her flair for self-dramatization:

> She wore heavy, primitive, exotic jewelry. She smoked when few women dared . . . , and didn't when many women did. And her clothes weren't clothes; they were costumes. Some of these garments she designed herself. They were made of coarse white fabrics splashed with vivid embroideries across breast and shoulders, falling in long skirts that curtained her lame leg and twisted foot. . . . She disguised it so well that some people never realized that she walked with a limp.

Maynard Dixon and Lange both maintained successful businesses through the boom years of the 1920s but were forced to retrench drastically at the onset of the Depression, when orders for his murals and her society photographs fell off rapidly. They economized by living in their studios. Lange, whose work until then had been largely conventional portraiture, now began to investigate Depression conditions, and some of her most famous work depicted lines of unemployed, humiliated men seeking food and relief in San Francisco. She said later that, although she had enjoyed portraiture, "I realized that I was photographing only people that paid me for it. That bothered me. . . . I had to really face myself. . . . I was aware that there was a very large world out there that I had not entered too well, and I decided I'd better."

Paul Schuster Taylor, a World War I Marine veteran and professor of economics at the University of California, Berkeley, admired some of these photographs in a show at the Oakland Museum. He used one in a *Survey Graphic* magazine article and then invited Lange to join him in working for the California Emergency Relief Administration, recently established as part of President Roosevelt's New Deal. Lange agreed and collaborated with Taylor, illustrating articles he was writing on the plight of migrant workers in California agriculture and their need for government-sponsored camps. They visited the overcrowded, makeshift huts, many of them made of canvas and scrap wood, and sometimes leaning against wrecked old cars, in which migrant farm workers were forced to live exhausting, insanitary, and undernourished lives. Clark Kerr, then a young social scientist, worked with them in California's Central Valley in 1934 and recalled that "they had complementary skills but contrasting personalities. She was always moving, mostly talking, reacting in a flash, living in the moment" whereas "Paul thought carefully about everything, spoke seldom, and then softly."

The head of the Farm Security Administration (FSA), a related New Deal Agency, saw her photographs and, equally impressed, invited Lange to work for his agency. "No one was ever given exact directions," she wrote later of the FSA photographers. "You were turned loose in a region, and the assignment was more like this: 'See what is really there. What does it look like, what does it feel like? What actually is the human condition?'" Much of her work in the following years, upon which her fame now rests, traced the exit of Southern and Midwestern farmers from their land, "tractored out" by the spread of farm machinery, or forced away when their land was ruined in the vast "dust bowl" storms of the 1930s. Her images, along with those of such fellow FSA photographers as Ben Shahn, Aaron Siskind, and Arthur Rothstein, have become the visual counterpart of John Steinbeck's *The Grapes of Wrath*. Like the novel, they show the enduring dignity, as well as the privation, in the migrants' faces, and the bleak solitude of deserted farm houses in the dust-bowl country. Unlike many of her contemporaries involved in documenting the human cost of the Depression, however, Lange was not drawn to radical left-wing politics, though she often sympathized with the work of American Communist Party organizers among the migrant workers. Neither was she the only woman involved in government photo-documentary work. As **Andrea Fisher** has shown in *Let Us Now Praise Famous Women*, *Esther Bubley, Marjory Collins, Pauline Ehrlich*, and many others also worked for the FSA and other agencies, each contributing photographs in her own distinctive idiom.

Lange, as even her close friends admitted, was a prickly personality, not easy to get along with. She was frequently at odds with Roy Stryker, the FSA administrator in Washington, partly because he specified that all the work she did while on the government's payroll become the property of the government, even such famous pictures as that of an exhausted migrant mother surrounded by her ragged children in a pea-pickers' camp. Indeed, she was required to send her rolls of film, as soon as they were exposed, to Washington, and often did not see the pictures themselves until weeks later when other government employees had developed and printed them. Some she sent to Ansel Adams, the pre-

Migrant Mother, Nipomo, California. *Photo by Dorothea Lange.*

mier California landscape photographer, whom she had befriended in 1934, and he recalled that packages of film would arrive from the deep South stinking of mildew and sometimes damaged by the humidity. When museums and publishers asked to buy copies of her photographs for shows, she had to plead with Stryker to send her the negatives and promise to return them at once since they were all officially government property. Lange and Stryker fell out over this issue. After 1936, she worked only irregularly for the Administration, then was fired once and for all in 1938, over the protests of other FSA photographers who recognized her exceptional gifts. But at least she was able to use some of her FSA photos in a book she and Taylor published in 1939, *An American Exodus*, for which he provided the text and she the illustrations. It charts the depopulation of the agricultural South and West and follows migrant workers west to California and the work camps.

Lange's close working relationship with Paul Taylor, meanwhile (he had also joined the FSA), developed into an equally intense personal relationship; in 1935, they both divorced and married one another. (Paul, who had married **Katharine Page Whiteside** in 1920, had three children.) With his encouragement, she applied to the Guggenheim Foundation after losing her government job and became the first woman to win one of its fellowships. With the money, she undertook a documentary study of farm life in obscure parts of rural America.

The outbreak of the Second World War prevented Lange and Taylor's book from gaining much acclaim. But the war did provide another opportunity for Lange's continuation of her career as a government photographer. After the Japanese attack on Pearl Harbor, she was recruited by the War Relocation Administration (WRA) to make a pictorial record of the deportation of Japanese-Americans away from the West Coast. In the panic which seized California in the first days of the war, white citizens, including the governor, Earl Warren, feared that Japanese immigrants and their American-born descendants were potential enemy agents, and although there was no hard evidence to support the alarm, Warren was able to get President Roosevelt's support for the drastic relocation policy. Lange herself thought it was a disgraceful violation of civil rights and in her photographs she made a point of showing the deportees' violated dignity, or captured such ironic moments as Japanese-American children saluting the flag and reciting the Pledge of Allegiance. The government was careful to use only those of her photographs which showed the evacuation of the West Coast cities and the deportees' arrival at Manzanar, in the dust-blown Owens Valley, as though the whole episode was good natured, orderly, and humane. They suppressed or confiscated pictures which showed that the deportees' guards were soldiers carrying guns. Whenever Lange entered the camps, she was accompanied by armed men who authorized or prevented her photographing of proposed subjects. Her husband Paul Taylor, meanwhile, joined a protest movement led by the philosopher John Dewey,

and petitioned President Roosevelt to give each individual a loyalty hearing rather than undertaking a mass deportation.

Lange's other wartime work included photographs of the booming shipbuilding industry in Richmond, California, near her Berkeley home, in collaboration with Ansel Adams. Adams had also photographed the Japanese relocation project and published a book about it, *Born Free and Equal*, but of the two he was less outraged, and more willing to see the deportations as a temporary expedient made necessary by wartime conditions. On the other hand, he was more scrupulous than Lange on an expedition to Utah in the early 1950s to photograph isolated Mormon communities. Taylor and Lange disguised the fact that they were on assignment for *Life* magazine rather than just working as sociologists, and when the Mormons saw themselves in the national magazine they were "absolutely horrified," Adams recalled. "Some wanted to sue. I was very embarrassed."

In the late 1940s, Lange was forced by ill health to stop working—she had a succession of severe stomach ulcers which were only inhibited by radical surgery. In the early 1950s, however, still undaunted, she resumed her career, working for *Fortune* and *Life* magazines, on such photo-essay projects as the inundation of a California valley for the sake of the San Francisco water supply, and the work of an Alameda County public defender. In addition, she helped to create a new photography magazine, *Aperture*, in which she was able to feature more of her work than the commercial magazines could use, and discuss its technical as well as artistic elements.

Paul Taylor traveled abroad frequently in the 1950s, often accompanied by Lange. She found it difficult pursue her work in Korea, Vietnam, Pakistan, Indonesia, Ecuador, and Egypt because she knew none of the languages and continued to be dogged by ill health. In America, she had relied on conversations with her subjects to break the ice before photographing them, in a way which was not possible in Asia. She also wondered whether it was possible to do justice to many brilliantly colorful Asian scenes shot solely in black and white. Even so, many of her photographs of Asians and Egyptians, especially of women and children, are strikingly effective.

By the early 1960s, Lange's reputation had grown to such a point that the Museum of Modern Art in New York decided to mount a retrospective of her life's work. At the same time, a local television station, KQED, made two documentaries of her life and work, celebrating her

Dorothea Lange, 1957. Photograph by Imogen Cunningham.

achievement. This full recognition had come almost too late, however, for in 1964 she was diagnosed with inoperable cancer of the esophagus. Her longtime friend Ansel Adams wrote that "the older she got the more beautiful she got. Absolute sexless beauty. Rather frightening sometimes." She was able to choose the photographs for the Museum of Modern Art show, and for her book *Dorothea Lange Looks at the American Country Woman* (1967), but she died, aged 70, in October 1965 before the show could begin or the book appear.

SOURCES:

Fisher, Andrea. *Let Us Now Praise Famous Women: Women Photographers for the U.S. Government from 1935 to 1944.* London: Pandora, 1987.

Hayan, Therese T., *et al. Dorothea Lange: American Photograph.* San Francisco, CA: Chronicle Books-San Francisco Museum of Modern Art, 1994.

Lange, Dorothea, and Paul S. Taylor. *An American Exodus: A Record of Human Erosion in the Thirties* (published in 1939). New Haven, CT: Yale University Press, 1969.

Meltzer, Milton. *Dorothea Lange: A Photographer's Life.* NY: Farrar, Straus, and Giroux, 1978.

Partridge, Elizabeth, ed. *Dorothea Lange: A Visual Life.* Washington DC: Smithsonian Press, 1994 (including cited essays and interviews by Linda Morris, Clark Kerr, Ansel Adams, and Sally Stein).

COLLECTIONS:

Oakland Museum, California; New York Public Library; Roy Stryker Papers, University of Louisville; Bancroft Library, University of California, Berkeley.

Patrick Allitt,
Professor of History, Emory University, Atlanta, Georgia

Lange, Elizabeth Clovis (1784–1882)

African-American religious founder. Name variations: Mother Mary Elizabeth Lange; Mother Mary Elizabeth. Born in the French colony of St. Domingue in 1784; died in 1882 in Baltimore, Maryland; daughter of Clovis Lange and Annette ("Dede") Lange; never married.

Immigrated to U.S. (1817); founded school for black Catholic children in Baltimore (1820s); with support of Father James Hector Joubert, founded Oblate Sisters of Providence, the first black Roman Catholic order in the United States (1829); ran schools and supervised teacher training; began the order's first mission school in St. Louis, Missouri (1880s).

Elizabeth Clovis Lange was born in the French colony of Saint Domingue in 1784. Her mother **Annette Lange** (known as Dede) was the natural daughter of Mardoche Lange, a Jewish plantation owner in Jeremie, Haiti. Her father Clovis had the same family name of Lange. Emigrating to Cuba from Haiti sometime before Toussaint L'Ouverture's Haitian Revolution, the family lived near the city of Santiago, but split up when Dede and Elizabeth Lange left Cuba for the United States in 1817. They landed in Charleston, South Carolina, where they stayed a short time before moving on to Norfolk, Virginia, and finally to Fells Point in Baltimore in the early 1820s. Dede Lange soon returned to the West Indies, but her daughter remained in Baltimore.

Lange's decision to stay in Baltimore was a brave one: she was a black Catholic French-speaking woman living in a Protestant-dominated, slave-holding state. Baltimore did have a French-speaking community, which included refugees from the French Revolution and the French island possessions in the West Indies, many of whom had fled the revolution there. By 1793, the Fells Point area had a sizable Haitian community of about 1,500, of whom approximately 500 were of African ancestry. The nucleus of religious activity for black and white Haitians was St. Mary's Seminary Chapel, run by the Sulpicians, themselves émigrés from revolutionary France. The black congregants met in the segregated "chapelle basse" below the church.

Soon after arriving in Baltimore, with the help of another refugee, **Marie Magdalene Balas,** Lange opened the first school for the city's French-speaking immigrants. No public education was provided for black children there, and while Maryland—unlike other Southern states—did not legally prohibit the education of blacks, it did not encourage it at all. There were a few small schools for black children operated by Protestant groups, but there was little available for the children of black Catholics.

The school had scant financial support, and Lange was forced to close it in 1827. She turned to the Sulpician fathers for advice, finding support from Father James Hector Joubert. Lange was a devout Catholic, and Father Joubert not only encouraged her in her educational plans, but also in her desire to become a member of a religious order. As existing orders only admitted white women, a new order for black women needed to be established. By giving the order an educational focus, Lange and Joubert hoped to attract women who could learn to teach and run Catholic schools for black children.

Archbishop Whitfield of Baltimore approved the founding of the new religious order, reassuring Lange that white people would not be offended to see black women in religious habits. Lange, Balas and **Rosine Boegue** began their novitiate on June 13, 1828, preparing for their religious vows. The three women established a school for black children in a rented house near the Sulpician Seminary, supported by money raised from members of the black community and the white Haitian community. The school moved to larger premises on Richmond Street later that year.

On July 2, 1829, in the house on Richmond Street, the first black Roman Catholic order in the United States was instituted, the Oblate Sisters of Providence. The first four members were Mother Mary Elizabeth, as Lange was now known, and Sisters Marie Francis, Mary Rose, and Mary Theresa (a former pupil, **Almeide Duchemin Maxis**). As well as making history with her new religious order, Lange was an educational pioneer with her school and teacher training facility, the first of its kind for black women in Baltimore. She was to become a dynamic, resourceful and influential figure in Baltimore's educational circles for the greater part of the 19th century.

The school on Richmond Street soon moved to Pennsylvania Avenue and became the Saint Frances Academy. Its annual examinations were overseen by faculty members from St. Mary's College and later by the Jesuits of Loyola College. Students competed for medals and awards and took part in concerts, recitals and choirs. The school was predominantly vocational, with sewing and other domestic arts on the curriculum, in addition to religious instruction. As well as running the school, the sisters began taking in widows and indigent elderly women unable to support themselves.

During the cholera epidemic of 1832, Lange and 11 of the Oblate Sisters volunteered to help minister to the sick in the almshouse, responding to an appeal for nurses. Unlike the Sisters of Charity, a white nursing order, the Oblates were never publicly recognized for this work.

In the 1840s, after Joubert's death, the convent experienced a financial downturn and the archbishop of Baltimore, seeing the poverty of the sisters, ordered them to disband. Lange refused, and the sisters took in washing and ironing, and worked outside the convent as domestics, in order to maintain the order.

Lange's fears that people might be shocked at the sight of a black woman in a religious habit were not unfounded. Some ridiculed the sisters or physically threatened them: in the 1860s, sisters teaching in Philadelphia were repeatedly forced from the sidewalks. There were also forces at large in the Catholic Church that were opposed to a black religious order, at a time when some theologians believed that black people had no souls. However, Lange's devotion to her church, and her service to the educationally deprived, won her the approbation of Pope Gregory XVI.

As well as running her educational order, Lange also took part in community outreach programs. During the Civil War, she became local superior of St. Benedict's school in Baltimore and subsequently organized the establishment of other schools in Baltimore, Philadelphia and New Orleans. In her final years, still dynam-

ic, she began the order's first mission school in St. Louis, Missouri. By the time of Lange's death in 1882, the Oblate order was established in the United States, the Caribbean, and Central America. More than 100 years after her death, there are attempts to make her the first African-American female to be canonized by the Roman Catholic Church.

SOURCES:

Hine, Darlene Clark, ed. *Black Women in America: An Historical Encyclopedia.* Brooklyn, NY: Carlson, 1993.

Paula Morris, D.Phil.,
Brooklyn, New York

Lange, Helene (1848–1930)

Intellectual leader of the League of German Women's Associations for the first 30 years of the 20th century who is still celebrated in Germany for her work in establishing schools for women. Born on April 9, 1848, in Oldenburg, Germany; died in Berlin on May 23, 1930; daughter of Carl Theodor Lange (a merchant) and Sophia Elisabeth (Niemeyer) Lange; attended the Women's High School of Oldenburg and began private instruction for the teacher's examination, 1872; lived with Gertrud Bäumer; never married; no children.

Employed in a pastor's house in southern Germany (1864); accepted position in a secondary school in Berlin (1876); was a signatory to the "Yellow Brochure" asking the Prussian government to establish schools to help prepare women for high school and university study (1887); was co-founder and first president of the German General Teachers' organization (1889); began a "practical" curriculum of study for women (1889); transformed the "practical" curriculum into a high school curriculum (1893); founded Die Frau (1893); was a co-founder of the League of German Women's Associations (1894); became president of the League (1901); engineered election of Gertrud Bäumer to presidency of the League (1910); served in the upper house of the Hamburg legislature (1919–20); awarded a medal by Prussian government for patriotic service to the state (1928).

Major works: (editor with Bäumer and others) Handbuch der Frauenbewegung *(5 vols., Berlin: Moeser, 1901);* Die Frauenbewegung in ihren modernen Problemen *(Leipzig: Quelle and Meyer, 1908);* Lebenserinnerungen *(Berlin: Herbig, 1928).*

Born in 1848 into a family which was conservative and evangelical in many ways, Helene Lange recalled that, paradoxically, her childhood bedroom was decorated with pictures of 19th-century liberal heroes, including the Italian nationalist Guiseppe Garibaldi. Her mother died when she was seven years old, leaving Lange to be raised with two brothers. When she became an employee at age 16 in the house of a Protestant minister in southern Germany, and when she worked as an au pair in Alsace during the following year, she was startled to discover that her word, as a woman, was taken less seriously than the word of any man.

Lange chose to enter the only professional career open to German women at the time, teaching. She started her own intensive study of philosophy, literature, history, religious history and ancient language. In 1872, she began taking private instruction to prepare for the teacher's examination, and in 1876 she accepted her first teaching job, at a private woman's secondary school in Berlin. There, she became prominent in the "conservative" wing of the Berlin feminist movement, in contrast to "radicals" such as *Helene Stoecker, Anita Augspurg, and *Lida Heymann.

Anita Augspurg.
See joint entry under Heymann, Lida.

Lange believed that each sex had its special "claim on culture" and that motherhood was the special claim of women. She argued that marriage, as the "victory of women over the polygamous instinct of men," was an unquestionable good. The wife was not only the center of the family's education but was also a coworker with her husband, filling the "occupation" of motherhood. But Lange added that marriage was also the source of much suffering and pain. While being given the responsibility for keeping up the home, the wife had no claim on the family finances.

I have the feeling that the education of women will not be really improved through a system controlled by men.

—Helene Lange

The solution, she wrote, was education. To Lange, "education is everything." For women, education was "self-emancipation and self-realization," opening doors to occupations in which few women were represented. When Lange joined and was elected president of the German General Teachers' organization in 1889—a position she would hold for more than 30 years—she began a course which would make her the major crusader for women's educational reforms in Germany. "I do not see how the time can become more favorable for women by patient waiting and ominous silence," she wrote. Central to all of her speeches and writing was the belief that in order to maximize the potential of women, "the education and refinement of women should be placed in the hands of women."

Lange argued that an entirely new system of schools, separate from education for men, should be created to prepare women for occupations and for university study, as they wished. Arguing that German girls were "raised mostly to be much too dependent on others," in 1889 she created a "practical" curriculum designed to prepare women for the business world. In 1893, she transformed her "practical curriculum" into a curriculum for a women's high school, including Latin, mathematics, the sciences, and basic economics.

Lange became a leader in efforts to create women's high schools throughout Germany. In 1887, she was part of the "Yellow Brochure" petition to the Prussian Government, asking for the establishment of schools to prepare women for high school and university study. Her work quickened after 1908, when the Prussian government decided to support efforts to increase the number of schools for women. Among the products of her efforts were a new women's high school in Hamburg, founded in 1910 but later renamed the Helene Lange High School, and two institutions she founded in 1917 in Hamburg, the Social Women's School and the Social Pedagogical Institute.

Helping German women enter universities was a more difficult problem. At the turn of the century, women could attend, but not graduate from, German universities; individual states in Germany paid their tuition to universities out of the country, such as Switzerland. Lange noted that "women could take classes in universities, but they are excluded on principle from passing the examination for graduating; not even a private examination is allowed them." This situation elicited from Lange the bitter observation that "Germany is the only and the last great nation of culture which leaves its women under the oppression of medieval fetters . . . keeping doors closed to them at the institutions of higher learning." "This murder of the mind," she added, "is committed daily in our country."

Declaring that "the time of the covert war of German men against women is over," Lange called for the "intellectual emancipation" of women. "Those who intellectually hunger should be offered the best food in Germany," she said of the university problem. Her work was a factor in the broadening of opportunities for women in German universities. In 1876, there were only about 100 women students in German universities; by 1913, the figure had reached 36,000.

Asked about the effect these changes would have on German men, Lange replied that "capable men need fear nothing." "As in the past," she predicted, "the majority of women will live their lives for their families." While unmarried women would select the same occupations that "they now select," a larger number of married women "will pursue their studies than is now the custom, perhaps even entering the professions," she predicted. She appealed to German men's sense of fairness, noting that "when men compete among themselves or with each other, only one thing is taken into consideration—the position is given to him who is most competent. Why is this not extended to both sexes?"

In 1893, Lange founded *Die Frau,* the major journal of the bourgeois (non-Marxist) women's movement. Never married, Lange called the teachers' organization which she headed her "dearest child" but described *Die Frau* as her "first love." Lange was also a cofounder of the League of German Women's Associations in 1894. In 1901, she became president of the League and would be its intellectual leader for some 30 years. In 1910, she engineered the election to that position of *Gertrud Bäumer, whom she had met in 1897 and who became her lifelong companion. (Bäumer would be the editor of *Die Frau* from 1921 to 1944.)

Within the League, Lange clashed with the "radicals" of the organization such as Stoecker, who wanted to give women the same sexual freedom accorded to men, and Augspurg and Heymann, who combined feminism and pacifism. Lange and Bäumer believed that German women had to "prove themselves fit" for leadership and trust in Germany. She said that the women's movement should stress "fundamentals" rather than "agitation," adding that the work of women in schools, the universities, and "the various occupational groups" should be directed toward showing that "women can do it."

Lange never belonged to a right-to-vote or suffrage society; she regarded voting not as an end in itself but as a means to the end of protecting women's interests. She feared that suffragists or "radical" efforts would provoke a backlash which would eradicate the progress German women had made. "The women's movement," she lectured her audiences, "must be politically neutral. Organizations which commit themselves to our work must content themselves with advancing causes and dare not make themselves political, or they will not be able to represent all streams of the women's movement."

When *Minna Cauer attempted to have the League declare itself in favor of women's suffrage, Lange—while admitting that "a quarrel within

our group is particularly unpleasant"—ruled Cauer out of order. She also opposed the abolitionist movement—the campaign of women's groups to end the tradition that each major German city contained a municipally sponsored bordello. Still, when a ban forbidding German women to join political associations was lifted in 1908, in 1909 Lange joined the Progressive Association, a liberal group based on the ideas of Friedrich Naumann, a political writer who was instrumental in the rightward shift of German liberalism in the years leading up to World War I.

Lange regarded World War I as a perfect opportunity to show that women would devote a year of service to Germany, matching men's military service through women's work on the home front. During the war, she led the women's movement into the National Service campaign, cooperating with the Red Cross, religious associations, and other organizations in enrolling women in factory jobs and other war-related occupations. At the end of the war, she served from March of 1919 to September of 1920 in the upper house of

Helene
Lange

the Hamburg legislature where, by virtue of her age, she was president of the body. She resigned from her legislative post when she and Bäumer moved their residence back to Berlin.

Honors began to flow to her in post-World-War-I Germany. Her 70th and 80th birthdays, in 1918 and 1928, were marked by special celebrations at some of the women's schools she had worked to found. She was made an honorary citizen of her native city of Oldenburg. In 1923, she received an honorary doctorate in law and economics from the University of Tübingen. The Prussian government recognized her as a patriotic German in 1928, when it awarded her a medal inscribed with the words "for service to the state."

Helene Lange died in 1930, three years before the Nazi accession to power in her country. She thus escaped the fate of her companion Bäumer, who was regarded by American and British troops, occupying her part of Germany after World War II, as a possible Nazi sympathizer. During the late 1940s and early 1950s, at a time when Bäumer was forbidden to publish by the military occupation, Lange was eulogized by German political leaders and, in ceremonies held at many of the schools she had helped to found, was lauded as Germany's premier school reformer of the 20th century.

SOURCES:

Baumer, Gertrude. *Studien über Frauen.* 3 vols. Berlin: Herbig, 1924.

Frandsen, Dorothea. *Helene Lange.* Stuttgart: Herderbucherei, 1980.

Gerhard, Ute. *Unerhört Die Geschichtre der deutschen Frauenbewegung.* Reinbeck bei Hamburg: Rowohlt, 1990.

Schultz, Hans Jürgen. *Frauen: Porträts aus zwei Jahrhunderten.* Stuttgart and Berlin: Kreuz, 1981.

SUGGESTED READING:

Evans, Richard J. *The Feminist Movement in Germany 1894–1933.* London and Beverly Hills: SAGE Publications, 1976.

Lange, Helene. *Higher Education of Women in Europe.* Translated by L.R. Klemm. NY: Appleton, 1901.

COLLECTIONS:

Correspondence, notebooks, diary, and other materials are contained in the Helene Lange Archiv, Berlin, Germany.

Niles Holt,
Professor of History, Illinois State University, Normal, Illinois

Lange, Mary Elizabeth (1784–1882).

See Lange, Elizabeth Clovis.

Langer, Susanne Knauth (1895–1985)

American philosopher, writer, and educator who was particularly concerned with art, logic and the mind.

Born Susanne Katerina Knauth on December 20, 1895, in New York, New York; died on July 17, 1985, in New London, Connecticut; daughter of Antonio Knauth (a lawyer) and Else (Uhlich) Knauth; Radcliffe College, A.B., 1920, A.M., 1924, Ph.D., 1926; graduate study at the University of Vienna, 1921–22; married William Leonard Langer, on September 3, 1921 (divorced 1942); children: Leonard C.R. and Bertrand W.

Awards: Radcliffe achievement medal (1950); D.Litt., Wilson College (1954); D.Litt., Mt. Holyoke College (1962); D.Litt., Western College for Women (now Western College, 1962); D.Litt., Wheaton College, Norton, Massachusetts (1962); LL.D., Columbia University (1964); D. Humane Letters, Clark University (1968).

Selected writings: The Cruise of the Little Dipper and Other Fairy Tales (Norcross, 1923); The Practice of Philosophy (Holt, 1930); Philosophy in a New Key (Harvard University Press, 1942); An Introduction to Symbolic Logic (Houghton, 1953); Feeling and Form (Scribner, 1953); Problems of Art (Scribner, 1957); Philosophical Sketches (Johns Hopkins Press, 1962); Mind: An Essay on Human Feeling (Johns Hopkins Press, vol. 1, 1967, vol. 2, 1972, vol. 3, 1982).

Some philosophers stand out for their commitment to a revolutionary approach to philosophy as a discipline. Among the likes of Socrates, Friedrich Nietzsche and Ludwig Wittgenstein, who devised and implemented their own prescriptions for better approaches to the most profound problems, we must count Susanne Langer, who argued that philosophy would be revolutionized in the 20th century by the burgeoning knowledge of symbols and how we use them. Langer argued that philosophy passes through cycles in which a particular approach becomes exhausted and is succeeded by another. For her, the growing understanding of symbols was the new awareness which could revitalize philosophy, providing fresh perspective on the traditional problems. Philosophy is often considered to advance as issues become clarified by new approaches and problems become resolved. But Langer contended that for long periods of history philosophers will argue over the same questions in the same ways. According to her, this is initially observed in ancient Greek philosophy (4th century BCE): the problems first addressed by Plato are not changed by his student Aristotle but approached in the same way. Because Aristotle comes to answers that oppose Plato's, between them they exhaust the potential for enlightening answers to their questions. Likewise, Langer believed that the philosophical problems first posed by Réne Descartes in the 17th century could no longer act as a fertile source of philosophical study due to the work of Immanuel Kant at the end of the 18th century. Descartes' position was that the mind and body are distinct substances mysteriously intertwined. We can progress no further with this than to say, with Kant, that all we know of the physical world, including our bodies, is structured by our minds. However, for Langer the new understanding of the pervasiveness of symbolic systems in our experience offers a fresh arena for philosophical discourse. Therefore, she devoted herself to the study of symbols and how they pervade human experience. In doing so, she linked together the diverse fields of the arts and sciences by considering how their methods are all similarly dependent on the manipulation of symbols.

Susanne Katerina Knauth was born in 1895 on the Upper West Side of Manhattan to Antonio and **Else Knauth**, who were German immigrants. Her father was a lawyer, who in his spare time played cello and piano and encouraged his daughter's love of music. She learned to play the cello and enjoyed this throughout her lifetime. Much of her education took place at home. Although she attended a French school in Manhattan, her schooling was interrupted by several years of illness: a druggist had filled a prescription for her incorrectly, and she suffered from cocaine poisoning. As a result, she was too ill to attend school and was tutored at home. In the summer, the Knauths went canoeing at Lake George.

Because the only language spoken in her home was German, when Susanne left home for Radcliffe College, after her father's death, it was the first time she spoke English in every aspect of her daily life. At Radcliffe, she had a distinguished undergraduate career, devising her own tricks for increasing her academic performance. For instance, although she had always been good at algebra, she had trouble with the spatial relationships of geometry. But by translating geometry into algebra in her head she was able to achieve excellence in every area of mathematics. This was very important, as much of her work involved logic and mathematics. Her problem with spatial understandings also made it difficult for her to remember some of the details from academic books and articles. So in her junior year she began to keep an elaborate set of card files for academic sources which she maintained and relied on for the rest of her life.

At Radcliffe, she met William Langer, a graduate student in history who went on to become a distinguished professor. Following their marriage in 1921, she did graduate work in logic at Radcliffe and spent one semester at the University of Vienna. The first book that she published, in 1923, was not philosophy but illustrated children's stories, *The Cruise of the Little Dipper and Other Fairy Tales.* She had two children, Leonard C.R. and Bertrand W., and went on to receive a master's degree in 1924 and a doctorate in 1926, remaining at Radcliffe as a tutor in philosophy.

In *The Practice of Philosophy*, published in 1930 with a preface by the esteemed philosopher Alfred North Whitehead (who had instructed her at Radcliffe), Langer argued for the importance of mathematics and logic to philosophy. According to her, philosophical technique is characterized by abstraction: extracting a concept from the variety of its occurrences. For example, looking at beauty in general rather than at any number of beautiful things in particular, and finding its general form, helps us to order our ideas for the pursuit of philosophical insight. Such analysis may solve problems or reveal them, and logic and mathematics are especially helpful because they concern meanings and ideas, rather than facts. "Logic is the science of forms as such, the study of patterns," she wrote. In *An Introduction to Symbolic Logic* (1937), she explains how our reasoning about things is symbolized in the study of logic.

A further argument from *The Practice of Philosophy* is that philosophical problems change over time and that the 20th century, with all its new mathematical and logical knowledge, brings a new age to philosophical thought.

> The progress of philosophy is not so much from premises to conclusions as from commonly accepted conclusions to their premises. Science grows in scope; philosophy increases in depth. It is the substructure, not only of science, but of all experience.

Philosophy can take its old understandings and renovate them, using new skills in mathematics and logic to discredit parts of it and to revitalize others. Thus, she did not consider even her own ideas to be final.

In 1942, Langer published *Philosophy in a New Key*, one of the bestselling books ever published by Harvard University Press. In it, she applied the method of philosophy prescribed in *The Practice of Philosophy* to the discipline of philosophy itself, by examining how reasoning has operated in the history of philosophy. She built on the argument that mathematical and logical knowledge will revitalize philosophy and began to take what she considered to be the new direction necessary for philosophical progress.

> As every shift of tonality gives a new sense to previous passages, so the reorientation of philosophy which is taking place in our age bestows new aspects on the ideas and arguments of the past. Our thinking stems from that past, but does not continue it in the ways that were foreseen. Its cleavages cut across the old lines, and suddenly bring out new motifs that were not felt to be implicit in the premises of the schools at all; for it changes the questions of philosophy.

Langer built on the philosophy of symbols developed by Ernst Cassirer, Whitehead, and Wittgenstein, and opposed the view popular among her contemporaries that moral statements, art and metaphysics (the study of what exists) are simply emotional expressions. According to Langer, there are two types of symbolism. Discursive symbolism is constructed from a given syntax and a vocabulary and provides literal meaning. This includes logic and mathematics and most of natural language. Non-discursive, or presentational, symbolism (for example, art) conveys meaning which is not literal and refers to no particular individual experience. Nevertheless, art is symbolic and not just expressive.

A screaming baby gives his feeling far more release than any musician, but we don't go into a concert hall to hear a baby scream; in fact, if that baby is brought in we are likely to go out. We don't want self-expression.

—Susanne Knauth Langer

Langer argued that the use of symbols distinguishes humans from animals:

> The symbol-making function is one of man's primary activities, like eating, looking, or moving about. It is the fundamental process of his mind, and goes on all the time.

It is not just that humans have a broader use of gestures and therefore a broader range of signals. Signals are only representative pictures of things. Symbols, on the other hand, may be used as signals, but they are abstractions which also may point to nothing in particular. They can represent things that are not in our immediate environment. A dog can only respond to "dinner" with the expectation that food will be forthcoming, that is, as a particular experience. But humans can consider "dinner," can take it as a concept for reflection: do we want dinner? how will we get it? etc. For us it can be more than a signal; it can be a symbol. "Symbols are not proxy for their objects, but are *vehicles for the conception of objects.*"

After her divorce in 1942, Langer spent five years teaching at Columbia and eight years at Connecticut College, occasionally taking sabbatical leave or acting as a visiting scholar at other colleges. In 1953, she published *Feeling and Form*, which develops the philosophy of art posited in *Philosophy in a New Key* into a comprehensive theory of aesthetics. Langer defined art as "the creation of forms symbolic of human feeling," and argued that it has four distinguishing characteristics: art is (1) created; (2) an expression of human—not personal—feeling; (3) symbolic; and (4) meant for contemplation.

Langer opposed the traditional view, known as self-expression theory, that art is an expression of personal feeling, "a symptomatic expression of currently felt emotions." According to this view, meaning must be representational; a symbol must make reference to some particular thing that can be experienced. Any other expression is simply an extension of emotion, like a laughter or a cry, and not a representation of anything experienced. Langer argued that although art may be used for personal expression, such as on a greeting card, this is only one use of art. Not any exclamation can be considered art. A baby's cry may be very expressive, but we would not consider it art. Moreover, if personal expression were the key to artistic creation, then art about negative feelings, such as despair, would be virtually nonexistent because such feelings interfere with one's ability to produce art.

Instead, art is an expression of the form of feeling, notes Langer, where feeling is considered to encompass a wide range of experiences:

> forms of growth and attenuation, flowing and stowing, conflict and resolution, speed, arrest, terrific excitement, calm or subtle activation and dreamy lapses—not joy or sorrow perhaps, but the poignancy of both—the greatness and brevity and eternal passing of everything vitally felt.

Feeling is "unlogicized mental life," that element of experience which escapes discursive symbolism, but which can be captured in the presentational symbolism of art. Art symbolizes our thoughts about the way emotions are experienced, but does not express emotion itself.

Feeling and Form is one of Langer's best-known works, and it continues to act as a resource in contemporary philosophy of art. She expands on its themes in other publications. *The Problems of Art* (1957) is a collection of letters and articles relating to her earlier work. *Reflections on Art: A Source Book of Writings by Artists, Critics and Philosophers* (1960) is an anthology of works by other writers who influenced the views presented in *Feeling and Form*.

When Langer retired from teaching, she looked to larger philosophical problems surrounding her theory of aesthetics. *Philosophical Sketches* (1962) is a collection of papers which she delivered to audiences on topics ranging from art to biology. Here, she expressed the view that mathematical study has been exhausted, and she argued that this opens up potential for exploring the use of symbols in less abstract sciences such as psychology.

She proceeded to work out a philosophy to address the reasoning processes of the sciences in her final and largest work, *Mind: An Essay on Human Feeling*. It was completed over many years of her retirement, living alone in a red farmhouse in Connecticut. Her home was not tidy but brimming with the sources that inspired her work. She kept fish and tadpoles in aquariums and jars—inspiration for the philosophy of biology developed in *Mind*. The house was filled with books in English, German, and French, and a grand piano sat in the same room where her cello and two violins resided in a glass case.

Susanne K. Langer

Even past the age of 70, Langer was described as "alert and erect with notable vitality" and frequently spent ten hours a day reading and writing, still relying on her intricate system of index cards. She claimed to have "a mind like fly paper" that sometimes became crowded with information, even as trivial as jingles or advertisements from childhood. In order to capture inspirations, she kept note cards by her bed and learned to write neatly in the dark.

Her spare time was spent on housework, reading poetry, and playing music in a string quartet with friends. She would have preferred more time to practice the cello but found that the necessary concentration detracted from her work, so she focused instead on philosophy. Langer often visited her sons and enjoyed the outdoors, frequently driving off in her station wagon to spend some time in her green canoe "The Creek Mouse." Each summer, she spent a week camping and canoeing with a friend, and believed that this revitalized her work.

Mind has over 1,000 pages, and was published in three volumes in 1967, 1972 and 1982. It concerns a question that arises out of *Feeling and Form*: why is it important that art have an organic, life-like form? She explored the methods of art, biology, social theory, and psychology, and the importance of imagery to these disciplines:

> There is value in images quite apart from religious or emotional purposes: they, and they only, make us aware of the wholeness and over-all form of entities, acts, and facts in the world; and little though we may know it, only an image can hold us to a conception of a total phenomenon, against which we can measure the adequacy of scientific terms wherewith we describe it.

So she built on her exposition of art from the earlier *Feeling and Form*, applying that book's theory of symbols to the life sciences. She also argued that biology and psychology are hindered by their adoption of the inorganic images of physics. The argument from *Philosophy in a New Key* has continued as well. Langer posited that the evolution of feeling distinguishes humans among animals, that the artist or the scientist is enabled by systems of symbols to come to understandings that surpass individual experience. She opposed the distinction between mind and body which obsessed philosophers from the time of Descartes, and she argued that feeling, including rational thought, is what is essentially human: we have no experience outside of our bodies. Susanne Langer died after a long illness on July 17, 1985, in New London, Connecticut.

Opposite page

Frances Langford

SOURCES:

Greer, William R. "Susanne K. Langer, Philosopher, is Dead at 89," in *The New York Times*. July 19, 1985, p. A12.

Lord, James. "A Lady Seeking Answers," in *The New York Times Book Review*. May 26, 1968, pp. 4–5, 34.

SUGGESTED READING:

Curran, Trisha. *A New Note on the Film: A Theory of Film Criticism Derived from Susanne K. Langer's Philosophy of Art*. NY: Arno Press, 1980.

Ghosh, Ranjan Kumar. *Aesthetic Theory and Art: a Study in Susanne K. Langer*. Delhi: Ajanta Publications, 1979.

Catherine Hundleby,
Ph.D. candidate in Philosophy at the
University of Western Ontario, Canada

Langford, Frances (1914—)

American singer and actress. Born on April 4, 1914, in Lakeland, Florida; daughter of Annie Newbern (a concert pianist); attended Southern College, Florida; married Jon Hall (an actor), on June 4, 1938 (divorced 1955); married Ralph Evinrude (a marine motor company magnate), on October 5, 1955 (died 1986); no children.

Filmography: Every Night at Eight *(1935)*; Broadway Melody of 1936 *(1935)*; Collegiate *(1936)*; Palm Springs *(1936)*; Born to Dance *(1936)*; The Hit Parade *(1937)*; Hollywood Hotel *(1938)*; Too Many Girls *(1940)*; Dreaming Out Loud *(1940)*; All-American Co-Ed *(1941)*; Mississippi Gambler *(1942)*; Yankee Doodle Dandy *(1942)*; Cowboy in Manhattan *(1943)*; This Is the Army *(1943)*; Follow the Band *(1943)*; Never a Dull Moment *(1943)*; The Girl Rush *(1944)*; Dixie Jamboree *(1944)*; Radio Stars on Parade *(1945)*; The Bamboo Blonde *(1946)*; Beat the Band *(1947)*; Make Mine Laughs *(1949)*; Deputy Marshal *(1949)*; Purple Heart Diary *(1951)*; *(appeared as herself)* The Glenn Miller Story *(1954)*.

Radio: "Hollywood Hotel" *(CBS, c. 1936–38)*; "The Texaco Star Theater" *(CBS, 1939–40)*; "American Cruise" *(NBC, 1941)*; "The Bob Hope Pepsodent Show" *(NBC, c. 1941–45)*; "The Bickersons" *(NBC, 1946–47; CBS, 1947–48, 1951)*.

Television: "Star Time" *(Dumont, 1950–51)*; "The Frances Langford-Don Ameche Show" *(ABC, 1951–52)*.

Album discography: The Bickersons *(with Don Ameche, Col CL-1692/CS 8492)*; The Bickersons *(with Don Ameche, Radiola 1151)*; The Bickersons Fight Back *(with Don Ameche, Col CL-1883/CS-8683)*; The Bickersons Rematch *(with Don Ameche, Col G-30523)*; Born to Dance *(CIF 3001)*; Collegiate *(Caliban 6042)*; Every Night at Eight *(Caliban 6043)*; Hollywood Hotel *(EOOOH 99601, Hollywood*

Soundstage 5004); I Feel a Song Coming On: 1935–37 *(Take Two TT 214);* Old Songs for Old Friends *(Cap T/ST-1865);* Rainbow Rhapsody *(Mer MG-25005);* The Return of the Bickersons! *(with Don Ameche, Radiola 3MR-4);* This Is the Army *(Hollywood Soundstage 408, Sandy Hook 2035);* Yankee Doodle Dandy *(Curtain Calls 100/13).*

The daughter of concert pianist **Annie Newbern**, Frances Langford was born in Lakeland, Florida, in 1914, and aspired to a career as an opera singer until a tonsillectomy in 1930 turned her from a soprano into a contralto. Switching her focus to popular music, she got her first break when a millionaire cigar manufacturer heard her sing at an American Legion party and signed her for a 13-week stint on a local radio show in Tampa, Florida. Rudy Vallee heard her, was equally impressed, and offered her a guest spot on his network radio show, which led to further radio performances, a couple of musical shorts, and a small role in the stage musical *Here Goes the Bride* (1933), which closed after seven performances.

The turning point in Langford's career came during an engagement at New York's Waldorf-Astoria when she was asked to perform at a private party for songwriter Cole Porter. Also present that evening was Paramount producer Walter Wanger, who hired her on the spot. She made her screen debut in *Every Night at Eight* (1935), as one of three singers (***Alice Faye** and ***Patsy Kelly** completed the trio) hoping to break into radio. Langford's solo, "I'm in the Mood for Love," became a huge hit for her, as did "I've Got You Under My Skin," a song from her subsequent movie *Born to Dance* (1936), which showcased the talents of ***Eleanor Powell**. Originally sung in the film by **Virginia Bruce**, "Under My Skin" was recorded for Decca by Langford and came to be associated with her. A series of pleasant musicals rounded out her early film career, ending with *Hollywood Hotel* (1937), based on the popular radio variety show hosted by Dick Powell, on which Langford was a frequent guest.

Frances Langford found her greatest audience through radio and recordings. Voted America's number one female singer in 1938, she continued to record for Decca, and in 1939 joined "The Texaco Star Theater," the popular radio show co-starring Ken Murray and Kenny Baker. In 1941, she began a long and successful association with Bob Hope, becoming a regular on "The Bob Hope Pepsodent Show." During World War II, she joined Hope on many of his

USO tours to entertain the overseas troops, logging over 250,000 miles. Dubbed "Sweetheart to the GIs," Langford frequently put herself in harm's way, journeying to the front lines to perform, and chancing long plane flights between Allied bases. "I've had my share of close calls on these trips," she admitted, "but the rewards are worth every nervous twinge." During the later years of the war, Langford wrote a syndicated newspaper column, "Purple Hearts Diary," in which she related her experiences visiting wounded GIs. Between tours, Langford warbled her way through a number of films, the best of which were *Yankee Doodle Dandy* (1942), in which James Cagney created an Oscar-winning portrayal of George M. Cohan, and *This Is the Army* (1943), based on Irving Berlin's rousing stage musical.

Following the war, the singer played nightclubs and displayed her considerable comedic skills in the popular network radio show with Don Ameche entitled "The Bickersons" (1946–48). A comedy about a battling couple, the show had its beginnings as a sketch on an episode of the Edgar Bergen-Charlie McCarthy radio show. In 1950, she and Ameche hosted the television show "Star Time," a variety-comedy series which lasted four months. The pair emceed a second television show in 1951 that featured Jack Lemmon in a recurring domestic sketch. In 1952, Langford entertained troops in Korea. By that time, her movie career was waning; her last appearance on the screen was a guest spot in *The Glenn Miller Story* (1954).

A petite blue-eyed blonde, Langford was married for 17 years to actor Jon Hall who had made one film with her in 1949, the forgettable Western, *Deputy Marshal*. The couple divorced in 1954, and in 1955 Langford married outboard-motor tycoon Ralph Evinrude, after which she retired to private life. Her only public appearances were on an occasional television special and at "The Outrigger," a club near the 200-acre resort facility she and her husband owned and operated at Jensen Beach, Florida. During the Vietnam War, Langford once again volunteered to entertain the troops, traveling overseas in 1966, both with and without her old friend Bob Hope. In 1967, she and Don Ameche appeared together for the last time, performing one of their classic "Bickersons" skits on television's "Hollywood Palace."

Frances Langford lived quietly in Florida during the 1970s and underwent successful open-heart surgery in 1978. The singer came out of retirement in 1989 to participate in the PBS documentary "Entertaining the Troops." She opened the 90-minute program by singing "It's Been a Long Long Time" and was part of a reunion segment with Hope and other World War II entertainers. She ended the group's reminiscences with "I'm in the Mood for Love," still displaying her noted singing style.

SOURCES:

Katz, Ephraim. *The Film Encyclopedia*. NY: Harper-Collins, 1994.

Lamparski, Richard. *Whatever Became of . . . ?* 1st and 2nd Series. NY: Crown, 1967.

Parish, James Robert, and Michael R. Pitts. *Hollywood Songsters*. NY: Garland, 1991.

Barbara Morgan,
Melrose, Massachusetts

Langgässer, Elisabeth (1899–1950)

German author whose posthumously published novel The Quest *(1950) is regarded by many critics as one of the finest German works dealing with the moral burden of Nazi inhumanity. Name variations: Elisabeth Langgasser; Elisabeth Langgaesser. Born on February 23, 1899, in Alzey; died in Karlsruhe on July 25, 1950; daughter of Eduard Langgässer and Eugenie (Dienst) Langgässer; had one brother; married Wilhelm Hoffmann (1899–1967), in 1935; children: (with Herman Heller) Cordielia (later, Cordelia Edvardson, a writer); (with Wilhelm Hoffmann) Annette and Franziska.*

Elisabeth Langgässer died during the summer of 1950 in a West Germany that had barely begun the process of physical and moral reconstruction after the devastations of World War II. At the time of her death, she had just completed the manuscript of her novel, *Märkische Argonautenfahrt* (*The Quest*). Although her work, which explored difficult moral choices, was highly praised by postwar critics, it faded from memory by the mid-1950s in a Germany more interested in appreciating its newfound prosperity than probing the troubling issues of individual and collective moral responsibility. By the 1990s, her writings were finally being rediscovered by scholars and readers alike. As her reputation soars to new heights, her work is now recognized as a major contribution to modern German literature. Influenced by Christian beliefs, Langgässer explores through her writings the persistent motifs of sin, grace, salvation and the dualistic nature of the world.

Elisabeth Langgässer was born in the Rhenish Hessian town of Alzey in 1899. Her mother Eugenie was Roman Catholic; her father Eduard, born Jewish, had converted to Catholicism at the time of his marriage. Eduard Langgässer had achieved success as a builder, and the family lived in middle-class comfort. Raised in a Roman Catholic environment, Elisabeth nevertheless soon became aware that the larger society often looked upon her as being different because of her half-Jewish parentage. By 1920, Langgässer was writing poems of merit, and in 1924 she published her first volume of verse, *Der Wendekreis des Lammes: Ein Hymnus der Erlösung* (The Changing Circle of the Lamb: A Hymn of Redemption). Throughout her writing career, her poetic vision would deepen and expand, and she published two more lyric cycles, *Die Tierkreisgedichte* (Poems of the Zodiac, 1935) and *Der Laubmann und die Rose* (The Leaf Man and the Rose, 1947). In totality, her poems reflect a belief in a divine geometry that leads to the ultimate truth of human existence, which Langgässer believed to be Christ or the Logos.

Langgässer grew up in the city of Darmstadt to which she had moved at age ten following her father's death, and she received her education at the prestigious Viktoriaschule. Unlike in nearby Frankfurt am Main, which was dedicated to commerce, the arts flourished in Darmstadt, and the young writer looked forward to a literary career. In the meantime, she earned a teaching degree and worked as a primary-school teacher in the Darmstadt area, including service at a school in the nearby village of Griesheim in the rural Oppenheim district. Determined to make her mark in the world of letters, she wrote in every spare minute. Langgässer also became one of the most enthusiastic members of a circle of writers that was linked to the literary journal *Die Kolonne*. The group included Günter Eich and Peter Huchel, and believed that literature could flourish in a realm beyond the tensions of daily political existence. This notion would result in a considerable degree of naïveté when the Nazi movement began to dominate the public life of Germany in the early 1930s. For years after the National Socialist party came to power, Langgässer would retain her belief that, because it was so patently a force for evil, the duration of the Nazi dictatorship would be a brief one.

The late 1920s were exciting, turbulent years for Langgässer. An unsuccessful love affair with Hermann Heller, a Jewish political scientist, resulted in the birth of a daughter Cordielia. Finding it difficult to achieve a balance between the multiple demands of her teaching career, motherhood, and a strong need to write, at times she found herself in despair, as when she confessed in a letter, "Yesterday I simply burst into tears. I couldn't stand the noise any more. . . .

One thing is certain, if you have a child then your day is completely full. Or a profession—then you have to have somebody else care for the child. Both our fathers ('women belong in the home') and Soviet Russia did absolutely the correct thing." Despite these difficulties, Langgässer was able to organize her energies successfully. In 1929, soon after the birth of her daughter, she had moved to Berlin where she continued to write and produced a successful series of dramatic scripts that were broadcast over Berlin Radio. In 1932, on the eve of the Nazi takeover, Langgässer received validation of her literary efforts when she was given the Deutsche Staatsbürgerinnenpreis (German Citizen's Prize) for her novella *Triptychon des Teufels* (The Devil's Triptych), which some critics compared to the classic prose of *Annette von Droste-Hülshoff. In 1933, the year the Nazi dictatorship was established, Langgässer published her first novel, the finely crafted *Proserpina, Welt eines Kindes* (Proserpina, A Child's World).

The Nazi grip on Germany increased with each passing year, and by 1935, when the infamous Nuremberg Laws were enacted to define German Jews as little more than barely tolerated aliens in the Reich, Langgässer had to accept the fact that the conditions of her life were becoming harsher with each passing day. One beacon of hope was her 1935 marriage to Wilhelm Hoffmann, with whom she raised Cordielia and had two more daughters, Annette and Franziska. In 1936, Langgässer published her second novel, *Der Gang durch das Ried* (The Path Through the Marsh), which clearly echoes her own predicament in a Nazi Germany that was becoming increasingly hostile to both practicing "full-blooded" Jews and Jewish "hybrids" who were Christian in religion but "alien in blood." The novel concerns a former soldier of the French army that had occupied the German Rhineland until 1930. Calling himself Jean-Marie Aladin, he is released from an insane asylum having lost all memory of his real name and past life. As he wanders aimlessly through the Rhenish region, his memory gradually returns. He is in fact Peter Schaffner, the runaway son of a German butcher. Years before, frightened by his father's threats to dismember and kill him, he had fled to France and there joined the French Foreign Legion. By way of a protagonist with a French-Arab name, Langgässer deflects a number of associations regarding Jews and German-Jewish *Mischlinge* (hybrids), like herself, onto Arabs and the French.

Only two months after the publication of *Der Gang druch das Ried*, it was banned by the

Nazi state. Reviews had been largely negative, with one characterizing the book in the following terms: "Everything is musty, grey, it smells of decay, it wallows in desire." Since the Nuremberg Laws had gone into effect in 1935, Langgässer had been trying to substantiate her claim that she was a full-blooded Aryan—an attempt that proved futile in view of the fact that her father had been born a Jew. Unable to prove her racial purity, she now found herself legally defined as a German-Jewish hybrid, a first-degree *Mischling*. On May 20, 1936, Langgässer was excluded from the Reichsschrifttumskammer (Reich Literature Chamber), a fatal blow to her literary ambitions because it meant she could no longer be published in Nazi Germany.

Over the next several years, while helping to support her family by anonymously writing advertising copy, she attempted to persuade Nazi authorities to reverse their decision. In a letter of August 1937 to Hans Hinkel, a leading Nazi cultural administrator, Langgässer argued that her artistic traits were in no way to be seen as Semitic and could in fact be traced back several generations on her mother's (Aryan) side. She also noted that not only had her career been assisted by the novelist *Ina Seidel, who enjoyed the full support of the Third Reich's literary establishment, but her writings had been rejected on several occasions by Jewish publishing firms and authors like Alfred Döblin. Furthermore, she informed Hinkel, "I would like to add that I am married to a man of pure Aryan background."

Despite the increasingly demoralizing blows that she endured over the next years, Langgässer refused to succumb to despair. Supported by her husband, she raised her three daughters in as normal an environment as possible under the inhumane conditions of Nazi Germany. Although her status as a first-degree *Mischling* placed her in a relatively secure position under the racist system of the Nuremberg Laws (at least when compared to those Germans now defined as full-blooded Jews), the future was at best uncertain. Particularly vulnerable was her oldest daughter Cordielia, who, because her father was Jewish, was defined as a full-blooded Jewess. Langgässer began work on a new novel even though she knew that it could never be published in Germany as long as the Nazis were in power. She wrote in secret, under danger of discovery, and was motivated to continue work on the manuscript by what she called "the gentle madness of artistic compulsion." It would be published in 1946 as *Der unauslöschliche Siegel* (The Indelible Seal).

Langgässer kept her threatened family intact during almost five years of war and destruction. By 1942, for Jews under German rule both inside the Reich and in the occupied territories of Europe, discrimination and hatred turned into systematic annihilation, the Holocaust. The year 1944 was catastrophic for Langgässer and her family, for in that year Cordielia was taken first to the "model" ghetto Theresienstadt-Terezin near Prague, and then to Auschwitz. Langgässer was conscripted to work in a cable factory in Berlin, despite the fact that her health was declining (she would later be diagnosed with multiple sclerosis). Although Langgässer, her husband and her two youngest daughters survived the bombing of Berlin in the closing months of the war, she was tormented, wondering if Cordielia was still alive.

Cordielia did survive Auschwitz, in part by chance and also possibly because she had worked as a secretary for the infamous Dr. Josef Mengele. Taken to Sweden after her liberation from the camp, she suffered from tuberculosis and was hospitalized for a long period. Langgässer did not receive word that her daughter was alive until 1946. Mother and daughter were not able to meet, however, until the fall of 1949, less than a year before Langgässer's death. Cordielia remained in Sweden, where she changed her name to **Cordelia (Edvardson)**. Their relationship was scarred by their mutual trauma, and in her powerful memoir, *Burned Child Seeks the Fire*, Cordelia analyzes the complex nature of her often angry feelings toward a mother whom she loved but also hated for being "blind" and "stupid."

As one of the very few writers of quality to have remained in Nazi Germany, Elisabeth Langgässer enjoyed considerable fame in the first years after the war. Several of her poems appeared in the first postwar anthology of verse published under the imprimatur of the U.S. Information Control Division. When in 1946 the novel she had written secretly during the Nazi era, *Der unauslöschliche Siegel* (The Indelible Seal) was published, most reviews were enthusiastic. Although she had written the novel as a believing Christian and her themes—central to explaining the existence of evil in modern times— were in many ways as old as humanity, Langgässer's literary techniques were modern, experimental, and unconventional. The book's representation of lesbian love, and what were termed other "erotic liberties," outraged some Catholic, and other conservative, literary critics, and the novel was effectively blacklisted by the Catholic Church.

Encouraged by the publication of this novel, Langgässer continued to write, concentrating for the next several years on short stories; many are of the highest quality. These stories deal with ordinary women and men in the Third Reich, individuals whose small and often thoughtlessly opportunistic deeds (and failure to act) made it possible for the Nazi regime to function and carry out much of its murderous agenda. Some, such as "Untergetaucht" (In Hiding) and "Saisonbeginn" (Start of the Season), recount the persecution of Jews. Possibly written under the influence of the American short story, which served to inspire many writers in postwar Germany, "Saisonbeginn" has a shocking ending, which depicts average and apparently "normal" Germans at a holiday resort all acting like Nazi travelers. Others, such as "Der Erstkommunionstag" (First Communion Day) and "Jetzt geht die Welt unter" (The World is Now Ending), portray the terrors experienced by civilians during air raids. Additional short stories from this period include such memorable works as "An der Nähmaschine" (At the Sewing Machine), which portrays the life of slave laborers under the Nazis, and "Lydia," about a Russian woman slave laborer in Germany.

In October 1947, Langgässer participated in the First Congress of German Writers, which for the first and last time before the full onset of the Cold War brought together writers from all the zones of a defeated and occupied Germany. The grand old lady of German letters, 83-year-old *Ricarda Huch, was chosen to be the honorary president of the congress, and, along with Communist writer *Anna Seghers (who had recently returned to Germany from exile in Mexico), Elisabeth Langgässer was celebrated as one of the "triumvirate of great contemporary women novelists." In her address to the congress, one of the high points of the entire meeting, Langgässer sharply criticized those writers who had remained in Nazi Germany and continued to publish during the years of dictatorship. These authors, who argued that they were part of an "inner emigration" were, she asserted, no more than part of an "enormous self-deception." She believed that the horrors unleashed by the Nazi regime demanded that writers be aware of their great moral responsibilities in the postwar world. For Langgässer, such responsibilities included a radical scrutiny of all aspects of a German language that had been profoundly debased by the Nazis and their accomplices, "terrible criminals and horrifying idiots [who had made possible] the destruction and demise of our continent."

Over the next several years, Langgässer was profoundly affected by her continuing struggle to renew her relationship with her daughter in Sweden, as well as by the rapidly deteriorating political situation of the Cold War. Although she rejected the philosophical underpinnings of Marxism, her relations with individual Communist writers and intellectuals remained cordial. She worked as an editor for the Communist-oriented *Aufbau* and for *Die Wandlung*, which leaned toward Western ideals. During this period, Langgässer had a particularly strong intellectual partnership with Ernst Niekisch. A strong-willed writer who had been an advocate of National Bolshevism during the Weimar Republic, Niekisch had been blinded and crippled as a result of his imprisonment and mistreatment by the Nazis. Despite her declining state of health from multiple sclerosis, Langgässer continued to write and was her family's sole means of support. In a letter written in January 1947, she described a situation of "Hunger, no shoes for the children or myself, a wearisome struggle from one day to the next . . . the temperature in the room where we lived ten degrees centigrade. In spite of this I started a new piece of work." In the summer of the same year, among her strategies to keep her family fed was Langgässer's

Elisabeth Langgässer

transaction with a Catholic priest: she traded a copy of her novel for the book's weight in flour.

In 1948, she left Berlin and returned to her home area of Rhenish Hesse. Although her health continued to deteriorate, she was determined to write at least one more novel. Langgässer completed her last manuscript in late June 1950 and wrote to a friend: "The novel is finished. But, alas, so am I." She died in the next month, on July 25, 1950, in Karlsruhe. Her novel, *Märkische Argonautenfahrt* (Argonauts of the Mark Brandenburg, known in America as *The Quest*), was published posthumously. In 1951, she was posthumously awarded the Georg Büchner Prize, West Germany's most prestigious literary award.

In *The Quest*, Langgässer adapted the classical story of the Argonauts to the situation in a shattered postwar Germany. This powerful work tells of seven pilgrims who set out from a still-smoldering Berlin to reflect on their existences at a Benedictine nunnery. In its narrative consciousness, rather than literal time sequence, *The Quest* is a highly complex work that relies on a kind of synchronicity in which the texts of the Old Testament of the Jews and the Christian New Testament, as well as the myths of the ancient Greeks and the Indian subcontinent, coexist in harmony, complementing and illuminating one another. As Sodom, Gethsemane, the epic story of Achilles at Troy, and Hiroshima pass before the reader, "everything was simultaneous, of equal importance, and wore before its face a mask which (apart from slight nuance) made one suspect that its lacquered, hastily painted canvas concealed identical features."

Writing of Langgässer's literary achievements, critic Peter Demetz points out that, in her later novels:

> the mystical impulse, or the drive to ask questions of religious import, clashes with her awareness of the historical moment she experienced; the timeless and the actual are fused in an irresistible language of sibylline fervor. . . . Her chapters on the sufferings of the last Berlin Jews huddled in the *Kleiderkammer* (clothes closet) of the Jewish Center before being sent east, her merciless view of life in a small Brandenburg village after the Soviet Army came, and her concluding story about the black marketeers hidden in the cellars have not been equaled in her time.

Although a small band of her contemporaries appreciated both the intensity and depth of her art, and she was briefly popular in the last few years of her life, Langgässer was arguably never fully understood at that time either by critics or by many of her readers. A difficult writer who wrote about the great moral dilemmas that arose during a terrible era in human history, she herself noted the reason why many of her contemporaries found it difficult to understand her message: "I was dismissed as a 'Christian writer'—which, of course, I am, but I would prefer 'Christian writer' without the connotations of literary triviality. And because I am dismissed in this way, I have attracted the aversion of liberals for who I am an emetic."

On the occasion of her premature death in 1950, the *Frankfurter Allgemeine Zeitung* lamented that Langgässer's passing represented a major blow to German letters, and called it "the most important loss to our literature since the death of Ricarda Huch." For a generation, neither Germany nor the rest of the Western world appeared capable of grasping the difficult and painful themes touched by this writer. Material prosperity and the morally simplistic dichotomy growing out of the Cold War made her work seem irrelevant or too convoluted for modern readers. This situation started to change in the 1980s, when her work began to be rediscovered in both Germany and the United States. Scholarship then uncovered a remarkable life lived in the face of countless terrors, and a body of literature of the highest quality.

SOURCES:

Angress, R.K. "The Christian Surrealism of Elisabeth Langgässer," in Melvin J. Friedman, ed. *The Vision Obscured: Perceptions of Some Twentieth Century Catholic Novelists*. NY: Fordham University Press, 1970, pp. 187–200.

Augsberger, Eva. *Elisabeth Langgässer*. Nuremberg: Hans Carl, 1962.

Borth, Richard Anthony. "Themes in the Short Prose Fiction of Elisabeth Langgässer," M.A. thesis, University of North Carolina at Chapel Hill, 1967.

Demetz, Peter. *After the Fires: Recent Writing in the Germanies, Austria and Switzerland*. NY: Harcourt Brace Jovanovich, 1986.

———. "Literature under the Occupation in Germany: Memories of a Contemporary," in Ernestine Schlant and J. Thomas Rimer, eds., *Legacies and Ambiguities: Postwar Fiction and Culture in West Germany and Japan*. Washington, DC: The Woodrow Wilson Center Press; Baltimore and London: The Johns Hopkins University Press, 1991, pp. 123–133.

———. *Postwar German Literature: A Critical Introduction*. NY: Pegasus, 1970.

Doster, Ute. *Elisabeth Langgässer, 1899–1950*. Marbach am Neckar: Deutsche Schillergesellschaft, 1999.

Edvardson, Cordelia. *Burned Child Seeks the Fire: A Memoir*. Translated by Joel Agee. Boston, MA: Beacon Press, 1997.

El-Akramy, Ursula. *Wotans Rabe: Elisabeth Langgässer, ihre Tochter Cordelia und die Feuer von Auschwitz*. Frankfurt am Main: Verlag Neue Kritik, 1997.

Gelbin, Catherine Susan. "The Indelible Seal: Race, Hybridity, and Identity in Elisabeth Langgässer's Writings," Ph.D. dissertation, Cornell University, 1997.

Gelbin, Cathy. "In Quest for a Unified Self: Race, Hybridity, and Identity in Elisabeth Langgässer's *Der gang durch das ried*," in *New German Critique*. No. 70. Winter 1997, pp. 141–160.

———. "'Es war zwar mein Kind, aber die Rassenschranke fiel zwischen uns': Elisabeth Langgässer und die Mutter-Tochter Beziehung," in *Zeitschrift für deutsche Philologie*. Vol. 117, no. 4, 1998, pp. 564–596.

Hetmann, Frederik. *Schlafe, meine Rose: Die Lebensgeschichte der Elisabeth Langgässer*. 2nd ed. Weinheim: Beltz & Gelberg, 1987.

Korn, Karl. *Rheinische Profile: Stefan George, Alfons Paquet, Elisabeth Langgässer*. Pfullingen: Neske Verlag, 1988.

Krüger, Horst. *A Crack in the Wall: Growing Up under Hitler*. Translated by Ruth Hein. NY: Fromm International Publishing Corporation, 1986.

Langgässer, Elisabeth. *Briefe 1924–1950*. Edited by Elisabeth Hoffman. 2 vols. Düsseldorf: Claassen Verlag, 1990.

———. *The Quest*. Translated by Jane Bannard Greene. NY: Alfred A. Knopf, 1953.

Lezzi, Eva. "'Gebranntes Kind such das Feuer': Über die Zerstörung von Kindheit und Mutterschaft durch Auschwitz," in *Zeitschrift für deutsche Philologie*. Vol. 117, no. 4, 1998, pp. 597–615.

Meyer, Franziska. "Women's Writing in Occupied Germany, 1945–1949," in Chris Weedon, ed. *Post-War Women's Writing in German: Feminist Critical Approaches*. Providence, RI: Berghahn, 1997, pp. 25–43.

Müller, Karlheinz. *Elisabeth Langgässer: Eine biographische Skizze*. Darmstadt: Gesellschaft Hessischer Literaturfreunde, 1990.

———. *Elisabeth Langgässer: Vortrag anlässlich der Ausstellungseröffnung, Elisabeth Langgässer, am 19. April 1994 in der Badischen Landesbibliothek*. Karlsruhe: Badische Bibliotheksgesellschaft, 1994.

Reinhold, Ursula, Dieter Schlenstedt, and Horst Tanneberger, eds. *Erster Deutscher Schriftstellerkongress 4.–8. Oktober 1947: Protokolle und Dokumente*. Berlin: Aufbau-Verlag, 1997.

Riley, Anthony W. "'Alles aussen ist innen': Zu Leben und Werk Elisabeth Langgässers unter der Hitler-Diktatur: Mit einem Erstdruck des frühen Aufsatzes 'Die Welt vor den Toren der Kirche (um 1925),'" in Wolfgang Frühwald and Heinz Hürten, eds., *Christliches Exil und christlicher Widerstand: Ein Symposon an der Katholischen Universität Eichstätt 1985*. Regensburg: Verlag Pustet, 1987, pp. 186–224.

Rippley, La Vern J. "The Cyclic Novellen of Elisabeth Langgässer," in *American Benedictine Review*. Vol. 21, 1970, pp. 88–97.

Schirmbeck, Heinrich. "Das Dilemma Elisabeth Langgässers," in *Frankfurter Hefte: Zeitschrift für Kultur und Politik*. Vol. 32, no. 8, 1977, pp. 50–58.

Schlant, Ernestine. *The Language of Silence: West German Literature and the Holocaust*. London: Routledge, 1999.

Thorsen, Kristine Anderson. "Divine Geometry: Elisabeth Langgässer's Lyric Cycles," Ph.D. dissertation, Northwestern University, 1988.

John Haag,
Associate Professor of History,
University of Georgia, Athens, Georgia

Lang-Köstlin, Josephine (1815–1880).

See Lang, Josephine.

Langley, Eve (1908–1974)

Australian writer. Born in Forbes, New South Wales in 1908; died in 1974; married Hilary Clark (an artist and art teacher); children: three.

Born in 1908 in New South Wales, writer Eve Langley moved to New Zealand in 1932, married and had three children. She subsequently returned to Australia where for some time she led a seemingly conventional life and was active in Sydney's literary circles. In later life, however, Langley turned reclusive, moving to the deserted bush near Katoomba in the Blue Mountains and residing in a shack she dubbed "Iona-Lympus." Adopting Oscar Wilde as an alter ego, she dressed as a man, wore a white topi, carried a knife in her belt, and became obsessed with guns. Langley is best remembered for her sequential novels, *The Pea Pickers* (1942) and *White Topee* (1954), the first of which was praised by Douglas Stewart as "the most delightful novel" ever written by an Australian. The books center on the protagonist-narrator Steve, who struggles to reconcile her intellectual need for freedom of thought and expression with her emotional need for a fulfilling relationship. Not until the end of *White Topee* does she finally come to grips with her conflicted psyche: "I really didn't want to be loved," she concludes. "What I really wanted was to be a man, and free for ever to write and think and dream." Langley's personal life remains a mystery, although it is assumed that her own struggles were not as clearly resolved as those of her literary protagonist.

Langley, Katherine (1888–1948)

Republican congressional representative from Kentucky, 70th–71st Congresses (March 4, 1927–March 3, 1931). Born Katherine Gudger on February 14, 1888, near Marshall, in Madison County, North Carolina; died on August 15, 1948, in Pikeville, Kentucky; daughter of James Madison Gudger, Jr. (a U.S. congressional representative); graduated from Woman's College, Richmond, Virginia; attended Emerson College of Oratory, Boston, Massachusetts; married John Langley (a politician), in 1903 (died 1932).

Born in Madison County, North Carolina, in 1888, Katherine Gudger was the daughter of James Madison Gudger, Jr., a well-known Democratic congressional representative. After graduating from the Woman's College in Richmond, Virginia, and attending Emerson College of Oratory in Boston, she taught voice and expression at the Virginia Institute in Bristol. In 1903, she married John Wesley Langley and moved with her new husband to Pikeville, Kentucky. When he was elected to Congress in 1906, she worked as his secretary and also became active in the Kentucky Republican Party.

In 1924, Katherine Langley succeeded to her husband's seat in the House of Representatives following his bootlegging conviction for conspiring to transport and sell liquor. In 1926, while he was serving time in the Federal Penitentiary in Atlanta, Langley successfully ran for the House seat from Kentucky's Tenth District, with the purpose of vindicating her husband's name and carrying on his work. She was appointed to several committees and in 1930 became the first woman to serve on the Republican Committee on Committees. She was also successful in her petition to President Calvin Coolidge to grant her husband clemency provided he informally

Katherine Langley

agree to forfeit the right to stand for public office. Unfortunately, John was not a man of his word and in 1930 declared his intention to run for his old House seat, betraying the president and his wife, whom he had not informed. Although Langley refused to have her name removed from the ballot, the public outcry cost her votes, and Democrat Andrew Jackson May won the seat. Following her husband's death in 1932, Katherine Langley served as railroad commissioner of the third Kentucky district, from 1939 to 1942. She died on August 15, 1948, in Pikeville, Kentucky.

SOURCES:
Office of the Historian. *Women in Congress, 1917–1990.* Commission on the Bicentenary of the U.S. House of Representatives, 1991.

Langton, Jane (fl. 15th c.)

English silk merchant. Flourished in 15th century in London.

A citizen of London, Jane Langton established and managed her own business, importing and marketing silk cloth. Her name appears in the household records of the English royal family as a trusted silk merchant. Langton had established herself in business after her husband died, as a means of supporting herself without being forced to remarry. She was a well-respected entrepreneur and earned substantial profits from her wealthy noble and bourgeois customers.

Laura York,
Riverside, California

Langtry, Lillie (1853–1929)

British courtesan and actress who rose from an obscure life on the Isle of Jersey to become celebrated, in her youth, as the most beautiful woman of her era. Name variations: Lily; The Jersey Lily. Born Emilie Charlotte Le Breton on October 13, 1853, on the Isle of Jersey; died in Monaco on February 12, 1929; daughter of William Le Breton (Anglican dean of Jersey) and Emilie Martin (a Londoner); tutored at home; married Edward Langtry, on March 9, 1874 (divorced 1885); married Hugo de Bathe, in 1899; children: (with Louis Battenberg) Jeanne-Marie Langtry (b. March 8, 1881, in Paris).

Made stage debut in She Stoops to Conquer *in London (December 15, 1881). Publications:* The Days I Knew *(1925).*

Lillie Langtry was born Emilie Charlotte Le Breton in 1853 on the Isle of Jersey (eleven miles long by five miles wide, a few miles off the coast of France). She was a roughneck and playmate of six brothers in a family with a glorious past. A Le Breton fought at the Battle of Hastings in 1066 beside William the Conqueror and was pictured in the Bayeux Tapestry. His descendants were feudal lords who prospered under King John Lackland, but in Lillie's day the family was circumscribed by money and the provincial nature of the island.

Her first romantic attachment, when she was about 13, led to a shocking discovery. She had fallen in love with a local boy from the island, whom her father William Le Breton, Anglican dean of Jersey, had forbidden her to see. Lillie pressed him for an explanation until she learned that the boy was her father's illegitimate son, her own half-brother.

A handful of English lords owned property in Jersey, and Lillie, as daughter of the dean, was considered a suitable companion for their daughters. She was by all accounts astonishingly beautiful, with reddish hair and deep blue eyes. Through the offices of Lord Suffield, who owned an estate on Jersey and was lord-in-waiting to Queen *Victoria, Lillie was introduced to London society at age 15. She found herself socially inept, graceless, and her clothes inferior even to the maids who dressed in tailored black dresses and crisp white aprons. When her weeks in London were over, she returned happily to Jersey.

Edward Langtry, the ne'er-do-well grandson of Belfast's wealthiest shipowner, was a 26-year-old widower living on the island. By her own admission, Lillie was attracted to his 80-foot yacht *Red Gauntlet*. Ambitious for money, excitement, and position, she set about to win him over. Soon after their marriage, on March 9, 1874, Edward sold his boat to generate the income with which to keep his costly bride. His ardor for her soon cooled, however, and he publicly compared Lillie unfavorably to his first, more docile wife **Jane Langtry**. The Langtrys did share a love of their racing yawl, and once, out of deference to Lillie who was sleeping in her cabin, Edward declined to fire a victory cannon when he passed a winning post. Waiting for her to awaken, he allowed two other boats to drift past him and win the race.

With Edward's money, Lillie bought Noirmont Manor, an estate on Jersey that she liked to think rivaled the feudal courts of her ancestors. She soon tired of its isolation, however, and the couple moved to Southampton where she contracted typhoid fever. She convinced her physician that she should convalesce in the city of London, which had no reputation for therapeutic properties, but great renown for its social ones.

In 1876, when she was 23, a chance meeting at the royal Aquarium with Lord Ranelagh, whom she knew from Jersey, led her into London society and the world of the Aesthetes. Devotees of a Romantic knightly past, they included in their number the architect and designer William Morris and the painter Edward Burne-Jones. Lacking furs, jewels, a proper maid and sufficient funds, Langtry knew she could not compete with women of fashion. Cleverly, she cultivated her own style and dressed down in simple clothes fashioned for her in Jersey, and arranged her hair with a loose knot at the nape of her neck and a fringe of bangs on her forehead.

When she appeared in drawing rooms where monied society entertained rising artists, she was a sensation. John Everett Millais was struck by her pale skin, high profile and Junoesque figure. Combining the qualities of a country girl with the spirit of a goddess, she appeared to embody the passions of the Arthurian Age, which the Aesthetes celebrated. Millais asked to be introduced to her and immediately sought to do her portrait. Soon, other artists and lords pressed in, asking her to model for them or to allow them to take her to dinner. In a corner of the room, George F. Miles took a tailor's bill from his pocket, sketched her in pencil, and soon had the sketch reproduced and advertised in shop windows.

As her celebrity grew, Edward Langtry was ignored. Having sought the sea in Jersey, he now found himself confined to London drawing rooms where he retreated into melancholy and drink. His uncomfortable role was to provide Lillie with funds and the respectability of being a married woman.

When Millais' portrait of her was exhibited at the Marsden galleries in 1877, she was established a "p.b." or professional beauty, a group of young women celebrated for being celebrated. Soon she was known as "The Jersey Lily," after a second painting Millais did of her. Langtry was sought after by society hostesses and was the subject of mass-produced photographs sold to the public. She attended two or three parties a night, accompanied by the hapless Edward. One woman described her as entering a room like "a beautiful hound set upon its feet."

Still unable to afford fashionable Paris gowns, Langtry wore a black mourning dress for her favorite brother who had just died. Frances Maynard, a young girl who met her at this time (and who would later succeed her as mistress to the prince of Wales as *Frances Greville, countess of Warwick, the richest woman in the kingdom), wrote: "She had dewy violet eyes, a complexion like a peach. How can words convey the vitality, the glow, the amazing charm that made this fascinating woman the center of any group she entered?" Langtry earned acclaim, and probably some money, by continuing to model for artists and photographers. Edward Langtry, whom Frances dismissed as "an uninteresting fat man," always accompanied her. James Whistler, Edward Poynter and George Frederic Watts produced some of the more famous portraits of Langtry at this time.

Mutual friends arranged for Lillie to meet Queen Victoria's son Edward, the prince of Wales (the future king Edward VII), at a dinner party, and soon they began an affair. When Edward openly flaunted their relationship, Langtry was lionized by hostesses. She was no longer intimidated by her social gaffes and felt they did not matter. She once asked Ulysses S. Grant, who was on a world tour, what he had done since the Civil War, oblivious to the fact that in the interim he had been president of the United States.

I would rather have discovered Mrs. Langtry than have discovered America.

—Oscar Wilde

The prince of Wales built a house for her in Bournemouth so they could rendezvous a hundred miles from London in relative privacy. At public receptions, she met the greatest politicians of the age, including Benjamin Disraeli and William Gladstone, who brought her books and offered to tutor her in English literature. Oscar Wilde, then a disheveled 22-year-old just down from Oxford, already possessed a prize for poetry and a gift for showmanship, and the two of them found they could use each other to advantage. Wilde walked through town holding a single white amaryllis to show his admiration for "The Jersey Lily," and she relied on him to educate her about art and the classics. She soon fell behind in her studies and declined to follow up on some of his more elaborate suggestions—such as driving through the park, enveloped in black, with "Venus Annodomini" written on her bonnet in sapphires.

Only one woman threatened Langtry's renown as the most sought-after woman in London—*Sarah Bernhardt. Bernhardt, who brought her Comédie Française to England in 1879, briefly captured the prince of Wales' attention, but the two women apparently admired each other and were soon friends. Lillie then became infatuated with a new man, Louis Battenberg, the prince's nephew, and soon found she was pregnant by him. Meanwhile, Edward Langtry's Irish estates were being ruined by political turmoil and the potato famine of the late 1870s. Lillie sent him off to America on some dubious business prospect during her confinement, and the two never lived together again. After her daughter **Jeanne-Marie Langtry** was born in Paris on March 8, 1881, Langtry gave her to her mother to raise as the child of one of her deceased brothers. With debts closing in on her, Lillie considered several professions to make money, including gardening, to make the most of her sobriquet The Jersey Lily, and the new field of product endorsement. Finally, she decided to capitalize on her looks and popularity by going on stage, although her friend *Ellen Terry warned that she was too pampered to endure such a rough life.

So at age 28, Lillie Langtry prepared for her stage debut. On December 15, 1881, she appeared in a supporting role in Goldsmith's *She Stoops to Conquer* at the Theater Royal in London. All the while, she was bedeviled by thoughts that actors were no better than tradesmen, and she was bored by long rehearsals, which seemed like physical labor. The prince of Wales, whose friendship she always retained, helped her by attending the opening with his wife, Princess *Alexandra of Denmark, who was perennially gracious and supportive of Langtry.

Some critics expressed surprise that the Jersey Lily had potential as an actress. Others said she would have to work hard to prove that she had real gifts. Lillie, however, was enough of a success that the prince soon persuaded the actor-manager Squire Bancroft to hire Langtry at a handsome salary. As if to remove the long-standing stigma from the acting profession, the prince opened his home, Marlborough House, to actors and openly socialized with them. Gladstone, now prime minister, who made a hobby of trying to rescue fallen women, gave Lillie volumes of Shakespeare and read scenes aloud to her.

Langtry had by now been replaced as the prince's favorite by Frances Greville. Embarked on a new phase of her life, Lillie attempted to sue Edward Langtry for divorce, but he threatened to create a scandal. She was forced to pay him a monthly allowance, which would be revoked if he attempted to contact her.

When Langtry felt she had sufficient experience, she organized her own troupe, which was managed by the erstwhile actress **Henrietta**

Lillie Langtry

Hobson, her business manager. After touring the provinces, the company traveled to the United States. Two days after the Jersey Lily's departure, Louis Battenberg was allowed to return to Great Britain from an extended tour of duty in the Middle East.

On her own and in greater need of money than respectability, Langtry's hardness and venality began to assert itself. A 22-year-old American millionaire named Freddie Gebhard wooed her with a diamond necklace and bracelet. Their relationship, her popularity with the public (but not with the critics), and an acrimonious break with Henrietta Hobson, kept gossip columnists busy promoting Lillie's name. Her fame was such that she stopped traffic in New York after her American debut in *Unequal Match* in 1882. When the troupe toured the West, she and Gebhard openly traveled together, prompting a congressman to demand that she be deported, and an editor in St. Louis to challenge Gebhard to a duel.

Fearing that the notoriety would hurt her in Britain, she decided to stay in the States and took the $100,000 she had earned from the tour and invested in real estate on Fifth Avenue and a private railroad car decorated with polished brass lilies. She became a citizen, which enabled her to divorce Edward in 1885 on grounds other than adultery, of which she of course was guilty. Still living in England, he knew nothing of the existence of his wife's daughter, who was now six, or of the divorce proceedings.

Langtry returned to Europe to see her daughter, to buy clothes in Paris, and to study acting in Paris with Sarah Bernhardt. "I despair of becoming a real actress when I work on the stage with her and I would gladly exchange my beauty, such as it is, for a soupçon of her great gift," she wrote a friend in New York.

During her years in America, Langtry was shunned by American society. Though the Four Hundred excluded her from their number, she enjoyed the rough and tumble of the American West. Cowhands staged an impromptu rodeo for her benefit and "Judge" Roy Bean traveled to Chicago to see her perform, then returned to Texas and named a town after her.

On her visits to England, she encouraged aristocrats who wooed her. Hugh, Lord Lonsdale, the "sporting earl," and Sir George Chetwynd came to blows over her while the three promenaded in London's fashionable Rotten Row. Newspaper headlines about this brawl between two married men ended any pretense Langtry might have had to respectability and alerted tradespeople, to whom she owed money, of her return. They soon sued her. At 30, the one shock she was unable to face was the passage of time. When Oscar Wilde presented her with a play he had written for her, about a woman with a grown illegitimate daughter, she claimed she was too young and thus passed up *Lady Windermere's Fan*. Meanwhile, her daughter was growing up uncertain as to whether she was Lillie's niece or daughter, a child of the prince of Wales or Edward Langtry, whom she had never seen. Gebhard treated her as his daughter, but Lillie broke with him in 1889, when Jeanne-Marie was

eight. Reportedly, Gebhard and Langtry fought over a visit from the prince of Wales while Lillie was gravely ill in London. Neither Langtry nor her daughter ever saw Gebhard again.

Now resettled in Britain, Lillie took as her next millionaire the disreputable Squire Abingdon, a Scot and amateur jockey who would beat her and then repent by giving her a ransom in diamonds, emeralds and sapphires. When a friend found Lillie hiding at home with a blackened eye, Langtry said, "I detest him, but every time he does it, he gives me a check for £5,000." The few respectable people who had stood by her through her past escapades now shunned her. When the squire found Langtry in a Paris hotel with a young Englishman, he destroyed their room in his rage, then beat them both savagely. Lillie spent ten days in the hospital, during which time she signed a complaint for the squire's arrest. To restore himself to her good graces, he had jewels delivered daily, then presented her with two thoroughbreds. She held on to the gifts, and her anger, until he gave her a 600-ton yacht that was more than the equal of the prince of Wales' new toy *The Britannia*. Like the prince, Langtry soon sold her vessel to concentrate on her racing stable. She collected £120,000 on a single race in October 1897. Husband and lover did less well. Edward Langtry died insane on October 15, 1897, in a Chestershire county asylum. After Lillie sent a wreath with a ribbon in her racing colors of turquoise and fawn, *The New York Times* noted in an editorial that it was a "piece of insolence so utterly reckless and original, and at the same time so ingenious and effective, that its moral and social aspects tend to or toward complete disappearance."

Langtry made one last marriage, to Hugo de Bathe, who was 19 years her junior. His father, the baronet Sir Henry de Bathe, promptly disinherited him, saying, "I wish I could die now so that the will could go into effect at once." He waited six years to die, and then Lillie became Lady de Bathe, while remaining on the stage. One afternoon at a party, Jeanne-Marie, who thought her father was dead, learned that Louis Battenberg was her father and politely left the party to return home to confront her mother with the lies she had told. Their relationship never recovered. Jeanne-Marie married a Scottish lord, had four children, and slowly cut Lillie from her life. After the death of Edward VII, who had loved Lillie when he was prince of Wales, the royal family received her, but her own daughter would not. Lillie Langtry died in Monaco on February 12, 1929, with only a paid companion by her side.

SOURCES:

Gerson, Noel Bertram. *Lillie Langtry*. London: Hale, 1972.

Langtry, Lillie. *The Days I Knew*. NY: George H. Doran, 1925.

SUGGESTED READING:

Birkett, Jeremy, and John Richardson. *Lillie Langtry: Her Life in Words and Pictures*. Poole: Blandford Press, 1979.

Brough, James. *The Prince and the Lily: The Story of Lillie Langtry—The Greatest International Beauty of Her Day*. NY: Coward, McCann & Geoghegan, 1975.

RELATED MEDIA:

Lillie (11 hours, 22 min. videocassette), seven-part series starring **Francesca Annis**, aired on Public Television.

Kathleen Brady,
author of *Lucille: The Life of Lucille Ball* (Hyperion) and *Ida Tarbell: Portrait of A Muckraker* (University of Pittsburgh Press)

Lan Ping (1914–1991).

See Jiang Qing.

Lanvin, Jeanne (1867–1946)

French fashion designer and perfumer. Born in 1867; died on July 6, 1946; eldest of 11 children; children: Marguerite later known as Countess Marie-Blanche de Polignac (b. 1887).

Jeanne Lanvin, one of the foremost names in couture during the 1920s, was born in 1867. A French dress designer who is remembered primarily for her classic perfume, Arpege, Lanvin was trained as a seamstress and began her career in a milliner's house on Rue du Faubourg Saint-Honoré. In 1885, she opened her own workroom in a tiny studio apartment in Paris. Her small fashion house, La Maison de Couture, had its beginnings in a few simple dresses she stitched for her sister and daughter. Fashioned from plain fabrics to which she added quilting and embroidery, the designs caught on with her customers who began ordering them for themselves and their daughters. Hence, Lanvin was credited with the first mother-daughter outfits, although she later became known for her wedding gowns and *robes de style* as well.

In 1926, the designer opened a men's boutique (the first of its kind) and in 1927 created the perfume Arpege for her daughter **Marie-Blanche de Polignac**. A devotee of modern art, Lanvin enlisted Art Nouveau artist Paul Tribe to help design the packaging for her new product. From a photograph, Tribe created the famous mother-daughter image that adorns the top of the perfume bottle, which also became the logo for the fashion house. Lanvin was renowned for her

sense of color, and found inspiration in her own art collection, which contained paintings by Vuillard, Renoir, Fantin-Latour, and Odilon Redon.

After Lanvin's death in 1946, her daughter Marie-Blanche de Polignac took over until 1958. The house, which continues, has included such designers as Spain's Antonio del Castillo (1950–1963) and Belgium's Jules-François Crahay (1963–1984), as well as **Maryll Lanvin** (1985–1989), wife of Bernard Lanvin, the son of Jeanne's nephew, and Claude Montana (1990–1992). Spanish designer **Cristina Ortiz** made her House of Lanvin debut in 1998.

SOURCES:

Ehlert, Athena. "Arpege—The Gift of a Gifted Mother," in *Victoria*. May 1995, p. 42.

Laodice (fl. 129 BCE)

*Queen of Parthia. Flourished around 129 BCE; daughter of *Cleopatra Thea (c. 165–121 BCE) and Demetrius II Nicator, Seleucid king (r. 145–138); sister of Antiochus VIII Philometor Grypus and Seleucus V; married Phraates II, king of Parthia.*

Laodice I (c. 285–c. 236 BCE)

Queen of Syria who fought fiercely to ensure that sons of her line would rule over Seleucid Asia. Born around 285 BCE; died around 236 BCE; daughter of Achaeus, a Seleucid prince, and an unknown mother; married Antiochus II, third Seleucid (that is, Macedonian) king of Asia; children: daughters, Stratonice III, Laodice II, and perhaps an unnamed third daughter; sons, Seleucus II and Antiochus Hierax (the Hawk).

Although one source claims that Laodice I was the daughter of Antiochus I, the second Seleucid king of Asia, she was more likely the daughter of Antiochus' brother, Achaeus. The name of Laodice's mother is unknown. So also is the year of her birth, although chronological considerations of a dynastic nature suggest that she was born around 285 BCE. If so, Laodice would have been about 20 when she married her cousin Antiochus II, the son of Antiochus I.

The mid-260s were a difficult time for Antiochus I, for the periphery of his empire had begun to break away from centralized authority. This process was exasperated by the disaffection of Seleucus I, the older of his two sons. Confronted with Seleucus' excessive ambition, Antiochus I had him executed. This personal tragedy, in conjunction with the waning of his physical vigor, stimulated Antiochus I to elevate his other son, Antiochus II, to the position of co-regent

(266). It was almost certainly within this context that Antiochus I then arranged for the marriage of Laodice to Antiochus II, both to consolidate dynastic interests within the Seleucid house and to promote the production of children to carry on the royal line.

With Antiochus II, Laodice had two sons, Seleucus II and Antiochus Hierax (the Hawk), two daughters, *Stratonice III and *Laodice II, and perhaps an unnamed third daughter. These daughters later functioned as diplomatic pawns in Antiochus II's losing battle to maintain control of his kingdom's frontiers. Stratonice would marry Ariarathes III of Cappadocia; Laodice II would marry Mithridates II of Pontus (both sub-kingdoms in modern Turkey). In addition, it is possible that a third daughter may have become the wife of Diodotus, a general appointed to Bactria (modern Afghanistan). Diodotus was originally loyal to Seleucid interests, but, after his province was cut off from the heart of the Seleucid Empire (in modern Syria) by the successful rebellion of the Parthians in 247, he eventually established an independent command in the east.

*U*rged on by his mother, Laodice, who should have restrained him instead, Seleucus inaugurated his reign with a murder.

—Justin

Despite the serious erosion of the Seleucid frontiers, however, when Antiochus II became sole monarch after the death of his father in 261, he occupied himself primarily with problems of more immediate importance to the core of his realm. What concerned Antiochus II was the Egyptian encroachment upon territories along the coasts of Aegean Turkey and Palestine that he considered his by dynastic right. Alexander the Great's Empire stretching from the Adriatic Sea to the Indus River had lasted but a short time after that conqueror's death in 323. By 270, what Alexander had briefly united had been divided among several states, chief among them being the Macedonian kingdoms in Europe, Asia and Egypt, ruled respectively by the Antigonid, Seleucid, and Ptolemaic dynasties (each founded by a general who had once served under Alexander). These rival monarchies owed their independent existences to the on-again, off-again wars waged chiefly among themselves.

By 261, to protect Egypt and to expand his sphere of influence, Ptolemy II, the reigning king of Egypt, had seized most of the coast of the eastern Mediterranean Sea, much of which had been at least for a time under a Seleucid master. To rec-tify this "injustice" to his territorial claims, in 259 Antiochus II (after having arranged for a temporary alliance with Antigonus II, the Macedonian king of Europe) launched the Second Syrian War against Ptolemy II. By 253, Antiochus II had achieved enough success in this conflict for Ptolemy II to offer peace—a peace to be secured through the marriage of Antiochus II to Ptolemy's daughter, *Berenice Syra. In order to sweeten the deal, Ptolemy II offered to Antiochus the lucrative revenues of Palestine, then being collected by Egypt, as Berenice's dower. Lusting after these revenues and worrying that a continuation of war could undermine interests further afield, Antiochus agreed to the peace and marriage—a decision which had profound implications for Laodice. Although royal polygamy was well established in the Macedonian tradition at this time, Ptolemy II would have none of it in this case. Fearing that the life of his beloved daughter would be endangered if Laodice remained at court, and wanting a son of Berenice Syra to succeed Antiochus II in lieu of the two heirs already produced by Laodice, the Egyptian king made it a condition of peace that Antiochus divorce Laodice.

This Antiochus did, even though he doted on Laodice. (However, being somewhat of an alcoholic playboy, he was certainly not faithful to her.) In order to soften the blow of rejection, Antiochus gave Laodice a substantial estate, consisting of several properties near Babylon and Borsippa. These provided for a comfortable "retirement," but, after leaving Antioch (the Seleucid capital), Laodice and her children had no intention of residing in the relative isolation of Mesopotamia. Rather, they took up residence in Ephesus. The Aegean seaport of Ephesus was far better placed both for the inauguration of political intrigue and for the successful flight that might become necessary if such intrigue went awry. Clearly, Laodice had no intention of abandoning her husband or his empire to Berenice Syra and any sons she might produce.

Within a year of her Seleucid marriage, Berenice did give birth to a son in whose person was the promise of a lasting peace between the Ptolemies and the Seleucids. Nevertheless (for whatever reason, but certainly at the instigation of Laodice), Antiochus abandoned Berenice Syra and Antioch for Ephesus and Laodice. On a personal level, Antiochus obviously preferred Laodice over Berenice Syra, but it is equally clear that Laodice must have been politically active on behalf of her sons and against Egypt. Otherwise, Antiochus' potentially foolhardy alienation of Ptolemy II and the revenues of Palestine is inexplicable. As far as the succession was concerned,

Laodice almost certainly pointed out to Antiochus' subjects that their well-being depended on a secure succession. Furthermore, she probably suggested that her sons were unlikely to give way before the claims of Berenice Syra's infant son, and that, because they were older, they had a much better chance of attaining their majority before Antiochus II died. In addition, it is also likely that Laodice used her location in Ephesus to approach Antigonus II in Macedonia, for that monarch could not have been at all happy about a Seleucid-Ptolemy alliance. As such, it is probable that Antigonus pulled out all the stops to convince Antiochus II that a union with Laodice was more in his long-term interest than one with Berenice Syra.

Although Antiochus II remained in Ephesus for several years after joining Laodice there, no open breech between Syria and Egypt developed, both because he did not officially divorce Berenice and because Ptolemy II, despite applying diplomatic pressure on Antiochus to return to his (second) wife, was apparently too far into physical decline for an aggressive move against Antiochus.

So things continued until January 246 BCE, when the death of Ptolemy II brought Berenice Syra's brother, Ptolemy III, to the Egyptian throne. Unwilling to tolerate the humiliation of his sister and kingdom, Ptolemy III pressured Antiochus II to honor the obligations which he had accepted in order to win the revenues of Palestine at the end of the Second Syrian War. Within months, this assertiveness appeared on the verge of paying off, for it seemed as though Antiochus was about to return to Berenice Syra in Antioch. In August, however, just before an imminent departure, Antiochus died suddenly—almost certainly the victim of poison. Immediately thereafter, Laodice had her son, Seleucus II, proclaimed king.

Thus throwing down the political gauntlet, Laodice acted decisively against her rival and her rival's son before their rescue could be effected by Ptolemy II. Both were murdered in Antioch, certainly at Laodice's instigation and perhaps even personally carried out by her son, Seleucus II. Thereafter, Ptolemy III invaded the Seleucid Empire, beginning the Third Syrian War (246–241). Although too late to save Berenice Syra, Ptolemy's incursion reasserted his control over much of the Palestinian and Anatolian coasts. Her sons being too inexperienced to confront Ptolemy III directly, Laodice championed their dynastic claims. In this role she functioned competently, forestalling the premature collapse of Seleucid power. One anecdote in particular testifies to both Laodice's position and ruthlessness. Concerned with the loyalty of Sophron, the commander of her Ephesus garrison, Laodice discussed her fears in front of one of her personal attendants, a woman named **Danae**, who, unknown to Laodice, was also Sophron's lover. After Danae warned Sophron about his imminent arrest, he betrayed Ephesus to Ptolemy III. When Laodice discovered how Sophron had been forewarned, she had Danae—hitherto an intimate—thrown to her death from a cliff. To a Laodice engaged in a war for the very survival of her line, nothing could excuse such perfidy.

Despite her leadership during the Third Syrian War, Laodice's ultimate impact upon the Seleucid was mixed at best. Perhaps emboldened by her success in maintaining the core of the Seleucid Empire against Egypt's aggression, Laodice refused to relinquish the reins of power once peace had been arranged. Despite the fact that her older son was well over 20 when a new pact ended this round of war with Egypt, Laodice refused to withdraw from public affairs. In fact, to ensure the extension of her own influence and perhaps imagining her influence over her younger son to be greater than over her older, Laodice incited Antiochus Hierax (only 14 at the time) to challenge Seleucus II's sole possession of the Seleucid throne. Laodice's encouragement of Antiochus Hierax provoked a debilitating civil war which ended only in 236, which even then was settled only after Seleucus II ceded to Antiochus Hierax his territorial claims north of the Taurus Mountains—thus effectively relinquishing all personal claims to Anatolia. Although the brothers thereafter are known to have co-operated at least occasionally, their rivalry certainly accelerated the disintegration of the Seleucid Empire.

When Laodice died is unknown. Nevertheless, given her willingness to pit her sons against each other for her personal advantage, it is unlikely that she lived to see their reconciliation in 236. It is even possible that her death precipitated this reconciliation.

William Greenwalt,
Associate Professor of Classical History,
Santa Clara University, Santa Clara, California

Laodice II (fl. 250 BCE)

*Queen of Pontus. Born around 260 BCE; daughter of *Laodice I (c. 285–c. 236 BCE) and Antiochus II, Seleucid king (r. 261–246 BCE); sister of Seleucus II and *Stratonice III; married Mithridates II of Pontus (a sub-kingdom in modern Turkey).*

Laodice III (fl. 200 BCE).

See Cleopatra I for sidebar.

Lao Fuoye (1835–1908).

See Cixi.

La Palme, Béatrice (1878–1921)

Canadian soprano and violinist who was the first Quebec singer to star in great opera houses after Emma Albani. Born Marie Alice Béatrix Beloeil near Montreal, Quebec, on July 27, 1878; died in Montreal on January 8, 1921; studied violin with Frantz Jehin-Prume; studied voice with Gustave Garcia; married Salvator Issauerl (a French tenor), in 1908.

Was first winner of the Lord Strathcona scholarship to the Royal College of Music in London (1895); made debut at Covent Garden (1903), Opéra-Comique in Paris (1905), Montreal Opera Company (1911), Century Opera House in New York (1913); retired to teach (1914); gave last public performance (1919).

Béatrice La Palme was born Marie Alice Béatrix Beloeil near Montreal, Quebec, in 1878. She began her musical career as a violinist and was the first winner of the Lord Strathcona scholarship to the Royal College of Music in London in 1895. There, she began studying voice with Gustave Garcia, and Dame *Emma Albani advised her to devote herself exclusively to singing. La Palme's Covent Garden debut occurred on July 18, 1903, when she replaced *Fritzi Scheff at the last minute as Musetta in *La Bohème*. She continued to perform in London until 1911, when she returned to Montreal with her husband Salvator Issauerl, the French tenor, whom she had married in 1908. She performed for two seasons there. In 1913, La Palme made her New York debut at the Century Opera House, where she sang 56 performances of 15 operas. In 1914, she was in Chicago for a season at Ravinia Park. Physical exhaustion and hearing problems as well as the uncertainty of World War I caused her to retire early at the age of 36. She then devoted her career to teach-

Laura La Plante

ing, joining her husband at the studio he had opened in Montreal in 1911. Unfortunately, no recordings of her work exist.

John Haag,
Athens, Georgia

La Pasionaria (1895–1989).

See Ibárruri, Dolores.

La Plante, Laura (1904–1996)

American actress who was the first woman to sing on screen. Name variations: Laura La Plante Asher. Born in St. Louis, Missouri, on November 1, 1904; died on October 14, 1996, at Woodland Hills, California; attended school in San Diego, California; married William Seiter (a director at Warner Bros.), in 1926 (divorced 1932); married Irving Asher (a producer), on June 19, 1934; children: (second marriage) Jill Asher; Tony Asher.

Selected films: The Great Gamble (The Big Plunge, serial, 1919); The Old Swimmin' Hole (1921); 813 (1921); The Big Round-Up (1921); Play Square (1921); Perils of the Yukon (serial, 1922); The Wall Flower (1922); The Ramblin' Kid (1923); Dead Game (1923); Burning Words (1923); Shootin' for Love (1923); Out of Luck (1923); Ride for Your Life (1924); Sporting Youth (1924); Excitement (1924); The Dangerous Blonde (1924); Young Ideas (1924); Butterflies (1924); The Last Worker (1924); Smoldering Fires (1925); Dangerous Innocence (1925); The Teaser (1925); The Beautiful Cheat (1926); The Midnight Sun (1926); Skinner's Dress Suit (1926); Poker Faces (1926); Her Big Night (1926); Butterflies in the Rain (1926); The Love Thrill (1927); Beware of Windows (1927); The Cat and the Canary (1927); Silk Stockings (1927); Thanks for the Buggy Ride (1928); Finders Keepers (1928); Home James (1928); The Last Warning (1929); Scandal Show (1929); Show Boat (1929); The Love Trap (1929); Hold Your Man (1929); Captain of the Guard (1930); The King of Jazz (1930); Lonely Wives (1931); God's Gift to Women (1931); Arizona (Men Are Like That, 1931); Little Mister Jim (1946); Spring Reunion (1957).

One of the top silent stars of the 1920s, Laura La Plante began her film career at 15, playing a bit part in one of the popular comedy shorts made by director-producer Albert Christie. Blonde and blue-eyed, with an impish grin, she gained notice with her performance in *The Old Swimmin' Hole* (1921) and subsequently signed a long-term contract with Universal. She was initially cast as the heroine in Westerns and adventure films, but found her niche as the girl-next-door in social comedies. Two notable departures from her usual vehicles were the spooky melodrama *The Cat and the Canary* (1927) and the original version of *Edna Ferber*'s *Show Boat* (1929), in which she played Magnolia. In this part-talkie film, La Plante became the first woman to sing onscreen.

Unlike many silent stars, La Plante's voice was as pleasant as her appearance, and she could have made a smooth transition to talkies had her personal life not taken her far from Hollywood. In 1936, after divorcing her husband of six years, director William Seiter, La Plante married producer Irving Asher and retired from films to live in London, where she appeared on stage. She and Asher returned to Hollywood in 1940, but La Plante was not seen on screen again until 1946, when she took a small role opposite Jackie "Butch" Jenkins in *Little Mister Jim*. In 1956, she starred in a CBS television drama, and the following year appeared as *Betty Hutton*'s mother in the film *Spring Reunion*. In later years, La Plante tended to laugh off her movie career. "That was so long ago I cannot even remember doing them."

SOURCES:
Katz, Ephraim. *The Film Encyclopedia.* NY: HarperCollins, 1994.
Lamparski, Richard. *Whatever Became of . . . ?* 1st and 2nd Series. NY: Crown, 1967.

Barbara Morgan,
Melrose, Massachusetts

La Pola (1795–1817).

See Salavarrieta, Pola.

Lara, Adelina de (1872–1961).

See de Lara, Adelina.

La Rameé, Louise (1839–1908).

See Rameé, Louise de la.

Larcom, Lucy (1824–1893)

American author and educator. Born on May 5, 1824 (some sources cite 1826), in Beverly, Massachusetts; died on April 17, 1893, in Boston, Massachusetts; daughter of Benjamin Larcom (a sea captain) and Lois (Barrett) Larcom; graduated from Monticello Seminary in Godfrey, Illinois, 1852; never married; no children.

Selected writings: Ships in the Mist *(1859);* The Sunbeam and Other Stories *(1860);* Poems *(1869);* Childhood Songs *(poems, 1873);* Wild Roses of Cape Ann and Other Poems *(1881);* A New England Girlhood, Outline from Memory *(1889, reprint. ed. 1924, 1986);* Easter Gleams *(1890);* As It Is in Heaven *(1891);* The Unseen Friend *(1892);* At the Beautiful Gate and Other Songs of Faith *(1892).*

Lucy Larcom was born in Beverly, Massachusetts, on May 5, 1824, the ninth of ten children of Benjamin and **Lois Larcom**. The Larcoms had lived in Beverly for generations, and Lucy grew up in the Puritan tradition that was a family hallmark. Her father, a sea captain with a strongly religious nature, was a marked influence on the young girl. His death in 1835 left the family without sufficient income, so they moved to Lowell, Massachusetts, where Lucy's mother supervised a dormitory set up by a textile company to house its female workers, called "mill girls." With the family still in need of further income, the older girls quit school to become mill girls themselves; soon, at age 11, Larcom did the same.

Although she was a fairly popular writer in her day, Larcom is now known primarily for her autobiographical *A New England Girlhood, Outline from Memory*, part of which describes the life Larcom and others lived as factory workers in the Lowell mills in the late 1830s and early 1840s. It is considered a classic portrayal of small-town life, as well as a valuable insider's look at mill life. Textile mills were a vital part of the Industrial Revolution, and the mill girls, many of whom at the time came from local farms and were the first in their families to leave the land, were an illustration of how that revolution changed (and would continue to change) society. Larcom's sisters became leaders in the mill community, and founded the *Operative Magazine*, in which Larcom's first poems were published. She also published poems in the *Lowell Offering*, another magazine produced by and aimed at mill girls. Mill girls established evening classes and lectures for their own educational improvement; Larcom participated in a German class and a botany class, and also in an "improvement circle" at which members' essays were read aloud. Work in the mills occupied most of their time, however (in 1846, lawmakers in Massachusetts would refuse to sign a law mandating a maxi-

Lucy Larcom

mum ten-hour workday). Many years later, Larcom would recall with regret that she had not been allowed to leave her work to see Charles Dickens when he visited the mills. Although those were the years that saw the beginnings of movements to organize workers and bargain for better conditions, such as the Lowell Female Labor Reform League led by *Sarah Bagley, Larcom did not participate in those movements, and for the most part *A New England Girlhood* portrays mill life favorably.

In 1846, Larcom quit the mills and moved to Illinois with her sister **Emeline Larcom**. She taught school in Looking Glass Prairie for three years and then, using the money she had saved, enrolled in Monticello Seminary in Godfrey, Illinois, in 1849. She graduated in 1852, and moved back to Beverly; in 1854, she won $50 in a poetry contest for her "Call to Kansas." From 1854 to 1862, while continuing to write poetry, Larcom taught English literature and rhetoric at Wheaton Seminary (now Wheaton College) in Norton, Massachusetts, where she revolutionized the school's teaching methods by using lectures and discussions rather than the standard approach of reciting from textbooks. She also suggested improvements for courses and founded the college newspaper.

In the years after 1862, Larcom divided her time between Beverly and Boston while publishing books of prose and of poetry. She was an editor of a children's magazine, *Our Young Folks*, from 1865 to 1873. A friend of John Greenleaf Whittier, she edited without credit three volumes published under his name, including *Child Life* (1871) and *Songs of Three Centuries* (1883). Her work became quite popular and was also published in magazines including *St. Nicholas*, *Youth's Companion*, and *The Atlantic Monthly*. She wrote a good deal of work aimed at children, although she did not have children of her own. Larcom's intense Christian faith was the most important inspiration for her poetry, which, in common with much Victorian art, was intended to "do good" for the reader. She had a particular fondness for the beauty of nature, seeing it as an expression of the divine, and many of her poems detail rural scenes of the people and environment of New England. Lucy Larcom died in Boston on April 17, 1893, and was buried in an unmarked grave in Beverly.

SOURCES:

Buck, Claire, ed. *Bloomsbury Guide to Women's Literature*. NY: Prentice Hall, 1992.

James, Edward T., ed. *Notable American Women, 1607–1950*. Cambridge, MA: The Belknap Press of Harvard University Press, 1971.

McHenry, Robert, ed. *Famous American Women*. NY: Dover, 1983.

Karina L. Kerr, M.A., Ypsilanti, Michigan

Laredo, Ruth (1937—)

American pianist, known for her performance of Russian music. Born Ruth Meckler in Detroit, Michigan, on November 20, 1937; daughter of Ben Meckler and Miriam (Horowitz) Meckler; granted diploma from the Curtis Institute of Music, 1960; married Jaime Laredo (the Bolivian violin virtuoso), in 1960 (divorced 1974); children: daughter Jennifer Laredo.

Ruth Laredo was born in Detroit, Michigan, in 1937 and studied with Rudolf Serkin at the Curtis Institute of Music in Philadelphia. Her debut took place in New York in 1962 with Leopold Stokowski and his American Symphony Orchestra. In 1965, she toured Europe with Serkin and his son Peter, receiving fine reviews. In 1960, she married the Bolivian violin virtuoso Jaime Laredo, and they played numerous recitals together; they divorced in 1974. Laredo was known and respected as a specialist in Russian music. Her performances and recordings of the solo piano compositions of Rachmaninoff and Scriabin were widely praised, and her recitals were invariably sold out.

John Haag, Athens, Georgia

Larentia, Acca (fl. 9th, 8th, or 7th c. BCE)

Legendary personage or minor goddess honored on a special Feast day in Rome and the subject of two traditions: one associates her with the stepmother of Romulus and Remus, the other depicts her as a prostitute during the reign of King Marcius Ancus. Pronunciation: AK-kah Lar-EN-tia. Name variations: Larentina, Laurentia, Fabula. As the stepmother of Romulus and Remus her floruit would fall before any one of several dates in the 9th and 8th centuries BCE that the Romans claimed as the foundation date of their city; as the prostitute and lover of Hercules her floruit would fall within the dates of the reign of King Ancus: 642–617 BCE. Married to herdsman Faustulus according to the former story; married to Carrutius or Tarrutius according to the latter. Honored by Roman festival day, the Larentalia or Larentinalia, on December 23.

Often it can be difficult to account for the figures of Roman mythology. The Roman mind was intensely religious, honoring dozens of named deities in many cult festivals throughout the year. Unlike the Greeks, however, the Romans did not readily conceive of their gods in human form; Italian divinities remained in the folk consciousness as abstractions of fertility or health, for example, and few legends or myths grew up around them. At a certain point in Roman history, however, the influence of Greek literature, with its varied and colorful tales of gods and heroes, made a profound impact on Roman tastes. This influence, coincident with Rome's growing conception of itself as a political power in the world, created in its educated citizens the need to explain the religious and historical foundation of the state in Latin literature. The result, though by no means insincere, is a fundamentally self-conscious mythology: even a single author can argue with himself over the versions or meanings of a story he is recounting to explain a religious custom or historical practice, and sometimes the native Italian or Etruscan origins of a mythical subject are conflated or confused with Greek subjects in the process.

This situation is responsible for the mixed accounts of the personage known most often as Acca Larentia, whose feast was celebrated at Rome into Imperial times at a shrine in the district of the city Velabrum. She is referred to in many ancient texts which offer slight variants, and differences in viewpoint, on her role, but the two basic stories to account for her honors are easily retold.

The first story makes Acca Larentia a figure in the history of Rome's foundation, intimately associated with its legendary founders, Romulus and Remus. Livy's and Plutarch's accounts of this association are probably the best known. During the reign of King Amulius of Alba, his niece **Rhea Silvia** became pregnant, claiming the god Mars as the father. She eventually delivered the twin brothers Romulus and Remus, whom the king, fearful for his succession, commanded to be exposed on the banks of the Tiber. The servant allotted for this task found that the river had overflowed its banks, and rather than wade out to where the stream was strong, left the boys in a basket in the stagnant pools of the flood. They did not drown, as he had hoped, but were instead stranded on a patch of dry land when the waters receded. Crying from hunger, they were heard by a she-wolf come down from the mountains to drink, who immediately began to suckle them.

As this wolf was gently licking the infants, the king's herdsman, Faustulus, happened by. He took the boys home to his wife Acca Larentia, who was grieving at the stillbirth of her own child. She nursed the twins, and thus gained her reverend position in the Roman religious year as the *alma mater* of the Roman state in the person of its founder, Romulus.

The second story of Larentia (for which the accounts of Macrobius, Plutarch, and Augustine are particularly full) says that she was a beautiful and well-known courtesan living in the days of Marcius Ancus, the fourth king of Rome. When the caretaker of the temple of Hercules found himself bored on a festival day, he began to throw dice to amuse himself. His game was to roll once for himself, and then once for Hercules, swearing that the winner should have a good dinner and a prostitute as reward. The hand that threw for Hercules won. True to his word, the caretaker locked dinner and Acca Larentia in the temple for the night. The next morning, Larentia claimed that Hercules had indeed visited her bed, and had offered her some advice in thanks for his pleasant evening. He told her that she should befriend and marry the first man she met upon leaving the building, and that he would provide her reward.

This tradition says that the lucky man first attracted by her charms that morning was a wealthy old (or young) gentleman named Tarrutius (or Carrutius). When he died, his estate passed to Larentia, and upon her death, in gratitude for the benefit she had received from the god, she left her wealth to the people of Rome. In exchange for this, King Ancus had her buried in the most frequented area of the city, the Velabrum, and instituted yearly honors to her in a shrine on the site.

The fact that neither of these two stories was deeply rooted in the collective memory of the Roman people allowed for several authors of the above accounts to speculate openly on their relative truthfulness as explanations for the rites of the Larentalia celebrated in December. Livy adds to his story of the wolf the opinion of some that this element originated because Larentia, Faustulus' wife, was rather loose in her morals, and had thus earned the nickname *lupa*, "wolf," which in common parlance was equivalent to "whore." Plutarch, in reporting the same tradition, takes the further step of linking the two Larentia stories. He postulates that there were, in fact, two women of that name, one the nurse of Romulus in the earliest days of Rome, the second the courtesan of Ancus' day (with the surname Fabula). He avoids the need to choose between them absolutely by adding the following flourish to the story of the latter Larentia's death: already esteemed as a benefactor and the mistress of a god, she one day vanished into thin air on the site of the former Larentia's grave in the Velabrum.

Ancient speculation on the relationship between the Lares (Roman household gods) and Larentia associated the rites of the Larentalia with chthonian beliefs; she also came to be known as the mother of the original *fratres arvales,* an important priestly college in Rome. The original characteristics of the minor goddess have also been a subject of scholarly debate in modern times, especially within the last century. Contemporary consensus shifts away from the identification of Larentia with the Lares. The modern analytical eye has also detected Greek and possibly Etruscan origins for the myths of Larentia reported in Classical sources, and students of comparative mythology have noticed its several points of similarity with quite unrelated myths from around the world. Such scholarship, however, does not lessen the force of the figure presented to posterity by the ancient Roman mythographer. His purpose was to ground the forgotten past in an accessible and memorable form: he explained obscurities, smoothed over omissions, and made vagueness concrete for the greater glory of Rome. All of the various stories about her offered great possibilities to the Roman imagination, a fact verified both by the frequent retelling of her story throughout Classical times, and the occasional appeal to her image in art and poetry.

SOURCES:

Augustine, Saint. *The City of God.* Translated by William M. Green. Vol. 2: *Books 4–7.* Loeb Classical Library. London: William Heinemann, 1963.

Dionysius of Halicarnassus. *Roman Antiquities.* Translated by Earnest Cary. Vol. 1: *Books I–II.* Loeb Classical Library. Cambridge, MA: Harvard University Press, 1990.

Gellius, Aulus. *Attic Nights.* Translated by John C. Rolfe. Vol. 2: *Books 6–13.* Loeb Classical Library. Cambridge, MA: Harvard University Press, 1982.

Grant, Michael. *Roman Myths.* NY: Scribner, 1971.

Latte, Kurt. *Römische Religionsgeschichte.* Handbuch der Alterumswissenschaft, fünfte Abteilung, vierter Teil. Munich: C.H. Beck'sche Verlagsbuchhandlung, 1960.

Livy. *Ab Urbe Condita.* Translated by B.O. Foster. Vol. 1: *Books I & II.* Loeb Classical Library. Cambridge, MA: Harvard University Press, 1988.

Macrobius. *The Saturnalia.* Translated by Percival Vaughan Davies. NY: Columbia University Press, 1969.

Ovid. *Fasti.* Translated by James George Frazer. 2nd rev. ed. by G.P. Goold. Loeb Classical Library. Cambridge, MA: Harvard University Press, 1989.

Pliny. *Natural History.* Translated by H. Rackham. Vol. 5: *Books XVII–XIX.* Loeb Classical Library. Cambridge, MA: Harvard University Press, 1952.

Plutarch. *Plutarch's Lives.* Translated by Bernadotte Perrin. Vol. 1: *Theseus and Romulus, Lycurgus and Numa, Solon and Publicola.* Loeb Classical Library. Cambridge, MA: Harvard University Press, 1982.

———. *The Roman Questions of Plutarch.* Translated by H.J. Rose. Oxford: Clarendon Press, 1924.

Varro. *On the Latin Language.* Translated by Roland G. Kent. Vol. 1: *Books V–VII.* Loeb Classical Library. Cambridge, MA: Harvard University Press, 1993.

RELATED MEDIA:

Coin portrait of Acca Larentia in Grant, *Roman Myths,* pl. 12.

Peter H. O'Brien,
teaches English and classics at
Boston University Academy, Boston, Massachusetts

Larentina (fl. 9th, 8th, or 7th c. BCE).

See Larentia, Acca.

Lark Ellen (1868–1947).

See Yaw, Ellen Beach.

Larkin, Delia (1878–1949)

Irish labor leader. Born Brigid Larkin in Toxteth, Liverpool, England, on February 22, 1878; died in Dublin, Ireland, on October 26, 1949; fifth child of James Larkin and Mary Ann (McNulty) Larkin; sister of James (Big Jim) Larkin (a labor leader); educated at Chipping Street elementary school, Liverpool; married Peter Colgan, on February 8, 1921.

Delia Larkin's public life as an organizer of Irish women workers was overshadowed by her more famous older brother James (Big Jim) Larkin, and it is only in recent years that her activities and contribution to Irish labor have begun to receive their due. Her parents were both from Northern Ireland and had immigrated to Liverpool shortly after their marriage in the mid-1860s. She was christened Brigid, although she was known all her life as Delia; her mother had signed her birth certificate with a cross, an indication she was illiterate. The family lived in Toxteth, one of the poorest parts of Liverpool, where overcrowding, sickness, poverty and high infant mortality were rife. Delia's elder sister Agnes died when she was a baby. Her father died in 1887 when Delia was nine and, like her older brothers Jim and Hugh Larkin, she had to go to work early in order to support the family. Though she never had the chance of further education, for the rest of her life she loved poetry and drama.

In Liverpool, Larkin worked as a nurse and as a teacher; at the time, neither occupation required a professional qualification. Her brother James had become actively involved in labor politics on the Liverpool docks, and in 1907 he went to Belfast as an organizer for the National

Union of Dock Laborers. In 1909, he founded the Irish Transport and General Workers Union (ITGWU). Delia also left Liverpool for Ireland, and by 1911 she had joined James and his family in Dublin. Although Delia was initially skeptical, it was decided to start a women's trade union as part of the ITGWU. The first advertisement for the Irish Women Workers Union (IWWU) appeared in the *Irish Worker* (the ITGWU's paper, in which Delia had a column) in the summer of 1911. That September, the union was launched, and in her column Delia declared: "All we ask for is just shorter hours, better pay than the scandalous limit now existing and conditions of labor befitting a human being."

As her biographer **Theresa Moriarty** has noted, women trade unionists were very isolated at the time. The membership never amounted to more than 1,000, and they lacked the organizational experience of their male colleagues. Larkin built up her union around the members' militancy and gave unstintingly of her energy and commitment. The union was based at the ITGWU headquarters in Liberty Hall in Dublin. Larkin was available there to members seven days a week and built up a united organization with strong loyalties. She arranged discussion groups and social events, outings, concerts, drama groups and dances.

The IWWU soon had branches in other Irish cities and towns, but most of the members worked for small firms; Jacob's biscuit factory in Dublin was the only workplace where the union could count its membership in the hundreds. The union won two small strikes in 1912 but was less successful the following year, when membership dropped to 700. At the end of August 1913, the IWWU became involved in the great lock-out of workers which followed the tramway strike. Over 300 women workers were locked out of Jacob's because they were wearing the IWWU badge in support of the tramway strikers. When James Larkin went to England to seek British support for the strike, Delia helped to organize support for the strikers at Liberty Hall. She also arranged to bring strikers' children to England to be looked after. This precipitated a major row with the Catholic archbishop of Dublin, who feared that the children's faith would be undermined.

After the lock-out ended, nearly 400 IWWU members were sacked. In order to raise funds, Larkin went on tour with a drama group comprising some of the sacked workers. Financially the tour was not a success, and this brought to a head tensions between the ITGWU

and the IWWU, tensions aggravated by divisions between James Larkin and his ITGWU rival William O'Brien. In September 1914, the IWWU was ordered to leave Liberty Hall, and in October James Larkin went to the United States. In July 1915, after further months of wrangling, Delia Larkin left Dublin for London, where she helped to nurse wounded soldiers. This did not indicate support for World War I. In the United States, her brother James was actively campaigning against the war, as was her brother Peter Larkin in Australia who was subsequently imprisoned.

Delia Larkin returned to Dublin in 1918 and worked for the insurance section of the ITGWU. Humiliatingly, she was excluded from membership of the IWWU. There also was a further outbreak of factionalism within the ITGWU in which she became involved. At this point, she considered going to Australia to stay with her brother Peter and his wife. A copy of her letter was intercepted by the Australian police who considered her "no improvement on her brothers." Shortly after this, at the height of the red scare, James was arrested in America for criminal anarchy and sentenced to three years. Delia agitated ceaselessly for both her brothers.

Delia Larkin largely disappeared from public view after her marriage to Peter Colgan in February 1921, although her apartment became a gathering point for young left-wing writers such as Liam O'Flaherty, Sean O'Casey, and Peadar O'Donnell. When her brother James returned to Ireland in 1923, she organized a drama group for the new union he set up, the Workers Union of Ireland. James lived with her and her husband in his last years, before dying in 1947. When Delia Larkin died in 1949, she was buried beside him and her brother Peter in Glasnevin cemetery in Dublin.

SOURCES:

Moriarty, Theresa. "Delia Larkin: Relative Obscurity" and "Larkin and the Women's Movement" in *James Larkin: Lion of the Fold*. Ed. by Donal Nevin. Dublin: Gill and Macmillan, 1998, pp. 93–101, 428–438.

Deirdre McMahon,
lecturer in history at Mary Immaculate College,
University of Limerick, Limerick, Ireland

Laroche, Baroness de.

See Quimby, Harriet for sidebar on Elise-Raymonde Deroche.

Laroche, Raymonde de (b. 1886).

See Quimby, Harriet for sidebar.

La Roche, Sophie von (1730–1807)

German novelist and publisher of a journal for women whose writings depict morally strong women capable of rising above all misfortune. Name variations: Sophie La Roche. Pronunciation: Roche rhymes with posh. Born Sophie Gutermann in the Bavarian town of Kaufbeuren, Germany, on December 6, 1730; died in Offenbach, Germany, on February 18, 1807; daughter of Georg Friedrich Gutermann (dean of the medical faculty at the university in Augsburg) and Regina Barbara (Unold) Gutermann; married Georg Michael Frank von La Roche, on December 27, 1753; children: out of eight only five survived infancy, Maximiliane von La Roche Brentano (1756–1793, mother of Bettine von Arnim); Fritz von La Roche (b. 1757); Luise von La Roche (b. 1759); Carl von La Roche (b. 1766); Franz Wilhelm von La Roche (b. 1768).

Wrote first novel Geschichte des Fräuleins von Sternheim *(1771, translated as* Memoirs of Miss Sophy Sternheim *in 1776); wrote* Rosaliens Briefe an ihre Freundin Marianne von St** *(Rosalie's Letters to Her Friend Marianne von St**, 1779–81); published her journal* Pomona für Teutschlands Töchter *(Pomona for Germany's Daughters, 1782–84); wrote the story* Die zwey Schwestern: Eine moralische Erzählung *(1784, translated as* Two Sisters*); wrote* Briefe an Lina *(Letters to Lina, 1785–87); published novel* Erscheinungen am See Oneida *(Event at Lake Oneida, 1798); in later years, wrote* Mein Schreibtisch *(My Writing Desk, 1799); published travelogues on Switzerland, France, Holland and England; wrote* Schönes Bild der Resignation *(Beautiful Image of Resignation, 1801), the anthology* Herbsttage *(Autumn Days, 1805), and* Melusinens Sommer-Abende *(Melusine's Summer Evenings, 1807). Many of her earlier works were published anonymously.*

Sophie Gutermann was born in the Swabian town of Kaufbeuren on December 6, 1730. Her father Georg Friedrich Gutermann was a well-respected physician who never failed to emphasize the importance of education to his children. Little is known about Sophie's mother **Regina Gutermann**, who would die when Sophie was 17. Being the oldest of the family's 13 children, Sophie profited the most from her father's mentoring efforts. He was a typical patriarch, who insisted on controlling the direction and content of her learning. Introduced to his library when she was two, Sophie found the colorful and decorative title pages of books fascinating. By age three, she could read well, but only the Bible and other religious tracts were permitted. Her family's interest in pietism and its close association

with the Swabian Pietists may have encouraged her to read the complete Bible at the age of five. As Sophie grew older, Georg tried to awaken her interest in natural science, astronomy, and history. While Regina taught her daughter the necessary domestic skills, Georg prided himself in providing her with a well-rounded education. But when Sophie expressed her desire to receive a systematic education, such as that available to young boys of her age, her father bluntly refused. It was almost impossible for him to envision his daughter as anything but a housewife and mother in the future. La Roche realized for the first time that she was powerless over her father's decrees; he was the benevolent, absolutist ruler taking care of his dependents and exercising full control over them.

Father and daughter experienced another conflict over her first fiancé, the Italian Gian Lodovico Bianconi (1717–1781). Sophie was 17 when she became engaged to Bianconi, the personal physician of Augsburg's prince bishop. Gian Bianconi hardly wanted a traditional wife; rather, he prepared her for the role of his companion. He encouraged her efforts to learn mathematics and music and introduced her to contemporary Italian literature. Following Regina's death, however, Georg broke off Sophie's engagement, because Bianconi insisted that their children be raised Catholic. Georg disagreed so vehemently on this point that Sophie had to distance herself from Bianconi despite her admiration for him. At her father's behest, she tore Bianconi's portrait into a thousand pieces. She was then sent away from Augsburg to Biberach for a change of scene. The only way in which she could ameliorate her father's despotic behavior was by vowing to forget what Bianconi had taught her.

In Biberach, while living with her paternal grandparents, she helped around the house and spent her leisure time reading and adjusting to the quiet life there. This acceptance is indicative of her flexibility. As long as she could turn to books for comfort, Sophie faced vicissitudes with equanimity. Learning was the one constant in her ever-changing life, and she hung on to it passionately. Through her reading, she developed a belief in the capacity of reason and virtue to provide happiness. Later, in her writings, she presented virtuous behavior as the ultimate guarantee for personal happiness. Through her friendship with her distant cousin Christoph Martin Wieland (1733–1813), she came to know more about literature and also began to feel an impetus to write. Wieland, who was a law student and had studied philosophy, was also searching for direction when he met the recently arrived Sophie in Biberach. Both found in the other a friend who could help ease their isolation. Wieland considered Sophie the embodiment of his ideal woman: she seemed to possess tenderness, sympathy, charm, intellect and beauty—qualities then highly valued. Sophie encouraged Wieland to express his feelings in poetry. She became his muse, while he became the only one who could speak to her soul. They poured out their thoughts and feelings in the letters they exchanged, and by now they were also engaged. Soon after, in 1752, Wieland left for Zurich, Switzerland, to study literature under the poet and literary critic J.J. Bodmer (1698–1783). Thereafter, the young man took little initiative in setting a marriage date, and Sophie was left to endure her father's constant inquiries about her matrimonial future. Neither her father, who thought that Wieland had no bright prospects, nor Wieland's mother, who could not imagine her son married to a worldly woman like Sophie, liked the idea of the marriage. Hence, the engagement was annulled by both parents. Even so, Christoph and Sophie remained friends and continued to help each other develop into mature writers.

Georg decided that she would marry Georg Michael La Roche (1720–1788), a respectable administrator and a liberal Catholic. After their marriage in 1753, the couple moved to Mainz, where Georg Michael served as private secretary to the first minister Count Anton Friedrich Heinrich von Stadion. Their life at court gave Sophie the opportunity to interact with the intellectuals of the city. She did not have to bother about mundane household chores and thus could devote her time to socializing. Her husband stayed in Count von Stadion's service for eight years while Sophie developed into an excellent hostess, entertaining the well-known figures of her day, including Johann Wolfgang Goethe. Georg Michael encouraged Sophie's interest in literature and philosophy, gave her a free hand in arranging social gatherings at their home, and, as a true believer in the ideals of the Enlightenment, made sure that Sophie kept informed of developments in music, painting, and English and French literature. Sophie realized that her marriage of convenience had in fact given her an independence that she had never known, and she would always appreciate Georg Michael for the freedom he gave her. When von Stadion retired in 1762, he moved to Warthausen near Biberach, and the La Roches settled there to be near him. Sophie continued offering her home as a meeting place for leading individuals of her day, while educating herself through books from Count von Stadion's library. Six years later, when Count von Stadion died, Georg Michael could no longer afford to maintain their comfortable lifestyle, and Sophie found herself alone and isolated. She resorted to corresponding with friends and acquaintances.

> *I still feel with my 68 years the great value of knowledge.*
>
> —**Sophie von La Roche**

While fulfilling her role as a woman of the court, La Roche had not forgotten that she was also a wife and a mother. She had given birth to eight children, only five of whom, however, survived infancy: **Maximiliane von La Roche Brentano** (b. 1756); Fritz (b. 1757); Luise (b. 1759); Carl (b. 1766) and Franz Wilhelm (b. 1768). When her two daughters were sent away to a convent in Strassbourg for schooling, Sophie became more lonely than ever, and she devoted her time to completing her first novel, *Die Geschichte des Fräuleins von Sternheim* (1771), which would be translated as *Memoirs of Miss Sophy Sternheim* (1776). Financial necessity was another incentive for her writing. Due to the La Roches' declining finances, their eldest son Fritz was also sent away for education in 1769 to study with Wieland.

Used to expressing her joys and frustrations in letters, La Roche dealt with the absence of her daughters by inventing a "paper maiden" in *Sternheim*. She created a fictional character whom she could bring up according to her own ideas. By presenting in her novel the necessity for women's education to make them independent and strong, Sophie indirectly gained legitimization for her writing. The profession of letters was then dominated by men. If a woman took up the pen, it was thought to be at the cost of her household duties. Hence only an overt proclamation of an altruistic purpose in her work could allow Sophie to continue her literary activities. The pedagogical aspect of *Sternheim* was successful in warding off any criticism of her "unfeminine" attempt to assume the public persona of a writer. Moreover, Wieland's introduction to the novel helped realize a positive reception by the critics. From the beginning, Wieland had encouraged Sophie to write this novel. During its ten-year gestation, he had made suggestions and corrections, supported her ideas and thus given her the confidence to keep working.

Sternheim's popularity was widespread. Its heroine Miss Sophie von Sternheim fascinated both male and female readers with her virtue, beauty, intelligence, independence, and sense of culture. Her moral uprightness, which proved to be a weapon against the corrupt men at court, gave middle-class readers a sense of superiority over the nobility. Those who appreciated such novels as Samuel Richardson's *Clarissa* or *Pamela* and J.J. Rousseau's *Émile* and *La nouvelle Héloïse* found *Sternheim* equally appealing. In addition, the novel's message was welcomed by upper-class and educated readers. Since this novel was in the form of letters written by three individuals, it presented its readers with different points of view, thereby giving the impression of an objective piece of work.

Sophie's second novel *Rosaliens Briefe an ihre Freundin Mariane von St.*** (*Rosalie's Letters to her Friend Mariane von St.***, 1780–81) was, like *Sternheim*, didactic in nature. But it was never as popular as *Sternheim*. With the advent of the Sturm-and-Drang (storm-and-stress) writers, like Goethe and Schiller, who advocated unrestrained love over self-imposed resignation, the literary climate changed. Sophie's *Letters* could not find an audience when Goethe's *The Sorrows of Young Werther* (1774) was the rage throughout Germany. Werther's self-destructive concept of love was completely at odds with Sternheim's reasonable love. Literary differences created personal discord between Goethe and Sophie. In addition, Werther's Lotte seemed to be based on Sophie's oldest daughter Maximiliane, for whom Goethe had expressed his admiration. All these factors brought about a complete break in Sophie and Goethe's relationship, though Sophie was able to renew her old friendship with Wieland and thus did not feel rejected by the literary establishment. Wieland would remain a source of support throughout her life.

The theme of women's education continued to preoccupy Sophie von La Roche. When she began her journal *Pomona für Teutschland's Töchter* in 1783, she became the first woman to publish an educational and literary monthly for women. In it, she never failed to emphasize the importance of learning alongside domestic virtues for women. *Pomona* included letters, poems, stories, essays and translations which celebrated the idea of women's education. Most of the contributions to the journal were written by Sophie herself, who had assumed the role of a maternal friend to her female readers. Her writing was also the family's only source of income after her husband lost his job at the conservative Trier court. It is not clear, however, as to why Sophie stopped publishing her journal after 1784. Either the pirated copies of her periodical robbed her of her subscribers, as she claimed, or she was making preparations to travel.

Her first trip was to Switzerland in 1784, followed by visits to France in 1785 and Holland and England in 1786. La Roche traveled on a minimum budget, either with a female friend or with one of her younger sons. As her husband continued to remain unwell after he lost his job, he stayed at home. During her journeys, Sophie recorded her keen observations in a diary and later published them in the form of travelogues. She wrote about the places and the people she visited, interspersing her observations with accounts of local history and economy. In Switzerland, she was charmed by her natural surroundings, whereas in France she admired the French culture and art. Dutch trade and industry brought out her appreciation for the hard-working people, while the beautiful English countryside, the political awareness of the English, and their economic well-being, made her admire most everything that was English. She described her social meetings with well-known personalities, including George III and Queen *Charlotte of Mecklenburg-Strelitz (1744–1818). Her writings about women in these countries illustrate her curiosity to learn about their differences and similarities to German women.

Traveling abroad gave La Roche an opportunity not only to learn about foreign lands and people but also to experience a sense of freedom. She could escape the demands of her household and family. In her writings, she acknowledges her gratitude to her husband for allowing her to travel. In her time, she was one of the few German women who had traveled extensively and who had met with so many important people. But she was unable to continue her travels for long. The deaths of her husband in 1788, her youngest son in 1791, and her daughter Maximiliane Brentano in 1793, robbed her of her enthusiasm to gather new experiences in foreign lands. In addition, her financial condition hardly permitted her to continue. The French occupation of the left shore of the river Rhein resulted in the cancellation of her widow's pension from the Trier court, and her literary neglect made matters worse. But once again she turned towards writing for solace and financial support.

From the letters she received from her oldest son Fritz and his wife, who were attempting to settle in America, Sophie created the basis of her next book *Erscheinungen am See Oneida* (Event at Lake Oneida, 1798). This German novel in an American setting tells of a French couple who settled near Lake Oneida in northern New York state. The book appealed to many readers who found the struggle of early settlers with nature fascinating. But Sophie's later books, such as *Schattenreise abgeschiedener Stunden in Offenbach, Weimar und Schönebeck im Jahr 1799* (Silhouettes of Departed Hours in Offenbach, Weimar and Schönebeck in the year 1799, 1799), *Mein Schreibtisch* (My Writing Desk, 1799), *Schönes Bild der Resignation* (Beautiful Image of Resignation, 1801), *Herbsttage* (Autumn Days, 1805), and *Melusines Sommerabende* (Melusine's Summer-Evenings, 1806), failed to gain a large readership. The younger generation did not respond to her ideas of arranged marriages, virtue and charity. La Roche's belief that a woman's place was ultimately within the home was rejected by the Romantics, who preferred (at least in their reading material) female companionship and intelligence resulting in the union of souls over the domestic virtues of a housewife.

Dejected by her pecuniary state, literary rejection and personal tragedies, Sophie von La Roche died in Offenbach in 1807. Nevertheless, her literary legacy was successfully passed on to her granddaughter *Bettine von Arnim, her daughter Maximiliane's daughter. Bettine continued her grandmother's literary endeavors by writing socially critical works in the epistolary genre.

SOURCES:

Blackwell, Jeannine. "Sophie von La Roche," in *German Writers in the Age of Goethe: Sturm und Drang to Classicism: Dictionary of Literary Biography*. Vol. 94. Edited by James Hardin and Christoph E. Schweitzer. Detroit, MI: Bruccoli, Clark and Layman, 1990, pp. 154–161.

Lange, Victor. "Visitors to Lake Oneida: An Account of the Background of Sophie von la Roche's Novel 'Erscheinungen am See Oneida'," in *Deutschlands literarisches Amerikabild*. Ed. by Alexander Ritter. NY: Georg Olms, 1977, pp. 92–122.

Mielke, Andreas. "Sophie La Roche: A Pioneering Novelist," in *Modern Language Studies*. Vol. 18, no. 1. Winter 1988, pp. 112–119.

Petschauer, Peter. "Sophie von Laroche, Novelist Between Reason and Emotion," in *Germanic Review*. Vol. 57, no. 2. Spring 1982, pp. 70–77.

Watt, Helga Schutte. "Woman's Progress: Sophie La Roche's Travelogues 1787–1788," in *Germanic Review*. Vol. 69, no. 2. Spring 1994, pp. 50–60.

SUGGESTED READING:

Lynn, James, ed. *The History of Lady Sophia Sternheim.* NY: New York UP, 1992.

COLLECTIONS:

Some of Sophie von La Roche's letters and manuscripts are at the Freies Deutsches Hochstift, Frankfurt am Main in Germany. Other collections can be found at the Deutsches Literaturarchiv Schiller Nationalmuseum, Marbach; the Stadtarchiv, Offenbach; the Wieland-Museum, Biberach; the Universitätsbibliothek, Freiburg; the Pfälzische Landesbibliothek, Speyer; the Zentralbibliothek, Zurich; the Hessisches Staatsarchiv, Darmstadt; the Stadtbibliothek Schaffhausen; and the Bayerische Staatsbibliothek, Munich.

Vibha Bakshi Gokhale,
author of *Walking the Tightrope: A Feminist Reading of Therese Huber's Stories* (Boston, Massachusetts)

La Rochefoucauld, Edmée, Duchesse de (1895–1991)

Catholic leader in the struggle to gain French women the right to vote, who was also a leading figure in the French literary establishment for more than 60 years.

Name variations: (pseudonym) Gilbert Mauge. Pronunciation: ed-MAY, doo-SHESS der lah-ROHSH-foo-COH. Born in Paris, France, on April 28, 1895; died in Paris on September 20, 1991, and was buried in the tomb of the family's château in Montmirail (Marne); daughter of Edmund, Comte de Fels, and Comtesse de Fels, who was a founder of the UNVF (Edmée's autobiography does not include the name of her mother nor the names of her children); privately educated; married Jean, Duc de La Rochefoucauld, on December 27, 1917; children: two sons, two daughters.

Married the heir to the La Rochefoucauld ducal title (1917); published her first book (1926); became an officer in the Union Nationale pour le Vote des Femmes (1927); was president of the UNVF (1930); reported on the Spanish Civil War (1938); became a member of the jury for the Prix Fémina (1944); published studies of Noailles, Fargue, Goll, and Valéry (1950s); assisted her brother André de Fels, publisher of the Revue de Paris (1961–70); elected to the Belgian Royal Academy of the French Language and Literature (1962); published a guide to the Cahiers of Paul Valéry (1964–66); failed to be elected to the Académie Française (1983); published her last book, at age 94 (1989).

Principal writings—all published in Paris unless noted: Fonction de X (Éditions du Sagittaire, 1926); Nombres (Émile-Paul, 1926); Merveille de la mort (Kra, 1927); Faust et Marguerites (Émile-Paul, 1927); The Unknown Quantity (London: The Fortune Press, 1928); La Vie humaine (Émile-Paul, 1928); Le Voyage de l'esprit (Sagittaire, 1931); Le Même et l'autre (Sagittaire, 1932); Spanish Women (NY: Peninsular News Service, 1938); La Femme et ses droits (Flammarion, 1939); Les Moralistes de l'intelligence (Hermann, 1945); La Vie commode aux peuples (Sagittaire, 1947); Chasse cette vivante (Sagittarie, 1948); Images de Paul Valéry (F.-X. Le Roux, 1949); Vus d'un autre monde (Gallimard, 1950); Le Soleil, la lune, les étoiles (Odilis, 1951); Plus loin que Bételgeuse (Odilis, 1952); Paul Valéry (Éditions universitaires, 1954); Choix de poèmes (Gallimard, 1955); Le dernier quart d'heure de Marcel Achard, Louis Amade, et al. *(La Table Ronde, 1955);* Anna de Noailles *(Éditions universitaries, 1956);* Pluralité de l'être *(Gallimard, 1957);* Léon-Paul Fargue *(Éditions universitaires, 1958);* Hommage à Jean de Pange, l'historien, le français, le chrétien *(B. Grasset, 1959);* Menton *(Hachette, 1962);* En lisant les cahiers de Paul Valéry *(Éditions universitaires, 1964–66);* La Nature et l'esprit *(Plon, 1965);* Claire Goll *(P. Seghers, 1967);* Femmes dramaturges *(Brussels: Palais des Académies, 1968);* Femmes d'hier et d'aujourd'hui *(B. Grasset, 1969);* Courts Métrages *(B. Grasset, 1970);* Spectateurs *(B. Grasset, 1972);* L'Angoise et les écrivains *(B. Grasset, 1974);* De l'ennui *(B. Grasset, 1976);* L'Acquiescement *(B. Grasset, 1978);* À l'ombre de Marcel Proust *(A.G. Nizet, 1980);* Courts Métrages II *(B. Grasset, 1980);* Flashes *(B. Grasset, 1982);* Flashes II *(B. Grasset, 1984);* Flashes III *(B. Grasset, 1989).*

Edmée, youngest of the two sons and two daughters of Edmund, Comte de Fels, was born to wealth and in due course married the scion of a family whose name had graced the rolls of the highest French nobility since long before the Crusades. If she had done no more than bear an heir and play Lady Bountiful for some high-toned charities, nobody would have expected more. Instead, she became a leader in the struggle for women's rights and made herself into a prominent figure in the French literary world, not a very forgiving environment. To the last days of her long life, she was a formidable personage, accomplished, highly intellectual, and, it seems, well-turned-out; as she wrote in her 90s, "[For a woman] to remain elegant despite her feelings of laziness and fatigue, doesn't this appear to be meritorious?"

Edmée's father was a diplomat for a time, notably as vice-resident at Tunis (then, the capital of the French protectorate of Tunisia), and for many years director of the prominent arts magazine *La Revue de Paris.* His father had been a Luxemburger who converted to Protestantism, moved to Denmark, and become a shipowner *(armateur).* Edmund was born in France and was converted back to Catholicism by the Abbé de Broglie. He was not an ardent Catholic, but he was generous to the Catholic Institute of Paris and founder of its library, named for him. He was a friend of a claimant to the throne, Louis Philippe Robert, Duc d'Orléans ("Philippe VIII"), and a contributor to *L'Oeuvre* during the First World War.

Edmée's maternal grandfather was a banker and industrialist who had loaned money to Ferdinand de Lesseps to build the Suez Canal. His daughter, Edmée's mother, the Comtesse de Fels, was cultured and a devout Catholic, an avid reader of writings by the mystics, although Edmée noted that she kept novels by *Colette in her bedside table. She had been brought up strictly and was rather austere. Edmée experienced pangs of jealousy seeing her mother dandle deprived children on her knees and kiss them, things she did not do to her own.

An 18th-century country château in the Beauce region southwest of Paris, pulled down and rebuilt during her childhood, was young Edmée's home much of the time. She loved gardens but not the country, preferring the townhouse in the Faubourg Saint-Honoré in Paris or the seaside at Deauville. Her father did not believe girls needed a high education, and consequently she felt frustrated. It was only after her marriage in 1917 that she took private lessons in Latin and mathematics. Still, her father favored good reading, being a devotée of the diarist Saint-Simon, and discussed Kant and Fichte and others with her. She learned the piano and painting, in later life taking lessons from Lucien Lévy-Dhurmer (1865–1953) and becoming a respected portraitist. Watched over by English and German nannies, she, like her mother, received a strict Catholic upbringing, but in the liberal Catholic tradition. She remained devout for life but not at all closed-minded. Religious bigotry was foreign to her.

As with most families in France, the Great War of 1914–18 took a toll. She lost a brother (an aviator) in 1916 and a suitor. On December 27, 1917, she married Jean, future **Duc de La Rochefoucauld,** who was, like her late brother, an aviator. After the war they settled into an affectionate if uninteresting life—"Each felt himself to be in a limited world"—during which she gave birth to two sons and two daughters. Certainly she experienced no grief at the hands of her mother-in-law, whom she later described as a humble, kind, very religious, and charitable woman who, despite her high status, did not own an automobile and traveled about Paris to her charities by tram or subway.

Edmée La Rochefoucauld became active in the feminist cause in December 1927, when she agreed to be vice-president of the Union Nationale pour le Vote des Femmes (UNVF), the principal Catholic women's rights organization. Several influences propelled her in this direction. Her mother, the Comtesse de Fels, had been a founder of the UNVF in 1920 and was on its central committee, and Edmée had heard Charles Loiseau speak "brilliantly" on feminism at her parents' home. She had numerous important political connections. Her father and later her brother André were directors of the *Revue de Paris,* and through André, a deputy in Parliament, she had links to the Paris press and the Alliance Démocratique (with the Fédération Républicaine, one of the two most important moderate-conservative political parties), of which he was vice-president; as well, her father-in-law was prominent in her uncle Jacques Piou's Action Libérale Populaire, the principal Catholic republican party, while her husband was its president. To all this might be added a lingering resentment over her early lack of education because she was a girl, writes **Christine Bard**, "a feeling of injustice since infancy, and a precociously critical mind which pierced the hypocrisy and contradictions of adults. . . . From the young girl who at age 15 taught the catechism to peasants to the suffragist evangelizing crowds of women there is a continuity which preserves the role devolving upon the male and female elites."

The UNVF's leaders were liberal Catholics running a Catholic version of the secularist Union Française pour le Suffrage des Femmes. Unlike the latter, it heavily emphasized the family and established hierarchies. Consequently, it differed with other feminists over Civil Code reforms. It experienced its own internal stresses over church-state relations and education and over the "family vote" projects often favored by conservatives which, for example, would give fathers more votes in proportion to the number of their children. It officially opposed *vote familiel* schemes or any others whereby women would not vote on the same basis as men, saying such matters should be taken up only after women received the vote.

La Rochefoucauld entered the UNVF during a crisis in 1926–27 which resulted in the founding by **Aimée Bazy** of a split-off organization, the Féderation Nationale des Femmes. The FNF was more *familiel* and, unlike the officially apolitical UNVF, politically oriented—although the UNVF sometimes gave electoral advice to voters. Bazy asked La Rochefoucauld to take the presidency of the FNF, but she politely declined. Instead, she accepted the call of the UNVF's president and co-founder, **Mme Levert-Chotard**, to be vice-president and take charge of the organization's first regular publication, a monthly, the *Union Nationale des Femmes: Défense des intérêts féminins, familiaux et professionels.*

La Rochefoucauld advanced rapidly, becoming secretary-general and in December 1930 president, succeeding Levert-Chotard. The UNVF became a more dynamic organization under her impulsion, attracting many enthusiastic young women, founding chapters in every département, and by 1939 boasting a membership of 100,000—an impressive number in a country not famous for high numbers of "joiners." She was aided by a coterie of highly capable women, including **Marie-Thérèse Moreau**, an attorney who gave technical advice and became secretary-general in 1930, **Henriette Chandé**, of *Paris Match*, **Muriel Brunhas-Delamarre**, **Suzanne Desternes**, and **Agathe Rouart-Valéry**, daughter of the poet Paul Válery, who himself wrote and spoke for the UNVF.

> *Future generations will never know the efforts and persistence that were required of the women who led the feminist movement.*
>
> —Suzanne Grinberg and Odette Simon-Bidaux, 1938

La Rochefoucauld strongly believed that if women were to win the vote, they must become educated in public affairs, show they could speak knowledgeably in public, and build an organization. The UNVF was more concerned with doing things than making a noise. Its methods were entirely peaceful, even sedate, but she recalled that she nevertheless reaped much acid criticism, notably in the press. The educative role—a tradition in the Catholic women's movement—was wide-ranging, with lectures and congresses devoted to the functioning of Parliament and the State, the State budget, urbanism, municipal government and finance, the national economy, professional training, etc. The UNVF also involved itself in public health, the rights of working women, and reform of the Civil Code. The object was to teach women how to vote and why, indeed, they should.

In the struggle in the late 1930s to reform the Code, the UNVF differed from secular feminists by a willingness to retain (with some revisions) the husband's role as "head" (*chef*) of the "natural hierarchy" of the family. To that extent some have questioned whether the UNVF was truly feminist, since it did not challenge all gender-defined roles. However that may be, in extreme old age La Rochefoucauld once defined feminism as "conquest of a part of the rights which men little by little have been led to accord one another." Earlier, in 1939, she had written that "the first and natural function of women is maternity." Unlike some other Catholic conservatives, however, she favored opening as many vocations to women as possible and even encouraging them to work if they wished—providing, of course, their jobs were not incompatible with women's "first and natural function." And, unlike many thoroughly egalitarian feminists, she favored legislation giving women special protections in the workplace. It is worth noting that in old age she observed, "It is the physical power of the man which has rendered the woman a slave despite her intelligence. And this for millenia." In short, she had no trouble in asserting that the "chiefs" of the "natural hierarchy" had egregiously abused their power, physical and legal.

The Chamber of Deputies voted for women's suffrage in 1919, 1932, 1935, and 1936, but the Senate refused to budge. Catholic leaders and laity, like most of French society, disagreed over the issue. Significantly, no Cabinet or party made it a priority. The Second World War changed minds. To La Rochefoucauld's fervent praise, Charles de Gaulle, as head of France's provisional government after the war, simply granted women the vote in 1944; they cast their first ballots in 1945. At her death in 1991, Edmée de la Rochefoucauld would be the last survivor of those who had led the fight for female suffrage to victory.

After the war, the UNVF became the Union Nationale des Électrices. La Rochefoucauld continued to write for its small monthly until 1964, when she gave it up. Since 1961, she had helped her brother André at the *Revue de Paris,* and she continued until it ceased publication in 1970. For a time after 1945, she also made a bid for a political career with the Republican Party of Liberty (PRL), which soon folded into de Gaulle's Assembly of the French People (RPF). She became a Gaullist municipal councillor in Montmirail (Marne), the family seat. When a place became vacant in Parliament for that district, she was planning to run when Jean Taittinger persuaded her to withdraw, opening the way to him for a brilliant career. Sexual and class prejudices against her certainly contributed to frustrating such political ambitions as she had. The same may have been the case when she failed (by one vote) to gain election to the Académie des Sciences morales et politiques. She had addressed it in 1938 on women's suffrage and on April 21, 1952, on seeking (with Hitler's example in mind) to install in international law a right of peoples to resist oppression and the waging of wars of aggression by their rulers.

As her political activity gradually faded after the war, she turned to what was her first love and most lasting interest: literature. Her

mother had called her a "'philosophe' the girl who had read Bergson." Her first books, timidly offered under the pseudonym Gilbert Mauge, were a surrealistic story, *Fonction de X* (1926), and some poems in *Nombres* (1926). Under her own name came a story, *Merveille de la mort* (1927), a pseudo-gothic tale, *Faust et Marguerites* (1927), and her only novel, *La Vie humaine* (1928). They were written in a "rather dense" style, she noted in her memoirs, which she abandoned when she turned thereafter to biography, criticism, poetry, essays on science (mathematics, astronomy, biology), philosophical and religious musings, and observations about her times and acquaintances. In short, she had found herself "caught in the literary gears," and after 1945 two years seldom passed without a book or two until her last, published at age 94.

To mention only a few, there were biographies of poets ***Anna de Noailles** (1876–1933), Léon-Paul Fargue (1876–1947), ***Claire Goll** (1891–1977), and Paul Valéry (1871–1945); observations in *Pluralité de l'être* (1957) and *Spectateurs* (1972); "encounters" with writers in *Courts Métrages* I, II (1970, 1980); a report on a visit to Spain in 1938 during the Civil War, translated as *Spanish Women* (1938), which the Loyalist government used for propaganda purposes; and *Femmes d'hier at d'aujourd'hui* (1966), a defense of celebrated women. Her last works were three volumes of *Flashes* (1982, 1984, 1989), an odd title for what she termed "pseudo-memoirs by fits and starts." Indeed, only the first contains some bits of autobiography, the remainder being short pieces or snippets on many subjects in a style reminiscent of Blaise Pascal's *Pensées.* Beyond doubt, her most lasting contribution was her indispensable three-volume commentary, *En lisant les cahiers de Paul Valéry* (1964–66), on her great friend's 29 volumes of notes and thoughts.

When not at her writing table, she painted portraits—notably of Valéry, André Maurois, Francesco Garcia Calderon, and Marshal Franchet d'Espérey—entertained writers such as Maurois, Jules Romains, Paul Morand, Noailles, Fargue, and especially Valéry from the 1920s on, gave dinners (entitled "Cells, Atoms, Stars") for scientific and literary luminaries, and lectured in Europe, South America, the United States, Canada, and French-speaking Africa. From 1944 until her death, she was a member of the jury for the prestigious Prix Fémina, noted for voting for works she loved and not for writers whose "turn" it was. She was made a commander in the Legion of Honor and, in 1962, a member of the Belgian Royal Academy of the French Language and Literature. In 1983, however, she failed election to the Académie Française.

Also in 1983, a reporter from the Manchester *Guardian* visited this incisive critic and astute observer of her time. He found her, at age 88, a "regal" personage, firm of step, living with a butler-chauffeur and "doom-faced" Spanish housekeeper in an "echoing" mansion in the fashionable Passy quarter. She was cordial, insisting upon sharing a new bottle of wine, but he found her "in a most courteous way overbearing of mind." When asked if rumored deals with publishers and cabals had a bearing on who won prizes, she answered "imperturbably, 'I am outside all that. *Voilà mon sentiment.*'" The reporter departed duly impressed by this *grande dame* from another age: "It was Sunset Boulevard—but with little sign of the sun setting."

SOURCES:

Bard, Christine. *Les Filles de Marianne: Les Féminismes, 1914–1940.* Paris: Fayard, 1995.

La Rochefoucauld, Edmée de. *En lisant les cahiers de Paul Valéry.* Paris: Éditions universitaires, 1964–66.

———. *La Femme et ses droits.* Paris: Flammarion, 1939.

———. *Flashes.* 3 vols. Paris: B. Grasset, 1982–89.

McMillan, James F. "Clericals, Anti-Clericals and the Women's Movement in France under the Third Republic," in *The Historical Journal.* Vol. 24, no. 2, 1981, pp. 361–376.

Obituaries: *Chicago Tribune,* Sept. 23, 1991; *The Guardian* (Manchester), Sept. 27, 1991; *Le Monde* (Paris), Sept. 23, 1991.

Rabaut, Jean. *Histoire des féminismes français.* Paris: Éditions Stock, 1978.

Smith, Paul. *Feminism and the Third Republic.* Oxford: The Clarendon Press, 1996.

SUGGESTED READING:

Brée, Germaine. *Twentieth Century French Literature.* Chicago, IL: University of Chicago Press, 1983.

Desternes, Suzanne. *Trente ans d'efforts au service de la cause féminine.* Paris: R. Laffont, 1959.

Duchen, Claire. *Women's Rights and Women's Lives in France, 1944–1968.* NY: Routledge, 1994.

Grinberg, Suzanne, and Odette Simon-Bidaux. *Les Droits nouveaux de la femme mariée.* Paris: Librairie du Receuil Sirey, 1938.

Irvine, William D. *French Conservatism in Crisis: The Republican Federation of France in the 1930s.* Baton Rouge, LA: Louisiana State University Press, 1979.

Klejman, Laurence, and Florence Rochefort. *L'Égalité en marche: Le Féminisme sous la Troisième République.* Paris: Presses de la Fondation nationale des sciences politiques, 1989.

Paul, Harry W. *The Second Ralliement: The Rapprochement between Church and State in France in the Twentieth Century.* Washington, DC: The Catholic University of America Press, 1967.

Weiss, Louise. *Mémoires d'une européenne.* Vol. 3: *Combat pour les femmes, 1934–1939.* Paris: A. Michel, 1978.

Wright, Gordon. *France in Modern Times: From the Enlightenment to the Present.* 5th ed. NY: W.W. Norton, 1995.

COLLECTIONS:

Paris: Bibliothèque Marguerite Durand.

David S. Newhall,
Professor Emeritus of History,
Centre College, Danville, Kentucky

La Rochejacquelein, Marie Louise Victoire, marquise de (1772–1857)

French royalist and author of Mémoires. *Name variations: LaRochejaquelein; Marquise de La Rochejacquelein. Born Marie Louise Victoire de Donissan or de Donnisson in Versailles, France, on October 25, 1772; died at Orléans, France, on February 15, 1857; married Louis du Vergier or Verger, marquis de La Rochejacquelein (1777–1815).*

Marie Louise Victoire, marquise de La Rochejacquelein, was a royalist and second wife of Louis du Vergier, marquis de La Rochejacquelein, the French Vendean leader who was killed in battle at Pontdes-Mathis, near St.-Gilles, France, on June 4, 1815. Her brother-in-law, Henri du Vergier, comte de La Rochejacquelein, had also been killed in battle at Nouaille, in March 1794. Mme La Rochejacquelein published her *Mémoires* of the Napoleonic Wars in 1815.

Larrieu, Francie (1952—)

American runner. Name variations: Francie Larrieu Smith. Born Francie Larrieu on November 23, 1952, in the San Francisco Bay area; sixth in a family of nine children; sister of Ron Larrieu, an Olympian 10,000 meter runner; attended the University of California, Los Angeles; married second husband Jimmy Smith (an exercise physiologist).

Once considered the greatest middle-distance runner in American history, Larrieu broke world records in the mile, 2 miles, 100, 1,500, and 3,000 meters.

Francie Larrieu read about track events on the back of a Wheaties box and set out to compete in the Junior Olympics. She was 13 when she entered her first meet in Santa Clara, California. But she failed to make the start in the 220-yard dash, because she was not certain it was an actual race. Instead, her furious coach entered her in the 660, which she won hands down.

In 1969, Larrieu qualified for her first U.S. track team. She was thought to be an incredible runner, but her stamina seemed to wane, and she was often sick. So she dropped out of competition until 1972, when her coach, Augie Argabright, persuaded her to run a 2½ mile race. Finishing ahead of some of the best long-distance runners in the nation convinced Larrieu she should return to the sport. She began running 100 miles a week and made her first Olympic team in 1972, the youngest member of the track-and-field squad. Awestruck, however, she failed to make the finals.

In 1975, at the Toronto Star-Maple Leafs Indoor Games, she won the 1,500 meter race and broke the world record. Not long after, Larrieu set another world record in the mile at 4:29 and broke her record in the 1,500 meter with a time of 4:09.8. A few weeks later at the U.S.-USSR indoor meet, Larrieu set a time of 4:28.5. She broke records in the mile, 2 mile, 100, 1,500 and 3,000 meters.

But the Olympic medal she had long sought eluded her. In 1976, a case of the flu put her on the Olympic sidelines; the 1980 political boycott did the same. But Francie Larrieu continued to set records throughout Europe, won 22 national championships, and set 17 outdoor American track records. After failing to make the 1984 Olympic team, she added a new coach, Robert Vaughan. Four years later, at age 36, she took part in the 1988 Olympics, finishing 5th in the 10,000 meters. Remarkably, Larrieu later increased her times at the 10,000, setting a new American record of 31:28.9 at the 1991 Texas Relays. Winning an Olympic medal had been the carrot throughout most of Larrieu's career. "But along the road," noted the 40-year-old competitor, "I just fell in love with running."

SOURCES:

Hollander, Phyllis. *100 Greatest Women in Sports.* NY: Grosset & Dunlap, 1976.

Jacobs, Helen Hull. *Famous Modern American Women Athletes.* NY: Dodd, Mead, 1975.

Karin L. Haag,
freelance writer, Athens, Georgia

Larrocha, Alicia de (1923—)

Spanish composer, one of the greatest pianists of the second half of the 20th century, and the most famous pianist in Spain and the Hispanic world. Name variations: Alicia de la Rocha. Born Alicia de Larrocha y de la Calle in Barcelona, Spain, on May 23, 1923; daughter of Eduardo de Larrocha and Maria Teresa de la Calle; studied with Frank Marshall (1883–1959) at the Granados Academy; married Juan Torra, on June 21, 1950; children: Juan Francisco and Alicia.

Began to study piano at Academia Marshall at age three; gave first public performance (1929); played with Madrid Symphony, age 11 (1934); made first international tour (1947); played in U.S.

(1954–55); awarded Grand Prix du Disque (1960); awarded Paderewski Medal (1961); performed in New York to great critical acclaim (1965); named Musical America's Musician of the Year (1977); awarded Deutscher Schallplatten Prize (1979); won the Spanish Order of Civil Merit and the Harriet Cohen Medal; became known for her incisive and unique interpretation of the classical piano repertoire.

When her aunt closed and locked the piano, her favorite plaything, three-year-old Alicia screamed in frustration. "I put my head on the floor and banged it," she recounted years later. "I was in a real temper, and I did it so hard that blood began to flow out." In face of the child's determination to play, her mother took Alicia to the nearby Academia Marshall, where Frank Marshall agreed to accept the young prodigy as a student. Thus began the training of Alicia de Larrocha, the celebrated musician who earned a place among the elite pianists of the 20th century.

Born on May 23, 1923, to Eduardo de Larrocha and **Maria Teresa de la Calle** in Barcelona, Spain, Alicia de Larrocha was surrounded by music. Her mother was an accomplished pianist and former student of Enrique Granados. Alicia's aunt taught at the Academia which Granados founded in 1909 and which his favorite student, Frank Marshall, directed following the master's tragic death in 1916. At age five, Alicia gave her first public performance. After several concerts in Barcelona over the next six years, she played a Mozart concerto with the Madrid Symphony Orchestra, conducted by Fernández Arbos. Meanwhile, her family and conservatory connections helped acquaint Alicia with the leading figures of Spanish music. She also met great virtuosos such as Artur Rubinstein when they played in Barcelona and visited the Academia.

The 1930s were, however, a time of travail for Spain, culminating in the Civil War of 1936–39. The young pianist found her life disrupted in many ways. Barcelona was a Republican center of resistance to Francisco Franco's ultimately victorious Nationalist forces. Fearing that the Loyalists would kill him in the anarchy that enveloped Barcelona, Marshall fled the country. So did many of the Barcelona artistic community, and Larrocha found herself on her own. Remembering the final days of the war, she recalled: "We had no food in the last six months; it was a tragedy. My father went to the mountains to get greens to eat because we had no wood, no bread, no oil."

Despite such interruptions, music had become "my life, though I confess I never thought

about giving concerts or making music my career. I just wanted music to be as much a part of my physiology as the heart, lungs, and other vital organs were. Music fulfilled a need, a craving, and that was it." She learned quickly and easily, often a piece in a single day. Yet Larrocha truly wanted to be an operatic or *lieder* singer. On the eve of the war, she had thrown herself into practice, only to find it caused polyps on her vocal cords. Nonetheless, she continued serious vocal training as late as 1950. Her music was not work but fun to her, and she had few professional ambitions. Spaniards considered music an avocation for enjoyment, and her mother had given up her musical career when she married. In fact, her mother sometimes worried that Alicia spent too much time at the piano, that she was missing life. But her parents still gave her freedom to play if and when she chose.

At the end of the war, Frank Marshall returned to Barcelona, and Larrocha resumed her studies with him. During the 1940s, she played occasional concerts in Spain, the Canary Islands, and Spanish Morocco but did not actively seek engagements. Her first foray north of the Pyrenees came in 1947, when she played in Paris, Geneva, Lausanne, London, Edinburgh, and Brussels. Three years later, she married pianist and teacher Juan Torra.

In 1954, conductor Alfred Wallenstein, who had heard Larrocha in Europe, invited her to perform with the Los Angeles Philharmonic Orchestra. That trip also afforded the opportunity to play with the San Francisco Symphony, under the baton of Enrique Jordá, and some Barcelona friends arranged her New York debut at Town Hall in 1955. These excursions brought her generally favorable reviews, but only in 1965 did she return to the United States. During the intervening decade, she had two children (Juan Francisco and Alicia), continued to tour Europe, made occasional records for Decca, taught at the Academia, and became its director when Marshall died in 1959. Her recording of Isaac Albéniz's *Iberia* for Columbia won the Grand Prix du Disque in 1960. A year later in London, she received the Paderewski Medal for pianists. Nevertheless, Larrocha mounted no publicity campaign to promote her career and did not pursue American concerts. "I didn't mind," she remarked. "I wasn't ambitious."

Then, in 1965, Herbert Breslin, a New York promoter, wrote to inquire about her interest in playing in the United States, even though he had only heard her records. Larrocha's husband feared that Breslin wanted them to advance him money for a promotional campaign, and the couple did not respond to the letter. But Breslin was so enthused about her artistry that he persisted, offering her several concerts with the New York Philharmonic Orchestra, which she accepted. Thus, at age 42, her career began its meteoric rise. To rave reviews, she played four times with the Philharmonic and gave a recital at Hunter College, the latter attended by Artur Rubinstein, Claudio Arrau, and *Ania Dorfmann. They listened to selections from *Iberia* by Albéniz and from *Goyescas* by Granados, plus sonatas by

Soler and Schubert, and Bach's *English Suite No. 2.* The New York Times' music critic Harold C. Schonberg reported that her performance was "pianistically flawless, with infallible fingers, brilliant sonorities, steady rhythm, everything." Larrocha had put the lie to the impression that she had little more than a Spanish repertoire. By the end of the year, following the death in 1965 of Dame *Myra Hess, critics and public acclaimed her the reigning female pianist.

Certainly Larrocha never considered herself a Spanish specialist nor restricted herself to any particular period, though her interest and study never went beyond Prokofiev. "In my choice of composers, I enjoy going from one to the other," she said. "I suppose I might be called a free spirit in this regard. I totally believe that in every period there are new moods, new idioms, and peoples are searching for new systems." Larrocha's training under Marshall had first emphasized Mozart, Bach, and the other great European composers. Such repertoire was essential before she began playing Spanish music.

Once she had built a foundation on those masters, Marshall had helped her dominate the great Spanish composers. By then, she was 17. Through him, wrote *New York Times* critic Donal Henahan in 1976, "she came to clairvoyant understanding of the music of Granados, Falla and Albéniz, the trinity of Spanish music." Larrocha understood that her nation's music required special techniques to display its color and rhythm. "Both Albéniz and Falla took the guitar as their instrumental model," she noted. "And this style has something to do with the same qualities that our great flamenco dancers have— it is the sense of excitement held tightly under control. There is no hysteria or flamboyance. . . . With this comes the quality of seduction, a certain arrogance or haughtiness."

The piano presented special challenges to Larrocha. At 4'9", she was tiny. "She is so short and so small," wrote Rickenbacker, "that her elbow hardly reaches the top of the woodwork of a concert grand, even when she wears high heels. In order to get both hands into the upper reaches of the keyboard she has to turn her body to the audience and stretch her arms straight out." Her small hands and short fingers required constant exercise to stretch beyond a nine-key span, whereas almost all concert pianists could easily span at least ten keys. Marshall developed exercises especially for her. While Larrocha never dreamed of longer fingers, she wished for a broader span: "I am always doing Chopin études, always stretching. The hands are my obsession."

Perhaps in part because of her small hands, she carefully worked out the fingering of new pieces, adjusting it to fit her physical limitations and to make certain that the necessary finger was available for the desired tone. "For me," she explained, "the fingering is very important. I may decide on using a certain finger to produce a particular tone, but if it doesn't work, then I have to change the fingering accordingly. That's why I don't advocate practicing away from the piano as some pianists do; a decision on fingering may not be practical at the concert hall, and by that time it's a little late to change."

Perhaps her small size endeared her to audiences. Certainly Larrocha made no appeal to them through flamboyant behavior. Entering the stage on a typical evening, she acknowledged the audience with a smile and immediately sat at the keyboard, ready to begin. But her calm exuded controlled emotion, similar to the Spanish music for which she was so famous. Her sedate and self-effacing public persona belied a naturally pessimistic and moody inner self. She refused to be swept up by the public adulation, particularly in the U.S., because she feared that it might stop as quickly as it started. She disliked listening to her own recordings: "I am so moody that what pleases me today may seem intolerable tomorrow." Yet such emotions made travel attractive, as it brought new faces and locations.

At the height of her touring between 1965 and 1980, she usually played between 100 and 125 engagements per year. This included several months in the States and a few concerts in Latin America before she returned to Europe. Usually, she traveled alone, practicing whenever possible. Her manager arranged for a piano in her hotel room. To avoid disturbing other guests, she used a mute on the strings. When possible, she practiced at the Steinway headquarters in New York or Hamburg. In Barcelona, she played a pre-Civil War Bechstein, perfectly suited to her.

For Larrocha, playing with so many different conductors and orchestras sometimes interfered with the full expression of her artistry. She often had only two or three days to practice with an orchestra. Through intuitive sensitivity, great conductors adapted to her genius; with good conductors, she had less flexibility. Her travels also brought occasional master classes with aspiring pianists. Larrocha gave few of them because she considered them useless; in a single class, she felt she could not know the students or really help them understand her.

The passing years brought new honors. For a decade, she played annually at New York's Mostly Mozart Festival, the only musician to be such a constant presence. So great was her popularity in New York that she could easily sell out a stand of six or seven concerts. Particularly moving to Larrocha was her reception by an ecstatic audience in Barcelona in 1971. She had not performed publicly in her native city for seven years, and when she entered to play Chopin's Second Concerto, the crowd gave her an ovation before she played, something extremely rare in Spain. In 1977, *Musical America,* the classical-music monthly, named her its musician of the year and cited her command of the Spanish repertoire and her mastery of the classical keyboard. Two years later, she played all five of Beethoven's piano concertos with André Previn and the Pittsburgh Symphony. That year, she also received the German Schallplatten Prize.

Despite her accomplishments, Larrocha remained surprisingly unaffected by her fame. As a private student, she had never participated in piano competitions, and that, Larrocha believed, made her less concerned with glory and wealth. Her real competition was with herself, to grow as a musician. More and more, she found her chief joy not in the applause of public performance but in the satisfaction of learning more about music and looking for something new in her own artistic abilities. She became a great pianist, in part, because she used her initial fame as an opportunity to expand her repertoire and to develop further as an artist.

Neither was she especially concerned about her rank among other pianists. Some critics such as Harold Schonberg saw her as an outstanding female pianist, but her virtuosity eventually made gender-based evaluations irrelevant. Unsurpassed in her renditions of complex, precise, delicate music, she also demonstrated artistic mastery of powerful, stormy pieces by Beethoven and Schubert. As Henahan of *The New York Times* observed: "Manly virility can become as great a bore in music as too much delicacy and poetic introspection. The 'greatest' pianists, no matter their sex, combine these and a universe of other qualities in their playing." To which he added, "There are, let us face it, few male pianists who play as strongly, let alone as fluently and accurately as de Larrocha." According to William Livingstone, in *Stereo Review* (1980), "the most outstanding characteristics of her playing are the unshakable rhythmic underpinning of all her interpretations and her uncanny ability to find a dance-like quality in whatever music she plays." Of the woman who gave Spanish piano music its international standing, *Newsweek*'s Hubert Saal wrote in 1972: "Today, mentioning her in the same breath with Rubinstein or Horowitz raises no eyebrows."

SOURCES:

Henahan, Donal. "It Skirts the Question to Call Her the Great 'Woman' Pianist," in *The New York Times.* July 21, 1974, D13.

———. "They're Mad about Alicia," in *The New York Times Magazine.* July 18, 1976, pp. 13–16.

Jacobson, Robert. "A Day with de Larrocha," in *Saturday Review.* October 30, 1971, pp. 68–69, 82.

Livingstone, William. "Alicia de Larrocha," in *Stereo Review.* Vol. 44, 1980, pp. 78–80.

Mash, Elyse. *Great Pianists Speak for Themselves.* NY: Dodd, Mead, 1980.

SUGGESTED READING:

Marcus, Adele. *Great Pianists Speak with Adele Marcus.* Neptune, NJ: Paganiniana, 1979.

Kendall W. Brown,
Professor of History, Brigham Young University, Provo, Utah

Larsen, Nella (1891–1964)

Award-winning novelist of the Harlem Renaissance, whose fiction exploring themes of gender, race, class, and sexuality heralded the later work of African-American women writers. Name variations: Nellie Larson; Nella Imes; Nellie Walker; (pseudonym) Allen Semi. Pronunciation: LAHR-suhn. Born Nellie Walker on April 13, 1891 (not 1893 as she later claimed) in Chicago, Illinois; died in her Manhattan apartment a few days before her body was found on March 30, 1964; daughter of Peter Walker, a cook and laborer, or Peter Larson or Larsen, a railway conductor (the two men might be one and the same), and Mary Hanson Walker Larson or Larsen (a seamstress); attended six years of public schooling; attended Fisk University, one academic year, 1907–08; Lincoln Hospital and Home Training School for Nurses, New York, diploma, 1915; Library School of the New York Public Library, certificate, 1923; married Elmer Samuel Imes, on May 3, 1919 (divorced 1933); no children.

Had two short pieces published in the Brownies' Book *(1920); worked as a library assistant, New York Public Library 135th Street Branch (1922); was a librarian at the 135th Street Branch (1923–26); published first two short stories (1926); published first novel,* Quicksand *(1928); published second novel,* Passing *(1929); awarded bronze medal, Harmon Foundation (1929); was first African-American woman recipient of Guggenheim Fellowship for creative writing (1930); traveled through Spain and France (1930–31); worked as a nurse, Gouverneur Hospital (1944–61); worked as a nurse, Metropolitan Hospital (1961–64).*

Publications: "Playtime: Three Scandinavian Games" and "Playtime: Danish Fun," in Brownies' Book *(Vol. 1, June 1920, pp. 191–192, 219); review of* Certain People of Importance *by Kathleen Norris, in* Messenger *(May 1923, p. 713); (under pseudonym Allen Semi) "The Wrong Man" in* Young's Realistic Stories Magazine *(January 1926, pp. 243–246); (under pseudonym Allen Semi) "Freedom," in* Young's Realistic Stories Magazine *(April 1926, pp. 241–243); "Correspondence," in* Opportunity *(September 1926, p. 295);* Quicksand *(NY: Alfred A. Knopf, 1928); review of* Black Sadie *by T. Bowyer Campbell, in* Opportunity *(January 1929, p. 24);* Passing *(NY: Alfred A. Knopf, 1929); "Moving Mosaic or N.A.A.C.P. Dance, 1929," excerpt from* Quicksand, *in* All-Star Benefit Concert for the National Association for the Advancement of Colored People, *Forrest Theater, New York, program booklet (December 8, 1929); "Sanctuary," in* Forum *(January 1930, pp. 15–18); "The Author's Explanation," in* Forum *(Supplement 4, April 1930, pp. xli–xlii).*

By 1920, the formerly white area of Harlem, occupying less than two square miles in New York City, had become home to about 200,000 black people. With the heroic service of African-Americans during the recently ended World War I still fresh on their minds, Harlem's residents vowed to continue the fight for democratic rights on their own behalf. One of the weapons would be the quantity and quality of creative work that marked the era of the 1920s known as the Harlem Renaissance or New Negro Movement. As Alain Locke put it in the introduction to his anthology of works by Harlem Renaissance writers published in 1925, "The pulse of the Negro world has begun to beat in Harlem." One of the major novelists associated with that quickening pulse was Nella Larsen, whose difficult youth and obscure old age did not lessen the impact of her creative work, both at the time of its publication and decades later.

The facts of Larsen's birth and childhood are sketchy, in part because as an adult she tended to invent, rather than report, her personal history, as her biographer Thadious Davis has shown. Her mother **Mary Hanson** was a white seamstress of Danish birth, and her father appears to have been a black West Indian immigrant named Peter Walker who worked in Chicago, Illinois, as a cook and laborer. The couple applied for a marriage license in Chicago in 1890, but there is no record that they married then. Their daughter Nellie Walker was born on April 13, 1891. Although Nella later wrote that her father died when she was two years old and that her mother then married a white man, Davis has speculated convincingly that Peter Walker changed his name to Peter Larson and then Larsen and began passing as white in order to take a better-paying whites-only job as a railway conductor. During the transition, however, the obviously non-white daughter Nellie could not stay in the household, and records indicate that a child named Nellie Larson lived in one of Chicago's institutions for unwed mothers and their children in 1900. From 1901 until 1907, Nellie Larson lived with the Peter Larson/Larsen family and attended elementary school and junior high before leaving Chicago to enroll in high school courses at Fisk University in Nashville, where she began using the name Nella Larsen.

Nella stayed at Fisk only one academic year, leaving in 1908 when familial support apparently ceased. The deterioration of family connections must have contributed to a feeling of exile to the margins, an uncomfortable but nevertheless valuable vantage point from which the future writer could "catch that flying glimpse of the panorama," as Nella called the hopes and activities of her generation. Very little is known of her life from 1908 until 1912, though she later claimed to have spent time with her mother's relatives in Copenhagen while a teenager. In 1912, she enrolled in the Lincoln Hospital and Home Training School for Nurses in New York City, where a student could work in exchange for vocational education. The program provided training for African-American women to become nurses, but only whites filled the administrative and physician positions. Despite the racial discrimination, Larsen was surrounded by a number of influential and dedicated African-American women, including *Adah Thoms, who helped transform nursing into a profession, and Larsen also began to meet prominent New Yorkers who would help usher in the Harlem Renaissance era.

Upon graduation in 1915, she stayed at Lincoln Hospital as a supervisor for several months before accepting a position in Alabama as head nurse at Tuskegee Institute's John Andrew Memorial Hospital and Nurse Training School. Finding the job of supervising the hospital's nurses and running a training program with insufficient funds frustrating, and the paternalistic atmosphere on campus restrictive, she returned to a supervisory position at Lincoln after only one year in the South. Two years later, she became one of the elite of African-American nurses employed by the New York Department of Health. While working with a nurses' organization supporting relief efforts during World War I, she met physicist Elmer Samuel Imes, son of an

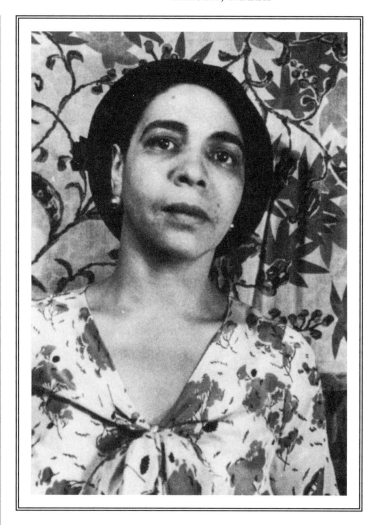

influential African-American family. With her marriage to Imes on May 3, 1919, Nella began to move in an interracial social circle of well-connected, highly educated professionals.

Discontented with her public-health work and feeling encouraged by the publication of two short pieces in the *Brownies' Book*, an African-American children's magazine edited by the highly educated ❦ **Jessie Redmon Fauset** (later considered a "midwife" of the Harlem Renaissance for her role in identifying and ushering into print new young writers), Larsen resigned from the Health Department. She began volunteering at the New York Public Library's 135th Street Branch in Harlem, where she soon landed a paid position as an assistant in the children's department. In the fall of 1922, she took a leave of absence to become the first African-American admitted to the library's training program, earning the certificate that led to an upgraded position and salary when she returned to full-time work at the 135th Street Branch in 1923. Her career move proved to be fortuitous, for the li-

Nella Larsen

Fauset, Jessie Redmon. See *Women of the Harlem Renaissance.*

brary served as a cultural center during the Harlem Renaissance, the period in the 1920s when an outpouring of African-American literature and arts gained notice and respect from both blacks and whites. In the library's assembly room, black writers gave readings from their work; in the library's little theater, black playwrights, directors, and actors produced live performances; and on the library's walls, black artists displayed their creations. Larsen met whites and blacks interested in the creative products of African-Americans, and she responded to the existence of an enthusiastic market by beginning to write fiction. *Young's Realistic Stories Magazine* published two of her short stories in 1926, shortly after she left her library job to concentrate on writing.

For the first time she suffered and rebelled because she was unable to disregard the burden of race. It was, she cried silently, enough to suffer as a woman, an individual, on one's own account, without having to suffer for the race as well.

—Nella Larsen, *Passing*

Alfred and *Blanche Knopf published her first novel, *Quicksand,* in 1928, and her second, *Passing,* a year later. Both books explore the tensions inherent in the lives of middle-class black women who desire freedom from society's racial and gender limits. At a time when most African-American women worked as low-paid agricultural laborers or domestics, with few educational opportunities and little if any access to birth control, a small minority of educated, middle-class black women founded clubs, schools, settlement houses, and other institutions designed to help uplift the race in general and their sisters in particular. Although their efforts accomplished much, they failed, at least during Larsen's lifetime, to break down all of the barriers to black women's full, autonomous participation in American society and culture. Those failures, evident in Larsen's lived experiences, fueled her creative imagination.

Critics have seen autobiographical elements in both of Larsen's books, particularly in reflections of her ambivalence about her own racially mixed heritage and women's expected behavior as wives and mothers. In *Quicksand,* for instance, the mixed-race female protagonist Helga Crane leaves her teaching position on the stultifying campus of a Southern black college to spend time with relatives in Copenhagen, where she is regarded as intriguing and exotic, but ends up back in the United States submerged in an oppressive marriage. In *Passing,* Larsen exposes the lies perpetrated by men and women of color who live in a racist, sexist, class-conscious, and homophobic society, perhaps similar to the kinds of deceptions the novelist herself seems to have practiced to obfuscate her humble and painful origins. Literary critic **Deborah McDowell** also has explicated the themes of black women's sexuality present in both novels. At a time when black women organized to counter the popular image of themselves as sexual savages—the legacy of the historical sexual exploitation of black women under slavery—Larsen broke new ground by attempting to represent black women's sexual desires in a realistic, though circumspect, way. In her sophisticated handling of society's white-black, male-female, lesbian-straight, urban-rural, North-South, elite-humble, married-single, creative-conventional, control-chaos dualities and her ambiguous endings, Larsen demonstrated a modernist sensibility, a need to shatter old patterns without necessarily constructing new ones to replace them.

Well-known critics such as W.E.B. Du Bois and Alain Locke noticed and praised Larsen's novels; friends such as the white writer and socialite Carl Van Vechten and the African-American writer and NAACP activist Walter White served as advocates for her work. In 1929, she received the Harmon Foundation's Bronze Award for Distinguished Achievement among Negroes in Literature, largely for her literary style and her willingness to tackle difficult topics in *Quicksand.* A year later, she became the first African-American woman to receive a Guggenheim Foundation fellowship, intended to underwrite a year's stay in Europe to research her planned third novel. Shortly before she left for Europe, however, Larsen's short story "Sanctuary" appeared in the *Forum* magazine, followed by charges that she stole the idea and format of the story from another author whose work had appeared eight years earlier. Larsen denied having plagiarized, but the incident harmed her reputation and her self-image. Though she began work on two or three additional novels and submitted a completed novel to her publisher, no more of her fiction appeared in print.

When she returned from Europe in 1932, she briefly joined her husband in Nashville where he was on the Fisk University faculty. Aware that Elmer was romantically involved with a white woman, Larsen divorced him in 1933. Having been rejected as a mixed-race daughter by parents who apparently chose to identify themselves as a white couple, she responded to Elmer's rejection and to the setbacks in her writing career in part by beginning to remove herself from the social and professional circle that had produced and supported the Harlem Renaissance. Although Larsen returned to New York after her divorce, she tended to avoid Harlem, which had suffered visibly as a result of economic hard times, and by 1937 she had cut herself off from all contact with literary friends. A kind of exile had been thrust upon her, first by her birth family and then by her husband, but in her mature years she fashioned her own exile, living somewhat reclusively in a small apartment on Manhattan's Lower East Side.

Larsen's alimony settlement sustained her throughout the Depression. But with Elmer's death in 1941, her livelihood ceased, and, identifying herself as the widow Mrs. Imes, she did some private duty nursing. In 1944, she went to work as a registered nurse at Gouverneur Hospital in New York where she eventually became night supervisor. Seventeen years later, at age 70, she joined the staff at Metropolitan Hospital where she worked until her death of heart failure in 1964. Because she lived the last years of her life apart from them, friends and acquaintances from the Harlem Renaissance era failed to note her demise, but hospital co-workers expressed sadness at the loss of a colleague whom they considered an excellent and caring nurse.

Larsen's life exemplified the triumphs and tragedies of a talented, intelligent woman of color driven to reach for—and accomplish—more than her upbringing promised. She invented a life of creative ambition that produced two enduring novels evocative of the limits she herself faced and fought. Ultimately thwarted by her own inner conflicts as well as by external circumstances, at mid-life Larsen reinvented herself, trading creative ambition for compassionate acceptance.

SOURCES:

Davis, Thadious M. *Nella Larsen, Novelist of the Harlem Renaissance: A Woman's Life Unveiled*. Baton Rouge: Louisiana State University Press, 1994.

McDowell, Deborah E., ed. "Introduction" in *Quicksand* and *Passing*, by Nella Larsen. New Brunswick, NJ: Rutgers University Press, 1986, pp. ix–xxxv.

Washington, Mary Helen. "Nella Larsen: Mystery Woman of the Harlem Renaissance," in *Ms.* Vol IX, no. 6. December 1980, pp. 44–50.

SUGGESTED READING:

Carby, Hazel. *Reconstructing Womanhood: The Emergence of the Afro-American Woman Novelist.* NY: Oxford University Press, 1987.

Lewis, David Levering. *When Harlem Was in Vogue.* NY: Knopf, 1981.

COLLECTIONS:

Letters between Nella Larsen and Carl Van Vechten and between Larsen and **Dorothy Peterson** are in the James Weldon Johnson Collection, Yale Collection of American Literature, Beinecke Rare Book and Manuscript Library, Yale University.

Cheryl Knott Malone,
lecturer, reference librarian, and bibliographer, Austin, Texas

Larson, Nicolette (1952–1997)

*American singer known for her Top-Ten hit "Lotta Love." Born on July 17, 1952, in Helena, Montana; died on December 16, 1997, in Los Angeles, California; one of three daughters and six children of Robert Larson and Josephine Larson; married Russ Kunkel (a drummer), in 1990; children: one daughter, **Elsie May Larson Kunkel** (b. 1990).*

Was a back-up and session singer in the Los Angeles country-rock scene (mid-1970s); sang on Tales from the Ozone *by Commander Cody and His Lost Planet Airmen, 1975; performed on dozens of other albums (1970s–1980s); was associated with Neil Young, Linda Ronstadt, Michael McDonald, Graham Nash and many other major West Coast artists; recorded six albums as solo artist; had Top-Ten hit, "Lotta Love" (1979); had a country-music career (1980s).*

Solo albums: Nicolette *(1978);* In the Nick of Time *(1979);* Radioland *(1980);* All Dressed Up and No Place to Go *(1982);* Say When *(1985);* Sleep Baby Sleep *(1994).*

Nicolette Larson was born in Helena, Montana, in 1952, one of three daughters of the six children of **Josephine Larson** and Robert Larson, who worked for the Treasury Department. The large family moved to a different U.S. city every few years, preparing Larson for the peripatetic life she was to lead as one of the most sought-after back-up singers and collaborators of the 1970s. Larson's family eventually settled in Kansas City, while Larson moved to San Francisco in 1974. Working for the Golden Gate Country-Bluegrass Festival, Larson was encouraged to pursue a professional music career, joining David Nichtern and the Nocturnes and playing clubs around the Bay area. A year later, at 21, she moved to Los Angeles, the center of the country-rock music scene, to find work as a session singer.

Her first break is said to have occurred when she was working at the coat-check counter of a Los Angeles nightclub and performed an impromptu duet performance with the club's sound engineer when the opening act canceled. It's likely, however, that by this point she had already come to the attention of Commander Cody and His Lost Planet Airmen, who invited her to sing on 1975's *Tales from the Ozone*. Larson went on to tour with Commander Cody and sing on another two of their albums.

By the late 1970s, Larson was touring and recording with many of the era's key musical figures, including **Linda Ronstadt**, Neil Young, **Emmylou Harris**, Michael McDonald, Willie Nelson, Jimmy Buffett, Christopher Cross, the Dirt Band, Hoyt Axton, the Beach Boys, Graham Nash and the Doobie Brothers. Ronstadt, who became a mentor and close friend, and who was instrumental in launching Larson's career, described Larson as "a fellow road warrior."

It was a period when female solo artists—who were more than just the derided "girl singers" of the 1960s—were actively sought by record companies for the first time (described by *The New York Times* critic John Rockwell in 1979 as "the current fad for women singers"). In 1978, with the support of Ronstadt and Neil Young, Larson was offered a record contract with Warner Bros., releasing her first single, "Lotta Love," later that year. The song was written by Neil Young, with whom Larson had earlier had a brief but intense romantic relationship. (They remained friends for the rest of her life. Larson sang on five Neil Young albums, dueting with him on the poignant title track of 1992's *Harvest Moon* and appearing with Young on *MTV Unplugged* in 1993.) According to Larson, she first heard "Lotta Love" after spotting an old tape on the floor of Young's car. When she told Young how much she liked it, he replied: "It's you." A radio hit, "Lotta Love" reached #8 on the pop charts, helping her debut album *Nicolette* to achieve gold status.

Larson recognized that, like Ronstadt, she was a greater singer than a songwriter. "I'm not an instinctive songwriter like Neil, who can sit down and write six songs a day," she said in 1979. "[But] I think I express myself as a singer just fine." "Lotta Love" was to prove Larson's biggest hit. Her second album, *In the Nick of Time*, and single "Rumba Girl," both stalled at #47 on the charts, though the album's duet with Michael McDonald, "Let Me Go Love," was a Top-40 hit.

After indifferent sales for her next albums, 1980's *Radioland* and 1982's *All Dressed Up and No Place to Go* (which spawned the single "I Only Want To Be With You"), Larson retreated from the rock scene. "Nicolette moved a lot of people with her depth of feeling at a time when it was easy to be cynical," Jackson Browne once said. Seeking a change in focus, Larson starred in the country musical *Pump Boys and Dinettes*; the resulting good notices won her a recording contract with MCA Nashville in 1983. Her first country album, . . . *Say When* (1985), was a commercial failure, but in 1986 Larson enjoyed success with "That's How You Know When Love's Right," a duet with Steve Wariner. A Top-Ten country hit, the single stayed in the charts for five months. Her subsequent career included a USO tour with **Valerie Carter** and **Lauren Wood**, and some television and movie acting, including the role of nightclub singer in the Arnold Schwarzenegger-Danny DeVito comedy *Twins*.

Larson's crystalline, strong, versatile voice was a distinctive presence on both pop and country radio. **Bonnie Raitt** called her "a sultry rodeo angel." Jimmy Buffett described hearing her "unmistakable voice" on a record playing in an Aspen restaurant: "The sun lit up the mountain and the sky was Caribbean blue, and the little girl with the big voice was coloring the Rockies."

Her awards included *Performance* magazine's Best Female Vocalist (1979), the Academy of Country Music's Best New Vocalist (1984), and *Cashbox* magazine's Best New Country Vocalist in 1985. In 1978, she won *Rolling Stone* magazine's critics' poll, the same year Ronstadt won the readers' poll. Ronstadt "was tickled," Larson recalled. "She said, 'We're both queens of the prom.'"

In 1990, Larson married renowned session drummer Russell Kunkel, giving birth to their only child, Elsie May, the same year. The birth of her daughter inspired the last album Larson recorded, 1994's *Sleep Baby Sleep*, a collection of lullabies and children's songs which included duets with Graham Nash and Linda Ronstadt. Larson remained a popular figure among her fellow musicians. Paul Gurion suggested that her "well-worn robe, the slippers, and the 'Aw Shucks' demeanor was a disarming disguise for an often probing wit that got right to the heart of the matter."

In December 1997, after being rushed to the UCLA Medical Center in Los Angeles with liver failure, Larson died from a condition known as cerebral edema, a build-up of toxic fluids in the brain. At a memorial concert in February 1998, fellow musicians paid tribute to the woman described by Dan Fogelberg as "a rare and wonderful singer."

SOURCES:

Classic Images (obituary). February, 1998.

The Day [New London, CT]. December 18, 1997.

Interview with John Rockwell. *The New York Times.* March 16, 1979.

New York Post (obituary). December 18, 1997.

Time (obituary). December 29, 1997.

Paula Morris, D.Phil.,
Brooklyn, New York

La Sablière, Marguerite de

(1640–1693)

French student of science and mathematics who was noted as a patron of savants. Name variations: Mme de la Sabliere. Born Marguerite Hessein in 1640 in Paris; died on January 5 (some sources cite January 8), 1693, in Paris; daughter of Gilbert Hessein and Margaret Menjot; educated by uncle (Antoine Menjot) and tutors; married Antoine Rambouillet (1624–1680), also seen as Antoine de Rambouillet, seigneur de la Sablière (a Protestant financier entrusted with the administration of the royal estates), on March 15, 1654 (died 1679); children: Anne de Rambouillet; Nicolas de Rambouillet; Marguerite de Rambouillet.

Although she did not contribute original works to science, Marguerite de la Sablière is nonetheless famed as a student and patron of the sciences and arts and hostess of a popular salon frequented by geniuses. "A woman of great intellectuality and of vast erudition," writes the Reverend Hugh Francis Blunt, "she may be regarded as the personification of that great charm which characterized the women of letters of the second half of the seventeenth century."

De la Sablière was born Marguerite Hessein in Paris in 1640, the eldest of four children of Huguenot banker Gilbert Hessein and **Margaret Menjot**. Margaret died when Marguerite was only nine years old; as a result, Gilbert and his brother-in-law Antoine Menjot lavished attention on the child. Menjot was a well-known philosopher and theologian in his own right, as well as king's physician. De la Sablière was tutored in Latin and Greek, mathematics and science, and was taught the art of entertaining by a cousin who was a countess.

At age 14, de la Sablière was married off to another cousin, the classically educated financier Antoine de Rambouillet, seigneur de la Sablière, partially to facilitate her father's impending second marriage. Three children, Anne, Nicholas and Marguerite, were born in the next four years. The de la Sablières' marriage broke down over the next decade, the causes rumored to be his wandering eye (including a liaison with *Ninon de Lenclos) and her small inheritance at the time of her father's death in 1661. Whatever the cause, on March 1, 1667, she (although an ardent Protestant) sought refuge in a Catholic convent. Her husband succeeded in gaining sole custody of the children, whom she recovered only after his death in 1679.

Abandoned and poor, de la Sablière lived with her brother Pierre Hessein, who was friends with a number of the great minds of the day. Her home became an important salon, a meeting-place for poets, scientists, writers, and brilliant members of the court of Louis XIV, and she received instruction in mathematics, astronomy, and physics from Giles Persone de Roberval and Joseph Sauveur, both members of the French Academy of Sciences. Famed writers Moliere, Fontanelle, and La Fontaine (who is said to have lived with her for a number of years) were her friends, as well as King John III Sobieski of Poland. La Fontaine had joined the group around 1673, and, for 20 years, Mme de la Sablière relieved him of every kind of financial anxiety. Another frequent visitor was the traveler and physician François Bernier, whose abridgment of the works of Pierre Gassendi was written for her.

The Abbé de Chaulieu and his fellow poet, Charles Auguste, Marquis de La Fare, were among her most intimate associates. La Fare sold his commission in the army to spend time with her. This liaison seems to have been the only serious passion of her life, and she was his mistress from 1676 to 1682, when she was abandoned for a second time. According to *Marie de Sévigné, La Fare's head was turned by his love of the theater, but to this must be added a new passion for the actress *Marie Champmeslé.

In 1685, de la Sablière converted to Catholicism and devoted herself to volunteer work for the Hospital for Incurables to atone for her worldly sins. She also began a lengthy correspondence with Abbot de Rancé. She died on January 5, 1693, at her home.

De la Sablière had vocal supporters throughout her life, as well as detractors. La Fontaine called her "his Muse," and Ninon de Lenclos thought her "one of the prettiest and most singular women of the world." However, she is most commonly remembered through Nicholas Boileau-Despréaux's *Satire contre les Femmes* where she is referred to as "this learned woman whom Roberval esteems and whom Sauveur frequents." She is pictured as having weakened her sight and ruined her complexion by her nightly observations of Jupiter. She was defended by Charles Perrault in his *Apologie des femmes* as a talented yet modest woman.

SOURCES:

Blunt, Rev. Hugh Francis. *The Great Magdelens*. NY: Macmillan, 1928.

Mozans, H.J. *Women in Science*. Notre Dame: University of Notre Dame Press, 1991.

Ogilvie, Marilyn Bailey. *Women in Science*. Cambridge, MA: MIT Press, 1986.

Kristine Larsen,
Associate Professor of Physics and Earth Sciences, Central Connecticut State University, New Britain, Connecticut

Lascaris, Irene (fl. 1222–1235).

See Irene Lascaris.

Lascelles, Ann (1745–1789).

See Catley, Ann.

Lascelles, Elizabeth (b. 1924).

See Collingwood, Elizabeth.

Lascelles, Patricia (1926—)

*Countess of Harewood. Name variations: Patricia Tuckwell; (nickname) Bambi. Born Patricia Elizabeth Tuckwell on November 24, 1926, in Melbourne, Australia; became second wife of George Lascelles, 7th earl of Harewood, on July 31, 1967. George Lascelles' first wife was *Marion Stein.*

Lascelles, Viscountess (b. 1948).

See Messenger, Margaret.

Laskaridou, Aikaterini (1842–1916)

Greek educator and feminist. Name variations: Ekatherina Laskaridou. Born in 1842; died in 1916.

Aikaterini Laskaridou, who was born in 1842, used her considerable wealth and education to improve the intellectual status of Greek women. Studying the educational systems in Western Europe, she attempted to recreate them in her own country, utilizing her own money to implement programs of study. She opened the first nursery school in the country and trained teachers to work in them. She championed the introduction of gymnastics into the curriculum of girls' schools and was instrumental in setting up workshops where poor women could receive a rudimentary education. Laskaridou wrote extensively on child rearing and education and also published a few short stories.

Lasker, Mrs. Albert D. (1900–1994).

See Lasker, Mary.

Lasker, Mary (1900–1994)

American philanthropist and champion of biomedical research whose greatest achievement was the National Cancer Act of 1971, a result of her prodding the Nixon administration into a "war on cancer." Name variations: Mary Reinhardt; Mrs. Albert D. Lasker. Born Mary Woodard in Watertown, Wisconsin, on November 30, 1900; died in Greenwich, Connecticut, on February 21, 1994; daughter of Frank Elwin Woodard (a banker and investor) and Sara (Johnson) Woodard; had a sister Alice Woodard; attended the University of Wisconsin; Radcliffe College, A.B. cum laude, 1923; postgraduate work at Oxford University; married Paul Reinhardt, in 1926 (divorced 1933); married Albert Davis Lasker (an advertising executive), on June 21, 1940 (died 1952); children: (stepchildren) Francis Brody; Edward Lasker.

Established the Albert and Mary Lasker Foundation (1942); founded the prestigious Albert Lasker Medical Research Awards given annually (1944); played a crucial role in convincing Americans it was socially acceptable to discuss the issue of cancer in public; received the Presidential Medal of Freedom (1969).

Born in 1900 into a prominent family in Watertown, Wisconsin (her father was a banker and investor), Mary Woodard grew up in a family that valued independent thinking. Mary's mother **Sara Johnson Woodard** was a civic leader who founded two public parks in Watertown. Sara Woodard kept current with the arts and sciences and was particularly interested in such areas as psychology and psychiatry. Mary was also drawn to such subjects; by age 12, she was reading such arcane texts as Hudson's *Law of Psychic Phenomena*. Although sheltered, her childhood was not always idyllic. Throughout much of it, Mary suffered from painful, recurrent ear infections, and she was severely ill with influenza during the pandemic of 1918–19 which killed more than 20 million worldwide. Although she made a full recovery from these illnesses and would live to age 93, she was always aware of her own, and others', mortality. This was underlined when both of her parents died suddenly of strokes while she was still young.

Mary Woodard first attended the University of Wisconsin and then earned a degree in art history and appreciation at Radcliffe College, graduating in 1923. After doing postgraduate work at Oxford University, she returned to the United States in 1924 and in 1926 married Paul Reinhardt, a New York City art dealer. Working at her husband's gallery, Mary became a savvy art dealer, selling paintings to museums and wealthy collectors, arranging exhibitions of Old Masters as well as contemporary art, and handling publicity for artists. After divorcing Reinhardt in 1933, Mary left the art market, having become "tired of being in a business where numerically few things were sold," she said. "I wanted to sell masses of things to masses of people. I found out that the things which people still bought in a depression were paper patterns."

Her new business, which she called Hollywood Patterns, produced inexpensive dress patterns which were marketed in packages adorned by photographs of the reigning Hollywood movie stars. Manufactured and sold by Vogue Patterns, the new brand was distributed to department-store chains which sold the patterns for an affordable 15 cents each. Mary earned one-third of a cent on each sale, which quickly turned into a substantial sum given the fact that many millions of women sewed their own dresses during the Depression era. Soon, she had become financially independent. Although she knew the value of money and developed a knack for making substantial amounts of it, Mary the banker's daughter also had a taste for luxury and enjoyed being surrounded by creature comforts and beautiful objects, particularly museum-class paintings.

On June 21, 1940, Mary Woodard entered into a world where cost was no object when she became the third wife of a legendary figure in the advertising world, Albert D. Lasker. President and sole owner of the immensely successful Lord & Thomas advertising agency, Albert had long been an influential personality by the time he first met Mary in the spring of 1939 at Manhattan's famed 21 restaurant. More than anyone else, Albert was able to persuade women to start smoking, convincing them that they could remain slim if they reached "for a Lucky instead of a Sweet." (This was in an age when there were no surgeon general's warnings about the health hazards from smoking.) He went on to make even more money organizing brilliantly effective advertising campaigns to increase sales of facial tissues, orange juice, and sanitary napkins. Even before he met Mary, Albert had been philanthropically generous, donating $1 million and his $3 million Lake Forest, Illinois, estate to the University of Chicago. Over the years, he also contributed millions in support of cancer research projects.

Soon after they first met, Albert asked Mary what she wanted most out of life. Her reply was simple. "To promote research in cancer, tuberculosis and the major diseases." By 1942, Mary

Lasker had persuaded her husband to sell his agency and retire. That year, they founded the Albert and Mary Lasker Foundation to assist and encourage medical research and public health administration. Starting in 1944, the foundation began to give Albert Lasker Medical Research Awards on an annual basis (with occasional exceptions), to honor and reward outstanding contributions to clinical and basic medical research. As the years went by, the Lasker Award came to be recognized in the medical research community as the American equivalent of a Nobel Prize; in fact by 1994, 51 Lasker Award honorees had won the coveted Nobel. Along with a cash award, the Lasker Award includes a reproduction of one of the great art works of antiquity, the Winged Victory of Samothrace.

In 1943, Mary watched helplessly while a beloved family cook died slowly from uterine cancer, then universally accepted as an incurable disease. Lasker was shocked to learn that current medical knowledge could offer no treatment to halt the progress of the malignancy. De-

*Mary
Lasker*

termined to do something, she was able to persuade a number of prominent individuals to donate funds for the American Cancer Society to establish its own research program. She also convinced a *Reader's Digest* editor to write several articles on cancer, hitherto an almost taboo topic in the media. The articles, which appeared with appeals to support the work of the American Cancer Society, raised the then handsome sum of $120,000, which enabled the organization to purchase support materials for its first large-scale fund-raising drive in 1945. Determined to see this campaign succeed, Mary Lasker paid the salaries of professional fund raisers who helped organize and execute the campaign. She gave the funding on the condition that 25% of the money raised be earmarked for cancer research programs. The 1945 campaign was a considerable success, raising $4.2 million.

Although her involvement in the American Cancer Society's 1945 fund-raising campaign had gone well, Lasker now turned her attention to Washington, D.C., firmly convinced that only the resources of the federal government could be relied on over the long run to support the kind of medical research that could eliminate cancer. In 1946, she and her husband achieved one of their first victories when they played a key role in setting up a research center authorized by the National Mental Health Act. In 1947, both Mary and Albert Lasker gave their support to the Wagner-Murray-Dingell bill for creating a national health insurance system for all Americans, but this never made it out of committee as a result of the vehement opposition mounted by the American Medical Association. Undismayed, over the next few years Mary Lasker mastered the art of lobbying and public relations, often getting ideas and advice from her husband, a past master of persuasion. After Albert Lasker died of cancer in 1952, Mary was even more determined to eradicate the disease. Inheriting both her husband's great wealth ($80 million) and the network of friendships and connections they had created over the years, she spent more time than ever on Capitol Hill to lobby for expanded medical research budgets.

On several occasions, she made major personal contributions to medical research by selling paintings from her superb collection, which included works by Matisse, Miro, Picasso, and Renoir. When a health appropriations bill was in danger of being vetoed by President Dwight Eisenhower, Lasker talked one of the president's golfing buddies into arranging a meeting between Eisenhower and Harvard cancer researcher Sidney Farber. The bill escaped the veto.

Lasker gained access to the new Kennedy administration by presenting *Jacqueline Kennedy with a $10,000 check for redecorating the White House. One Washington insider claimed that Lasker's charm and tenacity had turned "dozens of Congress members and Presidents into mush."

Soon after her husband's death, Mary Lasker established the National Health Education Committee, which published a number of books designed to inform the general public about major deadly and crippling diseases. Over the next decades, she would be involved in numerous organizations which she founded or energized, including the American Cancer Society (chair and honorary president), the United Cerebral Palsy Research and Education Foundation (vice-chair), the Research to Prevent Blindness Committee (trustee), the National Committee for Mental Hygiene (director), the American Heart Association (member of the advisory council), and a half-dozen others. Never a merely decorative board member, Mary Lasker received high praise from her friend *Eleanor Roosevelt, who noted, "Not only can she grasp an idea quickly when it is presented to her, but she sees where you can go with it."

Starting in the late 1960s, Lasker lobbied ceaselessly to expand federal support of cancer research. In December 1969, *The New York Times* printed a full-page advertisement paid for by the "Citizens Committee for the Conquest of Cancer" which asserted in large type: "President Nixon, You Can Cure Cancer. We lack only the will and the kind of money and comprehensive planning that went into putting a man on the moon. Why don't we try to conquer cancer by America's 200th birthday?" The Citizens Committee was a committee of one: Mary Lasker. Though she spent only $22,000 on the ad, the White House found itself swamped with at least 7,000 letters from the public demanding action on cancer research. In Washington in March 1970, Lasker began her campaign by persuading a receptive Senator Ralph Yarborough of Texas to create a panel of consultants to decide how best to approach the conquest of cancer. She was convinced that because the National Cancer Institute (NCI) was a division of the National Institutes of Health (NIH), which had a philosophy of emphasizing basic biomedical research rather than investigation of promising therapies, the entire thrust of cancer research in the United States had remained overly theoretical while every day lives were being lost.

Because Lasker and Yarborough had chosen the panelists, their central recommendation was preordained. The panel's report, completed in December 1970, proposed that an independent cancer agency be created along the lines of the "we'll land men on the moon within the decade" pattern NASA had adopted in the early 1960s. In effect, NCI was to be separated from NIH. The report argued that only an independent agency free of bureaucratic red tape could efficiently shape and direct such an effort, as well as command the visibility necessary to retain ongoing public and political support.

The panel's recommendations were embodied in legislation introduced in Congress in January 1971. The scientific community, however, was strongly opposed to the dismemberment of NIH. When the bill became trapped in a political morass in the Senate, Lasker enlisted the help of ⚜➤ **Ann Landers**, who, in her first ever "Dear Reader" column, urged the public to write lawmakers to support the bill. A sea of mail inundated Congress, and Senate staffers put up a sign reading: "Impeach Ann Landers." Senator Alan Cranston alone received 60,000 letters within five weeks. Although Mary Lasker and her "Little Lambs," a supportive circle of socialites, physicians, and congressional representatives, made a number of compromises, on balance the "Laskerites" won a substantial victory when the final legislative document was signed into law in December 1971, as the National Cancer Act. Although on paper NCI remained a division within NIH, in reality it became the first among equals, emerging much stronger in budgetary terms (it received an additional $800 million over the next five years). NCI would now be watched over by a special committee reporting directly to the president, and its budget would be submitted directly to his office. Even after the law went into effect, some in the medical community continued to criticize Lasker's fundamental philosophy of medical research, arguing that many of her goals, such as developing a vaccine against cancer, were based largely on wishful thinking and were simply scientifically unrealistic. Others disagreed with her ultra-optimistic point of view, based on her belief that "you can solve any problem if you have money, people, and equipment." Lasker responded vigorously to these and similar criticisms, arguing, "Nobody knows the full picture about many of these diseases, so how does anyone know what's an unrealistic demand and what isn't?"

Although a series of strokes in the early 1980s slowed her down, Lasker continued her struggle to find cures for the major killer diseases. In 1986, when the White House and many members of Congress were still largely in a state of denial regarding the AIDS epidemic, she focused national attention on the need for greater research into that emerging plague by persuading *Elizabeth Taylor to appear at a Congressional hearing. Always aware of the power of publicity, over the decades Lasker recruited effective lobbying allies and such media-savvy personalities as heart surgeon Michael E. DeBakey, actress *Irene Dunne, Hollywood mogul Louis B. Mayer, and actress *Jennifer Jones and her industrialist husband Norton W. Simon. By the end of her life, Lasker had earned three dozen honorary awards and degrees, including the highest award the United States can confer on a civilian, the Presidential Medal of Freedom. In the 1980s, Lasker also worked to increase research budgets to seek cures for diabetes, growth disorders, and osteoporosis.

Friends and strangers alike often commented on Mary Woodard Lasker's striking beauty, with her dark hair and violet-blue eyes. She had perfected the role of the society grande dame. At her Manhattan townhouse, which accommodated the stunning Lasker collection of French impressionist and modern art, she enjoyed being the provider of "a calm but interesting setting for people." And in the immaculate, all-white interior (which included her white cat Marshmallow) of her home in Greenwich, Connecticut, she took for granted the privileges known but to a select few.

In addition to her fight against deadly diseases, she supported urban beautification and was generous in providing funds for flowers planted in various locations in New York City. Lasker donated 300 Japanese cherry trees to the United Nations headquarters in Manhattan. In 1953, an article in *The New York Times* affectionately referred to her as "Annie Appleseed."

After spending much of her long life fighting to make the lives of all people healthier and less marked by pain and suffering, Mary Lasker died of pneumonia at her Greenwich home on February 21, 1994. For Lasker, it had been simply a matter of her being "infuriated when I hear that anyone's ill, especially when it's from a disease that virtually nothing is known about." One way to gauge the success of her efforts can be seen in the expansion of the budget of the National Institutes of Health, which grew from $2.4 million in 1945 to $11 billion in 1993. The National Cancer Institute's budget jumped from $18.9 million in 1950 to $1 billion in 1990. "I am opposed to heart attacks, cancer and stroke the way I am opposed to sin," she said.

SOURCES:

Altman, Lawrence K. "Why Many Trailblazing Scientists Must Wait Many Years for Awards," in *The New York Times*. September 26, 1995, p. B6.

⚜
Landers, Ann.
See Friedman, Esther Pauline.

Cohen, Gary. "A Tobacco Fortune for a Cancer Cure," in *U.S. News & World Report*. Vol. 116, no. 9. March 7, 1994, p. 21.

———— and Shannon Brownlee. "Mary and the 'Little Lambs' Launch a War," in *U.S. News & World Report*. Vol. 120, no. 5. February 5, 1996, pp. 76–77.

Culliton, Barbara J. "Recollections on the War on Cancer," in *Science*. Vol. 237. August 21, 1987, p. 843.

Gunther, John. *Taken at the Flood: The Story of Albert D. Lasker*. NY: Harper, 1960.

Lawford, Valentine. "Profiles: Mary Lasker," in *Architectural Digest*. Vol. 42. October 1985, pp. 188–195.

Mahaney, Francis X., Jr. "Mary Woodard Lasker: An Appreciation," in *Journal of the National Cancer Institute*. Vol. 86, no. 6. March 16, 1994, p. 406.

"Mary W. Lasker, Philanthropist For Medical Research, Dies at 93," in *The New York Times Biographical Service*. February 1994, pp. 304–305.

Rettig, Richard A. *Cancer Crusade: The Story of the National Cancer Act of 1971*. Princeton, NJ: Princeton University Press, 1977.

Siwolop, Sana. "The Fairy Godmother of Medical Research," in *Business Week*. No. 2955. July 14, 1986, p. 67.

Wetterau, Bruce. *The Presidential Medal of Freedom: Winners and Their Achievements*. Washington, DC: Congressional Quarterly, 1996.

COLLECTIONS:

Eleanor Roosevelt Papers, Franklin D. Roosevelt Library, Hyde Park, New York.

Vincent T. DeVita, Jr. Papers, Manuscripts and Rare Books Department, Swem Library, College of William and Mary, Williamsburg, Virginia.

John Haag,
Associate Professor of History,
University of Georgia, Athens, Georgia

Lasker-Schüler, Else (1869–1945)

German lyric poet of the 20th century, winner of one of Germany's highest literary honors, the Kleist Preis, who was forced by her Jewish heritage into exile during the Nazi era. Name variations: Elsa Lasker-Schuler or Schueler. Born Else Schüler on February 11, 1869, in Elberfeld, Germany; died on January 22, 1945, in Jerusalem; daughter of Aron Schüler (a banker) and Jeanette (Kissing) Schüler; married Berthold Lasker, in 1899 (divorced 1903); married Georg Levin also known as Herwarth Walden, in 1903 (divorced 1912); children: (first marriage) Paul Lasker (b. 1900).

Published her first poems in Die Gesellschaft *and* Das Magazin für Literatur *(1899); became famous as a poet and bohemian in Berlin cafes; received the Kleist Preis (1932); fled Germany (1933); reached exile in Israel (1939).*

On a cold day in January 1945, a small gathering in a Jerusalem cemetery stood listening to a poem read aloud in German, one of the few occasions during that period when the German language was spoken anywhere in public in Palestine. War had forbidden it, as German was the language of the enemies of Palestine, and World War II was not yet at an end. But in the peace that came with the end of a tormented life, the sound of German was the final irony to mark the passing of the elderly woman who was being buried there—Else Lasker-Schüler, author of the words being spoken.

> I know that I must die soon.
> Yet all the trees are radiant
> After summer's long-awaited kiss—
>
> My dreams grow gray—
> Never have I written a sadder ending
> In my books of rhymes.
>
> You pluck a flower for me—
> I loved it in the bud.
> Yet I know that I must die soon.
>
> My breath hovers over the river of God—
> Softly I set my foot
> On the path to my long home.

Recognized by many as the finest lyrical voice of 20th-century Germany, she had instilled a poetry into her native language that few possessed and had then been prevented from living in her native land. Driven to exile in Jerusalem, she was deprived there of hearing or speaking the language she cared about most. Provided with a pension adequate for her needs, she continually gave most of it away and spent her final years in an unheated furnished room, sleeping in an easy chair because she did not own a bed and did not want one. Prone since youth to a bohemian lifestyle, she spent her days sitting in cafes and her nights at the movies, still occasionally writing poetry, still appreciated by the other writers and artists in exile like herself, but growing increasingly eccentric in her behavior and her dress. Exiled in both language and land, she felt nowhere at home.

Else Schüler was born on February 11, 1869, in the German town of Elberfeld, the youngest of six children, three girls and three boys. Her father Aron Schüler was a banker, and her mother **Jeanette Kissing Schüler** devoted much time to literature. Else was the granddaughter of a rabbi, although her family was not especially religious. Of all her siblings, she was closest to her brother Paul, who was seven years her elder. He wrote poetry in Greek and Latin, and she adored him.

In school, Else was mercilessly teased by her Catholic and Lutheran classmates, reflecting the anti-Semitism that was escalating in Germany in those days. The children would taunt her with the words "Hepp, Hepp," which was thought to be a medieval abbreviation signifying "Jerusalem be damned." When her mother recognized the child's suffering, she decided to educate Else at home, a much happier experience. Jeanette Schüler fostered a free, joyful spirit in Else, affirming her imaginative skills, urging her to explore a world of sound and color, and encouraging her interest in poetry.

When Else Schüler was 14, her beloved brother Paul died. When she was 21, her mother died and was mourned by Else ever after. "When my mother died, the moon broke in two," she wrote. Else was 30 when she married Berthold Lasker, a Berlin physician eight years her senior, in 1899. That same year, she published her first poems in *Die Gesellschaft* and *Das Magazin für Literatur.* In the early days of her marriage, she rented a studio near the Tiergarten and began living a life separate from her husband. In 1900, she gave birth to a son, named Paul after her dead brother. When the boy was a year old, she separated from Lasker, and the couple divorced in 1903. Else Lasker-Schüler had by then taken to playing the role of the "Prince of Thebes,"

wearing extravagant baggy pants, flowing gowns, colorful rags, and cheap glass beads. She became notorious for frequenting cafes where she often shared opium and cocaine with her friends. The cultural elite of Berlin admired her poetry and welcomed her eccentric antics.

During the hours Else spent writing or sketching her fellow artists in the Café des Westens or the Romanisches Café, she met her second husband, Georg Levin, whom she married in 1903. An art historian, accomplished composer, and founder of the art society Verein für Kunst, Georg also established the highly successful cultural-literary journal *Der Sturm,* in which he published a number of his wife's poems. Else soon gave Georg a different name—Herwarth Walden—which turned out to be more lasting than their marriage. In the spring of 1910, Walden left her for another woman. The divorce became final in 1912.

In her early 40s at the time of her separation from her second husband, Lasker-Schüler became a nomad, wandering from hotel to rooming

Else Lasker-Schüler

house. Although she often wrote of her home-sickness for Elberfeld and Westphalia, she remained in Berlin, a city with which she had a love-hate relationship. Names, dates, and places were never as important to Else as the poetry of words, and she often reordered the facts of her life to fit her vision of herself, much as she would rearrange words to construct a poem. Biographers have had to dig to separate fact from fiction. It was only recently, for example, that documents revealed her actual date of birth to be 1869, rather than 1876 as she claimed. She also alleged that her father was an architect who built houses for the poor and allowed them to live in them at no cost, when he was in fact a banker. In Else's descriptions, her father's father, a simple rabbi, became a chief rabbi who conversed with Catholic bishops about matters divine, and her mother's ancestors came from Spain, not England. Lasker-Schüler also denied that Berthold Lasker was the father of her son Paul, claiming that he had been fathered by a Greek aristocrat by the name of Alcibiades de Rouan.

I am homesick for our garden and tower. What does the world want from me?

—Else Lasker-Schüler

Around the turn of the century, Lasker-Schüler became involved with the mystical poet Peter Hille, who introduced her to Die neue Gemeinschaft (The New Community). Founded by the brothers Heinrich and Julius Hart, the group included some 70 poets and philosophers who rejected materialism, similar to groups which sprang up in the 1960s in the United States. Members included the poet Peter Baum, theologian Martin Buber, and Gustav Landauer. Lasker-Schüler idolized Hille: "His brown eyes are two heavens, and that's why anybody who saw him became a believer." His death in 1904 was another great loss, but her relationship with him had led her away from the bourgeois world forever.

Lasker-Schüler wrote prolifically. In the first decade of the century, she published two books of poetry (*Styx* [1902] and *Der Siebente Tag* [1905]); two books of prose (*Das Peter Hille Buch* [1906] and *Die Nächte der Tino von Baghdad*); and a play (*Die Wupper* [1909]). The great German writer Thomas Mann once said, "The poet is not somebody who invents things, but somebody who creates something out of things as they are." According to Hille, the four elements in the work of Lasker-Schüler were the Judaic, the Arabic, the childlike, and the primordial, and she "took refuge in dreams of angels who resembled heavenly gardeners, in dreams of her mother and child, or in madness." At the same time, Lasker-Schüler celebrated the joy of life and sacred devotion to love. Her work was characteristic of the Art Nouveau movement. Its imagery used roses, lilies, hyacinths, and twisting flames, all meandering, climbing, winding, and springing up. Lasker-Schüler's unique universe of fantasy was created despite personal loss and exile, and the language of her poetry transcended frail human barriers to become sublime.

In 1913, Lasker-Schüler journeyed to Russia in the hope of securing the release of her friend, the writer and activist Johannes Holtzman. The former publisher of the anarchist journal *Kampf*, he had been sentenced to 15 years in prison for revolutionary intrigue in tsarist Russia, and had been committed to a mental institution in Moscow in 1912. Lasker-Schüler was appalled by the condition in which she found him but was forced to return to Berlin without winning his release. Holtzman later died of pneumonia in Moscow.

Lasker-Schüler loved many men. In 1912, she fell in love with the poet Gottfried Benn, who held her in great regard throughout his life. She also met Georg Trakl and later wrote two poems about their brief friendship. She had a longer association with the Viennese critic and satirist Karl Kraus, who recognized the greatness of her poetry and published some of it in his periodical, *Die Fackel*. When Lasker-Schüler had financial difficulties in 1913, Kraus published an appeal for contributions on her behalf. Throughout this period of poverty, prolific publishing, and intense relationships, she remained devoted to her son. Paulchen, as she called him, was bright and creative, and no matter how erratic her lifestyle, he remained at the center of her life. Part of her deprivations resulted from the expenses of sending him to a good boarding school.

During the 1920s, Lasker-Schüler traveled extensively in Germany, Austria, and occasionally to Prague, giving poetry readings and visiting friends. In 1925, when Paul was diagnosed with tuberculosis, she poured all her resources into securing the best medical attention for him, selling sketches and drawings as well as her poetry to provide for his care in the best sanatorium in Switzerland. That year, friends organized another collection for her sake, while she continued to write lyrical verse and to appear in Berlin cafes dressed in outlandish clothes. Paul's death in 1927 became her greatest loss.

Always in the parting year
You will die to me, my child . . . .

In 1932, Else Lasker-Schüler was aged 63 when she received the Kleist Preis, one of Germany's highest literary honors. Her pleasure in this recognition might have been greater had it not been accompanied by the sting of anti-Semitism then on the rise. As one critic wrote, reflecting a view held by all too many at the time, "The pure Hebrew poetry of Else Lasker-Schüler has nothing to do with us Germans." Later the poet spoke of being knocked down by bullies in uniform, a common experience for Jews in Berlin during that period. On April 19, 1933, the political ascent of the National Socialists led her to flee Berlin, without luggage and telling no one of her destination. She went to Zürich, where she spent six nights sleeping on a park bench until her identity was discovered. On May 23, Albert Einstein noted, "Frau Else Lasker-Schüler also belongs to those noble individuals whom blind hatred has driven into exile." The poet who had been a nomad by choice, henceforth became an exile of circumstance.

In 1934, she accepted an invitation from a Greek couple to visit Palestine. Summing up her initial reaction to the Holy Land in a letter to Ernst Ginsberg, she wrote, "Glorious land of the Bible, caravans continually passing my balcony. Quite different than one expects. But difficult." In July, she returned to Switzerland, where her economic situation remained perilous as the readings that provided her income were often canceled. In 1936, her play *Arthur Aronymous,* a plea for reconciliation and peaceful coexistence of Christians and Jews, was not well received by the Zürich press, and she became more disillusioned. She wrote to Ginsberg: "I would like to flee across the ocean. . . . I am homesick for our garden and tower. What does the world want from me?"

In 1937, she made a second visit to Palestine, where she found a literary following among other exiles from Nazi Germany. Some, like Martin Buber, were already known to her, but for the most part she was forced to make new friends. Giving readings of her poetry, which always revived her, she would dress in a favorite Hussar-style black velvet jacket, and emote with enthusiasm. In August of that year, she returned to Switzerland where she was supported largely by the wealthy industrialist Silvain Guggenheim. But the threat of war was flooding Switzerland with exiles in need of financial help, and her situation grew increasingly difficult. In April 1939, she left for Palestine once more for a short visit. Instead, the looming war intervened, and Else Lasker-Schüler never again saw Europe.

In Palestine, the poet found many who welcomed her. In a land where most people were quite poor, she received a comfortable pension, but she was an old woman in her 70s who had suffered many losses, and she failed to adjust to her new home. For the writer so finely attuned to language, her greatest loss was the language of her birth and of her poetry that she could not publicly speak. This loss was the subject of her final work, *Mein blaues Klavier* (My Blue Piano):

> I have a blue piano at home
> But I don't know a single note.
>
> It is standing in the dark of the cellar door
> Since the world turned savage.

The dedication of this last volume of poems reads, "To my unforgettable friends in the cities of Germany—and to those who like me are exiled and now scattered over the world. In loyalty!"

Since her death, Else Lasker-Schüler has regained her place as one of the preeminent poets of Germany. But in her lifetime, she became trapped in the irony of her heritage: recognized by many as the greatest lyrical poet of her time, she was forced by Nazi racial ideology from her homeland, unable to lay claim to the only culture she had known since birth. In her era, however, no contribution to the German language and literature by a "pure Aryan" managed to equal hers.

SOURCES:

Cohn, Hans W. *Else Lasker-Schüler: The Broken World.* Cambridge: Cambridge University Press, 1974.

Eger, Henrik. "Else Lasker-Schüler," in *Literary Exiles in the Twentieth Century.* Edited by Martin Tucker. NY: Greenwood Press, 1991, p. 407–410.

"Lasker-Schüler, Else," in *Lexikon deutschsprachiger Schriftsteller.* 2 vols. Leipzig: VEB Bibliographisches Institut, 1972–74, vol. 2, pp. 14–15.

Pfanner, Helmut F. *Kulturelle Wechselbeziehungen im Exil—Exile Across Cultures.* Bonn: Bouvier Verlag Herbert Grundmann, 1986.

Politzer, Heinz. "The Blue Piano of Else Lasker-Schueler," in *Commentary.* Vol. 9. April 1950, pp. 335–344.

Resch, Margit. "Else Lasker-Schüler," in *Dictionary of Literary Biography.* Vol. 66, part I. Edited by James Hardin. Detroit, MI: Gale Research, 1988, pp. 285–305.

Robertson, Ritchie. "Nationalism and modernity: German-Jewish writers and the Zionist movement," in *Visions and Blueprints: Avant-Garde Culture and Radical Politics in Early Twentieth Century Europe.* Edited by Edward Timms and Peter Collier. Manchester: Manchester University Press, 1988, pp. 208–220.

Schwertfeger, Ruth. *Else Lasker-Schüler: Inside This Deathly Solitude.* NY: Berg, 1991.

Serke, Jürgen. *Die verbrannten Dichter.* Weinheim and Basel: Beltz & Gelberg Verlag, 1978.

Zimroth, Evan. "The Black Swan of Israel," in *Tikkun*. Vol. 5, no. 1. January–February, 1990, pp. 35–39.

John Haag,
Associate Professor of History,
University of Georgia, Athens, Georgia

Laski, Marghanita (1915–1988)

British novelist and critic. Name variations: (pseudonym) Sarah Russell. Born on October 24, 1915, in London, England; died on February 6, 1988, in Dublin, Ireland; daughter of Neville J. Laski (a lawyer) and Phina Gaster Laski; granddaughter of Dr. Moses Gaster; niece of Harold Laski; educated in Manchester; Somerville College, Oxford, B.A., 1936; married John Eldred Howard (a publisher), in 1937; children: Rebecca Howard; *Jonathan Howard.*

Honorary fellow of Manchester Polytechnic (1971); member of Annan Committee of Inquiry in Future of Broadcasting (1974–77); served as vice-chair of the Arts Council of Great Britain (1982), and chair of its Literature Panel (1980–88); worked as journalist, critic, broadcaster and novelist; contributed to Oxford English Dictionary.

Selected novels: Love on the Supertax *(1944); (under pseudonym Sarah Russell)* To Bed with Grand Music *(1946);* Tory Heaven, or Thunder on the Right *(published as* Toasted English, *1949);* Little Boy Lost *(1949);* The Village *(1952);* The Victorian Chaise-Longue *(1953).*

Selected criticism: Mrs. Ewing, Mrs. Molesworth, and Mrs. Hodgson Burnett *(1950);* Jane Austen and Her World *(1969);* George Eliot and Her World *(1973);* From Palm to Pine: Rudyard Kipling Abroad and at Home *(1987).*

Born in London in 1915, Marghanita Laski was the daughter of **Phina Gaster Laski** and Neville J. Laski, a King's counsel. Her maternal grandfather, Dr. Moses Gaster, was the chief rabbi of the Portuguese and Spanish Jews in England, and Laski grew up influenced by his religious views, as well as by the political views of her uncle Harold Laski, a renowned liberal. After bouts studying fashion design and philological research, Marghanita decided on a career in journalism, taking her B.A. at Somerville, a women's college at Oxford University. She married publisher John Eldred Howard in 1937 and took jobs in publishing, diary farming, nursing and intelligence, eventually working as a radio and television broadcaster. It was not until the birth of her second child that she began writing books.

Between 1944 and 1953, Laski published six novels, including *Love on the Supertax* (1944),

The Victorian Chaise-Longue (1953), and *Little Boy Lost*, a 1949 novel made into a Bing Crosby melodrama four years later. Her first serious novel, *Little Boy Lost* was the story of a father's search for his son in France immediately after World War II. Laski was a versatile novelist: her first book, *Love on the Supertax*, was a science-fiction account of postwar England; her second, *Toasted English*, was a satire about a mock utopia in which the English caste system is revived. *The Village* (1952) was a comedy of manners about class consciousness, and her last—and most popular—novel, *The Victorian Chaise-Longue*, was a suspense thriller, described by the *San Francisco Chronicle* as "a little jewel of horror."

Laski's first work of biographical criticism was 1950's *Mrs. Ewing, Mrs. Molesworth, and Mrs. Hodgson Burnett*, a study of Victorian children's authors *Juliana Horatia Ewing, *Mary Louisa Molesworth and *Frances Hodgson Burnett. Laski's reputation as a critical biographer increased with the publication of *Jane Austen and Her World* in 1969. Laski also write critical studies of George Eliot (*Mary Anne Evans) and Rudyard Kipling, along with two religious studies and a play, *The Offshore Island* (1955). A prolific contributor to periodicals, Laski was also an adept lexicographer and editor, writing for the *Oxford English Dictionary* and numerous publications on both sides of the Atlantic, including *The Times Literary Supplement*, *The New Yorker*, *Atlantic Monthly*, *The New York Times Book Review* and the Manchester *Guardian*.

A respected figure in British letters, Marghanita Laski died on February 6, 1988, in Dublin, Ireland.

SOURCES:
Contemporary Authors Online. The Gale Group, 1999.

Paula Morris, D.Phil.,
Brooklyn, New York

Laskine, Lily (1893–1988)

French harpist who concertized and recorded widely in a career that spanned over eight decades. Born Lily Aimée Laskine in Paris, France, on August 31, 1893; died in Paris on January 4, 1988; daughter of a medical doctor and a mother who loved the arts and was an excellent pianist; had one brother; married Roland Charmy (a violinist, chamber musician and professor at the Paris Conservatoire), on August 30, 1938.

Won a first prize at the Paris Conservatoire (1906); joined the Paris Opéra as a harpist (1909), the first woman in the orchestra; awarded the Cross of the Légion d'Honneur (1936) and a Chevalier (1958) for her musical accomplishments.

Lily Laskine was born in Paris, France, in 1893. Her father was a medical doctor who had dreamed of becoming a musician and served as the house doctor of the Orchestre de la Société des Concerts. Her mother had studied with Chopin's last living pupil. Both of Lily's parents were of Russian descent, and both were interested in her musical career as well. Mme Laskine's approach was practical; aware that Lily was not taken with the piano, she asked if Lily would like to play the harp. From that moment, Lily was enthralled with the instrument. Mme Laskine then took her daughter to Alphonse Hasselmans, professor of harp, at the Paris Conservatoire, but he informed them that he never took beginners. Mme Laskine took Lily by the hand, turned on her heel, and said, "In that case, my daughter will not play the harp!" Hasselmans capitulated.

After three years of private instruction, 11-year-old Lily entered the Conservatoire in Hasselmans' class. At 6'3", Hasselmans was an imposing figure who intimidated the little girl, though she loved and admired him. Her mother, however, was more intimidating than Hasselmans and never let her daughter attend lessons alone. Lily Laskine's entire musical education was brief—those three years of private instruction followed by two years at the Conservatoire. In 1906, at age 13, she won first prize at the Conservatoire for her playing. "You have your first prize," her mother concluded. "You know how to play the harp as well as Hasselmans. Now manage by yourself." Laskine never studied with anyone else.

Although Mme Laskine was her fierce advocate, Lily was closest to her father whom she adored. Music was their bond. At age 14, Lily began her career as a soloist carefully supervised by her parents, especially her mother. Her talent was immediately recognized and offers came from all sides. Mme Laskine, however, was cautious, protecting her daughter from being overwhelmed.

In 1909, Laskine applied to the Paris Opéra for the harp position and was named as a substitute, not because of her ability but because of her youth. She was the first woman ever hired by the Opéra orchestra and, at 16, the youngest performer. From that point forward, she played with many orchestras. The conductor Serge Koussevitzky wanted the young harpist to follow him to the United States, where he was engaged to lead several orchestras. Dr. Laskine objected, however, suspicious of Koussevitzky's reputation as a seducer. Instead, Laskine joined the Orchestre Straram, where she began to play classical as well as solo repertoire. She thorough-

ly enjoyed being part of the orchestra. "All of that completed my life," she once said. "I would never have known a similar pleasure if I had confined myself to the role of a soloist." In 1930, she performed in the première of Maurice Ravel's *Boléro*, which was conducted by the composer, and was amused by his stage fright. As solo harpist, she joined the Orchestre National de France which was founded in 1934. She played under the great conductors of the era—Richard Strauss, Arturo Toscanini, Bruno Walter, Paul Paray, and Philippe Gaubert.

In 1938, Laskine married Roland Charmy, a violinist who also taught at the Paris Conservatoire. In 1948, she was appointed to a professorship while continuing to concertize and record. In addition to her activities as a classical musician, Laskine worked with such popular singers as *Edith Piaf and Maurice Chevalier, making recordings with them. She also worked on film scores with Delerue, Michel Legrand, and Francis Lai. For more than 30 years, she served as harpist for the Comédie Française. Laskine was interested in expanding the harp repertory, and her efforts were largely successful. Albert Roussel, Jacques Ibert, Henri Marelli, and Jean-Michel Damase were only some of the many composers who wrote compositions for her.

Lily Laskine played with many musicians, including her husband. Her most famous recordings, however, may be with the flutist Jean Pierre Rampal. Despite the fact that she played the works of every major composer as well as the works of popular artists, Laskine was probably best known for her interpretations of Mozart. At the Salzburg Music Festival in 1937, she gave a landmark performance of Mozart's concerto for flute and harp, a work she later recorded with Sir Thomas Beecham. She also performed works by lesser-known composers, expanding the repertoire. Laskine appeared on stage well into her 80s. Among her many honors were Officier de la Légion d'Honneur, Grand Officier de l'Ordre National du Mérite, Commandeur des Arts et Lettres, and the Grand Prix du Film Musical. When the harpist died on January 4, 1988, age 94, Rampal gave perhaps her best epitaph when he described her as, "Music in the form of a woman!"

SOURCES:

"Mlle Lily Laskine," in *The Times* [London]. January 6, 1988, p. 10.

Nordman, Marielle. "Lily Laskine" (translated by Jane Weidensaul), in *American Harp Journal*. Vol. 10, no. 2. Winter 1985, pp. 3–7.

Rensch, Roslyn. *The Harp: Its History, Technique, and Repertoire*. NY: Praeger Publishers, 1969.

———. *Harps and Harpists*. Bloomington, IN: Indiana University Press, 1989.

John Haag,
Associate Professor of History,
University of Georgia, Athens, Georgia

Lasthenia of Mantinea and Axiothea of Phlius

Two philosophical students of Plato and Speusippus in the 4th century BCE. *Lasthenia was from the Arcadian city of Mantinea; Axiothea was from Phlius, near Corinth. Both women, who travelled to Athens to become students of Plato, were born into wealthy Peloponnesian families.*

In antiquity it was said that both Lasthenia and Axiothea donned masculine clothes in order to study philosophy. If they did so, their reason was less to fool Plato (for the great philosopher was virtually unique during the 4th century BCE in his appreciation of the potential of the feminine intellect) than to avoid scandal. We know nothing of their contribution to the intellectual life of the Academy, but they obviously spent some period of time there, for when Speusippus followed his uncle Plato as the Academy's head, both women remained in Athens and associated themselves with the new master. Dionysius the tyrant of Syracuse, himself closely associated with the Academy and its members, hinted in a letter that there may have been more than a platonic relationship between Lasthenia and Speusippus (who was always characterized as being more intemperate and pleasure seeking than Plato). Whether true or not, this allusion to a covered-up scandal implies that those associated with the Academy knew exactly who these women were, but that most preferred to be discreet as to the secret of their gender for fear of whatever negative publicity might taint the reputation of the Academy among those not intimately associated with Plato's circle.

SUGGESTED READING:

Waithe, M.E., ed. *Ancient Women Philosophers*. Boston, MA: Dordrecht Press, 1987.

William Greenwalt,
Associate Professor of Classical History,
Santa Clara University, Santa Clara, California

La Suze, comtesse de (1618–1683).

See Coligny, Henriette de.

Lathrop, Julia Clifford (1858–1932)

American social worker and reformer who was appointed director of the U.S. Children's Bureau (1912), becoming the first woman to head a government bureau. Born in Rockford, Illinois, on June 20, 1858; died in Rockford on June 29, 1932; eldest of five children, two girls and three boys, of William Lathrop (a lawyer and politician) and Sarah Adeline (Potter) Lathrop; attended Rockford Seminary (later Rockford College); graduated from Vassar College, 1880; never married; no children.

A pioneer in the field of child and public-welfare administration, Julia Lathrop was born in 1858, the eldest of five children, and raised in Rockford, Illinois, where the family had settled in 1851. Her father William Lathrop, a descendant of nonconformist cleric John Lothropp, headed his own law firm and helped organize the Illinois Republican Party, serving in the state legislature and later as a congressional representative. Her mother **Sarah Potter Lathrop**, valedictorian of the first graduating class of Rockford Seminary, was an ardent suffragist and a cultural leader in the community. Following high school, Julia Lathrop attended Rockford Seminary for a year, then transferred to Vassar College. Graduating in 1880, she then worked as a secretary in her father's law firm and devoted her spare time to a number of reform movements. In 1889, she left Rockford to join *Jane Addams at the newly founded social-service settlement, Hull House, in Chicago, where she remained for the next 20 years.

During the depression of 1893, Lathrop was appointed by governor John P. Altgeld to serve on the Illinois Board of Charities. In that capacity, she investigated 102 county farms and poor-houses in the state, examining the facilities and interviewing directors and inmates. In the winter of 1893–94, she interrupted that work to investigate relief applicants in the Hull House district. Her stark descriptions of Cook County's charitable institutions, including the infirmary and insane asylum, were included in the publication *Hull-House Maps and Papers* (1895). Continuing her state-wide work, Lathrop traveled to Europe in 1898, and again in 1900, to study modern techniques of organizing and staffing charitable facilities. Her experiences became part of a handbook, *Suggestions for Visitors to County Poorhouses and to Other Public Charitable Institutions*, published in 1905. Within its pages, as well as in her other published articles and in a speech to the National Conference of Charities and Corrections in 1902, Lathrop expressed her objections to the indiscriminate grouping of the young and old and the physically ill and insane in the same state institutions, and suggested separate facilities for delinquent children and specialized hospitals for mental patients. Later, in 1909, Lathrop became a charter member of Clifford W. Beer's National Committee for Mental Hygiene.

In 1901, Lathrop resigned from the Board of Charities in protest over the staffing of state institutions with inadequately trained attendants and political appointees. She would serve the board again from 1905 until her plan for its reorganization along nonpartisan lines was adopted in 1909. In 1903, in order to facilitate an upgrading of institutional staffing, Lathrop joined Graham Taylor in developing a training program which became the Chicago School of Civics and Philanthropy in 1908. Lathrop both lectured at the school, and, with *Sophonisba Breckinridge, established its research department. She continued to serve the school as a trustee until it became part of the University of Chicago in 1920.

Julia Lathrop's ongoing concern with the rehabilitation of child offenders led her to a joint effort with Jane Addams and *Lucy L. Flower to find a solution to the problem through the juvenile court movement. In 1899, with the support of the Chicago Woman's Club and the Chicago Bar Association, the women secured legislation to establish the first juvenile court in the country. Constructed on a site across the street from Hull House, the court building housed a detention home and eventually, in 1909, a psychopathic clinic. Lathrop was instrumental in establishing a Juvenile Court Committee which raised money for the salaries of two probation officers for the juvenile court. She also had a hand in the formation of the Illinois Immigrants' Protective League in 1909, and would remain a trustee of the organization until her death.

Lathrop, who never married, was a thin-faced woman with dominant features. Her sincerity and vitality, however, often transformed her plainness, and she could be persuasive. As her friend Jane Addams noted, she had the ability "to evoke a sympathetic response from the most unpromising human mind."

In 1912, Lathrop was appointed by President William Taft to head the newly created Children's Bureau of the Department of Commerce and Labor, and in that post became the first woman to head up a federal bureau. Although her budget and staff were limited, the bureau embarked on a series of studies, the first of which was on infant mortality. After developing a system for uniform birth registration, the bureau undertook studies on child labor, pen-

sions for mothers, illegitimacy, juvenile delinquency, nutrition, and retardation. During World War I, it was additionally concerned with the children of soldiers and working mothers. With the passage of the Keating-Owen Child Labor Act in 1916, a Child Labor Division was set up within the bureau to enforce the mandate, and Lathrop appointed *Grace Abbott to administrate the division. Lathrop went on to campaign for the Sheppard-Towner Act, offering federal grants-in-aid to states for maternity and infant-care programs, which passed in 1921. That same year, suffering from a hyperthyroid condition, Lathrop resigned as director of the Children's Bureau and was succeeded by Abbott.

Lathrop remained active in retirement, living with her sister in Rockford, Illinois. She served as president of the Illinois League of Women Voters (1922–24) and was also on a presidential commission investigating conditions for immigrants at Ellis Island. She wrote articles and contributed a chapter to *The Child, the Clinic, and the Court* (1925). From 1925 to 1931, she served as an assessor on the Child Welfare Committee of the League of Nations. In the months just before her death in 1932, she was still at work, attempting to win a reprieve

Julia Clifford Lathrop

for a 17-year-old Rockford boy under sentence of execution for murder.

SOURCES:

James, Edward T., ed. *Notable American Women, 1607–1950.* Cambridge, MA: The Belknap Press of Harvard University Press, 1971.

McHenry, Robert, ed. *Famous American Women.* NY: Dover, 1983.

SUGGESTED READING:

Addams, Jane. *My Friend, Julia Lathrop,* 1935.

Barbara Morgan,
Melrose, Massachusetts

Lathrop, Mother Mary Alphonsa
(1851–1926).

See Lathrop, Rose Hawthorne.

Lathrop, Rose Hawthorne
(1851–1926)

American Catholic convert and founder of an order of sisters dedicated to caring for terminally ill and destitute cancer patients. Name variations: Mother Alphonsa; Rose Hawthorne. Born in Lenox, Massachusetts, on May 20, 1851; died in New York on July 9, 1926; youngest of three children of Nathaniel Hawthorne (the novelist) and Sophia Peabody Hawthorne (1809–1871); married George Parsons Lathrop, in 1871 (separated 1893); children: Francis Lathrop (1876–1881).

Hawthorne family moved to Europe (1853); returned to America (1860); Nathaniel Hawthorne died (1864); Sophia Peabody Hawthorne died (1871); Rose and George Lathrop converted to Catholicism (1891); Rose moved to the Lower East Side of New York and began her work with cancer victims (1894); along with Alice Huber, Rose became a Dominican, taking the name Sister Alphonsa (1899); founded sisterhood, Servants of Relief for Incurable Cancer; established home in Hawthorne, New York (1901); served there (1901–26).

There is an honorable tradition in Roman Catholicism of women caring for the poor, the special work of many orders of sisters. Though Rose Hawthorne Lathrop was the descendant of American Puritans, she converted to Catholicism and joined in this tradition, taking under her protection one of the most despised and outcast groups, penniless terminal cancer victims. After an early life which showed few premonitions of this vocation, she turned to it following the failure of her marriage, and devoted to it the last 32 years of her long life.

The youngest child of **Sophia Peabody Hawthorne* and the novelist Nathaniel Hawthorne, Rose was born in 1851 at the family's home in Lenox, Massachusetts, just after family fortunes had taken a turn for the better with the success of her father's *The Scarlet Letter.* When she was two, her family moved to England. Nathaniel had been at Bowdoin College with Franklin Pierce, and he wrote a campaign biography of his old friend when Pierce was a presidential candidate in 1852. As a reward for his help, President Pierce made Nathaniel American minister to Liverpool. Much of Rose's early childhood was spent in Britain, but there was also an excursion to the major cities of Europe and a long stay in Rome, during which her father conceived and wrote *The Marble Faun.* Despite his success as a writer, Nathaniel did not want his children or his wife Sophia to follow his example. When he overheard young Rose tell a friend that she was writing stories, he was angry: "Never let me hear of your writing stories! I forbid you." He deplored all literary work by women, saying that "it does seem to me to deprive women of all delicacy."

The Hawthornes were back in America by 1860, and Rose was only 13 when her father died in 1864. The family stayed in Concord at first, and Rose attended Dio Lewis' Seminary for Young Ladies in nearby Lexington, which specialized in healthy outdoor activities, but after two years it burned to the ground. Sophia Hawthorne then decided to return to Europe and the family settled in Dresden, Germany. Rose's brother Julian described Rose as an impetuous young woman:

> She was very critical of others, and would endow this or that person with virtues which they lacked or with faults of which they were innocent; vehemently repenting afterward, her errors of judgment, but prone as ever to repeat them. She had no girl confidantes; and in spite of her beauty and charm, she disturbed rather than won her male acquaintance.... If she ever had a love affair, it was in some region of the imagination beyond the scope of daily life.

In Dresden, the Hawthornes met George and Francis Lathrop, young Americans studying poetry and art, and the two families soon became friends. The relationship continued when both families moved to London to escape the Franco-Prussian War of 1870. After a flirtation with her elder sister **Una Hawthorne**, George fell in love with Rose. She reciprocated, and they were married in England, when both were aged just 20. In the same year, Sarah Hawthorne died of pneumonia and was laid to rest in London. Una decided to stay in Britain, while Rose and George returned to the United States.

George Lathrop was a talented poet and author who wrote the first critical biography of Rose's father, which was highly regarded at the time. He became assistant editor (under William Dean Howells) of the *Atlantic Monthly*, then editor of the *Boston Courier*. He also founded the American Copyright League in 1883 to protect the rights of British authors in America and Americans in Britain: it drafted what later became the basic international copyright laws. Rose Hawthorne Lathrop spent the first years of her marriage illustrating children's books, writing poetry (including a collection, *Along the Shore*, 1888), and later publishing an affectionate reminiscence of her father's life, *Memories of Hawthorne* (1897), but she doubted her literary talent and was afraid that what progress she made as a writer might be through the influence of her husband and the memory of her father rather than by her own merits.

Rose gave birth to a son Francis in 1876, and, after several restless years of moving from place to place, the Lathrops managed to buy back the Concord house where her parents had spent their happiest years. They also had their son baptized a Catholic, though neither of them had yet "gone over to Rome." When he was five, however, Francis caught scarlet fever and died. After his death, George Lathrop began to drink heavily. Always a lover of convivial drinking, he now began to deteriorate into alcoholism, though he was still working hard and winning praise in literary society. In 1877, Rose's sister Una had also died. She had been working at a social settlement house in the slums of east London, and her example seems to have been influential in Rose's later decision to work with incurables.

In 1891, influenced by their Italian memories and by a persuasive friend, Alfred Chappell, Rose and George converted to Roman Catholicism, much to the surprise of their Concord neighbors. Rose later wrote that her father himself had had a thoroughly Catholic sensibility, which had prepared her mentally for conversion. Within two years, however, and notwithstanding the powerful Catholic emphasis on the sanctity of marriage, she found her husband's continued drinking intolerable and decided to leave him. They were reconciled later in 1893 and together researched and wrote *A Story of Courage,* the history of a Catholic convent, the Visitation Order in America at Georgetown, many of whose distinguished members were also converts. Soon after its publication in 1895, however, Rose left George again, and they were never

subsequently reconciled. He died of cirrhosis of the liver in 1898, at age 47.

Among Rose's literary friends was *Emma Lazarus, the wealthy daughter of Jewish immigrants and author of the poem inscribed at the base of the Statue of Liberty. They had met at the New York literary salon of Richard Watson Gilder in the mid-1880s and become mutual admirers. But Lazarus developed cancer and died in her late 30s; and witnessing her painful death also helped lead Rose Hawthorne Lathrop to her life's vocation, the care of terminal cancer patients.

In the 1890s, many doctors shared the popular belief that cancer could be passed on from person to person like an ordinary infection, with the result that sufferers were often shunned even by their own families. Rose Hawthorne Lathrop was convinced from what she had seen that this view of cancer as contagious was false. In 1894, she began to prepare herself by volunteering as an unpaid nurse in a New York cancer hospital; for three months, she changed dressings, studied

Rose Hawthorne Lathrop

treatments, and did what she could to comfort the dying. The work was gruesome; many of the women she cared for had foul-smelling cancers on the surface of their bodies, and only by an intense act of will could Rose overcome her physical horror of what she saw and smelled. Emma Lazarus' sister **Annie Lazarus** had tried this work and found it intolerable. Rose was indignant to learn that cancer hospitals usually discharged patients once they were convinced that a cure was impossible. She became friendly with one woman in her ward, Mrs. Watson, only to discover her suddenly missing one morning following the doctor's diagnosis that her condition was terminal. The result of ejection for poor patients was often a death in the most squalid surroundings, sometimes in the poorhouse or even on the streets.

[As a child, Rose was] an innate patrician. . . . Ugliness, dirt, disharmony, revolted her, and she averted herself from them with a haughty disgust. In view of her after career, this trait of hers must be emphasized.

—Julian Hawthorne

Rose Hawthorne Lathrop had no formal medical training and never showed any interest in becoming a doctor. Instead, she wanted to give comfort and dignity to the dying by providing them with a clean, dry, safe place to stay in the last months of their lives, at no cost. To begin her experiment, she rented a small apartment on the Lower East Side of New York City and took in women cancer patients whom doctors had discharged as incurable. She also visited those still living with their families, changing their dressings and making them as comfortable as possible. In the early years, Rose had no accommodation for men, so they too had to be "out-patients."

Her friends and relatives were both impressed and dismayed by the work she had chosen. Several sent contributions of money and a few came to work with her occasionally, but found the work gruelling and painful. In 1897, Rose hired a permanent assistant, **Alice Huber**, who had come to New York from Kentucky to study art but now moved into the hospice and took on the cancer work full time. Their first patient was the same Mrs. Watson whom Rose had befriended earlier, and whereas the hospital had excluded her, she now became part of the new household until her death. Another early assistant and enthusiast for the work was James J. Walsh, a Catholic doctor and popular historian who later wrote a book about Rose Hawthorne

Lathrop and championed her cause among wealthy potential donors. Walsh also gave popular courses of public lectures and donated all the proceeds to the hospice.

Lathrop and Huber, coming from prosperous families, found their new situation a jolting change from earlier life. The sheer noise of street life all around them was unnerving to women who had grown up in spacious, silent surroundings. They had to give up all their leisurely diversions from earlier life. Rose wrote in *Christ's Poor*, her fund-raising journal:

> I don't believe there was anyone who loved fancy work, the reading of novels, painting, the theaters, chatting socially with friends about jolly matters, more heartily than I have done. I remember that on the day when I realized there would be no more time for me to paint in oils or water colors again if I attended faithfully to the work heaven seemed to be giving me to perform, it was as if a sword entered my bosom and I said, "O God, I cannot make that one sacrifice for You." But all the same I knew I should make it.

She was convinced that her Catholic faith gave her the strength to do this work and suggested to Huber that they wear plain dresses similar to those worn by nuns. This was partly to afford them a little more safety in the dangerous area where they worked but also partly a declaration that they were doing the sort of work the Catholic sisterhoods undertook. In recognition of her earlier preconversion life, Rose Hawthorne Lathrop at first chose the name "Daughters of the Puritans." Later, as they attracted new recruits, and with the enthusiastic assent of Archbishop Corrigan of New York, they became Third Order Dominican Sisters, taking the title "Servants for the Relief of Incurable Cancer." Rose now adopted the name of Sister Alphonsa, in honor of St. Alphonsus of Liguori, while Alice Huber became Sister Rosa, in honor of St. *Rose of Lima. When their ranks had swelled to eight nurses, they became Dominican sisters, dedicated to St. Rose of Lima.

Rose disliked the sternness of contemporary attitudes to charity and insisted on maintaining a humane environment. Experience soon told her that middle-class views (such as that poverty was the result of laziness and that generous charitable giving merely encouraged it) were hopelessly inadequate. "Severe theories will never satisfy a hungry person," she observed, "even if they eradicate poverty in the twenty-first century." Besides, "Christ did not ask us to eradicate poverty—on the contrary we are allowed to make it at home with us. The poor are a very valuable opportunity for kindness, and help for them is never degrading unless it is falsely given."

Rose was a skillful and inexhaustible fund raiser and as the years passed the Servants' funds began to swell (Mark Twain was one of many literary celebrities who contributed generously), enabling them to buy first a large Cherry Street house a few blocks from their first site, and later a hilltop estate, Rosary Hill, overlooking the Hudson River a few miles outside New York City. Further extensions and enlargements continued through the next two decades, and in the last years of her life Lathrop watched with relief as a fireproof building rose on Rosary Hill to replace its rickety and flammable predecessor. The cost of maintaining these establishments and trying to find accommodations for growing numbers of residents led to perpetual financial crises, but determined fund raising enabled the Servants to survive each one. They also raised money to give dignified funerals to their guests, since burial in Potter's Field was a source of particular dread to many. The little graveyard at Rosary Hill had as its centerpiece a stone cross donated by one of poet Henry Wadsworth Longfellow's three daughters.

Visiting Lathrop at Rosary Hill in the early 1920s when they were both in their 70s, her brother Julian observed: "I found her . . . naive and childlike, like the little girl who had been my playmate, but with this difference. The passions of her nature, doubtless as urgent as ever, centered no longer round her personal fate. . . . She lived, labored, and prayed only for those incarnations of mortal misery which she had drawn about her." But even then, in her black robes, "cheerfulness emanated from her like a fragrance." Rose Hawthorne Lathrop remained active to the end of her life despite deteriorating health, dying in 1926 at the age of 75.

Patrick Allitt,
Professor of History, Emory University, Atlanta, Georgia

Latife Hanim (1898–1975).

See Hanim, Latife.

Latimer, Elizabeth (d. 1395)

Baroness Latimer. Died on November 5, 1395; married John Neville, 3rd baron Neville of Raby, in 1382; children: John Neville, 6th baron Latimer (d. 1430).

Latimer, Elizabeth W. (1822–1904)

English-born author and translator. Name variations: Elizabeth Wormeley; Elizabeth Wormeley Latimer.

Born Mary Elizabeth Wormeley in London, England, on July 26, 1822; died in Baltimore, Maryland, on January 4, 1904; daughter of Ralph Randolph Wormeley (a rear admiral in the British Navy) and Caroline (Preble) Wormeley; married Randolph Brandt Latimer, in 1856; children: several.

Works: Forest Hill: A Tale of Social Life in 1830–31 (1846); Anabel: A Family History (1853); Our Cousin Veronica: or, Scenes and Adventures over the Blue Ridge (1855); (translator) L. Ulbach's Madame Gosselin (1878); (with A.R.W. Curtis) Recollections of Ralph Randolph Wormeley, Rear Admiral, R.N.; Written Down by His Three Daughters (1879); Salvage (1880); My Wife and My Wife's Sister (1881); Princess Amelie: A Fragment of Autobiography (1883); Familiar Talks on Some of Shakespeare's Comedies (1886); (translator) L. Ulbach's The Steel Hammer: A Novel (1888); (translator) L. Ulbach's For Fifteen Years: A Sequel to The Steel Hammer (1888); (translator with J.H. Allen) E. Renan's History of the People of Israel (1888–96); A Chain of Errors (1890); (translator) *George Sand's Nanon (1890); France in the Nineteenth Century, 1830–1890 (1892); Russia and Turkey in the Nineteenth Century (1893); England in the Nineteenth Century (1894); (edited) My Scrap-book of the French Revolution (1894); Italy in the Nineteenth Century and the Making of Austro-Hungary and Germany (1896); Spain in the Nineteenth Century (1897); Europe in Africa in the Nineteenth Century (1898); Judea from Cyrus to Titus, 537 B.C.–70 A.D. (1899); The Last Years of the Nineteenth Century (1900); (translator) J.C.L. de Sismondi's The Italian Republics (1901); (translator) The Love Letters of Victor Hugo, 1820–1822 (1901); Men and Cities of Italy (1901); The Prince Incognito (1902); (translator) G. Gourgaud's Talks of Napoleon at St. Helena with Gen. Baron Gourgaud, Together with the Journal Kept by Gourgaud on Their Journey from Waterloo to St. Helena (1903).

The daughter of American-born parents, Elizabeth Wormeley Latimer was born in 1822 in London, where her father, a naturalized British subject, served as a rear admiral in the British Navy. Latimer spent her youth traveling extensively and living in London and Paris. Although her education was sporadic, she grew up in the company of the socially prominent and made her debut in the court of Louis Philippe. When Latimer was in her 20s, the family returned to America and lived in Boston and Newport, Rhode Island. Encouraged in her writing by *Julia Ward Howe, Latimer published her first book in 1846. She followed up with several novels before her marriage to Randolph Latimer in 1865. The couple moved to Baltimore, Maryland, where for the next 20 years Latimer devoted herself to home and family. She returned to her literary career in 1878, turning out novels, magazine articles, translations, and histories for the next 30 years.

Latimer's novels are criticized for lacking well-rounded characters, though *Our Cousin Veronica* (1855), which utilized many of the author's experiences in England and Virginia, is cited by **Karen Steele** in *American Women Writers* for its vivid action and description. Latimer is better remembered for her histories, which reflect her own great love of the past and her fascination with the adventures of royalty, military figures, and explorers. Well researched and written in a lively, readable style, they were extremely popular and went through numerous editions. "In all of her histories," writes Steele, "one senses her desire to keep abreast of events in the world and, at the century's end, to sum up historical achievements." Elizabeth Latimer continued to write until her death on January 4, 1904.

SOURCES:
Mainiero, Lina, ed. *American Women Writers*. NY: Frederick Ungar, 1980.
McHenry, Robert, ed. *Famous American Women*. NY: Dover, 1983.

Barbara Morgan,
Melrose, Massachusetts

la Tour d'Auvergne, Madeleine de
(1501–1519).

See Madeleine de la Tour d'Auvergne.

La Tour du Pin, Henriette de
(1770–1853)

French writer. Name variations: Henrietta, Marquise de La Tour du Pin. Born Henriette-Lucy Dillon in Paris, France, in 1770; died on April 2, 1853; daughter of Arthur Dillon (1750–1794) and **Lucie de Rothe** (1751–1782, lady-in-waiting to Marie Antoinette); married Frederic-Séraphin, comte de Gouvernet, later Marquise de La Tour du Pin (1759–1837, a soldier, prefect, and minister to the court at The Hague), in 1787; children: Humbert (1790–1816); Séraphine (1793–1795); Charlotte, known as Alix (1796–1822, who married the comte de Liedekerke Beaufort); **Cécile de La Tour du Pin** (1800–1817); Aylmar (1806–1867); three others died in infancy.

"Her memoirs are every bit as fascinating as those of *Madame de Staël, *Madame de Genlis, and *Madame d'Abrantès," wrote John Weightman in *The Observer*. "She has an enchanting eighteenth-century liveliness as well as an indomitable spirit. She was obviously a remarkable woman." Henriette de La Tour du Pin wrote of the Revolution and the Age of Napoleon because she had experienced both events firsthand.

She was born in 1770, during the final years of the reign of Louis XV. Two years after her marriage at age 16 to Frederic-Séraphin, comte de Gouvernet, later Marquise de La Tour du Pin, the revolution of 1789 broke out, robbing her of her post as lady-in-waiting to Queen *Marie Antoinette** and prompting her family to flee to Albany, in upstate New York, to wait out the revolution and avoid the guillotine. Her father Arthur Dillon, whose second wife was **Comtesse de La Touche** (first cousin of Empress *Josephine), was executed by the Revolutionaries in 1794.

Following a return to France, Mme de La Tour du Pin was lady-in-waiting to Queen *Marie Louise of Austria** while her husband served Napoleon as prefect in Brussels (1801–12), then prefect in Amiens. He was also one of the Ambassadors Plenipotentiary of France at the Congress of Vienna and ambassador in Turin (1820–30).

Having fled the Revolution of 1830, she and her husband lived in Nice and Lausanne. Following the death of her husband in 1837, she settled at Pisa, in Tuscany, where she lived until her death on April 2, 1853. The mother of eight children, Mme de La Tour du Pin determined, at age 50, to document her life for her only surviving child.

SUGGESTED READING:
Memoirs of Madame de La Tour du Pin. Translated by Felice Harcourt. NY: McCall Publishing, 1971.

La Tules (c. 1820–1852).
See Barcelo, Gertrudis.

Latynina, Larissa (1934—)
Russian gymnast who won 17 Olympic gold medals. Born Larissa Semyonovna Latynina in the USSR on December 27, 1934; married with two children.

Won World championship in the combined (1958, 1962), in the balance beam (1958), in the horse vault (1958), for the floor exercises (1962); won Olympic gold medals in the individual all-around (1956, 1960), in the horse vault (1956), for the floor exercises (1956 [tied with Ágnes Keleti], 1960, 1964); won Olympic team gold (1956, 1960, 1964); won the *silver in the individual all-around (1964); won the silver in the balance beam (1960) and the bronze (1964); won the silver in the uneven bars (1956, 1960) and the bronze (1964); won the silver in the horse vault (1964) and the bronze (1960).*

Larissa Latynina, perhaps the greatest gymnast of them all, held the women's record for both individual and total world championship titles. Between 1956 and 1964, she won ten individual championships and five team titles. In the Olympics, Latynina accumulated six individual gold, three team gold, four silver, and four bronze medals. Her total of 17 Olympic medals topped any Olympian—male or female—in any sport. She was also the only gymnast in the world to have won medals in every event on the program in two Olympics. During these years, she also married and given birth to two children.

In the 1956 Melbourne Olympics, 22-year-old Latynina went head-to-head with 35-year-old *Ágnes Keleti of Hungary. That year, Keleti ended her Olympic career with three golds and two silver medals while Latynina began hers with four golds and one silver. In the floor exercises, the two tied for the gold medal (causing some to miscalculate Latynina's medal total, an erroneous 18). Four years later in Rome, Soviet gymnasts topped all rivals. The women won every event except the balance beam, and Larissa Latynina led the pack with three golds, two silvers, and a bronze. Her total domination of the sport was not halted until the 1964 Tokyo Olympics, with the arrival of *Vera Caslavska. Even so, Latynina added two golds, two silver and two bronzes to her total.

The intricacy of her routines and her technical brilliance revolutionized women's gymnastics. But the world had not yet begun to pay heed to the sport, making Larissa Latynina a relative unknown outside the Soviet Union. Upon her retirement, she became a coach for the Soviet national team.

Lauder, Estée (1910—)

American cosmetics entrepreneur. Name variations: Estee Lauder. Born Josephine Esty (changed to Esther on her birth certificate) Mentzer on July 1, 1910, in Corona, Queens, New York; youngest of two daughters of Max Mentzer (a businessman) and Rose (Schotz) Rosenthal Mentzer; graduated from P.S. 14; married Joseph Lauter (later changed to Lauder), in 1930 (divorced 1939, remarried 1943, died 1983); children: two sons, Leonard and Ronald.

Named by *Time* magazine as one of the top "100 Builders & Titans of the 20th Century," Estée Lauder founded a "little business" in the 1930s that grew into a cosmetics empire that at the end of the 20th century controlled 45% of the cosmetics market in U.S. department stores and sold in 118 countries. An ambitious, hard-working woman who personally oversaw every aspect of her business from testing to packaging, Lauder has become part of American business folklore.

Born Josephine Esther Mentzer, Lauder was the youngest of two daughters of **Rose Schotz Mentzer**, a Hungarian beauty, and her second husband Max Mentzer, a Czechoslovakian who had given up a privileged life to come to America. Rose, who was ten years Max's senior, brought six children to her second marriage, so Lauder had five half-brothers and a half-sister, in addition to her older sister **Renee Mentzer**, to whom she was very close. Lauder was raised in Queens, where her father ran a hardware store and she attended public school. Even as a child, she was preoccupied with beauty rituals and spent hours brushing her mother's hair and applying facial "treatments" to any female in the family who would sit still long enough. Probably the most influential person in her young life was her mother's brother John Schotz, a skin specialist from Hungary who came to America for a visit and was forced to stay because of the war. "Maybe I'm glorifying my memories," writes Lauder in her 1985 autobiography *Estée*, "but I believe today that I recognized in my Uncle John my true path." In the stable behind the Mentzer house, John produced a glorious "snow" cream, which Lauder slathered over her face and the faces of all her friends.

The second influence on Estée's career was Joe Lauter (later changed to Lauder), whom she met on a holiday and married in 1930. The couple settled in New York City and started a family while Lauder continued to experiment with her uncle's creams, improving them with her own personal touches. She sold her first products, a Cleansing Oil, a Creme Pack, and a Super-Rich All-Purpose Cream, to the House of Ash Blondes, a beauty salon she frequented on West 72nd Street. Her outlets gradually grew to include shops in New York as well as the hotels and resorts of Long Island. Lauder's early technique of demonstrating her products and providing free introductory samples became the trademark of her selling style; to this, she added a dollop of aggressive charm. "You simply cannot say 'no' to her," said one buyer.

While Lauder was caught up in her career, her marriage foundered, and in 1939, she and Joe divorced, though they remained good friends. Lauder then embarked on a number of romantic interludes, including one with Charles Moskowitz, an executive at Metro-Goldwyn-Mayer, but her ties to Joe and her young son Leonard remained strong. Four years after their divorce, she and Joe remarried, vowing never to be separated again for more than a few days. Joe also gave up his job and became a partner in the Lauder enterprise, handling the finances and production aspects of the business while Lauder oversaw sales. In 1944, a year after renewing their vows, the Lauders had a second son, Ronald.

The company was not the overnight success that some have come to believe. "I cried more than I ate," Lauder wrote of those early years. "There was constant work, constant attention to detail, lost hours of sleep, worries, heartaches. Friends and family didn't let a day go by without discouraging us." By 1946, however, with four products and their first substantial order from Saks Fifth Avenue, the Lauders had established an office in New York. The business took a decidedly upward turn in 1953, with the introduction of Youth Dew, a bath oil that doubled as a skin perfume and was distinguished by its lasting scent. The product took the cosmetics industry by storm and put Lauder solidly into the fragrance business. In the years since, Lauder has had equal success with such fragrances as Estée, Azurée, Aliage, Private Collection, White Linen, and Beautiful, all personally formulated and tested by her. The cosmetics portion of the business also flourished under several product lines, including Clinique (a hypoallergenic line for women with sensitive skins), Prescriptives (a customized makeup line), and the classic Estée Lauder products. In 1964, she launched a line of fragrances and skin-care products for men christened Aramis, the first of its kind. A customized cologne, JHL, named for her husband, would later be added to the men's line.

Lauder attributes much of her success to the fact that the business is very much a family affair. What is not handled by the family is entrusted to a hand-picked cadre of employees selected from the best and brightest in the industry. "You have to hire surrogate bosses, responsible thinking people who are able to move fast, take risks, and make judgments that would be similar to yours," she says. Lauder's oldest son Leonard has been involved with the business since high school; he began working full time for the company in 1958, fresh out of the navy. Admitting that it takes a cooperative effort to survive and grow in business, Lauder credits Leonard with making the company one of international repute.

Leonard's wife, **Evelyn Lauder**, a former teacher, began working for the company as a young bride, and became an integral part of the business. Lauder's younger son Ronald worked in the business for 17 years before moving on to international management. Lauder credits him with helping to expand the European markets and with introducing Prescriptives. Ronald's wife **Jo Carole Lauder** also worked for Estée before she took on museum work. As well, Lauder's grandchildren hold key positions in the company, insuring continuity if not innovation. But Lauder was never known as a trend-setter, writes **Grace Mirabella** in *Time* (December 7, 1998). "What you had with Estée Lauder was the quality of her view, of her demand for an ultrafeminine portrayal of the product. Every woman in every ad was the essence of femininity. Is that the kind of women we are talking about now? I'm not sure, but women know who Lauder is. Hers is a product with a focus—it's not MTV."

Lauder's passion for work was apparently balanced by a passion for living well. Her hard-earned compensations included homes in the south of France, Palm Beach, London, and New York, each elegantly decorated and complemented by an appropriate garden. "Being surrounded by color and fragrance is as important to me as eating," she writes. Even when she was working seven days a week, Lauder rarely turned down a social invitation; refreshed by an afternoon nap, she was out five nights a week on average. Lauder viewed her social and business life as complementary, one building on the other. She also liked to entertain in a grand manner, and her legendary parties, planned meticulously, honored such luminaries as Pablo Picasso, the Duke and *Duchess of Windsor, the Aga Khan, and Monaco's princess, *Grace Kelly.

Lauder, who turned the business over to her son in 1982 but remained chair of the board of Estée Lauder, Inc., has received numerous honors in recognition of her business achievements and philanthropy. *Harper's Bazaar* named her one of "100 American Women of Accomplishment" in 1967, and 575 business and financial editors recognized her as one of the "Top Ten Outstanding Women in Business" in 1970. Additionally, she has been awarded the Insignia of Chevalier of the Legion of Honor (1978), the gold medal of the City of Paris (1979), as well as the Crystal Apple from the Association for a Better New York (1977) in recognition of the three world-famous adventure playgrounds created through the Estée and Joseph H. Lauder Foundation. Lauder has also been active in National Cancer Care and the Manhattan League.

Lauder's husband Joe died suddenly in 1983, on the night of a gala celebration of the couple's 53rd wedding anniversary. Lauder was devastated. She remained active, however, until 1994, when she broke her hip. She has not been seen in public since that time, although her office at Lauder headquarters remains as she left it, as though she might return to occupy it at any moment.

SOURCES:

Kaltenborn, Ruth. "Estee Lauder—The Sweet Smell of Success," in *Palm Beach Life* [Palm Beach, Florida]. December 1974.

Lauder, Estée. *Estée: A Success Story*. NY: Random House, 1985.

Mirabella, Grace. "Estee Lauder," in *Time*. December 7, 1998, pp. 183–184.

SUGGESTED READING:

Israel, Lee. *Beyond the Magic*, 1984.

Barbara Morgan,
Melrose, Massachusetts

Lauderdale, duchess of (1626–1698).

See Murray, Elizabeth.

Lauenstein, Countess (c. 1803–1854).

See Sontag, Henriette.

Laughlin, Clara E. (1873–1941).

See Anderson, Margaret Carolyn for sidebar.

Laumann, Silken (1964—)

Canadian athlete and motivational speaker. Born Silken Laumann on November 14, 1964, in Mississauga, Ontario, Canada; daughter of Hans Laumann and Seigrid Laumann; sister of Danielle Laumann (b. 1961), also seen as Daniele; educated in Mississauga public schools; attended University of Victoria, 1984–86; University of Western Ontario, B.A., 1988; married John Wallace; children: William.

Won the bronze medal in double sculls with sister Danielle at the Olympics (1984); won two World Cup championships in rowing (1991); overcame difficult circumstances to win the bronze medal in single sculls at the Olympics (1992); won silver medal in single sculls at the Olympics (1996).

Born in Mississauga, Ontario, in 1964, Silken Laumann began sculling when she was 17, training on the Credit River with her older sister **Danielle Laumann**. Only two years later, the sisters won the bronze medal in double sculls at the 1984 Summer Olympics in Los Angeles. With such a quick rise to the top in her new sport, the sky seemed the limit for Laumann, who, unlike her sister, was determined to pursue an athletic career in earnest. However, in 1985, Laumann began to experience severe back pain whenever she rowed. Medical authorities determined that she suffered from a congenital curvature of the spine, which was aggravated by the movements involved in sculling. Despite the pain, Laumann was unwilling to abandon rowing. A disappointing finish in seventh place at the 1988 Olympic Games in Seoul, South Korea, shook her confidence, and she briefly considered giving up the sport.

In 1989, unhappy with the way Canadian women's rowing teams trained, Laumann began training with the men's rowing team, coached by Michael Spracklen. "I had worked hard before," she told *Maclean's* magazine, "but with Mike, I knew that I was putting my effort into something that would work." Two years later, competing as an individual racer in the women's heavyweight division, she won the World Cup of rowing. This honor is bestowed on the competitor who scores the largest total of points in a series of races. Competing in the 2,000-meter singles at the same competition, Laumann took the world championship, narrowly defeating Rumania's **Elisabeta Lipa**. These dual wins in 1991 made Laumann the woman to beat at the 1992 Summer Olympics in Barcelona.

However, in May of 1992, less than three months before the Summer Games, Laumann suffered severe injuries while warming up for a rowing competition in Essen, Germany. A German boat struck Laumann's boat, driving part of it into her right leg, breaking a bone and ripping nerves, muscles, and ligaments. For a brief time, it appeared the accident might end her rowing career. "The muscles on the outside of my right leg were peeled back and hanging down to the ankle," she told *Maclean's*. "I think that's why the doctors thought I would never row again. In a person of average fitness, they would have just cut the muscle off. The blood wouldn't get back up there, and the tissue would die. But my muscle has lived. It's basically astounding, and I guess I'm surprising a lot of doctors." No less astounding was the speed with which Laumann bounced back from this devastating injury. While still bedridden in the hospital, she began exercising to keep her upper body in shape. She underwent a number of operations and a skin graft. Before she was fully able to walk again, she returned to her scull, having missed less than a month of training.

Laumann's performance in the Barcelona Games was hailed by sports commentators and singled out as one of the most inspirational moments in the history of the Olympics. Still able to walk only with the help of a leg brace, she prepared for her event by stripping off the brace at the dock and lowering herself into her scull with pain evident on her face. She rowed to a bronze medal, finishing behind Elisabeta Lipa and **Annelies Bredael** of Belgium. "I chose to work on the premise that there was a little light at the end of the tunnel," said Laumann, "and that I could work towards that light." For much of the race, she was in fourth place, trailing **Anne Marden** of the United States. "With about 1,000 meters to go, I thought I was going to die," she later recalled. "I knew I couldn't win, but I wanted one of the medals. I said to myself, 'I'm not coming in fourth.' Fourth is the worst position—to just miss a medal." Laumann focused her attention on Marden, concentrating all her energies on overtaking the American. Just a few meters before the finish line, she pulled ahead of Marden and held on to third place.

Twice named Canada's female athlete of the year (1991 and 1992), Laumann received a number of honors during her years as a rower. She was given the Lou Marsh Award as Canada's outstanding athlete in 1991, received the Meritorious Services Cross in 1994, had a street named in her honor in her native Mississauga, and was awarded honorary degrees from several Canadian universities. In 1996, she was the subject of a made-for-television film, *Golden Will: The Silken Laumann Story*, and in 1997 she received the *Wilma Rudolph Courage Award.

In 1995, Laumann won gold medals in single and quadruple sculls at the Pan-American Games; officials later stripped her of these medals when drug tests detected an over-the-counter cold medicine she had taken during the week of the race. At the 1996 Summer Olympics in Atlanta, she rowed to a silver medal in the single sculls. Largely on the strength of her 1992 Olympic victory, Laumann started lecture tours in Canada and the United States, making about 30 speeches each year to young people.

In March of 1999, Laumann officially announced her retirement from competitive rowing. In a press conference in Victoria, British Columbia, where she lived with husband John Wallace and young son William, she said that she had lost the "competitive desire" she considered essential to success. Summing up her career, despite the adversity, Laumann had earlier noted, "There are not that many areas of your life where you can be one of the best in the world."

SOURCES:

Greenspan, Bud. *100 Greatest Moments in Olympic History*. Los Angeles, CA: General Publishing, 1995.

Johnson, Anne Janette. *Great Women in Sports*. Detroit, MI: Visible Ink, 1998.

Who's Who of Canadian Women, 1997. Toronto: Who's Who Publications, 1997.

Don Amerman,
freelance writer, Saylorsburg, Pennsylvania

Launay, Marguerite Cordier de, Mme de Staal (1684–1750).

See Staal de Launay, Madame de.

Launay, vicomte de (1804–1855).

See Girardin, Delphine.

Laura

Saint and abbess. Flourished when the Saracens held Spain, between the 9th to 11th centuries.

Saint Laura, who had been married before she became a nun, was the abbess of the convent of St. Mary of Culédor. Arrested by Saracens, Laura was thrown into a cauldron of boiling pitch. Her feast day is on October 19.

Laura (1308–1348).

See Noves, Laure de.

Laurence, Margaret (1926–1987)

Canadian writer who was one of the key figures in the development of 20th-century Canadian literature.

Born Jean Margaret Wemyss on July 18, 1926, in Neepawa, Manitoba, Canada; died in Lakefield, Ontario, Canada, on January 5, 1987; daughter of Robert Wemyss (a lawyer) and Verna (Simpson) Wemyss; attended public school in Neepawa and United College in Winnipeg, Manitoba; married John Laurence, known as Jack, in 1947 (divorced 1969); children: Jocelyn (b. 1952) and David (b. 1955).

Her mother died suddenly (1930); her mother's sister came to Neepawa to look after her and married Robert Wemyss, becoming her stepmother (1931); Robert Wemyss died (1935); submitted first story to a Winnipeg Free Press writing contest (1939); worked as a reporter for the Winnipeg Citizen (1947–48); moved to England with husband (1949), and then to British protectorate of Somaliland (1952); family returned to Canada (1957) and she began writing; separated from her husband (1960) and returned to England with her children; made a Companion of the Order of Canada (1971); returned to Canada (1973); awarded the Governor-General's Medal for fiction (1974); was chancellor of Trent University in Peterborough (1980–83).

Selected works: A Tree for Poverty: Somali Poetry and Prose (1954, reprinted 1970); This Side Jordan (1960); The Tomorrow-Tamer (1964); The Prophet's Camel Bell (1964); The Stone Angel (1964, reprinted 1968); A Jest of God (1966, reprinted 1974); Long Drums and Cannons: Nigerian Dramatists and Novelists, 1952–1966 (1968); The Fire-Dwellers (1969, reprinted 1973); A Bird in the House (1970, reprinted 1974); Jason's Quest (1970); The Diviners (1974).

The awareness of an ability to write came early to Margaret Laurence. From age seven, she wrote stories; at age twelve, she won Honorable

Mention in a children's writing competition conducted by the *Winnipeg Free Press,* a major Canadian newspaper. Often writing from her own experiences, she produced characters that were strong, individualistic, and tragic, and made her work a meditation on the human experience, not just in Canada but in the broader world as well. Laurence is regarded as one of the most influential Canadian writers of the late 20th century.

A deep influence on her early writing was the encouragement she received from her stepmother, **Margaret Simpson Wemyss,** for whom she was named, and who was also her aunt. In 1930, when Margaret Laurence was only four years old, her mother **Verna Simpson Wemyss** died. That year, Margaret Simpson Wemyss, eight years older than her sister Verna, returned to the small town of Neepawa to raise Verna's daughter. A clever and loving women, Margaret Simpson Wemyss had been a successful schoolteacher in Calgary; the following year, she married Margaret's father, Robert Wemyss, who was a lawyer. The bond between stepmother and daughter was young Margaret Laurence's salvation, since her father died when she was nine.

*W*hat I care about trying to do is to express something that in fact everybody knows, but doesn't say.
—Margaret Laurence

Neepawa was to serve as the model for the fictional town of Manawaka which is the setting for all of Margaret Laurence's Canadian stories. About 125 miles northwest of Winnipeg, Neepawa is the capital of the province of Manitoba, and located on a plateau overlooking a valley where two creeks merge to form the White Mud River. Encompassing fertile soil, the district was settled by Scottish pioneers who trekked westward from eastern Canada in the 1870s and 1880s in search of farmland. All the history of this small town became part of Laurence's Manawaka, but it was the cataclysmic events of her own time—the effects of the First World War, the hardships of the Great Depression, and the Second World War—that were to be shown with particular impact.

In 1944, Margaret was 18 when she left Neepawa to attend United College in Winnipeg. There she studied English and developed the foundations of her literary style, while publishing poetry and her first short stories in the college newspaper, where she was also the assistant editor in her final year. After graduation, Laurence worked for a year as a reporter for the *Winnipeg Citizen,* a labor-oriented newspaper, writing book reviews and a daily radio column.

In 1947, at age 21, she married John Laurence, a civil engineering student known as Jack. After his graduation in 1949, the young couple left Canada for England; a year later, they left England for Africa, where Jack Laurence had been hired for a dam and dike building project in the deserts of the British protectorate of Somaliland, now Somalia. When the British Colonial office discouraged Jack from taking his wife along, on the grounds that Somaliland would to be too rough and rugged a place for a woman, Jack described Margaret as "a kind of female Daniel Boone" and finally persuaded the authorities she should be allowed to go.

For the next two years, the couple lived in isolated desert camps, sometimes sleeping in tents and at other times in their vehicles. With none of the comforts of modern life, Margaret Laurence relished the experience of Somaliland. As she later wrote, "Nothing can equal in hope and apprehension the first voyage east of Suez, yourself eager for all manner of oddities." While Jack worked on dam constructions, she became intrigued by the Somali people, particularly their extensive oral literature, and set out to collect and translate examples of the tales and poems of this essentially nomadic people. In 1954, her translations were published as *A Tree for Poverty: Somali Poetry and Prose.*

In 1952, Laurence returned to England for the birth of her daughter, **Jocelyn Laurence;** the family then moved on to the Gold Coast, now Ghana, where David was born in 1955; they remained there until 1957. Shortly after David's birth, in August 1955, Laurence began drafting her first novel, *This Side Jordan.*

Ghana is the setting of both *This Side Jordan* and *The Tomorrow-Tamer,* a collection of short stories. The country achieved independence in 1957, only a few months after the departure of the Laurences, and the charged political atmosphere of the years leading up to that independence inform both works. *This Side Jordan* portrays the conflict between the two prevailing social groups within Ghanese society, one colonial British and one African, during this time. Built around the threat felt by the British administrators of an established textile company during the shift to African control, the story identified the British group as sympathetic to the goals of the Africans, but in retrospect Laurence believed she had been far more successful in probing the British mentality than she had that of the Africans. Reviewers gave her achievement a more positive assessment, however. And **Patricia Morley**, in her biography of Laurence, describes the novel and collection as "a sensitive portrait of social change in West Africa and the pressures it exerts on individuals and groups."

The Prophet's Camel Bell, published in 1964, is a travel memoir of the author's experiences in Somaliland from 1950 to 1952, later remembered by Laurence as her most difficult work. "I believe that fiction is more true than fact," Laurence once said. She preferred fiction for the expression of characters' thoughts, and for the exploration of themes that is possible only in fiction.

After returning to Canada in 1957, Laurence turned her attention to Hagar Shipley, a character who had developed out of her own prairie background. *The Stone Angel,* published in 1964, is the story of Hagar's struggle in her last days to reconcile herself with her past, and became the keystone of Laurence's career as well as a landmark event in Canadian literature.

The story involves two separate but interlocking strands, in which events of the present trigger memories of the past. Hagar is a 90-year-old grandmother needing hospital care who stubbornly refuses to leave her home. Memories progress from her childhood to her marriage to Bram Shipley, which removed her from her social class and isolated her from her family, through the birth of two sons and her desertion of Bram, the deaths of Bram and her favorite son, John, to her life on the West Coast with Marvin, her surviving son. As her health fails, Hagar desperately attempts to evade her fate by making a secret journey to a nearby beach, an event Laurence's biographer Morley defines as "a descent into Self which is healing." By the story's end, Hagar is prepared for death, having come to terms with the events and emotions of her life.

Hagar's history, in the fictional prairie town of Manawaka, is an amalgam of prairie-town life and Laurence's own experience growing up in Neepawa. "In raging against our injustices, our stupidities," Laurence said, "I do so as my family, as I did, and still do, in writing about those aspects of my town which I hated and which are always in some ways aspects of myself." The setting she created was to remain the background for all her fiction set in Canada. *A Jest of God,* published in 1966, is the story of Rachel Cameron, who, through the ordeal of events involving one summer in Manawaka, emerges from her extended childhood into a fragile but sustaining identity. Eight stories, written and published from 1962 to 1970, and later

assembled for publication as *A Bird in the House,* were built around the maturation of the protagonist, Vanessa MacLeod, and based on Laurence's own childhood. *A Jest of God* was later adapted for the highly acclaimed American movie *Rachel, Rachel,* starring **Joanne Woodward** and directed by Paul Newman.

In 1962, after separating from her husband, Margaret Laurence left Canada for England with Jocelyn and David. She remained there for the next decade, completing *The Stone Angel* and *A Jest of God.* She also wrote numerous book reviews for journals and newspapers, as well as *The Fire-Dwellers,* her fourth novel, and the Vanessa MacLeod stories. During this period, she made a trip to East Pakistan, now Bangladesh, to see her husband and attempt a reconciliation, but the effort was not successful and the couple divorced in 1969. Laurence was also commissioned to visit Egypt to write several travel articles on that country, and after returning to Canada held several appointments as writer-in-residence at various Canadian universities.

Margaret Laurence

A hallmark of Laurence's writing is her retrospective approach to the work, drawing from the deep wells of her remembered experience. The African years took literary shape in Canada during the five years that followed; the Manawakan novels were created in England in the 1960s, and the experience of her years in Vancouver, on the Canadian west coast (1957–62), goes into *The Fire-Dwellers,* set down half a decade later. *The Fire-Dwellers* concerns Stacey MacAindra, a women married to a struggling salesman and the mother of four. Only in *The Diviners* does Laurence confront Canadian life in a manner contemporaneous with the time of writing. The story of writer Morag Gunn, *The Diviners* is the climactic work of the Manawaka series, and brings together the Scottish descendants and the Indian half-breed outcasts of Manawaka by chronicling her relationship with Jules Tonnere.

From time to time, Laurence also found refreshment in writing for children, producing *Jason's Quest, Six Darn Cows, The Olden Days Coat,* and *A Christmas Birthday Story.* In 1968, she expressed her continuing interest in African literature in *Long Drums and Cannons,* her tribute to the upsurge of Nigerian writing in English between 1952 and 1966.

After returning to live in Canada in 1973, Laurence became active in political organizations promoting world peace. She also influenced and advised the next generation of Canadian writers through writer-in-residence programs and served from 1980 to 1983 as chancellor of Trent University in Peterborough, Ontario. Meanwhile, she garnered several Canadian writing awards, most notably the Governor-General's Medal for fiction in 1974.

Margaret Laurence died on January 5, 1987, at age 61. Throughout the body of her work, her concern had been with characters who display a powerful desire for freedom; but the freedom they attain tends to be partial and imperfect, resulting in isolation. Laurence once voiced the view that human beings "ought to be able to communicate and touch each other far more than they do, and this human loneliness and isolation, which occurs everywhere, seems to me to be part of man's tragedy. I'm sure one of the main themes in all my writing is this sense of man's isolation from his fellows and how almost unbearably tragic this is." It is this reflection on the human experience that makes her a writer of note throughout the world.

SOURCES:
Morley, Patricia. *Margaret Laurence.* Boston, MA: Twayne, 1981.

Thomas, Clara. *Margaret Laurence.* Toronto: McClelland and Stewart, 1969.

SUGGESTED READING:
Thomas, Clara. *The Manawaka World of Margaret Laurence.* Toronto: McClelland and Stewart, 1976.

Mark Vajcner,
freelance writer and researcher in
Canadian history, Winnipeg, Manitoba, Canada

Laurence, Mary (b. 1928).

See Wells, Mary.

Laurencin, Marie (1883–1956)

French artist, poet, book illustrator, and set designer.
Born in Paris, France, on October 31, 1883; died in Paris on June 8, 1956; buried in Père Lachaise cemetery; illegitimate daughter of Pauline Laurencin and Alfred Toulet; married Baron Otto von Waëtjen, on June 21, 1914 (divorced 1921); no children.

Entered the Lycée Lamartine (1893); studied porcelain painting at the École de Sèvres (1902–03); attended Académie Humbert (1903–04); met Georges Braque (1903); exhibited at Salon des Indépendants, Paris (1907); began six-year affair with Guillaume Apollinaire (1907); held first individual exhibit of her paintings, Galarie Barbazanges, Paris (1912); lived in Spain (1914–19); returned to Paris (1921); designed sets and costumes for "Les Biches," Ballet Russes (1923); awarded Legion of Honor (1937); published memoirs, Le Carnet des nuits (1942); adopted Suzanne Moreau (1954); inauguration of Marie Laurencin Museum, Nagano-Ken, Japan (1983).

There is a quality of child-like innocence that pervades the life and art of Marie Laurencin. Yet she was the only female artist associated with, and accepted by, the male-dominated, exclusive avant-garde art movements in early 20th-century Paris. In fact, it is difficult to envision the primly dressed, bourgeois-mannered young woman as an intimate of the aggressive, boisterous male artists and writers who comprised the inner sanctum of Pablo Picasso's studio, the Bateau-Lavoir, on the rue Ravignan in Montmartre. The bold artistic and literary productions of the group, which included Juan Gris, Matisse, Modigliani, Georges Braque, Max Jacob, and Guillaume Apollinaire, are in glaring contrast to the paintings of Marie Laurencin whose talent "ranged between a flutter and a coo," as she described it. She observed and listened to the creative giants of her time, the Cubists, Fauvists, Dadaists, Symbolists, and Surrealists, but she was not an imitator; she did "not try to compete with male artists on their own ground."

Marie
Laurencin

Apollinaire, poet and art critic, praised Laurencin's "typically French grace," her "vibrant and joyful" personality, and her feminine qualities. He believed, "The greatest error of most women artists is that they try to surpass men, losing in the process their taste and their charm." Laurencin was different, however, continued Apollinaire, "She is aware of the deep differences that separate men from women—essential, ideal differences. . . . Purity is her very element." This appraisal of a talented artist may have been, in part, colored by the fact that Laurencin and Apollinaire were lovers at the time. Marie did, no doubt, embody a feminine aesthetic which was greatly admired by her contemporaries. As her friend, the poet André Salmon, expressed it, "there is something of a fairy wand in the brush of Marie Laurencin." And with this delicate wand, she created a soft, pastel, feminine world that contrasted sharply with the vivid, arbitrary colors and geometric figures emanating from Picasso's flamboyant and daring coterie of male artists.

> *I*f I feel so distant from other painters, it is because they are men. . . . But if the genius of men intimidates me, I feel perfectly at ease with everything that is feminine.
>
> —Marie Laurencin

It is curious that Marie Laurencin was able to develop and sustain warm relations with male friends, because her formative years were devoid of male influences. She was an illegitimate only child whose father made only occasional "unwelcome intrusions" in her life, but she idolized, and also feared, her elegant, aloof, authoritarian mother, Pauline, who "spoke little and sang very well." **Pauline Laurencin** came from Normandy and was said to be of Creole stock. Marie was given her mother's surname and inherited the "frizzy hair, rather full lips, and almond eyes" attributed to Creoles at that time. She was tall and thin and rather awkward in her movements. Laurencin claims she was "*triste, laide, et sans espoir*" ("sad, ugly, and without hope") when she was young. Her absentee father, Alfred Toulet, a deputy to the National Assembly from Picardy, was already married to another woman when Marie was born. His infrequent visits disturbed Laurencin who "had a horror of all these masculine episodes—the louder voice, the kisses on the forehead" which struck her as rather crude. *Gertrude Stein, the most famous American expatriate, art connoisseur, and permanent resident of Paris, who knew and liked Marie, said the Laurencin women lived like two nuns in a convent, a rather sagacious observation for Pauline had intended to become a Carmelite nun.

Marie Laurencin was an indifferent student and preferred the study of music and literature to painting; she was an avid reader and had a library of over 500 volumes when she died. All her life she had close friends in the Parisian literary community. When she began drawing at an early age, her mother discouraged her efforts and regularly destroyed her drawings. Pauline wanted Marie to be a teacher, but after graduating from the Lycée Lamartine, Marie began to study painting. She first attended the École de Sèvres to learn porcelain painting, and she also took drawing classes in Paris from the famous flower painter **Madeleine Lamaire**. Laurencin entered the Académie Humbert in 1903 and did her first etchings. Here she met the brilliant Georges Braque, who admired her talent and eventually introduced her to Picasso. In the early 1900s, Laurencin did a series of self-portraits which reveal "her inherent narcissism." Some critics allege that all her portraits of women resemble herself; as one remarked, "for [Laurencin] all of nature is nothing but a room of mirrors."

The year 1907 was a watershed in Laurencin's life and art, for Braque introduced her to Picasso and his circle of associates which included the poet, and aspiring art critic, Guillaume Apollinaire. To be allied with this avant-garde circle would prove to be immensely beneficial to Marie at this early stage of her career, and she was the only female admitted into this exclusively male bastion. For decades, her name would be linked to Picasso, Gris, Modigliani, Max Jacob, Francis Carco, and André Salmon. Apollinaire had met Picasso in 1904, and their friendship merged the poet's Left Bank literary crowd with Picasso's Montmartre group. Laurencin's inclusion in this artists' enclave led to her meeting Apollinaire; Picasso, certainly in jest, told Apollinaire that he had found his poet friend a "fiancée" and arranged for them to meet at Clovis Sagot's art gallery in Paris. The attraction was immediate and mutual between "the prophet of the Modern Movement" and the quiet artistic novice. To Apollinaire, Laurencin became his "little sun, a feminine counterpart of himself," a "twin soul." They were inseparable and were lovers for the next six years.

At age 24, Marie still lived with her mother, as did the 27-year-old Apollinaire. Both were illegitimate, brought up by domineering women, and both were "hypersensitive, capricious, and moody." Apollinaire had already established his literary reputation among the Symbolists and was a "cosmopolitan erudite" figure in Paris; Laurencin was thoroughly Parisian, never happy or comfortable outside of her familiar surroundings. Tyrannical and possessive, Apollinaire provided Laurencin with intellectual stimulation and encouraged her work. They were more than lovers, according to Douglas Hyland, "they were alter egos who completed one another."

Apollinaire was known to want to fashion, to shape, his women, and Laurencin was no exception. He and his artist friends "were the catalysts that sparked Laurencin's unique artistic vision"; moreover, he recognized her stylistic strengths and encouraged her to follow them. Consequently, the period from 1907 to 1914 is considered by critics to have been her best years as a painter. Marie, too, admitted: "The little I learned was taught me by the men whom I call great painters, my contemporaries, Matisse, Derain, Picasso, Braque. . . . If I never became a Cubist painter it was because I never could. . . but their experiments fascinated me." Apollinaire launched Laurencin's career in the Paris art world, praised her work in his art columns, and ranked her among the great talents of the time.

If Apollinaire was understandably biased by his involvement with Marie, not everyone was so charmed by the young Parisian naïf. Picasso's mistress, *Fernande Olivier, remarked that Marie had "the air of a little girl who was naive and a little vicious . . . a homely yet piquant-looking creature." **Margaret Davies** claims that Laurencin seemed rather like "a child lost among sophisticated adults" in her relations with the Montmartre group. If Marie was viewed as an

Woman with Dove, *painting by Marie Laurencin.*

innocent among this unconventional bohemian set of hedonists, the fastidious, bourgeois, gourmand Apollinaire was also a distinct presence among them. Olivier claimed that because of his penchant for neatness he and Marie made love in an armchair to avoid wrinkling his bed covers—"his bed was sacred." Surprisingly, Laurencin and her lover never lived together, but Apollinaire did move out of his mother's house to live near Marie and her mother. And the lovers never married; both of their mothers strongly disapproved not only of their liaison but of their unorthodox, "ne'er-do-well" friends. One might reasonably assume that sex was only a part of Laurencin's and Apollinaire's mutual attraction; as an art critic, he promoted her work and encouraged her native talent, but his poems that dealt with their love affair are strikingly less sensual than those dealing with his other women. The Spanish poet, Ramon Gomez de la Serva, who knew Marie well, called her "*la froide mais angélique Marie*" ("the cold but angelic Marie").

Laurencin's association with the artistic avant-garde resulted in her being included in their exhibit at the Salon des Indépendants in the autumn 1907. Cubists, Fauvists, and Symbolists were shunned by the more academic art movements and thus were forced to organize their own "independent" exhibitions. That Marie was accepted as a full-fledged member of the artistic elite is evidenced by her presence at the famous banquet held in Picasso's studio to honor Henri "Le Douanier" Rousseau in 1908. The following year, Rousseau portrayed Laurencin and Apollinaire in his painting "The Muse inspiring the poet." Marie also used friends as subjects; in 1908, she did her celebrated canvas, *Apollinaire and His Friends*. Apollinaire occupies a prominent position at the center of the painting, surrounded by Marie, Picasso, Fernande Olivier, and his dog Frika. One critic described it as "a flat, primitivizing composition dominated by sharp contours and arabesques." It appealed, however, to Gertrude and Leo Stein who bought it; Picasso also owned one of Laurencin's Cubist-inspired paintings, *La Songeuse (The Dreamer)*. A year later, a larger, more ambitious painting of "friends," including Gertrude Stein and others, was completed. It belonged to Apollinaire, who hung it above his bed in the apartment he later shared with his wife **Jacqueline Kolb**. These two compositions show the Cubist influence on Laurencin's work during her early career, a distinct contrast to her later paintings in which soft pastels dominate, creating a kind of dream-like, fairyland quality. Laurencin cannot, however, be classified as a Cubist painter; this is evident in her two paintings, *Portrait of Mme Fernande X* and *Young Girls (Jeunes Filles)*, included in the Cubist exhibition of 1911. Linked to the Cubists, but not one of them, Laurencin continued to exhibit in their gallery shows. In 1912, her paintings hung among those of Marcel Duchamp, Juan Gris, Robert Delaunay, and others at the Galerie La Boëtie and the Galerie Barbazanges.

By 1912, Laurencin was gradually breaking away from her domineering lover. When Apollinaire realized he was losing Marie, he responded by writing poems with her as the subject; "Le Pont Mirabeau," "Cors de Chasse," and "Marie" are all reflections on their fading love. In one of his finest poems, "Zone," he mourns the loss which propelled him "into one of his great troughs of despair." Shattered and unable to be alone, Apollinaire moved in with friends. A mutual friend, **Louise Faure-Favier**, tried to get the lovers to reconcile, but Marie adamantly refused. Even so, the poet and his muse remained in contact after their affair ended, and Apollinaire continued to hope that Laurencin would reconsider. In 1915, he told his fiancée Jacqueline (later his wife) that "with Marie it was a cerebral affair." Apollinaire's biographer, Margaret Davies, seems to endorse his assessment, stating that Marie "was a specifically French phenomenon, the 'jolie-laide' (pretty-ugly), who manages to prove that mind can always triumph over matter." In his *La Poète assassiné* (1916), Apollinaire recounts their turbulent affair; the hero is Croniamantal, a poet, the heroine, Tristouse Ballerinette, is his mistress about whom he writes, "She has the somber and child-like face of those destined to make men suffer." With Laurencin, as Francis Steegmuller notes, Apollinaire had "the most complete physical and spiritual relationship" he ever experienced.

Apollinaire was devastated by the break-up of their affair, but Laurencin was not; in fact, she did not need him any longer. An established artist in her own right now, Marie had secured a distinctive place in the world of modern art. In 1913, she obtained a contract with the German art dealer Alfred Flechtheim and, more important, with the Parisian dealer Paul Rosenberg. In addition, seven of her works were exhibited in the Armory show in New York. Laurencin was free now of the philandering Apollinaire, and when her mother died in 1913, she was finally on her own, free of the two persons who had been the dominating influences in her life.

Her independence did not last long, however, for in June 1914, she married Baron Otto von

Waëtjen—a most inopportune time to marry a German national as war between France and Germany was imminent. Waëtjen was from a good noble family and had come to Paris to study art at the Académie Humbert. **Charlotte Gere** describes him as a competent artist in straight portraiture, though "little more than a competent plagiarist, without originality [or] imagination." But, she notes further, he considered his talent superior to Laurencin's.

After they married, Marie and Otto left for a beach on the Atlantic coast of France. When war broke out, they fled south to Bordeaux and then to Spain, where they would live for almost five years. Laurencin never saw Apollinaire again; he joined the French army in December 1914 and was sent to the front. He suffered a serious head wound two years later and never fully recovered. Apollinaire died in the influenza epidemic of 1918. During the war, he had sent poems to Laurencin in Spain through a friend in Paris. He missed his "muse," Marie missed Paris. Despite being involved with the avantgarde movement in Madrid, she was lonely and depressed. She was, however, able to study the works of Goya, and during this time her characteristic, mature style began to emerge. Laurencin was not inspired to paint while in exile—she was isolated from her beloved and familiar Paris and from her friends. However, she did have contact with Picabia and the Dadaists in Madrid and Barcelona, and she contributed several poems to the Dada review *391*. Untouched by her contacts with Dadaism, she was influenced by Spanish culture; several of Laurencin's postwar paintings include the Spanish-inspired figure of a young girl with a black shawl in her group scenes of dancers. At the end of the war, Marie and Otto left Spain for Düsseldorf (1919). Here she designed wallpaper for an Art Deco decorator and did the illustrations for a friend's novel. But Laurencin still had little inclination to paint. She was still an expatriate, still longing for "her" Paris.

In 1921, Marie returned to Paris and began divorce proceedings. Some of her acquaintances assumed that she divorced Otto because he was German. In fact, Otto was an alcoholic, and their marriage had deteriorated. Laurencin never allowed even close friends to be privy to her most intimate thoughts and actions; not even her mother or Apollinaire had fathomed the depths of her character. Laurencin's world was private and closed; her reality was of her own creation, reflected and re-created in her art. The von Waëtjen family in Germany had lost everything in the war. Quietly and consistently, Laurencin remained in touch with them, sending money when she could. Moreover, she kept in contact with Otto in Paris until he died in 1942.

Marie never remarried, but she had numerous male friends and several lovers. Apollinaire had been a philanderer, and her marriage to Otto had forced her to live in exile, cut off from her "natural" surroundings. Now her work would occupy her energies, and her close female friends, who made fewer demands on her than men, became important to her need for a more settled, stable lifestyle. **Nicole Grout**, a fashion designer and sister of the famous couturier Paul Poiret, was one of her intimate friends. Armand Lowengard, nephew of a well-known Paris art dealer, was Marie's devoted companion for many years; a scholar and graduate of Oxford, he wanted to marry her although his family disapproved. There were rumors that Marie had female as well as male lovers. Her name was associated with *Natalie Clifford Barney and the Princess **Violet Murat**. If true, Marie's relationships with Barney's openly lesbian circle of famous and talented women did not damage her reputation with the public.

Laurencin's artistic career of 50 years can be divided into three distinct periods, as can her life. The first phase dates from her introduction into Picasso's circle until the end of World War I, during which time she produced large, complex paintings in bold colors. The two versions of *Apollinaire and His Friends* and *Les Deux Soeurs (The Two Sisters)* all reveal Cubist influence, as interpreted by Laurencin, of course. Her last large canvas, *Society Ball,* was completed in 1913. No young artist could have been more fortunate than Marie, to have one's own "publicity agent" in the person of the well-connected Apollinaire who praised and publicized her work, including her among the best of the experimental artists of the time in his critiques written for avant-garde journals. Marie's association with Picasso, Gris, Modigliani, and other "moderns" also provided her entrée to Gertrude Stein's select gatherings. And with Stein, Laurencin also acquired another admirer of her individual style. Then, in her second creative phase, Marie turned to feminine portraits, employing "an entirely feminine aesthetic," as Apollinaire described it; virginal women with pale, ovalshaped faces, fair hair, and black, almond-shaped "fathomless" eyes.

This second phase of Laurencin's long career began when she returned to Paris in 1921; her most productive period was the two decades between the wars. From 1921 to 1937, Laurencin produced her most typical, and recognizable, work, which reveals her mature style. Marie had found her own artistic genre, and "her mood too shifted to one of lyrical melancholy." Her world was depicted in muted pastel hues of soft pink, pale blue, dove-grey, and a dominance of shades of white, and this world was "an orderly feminine one, in which it was difficult to imagine the male." Marie consciously and aggressively took charge of her art and of her life. She commenced a business arrangement with Paul Rosenberg who exhibited her pictures in his Paris gallery and received large commissions from the sale of her paintings. He also paid all her bills, relieving her of this banal burden. With her reputation re-established after a single exhibition on her return to Paris, Laurencin was suddenly financially secure. She achieved great success as a portrait artist and painted some of the most fashionable and famous people of the time, including the Baronne Gourgaud, *Coco Chanel, Lady Emerald Cunard (◀◈ Maud Cunard), and W. Somerset Maugham. Coco Chanel disliked her portrait, saying it did not look like her, but as one of Marie's critics remarked, "likeness was never the primary aim of Laurencin's portraiture." When Lady Cunard, an elegant London society hostess, expressed her displeasure at being portrayed on a horse, Laurencin threatened to replace the horse with a camel. The horse remained, for Marie always won artistic debates with her clients. The gentle, dream-like depiction of Lady Cunard hung in her fashionable residence in London and was greatly admired by her society guests. Laurencin had intended to paint her friend ◀◈ Adrienne Monnier, whose bookstore was one of the literary focal points of Paris, but Adrienne insisted that Marie include her nose in the painting—Laurencin portraits were often "noseless." "I don't see you with a nose," Laurencin informed her, and no portrait was done.

Preferring to paint slender, willowy young women, Marie charged double for portraits of men—except for Maugham, who was a personal friend. The Maugham portrait is not one of her more notable paintings, and Laurencin made a gift of it to Maugham; years later, he professed not to care for Laurencin's style, but he kept the painting. Marie also increased her price for those who bored her, and for brunettes since she preferred blondes. And she avoided painting children—they did not arouse her creative senses. Marie needed to relate to her subjects, to be "in sympathy spiritually" with them. In light of this, it is striking that so many of her portraits of women resemble one another and, as some critics claim, actually look more like the artist than themselves.

Laurencin's talent extended beyond portraiture. In 1923, she designed the set and costumes for Sergei Diaghilev's ballet, *Les Biches* (The Does, or Hinds), choreographed by *Bronislava Nijinska, sister of the famous Russian dancer Nijinsky. First performed by the Ballets Russes in Monte Carlo in 1924, it was also a resounding success in Paris and later in London and Berlin. A revival of the ballet in London in 1964 included exact reproductions of Laurencin's set and costumes which had contributed so much to the initial success of the Diaghilev ballet. Other famous artists, including Picasso, Matisse, and Juan Gris, also designed sets—at the time, art was not confined to canvas and stone or to displaying one's work in art galleries. To many of the Cubists, Symbolists, and others of the 1920s' avant-garde, art was wed to literature and to theater, and their interests were inclusive rather than exclusive. Laurencin's contribution to *Les Biches* led to further commissions, and she continued to produce stage designs and costumes for over two decades; her last involvement was with *Sleeping Beauty* for Ballets de Monte Carlo in 1947. She also collaborated with André Grout on the "Chambre de Madame" for the Exposition Internationale des Arts Décoratifs in Paris (1925). Laurencin was a multitalented artist, never limited to a single genre to express her imagination and creativity. Wallpaper, interior decoration, stage settings, costumes, portraits, paintings of flowers and landscapes were all within her realm of art.

In the 1920s and 1930s, Marie was one of the three most well-known women in France, along with *Colette and Coco Chanel. She exhibited in Paris, London, New York, and Berlin, and her paintings sold well. In 1925, she was able to acquire a country house in Champrosay and three years later purchased a large apartment in Paris. The Laurencin exhibits attracted admirers and buyers; in addition to portraits, she painted flowers and a few landscapes which attracted additional admirers and buyers. Laurencin also illustrated more than 20 books. In 1929, *Janet Flanner (writing under her famous nom-de-plume Gênet) penned her regular "Letter from Paris" for *The New Yorker* magazine: her subject, Laurencin's illustration of Lewis Carroll's *Alice in Wonderland*. Alice, Flanner notes, looked like Laurencin, and the Rabbit wore "a little pink Marie Laurencin hat and looks like a French poodle." She was not a great fan of Laurencin's portraits, either. This negative reaction was not widespread, however. Marie was in demand by both authors and publishers; she illustrated *Katherine Mansfield's *Garden Party* and books by André Gide and Marcelle Auclair (the founder of *Marie*

❧▶
Cunard, Maud. *See Cunard, Nancy for sidebar.*

❧▶
Monnier, Adrienne. *See Beach, Sylvia for sidebar.*

Claire fashion magazine in France). Respected and successful, Laurencin taught at an art academy in Paris from 1932 to 1935.

The third, and final, phase of Laurencin's extensive career is regarded by most critics as her "bad" period. Her work then is said to lack the delicacy of earlier periods, with "a much coarser use of form and color." Critics claim to observe a decline in quality, even in her portraits of women that frequently "verge on the saccharine." She was considered "dated" and too obviously stylized, too predictable. To a great extent, this is true; Laurencin had developed her own distinctive style, her own vision of reality, and she changed little in the depiction of her chosen subjects. Her artistic genre had brought her international recognition and financial rewards; her success was not based on imitating "popular" styles nor on following or reacting to modern trends. Instead, Laurencin insisted that she painted nature as she saw it, that she was a "natural painter," not an "instinctive" one.

The French government awarded Laurencin the Legion of Honor in 1937 and purchased her painting *The Rehearsal* which hangs in the Musée National d'Art Moderne in Paris. Two years later, Europe was embroiled in another war, but Laurencin risked her life to remain in Paris—she wanted to complete paintings she was working on. Invasion and occupation by the Germans was obviously less odious to her than living in exile again. Paris was her home, her artistic milieu, and a German presence could be tolerated better than a lonely, isolated existence in a foreign land. Like Natalie Barney, Marie regarded women as victims of war as much as men were, and she endured the privations suffered by civilians in Paris during the bleak years of Nazi occupation, 1940–44. The Germans requisitioned her large apartment, and she was forced to move into a smaller one and rent a studio. Despite the hardships, Laurencin continued to paint during the war, to design sets, and to exhibit her work. In 1942, a book of memories and reminiscences was published, entitled *Le Carnet des Nuits* (literally, The Notebook of Nights).

Laurencin suffered from a variety of ailments and serious bouts of depression for many years, but she continued to paint until she was nearly 70. Following the liberation of France and the end of the war, Marie tried, unsuccessfully, to reclaim her apartment. She went to court in 1951, but the case was not settled until 1955, when she finally regained possession. Before her claim was settled, she adopted her housekeeper, **Suzanne Moreau**, who had been

with her for almost 30 years. (After Laurencin's death, Suzanne would become the zealous guardian of her reputation, refusing scholars access to Marie's papers to protect her benefactor's much-cherished privacy.) Marie Laurencin died of a heart attack on June 6, 1956, and was buried in Père Lachaise cemetery in Paris, joining Apollinaire, Colette, Gertrude Stein, and other great cultural icons.

In 1983, the 100th anniversary of her birth saw the inauguration of the Marie Laurencin Museum in Nagano-Ken, Japan. Her paintings still sell well—*Jacqueline Kennedy Onassis owned one—and continue to be exhibited; in Paris, her work hangs among that of Dufy, Modigliani, Léger, and other famous artists of her time.

An artist and a poet's muse, she painted a world she viewed through her short-sighted eyes, was a friend of some of the greatest creative figures of the 20th century, and skillfully managed to fashion a personal life that met her need for privacy and independence. A long-time friend described Marie Laurencin as "a poetic being who managed to sustain the magic of childhood throughout her life," a life that was "a peculiar *mélange* of nun and libertine."

SOURCES:

Davies, Margaret. *Apollinaire*. Edinburgh and London: Oliver and Boyd, 1964.

Gere, Charlotte. *Marie Laurencin*. NY: Rizzoli, 1977.

Hyland, Douglas, and Heather McPherson. *Laurencin: Artist and Muse*. Birmingham, AL: Birmingham Museum of Art, 1989.

Steegmuller, Francis. *Apollinaire: Poet Among Painters*. NY: Farrar, Straus, 1963.

SUGGESTED READING:

Allard, Roger. *Marie Laurencin*. Editions de la Nouvelle Revue Française, 1921.

Day, George. *Marie Laurencin*. Paris, 1947.

Olivier, Fernande. *Picasso et ses amis*. Paris: Stock, 1933.

Shattuck, Roger. *The Banquet Years*. London: Farber, 1960.

Warnod, Jeannine. *Le Bateau-Lavoir*. Paris: Presses de la Connaissance, 1976.

COLLECTIONS:

Marie Laurencin's unpublished correspondence, notebooks, photographs, official documents, and exhibition catalogues are located in the Bibliothèque Jacques Doucet, Paris, France.

Jeanne A. Ojala,
Professor of History, University of Utah, Salt Lake City, Utah

Laurentia (fl. 9th, 8th, or 7th c. BCE).

See Larentia, Acca.

Laurette de St. Valery (fl. 1200)

French noblewoman and healer. Flourished in 1200, in Amiens, France; married Aléaume de Fontaines, of the petty nobility (died 1205).

Laurette de St. Valery was a woman of the lower nobility of Amiens, in northwestern France, who became a doctor. She married Aléaume de Fontaines. In 1202, after some years of marriage, her husband left her to join the Fourth Crusade; he died three years later in Constantinople. The widow Laurette spent the rest of her life learning medicine and practicing among the poor for free. She was a devout woman and believed that she could best serve God by serving the physical needs of the poor. For her charity and medical skills, she gained the respect and admiration of the people of Amiens and the surrounding area.

SOURCES:

LaBarge, Margaret. *A Small Sound of the Trumpet: Women in Medieval Life*. Boston: Beacon Press, 1986.

Laura York,
Riverside, California

Laurie, Annie (1863–1936).

See Black, Winifred Sweet.

Laval, Josée (c. 1911—)

French daughter of Pierre Laval who staunchly defended her father. Name variations: Josee or José Laval; Josée de Chambrun; Mme de Chambrun; Comtesse de Chambrun. Born around 1911; daughter of Pierre Laval (1883–1945, prime minister of France and open collaborator with the Germans) and Eugenie (Claussat) Laval (daughter of Chateldon's mayor); married Count Réne de Chambrun (French military attaché in Washington at the time of the fall of France in summer of 1940), in 1935.

"In marrying Comte René de Chambrun, Mlle. José Laval . . . married into the Roosevelts, Longworths, and Murats, which is pyramidal for the granddaughter of a jolly Auvergnat innkeeper," wrote *Janet Flanner in 1935. Josée Laval was born around 1911, the daughter of **Eugenie Claussat Laval** and Pierre Laval. Before he became prime minister of France and a Nazi collaborator, Pierre had been a provincial schoolteacher. Josée's family was poor during her childhood but extremely rich by the time she had reached her teen years.

After World War II, her father "was the most hated man in France," writes biographer Hubert Cole, "the focal point of the nation's shame and revulsion, its evil genius." On October 4, 1945, Charles de Gaulle's Provisional Government launched Pierre Laval's trial for treason. Even for a political tribunal, the proceedings were embarrassing. The jury screamed obscenities at the defendant, who was given no opportunity to introduce evidence. The prosecutor, several years previously, had volunteered to serve on Vichy's Denaturalization Commission, a vehicle for the deportation of Jews. After Laval's conviction, de Gaulle refused to order a retrial. On October 15, 1945, Pierre Laval nearly escaped the firing squad by swallowing poison in prison. Revived by a team of frantic doctors, he was shot several hours later.

Convinced that her father was the victim of a miscarriage of justice, Josée Laval fought for years to restore his reputation. She also published and wrote a preface for a collection of documents, *Laval parle*. Even Pierre Laval's enemies agreed that his trial had been scandalous and highly irregular. When some years later M. François-Ponset spoke before the French Academy extolling the virtues of Marshal Pétain and the villainy of Laval, Josée mailed a long statement to the French press which included letters from François-Ponset to her father, extolling his policies and political wisdom.

SUGGESTED READING:

Cole, Hubert. *Laval: A Biography*. Putnam, 1963.
de Chambrun, Réne. *I Saw France Fall*.

Lavallière, Eve (c. 1866–1929)

Popular and versatile French stage actress who became a nun. Name variations: Eugénie Lavallière; Eva Lavalliere; Eugénie Feneglio. Born Eugénie Pascaline Feneglio around 1866, in Toulon, France; died on July 10, 1929, in Vosges, France; children: (with Fernand Samuel, a theater manager) one daughter, Jeanne.

Raised in Toulon and Perpignan; apprenticed to dressmaker; became singer and actress in Paris at end of 19th century, most closely associated with Variété Theater; retired (1915); entered l'Ordre des Tertiaires Franciscains (1920s).

Born Eugénie Pascaline Feneglio in the seaport town of Toulon, France, around 1866, Eve Lavallière was the daughter of two poverty-stricken dressmakers. Her father made costumes for the Bijou Theater, while her mother sewed clothes for private customers at home. Her parents were alcoholics, constantly arguing and sometimes physically violent, and Lavallière and her older brother grew up in a dispiriting environment. She found escape as a child in attending church, in studying at l'École des Dames de Saint-Maur and in visiting the theater where her father worked, a combined fascination with religion and theatrics that was to inform her two chosen careers in life.

The family moved inland to Perpignan, throwing themselves on the charity of their relative, **Madame Garnier**. After Lavallière's father fatally wounded her mother and then shot himself, Madame Garnier sent the teenager to live at the local convent, but the girl soon ran away, apprenticing with a fashionable dressmaker. There the talented and ambitious young woman is said to have acquired the name Lavallière, after *Louise de La Vallière (1644–1710), mistress of Louis XIV. An aspiring actress, Lavallière formed a small amateur theater group with some friends, charging minimal admission to see works by Racine and Molière.

Moving to Paris, Lavallière adopted the first name Eve to go with her new persona. Poor and vulnerable, she found work singing cabaret in Montmartre bars. Her break came when she won an audition for the chorus line at the Variété. Before long, she was "the hit of Paris," according to *Janet Flanner in *Paris Was Yesterday*. Actress, singer and comedian, Lavallière became a well-known and much gossiped-about figure of Paris' glamorous nightlife. She had a daughter, Jeanne, with Fernand Samuel, the manager of the Variété, though whether she ever married Samuel or not is disputed; he died before World War I.

Her last performances were in 1914, when she created the title role in *Ma Tante d'Honfleur*. Despite plans to travel to the United States for a tour, Lavallière decided to retire from the theater, taking up residence at the château of Chanceaux-sur-Choiselles. Her dramatic flight from the theatrical world caused much speculation, including accusations of espionage on behalf of the Germans. In search of a religious life, Lavallière asked to join the Carmelite order of Avignon but was refused. After much searching for a religious order that would accept her, Lavallière went to Africa for a short-lived stint as a nurse in Tunis.

In the summer of 1929, Eve Lavallière, like her namesake Louise de La Vallière, died a nun, a member of l'Ordre des Tertiaires Franciscains in the Vosges.

SOURCES:
Flanner, Janet. *Paris Was Yesterday*. NY: Viking, 1972.
Murphy, Edward F. *Mademoiselle Lavallière*. NY: Doubleday, 1949.

Paula Morris, D.Phil.,
Brooklyn, New York

La Vallière, Louise de (1644–1710)

French mistress of Louis XIV from 1661 to 1667.
Name variations: Duchesse de La Vallière; Sister

Eve
Lavallière

(Soeur) Louise de la Miséricorde. Born Françoise Louise de la Baume Le Blanc in Tours, Touraine, France, on August 6, 1644; died in 1710; daughter of Laurent de la Baume Le Blanc (d. 1651, an officer who took the name of La Vallière from a small property near Amboise) and a mother (name unknown) who joined the court of Gaston d'Orléans at Blois; children: (with Louis XIV) Charles (December 1663–1666); a second child (January 1665–1666); daughter Marie Anne, known as Mlle de Blois (b. October 1666, who married Armand de Bourbon, prince of Conti, in 1680; Mlle de Blois' youngest child, the count of Vermandois, died on his first campaign at Courtrai in 1683); another son (b. October 1667).

Louise de La Vallière, favorite mistress of Louis XIV of France, was born in Touraine in 1644, of an ancient and noble family. Her father Laurent de la Baume Le Blanc, an officer, took the name of La Vallière from a small property near Amboise. When he died in 1651, her mother (name unknown) soon married once more

Louise de La Vallière

and joined the court of Gaston d'Orléans, duke of Orléans and brother of Louis XIII, at Blois. Louise was brought up at the court with the younger princesses, *Françoise d'Orleans, *Marguerite Louise of Orleans, and their stepsister *Anne Marie Louise d'Orléans Montpen-sier (daughter of Gaston's first wife *Marie de Bourbon). After Gaston d'Orléans' death in 1660, his second wife *Marguerite of Lorraine moved with her daughters to the palace of the Luxembourg in Paris, and with them went Louise, who was now a girl of 16. A skillful rider and fine musician, Louise was known for her sweet voice and even sweeter disposition. Her contemporaries noted that she was not a great beauty and was slightly lame, but she was easy-going and charming.

Through the influence of a distant relation, **Mme de Choisy**, La Vallière was named maid of honor to *****Henrietta Anne**, duchess of Orléans and daughter of Charles I, king of England, who was about her own age and had just married Philip I, duke of Orléans, Louis XIV's brother. Arriving from England, Henrietta joined the court at Fontainebleau and was soon on the friendliest terms with her brother-in-law, so friendly that there was some scandal. In an effort to avoid gossip, it was decided that the king should turn his attentions elsewhere. The person selected was Henrietta's maid of honor, Louise de La Vallière. Thus, after only two months in Fontainebleau, Louise became the king's mistress. The affair, begun on Louis' part as a decoy, developed immediately into genuine passion on both sides. It was the king's first serious attachment, and Louise—an innocent, religious-minded girl—brought neither coquetry nor self-interest to their association, which was diligently concealed.

But in February 1662, there was a serious breach between Louis and Louise when Louise loyally refused to gossip about Henrietta Anne's possible involvement with the Comte de Guiche. Louise fled to an obscure convent at Chaillot, but Louis soon followed. Louise's enemies—chief of whom was *****Olympia Mancini**—sought her downfall by bringing her liaison to the ears of Louis' queen *****Maria Teresa of Spain**. La Vallière was presently removed from the service of Henrietta and established in a small building in the Palais Royal, where in December 1663 she gave birth to a son Charles. He was given in charge to two faithful servants of Jean-Baptiste Colbert, France's minister of finances.

Concealment was practically abandoned after her return to court and, within a week of the queen-mother's death (*****Anne of Austria**) in January 1666, La Vallière appeared at mass beside Maria Teresa. But Louise's favor was already waning. She had given birth to a second child by Louis in January 1665, but both children were dead before the autumn of 1666. A daughter born at Vincennes in October 1666, who received the name of Marie Anne and would be known as **Mlle de Blois**, was publicly recognized by Louis as his daughter in letters-patent, making Louise a duchess in May 1667 and conferring on her the estate of Vaujours. In October of that year, she had a son, but by this time her place in

Louis' affections was forever usurped by the *****Marquise de Montespan**, who had long been plotting against her. La Vallière was compelled to remain at court as the king's official mistress, and even to share Mme de Montespan's apartments at the Tuileries. She made an attempt at escape in 1671, when she fled to the convent of Ste. Marie de Chaillot, but was forced to return. In 1674, she was finally permitted to enter the convent of the Carmelites in the Rue d'Enfer in Paris, taking her final vows, a year later, as Sister (Soeur) Louise de la Miséricorde; she spent 36 years there in penance and prayer.

La Vallière's *Réflexions sur la miséricorde de Dieu,* written after her retreat, was printed by Lequeux in 1767, and in 1860 her *Réflexions, lettres et sermons,* edited by M.P. Clement, appeared in two volumes. Some apocryphal *Mémoires* were printed in 1829 and the *Lettres de Mme la duchesse de la Vallière* (1767) is a bastardized version of her correspondence with the Maréchal de Bellefonds. Later biographical works include Arsène Houssaye's *Mlle de la Vallière et Mme de Montespan* (1860), Jules Lair's *Louise de la Vallière* (3rd ed., 1902, English trans., 1908), and C. Bonnet's *Documents inédits sur Mme de la Vallière* (1904). *****Madame de Genlis** and Alexandre Dumas wrote historical novels based on her life, and *****Elisabeth Vigée-Le Brun** used Louise's visage for her painting of a penitent *****Mary Magdalene**. A necklace with pendants has been named for her; it is usually spelled *lavaliere.*

Lavaur, Guirande de (d. 1211).

See Guirande de Lavaur.

Lavenson, Alma (1897–1989)

American photographer. Born Alma Ruth Lavenson in San Francisco, California, in 1897; died in Piedmont, California, in 1989; University of California, Berkeley, B.A., 1919; married Matt Wahrhaftig (a lawyer), in 1933 (died 1957); children: Albert (b. 1935); Paul (b. 1938).

A contemporary of *****Dorothea Lange**, *****Margaret Bourke-White**, and *****Marion Post Wolcott**, Alma Lavenson took up photography in 1919 and continued working until her death at age 92. Her portraits, still lifes, industrial, and architectural photographs reflect the development and trends in photography over a 70-year span.

Alma Lavenson was born in 1897 and spent her early years in San Francisco. When the 1906 earthquake destroyed the city, she moved with her family to Oakland. Following her graduation from the University of California at Berkeley in 1919, Lavenson went on a seven-month tour of Europe; during this time, she became interested in photography. In the 1930s, she exhibited in both her native San Francisco and in New York City, where she met and was influenced by *Imogen Cunningham and Alfred Stieglitz. Although not a member of Group f/64, Lavenson was represented in their first exhibition in San Francisco in 1932. She was also influenced by Ansel Adams, and took many photos in California and New Mexico. Later, in the 1960s and 1970s, she traveled and photographed in Europe, Asia, and Latin America.

Alma Lavenson was a frequent contributor to the magazines *Photo-Era* and *Camera Club*, and her photographs appeared in Sydney B. Mitchell's book *Your California Garden and Mine* (1947). She was also represented in Edward Steichen's *Family of Man* exhibition at the Museum of Modern Art in New York in 1955. In 1979, a retrospective of her work was held at the California Museum of Photography at the University of California, Riverside. Lavenson was married in 1933 to lawyer Matt Wahrhaftig and had two sons, Albert and Paul. She died in 1989 in Piedmont, California, where she had lived since 1935.

SOURCES:

Moreland, Kim, Leo Ribuffo, and Catherine Griggs. "Book Notes: American Photography," in *American Studies International*. October 1992.

Rosenblum, Naomi. *A History of Women Photographers*. NY: Abbeville Press, 1994.

SUGGESTED READING:

Ehrens, Susan. *Alma Lavenson Photographs*. Berkeley, CA: Wildwood Arts, 1991.

Barbara Morgan,
Melrose, Massachusetts

Laverty, Maura (1907–1966)

Irish novelist, playwright and broadcaster. Born Mary Kelly in Rathangan, County Kildare, on May 15, 1907; died on July 26, 1966, at her home in Dublin; second of thirteen children of Michael Kelly and Mary Ann (Tracey) Kelly; educated at Brigidine

Waterlillies by Alma Lavenson, 1932.

Convent, County Carlow; married Seamus Laverty also seen as James Laverty, on November 3, 1928; children: two daughters, Maeve Laverty and Barrie Laverty, and one son, James Laverty.

Awards: Irish Women Writers' Award (1942).

Selected publications: Never No More *(1942, rep. Virago, 1985);* Alone We Embark *(US:* Touched by the Thorn, *Longmans, 1943);* No More than Human *(Longmans, 1944);* Lift Up Your Gates *(US:* Liffey Lane, *Longmans, Green, 1946).*

When Maura Laverty started to write fiction in the early 1940s, her childhood experiences of growing up in rural County Kildare informed much of her writing. **Maeve Binchy** has noted the strength and force of her country characters and the amazingly intense village life. Laverty knew what it was like to go from comfortably well off to very poor. Her father Michael Kelly, who married when he was 57, owned a large farm, but lost it as a result of his gambling habit. To support the family, her mother **Mary Ann Kelly** became a dressmaker. Maura spent much of her childhood with her grandmother, who was immortalized as Delia Sally in Laverty's first novel *Never No More.*

Maura's adventurous streak asserted itself when, after leaving school, she went to Spain in 1925 to be a governess. She soon abandoned that notion and trained as a secretary, subsequently working for the diplomat Prince Bibesco, and then for the Banco Calamarte and the journal *El Debate.* She became engaged to a Hungarian, but when she returned to Dublin to announce the news to her family, she met James Laverty, then serving in the Irish army. They married after a whirlwind courtship. James, who would become a journalist, also had a profitable agency for the Irish Sweepstakes but this disappeared with the outbreak of the Second World War and with it the Lavertys' comfortable existence.

The idea for her first novel, *Never No More,* came when Laverty read an old cookery book by **Florence Irwin**, *Irish Country Recipes,* which brought back memories of her childhood in Kildare. Sean O'Faolain serialized the novel in his journal *The Bell.* After her death, the *Irish Times* would call it "one of the best books about an Irish childhood." However, her next three novels—*Alone We Embark* (1943), *No More Than Human* (1944), a sequel to *Never No More,* and *Lift Up Your Gates* (1946)—were all banned under Ireland's strict censorship laws, a fate Laverty shared with other leading writers of her generation. The director of Dublin's Gate The-

ater, Micheál MacLiammóir, wrote to Laverty of his "despair" that Ireland was "slowly being transformed by a pack of ignoramuses into a dank, damp little nursery."

It was MacLiammóir's fellow Gate director, Hilton Edwards, who suggested to Laverty that she adapt *Lift Up Your Gates* into a stage play. The novel was set in a Dublin tenement lane, behind two formerly grand Georgian houses, and follows the 14-year-old Chrissie Doyle as she traverses the lane on her paper round. As Doyle visits the various shops and apartments, Laverty describes the lives of her customers. The play, called *Liffey Lane* and produced in February 1951, was an enormous commercial and critical success. It was followed by two other plays which formed a trilogy, *Tolka Row* (October 1951), about a Dublin inner-city family moved to a new council estate, and *A Tree in the Crescent* (October 1952). Laverty's plays gave the Gate much-needed box-office success and all but kept the theater afloat in the 1950s. However, as Christopher Fitz-Simon wrote in his biography of MacLiammóir and Edwards, she was exploited ruthlessly by them in the matter of payment although she was badly off financially, with three children and a husband to support.

Broadcasting had become an increasingly important source of income for Laverty. She had a weekly radio program in which she answered letters on a variety of topics, especially cookery. Her cookery books, *Kind Cooking* (1946) and *Full and Plenty* (1961), were enormously popular with generations of Irish women. The pages

Maura Laverty

of her books, writes Binchy, "are full of spicy vapours which would cajole a dying man to eat, luscious pools of butter on speckled surfaces of seed cake, potato apple cakes oozing with sugar and butter."

Shortly after Irish television service began at the end of 1961, Christopher Fitz-Simon, who was working in the drama department, asked Laverty to adapt *Tolka Row*. The first episode aired in January 1964, and the show quickly became one of the most popular on Irish television. Laverty would write all the episodes until her death in 1966. As the first Irish television soap opera, its importance lay in its portrayal of the urban working class in a culture which was largely preoccupied with rural life. As one television executive observed, "It introduced one half of Ireland to the other half."

At the beginning of 1966 Laverty's health began to deteriorate. She had a serious operation, and also broke her hip, but continued to record her radio programs from her hospital bed. In May 1966, the 100th episode of *Tolka Row* was televised. At the end of July, Laverty was found dead at her home in Dublin; she had suffered a heart attack. Since the 1980s, a number of her books have been reprinted, including *Never No More* and her children's books, *Cottage in the Bog* (1992) and *The Queen of Aran's Daughter* (1995), which were illustrated by her daughter, the artist **Barrie Castle**.

SOURCES:

Binchy, Maeve. Introduction to *Never No More*. London: Virago, 1985.

Fitz-Simon, Christopher. *The Boys: A Double Biography*. Dublin: Gill & Macmillan, 1994.

Obituaries in *Irish Independent, Irish Press, Irish Times*, Dublin, 28–30 July 1966.

Sheehan, Helena. *Irish Television Drama: A Society and its Stories*. Dublin: RTE, 1987.

Deirdre McMahon,
lecturer in history at Mary Immaculate College,
University of Limerick, Limerick, Ireland

Lavin, Mary (1912–1996)

Irish writer. Born in East Walpole, Massachusetts, on June 11, 1912; died in Dublin, Ireland, on March 25, 1996; only child of Thomas Lavin and Nora (Mahon) Lavin; educated at Loreto Convent, Stephens Green, Dublin; University College Dublin, B.A. (honors), 1934, M.A. (1st class honors), 1938; married William Walsh (a lawyer), in September 1942 (died 1954); married Michael McDonald Scott, in 1969 (died 1990); children: (first marriage) Valentine Walsh; Elizabeth Walsh; Caroline Walsh.

Awards: James Tait Black Prize (1944); Guggenheim Fellowships (1959, 1962, 1972); granted honorary D.Litt, National University of Ireland (1968); American-Irish Foundation Award (1979); Aosdána (Irish Government, 1992).

Mary Lavin was born in 1912, the only child of Irish immigrants living in Massachusetts. Her parents returned to her mother's family home in Athenry, Galway, when she was ten. Later, the family moved to the east of Ireland, to Bective in Meath, where her father worked as an estate manager. Lavin retained close links with the area until her death, and it provided inspiration for her fiction. She studied English at University College Dublin and wrote her postgraduate thesis on *Virginia Woolf. Lavin published her first short story, "Miss Holland," in 1938, and in 1939 another story was published in *Atlantic Monthly*. Two years later, her first collection of short stories, *Tales from Bective Bridge*, was published and won the James Tait Black Prize. She continued to write steadily after her marriage in 1942 and the birth of her three daughters, publishing the short-story collections *The Long Ago* (1944) and *At Sally Gap* (1946), which included the novella *The Becker Wives*. She also wrote two novels, *The House in Clewe* (1945) and *Mary O'Grady* (1950)

Mary Lavin drew upon her own experiences for many of her stories: the tension in her parents' marriage, the people and the landscape around Bective, her school and student days in Dublin. The Irish academic and critic Augustine Martin has written of the disregard by many Irish writers of "that great provincial hinterland represented by Mullingar, Roscrea, Kilkenny and Athlone where the real dynamism of change and development is centred. . . . They bypass a whole provincial ethos in a blur of alternating grey and green." Mary Lavin was an exception to this, and Martin considered her an exemplary chronicler of this neglected, provincial Ireland. Writing, Lavin once said, was "only looking closer than normal into the human heart, whose vagaries and contraries have their own integral design." She observed the changes in Irish society in the first decades after independence; she never sentimentalized Irish rural life but saw with compassion its emotional and social problems, especially as they affected women. In *The Will* (1964), she describes a young girl who elopes with her lover and is rejected by her family, a rejection symbolized by her mother cutting her out of her will. This conflict, between those who seek and accept love, and those who turn their hearts and minds against it, is echoed in other stories. This leads to another theme, as Maurice Harmon has noted: self-deception, the self-deception of those who blind themselves to reality, who diminish themselves and those around them.

Mary Lavin's husband died suddenly in 1954, leaving her with three young children to support. She continued to write but included her children in her writing life as much as possible. Royalties were spent on travel, and one of her daughters recalled that by the age of 14 she was acquainted with the Vatican Museum in Rome. Lavin could write anywhere and was a well-known figure in the National Library in Dublin and in various cafés where she would sit with a mass of manuscript, wrestling with words, adding, pruning, and writing draft after draft until she was satisfied. The novelist **Maeve Binchy**, who taught Lavin's daughters early in her career, noted that Lavin demystified the business of writing. "She said that she regarded going to the National Library as going to the office, and that if she was late she would run . . . as anyone would run if they were going to be late for a job. She always said you could never be sure of inspiration but you should be sitting down quietly with your pen and paper ready in case it did strike."

In 1959, her *Selected Short Stories* were published, and she won the first of three Guggenheim fellowships for fiction. Lavin abandoned novel writing after 1957 and had a growing reputation as a master of the short story. She was variously compared to other Irish short-story writers such as Liam O'Flaherty, Sean O'-Faolain, and William Trevor, as well as to Balzac, Chekhov, and Saki. Lavin herself paid tribute to *Jane Austen whose work she had long admired for its precision. "I don't think a story has to have a beginning, middle and end. I think of it more as an arrow in flight . . . or a flash of lightning, lighting up the whole landscape all at once, beginning, middle and end." She was irritated by the wariness of most publishers towards the genre: "Publishers are definitely unfair to short story writers . . . since the essence of the short story is its conciseness, an addiction to change is an occupational disease and not the self-indulgence publishers think."

Lavin wrote compassionately about widows who refuse to be cowed by death and who are not afraid to seek new relationships and experiences. In 1969, she married for a second time. It was a happy marriage, and her husband Michael McDonald Scott was a considerable support to her. In her last stories, old age was a dominant theme, particularly the interlinking of genera-

Mary Lavin

tions—grandmothers, mothers and daughters—a process which had its rewards, but also, as Lavin the realist was aware, its share of tensions.

SOURCES:

Bowen, Zack. *Mary Lavin*. Lewisburg: Bucknell University Press, 1975.
Kelly, Angeline A. *Mary Lavin, Quiet Rebel: A Study of Her Short Stories*. NY: Barnes & Noble, 1980.
Peterson, Richard F. *Mary Lavin*. Boston: Twayne, 1978.

Deirdre McMahon,
lecturer in history at Mary Immaculate College,
University of Limerick, Limerick, Ireland

Lavoisier, Marie (1758–1836)

French scientific collaborator of her husband Antoine Lavoisier, the founder of modern chemistry. Name variations: Marie Anne Pierrette Paulze; comtesse de Rumford; countess of Rumford; Madame de Rumford. Born Marie Anne Pierrette (also seen as Pierette) Paulze in 1758; died on February 10, 1836; daughter of Jacques Paulze and Claudine (Thoynet) Paulze; had three brothers; married Antoine Laurent Lavoisier (1743–1794), the founder of modern chemistry, in 1771; married Benjamin Thomson, count of Rumford, in October 1805.

In an arranged marriage, Marie Lavoisier and Antoine Lavoisier enjoyed a relationship which developed into a successful scientific collaboration, but they were caught up in one of the most dramatic events in modern European history. Marie survived the French Revolution, which cost her husband his life, but was imprisoned for several months at the height of the Terror.

The 1788 dual portrait of the Lavoisiers by the great French painter Jacques Louis David, now in New York's Metropolitan Museum of Art, enlivens a moment in time of historic importance to modern civilization. The painting was completed only months before Antoine published his crowning scientific achievement in February 1789, *Traité élémentaire de chimie* (*Elementary Treatise on Chemistry*), the volume which laid the foundations of modern chemistry. The portrait gives every sign of presenting not Antoine Lavoisier as its leading figure, but rather his wife, who occupies the foreground of the canvas and is shown as small, somewhat plump, with a long, straight nose and lips that are tightly closed. In contrast to Marie, whose pose has been called protective and maternal toward her husband, Antoine, a wealthy and powerful member of the new nobility, is depicted as diffident and even docile. Some see the portrait as an indicator of the painter David's growing anti-establishment attitudes; others ask if it hints at tensions beneath the surface of a couple known to be close. Regardless, the portrait reveals two major figures in the intellectual life of France as they wished to be seen, at a time when their nation was poised on the brink of revolution.

Both Marie and Antoine Lavoisier were born into the highest reaches of the French bourgeoisie. Marie's father Jacques Paulze was director of the royal tobacco commission. After her mother **Claudine Thoynet Paulze**'s death, Marie was brought back to Paris from the convent where she had been sent for her education and served as hostess of her father's lavish entertainments. With her striking blue eyes, brown hair, and perfect complexion, she was both feminine and charming by age 13.

Antoine Laurent Lavoisier was born in Paris in 1743, more than a decade before Marie. He was a handsome man whose papers were brilliant analyses of various scientific problems, including the nature of thunder, the aurora, and the then still-prevalent belief, which he refuted, that by means of repeated distillation water was converted into earth. Where science was concerned, he was the man to watch in French intellectual life. By the time of his marriage to Marie, he would also be a wealthy man, having become a full titular member of the *Ferme Générale* (General Farm), the lucrative system of taxation carried on by a few privileged families on behalf of the French crown. Antoine's scientific interests left him little time to mix with fashionable women but through Jacques Paulze, who was also a member of the General Farm, Antoine met his daughter Marie. Antoine (15 years her senior) felt at ease in the company of the 13-year-old, who despite her age listened with interest as he talked about his scientific projects and displayed her musical talents on the harp and harpsichord while they spent many evenings in each other's company.

There was, however, another with interest in marrying Marie. The count of Amerval, a relatively impoverished 50-year-old aristocrat, hoped that by marrying her he would enter into a union that would be to his financial advantage. Marie's mother's uncle, the Abbé Terray, who was controller general of finance and the individual in charge of the General Farm tax system that provided the Paulze family's wealth, attempted to pressure Jacques to approve the marriage. Revealing the independent spirit that would characterize her long life, Marie called Amerval "a fool, an unfeeling rustic and an ogre." Jacques refused to grant permission for his daughter's marriage to a much older (and financially pinched) suitor, despite the fact that by doing so he risked losing his lucrative post as tobacco commission director. Jacques kept his job and, to forestall more meddling by his powerful uncle-in-law, he made clear his approval of Marie's marriage to Antoine.

The marriage contract, which was signed on December 4, 1771, stipulated that Marie would bring a dowry of 80,000 livres ($3,200,000). The groom brought much greater wealth into the marriage, which guaranteed that the couple's annual income would be about 20,000 livres ($800,000), providing for a life of considerable luxury. After their marriage ceremony (which took place on December 16, 1771, in the chapel of the Hôtel des Finances on the rue Neuve des Petits Champs), the couple moved into a house bought for them by Antoine's father on the fashionable rue Neuve des Bons Enfants, near the gardens of the Royal Palace. Antoine's father then bought him a title of nobility in 1772.

Although Marie was very likely pregnant in 1774, the couple remained childless. This allowed Marie, who was interested in her husband's scientific work, both the time and energy to assist him in his research. By 1775, when Marie was 17, she was already being referred to in correspondence as Antoine Lavoisier's "philosophical wife." By 1777, she was being tutored in chemistry by her husband's disciple and collaborator Jean Baptiste Bucquet. She learned English, a language her husband would never master, and translated many chemical works for him not only from English but also from other languages. Of her published translations, the most important is Richard Kirwan's 1787 *Essay on Phlogiston*, which appeared in Paris during 1788 and includes a few notes by Marie as well as commentaries by her husband and other French chemists who effectively refuted Kirwan's erroneous theories. She also studied drawing with the painter Jacques Louis David and made sketches of the Lavoisier laboratory.

One of her most important achievements was her assistance to Antoine in the preparation of the plates for his epoch-making book, *Elementary Treatise on Chemistry* (1789). She was often in his laboratory, assisting him by recording his scientific observations in large registers that served as raw data for his articles and books. An enthusiastic conversationalist and correspondent as well as a competent editor, Marie Lavoisier played a major role as an effective disseminator for the doctrines of the new chemistry that grew out of her husband's experiments.

After the couple moved to an apartment in the Arsenal where Antoine held the post of Régisseur des Poudres that placed him in charge of the French monarchy's production of gunpowder, Marie often presided over intellectual soireés, to which were invited many of Paris'

Marie Lavoisier with her husband Antoine.

most brilliant scientists and artists. A testament to the intensity with which the couple carried out their scientific pursuits, their laboratory was immediately adjacent to their apartment. Often working together with Marie, Antoine arose at six in the morning and worked until eight; they returned to the laboratory in the evenings, working there from seven until ten. At least one full day of the week—"the day of happiness"—was devoted entirely to scientific experiments.

In addition to the hours spent investigating the basic mysteries of chemistry in their laboratory, much of Antoine's time went to his job as director of the state gunpowder administration. When he took over the newly established agency in 1775, France was producing less than half of its annual requirements of gunpowder. Antoine's thorough reforms of the organization brought rapid improvements, and, by the time the American Revolution began in 1776, the French found it possible to supply the American rebels with sufficient powder to continue their resistance against the British crown. As quantities increased, prices dropped, and the quality of the gunpowder also improved markedly. Antoine wrote with pride in April 1789: "One can truly say that North America owes its independence to French gunpowder." He was often assisted and encouraged by Marie while carrying out this work, which at times proved life-threatening. In October 1788, while both of them were in a mill observing the grinding of a new type of gunpowder, the mill exploded, killing one of the organization's directors and a young woman standing nearby. Both Lavoisiers had been positioned behind a barrier at the time and consequently were not injured.

The Lavoisiers were in no immediate danger at the start of the French Revolution in the spring of 1789. In fact, Antoine's public record, as a highly respected government administrator and scientist as well as an advocate of economic and social reform, was exemplary. He had started a model farm to demonstrate the advantages of the latest techniques of scientific agriculture as early as 1778, was a member of the provincial assembly of Orleans, and participated in various schemes of local improvements, and during the famine of 1788 advanced money without interest to several towns for the purchase of barley to alleviate suffering. Once the revolution began, he was called on to participate in various reform efforts, including the creation of a new system of taxation, and served on committees overseeing changes in public education, public hygiene, coinage, and the casting of cannon. He was also a leading member of the commission appointed

to create a system of uniform weights and measures, a reform effort that resulted in the establishment of the metric system.

At first optimistic in his assessment of the revolution, in a letter dated February 5, 1790, Antoine Lavoisier informed his American friend and fellow scientist Benjamin Franklin that as far as he could judge, he regarded "our Revolution . . . as completed." From the very start of the revolution, however, the situation in Paris was precarious for members of the privileged elite classes like the Lavoisiers. In early August 1789, after a boat loaded with gunpowder was seen being prepared to leave the quay on the Seine near the Arsenal, suspicious local residents became convinced that this was evidence that the Régisseurs des Poudres were trying to deny the Paris populace access to gunpowder, thus threatening their ability to defend their newly acquired freedoms. A mob formed at the Arsenal demanding the arrest of Antoine and one of his colleagues, both of whom were taken to the Hôtel de Ville (City Hall). Fortunately for Antoine, he secured his release with a sufficiently convincing explanation of the situation, which was that the boat contained low-grade gunpowder for export, and another vessel, loaded with high-grade powder, was soon expected to arrive on the Seine from the factory at Essonnes. This began to calm frayed tempers, and after another tense day, when both Antoine and Marie found themselves to be virtual prisoners at the Arsenal, the mob dispersed.

During these increasingly troubled years, Antoine, assisted by Marie, continued to carry out his scientific investigations. Two sketches made by her (1790 and 1791) show experiments on human respiration and are of both artistic and scientific interest. No doubt because she had studied with Jacques Louis David, Marie Lavoisier's sketches depict her husband in bold Davidian poses that celebrate political republicanism as much as they depict prosaic scientific reality. Her sketches illustrate the ways in which politically inspired modes of representation could also be utilized when depicting other, quite different, forms of human activity.

By 1792, with the rapidly increasing radicalization of the French Revolution, Antoine Lavoisier had become an object of suspicion. As a Tax Farmer and prominent member of the Ferme Générale, he was linked to one of the most hated aspects of the Old Regime's discredited system of privilege and exploitation. Even his many years of work at the Arsenal as head of the government gunpowder monopoly were now open to criticism. The politician Jean Paul Marat accused Antoine of putting the city of Paris in prison as well as impeding the city's air circulation by means of the *mur d'octroi* (toll-house wall) erected at his suggestion in 1787. In August 1792, the Lavoisiers had to leave their apartment and laboratory at the Arsenal because mob violence made living there unsafe. In November of that year, the revolutionary government of the Convention ordered the arrest of the former Farmers General. Antoine was tried by the revolutionary tribunal at the height of the Terror in May 1794, and the perfunctory proceedings against him and 31 others took only a few hours to conclude. Of the 32 tried, 28 were found guilty and sentenced to death. In the afternoon of the same day, May 8, 1794, Antoine and the others who had been convicted, including Marie's father Jacques Paulze, were guillotined at the Place de la Revolution, now the Place de la Concorde. Without ceremony, the victims were buried in anonymous graves in the cemetery of the Parc Monceaux. The following day, Joseph Lagrange remarked: "It required only a moment to sever that head, and perhaps a century will not be sufficient to produce another like it."

Soon after the execution of her husband and father, Marie Lavoisier was arrested and jailed along with other heirs of dead Tax Farmers. Two months later, she wrote abjectly to her local revolutionary committee to declare her belief in the ideals and principles of the revolution and the French Republic. By this time, the dictator Maximillien Robespierre had been guillotined, and the Reign of Terror was over. In August 1794, she was released from prison. Now destitute, she had to be supported by a former servant who took pity on her plight. Although traces of the trauma she had endured would mark her personality for the rest of her life, over the next few years Madame Lavoisier slowly put the pieces of her shattered existence back together. With the end of the terrorist phase of the revolution, she inherited the bulk of her husband's wealth and began once more to entertain Parisian society. During this difficult period of adjustment, she carried on an intense love affair with an old family friend who was 20 years her senior, Pierre Samuel Dupont, a relationship that appears to have begun in the final, chaotic months before her husband's trial and execution. Although their strong personalities made a permanent stable relationship virtually impossible to achieve, even after their liaison had ended Dupont remained emotionally attached to Marie. In 1799, at the time of his departure for America, he addressed her in a letter which he never sent: "my dear lady,

your name will always be linked with mine." (In the New World, Dupont had an immensely successful business career as founder of the chemical company that still bears his family name.)

In October 1805, Marie Lavoisier married Count Rumford, whose title was Bavarian but who was in fact a colorful Massachusetts-born scientist named Benjamin Thomson. His accomplishments included service as a colonel in the British Army during the Revolutionary War. One of the most highly regarded scientific investigators of the day, Count Rumford studied the nature of light, demonstrated the mechanical nature of heat, and made practical discoveries in the area of the rational use of foods and fuels, resulting in more nourishing soups for feeding the poor and greatly improved fireplace designs. In a letter describing Lavoisier soon after he met her in 1801, Rumford praised "this amiable lady . . . [who is] . . . very sociable . . . [and who] . . . lives in elegant style, and is hostess to the greatest philosophers and the most eminent scientists and writers in Paris. And above all, she is kindness itself."

It soon became obvious to all of Paris that this union—of two highly intelligent and strong-willed individuals, both of whom were middle-aged and set in their ways—was very much a mismatch. Lavoisier lived to entertain friends in her charming house, surrounded by an English garden, in one of the most elegant districts of Paris. Rumford, on the other hand, desired the peace and quiet of his laboratory and his beloved rose garden. Both were stubborn and unwilling to compromise on even the most trivial matters, and they argued much of the time, sometimes in public. After he forbade the porter to let his wife's friends enter the house (forcing them to speak with their hostess through the mansion gate), she got her revenge by pouring boiling water over his exquisite rose bushes. After four years characterized by little wedded bliss, the marriage ended in 1809 with an amicable separation that left the oft-poor but famous scientist Rumford with a handsome financial settlement of between 300,000 and 400,000 francs.

For the next 27 years, Madame de Rumford, as she continued to be known, devoted herself entirely to entertaining her friends in grand style. In the words of historian François Guizot, she chose to entertain her distinguished guests—scientists, artists, and high society—with "a rather singular mixture of rudeness and courtesy." Most of her visitors were flattered to receive her invitations and usually ignored the fact that "her language could be brusque and she was subject to authoritarian whims." For a number of years before he was forced to return to America, one of her most favored party guests was her old lover Pierre Samuel Dupont. Several years after his return to the States, Dupont died in Wilmington, Delaware, of a chill caught while helping to put out a fire at his son's gunpowder works.

As Lavoisier's friends of the past began to die, she lived more and more alone. A relic from the Old Regime, she became ever more eccentric, a nature often commented on by the younger generation of French writers and intellectuals. The Delahante brothers, descended like Antoine Lavoisier from a family of pre-revolutionary Tax Farmers, wrote about their visits to her home on the rue d'Anjou. They began by noting the striking David portrait of Antoine and Marie Lavoisier, going on to describe Marie:

> This old Turk [who] was all that remained of the beautiful young woman depicted by David: it was Madame de Rumford, with her aged, masculine face, coiffed and rigged out in the most bizarre way. She greeted us in her abrupt manner, which was not unkind, asked us to sit down, and began asking us questions about our studies and pastimes. . . . After a few minutes she would suddenly get up from the love seat and go and stand with her back to the fireplace . . . pull up her skirts from behind as high as her garters and leisurely warm her enormous calves. . . . She often gave elegant balls that we enjoyed more than the visits, in spite of her active surveillance and the severity with which she chased us away from the buffet to have us dance the quadrille.

Marie Lavoisier died on February 10, 1836, having played an important role in the birth of modern chemistry. She had lived under and survived the various political and other vicissitudes of seven constitutions and eight forms of government in a turbulent era of French history.

SOURCES:

Alic, Margaret. *Hypatia's Heritage*. Boston, MA: Beacon Press, 1986.

Donovan, Arthur. *Antoine Lavoisier: Science, Administration, and Revolution*. Oxford, U.K. and Cambridge, MA: Blackwell, 1993.

Duveen, Denis I. "Madame Lavoisier, 1758–1836," in *Chymia*. Vol. 4, 1953, pp. 13–29.

Holmes, Frederic Lawrence. *Lavoisier and the Chemistry of Life: An Exploration of Scientific Creativity*. Madison, WI: University of Wisconsin Press, 1985.

Miller, Jane A. "Women in Chemistry," in G. Kass-Simon and Patricia Farnes, eds., *Women of Science: Righting the Record*. Bloomington: Indiana University Press, 1990, pp. 300–334.

Ogilvie, Marilyn Bailey. *Women in Science: Antiquity through the Nineteenth Century*. Cambridge, MA: MIT Press, 1986.

Perrin, C.E. "The Lavoisier-Bucquet Collaboration: A Conjecture," in *Ambix: The Journal of the History of Alchemy and Chemistry*. Vol. 36, no. 1. March 1989, pp. 5–13.

Poirier, Jean-Pierre. *Lavoisier: Chemist, Biologist, Economist*. Translated by Rebecca Balinski. Philadelphia, PA: University of Pennsylvania Press, 1996.

Schofield, Maurice. "Women in the History of Science," in *Contemporary Review*. Vol. 21, no. 1215, 1967, pp. 204–206.

Smeaton, W.A. "The Chemical Work of Horace Bénédict de Saussure (1740–1799), With the Text of a Letter Written to Him by Madame Lavoisier," in *Annals of Science*. Vol. 35, no. 1. January 1978, pp. 1–16.

———. "Monsieur and Madame Lavoisier in 1789: The Chemical Revolution and the French Revolution," in *Ambix: The Journal of the Society for the History of Alchemy and Chemistry*. Vol. 36, no. 1. March 1989, pp. 1–4.

Umesh, Nila. "The Woman Behind Antoine Lavoisier," in *Link* [New Delhi]. Vol. 31, no. 14–15. November 13–20, 1988, pp. 42–43.

John Haag,
Associate Professor of History,
University of Georgia, Athens, Georgia

La Voisin (d. 1680).

See French Witches for Catherine Deshayes.

Law, Ruth (d. 1970)

First American pilot to fly nonstop for 590 miles. Died in 1970.

In a plane that she had purchased from Orville Wright in 1912, aviator Ruth Law made news when she became the first woman pilot to perform a loop-the-loop. She was also the first woman to chance flying at night, a dangerous venture at the time. Law captured the spotlight once again on November 19, 1916, when she attempted to fly nonstop from Chicago to New York City.

In preparation for the undertaking, she had asked Glenn Hammond Curtiss, a major airplane manufacturer, to sell her a larger plane, one that could hold more fuel and was more conducive to longer flights. Curtiss refused, convinced that a woman could not pilot a large plane. Instead, Law had to use an older, smaller plane, one used for stunt flying at air shows. Her modified Curtiss biplane, named "Baby Machine," was outfitted with three important pieces of equipment that gave her an advantage: overhangs on the wing, which afforded greater altitude, a windshield to protect her from the wind (pilots flew in open cockpits then), and an extra fuel tank which gave her 53 gallons of fuel instead of the usual eight. But the extra fuel made the airplane heavier, so mechanics took the lights off the plane to lighten the load. Without lights, Law could not navigate well after sunset. She would have to get to New York before dark.

The night before departure, Law slept in a tent on the roof of a Chicago hotel to get accustomed to the cold. When she arrived at Chicago's Grant Park, on the shore of Lake Michigan, at four in the morning, she was so bundled up against the cold she was unrecognizable. She was wearing two pairs of woolen longjohns, two leather suits, and the properly feminine skirt over her pants. "I didn't look any more like a woman than anything at all," she later recalled. "A man, a workman with his lunch pail, came hurrying over, stretched out his hand, and said, 'Well, good luck, young feller. I hope you make it.'"

With a sizeable press contingent on hand, Law climbed into her cockpit. But the freezing weather made the engine hard to start, and she lost precious daylight hours. Finally, at around 8 AM, the crowd watched with fear as the plane took off. With the wind and the additional fuel, it appeared to be hard to control. Flying at the speed of 100 miles an hour, one mile above the earth, Law had no instruments to rely on. Instead, strips of survey maps mounted on rollers inside a glass-topped box kept her on course. She also had maps taped to her leg, a compass, a clock, and a speedometer.

During her flight, she had only one bad moment: her oil gauge registered no pressure as she flew over Cleveland. Since it was impossible to land, she simply kept on. Then at 2:00 PM, two hours away from her destination, she ran out of fuel over Hornell, New York, and had to land. Law had flown an unprecedented 590 miles nonstop in six hours, setting the American nonstop record. It was a staggering feat at the time. Then she ate lunch, refueled the plane, and continued on to New York City, where she was greeted by a large welcoming committee. In the days to come, Woodrow Wilson would sing her praises and a dinner would be held in her honor. One year later, **Katherine Stinson** would break her record.

Ruth Law spent the latter part of her piloting career barnstorming with a flying circus that bore her name, but gave up flying at age 31 at her husband's request.

SOURCES:
"The Time Machine," in *American Heritage*. November 1991, pp. 43–44.

SUGGESTED READING:
Brown, Don. *Ruth Law Thrills a Nation* (juvenile). Boston, MA: Houghton Mifflin, 1993.

Lawford, Patricia Kennedy (b. 1924).

See Kennedy, Rose Fitzgerald for sidebar.

Lawick-Goodall, Jane van (b. 1934).

See Goodall, Jane.

Ruth Law

Lawless, Emily (1845–1913)

Irish novelist and poet. Name variations: Honorable Emily Lawless. Born on June 17, 1845, in County Kildare, Ireland; died on October 19, 1913, in Surrey, England; daughter of Lord Edward Lawless, third Baron Cloncurry, and Lady Elizabeth Kirwan; had early education at home; D.Litt., Trinity College, Dublin; never married; no children.

Selected writings: Hurrish *(1886);* Major Lawrence FLS *(1887);* With Essex in Ireland *(1890);* Maelcho *(1894);* Grania *(1892); (poems)* With the Wild Geese *(1892); (biography)* The Life of Maria Edgeworth *(1904); (poems and prose)* The Point of View *(1909); (co-written with Shan E. Bullock and completed after Lawless' death)* The Race of Castlebar *(1913);* The Inalienable Heritage *(poems, 1914); (edited by Padraic Fallon)* Collected Poems *(1965).*

The oldest of eight children, Emily Lawless was born on June 17, 1845, on her father's estate in County Kildare, Ireland. The Lawless family was a part of the wealthy Anglo-Irish upper class; her father was Lord Edward Lawless, third Baron Cloncurry, who committed suicide when she was 14, and her mother, Lady **Elizabeth Kirwan**, was an acclaimed society beauty. Growing up into a fairly solitary woman with an affinity for the outdoors, Lawless lived most of her life at her father's estate and at her mother's, in County Galway, riding horses, gardening, swimming, and translating her observations of the natural world around her into the realistic settings of her novels and poetry.

Lawless' novels were serious efforts to address contemporary problems in Ireland, including peasant violence, and she was praised for her accurate depictions of Irish peasant life. Her writings, including *Hurrish*, which takes place in County Clare shortly before the start of the struggle for Irish Home Rule, reveal a strong nationalist vision of Ireland. The English politician W.E. Gladstone, who as prime minister in 1886 introduced the first bill for Home Rule, praised *Hurrish*, which was published that year, for showing "a living reality, the estrangement of the people of Ireland from the law." She also wrote a history of Ireland (1887) and a biography of the Irish novelist *Maria Edgeworth (1904), for the English "Men of Letters" series. Her most popular novel was the tragic *Grania* (1892), set on the bleak Aran Islands off the coast of County Galway, which due to its "remarkably feminist" slant is probably also the most likely to interest current readers. In the last years of her life, Emily Lawless moved to England, apparently because of the new political climate in Ireland. Her mental and physical health declined, and she died in Surrey, England, on October 19, 1913.

SOURCES:

Kunitz, Stanley J., ed. *British Authors of the Nineteenth Century.* NY: H.W. Wilson, 1936.

Todd, Janet, ed. *British Women Writers.* NY: Continuum, 1989.

Karina L. Kerr, M.A.,
Ypsilanti, Michigan

Lawrence, Andrea Mead (1932—)

American Alpine skier who was the first American— female or male—to win two gold medals in a single Winter Olympics. Name variations: Andrea Mead; Andy Mead. Born Andrea Mead in Rutland, Vermont, on April 19, 1932; daughter of Janet Mead and Bradford Mead; married Dave Lawrence (a skier), in 1951 (divorced 1967); children: five.

After Alpine skiing became popular in the United States in the early 20th century, the Winter Olympics did much to promote it. The success of the American women's Alpine ski team in the 1948 and 1952 games created public enthusiasm for the sport, and Andrea Mead Lawrence played a major role in that success.

Born Andrea Mead, known as Andy, in Rutland, Vermont, in 1932, she grew up in the backyard of Vermont's Pico Peak at a ski resort owned by her parents. By age three, she was skiing. Racing came naturally to Lawrence, who flew down the slopes. Although she had no formal coaching, she seemed to know intuitively what racing required. By age eight, she was winning local contests. Lawrence has always credited her mother for encouraging her to continue skiing after her father died when she was ten.

At 11, Andy finished second in the Women's Easter Slalom championships. She qualified for the U.S. Olympic team at age 14. In 1948, she was the youngest member of the U.S. Women's Alpine Olympic team in the St. Moritz, Switzerland, Winter Games (where America's *Gretchen Fraser took the gold in the slalom and Switzerland's **Antoinette Meyer** the silver). Inexperience cost Lawrence the bronze by just one-tenth of a second; she was shutout by Austria's **Erika Mahringer.**

In 1949, Lawrence won all the events held at the Federation International de Ski tryouts in Whitefish, Montana. The following year was an off year for the young skier, but in 1951 she won ten out of 16 races. In 1952, conditions were less than ideal at the Oslo Olympics; Norwegian soldiers had to shovel snow onto the course before the giant slalom. Nonetheless, Lawrence won the event by nearly three seconds over **Dagmar Rom** of Austria. Although Lawrence fell in the women's slalom on the first run, she recovered to finish the run, and her second run was perfect. The combined time of both runs put her in first place for her second gold; **Ossi Reichert** of Germany took the silver. In 1951, Andy married fellow skier Dave Lawrence. Her third child was just four months old when she competed in the 1956 Olympics and finished one tenth of a second behind the bronze medalist.

Lawrence was awarded the White Stag Trophy in 1949, the Beck International Trophy in 1952, inducted into the National Ski Hall of Fame in 1958, and named to the International Women's Sports Hall of Fame in 1983. At the 1960 Winter Olympics held in Squaw Valley, California, Andrea Mead Lawrence was chosen to ski the Olympic flame into the stadium.

After retiring from competition, Lawrence moved with her family to Aspen, Colorado, and became active in the community. Following her divorce in 1967, she moved with her children to the Mammoth Lakes area of the Sierra. There, Lawrence continued her involvement with community issues. She joined the Mono Lake Committee, helped form the conservation group Friends of Mammoth, and battled high-rise construction. She was a Mono County Supervisor from 1982 to 1999. Intent on coordinating all the environmental groups in the region, she also formed the Sierra Nevada Alliance.

SOURCES:

Condon, Robert J. *Great Women Athletes of the 20th Century*. Jefferson, NC: McFarland, 1991.

Woolum, Janet. *Outstanding Women Athletes: Who They Are and How They Influenced Sports in America*. Phoenix, AZ: Oryx Press, 1992.

Karin L. Haag,
freelance writer, Athens, Georgia

Lawrence, Elizabeth (1904–1985)

American landscape architect whose legendary gardens in Raleigh and Charlotte, North Carolina, provided a backdrop for her writings. Born in Marietta, Georgia, on May 27, 1904; died on June 11, 1985, in Annapolis, Maryland; daughter of Samuel Lawrence and Elizabeth (Bradenbaugh) Lawrence; grew up in North Carolina; graduated from Barnard; first woman to receive a degree in landscape architecture from the North Carolina State College of Design, 1930.

Received the Herbert Medal of the American Plant Life Society (1943) for her contributions to gardening and gardening literature; honored by the American Horticultural Society and the National Council of State Garden Clubs for A Southern Garden.

Selected writings: A Southern Garden: A Handbook for the Middle South *(University of North Carolina Press, 1942, rev. ed. 1967);* The Little Bulbs: A Tale of Two Gardens *(Duke University, 1957);* Rock Garden in the South *(Duke University, 1960);* Gardens in Winter *(Harper, 1961);* Lob's Wood *(1971); (author of introduction)* The Gardener's Essential *Gertrude Jekyll (Breslich and Foss, 1983);* Gardening for Love: The Market Bulletins *(Duke University, 1987); (edited by Bill Neal)* Through the Garden Gate *(a selection of her newspaper columns, University of North Carolina Press, 1990).*

On March 19, 1941, Elizabeth Lawrence—a Barnard graduate and trained landscape architect—wrote William Crouch, director of the University of North Carolina Press: "I have written a garden book for the Middle South based on my own records which I have been keeping for a number of years with a book in my mind, for there is no book for gardeners in our section, and there is need of one." The first edition of *A Southern Garden* appeared in 1942, received decent reviews, sold moderately for the next 15 years, then quietly went out of print. In 1957, the year of its demise, Lawrence published *The Little Bulbs* and took on a weekly gardening column for the *Charlotte Observer* which she would continue for the next 14 years. For years, though gardeners sang the praises of *A Southern Garden,* they were reluctant to hand out their hard-to-come-by copies. In 1967, when a revised edition was published with a new introduction, *Katherine S. White wrote in *The New Yorker:* "A Southern Garden is far more than a regional book; it is civilized literature by a writer with a pure and lively style and a deep sense of beauty." Minus its ten-year hiatus, *A Southern Garden* has been in print for over 50 years.

When the book was first published, Lawrence was writing of her garden in Raleigh. Six years later, she built a new house and garden in Charlotte. "Broad stone steps, planted with tiny treasures and flanked by a rock garden, led down from the terrace's edge to a wide walk of fine crushed gravel," wrote **Edith Eddleman** in her foreword to the new edition. "On one side of the walk, Carolina cherry laurels (*Prunus Laurocerasus*) pruned up high gave the illusion of a row of olive trees. Moving from the terrace to the path, I felt that I had journeyed from an alpine meadow to the Mediterranean."

It was Lawrence and her colleague *Caroline Dormon in Louisiana who encouraged oth-

Elizabeth Lawrence

ers to preserve the native wildflowers of the region. Sometime in the late 1940s, *Eudora Welty had put Lawrence's name on the mailing list of the *Mississippi Market Bulletin*, a free bimonthly made up of classified ads from rural families from several Southern states who had land, livestock, tools, produce, seeds, and plants to sell. Lawrence regularly ordered plants by way of the *Bulletin*, often initiating a prolonged correspondence with the flower sellers, usually women who dealt in "old timey" plants. Fascinated with the numerous rare plants, Lawrence set out to learn their botanical names. "Reading the flower lists is like reading poetry," she wrote, "for the flowers are called by their sweet country names, many of them belonging to Shakespeare and the Bible."

In 1962, Lawrence determined to meld the bulletins, plants, and correspondence into a book but died before the work was completed. Editor Allen Lacy, who sifted through a huge box filled with the material to fashion *Gardening for Love*, wrote in his introduction, the "book ranged widely into the whole history of gardening in the Western world, with references to Pliny and Virgil, to herbalists such as Parkinson and Gerard, and to more recent writers such as Thoreau and *Sarah Orne Jewett—and to Eudora Welty."

Sometimes called the *Jane Austen of gardening, Elizabeth Lawrence is to gardens, notes Lacy, what *M.F.K. Fisher is to food. "I do not suppose there is any part of the world in which gardens are not beautiful in spring," wrote Lawrence. "Travellers in other seasons are told, 'you should see our gardens in spring.' To which they reply, 'but we cannot leave our own then.'"

SOURCES:
Lawrence, Elizabeth. *A Southern Garden*. University of North Carolina Press, special edition, 1991.

Lawrence, Emmeline Pethick-
(1867–1954).

See Pethick-Lawrence, Emmeline.

Lawrence, Florence (1886–1938)

Canadian-born actress who was America's first movie star. Born Florence Annie Bridgewood in Hamilton, Ontario, Canada, on January 2 (some sources cite September 22), 1886; committed suicide in West Hollywood, California, on December 28, 1938; interred in an unmarked grave in Hollywood Memorial Cemetery; third child and only daughter of George Bridgewood (a British actor and impresario)

and Charlotte Amelia (Dunn) Bridgewood, an American actress known professionally as Lotta Lawrence; married Harry L. Solter (a director), in September 1908 (died 1920); married Charles Bryne Woodridge (a Denver business broker), on May 21, 1921 (separated 1929, divorced 1931); married Henry Bolton, in November 1931 (divorced 1932); no children.

Selected films: Daniel Boone (1907); Macbeth (1908); (as Juliet) Romeo and Juliette (1908); (title role) Salome (1908); The Heart of O. Yama (1908); A Smoked Husband (1908); The Barbarian Ingomar (1908); Romance of a Jewess (1908); The Call of the Wild (1908); The Devil (1908); The Zulu's Heart (1908); The Planter's Wife (1908); (as Cleopatra) Antony and Cleopatra (1908); The Song of the Shirt (1908); (as Katherine) The Taming of the Shrew (1908); The Ingrate (1908); After Many Years (1908); The Viking's Daughter (1908); Richard III (1908); The Valet's Wife (1908); The Test of Friendship (1908); An Awful Moment (1908); Mrs. Jones Entertains (1910); The Sacrifice (1910); The Salvation Army Lass (1910); The Lure of the Gown (1910); Deception (1910); The Drunkard's Reformation (1910); The Cardinal's Conspiracy (1910); Mrs. Jones' Lover (1910); Love's Stratagem (1910); The Joneses Have Amateur Theatricals (1910); At the Altar (1910); Confidence (1910); Resurrection (1910); The Right to Love (1910); Jane and the Stranger (1910); Mother Love (1910); The Broken Oath (1910); The Eternal Triangle (1910); The Call of the Circus (1910); Irony of Fate (1910); All the World's a Stage (1910); The Test (1911); Vanity and Its Cure (1911); The Burglar (1911); The Actress and the Singer (1911); Her Artistic Temperament (1911); The Wife's Awakening (1911); The Little Rebel (1911); The Gypsy (1911); The Slavey's Affinity (1911); The Maniac (1911); A Blind Deception (1911); The Players (1912); All for Love (1912); Flo's Discipline (1912); The Advent of Jane (1912); The Angel of the Studio (1912); The Closed Door (1913); The Spender (1913); A Girl and Her Money (1913); The Romance of a Photograph (1914); The False Bride (1914); The Honeymooners (1914); Pawns of Destiny (1914); Disenchantment (1914); A Singular Cynic (1914); Elusive Isabel (1916); The Way of a Man (1919); The Mended Lute (1919); The Slave (1919); The Unfoldment (1922); The Satin Girl (1923); Gambling Wives (1924); The Johnstown Flood (1926); The Greater Glory (1926); (extra) Secrets (1933).

Born Florence Annie Bridgewood in Hamilton, Ontario, Canada, in 1886, film star Florence Lawrence was the daughter of George

Bridgewood, a British actor, and **Lotta Lawrence**, an American actress. From the age of three, Florence appeared in her parents' tent show billed as "Baby Florence, the Child Wonder." Except for a brief interval when she lived with relatives in Buffalo, New York, Lawrence toured with the show until it folded in 1906. She and her mother then went to work for the fledgling Edison Vitascope film company, where Florence began to build her reputation with a role in *Daniel Boone* (1907). In 1908, Lawrence joined the Biograph company, a new enterprise started by D.W. Griffith, and was promoted simply as "The Biograph Girl." The company feared that if they used her real name, she might demand more than the $25 per week salary they were willing to pay. Lawrence appeared in a string of successful pictures at Biograph, including many directed by Griffith. In 1910, however, she was lured away from the studio by Carl Laemmle who was starting up his own company, Independent Motion Picture Company of America (IMP). He first starred Lawrence in *Love's Stratagem* (1910), a film directed by Lawrence's husband Harry L. Solter, whom Laemmle had also hired away from Biograph. At the time he hired Lawrence, Laemmle also set in motion an elaborate scheme that launched the film industry's star system. He first planted a newspaper story in which he reported that "The Biograph Girl" (Lawrence) had been killed in a streetcar accident. The next day, he ran an advertisement denouncing the malicious rumor his enemies had started concerning the death of Lawrence, who was now "The Imp Girl," very much alive and working for him. From then on, Lawrence used her own name, becoming the country's first named movie star. Laemmle would later lure *Mary Pickford away from Biograph, then proclaim, "Little Mary is an Imp now."

Fame proved to be fleeting for Lawrence. She left Laemmle in 1911 and for several years worked for producer Sigmund Lubin. Subsequently, she and her husband were briefly with the Victor Motion Picture Company. In 1915, Lawrence was seriously hurt while performing a scene in a burning building. Trapped, she could have jumped to safety but instead aided co-star Matt Moore. Lawrence injured her back and suffered facial burns which left scars. The following year, while attempting to return to film, she collapsed on the set and was completely paralyzed for the next four months. She then endured partial paralyzation for four more years. Lawrence was forced, for the most part, into retirement. She ended her career at MGM, drawing a small salary as an occasional extra. Contin-

Florence
Lawrence

ued illness, the death of her husband in 1920, and the failure of a second and third marriage left her despondent, and, in December 1938, she committed suicide by ingesting ant poison.

SOURCES:

James, Edward T., ed. *Notable American Women, 1607–1950*. Cambridge, MA: The Belknap Press of Harvard University Press, 1971.

Katz, Ephraim. *The Film Encyclopedia*. NY: HarperCollins, 1994.

McHenry, Robert, ed. *Famous American Women*. NY: Dover, 1983.

Barbara Morgan,
Melrose, Massachusetts

Lawrence, Frieda (1879–1956)

German baroness, writer, and wife of British novelist D.H. Lawrence. Name variations: Baroness Frieda von Richthofen; Frieda Weekley. Born Emma Maria Frieda Johanna von Richthofen in the French city of Metz, in Lorraine, in 1879; died in Taos, New Mexico, on August 11, 1956; second of the three daughters of Friedrich von Richthofen (a civil engineer) and Anna (Marquier) von Richthofen; sister of Else von Richthofen; attended convent schools; married Ernest Weekley (an English professor), on August 29, 1899 (divorced, May 28, 1914); married D(avid) H(erbert)

Lawrence (1885–1930, the novelist), on July 13, 1914 (died March 2, 1930); married Angelo Ravagli (a captain in the Italian army), on October 31, 1950; children: (first marriage) Montague "Monty" Weekley (b. 1900); **Elsa Weekley** *(b. 1902);* **Barbara "Barby" Weekley** *(b. 1904).*

On May 13, 1912, Frieda von Richthofen Weekley abandoned her husband and three young children and eloped with the British writer D.H. Lawrence, who at the time was struggling to get his literary career off the ground. Thus began their tumultuous 18-year relationship, during which Frieda came to view herself as his liberator. "It was given to me to make him flower," she wrote to her friend **Dorothy Brett** shortly after D.H. Lawrence's death in 1930. Indeed, Frieda influenced much of D.H.'s work after 1912, although some critics and scholars tend to ignore her impact. In *The von Richthofen Sisters*, Martin Green recognizes Frieda as a major force in both D.H.'s life and art. "She gave him sensual happiness, but she also gave him—by the same gift—a mission as a writer. She gave him her identity, her idea—which became his idea. She even helped him significantly with the work of translating that idea into literary terms."

Frieda von Richthofen was born in the French city of Metz, in Lorraine, in 1879, the second of the three daughters of **Anna von Richthofen** and Baron Friedrich von Richthofen. She grew up in a two-story farmhouse in Metz, where the baron was a civil engineer in the Prussian army of occupation. "It was a strange time," Frieda wrote about the occupation. "I knew that I had nothing in common with most people, an uneasy feeling, I ought to be like them and wasn't." Of the three von Richthofen sisters, dubbed the "three Graces" by the baron, Frieda was the self-proclaimed "wild" one, a robust roughneck with little patience for the classroom. Not as intelligent as her older sister *Else von Richthofen* or as beautiful as the younger **Johanna ("Nusch") von Richthofen**, Frieda had an untamed energy that she carried from childhood into her adult years. As a young girl, she became deeply attached to her father, a man who demanded the highest moral fiber in others but cheated in his marriage with a string of mistresses. "Her attraction to the baron's sensual aura of failure was the most immediate and aggrandized," writes **Janet Byrne** in her biography of Frieda, *A Genius for Living*. "She would always require that the men in her life allow her, in some form, to pity them; that they understand

her sense of herself as flawed; and that, as in her favorite myths, they give equal play to her attributes and the grandness of her faults."

By age 15, Frieda had blossomed into a comely young woman, with long, thick blonde hair, an aristocratic profile, and intriguingly unbalanced features. She developed a schoolgirl crush on her 21-year-old cousin and two years later entered into a chaste love affair with a Prussian lieutenant named Karl von Marbahr. She might have married him, but her mother disapproved of the match and sent her off to Berlin to forget him. (Frieda, however, never forgot Marbahr and 40 years later addressed part of her memoirs to him.) In the summer of 1899, Frieda married Ernest Weekley, a somewhat stuffy English academic 15 years her senior, whom she had met while on holiday in Freiburg. Although he seemed an unlikely choice, she was drawn to his dignity and respectability. Weekley, however, was shy with women, hardly a match for his irrepressible bride. The morning after a less than satisfying wedding night, Frieda seemed to sense that the marriage may have been a mistake. "So that's that. It's a sad affair, now the door has shut on my life and I must make the best of it," she solemnly recorded. The couple settled in Nottingham, England, where Ernest had a position as an English professor at University College. Within a period of five years, Frieda had three children—Monty (b. 1900), Elsa (b. 1902), and Barby (b. 1904)—whom she adored, though her relationship with Weekley so stifled her that she harbored thoughts of running away. Even a succession of new houses, each larger and better equipped, did little to quell Frieda's restlessness and her disdain for conventional English life.

With her husband preoccupied with his work, Frieda embarked on a series of extramarital affairs, the most notable of which was with the Freudian psychologist and free-love advocate Otto Gross who was brilliant, charismatic, and addicted to cocaine. The two met while she was a houseguest of **Frieda Gross** ("Friedel"), from whom Otto was separated. At the time, Otto was also having an affair with Frieda's sister, Else, who was now married to Edgar Jaffe, a political economy professor. (Else subsequently had a child with Gross, causing a rift between the sisters that would last for several years.) After their initial two-week liaison had ended and Frieda had gone home, Gross continued to pursue her through a series of passionate love letters. Calling her his "golden child" and "the woman of the future," he bestowed upon her a value she had never before acknowledged in herself. "I know now how people will be who are no longer stained by all the things I hate and fight," he wrote. "I know it through *you*, the only person who *today* has stayed free of chastity as a moral code and Christianity and Democracy and all those heaps of nonsense." Though Frieda briefly considered leaving Weekley for Gross, she eventually came to realize, as she recounted in her memoirs, that he "didn't have his feet on the ground of reality." She did take much of his philosophy of free love to heart, however, and in 1911, during another visit to Friedel Gross, embarked on an affair with Ernst Frick, an international anarchist who was later jailed for having detonated a bomb outside a Zurich police station in 1907.

Frieda first met D.H. Lawrence on March 3, 1912, when he came to the house to talk with Ernest about a job as a lecturer. (D.H. may have seen or known of Frieda before that time, as he went to high school and college in Nottingham, and his brother George also had a house there.) Initially, Frieda found him "obviously simple," hardly the "young genius" her husband had described. "His face was plump after convalescence from a months-long bout with pneumonia," writes Byrne, "his mustache and thick red hair were assiduously brushed, setting off lucid blue eyes, and he wore a freshly starched wing collar and black patent leather shoes." Although they spoke only briefly before lunch, they experienced an immediate and mutual attraction. "You are the most wonderful woman in all England," D.H. wrote Frieda after their meeting. "You don't know many women in England," Frieda replied. They probably made love soon after, though the date and circumstances are unknown. "But then, can I describe what it was like when we were first together?," Frieda wrote later. "It just had to be. What others find in other ways, the oneness with all that lives and breathes, the peace of all peace, it does pass all understanding, that was between us, never to be lost completely."

Shortly after their love affair began, Frieda also became D.H.'s reader, working on the early chapters of "Paul Morel" (a working title for the later *Sons and Lovers*). Over the next eight weeks, they saw each other regularly, on one occasion even traveling to London together and staying at the house of D.H.'s publisher Edward Garnett in Kent. As the relationship deepened, D.H. urged Frieda to tell Weekley, but she hesitated. When she finally did confront her husband, she only managed to confide her affairs with Gross and Frick, before dissolving into tears. Three agonizing days later, she left Weekley and their children and traveled with D.H. to Metz, where her father was celebrating his Jubilee year.

In Metz, Frieda began to have second thoughts and banished D.H. to a local hotel while she stayed with her family. Fueling her uncertainty was her guilt over leaving her children and the simmering fear that she might not see them again. There was also the very vocal disapproval of her parents, who were enraged at her behavior. The baron, who by now had fathered an illegitimate child with one of his mistresses, claimed to be morally offended. "You travel about the world like a barmaid," he later wrote her. While Frieda wavered, D.H. grew desperate and wrote to Weekley. "I love your wife and she loves me," he confessed. Weekley wrote Frieda asking for a divorce and telling her that she would never see her children again. Meanwhile, during one of their few rendezvous in Metz, Frieda and D.H. wandered into a military zone and were questioned by police who believed D.H. was a spy. The baron was forced to intercede and insisted that D.H. leave town. Parted from Frieda for several weeks, D.H. traveled to visit a cousin in the Rhineland, writing one of his most beautiful love poems to Frieda, "Bei Hennef," while en route.

The couple reunited in Munich, where they began life together in a small rented apartment outside the city. It was the first in a succession of rented and borrowed homes they would occupy. They were difficult years, plagued with problems that continually threatened to destroy the relationship, and indeed did stall it from time to time. Always at issue was Frieda's devotion to her children, which D.H. seemed unable or unwilling to understand or tolerate. There were also financial woes, personality clashes, petty jealousies, and, in later years, concerns over D.H.'s declining health. Outside the couple's personal realm, there were societal factors at play, as Alastair Niven points out in a biography of D.H. Lawrence in *British Writers*. "It was in every sense an unconventional liaison that shocked contemporary morality," he wrote, "for it not only disrupted the Weekley marriage but it cut across class." In the midst of her most difficult times with D.H., Frieda also bore the inequities of her womanhood, realizing that while D.H. could very well leave her, she could not leave him. "How could I earn a living?," she pondered during one miserable spell between them. "I was never taught anything which might earn me a living. . . . I am helpless. I am caught." She then quickly hedged. "I wish to be caught. We love each other."

In the summer of 1912, strapped for money and having to vacate the Munich flat, the couple set out on probably one of the most memorable adventures of their lives, a journey across the Alps to Italy, on foot. Having sent their few belongings ahead, they walked approximately ten miles a day, sleeping in hay-huts and chapels along the way, and occasionally spending a week or two at a farmhouse or cheap hotel. In rainy weather, they traveled by coach or train, but it was still a grueling and exhausting journey. Early in the trip, Frieda had her first outside affair, establishing a pattern of infidelity that marked her relationship with D.H., who also had his share of extracurricular liaisons. (D.H. was bisexual, though it is unknown whether he consummated any of his relationships with men during his years with Frieda.) Frieda's first betrayal consisted of a single night spent with Harold Hobson, who had joined them briefly on the first leg of the walking tour. John Worthen, in his biography of D.H. Lawrence, suggests that the encounter may have been Frieda's way of asserting her independence, of making it clear to D.H. that even though she had agreed to leave her husband and children for him, she was still her own woman.

The couple ended their trek in the village of Gargnano, Italy, where they spent the winter. D.H. worked feverishly rewriting "Paul Morel" into *Sons and Lovers*, wanting desperately to prove himself capable of supporting Frieda. Creative bursts of energy became typical of the writer, who conducted his entire literary career on the move and seemed to be able to work anywhere. Frieda once called him "a writing machine," referring to a fixation on work that often drove him to utter exhaustion and illness, through which Frieda patiently nursed him. "Often he was ill when his consciousness tried to penetrate into deeper strata," she wrote later, "it was an interplay of body and soul. . . . He demanded so much of me and I *had* to be there for him so completely."

Frieda's divorce from Weekley and marriage to D.H. were anticlimactic events, considering what the couple had already endured. The marriage ceremony, which took place on July 13, 1914, was an impersonal affair conducted at the Kensington Registry Office in London, with only a few friends in attendance, among them *Katherine Mansfield and John Middleton Murry, who would remain close friends with the couple. Although the Lawrences had hoped to return to Italy, the outbreak of World War I detained them in England where they were barred by regulation from leaving the country and were frequently under surveillance. They had "compounded their social unacceptability by going against the current of Anglo-German hostility," wrote Niven. "[D.H.] had the most profound horror at the way the war was conducted. It seemed to him an explosion of all the obscene, violent, destructive, and materialistic characteristics of Western machine-worshipping society, while at the same time he was equally outraged by the loss of young life." Though he was exempted from compulsory service due to his health, D.H. wrote: "The War finished me; it was the spear through the side of all sorrows and hopes." He frequently took his frustrations out on Frieda, chiding her for her Germanness, and intimating that his relationship with her might indeed jeopardize his success.

In the meantime, the publication of *Sons and Lovers* (1913) had established D.H. as a promising author and opened many doors. He and Frieda began to enjoy a social life and a widening circle of friends, including *Cynthia Asquith and *Ottoline Morrell, whose salons for artists, writers, and others of the intelligentsia brought them in contact with the entire Bloomsbury circle, many of whom D.H. ultimately found "conceited and self-centered." They moved back to London for a brief time in August 1915 and then took up residence in borrowed houses in the English countryside. D.H. finished *The Rainbow* (published in 1915), a spin-off of *The Sisters*, which had become too long for one volume. The book, for which he had enormously high hopes, was savagely attacked by most of the critics and was eventually declared obscene and ordered destroyed. D.H. was devastated, sure that his reputation as well as his earning power as a writer were over.

As the war dragged on, the Lawrences were strapped for money and remained under surveillance, which made Frieda fearful even to leave the house. One evening their cottage was ransacked, and the next day the Lawrences were expelled from Cornwall. They were taken in by friends in London, but were followed by detectives who eavesdropped at the apartment door. They then moved to a friend's empty cottage in Berkshire, where they continued to be stalked by the police.

After the war, the Lawrences deliberately exiled themselves from England. In December 1919, shortly after D.H. had completed *Women in Love* (published in New York in 1920), they left for Italy. They remained there until 1922, living in Florence, Capri, and a stucco farmhouse near Mount Etna in Sicily, which Frieda loved. "Living in Sicily after the war years was like coming to life again," she wrote. From Italy, the Lawrences ventured around the world: to Ceylon, Australia, America, Mexico, Europe, and

back to America, all within a mere two-year period (1922–24). Their arrival in America, which D.H. hoped might be their utopia, occurred on September 4, 1922. They first landed in San Francisco, then were met outside Sante Fe by *Mabel Dodge Luhan, the philanthropist and salon impresario who had become enchanted with D.H. after reading *Sons and Lovers* and actually paid for the Lawrences to come to America. Luhan took them to Taos, where they eventually established a home, and where Frieda returned after D.H.'s death. "By and large one may say that [D.H.] and Frieda found in Taos what Mabel had promised them they would," writes Green. "It *was* the place they had been looking for, the effective antithesis of the city and of civilization." Frieda claimed it was the Indians that gave them a deeper realization and connected them with the earth. Her husband "could never have written *Lady Chatterley* if he had not known Taos," she wrote later. D.H. agreed that New Mexico had "finally liberated him from the inherited inhibitions of Christianity."

The Lawrences' relationship went through a particularly shaky period around 1923. On a trip to Mexico in March of that year, the tensions between them reached the boiling point. D.H., whose increasing bouts of consumption made him ill and cranky, frequently demeaned Frieda in public, making hostile references to her increasing weight, which embarrassed him. "Her long-standing habits—chain-smoking, and sitting with her legs apart, like a 'slut,' though often long skirts concealed all but her ankles— were also frequent targets," wrote Byrne. Frieda, humiliated by her husband's tirades, was frequently at a loss for words. "When even silence failed to stanch a tirade, she went to Sanborn's, a local teahouse, for strawberry shortcake." That summer, having not seen her children in four years, Frieda left for England without D.H., who accused her of "chasing . . . those Weekley children." During the three-month separation, D.H. traveled across America, then, at Frieda's urging, joined her in England. They later returned to Taos, taking up residence on a rundown ranch ("Kiowa") given to them by Mabel Luhan. It was the first and only home they would ever call their own. D.H. took great pleasure in repairing and restoring the structure over a five-week period during the summer, and Frieda knitted, cooked, and churned her own butter. "It was very beautiful up here," D.H. wrote in a letter to a friend. "We worked hard, and spent very little money. And we had the place all to ourselves, and our horses the same. It was good to be alone and responsible."

In August 1924, D.H. suffered from a bronchial hemorrhage, signaling the onset of tuberculosis, which dominated the last five years of his life. He recovered sufficiently for the couple to spend the fall in Mexico, at a house in Oaxaca that they rented from a Mexican-born Scottish priest. D.H. worked on essays and a second draft of *The Plumed Serpent,* then was besieged with the flu, followed by bouts of typhoid and malaria. In late February 1925, he was told he was in the terminal stage of tuberculosis and was given a year or two at the most. "If I die," he told Frieda, "nothing has mattered but you, nothing at all."

By February 1925, however, D.H. was well enough to travel, and the couple returned to Europe again, visiting family in Nottingham and Baden-Baden, then going on to Italy where they rented a villa in Spotorno, near the Mediterranean. Their landlord was a married officer in the Italian army by the name of Angelo Ravagli, a strikingly handsome figure to whom Frieda was immediately drawn. She began an affair with Ravagli that continued at intervals over the next four years. D.H. was aware of the romance, although it did not seem to alter his feelings for Frieda, or hers for him. "The worst quarrels of their lives did not occur over her affairs (or his for that matter)," writes Worthen, "but over other people altogether; people he insisted on bringing into their lives, like Ottoline, or Mabel, or Brett, or—at other times—his sister **Ada Lawrence**; or over Frieda's daughters; or (at times) almost anyone with whom one of the two felt the other was siding with, against them. It was those who invaded their living space that mattered, not those who briefly occupied their beds."

From 1926 to 1928, D.H. was consumed with *Lady Chatterley's Lover,* the book for which he would become well known and the one that made him more money than he had made in his life. He also began to paint, producing a series of powerful renderings, many of them sexual in nature. In 1929, a solo show of his works in England was closed by the authorities because of excessive realism. He finished a second version of *Lady Chatterley's Lover* in the spring of 1927 ("verbally terribly improper," he called it), after which he suffered a third bronchial hemorrhage, his worst yet. As soon as he could travel, he and Frieda went to Bavaria and stayed in Frieda's sister Else's house, then returned to Italy, where he decided to publish *Lady Chatterley's Lover* himself. He rewrote yet a third version of the novel in a remarkable six-week period between November 1927 and January 1928.

For the next two years, Frieda's days were dominated by her husband's illness, which dictated where they lived and the quality of her life. Her very vitality infuriated D.H., but the challenge of it also seemed to revive him. They resided for the most part in Italy until mid-1928, then in France where D.H. eventually entered Ad Astra sanatorium in Vence. Although his condition did not improve, he insisted on leaving, and Frieda found a villa for them in Vence and hired a nurse to care for him. On March 1, 1930, he was taken by taxi to the new house, but the following afternoon he began to deteriorate and by that evening was dead. Frieda stayed alone with his body that night, singing his favorite hymns and folk songs.

"Then we buried him, very simply, like a bird we put him away, a few of us who loved him," wrote Frieda of his funeral. "We put flowers into his grave and all I said was 'Good-bye, Lorenzo,' as his friends and I put lots and lots of mimosa on his coffin. Then he was covered over with earth while the sun came out on to his small grave in the little cemetery of Vence which looks over the Mediterranean that he cared for so much." D.H.'s remains were eventually cremated and in April 1935 were brought back to the United States and placed in a chapel built at the New Mexico ranch.

Although the relationship had ended, it survived in D.H. Lawrence's writing, as did the writer's relationships with all the women in his life. But, as Martin Green points out, Frieda not only served D.H.'s characterizations and plots, but also functioned as his best critic. She had a substantial hand in refining the manuscript of *Sons and Lovers,* the book that established him as a writer. "I think L. quite missed the point," she wrote about the novel to publisher Edward Garnett. "[H]e is so often beside the point 'but "I'll learn him to be a toad" as the boy said as he stamped on the toad.'" As would become her pattern, Frieda argued with D.H. about the novel's language, and the motivation of the characters. She line edited for him, writing "hoyty-toyty" beside what she considered to be overblown phrases, and actually rewrote some of the new chapters which helped fortify the pivotal character of Miriam. (D.H. took one brief respite from his work on *Sons and Lovers* during which he wrote a comic play about Frieda's marital status called *The Fight for Barbara.* She countered with a parody of "Paul Morel" called "Paul Morel, or His Mother's Darling," but D.H. was not amused and the play disappeared.)

D.H. also characterized other members of Frieda's family. According to Green, Frieda's father is sketched as "the Baron" in the story "The Thorn in the Flesh," and some of his dubious ethics are portrayed in the character of Will in *The Rainbow* and *Women in Love*, as well as in the officer of "The Mortal Coil." Anna von Richthofen, Frieda's mother, turns up as Anna Brangwen in *The Rainbow*. D.H. exposed Frieda's complex relationship with her sister Else in *The Sisters*, although in the first draft the characters were blurred together, both becoming Frieda. "[T]hey are me, these beastly, superior arrogant females!," Frieda wrote to publisher Garnett. "Lawrence hated me just over the children[;] I daresay I wasn't all I might have been, so he wrote this!" Frieda fought constantly with D.H. over the rewrite of *The Sisters*. During one such battle, when D.H. announced that women had no souls and could not love, Frieda smashed him over the head with the plate she was wiping and left the room.

Immediately following D.H.'s death, Frieda seemed unable to cope. She was never adept at practical matters; even using the telephone befuddled her. In a letter of September 24, 1959, Aldous Huxley expressed his surprise at Frieda's helplessness. "She seemed such a powerful Valkyrie," he wrote, "but, as I found out when she came to London after D.H.'s death to deal with business and stay to herself in a hotel, she was amazingly incapable and, under her emphatic and sometimes truculent façade, deeply afraid. She had relied totally on D.H., and felt completely lost until she found another man to support her." Since a will that D.H. had drawn up in 1914 could not be located, it became necessary for Frieda to battle D.H.'s family for his royalty rights. The matter dragged on for two years and was finally settled in court, where John Middleton Murry produced the missing document that he and Katherine Mansfield had witnessed. During the trial, while her lawyer was sentimentalizing her relationship with D.H., Frieda interrupted him at one point, exclaiming: "But that's not true—we fought like hell!"

In May 1933, Frieda returned to the Kiowa Ranch at Taos with Angelo Ravagli, who had since separated from his wife. (He would not be formally divorced until 1950, after which he and Frieda would marry.) Frieda's relationship with Ravagli seemed as unlikely as her marriage to Weekley. Some, including Frieda's daughter Barby, theorized that the liaison represented a "return" to Weekley, while others believed that Ravagli was more of a father figure. It may be, however, that Frieda merely saw Ravagli as part of an intriguing experiment. "I want Dario [Ravagli] to come to America with me, to that small wild place in the Rockies; and I will see what happens to him there," she wrote in her second memoir. For his part, Ravagli was initially horrified at the loneliness of Taos and the primitiveness of the ranch. They began construction of a new house on the property, and Frieda started her memoir, *Not I, but The Wind . . .*, taken from the first line of a poem D.H. had written celebrating their love. The autobiography, published in October 1934, sold briskly and was reprinted several times. (A second volume, *And The Fullness Thereof. . .*, was never completed, but was published posthumously as *Frieda Lawrence: The Memoirs and Correspondence*.) Meanwhile, Ravagli served as handyman around the ranch and as Frieda's business partner as she undertook management of the Lawrence estate, a task that became increasingly complex over the years, due to reprint rights, film rights, collected editions and posthumous volumes.

From 1933 until the Second World War, Frieda and Ravagli often wintered in California, escaping the harsh winters of Taos. As early as the winter of 1936, when the couple visited Hollywood, Ravagli began frequenting dance halls with other women, to whom he confided that his relationship with Frieda was a contractual one. His infidelity, which increased over the years, seemed of little note to Frieda, who was more concerned with his help on the ranch, in planting and taking care of the animals. "As long as his interest in other woman was fleeting, she gave him free rein 'to have his flings,' insisting that, at fifty-seven, she was old and preferred to read at night," explains Byrne. The only one of Ravagli's affairs that seriously threatened Frieda was that with **Dorothy Horgan**, a younger married woman from New York, whom he pursued unsuccessfully for many years.

In 1939, Frieda bought a second house ("Los Pinos") in the village of El Prado, with two outbuildings, one to be used as a guest house and the other to serve as a workshop for Ravagli, who had taken up pottery. At Kiowa, Frieda entertained an ever-growing circle of friends, including **Rebecca James**, **Millicent Rogers**, and *****Georgia O'Keeffe** who collected erotica and loved D.H.'s paintings which Frieda displayed in a room built especially for that purpose. "I can remember very clearly the first time I ever saw her," O'Keeffe later recalled of Frieda, "standing in a doorway, with her hair all frizzed out, wearing a cheap red calico dress that looked as though she'd just wiped out the frying pan with it. She was not thin, and not young, but there was something radiant and wonderful about her."

During the 1940s, Frieda wrote several essays and letters to editors clarifying and refuting details that had been written about D.H. in a flood of articles and books. She also wrote a foreword for a publication of the first version of *Lady Chatterley's Lover*, which, like the other two versions, was also deemed obscene and seized.

In 1952, Frieda returned to England, a trip she dreaded in light of all that had happened there to her and D.H. It was, however, a happy occasion, made so by the opportunity to visit with all three of her children, their spouses, and her five grandchildren. She had even proposed a meeting with Weekley (now 89 and nearly blind), but it was called off when the children objected. Returning to Taos, Frieda began to sense her own mortality as more and more of her friends succumbed to illness. Though stricken with asthma, she retained much of her vigor and magnetism throughout her later years. **Amalia de Schulthess**, a sculptor from Beverly Hills who visited her in 1953, attested to that fact, noting that the atmosphere changed when she entered a room. "She was very powerful and intensely female," said de Schulthess. Nevertheless, sensing that her days were numbered, Frieda took up the matter of her estate and deeded the upper ranch to the University of New Mexico. Life remained good for her until April 1956, when she suffered a serious viral infection from which she never completely recovered.

Frieda Lawrence died on August 11, 1956, succumbing to a massive stroke she had suffered on August 8. Ravagli sent her off in grand style, burying her outside D.H. Lawrence's tomb and playing a recording of her recitations of several of his poems on a gramophone while the mourners enjoyed a picnic supper under lighted paper lanterns. Frieda no doubt would have found the tribute much to her liking. She also would have derived a great deal of pleasure from Penguin Books' successful defense of its unexpurgated edition of *Lady Chatterley's Lover* in a London court in 1960, after which D.H. Lawrence's popularity soared.

SOURCES:

Byrne, Janet. *A Genius for Living: The Life of Frieda Lawrence.* NY: HarperCollins, 1995.

Green, Martin. *The von Richthofen Sisters: The Triumphant and the Tragic Modes of Love.* NY: Basic Books, 1974.

Jackson, Rosie. *Frieda Lawrence.* San Francisco, CA: Pandora, 1994.

Niven, Alastair. "D.H. Lawrence," in *British Writers.* Vol. VII. NY: Scribner, 1984.

Tedlock, E.W., Jr., ed. *Frieda Lawrence: The Memoirs and Correspondence.* NY: Alfred A. Knopf, 1964.

Worthen, John. *Biography of D.H. Lawrence.* Nottingham, England: The University of Nottingham, 1997.

Barbara Morgan,
Melrose, Massachusetts

Lawrence, Gertrude (1898–1952)

*British singer, dancer, and actress, an idol of the interwar generation, who achieved, enhanced, and maintained her status as a "star" on both sides of the Atlantic for nearly 30 years. Born Gertrud (Gertie) Alexandra Dagmar Klasen on July 4, 1898, in Clapham, London; died of cancer on September 6, 1952, in New York; daughter of **Alice Louise (Banks) Klasen** and Arthur Klasen (a singer, known professionally as Arthur Lawrence); educated at various local schools and Miss Italia Conti's Stage School; married Frank Gordon Hawley, in 1918 (divorced 1927); married Richard Stoddard Aldrich, on July 4, 1940; children: (first marriage) **Pamela Hawley** (b. 1918).*

Grew up with extended family—grandparents, mother and stepfather—whose frequent moves through South London suburbs meant sparse education; made professional debut as child dancer in Babes in the Wood *at the Brixton Theatre, London (1908); attended Italia Conti's Stage School for four years (1911–14); met Noel Coward (1913); went to live with father (1914) and remained working as chorus member in a variety of shows in London and the provinces until engaged as understudy to Beatrice Lillie in* Andre Charlot's Revues *(1916–19); met and married talent scout Frank Gordon Hawley, 20 years her senior (1918); separated from Hawley and returned to work with Charlot, leaving daughter with her mother; did cabaret at Murray's Nightclub and various touring engagements (1920); met Philip Astley and began to socialize with wealthy members of the aristocracy, including Edward, prince of Wales; scored successes in several musical shows quickly becoming the talk and toast of London's West End (1921–24); made first appearance on Broadway in* Andre Charlot's Revue of 1924 *(1924); divided professional life (appearing in musicals, plays and films) between London and New York, with holidays in the South of France (1925–35); sent daughter Pamela to Roedean (exclusive boarding school for girls); declared bankrupt (1935); transferred to New York with* Tonight at 8:30 *(1936) and did not return to the British stage until 1944; met Richard Aldrich (1939); dubbed "the greatest feminine performer in the American Theater" when* Lady in the Dark *opened at the Alvin Theater (September 1941); hosted a weekly chat show over network radio and also broadcast a condensed version of* Pygmalion; *made wartime tour through Europe with ENSA (1944); made USO wartime tour of the Pacific (1945); began relationship with Daphne du Maurier during "September Tide" in London (1949); won a Tony Award for* The King and I, *playing at the St. James' Theater, New York (1951).*

Stage productions include: A to Z, *with Jack Buchanan, the Trix sisters and Beatrice Lillie (1921);* London Calling! *with Noel Coward (Duke of York's Theater, 1923);* Andre Charlot's Revue of 1924 *(Times Square, NY) and* Andre Charlot's Revue of 1926, *in which she sang "Poor Little Rich Girl";* Oh Kay! *(New York and London, 1926–27), singing "Do, Do, Do" and "Someone to Watch Over Me"; played Marie in* Candle-Light *(Southampton, England and Empire, NY, 1929); appeared as Amanda in* Private Lives *with Noel Coward and Laurence Olivier (London and NY, 1930–31), singing "Someday I'll Find You"; appeared as Sarah Casanove in* Behold We Live *with Gerald du Maurier (London, 1932); had nine roles in* Tonight at 8:30 *with Noel Coward (London and New York, 1935); appeared in* Susan and God *(1937),* Lady in the Dark *(1941),* September Tide *(1949), and* The King and I *(1951). Films include* Lord Camber's Ladies, Rembrandt, Men Are Not Gods, *and* The Glass Menagerie. *Made numerous recordings of songs, medleys and scenes.*

In July 1918, England was still at war and the German air-raids over London were increasing. It had been a hot day in London, and Gertrude Lawrence—newly married to "impresario" Frank Hawley and several months pregnant—was feeling distinctly unwell as she boarded the bus for work. Despite misgivings, her employer Andre Charlot had forgiven her the unprofessional behavior and pranks played during previous seasons and rehired her for the chorus of his revue *Tabs.* Lawrence was also understudy to her great friend and partner in mayhem, *Beatrice Lillie.* On this particular evening, Gertie arrived late to sign in at the theater. As she stepped through the stage door, an ashen-faced stage manager greeted her with "For God's sake! Where the hell have you been? Lillie's off. Went riding in Hyde Park and the horse threw her. Concussion, they say she's got. You've got to go on." Hardly able to grasp the significance of the opportunity, Lawrence squeezed herself into Lillie's costumes and, for the next two hours, held a packed audience in thrall. Charlot was delighted.

For several weeks thereafter, with her girth increasing as rapidly as her confidence, Gertie starred in the West End. On the night of her last performance, she went into labor and produced her first and only child, Pamela, less than 48 hours after taking three encores. Within weeks, her marriage was at an end, and she had gone back to live with her mother. The juxtaposition of these events shaped her life. The brief taste of stardom, of being able to capture the hearts, imagination, and applause of a doting audience, had strengthened her resolve to earn her own place at the top of her profession. The birth of her daughter, and the need to support her, gave Lawrence determination and focus. Until that year, she had been very much on the fringes of show business: a lucky, plucky "child actress and danseuse" as her card had read, with a strongly independent streak and an ambitious mother. The common aspiration of the chorus girl was to marry well and settle down to a comfortable life in the country, raising children and playing the gracious host. Lawrence already suspected that she was not cut out for that scenario.

Gertrude Lawrence had come into theater in a roundabout way. She was born Gertrud Alexandra Dagmar Klasen in 1898 in Clapham, a respectable, lower-middle-class area of South London and, though her great friend Noel Coward teased her about the exaggerated childhood accounts of a barefoot urchin, singing and dancing on street corners and gnawing fishheads in the gutter, the family's fortunes fluctuated rapidly. Proud Mrs. Banks, wife of a master builder, always believed that her daughter **Alice** had taken a sorry step down when she fell for the handsome, young entertainer of Danish extraction, Arthur Klasen, who sang under the name Arthur Lawrence. Apparently his appalling temper when under the influence of alcohol quickly drove Alice back to mother. She soon remarried, and Gertie adored her stepfather whom she always called Dad. Though undoubtedly loving and caring, it is not clear that Dad ever had a steady means of employment. He gambled on the horses, was usually out of pocket, and the family moved house frequently—always leaving debts behind. This involved a kind of ritual that Gertie long recalled. When the bills mounted up so high that a move was inevitable, "a van drove up and men smelling of sawdust and beer" repossessed the hired piano and other pieces. But Dad had always ensured that one of his creditors (usually the grocer) was properly reimbursed—so that the family would have an ally when making their final getaway. After dark, the grocer's boy would arrive with a cart, and Gertie would watch as her mother took down the curtains and packed their few possessions into parcels. Then the three fugitives would creep away into the night, heading for a new life in another part of town where landlords and shopkeepers were unaware of their distressed circumstances. Lawrence seems to have enjoyed the excitement and drama of these "Midnight Flits" and wasn't conscious of any of the demeaning aspects, probably because, as she recalled, they were always dressed proudly in their best clothes.

She cheerfully dedicated her own life to a series of elaborate and glorious imitations of life— imitations that were just a little better, a little brighter, than life itself. This was her fun. This was her mission. This was why she gave herself to us.

—Oscar Hammerstein

However, by the time Gertrude was ten, her mother had grown tired of relocating. Giving up hope that Dad would ever be anything approaching "a provider," Alice applied for a job as one of Robin Hood's Merry Men in the local Christmas show. As it happened, the management were also looking for a child who could sing, dance, and be relied on to turn up on time. Ambitious for her daughter and in need of the extra six shillings (80 cents) a week that this would bring, Alice landed parts for both herself and Gertie in the Brixton version of the pantomime *Babes in the Wood.* Realizing the need for child performers, both Alice and her daughter decided that Gertie should have some sort of training to open more doors into the profession. Miss **Italia Conti** had a basement studio in central London where she taught singing, dancing, elocution, and the rudiments of stagecraft. Gertrude's audition impressed Conti, who offered her one afternoon's classes free of charge for six weeks and the opportunity to stay on and become a pupil-teacher in lieu of fees, "if I showed promise," said Lawrence. She did.

Through hard work, Lawrence was offered more chorus work in Christmas shows in London and touring productions nationwide. Traveling north on the train to play an Angel in *Hannele,* she met the young man who was to have the most consistent influence on her life. "She gave me an orange and told me a few mildly dirty stories and I loved her from then onwards," recalled Noel Coward. He was 13; she was 14.

Not long after, on a trip to the seaside, Lawrence invested a penny in a gypsy fortune-telling machine. The card read: "A star danced, and you were born." Her fate was sealed. When she discovered that her real father Arthur Lawrence was topping the bill at a nearby theater she began to concoct a plan. One day, when

her mother was out for the afternoon, she packed her belongings in a small case, wrote a brief note to explain her whereabouts, and left home to join her father "on the road." Though he was more than a little surprised, he took her in, and she toured with him for nearly two years. But, by age 16, Gertie was on her own.

The outbreak of the First World War in 1914 brought business to box-offices everywhere, and, after a few false starts, Lawrence found herself working in the West End for three years running—in the chorus and understudying at the Vaudeville Theater in Andre Charlot's "intimate" revues. When the war finally drew to a close, Gertie's audacious personality provided many young officers returning from the front with all the fun and laughter they craved. Her dressing room was filled with flowers and admirers, and she was now becoming a star offstage as well. While performing cabaret in a nightclub called Murray's, she made some useful conquests, not the least being the dashing Captain Philip Astley. Well-bred and well-connected, Astley was carving out a career in the Household Cavalry. He fell deeply in love with Lawrence, and during their long relationship she was more or less reinvented. He guided her taste in clothes and style, and taught his eager pupil the behavior and jargon of the smart set to which he belonged. Lawrence emerged a gracious, polished, sparkling product of Mayfair, and her social passport into high society was issued without question.

And so began the Legend of Gertrude Lawrence. In 1921, she again took over from Beatrice Lillie, this time to star in Charlot's *A to Z* with Jack Buchanan. In *London Calling!,* Noel Coward (a co-author) and Gertrude Lawrence sang the timeless "You Were Meant for Me" and danced to the choreography of their friend Fred Astaire who happened to be in town. Already the toast of London, Lawrence went to New York. Andre Charlot borrowed several of the best songs from his past revues and wove them into a package acceptable for Broadway. The result was a magnificent vehicle for the talents of Gertie, Bea Lillie, and Jack Buchanan. But the "Big Three" (as they had become known) were not certain if their comparatively modest show would appeal to New Yorkers, who were more used to the Ziegfeld extravaganzas. As it turned out, the critics were ecstatic. When the show and tour finally finished 15 months later, plans were already being laid for the next edition of *Andre Charlot's Revue.* Advance sales amounted to $200,000, and the three stars were to be paid an enormous $2,500 per week when they returned to the States in

1925. At this point, Gertie seemed to lose any vestige of common sense about money. She spent freely and continuously.

All three performers were admired, but reviewers singled Lawrence out for special praise. One remarked that she danced with "magical lightness," sang true and clear (not a judgment universally shared), could convulse an audience with a touch of Cockney horseplay and move them to tears with a sentimental ballad—concluding "she is the ideal star." In the spring of 1925, the show began a long American tour during which Gertie seemed to conquer the hearts of the entire nation. She was 28 years old, rich, famous and pleased with her life. Anxious to capitalize on her success, she decided to stay on in New York when a new musical entitled *Oh Kay!* by P.G. Wodehouse and Guy Bolton, with music and lyrics by the Gershwins, was offered to her. Her triumph in this production both on Broadway and later in London secured her status as a star in her own right. It was her wistful rendition of the vintage song "Someone to Watch over Me" that stopped the show and possibly provoked Philip Astley to propose at last. Gertie's

Gertrude Lawrence

refusal indicates that she may have realized that being Mrs. Anybody was unlikely to bring her any kind of fulfillment. The theater was her life, her home, and her happiness. An engagement, however, was all right. Engagement would mean an attentive escort and respectability without responsibility. Perfect. So she became engaged to a New York banker, Bert Taylor, and at once turned her attention to her future career. This, she wisely realized, would have to include straight plays (there were no musical stars over the age of 40) and films (to widen her public following). The film *The Battle of Paris* (which included songs by Cole Porter) was described as a "floperetta" but the play *Candle-Light* was a hit—presumably because a comedy about the extramarital affairs of Viennese princes provided a welcome distraction from the grim realities of the Wall Street crash. Lawrence was delighted to find her photograph next to that of *Helen Hayes on the wall of fame at the Empire Theater, and Noel's cable read LEGITIMATE AT LAST. WON'T MOTHER BE PLEASED?

Not long after, Coward confided that he had a play forming in his head for both of them: *Private Lives*. The prospect thrilled Gertie, and they spent several weeks together honing the script and rehearsing in the South of France. Unfortunately, this meant that her daughter Pamela was more or less neglected once again. Though Lawrence was sensitive and loving, the role of "a real-life mother" eluded her. *Private Lives*—a hilarious and deceptively frivolous comedy about two people (Amanda and Elyot) who cannot live with or without each other—premiered in Edinburgh in August 1930. It was the third time Noel and Gertie had appeared together on stage, and they were to work together only once more (in *Tonight at 8:30* in 1935); yet theirs was perhaps the most successful light-comedy partnership of the century and never better expressed than in this play.

However, by the time the show finished in London and America, the main force driving Lawrence was the need to clear her burgeoning debts. Fortunately, she had an astute advisor in *Fanny Holtzmann—a fragile-looking lawyer and accountant whose toughness would be proved again and again over the next 20 years. But trying to curb Gertie's spending habits was virtually impossible. "She spends like an entire fleet of drunken sailors" said Holtzmann. Lawrence's generosity was legendary, her entertainment lavish, her tastes expensive. She never really changed her ways through all her financial crises (which included bankruptcy in 1935), she simply worked harder and earned more money with each venture. And there were many ahead.

During the "turbulent '30s," Lawrence had supreme success in the theater on both sides of the Atlantic but fairly limited success in movies. On the whole, her style was too broad and her discipline too loose for the screen. Perhaps her most forgettable film was *Mimi* (a celluloid version of *La Bohème*) in which she appeared with Douglas Fairbanks, Jr. The two were enjoying a robust affair at the time. Fairbanks, some ten years her junior, had admired her for many years. He adored her sense of fun, which he found "kind of rare," and appreciated that to her, "being a star was a full-time job." *Rembrandt*, co-starring Charles Laughton, was better received and remains her best screen performance.

While in America, Lawrence was deeply disturbed when her friend Edward VIII gave up the throne of England in favor of marriage to the woman he loved—*Wallis Warfield, soon to be the duchess of Windsor. To Lawrence, it represented a dangerous crack in the carefully constructed social order of Britain and the act was also indefensibly unprofessional. She and Noel vowed to be home in time to attend the Coronation of George VI—an event for which Gertie had her jewelry dipped in gold. She was always glad to have seen London in that summer of 1937: "It was wonderful—a last burst of splendour before the storm burst."

Back in New York, Holtzmann urged her to seek out an interesting new play that would keep her employed for as long as possible. *Susan and God*, by pioneering feminist playwright *Rachel Crothers, was just that. The 288 Broadway performances were followed by a tour of 27 cities (24 of which gave their keys to Lawrence) and a radio production. She became an American resident and, shortly after the show closed, met the man she was to marry. Richard Stoddard Aldrich was an ex-banker of conservative New England stock, a Harvard graduate, who just happened to be manager of a theater in Cape Cod—part of the "summer straw-hat circuit." Gertie appeared there in *Skylark*, a show in tryouts en route to Broadway. Their friendship began cautiously. He thought her at first a "spoiled prima donna"; she found him puzzling and stuffy. By the time Lawrence boarded the train for New York, there was more than a glimmer of romance between them. Lawrence, now 41, had experienced some loneliness during the past few years—the loneliness of the star too revered to approach. She was aware that she needed roots, and Aldrich was certainly "a very firm root." The wedding took place quietly on the Cape on July 4, 1940—Gertie's 42nd birthday. On hearing the news, actress *Constance

Collier quipped, "Poor man, he thinks he's marrying Miss Lawrence and will wake up to find he's married Myth Lawrence," while Aldrich's mother sighed reassuringly, "We will not mention it to anyone and naturally none of the people we know will mention it to us."

Meanwhile, the Second World War had broken out in Europe, and Lawrence's sense of patriotic duty, combined with her new status as "Mrs. A.," led her to fund-raise tirelessly for the British war effort and to organize the evacuation of 60 children from the English Actors' Orphanage to Canada. At the same time, she was being pursued by Messrs. Hart, Weill, and Gershwin to star in their major new musical *Lady in the Dark*. Newcomer Danny Kaye was also in the cast. His virtuoso number "Tchaikovsky" might have threatened a lesser actress, but, for the moment at least, Gertie was perfectly confident of her skill and command. On the first night, when the audience had finished applauding Kaye, she came slowly to the front of the stage and almost whispered her next song "Jenny." The effect was stunning— Lawrence's showmanship had triumphed once again. The show ran until 1943. This time America had entered the war, and Gertie was feeling the pressure of playing several roles simultaneously: leading lady, radio broadcaster, and American navy wife. Fiercely denying rumors of a rift in her marriage, Lawrence joined the British Services entertainment group ENSA and, in the summer of 1944, toured her own revue through England, Belgium and France. Back on the Cape, she completed and published her autobiography *A Star Danced* and went off on a promotional tour. But Lawrence longed to have a brilliant return to the London stage. That opportunity came from the pen of *Daphne du Maurier, daughter of one of Gertie's favorite co-stars, Gerald. The play was *September Tide*. During rehearsals, the pre-London tour, and the West End run, a deep friendship developed between the two women. Daphne slowly became infatuated with the moody, demanding, mercurial star and enthralled by her performance in the play. Later, in the winter of 1950, they vacationed together in Florida and according to du Maurier "behaved like two silly schoolgirls." When she was sent the snapshots of their holiday, reputedly du Maurier blushed at the "incriminating things" Lawrence had written on the back.

By that time, though, Lawrence was back on the Cape and having "a year off" to devote herself to Richard and consider her next foray onto Broadway. But Holtzmann was full of plans. Rodgers and Hammerstein were busy adapting *Margaret Landon's book *Anna and the King of Siam* to be ready for Gertie to start rehearsals early in 1951. The show presented huge vocal and physical challenges to her, and her behavior was increasingly erratic and unpredictable. Sheer determination saw her through the first months of the run of *The King and I*. The show collected several Tony Awards and many accolades, but Gertie's recurring bad health was beginning to worry those closest to her. Although she had had lengthy tests which revealed no problems other than exhaustion, she was repeatedly "off" and frequently giving almost embarrassingly bad performances. But she was determined to see out her two-year contract and would not even listen to Coward, who implored her to gracefully give up a show that required her to run four miles a night around the stage, wearing huge crinolines that weighed 75 lbs. each. In the fall of 1952, Lawrence finally collapsed when returning to her dressing room one afternoon. She was rushed to the hospital where the doctors diagnosed hepatitis. Although Richard was called to her bedside and friends were everywhere alerted, there was no reason to think the disease would be fatal. Then, early on the morning of September 6, her condition suddenly grew much worse. She fell into a coma and passed away shortly thereafter. The autopsy revealed that cancer had completely consumed her liver, though the primary source was never discovered. Gertrude Lawrence was 54.

Friends and fans throughout the world were devastated. On the evening of her funeral, the lights of Broadway, London, and Hollywood were dimmed for two minutes as a tribute. Five thousand mourners stood outside the Fifth Avenue Presbyterian Church to pay their last respects—another 1,800 were inside. Lawrence was buried in the Aldrich family plot in Upton, Massachusetts, beside the mother-in-law who had eventually come to love her.

SOURCES:

Aldrich, Richard Stoddard. *Gertrude Lawrence as Mrs.* London: Odhams Press, 1954.

Forster, Margaret. *Daphne du Maurier*. London: Chatto & Windus, 1993.

Lawrence, Gertrude. *A Star Danced*. London: Merritt and Hatcher, 1945.

Morley, Sheridan. *A Bright Particular Star*. Pavillion Michael Joseph, 1986.

SUGGESTED READING:

Berkman, Edward. *The Lady and the Law: A Biography of Fanny Holtzmann*. Boston: Little, Brown, 1976.

Coward, Noel. *Present Indicative*. London: Heinemann, 1937.

De Mille, Agnes. *Speak to Me, Dance With Me*. Boston: Atlantic-Little, Brown, 1973.

Bonnie Hurren,
freelance actor, director, and artistic director of
Show of Strength Theatre Company in Bristol, England

Lawrence, Janice (1962—)

African-American basketball player. Born on June 7, 1962, in Lucedale, Mississippi; graduated from Louisiana Tech University, 1984.

Won the Wade Trophy (1984); was a member of the U.S. team which won the gold medal in the Los Angeles Olympics (1984); played professional ball with the Women's American Basketball Association.

Janice Lawrence, who was born in Lucedale in 1962, saw basketball as a ticket out of Mississippi. On scholarship at Louisiana Tech, she became a valuable center-forward, averaging 20.7 points and 9.1 rebounds per game. She was particularly adept at steals and led her team in that category. In 1983, Lawrence was a member of the U.S. team that placed first at the Pan-American Games. She was also named to the U.S. World University Games team and the Kodak All-American team. While Lawrence played for Louisiana Tech, her team was inevitably in the Final Four and won two NCAA championships. No one was surprised when Janice Lawrence was chosen Most Valuable Player of the 1983 national tournament. In 1984, she was named to the 1984 U.S. Olympic basketball team which won the gold medal in Los Angeles. By the end of her college career, Lawrence had amassed 2,403 points, 1097 rebounds, and 194 assists. When the professional Women's American Basketball Association got underway in 1984, Lawrence was the first college senior chosen. She then played with a New York franchise for a short time.

SOURCES:

Markel, Robert, Nancy Brooks, and Susan Markel. *For the Record: Women in Sports*. NY: World Almanac, 1985.

Page, James A. *Black Olympian Medalists*. Englewood, CO: Libraries Unlimited, 1991.

Karin Loewen Haag,
Athens, Georgia

Lawrence, Marjorie (1908–1979)

Australian soprano who performed in a wheelchair after suffering the crippling effects of polio. Born Marjorie Florence Lawrence in Dean's Marsh, Victoria, Australia, on February 17, 1908; died on January 10, 1979, in Little Rock, Arkansas; daughter of William Lawrence and Elizabeth (Smith) Lawrence; studied with Cécile Gilly in Paris; married Thomas Michael King, on March 29, 1941.

Made debut at Monte Carlo (1932), Paris Opéra (1933–36), Metropolitan Opera (1935–49); was a professor of voice at Tulane University (1956–60) and became a director of the Southern Illinois University opera workshop (1960).

Born in 1908 in a country village, population 140, in Dean's Marsh, Australia, Marjorie Lawrence grew up surrounded by four brothers, one sister, and a profusion of sheep farmers. "I was an impossible child," she once noted. "I wanted to be a boy like my brothers." After early music study with the local parson, she was convinced by age 18 that she wanted a singing career, but her father said no. So she and her brother Cyril, who would become her manager, set out for Melbourne. While working as a seamstress for two years, Lawrence studied with Ivor Boustead. In 1929, she won a vocal competition sponsored by a Melbourne newspaper, prompting her father to consent to her study in Paris. Lawrence made her debut in Monte Carlo as Elisabeth in *Tannhäuser* (1932), her Paris debut as Elsa in *Lohengrin* (1933), and her Metropolitan debut as Brünnhilde in *Die Walküre* (December 1935).

In personality, Marjorie Lawrence was a far cry from the stalwart Wagnerian personas she interpreted. "For heaven's sake, don't let me catch you calling me a prima donna or diva," she instructed the editors of *Current Biography*. "And I'm not Madame Lawrence, or anything like that. I'm just Marjorie. I don't have a favorite recipe for kugelhupf or spaghetti. I hate critics and crowded rooms and stuffy people and I just can't wait until I get out in the fresh air with a good horse or my bike. How I love my bike."

Marjorie Lawrence made steady progress in her opera career and was a particularly athletic soprano. She was one of the few actresses who could follow Richard Wagner's instructions for *Götterdämmerung*. On the evening of January 12, 1936, her Brünnhilde leapt on her horse Grane and galloped to Siegfried's funeral pyre at the end of the opera. "The audience was taken by storm," wrote Olin Downs in *The New York Times*. Up until then, sedentary prima donnas had "led ancient nags across the stage by a bridle or left them in charge of a stable groom," noted *Current Biography*. Her physical strength was an asset in Richard Strauss' *Salomé*, when her *Dance of the Seven Veils* produced a similar effect. Jerome Bohm reported in the *New York Herald Tribune* in 1938, "It was a remarkable feat for an actress who has not been trained as a dancer to have surmounted an all but insurmountable problem so convincingly and to have sung the tremendous closing scene so convincingly." Then, Lawrence contracted polio in

1941, at age 31. She would spend the rest of her life in a wheelchair.

Lawrence's determination to continue her career after being confined to a wheelchair was equally amazing, all the more so in an era of nonexistent access for the disabled and a prevailing attitude that those who were physically challenged should stay out of public view. Concert and opera managers were reluctant to hire her, fearing a decline in her vocal abilities. She overcame this reluctance, only to have some claim that she exploited her handicap. Many, however, were more charitable. Of her 1943 comeback, critic Noel Straus wrote: "The long rest she has had did its share in giving freshness to the voice which was never before as absolutely firm in its tones, nor employed with such depth of feeling." Edward O'Gormann added, "I don't believe Miss Lawrence's voice has ever sounded as rich and as powerful . . . as it did last night." Some accommodations were made for her disability and special productions of *Tannhäuser* and *Tristan und Isolde* under Sir Thomas Beecham's direction were given. Her last professional role was as Amneris in *Aïda* in 1947 at the Paris Opéra.

After she left the stage, Lawrence turned to teaching at Tulane and Southern Illinois University (SIU). At SIU, the Marjorie Lawrence Opera Theater was established in her honor. In 1949, she wrote *Interrupted Melody: The Story of My Life*, detailing her career, and a 1955 movie based on the book is still considered one of the best "biopics" ever filmed. An Oscar went to *Sonia Levien and William Ludwig for Best Adapted Screenplay, along with an Oscar nomination for Best Actress to *Eleanor Parker (whose voice was dubbed by *Eileen Farrell).

SOURCES:

Rothe, Anna, ed. *Current Biography*. NY: H.W. Wilson, 1940.

Sadie, Stanley, ed. *New Grove Dictionary of Music and Musicians*. 20 vols. NY: Macmillan, 1980.

SUGGESTED READING:

Lawrence, Marjorie. *Interrupted Melody: The Story of My Life*. NY: Appleton, 1949.

RELATED MEDIA:

Interrupted Melody (105 min. film), starring Eleanor Parker, Glenn Ford, and Roger Moore, with a cameo by Eileen Farrell as a vocal student, script by William Ludwig and Sonya Levien, produced by MGM, 1955.

Lawrence, Mary Wells (1928—)

American advertising executive. Born Mary Georgene Wells Berg on May 25, 1928, in Youngstown, Ohio; daughter of Waldemar Berg and Violet (Meltz) Berg; attended Carnegie Institute of Technology, 1949; mar-

ried Harding Lawrence, on November 25, 1967; children: James Lawrence; State Lawrence; Deborah Lawrence; Kathryn Lawrence; Pamela Lawrence.

Honorary LL.D., Babson College (1970), Carnegie-Mellon University (1974).

Marjorie Lawrence

One of the few women in the 1960s to break into the male-dominated corporate ranks, Mary Wells Lawrence founded the legendary New York advertising agency Wells, Rich, Greene, Inc., in 1966 and turned it into a multimillion-dollar enterprise. The creative force behind such well-known commercial catch-phrases as "I can't believe I ate the whole thing," "Try it; you'll like it," "Plop, plop, fizz, fizz," and "Friends don't let friends drive drunk," the agency in its heyday attracted the world's largest and most sophisticated clientele. Kenneth Olshan, who spent his early career at the agency and later became its chair, calls Mary Wells Lawrence "a brilliant, charismatic and glamorous leader" and claims that the enterprise was unique from the onset. "Mary was an intuitive nurturer of clients and talent," he wrote in a 1998 article for *Advertising Age*. "If agencies have genders, ours was feminine. It felt more like a Mediterranean family than like the typical macho boys' clubs of our larger and traditional Madison Avenue competitors of the era."

Mary Wells Lawrence got her start writing retail-store copy, then struck out on her own. Instead of pursuing the usual woman-oriented commodities like cosmetics and food, Lawrence set her sights on such "hard" profitable accounts as Braniff, Chase, Ford, Hertz, ITT, Philip Morris, Ralston Purina, and the New York Stock Exchange. She also surrounded herself with the bright and talented and created an environment in which they flourished. "We were an ethnic melting pot," writes Olshan. "Sexism and prejudice of any kind were not allowed. We worked all hours and fought and argued over ideas. Even screamed and slammed doors. But we respected each other and rarely went home mad."

In addition to nurturing her staff, Lawrence created a family-like environment for her clients. There were client vs. agency softball games staged at Busch Stadium under the lights and intimate lunches with clients' spouses at Lawrence's apartment. Although the intensely personal approach alienated some potential clients, the Wells Rich Green agency never changed. "We stood out in a business increasingly dominated by bland, financially oriented communication conglomerates," said Olshan. The advertising community also recognized Lawrence's unique contribution. She was named to the Copywriters Hall of Fame Copy Club in 1969 and in 1971 was honored as Advertising Woman of the Year by the American Advertising Federation.

When it came time for Lawrence to retire, the agency worked to create a "seamless transition" which honored the traditional objectives of the company. Olshan served as chair of the organization for many years, after which it was acquired and reacquired by other corporations, eventually losing the culture and philosophy attributed to its founder. Mary Wells Lawrence retired to France.

SOURCES:

Bird, Caroline. *Enterprising Women*. NY: W.W. Norton, 1976.

Olshan, Kenneth S. "Forum: Olshan Tells Where Wells Went Wrong," in *Advertising Age*. March 2, 1998.

Barbara Morgan,
Melrose, Massachusetts

Lawrence, Susan (1871–1947)

British politician. Born in London, England, in 1871; died in 1947; daughter of an eminent lawyer and a judge's daughter; studied at University College, London, and Newnham College, Cambridge.

Member of London County Council (1910–28); elected to Popular Borough Council (1919); served as Labour member of Parliament (1923–24, 1926–31); served as parliamentary secretary to Ministry of Health (1929–31); served as chair of Labour Party (1929–30).

Although she never dedicated herself to women's issues during her political career, the feminist movement is indebted to Susan Lawrence. Simply by attaining the office of MP (member of Parliament) in Britain's Parliament of the 1920s, and functioning skillfully there, Lawrence and a handful of other women gave British society new reasons to respect women's abilities.

Born in London in 1871 to a privileged family and well educated, the tall, dignified, and intellectual young Lawrence exuded self-confidence. While still at Newnham College, she led the Conservatives in the college's Political Society, and shortly afterward was elected to a Conservative post on the London County Council. However, Conservative "indifference to low wages and the bad conditions of women [workers]" eventually motivated her to join the Labour Party, where she found her life's path.

Her sincerity, integrity, vigor, and dedication soon propelled her to national office. As an MP, her method was single-minded and her style heroic in her defense of the rights of the working classes; her attitude has been referred to as "daredevil" and "revolutionary." In committee work, this outlook kept her from listening well, but in parliamentary debate, to which she always contributed heavily, it gained her the respect of House members who found her speeches expert, forceful, and precise in relevant fact and detail. Yet her parliamentary career was truncated before its peak, when she was defeated in 1931. Ten years after that, still stalwart in her socialism, she was ousted from the party's executive committee.

Ninety percent of Lawrence's debate topics as an MP were welfare issues, but her politics never included distinctions between women's and men's concerns. In fact, she declared in 1918 that "women must combat the argument that women should organize themselves on a sex basis" and was angry when Labour Party women barred male speakers from one of their national conferences. For her, the class struggle required men and women to band together. In her later years, Lawrence was popular for her racy stories about Labour Party notables, and she remained greatly interested in social issues until the day she died.

SOURCES:

Harrison, Brian. *Prudent Revolutionaries: Portraits of British Feminists between the Wars.* Oxford: Clarendon Press, 1987.

Jacquie Maurice,
Calgary, Alberta, Canada

Lawrenson, Helen (b. 1907)

American editor and writer. Name variations: Helen Brown; Helen Brown Nordern. Born Helen Brown on October 1, 1907, in LaFargeville, New York, seven miles south of the Canadian border; daughter of Lloyd Brown (described by his daughter as an "unsuccessful promoter"); attended Bradford School and Vassar; married Heinz Nordern (a musician), in 1931 (divorced 1932); married a Venezuelan diplomat named López-Méndez, in 1935 (divorced 1935); married Jack Lawrenson (co-founder of the National Maritime Union), in 1940 (died, November 1957); children: one son and one daughter, Johanna.

Helen Lawrenson was the managing editor and film critic of *Vanity Fair* (1932–35) and a frequent contributor to *Vogue, Harper's Bazaar, Look, Esquire* and *Town and Country.* She was also the author of *Latins are Lousy Lovers.* Frank Crowninshield once said of "the dark and flashing Helen Brown Norden," that she was "an avowedly revolutionary spirit, a satirist of a bold, even Rabelaisian order, and the master of a highly personalized prose style. Unfortunately, she had so strong a distaste for writing that she rarely lifted her pen save under the direst compulsion." Her memoir *Stranger at the Party* (1975) details her career, her marriages, and friendships with *Clare Boothe Luce, Bernard Baruch, and Condé Nast.

Lawson, Louisa (1848–1920)

Australian feminist, publisher, editor, journalist, and poet. Born Louisa Albury on February 17, 1848, near Mudgee, New South Wales; died on August 12, 1920; second of twelve children of Harry Albury (a station hand) and Harriet (Wynn) Albury; attended Mudgee national school; married Niels Hertzberg Larsen also known as Peter Lawson (a Norwegian sailor), on July 7, 1866 (separated 1883); children: five, including Henry Lawson (a writer).

One of 12 children, Louisa Lawson was born in 1848 and grew up near Mudgee, New

South Wales. She was forced to leave school to care for her siblings. At 18, she married Niels Hertzberg Larsen, also known as Peter Lawson, a Norwegian sailor several years her senior. By some accounts, she was pressured into the marriage; whatever the case, it was never a particularly happy union. The couple joined the Weddin Mountain gold rush but later returned to New Pipeclay near Mudgee, where they were based until 1883, and where Lawson gave birth to five children, one of whom died in infancy. Since Peter was away from home much of the time, she raised the children on her own and also worked at various jobs to supplement the family income.

In 1883, having grown frustrated with a life of poverty, Lawson took her younger children and moved to Sydney, where she immersed herself in Spiritualism and the women's movement. In 1887, with her son Henry Lawson (who would later enjoy his own career as Australia's leading poet and short-story writer), she took over editing a radical newspaper, the *Republican.* The following year, she founded *Dawn,* the first Australian feminist journal, which gave rise to the Dawn Club, a suffrage society which, through an association with the Sydney School of Arts debating club, prepared women to speak publicly for the cause. Through the pages of *Dawn,* Lawson continued to focus attention on women's issues, including suffrage and job equity. In her editorials, she blamed prostitution on men and unfair laws and urged parents to educate their daughters so they would not be forced to take work as domestics. In 1889, Lawson established the Association of Women, merging her work with that of *Rose Scott and the Womanhood Suffrage League. She continued to speak out emphatically for the cause, gaining notoriety for declaring that woman must gain the vote "to redeem the world from bad laws passed by wicked men."

Injuries suffered in a tram accident in 1900 curtailed Lawson's activities, though she remained politically active, joining the Council of the Women's Progressive Association and continuing to encourage the appointment of women to public office. During this period, she was also involved in litigation over the piracy of her invention of a new buckle for fastening mailbags. She was eventually awarded compensation, but at a reduced amount.

After 1901, *Dawn* began to lose its edge and by 1905 was forced to close. Lawson was increasingly plagued by family problems. In 1894, she had helped her son Henry bring out his first collection, *Short Stories in Prose and Verse,* but the book was poorly produced and led to an estrangement between mother and son. Another son suffered from mental breakdowns, and Lawson also frequently quarreled with her daughter.

In later years, Lawson took up residence in a cottage in Marrickville and supported herself as a freelance writer, producing short stories which appeared in several Sydney newspapers. A collection of poems, *The Lonely Crossing*, was published in 1906. Lawson, who died on August 12, 1920, was featured on an Australian postage stamp during International Women's Year, in 1975.

SOURCES:

Radi, Heather, ed. *200 Australian Women*. NSW, Australia: Women's Redress Press, 1988.

Wilde, William H., Joy Horton, and Barry Andrews, eds. *Oxford Companion to Australian Literature*. Melbourne: Oxford University Press, 1994.

SUGGESTED READING:

Matthews, Brian. *Louisa*, 1988.

Ollif, Lorna. *Louisa Lawson: Henry Lawson's Crusading Mother*, 1978.

Laya (fl. c. 100 BCE).

See Iaia.

Laye, Evelyn (1900–1996)

British star of musical comedy. Born Elsie Evelyn Lay on June 10, 1900, in London, England; died in February 1996, in London, England; only child of Gilbert Lay (an actor and composer) and Evelyn Stuart (a singer and actress); attended school in Brighton and Folkestone, England; married Sonnie Hale (an actor), in 1926 (divorced 1927); married Frank Lawton (an actor), around 1934 (died 1969); no children.

Selected theater: made stage debut as walk-on in Mr. Wu *(Theater Royal, Brighton, 1915); London debut in* Honi Soit *(East Ham Palace, April 1916); appeared as Pyrrha in* Oh Caesar! *(Lyceum, Edinburgh, December 1916), Madeline Manners in* Going Up *(Gaiety, May 1918), Dollis Pym in* The Kiss Call *(Gaiety, October 1919), Bessie Brent in* The Shop Girl *(Gaiety, March 1920), Mollie Moffat in* Nighty Night *(Queen's Theater, London, March 1921), Mary Howells in* Mary *(April 1921); appeared in* The League of Nations *(Oxford, August 1921),* Fun of the Fayre *(London Pavilion, October 1921), as Sonia in a revival of* The Merry Widow *(Daly's Theater, May 1923), in the title role in* Madame Pompadour *(Daly's Theater, December 1923), as Alice in* The Dollar Princess *(King's Theater, Glasgow, December 1924), as Betty in* Betty in Mayfair *(Adelphi, London, November 1925), as Molly Shine in* Merely Molly *(Adelphi, September 1925); succeeded Winnie Melville as Princess Elaine in* Princess Charming *(Palace, March 1927); appeared as Lili in* Lilac Time *(Daly's Theater, December 1927); had leading role in* Blue Eyes *(Piccadilly, April 1928); appeared as Marianne in* The New Moon *(Drury Lane, April 1929); made New York debut in* Bitter Sweet *(Ziegfeld Theater, New York, November 1929); appeared as Belinda Warren in* Sweet Aloes *(Booth Theater, New York, March 1936), Princess Anna in* Paganini *(Lyceum, London, May 1937), Natalie Rivers in* Between the Devil *(Majestic Theater, New York, December 1937), Prince Florizel in the pantomime* The Sleeping Beauty *(Theater Royal, Birmingham, England, December 1938), Violet Gray in* The Belle of New York *(Piccadilly, August 1943), Katherine in* Three Waltzes *(Prince's Theater, March 1945, and tour); toured as Laura Kent in* Elusive Lady *(1946); toured as Lady Teazle in* The School for Scandal *(1948); appeared as Prince Charming in* Cinderella *(Palladium, Christmas 1948), Marina Verani in* Two Dozen Red Roses *(Lyric, May 1949); toured as Stella in* September Tide *(1950); appeared in* The Domino Revue *(Wimbledon, July 1953), as Mrs. Darling in* Peter Pan *(The Scala, Christmas 1953), as Marcelle Thibault in* Wedding in Paris *(Hippodrome, April 1954), as Lady Marlowe in* Silver Wedding *(Cambridge Theater, July 1957), as Lady Fitzadam in* The Amorous Prawn *(December 1959); succeeded Joan Bennett as Edith Lambert in* Never Too Late *(Prince of Wales, January 1964); appeared as Lady Catherine in* The Circle *(Ashcroft, Croydon, April 1965), as *****Annie Besant*** *in* Strike a Light *(Alhambra Theater, Glasgow, April 1966), as Mrs. Fitzmaurice in* Phil the Fluter *(Palace, November 1969), as Eleanor Hunter in* No Sex Please—We're British *(Strand Theater, June 1971); toured as Leonora Fiske in* Ladies in Retirement *(1976); toured in* Pygmalion *(1978); appeared in* Glamourous Nights *at Drury Lane (1992).*

Films: Luck of the Navy *(1929);* One Heavenly Night *(US, 1931);* Waltz Time *(1933);* Princess Charming *(1933);* Evensong *(1934);* The Night is Young *(1934);* Make Mine a Million *(1939);* Theater of Death *(1966);* Say Hello to Yesterday *(1971).*

Britain's "Queen of the Musical Comedy," Evelyn Laye graced the London stage for over 70 years, from her 1916 debut in an obscure revue, *Honi Soit*, to her appearance in the nostalgic *Glamourous Nights* at Drury Lane, at age 92. "I have never been able to give up the theater," she said drolly when she was well into her 80s. "I like the smell of it, the smell of the stage door, my dressing room, applying my make-up and of course, my audiences."

Laye was the only child of Gilbert Lay (she added the "e" later), an actor and composer, and **Evelyn Stuart**, a singer and player in Victorian pantomimes. As a baby, Laye slept in a cot in her mother's dressing room and, as a little girl, she began dreaming of her own stage career. When Laye was 13, her father, who at the time was managing the Pier at Brighton, wangled her the role of a ballet dancer in a charity show. At 15, accompanied by a chaperon, she toured the country in *Mr. Wu*, playing a mute Chinese servant. Her break came in 1916, when Robert Courtneidge cast her in his musical comedy *Oh Caesar!*, which also starred his daughter *Cicely Courtneidge** and her husband Jack Hulbert. Two years later, Laye debuted as a "Gaiety Girl," portraying the second lead in *Going Up*, which ran for 574 performances. She then starred in a revival of *The Shop Girl* (1920), literally stopping the show with a lively rendition of "Here Comes the Guards Brigade," which she sang while marching across the stage with a troop of bona fide guardsmen loaned out by the army for the occasion.

With her career on the rise, Laye was lured away from the Gaiety by impresario Sir Charles Cochrane who starred her *The League of Nations* and *Fun of the Fayre* (both in 1921). Around this time, she began a long courtship with actor Sonnie Hale, whom she married in 1926, despite her parents' disapproval. The couple divorced a year later when Hale fell in love with one of his co-stars, *Jessie Matthews**.

By 1929, Laye was the most prominent musical-comedy star in England and had also made her first film, *Luck of the Navy*. That year, she crossed the Atlantic to make her New York debut at the Ziegfeld Theater, appearing in Noel Coward's operetta *Bitter Sweet*. Brooks Atkinson of *The New York Times* found her nothing short of perfection. "What makes Evelyn Laye so rare a presence in the leading part is not merely her fragile beauty but the daintiness with which she acts and sings in the precise spirit of the play," he wrote. "As an actress she catches the ardor of the romantic love scenes of the first act, she trips through the dramatic episodes with a skill equal to Mr. Coward's composition. She has, moreover, a voice sweet in quality and full in tone." Producer Flo Ziegfeld was also impressed with Laye, so much so that he broke with tradition and put her name in lights on the theater marquee, even placing it above the show's title.

Having been devastated by the break-up of her marriage, Laye was more cautious about her relationship with actor Frank Lawton, whom she had met in 1928, but did not agree to marry until 1934. The couple were both in California at the time, working on films, and they eloped on a day off. Before returning to England in 1937, Laye revived her role in *Bitter Sweet* at the Shrine Auditorium in Los Angeles, and made another visit to Broadway, appearing in *Sweet Aloes*.

During World War II, when new stage productions were limited, Laye toured in variety shows and entertained soldiers at various military bases across the country. After the war, she found it difficult to rekindle her career, and she spent the greater part of the next ten years touring variety halls in the provinces. She finally scored a comeback success in 1954 as Marcelle Thibault in *Wedding in Paris*. "How delightful it is to have Evelyn Laye back with us!," exclaimed Frank Granville-Barker. "Once more she is in her rightful place as leading lady of British musicals, sweeping gaily across the Hippodrome stage with her usual vivacity, poise and assur-

Evelyn Laye

ance." In 1959, Laye enjoyed a two-year run in *The Amorous Prawn* and then in 1965 generated another burst of acclaim from the critics for her portrayal of Lady Catherine in W. Somerset Maugham's *The Circle.* "Miss Laye, whom I have never seen before, must be a dream to play with," wrote Hugh Leonard. "Her timing is faultless, she never hogs the stage . . . and she is that rare thing: a comedienne who doesn't try to be funny." Laye opened a new musical, *Phil the Fluter,* in 1969, but the show lasted only a few months. Her last West End performance was in *No Sex Please—We're British,* which won as much praise for the costumes as for any of the performances.

During her long career, Laye continued to make occasional films, notably *The Night is Young* (1934), a musical co-starring heartthrob Ramon Navarro. The Sigmund Romberg score contained the haunting ballad "When I Grow Too Old to Dream," which over the years became Laye's signature song. She went into production of her last film, *Say Hello to Yesterday* (released in 1971), shortly after the death of her husband in 1969.

Evelyn Laye continued to perform up until four years before her death. She was awarded the CBE in 1973 and was feted at the Strand Theater on her 80th birthday. To mark the occasion, her friends endowed the London Academy of Music and Dramatic Art with an Evelyn Laye Award, an annual prize for the best performance in a musical. Laye spent her final years in a nursing home in the West End, near so many of the theaters in which she had performed. She died there in February 1996.

SOURCES:
Bickerdyke, Percy. "Stars of Yesterday: Evelyn Laye," in *This England.* Summer 1996.
Morley, Sheridan. *The Great Stage Stars.* London: Angus and Robertson, 1986.

SUGGESTED READING:
Laye, Evelyn. *Boo, To My Friends,* 1958.

Barbara Morgan,
Melrose, Massachusetts

Layla al-Akhyaliyya (fl. 650–660)

Seventh-century Arab Muslim poet who was widely acclaimed for composing poignant elegies. Name variations: Laila or Layla bint al-Akhyal. Pronunciation: LAY-la al-ak-ya-LEE-ya. Born in the central part of the Arabian peninsula sometime before the middle of the 7th century; date or location of death is uncertain as reports contradict each other, but it seems most likely that she died shortly after the beginning of the 8th century; married Sawwar Ibn Awfa al-Qushayri.

In pre-Islamic Arabia, it was customary for women to lament the deaths of their relatives by singing, dancing, tearing their clothes, beating themselves, and reciting elegies which celebrated the merits of the deceased. Originally, these elegies were composed in rhymed prose. However, by the time the Prophet Muhammad received his first revelation in the year 610, a poetic genre devoted to this type of expression had developed. In Arabic, it is called *ritha'* (lamentation). Both men and women composed poems in the *ritha'* genre but, because the display of emotions while mourning was considered more appropriate to women, it has often been associated with female poets. One of the first Muslim women to become famous for her elegiac verse was Layla al-Akhyaliyya.

Layla was born in the central part of the Arabian peninsula to the 'Amir Ibn Sa'sa'a group of the tribe of 'Uqayl, sometime before the middle of the 7th century, and she married a man named Sawwar Ibn Awfa al-Qushayri. Beyond this, very few details about her life have been preserved. Historians generally regard the decade between 650 and 660 as the high point of her career.

Despite the lack of information, there can be no doubt that Layla al-Akhyaliyya was an important historical figure. The verses attributed to her reflect not only her own concerns, but also major challenges facing the Islamic community during her lifetime. The Prophet Muhammad had died in 632 and, for several decades following his death, Muslims could not agree on who was best suited to succeed him or how his successor's authority should be defined. Layla reportedly composed an elegy in memory of the third man to follow Muhammad as leader of the Islamic polity (caliph), 'Uthman Ibn 'Affan, whose death by assassination in 656 is considered a major turning point in Islamic history. It marks the beginning of the first civil war from which the Umayyad family emerged victorious and, in time, established an Islamic empire.

Unfortunately, only fragments of Layla al-Akhyaliyya's poetry are extant. These have been preserved in encyclopedic texts and biographical dictionaries which were compiled beginning in the 9th century—such as Ibn Qutayba's *al-Shi'r wa-'l-shu'ara'* (Poetry and Poets) and Abu Faraj al-Isfahani's *Kitab al-aghani* (Book of Songs).

By the time these works were written, Layla was most famous for her elegies mourning Tawba Ibn Humayyir, a warrior from her tribe who had been killed in battle. According to tradition, he had remained devoted to her throughout his lifetime despite her marriage to another man, and evidence suggests that she shared his romantic feelings. Layla al-Akhyaliyya's verses lamenting Tawba's death express deep sadness at a personal loss. She recited, "I swear I will still compose elegies for someone who dies after Tawba, and shed tears for someone against whom calamities have turned. By your life! There is no disgrace for a young man in death, if faults did not afflict him in life."

Although Layla is renowned for her elegies, she also engaged in at least one poetic exchange in the *hija'* (lampoon) genre. Part of her repartee with a 7th-century poet named al-Nabigha al-Jadi has survived.

Layla al-Akhyaliyya reportedly died at the beginning of the 8th century while traveling to visit her cousin, the famous commander Qutayba Ibn Muslim, who was on a military campaign in Khurasan (northeast Iran) on behalf of the Umayyad governor al-Hajjaj.

SOURCES:

al-Isfahani, Abu al-Faraj. *Kitab al-aghani* (*Book of Songs*). 24 vols, in progress. Cairo: Dar al-Kutub al-Misriyya, 1929–present.

The Cambridge History of Arabic Literature: Arabic Literature to the End of the Umayyad Period. Edited by A.F.L. Beeston, T.M. Johnstone, R.B. Serjeant, and G.R. Smith. Cambridge: Cambridge University Press, 1983.

Gabrieli, F. "Layla al-Akhyaliyya," in *Encyclopaedia of Islam.* 2nd ed.

Ibn Qutayba. *al-Shi'r wa-'l-shu'ara'* (*Poetry and Poets*). Beirut: Dar al-Thaqafa, 1964.

Kate Lang,
Assistant Professor of History,
The University of Wisconsin—Eau Claire

Layla bint al-Akhyal (fl. 650-660).

See Layla al-Akhyaliyya.

Lazarus, Emma (1849–1887)

American-Jewish poet, writer and scholar who committed herself to helping Russian-Jewish immigrants, and whose poem "The New Colossus," welcoming immigrants, is inscribed on the Statue of Liberty. Born on July 22, 1849, in New York City; died of Hodgkin's disease on November 19, 1887, in New York City; daughter of Moses Lazarus (a sugar refiner and businessman) and Esther Nathan Lazarus; educated privately, at home; never married; no children.

Part of a prosperous and distinguished family; remained in her parents' home throughout her life; began writing in her teens; published first poetry col-

lection (1866); met Ralph Waldo Emerson, an early mentor (1868); first heard about problems of Russian-Jewish immigrants (1881–82); wrote articles countering anti-Semitic attacks (1882); wrote "The New Colossus" (1883); traveled to Europe (1884, 1885–86); "The New Colossus" inscribed on the Statue of Liberty (1903).

Selected writings: Poems and Translations *(published privately, 1866, published commercially, 1867);* Admetus and Other Poems *(1871);* Alide: An Episode of Goethe's Life *(1874);* The Spagnoletto *(1876); assorted translations of medieval Spanish-Jewish poets (1879);* Poems and Ballads of Heine *(1882);* Songs of a Semite *(1882);* An Epistle to the Hebrews *(1882–83);* "The New Colossus" *(1883);* By the Waters of Babylon *(1887).*

Emma Lazarus lived a short and quiet life. She never openly rebelled against her parents, did not travel until she was over 30 years old, never married or had children, never stood on a speaker's podium. Yet, more than a century after her death, her name immediately brings a spark of recognition even to those who know little about the history of American women, or Jewish women, or that one woman with whom Lazarus' name is inextricably linked: the Statue of Liberty.

Emma was born on July 22, 1849, almost exactly one year after the first Woman's Rights convention was held at Seneca Falls, New York. It was a time of political and social turmoil in the United States. Abolitionists were debating states' rights advocates, and North and South were facing off for a major conflict. Across the ocean, a revolution was occurring in Germany which sent a wave of new immigrants to America, and gold had been discovered in California. But the young Emma lived a sheltered life, far from the politics raging around her. Her father Moses Lazarus was a prosperous Sephardic (Spanish) Jewish sugar refiner. He traced his ancestry back to the first 23 Jews to settle in New York in 1654, refugees from an earlier colony in Recife,

Emma Lazarus

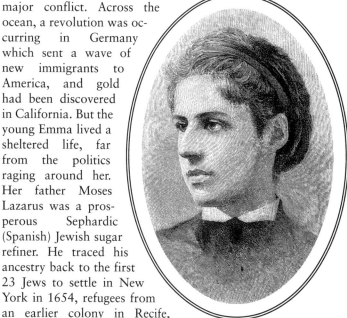

Brazil. Her mother **Esther Nathan Lazarus** also came from an old, distinguished line. The Nathan family began in America with Simon Nathan, an English Jew of Sephardic descent who came to the New World in 1773 and actively supported the American Revolution. Descendants of Simon Nathan married into the equally distinguished Seixus, Cordozo, and Lazarus families of Philadelphia and New York. Theirs was the rich society of uptown Manhattan, a refined and exclusive world of private education, elegant homes, fine china, and literary salons.

Emma was the fifth of seven children in the Lazarus household—eldest son Frank had been followed by six daughters. Considered too fragile and sickly for a school environment, Emma studied with tutors at home. By the time she was 13, her father Moses saw in her a unique talent and took personal charge of her education. He supervised her study of languages, literature, and the classics and encouraged her to write.

Until we are all free, we are none of us free.

—Emma Lazarus

Lazarus began writing poetry while still a child. By the time she was 17, she had enough for a small collection which her doting father had published at his own expense in 1866, for the benefit of family members. However, her work caught the attention of others in the literary world and was republished commercially one year later under the modest title *Poems and Translations*.

As a young woman, Lazarus was shy and rarely left home except for visits to family members. Until her poems brought her a small amount of acclaim, she seems to have had few friends outside her extended family circle. Her second book, *Admetus and Other Poems,* published in 1871, was well received both in the United States and in England, and gave her still more confidence. A novel, *Alide: An Episode of Goethe's Life,* written in 1874, was also reviewed well. Interspersed with these original writings, all heavily influenced by the literature she read, Lazarus spent considerable energy and talent on translations of other poets. Among her most successful translations were the poems of the German-Jewish poet Heinrich Heine, which first appeared individually, in newspapers and magazines, and then were published in book form in 1881. She also translated medieval Hebrew poetry. Although she had apparently studied some Hebrew, she depended mostly on the original German translations of these for her own renderings.

As she became well known, Lazarus established relationships with many male writers, including Henry James, John Greenleaf Whittier, James Russell Lowell, and John Burroughs. She discussed her own work with them as well as the works of others, mostly through letters. There is no clear evidence that Lazarus ever had any romantic attachments, though rumors and circumstance have linked her with two men. The first was her cousin Washington Nathan, a high-living socialite of her own age, considered very attractive to women. Washington Nathan was accused of murdering his father, Emma's maternal uncle, in 1870, but was acquitted for lack of evidence. Lazarus made no mention of this incident in her poetry and dedicated only one poem ("Lohengrin") to him.

The second man was Charles deKay, literary and art editor of *The New York Times* and also a poet. Lazarus had become close friends with his sister **Helena deKay Gilder** and her husband Richard Gilder, editor of *Century* magazine, and probably met him through that connection. She admired deKay's work and allowed him to escort her to many cultural events in New York City. Biographers have conjectured that Lazarus could not marry him, either because he was a Christian, or due to her unnaturally close relationship with her father. (No one suggested that it may have been deKay himself who rejected the match because she was Jewish.)

Although Emma's family never sought to deny their Jewish identity, they were quite assimilated into Christian society. Moses and Esther Lazarus belonged to the best non-Jewish clubs in New York City, engaged in business relationships with Christians, and from 1870 on, spent their summers in Newport, Rhode Island, completely at home in gentile high society. Emma herself showed no evidence of any strong religious feeling toward Judaism. The Lazarus name appeared on the membership list of Shearith Israel, the oldest and most respected synagogue in New York City, but neither Emma nor her family appear to have attended services. In a letter written in 1877, she explained that her "interests and sympathies" were with the Jews, but "my religious convictions and the circumstances of my life have led me somewhat apart from our people." Lazarus' writings suggest that she had absorbed and believed many of the anti-Jewish stereotypes of her non-Jewish friends and neighbors.

There is more probability that Emma's emotional dependence on her father, Moses Lazarus, was the reason for what was then genteelly called her "spinsterhood." In fact, Moses was charismatic and beloved, the pivotal member of a close and interactive family. None of Emma's five sisters married until after their father died in 1885, and his passing was considered to be an especially hard blow for Emma, acknowledged to be his favorite.

A hint of the conflicts Lazarus may have experienced due to this strong filial affection can be seen in her verse-play *The Spagnoletto*. The story is set in Renaissance Italy but tells of a woman who, defying her father, runs off with her lover. As a punishment to this disobedient and unfaithful daughter, the father commits suicide before her eyes. Two other works, "The Dance of Death" (later included in her book *Songs of a Semite*) and an essay on Shakespeare's *King Lear*, also touch on the theme of father-daughter devotion.

Lazarus' relationship with the aging philosopher and writer Ralph Waldo Emerson is one of the most well known of her friendships. The young poet first met him at a social gathering when she was 19 years old, and agreed to send him a copy of her first collection of poetry. He read it and wrote her encouragingly, praising her talents and giving her advice. Her second collection (*Admetus and Other Poems*) was dedicated to him. However, when Emerson compiled *Parnassus,* an anthology of important American poetry, he did not include a single poem of hers. Emma was bitterly disappointed and actually wrote him a letter accusing him of treating her "with absolute contempt." She claimed that "the opinions you have expressed to me in private" were completely contrary to "this public neglect" and "leaves me in utter bewilderment as to your real verdict."

Despite this angry letter, their relationship continued. In 1876, two years after the publication of her first novel, *Alide,* Emerson invited her to spend a week at his home in Concord, Massachusetts. This was a milestone for Lazarus for several reasons. It marked the resumption of a friendship with a man whom she—and indeed the whole nation—respected and admired. It was also a sign of real acceptance into the literary world, and a chance to meet other well-known figures in Emerson's famous circle. And finally, at age 27, this was the first trip Lazarus took alone, without any member of her family to accompany her.

Lazarus' visit to Concord was not the opportunity she had hoped. At 73, Emerson was tired and set in his ways. Although Emma did have a few brief talks with him, the more important outcome of that week was her developing friendship with **Lidian Emerson**, Emerson's wife,

and **Ellen "Nelly" Emerson**, his daughter, who was Emma's contemporary. Emerson had been a Protestant preacher, and Ellen a Sunday School teacher who, like Emma, had lived a fairly sheltered life. Ellen later wrote that her encounter with Emma Lazarus was "more interesting than I could have imagined." It was apparently her first (and possibly her only) meeting with what she called "a real unconverted Jew." Emma and Ellen continued their friendship over many years, although Emma made only one other visit to the Emerson home.

After her trip to Concord, Lazarus resumed her literary activities and her quiet life: social engagements with family and friends, summers at Newport, reading, translations, discussions on books and art. She became a frequent contributor to *The New York Times,* and to *Century* and *Critic,* well-known magazines of the day, as well as the *Jewish Messenger* and the *American Hebrew,* popular Jewish publications.

It was in 1882 that Emma Lazarus first became mobilized to the cause of the Russian Jews. Before that time, she had dabbled in Jewish history and written a few poems on Jewish themes. Emma had been encouraged along these lines by a family friend, Rabbi Gustav Gottheil, spiritual leader of Temple Emanu-el in Manhattan. The writings of George Eliot (***Mary Anne Evans**), and especially Eliot's novel *Daniel Deronda*, had also had a positive influence on her attitude toward her own people. However, Lazarus only wholeheartedly espoused their cause when it was taken up by her non-Jewish associates.

The pogroms (anti-Jewish riots) in Russia following the assassination of Tsar Alexander II in 1881 had generated much comment from New York's humanitarian community, both Jewish and Christian. Lazarus was genuinely touched by the plight of her co-religionists who, by 1882, were pouring into New York harbor and filling the run-down and overcrowded neighborhoods near the port in lower Manhattan. She was equally affected by the bigotry against Jews which emanated from many quarters, including her own upper-class Jewish circle. Christians feared that an influx of Jewish immigrants, considered "base" and undesirable, would have a negative influence on American society. Upper-class Jews, already well established in the United States, echoed those feelings, but had an additional—and realistic—concern. These impoverished and uneducated Jews, whom Lazarus would later describe in a poem as having crawled forth "from the loathsome recesses of the Jewry," posed a very personal threat to American "Hebrews" as they preferred to call themselves. Earlier Jewish immigrants, from Spain, England and Germany, had carefully cultivated an image of gentility and refinement. Now they were being lumped together with this new group of poor, dirty, and uneducated Jews. It was this concern which must have fueled Emma's indignation, at least partially, when she was shown an anti-Semitic article in the *Century*.

The article blamed the Jews and their own unacceptable activities for the Russian attacks on them, and accused all Jews of unethical behavior and crimes against society. Lazarus' response to this article was a point-by-point refutation and an accurate description of Eastern European Jewish life and its problems. However, she also made it clear that Russian Jewry needed to reform itself from within by means of education, both technical and religious. Her ideas were reflected in a series of 15 essays called *An Epistle to the Hebrews*, published in 1882 in the *American Hebrew*.

From that point on, for the next two years, Lazarus devoted herself to the cause of Russian-Jewish immigrants. Her attack on this problem was two-pronged. She founded the short-lived and little-known Society for the Improvement and Colonization of East European Jews, thus becoming one of the earliest American advocates of modern Zionism and the American spokesperson for the resettlement of Jews in Palestine. In addition, she began visiting the new immigrants, especially those who were being held in quarantine at Ward's Island, and tried to help them. Initially, her help consisted of small amounts of money, food, and clothing. Later, her belief in the need for occupational reeducation led to her establishment of the Hebrew Technical Institute.

The consensus of her biographers was that although Lazarus was sympathetic to the hardships of these unfortunate Jews, she did not identify with them. As a result, she never "connected" in any real sense but always felt—and was considered to be—an outsider. Nevertheless, she attended rallies to raise money for Russian Jews and wrote poems about the brotherhood of the Jewish people. In her poem "The Prophet," she challenged the more comfortable American Jews to acknowledge their kinship with the "caftaned wretch" who was also a part of their people. It is easy, Lazarus suggested, to feel close to men like Moses ben Maimon, Judah HaLevi, Moses Mendelssohn, great Jewish philosophers and writers, and others of their caliber and accomplishment. But those who have "faith in the fortune of Israel" must dare to unite with *all* Jews.

In "The Banner of the Jew" she called "Wake, Israel, wake!" to the needs of "the urgent hour."

As Emma described herself in a letter to a friend: "I have plunged . . . recklessly and impulsively" into the Jewish Question. This quiet and private woman even composed several speeches, although she was never unladylike enough to read them herself before an audience. Women public speakers were not yet acceptable in elite society despite the women's suffrage movement, and Emma submitted her written remarks to be read by male participants at the rallies.

This openly pro-Jewish stand was a courageous one in the upper-class world of the 1880s; in many respects even more courageous because Emma was a Jew herself. But the issue was very much alive during those months, being discussed in every newspaper and journal, and Emma was fortified in her beliefs by all her Christian friends. However she came to her commitment, there seems to be no doubt that through this issue Lazarus found a new meaning and pride in her Jewish identity and fully understood that the fate of Russian Jews was inextricably intertwined with her own. She published a new collection of poetry, *Songs of a Semite,* and wrote: "I have no thought, no passion, no desire save for my own people."

Just one year after she had proclaimed her devotion to the Jewish people, Emma embarked on her first trip to England and France, accompanied by her younger sister **Annie Lazarus**. She had many letters of introduction to European Jewish leaders and philanthropists, as well as to famous non-Jews such as writer Robert Browning and social reformer William Morris. With praise for *Songs of a Semite* still recent, she found that people were anxious to meet her and hear her opinions.

After her return from this successful and exciting trip, Lazarus was at the peak of her career. It was at this time that she was approached by the Bartholdi Pedestal Fund for the Statue of Liberty and asked to write a poem. The Statue of Liberty was a gift from France, sculpted by the artist Frédéric Auguste Bartholdi. Due to be delivered shortly, there was as yet no place for the enormous statue. It was with some sense of urgency, therefore, that a fund-raising auction was organized and all the noted writers of the day were asked to contribute to the cause.

At first Lazarus was reluctant, claiming that art needs inspiration and cannot be commissioned. However, a member of the fund-raising committee appealed to her emotions, asking her to consider what the statue might mean to the Russian-Jewish refugees who saw it for the first time. Emma agreed, and just one month before the scheduled auction, wrote the sonnet that would become her most famous work: "The Giant Colossus."

> Not like the brazen giant of Greek fame,
> With conquering limbs astride from land to land;
> Here at our sea-washed, sunset gates shall stand
> A mighty woman with a torch, whose flame
> Is the imprisoned lightning, and her name
> Mother of Exiles. From her beacon-hand
> Glows world-wide welcome; her mild eyes command
> The air-bridged harbor that twin cities frame.
>
> Keep, ancient lands, your storied pomp! Cries she
> With silent lips. "Give me your tired, your poor,
> Your huddled masses yearning to breathe free,
> The wretched refuse of your teeming shore.
> Send these, the homeless, tempest-tost to me.
> I lift my lamp beside the golden door."

Along with poems by Longfellow, Whitman, Bret Harte, and Mark Twain, Emma Lazarus' poem was sold at auction in December 1883. It was the only poem among the illustrious collection that was read out loud at the event. Then it was promptly forgotten. When the statue was finally brought over to New York in 1886, Lazarus was in Europe and had moved on to other concerns. First there was Emma's own failing health, but that was overshadowed by the death of her father, Moses Lazarus. He had passed away in March 1885 after a long illness.

Exhausted and depressed, Emma embarked on another trip to Europe with Annie, this one much longer than the first. While in England, she began a new novel, but her mood and poor health forced her to give up the project. Instead, she traveled through Holland, then on to Paris and Rome where she enjoyed viewing all the great art about which she had only read until then. When she returned to England, she fell ill once again and was chronically exhausted. She pushed herself to visit more galleries and continue her planned activities despite a growing weakness, but finally could no longer sustain the effort. At Annie's insistence, in July of 1887, Emma agreed to return home and was diagnosed with Hodgkin's disease, a form of cancer. She had just turned 38.

Lazarus continued writing poems, letters, and translations even after she was completely bedridden. Among her last published works was a series of poems about "Jewish reality and the Jewish dream" published in March 1887 under the title *By the Waters of Babylon*.

Emma Lazarus died in her home in New York City on November 19, 1887. In addition to her large family, many of the noted literati of New York came to her funeral and praised both her and her work. However, her poetry slowly slipped into oblivion. Her sister Annie refused to release much of Emma's later poems for republication because she considered it "sectarian propaganda" and felt it did not reflect her sister's true views. Annie had subsequently married a Christian and converted to Catholicism, and many people felt that she was embarrassed by her sister's works on Jewish themes.

It was not until 1901, 14 years after Lazarus' death, that a friend and admirer, **Georgina Schuyler**, rediscovered a copy of "The New Colossus" and began a campaign to have it placed on the pedestal of the Statue of Liberty, now permanently set on Bedloe's Island (present-day Liberty Island), outside New York harbor. It took Schuyler two years to overcome all the red tape involved in such a project, but on May 6, 1903, the 14 lines of Lazarus' sonnet, inscribed on a bronze plaque, were attached to the base of the statue. Schuyler wrote to her friends: "dear Emma's poem" is in place. Since that time, "The New Colossus" has been memorized by millions of schoolchildren, set to music, and been accepted as an integral part of America's culture and literature. It is a singular accomplishment for the modest poet who once wrote:

> Late Born and woman-souled I dare not hope
> The freshness of the elder lays, the might
> Of manly, modern passion shall alight
> Upon my Muse's lips . . .

SOURCES:

"Emma Lazarus," in *Encyclopedia Judaica*. 1972 ed.

James, Edward T., ed. *Notable American Women, 1607–1950*. Vol. 2. Cambridge, MA: Belknap Press of Harvard University Press, 1971.

Lefer, Diane. *Emma Lazarus*. NY: Chelsea House, 1988.

Young, Bette Roth. *Emma Lazarus in Her World: Life and Letters*. Philadelphia: Jewish Publication Society, 1995.

SUGGESTED READING:

Henry, Sondra, and Emily Taitz. *Written Out of History: Jewish Foremothers*. NY: Biblio Press, 1991.

Jacobs, H.E. *The World of Emma Lazarus*. NY: Schocken Books, 1949.

Schappes, Morris U., ed. *Emma Lazarus: Selections from Her Poetry and Prose*. IWO Jewish American Section, 1944 (reprinted NY: Emma Lazarus Federation of Jewish Women's Clubs, 1978).

COLLECTIONS:

Schappes, Morris U., ed. *The Letters of Emma Lazarus, 1868–1885*. NY: New York Public Library, 1949.

Emily Taitz,
adjunct professor of Women's Studies,
Adelphi University, Garden City, New York,
and co-author of *Remarkable Jewish Women:
Rebels, Rabbis and Other Women from
Biblical Times to the Present* (Jewish Publication Society, 1996)

Lazis, Asja (1891–1979).

See Lacis, Asja.

Lazutina, Larissa (c. 1966—)

Russian cross-country skier. Name variations: Larissa Lazhutina. Born around 1966.

Larissa Lazutina was a relay gold medalist in the 1992 (Albertville) and 1994 (Lillehammer) Olympics. In 1998, she won the silver in the 1500K cross-country classical race in Nagano, finishing 47:01.4 to teammate *Olga Danilova's 46:55.4. Two days later, battling blinding snow, Lazutina took the gold medal in the women's 5-kilometer classical cross-country race with a time of 17:39.9. She then added another gold medal in the 10-kilometer freestyle with a time of 46:06.9, and a gold medal in the 4x5-kilometer relay. Her teammates in the relay, with a time of 55:13.5, were Danilova, **Nina Gavriliuk**, and **Yelena Välbe**. Norway finished second (**Bente Martinsen, Marit Mikkelsplass, Elin Nilsen, Anita Moen-Guidon**) with a time of 55:38.0, and Italy third (**Karin Moroder, Gabriella Paruzzi, Manuela di Centa**, and **Stefania Belmondo**) with a time of 56:53.3.

Lea, St. (d. about 383)

Saint. Died around 383; a widow.

What is known of St. Lea comes from a letter that St. Jerome sent to St. *Marcella. From it we learn that Lea, following the death of her husband, gave up her life of wealth and privilege and retired to a Roman monastery, where she eventually rose to the position of superior. "Exchanging her rich attire for sackcloth, she ceased commanding others to obey all," he writes, "she lived in a corner with a few sticks of furniture; passed nights in prayer; instructed her companions by example rather than by protests and speeches; awaited her arrival in heaven to be rewarded for the virtues which she practised on earth." Jerome compares Lea's acceptance into Heaven to that of a recently dead consul, who enjoyed great wealth and admiration while he lived, but may encounter a lesser fate in the hereafter. "The fact is that he is plunged into outer darkness, while Lea, who was willing to be thought a dolt here below, has been received in the house of the Father, at the feast of the Lamb." Jerome goes on to encourage St. Marcella to renounce all that is of the flesh, "for our bodies will very soon be dust nor will anything else last longer."

SOURCES:

Englebert, Omer. *The Lives of The Saints.* Translated by Christopher and Anne Fremantle. London: Thames and Hudson, 1951.

Leach, Abby (1855–1918)

American educator who was instrumental in opening Harvard's doors to female scholars, which eventually led to the creation of Radcliffe College. Born on May 28, 1855, in Brockton, Massachusetts; died on December 29, 1918, in Poughkeepsie, New York; daughter of Marcus Leach and Eliza Paris (Bourne) Leach; educated at Brockton High School, Oread Collegiate Institute, the "Harvard Annex" (which later became Radcliffe College), Johns Hopkins University, and the University of Leipzig; private studies with Harvard professors; Vassar College, B.A. and M.A., both 1885.

Abby Leach was born on May 28, 1855, in Brockton, Massachusetts, the third of five children of **Eliza Leach** and Marcus Leach, a manufacturer of boots and shoes who was one of Brockton's leading citizens. Abby was a precocious child who read Latin for pleasure. She graduated from high school in 1869 and entered Oread Collegiate Institute in Worcester, Massachusetts, where she studied Greek. For a short while she taught at Brockton High School before beginning a five-year teaching career at Oread in 1873. Three years later, she became preceptress there.

In 1878, at age 23, Leach moved to Cambridge to study Greek, Latin, and English with professors at Harvard College. With some difficulty, she managed to convince William Watson Goodwin, professor of Greek, to take her on as a private student. He was so impressed by her skills that he persuaded Professor James Bradstreet Greenough of the Latin department and Professor Francis James Child of the English department to take her on as a private student as well.

Many believe that Leach's work was what convinced Harvard, in 1879, to open up instruction to women through the "Society for the Private Collegiate Instruction for Women," commonly called the "Harvard Annex," which later became Radcliffe College. While Leach continued her studies at the Annex, she also taught at the Girls' Latin School in Boston. In 1883, Leach became an instructor at Vassar College, teaching Greek and Latin. Vassar granted Leach bachelor's and master's degrees in 1885, based on her work at Harvard. She continued her studies at Johns Hopkins and also studied for a year at the University of Leipzig. In

1886, she became an associate professor at Vassar and, in 1889, was made full professor and head of the Greek department, a post she would hold for 29 years.

Leach was a resolute opponent of "expediency and compromise" in education and (by extension and because of her deep belief in the classical Greek ideals) in life. She had a tremendous impact on Vassar through her teaching, despite the damage to her career there wrought by strained relations with *Grace Harriet Macurdy, another member of the Greek department, and contributed several articles to various scholarly journals. One of her articles, "Fatalism in the Greeks," was republished as the chapter "Fate and Free Will in Greek Literature" in Lance Cooper's *The Greek Genius and Its Influence* (1917). She was also involved with several academic organizations; she sat on the committee of managers of the American School of Classical Studies in Athens from 1888 until her death, was president of the American Philological Association from 1899 to 1900, and was president of the Association of Collegiate Alumnae (later the American Association of University Women) from 1899 to 1901. Abby Leach died in her home of cancer, at age 63, on December 29, 1918.

SOURCES:

James, Edward T., ed. *Notable American Women, 1607–1950.* Cambridge, MA: The Belknap Press of Harvard University Press, 1971.

McHenry, Robert, ed. *Famous American Women.* NY: Dover, 1983.

Karina L. Kerr, M.A.,
Ypsilanti, Michigan

Leadbetter, Mary (1758–1826)

Irish-born poet and storywriter. Name variations: Mary Shackleton; Mrs. Leadbetter. Born Mary Shackleton at Ballitore, County Kildare, Ireland, in December 1758; died in Ballitore on June 27, 1826; granddaughter of Abraham Shackleton (1697–1771, a schoolmaster); married William Leadbetter, in 1791.

An Irish-born writer of Quaker birth, Mary Leadbetter became a friend and correspondent of Edmund Burke who had been a student of her grandfather's. She published *Poems* (1808), *Cottage Dialogues among the Irish Peasantry* (1811), and *Cottage Biography* (1822). Her best work, *Annals of Ballitore*, was published in 1862 as *The Leadbetter Papers* by R.D. Webb.

Leah.

See joint entry titled Rachel and Leah.

Leakey, Mary Nicol (1913–1996)

English archaeologist whose discovery of the Zinj skull and the Laetoli footprints furthered understanding of the origins of humanity. Born Mary Douglas Nicol in London, England, on February 6, 1913; died in Kenya on December 9, 1996; daughter of Cecilia (Frere) Nicol and Erskine Nicol (a landscape painter); attended private schools; married Louis Seymour Bazett Leakey (an archaeologist), on December 24, 1936 (separated 1968); children: Jonathan Leakey (b. 1940); Deborah Leakey (b. 1943); Richard Leakey (b. 1944, a renowned paleontologist); Philip Leakey (b. 1949).

Awards: Hubbard Medal of the National Geographic Society (1962), with Louis Leakey; Prestwick Medal of the Geological Society of London (1969), with Louis Leakey; Gold Medal of the Society of Women Geographers (1975); Linnaeus Gold Medal of the Royal Swedish Academy (1978); Elizabeth Blackwell Award (1980); Bradford Washburn Award (1980).

Father Erskine Nicol died (1926); undertook first archaeological field work, Hembury Fort (1930); met Louis Leakey (1933); asked to illustrate Louis Leakey's book Adam's Ancestors *(1933); directed first dig at Hembury (1934); traveled to Africa (1935); returned to England (September 1935); Louis Leakey secured funding from the Rhodes Trust (1936); traveled to Africa (1937); excavated Hyrax Hill (1937); excavated the Njoro River Cave (1937); Louis Leakey appointed curator of the Coryndon Museum, Nairobi, Kenya (1940); excavated Ngorongoro (1940); attended first Pan-African Congress of Prehistory and Paleontology (1947); secured funding from the Royal Society (1947); excavated Rusinga Island (1948); discovered* Proconsul africanus *(1948); secured funding from the Wenner-Gren Foundation for Anthropological research (1951); recorded Tanzanian rock paintings (1951); excavated the Olduvai Gorge (1951–58); discovered Zinj (July 17, 1959); Tanzanian government issued postage stamp honoring Mary and Louis Leakey (1965); separated from her husband (1968); death of Louis Leakey (October 11, 1972); elected member of the British Academy (1973); discovered early hominid footprints at Laetoli (1976).*

Selected publications: "Notes on the Ground and Polished Stone Axes of East Africa," in Journal of East Africa and Uganda Natural History Society *(1943); "Report on the Excavations at Hyrax Hill, Nakura, Kenya Colony," in* Transactions of the Royal Society *(South Africa, 1945); "Primitive Artifacts from the Kanapoi Valley," in* Nature *(1966); "Cultural Patterns in the Olduvai Gorge, Tanzania," in* After the Australopithecines *(K.W. Butzer and G.L. Isaac, eds. The Hague: Mouton, 1975); "3.6 Million Years*

Old Footprints in the Ashes of Time," in *National Geographic (1979);* Olduvai Gorge: My Search for Early Man *(London: Collins, 1979).*

Mary Leakey was born in London, England, on February 6, 1913, the only child of **Cecilia Frere Nicol** and Erskine Nicol, a popular landscape painter of Scottish descent. Mary inherited her father's talent for drawing, which later proved invaluable in her career. Her great-great-grandfather was John Frere, the late-18th-century geologist and archaeologist who first connected artifacts with extinct animals. Mary Leakey wrote, however, that she was unwilling to "stretch faith in genetic inheritance" and attributed her principle archaeological influence to her father, who was an amateur Egyptologist.

For most of the year, the family traveled on the Continent. Each summer was spent in London, where Erskine Nicol held an annual exhibition of his work. Aside from a brief sojourn at an elementary school in France, Leakey received little formal education; her father taught her to read and write. While in France, she visited the famous cave paintings of the Dordogne region, met Elie Peryony, and began to collect Paleolithic tools, which were not considered of value by the local museum at Les Eyzie. Abbé Lemozi, an avid amateur archaeologist and friend of the family, accompanied Leakey on visits to the cave paintings of Pêch Merle.

ℒouis could interpret finds, sometimes beyond the obvious, but it was Mary who really gave that team scientific validity.

—Gilbert Grosvenor, chair of the National Geographic Society

Mary Leakey's father died when she was 13 years old. Upon the family's return to England, her mother sought to further her daughter's education, but Leakey's tutors found her uncooperative and rebellious. She was also expelled from two convent schools. Since she "had never passed a single exam, and clearly never would," recalled Leakey, the chances of her being admitted to a university were non-existent. If Mary Leakey rebelled against the strictures of formal education, however, she thrived on independent learning. She set herself a rigorous course of self-study, which included sitting in on geology lectures at London University. She also attended the lectures of Sir Mortimer Wheeler at the British Museum.

In 1930, Leakey undertook her first archaeological field work at Hembury Fort, a Neolithic site in Devon, and published several drawings of the finds. Her efforts came to the attention of archaeologist *Gertrude Caton-Thompson, who asked Mary to illustrate a book on Egyptian excavations, *The Desert Fayoum.* In 1933, Caton-Thompson invited her to attend a lecture being given by Louis S.B. Leakey at the Royal Anthropological Institute. A fellow of St. John's College, Cambridge, Louis Leakey was an experienced archaeologist with three African expeditions to his credit. He asked Mary to illustrate his forthcoming book *Adam's Ancestors.*

What began as a professional collaboration soon blossomed into romance. She and Louis, she wrote, shared a fascination for "wild places, working in the field, and being alone among wild animals." However, Louis was ten years her senior and married, and his wife **Frida Leakey** was expecting their second child. At length, Louis broke the news to Frida, and reports of the impending divorce scandalized the Cambridge community. Mary was repeatedly asked to abandon the relationship for the sake of Louis' career. Deeply in love, she refused.

By 1934, Mary Leakey was directing her first archaeological dig at Hembury. A hominid skull was unearthed the following year, and the find resulted in her first publication. In April 1935, she joined Louis in Tanzania. Her first trip to Africa had a profound impact. "Africa," she later wrote, "had cast its spell." A year after the couple returned to England in September 1935, divorce proceedings were initiated (October 19, 1936), and Frida Leakey obtained custody of her two children. On December 24, 1936, Mary and Louis Leakey were married in Wares, England. By this time, it was clear that Louis' professional association with Cambridge University was at an end. The young couple planned to settle in Africa and pursue archaeological research. Because of his fluency in Kikuyu, Louis was able to secure funding from the Rhodes Trust for a two-year study of the Kikuyu tribe.

While he conducted his research on the Kikuyu, Mary Leakey began a dig at Hyrax Hill, a lava ridge about a half mile long, in Kenya. There, she discovered a Neolithic settlement and 19 burial sites. The Kenyan government declared the site a national monument, and several years later erected a museum nearby. In 1937, the Leakeys were invited to excavate a cave at the Njoro River, which yielded many Elementeitan artifacts. Among the finds were bowls, weapons, tools, and beads. At the Njoro River Cave, they also uncovered evidence of ritual cremation; each person was buried with a bowl, a mortar, and a pestle. The first archaeological site in Kenya to be dated using the radio-carbon method, its age was estimated by the Leakeys to be 960 BCE.

During World War II, Louis Leakey, like many British scholars, was employed by British intelligence; he smuggled guns to guerrillas in Ethiopia. In 1940, he also became the curator of the Coryndon Museum in Nairobi, and was the first curator to make the museum accessible to all races. Later, he became the curator of the National Museum of Kenya. For much of the war, Mary Leakey conducted research at Ngorongoro in northeast Tanzania, and at Olorgesailie in Kenya, using Italian prisoners of war as laborers. The Olorgesailie site yielded several cleavers and axes used for the slaughter of large mammals. She also unearthed the remains of 50 giant baboons, and theorized that they had been cornered and killed by early hominids. Eventually, the site was declared a national park. In 1947, the first Pan-African Congress of Prehistory and Paleontology was hosted by Louis Leakey in Nairobi. An excursion to one of Mary Leakey's digs was organized, and as a result the Royal Society in London agreed to fund her research for one year.

Working on Rusinga Island in the northeast corner of Lake Victoria in 1948, Mary Leakey made a spectacular discovery. She unearthed the skull, jaws, and teeth of what came to be known as *Proconsul africanus*. At the time, there was great speculation that the find represented the "missing link" in the evolution between apes and humans. *Proconsul africanus* was the first early ape skull ever discovered. Louis described the unearthing of the skull in his journal:

> Returned to the ape skull with Mary, Heselon, Nderitu and Zadok and got it out. It is very broken up and large parts are missing, but we have the whole jaw, most of the face, including the orbit on one side of the frontal and bits of parietal. . . . The form of frontal in an adult is almost infantile, as I fully expected it would be if, as I have argued so often, modern apes are very specialized in respect of supra-orbitals.

Mary reconstructed the fragmented skull with such skill that Louis remarked: "Mary has got it

Mary Leakey presents the skull of Proconsul *to the world's press at Heathrow Airport, 1948.*

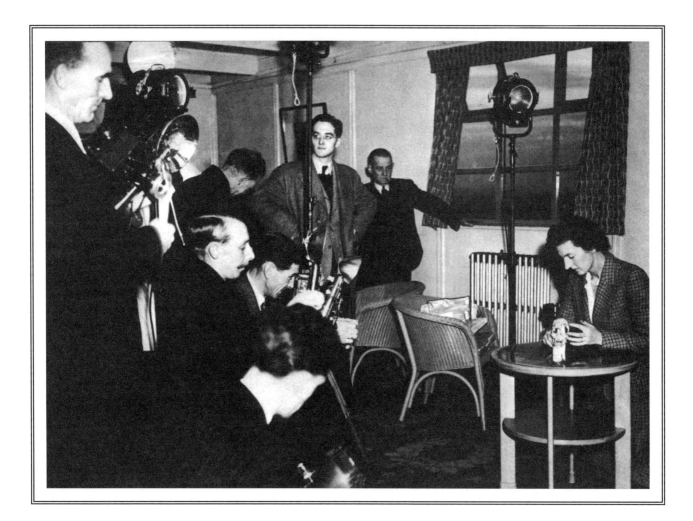

together perfectly, although many of the pieces were about the size of a match-head." Although *Proconsul africanus* did not prove to be a direct descendant of early hominids, the international press coverage surrounding the discovery persuaded the Kenyan government to fund Mary Leakey's research for the next several years.

In 1950, the Leakeys and their four children visited Europe and toured the recently discovered cave paintings at Lascaux, in France. Louis Leakey was awarded an honorary degree by Oxford University, an irony which would not have been lost on him given his past difficulties with Cambridge. As well, the couple met Alexander Wenner-Gren, founder of the Wenner-Gren Foundation for Anthropological Research. The foundation's agreement to fund Mary's research in 1951 gave her an opportunity to investigate Tanzanian rock paintings, which she had originally begun to record in 1935. The painted rocks depicted hunting scenes, humans dancing, bathing, and playing music. "No amount of stone and bone could have yielded the kinds of information that the paintings gave so freely," she noted. Leakey concluded that the artwork formed part of a cultural tradition dating back to the Paleolithic period. She was anxious to record the paintings before they were destroyed by local inhabitants, who chipped off pieces in the belief that they were magic. These paintings appeared in her book *Africa's Vanishing Art*.

From 1951 until 1958, Leakey and her husband devoted the bulk of their energies to the excavation of Bed II of the Olduvai Gorge, near the Kenya-Tanzania border. In 1959, they decided to refocus their efforts on Bed I. While walking her Dalmatian on July 17, 1959, Mary Leakey noticed a bone protruding from the surface of Bed I. It turned out to be part of a jaw bone. After painstaking work, she recovered a skull subsequently christened "Zinj" from the Arabic word for "Africa." The skull also became known as "Nutcracker Man" because of its large teeth. The find caused an international sensation. Contemporary scientists believed that the human species had evolved in Asia only a few hundred thousand years before. The discovery of Zinj proved them wrong. The skull was found to be 1.75 million years old.

International fame also brought controversy. Louis initially classified the skull as a new genus of the Homo family, the progenitors of Homo erectus. Noted paleoanthropologist Phillip Tobias disagreed. Instead, Tobias argued that the skull was from the earliest hominid period, Australopithecus. Thus, the skull came to be known as *Australopithecus boisei*. In December 1965, the Tanzanian government issued a postage stamp showing Zinj, along with Mary Leakey and Louis in the background.

In both Beds I and II, Mary Leakey unearthed other human remains which where contemporary, although different from *Australopithecus boisei*. These proved a puzzling find. Bed I also yielded the foundation of a dwelling, and she discovered tools which ranged from 2 to 8 million years of age. These discoveries were of decisive importance, wrote Jerrie McIntyre:

> Until these discoveries, few anthropologists believed that two hominid groups—an early Homo species and a robust australopithecine—could occupy the same territory at the same time. Both Louis and Mary Leakey attributed the toolmaking ability they had formerly credited to *A. boisei* to the larger-brained . . . hominids capable of "precision grip." The toolmaker was christened *Homo habilis* by Louis Leakey, Phillip Tobias, and John Napier; but some authorities still regard fossils from this group as gracile or "advanced gracile" Australopithecines.

As Louis' international reputation grew, his research became increasingly unorthodox, and his interests focused almost exclusively on spectacular finds. Unlike her husband, Mary Leakey preferred to work quietly behind the scenes and maintained a more conservative theoretical approach. "Not a careful scientist," writes John S. Major, "Louis invariably claimed too much credit for his finds made by Mary and others on his team, and he ascribed too much significance to each find." He also had a series of affairs. This caused friction between the two, and the Leakeys separated in 1968. Louis Leakey died of a heart attack on October 11, 1972.

At the Laetoli Beds, 30 miles from the Olduvai Gorge, Mary Leakey in 1976 made one of the most important finds in archaeological history. She and her assistants uncovered hominid footprints in the volcanic ash. The footprints were "so sharp," she wrote, "that they could have been left this morning." This discovery proved that early hominids were walking upright between 3.5 and 3.8 million years ago. By 1979, Leakey and her team had excavated 80 feet of the prehistoric trail and determined that three hominids had been present. As well, they unearthed the remains of 25 early hominids, though no tools were found.

Mary Leakey's findings shed new light on work being done by Donald Johanson, the discoverer of "Lucy," the most complete Pliocene hominid skeleton yet to be unearthed. Excavated in Ethiopia, "Lucy" is over 3 million years old, and Johanson claimed that she had been bipedal. A spirited debate arose within the archaeological community, however, concerning the mobility of early hominids. As Kenneth Feber and Michael Park note, Mary Leakey's work at Laetoli had important implications for Johanson's research:

> Even at this point some differences of opinion existed about just how bipedal these early hominids were. Estimates were based on inference from the structure of the bones; no one had actually seen them walking around. In 1976, however, the next best thing was unearthed. A group led by Mary Leakey uncovered a set of footprints at Laetoli. . . . The nature of the prints and their orientation to each other show no difference from the prints made by people today.

Unlike many of her archaeological colleagues, Leakey received her professional training in the field, rather than the classroom. She was a persistent and devoted archaeologist, with an eye for detail. Unfortunately, for many years her work was overshadowed by that of her husband, who was arguably the poorer scientist of the two. It was not until after his death that Mary Leakey emerged as an archaeologist of international stature in her own right. As Stephen Jay Gould commented, Mary Leakey has been the "unsung hero" of archaeology. Notes Charles Moritz:

> The name Leakey is synonymous in most people's minds with the successive dramatic discoveries of fossilized hominid bones and stone artifacts that have, over the years, pushed the true origins of man further and further back in prehistory.

In 1982, Mary Leakey lost the vision in her left eye due to thrombosis. As a result, she curtailed her field research. Nonetheless, her son Richard Leakey, his wife **Meave Leakey,** and their daughter **Louise Leakey,** continue the family tradition. Richard is the curator of the National Museum of Kenya and founder of the Louis Leakey Memorial Institute for African Prehistory. As of 1985, he was a member of the Kenyan Parliament, as well as assistant minister of Foreign Affairs.

Unlike her husband, Mary Leakey "never believed that knowledge of the past would help us to understand and possibly control the future. . . . Nature," she wrote, "will take its course, and man's activities will follow an irreversible pattern." Nevertheless, her contributions led to a more profound understanding of early human development. They also serve to remind us of the common ancestry which we all share. Mary Leakey died in Kenya on December 9, 1996, age 83. "Louis Leakey en-

joyed the limelight whether he was being applauded or criticized," said Gilbert Grosvenor, chair of the National Geographic Society. "Mary preferred a quieter life. Olduvai Gorge was probably heaven on earth to her."

SOURCES:
"African Queen," in *People Weekly*. December 23, 1996.
Cole, Sonia. *Leakey's Luck*. London: Collins, 1975.
Feber, Kenneth L., and Michael Alan Park. *Human Antiquity*. Mountain View, CA: Mayfield, 1989.
Gacs, Ute, Aisha Khan, Jerrie McIntyre, and Ruth Wienberg, eds. *Women Anthropologists*. CT: Greenwood, 1988.
Irwin-Williams, Cynthia. "Women in the Field: The Role of Women in Archaeology before 1960," in *Women of Science*. G. Kass-Simon and Patricia Farnes, eds. Bloomington: Indiana University Press, 1990.
Leakey, Louis Seymour Bazett. *By the Evidence: Memoirs, 1931–1951*. NY: Harcourt Brace Jovanovich, 1974.
Major, John S. "The Secret of 'Leakey Luck'," in *Time*. August 28, 1995.
Moritz, Charles. *Current Biography Yearbook 1985*. NY: H.W. Wilson, 1985.

SUGGESTED READING:
Leakey, Mary. *Disclosing the Past*. Garden City, NY: Doubleday, 1984.
Morell, Virginia. *Ancestral Passions*. Simon & Schuster, 1995.

Hugh A. Stewart, M.A.,
Guelph, Ontario, Canada

Leander, Zarah (1907–1981)

Swedish actress and singer who became the greatest screen idol of the Third Reich. Name variations: Sarah Leander. Born Zarah Stina Hedberg in Karlstad, Sweden, on March 15, 1907; died in Stockholm, Sweden, on June 23, 1981; married Nils Leander; married Vidar Forsell; married Arne Hülpers; children: daughter, Boel; son, Göran.

Ironically, the woman who was likely the greatest screen idol of the Third Reich was not German but a foreigner. Joseph Goebbels, Minister of Propaganda and Public Enlightenment, was profoundly displeased that the leading lady of National Socialist Germany was a Swedish actress and singer named Zarah Leander. After making ten films in Nazi Germany, Leander returned to Sweden in 1943 at a time when the war was turning against the Hitler regime. Her postwar career was burdened by accusations of having played a role in providing entertainment for a criminal state, but in her final years she emerged as the most important icon ever known in Germany's gay community.

Born in 1907 into a family of pastors (her father and generations of his ancestors were

Lutheran ministers), Zarah Hedberg exhibited musical precocity at age six by participating in a concert in her hometown of Karlstad. Soon after, she began to display equally impressive talent as a singer. In 1929, Zarah made her debut in several provincial theaters in productions by Ernst Rolf, Sweden's equivalent of Florenz Ziegfeld.

From 1930 through 1932, she regularly appeared on stage at Stockholm's Vasa-Theater as well as at the same city's Ekmanstheater. Regarded as both an accomplished actress and singer, she also performed outside of Sweden from this point on. In Vienna, beginning in September 1936, she starred in a highly popular operetta, Ralph Benatzky's *Axel an der Himmelstür* (Axel at Heaven's Gate). The production's director was Max Hansen, who had left Germany in 1933 after having allegedly "insulted the Führer." Hansen had discovered the unknown Zarah Leander while on a trip to Scandinavia. In addition to engaging her for Benatzky's operetta, he also brought her to the attention of talent scouts from UFA, the vast film studio that was Nazi Germany's version of Hollywood.

In 1936, Leander made her first German-language film. *Premiere,* an Austrian production, was lavish; in the film's most spectacular scene, Leander appeared in an ornate gown, holding the train of her dress and singing "Ich hab' vielleicht noch nie geliebt" (Perhaps I Have Never Loved Yet), while descending a seemingly endless staircase. Although *Premiere* was only moderately successful, Leander's talents convinced UFA executives that she was a property well worth signing. Her contract was both generous—200,000 reichsmarks for three films—and unusual, in that it stipulated that 53% of her salary was to be paid in Swedish kronor directly to her bank in Stockholm.

By 1936, it had become clear to Goebbels that, try as he might, Nazi Germany was without a replacement for several entertainment superstars who had either left the country, like *Marlene Dietrich (as an anti-Nazi, Dietrich would refuse to return to Germany), or had flatly refused to ever perform in German films, like *Greta Garbo. To find an actress of comparable star quality was now imperative, and, although it incensed him to do so, Goebbels set in motion his huge propaganda machine in order to create a superstar for a German people in need of diversion from the assault of daily propaganda. In the closing weeks of 1936, the state-controlled UFA studio began an extensive promotion of the still little-known Swedish actress.

A press campaign which reached 4,000 German newspapers, resulting in her face appearing on 80 magazine covers, created interest in the Berlin opening in February 1937 of Leander's *Premiere*. Canned slogans—easily inserted into the media because in the previous year all film criticism in the normal sense of the term had been banned—appeared "spontaneously" in virtually all German newspapers and magazines. The German reading public found themselves overwhelmed by such encomiums as "Zarah Leander, the great Swedish artist; a second Greta Garbo," "Zarah Leander, the great film and revue star, a captivating figure as singer and actress," and "Zarah Leander, the woman with the dark voice."

Photographs that accompanied the "suggested" press pieces revealed a woman with a face that was the incarnation of "ineffable sadness," a strong-boned visage with unforgettable languorous eyes. Some film historians have suggested that Leander's sad, yearning expression appealed to a German public which had become starved for romantic escapism. She also exuded a strength of personality that many likely longed for in an environment of relentless control and manipulation. The image portrayed by these photographic portraits of Leander was no accident; in fact, it represented the efforts of Franz Weihmayr, the superbly skilled cinematographer who would play a significant role in making all ten of her films for UFA visually memorable. The aggressive UFA publicity drive paid dividends almost immediately. Within the space of a few weeks, the previously little-known Swedish performer had become famous throughout the German Reich.

In her 1937 film *La Habañera*, Leander starred in the role of Astrée Sternhjelm, a young Swedish woman who visits Puerto Rico and falls in love with the bullfighter Don Pedro, whom she marries. The film ends with the now villainous Don Pedro losing his life, and his widow following the instincts of her blood by returning with her young son to her Nordic homeland. It was directed by Detlef Sierck (known as Douglas Sirk after he arrived in Hollywood), who fled to the United States soon after this film was completed because his Jewish wife, actress **Hildegard Jary**, was endangered in Germany. Both Leander's acting and singing in the film brought positive assessments by critics, including one who wrote in Berlin's *12 Uhr-Blatt:* "She touches us most of all when she sings 'La Habañera' in that deep voice."

In her next film, *Heimat* (Homeland), Leander played the role of a German opera singer

Zarah
Leander

who has become a celebrated artist. She returns home after a long absence to find herself still rejected by her father because of an affair she had years earlier that resulted in an illegitimate child. She regains the love of her father after her seducer, an unscrupulous banker, is caught being involved in illegal financial dealings and commits suicide. The film ends happily with the singer reconciled with her family. Leander's vocal talents blossomed in this vehicle, in which she sings an aria from Gluck's "Orfeo" as well as an excerpt from Bach's "St. Matthew's Passion." Not surprisingly, the muzzled critics again praised the singing Swedish actress. One characterized the entire film by noting:

> The return to one's roots is an instinct passed down from father to son in one of the noblest works yet produced by our national film industry. . . . Zarah Leander, suffused with patriotic feeling, and with a spare, intense style stripped of the slightest superfluous gesture, portrays a woman who has done wrong but who comes to her senses in time, who left the city of her birth but returns, in faith and good will. . . . With this performance, La Leander makes it clear that she is our most complete actress.

Emphasizing the folkish and nationalist elements in this film, Nazi film officials scheduled its premiere on June 25, 1938, in the Free City of Danzig, a territory that had been taken from the defeated German Reich at the time of the hated Treaty of Versailles. The Berlin premiere did not take place until September 1, 1938.

Two weeks before the start of World War II, Leander's 1939 film *Es war eine rauschende Ballnacht* (It Was a Wild Night at the Ball) premiered on August 15. The film, set in Tsarist Russia, casts Leander as Katharina Murakin, the wife of a wealthy merchant, who renews her youthful love affair with the composer Peter Ilyitch Tchaikovsky. The movie ends tragically when, just as the two lovers are about to be reunited, the composer falls victim to cholera and dies. This confection, which among other things ignores the historical fact that Tchaikovsky was gay, was popular with a German public uneasy about their future as the world once again was plunged into war. Writing in *Die Filmwelt*, critic H.E. Fischer gushed: "And Zarah Leander? Is it necessary to mention again that vibrant, fascinating voice? No. But it must be said that in this film she is more beautiful than ever, and truly moving in its numerous dramatic scenes. Another outstanding feature of the film is its photography, Franz Weihmayr is a master cameraman, one who creates music for the eyes. Every shot glows with an inner light of its own, and this is truly the mark of a master!"

By June 1942, when *Die grosse Liebe* (*The Great Love*) premiered in Berlin, Nazi Germany was fighting for its very existence in what was now the Second World War. Leander plays the role of Hanna Holberg, the star singer of Berlin's "Scala" music hall. Luftwaffe pilot Paul Wendlandt (played by Viktor Staal), spends the night with Hanna as the result of a surprise air raid and quickly realizes that he has fallen in love. After a series of complications, Hanna once again encounters Paul, this time in a military hospital where she works as a nurse. At the end of the film, firmly convinced that the war will soon end, she silently takes the wounded Paul's hand in her own. The continuing optimism about the war that was being fostered by the regime is reflected in one of the songs Leander sings in the film, entitled "Ich weiss, es wird einmal ein Wunder geschehen" (I Know That a Miracle Will Happen Someday). Another of the film's songs, "Davon geht die Welt nicht unter" (The World Will Not Die of This), reflects the same spirit of almost desperate optimism in the face of growing panic. Ironically, these songs were written by Bruno Balz while he spent three weeks in a Gestapo prison accused of homosexuality. This film would be Zarah Leander's greatest triumph in the Third Reich, representing not only a cinematic achievement but a major contribution by the UFA studios to German home-front morale, which was being severely tested; only two weeks before the film's premiere, a massive Royal Air Force bombing raid had reduced the heart of the city of Cologne to rubble in little over 90 minutes.

Although it was in many ways a typical UFA escapist film, *Die grosse Liebe* was also regarded by the studio heads and by Joseph Goebbels as a "war-education film," seamlessly blending the elements of popular entertainment and mass manipulation. Not only propagandistically, but financially as well, this film was considered a great success. Its original cost estimate had been a little over 1.5 million reichsmarks, and although its actual cost was 3.1 million, the film would earn over 9.2 million reichsmarks by November 1944 and, astonishingly, would be viewed by almost 28 million moviegoers.

Zarah Leander no doubt savored the immense popularity of *Die grosse Liebe,* and she began work on her next film soon after its premiere. As the highest paid, and very likely the most popular, German film actor, "die Leander," as she was referred to by fans, could reasonably look ahead to more triumphs. But the end of her German film career, and of Nazi Germany itself, was coming within view. Defeat loomed on the eastern front, and the staggering loss of the German Sixth Army at the battle of Stalingrad in January 1943 marked the beginning of the end of Hitler's Reich. Leander's tenth and last German film, *Damals* (Back Then), is relayed in flashbacks and tells of a passionate love, a fragile marriage, and a suspicion of murder. During the filming, she learned that UFA would no longer honor the clause in her contract requiring that 53% of her salary be transferred to her Swedish bank account. Leander then went on strike, refusing to participate in the film until the matter was resolved in her favor. Goebbels took this as a personal challenge, and he unsuccessfully tried to persuade her to accept a new arrangement, namely becoming a German citizen and exchanging her estates in Sweden for a manor and estate in East Prussia. The film had barely been completed when an Allied bombing raid brought ruin to Leander's Berlin villa. While it burned, she managed to throw her wardrobe to passersby on the street. *Damals* premiered in March 1943, and she made a few song recordings, but six weeks later Zarah Leander flew home to Sweden, never to return to Nazi Germany.

She received a cool welcome in her homeland. Many Swedes felt only hostility toward a performer they believed had given prestige to an inhuman regime, while enriching herself in the process. She ignored these reactions. Leander divorced her second husband and focused her energies on making profitable a fish cannery into which she had invested much of her fortune. In Nazi Germany, where she had been a superstar for half a decade, she was now *persona non grata.* Goebbels and the UFA executives who had earlier ignored Leander's professed indifference to politics and her hosting of parties which included many friends and acquaintances who were gay, now mounted a press attack on her. The Nazi media exposed her to be a "friend of the Jews," and it was reported that she had given an interview with the Swedish newspaper *Ny Dag* in which she acknowledged being friendly with Jews. She had also responded to a question about whether of not she might sing anti-German songs in her new revue by suggesting that this was entirely up to the director to decide. Despite these attacks, her songs continued to be broadcast by German radio stations, and her films were still being screened in many locations in the Reich. The SS even noted in one of its confidential intelligence reports that jokes were circulating among the German population in which Zarah Leander, after having been summoned to an engagement at the Führer's military headquarters, is requested to sing one of the hit songs from *Die grosse Liebe,* namely "I Know That a Miracle Will Happen Someday."

After several years of virtual internal exile on her rural Swedish estate, Leander reemerged to continue her career. At first she failed to gain entry into the postwar Austrian and Swiss film world, but by February 1949 she was again in Germany, on a concert tour of the Western occupation zones of that defeated nation. Although no longer youthful, she made appearances in a number of West German films throughout the 1950s, including *Cuba Cubana* (1952), *Ave Maria* (1953), *Bei Dir war es immer so schön* (It Was Always So Nice With You, 1954), and *Der blaue Nachtfalter* (The Blue Moth, 1959).

In September 1958, she began a successful run at Vienna's Raimund-Theater in Peter Kreuder's musical *Madame Scandaleuse,* a show that also pleased audiences in Berlin, Hamburg, and Munich. In 1964, she returned to Vienna to star in another Kreuder musical, *Lady aus Paris* (The Lady from Paris), and Leander was still performing at the end of the 1960s in Hamburg in *Wodka für die Königin* (Vodka for the Queen). She performed in musical comedies in Berlin during these years and even ventured into a joint Italian-German production. Leander also appeared in the new medium of television, including on the show "Star unter Sternen" (A Star under the Stars), and was featured on the program "TV Hören und Sehen" which screened a series on her life on the occasion of her 65th birthday in 1972.

In her final decades, Zarah Leander became the most important icon of Germany's gay community, a status she would hold even in the years after her death in Stockholm on June 23, 1981. The unusual nature of her voice, described by German filmmaker *Helma Sanders-Brahms as a "hermaphroditic voice, half man, half woman," was remarked on by other observers for its powerfully seductive aspects which were revealed as she sang erotic songs in the baritone range. The audiences who came to see her in the last years of her career were primarily comprised of gay males who forgave the aging star for her appearance; even with the prodigious help of wigs, jewelry and makeup, she could no longer disguise the ravages of time. During these years (she appeared on stage as late as 1978), she often performed at transvestite balls ("Tuntenbälle") such as the "Ball der Freunde" (The Friends' Ball) at the gay Club 70. At a time in West Germany when Paragraph 175 of the Criminal Code continued to stigmatize homosexuality, Leander's concerts were one of the few places where gay men could meet openly without fear of being arrested.

In the history of cinema, Zarah Leander was and will always remain a National Socialist star. A talented and ambitious artist, she took full advantage of the golden opportunity that opened up for her and other relatively unknown performers in Germany during the 1930s with the emigration of German superstars. Although she claimed to have no interest in politics, Leander's actions revealed an acute awareness of how Nazi Germany was ruled, and she successfully curried favor with some of the most powerful figures in that society. As a consequence, she was able to reap rich rewards from these arrangements, persuading herself (and others) that she had somehow remained separate from and free of their malignant power. Both during and after World War II, she held on to the belief that she had never played a role in the hideous nature of the Third Reich. Her memoirs indicate little if any introspection on these matters.

SOURCES:

Ascheid, Antje. "A Sierckian Double Image: The Narration of Zarah Leander as a National Socialist Star," in *Film Criticism*. Vol. 23, no. 2–3. Winter–Spring 1999, pp. 46–73.

Ascheid, Antje Ingrid. "Hitler's Heroines? Stardom, Womanhood and the Popular in Nazi Cinema," Ph.D. dissertation, New York University, 1999.

Currid, Brian Patrick. "The Acoustics of National Publicity: Music in German Mass Culture," Ph.D. dissertation, University of Chicago, 1998.

Koepnick, Lutz. "En-gendering Mass Culture: The Case of Zarah Leander," in Patricia Herminghouse and Magda Mueller, eds., *Gender and Germanness: Cultural Productions of Nation.* Providence, RI: Berghahn Publishers, 1997, pp. 161–175.

Kreimeier, Klaus. *The Ufa Story: A History of Germany's Greatest Film Company 1918–1945.* NY: Hill and Wang, 1996.

Kuzniar, Alice A. "Zarah Leander and Transgender Specularity," in *Film Criticism*. Vol. 23, no. 2–3. Winter–Spring 1999, pp. 74–93.

Leander, Zarah. *Es war so wunderbar! Mein Leben.* Translated by Anna-Liese Kornitzky. Hamburg: Hoffmann und Campe Verlag, 1983.

———. *So bin ich und so bleibe ich.* Gütersloh: Bertelsmann Lesering, 1958.

"Die Nazis und die Schauspieler," in *Theater heute.* No. 9, 1989, special issue.

Papen, Manuela von. "Opportunities and Limitations: The New Woman in Third Reich Cinema," in *Women's History Review.* Vol. 8, no. 4, 1999, pp. 693–728.

Rentschler, Eric. *The Ministry of Illusion: Nazi Cinema and Its Afterlife.* Cambridge, MA and London: Harvard University Press, 1996.

Romani, Cinza. *Tainted Goddesses: Female Film Stars of the Third Reich.* Translated by Robert Connolly. NY: Sarpedon, 1992.

Sanders, Ulrike. *Zarah Leander: Kann denn Schlager Sünde sein?* Cologne: Pahl-Rugenstein Verlag, 1988.

Schulte-Sasse, Linda. *Entertaining the Third Reich: Illusions of Wholeness in Nazi Cinema.* Durham, NC: Duke University Press, 1996.

Seiler, Paul. *Ein Mythos lebt: Zarah Leander.* Berlin: Graphische Werkstätten, 1991.

———. *Zarah Leander: Ein Kultbuch.* Reinbek bei Hamburg: Rowohlt Verlag, 1985.

———. *Zarah Leander: Ich bin eine Stimme.* Berlin: Ullstein Verlag, 1997.

Wistrich, Robert. *Who's Who in Nazi Germany.* London and NY: Routledge, 1995.

Zumkeller, Cornelia. *Zarah Leander: Ihre Filme, ihr Leben.* Munich: W. Heyne Verlag, 1988.

RELATED MEDIA:

Blackwood, Christian. *My Life for Zarah Leander (Mein Leben für Zarah Leander,* video), Christian Blackwood Productions, Bayerischer Rundfunk, 1987.

Cabaret's Golden Age, Vol. I, Flapper-Pavillion CD 9727, released 1991.

John Haag,
Associate Professor of History,
University of Georgia, Athens, Georgia

Lear, Evelyn (1926—)

American soprano. Name variations: Mrs. Thomas Stewart. Born Evelyn Shulman on January 8, 1926, in Brooklyn, New York; daughter of Nathan Shulman and Anna (Kwartin) Shulman; studied with John Yard, Sergius Kagen, and *Maria Ivogün; attended New York University, 1944–45; attended Hunter College, 1946–48; attended Juilliard School of Music, 1953–54; attended Hochschule für Musik, Berlin, Germany, 1957–59; married Dr. Walter Lear, in 1943; married Thomas Stewart (a baritone), on January 8, 1955; children: (first marriage) two daughters, Jan and Bonni.

Made debut in Berlin (1957), Salzburg (1962–64), Covent Garden (1965), Teatro Colon (1965), Metropolitan Opera (1967); received honorary title of Kammersaengerin, Senate of Berlin (1964); won Grammy award for role of Marie in Wozzeck *(1965); retired (1985).*

Evelyn Lear was born Evelyn Shulman in Brooklyn, New York, in 1926. A musician as well as a singer, she played the piano and perhaps learned her incredible breath control from playing the French horn. This ability made it possible for her to take on a wide range of roles from Mozart to Strauss. As a member of the West Berlin Opera ensemble, Lear made 33 recordings. She also appeared in Robert Altman's film *Buffalo Bill and the Indians* with Paul Newman, Joel Grey, and Burt Lancaster. Evelyn Lear was one of the few singers to have performed Sophie, Octavian, and the Marshallin in *Der Rosenkavalier,* Despina and Fiodiligi in *Cosi fan tutte,* and Cherubino and the Countess in *Figaro.* She also gave many performances of lieder until her retirement in 1985.

John Haag,
Athens, Georgia

Lear, Frances (1923–1996)

American magazine editor and feminist who founded Lear's *magazine "for the woman who wasn't born yes-*

terday." Born on July 14, 1923, in Hudson, New York; died on September 30, 1996, in New York City; adopted daughter of Herbert Adam Loeb (a businessman) and Aline (Friedman) Loeb; briefly attended Sarah Lawrence College, Bronxville, New York; married Norman Lear (a television producer), on December 7, 1956; children: two daughters, **Kate Lear**; **Maggie Lear**.

In the early 1960s, Frances Lear was an unquestioning, full-time housewife and mother when she read *Betty Friedan's groundbreaking treatise *The Feminine Mystique* which served as the catalyst for the modern women's movement. Lear became an ardent women's rights activist, working in the political arena with the National Organization for Women (NOW) and as a partner in one of the first executive-search firms dedicated to the placement of women. In 1988, after receiving an unprecedented divorce settlement from her husband of 30 years, television producer Norman Lear, Frances used a portion of the money to launch *Lear's,* the first mass-circulated magazine dedicated to women over 40. She would remain editor-in-chief of the magazine until it ceased publication in 1994, the same year she began a two-year battle with breast cancer.

Frances Lear was born in 1923 at the Vanderheusen Home for Wayward Girls in Hudson, New York, the daughter of an unwed mother and an unknown father. She spent the first 14 months of her life in an orphanage until she was adopted by Herbert and **Aline Loeb** of Larchmont, New York, who also changed her name from Evelyn to Frances. When she was 11, her adoptive father committed suicide after his clothing business fell victim to the Great Depression. Her adoptive mother, who remarried, died seven years later. Frances was educated in a series of boarding schools and briefly attended Sarah Lawrence College, but she dropped out at the age of 17 to head for New York City. For the next 15 years, she held a series of jobs in retailing and advertising; she also married and divorced twice. In those days, she said, you had to get married in order to sleep with a man.

At 33, Frances met and married Norman Lear, then a successful comedy writer, newly divorced. The couple settled in Encino, California, and while Norman and Bud Yorkin launched the sitcom "All in the Family," Frances took care of the couple's two daughters, Kate and Maggie. (Norman also had a daughter, **Ellen Lear**, from his previous marriage.) "I sewed and crocheted and gardened and wallpapered and cooked gourmet meals," she told **Dinah Prince** in an interview for *New York* magazine (December 15, 1986). "I loved being a mother." When Lear read Friedan's book, her initial reaction was one of anger; she interpreted it as a put-down of all the traditional values she held dear. Then she realized that, in actuality, Friedan was only prodding her to seek the recognition and sovereignty that she—and all women—deserved.

Lear worked with missionary zeal. In 1968, she joined the presidential campaign of Eugene McCarthy and also served as the national talent coordinator for the Democratic Party. She was active in the National Organization for Women and demonstrated with her husband for the passage of the Equal Rights Amendment (ERA). The Lears also used their new home in Brentwood to host fund-raising events for progressive political causes. In 1972, Frances founded Lear Purvis Walker & Company, a first-of-its-kind executive-search firm specializing in the placement of women. For several years, she chaired the Women's Lobby, a Washington-based feminist organization, and in 1976, she served a term on the advisory board of the National Women's Political Caucus. She also promoted the cause in print, contributing articles to *Newsweek*, *Vogue*, *Ms.*, and the *Harvard Business Review*.

Frances Lear

By the 1970s, Norman and Bud Yorkin's successful television shows—"All in the Family," "The Jeffersons," and "Maude" (whose title character, played by **Bea Arthur**, was thought to have been based on Frances)—had made Norman a multi-millionaire and a celebrity. Frances began to suffer a loss of identity that worsened during the 1980s when Norman founded his own civil-liberties group, People for the American Way, thus becoming more deeply involved in an area she had staked out as her own. In 1981, she vented her frustration in a piece for *The New York Times*, writing that in Hollywood "a woman is a nonperson unless she is under twenty-one, powerful, or a star. . . . Unless she is nailed to her husband, an industry wife is looked *through*, never at." Frances later explained her creeping sense of worthlessness to Prince: "I had very little self-esteem. I was depressed often. I tried very hard to be involved in things that brought me pleasure. But it wasn't enough. . . . Emotionally, I was a nonperson."

In her search to boost her self-confidence and to find a new "area of mastery," Lear first left her husband, moving to their duplex in Manhattan's posh Ritz Tower. When they subsequently divorced in 1986, she walked away with a settlement estimated at between $100 and $112 million, then the largest ever recorded. "I was very much a part of his thinking," she said. "Norman could not have done his shows without me." Lear next sought a new outlet for self-expression, a quest that was finally realized in her magazine *Lear's*. Conceived for the middle-aged woman, who in the past had been ignored in favor of her more youthful counterpart, the magazine was Lear's attempt to raise the self-esteem of women just like her. "I wanted to focus attention on this woman as something other than what she was perceived to be," she said in an interview for *Advertising Age* (October 23, 1989). "She was not this menopausal, depressed, empty-nested person whose life was finished."

Ignoring the naysayers who doubted she could pull it off, Lear invested $25 million in her new project and hired savvy professionals to bring her concept into reality. But despite her access to expertise, her inexperience proved to be a stumbling block, both during the two-and-a-half year period it took to get the magazine off the ground, and throughout the six years it was in publication. There were complaints about her inability to make crucial decisions in a timely fashion, her need to have total control over editorial policy, and her volatility. "She blew sometimes like a gale through a broken window," said Nelson Aldrich, one of a succession of editors at *Lear's*. "She could also be incredibly smart and inspiring," commented **Caroline Miller**, who would serve as the magazine's editor in its final days.

Lear blamed her unpredictable management style on manic depression, a disorder she battled off and on for years. "My illness makes me more volatile than other heads of companies," she told *Fortune* magazine in 1989. In her 1992 autobiography, *The Second Seduction*, Lear also revealed that she had battled alcoholism, addiction to prescription drugs, and had tried on at least three occasions to end her life. Writing that the odds were stacked against her from the beginning, Lear claimed that her adoptive mother only tolerated her to please her adoptive father, and that her stepfather had molested her from the age of 12.

Lear's sold out its first issue, which hit the newsstands on February 23, 1988, with an unprecedented number of ad pages and a circulation base of 250,000. After a year as a bimonthly, it went monthly with its first anniversary issue, featuring Lear on the cover. A typical issue contained articles on politics, finances, and automobiles, along with celebrity profiles and health and style reports. In the fashion spreads, Lear used older models, adhering to her theory that beauty endured well beyond the middle years. After two years, however, Lear abandoned her original concept and lowered the magazine's target age to 35, putting it in competition with standard women's magazines. Advertising revenues suffered as a result. When the magazine ceased publication in March 1994, it had a circulation of 500,000, but had lost an estimated $25 to $30 million during its six-year run.

Lear never spoke badly of her ex-husband, or revealed the details of their divorce. "I still love him," she confided to **Liz Smith** in 1992. "I don't want to go into detail on someone I care about." Norman was like-minded. "She had flamboyance and flair and a taste for elegance rare in this world," he said when Frances Lear died of breast cancer in September 1996. "She was an original from the day we met until the day the world said goodbye to her."

SOURCES:

Lipton, Michael. "Queen Lear," in *People*. October 14, 1996, pp. 101–102.

Moritz, Charles, ed. *Current Biography*. NY: H.W. Wilson, 1991.

Nemy, Enid. "Obituary," in *The Day* [New London, CT]. October 2, 1996.

Barbara Morgan,
Melrose, Massachusetts

Lease, Mary Elizabeth (1853–1933)

American Populist orator and politician whose fiery appeals for Kansas farmers to protest their economic condition made her a national figure during the early 1890s. Name variations: Mary Ellen Lease. Born Mary Elizabeth Clyens on September 11, 1853, in Ridgeway, Elk County, Pennsylvania; died in Callicoon, New York, on October 29, 1933; daughter of Joseph P. Clyens (a farmer of Irish descent) and Mary Elizabeth Murray Clyens; attended local schools in New York State and graduated from St. Elizabeth's Academy in Allegany, New York; married Charles L. Lease (a pharmacist), in January 1873 (divorced 1902); children: four.

Moved to Kansas to teach school at an Indian mission (1870); lived in Texas for a decade after marriage; admitted to the bar in Kansas (1885); became a candidate for local offices for the Union Labor Party (1888); identified with the People's Party (1890); campaigned for the Populist presidential ticket (1892); appointed to Kansas State Board of Charities (1893) but was removed from office the same year; moved to the East by 1896 and campaigned for William Jennings Bryan, the presidential candidate of the Democrats and the Populists; supported William McKinley and the Republicans (1900); pursued career as a lecturer; endorsed Theodore Roosevelt and the Progressive Party (1912); spent the last years of her life in obscurity.

Selected publications: The Problem of Civilization Solved *(1895).*

Mary Elizabeth Lease is famous in American history for a single sentence. During the 1890 election in Kansas, Lease reportedly told an audience of farmers that they should "raise less corn and wheat, and more hell." The phrase, quickly shortened to "less corn and more hell," came to symbolize the passion of the farm discontent that swept across the Great Plains and the South of the United States during the first half of the 1890s. Whether or not Lease actually made the celebrated statement is in dispute. This question represents one of the many ironies that surrounded her life.

She was born in Pennsylvania on September 11, 1853, to Roman Catholic parents of Irish background. Later in life, she would allow reporters to believe that she had been born in Ireland and had there acquired her devotion to Irish freedom from British rule. Her family moved to a farm in Allegany County, New York, where she went to nearby schools before graduating from St. Elizabeth's Academy in Allegany. Her father served in the Union army during the Civil War and reportedly died in a Confederate prison camp. She traveled to Kansas in 1870 to teach in the parochial school on the Osage Mission, located in the southeastern part of the state. There, in January 1873, she married a pharmacist named Charles L. Lease; the marriage took her outside the church of her youth. ***Annie LePorte Diggs**, another prominent woman in the Populist movement, said later that Mary Lease was "not over-weighted with reverence for the clergy of any sect."

During the next decade, the Lease family spent most of their time in Texas. Mary Elizabeth gave birth to four children, and studied law, despite the demanding rigors of rural life. According to Gene Clanton, she pinned sheets of notes above her wash tub to study while she scrubbed the laundry that she took in for half a dollar a day. When the Leases returned to Kansas in the mid-1890s, she was admitted to the Kansas bar, a notable achievement at a time when the state had few women attorneys.

Soon, she stepped into the world of politics. In a lecture on "Ireland and the Irishmen," Lease spoke out for the cause of the Irish people and their desire to be free of British dominance. She also gave speeches about woman suffrage and the temperance crusade against alcohol and saloons. Until this time, she had identified with the Republican Party because of its record in the Civil War; by 1888, however, she had joined the Union Labor Party, a small and struggling third party in Kansas. She addressed the state convention of the Union Laborites in Wichita in 1888, and sought to win election to county offices as one of the party's candidates that year and again in 1889.

In 1890, hard times, low crop prices for Kansas farmers, and growing unhappiness with the performance of the Republicans and the Democrats led many farmers to embrace the new People's Party in the state. Mary Elizabeth Lease became one of the most popular campaign speakers for the new organization. She plunged into a summer and fall of stump speaking that involved thousands of angry voters in a turbulent process that shook the Kansas political establishment.

All observers agreed that Lease was a compelling orator, whatever their opinion about her political views. Unfortunately, few of her speeches in 1890 were printed in Kansas newspapers. What remains are the assessments of her style by those who heard her speak. Republican editor William Allen White of Emporia recalled her speaking manner in his autobiography: She had "a golden voice—deep, rich contralto, a singing voice that had hypnotic qualities." In 1891, a reporter for the *Kansas City Star* captured a few of her words: "The great and common people of this country are slaves, and monopoly is master," she said. "The West and South are prostrate before the manufacturing East."

In 1890, she reportedly uttered her famous phrase about corn and hell. In later life, she denied having made the remark, and charged that critics in the press had created it to embarrass her. Even so, she did not dispute the comment at the time because, she decided, "it was a right good bit of advice." Clanton uncovered references to the remark in Kansas newspapers in 1891, but whether it originated with her or with her Republican enemies may never be known. Her opponents also claimed that her real name was "Mary Ellen Lease" so that they could transform her into "Mary Yellin' Lease."

And now I say to you as my final admonition, not knowing that I shall meet you again, raise less corn and wheat, and more hell.

—Attributed to Mary Elizabeth Lease

Populist success in the 1890 Kansas elections added to the fame that Lease had acquired. She became identified with ending the long political career of three-term Republican senator John James Ingalls, whom she had criticized for his record during the Civil War. She alleged, according to Clanton, that Ingalls "never smelled gunpowder in all his cowardly life. His war record is confined to court marshaling a chicken thief." During 1891, she toured the South as one of a number of Kansas Populists who sought to build support for their third party in Dixie.

When the Populists nominated James B. Weaver to run for president in 1892, he campaigned in the South with Lease at his side, calling her "Our Queen Mary." Her reception in the South, however, was anything but friendly. "The sight of a woman traveling around the country making political speeches," said one Democratic editor, was "simply disgusting." Another commentator focused on her looks. "She's got a face that's harder and sharper than a butcher's cleaver. I could take her by the heels and split an inch board with it. She's got a nose like an anteater, a voice like a cat fight, and a face that is rank poison to the naked eye." Annie Diggs observed correctly: "Seldom, if ever, was a woman so vilified and so misrepresented by malignant newspaper attacks." Diggs described her col-

league's appearance as "tall and stately in bearing" with "black hair, fair complexion, and blue eyes—and blue eyes that seem to feel the weight and woe of all the world."

Weaver did not win the White House in 1892, but the Populist Party did gain the governorship in Kansas for its state candidate, Lorenzo D. Lewelling. When he took office, Lewelling recognized what Mary Lease had done for the party and appointed her to chair the state's board of charities. The new governor expected his appointee to name people that he favored to the various patronage positions under her control. Since the People's Party was now cooperating with the Democrats against the Republicans, Lewelling's policy meant that Lease would see some Democrats placed in these patronage positions.

But for Lease, favors to Democrats involved bitter personal feelings. In addition to her father's death in a Confederate prison, two brothers had died while they served in the Union army during the Civil War. Like many in the North, she believed that the Democratic Party had prolonged the war because of its opposition to vigorous prosecution of the conflict and its sympathy for the Southern cause. Thus, she blamed the Democrats for the deaths of her male relatives and the poverty that her family confronted because of these losses. She opposed Lewelling on the issue of Democratic appointments, and political tension between them grew. Finally, in late December 1893, the governor removed her from the state board of charities.

A public controversy ensued. Populists charged that Lease was working with the Republican Party against her former allies. Lease replied that the governor and his associates were trying to kill her politically. The governor's attempt to remove her failed when the state's Supreme Court decided that she had not been given adequate reasons and fair notice. The furor contributed to the defeat that the Kansas Populists experienced in the 1894 state elections.

During the mid-1890s, Lease left Kansas for New York. There, she published her only book, *The Problem of Civilization Solved* (1895), in which she advocated colonization of the tropics as a cure for the ills of civilization. The book did not attract a large audience. By this time, Lease had also renounced her earlier endorsements of prohibition and woman suffrage.

Despite her problems with Kansas Populism, she was active on behalf of the national party during the presidential election of 1896. Lease was a very visible presence at the Populist national convention at St. Louis in July, and she made one of the seconding speeches for the presidential candidacy of William Jennings Bryan. During the fall campaign, she spoke publicly for Bryan, the nominee of the Democrats and the Populists, in her characteristically controversial style. In one address in New York, reported in *The New York Times* of September 5, 1896, she said of Queen *Victoria of England that she was "no longer regarded as made of common clay, but of common mud."

After 1896, however, Lease's allegiance to Populism ended, and she announced, "I am a full-fledged Socialist." But by the time William Jennings Bryan was preparing to run against the reelection of Republican president William McKinley in 1900, she had become "an advocate of Expansion and the progressive policy of Republicanism," by which she presumably meant that empire which the United States had acquired as a result of the war with Spain in 1898. She offered her speaking services to Joseph L. Bristow of the Post Office Department in a letter of June 9, 1900. She called herself someone who could conduct "active political work for the success of Republicanism and the downfall of Democracy." She guaranteed "that the dissatisfied with whom I may have an opportunity to labor will not vote for Bryan." The Republicans put her to work, and she campaigned for the Republican ticket in Nebraska and Kansas. "As the daughter of an old Union soldier," she said, "I feel that my place is with the Republican Party."

During the early 20th century, Lease continued to make a living as a touring lecturer for various causes. She filed for divorce from her husband in 1901, and the decree was granted in 1902, on the grounds of non-support. In 1908, she became a lecturer with the New York Board of Education. She supported Theodore Roosevelt and the Progressive Party in 1912. Once again, she returned to the role of third-party critic of the Democrats and the Republicans. The Democrats, she said in New York City, were "a stench in the nostrils of heaven" while the Republicans were "the slave of the money power."

Her services to the Roosevelt campaign were apparently offered on a paying basis, since she was complaining to the Progressive Party headquarters in May 1913 that she had not received her money. She reminded the Progressive leadership in a letter to F.H. Hotchkiss of May 12, 1913, that she "performed faithfully, capably and efficiently at a cost of tremendous physical and mental effort as the meetings were held in the open and necessitated great expenditure of strength in order to reach the throng." When the party protested that she had "donated" her services, she threatened to file a lawsuit in a follow-up letter of May 23, 1913. Both letters are now included in the papers of Theodore Roosevelt at the Library of Congress. The financial plight of the Progressive organization in 1913 makes it unlikely that she ever received any payment for what she did in 1912. Lease spent the last years of her life in seclusion. She gave occasional interviews up to 1918 and then dropped out of sight until her death.

SOURCES:

Clanton, Gene. "Intolerant Populist: The Disaffection of Mary Elizabeth Lease," in *Kansas Historical Quarterly*. Vol. 34, 1968, pp. 189–200.

———. *Kansas Populism: Ideas and Men.* Lawrence: University Press of Kansas, 1968.

———. *Populism: The Humane Preference in America.* Boston, MA: Twayne, 1991.

Diggs, Annie L. "The Women in the Alliance Movement," in *The Arena*. Vol. 6. July 1892, pp. 161–179.

"Mary Lease Dead; Long Dry Agitator," in *The New York Times*. October 30, 1933.

Mary Elizabeth Lease

SUGGESTED READING:

Hicks, John D. *The Populist Revolt*. Lincoln, NE: University of Nebraska Press, 1961.

COLLECTIONS:

Joseph Little Bristow Papers, Kansas State Historical Society, Topeka.

Mary E. Lease, Manuscript Biography, probably written by her, Kansas State Historical Society, Topeka.

Theodore Roosevelt Papers, Manuscript Division, Library of Congress, Washington, D.C.

Lewis L. Gould,
Eugene C. Barker Centennial Professor
in American History, University of Texas at Austin

Leavitt, Henrietta Swan

(1868–1921)

American astronomer who established a standard by which to chart the magnitude of the stars and discovered the period-luminosity of Cepheid variable stars during her 26-year career. Born on July 4, 1868, in Lancaster, Massachusetts; died on December 12, 1921, in Cambridge, Massachusetts; daughter of Reverend George Roswell Leavitt and Henrietta S. (Kendrick) Leavitt; educated at Cambridge public schools and Oberlin College; graduated from the Society for the Collegiate Instruction of Women (later Radcliffe College), 1892; never married; no children.

One of seven children of Congregationalist minister Reverend George Roswell Leavitt and **Henrietta Kendrick Leavitt**, Henrietta Swan Leavitt was born on July 4, 1868, and grew up primarily in Cambridge, Massachusetts. Although she was almost completely deaf, she did not allow that fact to interfere with her education and career. When she was 17, her family moved to Cleveland, Ohio, where she attended Oberlin College from 1886 to 1888, originally studying music. She transferred to the Society for the Collegiate Instruction of Women (also known as the "Harvard Annex," later Radcliffe College) in 1888; a senior-year course in astronomy so interested her that she enrolled in another after graduating in 1892. After spending some time traveling, Leavitt volunteered at the Harvard Observatory in 1895.

At first working as an assistant in the examination of variable stars (stars which become brighter or dimmer in a regular or irregular pattern over a period of time), Leavitt was made a permanent member of the observatory staff, which also included *Annie Jump Cannon and *Williamina Paton Fleming, in 1902. She was soon promoted by Edward C. Pickering, the head of the observatory and an important advocate for women in astronomy, to chief of the photographic photometry department. The use of photographs in astronomy, rather than sketches made at the telescope, had begun in the late 19th century, as photographic technology itself progressed; by the early years of the 20th century, it was recognized that photographic plates can detect wave lengths the human eye cannot, and thus they became invaluable to the science. Photometry is the measurement of the intensity of light, which in astronomy is used to assess the magnitude of stars. In 1907, Pickering instituted a major program to overhaul previous (naked eye) calculations of star magnitudes, beginning with the creation of a basic sequence of magnitudes, photographically determined, against which other stars could be measured. Leavitt was named to devise this basic sequence.

The result of her work, a standard of brightness known as the "North Pole Sequence," was achieved through her observation of a group of stars near the North Pole. Leavitt started by observing and determining the magnitudes of 46 stars, then used those magnitudes to analyze a much larger portion of the surrounding sky, eventually determining brightness down to the 21st magnitude. Her initial research involved studying over 300 photographic plates taken from 13 different telescopes; the standards were published in 1912 and 1917, and before her death she had fully sequenced 108 areas of the sky. In 1913, the International Committee on Photographic Magnitudes adopted Leavitt's system as the standard for their project, known as the Astrographic Map of the Sky, to catalog the position of the stars; her system was also used by J.C. Kapteyn in his statistical studies of star distribution.

Her most important work, however, took place in 1912, with her discovery of the period-luminosity relation of Cepheid variable stars. Cepheids are a type of variable star with a rigidly regular pattern of brightness and dimness (pulsation); Leavitt discovered that the length of the pulsation of a star is an indication of its luminosity. This knowledge was later expanded by astronomers such as Edwin Hubble (who would discover Cepheid variables outside this galaxy in 1923) and used to measure the distances between the Earth and distant stars and galaxies.

In 26 years of research, Leavitt discovered four novas (a faint star which suddenly increases in brightness by 10,000 or more times) and about 2,400 variable stars, which made up more than half of those known until 1930. Of the stars she discovered, 1,700 were found while studying photographs of the Magellanic Clouds (known now to be nearby galaxies of stars). She was also the first to notice that the fainter stars in a sequence were generally redder than the brighter stars, which brought up the question of whether they were genuinely redder or only appeared so because of particles in the atmosphere (a distinction now determined through photoelectrical technology). Henrietta Leavitt worked at the Harvard Observatory until her death from cancer on December 12, 1921, at the age of 52.

SOURCES:

Bailey, Brooke. *The Remarkable Lives of 100 Women Healers and Scientists.* Holbrook, MA: Bob Adams, 1994.

James, Edward T., ed. *Notable American Women, 1607–1950.* Cambridge, MA: The Belknap Press of Harvard University Press, 1971.

McHenry, Robert, ed. *Famous American Women.* NY: Dover, 1983.

Karina L. Kerr, M.A.,
Ypsilanti, Michigan

Lebedeva, Sarra (1892–1967)

Russian and Soviet sculptor. Born Sarra Dmitrievna Darmolatova on December 23, 1892, in St. Petersburg, Russia; died in Moscow on March 7, 1967; married Vladimir Vasilevich Lebedev.

Visited Paris, Berlin, and Italy in the years before World War I; lived in Moscow (1925–67); was a member of USSR Academy of Arts.

The sculptor Sarra Lebedeva produced art that was ideologically correct by Soviet standards of her day and a number of works that transcend time and place and continue to speak to contemporary audiences. During 1892 in St. Petersburg, Sarra Dmitrievna Darmolatova was born into a prosperous family of the intelligentsia. Educated at home by private tutors until she was 14, she then attended classes at the School for the Encouragement of the Arts and also traveled widely with her family. In Italy, she was impressed by the masterpieces of Renaissance sculptors, particularly Donatello. Although she initially studied painting and drawing at Mikhail Bernshtein's school in St. Petersburg, two years later she switched to a study of sculpting, joining the school of the well-known sculptor Leonid Shervud (1871–1954). In 1915, she married graphic artist Vladimir Lebedev, and it was through studying the books in his extensive library that she first became acquainted with the then-revolutionary art of Bracque, Matisse, and Picasso.

In the period after the Bolshevik Revolution of November 1917, Sarra Lebedeva was drawn into the artistic and literary circles that dominated the city of Petrograd (as St. Petersburg was then called). Among the individuals whom she and her husband knew during these years were Alexander Blok, Maxim Gorky, Vladimir Mayakovsky, and Vsevolod Meyerhold. Lebedeva, in common with other Russian artists of the period, found her imagination captured both by the political and aesthetic possibilities of the revolution. In 1918, she responded enthusiastically to Vladimir Lenin's Decree on Monumental Propaganda. Having pulled down the massive statues and monuments of the tsarist state, the Soviet dictatorship of the proletariat called on Russia's sculptors to play an active role in creating the physical presence of a new workers' state, above all else by erecting monuments to revolutionary heroes of past and present. Sarra Lebedeva contributed a number of innovative works to this scheme of mass propaganda through art, namely monumental busts of *Danton* and *Alexander Herzen,* as well as a relief depicting *Robespierre.*

Beginning in 1924, when she executed her bust of *Leonid Krassin,* Lebedeva took on the

$\mathcal{S}$arra
$\mathcal{L}$ebedeva

role of sculptor of high officials of the Soviet state. Her portraits of leading Bolsheviks, which included Pavel Dybenko, Semyon Budyonny, and Feliks Edmundovich Dzerzhinsky (chief of the dreaded Cheka [Secret Police]), are by no means always flattering to their subjects, for as art historian Mikhail Alpatov has suggested, "Lebedeva was a sharp-sighted observer, and her observation is sometimes ruthless and ironic." It was through these portraits that she secured her place in the history of Soviet art. To remain a complete artist, she also sculpted and drew nudes, although during the Stalin era the nude was virtually proscribed. Art historian Miuda Yablonskaya has described Lebedeva's nudes as demonstrating "a lyrical and expressive approach to both subject-matter and the medium itself, and are altogether more personal and intimate than the monumental and heroic approach that she adopted for her public commissions." Also worthy of further study by art historians are Lebedeva's figurines in porcelain and faience.

Lebedeva began living in Moscow in 1925. During the next few years, before the full weight of Stalin's dictatorship suffocated most of the creativity in Soviet art, she continued to produce original works of sculpture. She also kept in touch with developments in the West, making trips to Berlin, London, and Paris between 1925 and 1928. In the 1930s, she remained true to much of her artistic vision, producing striking portraits not only of political leaders but also of prominent artists and intellectuals, including the ill-fated Jewish actor Solomon Mikhoels (1939). In 1936, at the start of Stalin's bloody Great Purge, Lebedeva executed a memorable work, the bronze *Girl With a Butterfly* (State Tretyakov Gallery), which Matthew Cullerne Bown has described as "a deeply charming work, a monumental meditation on the sculptor's absolutes of motion and stillness, weightlessness and gravity."

During the suffering of World War II, known to the people of the Soviet Union as the Great Patriotic War, Lebedeva captured in her sculpture the spirit of resolve that enabled her society to prevail over fascism. Particularly powerful is her 1942 *Portrait of Colonel Yusupov* (State Tretyakov Gallery), which was carried out by the artist at the wounded officer's hospital bedside. Another extraordinary work from this period is her *Portrait of Vladimir Tatlin*, which was created in 1943–44 (Russian Museum). Her 1961–63 work in limestone, *Portrait of Boris Leonidovich Pasternak* (State Tretyakov Gallery), depicts the author whose banned novel *Doctor Zhivago* became a cause celebre in both the West and the Soviet Union in the late 1950s. Sarra Lebedeva re-

tained her artistic energies to the end of her life, and died in Moscow on March 7, 1967.

SOURCES:

Bown, Matthew Cullerne. *Art Under Stalin*. NY: Holmes & Meier, 1991.

Milner, John. *A Dictionary of Russian and Soviet Artists 1420–1970*. Woodbridge, Suffolk, UK: Antique Collectors' Club, 1993.

Musee Rodin, Paris. *Trois sculpteurs sovietiques: A.S. Goloubkina, V.I. Moukhina, S.D. Lebedeva*. Paris: Musee Rodin, 1971.

Volkov, Solomon. *St. Petersburg: A Cultural History*. Translated by Antonina W. Bouis. NY: The Free Press, 1995.

Yablonskaya, M.N. *Women Artists of Russia's New Age 1900–1935*. Edited by Anthony Parton. NY: Rizzoli International, 1990.

John Haag,
Associate Professor of History,
University of Georgia, Athens, Georgia

Leblanc, Georgette (c. 1875–1941).

See Anderson, Margaret Carolyn for sidebar.

Le Blond, Elizabeth (1861–1934)

English mountaineer who was one of the first women to climb without a guide. Name variations: Mrs. Main; Mrs. Aubrey Le Blond. Born Elizabeth Hawkins-Whitshed in 1861; died in 1934; grew up in Ireland; married Fred Burnaby (a soldier who died in 1882); married a man named Main (died); married Aubrey Le Blond.

Widowed at 21, Elizabeth Le Blond began mountain climbing for consolation and made some notable first ascents in Chamonix and in the Engadine. She was also the first president of the Ladies' Alpine Club in 1907 and was elected for a second term in 1932. In 1900, she and Lady **Evelyn McDonnell** dispensed with the services of guides and climbed Piz Palu, a feat, said mountaineer *Dorothy Pilley, that was "hushed up and regarded as somewhat improper."

Lebron, Lolita (1920—)

Puerto Rican nationalist and terrorist. Born in 1920 in Puerto Rico; children: two.

On March 1, 1954, Lolita Lebron, a 34-year-old Puerto Rican seamstress, nationalist, and mother of two, led three men into the gallery of the U.S. House of Representatives, unfurled a Puerto Rican flag, and yelled "Viva Puerto Rico!" While members of the House looked up in surprise, Lebron dropped the flag, produced a Luger, and fired randomly into the assembly, as did her three companions (later identified as Irving Flores Rodriguez, Rafael Cancel Miranda, and Andres Figueroa Cordero). Although most of the representatives were able to scramble for cover, five were wounded, the most seriously being Alvin M. Bentley of Michigan, who sustained puncture wounds to his lungs and diaphragm. All would recover from their injuries.

Only minutes after the shooting, the terrorists were captured and placed under arrest. Lebron and her companions were sentenced to 75-year prison terms. For the next 25 years, some in the Hispanic community considered Lebron a political prisoner and freedom fighter. A Spanish colony until it was ceded to the United States at the end of the Spanish-American War (1898), Puerto Rico has been a self-governing commonwealth since 1952. A separatist movement against what is perceived as U.S. colonialist control of the Puerto Rican nation, which is what Lebron and her associates were protesting with their weapons, exists with little popular support. (Oscar Collazo and Griserio Torresola had also been acting in the name of the Puerto Rican independence movement when they staged an armed attack on Blair House in 1950, attempting to assassinate President Harry Truman at his temporary residence. Torresola was killed, and Collazo was wounded, tried, and sentenced to death. His sentence was later changed to life in prison.)

Puerto Rican voters rejected a referendum for independence in 1967, choosing to retain the island's commonwealth status. In September 1979, President Jimmy Carter, reacting to pressure from Puerto Rican minority groups, commuted the sentences of Lebron and the others, including Collazo, and freed them. (Cordero had been released years earlier because of terminal cancer.) Upon release, Cancel Miranda, who had mellowed over the years, said he was still a nationalist but "would rather hug people than fight them." Lebron, however, told journalists that she was an unrepentant independentista, and that she had no remorse over her actions. She continues to speak at pro-independence rallies in Puerto Rico and in the United States. In 1993, Puerto Rico again held a referendum to choose between U.S. statehood, independence, or the maintenance of commonwealth status. Both independence and statehood were rejected by voters.

Lebrun, Franziska (1756–1791)

German composer, singer, and pianist who performed throughout Europe and whose popular compositions included a set of sonatas published in London in 1780. Name variations: Franziska LeBrun; Francesca LeBrun; Franziska Danzi LeBrun; Franziska Dorothea Danzi. Born Franziska Danzi in Mannheim, Germany, and baptized on March 24, 1756; died on May 14, 1791, in Berlin; daughter of Innocenzo Danzi (a violinist); sister of the noted composer Franz Danzi; sister-in-law of Maria Margarethe Danzi (1768–1800); married Ludwig August Lebrun (1746–1790, an oboist and composer), in 1778; children: Sophie Lebrun Dulcken (b. 1781, a singer and pianist better known as Mme Dulcken); Rosine Lebrun Stenzsch (1785–1855, a singer, pianist, and actress in comedy).

Made debut as Sandrina in Sacchini's La contadina in corte in Schwetzingen (1772); made London debut at King's Theater (1777); sang in inaugural season of La Scala (1778); became leading soprano at Mannheim Court opera and celebrated prima donna throughout Europe; composed two widely published sets of sonatas for piano and violin (1779–81).

Works include: Six sonatas for fortepiano and violin, op. 1 and 2.

A contemporary of Wolfgang Amadeus Mozart, Franziska Lebrun was born Franziska Danzi in 1756 into a musical family living in Mannheim, Germany. Her exact date of birth is unknown, but her baptism is recorded as having taken place on March 24 of that year. Her Italian-born father Innocenzo Danzi was a musician, and her younger brother Franz Danzi was to become a well-known composer. Her daughters **Sophie Lebrun Dulcken** and **Rosine Lebrun** would follow in the family's musical footsteps, as would three of her granddaughters and a great-granddaughter.

The city of Mannheim was celebrated throughout late 18th-century Europe for its musical traditions and the virtuosic quality of its orchestra, of which Franz Danzi was a member. Commentator Charles Burney wrote in 1775 that "there are more solo players, and good composers in this, than perhaps in any other orchestra in Europe."

The young Franziska made her operatic debut on August 9, 1772, at age 16. She sang the role of Sandrina in Sacchini's *La contadina in corte* at the "little theater" in Schwetzingen, the summer residence of the Elector Palatine. Burney, who was present at the performance, described her as "a German girl whose voice and execution are brilliant."

After the success of this debut, Franziska soon became principal soprano and "virtuoso da camera" of the Mannheim court opera, where she created lead roles in Holzbauer's *Günther von Schwarzburg* (1777) and Schweitzer's *Rosamunde* (1780). As well as appearing in Mannheim, she began touring as an opera star. Elector Karl Theodor granted her a year's leave of absence, and she made her London debut as Ariene in Sacchini's *Cresco* at the King's Theater on November 8, 1777. Her first season there included roles in works by J.C. Bach and Tommaso Giordano.

After London, she traveled to Paris to appear at the Concert Spirituel, and then to Milan, where she received the great honor of singing in the first season of the Teatro alla Scala, which opened on August 3, 1778. This invitation may have been brought about by Mattia Verazi, the court poet at Mannheim and librettist for La Scala's inaugural opera, Salieri's *Europa riconosciuta*.

Sometime in 1778, Franziska married Ludwig Lebrun, an accomplished and highly regarded oboist who had played in the Mannheim orchestra since 1764, when he was just 15. Ludwig's father Alexander Lebrun had also been an oboist, enjoying a 23-year tenure in the Mannheim orchestra. Ludwig frequently absented himself from the orchestra in order to accompany Franziska on her professional engagements around Europe. Traveling with her to London, Paris, Vienna and Italy, Ludwig sometimes gave solo concerts and sometimes performed with Franziska; he also composed music for the oboe, and some ballet music for the King's Theater in London, possibly for operas in which Franziska Lebrun, as she was now known, was appearing.

Franziska Lebrun returned to London for the 1779–80 and 1780–81 seasons, adding roles by Sacchini, Bertoni, Grétry and Rauzzini to her repertoire. During this sojourn in London, she began composing, publishing two sets of six keyboard sonatas with violin accompaniment that were later reprinted in several editions in Paris, Offenbach, Mannheim, Berlin, Amsterdam and Worms. In recent years, some of these compositions have been recorded and others have been reprinted in volume XV of the series *Denkmäler der Tonkunst in Bayern*. Lebrun was also a noted teacher, her pupils including Maria Margarethe Marchand (***Maria Margarethe Danzi**), who eventually married her brother.

By 1782, Lebrun was one of the highest paid prima donnas in Europe. The Mannheim court moved to Munich, and in addition to singing there, she continued to tour Europe as an opera star and concert artist. She appeared in Verona and Vienna and spent a year in Naples

(1786–87), returning to Munich for Carnival in 1787, when she performed in Vogler's *Castore e Polluce*. In 1789 and 1790, she traveled to Berlin to appear as a guest artist. While there, her husband died, and Lebrun gave her last performance, in Reichardt's *Brenno*, in 1790. Remaining in Berlin, Franziska Lebrun died there on May 14, 1791. Like Mozart, who would outlive her by only a few months, she was just 35 years old.

Paula Morris, D.Phil.,
Brooklyn, New York

Le Brun, Elisabeth Vigée (1755–1842).
See Vigée-Le Brun, Elisabeth.

Le Brun or Lebrun, Mme. (1755–1842).
See Vigée-Le Brun, Elisabeth.

Lecavella, Mabilia (fl. 1206)
German merchant. Flourished in 1206 in Genoa.

Mabilia Lecavella worked in the business of long-distance trade from her native town of Genoa. Her name is preserved in a contract dated 1206 which she signed with a male trader, Rubaldus Galetta of Genoa. The contract stipulated a partnership between the business owners, in which Mabilia was to import fine linen and canvas from Swabia (southern Germany) and other regions, and arrange for its transport to Genoa. Then Rubaldus would arrange for its shipment to Sicily, where he must have had connections, and see to its sale there for a quarter of her total profits. Such complex business arrangements were not unusual for successful women like Lecavella, who operated their own companies and often traded internationally.

SOURCES:
Anderson, Bonnie S., and Judith P. Zinsser. *A History of Their Own*. Vol. I. NY: Harper & Row, 1988.
Uitz, Erika. *The Legend of Good Women: The Liberation of Women in Medieval Cities*. Wakefield, RI: Moyer Bell, 1988.

Laura York,
Riverside, California

Leclercq, Agnes (1840–1912).
See Salm-Salm, Princess.

Leclercq, Carlotta (c. 1840–1893)
English actress. Born around 1840; died in 1893; sister of *Rose Leclercq (c. 1845–1899).

Carlotta Leclercq appeared as Ariel in *The Tempest*, Nerissa in *Merchant of Venice*, and

Rosalind in *As You Like It*. She also toured England and America with Shakespearean actor Charles Albert Fechter.

Leclercq, Rose (c. 1845–1899)

*English actress. Born around 1845; died in 1899; sister of *Carlotta Leclercq (c. 1840–1893).*

Rose Leclercq was known for her broad style of comedy. She appeared as Mrs. Page in *Merry Wives of Windsor* and the queen in *Tosca*.

Le Clercq, Tanaquil (1929—)

American ballerina. Name variations: LeClercq. Born on October 2, 1929, in Paris, France; only daughter of Jacques Georges Clemenceau Le Clercq (a writer and professor) and Edith (Whittemore) Le Clercq; attended the Lycée Français de New York for three years; taught by private tutors from age 12; studied dance at the King-Coit School in New York; studied with Michael Mordkin; attended the School of American Ballet; married George Balanchine (choreographer and founder of the New York City Ballet), on December 31, 1952 (divorced 1969); no children.

Distinguished by her exquisite technique, her unique style, and her astonishingly long limbs, Tanaquil Le Clercq had a dazzling career with the New York City Ballet from its inception in 1948 until 1956, when a bout with polio put an end to her career and nearly took her life. Considered to be the quintessential Balanchine ballerina, Le Clercq was also the wife of the famous choreographer for 16 years.

The daughter of Austria-born Jacques Le Clercq and Edith Whittemore Le Clercq, Tanaquil was born in Paris in 1929 and named after the legendary *Tanaquil, wife of the Roman ruler Tarquin. Jacques had used the unusual name as a pseudonym when he was a young writer, calling himself Paul Tanaquil. "Tanny," as she was called by her friends, was raised in New York, where her father became a professor of romance languages at Queens College. From the age of four, when her talent for dancing was discovered, her life centered on ballet training. At age seven, she was a student of Michael Mordkin, then considered by many the best teacher in America. At 12, she accepted a scholarship to the School of American Ballet in New York City, where she first met George Balanchine, her future husband. Her initial impression of the famous choreographer was hard-

ly favorable; she saw him as an "old fogy" and a somewhat lackluster teacher. Tanaquil soon warmed to her mentor, however, and under his tutelage refined her technical skills. At 17, she danced her first professional solo role, the lead in the choleric section of *The Four Temperaments*.

By 1948, Le Clercq was a principle dancer with Balanchine's fledgling New York City Ballet, having won acclaim in a number of roles, among them Ariadne in the ballet-cantata *The Triumph of Bacchus and Ariadne*, a collaborative effort of designer Corrado Cagli, composer Vittorio Rieti, and, of course, Balanchine. (Irving Penn created a stunning photograph for *Vogue*, featuring Le Clercq as Ariadne, with the three collaborators seated at her feet.) She also danced in *Bourrée Fantasque*, *Symphony in C*, *Orpheus*, *Afternoon of a Fawn*, and *La Valse*. "What precocious sense of the transience of beauty and gaiety enabled her to dance this role with such infinite delicacy and penetration?" queried critic **Lillian Moore** after seeing her performance in *La Valse*. "Fleet, fragile, touchingly young, incredibly lovely, she brought it a haunting quality which lifted it into the realm of poetry." In England, where Le Clercq performed during a tour in 1948, the London *Daily Mail* called her "a remarkable dancer, particularly with her arms and hands," and went on to compare her "fluttering quality" to that of *Anna Pavlova.

Le Clercq and Balanchine were married on December 31, 1952, shortly after the annulment of his fourth marriage to ballerina *Maria Tallchief. Le Clercq, then 23, had the brightest future of any dancer of her day and was also one of the hardest working, practicing every day, including Sundays, and appearing in two or three ballets six nights a week. She once compared the rigors of dancing to "training a racehorse and being a racehorse at the same time." In October 1956, Le Clercq was touring with the company in Copenhagen when she contracted poliomyelitis. Doctors were barely able to save her life, let alone her career.

The dancer, paralyzed from the waist down, arrived home in a wheelchair, despondent. Balanchine, nearly blaming himself for what had happened, frequently recalled a ballet he had created for Le Clercq years earlier, when she was 15. *Resurgence* was set to music from Mozart and presented at the Waldorf-Astoria Hotel as a benefit for the March of Dimes, a charity devoted to curing polio. The piece took place in a ballet classroom, where students were hard at practice but also rejoicing in their youthful vitality. Into the scene there suddenly appeared a grotesque, black-clad monster—the evil Polio—who reached out and touched one of the girls, who fell paralyzed to the floor. The girl was Tanaquil; the evil Polio was Balanchine. "It was an omen," he said. "It foretold the future." The ballet ended with the girl's miraculous recovery, a "balletic finale," said Balanchine. "Nothing like that ending will happen in Tanny's real life," he sadly added.

Balanchine took a year off from the New York City Ballet to care for his wife. With time, Le Clercq broke out of her depression and in 1962 was able to assist **Patricia McBride** in her preparation for a revival of *La Valse*. She also wrote a book, *Mourka: The Autobiography of a Cat* (1964), about the couple's pampered cat Mourka, who was trained by Balanchine to perform *jetés* and *tours en l'air*. A second book, *Ballet Cookbook*, was published in 1967. In the meantime, Balanchine's obsession with yet another dancer, *Suzanne Farrell, was undermining the marriage. In 1969, the choreographer obtained a Mexican divorce from Le Clercq so he could marry this latest paramour, who was 40 years his junior. (Unwittingly, Farrell had foiled the plan by marrying dancer Paul Mejia in the interim.) In 1970, Le Clercq accepted an invitation to teach ballet at the Dance Theater of Harlem.

On November 24, 1998, Le Clercq was honored at a gala celebrating the New York City Ballet's 50th anniversary. The event, which was preceded by an alumni reunion, included a reenactment of the company's famous first program at the City Center on October 11, 1948, and included three of the ballets that had been part of Le Clercq's stunning repertoire: *Concerto Barocco*, *Symphony in C*, and *Orpheus*.

SOURCES:

Candee, Marjorie Dent, ed. *Current Biography*. NY: H.W. Wilson, 1953.

Hunt, Marilyn. "New York City Ballet Turns Fifty," in *Dance Magazine*. November 1998, Vol. 72, no. 11, p. 34.

Taper, Bernard. *Balanchine: A Biography*. NY: Times Books, 1984.

Barbara Morgan,
Melrose, Massachusetts

Lecouvreur, Adrienne (1690–1730)

Celebrated French actress whose premature death left many questions. Born on April 5, 1690 (some sources cite 1692), at Damery, Marne, France; died on March 20, 1730, in Paris; daughter of Robert Couvreur (a hatter); mother's name unknown; mistress of Maurice of Saxony; children: three daughters, one of whom was the grandmother of Maurice Dupin de Francueil, the father of George Sand.

Adrienne Lecouvreur was the daughter of a hatter who established himself in Paris in 1702. Though she had an unhappy childhood, her talent was discovered when she performed in private theatricals while employed as a laundress. For a number of years, starting at age 14, she journeyed with traveling companies from town to town, acquiring in this haphazard apprenticeship a thorough knowledge of her art.

While on tour, the 16-year-old fell in love with a baron and became engaged, but she suffered the first of her many tragedies when the baron died. The youthful Lecouvreur had three more lovers: the noble Philippe le Ray, the actor Clavel, and the soldier Comte de Klinglin. Though her stationery would bear the motto *Que Faire au Monde sans Aimer* (What is living without love?), she was unsuccessful at amours throughout her short life, perhaps because she was an accommodating lover. She once wrote to Clavel:

> Your welfare is far more precious to me than my own. So always follow the course that seems most pleasant to you. If ever I lose you and you are still happy, I shall have the joy of knowing I have not been a bar to your happiness.

Clavel took her at her word. Seeing before him an itinerant actress with no prospects, he married another woman who had a few thousand francs. But Adrienne's acting as well as her beauty became the talk of the provinces. Word of her potential drifted to Paris, and when Marc Antoine La Grand, *sociétaire* of the Comédie Française, came to see her act, he engaged her at once.

In 1717, age 25, Lecouvreur appeared at the Comédie Française in the title role of Crébillon's *Electre* and as Angélique in Molière's *George Dandin*. Her success was so great that she was immediately welcomed as a regular into the Comédie Française; for 13 years, she was the queen of tragedy there, attaining a popularity never before accorded an actress. She is said to have played no fewer than 1,184 times in 100 roles, of which she created 22. Soon recognized as the first French actress of her day, she excelled in both tragedy and comedy.

Lecouvreur owed her success largely to her courage in abandoning the stilted style of her predecessors; her delivery was natural, with a simplicity that delighted and moved her public. She revolutionized acting, diction, and costuming. When the popular actor Michel Baron returned to the stage at age 67, she gained a powerful co-conspirator in her attempt to change the stage traditions of generations. Lecouvreur's voice was soft, musical, and penetrating; she

*A*drienne
*L*ecouvreur

spoke as people spoke and her emotions were astutely human. She put conversational meaning into the rhymed couplets, shunned theatrical costuming, and dressed as her characters might dress. When she was not speaking, contrary to the fashion of the time, she continued to act, replacing statuesque poses with inventive stage business. Until then, French actors recited grandiloquently or in singsong metric, then stood stock-still, blankly staring into the wings, while their fellow actor responded in like manner.

Despite the latitude in her lifestyle (she already had two illegitimate daughters), Adrienne's social successes were many. She was on visiting and dining terms with half of the court of Philippe the Regent (later known as Philip V, king of Spain), and her salon was frequented by many notables and artists, among them a young writer named François Marie Arouet, who preferred to be known simply as Voltaire. He adored her. One lovesick reporter for the 1719 *Mercure* joined Voltaire in praise:

> Without being tall, she is exquisitely formed and has an air of distinction. No one on earth has greater charm. Her eyes speak as eloquently as her lips, and often they supply the place of words. In brief, I can compare her only to a flawless miniature. Her head is well

poised on shapely shoulders. Her eyes are full of fire; her mouth is pretty; her nose slightly aquiline. Her face is wonderfully adapted to express joy, tenderness, pity, fear, sorrow.

But Lecouvreur was not as amused as her admirers; she wrote to a friend, "I spend three-fourths of my time in doing what bores me." Then, in 1721, she fell in love and became mistress to the military leader Comte Maurice of Saxony, one of the 163 children of Augustus the Strong, king of Poland. With Maurice, Adrienne had her third child, a daughter, who would be the paternal great-grandmother of *George Sand. When the duchy of Courland lost its duke and Maurice, count of Saxony, spied a potential dukedom, Lecouvreur sold her plates, furnishings, and jewels to raise 40,000 francs for his ill-starred adventures and brief sojourn as the duke of Courland. (Russia would not recognize him.)

Like his father Augustus, the count sought the comfort of other women. None was more dangerous than **Françoise de Lorraine**, duchess of Bouillon. When Maurice rebuffed the duchess, claiming he was still in love with Lecouvreur, Adrienne was thrilled; the duchess was not. In July 1729, Lecouvreur received an anonymous note, requesting her presence at the corner of the Luxembourg Gardens at 11 the following morning. There she met a young man in cleric garb, a hanger-on of the Bouillon household. Abbe Bouret warned her that the duchess had tried to bribe him, and produced the box of poisoned bonbons that he was to send her as a gift from a humble admirer. As Adrienne escorted the abbe and the candy to the police, they fed one of the bonbons to a stray dog; it died within 15 agonizing minutes. But the Bouillon family had a great deal of influence. Even though Bouret stuck to his story under cross examination, he was thrown in prison until he confessed that his accusations were lies.

The duchess of Bouillon, now happily cleared of all suspicion, or so she thought, attended a performance of Lecouvreur's Phedre, and mockingly applauded her rival from a box seat. When Lecouvreur came to the line, "I know my own faults; but I am not one of those brazen women who, calm even in the exposure of their crimes, can face the world without a blush," she turned toward the duchess. That night, when the duchess emerged from the theater, she became the center of gossip and was greatly humiliated. Many Parisians were convinced that she would find a way to revenge this latest insult.

On March 20, 1730, the 40-year-old Adrienne Lecouvreur was suddenly stricken seriously ill, and a priest was sent for. In the eyes of the church, however, she was an actress and therefore immoral. The priest demanded she denounce her allegiance to the stage, and banish all earthly thoughts, before he could grant Extreme Unction. But when he asked, "Do you place your hope in the God of the Universe?" she glanced toward Maurice and whispered, "*There is my Universe, my Hope, my God.*" That day, denied the last rites of the church, she died suspiciously and unabsolved. Contemporary writers were convinced that she had been poisoned by the duchess of Bouillon; some declared that the poison was sent in a bouquet from another humble admirer. But the truth of these speculations has never been established.

Her remains were refused burial in consecrated ground. In protest, Voltaire wrote a poem about her death, expressing his indignation at the barbarous treatment accorded the woman whose "friend, admirer, lover" he was. His efforts landed him in so much hot water that he was obliged to leave Paris. Friends buried her secretly at night near the rue de Bourgogne.

Adrienne Lecouvreur is the most sympathetic figure in the history of the French stage. As an actress with a delicate, refined style she brought soul to a brilliant but artificial theater; as a gentle, lovable woman, her short life and sad end are filled with romance. In 1849, Eugène Scribe and Ernest Legouvé made her life the subject of the well-known tragedy, *Adrienne Lecouvreur,* which achieved great acclaim because of the performance of the renowned actress *Rachel* in the title role.

Leczinska, Maria (1703–1768).

See Marie Leczinska.

Lederer, Eppie.

See joint entry under Friedman, Esther Pauline and Pauline Esther.

Lederer, Esther P.F.

See joint entry under Friedman, Esther Pauline and Pauline Esther.

Ledoux, Jeanne Philiberte
(1767–1840)

French painter. Born in Paris, in 1767; died in 1840.

What little is known about French painter Jeanne Ledoux comes from salon records, which document that she was one of several women students of Jean Baptiste Greuze (1725–1805), and that she exhibited in the salons held between 1793 and 1819, after which she disappears from public record. According to **Ann Harris** and **Linda Nochlin**, the subject matter of Ledoux's paintings also help identify her as Greuze's pupil. "She did not attempt the elaborate moral tales in genre settings for which Greuze is best known," they write. "Instead she exploited the popularity of his head studies of beautiful young women and children, often depicted with animals, whose perfectly rounded features are frequently tinged with melancholy induced by the death of a pet sparrow or the temporary absence of a lover." The titles of two paintings exhibited in the Salon of 1819, *Little Girl Holding a Dove* and *Young Boy near an Apple with a Fistful of Sticks*, are indicative of Ledoux's preoccupation with children, as is *Portrait of a Boy* (Louvre, Paris), a work that exudes the sentiment and idealism found in so much of Greuze's work.

Harris and Nochlin also point out that in her later work, Ledoux adopted a less romantic, more straight-forward style, as evidenced in her *Portrait of Greuze* (Musée des Beaux-Arts, Dijon), a work based on Greuze's own *Self-Portrait*. In this painting, Ledoux abandoned formal composition for a more informal sketch. "She uses a rectangular format, simplified his clothing, lightens the tone, and leaves much of his jacket as sketchy underdrawing. The result is a more accessible, human image." In another work, *Portrait of a Boy* (The Baltimore Museum of Art), painted around 1800, the artist used a more direct technique, making the portrait more intimate than the earlier Louvre portrait.

Since Ledoux never exhibited any large history paintings or portraits of notables, it is assumed that she enjoyed a modest career as a portraitist, catering to a middle-class clientele. Many of her paintings remain with the descendants of her original patrons, thus further complicating efforts to identify and study her oeuvre. In addition, many of her works are not signed or dated, and thus, some may have been mistakenly attributed to the better-known Greuze.

SOURCES:
Harris, Ann Sutherland, and Linda Nochlin. *Women Artists 1550–1950*. Los Angeles County Museum of Art: Knopf, 1976.

Barbara Morgan,
Melrose, Massachusetts

Leduc, Violette (1907–1972)

Noted French author whose candid autobiography, **La Bâtarde,** *was a literary sensation in 1964. Name variations: Violette Le Duc. Pronunciation: Vee-o-*

Portrait of a Boy *by Jeanne Philiberte Ledoux.*

LET Le-DUKE. Born on April 7, 1907, in Arras, France; died of cancer in Faucon, France, on May 28, 1972; illegitimate daughter of Berthe Leduc (a servant) and Andre Debaralle (the son of Berthe Leduc's employer); attended boarding school, 1923–26; married Gabriel Mercier, in 1939.

Death of grandmother (1916); marriage of her mother (1920); expelled from boarding school (1926); ended love affair with her former teacher, met Maurice Sachs, and began writing for women's magazines (1934); fled to Normandy during World War II and began work in black market (1942); returned to Paris (1944); met Simone de Beauvoir (1945); endured mental breakdown and confinement in psychiatric hospital (1957); published bestseller, La Bâtarde (1964).

Selected works: L'Asphyxie (In the Prison of Her Skin, 1946); L'Affamée (Ravenous, 1948); Ravages (1955); La Bâtarde (The Bastard, 1964); Thérèse et Isabelle (1966).

Violette Leduc emerged from a catastrophically unhappy childhood and chaotic years as a young adult to become a significant figure on the French literary scene in the years after World War II. Although she only began writing at the age of 35, and although her early works received little popular or critical acclaim, she was recognized early on as a significant talent by *Simone de Beauvoir. Her frank autobiography, *La Bâtarde,* which appeared in 1964, put her at the center of one of France's great literary controversies, as critics split in their assessment of this shocking account of her life.

Leduc stood apart from the most important trends in French literature in the post-World War II years. She had no interest in themes of political engagement that attracted such existentialist literary figures as Beauvoir and Jean-Paul Sartre. She was similarly unattached to the rebellion in literary forms known as the "New Novel" and personified by Alain Robbe-Grillet and *Nathalie Sarraute. Leduc's obsessive interest in her own life story dominated her writing. As **Isabelle de Courtivron** notes, "the relentless personal voice remained the organizing principle of all her works." Leduc disturbed many critics and readers with her detailed descriptions of sex between women. In interviews she gave after the publication of *La Bâtarde,* she declared her belief in the right of women to write candidly about their physical desires and experiences.

My mother never held my hand.

—**Violette Leduc**

Leduc's themes have become increasingly relevant in recent years in light of feminist criticism. She has been described as an authentic female voice in presenting an autobiography that does not, like most male verities, focus on achievement but rather explores self-consciousness and self-understanding. The digressions and fragments of recollection in her writing have been seen as reflecting the typical experiences of women. Similarly, her focus on female adolescence, her candid description of lesbian lovemaking, and her painful and prolonged dependence on her mother can be seen as genuine aspects of the female experience.

But the richness of Leduc's writing has also invited critical examination from a psychoanalytic approach as well as from students of the elements of gender in literature. And there have been more conventional efforts to tie Leduc to the ongoing development of French literature. Thus, in recent years **Bonnie Engdahl** has considered the psychological ramifications of Leduc's use of wound images, tying this literary device to the symptoms of autism; and **Eileen Boyd Silvert** has examined the way in which Leduc constructed a literary world in which women took on the role of male authority fig-

ures. Meanwhile, de Courtivron, who leads the field in studying Leduc, has devoted much of her work to a consideration of Leduc's ties to the various strands of France's 19th- and 20th-century literary tradition such as surrealism. She notes that, while numerous French male writers had drawn upon their personal defiance of bourgeois norms as a basis for their writing, Leduc was the first woman to do so.

In 1996, **Michele Zackheim** approached Violette Leduc's complex life from a new direction by making her the centerpiece of a novel, *Violette's Embrace.* In this book, a longtime student of the author's work supposedly visits Leduc's haunts in Paris and the French countryside. Zackheim also creates a character named Lilli Jacobs, a friend of Leduc who possesses both a wealth of memories and a set of documents pertaining to the controversial writer.

Violette Leduc was born in Arras in northern France on April 7, 1907. Her unhappy childhood, which was to play a key role in her literary work, began with the circumstances of her birth. The illegitimate child of a servant, **Berthe Leduc**, and the son of the wealthy family for whom Berthe worked, Violette was deprived from birth of any hint of maternal love. Her sense of being an outsider in her own family grew when, in 1920, Berthe married and, three years later, became the mother of a legitimate child, Violette's half-brother.

Violette's childhood was barren in a way that left lasting scars on her personality, and, writes **Margaret Crosland**, "nothing was ever to destroy her desperate feelings of insecurity and the awareness that she could not grow up." She was physically unattractive, and her mother gave her none of the affection that Violette craved. Berthe also filled her daughter's ears with complaints about men and pregnancy. As Leduc recalled in her autobiography, at the breakfast table "my mother would tell me about the horrors of life," giving me "the gift of mistrust and suspicion." In Berthe's eyes, as her daughter recalled hearing it repeatedly, "men were swine, all men were heartless."

Two factors helped to some degree to lighten the girl's burdens. First, she had a positive relationship with her grandmother. Second, Berthe's marriage brought a measure of affluence to herself and Violette, permitting the young girl to be sent off to a boarding school with the opportunity for a good education. Both of these forces in Violette's life proved disappointing, however. Her grandmother died when the girl was only nine years old, and Violette's

Violette
Leduc

boarding-school experience came to an early and ugly end when she was expelled after two amorous relationships with women.

One of her lovers was a classmate at school, and their link soon ended. A more lasting tie was the one she developed with one of her teachers. Violette and Hermine remained lovers for more than a decade as the young woman moved to Paris, dropped out of school, and went to work as a secretary. Her future literary career was foreshadowed by her employment with a prominent publisher. This brought her into contact with some of France's most important writers.

An early literary mentor appeared in Leduc's life in 1934, when she had already begun writing for French women's magazines. Maurice Sachs, a shadowy figure who combined links to both France's criminal world and its literary community, intrigued her with his elegant lifestyle and his circle of acquaintances in Parisian literary society. Notes de Courtivron: "She gave Maurice Sachs her adoring friendship and he, flattered by her attention, took her under his disreputable wing." Her tie to Sachs grew stronger after the outbreak of World War II. The onset of the war had led Leduc to a sudden marriage to an old friend, Gabriel Mercier, which quickly collapsed. Mercier was one of a long line of homosexuals to whom the sexually uncertain woman was attracted throughout her adult life.

In 1942, Sachs convinced Leduc to accompany him to a rural hiding place in Normandy, where, in the village of Anceins, the two of them spent most of the remainder of the war. Sachs engaged in a variety of enterprises, including trading on the black market. He also offered aid to Jewish refugees fleeing the German occupation of France. Leduc was drawn into his black marketeering, but, even more significantly, she now began serious work as a writer. Sachs pushed her into this activity, insisting that she record her numerous, painful memories from childhood in durable form. Sachs was arrested, transported to Germany, and apparently murdered by the Nazi authorities by the close of the war, although the exact circumstances of his demise remain uncertain. Leduc received word of his death in 1945. She returned to Paris where a second literary mentor, Simone de Beauvoir, entered her life and directed her activity.

Beauvoir gave the new author's career a major boost by publishing portions of Leduc's *L'Asphyxie* in *Les Temps Modernes*. *L'Asphyxie* was the book that Sachs had pushed Leduc to complete in their wartime hideaway. *Les Temps Modernes* was the vibrant postwar journal for French intellectuals created by such figures as Jean-Paul Sartre and Beauvoir herself. Beauvoir also encouraged one of France's most prestigious publishing houses, Gallimard, to consider the book. Gallimard accepted *L'Asphyxie* and soon afterward took Leduc's second book, *L'Affamée*, as well. When the publisher insisted on cutting a large portion of Leduc's third book, *Ravages*, due to its sexually explicit nature, Beauvoir took up Leduc's cause in an unsuccessful effort to restore the deleted passages.

The tie between Beauvoir and Leduc continued for decades. The former displayed a complex set of reactions to Leduc, once describing her as "an amiable pest, sometimes a bore . . . usually too pathetic to criticize." In her voluminous correspondence, Beauvoir never referred to her new acquaintance by name but instead designated her as "the ugly woman." Nonetheless, the established and prestigious existentialist author pushed Leduc to work intensively and consistently, and she even kept Leduc solvent with regular monetary payments each month. According to de Courtivron, "as her principal literary adviser and her most discerning reader,"

Beauvoir "took Leduc from writing down random childhood associations to creating full-fledged literary works."

The rising author's acquaintance with Beauvoir brought her into a wider circle of French literary figures in the period after World War II. Leduc had a particularly tangled and painful link with Jean Genet. She developed a strong infatuation for this homosexual writer whose early life had been marked by criminal episodes. Genet refused to return Leduc's feelings, and it required Beauvoir's emotional support to keep the devastated woman from sinking into an even deeper depression than the one she normally endured.

Leduc's early works, such as *L'Asphyxie* and *L'Affamée,* tapped her life experiences without taking actual autobiographical form. The first was an adult narrator's recollections of her childhood. Consisting of 23 brief chapters, it shifts back and forth from descriptions of her family and her early acquaintances to bits of conversation and assorted anecdotes. Designated by Leduc as a novel, it takes the semi-fictional heroine as far as her initial period in boarding school. It began with a sentence that provides insight into the pain Leduc was to carry all her life: "My mother never held my hand." The second book describes a fevered relationship between the narrator and an older woman designated as "Madame." Beauvoir's biographer **Deidre Bair** considers it a work "about Leduc's thinly disguised passion" for Beauvoir, Leduc's famous and glamorous mentor. It is filled with savage imagery in which the heroine is sometimes the perpetrator of violent acts, sometimes their victim. The book stated clearly Leduc's lifetime conviction that "my ugliness will set me apart until I die," and it carries this theme forward with violent fantasies in which the heroine destroys mirrors.

Beauvoir kept tight restrictions on the relationship that was so crucial for Leduc. She permitted meetings between the two of them only according to a predetermined biweekly schedule. Leduc found that Beauvoir also avoided any personal interaction by spending every minute of their time together criticizing the former's writing. Beauvoir avoided the most famous literary gathering places in Paris, the Brasserie Lipp and the Flore, if she spotted Leduc sitting inside. Leduc had a history of suicide attempts, and she reportedly made another at this time by trying to leap in front of a truck in reaction to Beauvoir's indifference to her. Meanwhile, Beauvoir tapped what she had learned of Leduc's experiences, as well as her own experiences, for the section on lesbianism she included in her classic book on women, *The Second Sex*.

Despite the advantage of having a distinguished literary patron, Leduc was disappointed to find that there was no substantial popular response to her books. She continued to write in a small studio in a poor section of eastern Paris. Burdened as well by an unrequited infatuation with a homosexual businessman, Jacques Guérin, Leduc went over the edge into the depths of serious mental illness in 1957. Beauvoir, by now the supervisor of both Leduc's literary production and private life, took her to a psychiatric clinic, but Leduc remained burdened by mental illness for the rest of her life.

The author found herself in the public eye for the first time in 1964 with the publication of *La Bâtarde*. Encouraged by Beauvoir to write an autobiography, Leduc had been working since the late 1950s on the book, which recounted her life from birth until the close of World War II. It not only sold well, but it became the object of public scandal. Its frank discussions of her lesbian affairs as well as other facets of her life such as her illegitimate birth and her physical ugliness—topics which earlier female authors had avoided—disturbed critics writing for the conservative press. Beauvoir, who thought the book might well win one of France's prestigious literary prizes such as the Prix Goncourt, was willing to enhance its chances for such an honor by writing a preface for *La Bâtarde*.

The book combines the author's recollections with an account of her present circumstances as Leduc describes for the reader the moments in which she is writing. It also shifts among various viewpoints: the author's narrative, fragments of recalled conversations, and the author's dialogues with herself. In some passages describing her adult years, Leduc moved away from the preoccupation with her own experiences and provided a vivid account of Parisian life in the 1920s and 1930s. Nonetheless, the striking passages that evoked so much controversy were extraordinarily personal. Leduc recounts, for example, how she induced her lesbian lover to engage in sex in front of a wealthy male observer. She also describes her wartime experiences in a manner likely to shock the reader. Her account of the occupation years scarcely mentions the Germans, and she appears to have no concern about the great events of the time or the horrors perpetrated on her fellow citizens.

The nature of this memorable autobiography contrasts sharply with that of other Frenchwomen who wrote accounts of their lives at this time. Both Simone de Beauvoir, Leduc's mentor, and *Clara Malraux produced such works, but their books combined their personal stories with elements from the contemporary political and intellectual scene.

The possibility that the book might receive one of France's prestigious annual literary awards for fiction led to an acrimonious dispute over the propriety of granting such an award to Leduc. In the end, possible embarrassment for the prize-giving committees was avoided by an adroit compromise: the book was categorized as autobiography rather than fiction and removed from contention.

The success of *La Bâtarde* brought Leduc a degree of critical and popular recognition that had escaped her in earlier decades. Henri Peyre, professor of French literature at Yale and a noted literary critic, hailed it as "a courageous confession and a work of art" which was "sumptuous with images worthy of Rimbaud." The critic for London's *Sunday Times* compared Leduc's book to the *Confessions* of Jean-Jacques Rousseau and suggested it would tear down the barriers against candor in women's autobiography. Her new success also brought her a movie role, offers to write for *Vogue* magazine, and a place on the Parisian social scene.

In her few remaining years, Leduc continued to produce explicitly erotic works of fiction such as *Le Taxi*, which concerns incest between young teenagers. The passages that had been cut from *Ravages* were also now publishable in light of her recent literary success. These appeared in a separate volume under the title *Thérèse and Isabelle*, and the book subsequently became the basis for a film. Leduc also continued the formal story of her life with two more autobiographical volumes—*La Folie en tête* (1970) and *La Chasse à l'Amour* (1973)—following *La Bâtarde*. But these received nothing like the critical and popular response of the earlier work.

Some students of Leduc's life and work believe that she found an unaccustomed degree of happiness—or at least serenity—in her final years. In an interview given in 1970, she continued her longstanding candor about her physical appearance, stating, "I have been ugly. I'm still ugly." But she claimed to have no regrets and to be consoled by old age. "If I had been beautiful, I would have had a lot, but right now I would be forced to give up so much of it."

Violette Leduc spent her final years in an old house that she bought in southern France near Mount Ventoux. It was there that she died of cancer on May 28, 1972. According to Margaret Crosland, Leduc had planned a final volume of memoirs that would describe "a fascinating subject: her reactions to success." But "life had cheated her of so much and now it cheated her of her farewell performance."

SOURCES:
de Courtivron, Isabelle. *Violette Leduc*. Boston, MA: Twayne, 1985.

Engdahl, Bonnie. "Autistic States and Transitional Phenomena: Violette Leduc's *La Bâtarde*," in *The American Journal of Psychoanalysis*. Vol. 54. June 1994, pp. 159–171.

Evans, Martha Noel. *Masks of Tradition: Women and the Politics of Writing in Twentieth-Century France*. Ithaca, NY: Cornell University Press, 1987.

Francis, Claude, and Fernande Gontier. *Simone de Beauvoir: A Life . . . A Love Story*. Translated by Lisa Nesselson. NY: St. Martin's Press, 1982.

Sartori, Eva Martin, and Dorothy Wynne Zimmerman, eds. *French Women Writers: A Bio-Bibliographical Source Book*. Westport, CT: Greenwood Press, 1991.

Silvert, Eileen Boyd. "Permeable Boundaries and the Mother-Function in *L'Asphyxie*," in *Tulsa Studies in Women's Literature*. Vol. 11. Fall 1992, pp. 289–307.

SUGGESTED READING:
Crosland, Margaret. *Women of Iron and Velvet and the Books They Wrote in France*. London: Constable, 1976.

Hall, Colette. "*L'écriture féminine* and the Search for the Mother in the Works of Violette Leduc and Marie Cardinal," in *Women in French Literature*. Edited by Michel Guggenheim. Saratoga, CA: ANMA Libri, 1988.

Hughes, Alex. *Violette Leduc: Mothers, Lovers, and Language*. London: W.S. Maney, 1994.

RELATED MEDIA:
Therese and Isabelle (118 min. film in French with English subtitles), starring **Essy Persson** and **Anna Gael**, produced and directed by Radley H. Metzger, screenplay by Jesse Vogel; Audubon Films, 1968.

Neil M. Heyman,
Professor of History,
San Diego State University, San Diego, California

Lee, Agnes (1841–1873).

See Lee, Mary Custis (c. 1808–1873) for sidebar.

Lee, Agnes Rand (1878–1972).

See Käsebier, Gertrude for sidebar on Agnes Freer.

Lee, Alice Hathaway (1861–1884).

See Roosevelt, Alice Hathaway Lee.

Lee, Ann (1736–1784)

British-born religious figure and founder of the United Society of Believers in Christ's Second Appearing, commonly known as the Shakers, who is believed by her followers to be the second, and female, incarnation of Christ. Name variations: Ann Lees; Mother Ann Lee; Ann Lee Standerin; Ann Stanley. Born Ann Lees on February 29, 1736, in Manchester, England; died near Watervliet, New York, at the Shaker colony of Niskeyuna on September 8, 1784 (The Albany Gazette's obituary mistakenly reports her death as having occurred on September 7); daughter of John Lees (a blacksmith and tailor) and Ann (Beswick) Lees; married Abraham Standerin (later called Stanley), on January 5, 1761; children: Elizabeth (d. 1766), and three who died in childbirth or infancy.

Began attending revival meetings led by Quakers Jane and James Wardley (1758); had revelation that she was the second coming of Christ (1770); sailed for the New World (1774); helped establish the first Shaker colony at Niskeyuna, New York (1776); took missionary tour through New England (1781–83).

In the United States, the history of women and the history of religion are intrinsically intertwined. This distinctive connection influenced many issues ranging from definitions of women and their social roles within society, to the very events and social values that not only shaped their lives but also had an impact on the lives of all Americans. During the greater part of American history, church participation was one of the few public opportunities available and accessible to women. As **Arabella Stuart Wilson** notes, religious work gave women "a sphere of activity, usefulness, and distinction, not, under present constitution of society, to be found elsewhere." For this reason, among others, women largely outnumbered men as converts in the great awakenings, and it was predominantly women who remained active in religion and who continued to be involved in religious movements. Consequently, American history is filled with women, like Ann Lee, who made remarkable religious, social, and political contributions and who shaped and formulated the religious experience of America.

Ann Lee was born Ann Lees in Manchester, England, on February 29, 1736, the second of John Lees and **Ann Beswick Lees'** eight children. John was a blacksmith who worked at night as a tailor to support his family. Of Ann Beswick Lees almost nothing is known, although Shaker tradition maintains that she was "counted a strictly religious, and very pious woman." John, a later convert to his daughter's movement, was likewise regarded "though poor, [as] respectable in character, moral in principle, honest and punctual in his dealings, and industrious in business." Ann, like the majority of children of her class and time, received no formal schooling (she would, in fact, remain illiterate her entire life) and went to work at the burgeoning textile mills at age eight. Like her contemporaries, Lee worked twelve hours a day, six days a week, moving about in various textile jobs, from spinner, to cutter, to dyer. At age 20, she gained a much less dangerous and physically damaging job as a cook in the Manchester Infirmary, which was also the local insane asylum. Her early childhood and young adulthood were made more difficult by the added responsibilities of raising her siblings and keeping house for her family following the early death of her mother.

At the time of Lee's birth, Manchester possessed the highly charged atmosphere of the Evangelical Revival that swept England in the 1740s and 1750s. Such famous preachers as George Whitefield, and James and Charles Wesley of the Methodist movement, as well as many other sectarians ministers, visited and held revivals in Manchester. While each individual and each sectarian movement carried a slightly different message of God and salvation, all preached of the necessity of experiencing a "new birth" in the holy spirit and a moving personal experience with religion in order to gain salvation and a oneness with God. It was this context of Evangelicalism and revival that cultivated and nurtured Lee's growing distance from her family's Anglican Church and the development of her own highly personal religious beliefs and message.

It was within this climate that James and **Jane Wardley** founded a sectarian group in 1747. Originally Quakers, the Wardleys experienced visions that led them to separate from the Society of Friends and develop a unique form of expressive worship, probably influenced by the French Camisards who had immigrated to the Manchester area in 1685 after the revocation of the Edict of Nantes. The practices of this new sectarian group involved physically expressing the presence of the holy spirit through chanting and dancing. The Wardleys and their growing number of followers believed that religious fervor was a gift of the holy spirit and the experience of this gift led to the emotive and physical style of worship that gave the group its name, the "Shaking Quakers," later the Shakers. The Wardleys also prophesied that the second coming of Christ would be soon and, most significantly, in the guise of a woman.

Lee joined this group in 1758, at age 22, and rose slowly in the movement. It was only following her arranged marriage on January 5, 1761, to Abraham Standerin (later called Stanley), an apprentice of her father's, and her subsequent and speedy loss of three children in childbirth and in-

fancy, and the loss of a fourth, Elizabeth, in 1766, that Ann began to truly question her life and beliefs. According to the Testimonies, a collection of memories and narratives compiled by the Shakers following her death, Lee began "laboring" in an effort to find the holy spirit and new birth. She particularly dreaded sexual intercourse and, after seeking the advice of Jane Wardley, proclaimed her desire to lead a celibate life. Her husband, while not participating in her beliefs or in the movement, agreed.

Lee began active and increased participation with the Shaking Quakers in worship services and started preaching in public. She quickly drew the attention and disapproval of the authorities (it was considered blasphemous for a woman to speak out in such a way) and was arrested and fined countless times and, on occasion, jailed. After disturbing a service at the Anglican Cathedral in Manchester in 1770, Lee was locked up for the fourth time in the insane asylum. During this incarceration, she experienced a series of visions. First, she saw Adam and *Eve in the Garden of Eden, and it was revealed to her that she had been correct—sex was the root of all evil and the ultimate reason for humankind's separation from God. Second, and more significant than these revelations, Lee had a vision of Jesus who revealed to her that she was the next manifestation, the second appearance of Christ sent to bring completion and fulfillment and to serve as the full incarnation of the divine. According to her accounts of these visions, Christ had suffused her being, making clear that she was his female counterpart. God was both male and female as were the humans that God created. Jesus was the male messiah and the Catholicism that followed him failed to bring complete purity to the world. Now the second appearance of Christ had occurred in a female messiah, Ann Lee. With her, women and men were again equals, and Eden could therefore be restored.

Her visions and her new birth revitalized and recreated Ann Lee. She was immediately recognized by the Shaking Quakers as the fulfillment of their prophecies and, as the head of their so-

ciety, recognized and regarded as their "Spiritual Mother," Ann the Word, or Mother Ann. Her family, including her husband, father, and siblings, joined the order and all adhered to her revelations, that the weakness of the flesh caused all sins and depravity among humankind and that the millennium had arrived.

Life for the group in Manchester became increasingly difficult the more Lee and her followers preached in public and spoke of the second appearance or coming as an established fact. Already a difficult concept, their assertion was made more difficult by their belief that Ann was this second appearing. The Shakers were arrested continuously for creating public nuisances, disturbing the peace, and interrupting various religious services. As rumors about the Shakers' beliefs and form of worship spread, charges of heresy, witchcraft, and fanaticism soon followed. In 1774, Lee declared that the group must journey to America to establish the true church and to search out the "people of God in America" whom she had seen in a vision.

Do all your work as though you had a thousand years to live, and as you would if you knew you must die tomorrow.

—Mother Ann Lee

Lee and a small group of followers, including her brother William, niece Nancy, foster brother James Whitaker, and husband, set sail on May 19, 1774, from Liverpool aboard the *Mariah*. Landing in New York City, the group remained there for 18 months, attempting to gather funds and to locate the exact spot for their proposed colony. During this period, Lee's husband left her and the Shakers. The first colony was subsequently established at Niskeyuna, near Watervliet, New York, in the summer of 1776.

The early years of the colony were difficult, as were the early years of all new settlements in the wilderness of America. While the first four years brought no new converts, they were formative in laying the groundwork of the colony, the rules of conduct and beliefs. A communal form of living, accompanied by the physical separation of men and women except in meetings, worship, and dining, was established. All property was held in common, and governance was concentrated in the hands of a select group of Elders, comprised of an equal number of men and women, chosen by the ministry. The construction of buildings and the cultivation of the land was accomplished, and the Shakers, through the benefits of communal labor, quickly produced an abundance of crops for sale and became leaders in the market of garden seeds and medicinal herbs, providing a source of income for their movement and expansion.

While many, if not all, of the communitarian movements and groups of the late 18th and 19th centuries were millennial, in that they awaited the coming of the millennium (the 1,000-year reign of Christ), the Shakers were post-millennial. They believed they were living in the after days and fully expected that soon God would gather in the elect and then, in the spirit realm, convert and save all humankind. Shaker traditions, such as never leaving a task unfinished and hanging up their chairs before retiring at night, all reflected this sense of immediacy. The belief that they were living in the after years in immediate expectation of heaven provided further argument for their practice of celibacy, as there was no need to have offspring. This was predicated both on Lee's visions and on Jesus' saying that "in resurrection they neither marry, nor are they given in marriage, but are as the angels of God in heaven."

The Shakers were particularly revolutionary for their time. They questioned and overturned the basic societal systems of their day, not only in their belief that the second coming had occurred in the shape of a woman, but in their belief in the equality of women, their total lack of a system of class and wealth, and their dismissal of accepted norms of social interaction in their rejection of marriage and traditional family life. For Shakers, one of the first rules was that men and women should be treated as equals in all matters from spiritual to the governance of the community. "The order of nature requires a man and a woman to produce offspring," said Lee. "He is the Father and she is the Mother; and all the children, both male and female, must be subject to their parents . . . but when the man is gone, the right of government belongs to the woman. So it is with the family of Christ." Because Shakerism encouraged characteristically "female" traits such as passivity, piety, obedience, and chastity, it raised the status of these traits, and thereby that of women. While Shakerism proclaimed equality of sexes, it was the elevation and admiration of society's stereotypical "female" traits that raised women within the community to levels of equality and leadership. The fact that celibacy was practiced by both sexes eliminated the classical association of the evilness of the flesh with the temptation of women. In this way, the movement carried an implicit emancipatory message to Lee's female followers, for it gave them a voice not merely in the religion but in the day-to-day life of the colony.

Shaker beliefs, such as their open confession of sin regardless of class and rank, their style of communal living, and their renunciation of marriage, appeared to their neighbors to undermine the whole social order and created acute unease in the area. The fact that the Shakers were also spiritualists, believing they could communicate with the dead, did not alleviate tensions. In addition, the Shakers were pacifists in the time of the American Revolution, and, with the expansion of wartime activity in the area, rumors began to spread that the Shakers were harboring British spies and selling food and secrets to the enemy. The Shakers were, therefore, persecuted as loyalists. Two early converts, Joseph Meacham and Clavin Harlow, were arrested in July 1780 on suspicion of supplying food to the British army, and, in August, Ann Lee, her brother William, and James Whitaker were arrested as spies. While the others were eventually released, Lee was held without trial until December 1780 and was only released with the assistance of Governor George Clinton.

Undeterred by the growing resentment in the area, and encouraged by the growing number of new members, Lee and a small group of followers set out on a missionary trip in the spring of 1781 in order to search out "the people of God" who had brought her to America in the first place. In keeping with Lee's opinions about the symbolism of time, the mission set out on the same day that they had sailed from Liverpool, May 19th. This trip, which ranged through Massachusetts and Connecticut, had as its focal point a long stay in Cambridge. The place of residence for the Shakers in Cambridge was called the "Square House," the home of the late Shadrack Ireland, once a disciple of George Whitefield. Ireland, an eclectic preacher and charismatic, had originally built the house for his "spiritual Wives." Eventually, Ireland's followers were converted, and Lee declared that the people for whom she had been searching had been found. After much conversion and preaching while facing an equal amount of mob violence and intolerance, the small group made its way back to Niskeyuna, arriving in September 1783. Ann's brother William died the following summer, on July 21, 1784, most likely from wounds received from those mobs. Ann Lee died six weeks later, on September 8, 1784. Reportedly, her last words were: "I see Brother William coming in a glorious chariot to take me home."

The church organized after Lee's death was called "The United Society of Believers in Christ's Second Appearing," or "the Millennial Church." The Shaker movement spread, and new colonies were established in New England and later in Ohio, Kentucky, and Indiana. By 1830, there were 20 well-established and thriving groups. The movement reached its peak between 1830 and 1860.

Lee's illiteracy prevented her from leaving any personal chronicles. The only extant contemporary records of her life are the brief official records of church and government that log not the woman but official events: baptism, marriage, prison, immigration, and death. The only other evidence is the accounts written by friends and followers, with the obvious bias they entail, and the polemical literature of her enemies, with their own biases. The paucity of information specifically about Ann Lee is common for many women of her time and for history in general. While Ann Lee left behind only a few tangible records, she left an indelible imprint on American history and society. A role model for a number of other female spiritual leaders, she left behind a religious movement that lasted for over 100 years after her death, a movement that served as a pattern and example to countless other communities over the course of American history.

SOURCES:

Bednarowski, Mary Farrell. "Outside the Mainstream: Women's Religion and Women Religious Leaders in Nineteenth-Century America," in *Journal of the American Academy of Religion*. Vol. 48, 1980, pp. 207–231.

Marini, Stephen A. "A New View of Mother Ann Lee and the Rise of American Shakerism," in *The Shaker Quarterly*. Vol. 18. Nos. 2 and 3, 1990, pp. 47–62, 95–111.

Wells, Seth Y., ed. *Testimonies of the Life, Character, Revelations and Doctrines of Mother Ann Lee, and the Elders with Her, through Whom the Word of Eternal Life was Opened in this Day of Christ's Second Appearing, Collected from Living Witnesses in Union with the Church and Ministry of Mother Ann Lee*. Albany: Packard & Van Benthuysen, 1816.

SUGGESTED READING:

Andrews, Edward D. *The People Called the Shakers: A Search for the Perfect Society*. NY: Oxford University Press, 1953.

Humez, Jean M., ed. *Mother's First Born Daughters: Early Shaker Writings on Women and Religion*. Bloomington: Indiana University Press, 1993.

Procter-Smith, Marjorie. *Shakerism and Feminism: Reflections on Women's Religion and the Early Shakers*. Old Chatham, NY: Center for Research and Education, Shaker Museum and Library, 1991.

COLLECTIONS:

Shaker Manuscript Collection, rare Books and Manuscripts Division, New York Public Library; manuscripts and Special Collections Division of New York State Library, Albany; Shaker Museum and Library, Old Chatham, New York; Edward Denning Andrews Memorial Shaker Collection, Winterthur Library.

Amanda Carson Banks,
Senior Information Officer, The Divinity School,
Vanderbilt University, Nashville, Tennessee

Lee, Anne Carter (1839–1862).

See Lee, Mary Custis (c. 1808–1873) for sidebar.

Lee, Brenda (1944—)

American pop and country-music singer. Born Brenda Mae Tarpley on December 11, 1944, in Lithonia, Georgia; daughter of Reuben Lindsey Tarpley and Grayce (Yarbrough) Tarpley; graduated from Hollywood Professional School, 1963; married Charles R. (Ronnie) Shacklett, on April 24, 1963; children: two daughters, Julie Leann Shacklett and Jolie Shacklett.

Albums include: Brenda Lee (1960); This Is Brenda (1961); Emotions (1961); Brenda Lee, All the Way (1961); Sincerely, Brenda Lee (1962); That's All, Brenda (1962); All Alone Am I (1963); Let Me Sing (1964); By Request (1964); Top Teen Hits (1965); Versatile (1965); Too Many Rivers (1965); Bye Bye Blues (1966); Ten Golden Years (1966); Merry Christmas, From Brenda Lee (1967); Thanks a Lot (1967); Coming On Strong (1967); Here's Brenda Lee (1967); Reflections in Blue (1967); For the First Time (1968); Johnny One Time (1969); Brenda Lee Now (1975); LA Sessions (1976); Take Me Back (1980); Even Better (1980); Anthology 1956–1980 (1991).

Brenda Lee, who began singing on the radio in Conyers, Georgia, at age six, established an international career before the age of 20. She was born Brenda Mae Tarpley in Lithonia, Georgia, the daughter of Reuben Lindsey Tarpley and **Grayce Yarbrough Tarpley**. While still a child, she appeared on the radio show "Jubilee USA" with Red Foley and on television with Steve Allen and Perry Como. In 1955, she signed a recording contract with Decca and was put under the wing of Owen Bradley, who produced for *Patsy Cline and later *Loretta Lynn. Lee had minor hits with "One Step at a Time" and "Dynamite," then hit the pop and R&B charts with "Sweet Nothin's," which reached #4 in 1960. That same year, "I'm Sorry," a ballad at first thought too adult for the 15-year-old, was the #1 record for three weeks and sold over 10 million copies. She reached #1 again two months later with "I Want to Be Wanted," and in 1961 had four singles in the top ten: "You Can Depend On Me," "Emotions," "Fool Number One," and "Dum Dum." By the time she was 21, "Little Miss Dynamite," as the tiny singer came to be known, had cut 256 sides for Decca and had made several successful appearances in Europe.

As the early rock 'n' roll era faded, Lee made a successful crossover to country music, scoring with "If This Is Our Last Time" (1971), "Nobody Wins" (1974), and "Broken Trust" (1980), which she recorded with the Oak Ridge Boys. She continues to record and make club appearances and in 1988, along with *Kitty Wells and Loretta Lynn, was a guest on k.d. lang's *Shadowland* album. In 1991, MCA released a 40-song, double CD album, *Anthology 1956–1980*, which contains all of Lee's rock 'n' roll and country hits, and also includes some obscure cuts like the rockabilly "Let's Jump the Broomstick," a cover of *Edith Piaf's "If You Love Me (Really Love Me)," and "Is It True?," a 1964 tune featuring guitarist Jimmy Page.

Lee, who married her high school sweetheart Ronnie Shacklett in 1964, has two daughters, Julie and Jolie. Among her numerous honors is the National Academy of Recording Arts and Sciences' Governors Award, which she received in 1984.

SOURCES:

Clarke, Donald, ed. *The Penguin Encyclopedia of Popular Music.* NY: Viking, 1989.

Romanowski, Patricia, and George-Warren Holly, eds. *The New Rolling Stone Encyclopedia of Rock & Roll.* NY: Fireside, 1995.

Lee, Gypsy Rose (1914–1970)

Celebrated American ecdysiast and writer who turned the striptease into an art form, was accepted as a legitimate actress, and whose memoirs of growing up in show business were turned into the musical Gypsy. Born Rose Louise Hovick, but known as Louise Hovick, on February 9, 1914, in Seattle, Washington; died on April 26, 1970, in Los Angeles, California; daughter of John Hovick and Anna Thompson Hovick (known as Rose); sister of June Havoc (b.

Brenda Lee

1916); attended public schools and was tutored when touring with her mother and sister; married Arnold Mizzy (divorced 1938); married Alexander Kirkland (divorced 1944); married Julio de Diego (divorced 1951); children: (with film director Otto Preminger) Erik Lee Preminger.

Brought up in show business from the time of her parents' divorce (1918); at first sang and danced with her younger sister June throughout the Northwest; led a more settled existence during mother's two subsequent but short-lived marriages; auditioned for various vaudeville circuits (early 1920s); won a contract with the Pantages circuit through the West and Midwest, but remained in the chorus line backing up her younger sister June; June eloped with one of the chorus boys (1929); Rose soon built a new act around Louise, but by now vaudeville was dying in the surge of radio and feature films and was being replaced by its bawdier stepchild, burlesque. Mama Rose, undaunted, soon managed to get Louise star billing at a burlesque theater in Toledo, Ohio, where Louise performed her first, modest striptease and adopted the name Gypsy Rose Lee. From this point on, Gypsy took control of her own career, developing a trademark, almost balletic striptease act appreciated in terms of sophistication and entertainment value more than prurience. Gypsy went on to even wider audiences in feature films and on radio, wrote two novels and a play, and published her memoirs, which were turned into Gypsy, *one of the most successful Broadway musicals of all time (1959), and later successfully adapted for film and television.*

Selected filmography: (as Louise Hovick) You Can't Have Everything, Ali Baba Goes To Town *(1937);* Sally Irene and Mary, The Battle of Broadway, My Lucky Star *(1938); (as Gypsy Rose Lee)* Stage Door Canteen *(1943);* Belle of the Yukon *(1944);* Babes in Baghdad *(1952);* Screaming Mimi, Wind Across The Everglades *(1958);* The Stripper *(1963);* The Trouble With Angels *(1966).*

Selected publications: two mystery novels, including G-String Murders, *which was adapted for the screen as* Lady of Burlesque, *starring *Barbara Stanwyck (1943); a play was also adapted for film as* Doll Face *(1946);* Gypsy *(1957, autobiography).*

On a summer's evening in 1918, the worthy gentlemen of the West Seattle Knights of Pythias Lodge were treated to some after-dinner entertainment, provided courtesy of their fellow lodgemember Charlie Thompson. Charlie's daughter, Anna Thompson Hovick, who preferred to be known as Madame Rose, played the piano while her two daughters sang and danced.

The younger of the girls, two-year-old June (later known as ✤▸ June Havoc), was obviously the most talented, while the older one, four-year-old Louise, seemed awkward and uncomfortable. Nonetheless, the gentlemen gave the girls a hearty round of applause while their mother beamed proudly.

Mama Rose was determined that at least one of her girls would have the show-business career she had been denied, first by her father and then by her first husband, John Hovick. When she and John were divorced in 1918, Rose prevailed on her father to arrange for appearances for the girls at fraternal lodges and benevolent societies throughout Seattle. Charlie Thompson did not realize what his daughter was up to until it was too late, and Rose was troop-

---

✤▸ Havoc, June (1916—)

American actress. Name variations: Baby June. Born Ellen Evangeline Hovick on November 8, 1916, in Seattle, Washington; daughter of John Hovick and Anna Thompson Hovick, known as Rose Hovick; sister of Gypsy Rose Lee (1914–1970); attended public schools and was tutored when touring with her mother and sister; married at 13; married William Spier (a director).

Filmography: Four Jacks and a Jill *(1941);* My Sister Eileen *(1942);* No Time for Love *(1943);* Casanova in Burlesque *(1944);* Sweet and Low Down *(1944);* Brewster's Millions *(1945);* Gentleman's Agreement *(1947);* Intrigue *(1947);* The Iron Curtain *(1948);* When My Baby Smiles at Me *(1948);* Chicago Deadline *(1949);* The Story of Molly X *(1949);* Mother Didn't Tell Me *(1950);* Once a Thief *(1950);* Follow the Sun *(1951);* Lady Possessed *(1952);* Three for Jamie Dawn *(1956);* The Private Files of J. Edgar Hoover *(1977);* Can't Stop the Music *(1980);* Return to Salem's Lot *(1987).*

June Havoc began performing in vaudeville at the age of eight with her sister Louise, under the guidance of their mother. The act became a popular one on the vaudeville circuit in the West and Midwest until June left the act in 1929. **Rose Hovick** then built a new one around her older daughter that toured burlesque houses, where Louise, now *Gypsy Rose Lee, learned the fine art of the striptease.

Though Havoc went on to make movies, her Hollywood career never completely clicked. She had more success on the New York stage in *Pal Joey* (1940) and *Mexican Hayride,* for which she won a Donaldson Award in 1944. She also wrote and directed *I, Said the Fly* and the successful Broadway play *Marathon 33,* starring *Julie Harris. June's memoirs were published as *Early Havoc* (1959) and *More Havoc* (1980). Residing in Westport, Connecticut, Havoc was active in the causes of the arts and animals.

ing her girls up and down the West Coast looking for a break into show business.

The two girls led an unconventional life, living out of seedy hotel rooms on the fringes of vaudeville and leading a more settled existence during the two occasions their mother remarried. After the second marriage ended, however, the girls lived more or less permanently on the road.

Louise (originally named Rose Louise), writing years later as Gypsy Rose Lee, would describe her mother as "charming, courageous, resourceful, ambitious. She was also, in a feminine way, ruthless." For more than ten years, Louise was forced to the background while Rose concentrated on developing a career for June. "While Louise was the most beautiful child alive, she had no flair for singing and less for dancing," wrote June. "I must have seemed a more likely prospect from the very beginning."

If you wanna grind it,

Wait 'til you've refined it.

—The stripper Tessie, from the musical *Gypsy*

Show business, in the 1920s, meant vaudeville—live variety shows made up of acts by singers, dancers, acrobats, and comedians. Vaudeville had developed from the old minstrel shows of the late 19th century, and it reigned supreme as the most popular form of mass entertainment, with acts booked onto a number of circuits, or "wheels," that covered the entire country. Performers were required to do up to six shows a day, six days a week; to live out of trunks and suitcases; to put up with abusive, sometimes belligerent audiences and theater managers, only to travel through the night by train or bus to start all over again at the next stopover. They were paid in cash, under a bookkeeping system that was riddled with inaccuracies and outright cheating, and could be fired on the spot for questioning or complaining. Unions were unknown, radio was not yet seen as an entertainment form, and motion pictures were still a novelty.

It was in this milieu that Mama Rose brought up her girls with ferocious determination, finally winning them a booking on the Alexander Pantages circuit, one of the country's largest, covering the West and Midwest. Mama Rose built a new act around June, hiring six boys to form "Dainty June and her Newsboy Songsters," with Louise as the seventh newsboy. Louise did her best, but when her two left feet became painfully obvious, her mother threatened to send her home to Seattle to live with relatives. Terrified, Louise promised to try harder

and managed to stay with the act. "Dainty June" was a huge success on the circuit, especially when Rose added a barnyard number complete with live animals, and Louise performed as the back end of a cow that pranced around the stage while June sang.

Soon, the act became so popular that it was given a contract with the most prestigious circuit of them all, the Orpheum, at $1,250 a week, playing the best houses in Chicago, Buffalo, Detroit and other top venues. Mama Rose's "grouch bag," a capacious leather sack attached to her belt and suspended between her legs, at one point was stuffed with $25,000 in cash. But Louise continued to languish in June's limelight, even after Rose somehow arranged for her to appear in a skit opposite the most famous vaudeville performer of the day, *Fanny Brice. Petrified and with little time to rehearse, Louise blew her lines and was a complete flop, glad to flee back to the anonymity of a cow's hindmost.

By 1929, June was 13 years old and still playing "Baby June." Rose insisted on dressing her in little girls' clothes, even off stage, constantly referred to her as "The Baby," and refused to let her learn a new, more mature act. The last straw came when Rose arranged an audition with Roxy Rothafel, the Steven Spielberg of the vaudeville world and the man who would later conceive and develop Radio City Music Hall. Rothafel quickly recognized June's talent, and just as quickly realized that no future career for June was possible as long as her mother was involved. He offered June a contract on the condition that "Dainty June and her Newsboy Songsters" was abandoned and the development of June's career was turned over to him. Her mother refused, accusing Rothafel of being an evil, selfish man trying to separate a mother from her daughter. Shortly afterward, on New Year's Eve of 1929, after the last performance of the night in Topeka, Kansas, June ran away from the act with one of the Newsboys who, it turned out, she had secretly married some months before. (June would later metamorphose into June Havoc and develop a moderately successful career as a stage and screen actress.) With the act now dead, Rose took Louise home to Seattle.

But not for long. Within months, Rose was planning a new routine around Louise, this time with six girls. The act hit the road and went through various incarnations, from "The Madame Rose Debutantes" to "Madame Rose's Dancing Daughters" to "Rose Louise and her Hollywood Blondes," the latter after Louise sug-

Gypsy
Rose
Lee

gested they all dye their hair. That act was the first time Louise's name was given top billing.

By the early 1930s, however, it was clear to everyone but Mama Rose that vaudeville was dying at the hands of radio and the burgeoning film industry. Quality bookings were becoming harder to find, but Rose refused to close the act down and accepted play dates in houses offering acts from the raunchier stepchild of vaudeville, burlesque. Burlesque shows featured scantily clad women chased around the stage by bawdy comedians spewing seltzer bottles and double-entendres, and something neither Rose nor Louise had seen before—the striptease. Louise's chaste act may have seemed out of place to an audience expecting bare flesh and sexual innuendo, but for the management it was a way to legitimize their shows and keep the censors off their backs. These new venues were to give Louise an opening that would shape her career.

Her chance came in Toledo, Ohio, when the star ecdysiast got into a violent disagreement with a boyfriend, bashed him over the head, and ended up in jail. The management needed a quick replacement, and Rose knew just who that might be. Louise was horrified when her mother volunteered her, but Rose told her all she had to do was sashay back and forth across the stage a few times and drop a shoulder strap. Louise, who had watched the veteran strippers enough times and listened to their banter, knew there was more to it than that. The afternoon before her debut, she watched grimly as a worker put her new professional name up on the marquee—Gypsy Rose Lee. She told an interviewer years later that the Gypsy came from a song she had used in her act for years, "Little Gypsy Sweetheart." She couldn't remember where the Lee came from.

Opening night arrived, and, with Rose stationed in the wings, Gypsy took her place on stage, dressed in a tightly fitted gown made of a sheer, revealing material. "Hold your stomach in, honey," Rose whispered from offstage as the drumroll started, "and your shoulders back!" Many years later, Gypsy remembered it all perfectly:

> The spotlight blinded me for an instant, then my nervousness was gone and I began parading back and forth on the stage as I had seen the others strippers do. I lifted the sides of the full net skirt and made it swirl around me. . . . [T]hen, just as the music came to an end, I dropped the shoulder straps and the lavender net dress fell to the floor. Wrapping the curtain around me, I disappeared into the wings. I stood there for a long moment holding on to the scenery and trying to get my breath.

The applause may have been modest, but Gypsy's career was launched, along with freedom from her mother's control. Over the next year, Lee refined her act by putting more emphasis on the tease than on the strip, and by drawing on her vaudeville background to come up with a running patter of jokes and amusing observations. She developed the habit of seeking out a bald gentleman in the audience and calling out to him "Darling! Sweetheart! Where have you

been all my life!," then descending into the audience to plant a kiss on his bald pate. As she removed the pins from the outer layer of her costume, each would be dropped into the tuba in the orchestra pit, followed by appropriate squawks and honks from that venerable instrument. And she always ended her act with a deft removal of the last layer and a quick flash of her lacy undergarments before wrapping herself in the curtain at the side of the stage and blowing a kiss at the blackout. Her costumes, rather than being outrageous or provocative, were elegant and sophisticated, and she let the audience see only enough of what was underneath to keep them interested. "Miss Lee," observed one critic, "never takes off more than she has on." The act began to draw a more discerning audience, who appreciated Gypsy's work almost as an art form. In 1931, she came to New York, opening at the prestigious Republic Theater, and took Broadway by storm.

By the time she was 21, Gypsy was earning $900 a week and playing long runs at some of New York's best theaters. Typical of the patter she developed as she shed various garments was:

> When I lower my gown a fraction, . . .
> I'm not thinking of your reaction.
> I'm thinking of . . . The Apples by Cezanne.

Gypsy had a remarkable knack for publicity. When she first opened in New York in 1931, she noticed the powerful New York Mirror columnist, Walter Winchell, in the audience. The next morning, Winchell received a note from her apologizing for her poor performance of the previous evening and promising that if he returned that night, he'd see a better show. Winchell returned to see not Gypsy's usual routine but one she'd written just that afternoon based on Winchell's column of that morning. From then on, Gypsy got at least one mention every week in Winchell's writing. Soon, Variety reported that "Miss Lee has received more free space in two months then the rest of the burlesque business, including everybody in it, usually gets in two years."

For the next 25 years, Lee toured with much the same act, earning up to $10,000 a week for her talents. She became a national celebrity and even embarked on a short-lived film career when Darryl Zanuck put her under contract. But the government's film censor, Will Hays, would not allow "that strip woman" to appear on screen under the name Gypsy Rose Lee, and no one had ever heard of Rose Louise Hovick. Besides, Gypsy was well aware of her own limitations, and even she admitted that acting in front of a camera was

From the movie Gypsy, *starring Natalie Wood, based on the life of Gypsy Rose Lee.*

one of them. "When I saw my last picture in Hollywood," she told the *New York World Telegram* in 1938, "I knew it was the end. . . . I said, 'Gypsy, if that's you, you'd better go fast.' I didn't meet with much resistance from the studios." Nevertheless, Lee would return to Hollywood and appear in seven more films, including *Stage Door Canteen,* under the name by which everyone knew her. In addition, she wrote two popular murder mysteries (including *The G-String Murders* with **Craig Rice**), a play and, in 1957, published her memoirs, the rights to which she sold to Broadway producer David Merrick. By 1959, the musical *Gypsy*, starring *Ethel Merman as Mama Rose, with a book by Arthur Laurents, music by Stephen Sondheim, and lyrics by Jule Styne, had opened to rave reviews and was on its way to becoming one of the most popular musicals in Broadway history.

Lee was equally adept at keeping her private life out of the public eye. Few people knew of the court suit Mama Rose brought against her two daughters for non-support in 1941 (settled quietly out of court); or, of Gypsy's constant worries about money which kept her touring past the age when even she admitted any self-respecting stripper should quit (her last striptease came in Fort Lauderdale, Florida, in 1958, when she was 44 years old); or, of her unfulfilling relationships with men. She was married and divorced three times—to a dental-supply manufacturer whom she divorced in 1938, a Broadway matinée idol whom she divorced in 1944 after three months (her son Erik was born in 1945), and a Spanish sculptor-painter to whom she was married for the longest time, six years, before divorcing him in 1951. She told *New York Post* columnist Sidney Skolsky in 1967, "The first year of marriage, you're exploring everything new together. The second year, you're reliving the first year. The third year, it's just plain normal married life." There were several affairs in between marriages, notably with Broadway impresarios Mike Todd and Billy Rose. By the time her son Erik, who lived and toured with her, was ten years old, Gypsy had largely given up on finding a long-term relationship and devoted her time to seeing Erik into manhood. It wasn't until Erik turned 18 that he discovered he had been born out of wedlock and was not a product of Gypsy's second marriage. Confronted, Gypsy confided to Erik that his father was film director Otto Preminger. Erik, in his own memoirs of growing up with Gypsy, quotes her as telling him that she "picked" Preminger as a suitable father for the child she wanted. "It was after Mike [Todd] left me," she said to him. "I felt so alone that I decided to have something no one would ever be able to take away from me." Erik and Otto Preminger met as father and son in the late 1960s and, in 1971, Preminger publicly acknowledged his paternity and legally adopted Erik.

In the mid-1960s, Lee sold her New York townhouse and moved to Los Angeles, where she purchased a home perched high in Beverly Hills and devoted her time to gardening and to the latest collection of dogs which had been her constant companions since her touring days with Mama Rose. ("Show me someone who doesn't like animals," Lee always said, "and I'll show you a treacherous person.") She appeared very little in public, although she did tour Vietnam for the State Department to entertain American troops and agreed to several guest slots on television chat shows. Erik recalls these years as some of her happiest. But in late 1969, Lee was diagnosed with advanced lung cancer. She died of the disease on April 26, 1970. She was 56 years old.

Although her life was relatively short, Gypsy Rose Lee managed to fill those years with successful careers as a performer, a writer, and a single mother. Near the end, as Erik shepherded her past the other patients at the radiation clinic where she went for treatments, she told him quietly, "I've had three wonderful lives, and these poor sons-a-bitches haven't even lived once."

SOURCES:

Havoc, June. *Early Havoc*. NY: Simon & Schuster, 1959.

Lee, Gypsy Rose. *Gypsy: A Memoir*. NY: Harper Brothers, 1957.

Preminger, Erik Lee. *Gypsy and Me: At Home and on the Road with Gypsy Rose Lee*. Boston, MA: Little, Brown, 1984.

SUGGESTED READING:

Zeidman, Irving. *The American Burlesque Show*. NY: Hawthorn Books, 1967.

RELATED MEDIA:

Gypsy (musical), produced by David Merrick, starring Ethel Merman as Mama Rose, with a book by Arthur Laurents, music by Stephen Sondheim, and lyrics by Jule Styne, opened on Broadway on May 21, 1959.

Gypsy (98 min. film), starring *Rosalind Russell, *Natalie Wood, and Karl Malden, directed by Mervin LeRoy, Warner Bros., 1962.

"Gypsy," TV-movie starring Tyne Daly, 1994.

Norman Powers,
writer-producer, Chelsea Lane Productions,
New York, New York

Lee, Hannah Farnham (1780–1865)

American writer. Born Hannah Farnham Sawyer in Newburyport, Massachusetts, in 1780; died in Boston, Massachusetts, on December 17, 1865 (also seen as December 28); daughter of Micajah Sawyer (a physician); married George Gardner Lee, in 1807 (died 1816); children: three daughters.

Selected works: Grace Seymour *(1830);* Memoir of Hannah Adams *(1832);* The Backslider *(1835);* The Contrast; or, Modes of Education *(1837);* Three Experiments of Living *(1837);* Elinor Fulton *(1837);* Fourth Experiment of Living: Living Without Means *(1837);* The Harcourts *(1837);* Living on Other People's Means; or the History of Simon Silver *(1837);* New Experiments: Means Without Living *(1837);* Historical Sketches of Old Painters *(1838);* The Life and Times of Martin Luther *(1839)*; Rosanna; or, Scenes of Boston *(1839)*; The Life and Times of Thomas Crammer *(1841)*; Tales *(1842)*; The Huguenots in France and America *(1843)*; The Log Cabin; or, The World before You *(1844)*; Sketches and Stories from Life: For the Young *(1850)*; Familiar Sketches of Sculpture and Sculptors *(1854)*; Memoir of Pierre Toussaint *(1854)*.

Widowed after nine years of marriage and left with three daughters to support, Hannah Farnham Lee is believed to have turned to writing in order to keep her family afloat. Most of her early works focus on the difficulties women face in earning their own living and surviving on limited means, including her first novel, *Grace Seymour* (1830), which was published when she was 50. In it, she introduced the strong, virtuous heroine that came to dominate the 20 domestic novels she turned out between 1830 and 1854. In her later career, Lee also produced nonfiction historical works, educational in nature.

The book that established Lee as a writer, *Three Experiments of Living*, was published in 1837, during America's first serious economic depression. It was so popular that Lee's Boston publisher issued it three times that year, under slightly different titles. The novel, and its sequel *Elinor Fulton* (1837), focus on the Fultons, a family caught up in materialism. When they lose their money, they nearly fall apart, but are kept together by their virtuous daughter Elinor, who, as the main character of the second novel, supports her mother and siblings while her father attempts to reestablish his medical practice in the West. Like most of Lee's heroines, Elinor is endowed with the ability to make money and to spend it wisely.

Having established her reputation, Lee turned to nonfiction, specializing in history and art. In the first of these, *Historical Sketches of Old Painters* (1838), she wrote of artists, including Leonardo da Vinci, Michelangelo, and Antonio Correggio. Called in its day a "romantic biography," the work was enormously popular and reissued four times between 1839 and 1854, by various publishers in Boston, Philadelphia, and England. Lee's subsequent nonfiction, including *The Life and Times of Martin Luther* (1839), *The Life and Times of Thomas Crammer* (1841), *The Huguenots in France and America* (1843), *Familiar Sketches of Sculpture and Sculptors* (1954), and *Memoir of Pierre Toussaint* (1851), also sold well, although by modern-day standards, according to **Lina Mainiero**, they are unoriginal and overly didactic.

Hannah Lee's personal life remains a mystery. The daughter of a prominent physician in Newburyport, Massachusetts, she lived most of her life in Boston and died there on either December 17 or 28, 1865. Never considered a major writer even at the height of her popularity, Hannah Lee had already slipped into obscurity by the time of her death.

SOURCES:

Mainiero, Lina, ed. *American Women Writers*. NY: Frederick Ungar, 1980.
Weatherford, Doris. *American Women's History*. NY: Prentice Hall, 1994.

Lee, Harper (1926—)

American author of the 1960 Pulitzer Prize-winning novel To Kill A Mockingbird, *which presented a loving, yet uncompromising, portrait of the morality of the American South where whites ruled by oppressing blacks. Name variations: Nelle. Born Nelle Harper Lee on April 28, 1926, in the small town of Monroeville in southwestern Alabama; daughter of Amasa Coleman Lee and Frances (Finch) Lee; educated in the public schools; attended Huntingdon College, 1944–45; studied law at the University of Alabama, 1945–49; studied one year at Oxford University; never married; no children.*

Awards: Pulitzer Prize for Fiction, Alabama Library Association award, Brotherhood Award of National Conference of Christians and Jews, first in "The Best of the Year" list in The New York Times Book Review *(all 1961), and Bestsellers' Paperback of the Year award (1962), all for* To Kill A Mockingbird.

Grew up in Monroeville, broke off her legal studies and moved to New York to become a writer; worked as airline reservations clerk with Eastern Airlines and British Overseas Airlines (1950s), quit job to devote full time to writing; returned to Alabama to help nurse her ailing father and wrote short stories that became To Kill A Mockingbird, *which was published to universal acclaim (1960).*

As a child, Nelle Harper Lee had short cropped hair, wore coveralls, went barefoot, and "could talk mean like a boy," in the words of her Monroeville neighbor **Marianne Moates**. She could also beat up boys her own age, including her dear friend Truman Capote who spent summers next door. Nelle, named after her maternal grandmother Ellen, and nicknamed "Dody," was the third daughter in her family. The first born, a boy, had died in infancy.

Her father, Amasa Coleman Lee, was born in Georgiana, Alabama, in 1880. In 1913, he came to Monroeville as a legal apprentice, was later admitted to the bar, and in 1916 became a partner with the firm of Barnett and Bugg. From 1929 to 1947, he was editor of the local weekly *Monroeville Journal*. A relative of Capote's recalled Amasa Lee, who was the prototype for *To Kill a Mockingbird*'s Atticus Finch: "He was a tall, angular man, detached, not particularly friendly, especially with children. In fact, most of us kids were quite intimidated by him and his rather formal ways. He was not the sort of father who came up to his children, ruffled their hair, and made jokes for their amusement."

Nelle's mother was an accomplished pianist who delegated domestic responsibilities to Haddy, their live-in African-American housekeeper. **Frances Finch Lee** was heavy-set, but carried herself with considerable grace and wore her platinum-blonde hair in two thick braids that she coiled on top of her head. She sat on her front porch doing crossword puzzles as quickly as she could move her pencil, but her mind was not always clear. She frequently wandered up and down the street saying strange things to neighbors and twice tried to drown Nelle, who was saved by one of her sisters.

The Lee home was a white, one-story house with a porch that went the length of the front. The house was comfortable but sparsely furnished with wooden chairs, iron bedsteads, and bare floors of highly polished pine. Fig trees, crape myrtles, and pecan trees grew in the yard. A hedge separated the Lee home from that of the Faulks, three middle-aged sisters and their taciturn elder brother who each summer played host to their young cousin Truman Capote. As Lee was too rough to play with little girls, and Capote was too soft for the town's boys, the two became best friends and used to slip through the gaps in the hedge to visit each other. They sat up in her treehouse in a chinaberry tree and read about Tarzan, Tom Swift, and the Rover Boys, and later Sherlock Holmes. Capote told writer Lawrence Groble that instead of going to movies, they would go to the courthouse and watch her father try cases. Lee herself recalled going upstairs to watch her father from the balcony, unless the "colored" people were attending a trial because that was usually the seating area assigned to them.

She and Capote were gifted children in a small unpaved town that prized conformity. When Truman demonstrated that he knew how to read in kindergarten, the teacher hit his hand with a ruler. Nelle would reassure him by saying, "It's alright, Truman, that you know everything,

even if the teachers don't understand." She would later describe the dilemma of an educated child in a poor country school in *To Kill a Mockingbird*. Lee herself began writing stories at the age of seven, but never with an idea of publishing. Capote, meanwhile, was observing those around him and storing anecdotes for future tales. He told Groble that his first published story, "Mrs. Busybody," was based on Nelle's mother; his source was so obvious that it upset the town when it was published in the *Mobile Register*.

Harper Lee would later say of her childhood, "I was lonely because I didn't fit into anyone else's pattern and nothing can be more excruciating than that kind of loneliness. I had a robust childhood and, as I remember, a vigorous one. It was a childhood of terrible unhappiness, but it was not specifically unhappy. I suppose it was more or less normal, at least I found sufficient entertainment to fill each day."

She went to Huntingdon College in Monroeville, attended Oxford University for a year, then studied law at the University of Alabama, but broke off her studies in 1950 a few months before completing them to go to New York to become a writer. Capote had burst on the literary scene there in 1947 with his *Other Voices, Other Rooms*, the lyrical novel of a boy who accepts his homosexuality. Lee had helped inspire Idabel, the tomboy-ish girl in the book.

In New York, she sublet Capote's apartment and worked first as a book saleswoman, then as a flight reservations clerk for Eastern Airlines, because it had direct service to Alabama, and then for BOAC. The jobs financed a long and dedicated apprenticeship that consisted of writing for four hours each night, reading her work and discarding what she wrote. She realized that her aborted law studies had taught her to be clear and brief. The law also gave her story ideas. "You would be amazed at the depravity of human nature," she later told an interviewer for the *New York Herald-Tribune*.

Lee remained close to Capote, who was a darling of the literary and social world during the 1950s, and his friends became close to her as well. One Christmas, composer Mike Brown jotted down a promise, wrapped it in a red ribbon, and gave it to her as a present: "Miss Nelle Harper Lee gets enough time off to read and write whenever she wants to." He provided monthly loans of $100 so that Lee could quit her job and write full time. Aside from writing, she filled her days collecting memoirs of 19th-century clerics and pursuing interests such as golf, crime, and music.

Harper
Lee

Soon afterward, her widowed father, who was in his late 70s, suffered a series of heart attacks. Lee returned to Atlanta to look after Amasa Lee by day while her sister **Alice Lee**, a tax attorney, was at work. In the evenings, Lee went to the law office to write. Such behavior was hard for others to understand. "My aunt told me I was the laziest girl she had ever seen," Lee said when the book came out. "All I did was sit around and concentrate." The night she wrote a scene about an evil man chasing kids, she scared herself so badly that she ran all the way home.

On weekends, Lee mentally planned her writing on the golf course. She played regularly enough to score in the high 80s. "In Monroeville they're Southern people and if they know you are working at home, they think nothing of walking right in for coffee," she explained. "Your schedule is absolutely enforced by others. You just can't tell people you're busy working because they don't think writing is work. . . . But they wouldn't dream of interrupting you on the golf course."

As far as a sense of happiness is concerned, I was never happier than when I was writing the book.

—Harper Lee

During this time in Monroeville, she wrote three essays and a short story about an angry old woman who guarded her camellias from children, which later became a chapter in *Mockingbird*. She submitted the work to the agent Maurice Crain. Crain advised her to write a novel based on the story of the children and their father. "Until then," she said, "I thought I had done a story that was a slap-bang portrayal of a perfectly horrid old lady." She quickly drafted half of a novel, which Crain sold to J.B. Lippincott. "As far as a sense of happiness is concerned, I was never happier than when I was writing the book. I think the thing I've always wanted to be by myself," Lee said. She drafted the manuscript three times before she was satisfied.

While awaiting publication, she traveled by train with Capote to Kansas, where he was researching the unsolved murder of the Clutter family for *The New Yorker* magazine. While the crime they investigated was serious, their work had an aspect of the Rover Boys adventures and Sherlock Holmes stories they had savored in their childhood. Lee's help was crucial, because in the beginning she fit in much better with the local people than the short, plump Capote, who spoke in a high-pitched voice and giggled. Lee was 34, solidly built, and looked like her father, with his square, angular face. She had a strong, thin mouth, dark eyes, heavy eyebrows and black hair, which she wore short. "Nelle walked into the kitchen and five minutes later I felt I had known her for a long time," said a columnist for the local paper in Kansas.

Neither Lee nor Capote took notes during the interviews so that people would speak to them more spontaneously, as if they were having intimate conversations. But afterward, they hurried to their hotel rooms to write down their recollections. The two then compared what they had learned so that the story would be accurate.

Still, in order to get the facts straight, they once interviewed the same person three times in one day. Capote's article became the nonfiction novel *In Cold Blood,* which was published in January 1966 and established him as an authority on the criminal justice system.

By that time, Lee was famous in her own right. When *To Kill a Mockingbird* was published in 1960, it hit with stunning force. *Mockingbird* is two entwined stories. The first is of childhood adventures and brushes with danger, and features Scout, Jem, and Dill, a character based on Capote. The second, greater tale is of a black man falsely accused and convicted of rape. *Mockingbird* is a loving, candid portrait of the South. The book is set in 1935, yet its message was still true in 1960, a century after the Civil War: the black man had remained the slave of the white man's whims. In many ways, the novel continues to be significantly relevant.

Mockingbird was at the top of the bestseller list for 40 weeks, offered by four major book clubs. It was published in ten languages and went through a dozen printings. Reviewers were universally respectful and enthusiastic. The *Vogue* reviewer wrote, "Funny, happy and written with unspectacular precision, *To Kill a Mockingbird* is about conscience—how it is instilled in two children, Scout and Jem Finch; how it operates in their father, Atticus, a lawyer appointed to defend a Negro on a rape charge; and how conscience grows in their small Alabama town." *Time* observed, "Novelist Lee's prose has an edge that cuts through cant, and she teaches the reader an astonishing number of useful truths about little girls and about Southern life."

The novel was published as the civil-rights movement exploded across the South and became part of the national zeitgeist (spirit). Blacks were staging sit-ins demanding to be served at Southern lunch counters. "All I want is to come in and place my order and be served and leave a tip if I feel like it," said a black college graduate in Charlotte, N.C. In Montgomery, Alabama, a thousand black students gathered on the steps of the former Confederate Capitol building to protest segregation. By 1963, when the movie version of *Mockingbird* came out and Gregory Peck won the Academy Award for best actor, blacks and whites from the North were dying, some with the collusion of white Southern sheriffs, in attempts to register blacks to vote in the South.

Most of her neighbors in Monroeville were proud of Lee's achievement and were happy when reporters and filmmakers came to town to write about them. In May 1961, when *Mocking-*

bird won the Pulitzer Prize for fiction, the Alabama state legislature attempted to pass a resolution praising her, the daughter of a former state representative, for her achievement. It was blocked, however, by state senator E.O. Eddins who a few years earlier had managed to have a children's book banned from state libraries because in it a white rabbit married a black rabbit. The *Montgomery Advertiser* noted he had bagged "one black rabbit and one mockingbird."

Lee spent the first year after publication observing the filming of *Mockingbird* and caring for her father, who would die in 1963. But as early as May 1961, she told a reporter that she was thinking through her second novel. Lee said she would set it in the South because it was the last refuge of genuine eccentrics who have had time and room to develop their own individuality. "I don't mean that in a Gothic sense. They are very pleasant," she told **Harriet Stix** of the *New York Herald Tribune*. But work on a second novel did not go well. "I'm in a perpetual state of stuckness," she said in May 1964, four years after publication of *Mockingbird*. "I'll be so glad when it's over."

She admitted that at one point she threw the manuscript through the window of her second-floor workroom, then ran downstairs and gathered up the pages. She worked full days on the book, rewriting and discarding what she'd written, completing two pages a day. She finished a draft and expected to have a new novel out in 1965, but the book never came to light. She avoided the celebrity life that took up increasing amounts of Truman Capote's creative energies, but occasionally lunched with friends of his like the socialite ❧▶ **Babe Paley**. When writers for *People Weekly* interviewed Capote in 1976 about the slow progress of his work, they called Lee for comment. "We are bound by a common anguish," she said. Eventually, she stopped giving interviews, but she remained pleased with the success of *Mockingbird*. She said in 1996, "To my surprise and gratitude, *Mockingbird* seems to be meaningful to a new generation, one far removed from the miseries of the time it was first published." After *Mockingbird*, Harper Lee never published again.

▶❧
Paley, Babe. *See Cushing Sisters.*

From the movie To Kill a Mockingbird, *starring Mary Badham and Gregory Peck.*

SOURCES:

Contemporary Authors. Vol. 13–16. Detroit, MI: Gale Research.

Clarke, Gerald. *Capote: A Biography.* NY: Simon & Schuster, 1988.

Grobel, Lawrence. *Conversations with Capote.* NY: New American Library, 1985.

Moates, Marianne M. *A Bridge of Childhood.* NY: Henry Holt, 1989.

New York Herald Tribune. May 3 and May 24, 1961.

New York Post. November 2, 1960.

Paine, Albert Bigelow. *Life and Lillian Gish.* NY: Macmillan, 1932.

People Weekly. May 10, 1976.

Rudisill, Marie, with James C. Simmons. *Capote.* NY: William Morrow, 1983

RELATED MEDIA:

To Kill a Mockingbird (129 min. film), starring Gregory Peck, Brock Peters, **Mary Badham**, Phillip Alford, Robert Duvall, and John Megna, directed by Robert Mulligan, screenplay by Horton Foote, based on the novel by Harper Lee, produced by Alan Pakula, 1962 (won Academy Awards for Best Screenplay for Foote and Best Actor for Peck).

Kathleen Brady,
author of *Lucille: The Life of Lucille Ball* (Hyperion)
and *Ida Tarbell: Portrait of A Muckraker*
(University of Pittsburgh Press)

Lee, Harriet (1757–1851)

English writer and novelist. Born in London, England, in 1757; died at Clifton, near Briston, England, on August 1, 1851; daughter of John Lee (d. 1781, an actor and theatrical manager); mother an actress whose name is unknown; sister of dramatist Sophia Lee (1750–1824).

Harriet Lee and her sister *Sophia Lee were born in London. Their mother died at an early age, and, following their father's death in 1781, they moved to Bath. There, Sophia set up a girls' school with Harriet's help. In 1786, Harriet Lee published a novel written in the form of letters, *The Errors of Innocence. Clara Lennox* followed in 1797. Her chief work is the *Canterbury Tales* (1797–1805), a series of 12 stories which became quite popular. Lord Byron dramatized one of the tales, "Kruitzner," as *Werner, or the Inheritance.*

Lee, Holme (1828–1900).

See Parr, Harriet.

Lee, Ida (1865–1943)

Australian historian. Name variations: Ida Marriott. Born on February 11, 1865, in Kelso, New South Wales; died on October 3, 1943; third of eight children of George Lee (a grazier) and Emily Louisa (Kite) Lee; married Charles John Bruce Marriott (a secretary of the Rugby Football Union), on October 14, 1891; children: one.

Born in 1865 into a pioneering family in New South Wales, Ida Lee grew up in Leeholme, Kelso, where she rode to school on horseback. In 1891, she married Charles Marriott, after which she made her home in England. Though known for her historical accounts, Lee's first work was a volume of poetry, *The Bush Fire and Other Verses*, published in 1897. She then developed an interest in history, haunting British libraries, particularly the Admiralty, where she became fascinated with log-books, journals, and disregarded charts. In 1906, under her maiden name, she published *The Coming of the British to Australia 1788 to 1829*, after which she turned her attention to the obscure navigator John Hayes, researching his life from letters, family records, and newspapers of the period. The resulting work, *Commodore Sir John Hayes, His Voyage and Life*, published in 1912, led to chronicles of other notable ocean voyages, including *The Logbooks of the "Lady Nelson"* (1915), *Captain Bligh's Second Voyage to the South Sea* (1920), *Early Explorers in Australia* (1925), and *The Voyage of the Caroline* (1927), her last book, although she continued to research through correspondence with various museums and libraries. In an article in the *Geographical Journal* (April 1934), Lee put forth the theory that the British first sighted Australia in 1682, a fact she discovered from an original letter (found in the India Office) from the captain of the ship *Trial*, which was grounded on the Tryal rocks off the West Australian coast. Cited for her original research, Lee was elected a fellow of the Royal Geographical Society of London in 1913, and an honorary fellow of the Royal Australian Historical Society in 1918. She died on October 3, 1943.

SOURCES:

Radi, Heather, ed. *200 Australian Women.* NSW, Australia: Women's Redress Press, 1988.

Wilde, William H., Joy Horton, and Barry Andrews, eds. *Oxford Companion to Australian Literature.* Melbourne: Oxford University Press, 1994.

Lee, Jennie (1904–1988)

Scottish politician who held several high offices in the British Labour Party and pursued a left-wing socialist program in Parliament for solutions to social problems. Name variations: Jennie Bevan; Mrs. Aneurin Bevan; Baroness Lee of Asheridge. Born Jennie Lee on November 3, 1904, in Lochgelly, Fifeshire, Scotland; died on November 16, 1988, in London, England; daughter of James Lee (a coal miner) and

Euphemia Grieg; Edinburgh University, M.A., 1926, LL.B, 1927; married Aneurin Bevan, on October 24, 1934; children: none.

Elected to British Parliament for North Lanark (1929); defeated (1931); traveled as a lecturer, journalist and author (1931–40); worked in Ministry of Aircraft Production (1940–45); elected to British Parliament for Cannock (1945) and held seat until retirement (1970); served on National Executive Committee of Labour Party (1958–70); appointed parliamentary secretary, Ministry of Public Building and Works (1964–65); appointed parliamentary under-secretary of state for Education and Science (1965–67); was chair of the Labour Party (1967–68); appointed minister of state (1967–70); created Baroness Lee of Asheridge (1970).

Selected publications: Tomorrow Is A New Day *(Crescent Press, 1939, republished as* This Great Journey, *Farrar & Rinehart, 1942);* Our Ally, Russia *(W.H. Allen, 1941);* My Life With Nye *(Jonathan Cape, 1980).*

Jennie Lee was only 24 years old when she took her seat in Parliament. Becoming the youngest member in the House of Commons was an astonishing accomplishment for any politician, but for it to be done by a woman in 1929 made it all the more remarkable. Her passionate socialism brought her into a natural alliance with Aneurin Bevan, who came from a background similar to her own. They would marry in 1934, and when both were elected to the House of Commons in 1945, they would become the first husband and wife parliamentary team. A lecturer, politician, journalist and author, Jennie Lee was never simply the distaff side of a political team.

Lee was born on November 3, 1904, in Lochgelly, Fifeshire, Scotland. Her grandfather Michael Lee was a renowned trade unionist, pioneer founder of the Fife Miners' Association and a member of the Scottish Miners' Executive. Her father James Lee was a miner and an active trade unionist who held membership in the Independent Labour Party, and her mother **Euphemia Grieg** was the daughter of hotel owners in the nearby town of Cowdenbreath. For several years during Jennie's childhood, her family were proprietors of the Arcade Hotel, which she said was her childhood nursery. In 1912, her parents left the hotel business, and her father returned to coal mining and union activities. Her home environment introduced this coal-miner's daughter to socialism at an early age. Jennie's politics and warm-hearted brand of socialism were pro-foundly influenced by James Lee's commitment to social change. Her earliest impressions were of a neat, well-kept four-room home where socialist politics were served along with the traditional oatmeal and home-baked scones.

Jennie Lee received her early education at Cowdenbreath Elementary School where she earned a first place in the final examinations. This enabled her to attend Cowdenbreath Secondary School instead of going to work. Desiring more education, she eventually attended Edinburgh University with the aid of grants from the Fife Education Association, the Carnegie Trust, and numerous other scholarships and prizes won by her proven success in the university classroom. Although she was more interested in socialist activities, she seriously applied herself to her studies and was graduated in 1926 with a master's degree in education and a teaching certificate.

Her last year at Edinburgh University was the year of the General Strike in Great Britain. Lee divided her time between school and working at the strike headquarters, and spent her summer in Ireland raising money for miners' soup kitchens. She then returned to Edinburgh and in 1927 received an LL.B degree. For two years, she worked as a schoolteacher in the Scottish mining areas to support her family, since her father, like other miners who backed the General Strike, had been blacklisted by the mine owners. Lee admitted she had no bent for teaching, was too impatient, and did not believe in what she was doing. The misery, poverty and conditions endured by mining families in their schools, homes and jobs convinced her that she could not effect any change in a classroom. She passionately wanted to help the working classes.

In 1928, the Independent Labour Party, impressed by her convictions, propaganda skills, and background, asked her to be their candidate for North Lanark in the next general election. Despite her youthful age and lack of political experience, she was persuaded to accept the offer. Prior to the expected general election, the incumbent died, necessitating a by-election. In March 1929, Jennie Lee became a member of the British Parliament with a majority of 6,578 votes. The following year, the Labour Party won the general election and formed its second government under Prime Minister Ramsay MacDonald.

Lee quickly gained something of a national reputation at Westminster. Being a woman made her unique, but her youth, attractive "Salvation Army lass" image, engaging Scottish accent and near revolutionary passion made her a favorite of the media. Her colleagues in the House of Commons admired her. Just a few weeks after taking her seat, she broke with tradition by assuming an active role in the budget debate. Having come to London because she resented the slums, poverty, and unemployment plaguing Scotland, she became identified with the left wing of the Labour Party. She had passion and a socialist viewpoint and rapidly became a forceful exponent of the Labour Party policies. Lee was an industrious parliamentarian who visited her South Lanark constituents on weekends and spent many hours weekly answering their letters and working on policy matters. In 1929, she traveled to Vienna to study the Austrian Socialist Youth Movement. The following year, she accompanied Labour Party members John Strachey, Aneurin Bevan and George Strauss to study mining and industrial towns in the Soviet Union.

Politics for me, means the fight against poverty.

—Jennie Lee

The Labour government of Prime Minister MacDonald proved ineffectual in finding an economic solution to the worsening Great Depression. Jennie Lee and a few other Labourites tried to influence their party to stay with its own policy and forgo compromises with the Liberal and Conservative parties. By 1931, conditions were so bad that Labour demanded that the rich should bear the burden of higher taxes and investment reductions. Failing to gain support for this policy, the Labour Cabinet resigned, and MacDonald, at the king's request, formed the National Government, a coalition government to fight the Depression. MacDonald's decision split the Labour Party, but on October 28, 1931, the National Government coalition handily won the general election, 554 seats to 61. Jennie Lee was one of many members of Parliament who lost her seat.

During the intraparty fighting following the Labour Party split, Lee went with the Independent Labour Party faction. She stood for election to the House of Commons in 1935 and in a by-election in 1943, but she would not regain a seat in Parliament until after World War II. Lee became a lecturer and free-lance journalist. Starting in December 1931, she frequently made lecture tours to the Soviet Union, Europe, and the United States. She disregarded protocol or agent's schedules to carry her message to the working classes in the countries she visited. In America, she spoke to such diverse groups as Appalachian coal miners and Southern cotton workers while advocating unions without color restrictions. Her journalistic career included articles pub-

lished in the *New Republic* in America and in numerous British newspapers and periodicals. She covered politics in the Soviet Union and the Popular Front election of 1936 in France.

After a friendship of five years and an engagement of barely a month, Jennie Lee married Aneurin Bevan on October 24, 1934, in a ceremony at Holborn Registry Office in London. Lee recalled that when they had first met his mind was totally absorbed with other matters, and his clothes, black suit and striped trousers, were so out of character that she had shuddered. But she came to admire his personality, brilliant mind, and socialist convictions. They were an unconventional couple from the beginning. Both had doubts about the institution of marriage but neither wanted to offend the conformist values of their constituents. Nye, as he was known by his friends, purchased a special marriage license in hope of avoiding the press, and the bride had no wedding ring or cake. They became deeply attached to each other, and despite their meager incomes, lived a rich and happy life together. They would eventually have a home in London and a small farm in Buckinghamshire. Lee's parents came to live with them and to run the household for the active couple. Bevan loved to tell his friends that he had to marry Jennie in order to get his mother-in-law; it was a close-knit family with true affection.

Lee remained active in journalism, lecturing and politics following their marriage. In 1929, she had published her autobiography, *Tomorrow Is a New Day,* and in 1941 she published *Our Ally, Russia.* During World War II, she served for a short time as lobby correspondent for the *Daily Mirror.* Shortly after the surrender of France in 1940, she accepted Lord Beaverbrook's suggestion that she work at the Ministry of Aircraft Production. She served as a shop-floor supervisor whose responsibility was to keep the high-speed production lines moving. Because of her oratorical skills, she was sent to the United States in the autumn of 1941 by Brendan Bracken on a propaganda tour to win support for Britain, and was in California when Japanese forces attacked Pearl Harbor. In 1942, she resigned from the Independent Labour Party in a disagreement with its radical antiwar position.

Following the war, Lee made peace with and rejoined the Labour Party she had left in 1931. In the Labour Party landslide victory of July 1945, she was elected to Parliament from the Midlands constituency of Cannock with a majority of nearly 20,000 votes. Lee remained politically rebellious, and in 1946 was one of 59

Labourites who signed an amendment to a speech by King George V when he opened Parliament. Favoring encouragement and collaboration with countries pursuing socialism, the amendment was a criticism of Foreign Secretary Ernest Bevin's foreign policy views, and the signers believed that a democratic and constructive socialism could serve as compromise to the inevitable destructive conflict between American capitalism and Soviet communism. Both Lee and her husband were romantic leftists who sincerely believed politics was much more than a political exercise. As with the 1946 amendment, they fought for a type of socialism that was not in the mainstream of the Labour Party.

Lee found herself, in the years following the war, moving towards a personal decision concerning her husband and politics. She concluded that Nye was doing the things she hoped to accomplish, but with much more success than she could have. The public view of Nye as an aggressive man was, to her, offset by her knowledge that he possessed a vulnerable innocence that could destroy him politically. She believed she could prevent him from laying himself open to attacks from his enemies outside and inside the Labour Party. Bevan was a brilliant, self-educated man, but he sometimes lacked the discipline needed in politics. Though her temperament made the decision difficult, she realized that she was married to an exceptional man and that she could contribute more to the cause of socialism as the wife of Aneurin Bevan than as the politician Jennie Lee. Her decision was a true sacrifice for a woman who had broken into the male club and entered marriage in a spirit of equal partnership. With her formal education, she helped him with his writing and speeches. She always had his ear, and there were many of their colleagues who felt her advice was too negative. All her life, Lee was a rebel who remained opposition-minded in the belief that the Labour Party had lost its sense of direction and was drifting toward conservatism. It is doubtful that she influenced her husband's politics dramatically, but she was certainly an irritant when it came to his attitudes toward rivals and enemies.

As Bevan rose politically, Lee remained his most ardent supporter even as she quietly pursued her own career in Parliament. Uniquely, they were two politicians of similar sympathies who shared companionship and home but in public did not normally operate as a political duo. Bevan was minister of health in the 1945 Labour government of Clement Attlee, and became minister of labour in January 1951. He soon resigned in protest over cuts in social ex-

penditures when Attlee increased expenditures for rearmament. Although a colorful personality, brilliant speaker, spontaneous debater, and charming man, Bevan was sometimes rude and very stubborn. His political radicalism became a divisive force and his views created a wing of the Labour Party known as "Bevanism." He was defeated as party leader in 1955 by Hugh Gaitskell. Accepting his party's choice, Bevan moderated his opinions on foreign policy and colonial affairs. At the time of his death from abdominal cancer in 1960, the view of socialism he and Lee shared was in general decline. (Their ideals had a brief resurrection nearly two decades later when Michael Foot, Bevan's biographer and socialist kinsman, was elected and served as party leader for a short time.)

Jennie Lee became the loyal guardian of Nye's memory and achievements. Retaining her seat from Cannock in Parliament, she had confined herself to the role of a backbencher during the height of Nye's influence. She now resumed her own political career and in 1964, at the age of 60, was appointed to the Cabinet as minister for the arts by Labour Prime Minister Harold Wilson. It was a new office, and the energetic Lee threw herself into the job: government spending

Jennie Lee

on the arts doubled during her four-year tenure. One of her greatest achievements was the Open University, originally called the "University of the Air" by Wilson, but renamed by Lee. Using television and a regular faculty, the Open University was created to provide education through a correspondence program. It was a special sponsorship for Jennie Lee, who protected it from financial problems while proudly maintaining the academic standards of universities. She proved that socialism was concerned with eliminating spiritual as well as social poverty.

Lee remained a committed socialist while in office, once even threatening to resign over planned social security cuts. The government compromised and agreed to trim the defense budget as well. In 1966, she was made a privy counsellor. Having served on the National Executive Committee of the Labour Party since 1958, she received a great honor when she was elected party secretary in 1967. She also served as parliamentary secretary at the Ministry of Public Buildings and Works from 1964 to 1965, and minister of state from 1967 to 1970. In 1970, she lost her seat in the general election and was created a life peer as Baroness Lee of Asheridge.

In retirement, Lee enjoyed the theater, gardening, walking and reading, while remaining an enthusiastic champion of socialism, the trade-union movement, and the struggle against poverty. She had published her autobiography, *This Great Journey*, in 1963. In 1980, she authored a book about life with her husband, *My Life With Nye*. She was awarded an honorary LL.D from Cambridge University in 1974, made an honorary fellow of the Royal Academy in 1981, and received an honorary doctorate from Edinburgh University in 1982.

Jennie Lee died at age 84 of an undisclosed illness in London, England, on November 16, 1988. Her lifetime endeavors and her epitaph may have been defined in her own words: "Politics, for me, means the fight against poverty."

SOURCES:
Campbell, John. *Aneurin Bevan and the Mirage of Socialism*. NY: W.W. Norton, 1987.
Foot, Michael. *Aneurin Bevan: A Biography 1897–1945*. London: MacGibbon & Kee, 1962.
———. *Aneurin Bevan: A Biography 1945–1960*. NY: Atheneum, 1974.
"Jennie Lee," in *Current Biography*. NY: H.W. Wilson, 1946, pp. 337–340.
Lee, Jennie. *My Life With Nye*. London: Jonathan Cape, 1980.
———. *This Great Journey*. NY: Farrar & Rinehart, 1942.
———. *Tomorrow Is A New Day*. NY: Cresset Press, 1939.

SUGGESTED READING:
Bevan, Aneurin. *In Place of Fear*. London: MacGibbon & Kee, 1952.
Brome, Vincent. *Aneurin Bevan*. NY: Longmans, 1953.
Krug, Mark M. *Aneurin Bevan: Cautious Rebel*. NY: Thomas Yoseloff, 1961.
Lee, Jennie. *Our Ally, Russia*. London: W.H. Allen, 1941.

Phillip E. Koerper,
Professor of History, Jacksonville State University,
Jacksonville, Alabama

Lee, Mary (1821–1909)

Irish-born Australian suffragist. Born Mary Walsh on February 14, 1821, in Monaghan, Ireland; died on September 18, 1909, in North Adelaide, Australia; daughter of John Walsh; married George Lee (an organist and vicar-choral of Armagh Cathedral), in 1844 (died around 1879); children: seven, including Adelaide Lee.

Mary Lee, born Mary Walsh in 1821 in Monaghan, Ireland, married George Lee, an organist and vicar-choral of Armagh Cathedral, in 1844. The couple had seven children. Following the death of her husband around 1879, Mary sailed with her daughter Adelaide to care for her sick son, then living in South Australia. Although the young man died a year later, Lee remained in Australia, since she could not afford the trip home, and became one of the country's leading proponents of political and social reform. As early as 1883, she was active in the women's division of the Social Purity Society, which was successful in raising the sexual age of consent to 16. Becoming secretary of the Adelaide branch of the Social Purity Society, Lee directed the campaign for women's suffrage, calling it her "crowning task." "If I die before it is achieved," she said, "like Mary Tudor and Calais, 'Women's enfranchisement' shall be found engraved upon my heart." Her arguments, set forth in speeches, newspaper articles, and correspondence, were filled with historical, literary, and Biblical allusions.

By 1888, the Purity Society became the Women Suffrage League and, as such, sought enfranchisement on equal terms with men, without claiming access to parliamentary representation. From 1888 to 1892, Lee worked with League president Edward Stirling, who had first introduced a resolution for female suffrage in the South Australian Parliament in 1885. In 1892, when **Mary Colton** (1822–1898) became president, Lee became a devoted helpmate. Lee spoke at Suffrage League meetings, at Democratic clubs, and at Woman's Christian Temperance Union meetings (despite her views against total abstinence). With the League's council, she planned strategy, organized petitions, and solicited membership subscriptions. In 1891, following the endorsement of several churches and the United Labor Party, public interest in suffrage grew, as did Lee's confidence. Although she privately admitted that she was devastated by the frequent criticism of her "advanced" views, she could be outspoken, even abrasive, in her approach. In 1893, she called the Labor Party "a lot of nincompoops" when they supported a suffrage bill burdened by a conditional referendum. In 1894, after six separate bills, a seventh unencumbered suffrage bill finally passed. Lee then organized a colony-wide suffrage petition which was presented to Parliament in August 1894. In December of that year, the Constitution Amendment Act was passed, giving South Australian women the parliamentary vote. Subsequently, they won the right to a postal vote and the right to run for office.

Lee also supported trade unions for women and was the first secretary of the Working Women's Trade Union, founded in 1890. In 1893, she was elected the organization's vice-president and as such was a delegate to the Trades and Labor Council, where she served on the Distressed Women's and Children's Committee. In 1895, she was invited by two trade unions to run for Parliament, but she declined, claiming she could work better without obligation to a particular party. In 1896, on Lee's 75th birthday, the premier awarded her a purse of sovereigns, publicly donated, and acknowledged that the passage of women's suffrage was largely due to her "persistent advocacy and unwearied exertions."

Also in 1896, Mary Lee was appointed first female official visitor to the lunatic asylums, a post she served for the next 12 years. In these later years, however, she was plagued by poverty and an appeal for relief funds launched by an Adelaide paper brought little response. By the time of Lee's death in 1909, her achievements had mostly been forgotten.

SOURCES:

Radi, Heather, ed. *200 Australian Women.* NSW, Australia: Women's Redress Press, 1988.

Lee, Mary Custis (c. 1808–1873)

American aristocrat from Virginia and wife of Robert E. Lee. Born around 1808 in Arlington, Virginia; died in Virginia in 1873; daughter of George Washington Parke Custis (1781–1857, grandson of Martha Washington by her first marriage) and Mary Lee (Fitzhugh) Custis; great-granddaughter of Martha Washington (1731–1802); married Robert E. Lee (1807–1870, the Confederate general), in 1831; children: (four daughters) Mary Custis Lee (1835–1918); Anne Carter Lee (1839–1862); Eleanor Agnes, known as Agnes Lee (1841–1873); and Mildred Childe Lee (1846–1905); (three sons) Custis Lee; William Henry Fitzhugh ("Rooney") Lee; and Robert E. Lee, Jr.

Mary Custis was the great-granddaughter of *Martha Washington. Mary's father, George Washington Parke Custis, was Martha's grandson by her first marriage, and he was raised at Mt. Vernon by Martha and her second husband George Washington who had adopted the boy and influenced him until Washington's death in 1799. With his inherited fortune and vast landholdings (nearly 20,000 acres), George Custis began building his home, the now famous Arlington House, on a green hillside not far from the Potomac, completing the first two wings in 1804, the year of his marriage to **Mary Fitzhugh Custis**. Their daughter Mary, born around 1808, grew up in the stately Greek Revival house with its eight pillars, each five feet in diameter at the base.

Besides serving in the War of 1812, George Custis was a planter, painter, writer, and playwright; in 1831, he painted a still-extant portrait of his wife. His stories, published in the *National Intelligencer,* would be collected and released in book form by his daughter Mary as *Recollections of Washington.* George Custis also despised slavery, calling it "the mightiest serpent that ever infested the world." Though a slaveowner by birth, he freed a number of slaves in his lifetime. His wife and daughter held similar views. Before the slaves were released, mother and daughter conducted classes to help educate them to survive as freedmen, though it was against Virginia law to do so. But the Custises were gradualists, not outright abolitionists, preferring to go slow and resolve federal issues in order to save the Union.

In 1831, Mary Custis married Robert E. Lee, also of Virginia, who had graduated from the U.S.

Mary Custis Lee

Military Academy three years previous. The couple had seven children: four daughters, ◄❧ Mary Custis Lee, ◄❧ Anne Carter Lee, ◄❧ Agnes Lee, and ◄❧ Mildred Childe Lee, and three sons, Custis Lee, William Henry Fitzhugh ("Rooney") Lee, and Robert E. Lee, Jr. They were a close-knit family. The children grew up at Arlington House, riding, sledding, skating, swimming, and playing "amid jasmine and lilac and honeysuckle and grape arbor and rose garden and herb border and woods and orchards," writes Gene Smith. The Lee girls followed in the footsteps of their mother and grandmother, teaching slaves to read.

Following her father's death in 1857, Mary Custis Lee inherited Arlington House, soon known as the Lee mansion, but war clouds were looming. South Carolina seceded from the Union in 1860, and in 1861 Robert E. Lee resigned from the U.S. Army and accepted a commission as a general in the army of the Confederate States of America.

Mary's father George had remained a Federalist until the day he died, believing in a strong central government rather than states' rights.

Robert E. Lee also hated slavery, considering it "a moral and political evil," and thought secession "unconstitutional," but he believed it his duty to side with his native state. His personal code of honor and duty led him to proclaim that "loyalty to Virginia ought to take precedence over what is due the federal government." In 1861, Mary Custis Lee had to abandon her house, family heirlooms and papers when she accompanied her husband south. During the war, she and her daughters knitted socks and gloves for soldiers and served the wounded in military hospitals. In 1862, Mary's 23-year-old daughter Anne contracted typhoid and died; she was buried in the Jones Springs cemetery in Warrenton, North Carolina.

In 1865, Robert E. Lee surrendered at Appomattox Courthouse. The federal government wanted to be sure the Lees of Virginia never returned to live at Arlington House, and so the house and its grounds were turned into a burial ground: Arlington National Cemetery. In 1865, Robert E. Lee was appointed president of Washington College (later Washington and Lee University), in Lexington, Virginia, and the family

---

❧▶ Lee, Mary Custis (1835–1918)

Daughter of the Lees of Virginia. Born Mary Custis Lee in 1835; died in 1918; daughter of Robert E. Lee (1807–1870, the Confederate general) and *Mary Custis Lee (c. 1808–1873); tutored at home, then attended a female academy; never married; no children.

Mary Custis Lee, born in 1835, was the bright, critical, independent daughter, who traveled to more than 24 countries, including Australia, Japan, India, Europe, Africa. She was in London at the outbreak of World War I, when she told a reporter: "I am a soldier's daughter and what I can foresee of this war and the misery which must follow have made me nearly a peace advocate at any price." Mary died soon after the armistice.

SUGGESTED READING:

Coulling, Mary P. *The Lee Girls.*

❧▶ Lee, Anne Carter (1839–1862)

Daughter of the Lees of Virginia. Born Anne Carter Lee (named after her father's mother, Ann Carter Hill) in 1839; died of typhoid in 1862, age 23; daughter of Robert E. Lee (1807–1870, the Confederate general) and *Mary Custis Lee (c. 1808–1873); tutored at home, then attended a female academy; never married; no children.

❧▶ Lee, Agnes (1841–1873)

Daughter of the Lees of Virginia. Born Eleanor Agnes Lee in 1841; died of an intestinal disorder in 1873, age 32; daughter of Robert E. Lee (1807–1870, the Confederate general) and *Mary Custis Lee (c. 1808–1873); tutored at home, then attended a female academy; never married; no children.

❧▶ Lee, Mildred Childe (1846–1905)

Daughter of the Lees of Virginia. Born in 1846; died of a stroke in 1905; daughter of Robert E. Lee (1807–1870, the Confederate general) and *Mary Custis Lee (c. 1808–1873); tutored at home, then attended a female academy; never married; no children.

Mildred Childe Lee, who was born in 1846, adored her father and he adored her, calling her "Precious Life" which he would later shorten to "Life." They spent hours touring the countryside together on horseback. When he died, Mildred stopped riding and would not visit his beloved horse Traveller. In 1905, while in New Orleans for the Mardi Gras, Mildred was found unconscious in her room from a stroke. She died the following morning, age 59.

SUGGESTED READING:

Coulling, Mary P. *The Lee Girls.*

---

moved with him. Robert E. Lee died five years later, on October 12, 1870.

The general had urged his sons to marry, but not his daughters, and suitors from the all-male college were discouraged. Robert E. Lee often spoke of how his girls would stay with their parents, taking care of them into their sunset years, and, indeed, none of them would marry. Mildred, who tended the chickens, wrote a friend: "My chickens are a great comfort. I am often dreadfully lonely." In 1873, Agnes Lee died. Her mother Mary Custis Lee died one month later. She was buried at Lexington, as were all the Lees, except for Anne. Over the years, Anne's burial ground in North Carolina became a lovers' lane and the object of vandalism; her obelisk was toppled. In October 1994, the remains of Anne Carter Lee were moved to Lexington to rest beside her family.

SOURCES:

Kennedy, Roger. "Arlington House, a Mansion That was a Monument," in *Smithsonian*. October 1985, pp. 157–165.

Smith, Gene. "General Lee's Daughters," in *American Heritage*. July–August, 1996, p. 110.

SUGGESTED READING:

Connelly, Thomas L. *The Marble Man*. NY: Alfred A. Knopf, 1977.

Dowdey, Clifford. *Lee*. Boston, MA: Little, Brown, 1965.

Flood, Charles B. *Lee: The Last Years*. Houghton Mifflin, 1981.

Freeman, Douglas L. *R.E. Lee*. 4 vols. NY: Scribner, 1934–35.

Lee, Robert E., Jr. *Recollections and Letters of General Robert E. Lee*. NY: Doubleday, 1909.

Sanborn, Margaret. *Robert E. Lee*. 2 vols. Philadelphia, PA: Lippincott, 1966–67.

Lee, Mary Custis (1835–1918).

See Lee, Mary Custis (c. 1808–1873) for sidebar.

Lee, Mildred Childe (1846–1905).

See Lee, Mary Custis (c. 1808–1873) for sidebar.

Lee, Patty (1820–1871).

See Cary, Alice.

Lee, Peggy (1920—)

American jazz stylist, songwriter, and actress, defined by Down Beat *as the "greatest white female jazz singer since Mildred Bailey." Born Norma Deloris Egstrom (some sources cite Norma Jean Engstrom) in Jamestown, North Dakota, on May 26, 1920; one of seven children of Marvin Egstrom (a station agent for a railroad) and Selma Egstrom (who died when Lee was four); married David Barbour (a guitarist), in 1943 (divorced 1952); married Brad Dexter (an actor), on January 4, 1955 (divorced); married Dewey Martin (an actor), on April 25, 1956 (divorced 1959); children: (first marriage) daughter, Nicki Lee Foster.*

Began singing on local radio stations in high school, then in nightclubs in Chicago and California; hired to sing with Benny Goodman's band (1941), and became nationally known after appearances on network radio, in several musical films, and a string of bestselling records; began writing songs in collaboration with first husband; also wrote partial scores for motion pictures, was nominated for Best Actress for her appearance in Pete Kelly's Blues *(1955), and continued an active nightclub career into the mid-1980s; suffered a stroke (October 27, 1998).*

Partial discography: "Let's Call It a Day," "Why Don't You Do Right," "Fever," "Alright, Okay, You Win," "Hallelujah, I Love Him So," "The Best Is Yet to Come," "Is That All There Is?"

Songwriter: "Mañana," "Golden Earrings," "It's A Good Day," "I Don't Know Enough About You"; also wrote "We Are Siamese" and "He's a Tramp" (music and lyrics for the movie Lady and the Tramp*); also wrote music for other films, including* Johnny Guitar, About Mrs. Leslie, *George Pal's* Jack and the Beanstalk, Sharkey's Machine, The Time Machine, *and* The Russians Are Coming, The Russians Are Coming.

Filmography: The Powers Girl *(1943); (guest singer)* Stage Door Canteen *(1943);* Mr. Music *(1950);* The Jazz Singer *(1953); (lyricist and character voices)* Lady and the Tramp *(1955);* Pete Kelly's Blues *(1955); (lyricist and character voice)* Tom Thumb *(1958); (character voice)* Pieces of Dreams *(1970).*

Bandleader Benny Goodman found himself with a problem one day in 1941. Just before he was to open a major gig at Chicago's swank College Inn, his singer had defected to Artie Shaw, and Goodman was on the hunt for a replacement. Thus he found himself at another Chicago nightspot, The Buttery, listening to one of the candidates suggested to him, a tall, slim blonde who stepped on stage and confidently embarked on a rendition of "Those Foolish Things." Long before she was done, Goodman knew he'd need no further auditions. Peggy Lee was hired on the spot. No one was more surprised than she was. "He was just staring at me and chewing his tongue," she remembered many years later, adding that she was sure Goodman did not care for her. But that night at The Buttery a national career was launched for a singer, songwriter, and actress who, just a few years earlier, had been heard only on a local radio station in her native North Dakota.

Before singing on Valley City's KVOC, Peggy Lee had been plain Norma Egstrom from Jamestown, one of the tiny railroad towns strung out along the windswept northern plains of North Dakota. Born in 1920, she was the youngest of the seven children of Marvin and **Selma Egstrom**, hard-working descendants of the sturdy Scandinavians who populated the plains during the last half of the 19th century. Like almost everyone else in Jamestown, Marvin worked for the Great Northern railroad, as a depot master. His remarriage, shortly after Selma died, marked the beginning of a troubled childhood for the Egstrom children, especially little "Hootchie," as everyone called Norma.

If that's all there is, my friend,
Then let's keep dancing.

—Peggy Lee

Marvin's unexpected choice for a new wife was **Min Schaumberg**. Even at a distance of 60 years, Lee's shorthand description of her stepmother retained the fear which seized a six-year-old girl. "Obese," Lee remembered. "Strong as a horse. Florid face, bulging thyroid eyes, long black hair to her waist pulled back in a bun. Heavy breathing." Even men were afraid of Min, including her new husband, who spent more and more time away from home and turned to alcohol for solace. The children had no such freedom. Min routinely beat them, especially Norma, whom she particularly disliked. Min's favorite weapon was a willow switch, which she often made Norma cut herself before using it on the child with enough force to break the skin. By the time the railroad transferred the Egstroms to a nearby town, even drearier than Jamestown, Lee had already helped an older sister run away from home—for which, of course, she was beaten.

By the time she was 11, Lee had been put to work, finding jobs tending cows, doing housework, or babysitting and cooking for other families. The abuse from Min finally came to an end when the railroad once again transferred Marvin to another railroad town, but offered Min a job elsewhere. Although the enforced separation became permanent, Marvin's drinking had gotten worse and Lee, now 14, often ran the depot for him. But by the time she was in high school, music came to the rescue.

"I had always sung," Lee once wrote. "I sang before I could talk. Although I was alone a lot, I was never really alone because there was always music." There had been the radio, of course, and a tiny theater where she had seen some of the opulent movie musicals of the day. Then, too, there was Doc Haines and his Orchestra, who came to town one year to play a dance at Lee's high school. Doc Haines, despite the mature name, was a college student only a few years older than Lee, but he had a good enough ear to suggest that she sing for him on his weekly radio show on KVOC in Valley City, to which she hitchhiked every weekend. Lee was paid 50 cents per appearance, and Doc Haines was soon calling her his "little blues singer." She moved back to Jamestown after graduating and found two jobs, one working in the coffee shop of the town's only hotel, and the other singing on KRMC, which had studios upstairs. Then came the chance to audition for KDAY in Fargo, the state capital, where a customer who frequented the coffee shop knew the station manager. The audition was successful, and Norma Egstrom had a new job with a new name, Peggy Lee, devised by the station manager who wanted something more sophisticated.

To Lee, Fargo seemed like the biggest city in the world, but she had little time to enjoy it. She took a job slicing and wrapping bread in a bakery from four in the afternoon until four in the morning, then slept until nine before going to the radio station in time to sing on the "Noonday Variety Show" at $1.50 an hour. For extra money, she played Freckled Face Gertie on the "Hayloft Jamboree" and sometimes sang with the Georgie Porgie Breakfast Food Boys, as well as working in the record library, where she became familiar with all the leading composers of the day—Harold Arlen, Jerome Kern, Cole Porter, Richard Rodgers and Lorenz Hart.

In 1937, Lee took the biggest chance of her life and moved to California, where a friend from Jamestown had a place for her to stay. But work was even harder to find than back home, and the $18 in Lee's purse on her arrival disappeared with alarming speed. She took a job as a short-order cook and even worked as a barker at an amusement park before landing a singing job at a seedy nightspot, the Jade Club, known for hiring out-of-work singers desperate for a few dollars and a few hours' work. The club's clientele was quick to spot a naive smalltown girl, and one patron nearly succeeded in abducting Lee into a prostitution ring before the owner of the Jade Club came to her rescue. Badly frightened and plagued by throat trouble that only worsened the more she sang, Lee finally gave up and went back to Fargo, where she discovered she had tonsillitis. The ensuing operation was botched, leaving Lee open to infections that would plague her for years to come.

Once again in familiar territory, Lee soon found a new audience—the students from the University of North Dakota who crowded into the Coffee Shop at Fargo's Powers Hotel every weekend. A cross between an actual short-order restaurant and a pop nightclub, the Coffee Shop was Fargo's version of the Jade Club, with a cleaner, younger audience that loved the blend of blues, jazz, and pop that Lee had picked up in her travels through the underside of Los Angeles nightlife. She packed them in every weekend, singing their requests for $15 a week. But a love affair with a married man ended badly, and Lee felt compelled to leave once again, this time for St. Louis after she auditioned for Will Osborne and his orchestra. The new city treated her no better than Los Angeles had. Her throat began bothering her again, leading to another operation that only made the condition worse; and after only a few engagements, the band broke up, leaving Lee stranded with its manager and pianist. Undaunted, the three made their way back to California and to the very place where Lee had

fared so badly less than two years before—the Jade. But this time, things would be different.

In the audience one night was a young songwriter named Jack Brooks, who in a few years' time would write the pop standard "That's Amore." Impressed with Lee's style, Brooks invited her to audition at The Doll's House, a nightery in Palm Springs owned by a friend, Frank Bering. Bering was a successful hotelier who also owned the elegant Ambassador Hotel in Chicago, and who numbered among his acquaintances Fred Mandel, the millionaire owner of Chicago's leading department store of the time, not to mention the Detroit Tigers baseball club. Bering hired her, the Mandels were impressed with her singing, and, before long, Lee found herself the featured attraction at Chicago's ritzy Ambassador Lounge, living in a luxurious suite with maid service, a different gown for each night's performance, and $75 a week in spending money. The Mandels introduced her to the best of Chicago society, which quickly formed the backbone of her nightly audience at

the Ambassador. After barely a year, she joined Benny Goodman's band.

Goodman had already taken the country by storm, starting with his legendary appearances at The Palomar Ballroom in Los Angeles in 1937 (just when Lee was arriving for her ill-fated Jade Club experience), at New York's Paramount Theater later the same year after a cross-country tour, and the historic Carnegie Hall concert of 1938. By 1939, when he was all of 29 years old, Goodman had audaciously published his life story; and in 1941, when Lee was hired, he had settled into a long reign as the "The King of Swing." In later years, Lee would always wonder why Goodman did not fire her, especially after the reviews of her first night's performance at the College Inn appeared—"sweet sixteen and will never be missed" being one of the milder comments. She even offered to quit, but Goodman refused and told her to show up two days later for a recording session for Columbia, turning a deaf ear to Lee's confession that she had never been in a recording studio and assigning her "Elmer's Tune"—a notoriously difficult number with frequent rhythm-and-pitch changes.

Audiotape was still years in the future. Sessions were recorded straight to a wax master disc, and a mistake meant scrapping the master and starting over from the top. Understandably, Lee was apprehensive. But the band's pianist came to her rescue. He told her to arrive at the studio early, rehearsed her, and even inserted in the score a pitch-setting tone that, to the ordinary ear, sounded like merely a piano riff during the band's opening bars. "You catch it from that," he told Lee, "that'll be the cue, count four, and go!" It was the first of literally hundreds of recordings that would turn Peggy Lee into a national phenomenon, notably when she recorded "Why Don't You Do Right?" for Goodman, the record that established her reputation as a jazz artist. Goodman paid her the usual ten dollars to record it, with all rights forfeited.

By the time Lee arrived in New York with the band, word had gotten around. Playing the New Yorker Hotel's Terrace Room, her audience would routinely include Duke Ellington (who nicknamed her "The Queen"), Fats Waller, and other notables of the jazz-and-blues scene, along with some of Broadway's and Hollywood's leading names—*Joan Crawford, Gary Cooper, *Lynn Fontanne and Alfred Lunt. New York's nightbirds loved Lee's warm, personal delivery, which some compared to *Billie Holiday; and she was singing with some of the best sidemen in the business, for Goodman wanted only the cream of the crop in

his band and dismissed prevailing racial attitudes by hiring such African-American jazz greats as Cootie Williams, Lionel Hampton, Charlie Christian and Teddy Wilson. "If you don't feel a thrill when Lee sings," jazz critic Leonard Feather once wrote, "you're dead, Jack."

It was the band's guitarist, however, to whom Lee was paying the most attention. Goodman had hired David Barbour shortly after Lee joined the band, and it was obvious to everyone that the relationship was becoming more than professional. "My feelings for David grew and grew," Lee once wrote. "When I noticed he didn't eat very much, I would fix up his meals at the coffee shop counter; a little salt and pepper, a little butter, a little coaxing." The reason for Barbour's lack of appetite soon became apparent when, one night, he was late for the stage call. Running to his room, Lee found him close to passing out from drink. Despite his alcoholism, Lee was in love and married Barbour in Los Angeles in 1943, shortly after Goodman had fired him—not because of the drinking, the gossip went, but because Goodman was jealous. The rumors persisted, and even years later Lee would still feel compelled to deny there had every been any romantic attachment with Benny Goodman. "We were always just friends," she insisted.

Although her marriage would be plagued by Barbour's disease, it seemed to provide the love and security Lee hadn't felt since the death of her mother. She was careful to point out in later times that her husband had never been abusive to her and had had a "lovely, quiet disposition." A daughter, Nicki, was born to the couple in 1944. During the next several years, Barbour would encourage Lee's ambitions as a lyricist and write the melodies and arrangements for the tunes Lee said were largely based on her first real experience with a loving relationship—songs such as "It's a Good Day" and "I Don't Know Enough About You." Their most famous collaboration was the wildly successful "Mañana," a playful samba melody the couple wrote while vacationing in Mexico after one of the many operations for stomach ulcers and liver ailments that Barbour was forced to undergo. It was recorded with *Carmen Miranda's Brazilians doing backup vocals and, Lee claimed, was the first song to use a fadeout at the end, rather than coming to a coda and finale.

Lee's life took new turns in other ways during her marriage. She dabbled in politics, campaigning for Harry Truman in 1948, and served on the board of directors for the U.N.-based Meals for Millions program, which distributed food supplies to famine victims. In the late 1940s, she was introduced to Ernest Holmes, the founder and proponent of "The Science of Mind," a blend of psychology and spirituality and a precursor of many similar systems which have since come to prominence. "It wasn't until I met Ernest Holmes," Lee said, "that I realized we live in a universe that is primarily spiritual, and that it's possible to get everything we need . . . through the scientific application of prayer and meditation." Her beliefs were no doubt a great comfort during the later years of her marriage to Barbour, as his alcoholism grew more serious and his health more precarious. Finally, it was Barbour who pleaded with Lee for a divorce, saying he was afraid of unintentionally hurting Nicki one day. Under the laws then current, it was Lee who had to file and serve the papers which, ironically, occurred on the same night she recorded "Let's Call It a Day," a bittersweet song about the end of an affair which became all the more effective because of her own sadness. She and David were divorced in 1952, and two subsequent marriages—to Brad Dexter and Dewey Martin, both actors—were short-lived.

Despite such personal disappointments, Lee had become one of the country's most popular artists. No longer just a "girl singer" for a big band, she had established herself as a solo artist with a blues-tinged, seductive style that led one critic to label her "the queen of sultry." By the late 1940s, Lee was much sought after for the national radio shows of such stars as Bing Crosby (with whom she did two Hollywood musical films), Perry Como, and her old friend from her Chicago days, Jimmy Durante. She had a lucrative recording contract with Capitol, under which she would give new interpretations to such standards as "I've Got You Under My Skin" and "Love Me or Leave Me." She had become versatile enough to record a spoof song like "Caramba! It's the Samba!" and, in the same session, turn out a sexy, sassy version of "Them There Eyes." Danny Thomas, with whom Lee appeared in 1953's *The Jazz Singer,* told an interviewer, "There's nobody like her. She drops her head down, leans on the piano and just falls back to it as she's finishing. Lee's style is *her.*" In 1958, Lee's version of Little Willie John's "Fever," with only percussion and bass backing her up, took the nation by storm; that same year, she was nominated for an Oscar for Best Actress for her performance as the alcoholic singer Rose in Jack Webb's *Pete Kelly's Blues.*

Lee's voice had become so familiar that movie audiences flocked to theaters to see an animated feature in which she did four of the voices, collaborated on much of the score, and even did some of the sound effects. The film was Disney's 1955 release *Lady and the Tramp,* the story of the dainty spaniel Lady who falls for the rough-and-ready mutt named Tramp. Lee found the experience a creative challenge. "Walt [Disney] let me have all the freedom anyone could possibly have," she recalled. "Every person who worked on that film was touched by Mr. Disney's genius." Lee went on to write music for many other classic films—*Johnny Guitar,* George Pal's *Jack And The Beanstalk* (for which she wrote the theme and to which she contributed a character voice) and, in later years, *Sharkey's Machine* and *The Russians Are Coming, The Russians Are Coming.*

By late 1958, the stress of her workload began to have its effects. Lee's old throat problems re-emerged, and she was forced into a seven-month retirement, only to return in 1959 in an entirely new venture, as part owner of New York's legendary supper club, Basin Street East. It would become a New York fixture for years to come, prompting *Newsweek* to comment that Lee was "singlehandedly reviving the supper club business" that had been in decline since before the Second World War. In addition to months-long appearances at the club, Lee embarked on a string of television specials and traveled to Europe for dates in Paris and London, among other places. But during a performance in New York in the early 1960s, Lee had to be rushed to the hospital after collapsing on stage from what turned out to be double pneumonia and pleurisy. Even worse, she was diagnosed with diabetes. Another lengthy recuperation followed, during which Lee collaborated with composer Paul Horner and playwright William Luce on a musical version of her life, *Peg,* which closed after negative reviews and just three performances at Broadway's Lunt-Fontanne Theater.

But there was always the recording studio, and Lee's next national hit may have reflected her bitterness at the disappointment of a Broadway flop. It was 1969's "Is That All There Is?", written by Jerry Leiber and Mike Stoller (who had also come up with "You Ain't Nothin' But a Hound Dog" some years earlier for Elvis Presley), and Lee had a tough time convincing Capitol to let her record it, let alone release it. "They said it was too far out," Lee later remembered, although Capitol could hardly be blamed on the evidence of the lyrics. A spoken litany of life's disappointments—from a little girl's discovery that a circus wasn't all she thought it would be, to an old woman facing death with bored resignation—its only sung portion included the refrain:

If that's all there is, my friend,
Then let's keep dancing.

Lee's instincts, of course, were right on target, and she traded Capitol's insistence that she appear in a television special for their agreement to release the song. It remained at the top of the charts for months in 1969 and was re-released in 1973.

A much more serious battle awaited Lee, after the Disney Company announced the first release on videocassette of *Lady and the Tramp* in 1988. She had been paid only $3,500 for her work on the film, plus a $500 honorarium for promoting one of its many re-releases in theaters, and Lee felt she was entitled to a portion of the estimated $9 million Disney would make from a technology that had not existed in 1955. She sued Disney on the basis of a clause in her original contract that prevented Disney from selling any "transcriptions" of the film without her express consent, arguing that a videocassette qualified as a transcription. The court agreed, awarding her $3.8 million dollars and setting a precedent protecting artists' rights in their work, no matter in what future form that work is exploited. By the time the suit was settled in 1991, Lee was confined to a wheelchair, the result of her diabetes, double-bypass heart surgery, and a fall. She admitted that the trial had been hard for her, but told reporters that the settlement money would ensure a secure future for her three grandchildren, who were by then in their 20s.

With her retirement permanent, and before she suffered a stroke in 1998, Lee managed an art gallery with her daughter Nicki, enjoyed the success of several re-releases of her hundreds of recordings, and was honored at a "Celebrate Peggy Lee" concert in 1994, at which several singers influenced by her style paid her melodic tribute. It all proved something Jimmy Durante had told her years earlier, even though he knew nothing of her abused childhood. "Someday," he said, "you'll feel something come back from the audience, and then you won't ever feel afraid again."

SOURCES:
"Black Coffee (review)," in *Down Beat*. Sept. 23, 1953.
Hoefer, George. "Peggy Lee: Girl in the Middle," in *Down Beat*. Vol. 26, no. 11. May 28, 1959.
Lee, Peggy. *Miss Peggy Lee: An Autobiography*. NY: Donald Fine Books, 1989.
"No Pussycat in Court, Peggy Lee Nips Disney for $3.8 Million," in *People Weekly*. Vol. 35, no. 13. April 8, 1991.
Stark, John. "The Peggy Lee Songbook (review)," in *People Weekly*. Vol. 34, no. 13. October 1, 1993.

Norman Powers,
writer-producer, Chelsea Lane Productions, New York

Lee, Sarah (1791–1856)

English writer and artist. Name variations: Sarah Bowdich; Mrs. T.E. Bowdich. Born Sarah Wallis in Colchester, England, on September 10, 1791; died in Erith, Kent, England, on September 22, 1856; daughter of John Eglintin Wallis; married Thomas Edward Bowdich (a naturalist), in 1813 (died 1824); married Robert Lee, in 1829.

An English writer and artist, Sarah Lee was born Sarah Wallis in 1791 in Colchester, England. In 1813, she married the naturalist Thomas Edward Bowdich and accompanied him to Africa in 1814, 1815, and 1823. Following his death in 1824, she married Robert Lee. A popularizer of natural science, Sarah Lee wrote *Taxidermy* (1820), *Excursions in Madeira and Porto Santo* (1825), *Memoirs of Baron Cuvier* (1833), and *Adventures in Australia* (1851). She also wrote and illustrated *The Fresh-water Fishes of Great Britain* (1828).

Lee, Sophia (1750–1824)

English novelist and dramatist. Born in London, England, in 1750; died at her house near Clifton, Bristol, on March 13, 1824; daughter of John Lee (d. 1781, an actor and theatrical manager); mother was an actress whose name is unknown; sister of novelist Harriet Lee (1757–1851).

Sophia Lee's first dramatic work, *The Chapter of Accidents*, a one-act opera based on Diderot's *Père de famille*, was produced by George Colman at the Haymarket Theatre on August 5, 1780. The proceeds were spent in establishing a school at Bath, where Lee made a home for her sisters, including the writer ***Harriet Lee**. Sophia Lee's subsequent productions included *The Recess, or a Tale of other Times* (1785), a historical romance, and *Almeyda, Queen of Grenada* (1796), a tragedy in blank verse which opened at the Drury Lane with ***Sarah Siddons** in the lead. She also contributed to her sister's *Canterbury Tales* (1797). *Recess*, with its "underlining of women's 'lost' lives or invisibility in history, its treatment of madness and oppression, and its use of Gothic conventions," writes **Joanne Shattock**, has "attracted the attention of . . . critics who liken it to better known Gothic novels by ***Ann Radcliffe**, who very much approved of it."

SOURCES:
Shattock, Joanne. *The Oxford Guide to British Women Writers*. Oxford: Oxford University Press, 1993.

Lee, Vernon (1856–1935).

See Paget, Violet.

Lee-Gartner, Kerrin (1966—)

Canadian skier. Born on September 21, 1966, in Trail, British Columbia, Canada; grew up in Rossland, British Columbia.

Kerrin Lee-Gartner grew up in Rossland, British Columbia, five houses down from the parents of *Nancy Greene, the popular 1969 giant slalom gold medalist. But after ten years on the world-cup circuit, Lee-Gartner had managed only one third-place finish. Then on February 15, 1992, in Albertville, on what was considered the steepest, most difficult, and longest course ever designed for the downhill, Kerrin Lee-Gartner had the race of her life. With a time of 1:52.61, she brought home the first Olympic gold medal for a Canadian skier, male or female, in the downhill. **Hilary Lindh** of the United States won the silver with 1:52.61 while **Veronika Wallinger** of Austria won the bronze with 1:52.64. Before her win, Lee-Gartner had endured several injuries. She had been chosen for the Canadian Women's Ski Team at age 16, but her hopes for a successful World Cup tour in 1985 had been dashed when she had a serious accident and underwent reconstructive knee surgery. In February 1989, she had been off her skis for six months following another accident.

Leech, Faith (b. 1941).

See Fraser, Dawn for sidebar.

Leech, Margaret (1893–1974)

American historian who was the first woman to receive the Pulitzer Prize for history, and the only woman to win the Pulitzer Prize for history twice (1942 and 1960). Name variations: Mrs. Ralph Pulitzer. Born Margaret Kernochan Leech on November 7, 1893, in Newburgh, New York; died on February 24, 1974, in New York, New York; daughter of William Kernochan Leech and Rebecca (Taggert) Leech; attended private schools in Newburgh and Poughkeepsie, New York; Vassar College, B.A., 1915; married Ralph Pulitzer (a newspaper publisher), on August 1, 1928 (died June 14, 1939); children: Susan Pulitzer Freedberg; Margaretta Pulitzer (died in infancy).

The winner of two Pulitzer Prizes for history, one for her comprehensive study of the nation's capital during the Civil War, *Reveille in*

Washington (1941), the other for her biography of President William McKinley, *In the Days of McKinley* (1959), historian Margaret Leech was born in Newburgh, New York, in 1893 and began writing at a young age. In 1901, at age eight, she composed a short poem on the occasion of McKinley's assassination:

> I am oh so sorry that our President is dead,
> And everybody's sorry, so my father said;
> And the horrid man who killed him is a-sitting in his cell
> And I'm glad that *Emma Goldman doesn't board at this hotel.

Leech attended private schools and graduated from Vassar College in 1915. Her first job was with the Condé Nast publishing company, answering letters from disgruntled subscribers who had not received their magazines. She later worked for various World War I fund-raising organizations and was on the staff of *Anne Morgan's American Committee for Devastated France.

During the 1920s, Leech began writing novels, Her first, *The Back of the Book* (1924), concerning a refined young woman working in New York, drew extensively from her own experiences. A second novel, *Tin Wedding* (1926), written from the point of view of a woman on her tenth wedding anniversary, and a third, *The Feather Nest* (1928), about possessive mother love, followed in rapid succession. All three books were praised for their sound characterizations, their perceptive selection of detail, and their grace and clarity of style, qualities that Leech would develop more fully in her later

Margaret Leech

work. In 1928, Leech deviated from the novel form to collaborate with Heywood Broun on *Anthony Comstock: Roundsman of the Lord*, a biography of the famous reformer and crusader against obscenity. Based on solid research, the book was praised as factual as well as lively and witty, and became the first choice of the Literary Guild for that year.

Also in 1928, Leech married Ralph Pulitzer, publisher of the New York *World* and son of Joseph Pulitzer who founded the Pulitzer Prize. Her marriage, combined with her own stature as a writer, gave her access to an even wider literary circle, which grew to include publishers, playwrights, journalists, and actors. The Pulitzers had two daughters: Margaretta, who died in infancy, and Susan.

Following a collaboration with **Beatrice Kaufman** on an unsuccessful play, *Divided by Three* (1934), Leech embarked on the gargantuan project that would ultimately bring her fame. For a period of five years beginning in 1935, she investigated life in Washington, D.C., during the Civil War. Conducting her research at the New York Public Library and the Library of Congress, she examined letters, memoirs, photographs, newspaper articles, and government documents. The resulting *Reveille in Washington, 1859–1865*, which was serialized in the *Atlantic Monthly* before being published in book form in 1941, brought into vivid perspective a disquieting time in American history. "Despite its color and dramatic vigor," wrote MacKinlay Kantor, "few other histories of any nation or period bear more hammer-marks of an implacable concern for the grim and bitter truth." The book became a bestseller and received the Pulitzer Prize for history in 1942.

Leech worked 12 years on her second book, *In the Days of McKinley* (1959), which John Morton Blum called a "first-rate study of a second-rate President." Working slowing and "most ostentatiously," as she put it, Leech provided a graphic and comprehensive portrait of an epoch in American history as well as a fresh and independent view of her subject. "Miss Leech's engaging volume is not the last word on McKinleyism," wrote William Miller in the *New York Herald Tribune* (November 1, 1959), "but on McKinley himself it provides illuminating and pleasurable reading." In addition to receiving a second Pulitzer Prize for her book on McKinley, Leech was also awarded the Bancroft Prize by Columbia University.

Leech, who was widowed in 1939, was described as a direct and brisk woman. When not at work, she enjoyed travel, the theater, and good conversation. Her overwhelming pleasure, however, was in research and writing. "There's a challenge in taking something obscure and trying to find out what you can," she told Lewis Nichols. Margaret Leech died on February 24, 1974.

SOURCES:

Kantor, MacKinlay. *New York Herald Tribune Books.* August 31, 1941.

Moritz, Charles, ed. *Current Biography.* NY: H.W. Wilson, 1960.

Nichols, Lewis. *The New York Times Book Review.* November 1, 1959.

Read, Phyllis J., and Bernard L. Witlieb. *The Book of Women's Firsts.* NY: Random House, 1992.

Barbara Morgan,
Melrose, Massachusetts

Lefanu, Alicia (1753–1817)

English playwright. Name variations: Le Fanu. Born in 1753; died in 1817; daughter of *Frances Sheridan (1724–1766, novelist and dramatist) and Thomas Sheridan (a well-known actor-manager); sister of Richard Brinsley Sheridan (1751–1816) and *Elizabeth Lefanu (1758–1837); married Joseph Lefanu or Le Fanu (1814–1873, a novelist, journalist, and brother of Henry and Philip Lefanu, a divine), in 1776.

Alicia Lefanu wrote *The Flowers: A Fairy Tale* and the comedy *Sons of Erin* which was performed in London in 1812.

Lefanu, Alicia (c. 1795–c. 1826)

English writer. Name variations: Le Fanu. Born around 1795; died around 1826; daughter of Henry Lefanu or Le Fanu (brother of Joseph and Philip Lefanu) and *Elizabeth Lefanu (1758–1837).

Alicia Lefanu published the *Memoirs of Mrs. *Frances Sheridan* in 1824. She also wrote *Rosara's Chains: A Poem* (1812), *The Indian Voyage* (1816), *Strathallan* (1816), and *Helen Monteagle* (1818).

Lefanu, Elizabeth (1758–1837)

English writer. Name variations: Le Fanu. Born in 1758; died in 1837; daughter of *Frances Sheridan (1724–1766, novelist and dramatist) and Thomas Sheridan (a well-known actor-manager); sister of Richard Brinsley Sheridan (1751–1816) and *Alicia Lefanu (1753–1817); married Henry Lefanu (brother of Joseph and Philip Lefanu); children: *Alicia Lefanu (c. 1795–c. 1826).

Lefanu, Nicola (b. 1947).

See Maconchy, Elizabeth for sidebar.

Lefaucheux, Marie-Helene

(1904–1964)

French feminist and representative to the United Nations. Born Marie-Helene Postel-Vinay in Paris, France, on February 2, 1904; died in a plane crash in the United States, on February 25, 1964; daughter of Marcel Postel-Vinay and Madeleine (Delombre) Postel-Vinay; attended elementary schools in Paris; graduated from the École des Sciences Politiques; studied piano at the École du Louvre; married Pierre-Andre Lefaucheux (a lawyer, civil engineer, and president and general director of the Renault Automobile Works), in 1925.

A French housewife and "pianist of distinction," Marie-Helene Lefaucheux was thrust into public life in the 1940s, during the German occupation of France. With her husband Pierre-Andre Lefaucheux, a lawyer and civil servant, she became active in the Resistance, serving as vice president of the Paris Committee of Liberation and conducting welfare work among prisoners and deportees. When her husband was arrested and deported to Germany by train, Lefaucheux followed on her bicycle to ascertain its destination. She subsequently orchestrated her husband's escape from Weimar prison camp, for which she was awarded the Croix de Guerre and the Rosette de la Resistance. (Pierre-Andre later became president and general director of the Renault Automobile Works.)

Following France's liberation, Lefaucheux was elected to the Consultative Assembly, the first interim parliament of the provisional French government; she was representing the Organisation Civile et Militaire. In the November 1945 election, she was returned to the Constituent Assembly as a deputy. She was also elected to the Municipal Council of Paris, where she served as vice president. In 1946, she was elected to the Council of the Fourth French Republic under the terms of the new constitution, and she later represented metropolitan France in the Assembly of the French Union, serving as vice president from 1959 to 1960.

Lefaucheux was the only female member of the French delegation to attend the First General Assembly of the United Nations in 1946, and represented France on the UN Commission on the Status of Women. She was also a founder of the Association des Femmes de l'Union Français,

Marie-Helene Lefaucheux

an organization concerned with the welfare of Africans and Algerians. "The women of France have their rights," she said. "It is for us to see that other women in other parts of the world are helped and encouraged." From 1954 to 1964, Lefaucheux served as president of the National Council of Women and was elected president of the International Council of Women in 1957. She retired in 1964 and was killed in a plane crash the following year.

SOURCES:

Rothe, Anna, ed. *Current Biography.* NY: H.W. Wilson, 1947.

Uglow, Jennifer. *The Macmillan Dictionary of Women's Biography.* 2nd ed. London: Macmillan, 1989.

Lefebvre, Anne (1654–1720).

See Dacier, Anne.

Lefebvre, Catherine

(c. 1764–after 1820)

French heroine of Sardou's comedy. Name variations: Lefevre; duchesse de Dantzig or Duchess of Dantzig; Madame Sans-Gêne or Sans-Gene. Born Catherine Hubscher around 1764; died after 1820; married François Joseph Lefebvre ((1755–1820), duc de Dantzig (a French general), in 1783.

Catherine Hubscher married François Joseph Lefebvre, a common soldier, and served as laundress for his company. Though her husband was created marshal of the French empire, besieged and captured Danzig, and was appointed peer of

France around 1814 by Louis XVIII at the Restoration, it was said that Catherine remained a frank, unpretentious woman of the people. She was the basis for the heroine in Victorien Sardou's 1893 comedy *Madame Sans-Gêne*.

Leffler, Anne Charlotte (1849–1892).

See Edgren, Anne Charlotte.

Le Gallienne, Eva (1899–1991)

English-born actress, director, and producer who formed New York's Civic Repertory Theater, an attempt to establish a repertory tradition in the American theater, and worked nearly continuously throughout her long career. Name variations: E. Le G. Born January 11, 1899, in London, England; died on June 3, 1991, in Weston, Connecticut, of heart failure; daughter of Julie Nørregaard (a Danish journalist) and Richard Le Gallienne (English poet and novelist); never married; no children.

After graduating from London's Academy of Dramatic Arts, made her West End stage debut (1914) and soon crossed the Atlantic to appear to great acclaim on Broadway, where she became one of the most famous leading ladies of her day; turned to directing and formed New York's Civic Repertory Theater (1926), the first of three ultimately unsuccessful attempts to establish a repertory tradition in the American theater; made few film appearances, though nominated for an Oscar for her work in Resurrection *(1980); wrote two autobiographies and a novel for children.*

Filmography: The Player King *(1955);* The Devil's Disciple *(1959);* Resurrection *(1980).*

There was a certain irony to Eva Le Gallienne's last appearance on Broadway, a part of the world over which she had hovered, sometimes like a loving mother and sometimes like a scolding muse, for nearly seven decades. In that time, she had tried with sporadic success to coax the theater away from its commercial instincts and onto the path of Truth and Beauty. Now, in 1982, Le Gallienne had agreed to direct a revival of her adaptation of *Alice in Wonderland* and to take the part of the White Queen. So it was that she found herself on opening night suspended by wires over the stage in a white flounced gown and white, powdery makeup, waving her scepter and issuing her contradictory orders in a high, cackling voice to a bewildered Alice below—a cockeyed parody of her past efforts as leading lady, producer, and director to keep the theater on the straight and narrow. Her secretary later

reported that after Le Gallienne had taken the curtain calls demanded by a respectful audience, she returned wearily to her dressing room and sighed, "I don't want to work in the theater anymore. It's not my theater."

Seventy years earlier, she had written to a cousin, "I *do* wish to become a great actress, you don't *know* how I wish it!" She was only 15 then, but had been enjoying the theater and hobnobbing with thespians since early childhood under the guidance of her mother, the Danish journalist **Julie Nørregaard**. Julie had been separated for several months from her husband, the English poet and novelist Richard Le Gallienne, when Eva was born on January 11, 1899. Richard, a public defender of women's rights and freedoms like Nørregaard, was also a chronic womanizer and had been discovered in bed with a paramour by an indignant Julie less than a year after their marriage in February of 1897. Eva knew her father only through the letters her parents exchanged and from recollections of a half-sister, **Hesper Le Gallienne**, from an earlier marriage of Richard's. Eva did not meet her father until she was a grown woman in America.

Julie began taking Eva to the theater early on; Le Gallienne could recall seeing Charles Kingsley's *The Water Babies* at London's Drury Lane when she was just three. Eva spent much of her childhood, however, in Paris, where Julie took a newspaper job in 1904. "All around one is harmony of line and a richness of life, and beauty," Le Gallienne later said of growing up in Europe's cultural headquarters of the new century. Not long after they arrived in France, Julie took Eva to see the great *Sarah Bernhardt play the Prince in a production of *Sleeping Beauty*, presented in Bernhardt's own theater on the Place du Chatelet. Le Gallienne was mesmerized as soon as Bernhardt made her entrance as the Prince, "as though he lived more intensely, more joyously, more richly than other people," she wrote years later. In a tribute to Bernhardt, Julie named the millinery shop she opened in 1907 Madame Fédora, after one of Bernhardt's most successful plays. The shop did well enough to enable Le Gallienne to attend the theater several times a week with her mother, to spend summers with Julie's family in Denmark, and to attend a private girls' school. When she entered the Collège Sévigné at seven years of age, Eva was intimately familiar with London, Paris, and Copenhagen; had been reading for two years; and could speak, read and write French, English and Danish.

Among her mother's friends were the Favershams, an English acting and producing couple whose summer home in the English countryside, Chiddingford, had become an annual gathering place for theater notables. Julie and Eva were first invited in 1910. Among the guests were producer Herbert Beerbohm Tree and his leading lady at Tree's His Majesty's Theater, *Constance Collier. Collier became the first of Le Gallienne's several adolescent infatuations, and it was to Collier that Le Gallienne initially confided her intention to be an actress. Eva's earliest acting lessons were from Collier, who coached her in Shakespeare and taught her, Le Gallienne later said, to "bring out the music without losing the meaning." Le Gallienne took Collier's tutoring so successfully to heart that Will Faversham was inspired to offer her a small walk-on in an upcoming New York engagement, but Julie insisted that Eva's education came first and enrolled her daughter in a finishing school. Le Gallienne complained that the teachers were dull and boring, and that the school's policy of not allowing the girls to kiss one another was barbaric.

Late in 1913, Le Gallienne met the woman she had admired from a distance since she was a child. Julie, who had now moved back to London, interviewed Sarah Bernhardt for a newspaper article, struck up a friendship, and brought her daughter backstage one evening after a performance of Bernhardt's *Jeanne Doré*. Eva found herself speechless, but fared better on a second visit in 1914. "She soon put me at my ease," Le Gallienne later wrote of her idol, "asking me many questions, gradually drawing me out. She kept my hand in hers and I looked with wonder at the sensitive, nervous fingers, heavy with rings, the tips painted scarlet to the middle knuckle." The formidable Bernhardt had become such an institution that every aspect of her career and her productions were under her direct control, a professional status admired by Le Gallienne as much as Bernhardt's volcanic acting style. Bernhardt's productions, Le Gallienne later wrote, "had a tidy, organized brilliance that was somehow very French."

After surviving finishing school, Le Gallienne finally began her stage education in earnest at London's Academy of Dramatic Arts, where she studied movement, elocution, and techniques for acting both classical and modern drama. Even better, she appeared professionally on stage for the first time in 1914's *Monna Vanna*, in which Constance Collier played Maurice Maeterlinck's 15th-century Italian heroine. Le Gallienne was given a non-speaking part as a pageboy. "I wasn't a bit frightened," she boasted in a letter written after opening night, "and I felt quite at home and not a bit self-conscious. I tried to forget everything and live in the play, and I succeeded." Le Gallienne had her first speaking part as a Cockney maid in the comedy *The Laughter of Fools* the following year. Although she prepared for and played the role entirely seriously, the audience began chuckling from her first entrance and brought her back for a solo curtain call at the end. Her first notice in a London newspaper deemed her "a brilliant new comedienne," but wartime Zeppelin raids over London forced the show's early closing. Many English actors had decided their careers were safer in America, Constance Collier among them, and it was at Collier's suggestion that Julie and Eva sailed for New York in July of 1915.

> The theater should be free to the people just as the Public Library is free, just as the museum is free.
>
> —Eva Le Gallienne

Le Gallienne had the good fortune to arrive in New York at a time when theater audiences were seeking relief from the bad news in Europe with light-hearted romantic comedies and sentimental Cinderella tales that had plenty of parts for eager ingenues. One such production was *Mrs. Boltay's Daughters*, in which Le Gallienne made her American stage debut in the unlikely role of an African-American maid, having quickly learned black dialect as interpreted to her by a white actress playing one of the daughters of the title. Her performance, she later wrote, was "an astonishing portrait of a colored maid with very bright blue eyes shining out of a smeary, chocolate-colored face and speaking grotesquely bewildering dialect: part British, part Cockney, with here and there a dash of Irish." She fared better as another Cockney maid in *Bunny*, in which *The New York Times* noted that she "arrives on stage with a flourish, acting . . . with high spirits and no little skill." The *Times* was even more laudatory in its review of her work in *The Melody of Youth* as an Irish lass, and was positively effusive by the time she starred in her first leading role in *Mr. Lazarus*, in which she played a serving maid in a boarding house who becomes a beautiful socialite through the kindness of a stranger. "Miss Le Gallienne plays with a delicacy of which she has hitherto remained unsuspected," wrote the *Times'* John Corbin. But Le Gallienne found the role exhausting because, she said, "not being a master of technique and the tricks of my trade, I simply have to throw myself heart and soul into the part . . . in order to create the illusion." This was to become, in fact, precisely her technique throughout her long career, a complete absorption in the role at hand. "When I play, I am two different people," she wrote to a cousin in Denmark in 1916. "All day long, whatever I may be doing or whoever I may be with, I live with the character . . . 'til it becomes another self." Indeed, when actress **Mariette Hartley** studied under Le Gallienne nearly 50 years later, the older woman told her that the aim of an actor is total surrender of the self. Le Gallienne described the first time she had played Juliet, "waking up" later to find her cheeks streaming with Juliet's tears. It was after these moments, Le Gallienne told Hartley, when Bernhardt would murmur "*Dieu était là*" ("God was there").

But in 1916, her 17-year-old self was very much on her mind. With the intense self-appraisal of that age, Le Gallienne was noticing something else that seemed at odds with her peers. She confided to the same Danish cousin that she seemed to have no romantic interest in boys, describing her male friends as "comrades" but nothing more. "There must be something peculiar with me, for I never give it a thought," she wrote. Nor had she thought much about her infatuations with older women like Constance Collier and her worship of Sarah Bernhardt, whose friendship she renewed when Bernhardt toured America in 1916. She attended every performance of the 76-year-old Bernhardt's *Jeanne d'Arc* at the Empire Theater and never forgot the moment in the play when Jeanne tells the judges at her trial that she is 18 years old. "Everyone in the audience believed her," recalled Le Gallienne, "and rightly, for at that moment, it was true." Then there was Le Gallienne's friendship with *Eleanora Sears, a star athlete who had scandalized society by sitting astride a horse to play polo with men and by baring her arms with rolled-up sleeves on the tennis court; and with Russian émigré actress *Alla Nazimova, whose work Le Gallienne much admired. Adding to Eva's collection of strong-willed, independent women was the great *Ethel Barrymore, with whom Le Gallienne toured in two plays, playing Barrymore's daughter in both. Eva especially admired Barrymore's skill in drawing laughs with even the most banal line, and for her withering gaze out into the house when latecomers arrived in the audience—a look Le Gallienne quickly added to her own repertoire of expressions. Le Gallienne's affections finally settled on a woman of her own age, **Mary Duggat**. "Mimsey," as Le Gallienne called Duggat, had been among the company of a short-lived play in which Le Gallienne starred in 1917, and traveled with Le Gallienne during her tour with Ethel Barrymore. The two lovers were inseparable, Le Gallienne

spending more time with Mary than at home with Julie, and taking Mary along with her to lunch with Richard Le Gallienne, now officially divorced from Julia and remarried to an American. Neither parent expressed surprise at their daughter's lesbianism. Julie, in fact, left Eva and Mary on their own in New York by returning to England to resuscitate her writing career.

Le Gallienne's reaction to the actors' strike of 1919 gave the first indication of the argument she would have with the theater in years to come. The strike was delaying the opening of *Lusmore*, in which Le Gallienne was to play a blind girl. She had been excited about the role and felt it was held captive by banal labor disputes, even though she was a member of the fledgling Actors' Equity. It was of little consequence to her that the strike, which finally legitimized Equity as the profession's collective voice, was intended to break the despotic power of producers over actors. "It seems almost incredible," she complained, "that a beautiful, artistic production . . . should be stopped by carpenters and moving men. Such is democracy!"

Lusmore, when it finally opened, proved unsuccessful and closed in a month, but Le Gallienne quickly returned to work as Elsie Dover in *Not So Long Ago*, a Victorian romance that opened at the Booth Theater in May of 1920. "Miss Le Gallienne works as an artist in her medium," critic H.T. Parker wrote from Boston, where the show had played before moving to New York. She was, he said, "a youthful actress . . . who can define, disclose and differentiate character; who has plentiful charm, personality, and high spirits; and who keeps them steadily in service of the play and to the part." The show's producer, Lee Shubert, signed Le Gallienne to a three-year contract before sending it out on tour. Duggat chose not to accompany her, and Le Gallienne was devastated to learn on her return to New York that Mary had unexpectedly married. She took comfort with Nazimova, who had by now forsaken the stage for Hollywood and was living in grand style in her "Garden of Alla" on Sunset Boulevard. Le Gallienne found the glitter and commercialism of the film business disturbing (she would venture into film only three times in her career) and soon returned to New York and the stage role that would permanently establish her as the most respected actress of her day on the legitimate stage.

The play was Ferenc Molnar's melodrama-cum-fantasy *Liliom*, and the role was as the beatific Julie, a circus worker who redeems her abusive lover. (The play would be the basis for

Eva Le
Gallienne,
1927

the Rodgers and Hammerstein musical *Carousel*.) The drama was being staged by the Theater Guild, formed just after World War I by a group of Greenwich Village intellectuals devoted to the theater. By 1922, the Guild had almost singlehandedly saved Broadway from its slide into self-congratulatory provincialism by staging works from outside the dramatic mainstream. Molnar's play, then somewhat controversial for its frank treatment of physical abuse, had been brought to the Guild's attention by Joseph Schildkraut, a European-trained actor and a tremendously popular leading man on the New York stage. Schildkraut insisted on having Le Gallienne play opposite him. There was trouble almost as soon as rehearsals began, for Schildkraut was notorious for seducing his leading ladies. Le Gallienne had to turn increasingly to physical resistance to fend him off, on one occasion biting Schildkraut's hand when it strayed to her breast during a love scene. "It got to the point where Eva, in a rage, decided to leave the theater altogether," remembered Guild president *Theresa Helburn. "Never were there two such contrasting personalities as [Schildkraut] and Eva Le Gallienne."

Le Gallienne grew increasingly nervous and began to lose her voice as opening night approached, resorting to sucking on lemons to soothe her throat as the audience began to fill the old Garrick Theater on 37th Street the night of April 20, 1921. But her performance was a triumph and firmly placed her in the company of Ethel Barrymore, *Lynn Fontanne, and *Katharine Cornell as one of America's most famous leading ladies. "Her acting moved me as can only music," drama critic John Mason Brown told his readers the morning after *Liliom*'s opening. "One was not arrested by detail, it was all spirit—spirit on its way heavenward." *Liliom* was such a success that it had to be moved to the larger Fulton Theater, where it took up residence for more than a year. Near the end of its lengthy run, Alexander Woollcott wrote in *The New York Times*: "Miss Le G. is far better than in the first week of the run," but the truth was that Le Gallienne found herself struggling to keep her performances fresh. When not at the theater, she spent almost all of her time in an apartment she'd taken on lower Fifth Avenue, avoiding publicity and "living like a hermit," as she wrote to her mother, although she did not reveal to Julie that alcohol was becoming an increasingly important source of comfort. Throughout her life, in fact, Le Gallienne would be prone to periodic fits of alcoholism at times of stress or depression, and rescued by ex-lovers and friends who nursed her temporarily away from the addiction.

Liliom finally closed early in 1922. Le Gallienne agreed to tour with the show for several months, then traveled to Europe that summer with ❧ Mercedes de Acosta, a socialite, sometime author, and Le Gallienne's new paramour. Le Gallienne's relationship with de Acosta would continue for several years, extending into her professional life when the two women raised money to produce de Acosta's play *Sandro Botticelli*, based on the love affair between the Renais-

❧▶

de Acosta, Mercedes. See Garbo, Greta for sidebar.

sance painter and *Simonetta Vespucci. The production drew an audience only because Le Gallienne disrobed in the play's most famous scene, her breasts discreetly covered by a luxurious wig and everything below by a carefully placed chair. The play was universally panned, although Le Gallienne was much admired for her bravery.

On a second trip to Europe with de Acosta in 1923, Le Gallienne saw *Eleonora Duse perform in London and became an ardent fan of the great Italian actress who, like Bernhardt before her, played a wide variety of roles with her own touring repertory company. The two finally met in New York, just after Le Gallienne had agreed to the role of the indecisive Princess Alexandra in her second Molnar play, *The Swan*. Duse was shocked to hear that Le Gallienne would be required to play the same character eight times a week for as long as the producers chose. "It's barbaric!," Duse exclaimed. "You will kill your soul!" She advised Le Gallienne to refuse the offer and join a Russian troop of actors. "They are the only true ones," she said.

The Swan opened at the Cort Theater in October of 1923 to great acclaim. Le Gallienne was praised for her portrayal of the wayward young princess, a performance "admirable for its artistic restraint," said Woollcott, "its renunciation of all easy and obvious effects, and for the potency of its inward fires." But Duse's warning stuck in Le Gallienne's mind. She told friends she wanted "a wide range of experience embracing to the greatest possible degree the finest dramatic material." She wanted, in short, her own repertory company. Her first experiments were encouraging, critics praising her successful effort to raise money for, produce, and direct Hauptmann's *The Assumption of Hannele* in 1924 using many of the cast members of *The Swan*, in which she was still playing. When another actors' strike hit Broadway in the summer of that year, Le Gallienne's production of Ibsen's *The Master Builder* at a summer theater outside Philadelphia played to full houses. Again, she produced and directed herself, as well as taking the role of Hilda Wangel, the first of several Ibsen heroines she would bring to the stage. The production was such a success that Le Gallienne brought it to Broadway for the 1925–26 season, where the play had not been seen for nearly 20 years, when Nazimova had played Hilda. Halfway through *The Master Builder*'s run, Le Gallienne opened a second Ibsen play, *John Gabriel Borkman*, playing the domineering Ella Rentheim at the Booth in the afternoon and Hilda at night at the Princess Theater. In the swirl of acclaim, Le Gallienne somehow found

time to gain her American citizenship and buy the home in Weston, Connecticut, that would be her refuge for the rest of her life. She named it Toscairn. It sat on ten acres of rocky New England soil, from part of which Le Gallienne wrested the garden of which she became justly proud.

In May of 1926, Le Gallienne finally announced her plan for the Civic Repertory Theater, "presenting the finest plays . . . at the lowest possible prices." No seat in the house, she said, would cost more than $1.50 for evening performances and $1.00 at matinees. "I could not see why America should not have its own repertory theater subsidized by private capital in the same way that its opera companies and symphony orchestras are," she wrote. "Why should the drama be the only neglected art?" Her backing for the Civic came from banker Otto Kahn, from John D. Rockefeller, and from publishing heiress Mary Curtis Bok (*Mary Zimbalist), among others, all of whom responded favorably to the woman Le Gallienne picked to act as her principal fund raiser and personal representative, none other than Mary Duggat. Like her relationship to the theater itself, Le Gallienne's loyalty to friends and former lovers was deep and abiding, most of them remaining a part of her extended family throughout her long life.

The Civic's home was to be an aging theater on West 14th Street, the center of New York's entertainment industry for the previous 50 years but now heavily commercialized. Le Gallienne announced an ambitious opening season of six plays, in addition to the two Ibsen works already running uptown. The new productions included a costume drama called *Saturday Night*, the melodrama *Cradle Song*, Goldoni's *La Locandiera*, as well as Shakespeare's *Twelfth Night*, Chekhov's *The Three Sisters* (which had never been performed in English in the United States), and *Susan Glaspell*'s sociological study of greed, *The Inheritors*.

The Civic's opening night, October 15, 1926, was a disaster. Le Gallienne had unwisely chosen to open with *Saturday Night*, with its 43 speaking parts and a bewildering array of costume and set changes. The curtain did not go up until nine; each scene change, using an inexperienced crew of Italian immigrants, took up to 15 minutes; and Le Gallienne was so flustered by the confusion and audience unrest that she uncharacteristically fumbled her lines. "It was more frightful than anything in the world," wrote Noel Coward, whose own work, *The Vortex*, was playing uptown. "Eva was terrible, the production awful, and the play lousy." The next night's work, *The Three Sisters*, went much better; and by April of 1927, Le Gallienne had mounted all six new productions with few problems and had accomplished her goal of working in a wide range of material. During a typical week in December of 1926, for example, she was rehearsing *Twelfth Night*, playing the earthy mistress of an Italian inn for *La Locandiera*, Masha in *The Three Sisters*, Hilda in *The Master Builder*, and Ella in *Borkman*. Her nurturing of the Civic soon led everyone to call her "The Abbess of 14th Street." Critics were enthralled. "The Civic has recaptured the . . . lost charm,

the lost *pleasure* in the theater," burbled the normally acerbic Woollcott, while Robert Benchley advised his *New Yorker* readers: "One really ought to go there once a week just to recapture the feeling of theatergoing." A few were less fulsome with their praise, although Brooks Atkinson admitted in later years: "Thousands of theatergoers got their theater education in the battered, cheerless, 14th Street Theater that always smelled of disinfectant."

During its ten-year life, the Civic presented 37 productions, including four premieres. Among the new material was Le Gallienne's version of *Alice in Wonderland*, which she staged using moveable sets mounted on trolleys to retain the fluid craziness of Carroll's book. Among the cast was Schildkraut, playing the Queen of Hearts, and two students of Le Gallienne's at the time—Burgess Meredith as the Dormouse and *Julie Harris* as the White Rabbit. Of the Civic's 37 works, Le Gallienne directed 33 and acted in all but six, all the while refining her already considerable acting and directing skills. In rehearsal, she conducted numerous read-throughs of the work at hand until she was sure the entire company had arrived at what she called "a unified conception" of the play, after which she seldom intruded into whatever methods each actor used to remain faithful to that conception. "She seldom, if ever, spoke to an actor from the auditorium during rehearsal," company member Paul Ballentyne later recalled. When it did become necessary, Ballentyne said, "she would climb up the steps, cross the orchestra pit, take the actor by the arm, walk slowly upstage, talking to him or her."

The Civic's audiences, as Atkinson noted, were not the smart set that swooped into the big Broadway houses in tuxedos and gowns, but solidly middle-class secretaries, truck drivers, bakers and sales clerks who could afford the theater's modest admission. But the low prices meant that the Civic was losing money even when the house was full. Le Gallienne found, too, that playwrights were often reluctant to sandwich their new works into the Civic's repertory, since more money could be made with a long run in a Broadway house; as well, keeping actors on staff for more than a few months was a constant problem. Broadway itself changed during the Civic's existence, presenting by the early 1930s the kind of new, socially pointed works by authors like Clifford Odets and Maxwell Anderson that had once been the Civic's specialty. By 1935, running at $94,000 in the red and with the Depression bringing smaller and smaller houses, Le Gallienne was forced to close the Civic after appeals for government funding or support from Actors' Equity failed.

Le Gallienne did not appear on a New York stage again for seven years, clinging to her beloved repertory by performing in summer stock. She returned to Broadway in the 1942 murder mystery *Uncle Harry*, once again playing opposite Schildkraut, with whom she revived her production of *The Cherry Orchard* two years later. In 1946, she announced her second acting company, the American Repertory Theater (ART). Admitting that another of the Civic's problems had been its dependence on a single personality, she joined forces with former Guild president *Cheryl Crawford and with *Margaret Webster, a fellow English émigré whom she had known from her childhood days with the Favershams in England. The press announcement was pure Le Gallienne, pointing out that ART would "be for the drama what a library is for literature or a symphony orchestra for music."

The company had sold some $290,000 worth of stock to 142 investors and listed 5,000 subscribers by the time it mounted its first production, *Henry VIII*, in November of 1946. But once again Le Gallienne's high hopes for The Drama were flummoxed by rank commercialism, mainly high union costs when ART agreed to demands that the number of union workers remain constant, no matter the size of the show, and to a 50% pay raise demanded by the musicians. Critical reception of the other shows in ART's repertory, J.M. Barrie's *What Every Woman Knows* and Le Gallienne's revival of *John Gabriel Borkman*, was cool. Cheryl Crawford resigned after the first season, leaving Le Gallienne and Peggy Webster to struggle on into a second with *Hedda Gabler* and a new production of *Alice in Wonderland*. Critic George Jean Nathan, never as admiring of Le Gallienne as some of his peers, found the plays disappointing and without passion, calling the 1947–48 season "ice-time of 1948." With debts amounting to $340,000, ART shut down.

Denied her vision of the theater for a second time, Le Gallienne refused to appear on Broadway for ten years, turning again to summer stock, to recording the classics for America's phonographs, and to teaching at *Lucille Lortel's White Barn Theater, not far from her home in Connecticut. She also turned to the new medium of television, appearing in eight much-praised specials between 1955 and 1962. She disliked working in the two films she accepted, as Gertrude opposite Richard Burton's Hamlet in 1955's *The Prince of Players* and in G.B. Shaw's *The Devil's Disciple* in

1959. "There's no opportunity to play a whole scene," she complained. "It's done in scraps and bits. It's nothing but technical." She was finally enticed back to Broadway in 1958 for a play that closed after one performance when a plagiarism suit was filed against its author, while the next year's *The Southwest Corner* closed after only 36 performances.

It was work off-Broadway that led to Le Gallienne's third attempt at a national repertory. She had accepted the role of Queen *Elizabeth I in Schiller's *Mary Stuart* for the Phoenix Theater Company in Greenwich Village, playing opposite *Irene Worth in the title role. Directed by Tyrone Guthrie, it was her greatest success since the Civic Repertory days. After winning the Outer Critics Circle award for the touring production of the show, Le Gallienne led the effort to form a permanent touring enterprise called the National Repertory Company and launched its first season in 1959 by playing Elizabeth both in the Schiller play and in Maxwell Anderson's *Elizabeth the Queen*. Although she was honorary president of NRT, she was happy this time to leave the administration and finances of the company to others while the company traveled 40,000 miles in its first, 26-week season and played to an estimated quarter million people in 58 cities. Le Gallienne's work was said to be her finest in years; but still, the NRT finished that first season $150,000 in debt, struggling on for three more years before it was finally disbanded. Le Gallienne promptly rejoined Ellis Rabb's Phoenix Theater for another season until it, too, collapsed under financial strains. Retiring to the beloved sanctuary in Connecticut, Le Gallienne spent her time collecting her memoirs of Eleonora Duse into *The Mystic in the Theater* (1965) and began work on her second autobiography, *With a Quiet Heart*. (Her first, *At 33*, had been published in the 1930s.) But the theater held one more role in store to reward Le Gallienne for her years of devotion.

In 1975, she accepted an offer from the Kennedy Center to appear in its Bicentennial revival of *The Royal Family*, the *Edna Ferber-George Kaufmann play loosely based on the Barrymores. Her stunning performance as the imposing family matriarch Fanny Cavendish helped carry the production to Broadway in 1976, then on to a 23-week tour and a television adaptation for which Le Gallienne won an Emmy. Audiences were especially moved by Le Gallienne's inventive reworking of Fanny's death scene at the close of the play. As originally written, Fanny expires peacefully while sitting in a chair; Le Gallienne's Fanny, however, paced the room rehearsing a new part and collapsed while still in service to the stage.

Fanny Cavendish was the first of three memorable elderly women Le Gallienne brought to life. The second was **Ellen Burstyn**'s Grandmother Pearl, a flinty Kansas farm woman in the 1980 film *Resurrection*. "She went straight to the woman," wrote film critic Stanley Kauffmann in *The New Republic*. "The result is a lovely paradox, a fresh and strong performance of a tired and failing old lady." Le Gallienne was nominated for an Oscar for her work in the film. The third role was as Grandie in the 1981 Broadway production of **Joanna Glass**' *To Grandmother's House We Go*, in which she was, as Frank Rich wrote in the *Times*, "as lyrical as Juliet." The play's director, Clifford Williams, marveled at the Le Gallienne style, noting: "Every little thing is planned . . . a touch, a smile—yet nothing ever looked planned. Nothing is an accident."

But by the time of the ill-fated 1982 revival of *Alice in Wonderland*, Le Gallienne seemed to be losing interest in her beloved theater. Her secretary said that Eva, directing the production, seemed distant, remaining uncharacteristically silent as major revisions were made in her adaptation of 50 years before. The production had a short run and was the last time Le Gallienne would appear on a stage. By the time she traveled to California in 1984 to act in an episode of the popular dramatic series *St. Elsewhere*, it was apparent that 85-year-old Le Gallienne's health was failing and that her memory had become impaired. She had trouble remembering her lines and the names of her fellow players and was exhausted by the end of shooting.

Le Gallienne's final years in Connecticut were often difficult ones. At first she was able to tend to simple gardening tasks and to enjoy her vast collection of theatrical books ranged around the famous study where she had entertained so many friends and students. But her health declined precipitously in the late 1980s. With little short-term memory, she was sometimes unable to recognize the doctor who attended her nearly every day, but lucidly recalled her memories of Bernhardt and Duse for Ellen Burstyn, who videotaped them for posterity, and happily welcomed Mariette Hartley with open arms and a gleeful shout of, "I remember you!" She survived three operations for a troublesome hernia and was plagued by a host of other ailments as her body began to fail her. On the evening of June 3, 1991, the theater world learned that Eva Le Gallienne had died peacefully at home that afternoon, three months short of her 92nd birthday.

Le Gallienne's passionate love of the theater was that of a faithful suitor whose affections are not always returned. She never won a Tony, for example, until late in life, when she was given a special lifetime achievement award. But in her quest for a pure theater untainted by commercial concerns, she offered to her beloved, as Brooks Atkinson once noted, "a plausible, enlightened idea that it has never been able to forget." Her most precious gift, however, was kindling that love in others, especially the hundreds of young actors she taught over the years. "Many years ago," she told one student, "Duse took my hand. And now, I've taken your hand; and now, you are taking the hand of others."

SOURCES:
Atkinson, Brooks. *Broadway*. NY: Macmillan, 1970.
Hartley, Mariette, and Anne Commire. *Breaking The Silence*. NY: Putnam, 1990.
Schanke, Robert. *Eva Le Gallienne: A Bio-Bibliography*. NY: Greenwood Press, 1989.
———. *Shattered Applause: The Lives of Eva Le Gallienne*. Foreword by *May Sarton. IL: Southern Illinois University Press, 1992.
Sheehy, Helen. *Eva Le Gallienne: A Biography*. NY: Knopf, 1996.

Norman Powers,
writer-producer, Chelsea Lane Productions, New York

Leginska, Ethel (1886–1970)

English-born pianist who had a notable career in the U.S. as a composer, conductor, and a performer. Name variations: Ethel Liggins. Pronunciation: Le-GIN-ska (g as in "go"). Born on April 13, 1886, in Hull, England (some sources cite April 12); died in Los Angeles, California, on February 26, 1970, of a stroke; daughter of Thomas Liggins and Annie (Peck) Liggins; attended music schools in Frankfurt (Hoch Conservatory), Vienna, and Berlin; married Roy Emerson Whittern (also known as Emerson Whithorne), in 1907 (divorced 1916); children: one son, Cedric.

Made London debut (1902); had first nervous breakdown (1909); made New York debut (1913); began career as composer (1914); began role as speaker for feminist causes (1915); launched career as conductor (1924); made American debut as conductor (1925); had severe nervous breakdown followed by her retirement from solo performing, and founded Boston Philharmonic Orchestra (1926); toured Europe as conductor (1930); conducted premier of her opera Gale (1935); relocated permanently to Los Angeles (1940); conducted premier of her opera The Rose and the Ring (1957).

Major works: (opera) Gale, The Rose and the Ring, (orchestra) 2 Short Pieces, Quatres sujets bar-

bares, *and* Fantasy; *(chamber music)* From a Life, Triptych, 6 Nursery Rhymes, *and* 3 Victorian Portraits.

Ethel Leginska had a significant impact on several branches of the world of music. Starting as a successful pianist in Europe and the United States, by her late 20s she took up composing and, a decade thereafter, began a notable career as a conductor. Although she continued to work extensively in Europe, her career in writing music and in leading orchestras was centered within the American musical scene.

The role of women in the American musical world was in rapid transition at the close of the 19th century. Whereas women performers were a rarity and women's orchestras unknown as late as the 1870s, within two decades women were creating and seizing new opportunities in these areas. In the 1890s, as **Judith Tick** has written, there were a number of "historic firsts in the composition and performance" of women's works: "the first orchestra composition by a woman to be performed by a major American symphony orchestra; the first symphony, the first concerto, and the first large-scale choral composition." Pianists like *Teresa Carreño (a grandniece of Simon Bolivár), *Julia Rivé-King, and *Fannie Bloomfield Zeisler toured extensively. So-called "lady orchestras" likewise became common. Nonetheless, the orchestras at the center of American music continued to exclude women. The first female conductors in the United States, who began to appear around the turn of the century, were compelled to work with female ensembles: **Caroline B. Nichols** and the Fadette Women's Orchestra of Boston, and **Emma Roberto Steiner** with various light opera companies.

"During the 1920s," writes **Carole Neuls-Bates**, "American musical life underwent great expansion in keeping with the economic boom experienced by the country as a whole." In this era of newly constructed concert halls and newly founded symphony orchestras, women found widening opportunities. Talented women were now being trained at recently established musical conservatories such as the Eastman School in Rochester, New York, and the Juilliard School in New York City. Although still excluded from mainstream orchestras, women musicians founded their own organizations. Almost 30 such organizations performed in the United States from the 1920s through the 1940s. In addition, new orchestras that mixed male and female performers now began to appear. It was in this environment that Ethel Leginska rose to prominence as a founder and conductor of symphony orchestras.

The future musician was born in Hull, England, on April 13, 1886, the daughter of Thomas and **Annie Peck Liggins**. Little has been recorded about her youth, but she apparently responded to music even as an infant, was recognized at an early age as a gifted pianist, and, after initial training, gave entire recitals when she was only seven. A local family, the Wilsons, who had made a future in shipping, took Ethel under their wing, providing her with the opportunity for study in centers of music on the Continent. She started with training at the Hoch Conservatory in Frankfurt, where she worked under the direction of the noted Dutch pianist James Kwast. She probably received her most important training for her later career during the three years she studied in Vienna with Theodore Leschetitzky, a celebrated pianist and teacher whose pupils included Ignace Jan Paderewski. She then completed her musical apprenticeship in Berlin. It was during these years that she dropped her original family name to become Ethel Leginska. The new name suggested a continental heritage that was apparently designed to help her career. The musical stage of the time was dominated by performers of Russian or Polish background, and the phrase "Ethel Liggins from Hull" seemed less likely to attract audiences than its contrived, Slavic equivalent.

Leginska achieved quick recognition as a performer in her own country and elsewhere in Europe. Her debut as a soloist came in England in 1902, when, only 16 years old, she gave a successful performance at Queen's Hall in London. In 1907, she married an American, Roy Emerson Whittern, who was also studying music in Europe as a pupil of Theodore Leschetitzky. She and Whittern, who changed his name to Emerson Whithorne when he began a career as a composer, had a son Cedric in the year following their marriage. For a time, her husband acted as her manager.

A tribute to Leginska's growing reputation can be found in frequent references to her as the "Paderewski of women pianists." Sadly, in 1909, at an early stage in her career and personal life, she suffered the first in a series of nervous breakdowns that were to cause her difficulty over the following two decades. Leginska's personal life was marked by recurring difficulties. In 1912, she separated from her husband. In 1916, the marriage was apparently dissolved, although some sources indicate that the proceedings were not complete until 1918. The divorce involved a bitter custody dispute over the couple's only child. Leginska lost despite her claims that her husband had deserted her and that she could earn enough to support a one-parent family.

Even so, Leginska was able to make a successful debut in the United States, playing at Aeolian Hall in New York at the start of 1913. After that, she spent most of her time in America and appeared regularly on the New York concert stage. The critics hailed her talents, and she was particularly well known for her repertoire of works by the great German composers from Bach through Schubert, as well as for her all-Chopin programs. She sometimes presented these demanding performances without giving herself or the audience an intermission. But even early in her career, Leginska's failure to appear at some scheduled performances, attributable probably to her personal difficulties, led some in the musical world to dub her "the disappearing pianist."

We will never be original . . . until we . . . trust our own way instead of the eternal beaten paths on which we are always asked to poke along.

—Ethel Leginska

While in the States, she took a number of positions that marked her as one of the leading feminists of the musical world. Eschewing the bare-shouldered evening gown that was the standard dress expected of a female performer, she insisted on performing in a more comfortable (and warmer) costume. It consisted of a black silk shirt, black velvet jacket, a white vest, and a skirt of everyday length. Her short hairstyle also departed from the norm for female performers but offered her the freedom of movement she required while playing. Leginska likewise became an outspoken advocate for such measures as effective child care that would aid professional women in pursuing their careers. She was also canny about publicity. In 1916, when she injured her finger in a door, she sent an X-ray taken of the bruised digit to a music magazine and had the satisfaction of seeing it appear in a subsequent issue.

In the mid-1920s, Leginska's emotional difficulties and her corresponding inability to honor her concert engagements became too burdensome for her to continue that part of her career. A series of dramatic events in 1925 and 1926 made it impossible for her to hide her growing mental problems from the public. In late January 1925, though she set out in a taxi for an appearance before a crowd of 2,000 at Carnegie Hall, Leginska disappeared suddenly in New York City. A substitute performer was found at the last minute to take her place. When a friend notified the authorities, the police began a four-day search for her. In the end, they learned that she had suffered a nervous breakdown and fled to Boston. Leginska later recounted how, on this occasion, she had wandered the city in a daze, with "music singing" in her head. The distraught pianist then stopped at a friend's apartment to write down the tune. It is possible that the tepid reviews Leginska had received from New York critics for her recent debut as a conductor contributed to this emotional crisis.

In October 1926, a similar series of events took place. Leginska failed to appear before a crowd of 1,500 patrons at a scheduled People's Symphony Concert in New York City. Violinist Francis MacMillen filled in for her, and the crowd of ticket holders learned of the change only when they confronted a sign at the entrance to the auditorium. Following this latest breakdown, Leginska attempted to blame her manager for failing to cancel her engagement; she claimed she had asked him to do so well in advance of the concert. But this effort to conceal her emotional turmoil faded when she announced the cancellation of a recital scheduled for late November in Aeolian Hall. Ironically, it was there she had made her successful American debut in 1913. Trying to resume her concert career with a tour of the Midwest led to a new fiasco on January 20, 1926, when she abandoned a performance scheduled to take place before an audience of 4,000 in Evansville, Indiana. She had given a hint of her state of mind the previous day when she complained loudly of the city's yellow cabs, the lack of a symphony orchestra to accompany her, and the concert hall, which she described as "an old barn."

At this point, the troubled performer consulted doctors in Buffalo, where she was staying with friends. They diagnosed her condition as "a severe nervous breakdown," and they called upon her to rest and stay away from the concert stage for at least a year. Although she played the piano in conjunction with her subsequent work as a conductor, after this diagnosis Leginska no longer attempted to sustain a career as a soloist.

The pianist had switched her focus to composing around 1914, studying with Ernest Bloch in New York. Much of her energy over the next decade went into this effort. Her compositions included *Four Poems* for string quartet, which debuted in London in 1921, and a four-movement suite, *Quatre sujects barbares*, completed in 1923. Her most substantial work as a composer was completed by the end of the 1920s. Neuls-Bates has described her music as "progressive in its rhythmic intensity, its free approach to tonali-

ty, and its use of vocal declamation." Leginska's more substantial compositions were played by orchestras on both sides of the Atlantic.

The once successful pianist also became interested in conducting an orchestra, a vastly more radical departure from accepted practice than merely performing as a soloist with a traditional symphony orchestra. Notes **Christine Ammer**: "Traditionally such control, especially over an all-male orchestra, requires a forcefulness that was encouraged only in men." In the early 1920s, Leginska studied conducting in London where she worked under the direction of Eugene Gossens, then moved to Munich where she studied with Robert Heger. She appeared as a guest conductor in a number of European musical centers in 1924, including Munich, Paris, London and Berlin. A female conductor was still a novelty in the musical world of this time, and Leginska apparently obtained work as a conductor by agreeing to perform as a pianist on the same programs. Nonetheless, as Ammer notes, Leginska had the required qualities of a successful conductor: "superb musicianship" as well as "a vivid personality, which can command both the orchestra and the attention of the audience." Her gift for publicity remained in force, and she made it a point to inform the public in the United States, in both interviews and press releases, that she had been the first woman to conduct such esteemed orchestras as the Berlin Philharmonic. It seems likely, however, that another female conductor from America, the Dutch-born *Antonia Brico, had taken the podium in Berlin sometime earlier.

On January 9, 1925, Leginska made her American debut as a conductor, appearing with the New York Symphony Orchestra at Carnegie Hall. This was, in fact, the first time a woman had conducted in the famous New York concert hall. The critic for The New York Times was conspicuously unenthusiastic in assessing Leginska's skills, although he noted the warm response she received from the audience. In short order, however, she received a subsequent engagement in Boston, and Leginska enjoyed particular acclaim for her appearance later in the year at the Hollywood Bowl in Los Angeles.

Pursuing her career as a conductor, Leginska founded several orchestras in the last part of the 1920s: the Boston Philharmonic, the Boston Woman's Symphony, and the Boston English Opera Company. The Boston Philharmonic, which performed for only a single season, was a predominantly male ensemble. It was intended to provide good music to a mass audience at rock-bottom prices, and its performances received favorable reviews from Boston's leading critics. The Boston Woman's Symphony, founded in 1927, had a longer life span: it conducted extensive national tours in 1928 and 1929 and survived through 1930. The Woman's Symphony sometimes employed a small number of male musicians, Leginska explaining that a lack of some female instrumentalists from the Boston region made it necessary to use men rather than incurring the cost of bringing in women players from out of town. She also served as director of the Woman's Symphony Orchestra of Chicago.

Her developing talent at the podium won reluctant praise from American critics, many of whom still looked upon a female conductor as a slightly unwelcome novelty. The critic for The Boston Transcript captured the appeal of the Women's Symphony and Leginska's role in directing the ensemble. "In solidity of tone, vigour, and self-confidence . . . this orchestra ranks high among orchestras everywhere." It presented worthy programs "under the firm leadership of Ethel Leginska, that distractingly versatile but surpassingly musical person." According to Arthur Elson, who wrote a study of women in music at this time, Leginska was everywhere "acclaimed as a dynamic conductor of much skill, individuality, authority, and magnetism."

Apart from leading her own orchestras, Leginska continued to work effectively as a guest conductor. In December 1928 at the Boston Opera House, she conducted the National Opera Company in a performance of Rigoletto. In 1930, she had a successful tour conducting various European orchestras. In 1933, she conducted Beethoven's Ninth Symphony before an appreciative audience in Havana. In leading her own orchestras, Leginska filled the dual role of conductor and soloist when it came to works like Liszt's Hungarian Fantasia and Mendelssohn's Concerto in G Minor. For these performances, she stood in front of her musicians for the introduction, moved unobtrusively to the piano for her solos, then stood at the piano to direct the subsequent orchestral passages.

Neuls-Bates attributes particular significance to Leginska's work with the Boston Woman's Symphony Orchestra during its four years of existence. The organization's two extended tours in the eastern United States, one in 1928 and a second the following year, let it display its abilities to audiences as far as Chicago and St. Louis. Accomplished women musicians thus had an unprecedented opportunity to demonstrate their talents and, according to Neuls-Bates, give "encouragement to countless women to take up orchestral instruments." The tours were based on a rigorous schedule of traveling and performances, the 1928 tour presenting 55 concerts in only 43 days.

Leginska's work as a composer continued in the early part of the 1930s, during which time she wrote two operas. The first, The Ring and the Rose, received its initial performance only in 1957, but the second, Gale, was staged by the Chicago Civic Opera Company in 1935. Leginska herself took the podium for the premier performance of *Gale*. In the late 1930s, as her status as a female conductor lost its novelty, Leginska turned, perhaps reluctantly, to teaching. She established studios in London and Paris, then settled permanently in Los Angeles. Noted performers who studied with her included James Fields, Daniel Pollack, and Bruce Sutherland. Leginska still took the baton on occasion, leading the orchestra at concerts where her students were presented to the public. This multitalented woman, who had battered down numerous barriers in the musical world, died of a stroke in Los Angeles on February 26, 1970. Her work as a teacher had continued to the time of her death. According to Ammer, Ethel Leginska was "one of the most colorful women musicians of her time."

SOURCES:

Ammer, Christine. *Unsung: A History of Women in American Music*. Westport, CT: Greenwood Press, 1980.

Anderson, E. Ruth, comp. *Contemporary American Composers*. 2nd ed. Boston: G.K. Hall, 1982.

Bowers, Jan, and Judith Tick, eds. *Women Making Music: The Western Art Tradition, 1150–1950*. Urbana, IL: University of Illinois Press, 1986.

Elson, Arthur. *Woman's Work in Music*. Boston, MA: L.C. Page, 1931.

Sadie, Julie Anne, and Rhian Samuel. *The Norton-Grove Dictionary of Women Composers*. NY: W.W. Norton, 1995.

Sicherman, Barbara *et al.*, eds. *Notable American Women: The Modern Period: A Biographical Dictionary*. Cambridge, MA: The Belknap Press of Harvard University Press, 1980.

SUGGESTED READING:

Greene, David Mason. *Greene's Biographical Encyclopedia of Composers*. Garden City, NY: Doubleday, 1985.

Slonimsky, Nicolas. *Music since 1900*. 5th ed. NY: Schirmer Books, 1994.

Thompson, Oscar. *The International Cyclopedia of Music and Musicians*. London: J.M. Dent, 1975.

Neil M. Heyman,
Professor of History, San Diego State University,
San Diego, California

Legnani, Pierina (1863–1923)

Italian ballerina. Born in Italy in 1863; died in 1923; studied in Milan.

Pierina Legnani made her debut at La Scala, Milan, and then appeared with some success in Paris, Madrid, and London. It was in Russia, however, that she found fame. While performing with the Imperial Ballet at the Maryinsky Theater in St. Petersburg in 1893, in the ballet *The Tulip of Haarlem*, she executed 32 consecutive *fouettés*, for the first time in the history of the Imperial Ballet, earning her the title "Prima Ballerina Assoluta." Legnani remained at the Russian theater for the next eight years, and her

Pierina Legnani

amazing athletic accomplishments spurred Russian dancers to aspire to technical brilliance. Wrote *Agnes de Mille: "Legnani could perform an entire thirty-two bar adage on full point standing in the center of the floor without support. Her turn-out was so complete that she could balance a glass of vodka on the flat of her ankle while revolving in second position." While in St. Petersburg, Legnani danced as Odette in *Swan Lake*; she also appeared in *Caterina, Coppélia, The Talisman, The Halt of Cavalry, Bluebeard, Camargo*, and *Raymonda*. Following her Russian sojourn, she danced in Italy and France and in some of the Alhambra ballets in London.

SOURCES:

de Mille, Agnes. *The Book of the Dance*. NY: Golden Press, 1961.

Lehane, Jan (b. 1941).

See Court, Margaret for sidebar.

Lehmann, Beatrix (1903–1979).

See Lehmann, Rosamond for sidebar.

Lehmann, Inge (1888–1993)

Danish geophysicist and mathematician who in 1936 discovered the existence of the inner core of the Earth. Born on May 13, 1888, at Osterbro by the Lakes in Copenhagen, Denmark; died in Copenhagen on February 21, 1993; daughter of Alfred Georg Ludvig Lehmann (a professor of psychology) and Ida Sophie (Torsleff) Lehmann; sister of Harriet Lehmann; University of Copenhagen, master's degree, 1920; also studied at Cambridge University and University of Hamburg; master of science degree in geodesy, 1928; honorary doctorates from the University of Copenhagen and Columbia University.

By studying the shock waves generated by earthquakes, was able to theorize that the Earth has a solid inner core, a finding that was substantiated by other scientists; was chief seismologist of the Royal Danish Geodetic Institute (1928–53); retired (1953).

In 1971, the Danish geophysicist Inge Lehmann was awarded the William Bowie Medal of the American Geophysical Union in recognition of her "outstanding contributions to fundamental geophysics and unselfish cooperation in research." Lehmann, who had never earned a Ph.D., was one of the few women in her field for decades, and it took her determined nature to hold her own in a male, credentialed world where large egos were often the norm. "You should know how many incompetent men I had to compete with—in vain," she recalled. Lehmann nonetheless became one of the most innovative scientists of the 20th century. Born in the Victorian age, she lived to see both the birth and death of the Soviet Union, two World Wars, the coming of the Atomic Age, and the onset of a new world of computers and the Internet.

Lehmann was born in 1888 at Osterbro by the Lakes in Copenhagen, Denmark, the daughter of Alfred Lehmann and **Ida Torsleff Lehmann**. Inge's father was a professor of psychology at the University of Copenhagen and a pioneer in the study of experimental psychology in Denmark. She was sent to one of Denmark's most liberal and enlightened schools, the first coeducational institution in the country, which was founded and run by **Hanna Adler**, the aunt of Niels Bohr, a future Nobel Prize winner. From 1907 through 1910, Lehmann studied mathematics at the University of Copenhagen. During the 1911–12 academic year, she continued her mathematical studies at Cambridge University, returning to Denmark to begin work as an actuary. Her actuarial career lasted from 1912 through 1918, when she returned to the University of Copenhagen; two years later, she was awarded a master's degree. She took additional courses in mathematics at the University of Hamburg soon after.

In 1925, Lehmann began her career as a seismologist, working as a staff member of the Royal Danish Geodetic Institute. Decades later, she recalled being "thrilled by the idea that these instruments could help us explore the interior of the Earth, and I began to read about it." She helped install seismographs in her Copenhagen office and learned all she could about the nascent science from seismologists in Belgium, France, Germany, and the Netherlands. In 1928, after earning a master of science degree in geodesy (applied mathematics relating to the measurement of the Earth), Lehmann was promoted to the post of chief seismologist of the Royal Danish Geodetic Institute. One of the responsibilities in her heavy workload was the supervision of all aspects of Denmark's seismology program, which included writing the institute's bulletins and overseeing the operation of seismographic stations throughout Denmark and in Greenland. In addition, Lehmann continued independent research projects. From her first scientific essay (1926) to her last (1987), she published a total of 59 papers, many of which made significant contributions to her field.

A major earthquake in New Zealand in June 1929 produced sufficient data on European, including Danish, seismographs to be of great value for investigating the problem of whether the Earth had a liquid or solid inner core. The Danish seismographic network Lehmann was in charge of provided excellent data for such an investigation. In comparing a number of these recordings, she could clearly see onsets of various seismic waves through the Earth's core. This enabled her to make the necessary imaginative jump to conclude that the Earth had a tripartite structure, having a seismically distinct and solid inner core. This conclusion, which had taken Lehmann years of slow, painstaking effort, was published in her classic scientific paper of 1936, titled simply "P'." In 1938–39, her work was validated in papers published by seismologists Beno Gutenberg, Charles F. Richter, and Harold Jeffreys.

At the time of Lehmann's death in 1993, her aunt's grandson, Nils Groes, would remember Lehmann in her garden where she:

sat in the lawn with a big table filled with cardboard oatmeal boxes. In the boxes were cardboard cards with information on earthquakes and the times for these and the times for their registration all over the world. This was before computer processing was available, but the system was the same. With her cardboard cards and her oatmeal boxes, Inge registered the velocity of propagation of the earthquakes to all parts of the globe. By means of this information, she deduced new theories of the inner parts of the Earth.

After her retirement in 1953, Lehmann continued her scientific work and the writing and publication of papers. She visited research centers around the world, sharing decades of knowledge with scientists of her generation as well as the next. With a strong social conscience, she was concerned about the poor in Denmark and the conditions of refugees throughout Europe and the world. She also enjoyed attending art galleries in each country she visited. Among her favorites activities were hiking, skiing, and mountain climbing, particularly in the Alps. Having never received a Ph.D. degree, she was pleased to be awarded honorary doctorates both by her alma mater, the University of Copenhagen, as well as by New York's Columbia University. Other honors she received included being chosen as a foreign member of the prestigious British Royal Society in 1969. In her final years, Lehmann's research resulted in papers on the role of seismographic evidence in evaluating data generated by nuclear explosions, a subject of vital importance for the accurate monitoring of a comprehensive nuclear test-ban treaty. At the end of her life, while hospitalized, Lehmann told Nils Groes "that all day she had been thinking about her own life and she was content. It had been a long and rich life full of victories and good memories." She died in Copenhagen on February 21, 1993, three months shy of her 105th birthday.

SOURCES:

Bolt, Bruce A. "Inge Lehmann," in *Physics Today*. Vol. 47, no. 1. January 1994, p. 61.

———. *Inside the Earth: Evidence from Earthquakes*. San Francisco, CA: W.H. Freeman, 1982.

——— and Erik Hjortenberg, "Inge Lehmann (1888–1993)," in *Bulletin of the Seismological Society of America*. Vol. 84, no. 1. February 1994, pp. 229–233.

Brush, Stephen G. "Discovery of the Earth's Core," in *American Journal of Physics*. Vol. 48, no. 9. September 1980, pp. 705–724.

Fowler, C.M.R. *The Solid Earth: An Introduction to Global Geophysics*. Cambridge, UK and NY: Cambridge University Press, 1990.

Jacobs, J.A. *Deep Interior of the Earth*. London: Chapman & Hall, 1992.

Jeffreys, Bertha Swirles. "Inge Lehmann: Reminiscences," in *Quarterly Journal of the Royal Astronomical Society*. Vol. 35, no. 2. June 1994, pp. 233–234.

Lehmann, Inge. "P'," in *Bureau Central Seismoloque International*, Ser. A, *Travaux Scientifique*. Vol. 14, 1936, pp. 87–115.

Runcorn, S.K. *et al.*, eds. *The Earth's Core: Its Structure, Evolution, and Magnetic Field: A Discussion*. London: The Royal Society, 1982.

Schwarz, Joel. "Inge Lehmann, 1888–1993, Danish geophysicist," in Emily J. McMurray *et al.*, eds., *Notable Twentieth-Century Scientists*. 4 vols. Detroit, MI: Gale Research, 1995, Vol. 3, pp. 1216–1217.

Williams, C.A., and J.A. Hudson, "Inge Lehmann (1888–1993)," in *Quarterly Journal of the Royal Astronomical Society*. Vol. 35, no. 2. June 1994, pp. 231–233.

Yount, Lisa. *A to Z of Women in Science and Math*. NY: Facts on File, 1999.

John Haag,
Associate Professor of History,
University of Georgia, Athens, Georgia

Lehmann, Lilli (1848–1929)

German soprano who was famed for her interpretive skill. Born in Würzburg, Germany, on November 24, 1848; died in Berlin, Germany, on May 17, 1929; daughter and student of Marie Loewe; sister of **Marie Lehmann** *(1851–1931, a soprano); married Paul Kalish (a tenor), in 1888.*

Made debut in Prague (1865); took part in first complete performance of Der Ring *at Bayreuth (1876); was a permanent member of the Royal Opera (1870–85); made debut at the Metropolitan Opera (1885); retired (1892) but continued her career as a teacher.*

Lilli Lehmann was born in Würzburg, Germany, in 1848, the daughter of **Marie Loewe**, with whom she later studied. In 1876, Lehmann took part in the first complete performance of Richard Wagner's *Der Ring* at Bayreuth. An innovation at the time, this cycle would become an operatic standard in theaters throughout the world and performance at Bayreuth would be reserved for opera's finest singers. Lehmann was a member of the Royal Opera in Berlin for 15 years, from 1870 to 1885. Because recognition came slowly, she broke her contact with Berlin to debut as Carmen at the Metropolitan Opera in New York on November 25, 1885. During her first season there, she sang Brünnhilde from *Die Walküre,* Bertha from *La prophète,* and Venus from *Tannhaüser,* among other roles. She also took part in the first American performances of Karl Goldmark's *Die Königin von Saba* on December 2, 1885, and of *Merlin* on January 3, 1887. Continuing her role as a Wagner pioneer, Lehmann took part in the first performances of *Götterdämmerung* on January 25, 1885, of *Tristan and Isolde* on December 1, 1886, of *Siegfried* on November 9, 1887, and of the first complete cycle of the Ring in March

1889. On her return to Germany, Kaiser Wilhelm II penalized her for overstaying her leave in America; she was not allowed to perform in Germany until 1891.

Lehmann's experience of working directly with the composer in the first production of the Ring cycle gave her interpretation of Wagner's work an authority which was influential in New York opera. She appeared at the Met for seven seasons, retiring from there in 1902 after a final American concert tour. She then appeared at, and was artistic director of, the Salzburg Festival for a number of years (1902–10). Lilli Lehmann became a successful teacher; *Geraldine Farrar and *Olive Fremstad were among her pupils. She wrote a manual, *Meine Gesangskunst* (*How to Sing*), in 1902, and edited arias and songs. Her autobiography *Mein Weg* was published in Leipzig in 1913.

SUGGESTED READING:
Lehmann, Lilli. *Mein Weg* (*My Path through Life*), 1913.

John Haag,
Athens, Georgia

Lilli Lehmann

Lehmann, Liza (1862–1918)

English composer, pianist, singer, and first woman in England to be commissioned to write a musical comedy. Name variations: Fredrika; Mrs. Herbert Bedford. Born Elizabeth Nina Mary Lehmann in London, England, on July 11, 1862; died in Pinner on September 19, 1918; daughter of Rudolph Lehmann (a painter) and Amelia Lehmann (a singer); married Herbert Bedford (a painter and composer), in 1894.

Liza Lehmann was born Elizabeth Nina Mary Lehmann in London, England, in 1862. She grew up in an artistic family: her father Rudolph Lehmann was a painter; her mother **Amelia Lehmann** was a singer. Liza studied voice with her mother and then with Albert Bandegger and *Jenny Lind. Her musical education was quite good; her parents sent Lehmann to the Continent where she studied composition under Raumkilde in Rome and Freudenberg in Wiesbaden before returning to London to study with Hamish MacCunn. In November 1884, Liza Lehmann debuted as a singer at the Monday Popular Concerts. Her career was encouraged by Joseph Joachim and *Clara Schumann, two of the best-known concert artists of the time. In fact, Schumann accompanied Lehmann in a concert with the Philharmonic in 1888. In 1894, Lehmann gave up concertizing when she married Herbert Bedford, deciding to concentrate her energies solely on composing. She was the first woman in England ever to be commissioned to write a musical comedy or operetta, resulting in *Sergeant Brue*. Lehmann taught at the Guildhall School of Music in 1913. Her music was largely vocal, as she composed many songs and two operas in addition to *Sergeant Brue*. She is best remembered for *In a Persian Garden* (1896), a song-cycle for four voices based on the *Rubyaiyat of Omar Khayyam*, which included the song "Myself When Young."

John Haag,
Athens, Georgia

Lehmann, Lotte (1888–1976)

German soprano acclaimed for her Leonore in Fidelio *and her lieder recitals. Born on February 27, 1888, in Perleberg, Germany; died on August 26, 1976, in Santa Barbara, California; daughter of Carl Lehmann (secretary to the Ritterschaft, a benevolent society) and Marie (Schuster) Lehmann; attended Ulrich High School in Berlin; studied at Berlin Hochschüle für Musik with Helene Jordan, Erna Tiedke and Eva Reinhold (1904); studied with great Wagnerian soprano Mathilde Mallinger (1908–09); married Otto*

Krause (an insurance executive), on April 28, 1926 (died, January 1939); children: (stepchildren) Manon, Hans, Ludwig, Peter.

Debuted as Second Boy in Die Zauberflöte *(The Magic Flute), Hamburg Opera (1910); debuted in London as Sophie in* Der Rosenkavalier, *Drury Lane (1914); sang with Vienna State Opera (1916–37), where she created roles of Young Composer in Strauss' revised* Ariadne auf Naxos, *the Dyer's Wife in* Die Frau Ohne Schatten *(1919) and Christine in* Intermezzo *(1924); made Covent Garden debut as Marschallin in* Der Rosenkavalier *(1924); appeared in Buenos Aires (1922), in Paris (1928–34), in Chicago (1930–37), in Salzburg (1926–37); debuted at the Metropolitan Opera as Sieglinde (1934); performed 12 seasons at the Met until 1945; gave recitals until 1951; taught privately and as director of Music Academy of the West in Santa Barbara; was an honorary member of Vienna State Opera.*

Selected writings: Verse in Prosa *(early 1920s);* Orplid, mein Land *(1937);* Anfang und Aufstieg *(1937, published as* Wings of Song *in English);* More Than Singing: The Interpretation of Songs *(1945);* My Many Lives *(1948);* Five Operas and Richard Strauss *(1964);* Eighteen Song Cycles *(1971).*

Lotte Lehmann was born in 1888, in Perleberg, Germany, the daughter of Carl Lehmann, a secretary to the Ritterschaft, a benevolent society, and **Marie Schuster Lehmann**. Lotte and her brother spent their early years in Perleberg before Carl was transferred to the Prussian capital, Berlin. There, Lotte attended Ulrich High School intent on a career in teaching. A friend of Marie Lehmann noticed Lotte's superb singing voice and recommended a vocal coach. Lehmann's father, however, insisted that she renounce her ambitions to become a professional singer, and some of her early teachers also discouraged her from pursuing singing as a career, telling her she had no vocal talent. With great determination, however, Lehmann pursued her vocal studies, initially with **Helene Jordan, Erna Tiedke** and **Eva Reinhold** at the Hochschüle für Musik in Berlin. In 1908, she began studies with the great *****Mathilde Mallinger**, who had created the role of Eva in Wagner's *Die Meistersinger* in Munich in 1868, a teacher Lehmann found both inspiring and sympathetic. She was also taken under the wing of a wealthy family, and with their assistance and encouragement was offered her first singing contract by the Hamburg Opera.

Lehmann made her debut on September 2, 1910, performing the role of Second Boy in Mozart's *Die Zauberflöte (The Magic Flute)* in Hamburg. Her first solo role of note was Aennchen in Nicolai's *Die lustigen Weibe von Windsor*. Persistent, good natured and hardworking, Lehmann's real break came with her performance of Elsa in *Lohengrin* under a young and demanding Otto Klemperer. She was soon singing more important parts in Hamburg, achieving a total of 56 different roles before she moved to Vienna, the cultured Habsburg capital, at the end of 1916 to take up a contract at the prestigious Vienna Staatsoper. Klemperer was to become one of her great admirers, along with Arturo Toscanini, Bruno Walter and Franz Schalk.

It was in Vienna that Lehmann made her name as a lyric-dramatic soprano of the highest quality. After only two months there she came to the notice of Richard Strauss, who admired her natural manner and the warm timbre of her voice. When the company's star *****Marie Gutheil-Schoder** appeared lackluster and careless in rehearsals for Strauss' revised version of *Ariadne auf Naxos*, the composer suddenly offered the new role of the Young Composer to Lehmann. She went on to create the roles of the Dyer's Wife in *Die Frau Ohne Schatten* (1919) and Christine in *Intermezzo* (1924, in Dresden) at the composer's request. Lehmann was also given important roles, including Eva and Elsa, in many Wagner operas, and she soon established herself as one of the finest Wagnerian singers of her generation.

Lehmann was perceived as a quintessentially Viennese singer, charming, accomplished, elegant and bright, and her voice was large, with dramatic power. She became much more than just one of the leading lyric-dramatic sopranos of her day: she was one of the greatest voices of the 20th century. During the course of her career, she learned nearly 100 operatic roles and gave over 1,600 performances.

She made her London debut as early as 1914, singing Sophie in Strauss' *Der Rosenkavalier* at Drury Lane under the baton of Sir Thomas Beecham, but the time of her greatest fame in Britain was the 1920s and 1930s. After her Covent Garden appearance as the Marschallin in *Rosenkavalier* in 1924, under Bruno Walter, she sang there every season until 1938. Roles included Mozart's Countess and Donna Elvira, as well as Beethoven's Leonore in *Fidelio*, which she first sang in 1927 at the Beethoven Festival in Vienna. The Marschallin was to become a role with which she was closely associated in opera houses around the world. Alden Whitman wrote that the part "became synonymous with her name," while Harold C. Schonberg asserts that in this role "she was The One: unique, irreplaceable, the standard to which all must aspire." Although she is now thought of predominantly as an interpreter of German roles, Lehmann also excelled at many of Puccini's heroines; the composer himself had a high regard for her Suor Angelica. She also performed Verdi's Desdemona, Massenet's Manon and Charlotte, Tchaikovsky's Tatyana and the heroines of Korngold's *Die tote Stadt* and *Das Wunder des Helianes* during her career in Vienna and London.

Lotte Lehmann toured South America for the first time in 1922. Her U.S. debut took place on October 28, 1930, with the Chicago Civic Opera, her Metropolitan Opera debut following on January 11, 1934. In both appearances, she sang the part of the Wagnerian heroine Sieglinde in *Die Walküre*. Lehmann retained links with Vienna until Hitler's Anschluss, when Germany took over the country. Her professional rivalries in Vienna and her distaste for the Nazi regime and its intolerance led to a severing of ties with both Germany and Austria, and she immigrated to the United States. She sought American citizenship in 1938 and was naturalized some time afterwards, probably in 1945. (Lehmann had

Lotte
Lehmann

married the Viennese Otto Krause in 1926, but this marriage was short-lived, and the couple had no children.)

Lehmann's beautiful voice, natural theatrical gift and attractive stage personality won her many influential admirers, but she often felt at a disadvantage because of her lack of physical beauty, as well as her lack of political connections. Acutely sensitive to being overshadowed by other singers, and aware of the restrictions of her voice (she had some difficulty with breath control and a lack of body in her top notes), Lehmann could be resentful and insecure around other female stars. She had a series of well-known rivalries with other pre-eminent singers of her day, beginning with *Elisabeth Schumann in Hamburg (although they were eventually to become friends) and continuing with *Maria Jeritza and *Viorica Ursuleac in Vienna. At the Met, Lehmann often harbored resentments over unfair casting, and perceived *Kirsten Flagstad to be her great rival for public and critical affections, as well as for preferred roles, despite the fact that their voices were different in almost every way.

After her emigration to the United States, Lehmann continued to appear at the Met with growing success, singing the roles of Tosca, Elisabeth in Tannhäuser, and the Marschallin, until her farewell performance in that favorite role on February 23, 1945. Her last appearance in San Francisco the following year was also in the role of the Marschallin.

Her concert career had begun in the years following World War I, and she had performed to great acclaim at the Salzburg Festival during the 1930s with Bruno Walter as her accompanist. As Lehmann's opera career dwindled, she performed a growing number of song recitals. She regarded lieder as "the ideal union of poetry and melody." Her repertoire was extensive, with a preference for Schumann, and she enjoyed an easy rapport with audiences. Her recording career, which began in 1917, continued until 1946 and included readings of Goethe and Heine as well as operatic and concert repertoire. A recording was also made of Lehmann's farewell performance in New York's Town Hall on February 16, 1951, a recital that inspired an intensely emotional audience reaction and headlines around the world. "After forty-one years of anxiety, nerves, strain and hard work," she told her fans, "I think I deserve to take it easy." She retired to her home in Santa Barbara that year, giving one other public performance on August 7.

Lehmann, who as a child had literary as well as musical aspirations, published several books,

including verses, the novel *Orplid, mein Land* (1937), two books of memoirs, *Anfang und Aufstieg* (published in English as *Wings of Song*, 1937) and *My Many Lives* (1948), and a book on the interpretation of song, *More Than Singing* (1945). In 1948, she appeared in the MGM film *Big City* and, in 1950, held an exhibit of her watercolors at the Schaeffer Galleries in New York. After her retirement, Lehmann taught singing in Santa Barbara and London, enjoying her work with young singers and eagerly communicating to them both her vocal techniques and hard-earned career experiences. As well as giving private lessons and master classes, Lehmann became the director of the Music Academy of the West. In 1962, she co-directed a new production of *Der Rosenkavalier* at the Met. She was also busy painting and writing, and published *Five Operas and Richard Strauss* in 1964 and *Eighteen Song Cycles* in 1971. Lotte Lehmann died in Santa Barbara on August 26, 1976.

SOURCES:
Lehmann, Lotte. *More Than Singing: The Interpretation of Songs.* New York, 1945.
———. *My Many Lives.* New York, 1948.

SUGGESTED READING:
Jefferson, Alan. *Lotte Lehmann, 1888–1976.* Julia MacRae Books, 1988.

Paula Morris, D.Phil.,
Brooklyn, New York

Lehmann, Rosamond (1901–1990)

British novelist, short-story writer, translator, and editor who articulated themes exploring women's sexualities and creative expression. Born Rosamond Nina Lehmann on February 3, 1901, in Fieldhead in Bourne End, Buckinghamshire, England; died on March 12, 1990, in London; daughter of Alice Mary (Davis) Lehmann (an American) and Rudolph Chambers Lehmann (a poet, writer, editor of Punch *until 1919, and member of Parliament, 1906–14); educated privately in family home, Fieldhead, and at Girton College, Cambridge, 1919–22; married Walter Leslie Runciman, in 1922 (divorced 1927); married Wogan Philipps (a painter and member of House of Lords), in 1928 (divorced 1942); had intimate friendship with Cecil Day-Lewis (a poet and writer), 1941–50; children: (second marriage) Hugo Philipps (b. 1929);* **Sally Philipps Kavanagh** *(1934–1958).*

Awards, honors: president of English Center and International vice-president of International P.E.N.; a fellow of the Royal Society of Literature (member of Council of Authors); Commandeur dans l'Ordre des Arts et Lettres (1968); Commander of the British Empire (CBE) for service to literature (1982).

Selected fiction: Dusty Answer *(1927);* A Note in Music *(1930);* Invitation to the Waltz *(1932);* The Weather in the Streets *(1936);* The Ballad and the Source *(1944);* The Gipsy's Baby and Other Stories *(1946);* The Echoing Grove *(1953);* A Sea-Grape Tree *(1976).*

Other writings: A Letter to a Sister *(1931); (play, first produced in London, 1938)* No More Music *(1939); (editor with others)* Orion: A Miscellany 1–3 *(3 vols., 1945–46); (translator from the French)* Genevieve *by Jacques Lemarchand (1947); (translator from the French)* Children of the Game *by Jean Cocteau (1955); (with W. Tudor Pole)* A Man Seen Afar *(1965); (autobiography)* The Swan in the Evening: Fragments of an Inner Life *(1967); (with W. Tudor Pole)* Zeuge im Leben Jesu *(1969); (with Cynthia Hill Sandys)* Letters from Our Daughters *(1972); (editor with Sandys)* The Awakening Letters *(1978).*

In her novel *The Weather in the Streets* (1936), Rosamond Lehmann depicts a contemporary working woman, Olivia Curtis, experiencing the euphoric joy of passionate love with a man, but her lover is married to another woman. Despite her liberated modernity, Olivia suffers socially and economically. She loses her sense of personal identity. Is she an independent woman or a mistress? Her passion dissipates; she is disillusioned. Olivia pays for the affair; the man does not. Lehmann has crafted the seductive strategies of conventional romance fiction to indict a culturally constructed idea of love as well as the romantic literary genre it engenders.

It does all come out of the unconscious, my unconscious, which is very well stocked—with images, memories, sounds, voices, relationships. There comes a moment when they seem to coalesce and fuse, and suddenly something takes shape, like seeing a whole landscape with figures, or a whole house with all its rooms.

—Rosamond Lehmann

Lehmann's stories have drawn a large readership of women since the popular and critical success of her first novel, *Dusty Answer,* in 1927. Indeed, a half-century of conventional masculine literary assessment of her work praised its technical virtuosity, its lyrical rhapsodies, its rich psychological insight, yet relegated it to the margins as "women's literature." However, reassessments by late 20th-century critics have come to recognize that her novels use the mechanics of traditional romance in order to question the dominant cultural ethos and challenge masculine hierarchies. For instance, the critic **Judy Simons** praises Lehmann's exploration of the emotional and erotic lives of women "caught in a culture that appears to liberate but in fact imprisons them." Simons continues: "Lehmann is also an acute social historian, a bitter analyst of the British class system and of its impact on gender and identity." During the 1980s and '90s, *The Weather in the Streets* was assigned reading in women's studies courses in Britain and the United States. In 1983, the BBC produced television films of Lehmann's novel *Invitation to the Waltz* (1932) and its sequel *The Weather in the Streets.*

Rosamond Nina Lehmann was born on February 3, 1901, in Bourne End, Buckinghamshire, the second child of **Alice Davis Lehmann** and Rudolph Chambers Lehmann. Rudolph Lehmann was a talented poet and athlete, the heir of Scottish intellectual and artistic traditions represented by his grandfather, Robert Chambers, of *Chambers' Encyclopaedia.* He courted and married his American wife, Alice Davis, while coaching the crew team at Harvard University in Cambridge, Massachusetts, in the 1890s. Rosamond Lehmann's father was first a contributor to and then an editor of *Punch,* the British humor magazine, from which he retired in 1919. He was elected as a Liberal Party candidate from Harborough to Parliament in 1906 and again in 1910, after which he withdrew because of declining health. Rosamond was one of four children, three girls and a boy. Her younger sister ❧➤ **Beatrix Lehmann** became a widely admired actress and novelist, and her younger brother John Lehmann became a well-known writer, critic, as well as founder and editor of *New Writing* and editor of *London Magazine.*

Rosamond Lehmann came from an unusually privileged and talented family. Her childhood was the protected site of innocence, albeit uneasy and anxious, to which she returned for inspiration in her fiction. Her father built their home, Fieldhead, on the River Thames in Bourne End in Buckinghamshire. Its property and vast gardens encompassed a horse stable, a dog kennel, a boathouse, and a brick pavilion built as a school for the education of Rosamond, her sisters, and about 20 selected girls in the neighborhood. Her childhood was highly regulated by parents, teachers, nannies, and governesses, and punctuated by the Boat Races, the annual rowing competition between Cambridge and Oxford. Lehmann reproduced fragments of her childhood in much of her fiction and also in her autobiography, *The Swan in the Evening* (1967), in which she remembers: "Myself in extremis, floored; myself saved, rejoicing: each of these opposed conditions deemed while it lasts, to be perpetual; yet even then a shadowy third, an onlooker, watching, recording, in the wings." Lehmann credited her father with identifying her early talent as a poet. Humorous, whimsical, generous, and declining with Parkinson's disease in his 60s, he encouraged her to write verse and short stories.

In 1919, at age 18, Lehmann left the shelter of her family to study at Girton College, Cambridge. Her protected upbringing was immediately pierced by the disillusionment and cynicism generated during the intellectual aftermath of the First World War. She was among the first wave of women allowed to study and sit for university exams, although degrees were not yet conferred on women by Cambridge University. As a student, she joined a cohort of young men attending university who, as returned veterans, went about examining the assumptions of a society that had thrown them into the devastating conflict of the Great War. Several years later, Lehmann would record her Cambridge years in *Dusty Answer*, a novel that won instant fame in both Britain and the United States for its lyrical prose and delicate treatment of sexuality in general and particularly adolescent lesbianism, a subject rarely raised in public discourse.

Shortly after leaving Cambridge, Rosamond Lehmann married Leslie Runciman and moved to Newcastle, where her husband went to work in his father's shipping business. Striving to offset her unhappiness in both her marriage and its setting, a northern provincial town, Lehmann began to write *Dusty Answer*. Her marriage dissolved in 1927. In her second novel, *A Note in Music* (1930), Lehmann describes two early middle-aged women reconciling to emotionally stultifying marriages: "'I was brought up to believe in matrimony,' [Grace, the heroine] said, 'and monogamy, and pure womanhood waiting for pure love to come and lead it off to a pure home. A spade was called anything but a spade. I was a very slow developer. By the time I started to wake up and think for myself, it was too late: I'd lost my chance.'"

In 1928, Lehmann married the Honorable Wogan Philipps, a painter and eventually the first Communist to have a seat in the House of Lords. Lehmann's biographers agree that Wogan Philipps aptly bridged the chasm between Lehmann's traditional Edwardian childhood and the artistic avant-garde then flourishing in Bloomsbury. Their son Hugo was born in 1929, and their daughter Sally in 1934.

Lehmann, Beatrix (1903–1979)

English actress and author. Born in Bourne End, Buckinghamshire, England, in 1903; died in 1979; daughter of Alice Mary (Davis) Lehmann (an American) and Rudolph Chambers Lehmann (a poet, writer, editor of Punch *until 1919, and member of Parliament, 1906–14); sister of *Rosamond Lehmann (1901–1990).*

Beatrix Lehmann made her stage debut at the Lyric, Hammersmith, in 1924. In 1946, she became director-producer of the Arts Council Midland Theater Company. She also wrote short stories, two novels, and appeared in films.

Ipsden House, the home in Oxford that Lehmann established with Wogan Philipps, became a center of hospitality for the artists and writers who were among the younger generation of the Bloomsbury crowd. Her friends included Leonard and *Virginia Woolf, *Vanessa Bell and Duncan Grant, Lytton Strachey and *Dora Carrington, as well as W.H. Auden, Christopher Isherwood, and Stephen Spender. According to Spender, Rosamond Lehmann was "one of the most beautiful women of her generation." One of her biographers, **Ruth Siegal**, records that the painters Vanessa Bell and Duncan Grant had her sit for them, Cecil Beaton photographed her, Bernard Berenson lavished praise on her, and her exceptional beauty impressed **Julian Bell** and Christopher Isherwood when they first met her.

Lehmann's next novel, *Invitation to the Waltz* (1932), describes a 17-year-old girl's awakening into imaginative empathy and self-conscious isolation. The upper middle-class Olivia Curtis attends a "coming-out" dance in an aristocratic upper-class circumstance. The shadow of the First World War falls on the heroine: "She had a moment's dizziness: a moment's wild new conscious indignation and revolt, thinking for the first time: This was war—never, never to be forgiven or forgotten, for his sake." Olivia is presented with a variety of age groups, social classes, and points of view, which, according to the literary biographer, **Diana E. LeStourgeon**, provide "[h]ints of tragedy, of illness, of despair, of cruelty, and of lust. . . . The dark side of life is there, always balancing the lighter, though never, because Olivia is young and still undisillusioned, overwhelming it."

In 1936, Lehmann produced *The Weather in the Streets*, a pessimistic sequel to *Invitation to the Waltz*. Olivia, now divorced, self-sufficient, and working in London, falls in love with a married man and aristocrat. Siegal contends that Lehmann uses a clandestine relationship in order to complicate and intensify the problems of a woman's sexuality: "how the state of being in love consumes a woman's will and obliterates her sense of self; how she constricts her world to the single reality of her love: 'being in love with Rollo was all important, the times with him the only reality.'"

Confronting the threat of fascism both on the Continent and at home, many British intellectuals turned to leftist politics in the 1930s. Nevertheless, Lehmann refused either to change her politics or to overtly infuse politics into her writing. Surrounded by friends who were socialist and communist, she remained staunchly a fair-minded, middle-of-the-road liberal—although speaking out in the mid- and late-'30s in anti-fascist organizations and meetings. She wrote passionately in support of the Republican cause in Spain. Her husband Wogan Philipps volunteered as an ambulance driver for Spanish Medical Aid in 1936, was wounded, and returned to Ipsden House to declare his formal membership in the Communist Party. Ruth Siegal, Lehmann's biographer and friend, characterized him as a political fanatic. Lehmann separated from her husband in 1941 and divorced him in 1942.

Leaving Ipsden House, Lehmann established a home with her children in London, then in the Berkshire hills, and later, after the financial success of *The Ballad and the Source* (1944), in a rambling Georgian manor house in Wittenham near Abingdon and the River Thames. In the early 1940s, she began an intimate, romantic relationship with the married poet and writer, Cecil Day-Lewis; they shared life at Little Wittenham. The affair ended bitterly in 1950 when Day-Lewis divorced but married a much younger woman, actress **Jill Balcon**. Thereafter, Lehmann resided in London.

In 1938, Lehmann's play, *No More Music*, was produced in London. Berthold Viertel directed Rosamond's sister Beatrix in the lead, and though *Elizabeth Bowen predicted that the play would have a regular run, it failed. The stories that Lehmann wrote during the first years of the Second World War for her brother John's prestigious magazine *New Writing* were collected in a volume entitled *The Gipsy's Baby and Other Stories* (1946). The stories are intense, crafted explorations of social class and gender from the subjective perspectives of women at home during war. In "A Dream of Winter," for instance, a mother, feverish with influenza, expresses anxiety and responsibility for having removed a beehive from the eaves: "One performs acts of will,

and in doing so one commits acts of negation and destruction. A portion of life is suppressed forever. The image of the ruined balcony weighed upon her: torn out, exposed, violated, obscene as the photograph of a bombed house."

For a short period in 1943, Lehmann—together with Day-Lewis, Edwin Muir, and Denys Kilham Roberts—edited the hardcover journal, *Orion*. Three issues were produced. In 1946, after the war, her brother set up a publishing firm, John Lehmann Limited. Rosamond was a director and official advisor. In 1947, the firm was bought out; John Lehmann was retained as its managing director and Rosamond as its salaried reader.

In her fifth novel, *The Ballad and the Source*, Lehmann created the powerful, mythical character of Sibyl Jardine, an aging enchanter bent on attempting to mold yet a third generation to her will. Harking to Victorian origins and sweeping through the eras of the First and Second World Wars, *The Ballad and the Source* embodies a desire to explore the past in order to give "meaning and spiritual fortification in the dissolving present," John Lehmann's agenda for *New Writing*. Of Lehmann's novels, it is the most overtly feminist. The intimate love of young women for one another reverberates in the memories of grandmothers and in the honest sexual attraction between granddaughters, one of whom determines to train as a physician, declaring: "I shall have a different sort of life from other people, . . . I shall never fall in love." Sibyl Jardine enjoins her young interlocutor, Rebecca Landon, not to forget the debt 20th-century women will owe the generations of feminists who have preceded them:

> "One day, Rebecca, women will be able to speak to men—speak out the truth, as equal, not as antagonists, or as creatures without independent moral rights—pieces of men's property, owned, used and despised. . . . When you are a woman, . . . living . . . a life in which all your functions and capacities are used and *none* frustrated, spare a thought for Sibyl. . . . Say: 'She helped to win this for me.'"

The narrative is a maze of stories woven by Sibyl Jardine and the dying seamstress Tilly; they are refracted through the storytelling of Rebecca Landon, a young woman awakening to imaginative creativity. The critic Judy Simons asserts that Lehmann's exploration of narrative self-reflection and reflexivity in this novel is surprisingly post-modern.

In *The Echoing Grove* (1953), Lehmann reasserts the importance of intimacy between

Rosamond
Lehmann

women. She describes the reconciliation of two sisters after the death of a man who had been husband to one and lover to the other. In her last novel, *A Sea-Grape Tree* (1976), about psychic healing, the character Sibyl Jardine is resurrected under her *nom de plume*, Sibyl Anstey. Although

dead, she lives in spiritual medium, dominating the narrative and the young heroine until they reconcile.

In 1958, Lehmann's daughter, Sally, who had married the writer Patrick Kavanagh and moved to Jakarta, died of poliomyelitis. In 1967, Lehmann wrote: "Nowadays I measure my life by Sally, not by dates. There was the time before her birth; the time of her life span; the time I am in now, after she slipped away from us." Soon after Sally's death, Lehmann had a mystical experience that convinced her that Sally had contacted her from a world on the other side of death. The experience changed her life. Lehmann began to read widely in the field of psychic phenomenon. She recounted her spiritual encounter with her daughter first in a psychic journal, where she felt she was whispering to the converted, and then more bravely in her autobiography, *The Swan in the Evening,* in 1967. In 1971, the College of Psychic Studies published letters from Sally which were transcribed by the clairvoyant medium, Baroness **Cynthia Sandys.**

In *The Swan in the Evening: Fragments of an Inner Life,* Lehmann explained why she would never write a proper autobiography and describes the source of her creativity:

> [S]o much of my "life story" has gone, in various intricate disguises, and transmuted almost beyond my own recognition, into my novels, that it would be difficult if not impossible to disentangle "true" from "not true": declare: "This is pure invention. This partly happened, this very nearly happened, this did happen"—even if I could conceive it to be a worth-while operation.

Lehmann wrote fictions of womanhood, writes Simons, "as they map out the territory for an expanding feminine consciousness on its journey of development through the twentieth century."

Rosamond Lehmann lived to enjoy renewed fame with the republication of her works by Penguin and Virago in the 1980s. She died in London on March 12, 1990, at the age of 89.

SOURCES:

Lehmann, Rosamond. *The Ballad and the Source.* London: Collins, 1944 (reprinted with an introduction by Janet Watts, London: Virago, 1982).

———. *The Gipsy's Baby and Other Stories.* London: Collins, 1944 (reprinted with an introduction by Janet Watts, London: Virago, 1982).

———. *Invitation to the Waltz.* London: Chatto & Windus, 1932 (reprinted with an introduction by Janet Watts, London: Virago, 1981).

———. *A Note in Music.* London: Chatto & Windus, 1927 (reprinted with an introduction by Janet Watts, London: Virago, 1982).

———. *A Sea-Grape Tree.* London: Collins, 1976 (reprinted with an introduction by Janet Watts, London: Virago, 1982).

———. *The Swan in Evening: Fragments of an Inner Life.* London: William Collins, 1967 (reprinted London: Virago, 1977).

———. *The Weather in the Streets.* London: Collins: 1936 (reprinted with an introduction by Janet Watts, London: Virago, 1981).

LeStourgeon, Diana E. *Rosamond Lehmann.* NY: Twayne, 1965.

Siegal, Ruth. *Rosamond Lehmann: A Thirties Writer.* NY: Peter Lang, 1989.

Simons, Judy. *Rosamond Lehmann.* NY: St. Martin's Press, 1992.

SUGGESTED READING:

Gindin, James. "Rosamond Lehmann: A Revaluation," in *Contemporary Literature.* Vol. 15, no. 2. Spring, 1974, pp. 203–211.

Lehmann, John. *The Whispering Gallery: Autobiography I.* London: Longmans, 1956.

———. *I Am my Brother: Autobiography II.* London: Longmans, 1960.

Tindall, Gillian. *Rosamond Lehmann: An Appreciation.* London: Chatto & Windus, 1984.

COLLECTIONS:

Papers of Rosamond Lehmann are located in the King's College Library, Cambridge.

Manuscripts of Rosamond Lehmann are held by the Harry Ransom Humanities Research Center, the University of Texas at Austin.

RELATED MEDIA:

"Invitation to the Waltz," BBC-TV film, 1983.

"The Weather in the Streets," BBC-TV film, 1983.

Jill Benton,
author of *Naomi Mitchison: A Biography,*
and Professor of English and World Literature at
Pitzer College, Claremont, California

Lehnert, Josefine (1894–1983).

See Pascalina, Sister.

Leicester, countess of.

See Montfort, Amicia (fl. 1208).

See Eleanor of Montfort (1215–1275).

See Knollys, Lettice (c. 1541–1634).

Leichter, Käthe (1895–1942)

Austrian reformer who was one of the most gifted women in the Austrian Social Democratic movement.

Name variations: Kathe Leichter; (pseudonyms) Anna Gärtner; Maria Mahler. Born Marianne Katharina Pick in Vienna, Austria, on August 20, 1895; died near Magdeburg in February 1942; daughter of Josef Pick (a prominent attorney); sister of Vally Weigl (1889–1982), an Austrian-U.S. composer and music therapist; attended the Beamten-Töchter-Lyzeum, the University of Vienna (1914); doctorate from University of Heidelberg (1918); married Otto Leichter (1897–1973, a journalist and Socialist politician), in 1921; children: two sons, Heinz (b. 1924) and Franz (b. 1930).

Käthe Leichter was born Marianne Katharina Pick in Vienna, Austria, into a wealthy assimilated Jewish family on August 20, 1895, and grew up in a fashionable apartment house, Rudolfsplatz, 1, in the Inner City. Her sister would one day gain fame as the composer *Vally Weigl. From her earliest years, Käthe showed interest in the pressing issues of her day. As was then true of many Jewish intellectuals, she was attracted to the ideals of Marxian Socialism, which promised the creation of a world free of war, economic exploitation, imperialism and sexism. After attending Vienna's esteemed Lyceum for the daughters of higher civil servants, in the fall of 1914 she enrolled at the University of Vienna to begin a course of study in political science. At the time, women could enroll in such courses but could not receive a doctorate (this would be changed after the end of World War I, in 1919).

When the antiwar activist Fritz Adler assassinated the Austrian prime minister, Count Karl von Stürgkh, in October 1916, Käthe was transformed, moving rapidly to a radical Marxist internationalist position. Determined to receive a degree for her studies, Käthe obtained special permission to enroll as a regular student in the fall of 1917 at the University of Heidelberg. She received her doctorate from Heidelberg with honors in the summer of 1918, having learned much more than abstract political theory at that distinguished German institution. War-weary students, radicalized by three years of stalemate and homefront privations, and inspired by the apparent successes resulting from the Bolshevik Revolution in Russia in November 1917, joined radical cells and attempted to spread the gospel of social transformation throughout Central Europe. It was a profoundly idealistic young woman who took these ideas and ideals back with her to a defeated Vienna in the fall of 1918.

The ideals of the Bolshevik Revolution failed to conquer Germany in 1918–19, and in Austria and Hungary, as well, the forces of the extreme Leninist left were largely discredited by the fall of 1919. But starting in 1920, Vienna became a separate political entity within Austria, and a vast social experiment began. For almost 15 years, "Red Vienna" was able to push forward ambitious projects in public housing and public health that greatly advanced the welfare of the working classes of the former Habsburg metropolis. At the center of these reforms was a group of idealistic and dedicated intellectuals, many of them of middle-class Jewish origin, who were convinced that Vienna could point the way to an invigorated form of Marxism that was neither dictatorial like that of Leninist (or Stalinist) Russia, nor devoid of energy and ideas like the

German Social Democratic Party that many identified with the defeat of 1918.

In 1921, Käthe married fellow Socialist Otto Leichter, a talented journalist and Social Democratic Party official, and worked at Vienna's Worker's Chamber (*Arbeiterkammer*), which oversaw the broad system of social welfare initiated by the party. During the 1920s, Käthe Leichter wrote articles for the party press and collected materials for large-scale sociological studies of the working conditions of the Austrian working class. By the late 1920s, Käthe and Otto Leichter had become leaders of the "New Left" faction within the Austrian Social Democratic Party, engaging in numerous and often vigorous debates with the more conservative elements in the movement. In their private life, the couple enjoyed the company of their two sons Heinz and Franz.

But these personal joys began to be clouded in the early 1930s by the economic depression and the rapid rise of radical movements, particularly National Socialism. The Leichter family, being both Socialist and Jewish, was threatened by these developments but both Otto and Käthe remained convinced that their ideals would prevail. They refused to emigrate or to abandon their Marxist ideological position. When the Austro-Fascist dictatorship of Engelbert Dollfuss was established in February 1934 and the Social Democratic Party was banned, both Leichters remained in Vienna although their economic status became precarious.

Otto was soon involved in the underground work of the Socialists, who renamed themselves "Revolutionary Socialists," while Käthe assisted her husband, often using the pseudonyms "Maria," "Maria Mahler," and "Anna Gärtner." She was particularly active in the educational committee of the Revolutionary Socialist leadership group. One of her reports on trade union activity was smuggled out of Austria and appeared in print in Brussels in 1936 under her pseudonym "Maria Mahler."

Ever the optimist, a few days after the Nazi annexation of Austria, she told friends, half-seriously:

> Everything has its good side. Without Dollfuss, Schuschnigg and Hitler, I would have remained at my desk at the Arbeiterkammer, and friends would have celebrated my fiftieth birthday in the Vienna *Rathauskeller* with good food and bad speeches, and then slowly but surely have begun to regard me as one of the party's "Old-Timers." This way, however, I will have to start my life over again from point A.

A few weeks later, Leichter was a prisoner of the Gestapo. She had hoped to stay in Vienna to be with her aged mother, and while her husband and two sons were able to escape, first to France and finally, in 1940, to the United States, the Nazis refused to grant her permission to emigrate, regarding her as one of their "biggest catches"—a prominent Jewish female Socialist intellectual. Arrested in May 1938 as her emigration papers were being prepared, she was accused of high treason in September of that year. The sentence of four months' imprisonment, passed on her in October 1939, raised false hopes, since she was not released when her time was served. She was moved instead to the infamous Ravensbrück concentration camp, where her unwillingness to recant her views meant that only a miracle could save her. Her husband and many supporters around the world attempted to secure her release, but the Viennese Nazi authorities continued to perceive her as a dangerous foe. Near Magdeburg in February 1942, as they were being ostensibly transferred from Ravensbrück, Käthe Leichter was gassed to death in a railway train along with 1,500 other Jewish female prisoners.

SOURCES:

Leichter, Käthe. *So leben Wir: 1320 Industriearbeiterinnen berichten über ihr Leben.* Vienna: Verlag "Arbeit und Wirtschaft," 1932.

———. *Wie leben die Wiener Heimarbeiter?* Vienna: Verlag "Arbeit und Wirtschaft," 1928.

Leser, Norbert, ed. *Werk und Widerhall: Grosse Gestalten des österreichischen Sozialismus.* Vienna: Verlag der Wiener Volksbuchhandlung, 1964.

Lewis, Jill. *Fascism and the Working Class in Austria, 1918–1934: The Failure of Labour in the First Republic.* NY: Berg, 1991.

Röder, Werner, and Herbert A. Strauss, eds. *Biographisches Handbuch der deutschprachigen Emigration.* 4 vols. Munich: K.G. Saur, 1980.

Spiegel, Tilly. *Frauen und Mädchen im österreichischen Widerstand.* Vienna: Europa Verlag, 1967.

Steiner, Herbert, ed. *Käthe Leichter: Leben und Werk.* Vienna: Europa Verlag, 1973.

Weinzierl, Erika. *Emanzipation? Österreichische Frauen im 20. Jahrhundert.* Vienna: Verlag Jugend & Volk, 1975.

Widerstand und Verfolgung in Wien 1934–1945: Eine Dokumentation. 2nd ed. 3 vols. Vienna: Österreichischer Bundesverlag, 1984.

John Haag,
Associate Professor of History,
University of Georgia, Athens, Georgia

Leider, Frida (1888–1975)

German soprano who was a leading interpreter of Wagnerian roles. Born on April 18, 1888, in Berlin, Germany; died on June 4, 1975, in Berlin; daughter of a Berlin doctor; studied with Otto Schwarz; married Rudolf Deman (the violinist).

Made debut in Berlin (1915); was a member of the Berlin State Opera (1923–40); appeared at Covent Garden (1924–38); appeared at Bayreuth (1928–38); made debut at Metropolitan Opera (1933); appeared at the Paris Opéra (1930–32); taught voice following her retirement after World War II.

Frida Leider was born in Berlin in 1888, the daughter of a doctor. Initially, she studied medicine, before studying voice with Otto Schwarz. In order to support her ambitions as a singer, Leider worked as a clerk in the Berliner Bank; few of her colleagues suspected she would become famous as a singer of Wagnerian opera. After a series of small roles beginning in 1915, Leider was engaged by the Berlin State Opera. Performances at the Teatro alla Scala, in Paris, Vienna, Munich, Amsterdam, and Brussels soon followed. Each year, from 1924 to 1938, she was a guest artist at Covent Garden, and from 1928 to 1938 one of Bayreuth's greatest guest stars. Her performances as Brünnhilde and Isolde made many feel she was the most important Wagnerian soprano of her generation. In 1928, Leider appeared with the Chicago Opera Company as a principal, remaining for four seasons. On January 16, 1933, she made her debut as Isolde at the Metropolitan Opera, where she remained through 1934.

Despite her fame as the quintessential Wagnerian soprano, Leider experienced professional problems in Germany because her husband, the violinist Rudolf Deman, was Jewish. The concertmaster of the Berlin State Opera, he was forced to flee to Switzerland in 1940. At that point, Leider ended her career in Berlin and joined her husband. They were able to survive the war in exile thanks to the generosity of their good friend, tenor Lauritz Melchior. After the war, Leider and her husband returned to Berlin, but she did not return to the stage. She directed the Berlin State Opera's voice studio and in 1948 accepted a professorship at the Berlin Hochschule für Musik. When Leider died, her obituary summed up her career:

> In the early morning hours of June 4, 1975, the Berlin Kammersängerin Professor Frida Leider, honorary member of the Deutsche Oper Berlin, died. She was one of the most important personalities in the music history of the first half of our century. Without her the Wagner repertoire during these years would not have been possible. Seldom has the fusion of text and music, seldom the art of phrasing and dramatic expression cele-

brated such triumphs as the years that this great soprano was gracing our opera stages.

The Nazis temporarily terminated Frida Leider's career, but they were unable to obliterate it.

SOURCES:
Leider, Frida. *Playing My Part.* NY: 1966.

John Haag,
Athens, Georgia

Leigh, Augusta (1784–1851).

See Lamb, Caroline for sidebar.

Leigh, Carolyn (1926–1983)

American lyricist for many Broadway musicals, including Wildcat *and* Little Me. *Born Carolyn Paula Rosenthal in the Bronx, New York, on August 21, 1926; died in New York City on November 19, 1983; daughter of Henry Rosenthal and Sylvia Rosenthal; attended Hunter College High School; attended Queens College and New York University; married David Wyn Cunningham Jr. (an attorney), in 1959 (divorced).*

Martin Gottfried wrote that Carolyn Leigh was one of the three major lyricists to emerge in the musical theater during the late 1950s and early 1960s, along with Fred Ebb and Sheldon Harnick. Leigh's most successful collaborator was composer Cy Coleman, with whom she wrote songs for the musicals *Wildcat* and *Little Me*, as well as a string of popular hits. After their association ended in the 1960s, Leigh went on to collaborate on the musicals *How Now, Dow Jones* and *Smiles* before a heart attack ended her life at age 57.

A lifelong New Yorker, Carolyn Leigh was born in 1926 in the Bronx and, after attending Queens College and New York University, wrote radio and advertising copy before landing a job as a lyricist for a music publisher in 1951. Her popular success dates from 1954, when she wrote the lyrics for "Positively No Dancing" (music by Martin Roman), and "Young at Heart" (music by Johnny Richards), a song that Frank Sinatra turned into a standard. That same year, she collaborated with Mark Charlap on nine songs for what was to have been a small musical production of *Peter Pan*, including "I'm Flying," "I Won't Grow Up," and "I've Got to Crow." While the show was still on tour, the producers decided to turn it into a full-scale musical and hired composer Jule Styne to expand the score. He brought in his own lyricists, *Betty Comden and Adolph Green, who unwittingly stepped on Leigh's Broadway debut.

$\mathcal{F}$rida
$\mathcal{L}$eider

Leigh began her relationship with Cy Coleman in 1957, and, a year later, they scored their first runaway hit with "Witchcraft," another big seller for Frank Sinatra. Their second hit, "Firefly" (1958), was popularized by Tony Bennett, who subsequently hit the charts with a number of other Coleman-Leigh songs, including "It Amazes Me" (1958) and "The Best is Yet to Come" (1961).

In 1960, Coleman and Leigh collaborated on their first Broadway musical, *Wildcat*, a vehicle for *Lucille Ball. A hoedown number, "What Takes My Fancy," stole the show, and "Hey, Look Me Over" went on to become Ball's signature song. Gottfried, however, points to a lesser-known song from the show, "High Hopes," as containing some of Leigh's most gentle and metaphoric lyrics.

Unfortunately, Ball withdrew from *Wildcat* after 171 performances, signaling the show's demise. Leigh and Coleman immediately undertook their second Broadway collaboration, *Little Me* (1962), a show written by Neil Simon for Sid Caesar, who was returning to the stage following his enormous success on television. In the show, Caesar played seven different characters of different ages and nationalities, all paramours of the character Belle Pointrine, a girl of questionable virtue who rises from poverty to become a movie star. Although the show had only a moderate run (257 performances), it is considered Leigh's best work, perhaps because her lyrics complemented Simon's libretto so succinctly. When the show was revived on Broadway in 1982, Frank Rich of *The New York Times* wrote: "Every song in *Little Me* is tuneful, literate, dexterously crafted." Two of the musical's songs, "I've Got Your Number" and "Real Live Girl," achieved national popularity, although they lost much of their charm when taken out of context. Another song, "Here's to Me," became such a favorite of *Judy Garland's that she requested it be played at her funeral.

Coleman-Leigh songs were the products of constant bickering and vitriolic disagreements. "It's the best way for me," Leigh once told an interviewer. "He writes a song and plays it for me and I don't like it and I say, 'Cy, no, I won't write for *that*.'" When Coleman hated Leigh's lyrics, he didn't much bother to mince words either. "I wouldn't link eight notes to that if it were the last lyric on earth," he once told her. After the initial barbs, the two would discuss, argue, rewrite, and polish. The collaboration eventually wore itself out and ended in the 1960s, although the artists reunited to write two songs for a revival of *Little Me* in 1982.

While Coleman went on to write a string of successful musicals, including *Sweet Charity* (1966) with *Dorothy Fields, *On the Twentieth Century* (1978) with Comden and Green, and *Barnum* (1980) with Michael Stewart, Leigh never quite hit full stride again. She collaborated with Elmer Bernstein on *How Now, Dow Jones* (1967), an inane musical about big business, in which Leigh's songs lacked their usual warmth and upbeat spirit. Her last effort was *Smiles*, composed by Marvin Hamlisch.

Leigh also liked to perform her own songs and made occasional club appearances. Her last was at Michael's Pub in Manhattan in November 1980. The lyricist died in Lenox Hill Hospital in 1983.

SOURCES:

Ewen, David. *American Songwriters*. NY: H.W. Wilson, 1987.

Gottfried, Martin. *Broadway Musicals*. NY: Harry N. Abrams, 1979.

Hischak, Thomas S. *Word Crazy*. NY: Praeger, 1991.

Barbara Morgan,
Melrose, Massachusetts

Leigh, Frances Butler (1838–1910).

See Kemble, Fanny for sidebar.

Leigh, Janet (1927—)

American actress who was nominated for an Academy Award for her work in Psycho. *Born Jeanette Helen Morrison on July 6, 1927, in Merced, California; attended the College of the Pacific; married John Carlyle, in 1942 (annulled); married Stanley Reames, in 1946 (divorced 1948); married Tony Curtis (an actor), in 1951 (divorced 1962); married Robert Brandt (a stockbroker), in 1962; children: (third marriage) Kelly Lee Curtis; Jamie Lee Curtis (an actress).*

Selected filmography: The Romance of Rosy Ridge *(1947);* If Winter Comes *(1948);* Words and Music *(1948);* Act of Violence *(1949);* Little Women *(1949);* The Doctor and the Girl *(1949);* The Forsyte Saga *(1949);* The Red Danube *(1949);* Holiday Affair *(1949);* Strictly Dishonorable *(1951);* Angels in the Outfield *(1951);* Two Tickets to Broadway *(1951);* It's a Big Country *(1952);* Just This Once *(1952);* Scaramouche *(1952);* Fearless Fagan *(1952);* The Naked Spur *(1953);* Confidentially Connie *(1953);* Houdini *(1953);* Walking My Baby Back Home *(1953);* Prince Valiant *(1954);* Living It Up *(1954);* The Black Shield of Falworth *(1954);* Rogue Cop *(1954);* Pete Kelly's Blues *(1955);* My Sister Eileen *(1955);* Safari *(1956);* Jet Pilot *(1957);* Touch of Evil *(1958);* The Vikings *(1958);* The Perfect Furlough *(1959);* Who Was That Lady? *(1960);* Psycho *(1960);* Pepe *(1960);* The Manchurian Candidate *(1962);* Bye Bye Birdie *(1963);* Wives and Lovers *(1963);* Kid Rodelo *(1955);* Harper *(1966);* Three on a Couch *(1966);* An American Dream *(1966);* Grand Slam *(1968);* Hello Down There *(1969);* One Is a Lonely Number *(1972);* Night of the Lepus *(1972);* Boardwalk *(1979);* The Fog *(1980).*

Although she will forever be remembered for her bloody shower scene in Alfred Hitchcock's shock film *Psycho* (1960), Janet Leigh actually began her career playing sweet ingenues in the studio films of the 1940s and 1950s. The daughter of an insurance and real-estate agent, Lee was a personal discovery of actress *Norma Shearer, who saw her photograph on the desk of a ski lodge where Leigh's parents were working and took it to MGM. After giving Leigh a screen test, studio chief Louis B. Mayer decided to co-star the newcomer with Van Johnson in *The Romance of Rosy Ridge* (1947), even though she had no acting experience. "They were looking for a naïve young country girl," Leigh said, "and I was sure naïve and young."

Janet Leigh (right), during filming of The Fog, *with Adrienne Barbeau (left), John Carpenter (center), and Jamie Lee Curtis (top).*

Leigh, Vivien (1913–1967)

Two-time Academy Award-winning British actress who achieved international stardom for her portrayal of Scarlett O'Hara in Gone With the Wind. *Name variations: Lady Olivier. Born Vivian [sic] Mary Hartley in Darjeeling, India, on November 5, 1913; died in London, England, on July 7, 1967, of tuberculosis; only child of Gertrude and Ernest Hartley; convent-educated in England, Switzerland, France, and Ger-*

many before entering the Royal Academy of Dramatic Arts in London; married Hubert Leigh Holman (a barrister), in 1932 (divorced 1940); married Laurence Olivier (an actor), in 1940 (divorced 1960); children: (first marriage) daughter, Suzanne.

Appeared in her first film (1934); made her stage debut (1935) and appeared in a number of successful light dramas in the West End before achieving international stardom after her successful campaign to win the role of Scarlett O'Hara in David O. Selznick's Gone With the Wind (1939), for which she won the Academy Award for Best Actress; won a second Oscar (1951) for her portrayal of Blanche DuBois in the film version of Tennessee Williams' A Streetcar Named Desire; suffered from mental illness later in her career, eventually being diagnosed as a manic depressive.

Filmography: The Village Squire (1934); Things Are Looking Up (1935); Look Up and Laugh (1935); Gentleman's Agreement (1935); Storm in a Teacup (1937); Fire Over England (1937); Dark Journey (1937); A Yank at Oxford (1938); Sidewalks of London (1938); Gone With the Wind (1939); Waterloo Bridge (1940); Twenty-One Days (1940); That Hamilton Woman (1941); Caesar and Cleopatra (1946); Anna Karenina (1948); A Streetcar Named Desire (1951); The Deep Blue Sea (1955); The Roman Spring of Mrs. Stone (1961); Ship of Fools (1965).

Everyone remembered the first time they saw her. Laurence Olivier recalled his initial sight of "that exquisite face" in 1935, glimpsed across a crowded London restaurant. Producer David O. Selznick never forgot the firelight flickering over green eyes and dark hair the evening cameras rolled for the first time on his epic *Gone With the Wind*. And director George Cukor remembered laughing at the proper British girl reading for the part of a Southern belle in Selznick's film, until her stunning beauty and desperate ambition silenced him. "Where else shall we look for such a combination of intelligence, beauty, and emotional sympathy," an awestruck Londoner once wondered, "lit up as they are by shafts of sprightliness and humor?"

Vivien Leigh accepted these praises with the grace of a queen receiving the adoration of her courtiers, although her early life gave no hint of such an exalted status. She had been born plain Vivian Hartley and had been educated in a series of convent schools in England and on the Continent, the proper education for the daughter of **Gertrude Hartley** and a British solicitor, Ernest Hartley. The only exotic feature of her early life had been her birth in India. Although Ernest's

practice was in Calcutta, Gertrude had decided to retire to the cooler climate of Darjeeling to give birth to what was to be her only child on November 5, 1913. Six years later, Vivian left India to enter the Catholic school Gertrude had chosen for her, at the Convent of the Sacred Heart in Roehampton, England, where the girls rose at 6:30, attended Mass at 7:15, and breakfasted on bread and butter at 8:00. She remained at Roehampton for eight years, with only occasional visits from her parents. Among Vivian's friends at Roehampton was ***Maureen O'Sullivan**, whose interest in acting attracted Vivian and whose later career would inspire Vivian's own. With Maureen and other girls interested in the theater, Vivian traveled to London's West End and settled on George Robey as her favorite actor, attending 16 performances of one of his plays and obtaining an autographed picture each time.

By the time Vivian left Roehampton in 1928 to continue her studies at a French convent school in Dinard, she could play the violin, cello, and piano, and had appeared as Miranda in the school's production of *The Tempest* and Mustardseed in *A Midsummer Night's Dream*. She spent only a year in Dinard, however, before persuading Gertrude to enroll her in her first nonconvent school in Paris, where she was allowed to attend performances of the Comedie Française, take elocution lessons from one of the company's leading actresses, and gain a proficiency in both French and Italian. By 1931, the Hartleys had left India for good and settled back in England while their daughter finished her formal education in Biarritz, where she added German to her languages.

During her last school years, Vivian had been much influenced by a biography of the late 19th-century actress ***Lillie Langtry**, and by the fact that her former schoolmate Maureen O'Sullivan was now appearing in the West End. Vivian proposed to Ernest that she be allowed to enroll in London's Royal Academy of Dramatic Arts, which accepted her for its spring term in 1932. In the meantime, she had met through family friends a dashing London barrister named Hubert Leigh Holman, who, she told a friend, had the manner and physical attributes of a matinee idol. After only one term at RADA, Vivian left the school to become Mrs. Leigh Holman on December 20, 1932.

But her subsequent duties as the wife and official hostess for a successful London barrister seemed a dull substitute for a life on the stage. Although she had become pregnant shortly after their marriage, Vivian convinced Holman in the

spring of 1933 to let her resume her studies at RADA. The couple's daughter, Suzanne, born on October 12, 1933, was given over to the care of a nanny while Vivian completed her final year of dramatic studies and began looking for work. Her first paying job as an actress was a small part as a schoolgirl (she was identified in the credits as "The Girl Who Sticks Her Tongue Out") in *Things Are Looking Up*, for which she was given one line of dialogue and 30 shillings a day. While working on the film, Vivian met actor John Gliddon, who had been to America and been much impressed with the money being made by Hollywood agents who identified and developed young actors into screen stars, unlike the much more modest and discreet British system of the time, in which screen work was looked upon with some disdain by legitimate stage talent. Once he had left the acting profession to become an agent himself, one of Gliddon's first contracts was with Vivian. It was Gliddon who suggested she burnish her rather pedestrian name by changing the "a" in her first name to an "e" and taking her husband's middle name as her own professional surname. Shortly after signing with Gliddon, Vivien celebrated by going to the theater and watching an exciting young actor named Laurence Olivier, whom she reportedly told a friend she would marry one day and whom she even ventured backstage to meet. Olivier still remembered many years later the light kiss Vivien bestowed on his shoulder as she left his dressing room.

> $\mathcal{P}$eople who are very beautiful make their own laws.
>
> —Vivien Leigh

Gliddon found his new client a larger role in her second film, *The Village Squire*, which brought Leigh her first notices and prompted one reviewer to note: "Vivien Leigh shows promise." Still with his eye on Hollywood, Gliddon signed her for *Gentleman's Agreement*, produced by the British subsidiary of Paramount (not to be confused with the movie version of *Laura Z. Hobson*'s *Gentleman's Agreement*, filmed in 1947). By the time Gliddon secured Vivien's first professional role on the West End stage (in 1935's *The Green Sash*), he had already snagged her first major motion picture, *Look Up and Laugh*, one of a string of so-called "Ealing comedies" produced by Associated Talking Pictures. Vivien played a supporting role opposite *Gracie Fields, a popular comedian of the time who predicted Leigh would one day be a star. Despite the compliment, Vivien had grown quite self-conscious about her appearance on screen, being particularly sensitive about her hands, which she felt were too large, and her neck, which she felt was too long—a sensitivity not helped by *Look Up and Laugh*'s cinematographer, who delighted in calling her "the swan."

Though her film work was both gratifying and profitable, it was the stage that first made Leigh a star. While she was finishing work on *Look Up and Laugh*, she was cast in a West End costume drama, *The Mask of Virtue*, in which she first caught the eye of the mainstream British press. The reviews following the play's opening

in May of 1935 made Leigh famous to such an extent that she was dubbed the "Fame in a Night Girl." Such headlines as "New Star to Win All London" and "A Young Actress' Triumph" were typical, while *The Daily Mail* called her reception by the opening-night audience "one of the biggest personal ovations a newcomer has had on the London stage for quite a long time." One of those who read her notices with interest was Alexander Korda, the British film producer most well-connected with Hollywood. Korda's deal with United Artists was profitable enough for him to undertake building Britain's first new film studio in decades, at Denham, which was at the time the only facility able to shoot color. Although John Gliddon negotiated a profitable, five-year contract for her with Korda which was the talk of the industry, it would be some time before the producer would offer her a role in one of his films.

In the meantime, Leigh enjoyed the fame brought by *The Mask of Virtue*, appearing at parties where she was introduced to the likes of John Gielgud, Noel Coward and Douglas Fairbanks; posing for an extensive photo spread shot by Cecil Beaton; and once again meeting Laurence Olivier at a party celebrating the pregnancy of his wife, actress ✥▶ Jill Esmond. Leigh was offered a number of stage roles, including two of Shakespeare's queens—in *Henry VIII* and in *Richard III*—before Korda finally offered her a part as the love interest in the sort of costume drama for which he would later become famous. Vivien was to play a lady-in-waiting to Queen *Elizabeth I in *Fire over England,* and her co-star was none other than Laurence Olivier. (The great *Flora Robson played the imperious Elizabeth.)

The film went into production late in 1936 at Korda's new Denham studios, with Olivier playing Ingolby, the dashing sailor who falls in love with Vivien's character, Cynthia, as England prepares to meet the Spanish Armada. It did not take long for cast and crew to notice that Leigh remained on the set even after her scenes for the day were completed, bringing cups of tea to Olivier; or for more observant gossips to note that both of the actors' spouses were conveniently occupied in other pursuits—Holman being away on a sailing trip to Denmark, and Jill Esmond at home awaiting the birth of her baby. After her second picture for Korda, 1937's *Dark Journey*, Holman and Vivien happened to meet Olivier and Esmond on a vacation in Italy, the two couples spending much time together. While shooting her third film for Korda, the comedy *Storm in a Teacup*, Olivier was a frequent visitor to the set while Vivien reportedly rebuffed the ardent advances of her leading man, Rex Harrison. It was also while making that picture that she famously refused the director's suggestion of a pratfall by drawing herself up to full height and pointing out, "But I am an *English* actress!"

By the time she and Holman took a much-needed break in Switzerland, Vivien had set two goals for herself. One was to appear as Ophelia opposite Olivier's Hamlet in a special production to be given at the Danish castle traditionally said to be the Elsinore of Shakespeare's tragedy. The other was to play the heroine in the film version of a book she avidly consumed during her vacation. Called *Gone With the Wind*, it was written by an American author named *Margaret Mitchell.

As if in answer to her first wish, Korda cast Leigh and Olivier as the two romantic leads in *Twenty-One Days*, a suspense film with a script by Graham Greene based on a John Galsworthy short story. The two stars rehearsed together in the studio car that ferried them back and forth each day, and by the time a break in filming allowed Olivier to travel to Denmark for Hamlet, Vivien went with him as Ophelia. It was during the play's run that their affair deepened, despite the fact that Jill Esmond had traveled with her husband to Denmark. "[Vivien and I] could not keep from touching each other," Olivier later recalled, "making love almost within Jill's vision." John Gielgud, who was also in the cast, was assigned the task of taking Jill Esmond for long drives in the country while Olivier and Leigh explored their relationship in private and planned for their future.

Resuming production on *Twenty-One Days* on their return to England, Vivien suggested to Holman, who considered her affair with Olivier a brief infatuation, that a separation might be appropriate. Holman genially agreed, believing that patience would win the day and bring Vivien back to him. By late 1937, Vivien and Olivier had taken a house together in London's fashionable Mayfair district purchased with Olivier's advance for *Twenty-One Days*. At a press conference called to mark the completion of shooting on the picture, Leigh neatly side-stepped questions about her romance with Olivier but irritated Korda by talking volubly about *Gone With the Wind* rather than the film she had just finished for him. "I have never been so gripped by anything in my life," she enthused. "It's the finest book I've ever read, what a grand film it would make!" Then, noting that the film adaptation was already in pre-production in Hollywood, Leigh added, "I've cast myself as Scarlett O'Hara! What do you think?"

❧▶ Esmond, Jill (1908–1990)

English actress. Name variations: Jill Esmond Olivier. Born Jill Esmond-Moore in London, England, on January 26, 1908; died in 1990; daughter of Henry Vernon Esmond and Eva (Moore) Esmond; studied at the Royal Academy of Dramatic Art; married Laurence Olivier (an actor), in 1930 (divorced 1940); children: Tarquin Olivier.

In 1922, age 14, Jill Esmond made her stage debut at the St. James's Theater as Nibs in *Peter Pan*; she played the same part at the Adelphi in 1923 and 1924. In 1925, she appeared as Sorel Bliss at the Ambassador in *Hay Fever*. In March 1929, she made her first appearance in New York at the Booth Theater as Joan Greenleaf in *A Bird in the Hand*, a role she had been playing in London throughout the previous year. Other stage roles included Sybil Chase in *Private Lives*, Laura Hudson in *Men in White*, Ann Hammond in *Ringmaster*, Olivia in *Twelfth Night*, Blanche Monnier in *I Accuse*, Angela Brent in *Tree of Eden*, and Edith de Berg in *The Eagle Has Two Heads*. After traveling to Hollywood in the 1930s with her husband, actor Laurence Olivier, Esmond would appear in a number of films, including *This Above All, The White Cliffs of Dover, Random Harvest, Journey for Margaret, Casanova Brown*, and *A Man Called Peter*. Following her divorce from Olivier in 1940, she continued to live in Los Angeles for the duration of World War II.

The story of Vivien Leigh's successful drive to win the role of Scarlett has long been the stuff of Hollywood legend, from the series of London head shots she sent to Selznick, complete with hoopskirt, parasol and ring curls, to her whirlwind trip to Los Angeles to visit Olivier while he was shooting his first American picture, *Wuthering Heights*, based on *Emily Brontë's novel. Olivier saw to it that he and Vivien dined one evening with Olivier's agent, Myron Selznick, who conveniently happened to be David Selznick's brother. By 11 PM that December night in 1938, Myron had taken her to the back lot where David had assembled a collection of left-over sets from old silent movies, dressed them up to look like Civil War Atlanta, and set them alight for one of the film's most famous scenes. At the time, *Paulette Goddard was the odds-on Scarlett favorite of Hollywood wags after Selznick's much-publicized yearlong search for his heroine in which every actress from *Katharine Hepburn to *Lucille Ball had been tested. But moments after Myron had introduced Vivien to his brother, she was whisked off for a reading with the film's then-director, George Cukor (who would later be replaced by Victor

Fleming, fresh from *The Wizard of Oz*). By late December 1938, *Hedda Hopper reported to her readers that "the cute English vamp Vivien Leigh is in our midst, but not doing a picture," although at Selznick's request she did not mention Leigh had shot three tests for Scarlett. "She was a brilliant actress," said *Kay Brown, head of Selznick International in New York. "They tested her, silent tests, wardrobe tests, she was just the ideal. She was the most glowing, vibrant, dynamic woman I had ever met." On Christmas Day, 1938, Cukor told Leigh that she had the part but warned her to say nothing until the official studio announcement; and in early January 1939, John Gliddon received a telegram in London saying that Leigh "might possibly make an important picture at Selznick International" and asking him to cancel any existing commitments Gliddon had for her in England, promising that Selznick would make up his losses.

Selznick made his official announcement on January 13. "Miss Leigh was selected to play Scarlett," he said in his press release, "because she has the dark hair and green eyes of Miss Mitchell's description, and because her intelligence, determination and talent foretokened success in the most difficult assignment a Hollywood actress ever faced." Selznick had carefully elicited a supportive response from Margaret Mitchell herself, who said it would be easier for audiences to accept an actress unknown to them as Scarlett, but others objected strenuously to having a British actress playing a Southern plantation belle. One of the milder telegrams that flooded Selznick's office called his decision "an outrage to the memory of the heroes of 1776 who fought to free this land of British domination," while a correspondent for the fan magazine *Movie Mirror* wrote, "Why not cast Chiang Kai-shek and change the part to *Gerald* O'Hara!" While the fury raged, Leigh spent four hours a day for the next two weeks working on her Southern accent with a dialogue coach, did her final wardrobe tests, and was ready for her first day's shooting on January 26, 1939, on the front porch of Tara, newly constructed after the burned rubble from Selznick's "Atlanta" had been cleared away.

Scarlett appears in 90% of the 3½-hour film's scenes, and there was some worry that Vivien's stamina would give out over the ten weeks of the shoot, complicated by the fact that her heavy costuming left her limp in the brutally hot lighting required by the new Technicolor process. But as would be the case throughout her career, Leigh won the respect of cast and crew for her professionalism throughout a grueling schedule that often required her to be in makeup by five in the morning. On the few days she was not working, Vivien discussed her interpretation of the role with Cukor, with whom she formed a close friendship. Nor did she object when Selznick suggested that Olivier move out of the house she had rented on Crescent Drive, to be replaced by a personal assistant. Nearly a year after she began work on the film, *Gone With the Wind* had its world premiere in Atlanta on December 15, 1939, followed by openings in New York and Los Angeles. Despite the earlier outcry at her selection for the role, audiences fell in love with Leigh's Scarlett, and continued to do so over 60 years later. Bosley Crowther told his *New York Times* readers that Vivien Leigh was "as fine an actress as we have on the screen today. Maybe even the finest." His peers agreed, according Leigh the New York Film Critics Award for best female performance of 1939; while at the Academy Awards ceremony in February of 1940, Leigh was given the Oscar for Best Actress, quipping in her acceptance speech that if she thanked everyone who had helped her, her remarks would be as long as the film itself.

There were momentous changes in Leigh's personal affairs at this time, too. In January of 1940, Holman finally agreed to a divorce just days after Olivier received the same news from Jill Esmond, allowing Vivien and Olivier to marry in August of that year in California, when both divorces became final. Vivien would remain close to Holman despite the end of their marriage, visiting him often, sending Christmas cards and birthday gifts, and frequently taking their daughter Suzanne on vacations to the Continent and America. One close friend ventured the opinion that Leigh "seemed to suffer from an enormous guilt" for her open and very public adultery with Olivier before her divorce from Holman, and suggested that it may have been a factor in the mental illness that troubled Vivien in later life. To the public, however, Vivien Leigh and Laurence Olivier seemed the very embodiment of show business royalty, especially after they appeared in their second (and last) film together, 1941's *That Hamilton Woman*, a Korda picture based on the notorious affair between Lord Horatio Nelson and *Emma Hamilton. With England now in the midst of war, Korda's shoot was a hurried one, with little money to spare—so much so that in the last days of filming at Korda's Denham studios, only the half of Vivien's face that was lit was made up. Although some overly patriotic Britons thought that, as one of them put it, "history should not be told through the eyes of a trollop," Leigh's performance convinced film critics that her formidable

From the movie Gone With the Wind, *starring Vivien Leigh.*

range could easily encompass an American Southerner and an English Regency mistress. The reviewer for *The Daily Telegraph* wrote that her work was "easily the finest performance Miss Leigh has given us, and it confirms her position among the finest actresses of the screen."

Winston Churchill, whom it was said had suggested the film to Korda, was so taken with *That Hamilton Woman* that he screened it at least six times, including an oceanbound showing on the way to his Atlantic Charter meeting with Franklin Roosevelt in 1941.

Although *That Hamilton Woman* would be their last work together on screen, Leigh and Olivier appeared frequently together on the stage, their first love. Many of the productions were mounted by the company formed for that purpose by Olivier, which became known for innovative (some said heretical) presentations of classic works. Their version of *Romeo and Juliet,* for example, was presented on a specially built revolving stage and was played in the round, a novel technique at the time that did little to win critical approval, either in London or in New York, where the *Herald Tribune* critic Richard Watts wrote: "Miss Vivien Leigh and Mr. Laurence Olivier must expect to have their local sojourn . . . taken as a spectacular personal appearance by Heathcliff and Scarlett O'Hara than as an earnest interpretation of the star-crossed lovers in Shakespeare's tragedy." Reviewers also objected to Leigh's vixenish portrayal of Juliet and Olivier's interpretation of Romeo as a sexually naive schoolboy. The play closed in New York after only 34 performances and was said to have lost $100,000.

While Olivier returned to films to make up their losses, Leigh toured the British provinces in a production of Shaw's *The Doctor's Dilemma,* which finally arrived to great acclaim in the West End, where it ran for 13 months. Shaw, then in his late 80s, did not venture to see the production himself but eventually asked to meet Vivien when he learned of her interest in playing *Cleopatra (VII) in a film version of his *Caesar and Cleopatra*. "Do you think I'm good enough?," Vivien disingenuously asked him. "You are the *Mrs. Pat Campbell of our age," the spry old man replied, giving his blessing to the picture which began shooting in 1944, after Leigh had toured North Africa and the Mediterranean entertaining British troops with poetry, songs, and scenes from Shakespeare. Once again, war intruded on the production. Filming stretched over 21 months, being continually interrupted by air raids, power shortages, and troop call-ups which thinned the crew's ranks. Tragedy marred the set, too, when a pregnant Vivien slipped and fell during one scene and was later found to have miscarried her child. It was the second of three such incidents, an earlier pregnancy shortly after her marriage to Olivier and a third in 1956, ending the same way.

By war's end, Leigh had become Lady Olivier, with the knighthood conferred on her husband, and had begun her own, 16-year reign as Britain's first lady of the stage with such roles as Sabina in Olivier's London production of *The Skin of Our Teeth,* as Lady *Anne (of Warwick)

in his *Richard III* and most famously as Cleopatra in alternating productions of Shaw's play and Shakespeare's *Antony and Cleopatra* mounted for the 1951 Festival of Britain, later brought to Broadway (where it was dubbed "Two on the Nile"). This time, the critics were thrilled with her work. "She is . . . intelligent, audacious, and courageous," wrote the *Times*' Brooks Atkinson of her two Broadway Cleopatras, although Vivien's old friend John Gielgud put it more simply by saying, "There was so much Vivien in it." Few except her closest friends knew that her health was suffering, with recurring bouts of the tuberculosis which had plagued her as a child and, beginning in the 1950s, the erratic mood swings which characterize the manic-depressive, a disease not diagnosed accurately until some years later by a therapist in New York.

Neither of these afflictions were evident in her luminous portrayal of Blanche DuBois in both the London stage and the Hollywood film versions of *A Streetcar Named Desire*. Although Tennessee Williams' play, with its references to rape, homosexuality, and incest, had been deemed "low and repugnant" in an official bill passed by the House of Commons, Olivier had purchased the British rights to it, and Leigh had agreed to the role after meeting with Williams. Many of her admirers felt it was a part far below the woman Korda himself had once called "the epitome of an English lady." Realizing Blanche was one character that would rely solely on her acting ability and not on her aristocratic looks, Leigh's first step in preparing for the role was bleaching her hair blonde and wearing excessive amounts of makeup, much to her public's dismay. To add to the tension, the play was being directed by Olivier himself at a time when relations between them had become distant. Nevertheless, she was praised for her work over the play's West End run of 326 performances and was persuaded to reprise Blanche in the film version opposite Marlon Brando's Stanley, Karl Malden's Mitch and *Kim Hunter's Stella—all of whom were dedicated followers of Lee Strasberg's "Method" technique. Leigh found she had to combine her traditional English practice of building a character on a foundation of external mannerisms with Strasberg's intensely psychological training, a blend of "role and soul," as one reviewer put it. Leigh was so successful that she was awarded her second Oscar for playing an American Southerner, with some noting that Blanche could be seen as Scarlett's dark, tragic older sister.

Vivien's deteriorating physical and mental health became widely publicized during the first weeks of shooting for 1953's *Elephant Walk,* a love story set in India. Hospitalized in London after filming her exterior scenes in Sri Lanka, Leigh was unable to travel to Hollywood for the rest of the production and was replaced by *Elizabeth Taylor (although discerning viewers can still make out Leigh's silhouette in exterior long shots which were deemed too expensive to reshoot in Ceylon with Taylor). Vivien had recuperated enough to appear in the film version of Terence Rattigan's *The Deep Blue Sea* during 1954, directed by Anatole Litvak for Korda at Shepperton, where Olivier also happened to be directing and starring in his *Richard III.* The

two were often seen having lunch together in the studio commissary, but Vivien later confided to Rattigan that her marriage to Olivier had become troubled. Both of them appeared on stage at the 1955 Stratford Festival in *Macbeth, Titus Andronicus,* and *Twelfth Night,* all of which received the usual grumbling from critics still unused to Olivier's creative interpretations of Shakespeare's work.

Hospitalized again for pleurisy after the Festival, she was strong enough to embark with Olivier on "The Shakespeare Memorial Tour"

Vivien Leigh in
A Streetcar
Named Desire,
1951.

through Europe in 1957 and create a stir later that year by speaking out in that bastion of male privilege, the House of Lords, against the planned demolition of the West End's venerable St. James's Theater. As Lady Olivier, she was allowed a seat for distinguished visitors during the debate and became the first woman, with the exception of the queen, to speak to that august body by rising to declare, "My Lords, I wish to protest against the St. James's Theater being demolished." After the shock had worn off somewhat, Leigh was icily asked to leave, to which she replied, "Certainly. I have to get to the theater." (She was appearing in a new production of *Titus Andronicus* at the time.) The St. James's was eventually torn down, but Vivien's efforts, along with those of other distinguished members of her profession, influenced future legislation earmarking many of London's remaining old theaters as landmarks.

No one could have known that Olivier's production of *Titus Andronicus* was the last time Vivien would appear with him on a stage. Although both of them attended the wedding ceremonies for Vivien's daughter Suzanne in late 1957, Olivier had already left her and had begun an affair with actress *Joan Plowright. Leigh told a friend that there would have been no such separation if she had not been so ambitious about her career. The two saw little of each other over the next few years, and Vivien began her own affair with actor John Merivale, who shared her house on London's Eaton Square.

Three years later, as Vivien was preparing to walk on stage in New York in Christopher Fry's *Duel of Angels*, she was handed a telegram from Olivier asking for a divorce. The actor who played the male lead opposite her in the play never forgot that night. It was, he later said, "without a shadow of a doubt, her best performance. She was devastating. It was as if she realized she was on her own from now on." The next day, Olivier received a telegram back from her. "Lady Olivier," it read, "wishes to say that Sir Laurence Olivier has asked for a divorce in order to marry Miss Joan Plowright. She will naturally do whatever he wishes." Her divorce from Olivier became final in December of 1960. He married Plowright the following March. Thirty years later, still married to Plowright, Olivier confessed that his regret over the end of his marriage to Vivien was still acute. "My fault, of course," he told an interviewer. "The worst part of me . . . is my guilt complex. I feel almost responsible for the fall of Adam and Eve." Shortly before Olivier's death in 1989, a friend reported finding the great actor alone at home, watching one of Leigh's films with tears in his eyes.

Vivien sought some measure of peace in her work, starring in two well-received films, José Quintero's bitter *The Roman Spring of Mrs. Stone* in 1961 and Stanley Kramer's flawed 1964 adaptation of *Katherine Anne Porter's *Ship of Fools*, which was saved in good measure by Leigh's touching portrayal of Mrs. Treadwell. She toured Australia and New Zealand in repertory productions of *Twelfth Night*, *Duel of Angels* and *La Dame aux Camelias*, and received her first Tony award in America for her work in the 1963 musical *Tovarich*, in which she was required to speak and sing in a Russian accent as the Grand Duchess Tatiana Petrova. But her physical state was rapidly deteriorating, to say nothing of repeated and paralyzing bouts of depression. In late 1966, Leigh collapsed at her home on London's Eaton Square in the midst of preparations for the London debut of Edward Albee's *A Delicate Balance*. Subsequent X-rays revealed a large, tubercular spot on one lung which doctors were unable to heal. The disease claimed her life on July 7, 1967.

The tributes to Vivien Leigh's career and life were long and many, on both sides of the Atlantic, and, on the weekend following her death, marquee lights in all of the West End's theaters were dimmed for an hour. But it was Gertrude Hartley who gave the most touching homage to the daughter she had outlived. In the small park opposite Vivien's home on Eaton Square, Gertrude placed a simple wooden bench inscribed with words from Vivien's favorite Shakespearean play, *Antony and Cleopatra*. "Now boast thee, Death," it read, "in thy possession lies a lass unparallel'd."

SOURCES:

Anderson, Christopher. "A Lunch with Lord Larry," in *Ladies' Home Journal*. Vol. 106, no. 12. December 1989.

Molt, Cynthia. *Vivien Leigh: A Bio-Bibliography*. Westport, CT: Greenwood Press, 1992.

Vickers, Hugo. *Vivien Leigh*. London: Hamish Hamilton, 1988.

Norman Powers,
writer-producer, Chelsea Lane Productions, New York

Leigh-Smith, Barbara (1827–1891).

See Bodichon, Barbara.

Leighton, Clare (b. 1899).

See Brittain, Vera for sidebar.

Leighton, Margaret (1922–1976)

British actress who won two Tony awards. Born on February 26, 1922, near Birmingham, England; died on January 13, 1976; eldest daughter and one of three children (two girls and a boy) of Augustus George Leighton (a businessman) and Doris Isobel (Evans) Leighton; attended the Church of England College, Edgbaston, Birmingham, England; married Max Reinhardt (a publisher), in 1947 (divorced 1955); married Laurence Harvey (an actor), in 1957 (divorced 1961); married Michael Wilding (an actor), in 1964.

Selected theater: made acting debut as Dorothy in Laugh With Me (Birmingham Repertory Theater, September 4, 1938); joined the Old Vic Company, 1944; made London debut as the Troll King's Daughter in Peer Gynt (New Theater, August 1944); appeared as Raina in Arms and the Man (September 1944), Queen Elizabeth in Richard III (September 1944), Elena in Uncle Vanya (January 1945); made New York debut with the Old Vic Company as Lady Percy in Henry IV (May 6, 1946); appeared as Harriet Marshall, Wilhelmina Cameron, and Hope Cameron in The Sleeping Clergyman (1947), Tracy Lord in The Philadelphia Story (1949), Celia Coplestone in The Cocktail Party (1950), Masha in The Three Sisters (1951), Lady Macbeth in Macbeth (Shakespeare Memorial Theater, 1952), Ariel in The Tempest (Shakespeare Memorial Theater, 1952), Rosalind in As You Like It (Shakespeare Memorial Theater, 1952), Orinthia in The Apple Cart (1953), Lucasta Angel in The Confidential Clerk (1953), Mrs. Shankland and Miss Railton-Bell in Separate Tables (1954, New York, 1956), Rose in Variations on a Theme (1958), Beatrice in Much Ado About Nothing (New York, 1959), Elaine Lee in The Wrong Side of the Park (1960), Ellida in The Lady from the Sea (1960), Hannah Jelkes in The Night of the Iguana (1961), Pamela Pew-Pickett in Tchin-Tchin (New York, 1962), She in The Chinese Prime Minister (1964), Stephanie in Cactus Flower (1967), Birdie in The Little Foxes (New York, 1967), Cleopatra in Antony and Cleopatra (Chichester Festival, 1969), Lettice Mason in Girlfriend (1970), Mrs. Malaprop in The Rivals (1971), Elena in Reunion in Vienna (1971), Matty Seaton in A Family and a Fortune (1975).

Filmography: Bonnie Prince Charlie (1948); The Winslow Boy (1948); Under Capricorn (UK/US, 1949); The Astonished Heart (1950); The Elusive Pimpernel (The Fighting Pimpernel, 1950); Calling Bull-Dog Drummond (1951); Home at Seven (Murder on Monday, 1951); The Holly and the Ivy (1952); The Good Die Young (1953); The Teckman Mystery (1954); Carrington V.C. (Court Marshal, 1954); The Constant Husband (1955); The Passionate Stranger (A Novel Affair, 1957); The Sound and the Fury (US, 1959); Waltz of the Toreadors (The Amorous General, 1962); The Third Secret (1964); The Loved One (US,

1965); Seven Women (US, 1966); The Madwoman of Chaillot (1969); The Go-Between (1971); Zee & Co. (X Y & Zee, 1972); Lady *Caroline Lamb (1972); A Bequest to the Nation (The Nelson Affair, 1973); Galileo (US/UK, 1975); From Beyond the Grave (1975); Dirty Knights' Work (1976). Television: "Great Expectations" (1976).

The daughter of a British businessman, Margaret Leighton knew from an early age that she wanted a career on the stage. "In ignorance, I just liked the idea of it," she said, "and I felt sure I could make a living at it." She left school at age 15 to audition for Sir Barry Jackson at the Birmingham Repertory Theater. Jackson hired her as a stage manager and gave her a small role in Laugh With Me (1938), which served as her professional debut. In January 1941, Leighton left for a stint with the Basil C. Langton's Traveling Repertory Company but returned to the Birmingham Repertory in 1942. For the next two years, she immersed herself in the plays of Shakespeare, Shaw, and Chekhov, rehearsing days and playing nights. "I was convinced that the entire world existed within that theater and the two streets I walked through to get there," she said in a later interview with the New York World-Telegram (June 10, 1946).

In 1942, at the invitation of Ralph Richardson and Laurence Olivier, Leighton joined the Old Vic Company at the New Theater. (The original theater had been bombed in 1941.) She made her London debut with the company in August 1944, playing the Troll King's Daughter in Peer Gynt. In her next performance, as Raina in Arms and the Man, the young actress captured the attention of critics. "Margaret Leighton, tall, slender and fair . . . was an enchanting Raina, with a shy humour lurking behind the romantic dignity," reported **Audrey Williamson**. Leighton went on to a variety of roles, including Queen Elizabeth (*Elizabeth Woodville) in Richard III, Yolena in Uncle Vanya, Roxanne in Cyrano, and Sheila Birling in An Inspector Calls. She made her New York debut with the Old Vic in May 1946, playing Lady Percy (*Elizabeth Percy [1371–1417]) in Henry IV (Part I and II), and stayed on with the company for some time in repertory. By the time of her return to England, she had matured considerably as an actress. "She had crossed more than the ocean," wrote W.A. Darlington, "she had put behind her that invisible line which divides promise in an artist from achievement. She had always been good to look at, but good looks matter surprisingly little on the stage unless they are illuminated from within; as she now was."

The year 1947 was a banner one for Leighton. She earned critical acclaim for undertaking three roles in a single play, *The Sleeping Clergyman*, in which she portrayed a betrayed young woman, a murderess, and an international pacifist. "Margaret Leighton, appearing in three nicely contrasting roles, merges as an actress of exceptional versatility and delightful stage presence," reported *Theater World*. "One noticed in her an ability to change with complete

naturalness even the timbre of her voice." The year also marked Leighton's film debut in *Bonnie Prince Charlie*, and her marriage to the publisher Max Reinhardt (not to be confused with the German director). Although her film career always remained secondary, she went on to make a number of memorable movies, including *The Go-Between* (1971) for which she received an Academy Award nomination for Best Supporting Actress.

Meanwhile, Leighton's stage career was marked by her continual growth and refinement

Margaret Leighton and John Gielgud in Much Ado About Nothing, *1959.*

as an actress. In 1951, she appeared in a remarkably successful London revival of Chekhov's *The Three Sisters*, with a cast that included Sir Ralph Richardson and *Celia Johnson. "The most exciting performance is Miss Leighton's," reported William Hawkins in the New York *World-Telegram and Sun*. "This actress made her mark on Manhattan five years ago with Olivier and Richardson in the Old Vic. Since then she has grown in command and expressiveness, until she is most striking."

In 1952, Leighton joined the Shakespeare Memorial Theater Company at Stratford-on-Avon for the season. She turned in a number of winning performances, included one as Lady Macbeth (*Gruoch). Kenneth Tynan described her in the famous sleepwalking scene as "gaunt, pasty, compulsive," but also noted that "to cast a woman as attractive as Miss Leighton in the part is like casting a gazelle as Medusa." The season at Stratford also impacted on Leighton's personal life. The actress began a lengthy and passionate affair with actor Laurence Harvey, which eventually resulted in her divorce from Reinhardt in 1955. She would marry Harvey in 1957.

In 1954, Leighton turned in a much-lauded performance in the Terence Rattigan double bill, *Separate Tables*, playing Mrs. Shankland in *The Window Table* and Miss Railton-Bell in the second offering, *Table Number Seven*, two very different personas. "Miss Leighton's cold, regal, artful portrait of the worldly woman is brilliant enough by itself," wrote Brooks Atkinson of *The New York Times*. "But it seems all the more remarkable when she comes on in the second play as the lifeless young woman with the tearful voice and the futile mannerisms." The actress repeated her performance in New York in 1956, winning a Tony award for her effort. She received a second Tony, as well as a Variety Award and a Newspaper Guild Page One Award, for her performance as Hannah Jelkes in Tennessee Williams' *The Night of the Iguana*, which opened at New York's Royale Theater in December 1961. Around this time, Leighton's marriage to Harvey ended, and in 1964 she wed actor Michael Wilding.

Margaret Leighton continued to work steadily in England and America throughout the mid-1970s, even after she was diagnosed with multiple sclerosis in 1970. In 1972, she performed as Elena in *Reunion in Vienna* to rave reviews. The actress was named Commander of the British Empire (CBE) in 1974 and a year later performed in her last play, *A Family and a Fortune*, with Alec Guinness. By this time, she

was confined to a wheelchair, but despite great pain she stayed for the year's run of the play. Leighton died on January 13, 1976.

SOURCES:

Candee, Marjorie Dent, ed. *Current Biography*. NY: H.W. Wilson, 1957.

Hartnoll, Phyllis, and Peter Found, eds. *The Concise Oxford Companion to the Theater*. Oxford and NY: Oxford University Press, 1993.

Morley, Sheridan. *The Great Stage Stars*. London: Angus and Robertson, 1986.

Barbara Morgan,
Melrose, Massachusetts

Leijonhufvud, Margareta (1514–1551).

See Margareta Leijonhufvud.

Leiningen, princess of.

See Mary of Baden (1834–1899).
See Feodore of Hohenlohe-Langenburg (1866–1932).
See Marie of Russia (1907–1951).
See Kira of Leiningen (b. 1930).

Leinster, countess of.

See Kielmansegge, Sophia Charlotte von (1673–1725).

Leinster, duchess of.

See Lennox Sisters for Emily Lennox.

Leitch, Cecil (1891–1977)

British golfer who was the foremost woman player of her day and one of the game's greatest personalities.

Name variations: Charlotte Leitch. Born Charlotte Cecilia Pitcairn Leitch on April 13, 1891, in Silloth, Cumberland, England; died at home in London on September 16, 1977; daughter of John Leitch and Catherine Edith (Redford) Leitch; had four sisters; never married.

At age 17, Charlotte Leitch made a dramatic debut in golf at the British Ladies' championship at St. Andrews (1908). Twenty years later, she retired from competition, having won the French championship five times, the English championship twice, and the Canadian championship once. She was elected to the American Golf Hall of Fame in 1967.

She was born Charlotte Cecilia Pitcairn Leitch in 1891 in Silloth, Cumberland, England, into the comfortable circumstances of a physician's family. Not only Cecil, as she came to be known by family and friends at an early age, but all of her sisters grew up to be championship golfers, with Edith (**Edith Guedalla**) and May (**May Millar**) going on to be acclaimed as English Internationals. Though Cecil lost in the semifinals in her golfing debut at the 1908 British Ladies' championship, she had made her mark by playing decisively and powerfully. She employed a rather unorthodox flat swing and palm grip that enabled her to produce shots of exceptional accuracy and distance. In 1910, she defeated the leading amateur of the day, Harold Hilton, in the first challenge match to test the disparity between men and women players; the upset received at least as much attention in suffragist circles as in the golfing world.

After World War I, Leitch won the first postwar British championship in 1920. Later that same year, she was upset by *Joyce Wethered, and for the next several years the duels between these two superb golfers provided the British press with one front-page story after another. Although she was defeated in the 1925 British Open played at Troon, succumbing to Wethered at the 37th hole in the final, Leitch regarded this as her greatest match. She regained the title the next year and retired from the game in 1928.

An accomplished writer as well as golfer, Leitch regularly contributed articles to newspapers and magazines on all facets of the game. She also published three books, *Golf for Girls* (1911), *Golf* (1922), and *Golf Simplified* (1924). She served for a number of years on the council of the Ladies' Golf Union, but after her retirement from the game concentrated on making a career for herself in business. Leitch first went into the antiques market but soon found employment with the Cinema House organization, concentrating on the importation of foreign motion pictures into the United Kingdom. In addition, she was active in several aspects of YWCA work and was also a productive member of the Embroiderers' Guild for many years. Perhaps her proudest achievement after retiring from competition was her work for the Women Golfers' Museum, for which she amassed an impressive collection of books and memorabilia. In the final years of her long life, she was often to be seen at both amateur and professional women's matches. Leitch died in her London home on September 16, 1977.

Cecil Leitch

SOURCES:

Millar, M.S. "Leitch, Charlotte Cecilia Pitcairn (Cecil)," in Lord Blake and C.S. Nicholls, eds. *The Dictionary of National Biography 1971–1980*. Oxford and NY: Oxford University Press, 1986, pp. 496–497.

Steel, Donald, and Peter Ryde. *The Encyclopedia of Golf*. NY: Viking Press, 1975.

Wilson, Enid. *A Gallery of Women Golfers*. London: Country Life, 1961.

John Haag,
Associate Professor of History,
University of Georgia, Athens, Georgia

Leitch, Charlotte (1891–1977).

See Leitch, Cecil.

Leitch, Moira (fl. late 1300s)

Paramour of the king of Scotland. Flourished in the late 1300s; paramour of Robert II (1316–1390), king of Scotland (r. 1371–1390); children: (with Robert II) John Stewart, sheriff of Bute.

Leitzel, Lillian (1892–1931)

German-born aerial gymnast. Name variations: Lillian Pelikan. Born Leopoldina Alitza Pelikan in Breslau, Germany, in 1892 (some sources cite 1891); died on February 13, 1931, in Copenhagen, Denmark; daughter of Nellie Pelikan (an aerial performer); attended school in Breslau, Germany; married Clyde Ingalls (an executive with Ringling Brothers-Barnum & Bailey Circus), in 1920 (divorced 1924); married Alfredo Codona (a trapeze artist), in July 1928; no children.

Born in Breslau, Germany, in 1892, into a bohemian circus family, Lillian Leitzel followed in the footsteps of her mother **Nellie Pelikan**. Nellie performed an aerial act with her two sisters, billed as the "Leamy Ladies" (derived from the name of their American manager, Edward Leamy). Lillian, who was christened Leopoldina Alitza Pelikan but nicknamed Litzl (from which she took her stage name), was doted on by her mother, who had high expectations for her daughter. In addition to early training in acrobatics, Lillian was given dancing and music lessons and was taught to speak four languages. Eventually, Lillian joined the Leamy Ladies, performing with the act in a New York engagement with the Barnum & Bailey Circus in 1908. When her mother returned to Europe in 1911, Lillian remained in the United States, performing for a number of years on the vaudeville circuit. In 1914, she was hired by Ringling Brothers Circus, which featured her in their center ring. She appeared with the Ringling-owned Barnum & Bai-

ley Circus in 1917, and with Ringling again in 1918. By 1919, when the Ringling and Barnum circuses merged, Lillian Leitzel had perfected her extraordinary aerial act and was the featured attraction of "The Greatest Show on Earth."

Standing 4'9" and weighing only 95 pounds, Leitzel appeared fairylike but possessed incredible upper-body strength. Her routine, heralded by drums and cymbals and a command for all vendors to retire from the seats, began with a performance on the roman rings suspended high above the center ring. After a brief return to the ground for a bow, Leitzel was again hoisted by a rope to the dome of the big top for her finale. As the orchestra embarked on a frenetic rendition of "Flight of the Bumblebee," Leitzel, clutching a single rope with one hand, whirled her entire body around like a propeller, while the audience, necks craned upward, breathlessly counted out each revolution to 100 (60 in later years). Although her mother was credited as the first person to perform this unusual feat, it was Leitzel who perfected it into a dazzling and seemingly effortless acrobatic ballet.

$\mathcal{L}$illian
$\mathcal{L}$eitzel

Leitzel was married in 1920 to Ringling executive Clyde Ingalls, from whom she was divorced in 1924. Four years later, she wed Alfredo Codona, who was also an outstanding trapeze artist. On Friday, February 13, 1931, Lillian Leitzel was fatally injured during a performance in Copenhagen, Denmark, when the swivel on one of her rings broke, and she fell some 29 feet to the ground. She died of her injuries two days later and was cremated. Her ashes were returned to Inglewood, California, for burial.

SOURCES:
James, Edward T., ed. *Notable American Women, 1607–1950*. Cambridge, MA: The Belknap Press of Harvard University Press, 1971.
McHenry, Robert, ed. *Famous American Women*. NY: Dover, 1983.

Barbara Morgan,
Melrose, Massachusetts

Lejeune, C.A. (1897–1973)

Britain's first full-time film critic, whose writings for The Observer *covered more than three decades of filmmaking. Born Caroline Alice Lejeune in Didsbury, Manchester, England, on March 27, 1897; died in 1973; daughter of Adam Edward Lejeune and Jane Louisa (MacLaren) Lejeune; had four sisters and three brothers; graduated from the University of Manchester, 1921; married Edward Roffe Thompson; children: son, Anthony.*

Caroline Alice Lejeune was born in Didsbury, Manchester, England, in 1897, the daughter of a German-born Nonconformist minister of Huguenot ancestry. Her father died before she was two, and she grew up in a large house with her mother **Jane MacLaren Lejeune**, servants, a nanny, four sisters, and three brothers. Caroline began attending Oxford University, which she disliked, and transferred to the University of Manchester, graduating in 1921. By this time, she was contributing music reviews to the *Manchester Guardian*, made possible because C.P. Scott, the newspaper's editor, was a close friend of Caroline's mother Jane. At age 24, Caroline, henceforth known as C.A. Lejeune, decided to become a film critic. In a country which then had no full-time film critics, much less any women film critics, this was a bold decision. From 1922 to 1928, Lejeune was a film critic for the *Manchester Guardian*, signing her column C.A.L. In 1928, she began working for *The Observer*, a position she would hold until her retirement in 1960.

Many of Lejeune's reviews in *The Observer* remain of contemporary interest for their acute and perceptive commentaries on an emerging art form. When she began writing film reviews in the early 1920s, the medium was silent and in many ways primitive. But changes came quickly, and these were noticed with insight by Lejeune. Unafraid of film innovations, she welcomed the appearance of sound in films during the late 1920s, when other critics remained skeptical or even hostile to this revolution in filmmaking. From the start, she recognized the importance of newly emerging cinematic styles, including those in the powerful films being made in Soviet Russia, particularly Sergei Eisenstein's landmark *Battleship Potemkin*. Skilled at cultivating friendships, she was on close terms with many of the great personalities of the British prewar cinema, including Alfred Hitchcock and Alexander Korda.

For all of her sophistication about films, Lejeune was essentially a homebody, who enjoyed her family, friends, and garden to the fullest. After her retirement in 1960, she never again went to the cinema. (Even while she served as one of Britain's most influential film critics, Lejeune had never gone to film festivals on the Continent or made a pilgrimage to Hollywood.) Her books, well-received in her day, are still of value to readers.

SOURCES:
Hartley, Jenny. *Hearts Undefeated: Women's Writing of the Second World War*. London: Virago Press, 1995.
Lejeune, Anthony, ed. *The C.A. Lejeune Film Reader*. Manchester: Carcanet, 1991.
Lejeune, C.A. *Cinema*. London: A. Maclehose, 1931.
———. *Thank You For Having Me*. London: Tom Stacey, 1971.
Powell, Dilys. "Lejeune, Caroline Alice," in Lord Blake and C.S. Nicholls, eds. *The Dictionary of National Biography 1971–1980*. Oxford and NY: Oxford University Press, 1986, pp. 497–498.
Rosenthal, Alan. "The Film Criticism of C.A. Lejeune." M.A. thesis, Stanford University, 1962.

John Haag,
Associate Professor of History,
University of Georgia, Athens, Georgia

Lejonhufvud, Margareta (1514–1551).

See Margareta Leijonhufvud.

L.E.L. (1802–1838).

See Landon, Letitia Elizabeth.

Le Mair, H. Willebeek (1889–1966)

Dutch illustrator of children's books. Name variations: adopted the name "Saida" after her marriage. Born Henriette Willebeek Le Mair in Rotterdam, the Netherlands, on April 23, 1889; died in 1966; married Baron van Tuyll van Serooskerken, in 1920.

Selected works as illustrator: Premières Rondes Enfantines *(1904);* Our Old Nursery Rhymes *(1911);* Little Songs of Long Ago *(1912);* The Children's Corner *(1914);* Little People *(1915);* Dutch Nursery Rhymes *(1917);* A Child's Garden of Verses *(1926);* Twenty Jakarta Tales *(1939);* Christmas Carols for Young Children *(1946). Also illustrated the "Little Nursery Rhyme Books" series:* Grannie's Little Rhyme Book; Mother's Little Rhyme Book; Auntie's Little Rhyme Book; Nursie's Little Rhyme Book; Daddy's Little Rhyme Book; Baby's Little Rhyme Book; Piano Album of Children's Pieces; Baby's Diary; A Gallery of Children *(1925).*

The daughter of a wealthy corn merchant, illustrator H. Willebeek Le Mair was born in 1889 and raised in Rotterdam. As a child, she was greatly influenced by her artistic parents, who composed verses for her to illustrate. Her first book, *Premières Rondes Enfantines* (1904), was published when she was 15, during a stay in France. At that time, she also received some instruction from the leading French illustrator Maurice Boutet de Monvel, who in his own day had been inspired by the great English illustrator *Kate Greenaway.

Around 1910, Le Mair opened an exclusive school in her home. In addition to teaching, she used her young students as models, further developing her distinctive style. In 1911, she began one of her first commissions, a series of nursery-rhyme illustrations for Augener, an English music publisher. The series, which included *Our Old Nursery Rhymes* (1911), *Little Songs of Long Ago* (1912), and *Old Dutch Nursery Rhymes* (1917), was well received by the critics. "Since the days of Kate Greenaway I know of no one who has caught so well the spirit of childhood as Miss Willebeek Le Mair," wrote the reviewer for *Studio.* Augener also published several other books illustrated by the artist, including a group of six small rhyme books, as well as *Schumann's Piano Album of Children's Pieces, Baby's Diary,* and 11 sets of children's postcards (each containing 10 postcards).

In 1925, Le Mair created illustrations for *A Gallery of Children,* written by A.A. Milne. She subsequently illustrated Robert Louis Stevenson's *A Child's Garden of Verses, Twenty Jakarta Tales,* and, her own particular favorite, *Christmas Carols for Young Children.* Le Mair, who had developed an interest in Eastern philosophy and art from her girlhood travels to Arabia, married Baron van Tuyll van Serooskerken in 1920, and with her husband converted to Su-

fism, an Eastern religion of universal brotherhood and love. Along with her work as an illustrator, she spent much of her time helping the poor and supporting various charitable causes.

SOURCES:
Dalby, Richard. *The Golden Age of Children's Book Illustration.* NY: Gallery Books, 1991.

Barbara Morgan,
Melrose, Massachusetts

Le May Doan, Catriona (1970—)

Canadian skater who was the first Canadian woman to win an Olympic gold medal in speedskating. Born Catriona Le May in Saskatoon, Saskatchewan, on December 23, 1970; married Bart Doan (a rodeo rider).

Was Saskatchewan Female Athlete of the Year (1994); won gold and silver medals in the 500 meters at the World Sprint championships (1996); won the silver medal at the World Sprint championships (1997); won the gold medal in the 500 meters and the bronze in the 1000 meters at the Nagano Olympics (1998).

Catriona Le May Doan was the first Canadian woman to win a gold medal in speedskating. In 1998, in Nagano, the 5'7" skater won the gold medal in the 500 meter race in 1:16.60. She also took a bronze medal in the 1000 meters with a new Olympic record of 1:17.37; *Marianne Timmer* broke the same record a few minutes later with a 1:16.51 for the gold medal. USA's *Chris Witty* finished second.

Lemel, Nathalie (1827–1921).

See Michel, Louise for sidebar.

Lemlich, Clara (1888–1982)

American labor leader. Name variations: Clara Lemlich Shavelson. Born in the Ukraine, Russia, in 1888; died in Resada, California, on July 12, 1982; immigrated to the United States in 1903; married; children: three.

Co-founded Local 25 of the International Ladies Garment Workers' Union (ILGWU, 1906); led the 1909 "Uprising of the 30,000" strike; organized for the industrial section of the New York Woman's Suffrage Party (1910–12); co-founded Communist Party-USA.

Born in the Russian Ukraine in 1888, Clara Lemlich learned to fight at an early age. Forbidden by her Orthodox Jewish scholar father to learn how to read, young Clara secretly worked for a local tailor so that she could pay a tutor. By the time her family fled Russia in 1903 during the Kishinev pogrom, Lemlich was literate in both Yiddish and Russian and well-read in the revolutionary tracts of her day. Upon her arrival in America, she went to work in a New York City shirtwaist shop; she was 15 years old. Lemlich dreamed of becoming a doctor and spent her evening hours at the New York Public Library reading on her own, as school was out of the question. For Lemlich's family, like many immigrant families, the income of all, including children, was needed just to survive.

However, Clara Lemlich intended to do more than just survive. Frustrated by the long hours, low pay and exploitative conditions of her workplace, in 1906 Lemlich joined with several other young garment workers in the formation of the International Ladies Garment Workers' Union (ILGWU) Local 25. Her radical politics were very much a part of her trade-union philosophy. After being involved in numerous small strikes at the same time that she was attending classes in Marxist theory at the Rand School, Lemlich demonstrated her abilities as a leader and fighter in the massive strike of shirtwaist workers in 1909.

On November 22, 1909, a meeting was called to discuss a general strike in support of three striking shirtwaist firms, one of which employed Clara Lemlich. Organizers were amazed when hundreds of workers, primarily young Yiddish-speaking immigrant women, came to the meeting. Speaking in Yiddish, the 19-year-old Lemlich made an eloquent appeal for a general strike. Her plea was met with a resounding cheer, and what came to be known as "the Uprising of the 30,000" strike began. Lemlich had been out on strike since September, arrested several times, and beaten so badly by company thugs that she suffered six broken ribs. Nonetheless, she and eventually thousands of women garment workers carried on. Aided by the New York Women's Trade Union League and local Socialists, the strike lasted until February 1910. Although little was won from the employers, the strike did bring to the public's attention the horrific conditions under

Clara Lemlich

which many women worked. Even more important, perhaps, was the event itself. "They used to say you couldn't even organize women," Lemlich later said. "Well, we showed them!"

After the 1909 strike, Clara Lemlich was blacklisted from working in any garment shop in New York City. She spent some time as an organizer for the industrial section of the Woman Suffrage Party, the Wage-Earners' Suffrage League. However, by 1912, Lemlich and league head *Mary Ritter Beard had an apparent falling out. A year later, Lemlich married a printer who was also a Russian immigrant and a Bolshevik. Together, they had three children, and Lemlich remained active. She organized a rent strike which resulted in her family's eviction and, as a member of the Communist Party, was active in unemployment councils and hunger marches during the 1930s. After her husband grew ill, Lemlich returned to work in the garment trade and once again was a member of the ILGWU. Although she was not initially recognized for her early labor activities, the union gave her an honorary pension when she retired in the 1950s, in recognition of the ex-teenager who, with "fire in her mouth," had led a strike of 30,000 women in search of economic justice.

SOURCES:

Glenn, Susan A. *Daughters of the Shtetl: Life and Labor in the Immigrant Generation.* Ithaca, NY: Cornell University Press, 1990.

Orleck, Annelise. *Common Sense and a Little Fire: Women and Working-Class Politics in the U.S. 1900–1965.* Chapel Hill, NC: University of North Carolina Press, 1995.

Tax, Meredith. *The Rising of the Women: Feminist Solidarity and Class Conflict, 1880–1917.* NY: Monthly Review Press, 1980.

Kathleen Banks Nutter,
Manuscripts Processor at the Sophia Smith Collection, Smith College, Northampton, Massachusetts

Lemmon, Sarah Plummer

(1836–1923)

American botanist. Born Sarah Plummer in New Gloucester, Maine, in 1836; died in Stockton, California, in 1923; attended the Female College, Worcester, Massachusetts; attended Cooper Union, New York City; married John Gill Lemmon (a botanist), in 1880 (died 1909).

Sarah Plummer was born in New Gloucester, Maine, in 1836. She was a hospital nurse during the Civil War, after which she moved to California. Her interest in plants began with her marriage in 1880 to botanist John Gill Lemmon, and she developed into a noted collector and painter. A series of 80 sketches of flowers she made in the field won a prize at the World's Exposition in New Orleans in 1884–85, and she also created a series of watercolor paintings of flora found on the Pacific slope. She is credited with several scientific papers, and contributed occasionally to her husband's works. A new genus of plants that she discovered in 1882 was later named *Plummera floribunda* in her honor.

Lemnitz, Tiana (1897–1994)

German soprano. Born Tiana Luise Lemnitz in Metz, Germany, on October 26, 1897; died in 1994; daughter of a military bandmaster; studied with Anton Kohmann.

Made debut (1920); appeared at Aachen (1922–28), Hanover (1928–33), Dresden (1933–34), Berlin Staatsoper (1934–56), Covent Garden (1936–38); was director of the Berlin State Opera Studio.

One of the performers who helped reopen the Opera at the Admiralspalast in East Berlin after World War II, Tiana Lemnitz sang at the opening performance in 1945. She was born in 1897 in German Alsace, the tenth of eleven sisters and the daughter of a military bandmaster. Her first engagement was with the Aachen Opera in 1922. Lemnitz quickly moved into the ranks of German opera and soon became a permanent member of the Berlin Opera. Between 1928 and 1934, while she was a guest artist at Dresden, Richard Strauss asked her to sing Arabella in the premiere of his new opera. Lemnitz was the first and last Arabella in performances conducted by the composer himself in Berlin. In 1936 and 1938, Lemnitz appeared as Eva in *Die Meistersinger* and as Octavian in *Der Rosenkavalier,* one of her most celebrated roles. The war interrupted her career when the Berlin Staatsoper and all theaters in the Third Reich were closed in 1944. After the war, she continued to perform in Europe and America, retiring from the stage in 1960. Lemnitz then became director of the Berlin State Opera Studio and took a small number of pupils.

John Haag,
Athens, Georgia

Lemoine, Marie Victoire
(1754–1820)

French painter. Born in France in 1754; died in 1820; never married; no children.

Art scholars have yet to devote any meaningful research to the life and work of French painter Marie Victoire Lemoine, who was born in 1754. What little is known is that she studied with F.G. Ménageot (1744–1816), an academic history painter and portraitist who established a studio in Paris in 1774, and that she exhibited some 20 paintings in the Salon de la Correspondance in 1779 and 1785, and in the official Academy Salon between 1796 and 1814. Of the works attributed to her, which include portraits, miniatures, and genre pictures of children, only three self-portraits can be located. Her paintings of children, described variously as "young girl holding a dove," "small boy playing a violin," and "young girl cutting lilac," were apparently highly sentimental and may have been influenced by the work of Jean-Baptiste Greuze (1725–1805) who was known for his moralistic genre paintings.

Lemoine's best-known painting, *Interior of the Atelier of a Woman Painter,* was initially exhibited in the Salon of 1796 and now hangs in The Metropolitan Museum of Art in New York. "This unashamedly ambitious tour de force declares Lemoine's ability to work on a large scale," write **Ann Harris** and **Linda Nochlin,** "to orchestrate an elaborate composition, to combine portraiture and genre, to provide moral in-

Interior of the Atelier of a Woman Painter by Marie Victoire Lemoine.

struction, and even to paint still life." The work depicts two young women artists, one standing at an easel on which rests an unfinished painting and the other posed at a stool at her feet working on a sketch. Originally, the two women in the painting were identified as *Elisabeth Vigée-Le Brun and Lemoine, the former seemingly instructing the latter who is seated. However, since there is no evidence that Vigée-Le Brun was ever Lemoine's teacher, the painting may be some kind of tribute to her. "The picture does not have the merit of verity," contends **Germaine Greer**, "for it does not depict the interior of Vigée-Le Brun's shabby studio, nor is it a likeness of the artists who were both in their forties. It is rather a propagandist gesture and forms perhaps part of the background to the petition of artists and savants which made possible Vigée-Le Brun's return to Paris after her flight in 1791." Whatever the case, the picture did not have much of an impact, as Lemoine enjoyed only modest success during her lifetime. Greer also makes the observation that since the artist simply signed her work "Lemoine," some of her paintings may have been attributed to the male artist Jacques Antoine Marie Lemoine.

SOURCES:

Greer, Germaine. *The Obstacle Race*. NY: Farrar, Straus and Giroux, 1979.

Harris, Ann Sutherland, and Linda Nochlin. *Women Artists 1550–1950*. Los Angeles County Museum of Art: Knopf, 1976.

Barbara Morgan,
Melrose, Massachusetts

Lemp, Rebecca (d. 1590)

German woman, mother of six, burned as a witch. Burned at the stake as a witch in Nördlingen, Swabia, Germany, in 1590; married Peter Lemp (an accountant); children: six.

The respected wife of an accountant and the mother of six children, Rebecca Lemp fell victim to two ambitious local lawyers and a burgomaster and was one of dozens of women accused of witchcraft in Nördlingen, Germany, in 1590. Arrested and jailed while her husband was out of town, Lemp was certain she had nothing to fear because she had done nothing wrong. She soon learned otherwise and sent a letter to her husband pleading, "Don't hide thy face from me, thou knowest my innocence. In God's name, do not leave me in this anguish which is choking me." Although Peter Lemp supported his wife and attested to her innocence, she was brutally tortured on five occasions and eventually confessed. She attempted to smuggle another note to her husband, in which she requested some poison so she could end her suffering. The note was intercepted, however, and Lemp was further charged with attempted suicide. She was forced to write a confession to her husband, to which he responded with an impassioned letter defending his wife. It was ignored, however, and she was tortured yet again and finally burned at the stake. In addition to Rebecca Lemp, some 32 other highly respected women were burned as witches in Nördlingen.

Lempicka, Tamara de (1898–1980)

Polish portraitist, influenced by Cubism, and star of the Art Deco movement. Name variations: Baroness Kuffner; Baroness Tamara de Lempicka-Kuffner; La Belle Polonaise. Born Tamara Gorska in Warsaw, Poland, in 1898; died in Cuernavaca, Mexico, on March 18, 1980; daughter of Boris Gorski (an attorney for a French trading company) and Malvina (Decler) Gorska; student of Maurice Denis and André Lhote in Paris; married Tadeusz Lempicki (a Petrograd attorney), in 1916 (divorced 1928); married Raoul Kuffner (an Hungarian baron), in 1933 (died 1962); children: (first marriage) daughter Baroness Kizette de Lempicka-Foxhall.

Selected paintings: Woman in Black Dress *(1923)*; The Two Friends *(1923)*; Autoportrait *(also known as* Tamara in the Green Bugatti, *1925)*; Portrait of Marquis Sommi *(1925)*; Reclining Nude *(1925)*; Portrait of the Marquis d'Afflitto *(1925)*; Portrait of the Duchess de la Salle *(1925)*; Portrait of Prince Eristoff *(1925)*; Seated Nude *(1925)*; The Model *(1925)*; Group of Four Nudes *(1925)*; Portrait of Count Fürstenberg Herdringen *(c. 1925)*; Kizette on the Balcony *(1927)*; Kizette in Pink *(1927)*; Portrait of H.I.H., the Grand Duke Gabriel *(1927)*; The Young Ladies *(c. 1927)*; Andromeda *(1927–28)*; Beautiful Rafaela *(1927)*; Spring *(1928)*; High Summer *(1928)*; Portrait of a Man (Incomplete) *(Musée National d'Art Moderne, Paris, 1928)*; Portrait of Arlette Boucard *(1928)*; The Girls *(1928)*; Girl with Gloves *(Musée National d'Art Moderne, Paris, 1929)*; Women Bathing *(c. 1929)*; Portrait of Nana de Herrera *(1929)*; Portrait of Dr. Boucard *(1929)*; Lady in Blue with Guitar *(1929)*; St. Moritz *(1929)*; Portrait of Madame M. *(1930)*; Sleeping Woman *(1930)*; Idyll *(1931)*; Calla Lily *(1931)*; Portrait of Madame Boucard *(1931)*; Portrait of Ira P. *(n.d.)*; Portrait of Marjorie Ferry *(1932)*; Portrait of a Man, Baron Kuffner *(1932)*; Adam and Eve *(1932)*; Portrait of Pierre de Montaut *(1933)*; Portrait of Suzy Solidor *(1933)*; Sleeping Woman *(1935)*; Old Man with Guitar *(1935)*; Mother Superior *(Musée des Beaux-*

Arts in Nantes, 1939); Lady in Blue (1939); Key and Hand (1941); Calla Lily (1941); Surrealist Landscape (n.d.); Surrealist Hand (n.d.); Lady in Yellow (n.d.); The Orange Turban (1945); Amethyst (1946); Mexican Girl (1948); Venice in the Rain (1960); Calla Lily (1961). Exhibited in numerous private and joint shows (1923–1980); awarded Prix d'honneur at the Exposition Internationale in Bordeaux. Signed TJL or T.DE LEMPICKA; DE LEMPICKA.

Dubbed "the steely-eyed goddess of the automobile age" by *The New York Times*, the quintessential Art Deco portraitist Tamara de Lempicka was a darling of the haute monde—tall, slender, and enigmatic. "Like Greta Garbo, with whom she was acquainted," wrote her biographer Gilles Néret, "this star of Art Deco painting did everything she could to cover her tracks, leaving behind but few biographical cast-offs in an abundance of mysterious silence. Carefully selected cast-offs." But this high-profile artist of the post-Cubist 1920s and neo-classicist 1930s had been confined to history's attic until a 1973 retrospective of her works was held at the Galerie du Luxembourg in Paris. In 1994, **Barbra Streisand** sold Lempicka's *Adam and Eve* at auction for $1.8 million, a painting she had originally purchased for $135,000 ten years before. "Indeed," writes Edward Lucie-Smith, "since the rediscovery of her work in the early 1970s, Lempicka, even more than either [Jean] Dupas or [Raphael] Delorme, has come to be thought of as *the* Art Deco painter, almost to the exclusion of all rivals."

That Tamara de Lempicka was a woman of amazing will is known and has been verified. Born Tamara Gorska in 1898 in Warsaw, Poland, the daughter of well-to-do parents, she took over at the first opportunity. She was the middle child, with an older brother Stanczyk and a younger sister Adrienne. When Tamara was 12, her mother commissioned a famous painter to do a portrait of her dominant daughter. Lempicka hated the sittings as well as the result. Convinced she could do better, she commandeered Adrienne to sit while she painted her portrait. The result, she felt, was far more salutary.

In 1911, bored with school, the 13-year-old finagled a year off by inventing an illness and, with her grandmother, did the grand tour of Italy. There, her love of art was intensified. In 1914, the year that Franz Ferdinand, heir to the Austro-Hungarian throne, was assassinated, her mother remarried. Once again, Tamara rebelled. That summer, while armies throughout Europe mobilized, Lempicka left her school in Lau-sanne, Switzerland, and went to stay with her Aunt Stefa in Petrograd (St. Petersburg) rather than return home for the summer holidays. By August, the Russians and Germans were at each other's throats, and World War I had begun.

Privations had yet to occur, however, for those with money, and Aunt Stefa was rich; Tamara took to her lifestyle immediately and determined that she too would have a comfortable existence. At 17, she fell in love with a Petrograd attorney, Tadeusz Lempicki, and married him in the Chapel of the Knights of Malta in Petrograd in 1916. But 1917 was not a good year to be in Russia's capital city, especially for those living lavishly. Most Russians were coping with deplorable conditions. It was a year of turbulence and confusion. In February, there were "bread riots" in Petrograd that quickly developed into the March Revolution. This led to the abolition of the monarchy and the establishment of a Provisional Government led by Alexander Kerensky and comprised of members of the Fourth *Duma*. Following an unsuccessful offensive by the Russian army against the Austrians and Germans in July, street demonstrations broke out. The government brought in reliable troops to put down this event of the "July Days," and Kerensky's

Tamara de Lempicka

government became discredited. Then the Bolshevik Party of V.I. Lenin seized control of Petrograd in November. Lenin's "November Revolution" easily succeeded in taking power with the help of the Red Guard, a militia formed from factory workers.

By the close of 1918, Lenin's party had established a dictatorship based upon a new secret police, the Cheka. His opponents had formed "White" armies to fight his "Reds." When Lenin was nearly assassinated by a political opponent in September 1918, his colleagues launched a "Red Terror," in which thousands of enemies of the new government were executed. Tamara's husband Tadeusz was one of those caught in the net. Arrested by the Cheka, he was imprisoned in December of 1918; Tamara fled to Copenhagen where she eventually secured his release with the help of the Swedish consul in Petrograd. As homeless refugees, the couple immigrated to postwar Paris. There they lived in a small room in a cheap hotel, where their daughter Kizette was born. Tadeusz, who had grown moody and bitter due to his ordeal, was also a womanizer, and the marriage suffered; they would eventually divorce in 1928.

I live on the fringe of society, and the rules of normal society have no currency for those on the fringe.

—Tamara de Lempicka

Since Tadeusz spent well but earned little, Lempicka sold her jewels to support the family. Encouraged by her sister Adrienne, who was also in Paris taking up architecture, Lempicka began to study painting with post-symbolist Maurice Denis at the Académie Ranson, in hopes of earning an income with her still-lifes and portraits. It was her second teacher, the muted-Cubist André Lhote, who had the most influence. He instilled in Tamara the need to modify Cubism, to retain its commercially acceptable aspects but leave forms of objects intact. By simplifying Cubism, claims Gilles Néret, Lhote was really indulging in geometrism. Lhote maintained that a human body was like any other object. "This was what he called the 'plastic metaphor,'" writes Néret, "a metaphor which Tamara used time and again [in her paintings] . . . in her harems populated by provocative idiots; in her nudes, which are also allegories of lasciviousness; or in her portraits characterized by the haughty expression typical of a certain caste."

Lempicka's first paintings were sold by the Gallerie Colette Weill. Meeting with immediate financial success, she began to acquire impressive contacts with the Salon des Indépendants, the Salon d'Automne, and the Salon des Moins de Trente Ans. "After every two paintings sold," claimed her daughter Kizette, "she would buy a bracelet, until one day she would have covered herself in diamonds and jewels from her wrists to her shoulders." Once again, the family began to move into the upper strata. Lempicka traveled, enjoying the best hotels. She also began to surround herself with the cultural elite, living a bohemian life in Auteuil on the rich fringe, while "loving art and high society in equal measure," wrote her friend Jean Cocteau. "She had her own law," the law of the 1920s, Kizette observed:

> She was only interested in those she considered the better class of people: the aristocracy, the wealthy, the intellectual elite. She had the feeling, typical of all talented people, that she deserved everything which came her way, and this gave her the freedom to mingle only with those who could help her or nourish her ego in some way or other. She lived on the Left Bank, as was proper for an artist, despising everything that was bourgeois, mediocre or "pretty." She dressed luxuriously so as to dazzle her fans, while shrouding her past in a veil of mystery. Quite deliberately, she cultivated uncertainty as to her age, her life in Poland and Russia, and even her family. The Polish girl of good family, the child bride, the émigrée, the young mother—all disappeared behind her canvases . . . to emerge once more as the modern, bewitching, sophisticated—not to say decadent—beauty.

She would later complain to her daughter that the days became too short. "Sometimes I would go out in the evening, not come home until two, and then paint until six by the light of a blue lamp."

Repelled by the banality of the art surrounding her, Lempicka staked everything on style. She was fascinated with technique and wanted to become an artisan. "My goal was *never to copy,*" she said. Instead, she set out "to create a new style, bright, luminous colours and to scent out the elegance in my models." Her portraits were of Russian emigres, impoverished nobility, and the *neauveau riche,* flavored with homoeroticism.

In 1925, Lempicka established her reputation as a leading Art Deco artist at the Exposition Internationale des Artes Décoratifs et Industriels Modernes, the first Art Deco exhibition in Paris for furniture, fashion, painting, and apparel. A synthesis of Cubism and design, Art Deco would later be called degenerate art by Joseph Goebbels, becoming the fuel for Nazi bonfires. While American fashion magazines became aware of Lempicka's grand-dukes, marquesses,

Autoportrait
(Tamara in the
Green Bugatti),
1925.

and intimidating duchesses, exhibitions were held at the Salon the Tuileries and the Salon des Femmes Peintres. Her self-portrait *Autoportrait* (also known as *Tamara in the Green Bugatti*), which she painted for the cover of the magazine *Die Dame,* was celebrated. This blend of woman and machine was hailed as the perfect portrait of the age. Noted the magazine *Auto-Journal* in 1974: "She is wearing gloves, and a helmet. She is inaccessible, a cool, disconcerting beauty, behind which a formidable being can be glimpsed—this woman is free!"

"I was the first woman to paint cleanly," Tamara told her daughter, "and that was the basis of my success. From a hundred pictures, mine will always stand out. And so the galleries began to hang my work in their best rooms, always in the middle, because my painting was attractive. It was precise, it was 'finished.'" She was a devotee of Jean Ingres, especially his eroticism and distortions of the human form. This influence can easily be seen in her *Women Bathing,* evocative of Ingres' *The Turkish Bath.*

As the critics raved, mother and daughter went to Italy to study the classical masterpieces, and the Bottega di Poesia in Milan held Tamara's first Italian exhibition. While there, she took a lover, the Marquis Sommi Picenardi. (The bisexual Lempicka also had many affairs with women, often with her models. The affair with **Rafaela**, model for the painting *Beautiful Rafaela,* cited by the *Sunday Times Magazine* as "one of the most magnificent nudes of the century," would last one year.) While in Italy, she was eagerly pursued by Gabriele d'Annunzio, Italy's premiere poet and playwright, who, wanting to add Lempicka to his stable of mistresses, commissioned his portrait with sittings at his villa Il Vittoriale in Gardone. Though the portrait was never finished, the relationship soon was. Lempicka was far more eager to paint his portrait than to be involved with the by now elderly d'Annunzio. The brief flirtation, which was never consummated, would be detailed by d'Annunzio's housekeeper-mistress **Aelis Mazoyer.** Published in 1977, Mazoyer's book sold well in Europe and also served to revive Lempicka's popularity. The offbeat play *Tamara,* which opened in Toronto in 1981, was based on the book. The audience was handed champagne and found itself circulating throughout a building, amassing in different rooms where scenes were played out. The 1984 Los Angeles version, which at one point starred **Anjelica Huston**, ran for nine years.

In 1927, Lempicka's painting of her daughter, *Kizette on the Balcony,* won first prize at the prestigious Exposition Internationale des Beaux-Arts in Bordeaux. Another, *Kizette's First Communion,* won the bronze medal at the Exposition Internationale in Poznan, Poland. The following year, Lempicka became the mistress of Baron Raoul Kuffner, an Austro-Hungarian royal and one of the major collectors of her works; they met when he commissioned a portrait of his mistress, the Andalusian dancer **Nana de Herrera.** Lempicka moved into a spacious apartment, designed by Mallet-Stevens, in a three-story townhouse on the rue Méchain.

Here, she entertained the elite of Paris, along with the ambassadors of Greece and Peru, her goings and comings fully detailed by the Paris press. Lempicka's dominance, self-assurance, beauty, and high fashion made her the center of her universe.

But in 1929, when the stock market crashed and nationalists and socialists thrived, the climate for art and its patrons changed. It was no longer acceptable just to paint moneyed portraits for moneyed classes; art must be for the common folk. Surrealists and abstract artists were considered elitist. Great murals of herded, laboring humanity were now the vogue. Lempicka "saw herself as the herald of the strong," wrote Néret, "and the great triumph of her art was to reassure." But her portraits were far from plebeian. There was an arrogance in her sitters, a menacing quality. The nudes, notes Giancarlo Marmori, were "dripping with carnal presence." They were women, as Renoir categorized, not rising from the sea, but rising from the bed. Writes Néret:

> Tamara's heroes seem to be the last representatives of a decadent world which is falling apart, in which they no longer appear as anything but shadows, parading their boredom and conceit. The first is preparing for war, the second is creating a demand and fighting depression, while these last are closing the door on a world which will soon cease to exist. And it was here that the drama of Tamara de Lempicka would be played out, she too [would be] condemned like the others to disappear along with her creatures.

After the **Baroness Kuffner** died of leukemia, Lempicka married the baron in 1933, at the urging of her mother. He brought to the marriage a title, money, and culture, and their by-product: sought-after stature. From 1931 to 1939, Lempicka continued to work, with many exhibitions in Paris galleries. Those who were eager for her to paint their portrait had to stand in line. With high unemployment, a world in chaos, and the threat of Nazi Germany, Lempicka urged her husband to sell his estates in Austro-Hungary so they could emigrate to America.

In 1939, the Kuffners, minus Kizette who was at school in Europe, began a long sojourn in America, taking a house in Beverly Hills. For publicity, Lempicka held a competition in 1940 at the University of California-Los Angeles (UCLA) for a model for her painting *Susannah and the Elders;* she also sponsored her own solo exhibitions at the Paul Reinhart Gallery in L.A., at the Julian Levy Gallery in New York, the Courvoisier Galleries in San Francisco, and the

Milwaukee Institute of Art. Her new circle included such Hollywood stars as *Dolores del Rio, Tyrone Power, and George Sanders.

By the time the Kuffners moved to New York in 1943, her production had slowed. "It turned out as Cocteau had predicted; her social life began to corrupt her art," noted Kizette, who had arrived in America in 1941. "Once she set foot in New York, Tamara de Lempicka disappeared. What was left was a chic curiosity named Baroness Kuffner." She became known as "Hollywood's favorite artist" and the "baroness with the paintbrush." With America's attraction to titles, she was no longer a painter who had married a baron; she was a baroness who had taken up painting.

After a long silence, in 1960 Lempicka attempted to reclaim her artistic reputation by venturing into the world of abstract art, jettisoning what she was best at, representational. She was not successful. Exhibited at New York's Iolas Gallery in New York in 1962, her new paintings were met with a critical yawn. She never exhibited again.

When her husband died of a heart attack in 1962, a distraught Lempicka moved to Houston to be near Kizette, who had married a Texas geologist and had two daughters. Before long, Lempicka was running the household. In 1974, she moved to Cuernavaca in Mexico, controlling her daughter and grandchildren long distance by constantly modifying her will. When Kizette's husband died in 1979, Kizette moved to Cuernavaca to care for her seriously ill mother. After Lempicka died in her sleep on March 18, 1980, her daughter fittingly scattered her ashes over the crater of an active volcano, Mt. Popocatépetl. Writes Giancarlo Marmori:

> It would be too restrictive just to include Tamara de Lempicka in a catalogue of post-Cubist and classico-deco art. The psychological and physical intensity of her subjects, their meta-anatomies and tics, not to say their grimaces, are her way of introducing the very specific exaggeration of the "Neue Sachlichkeit." The exaggeration, and also the hypocrisy. We find ourselves face to face not with an elegant anthropomorphic decoration or with fresco silhouettes for the [French liner] Normandie or the Palais de Chaillot (alias the Palais du Trocadéro), but with extremely lively creatures whose innermost emotional life is sometimes brutally laid bare.

SOURCES:
Lempicka-Foxhall, Baroness Kizette de and Charles Phillips. *Passion by Design: The Art and Times of Tamara de Lempicka.* Oxford: Phaidon Press, 1987.

Lucie-Smith, Edward. *Art Deco Painting.* NY: Clarkson Potter, 1990.
Néret, Gilles. *Tamara de Lempicka, 1898–1980.* Köln, Germany: Benedikt Taschen, 1992.

RELATED MEDIA:
Tamara: a Living Movie (play) opened in Toronto, Canada, in 1981; ran in Los Angeles, 1984–93; ran in New York, 1987–89.

Lenclos, Anne de (1623–1705).

See Lenclos, Ninon de.

L'Enclos, Ninon de (1623–1705).

See Lenclos, Ninon de.

Lenclos, Ninon de (1623–1705)

Perhaps the most famous of French 17th-century courtesans, who enticed clients and lovers with an irresistible mixture of wit, charm and intellect, struggling throughout to gain financial independence and overcome the social stigmatism attached to her nonconformist lifestyle. Name variations: *true first name "Anne" but usually called "Ninon"; last name sometimes given as "L'Enclos" or "Lanclos," the historically correct spelling.* Pronunciation: *nee-NŌ duh lā-KLO.* Born Anne de Lanclos on January 9, 1623, in Paris, France (some sources erroneously cite November 11, 1620); died in Paris on October 17, 1705; daughter of Henri de Lanclos (a minor nobleman) and Marie-Barbe de la Marche; given some education at home by her father, but largely self-taught; never married; children: (with Louis de Mornay, marquis de Villarceaux) a son, Louis de Mornay (1652–1730), later chevalier de La Boissière.

Forced by unfortunate circumstances into prostitution, moved from lover to lover until late in life, slowly attaining a degree of social acceptance, thanks to a reputable intellect and the ability to maneuver adroitly within the bounds of permissible behavior; voluntarily entered into convents (1643 and 1648); forcibly committed into a refuge-home for "fallen women" (1656); always emerged from these socially cleansing retreats with a slightly increased degree of respectability; attained complete financial independence (1670s); hosted a small but well-known salon during the last decades of her life, entertaining both the high Parisian nobility and respected men of letters.

Late at night in the modest Paris apartment of a pretty young girl who was resting in her bedchamber, a small man clad all in black entered unexpectedly, waking the sleeper. The nocturnal visitor's eyes were fiery, his face spiritual, and he introduced himself as one who had power over the fate of men. Indeed, he had come to hear the girl's wishes for her own destiny, offering her either supreme greatness, vast riches, or eternal beauty. The 18-year-old brunette chose the latter, but had to pledge secrecy and sign the man's old black book with its crimson pages. *Noctambule,* for so he called himself, then gave her the power to charm any man, a power he had in 6,000 years only accorded four other women—Semiramis (**Sammuramat*), Helen, **Cleopatra (VII)*, and **Diane de Poitiers*. "You will always be young and fresh," he promised. "Never will your lovers leave you first. You will not age. You will excite passion at an age in which other women are surrounded only by the horrors of decrepitude." Three days before her death, *Noctambule* returned. Drawing back the bed-curtains, he produced the leather-bound volume with her signature on its blood-red pages. Stricken with terror, Ninon de Lenclos cried out in mortal anguish, realizing she had sold herself to none other than Lucifer himself. . . . Or so one of any number of legends embellishing the famous courtesan's life goes. In fact, one of the prime challenges in reconstructing her life is the separation of fact from fiction. Who, then, was this remarkable woman who engendered such a fascinating but enigmatic legacy?

The mystery begins with Ninon's birth. The parish register of Saint-Jean-en-Grève in Paris, France, documents the baptism of one Anne de Lenclos on November 11, 1620, the date of birth given by most older biographies. Her most recent scholarly biographer, however, plausibly argues that the girl born in 1620 was most surely an older sister who died in infancy, and establishes Ninon's correct date of birth as January 9, 1623. All in all, very little is known about her family background, and much has been distorted by tendentious and unscholarly early biographers. Ninon's father, a talented but impoverished lute-player of dubious noble extraction—he styled himself "squire"—was Henri de Lanclos, seigneur de la Douardière; her mother one **Marie-Barbe de la Marche**, a distant relation of the aristocratic Abra de Raconis family. The fate of Ninon's two

Ninon de Lenclos

brothers, Charles (born 1617) and Léonor (born 1619), is shrouded in obscurity.

Despite his relatively humble origins, Henri de Lanclos had powerful and well-placed patrons, so necessary for survival in 17th-century France. These included Charles II de Lorraine, second duc d'Elbeuf (1596–1657), and Timoléon d'Epinay, marquis de Saint-Luc, governor of Brouage and vice-admiral of France (c. 1580–1644). In 1632, while he was captain of a company in the regiment of Saint-Luc, all sources consistently describe Lanclos as leading the life of a debauched and disreputable minor noble. While it seems clear that his maverick behavior influenced Ninon in the same direction, early biographers go too far in attributing to Lanclos a "philosophical" influence on his daughter. Ninon's mother was supposedly extremely pious and of limited intelligence, but this is another literary construction of the 18th century, designed to explain Ninon's free-thinking non-conformism as a function of an inner intellectual struggle brought on by the antithesis of the philosopher-father and the bigot-mother.

Henri de Lanclos' real character is revealed in a sordid episode at stark odds with his legendary intellectualism. In January 1631, he was accused in a shabby affair of adultery, in the course of which he and some hangers-on violently beat up a female witness and then assassinated Louis du Maine, baron de Chabans, whom Lanclos believed was behind an imminent guilty verdict in the case. In December 1632, he fled the law, even before the Paris courts had issued a warrant for his arrest (July 23, 1633). First hiding out with powerful patrons, he later left the country. Thereafter his exact whereabouts and future career remain obscure; perhaps he died in 1649 in the battle of La Bouille, near Rouen. Lanclos' only real positive legacy to his daughter was a love for music and a gift for lute-playing. As for his moral influence, the overtly sexual nature of Lanclos' relationships with his mistress and wife, characterized by open caresses and witnessed by young Ninon, can hardly have failed to have contributed to the formation of her own liberal attitude toward contemporary sexual mores.

After the flight of her father, Ninon continued to live with her mother in the rue des Trois Pavillons, under rather straitened circumstances, Lanclos having been a spendthrift who apparently left them penniless. To help make ends meet, her mother sent Ninon out to play the lute for money in the fashionable and aristocratic Marais quarter of Paris. By virtue of her intelligence, wit and social graces—Ninon sang and danced well, played the clavecin, guitar and theorbo, too—she was accepted into the good social circles of the Marais, and soon frequented local salons. This formative experience was significant, for it taught Ninon proper behavior in polite society—the savoir-faire necessary for the success of her future career.

Ninon's first lover—not client—was the impoverished but seductive Charles-Claude de Beaumont, vicomte de Chaumusy, sieur de Saint-Etienne. Believing Saint-Etienne might marry Ninon, her mother granted him broad liberties with the young girl. Regrettably, all matrimonial hopes came to nought: Ninon and her mother had gambled heavily and lost. For the relationship with Saint-Etienne had been premarital—therefore illicit—and Ninon had lost her virginity, virtually destroying any chance for a good marriage. Indeed, in 17th-century France, roughly 90% of all girls took their matrimonial vows as virgins. Thus, Ninon's behavior, in defiance of all religious and social norms, had already marked her out as a marginal member of society.

For a short time, Ninon appears to have had an insignificant platonic affair of sentimental value with one Henri de Lancy, baron de Raray, captain of the gendarmes of Gaston d'Orléans. But by the time she was 18, family finances had deteriorated to the point that her mother felt impelled to sell the attractive girl's favors to Jean Coulon, councillor at the Paris Parlement and a neighbor in the Marais. Coulon was a Frondeur—or rebel against central authority during the minority of Louis XIV—and reputed to be very much a libertine. He was married to an equally unfaithful wife. When it had become apparent that he had taken an interest in Ninon, she did her best to keep the previous liaison with Saint-Etienne secret. But to no avail, for Ninon was soon found out and expelled from the polite society of *honnêtes-femmes* (virtuous women) she had frequented in the Marais, not to be readmitted until decades later.

The affair with Coulon was arranged in a business-like manner, and it was agreed he would keep her at a decent rate of 500 livres per month, common whores earning only 3–4 livres a meeting. The relationship lasted until 1650. So, from 1641 on, Ninon was publicly considered a courtesan. Dictionaries of the period indicate that contemporaries distinguished closely between *prostituées* and *courtisanes*. The term *prostitute* (and its derogatory variant *putain,* or whore) designated the lowest class of woman who sold her body for profit, and was universal-

ly defined in negative moral and social terms. Conversely, *courtisane* denoted a "kept woman who makes her living by making love," and was even considered somewhat respectable. Most important, courtesans were largely tolerated and unmolested by the law.

> The misfortunes of her youth . . . had made her a courtesan. The need for affection, attraction of pleasures, and taste for liberty had determined her to move from man to man. By sleeping with her clients and favorites, she sought her profit or her pleasure. . . . Her aim was . . . to escape the destiny of vulgar prostitutes.
>
> —Roger Duchêne

During her association with Coulon, Ninon soon added another paying lover-protector, François-Jacques comte d'Aubijoux (died 1656). Aubijoux, like Coulon an opponent of Cardinal Richelieu's absolutist policies, had been wounded in the rebellious army of Montmorency (1632) and was a key figure in the plot of Cinq-Mars (1642). Forced to flee France after the plot's failure, Aubijoux returned to Paris in 1643, after the Cardinal's death. Ninon's liaison with Aubijoux was significant because it improved somewhat her social acceptance in higher society. He was of an ancient and prestigious family, a seigneur with 40,000 livres per annum income, and, by 1645, king's lieutenant in Languedoc and governor of Montpellier. The relationship also improved her finances, for Ninon now disposed of a combined annual income, from Coulon and Aubijoux, of some 12,000 livres. By comparison, when the president of the Paris Parlement separated from his wife, he provided her with an annual allotment of 15,000; the famous playwright Pierre Corneille was given a pension of 2,000 livres per annum by the king, and Jean Racine only 600. By all standards, therefore, Ninon was quite comfortably well off. Notwithstanding, having two paying lovers was a clear indication of her status as a professional courtesan.

Coulon and Aubijoux were attractive and self-confident men in the prime of manhood, accustomed to spending money on the good things in life. Like many another epicurean noble, they took pleasure in fine horses, fashionable attire, an excellent cook—and the caresses of women such as Ninon, which they unabashedly enjoyed.

But in the end they were clients, and as such failed to satisfy Ninon's personal desires. One year into her relationship with Coulon, she met her first real love, Gaspard de Coligny, duc de Châtillon. Coligny was bisexual and the young lover of Louis II de Bourbon, duc d'Enghien (1621–1686, later the Great Condé) during the middle 1640s. Again transgressing the accepted moral code, Ninon took the initiative in this short, and apparently rather carnal, affair, but was soon jilted. The experience prompted her resolve to be the first to terminate all love affairs in the future. Coligny was followed by César Phoebus, comte de Miossens (1614–1676, maréchal d'Albret by 1653), said to be a particularly virile lover. Louis II de Bourbon, prince de Condé and victor of Nördlingen and Rocroi (1643–45), succeeded Miossens but failed to match his reputation in the alcove with that on the battlefield.

Ninon's mother died in the spring of 1643. Bereft of all family support, Ninon decided to enter a convent for a time, as a form of social rehabilitation and to augment her status vis-à-vis future clients. Taking such a step was not unknown among famous courtesans of the day. By 1644, Ninon had returned from seclusion, adroitly benefiting from her stratagem. Some sources contend that she had a relationship with the archbishop, Alphonse-Louis du Plessis de Richelieu (died 1653, brother of the famous cardinal), while at the convent. Though this appears dubious, he did visit Ninon frequently, indicating her social acceptability. She was also presented with a house worth 8,000 écus, by one Marc-Antoine Perrachon, future councillor and secretary of the king (1653). Ninon did not accord Perrachon any favors, it is said, and returned the gift once the donor became obtrusive. This was a significant act, because through it she had declared her personal independence. Indeed, according to Duchêne it was "the point of departure of a new life. Henceforth, she was a free woman, disposing of herself as she saw fit." At least, one should add, from a point of view of moral volition, and as long as she had enough paying lovers to choose from to assure a comfortable existence. For without a dowry and with her personal history, marriage to a suitable husband was hardly feasible.

In 1648, she traveled to Lyons for reasons unknown. Some authors have speculated that she sought treatment for a venereal disease, another version has it that she was pursuing a lover. Most probably, she was fleeing the capital troubled by the Frondist insurrection. Returning to Paris the following year, from about the age of 25 on she could not be bought; she would choose whom she liked and accept their favors, and long was to be the list of men whose advances she rejected—her "martyrs." Meanwhile, Paul Scarron, the famous poet and dramatist, was the first to publicly acclaim Ninon and her charms—both physical and intellectual—in his *Recueil de quelques vers burlesques*, published in 1648:

> Oh beautiful and charming Ninon,
> To whom no-one will ever reply "No,"
> Such is the authority
> Acquired in all places by a young woman
> When, along with wit, she possesses beauty . . .

Ninon proceeded to benefit from the relatively relaxed morals characteristic of French society during the early Regency of *Anne of Austria (1601–1666). Ninon took a new lover for a time, Pierre marquis de Villars-Orondate (1619–1698), later ambassador to Spain (1659) and known for his martial prowess; and she set up a reserve client-paymaster—Coulon and Aubijoux were still keeping her—one Léon Fourreau, on whose purse she drew heavily. Sometime before 1650, Ninon accosted Philippe de Montaut-Bénac, duc de Montaut, known as the duc de Navailles (1619–1684), whom she invited to her couch simply because he appealed to her—again reversing the usual gender roles. Through her psychologically refined coquettish behavior, she had perfected the art of attaining moral domination over the men with whom she had intercourse—clients, "martyrs," and favorites. It was she who decided the moment and nature of the encounter, always reinforcing her status of high-class courtesan, as against common prostitute.

By 1650, Ninon had managed her income well enough that she was almost capable of doing without any clients at all; the pressure of necessity was much reduced, and she had nearly attained her goal of complete financial independence. June of the year found her moved from the rue des Trois-Pavillons, where she had lived with her mother, to the rue des Douze-Portes, next to the Temple in the faubourg de Saint-Germain. The year also marked the crossing of a significant threshold of social acceptance, for most of her contemporaries seem to have believed that she had completely forsaken the outright sale of her favors.

During the early 1650s, Ninon indulged in a number of "caprices," a succession of lovers she took for her own pleasure and amusement: Henri de Sévigne (1623–1651), husband of the famous *Marie de Sévigné; Antoine de Rambouillet, marquis de La Sablière (1624–1680), husband of *Marguerite de La Sablière; and Henri-François, marquis de Vassé. She also narrowly escaped being locked up by the authorities, for early in 1651 the queen-mother, Anne of Austria, threatened her with forced entry into the convent. While the exact circumstances of this episode are not exactly known, Ninon the religious skeptic had probably gone too far with her nonconformist behavior during the period of the fast, or perhaps her earlier alliances with a number of Frondeurs had rankled. In any case, the threat was never realized, and any number of anecdotes—such as that of Saint-Simon—exist to adorn her supposed interview with Anne. The famous memorialist of court life under Louis XIV wrote that the queen-mother, finally exasperated with Ninon's blatant behavior, sent off a *lettre de cachet* commanding her to enter a convent, but without specifying a certain religious order. Upon receipt of the royal warrant, Ninon impudently informed the bearer which convent she preferred, and in which town; the queen, impressed with this show of spirit, withdrew her letter, leaving Ninon in peace.

From 1651 to 1656, Ninon was the mistress of Louis de Mornay, marquis de Villarceaux, an aristocrat not only exceedingly rich and a holder of many offices, but also high in favor at court. He was to be her last "paymaster." Villarceaux was 33 when the relationship began; it was to become the only real love match of her life. During this period, Ninon often left Paris and lived at the country château, near Meulan, of a rich friend of the marquis, one Charles de Valliquierville. It was there she secretly gave birth, sometime in July–August of 1652, to their son, Louis de Mornay, later chevalier de La Boissière. (He would become a naval officer and die on July 14, 1730, in Toulon.) The matter was delicate, for Villarceaux was married and could hardly recognize the boy at the time—though he would do so by officially registering him with the Parlement de Paris on November 29, 1690, a year before his death and long after the break with Ninon.

In the autumn of 1652, having restored her beauty, Ninon returned to Paris, where she reportedly received an invitation from the president of the Parlement of Paris to play the lute for him and his wife—a sign of social acceptance. At first, it seems Ninon lived with Villarceaux in the town house of the latter's friend, one Boisrobert, but on January 10, 1654, she moved to the rue de Richelieu, renting a house for 500 livres per annum. Ninon had become quite accepted and even fashionable in Paris, having

been the subject of at least one collection of flattering poems. Nonetheless, she still had to take care not to cross the bounds of propriety and cause another scandal. Another pregnancy followed, and during the summer of 1654, Ninon again left the city to deliver Villarceaux's second child, who did not live. In June of the following year, she assured the financial future of her surviving son with an endowment; Villarceaux would prudently do the same in 1657, using Valliquierville as an intermediary.

By 1654—Ninon was now 31—it appeared the young woman who had in desperation offered to sell her charms 13 years earlier, and been expelled from the good circles of the Marais, had come a long way socially. Duchêne described her situation:

> She is rich enough to offer herself, should she so desire, to a lover of her choice. She is intelligent and no one is bored in her company. She can play the lute exceedingly well. She can converse. She can even discuss Herodotus, Plato or Epicurus. She is an expert on moral discourse. Yet, be that as it may, she is still a courtesan whom ladies of rank refuse to meet.

The "constance" of her relationship with Villarceaux was not applauded by the circle of libertines around Ninon; her close friend, Charles de Marguetel de Saint-Denis, seigneur de Saint-Evremond (c. 1614–1703), even noted that the brilliance of her eyes and mouth was always in direct proportion to the number of her lovers. Indeed, the sensuous Ninon could not be satisfied by one man for long. So, in 1655, surrounded by a circle of young, admiring seigneurs, she took up with Miossens again, provoking a mad fit of jealousy in Villarceaux. And by March of 1656, royal patience with Ninon's behavior had also run out. She had finally lost in the double game of libertinage and trying to keep up appearances. As a public disgrace to morality, she was committed to the Madelonnettes on order of the queen-mother, who was scandalized by Ninon's candid impiety and licentiousness, all within sight of the Louvre.

Prostitution, the major cause of which appears to have been female unemployment, was at that time widespread in Paris and the provinces, and it is well known that many Versailles aristocrats frequented the capital's whores. Theoretically prohibited by law as early as 1560 due both to the spread of syphilis and a general concern for health and hygiene, it was still widely tolerated. Indeed, by 1780 the bourgeois annalist Louis-Sébastien Mercier was to count 30,000 common whores and 10,000 luxury prostitutes in Paris alone. Nonetheless, legislation became increasingly repressive during the reign of Louis XIV, prostitutes being treated as just one category of deviant within the overall scheme of social control typical of the *ancien régime.* Significantly, execution of the applicable decrees was entrusted to the lieutenant general of police in Paris. On rare occasions deported to the colonies, prostitutes in most cases were committed to one of a whole array of more or less penal institutions designed to reform their lifestyles.

The Madelonnettes, on the rue des Fontaines, to the north of the Marais, was such an institution. Having Ninon committed there meant treating her like a simple prostitute and demanding penitence. Fortunately, after but a short stay under the nuns' austere regime, Ninon's friends at court—the opposition to the moralizing party of the so-called *dévots*—obtained her transfer to a convent at Lagny, where conditions were somewhat less harsh. Situated on the Marne, 30 kilometers from Paris, Lagny was an ancient abbey founded in 644 by the Benedictine order, which had belonged since 1641 to the order of Saint Maurice. Little is known of the life Ninon led there, except that she was soon granted permission to receive visitors, the most famous of whom was Queen *Christina of Sweden, who made it a point during her stay in Paris to seek out the famous courtesan.

Ninon's fidelity during the Fronde seems to have been in her favor, for she was released thanks to the intercession of her friends—notably the Maréchal d'Albret—and returned to Paris in the spring of 1657. Though neither penitent nor converted to the moral values of her detractors, she now understood that her situation would remain subject to scrutiny, and that she therefore would have to monitor more prudently her public behavior and speech. This was to include the faithful, if hypocritical, attendance of the mass and observation of church holidays and customs. Moving from the rue de Richelieu as a sign of her resolve to take up a new life, she took up residence at the rue des Tournelles, not far from the Place Royale, scene of her debut as a lute-player and near the home of her dear friend, the poet Scarron. Here she was to remain the rest of her life. Ninon's new home was hardly a sumptuous aristocratic town-house, but more typical of the comforts of the middling bourgeoisie, requiring the services of just four servants: a cook, kitchen help, valet, and chambermaid. Its modest size permitted only a limited number of guests, so the salon she kept was rather intimate and low-key.

At this time, much ado was made about the ostensible letters written by Christina of Sweden, urging Louis XIV to invite Ninon to Versailles, and arguing that the young king's education could only be accomplished by associating himself with a woman of like wit and intelligence. One biographer interpreted such talk as an indication of public sympathy for and renewed social acceptance of the punished courtesan. In fact, many contemporaries stressed that her moral weaknesses seem to have been forgotten in favor of her capacity to set an example of savoir-faire in her famous salon. Henceforth, she was portrayed mostly in a positive light that downplayed her early career, as a variety of popular poets and playwrights celebrated her beauty, musical talents and—more important—her intellect. Duchêne even speculates that when *Madeleine de Scudéry, well-known for her irreproachable morals, included a flattering portrait of Ninon in her writings, this was because she perceived the former courtesan as a feminist ally.

During the decade from 1661 to 1671, Ninon slowly but surely gained favor in the best social circles, adopting the more dignified appellative of *Mlle de Lanclos.* Her respectability was enhanced by the comforts of financial security, for having astutely invested her accumulated capital in various municipal funds, during the last 30 years of life she enjoyed an annual income of some 7–8,000 livres. She took her last known lover—her last *caprice,* as she put it—in March 1671. The 23-year-old Charles de Sévigné (1647–1713) was none other than the son of Henri de Sévigné, a previous beau, and Ninon was three years younger than Madame de Sévigné, her lover's mother. The liaison lasted three weeks and was strongly disapproved of by Madame de Sévigné, especially due to Ninon's known religious cynicism. Indeed, she was never able to clear herself completely of a bad reputation concerning her heterodox religious views, and as late as 1696 a popular song appeared noting her irreligion.

Saint-Simon—who devoted an entire chapter of his memoirs to her "singular character"— left a vivid impression of Ninon's salon during the early 1690s, independently confirmed by the Duchesse de Montpensier (*Anne Marie Louise d'Orleans Montpensier). His portrait features "Mlle de Lanclos" entertaining with decorum the cream of court and town, with politics and religion as strictly prohibited subjects:

> Everything about her was done with seemliness and that outward show of modesty, which is often lacking, even with high-born princesses. . . . For this reason, she num-

bered among her acquaintances the noblest and most fastidious men at Court, so that it became the fashion to be received at her house. . . . There was never any gaming, nor vulgar laughter, nor quarrelling, nor mocking at religion and politics; but much witty, polished talk of matters old and new . . . for the tone was always light, well-mannered, and restrained. She knew how to begin a conversation and was well able to maintain one, because she was intelligent and well-versed in the affairs of every period.

Most significantly for her personal satisfaction, and though it had taken her over five decades, during the last years of her life, Ninon overcame the ultimate social barrier: she had finally been accepted, was frequented and invited by the *women* of the best society.

"Sound in mind and body to the end," according to Saint-Simon, Ninon de Lenclos died at her home on October 17, 1705, after a brief illness of three days, having gone to confession previously that month. As early as 1725, Châteauneuf was to write of her: "Ninon understood early that there can be only one and the same moral code for both men and women." In effect, she had rebelled against, and attempted to put out of effect, the double standard.

SOURCES:

Biographie universelle, ancienne et moderne. Paris: Chez L.G. Michaud, 1819.

Biographie universelle ou dictionnaire historique. . . . Edited by F.-X. De Feller. Paris: J. Leroux, Jouby et Cie., 1849.

Cabourdin, Guy and Georges Viard. *Lexique historique de la France d'Ancien Régime.* 2nd ed. Paris: Armand Colin, 1981.

Dictionnaire de l'Académie française. 2nd ed. Paris, 1695. Genève: Slatkine Reprints, 1968.

Dictionnaire du Grand Siècle. ed. François Bluche. Paris: Fayard, 1990.

Duchêne, Roger. *Ninon de Lenclos, la courtisane du Grand Siècle.* Paris: Fayard, 1984 [translated by William Chew].

Erlanger, Philippe. *Ninon de Lenclos et ses amis.* Paris: Librarie Académique Perrin, 1985.

Furetière, Antoine. *Dictionnaire universel, contenant généralement tous les mots français tant vieux que modernes et les termes de toutes les sciences et des arts.* Rotterdam, 1690. Genève: Slatkine Reprints, 1970.

Richelet, Pierre. *Dictionnaire françois, contenant les mots et les choses, plusieurs nouvelles remarques sur la langue françoise . . . Genève, 1680.* Genève: Slatkine Reprints, 1970.

St. Simon, Duc de. *Saint-Simon at Versailles.* ed. and tr. Lucy Norton. Harmondsworth: Penguin, 1985.

SUGGESTED READING:

Arnaud, Lella. *Ninon de Lenclos.* Paris: n.p., 1958.

Austin, Cecil. *The Immortal Ninon: A Character-Study of Ninon de l'Enclos.* London: George Routledge, 1927.

Bret, Antoine. *Lettres de Ninon de Lenclos.* Nouvelle ed. Paris: Garnier, 1870.

Bret, M. (Antoine). *Ninon de Lenclos.* London: Humphreys, 1904.

Brierre, Annie. *Ninon de Lenclos: Courtisane et grande dame de Paris.* Lausanne: Rencontre, 1967.

Correspondance secrète entre Ninon de Lenclos, le marquis de Villarceaux et Mme de M. Paris: Louis, 1797.

de Tinan, Jean. *L'exemple de Ninon de Lenclos amoureuse.* Bruxelles: n.p., 1921.

Douxmenil. *The Memoirs of Ninon de Lenclos; with her letters to Mons. de St. Evremond, and to the Marquis de Sévigné. Collected and translated from the French, by a lady.* London: R. and J. Dodsley, 1761.

Girardet, Philippe. *Le destin passionné de Ninon von Lenclos.* Paris: A. Fayard, 1959.

Goudal, Jean. *Ninon de Lenclos. Une grande courtisane au siècle de Louis XIV.* Paris: Hachette, 1937.

Lenclos, Anne, called Ninon de. *Correspondance authentique de Ninon de Lenclos, comprenant un grand nombre de lettres inédites et suivi de La coquette vengée. Avec une introd. et des notices par Emile Colombey [Réompression de l'édition de Paris, 1886].* Genève: Slatkine Reprints, 1968.

Lettres de Ninon de Lenclos au marquis de Sévigné, avec sa vie. Londres [i.e. Paris]: n.p., 1782.

Life, letters and philosophy of Ninon de L'Enclos. Chicago: Lion Publishing, 1903.

Magne, Emile. *Ninon de Lenclos. Portraits et documents inédits.* Paris: Librairie Nilsson, 1912.

Roche, France. *Ninon de Lenclos: femme d'esprit, homme de cour.* Paris: Editions R. Laffont, 1988.

Rowsell, Mary C. *Ninon de L'Enclos and her century.* NY: Brentano's, 1910.

Tallemant des Réaux, Gédéon. *Collection des plus belles pages; Historiettes.* Paris: Société du Mercure de France, 1906.

Tinan, Jean de. *L'exemple de Ninon de Lenclos amoureuse.* Bruxelles: Editions de la Chimère, 1921.

William L. Chew III,
Professor of History, Vesalius College, Vrije
Universiteit Brussel, Brussels, Belgium

Leng, Virginia (1955—)

English equestrian who was the first woman to win an individual Olympic three-day event. Name variations: Ginny Leng; Virginia Holgate. Born Virginia Holgate in February 1955; daughter of an officer of the Royal Marines and Heather Holgate; married.

Was the first woman to win an individual Olympic three-day event medal (1984); took the gold medal at the European championships for individual on Priceless (1985), on Night Cap (1987), on Master Craftsman (1989), as well as team gold (1981, 1985, 1987, 1989); won the gold medal at the World championships for individual on Priceless (1986), as well as team gold (1982 and 1986); won Badminton on Priceless (1985), and on Master Craftsman (1989); won Burghley on Priceless (1983), on Night Cap (1984), on Priceless (EC, 1985), on Murphy Himself (1986), on Master Craftsman (EC, 1989); won the Olympic bronze individual on Priceless (1984), and team silver (1984); won the bronze individual medal on Master Craftsman (1988), and team silver (1988).

Virginia Leng was born in 1955 and spent her childhood in Malta, Singapore, the Philippines, Canada, and Cyprus, as her father was an officer in the Royal Marines. At age three, while seated on a horse, she hopped over her first fence. From age 13 to 16, she attended school in Kent and acquired her first horse, Dubonnet. By age 18, Leng had won a team medal with Dubonnet at the 1973 Junior European championships in Pompadour, France; she also entered her first Badminton, England's premier three-day event, in 1974.

Having added Jason to her horse stable, Leng finished second at the French championships at Haras du Pin on Jason, and took the Canadian senior pre-Olympic three-day event at Bromont, near Montreal, in 1975, putting her on

*V*irginia *L*eng

the "long list" for the 1976 Olympic Games at Montreal. But in a fall at Ermington, Leng shattered her arm in 23 pieces; amputation was considered. At the same time, Jason broke a blood vessel and could no longer compete. Despite this, Leng was determined to compete that autumn at Burghley on another horse, Tio Pepe. In contention at first, on the final day horse and rider were eliminated for missing a show jump. The dreadful luck continued. In 1977, Tio Pepe broke down on both front legs in the steeplechase.

Two years earlier, Leng had acquired Priceless and Night Cap, both from the same sire. Though she credits Dubonnet for the start of her career, she credits Priceless with the beginning of her success. "Priceless was really the turning point," she says. As a six-year-old, Priceless won Bramham.

When her father died in 1981, Leng had to find a sponsor or give up. "I got myself a little portfolio, and went on the train to London about once a week for six months. I selected firms from the Yellow Pages, and knocked on doors, which was quite embarrassing. Most people were charming, and would pat me on the head and say, 'Sorry, we can't help, but have a cup of coffee.'" Someone encouraged her to try British National Bank. "In the end the only reason I succeeded was because the chairman's wife was fond of horses! And through various changes of name, Citybank Savings have looked after me ever since."

That same year, Priceless was 6th in the European championships at Horsens, Denmark, and the British team won the gold medal. Over the next seven years, Ginny Leng won a daunting series of major events. She was the first woman equestrian to medal in the Olympics, taking the bronze for the individual three-day event on Priceless in the 1984 Summer Games at Los Angeles under her maiden name Virginia Holgate; she also took the bronze on Master Craftsman at the 1988 summer games in Seoul, Korea, under her married name Leng.

Virginia Leng was surrounded by a dedicated team. Her mother fed the horses and did much of the road work, while **Dorothy Wilson** oversaw their preparation for each event. Pat Manning and Ferdi Eilberg were her dressage trainers, and Pat Burgess and Nick Skelton prepared her for show jumping. As well, Leng's early cross-country training was managed by **Sally Strachan** (whose sister **Clarissa** won team gold medals at the World and European championships). "I learned a lot, too, from watching *Lucinda Green,**" says Leng. "I used to play videos of her riding across country over and over again, and in slow motion. I studied her through all the phrases of the jump and noted her position and balance."

In 1988, Leng took a flyer off Murphy Himself in the Badminton competition. He was, she felt, "too strong a horse for her." Even so, she still took third place and went on to the Olympics at Seoul. But that winter, during a visit to the United States, she thought something was "not quite right" with her foot. Nine months after the fall, she had surgery for a broken ankle—just in time for the 1989 season.

Leng would not push a horse and would never run it on poor turf, especially if the horse had an ailment, such as a sore knee. The proof of her convictions came in 1989, when the selectors demanded that all horses contending for the Burghley team (who would then compete in the European championships) also run in the British Open, which would be held three-and-a-half weeks before Burghley. Since the ground was much too firm after a dry summer, Leng was resolute and would not allow Master Craftsman to run. In the end, the selectors reversed themselves. Master Craftsman led Great Britain to another gold at the European championships.

SOURCES:

Watchen, Guy. *Great Horsemen of the World.* London: Trafalgar Square, 1991.

L'Engle, Madeleine (1918—)

American writer of the popular A Wrinkle in Time *and* "Crosswick journals." *Name variations: Madeleine Camp, Madeleine Camp Franklin L'Engle. Pronunciation: Leng-el). Born Madeleine L'Engle Camp on November 28, 1918, in New York, New York; daughter of Charles Wadsworth Camp (a foreign correspondent and author) and Madeleine Barnett Camp (a pianist); educated at Smith College, B.A. (with honors), 1941; attended New School for Social Research, 1941–42; Columbia University, graduate study, 1960–61; married Hugh Franklin (an actor), on January 26, 1946 (died September 1986); children: Josephine Franklin Jones (who married Alan W. Jones); Maria Rooney; Bion Franklin.*

Had active career in theater (1941–47); taught with Committee for Refugee Education during World War II; taught at St. Hilda's and St. Hugh's School, New York (1960–66); librarian and writer-in-residence, Cathedral of St. John the Divine, New York (1966—); was a member of the faculty at University of Indiana, Bloomington (summers 1965–66, 1971); was a writer-in-residence, Ohio State University, Colum-

bus (1970), and University of Rochester, New York (1972); lecturer.

Awards, honors: Newbery Medal from the American Library Association (1963), Hans Christian Andersen Award runner-up (1964), Sequoyah Children's Book Award from the Oklahoma State Department of Education, and Lewis Carroll Shelf Award (both 1965), all for A Wrinkle in Time; *Book World's* Spring Book Festival Honor Book, *and one of* School Library Journal's Best Books of the Year *(both 1968), both for* The Young Unicorns; *Austrian State Literary Prize (1969), for* The Moon by Night; *University of Southern Mississippi Silver Medallion (1978) for "an outstanding contribution to the field of children's literature"; American Book Award for paperback fiction (1980) for* A Swiftly Tilting Planet; *Smith Medal (1980); Newbery Honor Book (1981) for* A Ring of Endless Light; *A* Ring of Endless Light *was selected one of New York Public Library's Books for the Teen Age (1981), as was* Camilla *(1982); Sophie Award (1984); Regina Medal from the Catholic Library Association (1984);* A House Like a Lotus *was exhibited at the Bologna International Children's Book Fair (1985); Adolescent Literature Assembly Award for Outstanding Contribution to Adolescent Literature from the National Council of Teachers of English (1986).*

Selected writings: The Small Rain: A Novel *(Vanguard, 1945, also published as* Prelude, *Vanguard, 1968);* Ilsa *(Vanguard, 1946);* And Both Were Young *(Lothrop, 1949);* Camilla Dickinson *(Simon & Schuster, 1951);* A Winter's Love *(Lippincott, 1957); (illustrated by Inga)* The Twenty-Four Days before Christmas: An Austin Family Story *(Farrar, Straus, 1964);* The Arm of the Starfish *(Farrar, Straus, 1965);* The Love Letters *(Farrar, Straus, 1966);* Lines Scribbled on an Envelope and Other Poems *(Farrar, Straus, 1969); (illustrated by Symeon Shimin)* Dance in the Desert *(Farrar, Straus, 1969);* Intergalactic P.S.3 *(Children's Book Council, 1970);* The Other Side of the Sun *(Farrar, Straus, 1971);* Dragons in the Waters *(sequel to* The Arm of the Starfish, *Farrar, Straus, 1976); (editor with William B. Green)* Spirit and Light: Essays in Historical Theology *(Seabury, 1976); (poetry)* The Weather of the Heart *(Shaw, 1978);* Walking on Water: Reflections on Faith and Art *(Shaw, 1980);* A Severed Wasp *(sequel to* A Small Rain, *Farrar, Straus, 1982);* And It Was Good: Reflections on Beginnings *(Shaw, 1983);* A House Like a Lotus *(sequel to* The Arm of the Starfish, *Farrar, Straus, 1984);* A Stone for a Pillow: Journeys with Jacob *(Shaw, 1986);* Certain Women *(1992);* Glimpses of Grace: Daily Thoughts and Reflections *(1996);* A Live Coal in the Sea *(Farrar, Straus, 1996).*

"The Austin Family" series: Meet the Austins *(Vanguard, 1960);* The Moon by Night *(Farrar, Straus, 1963);* The Young Unicorns *(Farrar, Straus, 1968);* A Ring of Endless Light *(Farrar, Straus, 1980).*

"Time Fantasy" series: A Wrinkle in Time *(Farrar, Straus, 1962);* A Wind in the Door *(Farrar, Straus, 1973);* A Swiftly Tilting Planet *(Farrar, Straus, 1978);* Many Waters *(Farrar, Straus, 1986).*

"Crosswicks Journals" (autobiography): A Circle of Quiet *(Farrar, Straus, 1972);* The Summer of the Great-Grandmother *(Farrar, Straus, 1974);* The Irrational Season *(Seabury, 1977);* Two Part Invention *(Farrar, Straus, 1988). Contributor of articles, stories and poems to periodicals, including* McCall's, Christian Century, Commonweal, Christianity Today, *and* Mademoiselle.

Madeleine L'Engle was born Madeleine Camp in New York City in 1918, the only child of Charles Wadsworth Camp, a foreign correspondent, playwright and critic, and **Madeleine Barnett Camp**, a talented pianist. L'Engle's childhood was spent in a creative but isolated environment. Her mother, who was almost 40 when L'Engle was born, did not agree with Charles Camp's more proscribed notion of child-rearing. L'Engle experienced what she later called "a strict English childhood"; she was encouraged to write, draw and play the piano, but mixed little with other children.

Her father's ill health (he was "gassed in the trenches of France" during World War I, wrote L'Engle) resulted in a move to Switzerland when she was 12. Introspective, awkward and slightly lame, L'Engle was placed in a series of austere boarding schools, in which she found solace by withdrawing even further into her private imaginative world. She learned "to shut out the sound of the school and listen to the story or poem I was writing when I should have been doing schoolwork. The result of this early lesson in concentration is that I can write anywhere."

She returned to the United States to attend college, graduating from Smith with honors in 1941. Deciding to work in the theater, she assumed the family name of L'Engle, and took a job as secretary and touring actress for *Eva Le Gallienne, but she gave up her stage career permanently after marrying actor Hugh Franklin in 1946. (Beginning in 1971, Hugh portrayed Dr. Charles Tyler, husband of Phoebe Tyler [**Ruth Warrick**], on the television soap opera "All My Children" for many years.)

By the time of her marriage, L'Engle had already begun writing seriously. Her first published novel, *The Small Rain* (1945), drew on the loneliness of boarding-school life and spoke to the discipline needed—and comfort found—in an artistic life. While continuing to write adult books, L'Engle published *And Both Were Young*, her first children's book, in 1949. The 1950s, however, were largely unproductive creatively, as L'Engle suspended her writing career to raise her children and work on the renovation of their home in rural Connecticut, where they also ran a general store. "My love for my family and my need to write were in acute conflict," she said. After a succession of rejection letters, she decided to renounce writing entirely on her 40th birthday in 1958. The decision was quickly reversed. "I had to write," L'Engle realized. "If I never had another book published, and it was very clear to me that this was a real possibility, I still had to go on writing."

Although her fortunes soon changed, L'Engle had some difficulty finding a publisher for her 1962 juvenile novel *A Wrinkle in Time.* Over 26 publishers rejected the book over a two-year period. Hard to pigeonhole as either science fiction or fantasy, *A Wrinkle in Time* was described to L'Engle as "too difficult for children." She admitted that it was "written in the terms of a modern world in which children know about brainwashing and the corruption of evil. It's based on Einstein's theories of relativity and Planck's quantum theory. It's good solid science, but also it's good, solid theology." *A Wrinkle in Time* is the story of Meg Murry, who must use time travel and ESP to rescue her scientist father from It, a disembodied brain on another planet; she must also learn the power of love in order to release him. **Ruth Hill Viguers** in *A Critical History of Children's Literature* calls it "a book that combines devices of fairy tales, overtones of fantasy, the philosophy of great lives, the visions of science, and the warmth of a good family story."

When her manuscript was finally accepted by Farrar, Straus, L'Engle was warned not to expect high sales. Defying all expectations, *A Wrinkle in Time* was a hit with the public, and won the Newbery Medal in 1963 and the Lewis Carroll Shelf Award in 1965; it was also a runner-up for the Hans Christian Andersen Award in 1964. Continuing both the characters of the book and its central theme of good versus evil, L'Engle wrote three further books in this "Time Fantasy" series. L'Engle's spiritual themes also found their way into her adult writing, from 1996's *Glimpses of Grace: Daily Thoughts and Reflections* to novels like 1992's *Certain Women.*

At the same time, L'Engle had begun work on a second series for young readers based around

the adventures of protagonist Vicky Austin, beginning with 1960's *Meet the Austins*. Subsequent books in the series, written between 1963 and 1987, are *The Moon by Night*, *The Twenty-Four Days before Christmas*, *The Young Unicorns*, *A Ring of Endless Light* and *Troubling a Star*.

In 1966, L'Engle became a librarian at the Cathedral of St. John the Divine in New York City. The dark, tiny library contained row upon row of dusty volumes, a mahogany fireplace, and, generally, one or two of L'Engle's dogs. "I walk into that . . . room every and day and my heart just sings," she wrote. "It's a beautiful room with high ceilings and paneled walls and great bay windows which look across the Cathedral close to the Cathedral building itself. And there I am at my lovely desk which sort of puts me (no matter who I am) in the position of being somebody who's there and can be talked to. The first thing I did was to keep the teapot going so that people could have a cup of tea."

L'Engle did much of her writing there, including some of her Crosswick journals and her books that wrestled with the question of religious faith. She considers herself "a very rebellious Christian. I fight against the establishment constantly. I'm also involved in it. I infiltrate from within." During her prolific career, she has written three plays, numerous articles and stories, and several autobiographical pieces. Her Crosswick journals have an avid following. By the 1980s, L'Engle was one of the bestselling children's authors in the United States, and several of her juvenile books are now considered children's classics. Wrote L'Engle: "In a letter I received, a child asked me, 'How can I stay a child forever and never grow up?' And I replied, 'I don't think you can, and I don't think it would be a good idea if you could. What you can do, and what I hope you will do, is stay a child forever and grow up.'"

SOURCES:

Garrett, Agnes, and Helga McCue. *Authors and Artists for Young Adults.* Vol. 1. Detroit, MI: Gale Research, 1989.

L'Engle, Madeleine, and Avery Brooke. *Trailing Clouds of Glory.* Westminster Press, 1985.

Newquist, Roy. *Conversations.* Rand McNally, 1967.

Rausen, Ruth. "An Interview with Madeleine L'Engle," in *Children's Literature in Education 19.* Winter 1975.

Paula Morris, D.Phil.,
Brooklyn, New York

Lenglen, Suzanne (1899–1938)

French tennis champion, winner of the Wimbledon title six times, who was considered the greatest female player in the history of the game. Pronunciation: Lawn-GLEN. Born Suzanne Rachel Flore Lenglen in Compiègne, France, on May 24, 1899; died in Paris, France, on July 4, 1938; daughter of Charles Lenglen (a wealthy businessman) and Anais Lenglen; never married; no children.

Was coached as a championship contender in tennis from age 11; won her first Wimbledon championship (1919); won gold medals in singles and mixed doubles in the Olympic competition (1920); won six French titles; won six Wimbledon titles (1920, 1921, 1922, 1923, 1925); collected 269 out of 270 match titles (1919–26).

Charles Lenglen, a wealthy businessman vacationing with his family on the Riviera in the summer of 1910, bought his 11-year-old daughter a tennis racquet. That autumn, he accompanied her to a tennis club in Nice and recognized her superior athletic ability. At the beginning of the 20th century, when most athletes were casual about fitness, excelling on the basis of innate ability rather than superior training, Charles Lenglen took a different approach. He decided that his daughter would be a tennis champion.

Suzanne Lenglen practiced for hours on the tennis courts. Her father would put a French franc on the ground to use as a target for her serves. Suzanne became so adept at placing her serve that she was capable of hitting the small coin five times in succession. But her parents, watching from the sidelines, were rarely satisfied. "Stupid girl!" her father would yell. "Keep your eye on the ball!" "Move, move, move!" her mother, **Anais Lenglen**, would add. By early adolescence, Lenglen was one of the best tennis players in the world. Her feats would dominate the tennis world from 1919 to 1926, and she became a sports legend, known worldwide for her fantastic play and ferocious temper. She was, wrote one biographer, "athletically formidable and emotionally tattered."

Suzanne Lenglen was born in Compiègne, France, on May 24, 1899. Once her tennis training began, she spent hours each day swimming, jumping, and sprinting to improve her general physical condition; the rest of the day was used to hone her tennis skills. Intense and systematic training formed the core of her daily existence. Papa Lenglen taught Suzanne the aggressive serve-and-volley style typical of men's tennis. Her successes were praised and her failures ridiculed.

When Suzanne was 15, she won the local tournament, sponsored by the prestigious Carlton Club of Cannes, and the international competitions held at the Stade Français in St. Cloud. Papa Lenglen had planned for her to become a Wimbledon champion in 1915, but World War I intervened. In 1919, the war had ended when she faced *Dorothea Lambert Chambers, 40 years old and a seven-time Wimbledon winner, on Wimbledon's courts. Half her opponent's age, Lenglen won 10-8, 4-6, and 8-6 in an era before tiebreakers. She also introduced an entirely new style of play into women's tennis, volleying and going frequently to the net. Her forehand was severe, and above all, after hours of aiming at a coin, she had exceptional control of the ball, able to place it wherever she chose. Her style of play so outshone her opponents that she rarely had to fear losing a match. After 1919, no one doubted that Suzanne Lenglen was Queen of the Courts.

Lenglen brought other changes to the tennis world in addition to her powerful style of play. Few players have had such an influence on tennis sportswear as this French athlete. Modern-day women take comfortable clothing that allows freedom of movement for granted, hardly aware that this type of freedom was not attained until the 1920s. It could also be said that the revolution in women's dress brought about other demands for social change. After World War I, the corset, the bustle, and the trailing skirt were abandoned by women in all walks of life who preferred to dress both safely and sensibly. Sports clothes "symbolized the new status of women," noted one historian. "It was the final proof of their successful assertion of the right to enjoy whatever recreation they chose, costumed according to the demands of the sport rather than the tabus of an outworn prudery."

As the sport of the affluent, tennis was especially bound by social convention. In the Victorian era, women playing lawn tennis wore garden party dresses with elaborate flounces, ornamental sleeves, high necks, and cinched waists over bustles, corsets, petticoats, and long drawers. Materials of silk or wool, and even lavish fur trim, were common; for a long time, the only concession to athletic demands was the wearing of shoes with soles of India rubber. The eventual adoption of all-white attire was actually due to Victorian prudery. In the late 19th century, society did not wish to acknowledge that ladies might perspire in public, but since players of the game often worked up a sweat, white clothes minimized the visibility of sweat stains. Hats were also common on court, for both men and women. Though the bustle gradually disappeared, corsets remained because the hour-glass figure was the rage. In 1905, *May Sutton caused a stir at Wimbledon when she became so warm that she rolled back her sleeves and revealed her wrists. Wimbledon champion *Elizabeth Ryan recalled that in the years leading up to World War I, when corsets hung about the dressing room after women finished playing, "It was not a pretty sight as many of them were blood-stained from the wounds they had inflicted."

Thus, in 1919, with Lenglen's first appearance at Wimbledon, it was difficult to tell which caused the greater stir: her athletic style of play or her tennis outfit. She wore a flimsy, one-piece cotton frock. The pleated skirt, which was very short for the period, reached only to mid-calf, while her short sleeves revealed her elbows, and she wore no petticoats or corsets. The costume was considered shocking and indecent, although it had to be admitted that it helped Lenglen to play her powerful game unhindered. The following year, Lenglen defeated Chambers at Wimbledon for a second time; this time, Lenglen's hair was bobbed, and around her head she wore two yards of brightly colored silk promptly labeled the "Lenglen Bandeau." Bobbed hair was still generally considered immodest, and Lenglen was said by some to dress like a prostitute; very soon, however, women both on and off the court were wearing short-sleeved frocks, bobbed hair, and colorful bandeaux. In 1923, Lenglen began wearing silk tennis dresses and hip-length silk cardigans with matching bandeaux, rarely appearing twice in the same color scheme. Sometimes she added shiny silk stockings. By then, the fashion industry was paying close attention to whatever she wore, because millions of women were quick to follow her example.

> [Lenglen was] a genius on the courts with all the temperament of a great artiste.
>
> —Robert J. Condon

For Lenglen, her clothing represented her view of herself as an athlete. After World War I, the famous Russian ballet company led by Serge Diaghilev relocated to nearby Monte Carlo, where Lenglen saw many productions. Influenced by her love of the dance, Lenglen compared her leaps on the courts to those of ballerinas onstage, and saw the freedom allowed by shorter skirts and sleeveless dresses as a means of bringing the flowing movements of ballet to the tennis court. The silk chiffons of her bandeaux and long matching neck scarves were copied from ballerinas and the modern dancer *Isadora Duncan, whose avant-garde costuming was the epitome of style and freedom. Once Lenglen dominated the courts, restrictions on women's dress were considerably lessened everywhere.

If shocked at first, the public learned to adore Lenglen's spectacular leaps. It seemed as if half her time on court was spent airborne. Of her unorthodox style, she said:

> My method? I don't think I have any. I just throw dignity to the winds and think of nothing but the game. I try to hit the ball with all my force and send it where my opponent is not. I say to myself, "Let the other one do the running about but run as fast as you can yourself if you have to."

After her first win at Wimbledon, Lenglen captured the title every year up to 1923, and again in 1925, missing the 1924 match due to illness. She also won six French championships. In 1921, she easily beat *Molla Mallory, the veteran American champion, in the French Hard Court championships.

The Americans wanted Lenglen to play on their courts, but her parents were not particularly anxious to travel to the United States. After considerable debate, the invitation to the matches at Forest Hills was accepted. Lenglen, who had shown signs of frail health since childhood, became ill during the Atlantic crossing, but once she arrived at Forest Hills she was her usual imperious self, insisting on wine before her matches although consumption of alcoholic beverages was prohibited throughout the country by the Volstead Act. The tennis officials met her demands, willing to even break the law if it would keep the French champion happy.

Molla Mallory wanted to avenge her defeat in France, and the public went wild over the promise of a match between two female champions. The contest was of short duration, however, as Lenglen had a coughing spasm and left the court, defaulting to Mallory. On doctor's orders, the rest of the tour was canceled, and Lenglen sailed back to Europe five days later. She would not return to the United States until the end of her career.

After this setback, Lenglen continued to win game after game. From 1919 to 1926, she won 269 of 270 matches. No one rivaled her accuracy and placement. Along with her high athletic leaps to return a volley, she calculated her movements about the court as if it were a chessboard. When Lenglen met Mallory in a match following Forest Hills, she quickly disposed of her American opponent 6-2, 6-0. The popularity of her game was also the first challenge to the supremacy of male tennis. Bill Tilden, the best-known male player of the era, admitted that more people came to Lenglen's games than to his.

Fans of the game were also eager to witness Lenglen's famous outbursts, when she would quarrel with officials, stomp her foot, and sob rackingly. She sometimes also exhibited a violent spell of coughing. In 1926, her arrogance at Wimbledon became legendary after Queen *Mary of Teck asked that the mixed-doubles match Lenglen was to play be rescheduled to suit royal convenience. Although many tennis players would have been thrilled that the queen wanted to be in the audience for their match, Lenglen was furious at being asked to wait. When the queen reached the royal box, Lenglen remained in the locker room until her teammate, Jacques Borota, entered the women's locker room (blindfolded) to beg her to play. Lenglen finally made her appearance, but the British were infuriated by this insult to their queen and watched the match in total silence. Unnerved, Lenglen got into an altercation with the officials and then flounced off the court, withdrawing from the tournament. The international incident forced the French government to apologize to the British government for the conduct of Mlle. Lenglen.

Such incidents only fueled Lenglen's popularity. That same year, when she was scheduled to play the American champion *Helen Wills at Cannes, the event was the talk of the sports world for months in advance. The playing styles of the two women were entirely different. Helen Wills had a deep, forcing service, a strong overhead, and was a skilled volleyer; she won her matches almost entirely from the baseline. Power and court tactics were her strengths; the length and pace of her groundstrokes were incredible. Wills was not especially fast or nimble, however, and opponents who abstained from those driving exchanges could be successful. Lenglen did not have Wills' power, and she went to the net more often, but her strength was in her ability to place the ball. In emotional terms, while Lenglen was highly nervous and often burst into tears during a match, Wills was known as "Little Miss Poker Face" for her emotional control. In preparation for the match at Cannes, special grandstands were built, and 3,000 spectators poured in from around the world. When Wills lost to Lenglen 6-2, 6-0, a humiliating defeat, many felt that the American had made the fatal mistake of trying to out-think her French opponent, whose chess-like strategy could be as devastating as her athletic prowess.

Aside from Mary of Teck, royalty fawned over her, and thousands packed into arenas to watch her play. While most players had to take the train, she rode to her tournaments in limousines, and top designers vied with one another to fashion her tennis wear. But Lenglen was a complex and sometimes tragic figure, completely dominated by her parents. Plagued with poor health, she was tense and moody. She could sulk, pull out of matches, and disappoint enormous crowds. She often claimed illness in order to get out of a match only to go dancing that night. Too often, such incidents made front page news worldwide. The frequent bouts of public hysteria surely sapped her physical and emotional strength, but when Lenglen appeared on court she resented every point scored against her. In

Suzanne
Lenglen

playing, she was determined never to give an inch, and the crowds loved it.

At the height of her career, many were drawn to the idea of a match between Lenglen and Tilden, the reigning male tennis star.

Lenglen once played a practice match with Tilden, in which she was reportedly beaten, but when word of her defeat was leaked to the press she was furious. Lenglen denied that she had been trying to play her best, and it became clear that there would never be a real match.

After the Wimbledon fiasco in 1926, with Lenglen at the height of her powers, she announced her withdrawal from amateur competition to play as a professional and signed with Charles C. Pyle to tour the U.S. for a series of exhibition matches. By the time she retired in the late 1920s, she had made a fortune. Meanwhile, from 1919 to 1926, the years of her amateur reign, she had redefined the role of the female athlete. Women champions were now expected to demonstrate great physical prowess, and even to defy conventional forms of social behavior and dress. On the courts, first and foremost, anemic playing had been permanently shelved.

After her withdrawal from professional competition, Lenglen founded a tennis school where she taught upcoming players. She was approaching 30, and the intensity of her career continued to take its toll. Lenglen had never been healthy, although whether this was due to emotional volatility or a weak constitution, no one could be certain. Part of her difficulties may have stemmed from never having been allowed to develop as a free and independent adult. Once, when Suzanne's mother was questioned by reporters about why the athlete had once again gone dancing shortly after withdrawing from a competition on grounds of ill health, Anais Lenglen told them, "*Suzanne est coquette toujours*" (Suzanne is always a tease). In retirement, her health did not improvement. Still, when she died of pernicious anemia, on July 4, 1938, at age 39, many were caught by surprise.

All of France mourned Suzanne Lenglen. Her funeral was almost a state occasion. King Gustav V of Sweden, 80 years old and a tennis enthusiast, sent the Swedish minister to represent him. France's premier Edouard Daladier attended, as did various ministers and members of government. Jean Borotra, Jacques Brugnon, Bernard Destremeau, and Christian Boussus—all famous French tennis players—attended the funeral mass at the church of Notre Dame de l'Assomption. The U.S. Lawn Tennis Association was represented by Russell Kingman, flowers poured in from around the world, and Lenglen's tennis pupils came to their teacher's funeral mass. The day before the funeral, July 5, 1939, Madame Lenglen was notified that Suzanne would be awarded the Legion of Honor, and a statue was planned in her honor at the Stade Roland Garros in Auteuil, France. She was buried in the family plot in Saint-Ouen Cemetery.

At her death, Suzanne Lenglen was considered to be the greatest woman tennis player of all time. Despite the emergence of later tennis greats

such as *Chris Evert, *Margaret Smith Court, *Steffi Graf, *Althea Gibson, *Martina Navratilova, and *Billie Jean King, her claim to the title has rarely been challenged; no one has achieved the margin of victory that Lenglen held. In almost 300 matches, as both an amateur and a professional, she lost only five times, a record that remains unequaled. In 1974, decades after her death, she was voted the greatest woman player in tennis by an international panel of sportswriters, receiving more votes than Wills, Gibson, or King.

SOURCES:

Bressan, Serge. *Le Sport et les Femmes*. Paris: La Table Ronde, 1981.

Condon, Robert J. *Great Women Athletes of the 20th Century*. Jefferson, NC: McFarland, 1991.

Edschmid, Kasimir. *Portraits und Denksteine*. Vienna: Kurt Desch Verlag, 1962.

Englemann, Larry. *The Goddess and the American Girl: The Story of Suzanne Lenglen and Helen Wills*. NY: Oxford University Press, 1988.

Grimsley, Will. *101 Greatest Athletes of the Century*. NY: Bonanza Books, 1987.

"Many Tennis Stars at Lenglen Service," in *The New York Times*. July 7, 1938, p. 19.

The New York Times. "Mlle. Lenglen." July 5, 1938, p. 16.

"1920's Woman Star Held Greatest Ever in Tennis," in *The New York Times*. March 31, 1974, section V, p. 6.

Robertson, Max, ed. *The Encyclopedia of Tennis*. London: George Allen & Unwin, 1974.

Soderberg, Paul *et al.*, eds. *The Big Book of Halls of Fame in the United States and Canada: Sports*. NY: R.R. Bowker, 1977.

"Suzanne Lenglen, Tennis Star, Dies," in *The New York Times*. July 4, 1938, p. 13.

Karin L. Haag,
freelance writer, Athens, Georgia

Lenin, Nadezhda or Nadya (1869–1939).

See Krupskaya, Nadezhda.

Lenja, Lotte (1898–1981).

See Lenya, Lotte.

Lennart, Isobel (1915–1971)

American writer who wrote Funny Girl *for Broadway and the screen. Born on May 18, 1915, in Brooklyn, New York; died in an automobile accident on January 25, 1971, in Hemet, California; married John Harding (an actor); children: one son, one daughter.*

Screenplays: The Affairs of Martha *(1942);* A Stranger in Town *(1943);* Anchors Aweigh *(1945);* It Happened in Brooklyn *(1947);* The Kissing Bandit *(1948);* Holiday Affair *(1949);* East Side, West Side *(1949);* It's a Big Country *(1951);* Skirts Ahoy! *(1952);* The Girl Next Door *(1953);* Meet Me in Las Vegas *(*Viva Las Vegas, *1956);* Merry Andrew *(1958);* The

Inn of the Sixth Happiness *(1958); The Sundowners (1960); Please Don't Eat the Daisies (1960); Two for the Seesaw (1962); Period of Adjustment (1962); Fitzwilly (1967); Funny Girl (1968). Playwright: (Broadway) Funny Girl.*

A native New Yorker, Isobel Lennart was born in 1915 and moved to Hollywood when she was in her early 20s to work in the motion-picture industry. By the time she was 27, she was on the writing staff at Metro-Goldwyn-Mayer Studios and had had her first screen credit. Though always thought of as a "serious writer" by her colleagues at the studio, Lennart wrote primarily light comedies and musicals.

Hollywood in the 1930s saw the heyday of political activism. The 1929 stock-market crash and the Depression that threw millions of women and men out of work gave rise to serious questioning about the viability of capitalism. There was no social security then, nor was there unemployment compensation; millions of working-class Americans were destitute. Many intellectuals and artists joined the Communist Party in the hopes of building a better future for the working class, and Isobel Lennart was one of them, joining in 1939. She resigned after Stalin signed his infamous pact with Hitler, but rejoined when Germany invaded Russia. When it became known that Stalin was murdering millions of his own people, Lennart renounced the party for the last time.

Around 1953, Senator Joseph McCarthy initiated the Communist witch hunts through the congressional House Un-American Activities committee (HUAC). Known or alleged Communist Party members were subpoenaed to testify before the committee. Those who refused to testify or those who refused to name other members as Communists went to jail. In the hysteria of these early Cold War years, being branded a Communist often ended a person's career. Though many prestigious writers like Dashiell Hammett and Dalton Trumbo went to jail for refusing to testify, other members of the Hollywood community, like the future president Ronald Reagan, voluntarily cooperated with the committee. Isobel Lennart apparently was one of those who volunteered to testify. Through the remaining years of the "blacklisting," as it is known in Hollywood, and possibly because of her cooperation, Lennart continued to work.

The movies Lennart wrote during the 1950s gave no hint of the heartbreak that went on behind the scenes in Hollywood. She was still an MGM staff writer, although she was sometimes "loaned" to other studios, and writing on staff meant she was assigned projects; they were did not originate with her. In those days, Americans wanted light romantic comedies and musicals, and that was just what Hollywood gave them. Lennart wrote musicals like *Skirts Ahoy!* (1952), about three WAVES on leave (*Esther Williams, Joan Evans and *Vivian Blaine), and *Merry Andrew* (1958), in which schoolteacher Danny Kaye falls in love with circus aerialist *Pier Angeli. Lennart also wrote two romantic comedies with essentially the same plot and cast with the same leading man. In *The Girl Next Door* (1953), cartoonist Dan Dailey falls in love with his neighbor, a singer played by *June Haver. In *Meet Me in Las Vegas* (1956), rancher Dailey falls in love with a ballerina, **Cyd Charisse.**

In the early 1960s, with the coming of the Vietnam War, the mood in America shifted, and Hollywood reacted with more serious fare. Though Lennart adapted comedies like *Please Don't Eat the Daisies* (1960) and *Two For the Seesaw* (1962), she also adapted *The Sundowners* (1960), a serious story about poor migrant workers who struggle and survive in the rugged Australian outback. She received an Academy Award nomination for her work on this film.

In 1962, Lennart adapted for the screen the Tennessee Williams play *Period of Adjustment.* Directed by George Roy Hill, the drama follows two newlywed couples (**Jane Fonda** and Jim Hutton, Anthony Franciosa and **Lois Nettleton**) as they go through a "period of adjustment," learning to cope with being married. Lennart's adaptation of the play was met with critical accolades.

Throughout her career, Lennart always dreamed of writing for the Broadway stage. In 1963, she wrote the musical *Funny Girl*, about the legendary vaudeville comedian *Fanny Brice. When it premiered in New York it was a smash hit and made the up-and-coming **Barbra Streisand** a household name. Lennart subsequently adapted the play for the screen. It was equally a success at the box office, and Streisand won an Academy Award for her performance. Ironically it is for this, her last screenplay, that Lennart is most known. Isobel Lennart died in an automobile accident on January 25, 1971, in Hemet, California, a town outside Los Angeles. She and her husband, John Harding, were returning home from a visit to their daughter in Prescott, Arizona. Lennart was 55.

SOURCES:

Morsberger, Robert E., Stephen O. Lesser, and Randall Clark. *American Screenwriters*. Detroit, MI: Gale Research, 1984.

Deborah Jones,
Studio City, California

Lennox, Caroline (1723–1774).

See Lennox Sisters.

Lennox, Charlotte (1720–1804)

English-American novelist and poet. Born Charlotte Ramsay in New York in 1720; died in England on January 4, 1804; daughter of Colonel James Ramsey (lieutenant-governor of New York); married Alexander Lennox, in 1748; children: a daughter and a son.

Charlotte Lennox was born in New York in 1720. Moving to London in 1735, and unprovided for at the time of her father's death, 15-year-old Charlotte began to earn a living with her writing, along with an unsuccessful attempt as an actress (1748–50). She remained the breadwinner after she married Alexander Lennox, said to be a ne'er-do-well, and had two children.

Over the years, Lennox became friends with Samuel Richardson and Samuel Johnson, whose admiration for her, thought some, "exceeded his judgment." While discussing the talents of **Elizabeth Carter**, *Hannah More, and *Fanny Burney, Johnson once remarked: "Three such women are not to be found; I know not where to find a fourth, except Mrs. Lennox, who is superior to them all." Lennox's major works include *The Life of Harriot Stuart* (novel, 1751); *The Female Quixote; or the Adventures of Arabella* (novel, 1752); and *Shakespear illustrated; or the novels and histories on which the plays . . . are founded* (1753–54), in which she maintained that Shakespeare had spoiled the stories he borrowed for his plots by adding unnecessary intrigues and incidents. *The Sister,* a comedy produced at Covent Garden on February 18, 1769, had a stormy first night and was withdrawn by the following day. The hostile reception, said Oliver Goldsmith, who wrote its epilogue, was caused by Lennox's criticism of Shakespeare. Despite its initial failure, *The Sister* was translated into German, and Sir John Burgoyne borrowed three of its characters for his successful 1786 play *The Heiress.* Charlotte Lennox also edited 11 editions of the monthly *Lady's Museum* and translated many books from the French, including the memoirs of the Duc de Sully, the countess of Berci, and *Madame de Maintenon.

Lennox, countess of.

See Montgomery, Margaret (fl. 1438).

See Stuart, Arabella for sidebar on Cavendish, Elizabeth.

See Isabel (d. 1457?).

See Hamilton, Elizabeth (c. 1480–?).

See Stewart, Anne (fl. 1515).

See Douglas, Margaret (1515–1578).

See Stewart, Elizabeth (fl. 1578).

Lennox, duchess of.

See Stuart, Frances (1647–1702).

Lennox, Emily (1731–1814).

See Lennox Sisters.

Lennox, Louisa (1743–1821).

See Lennox Sisters.

Lennox, Margaret.

See Douglas, Margaret (1515–1578).

Lennox, Sarah (1745–1826).

See Lennox Sisters.

Lennox Sisters

Four aristocratic daughters of the duke and duchess of Richmond.

Lennox, Caroline (1723–1774). English peeress. Name variations: Lady Holland; Caroline Fox. Born in March 1723 in London, England; died in July 1774 in London; daughter of Charles Lennox, 2nd duke of Richmond, and Sarah Cadogan (d. 1751); great-granddaughter of Charles II, king of England, and Louise de Kérouaille; married Henry Fox, in 1741; children: Stephen Fox (b. 1748); Charles Fox (b. 1749).

*Lennox, Emily (1731–1814). Duchess of Leinster. Name variations: Lady Kildare; Emily Fitzgerald. Born Emilia Mary Lennox in October 1731 in London, England; died in March 1814 in London; daughter of Charles Lennox, 2nd duke of Richmond, and Sarah Cadogan (d. 1751); great-granddaughter of Charles II, king of England, and Louise de Kérouaille; married James Fitzgerald, earl of Kildare and duke of Leinster, in 1747; married William Ogilvie, in 1774; children: (first marriage) George Fitzgerald (b. 1748); William (b. 1749), later duke of Leinster; **Emily Fitzgerald** (b. 1752); Charles Fitzgerald (b. 1756); **Charlotte Fitzgerald** (b. 1758); Henry Fitzgerald (b. 1761); **Sophia Fitzgerald** (b. 1762); Edward Fitzgerald (b. 1763); Robert Fitzgerald (b. 1765); Gerald Fitzgerald (b. 1766); **Fanny Fitzgerald** (b. 1768); **Lucy Fitzgerald** (b. 1770); George Fitzgerald (b. 1771); and five others who died young; (second marriage) **Cecilia Ogilvie** (b. 1775); **Mimi Ogilvie** (b. 1778).*

Lennox, Louisa (1743–1821). English peeress. Name variations: Louisa Lennox Conolly. Born in November 1743 in London; died in 1821 in Castletown, Ireland; daughter of Charles Lennox, 2nd duke of Rich-

mond, and Sarah Cadogan (d. 1751); great- grand-daughter of Charles II, king of England, and Louise de Kérouaille; married Thomas Conolly, in 1758; no children of her own but adopted her sister Sarah's daughter Emily Louisa Napier (b. 1783).

Lennox, Sarah *(1745–1826).* **English peeress.** *Name variations: Lady Bunbury; Sarah Napier. Born in February 1745 in London; died in August 1826 in London; daughter of Charles Lennox, 2nd duke of Richmond, and Sarah Cadogan (d. 1751); great-granddaughter of Charles II, king of England, and Louise de Kérouaille; married Thomas Charles Bunbury, in 1762; married George Napier, in 1781; children: (with Lord William Gordon)* **Louisa Bunbury** *(b. 1768); (second marriage) Charles Napier (b. 1782); Emily Louisa Napier (b. 1783); George Napier (b. 1784); William Napier (b. 1785); Richard Napier (b. 1787); Henry Napier (b. 1789);* **Caroline Napier** *(b. 1790); Cecilia (b. 1791).*

The four eldest daughters of Charles Lennox and **Sarah Cadogan**, the duke and duchess of Richmond, were renowned for their beauty and intelligence. The sisters' voluminous surviving correspondence, spanning the late 18th and early 19th centuries, provides a window into the daily lives of the elite in the Georgian period of British history. Caroline, Emily, Louisa, and Sarah were four of the seven surviving children of the duke and duchess, a loving couple devoted to their children. Charles' father was the illegitimate son of King Charles II and *****Louise de Kérouaille** and half-brother to George II, so the Lennox family claimed royal heritage and its privileges. The duke was Lord of the Bedchamber to his half-uncle George II, and the girls' childhood was divided between the ducal country house of Goodwood, Richmond House in London, and the royal palaces, where the king was exceptionally fond of them.

In 1741, the eldest daughter, Caroline, fell in love with Henry Fox, a member of Parliament, Prime Minister William Pitt's greatest rival, and an old friend of the Lennox family. The duke refused to permit their marriage because Henry was a commoner. Unable to change her parents' minds, Caroline and Henry eloped in May, provoking a major scandal in London society. Outraged by Caroline's disobedience, Charles Lennox forbade his family any communication with her or the Foxes. Only after the birth of her first child in 1748 was Caroline reconciled with, though never forgiven by, her parents. Another son followed in 1749, and the Fox couple remained happily married despite their initial difficulties.

By 1748, Emily Lennox was also happily married. Unlike Caroline, Emily had chosen a husband, James Fitzgerald, earl of Kildare in Ireland and later duke of Leinster, who was welcomed as a son-in-law by her parents. The wealthy Fitzgeralds were Ireland's largest landholders and consequently were important players in Irish politics. After her marriage at age 16 in 1747, Emily left her younger sisters at Richmond House for the Fitzgerald estates and Kildare House in Dublin, center of Irish society and politics. Over the next 20 years, Emily would raise a large family, giving birth to 18 children, of whom six sons and a daughter survived to adulthood.

Caroline Lennox

When Charles Lennox died in 1750, Sarah Cadogan moved with her unmarried children to the Fox household in London. She did not long survive her husband, dying in 1751. Her orphaned daughters Louisa, Sarah, and Cecilia were then taken to Ireland to live with their older sister Emily, as their mother's will stipulated, until they were old enough to marry (about age 15 in the late 18th century). Although they spent some time each year in Dublin, most of the time Emily kept her younger sisters at Carton, the earl's magnificent country manor in County Kildare.

Lady Emily was the most intellectual of the Lennox sisters. She read widely and had strong interests in British politics, philosophy, and theology. She was particularly drawn to the new Enlightenment philosophies of such writers as Jean-Jacques Rousseau; one source claims that she unsuccessfully invited Rousseau to educate her children according to his new theories. However, her accomplishments fell short of her ideals, as she did not provide an outstanding education to her children or younger sisters. The Lennox girls were not educated beyond the usual accomplishments thought necessary for aristocratic women—reading, writing, music, and embroidery, along with religious instruction—and much of their time was spent on adult amusements like hunting, riding, concerts, operas, and formal parties. As they matured, the beautiful Lennox sisters made an impression on Dublin society—tall and fair, with cheerful and outgoing personalities, they were always noticed and often written about when they appeared in public.

In 1758, Emily and her husband James arranged a marriage for 14-year-old Louisa to the Right Honorable Thomas Conolly of Castletown. Nine years her senior, Conolly was a member of Parliament and for a long time Speaker of the Irish House of Commons, with close political ties to Emily's husband James Fitzgerald. The couple moved to London briefly after the wedding, returning to the Conolly manor at Castletown in Kildare in 1759. Unlike her sisters, Louisa remained childless, although her desire for motherhood would lead her to adopt one of Sarah's infant daughters, **Emily Louisa Napier**, in 1784.

When Sarah turned 15, in accordance with the terms of her mother's will, she left for London, where she would live under the guardianship of her beloved sister Caroline and Henry Fox. There she was reacquainted with her great-uncle George II, to whom she was formally presented at court. Widely regarded in her time as the most handsome of the Lennox women, Sarah also drew the attention of the prince of Wales, the future George III, who fell in love with her. Sarah did nothing to encourage his feelings—revealing a lack of ambition for a royal position—but her guardians did everything they could to promote the marriage. George's infatuation continued after his accession as George III in 1760, but he was ultimately convinced by his advisors to marry *Charlotte of Mecklenburg-Strelitz, a German princess, for political reasons. Sarah became involved in several brief and harmless affairs over the next few years, but until 1762 no serious matches were considered, despite her many admirers.

In that year, the Foxes approved a match for her with Thomas Charles Bunbury, the wealthy young heir to the baronetcy of Bunbury and member of the House of Commons. They married in June, but their initial infatuation quickly faded; Sarah found herself neglected and bored at the Bunbury estate, Barton House in Suffolk; her husband was preoccupied with horseracing and gambling. The same year saw Caroline raised to the title of Baroness Holland by the king, a year before Henry Fox, already secretary of state and speaker of the House of Commons, was made Baron Holland. But royal favor was short-lived, and in 1765, Caroline and Henry sought to escape Henry's political enemies in Parliament by taking Sarah and Louisa to Paris. When they returned to England, Henry Fox was dismissed from his post in the royal administration, a major downturn in fortune for the Foxes.

On a second trip to Paris in 1767, Sarah became involved in a brief affair with Armand de Gontaut, duke of Lauzun. After it ended, she fell in love with a distant cousin, Lord William Gordon. Her relationship with him, which was widely gossiped about in London, led to her first pregnancy and the birth in December 1768 of Louisa Bunbury. Although Sarah's husband agreed to raise the child as his own, Sarah was not content to go back to her life as Bunbury's wife, and in 1769 she stunned her family and acquaintances by leaving her husband for Lord Gordon.

After a few months, however, Sarah and William Gordon parted for good, and Sarah and her daughter were taken in by her brother Charles Lennox, 3rd duke of Richmond. In letters to each other, her family condemned her behavior because of the dishonor she brought to the Lennox name and did not speak of her openly, yet at the same time their letters to Sarah show their love and loyalty for her. She lived in a separate house on the Richmond estate with her daughter through the 1770s, rarely appearing in public and visited only by her family. Her actions had cost Sarah the esteem of the English elite, and her prospects for regaining their respect looked dim.

The early 1770s proved a trying and sometimes tragic period for the entire family, beyond the scandal of Sarah's failed marriage. In 1773, Emily was left a widow with 12 surviving chil-

Emily Lennox

Louisa Lennox

 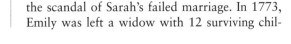

dren after the sudden death of the duke of Lein- ster. Her remarriage the next year to her chil- dren's tutor, William Ogilvie, shocked Dublin's elite, who disapproved of the daughter of a duke marrying beneath her rank. Her family was also disappointed, but, as with Sarah, they remained loyal and supportive. That summer, shortly after Emily's remarriage, the Lennoxes were saddened by the unexpected deaths of both Henry and Caroline Fox.

The next year Lord Bunbury sued for di- vorce from Sarah on the grounds of her adultery with William Gordon. After an extended divorce trial before Parliament, the king, Sarah's old suit- or George III, declared that Sarah's adulterous behavior with Gordon and others justified Bun- bury's divorce from her, and Sarah and Bunbury were both freed to remarry. By 1780, she was once again in love, this time with Colonel George Napier, a recently widowed British army hero who had fought in the American Revolutionary War. In 1781, they married and returned to Lon- don, where Sarah, age 37, re-entered high soci- ety. Although her sisters were pleased that she had re-established her good name, their brother, the duke of Richmond, strongly disapproved of her marriage to a poor ex-colonel. But it proved strong and long-lasting, although they had little money, and Sarah had eight children with her second husband. Sarah let one of her daughters, Emily Louisa Napier, born in 1783, be adopted by her sister Louisa when it became clear Louisa would not have any children of her own.

During the 1780s and 1790s, the Lennox sis- ters and their husbands divided their time be- tween Ireland, England, and Paris. Emily in par- ticular spent most of her time in Paris, then, as her health began to fail, she and Ogilvie settled in London, where Lord Conolly helped Ogilvie ob- tain a seat in Parliament. Both Sarah and Emily were rarely parted from their husbands in their last years, and occupied themselves with raising their large families. The sisters remained as close and supportive of one another in their later years as they had been as children, as their many sur- viving letters and frequent visits attest. Both Emily and Sarah found great satisfaction as moth- ers, and earned the acclaim of their contempo- raries by raising sons honored as heroes for their military achievements in the Napoleonic Wars.

Louisa shared a home in London with Sarah after the two women were widowed, Louisa in 1803 and Sarah the next year. As Emily, aging and in poor health, had already retired perma- nently to her Grosvenor Place house in London, the three sisters were reunited in their final years. With their children grown, the women passed their days in leisure by gar- dening, reading (or being read to, as Sarah and Emily both became blind), visiting family and friends, and corresponding with ac- quaintances in France and Ireland. Emily died at age 83 in 1814. Her younger sisters survived her for a number of years; Louisa died in 1821 at age 78, and Sarah died in 1826, age 81.

$\mathcal{S}$arah $\mathcal{L}$ennox

SOURCES:
Curtis, Edith R. *Lady Sarah Lennox: A Irre- pressible Stuart*. NY: Putnam, 1946.
Fitzgerald, Brian. *Emily, Duchess of Leinster: A Study of Her Life and Times*. London: Staples Press, 1949.

SUGGESTED READING:
Tillyard, Stella. *Aristocrats: Caroline, Emily, Louisa and Sarah Lennox*. NY: Farrar, Straus, 1994.

Laura York,
Riverside, California

Le Noir, Elizabeth Anne
(c. 1755–1841)

English poet and novelist. Born Elizabeth Anne Smart around 1755; died in Caversham, England, on May 6, 1841; daughter of Christopher Smart (a poet); mar- ried Jean Baptiste le Noir de la Brosse, in 1795.

Elizabeth Anne Le Noir, daughter of the poet Christopher Smart, was a novelist and poet in her own right, a favorite of *Mary Russell Mitford. Le Noir wrote *Village Annals* (1803), *Village Anecdotes* (1804), and *Miscellaneous Poems* (1825).

Lenor Telles de Menezes (c. 1350–1386).
See Leonora Telles.

Lenora.
Variant of Leonora.

Lenore of Sicily (1289–1341)

*Queen of Sicily. Name variations: Eleanor of Naples. Born in August 1289; died on August 9, 1341; daugh- ter of *Marie of Hungary (d. 1323) and Charles II,* duke of Anjou (r. 1285–1290), king of Naples (r. 1285–1309); married Frederick II (1271–1336), king of Sicily (r. 1296–1336), in May 1302; children: *Elizabeth of Sicily (d. 1349); Peter II, king of Sicily (r. 1337–1342).

Lenormand, Marie Anne Adélaïde (1772–1843)

French fortuneteller. Name variations: popularly known as La Sibylle du Faubourg Saint-Germain. Born in Alençon, France, on May 27, 1772; died in Paris on June 25, 1843.

A French fortuneteller, Marie Anne Adélaïde Lenormand became celebrated when she predicted the marriage of *Josephine de Beauharnais and Napoleon Bonaparte. Her clients included *Germaine de Staël, the great French actor Talma, and Alexander I, the tsar of Russia. Lenormand wrote a number of books on subjects connected with her profession.

Lenshina, Alice (1924–1978).

See Mulenga, Alice.

Lenski, Lois (1893–1974)

American illustrator and author of children's books. Born in Springfield, Ohio, on October 14, 1893; died in Tarpon Springs, Florida, on September 11, 1974; fourth of five children, three girls and two boys, of Richard Charles Lenski (a Lutheran minister) and Marietta (Young) Lenski; Ohio State University, B.S., 1915; additional study at Art Students League, New York, NY, and Westminster School of Art, London, England; married Arthur S. Covey (an artist and mural painter), in 1921 (died 1960); children: Stephen; (stepchildren) Margaret and Laird.

Awards, honors: Litt.D., Wartburg College (1959); L.H.D., University of North Carolina at Greensboro (1962); Ohioana Medal for Bayou Suzette (1944); John Newbery Medal for most distinguished contribution to literature for American children, for Strawberry Girl (1946); Child Study Association of America Children's Book Award for Judy's Journey (1947); D.Litt., Capital University (1966), Southwestern College (1968); University of Southern Mississippi Special Children's Collection Medallion (1969); Catholic Library Association, Regina Medal (1969), for her lifetime work in the field of children's literature.

Selected writings—for children, all self-illustrated, except as noted: Skipping Village (Stokes, 1927);

Alphabet People (Harper, 1928); A Little Girl of Nineteen Hundred (Stokes, 1928); Two Brothers and Their Animal Friends (Stokes, 1929); The Wonder City: A Picture Book of New York (Coward, 1929); Two Brothers and Their Baby Sister (Stokes, 1930); The Washington Picture Book (Coward, 1930); Spinach Boy (Stokes, 1930); Benny and His Penny (Knopf, 1931); Grandmother Tippytoe (Stokes, 1931); Arabella and Her Aunts (Stokes, 1932); Johnny Goes to the Fair (Minton, Balch, 1932); The Little Family (Doubleday, 1932); Gooseberry Garden (Harper, 1934); The Little Auto (Oxford University Press, 1934, also published as The Baby Car, 1937); Surprise for Mother (Stokes, 1934); Little Baby Ann (Oxford University Press, 1935); Sugarplum House (Harper, 1935); The Easter Rabbit's Parade (Oxford University Press, 1936); Phebe Fairchild: Her Book (Stokes, 1936); A-Going to the Westward (Stokes, 1937); The Little Sail Boat (Oxford University Press, 1937); Bound Girl of Cobble Hill (Lippincott, 1938); The Little Airplane (Oxford University Press, 1938); Oceanborn Mary (Stokes, 1939); Susie Mariar (Oxford University Press, 1939); Blueberry Corners (Stokes, 1940); The Little Train (Oxford University Press, 1940); Animals for Me (Oxford University Press, 1941); Indian Captive: The Story of *Mary Jemison (Stokes, 1941); The Little Farm (Oxford University Press, 1942); Bayou Suzette (Stokes, 1943); Davy's Day (Oxford University Press, 1943); Forgetful Tommy (Greenacres Press, 1943); Puritan Adventure (Lippincott, 1944); Spring Is Here (Oxford University Press, 1945); Strawberry Girl (Lippincott, 1946); The Little Fire Engine (Oxford University Press, 1946); Judy's Journey (Lippincott, 1947); A Surprise for Davy (Oxford University Press, 1947); Boom Town Boy (Lippincott, 1948); Mr. and Mrs. Noah (Crowell, 1948); Cotton in My Sack (Lippincott, 1949); Cowboy Small (Oxford University Press, 1949); I Like Winter (Oxford University Press, 1950); Texas Tomboy (Lippincott, 1950); Papa Small (Oxford University Press, 1951); Prairie School (Lippincott, 1951); Peanuts for Billy Ben (Lippincott, 1952); (with Clyde R. Bulla) We Are Thy Children (Crowell, 1952); We Live in the South (Lippincott, 1952); Mama Hattie's Girl (Lippincott, 1953); On a Summer Day (Oxford University Press, 1953); Corn-Farm Boy (Lippincott, 1954); Project Boy (Lippincott, 1954); (with Bulla) Songs of Mr. Small (Oxford University Press, 1954); We Live in the City (Lippincott, 1954); (with Bulla) A Dog Came to School (Oxford University Press, 1955); San Francisco Boy (Lippincott, 1955); Berries in the Scoop (Lippincott, 1956); Big Little Davy (Oxford University Press, 1956); Flood Friday (Lippincott, 1956); (with Bulla) Songs of the City *(E.B. Marks, 1956)*; We Live by the River *(Lippincott, 1956)*; Davy and His Dog *(Oxford University Press, 1957)*; Houseboat Girl *(Lippincott, 1957)*; *(with Bulla)* Little Sioux Girl *(Lippincott, 1958)*; Coal Camp Girl *(Lippincott, 1959)*; We Live in the Country *(Lippincott, 1960)*; *(with Bulla)* When I Grow Up *(Walck, 1960)*; Davy Goes Places *(Walck, 1961)*; Policeman Small *(Walck, 1962)*; We Live in the Southwest *(Lippincott, 1962)*; Shoo-Fly Girl *(Lippincott, 1963)*; The Life I Live: Collected Poems *(Walck, 1965)*; We Live in the North *(Lippincott, 1965)*; High Rise Secret *(Lippincott, 1966)*; Debbie and Her Grandma *(Walck, 1967)*; Deer Valley Girl *(Lippincott, 1968)*; Adventures in Understanding *(adult, Friends of Florida State University Library, 1968)*; Lois Lenski's Christmas Stories *(Lippincott, 1968)*; Debbie and Her Family *(Walck, 1969)*; Debbie Herself *(Walck, 1969)*; Debbie and Her Dolls *(Walck, 1970)*; Debbie Goes to Nursery School *(Walck, 1970)*; City Poems *(Walck, 1971)*; Debbie and Her Pets *(Walck, 1971)*; Florida, My Florida: Poems *(adult, Florida State University Press, 1971)*; Journey into Childhood: Autobiography of Lois Lenski *(adult, Lippincott, 1972)*.

Illustrator: Kenneth Grahame, The Golden Age *(John Lane, 1921)*; *Vera B. Birch*, The Green-Faced Toad *(John Lane, 1921)*; *Grahame*, Dream Days *(John Lane, 1922)*; *Padraic Colum*, The Peep-Show Man *(Macmillan, 1924)*; *Veronica S. Hutchinson, ed.*, Chimney Corner Stories *(Putnam, 1925)*; *Henry Drummond*, The Monkey Who Would Not Kill *(Dodd, 1925)*; *Caroline D. Emerson*, A Merry-Go-Round of Modern Tales *(Dutton, 1927)*; *May Lamberton Becker, ed.*, Golden Tales of Our America *(Dodd, 1929)*; *Emerson*, The Hat-Tub Tale; or, The Shores of the Bay of Fundy *(Dutton, 1928)*; Sing a Song of Sixpence *(Harper, 1930)*; *Hugh Lofting*, The Twilight of Magic *(Stokes, 1930)*; *Watty Piper, ed.*, Mother Goose Rhymes *(Platt, 1931)*; *Piper, ed.*, Jolly Rhymes of Mother Goose *(Platt, 1932)*; *Phil Stong*, Edgar, the 7:58 *(Farrar, Straus, 1938)*; **Dorothy Thompson*, Once on a Christmas *(Oxford University Press, 1938)*; *Maud Hart Lovelace*, Betsy-Tacy *(Crowell, 1940)*; *Cornelia Meigs*, Mother Makes Christmas *(Grossett, 1940)*; *Lovelace*, Betsy-Tacy and Tib *(Crowell, 1941)*; *Lovelace*, Betsy and Tacy Go Over the Big Hill *(Crowell, 1942)*; *Lena Barksdale*, The First Thanksgiving *(Knopf, 1942)*; *Lovelace*, Betsy and Tacy Go Downtown *(Crowell, 1943)*; *Clara Ingram Judson*, They Came from France *(Houghton, 1943)*; *Piper*, The Little Engine That Could *(Platt, 1945)*; *Mary Graham Bonner*, The Surprise Place *(Ryerson Press, 1945)*; *C.R. Bulla*, The Donkey Cart *(Crowell, 1946)*; *Alan Chaffee, adaptor*, Pinocchio *(Random House, 1946)*.

Born in 1893 in Springfield, Ohio, Lois Lenski grew up in the small town of Anna, Ohio, where her family moved when she was six. She later recalled it as a delightful horse-and-buggy town of a bygone era, the perfect place to spend a childhood. Her mother and father instilled in her a strong work ethic and a respect for knowledge. "My parents had a strong positive attitude toward learning and education," she said. "The most important thing was to learn, work hard and learn, read books, study . . . there is so much to learn."

As a small child, Lenski adored sewing and aspired to be a dressmaker. By third grade, however, she had discovered her talent for drawing and changed direction. Most of her early work was copied or traced from magazine covers and catalogues; she did not tackle original art until college. Along with her sketching, Lenski began reading voraciously, particularly Dickens, who inspired much of her own later writing. At Ohio State, she majored in education but took her electives in art, including courses in design, let-

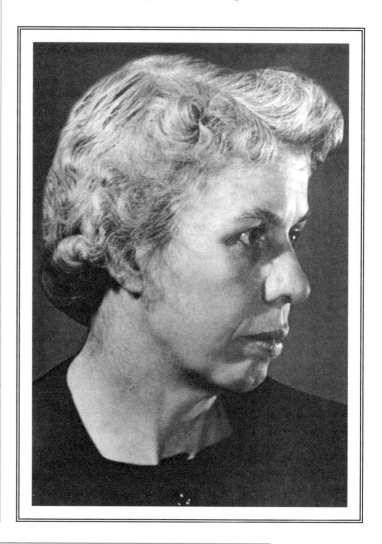

Lois Lenski

tering, and drafting. After college, she went to New York, where she attended the Art Students League and concentrated on the creative aspects of her training. Lenski also frequented the free night art class held at the School of Industrial Art, taking an illustration class taught by artist and mural painter Arthur Covey. There, she began illustrating stories and poems of her own choosing. Gradually, she amassed a portfolio—mostly drawings of children and children's activities—and began making the rounds of publishers. Her first professional illustrations were for the *Children's Frieze Book*, a paperback coloring book of nursery-rhyme figures, with a landscape background that was intended to be cut out and mounted in a continuous frieze. Lenski also continued to work on book ideas, the first manuscript of which she burned in frustration.

In 1921, following a year at London's Westminster School of Art, Lenski returned to New York and married Arthur Covey, who brought to the union his two children, Margaret and Laird, from a previous marriage. (The couple would later have another child, Stephen.) Lenski found marriage and mothering an exhausting job that sapped the strength she had once devoted to her work. She eventually learned to make time for herself, although it meant giving up her beloved gardening and doing the housework at night. Still searching for direction, she began to keep a sketchbook with her at all times, in which she soon recorded words and feelings as well as drawings. Then she kept a notebook along with her sketchbook, and thus an author was born. Her first books were nursery rhymes, verse, and little stories for young children.

From her studio on the 113-acre farm the family purchased in 1929, Lenski turned out a steady stream of books over the next several decades. "Although the years were lonely ones," she wrote, "as I worked alone, having no contacts at all with other writers, yet I was reaching my hand out and touching the lives of hundreds of thousands of children." For a number of years, Lenski focused on the past, creating historical books for older children. During the 1940s, however, she made several trips into the South, which led to a series of regional books about children from Louisiana (*Bayou Suzette*), Florida (*Strawberry Girl*), and the North Carolina mountains (*Blue Ridge Billy*). In 1946, she received the Newbery Medal for *Strawberry Girl,* and although she was grateful that the book had been singled out for honor, she felt that it represented only a small part of what she was attempting to accomplish with the series. "It is my hope," she explained at the time, "that young

people reading my regional books, will share the life of these people as I shared it, and living it vicariously, through the means of a vivid, dramatic, authentic, real-life story, will learn something of tolerance toward people different from themselves."

Lois Lenski was the recipient of numerous awards throughout her career, including the Regina Medal (1969) for her lifetime work in the field of children's literature. Lenski died in 1974, at age 80, in Tarpon Springs, Florida.

SOURCES:
Commire, Anne, ed. *Something about the Author.* Vol. 26. Detroit, MI: Gale Research.

Barbara Morgan,
Melrose, Massachusetts

Lentz, Irene (1901–1962).

See Irene.

Lenya, Lotte (1898–1981)

Austrian-born actress and singer who originated the role of Jenny in the Kurt Weill-Bertolt Brecht musical, The Threepenny Opera. *Name variations: Lotte Lenja. Born Karoline Wilhelmine Charlotte Blamauer on October 18, 1898, in Vienna, Austria; died on November 27, 1981, in New York; daughter of Franz Blamauer and Johanna Blamauer; married Kurt Julian Weill (a composer), on January 28, 1926 (died April 3, 1950); married George Davis (a magazine editor and journalist), on July 7, 1953 (died November 25, 1957); married Russell Detwiler, in 1962 (died 1969); married Richard Siemanowski, in 1971 (divorced 1973); children: none.*

Films: Die Dreigroschenoper *(The Threepenny Opera, German, 1931);* The Roman Spring of Mrs. Stone *(1961);* From Russia with Love *(1963);* The Appointment *(1969);* Semi-Tough *(1977).*

In the opening-night audience at a much anticipated 1977 revival of the Kurt Weill-Bertolt Brecht musical *The Threepenny Opera* at New York's Lincoln Center, a thin, elderly woman, her strong features accentuated by a bright red smudge of lipstick on her wide mouth, observed the performance with great concentration. When the curtain fell, she modestly declined to render her opinion of the performance to admirers who gathered eagerly around her; but the next day, she wrote her decidedly unfavorable views down for a friend, the theater critic John Simon. "I know the text fairly well; three quarters of the singers I could not understand," she complained to him. "They all sounded like they had hot potatoes in their mouths." Her familiarity with the text was surely understated, for Lotte Lenya had appeared in the original German production of *The Threepenny Opera* (*Die Dreigroschenoper*) in 1928, as well as in the 1931 film version and in a 1953 production of the show in New York. On several occasions, she had recorded selections from the score, and she was the executor of Kurt Weill's estate, having been married to him not once, but twice. Lenya had been the chief proponent of Weill's talent after the two of them arrived in New York in the 1930s and had overseen scores of productions of his works after his death 20 years later, all the while pursuing her own career on the musical stage and on film. "She was not only the keeper of her husband's flame," Simon wrote after her death, "she was also . . . an inextinguishable flame herself." Even more remarkable, Lotte Lenya managed to establish her own reputation while living much of her life in the shadow of far more visible men.

The first of these was her father Franz Blamauer, who was driving a delivery wagon for a florist in turn-of-the-century Vienna when his second daughter, Karoline, was born on October 18, 1898. The first child born to Franz and **Johanna Blamauer**, a laundress, had also been named Karoline, and had been the delight of her father, who lovingly nicknamed her "Linnerl," the Viennese diminutive for Karoline. Franz took great pride in his daughter's talent for singing and dancing, and was devastated by her death before her third birthday of a childhood illness. His grief was not eased by the birth of a son, named after himself, shortly afterward. By the time the second Karoline arrived, Franz had taken to drinking and beating Johanna, behavior which he came to focus increasingly on this new Karoline, who was nothing at all like his beloved first daughter, physically or temperamentally. "For me," Lenya wrote many years later, "the second Linnerl who looked so different and only reminded him of his dead beloved, he had only a maniacal hatred." Franz almost never turned his anger or his fists against his son or two other children, Maria and Maximillian, born before 1906, but singled out Lotte to drag from her bed in the family's two-room flat when he returned home after a night's drinking. Lenya always remembered her mother as her source of protection and support. It was Johanna who, noticing that Lotte did well in her studies, made sure she was enrolled in classes for gifted children at a school near the family's flat in Vienna's Hitzig district, at which Lotte later claimed she acquired her first appreciation for the arts and music.

The future Lotte Lenya made her first public appearance in what was billed as a circus but was actually little more than a dusty circle surrounded by a few bench seats set up in a field near her home to entertain passersby. This "circus" was run by a couple who had befriended Lenya as she passed to and from school each day. Asked to replace their ailing daughter, Lotte was fitted out with a peasant's costume and tambourine, dancing and singing for an audience which included her father. It was one of the few times Franz expressed pride in his daughter's abilities.

By 1912, when she was 13, Lenya left school and her abusive home environment for a life on the streets, where she joined the ranks of the "sweet young things"—Vienna's euphemism for child prostitutes. In later life, Lenya never tried to hide this period of her childhood and referred to it matter-of-factly as one of the few ways a poor girl could find a warm bed and a meal away from a tortuous home life. Although Lenya was not an especially attractive child, with mousy hair, pale skin, and a wide mouth further marred by an overbite, Johanna was not surprised at her daughter's activities, having commented on her sensuality at an early age by predicting that men would like her. Franz may have also known of his daughter's attractions, for when she left Vienna to live with an aunt in Zurich the next year he predicted she would become a full-time prostitute. Johanna was more practical. "Be smart, Linnerl," she said at the train station, "and don't come back if you can help it."

Oh, yesterday! That is the past already!
—**Lotte Lenya**

Life was more genteel in Zurich, where Lenya's Aunt Sophie kept house for a prosperous doctor. Even later, when the gentleman objected to having his peace disturbed by a gangly, noisy teenager and Lenya moved in with a friend's family nearby, her life was far more comfortable than in Vienna. It was in Zurich that she took her first formal dance classes, discovering that while ballet might not suit her, other talents lay waiting. "My body, feet, face, entire nature were against . . . the attitude of formal ballet," Lenya once said. "Instinctively, I seized instead on pantomime, improvisation, free movement, to give a sense of character. And in these I found myself." Her dance teacher came to the same conclusion and found her a walk-on role as a flower girl in a production of Glück's opera *Orfeo* at Zurich's Stadttheater during Christmas of 1913. By the outbreak of World War I, in August of 1914, Lenya had convinced the theater to give her a permanent contract and the secure income it brought.

Zurich was something of a boomtown during the war, becoming a major transfer point for troops, weapons, and the money to pay for them. "I never saw a really poor Swiss in all my time there," Lenya later said. "Every second house, it seemed, was a bank." Now boasting a job and her own apartment, she enjoyed the high times just like everyone else, becoming a denizen of the city's lively nightclub circuit on the arm of one or another soldier passing through on the way to the front. "The rumors about her loose life were widespread," one of Lenya's friends remembered many years later. "The nice thing about her was that she was always in good spirits, but there was around her an atmosphere of something forbidden and, I should say, *very* interesting."

More significantly, she managed to find a place in the cast of the Stadttheater's repertory company, the Schauspielhaus, where she was taken under the wing of the second male to have a drastic influence on her life. He was Richard Révy, the theater's producer and director, who introduced her to the theater's classical roles and came up with a more sophisticated name for her, "Lenja" (to become later, in America, "Lenya"), which he said made her sound like a Russian aristocrat. Her middle name, Charlotte, was shortened to Lotte. Also with Révy's guidance, Lenya was frequently seen at Zurich's Café Voltaire, the hub of Europe's avant-garde and the birthplace of Dadaism, where she met such artistic revolutionaries as Saint-Saëns and the poet Max Jacob. Through her acquaintances from the Café Voltaire, Lenya found work as an extra in a string of theatrical productions, among them a walk-on in a 1918 presentation of Strauss' *Der Rosenkavalier*, directed by the composer himself. In 1919, with the war at an end, Révy suggested that Lenya might have better luck in Berlin which, despite Germany's defeat, was an even more tempestuous center than Zurich for new forms of creative expression. Fully expecting to finally make a name for herself, Lenya worked up a dance routine with a friend and took it to Berlin in 1921.

With the social and political upheavals of Weimar Germany and Adolf Hitler's nascent National Socialist Party as a backdrop, Lenya spent a year looking for work after her friend gave up the effort and returned to Zurich. She survived by hocking pieces of jewelry that had been given to her by one of her Swiss lovers, allowing her to indulge in the freewheeling atmosphere of Berlin's cabarets and nightclubs, where anything and anyone could be had for a price. It was during these years that she refined the techniques that would mark her later stage presence—the half-talking, half-singing vocal style popular at the time, perfect for a voice which even Lenya admitted was "an octave below laryngitis," and the slinky, sinuous movements that showed her long legs off to best advantage. It was probably during this period, too, in the midst of Weimar Berlin's lively homosexual community, that Lenya began to fully express her bisexuality by taking a number of female partners. "She had tremendous sex appeal," one of her friends from the Berlin days once noted, "which is amazing since she also had none of the usual physical attributes we think of as attractive. But it was her charm, and although she didn't look sexy, she apparently just exuded sex—plain, raw sex."

Her only work during the period was an appearance as the wise-cracking maid Maria in a 1922 production of Shakespeare's *Twelfth Night*, her first speaking role and the first time she appeared on a program under the name Lotte Lenja. After two more years without work, Lenya was hired by German playwright George Kaiser, whom she had met in Zurich when Révy staged one of Kaiser's popular expressionist plays. Kaiser, known for his support of struggling young actors, now took Lenya to his country home, Grünheide, outside Berlin, to work as an *au pair* for his two children. One day Kaiser sent her off in a rowboat across Grünheide's lake to meet a young composer at the train station with whom he was developing an opera. Thus it was that Lenya met Kurt Weill, the man who would shape the rest of her creative life.

Weill, Jewish and the son of a cantor, was two years younger than Lenya but was already making a name for himself as a composer of considerable talent. He had been writing music since childhood and, at 17, had been an accompanist for the opera company in his hometown of Dessau, near Leipzig. By the time he met Lenya in 1924, he had been a conductor for various small orchestras around Germany and was studying music in Berlin while earning a living as a piano teacher and by playing evenings at beer gardens and music halls. The two had actually met two years before, when Lenya had auditioned for a pantomime Weill had written, although she had only heard his voice from the darkness of the pit. Lenya claimed for some years after their second meeting that Weill had proposed to her as she rowed him across the lake to Grünheide, it being a case of love at first sight. Many years later, however, she admitted it was nothing of the sort and, when pressed, would say that while her respect and devotion for Weill were deep and abiding, she had been incapable of loving any of her men, Weill included. "If you talk about love," she said, "that takes a little time." Nonetheless, Lenya visited Weill frequently in Berlin, spending weekends with him attending concerts or the theater. Through him, she met such musical luminaries as Otto Klemperer, Bruno Walter, Serge Koussevitzky, and Maurice Ravel, and attended the premieres of three of Weill's works performed by the Berlin Philharmonic under the baton of Erich Furtwängler. Their affair, at least as measured by their correspondence at the time, became increasingly passionate. "You need a human being who belongs to you," Weill wrote to her in 1925. "This someone has to be me! How will you answer?" The answer was yes. The two were married in a civil ceremony in Berlin on January 28, 1926.

The marriage came at a propitious time, for shortly afterward Weill met Bertolt Brecht, that bombastic, pugnacious exponent of theater as a vehicle for political and social criticism. Weill had been impressed by Brecht's radio play, *Man on Man,* while Brecht had heard several of Weill's compositions and thought of the young composer as a librettist for a work he had been commissioned to write for the 1927 summer festival at Baden-Baden. This first collaboration was *Mahagonny Songspiel,* based on five of Brecht's poems about a utopian society run amok. The "little Mahagonny," as it is sometimes called, would be the predecessor of Weill's and Brecht's full-length opera, *Aufsteig und Fall der Stadt Mahagonny* (*The Rise and Fall of the City of Mahagonny*), to be presented in Berlin three years after the *Songspiel.* Weill arranged for Lenya to audition for Brecht as work on the *Songspiel* progressed, and Brecht was sufficiently impressed to give her the role of Jessie, one of two blowsy women who accompany the work's two heroes to establish the new utopia. Although reviews from Baden-Baden were mixed, those for Lenya were distinctly positive, especially for her commanding stage presence during Jessie's "The Alabama Song." (Brecht and Weill borrowed freely from American musical forms and legend, although the settings of their productions were geographically vague.)

Lotte Lenya

Finding their work together congenial, Weill and Brecht collaborated next on the work for which they are chiefly known, *Die Dreigroschenoper* (*The Threepenny Opera*), a name chosen because of the show's small budget. Based on John Gay's 18th-century social satire, *The Beggar's Opera*, Weill and Brecht told their tale of Victorian gangland warfare through a mixture of song, spoken dialogue, and musical interludes. Lenya was cast as the prostitute Jenny, who guides the enraged J.J. Peachum to the brothel where his daughter has been hidden by her lover, MacHeath—nicknamed in the show "Mackie Messer" and "Mack the Knife." The production was directed by Brecht himself. The opening-night audience was at first uncertain of the work's unusual structure, but by the end of the evening, a standing ovation rang through the theater and reviewers especially mentioned Lenya for her mesmerizing presence. The show became such a hit that it was soon being mounted all over Germany and was made into a film by G.W. Pabst, giving Lenya even wider exposure. Brecht was impressed enough with her stage talents that he recommended her for a production of the Oedipus cycle which he produced and saw that she was cast in a play written by his then-lover *Marieluise Fleisser. "Lotte Lenja appeared fresh, clear and highly dramatic," wrote one critic of her work in *The Pioneers of Ingolstadt*, "and she acted with magnificent vitality." Another noted that "a whole world is visible in the way she moves."

The premier of *The Rise and Fall of the City of Mahagonny* in Leipzig on March 9, 1930, literally brought the house down, in a flurry of fistfights and shouting. Hitler's National Socialists were suspicious of the opera, interpreting its message of false hope in a promised utopia as a direct slap at their own party platform of a bright future for a purely "Aryan" Germany. The Nazis made sure they were well-represented that opening night, and Lenya recalled years later the mounting tension, "something strange and ugly," that spread throughout the house as the show progressed. The fighting had spread onto the stage by the time the police arrived to clear the theater. The Nazis disrupted performances of the work all over Germany in similar fashion. Hitler's election as chancellor in January of 1933 and the resulting Nazi control of the Reichstag meant that government reprisals against the Jewish Weill and the Marxist Brecht would assume more menacing forms than fistfights. Both men fled to Paris in March of that year.

Lenya often entertained friends years later with exciting tales of midnight border crossings and fake identity papers, but the truth was that, at the time Weill decamped to Paris with his current mistress **Erika Neher**, she was in the south of France enjoying a passionate holiday with another of her own lovers, an Italian opera tenor. ("But I *don't* cheat on Kurt," she once insisted. "He knows *exactly* what's going on.") The two were reunited in Paris while Lenya appeared in a ballet for which Weill and Brecht had composed the scenario, *The Seven Deadly Sins*, choreographed by George Balanchine. Lenya had conveniently stopped in Berlin on her way to Paris to close out Weill's bank accounts and bring a few of his personal possessions. The ballet was not well received, although the American composer Virgil Thomson thought that Lenya was "beautiful in a new way, a way that nobody has vulgarized so far." After the ballet's rapid demise, Lenya and Weill divorced. Weill remained in Paris while Lenya returned to her opera tenor, with whom she spent much time gambling in Monte Carlo. But their letter-writing never stopped, Lenya at one point inquiring, "Could you find me a nice American who would marry me right away for an American passport?" In 1935, deciding that she could not live apart from Weill, Lenya rejoined him in Paris and later sailed with him for New York, where Weill had a commitment for a production of his epic *The Eternal Road*, drawn from stories of the Old Testament.

Weill arrived in New York amid great fanfare, while Lenya, known only to a few American artists who had visited in Europe, was forced to spend much of her time in his considerable shadow. Settled in style at the St. Moritz, overlooking Central Park, Lenya worked on improving her imperfect English. She also became an American citizen, thanks to a forgiving judge who chose to ignore her notion that Abraham Lincoln was the first president of the United States. "I'm lucky he asked me that one," Lenya said later with complete seriousness. "If he'd asked me anything else about the Presidents, I'd have answered wrong."

It was because of Weill that she was given her first New York appearance at Town Hall, in *An American Evening in Honor of Kurt Weill*, for which she was billed as "Madame Lotte Lenja, Chanteuse"; and it was through Weill that she became friends with the Gershwins, Moss Hart, Maxwell Anderson, and other geniuses of the American stage. Her first American dramatic role was in the Broadway production of Weill's *Eternal Road*, a massive, four-hour epic with a three-story set and a huge cast which premiered in 1936. She played *Miriam the

Prophet, Moses' sister, but was lost in the panoply and received only one passing mention in the trade press for her efforts.

Meanwhile, Lenya and Weill had decided to rejuvenate their marriage, which by now both accepted in the nature of a deep friendship. Lenya owed much of her artistic life to him, just as Weill considered her his muse. "My melodies always come to my inner ear in Lenya's voice," he once said. They were married for the second time early in 1937 in a civil ceremony in Westchester County, moving into a duplex apartment on East 62nd Street which they purchased with proceeds from Weill's work on the scores of several Hollywood films. But as Weill's first American collaboration, with Maxwell Anderson, produced the musical *Knickerbocker Holiday* in 1938 (featuring Weill's memorable "September Song"), Lenya was still looking for work. With features some described as "equine," and her heavily accented, husky voice, she was not easy to cast. It wasn't until 1940 that Lenya finally landed a singing engagement at Le Ruban Bleu, a New York nightclub that specialized in European talent, where she inevitably sang a selection of Weill's songs and introduced a new one he had written for the occasion, "The Right Guy for Me." The appearance marked the beginning of her career in America as an artist in her own right, audiences being particularly impressed with the stage presence and smoky sensuality that had served her so well in Europe.

With the proceeds from the sale of the film rights to *Lady in the Dark,* the 1941 musical Weill had written with Moss Hart, the couple bought a country home in Westchester's New City, which they called Brook House. Here, Lenya indulged in a hitherto unexpressed domesticity, shopping for antiques and decorating the place in genteel country fashion. The year 1942 brought her first important notice from American drama critics, for her work in Maxwell Anderson's *Candle in the Dark,* the story of an American actress (played by *Helen Hayes) who rescues her French lover from the concentration camps. Lenya's role was a small one, as a refugee who works as Hayes' maid, but she managed to use it to great effect. More than one reviewer noted that she nearly stole the show from Hayes. "To come upon such an actress is an unexpected bonus," enthused one critic. While Lenya toured with the show during 1942, Weill wrote a part especially for her in his *Much Ado about Love,* a story set in Renaissance Florence based on the life of Benuto Cellini. The show, unfortunately, was in trouble as soon as it opened in tryouts, Lenya's performance as a duchess being especial-ly criticized. Even George S. Kaufman, called in for emergency surgery, was unable to rescue the musical, renamed *Firebrand of Florence* when it opened on Broadway in 1944, only to close after a few weeks.

After working at a feverish pitch ever since their arrival in America, and ignoring his doctor's warnings about high blood pressure, Weill collapsed from a heart attack early in 1950 and never fully recovered. Lenya was at his bedside when he died on April 3. She had never imagined life without the quiet, dignified man she may not have loved, but to whom she had given the tenderness and respect due a best friend. "As he died, I looked at him and asked myself, did I ever really know him?" she said. For three years after his death, she virtually disappeared from the stage. Those who saw her during the period were struck by the change in her usual good spirits. "It wasn't merely her appearance," noted George Davis, a magazine editor and journalist whom Lenya had met nearly 20 years before. "Her face was veiled by apathy. Here was a person who had lost interest in everything. She had abdicated from life."

It was Davis who, a year later, convinced Lenya to come out of seclusion to appear in a recital version of *The Threepenny Opera* at Town Hall; it was Davis who helped her with the mass of legal issues facing her as the executor of Weill's estate and archives, and who prevailed on her to begin recording her memoirs of her years with the composer; and it was Davis whom Lenya married in New York on July 7, 1953. "George married me out of friendship," she later said, "so I wouldn't be alone. It was a gesture of kindness because I was so lost." Shortly afterward, with great trepidation, she agreed to appear in a fully staged version of *The Threepenny Opera* at the Theater de Lys (now the *Lucille Lortel Theater) on Christopher Street in Greenwich Village. Fearing that no one would travel so far downtown, still stung by the negative reviews she had received for *Firebrand of Florence,* and terrified at the responsibility of appearing in the first full production of Weill's and Brecht's work in America, Lenya paced nervously up and down an alleyway outside the theater as the seats inside began to fill on opening night, March 10, 1954—26 years after she had played Jenny in the original German production. She needn't have worried, for the audience response and the reviews the next morning were full of praise for the production in general and her work in particular. "Lotte Lenya helps to tell the story without making a personal incident out of her presence in it," wrote Brooks Atkinson in

The New York Times, in admiration of her seamless work with the rest of the cast to give Weill's score—particularly "Mack the Knife" and her rendition of "Pirate Jenny"—a new audience. The production ran for a record 2,700 performances, grossing more than $3 million for its investors.

In the midst of professional success, however, Lenya's marriage was in trouble. Although she had been fully aware and accepting of George Davis' homosexuality, Lenya had not been prepared for his predilection for young men who often beat and robbed him; and Davis' alcoholism, of which she had also been aware, worsened to the point where he could no longer write or work. While on a trip to Germany in 1957 to record the score of *Threepenny* (on a previous trip in 1955, Lenya had been reunited with Brecht for the first time in nearly 20 years), Davis was hospitalized and died of alcohol-related illness.

Lenya spent the next three years recording more of Weill's music for American and European labels, performed in a New York City Ballet revival of *The Seven Deadly Sins,* and appeared in her first film in nearly 30 years, 1961's *The Roman Spring of Mrs. Stone,* based on the Tennessee Williams story. She portrayed the manipulative Contessa, the madam of a ring of male prostitutes who preys on the loneliness of the newly widowed Mrs. Stone, played by *Vivien Leigh (Leigh's last film appearance). "I loved doing it," Lenya told the press after shooting was completed. "So wicked and stark and old, this Contessa. But she was not all that vicious. She split fifty/fifty with her callboys. That's not bad for an agent." Her work in the picture won her a nomination for Best Supporting Actress (which went to *Rita Moreno for *West Side Story*).

Lenya's newfound movie fame no doubt brought the crowds back to the Theater de Lys later in 1961, where she opened in *Brecht on Brecht,* reading selections from Brecht's poetry and dramatic writings, as well as singing several of her favorite songs from *Threepenny.* In the audience one night was a young artist named Russell Detwiler, in whose company Lenya was seen for much of 1962, culminating in her announcement that they had been married in November of that year. She was 63 at the time; Detwiler was 37. Detwiler, like Davis before him, was gay and an alcoholic, although the results of his drinking were even more disastrous than Davis'. He often went on angry rampages, smashing the artwork Lenya had begun collecting under Davis' guidance and attacking a new

car Lenya had given him with a baseball bat. "I've married a child," she tried to explain to her friends, "and the result I've brought on myself." Her career, however, flourished.

She gave a small but memorable performance as the murderous Rosa Klebb in the 1963 James Bond film, *From Russia With Love,* in which she famously attacked Sean Connery with sensible shoes that sprouted lethal daggers. She confessed she was never happier than when she was engaged in work that had nothing to do with Weill, for presenting his work made her, she said, "as nervous as a cat. I feel a crushing responsibility." In 1965, she returned to the European stage for a production of Brecht's anti-militarist *Mother Courage.* The following year, she secured her reputation with her performance as Frau Schnieder in John Kander and Fred Ebb's *Cabaret,* drawn from the Berlin stories of Christopher Isherwood. Joe Masteroff's book was centered around a nightclub in Weimar Berlin, not unlike the ones Lenya had herself frequented, and told the story, among others, of the landlady Schnieder's love for the Jewish grocer in her neighborhood as the Nazi war machine is beginning its ominous rumbling—events Lenya had also personally witnessed 30 years before. "The Pineapple Song," her duet with Jack Guilford's grocer, was especially memorable. "She has a voice that could sandpaper sandpaper," Harold Schonberg wrote in the *Times,* "and half the time she doesn't even attempt to sing, but she can put into a song an intensity that becomes almost terrifying." *Cabaret,* along with her appearance in the Bond film, rescued Lenya from the obscurity of a wartime legend and brought her a new, younger audience that had not even been born when she first stepped on stage in Zurich.

Throughout her newfound success, Lenya dealt as best she could with Russell Detwiler's excesses. In October of 1969, Detwiler fractured his skull and died after what had apparently been a fall caused by a narcotic seizure. Lenya claimed that despite Detwiler's behavior, she had loved him the most of all her three husbands because, she said, he was the one who needed her most.

Two years later, Lenya married her fourth, and last, husband, a documentary filmmaker named Richard Siemanowski, whom she had met when he approached her about making a film of her life with Weill. They were married in June of 1971 and, after hardly seeing each other as Lenya toured and recorded in Europe, divorced in 1973. The film was never made. Shortly after the divorce, Lenya began complaining of stomach pains but continued to accept offers of work—notably as the aggressive masseuse, Clara Pelf, in 1977's *Semi-Tough*. Later that same year, she was admitted to a New York hospital for what was said to have been a hysterectomy, but was actually an operation that revealed cancer of the bladder. The treatment was long and painful, forcing Lenya to forego public appearances, although she continued to scrutinize plans and casting for productions of Weill's and Brecht's work. (Around 1960, she had engaged in a fierce legal battle with Brecht's widow *Helen Weigel over royalties.) But the progress of the disease, which soon spread throughout her body, halted even those activities. On November 27, 1981, Lotte Lenya died at the age of 83.

Although Lenya's career had to wait until her sixth decade to blossom, it never occurred to her to complain. In one of her last interviews, two years before her death, Lenya's wry humor was still very much in evidence. "I'm not so remarkable, really," she said. "I never cared about age." Then, after a thoughtful puff from one of her ubiquitous cigarettes, she added, "I think it's better to live to eighty-one than to die beautifully at twenty-five, don't you think?"

Lotte Lenya in Brecht on Brecht, *1962.*

SOURCES:

Simon, John. "Lotte Lenya," in *The New Leader*. Vol. 72, no. 9. May 15, 1989.

Spoto, Donald. *Lenya: A Life*. Boston, MA: Little, Brown, 1989.

Symonette, Lys, and Kim H. Kowalke. *Speak Low (When You Speak Love): The Love Letters of Kurt Weill and Lotte Lenya*. Los Angeles, CA: University of California Press, 1996.

Norman Powers,
writer-producer, Chelsea Lane Productions, New York

Léo, André (1832–1900)

French novelist, journalist, and feminist who founded France's first general feminist organization. Name variations: Andre Leo; André Léo was the pen name of Léodile Béra (also given as Léonide or Léonie Béra, Léonie or Léodile Bréa; Léodile Champseix or Champceix). Pronunciation: ON-dray LAY-o. Born Léodile Béra in Lusignan (some sources cite Champagné-Saint-Hilaire) in the department of Vienne in western France in 1832; died in 1900, possibly in Paris; daughter of the wife of a retired naval officer, who was at the time a notary and justice of the peace; mother's name unknown; described as well-educated; married Grégoire Champseix or Champceix (1817–1863), in 1852; married Benoît Malon (1841–1893), in 1873; children: (first marriage) twin sons, André and Léo, and possibly a daughter.

Moved with her self-exiled family to Switzerland and married; returned to France (1860) and became a successful novelist; founded France's first general feminist organization (1866); was heavily involved in the Franco-Prussian War and the Paris Commune in relief efforts and journalism (1870–71); fled to Switzerland (1871) and wrote for socialist papers; returned to France (1880) and continued as a novelist.

Principal writings (published in Paris unless otherwise noted): Un Mariage scandaleuse *(Achille Faure, 1862, new ed. Marpon-Flammarion, 1883);* Une Vieille Fille *(1864);* Les Deux Filles de M. Plichon *(1864);* Observations d'une mère de famille à M. Duruy *(1865);* Une Divorce *(Le Siècle, 1866);* L'Idéal au village *(Hachette, 1867);* Double Histoire: Histoire d'un fait divers *(Hachette, 1868);* La Femme et les moeurs: Liberté ou monarchie? *(1869, Du Lérot, 1990);* Aline-Ali *(Librairie Internationale, 1869);* Legendes corréziennes *(1870);* La Guerre sociale: Discours prononcé au Congrès de la Paix à Lausanne 1871 *(Neufchâtel: G. Guill, 1871);* Marie *(Le Siècle, 1877);* L'Épouse du bandit *(Le Siècle, 1880);* L'Enfant des Rudères *(Le Siècle, 1881);* Grazia *(n.d.);* La Justice des choses *(1891);* Le Petit Moi *(Dreyfous, 1891);* La Famille Androit *(Duruy, 1899);* L'Éducation nouvelle *(Duruy, 1899); anticlerical pamphlet,* Coupons le cable *(n.d.).*

Translations: The American Colony in Paris in 1867 *(Boston: Loring, 1868, 1900, 1983); "Woman and Morals," partially trans. in Kate Newell Doggett,* The Agitator *(1869).*

Journalism: La Coopération *(Paris, printed in Brussels, Sept. 9, 1866–June 4, 1868);* Le Mirabeau *(Brussels, Dec. 1, 1867–May 8, 1880);* L'Égalité *(Switzerland, March 2, 13, 1869);* Le Droit des femmes *(1869);* L'Agriculteur *(1870);* La République des travailleurs *(Jan. 8–Feb. 4, 1871);* Le Rappel *(March 18–May 23, 1871);* La Commune *(1871)* La Sociale *(March 31–May 17, 1871);* Le Reveil internationale *(Geneva, Oct. 1–9, 1871);* La Révolution sociale *(Switz., Oct. 26, 1871–June 4, 1872);* L'Almanach du Peuple *(Switz., 1872, 1873); other socialist papers in Switzerland to 1880;* L'Ordre sociale *(1880, no. 6);* L'Aurore *(c. 1897–c. 1900).*

André Léo, whose given name was Léodile Béra, was born in 1832 to the wife of a retired naval officer, currently a notary public and justice of the peace, living in Lusignan (or in some sources Champagné-Saint-Hilaire) in the department of Vienne in western France. Described as "well-educated," she moved to Switzerland with her Republican family after Napoleon III's 1851 coup d'état leading to the Second Empire (1852–70). There, in 1852, she married Grégoire Champseix, a disciple of the utopian socialist Pierre Leroux (1797–1871). Champseix had fled to Lausanne in 1851 to escape a three-year sentence for trying to incite a revolt in Corrèze against the coup. He became a college professor in Lausanne, then moved to Geneva, where he administered the socialist paper *L'Espérance*. With Champseix, Léo had twin sons, André and Léo, and possibly a daughter.

When the family returned to France after the amnesty of 1860, she began to publish novels under the pen name André Léo, works much influenced by Leroux's humanitarian egalitarianism and by his good friend *George Sand. Her first, *Un Mariage scandaleuse* (1862), was a success and was followed by *Une Vieille Fille* (1864), *Les Deux Filles de M. Plichon* (1864), *Une Divorce* (1866), *Aline-Ali* (1869), and a memorial to her husband, who died, worn out by illness, in 1863, *Légendes corréziennes* (1870). Critics compared her favorably to Sand. Her novels centered on the theme of the equality of women and men caught within a social order which subjugated women in the workplace with unequal pay and in marriages all too often made unhappy because they were (in the middle and upper classes) little more than property transactions motivated by "pride and cupidity."

Léo was the principal organizer of France's first successful general feminist organization, the Society for the Claiming of the Rights of Women (1866). Early participants included *Maria Deraismes, *Louise Michel, *Paule Mink, Noémie and Élie Réclus, Maria Verdure, Eliska Vincent, Louise David, and Mme. Jules Simon. Because of the variety of views represented, the society chose to emphasize education for females equal to that of males in order to hasten legal recognition of equal rights for women. (In 1870, Deraismes and Léon Richer would break off to found the Association for the Rights of Women, and in 1881 the remnants of André Léo's organization would fuse with it to form the Society for the Amelioration of Woman's Condition and the Demand of Her Rights.) In the late 1860s, Léo's salon was a gathering place for radicals and feminists from Europe and North America. With Deraismes and Mink, in 1868 she began speaking in public (now that it was legal for women), e.g., at the Vaux-Hall, in favor of political rights for women. She also helped Deraismes and Richer found the weekly *Le Droit des Femmes* (1869), which became the longest-lived women's publication of its time. In 1869, Léo published her only "theoretical" work, *La Femme et les moeurs: Liberté ou monarchie?*, which called for absolute equality for women as the true fulfillment of liberty, in contrast to the existing male "monarchy."

The Franco-Prussian War, including the siege of Paris (Sept. 1870–Jan. 1871) and the ensuing revolt by leftist republican Paris against the National Assembly (the Paris Commune, March–May 1871), found Léo intensively engaged as a journalist and political activist. Early in the war, she, Louise Michel, and **Adèle Esquiros**, with shocking boldness, personally presented to the Paris commander, General Trochu, an open letter by the historian Jules Michelet endorsed by thousands of signatures calling for the release of several followers of Auguste Blanqui (the famous left-wing rebel) who had been condemned to death. Surprisingly, they won a stay of execution (Sept. 2). Two days later, the Empire fell and the Third Republic was proclaimed. During the ensuing siege, Léo was active in Jules Allix's Committee of Women, which tried to set up communal workshops giving women jobs and food, and in the Society for the Relief of Victims of the War, which supplied (when allowed to by antifeminist officers) ambulances and nurses to the defenders. She initially opposed the idea of women's battalions but finally supported it dur-

ing the Commune. With a crowd of women and students, she and Michel led a demonstration in favor of an attempt—a chimerical project—to send relief to besieged Strasbourg; she and Michel were arrested and questioned but soon released. She also joined the huge left-wing demonstration on January 21, 1871, protesting the surrender. During the siege and the Commune, Léo was a member of the Montmartre Vigilance Committee with Louise Michel and Paule Mink, founded a society ("La Solidarité") to aid the needy in the 17th arrondissement, and spoke on socialism to the proliferating political clubs. But whether she actually joined the Union of Women for the Defense of Paris and the Care of the Wounded, founded in April by Karl Marx's friend *Elizabeth Dmitrieff as a section of the First Workingmen's International, is a matter of debate; it is certain that she did not approve of its authoritarian methods.

It was as a journalist, however, that André Léo was most prominent. After the fall of the Empire, she, Élie Réclus, and Benoît Malon (1841–1893) founded a weekly, *La République des Travailleurs*, an organ of the International. It became a daily in February 1871, preaching liberation of the workers by the workers. She also wrote for *La Commune* and for *La Sociale* (March 31–May 17), which she founded with **Anna Jaclard**, Eugène Vermersch, and Alphonse Humbert. Léo beseeched the peasants to join with the workers and not be deceived by the lies spread about by the government about the Commune: "What Paris wants in the last resort is the land for the peasant, the tool for the worker, and work for all." She defended and promoted the role of women—an important one—in the siege and the Commune. Most strikingly, despite her soaring idealism and socialist ideology, she criticized, writes **Edith Thomas**, in "lucid and practical" articles, the Commune's Central Committee for its endless chattering about grand reforms. She maintained, justly, that the Commune first had to win over the provinces and successfully repel the government's forces before most reforms could be undertaken. Sadly for her, lucidity and practicality were not hallmarks of the great Paris uprising.

Following the bloody crushing of the Commune in late May, Léo, facing arrest, fled to Switzerland with Malon in June 1871. She was condemned in absentia along with Anna Jaclard, Elizabeth Dmitrieff, and *Marguerite Tinayre. Léo, with Paule Mink and other Communard women, attended the Fifth Congress of the League of Peace and Liberty in Lausanne that September, where she delivered a ringing defense

Jaclard, Anna. See Kovalevskaya, Sophia for sidebar.

of the Commune which the chair finally felt obliged to shut off.

Through the 1870s, she contributed to various, mostly ephemeral, socialist papers. Sympathetic toward the ideas of the anarchist Michael Bakunin, she expressed her suspicion of Marx's centralizing tendencies while nevertheless deploring the divisions in the socialists' ranks. In 1873, she may have married Malon, a father of French socialism, and the founder of "integral socialism," a non-Marxist, humanitarian variety. They returned to France in 1880 after the amnesty, where Malon founded *La Revue socialiste,* France's leading socialist paper until 1914. Léo resumed novel writing, but critics, mostly very conservative, now wrote her off as a radical revolutionary. Her last years, after Malon's untimely death from cancer in 1893—they may have been separated from 1878 on—found her ignored and unhappy. During the Dreyfus Affair in the late 1890s, she joined the staff of *L'Aurore,* but death found her in 1900 at age 68. In her will she left a sum to endow the first town in France to "try the collectivist system by purchase of a communal land, worked in common with division of the product."

André Léo remained true to the humanitarian socialist principles she first imbibed from her husband and Pierre Leroux. Marxists regarded her as an "anarchist" who was too "individual," anarchists thought her too moderate, and bourgeois critics, after 1870, shunned her as a "rabid revolutionary." There was no "category" for her, writes Thomas. Her feminism was steadfast and logically consistent. The true revolution bringing liberty for all was impossible without ending women's "slavery." "When it comes to woman," wrote Léo, "the man does not want to be logical and seems not to be able to be so" (*La Femme et les moeurs*). As a novelist, she has probably been unjustly neglected. As a journalist, she was in the front rank during the Franco-Prussian War and the Commune and was, during that crisis, the most important woman in the profession.

SOURCES:
Bellet, Roger. "André Léo, écrivain-idéologue," in *Romantisme.* Vol. 22, no. 77, 1992, pp. 61–66.

Bidelman, Patrick K. *Pariahs Stand Up! The Founding of the Liberal Feminist Movement in France, 1858–1889.* Westport, CT: Greenwood Press, 1982.

Decaux, Alain. *Histoire des françaises.* Vol. 2: *La Révolte.* Paris: Librairie Académique Perrin, 1972.

Dictionnaire biographique du mouvement ouvrier français. Sous la direction de Jean Maitron. Paris: Éditions Ouvrières, 1964—.

McMillan, James F. *Housewife or Harlot: The Place of French Women in French Society, 1870–1940.* NY: St. Martin's Press, 1981.

Moses, Claire. *French Feminism in the Nineteenth Century.* Albany: State University of New York Press, 1984.

Offen, Karen. "Léo, André," in *An Encyclopedia of Continental Women Writers.* Ed. Katherine M. Wilson. NY: Garland, 1991.

Perrier, A. "Grégoire Champseix et André Léo," in *L'Actualité de l'histoire.* Vol. 30, 1960, pp. 38–39.

Rabaut, Jean. *Histoire des feminismes français.* Paris: Stock, 1978.

Sowerwine, Charles. *Sisters or Citizens? Women and Socialism in France since 1876.* Cambridge: Cambridge University Press, 1982.

Thomas, Edith. *The Women Incendiaries.* Translated by James and Starr Atkinson. NY: George Braziller, 1966 (originally *Les Pétroleuses.* Paris: Gallimard, 1963).

SUGGESTED READING:
André Léo, un journaliste de la Commune. Aigre: le Lérot rêveur, 1987.

Edwards, Stewart. *The Paris Commune 1871.* London: Eyre & Spottiswoode, 1971.

Horne, Alistair. *The Fall of Paris: The Siege and the Commune, 1870–71.* NY: St. Martin's Press, 1965.

Lambertz, Sigrid. *Die femme de lettres im Second Empire: Juliette Adam, André Léo, Adèle Esquiros und ihr Auseinandersetzung mit dem weiblichen Rollenbild im 19 Jahrhundert.* St. Ingbert: Rohrig Universitsverlag, 1994.

Moreau, Thérèse. "Un divorce: André Léo [Léonie Béra] et la révolution bourgeoise," in *Les Femmes et la Révolution français.* Vol. 3. Toulouse: Presses universitaires du Mirail, 1991, pp. 179–184.

DOCUMENTS:
Léo, André. "Mémoires." Amsterdam: International Institute of Social History. Descaves Collection.

Paris: Archives de la Préfecture de Police, Dossier B/A 1008.

David S. Newhall,
Professor Emeritus of History, Centre College, Danville, Kentucky, and author of *Clemenceau: A Life at War* (Edwin Mellen Press, 1991)

Leoba (700–779).

See Lioba.

Leobgyth (700–779).

See Lioba.

Leocadia (d. about 303)

Spanish saint. Died around 303.

A popular Spanish saint, Leocadia lived in Toledo when Dacian, an agent of Diocletian, arrived to enforce the Roman emperor's edicts against Christianity. A Christian, Leocadia was brought before Dacian and told to disavow her faith. She refused, and he had her beaten and thrown into a dungeon. When Leocadia heard about the tortures being endured by 13- or 14-year-old *Eulalia in Mérida by the same persecutors, she prayed for God to take her from a world of such horrors. She died while in prison. Her feast day is on December 9.

Leodegundia (fl. 10th c.)

Spanish poet. Flourished in 10th century Spain.

Leodegundia was a Spanish noblewoman. Little is known about her, except that she was an accomplished writer and poet, and probably spent most her time at the royal court. Her work is identified with a popular group of painters, illuminators, and writers who flourished in Spain in the 10th century. Mozarabic in style, her work reflected that complex blend of Christian European and Eastern Arabic cultures, images, and traditions which came to define most Spanish art in the Middle Ages.

Laura York,
Riverside, California

Léon, Pauline (1758–?).

See Lacombe, Claire for sidebar.

Leon, queen of.

See Berengaria of Castile (1180–1246).

Léon and Castile, queen of.

See Sancha of Leon (1013–1067).

See Urraca (c. 1079–1126) for sidebar on Constance of Burgundy (1046–c. 1093).

See Agnes of Poitou (1052–1078).

See Urraca (c. 1079–1126).

See Bertha of Burgundy (d. 1097).

See Berengaria of Provence (1108–1149).

See Ryksa of Poland (d. 1185).

See Beatrice of Swabia (1198–1235).

See Eleanor of Castile (1241–1290) for sidebar on Joanna of Ponthieu (d. 1279).

See Yolande of Aragon (d. 1300).

See Constance of Portugal (1290–1313).

See Maria de Molina (d. 1321).

See Guzman, Leonora de for sidebar on Maria of Portugal (1313–1357).

See Blanche of Bourbon (c. 1338–1361).

See Castro, Juana de (d. 1374).

See Joanna of Castile (1339–1381).

See Eleanor of Aragon (1358–1382).

See Beatrice of Portugal (1372–after 1409).

See Catherine of Lancaster (1372–1418).

See Maria of Aragon (1403–1445).

See Eleanor of Navarre for sidebar on Blanche of Navarre (1424–1464).

See Isabel of Portugal (1428–1496).

See Joanna of Portugal (1439–1475).

See Isabella I (1451–1504).

Leonarda, Isabella (1620–1704)

Italian composer. Born into a noble family on September 6, 1620, in Novara, Italy; died in Novara in 1704; entered the Convent of Saint Ursula of Novara in 1636; studied with Gaspare Casati.

Composed two motets for two voices (1645); became Mother Superior of Saint Ursula Convent (1693); became Madre Vicaria of the convent (1693); published a book of motets (1700); over 200 of her works in 20 volumes survive.

Like many women composers of an earlier age, Isabella Leonarda was a nun, and most of her compositions were sacred vocal music. Born into nobility in 1620 in Italy, she was 16 when she began her religious vocation in the Ursuline convent in her native city of Novara. Her parents most likely chose the religious life for her. Leonarda's studies with Gaspare Casati had begun a year earlier and continued until 1641. Her first compositions, two motets for two voices, appeared in Casati's *Third Book of Sacred Concerts*. Though never known as a performer, Leonarda composed litanies, psalm settings, vespers, responses, and four masses. No doubt convent life stimulated her musical creativity, as from medieval times onwards convents were havens where talented women could express their talents freely. In the early 1690s, Leonarda composed a sonata for solo violin and organ continuo, which means she was among the first Italian women to compose in these new instrumental Baroque genres. A prolific composer, Leonarda created works that were known and admired throughout Europe.

John Haag,
Athens, Georgia

Leone, Lucile Petry (d. 1999).

See Petry, Lucile.

Leonida (1914—)

Georgian princess. Name variations: Leonida Kirby. Born Leonida Bagration-Moukhransky on September 23, 1914, in Tiflis, Georgia, Russia, into a Georgian royal family; daughter of George, prince Bagration-Mukhranski, and **Helen Sigismondovna Zlotnicka***; married Sumner Kirby, on November 6, 1934 (divorced 1937); married Vladimir Cyrillovitch (1917–1992, great-grandson of Tsar Alexander II of Russia), on August 13, 1948; children: (second marriage) Marie Vladimirovna (b. 1953).*

Leonor.

Variant of Eleanor, Ellen, Helen, or Leonora.

Leonor of Aragon (1358–1382).

See Eleanor of Aragon.

Leonor of Austria (1498–1558).

See Eleanor of Portugal.

Leonor of Castile (d. 1415).

See Joanna of Navarre for sidebar on Eleanor Trastamara.

Leonor of Navarre (1425–1479).

See Eleanor of Navarre.

Leonor of Portugal.

See Eleanor of Portugal (1328–1348).
See Eleanor of Portugal (1434–1467).
See Eleanor of Portugal (1458–1525).
See Eleanor of Portugal (1498–1558).

Leonor of Portugal (1211–1231)

Queen of Denmark. Born in 1211; died on May 28, 1231; daughter of *Urraca of Castile (c. 1186–1220) and Alfonso or Alphonso II the Fat (1185–1223), king of Portugal (r. 1211–1223); married Valdemar or Waldemar the Younger (1209–1231), king of Denmark (r. 1215–1231), on June 24, 1229; children: *Sophie Valdemarsdottir (d. 1241).

Leonor Teles de Meneses (c. 1350–1386).

See Leonora Telles.

Leonora.

Variant of Eleanora, Ellen, Helen or Leonor.

Leonora Christine (1621–1698).

See Ulfeldt, Leonora Christina.

Leonora de Guzman (1310–1351).

See Guzman, Leonora de.

Leonora d'Este (1537–1581).

See Este, Eleanor d'.

Leonora of Aragon (1405–1445)

Queen of Portugal. Name variations: Eleanor of Aragon. Born in 1405; died on February 19, 1445, in Toledo; daughter of *Eleanor of Alburquerque (1374–1435) and Ferdinand I, king of Aragon (r. 1412–1416); sister of Maria of Aragon (1403–1445, mother of Henry IV, king of Castile); married Duarte I also known as Edward I (1391–1438), king of Portugal (r. 1433–1438); children: Joao or John (1429–1433); Filippa (1430–1439, died of the plague); Afonso also known as Alphonso V

(1432–1481), king of Portugal (r. 1438–1481); Maria (1432–1432); Fernando or Ferdinand (1433–1470), duke of Viseu; Duarte (1435–1435); Caterina (1436–1463); *Joanna of Portugal (1439–1475); *Eleanor of Portugal (1434–1467, who married Frederick III, Holy Roman emperor).

Leonora of Aragon (1450–1493)

Duchess of Ferrara. Name variations: Eleanora of Aragon; Eleanora d'Este; Leonora of Naples. Born on June 22, 1450; died of a gastric infection on October 11, 1493 (some sources cite 1492); daughter of Ferdinand also known as Ferrante I, king of Naples (r. 1458–1494), and *Isabel de Clermont (d. 1465); married Ercole I d'Este, 2nd duke of Ferrara and Modena (r. 1471–1502), on June 22, 1473; children: *Isabella d'Este (1474–1539); *Beatrice d'Este (1475–1497); Alfonso I d'Este (1476–1534), 3rd duke of Ferrara and Modena, who married *Lucrezia Borgia; Ferrando (1477–1540); Ippolito I (1479–1520, cardinal); Sigismondo (1480–1524). Ercole I also had two illegitimate children: *Lucrezia d'Este (d. 1516/18) and Giulio (1478–1561).

Leonora of Savoy (fl. 1200)

Ferrarese noblewoman. Name variations: Leonora di Savoia; Leonora d'Este. Flourished around 1200; second wife of Azo also known as Azzo VI d'Este (1170–1212), first lord of Ferrara (r. 1208–1212); children: Beata Beatrice I d'Este (d. 1226). Azzo's first wife was a woman of the Aldobrandeschi (name unknown) who gave birth to Aldobrandino I d'Este (d. 1215); his third wife was Alisia of Antioch, the mother of Azzo VII Novello (d. 1264).

Leonora Telles (c. 1350–1386)

Mistress and then queen of Ferdinand I of Portugal who served as regent following his death until overthrown in the Revolution of 1383–85. Name variations: Leonora Teles de Meneses; Lenor Telles de Menezes; Eleanor Tellez de Meneses. Born Leonora Telles de Meneses in Trás os Montes around 1350; died on April 27, 1386, at Cloister Tordesillas, Valladolid; interred at Cloister Mercede, Valladolid; daughter of Martin Afonso Telles de Meneses and Aldonza de Vasconcelhos also spelled Aldonsa de Vasconcelos; married João Lourenço also known as John Lorenzo da Cunha; married Fernando also known as Ferdinand I (1345–1383), king of Portugal (r. 1367–1383), in 1372 (died on October 22, 1383); regent of Portugal, 1383–1384; children: (first mar-

riage) Alvaro da Cunha; (second marriage) Beatrice of Portugal (1372–after 1409, who married John I of Castile and Leon); Pedro (1380–1380); Alfonso (1382–1382).

Death of Peter I of Portugal (1367); murder of Peter the Cruel (Pedro the Cruel) of Castile by his half-brother, Henry II of Trastamara; marriage of Leonora's daughter Beatrice and John I of Castile (1382); Portuguese defeat Castilians at battle of Aljubarrota (1385); Portuguese cortes proclaims John I of Aviz king (1385).

Leonora Telles was born in the mid-14th century, around 1350, to an aristocratic Portuguese couple, Martin Afonso Telles de Meneses and **Aldonsa de Vasconcelos**. Her uncle was the count of Barcelos, John Alphonso Telo, a dominant figure at the court of Ferdinand I, king of Portugal. As a young woman, Leonora married a cousin and minor noble, John Lorenzo da Cunha, and a son, Alvaro da Cunha, was born to them. Meanwhile her married sister, ❧▶ **Maria Telles**, lived at court as a lady-in-waiting to the *Infanta* (princess) *Beatrice of Portugal (c. 1347–1381).

Eventually Leonora Telles left her husband and child in northeastern Portugal and went to visit her sister Maria in Lisbon. Lodged at the palace, Leonora attracted the king's amorous attention, but shrewdly did not give in to his enticements. Ferdinand I was "handsome, liberal and impetuous," and as yet unmarried, although he was engaged to a Castilian princess, Henry II's daughter ❧▶ **Eleanor Trastamara**. Eleanor was still a child and unable to wed until she reached puberty. Leonora Telles had likely not traveled to Lisbon with any inkling that she would become the object of the king's desires, although her uncle, the count of Barcelos, was ambitious to enhance his power and influence over the ruler. But neither did she flee back to her husband and child. Once the monarch's passions became clear, her uncle recognized the situation's potential. He advised his niece in an ambitious game: entice Ferdinand until he broke with his betrothed princess Eleanor Trastamara and made Leonora Telles queen.

Of course, Leonora's own marriage made her situation even more complicated, as did the opinion of the Portuguese aristocracy and people. Puzzled by Leonora's delay in Lisbon and perhaps aware of rumors about her affair with the king, her husband John Lorenzo da Cunha insisted that she return home. When she informed the king that she must depart, he avowed his love for her and his determination

❧▶ **Telles, Maria** (d. 1379)
*Duchess of Valencia. Name variations: Maria de Menezes; Maria de Telles. Murdered by her husband in 1379; daughter of Martin Afonso Telles de Meneses and Aldonza de Vasconcelos also spelled Aldonsa de Vasconcelos; older sister of *Leonora Telles (c. 1350–1386); married John (c. 1349–1397), duke of Valencia, in 1376.*

to make her his queen. Almost immediately the count of Barcelos began negotiating the annulment of his niece Leonora's marriage. John Lorenzo refused to cooperate but, fearing for his life, took refuge in Castile. With him out of the way, Barcelos and the king easily secured the desired annulment.

It was more difficult, however, to keep the scandal from arousing public ire. Dissident Portuguese nobles, envious of Barcelos' influence, complained that Ferdinand I was insulting Henry II, the king of Castile. A group of aristocrats, including Prince Denis, Ferdinand's half-brother by their father Peter I's mistress, *Ines de Castro, provoked a public protest in Lisbon. Led by a tailor named Fernão Vasques, a crowd of 3,000 in Lisbon denounced the couple's behavior. Vasques called Leonora Telles a *bruxa* (witch) and proclaimed the people ready to prevent the king's marriage to such an evil woman. To forestall violence, Ferdinand I announced that he would never marry Leonora Telles and that he would make a public proclamation the following day. Instead, the lovers snuck out of the city, fearing a riot. Never one to let an affront pass, Leonora Telles made sure that Vasques paid with his life for his temerity. By this time Leonora was probably the king's mistress; in the public mind, she certainly was. According to some accounts, they were secretly wed in late 1371, although Ferdinand was too afraid to reveal the marriage. Meanwhile, he sent an ambassador to Henry II of Castile, announcing his intention to break the engagement with the princess, Eleanor Trastamara.

With the rebels suppressed, the royal couple celebrated their wedding in Oporto in 1372. Leonora Telles quickly took care of her relatives. She raised her uncle Barcelos to count of Ourém and made his son count of Barcelos. Her brother John Alphonso Telles de Meneses became admiral of Portugal and another brother, Gonçalo Telles de Meneses, count of Neiva. Many Portuguese nobles hated the queen but

◀❧
Eleanor Trastamara. *See Joanna of Navarre for sidebar.*

kept silent. A few, such as Prince Denis, left the court. Having gained her objective, the queen "then became hypocritically docile, seeking to captivate the nobility with her generosity and kindness." In February 1372, she gave birth to a royal princess, *Beatrice of Portugal (1372–after 1409).

On the international front, her presence on the throne gave Henry II a pretext for declaring war against Ferdinand. Declaring that Ferdinand had insulted Castile by breaking off the engagement, Henry II ordered his army across the border. Dynastic rivalries between the Western European monarchies provided the real motive behind the conflict. This was the era of the Hundred Years' War between England and France, whose monarchs needed allies in the Iberian peninsula. Henry II of Castile had aligned himself with the French, and John of Gaunt, duke of Lancaster, countered by offering support to Ferdinand I in 1372. As husband of ◄ Constance of Castile (1354–1394), Peter the Cruel's daughter, John of Gaunt claimed that he and his wife were the legitimate rulers of Castile rather than the fratricidal Henry II. Juan Fernández Andeiro, a Galician knight, represented Lancaster in Portugal and quickly became an intimate of Leonora Telles, if medieval accounts are to be believed. He promised English troops to protect Ferdinand from Henry's army, but they did not arrive on schedule. Castilian forces laid siege to Lisbon. Unprepared to defend their kingdom, Ferdinand and Leonora had to sign the ignominious peace of Santarém on March 19, 1373, that required the Portuguese monarchy to ally itself with Henry II.

Constance of Castile. See Castro, Ines de for sidebar.

As soon as King [Ferdinand] had died and Queen [Leonora] had been proclaimed regent, riots broke out in many towns, including Lisbon . . . and a powerful revolutionary movement took over Lisbon, Oporto and many other towns.

—Derek Lomax and R.J. Oakley

With peace temporarily restored, Leonora apparently set out to remove the principal domestic threats to her power. Ferdinand's father, Peter I, had left three illegitimate sons by two mistresses. The aforementioned Denis, count of Villar-Dompardo, and John, duke of Valencia, were the sons of Ines de Castro, while *Teresa Lorenzo had given birth to John (I of Aviz), master of Aviz. Denis had abandoned Portugal and gone to Castile. His brother John of Valencia was

married to Leonora Telles' own sister Maria. The queen allegedly spread rumors that her sister was unfaithful to John of Valencia, meanwhile suggesting to John that he might become king of Portugal by marrying Princess Beatrice. Taking the bait, John of Valencia murdered his wife Maria, only to have the queen publicly shun him. He fled to Lisbon, freeing Queen Leonora Telles of her second main nemesis.

She then turned her ire against John of Aviz and Gonçalo Vasques de Azevedo. The latter had detected the queen's sexual affair with Andeiro, and she feared he would make it a public scandal. Leonora Telles consequently persuaded her husband, who was still "completely dominated by that woman who had bewitched him," to arrest his half-brother John of Aviz and Vasques de Azevedo. She then sent a dispatch to the castle in Evora where they were imprisoned, ordering the jailer to execute them immediately. He hesitated, however, fearful of acting without clear orders from the king. When her strategy failed, she reportedly changed tactics, petitioning for their release to make it appear that she found their arrest unreasonable.

In 1379, Henry II of Castile died, leaving John I of Castile as his successor and rekindling international intrigue. Lancaster and Andeiro secretly petitioned Ferdinand to form a new anti-Castilian alliance with the English. Andeiro's influence with Leonora Telles and her control over the king eventually led Ferdinand to break the treaty of Santarém. The war went badly for all sides; the English Parliament refused to fund the duke of Lancaster's forces, and on August 10, 1381, the Portuguese and Castilian officers secretly agreed to end hostilities. As part of the pact, Ferdinand and Leonora's daughter Beatrice was to marry the son of John I of Castile.

The next two years undid much of what Leonora Telles' ambition had managed to achieve. In July 1382, she gave birth to a son and heir to the Portuguese throne, but he lived only a few days. Beatrice thus stood to inherit, but her gender and age did not provide good security. To protect the family's interests, Leonora and Andeiro renegotiated the dynastic alliance between Castile and Portugal in the spring of 1383. John I of Castile's wife *Eleanor of Aragon (1358–1382) had died, and he agreed to marry Beatrice himself, hoping the alliance would eventually make him effective ruler of both Castile and Portugal. In May, he married her, and she departed for Spain. More disastrous for Leonora Telles was the death of King Ferdinand on October 22, 1383.

This left Portugal without a ruler, as the king's only surviving child, the 12-year-old Beatrice, was now married to John I of Castile. Fearing that one of Ines de Castro's sons might try to seize the Portuguese crown, John I of Castile ordered their arrest. He then had himself and Beatrice proclaimed monarchs of Portugal and moved his army across the border. Meanwhile, Leonora Telles had appointed herself regent and governor. Yet Portuguese nationalists resented both Spanish attempts to control their country and Leonora's foreign advisors such as Andeiro. The queen herself was very unpopular and had no real power base. With the country anxious about the impending Castilian invasion, riots broke out in Lisbon and other important cities. John of Aviz broke into the royal palace and killed Andeiro on December 6, 1383. This unleashed a wave of popular resentment against the queen, and she feared that John of Aviz would kill her also. Nonetheless, he did not intend to seize power and allowed Leonora to continue governing as regent. Thus freed from immediate danger, Leonora Telles appealed to her son-in-law John I of Castile for aid, encouraging him to seize Portugal. John I of Castile and Leonora met in Santarém, where she conferred the regency upon him. In so doing, she deprived herself of any real political influence, and left the field to the men. Some Portuguese nobles sided with John I of Castile, but most Portuguese supported John of Aviz. In 1384, the Castilian army advanced on Lisbon and laid siege to it but eventually withdrew when plague infected their camp. The following year, the Portuguese devastated John I of Castile's army at the battle of Aljubarrota. Meanwhile the Portuguese cortes (medieval assembly) offered the crown to John of Aviz, completing the Revolution of 1383–85 and establishing the Aviz dynasty on the Portuguese throne.

For a while Leonora Telles tried to cooperate with John I of Castile, but he refused to permit her any real influence at his court. Frustrated and vengeful, she apparently took one of his cousins, Pedro de Trastamara, as her lover and pressed him to assassinate the king. When the plot was discovered, John I of Castile sent Leonora to a convent in Tordesillas, where she spent the brief remainder of her life. She died on April 27, 1386, and her body was eventually interred in the cloister of the Mercedarian convent of Valladolid.

SOURCES:

Bernardino, Teresa. *A Revolução Portuguesa de 1383–1385*. Lisboa: Publicações Europa-América, 1984.

Caetano, Marcello. *A Crise Nacional de 1383–1385*. Lisboa: Verbo, 1985.

Livermore, H.V. *A New History of Portugal*. Cambridge: Cambridge University Press, 1969.

Lopes, Fernão. *As Crónicas de Fernão Lopes Seleccionadas e Transpostas em Português Moderno*. 3 ed. Lisboa: Gadiva, 1993.

———. *The English in Portugal, 1367–87 : Extracts from the Chronicles of Dom Fernando and Dom João*. Transl. by Derek W. Lomax and R.J. Oakley. Warminster, England: Aris & Phillips, 1988.

Kendall W. Brown, Professor of History, Brigham Young University, Provo, Utah

Leonowens, Anna (c. 1831–1914)

English governess to the children of the king of Siam (Thailand) during the 1860s, who brought many reforms to his kingdom, fought against the oppressiveness of polygamy and the harem system, wrote several books on harem life, and gained international renown as the principal character in The King and I.

Born either Anna Harriette Edwards on November 6, 1831, in India or Anna Harriette Crawford on November 5, 1834, in Caernarvon, Wales, depending on the account; died in 1914; daughter of either a Private Edwards or a Captain Crawford, who died in military service, and a mother who may have been Anglo-Indian; educated in England until she returned to India, at age 14; married Thomas Leon Owens, on December 25, 1849 (died May 1859); children: Selina (b. 1851) and a second child, both of whom did not survive; Avis (b. 1854); Louis (b. 1855).

Widowed (1859); traveled to Siam, where she served as governess to the children and wives of the royal family (1862–67); published The Romance of the Harem *and other books which appeared as* Siamese Harem Life *and* The Romance of Siamese Harem Life; *lectured in later years to support herself; immortalized by the publication of* Anna and the King of Siam *by Margaret Landon (1944), which became the basis for the Rodgers and Hammerstein musical and movie* The King and I.

In 19th-century England, one of the few respectable professions open to women was that of governess. A governess was required to be a woman of gentle birth, because in theory her social status was equal to her employer's. Governesses were usually hired to instruct upper-class female children, as few schools for girls existed, although sometimes they taught young boys as well. Life as a governess could be relatively easy or very difficult depending on circumstances. In some cases, the governess was a virtual member of the family; in others, she received less consideration than a servant. Women chose to become governesses for a variety of reasons, though poverty often played a role. The death of a father or a husband might alter a woman's economic status and require her to seek employment. Daughters of the clergy, of army or navy officers, or of any member of the gentry were acceptable candidates. In 1850, there were some 20,000 governesses in England. English governesses were sought after as status symbols. Throughout the world, these women educated generations of young people.

One of the most famous governesses in the British tradition was Anna Leonowens, who spent five years as teacher to the children and wives of the king of Siam (modern-day Thailand), influencing their country in its early years of exposure to the West. Her story is complex because she probably reinvented her past in order to satisfy the strict Victorian code for employment as a governess.

The reinvention began with her alleged parentage. According to Leonowens' own account, she was born in Caernarvon, Wales, on November 5, 1834, the daughter of a captain in the army named Crawford; when she was six years old, the family sailed for India, where her father died in active military service. Accounts that are probably more factual establish that she was born in India on November 6, 1831, the second daughter of a poor army sergeant named Edwards, and a mother who may have been the child of an Anglo-Indian marriage, making her own heritage racially mixed. Her father died three months after Anna was born, and her mother married another soldier, a corporal, who was soon demoted to private. Anna and her sister, Eliza, were sent to England at a very young age to be educated, and returned to India as teenagers.

Anna Leonowens

There are two distinct versions of Leonowens' teenage years as well. By her own account she met a Reverend Mr. George Percy Badger after her return to India at age 14. Since life with her mother and stepfather was uncongenial, she accepted an invitation to accompany the Badgers on a tour of the Levant. According to this version, Badger was a distin-

guished orientalist, who taught her Arabic and engaged a tutor to teach her Persian. According to the more titillating version, the 30-year-old Mr. Badger had no wife, and Anna's travels with him were unchaperoned.

Records establish that Anna married Thomas Leon Owens on Christmas Day, 1849, just after turning 18. The couple had a daughter, Selina, born in India in 1851, who seems not to have survived; a second child, possibly born in Australia, also did not live. Avis was probably born in 1854, and Louis in 1855.

Thomas Leon Owens died in May 1859 in Malaya (Malaysia), at age 32. His occupation was listed at the time as "hotel master" in Penang, one of the British straits settlements along with Singapore and Malacca. On the death certificate his name appeared as Thomas Leonowens. It is not known if the alteration was made then for the first time, but it is the form of the name that his widow adopted, and thus entered history as Anna Leonowens.

All the discrepancies described above are probably rooted in the needs of a woman suddenly thrust on her own to conform to the strictest Victorian standards of behavior. Within the hierarchy of the British class system, for instance, her opportunities as the daughter of a "Captain Crawford," a gentleman of respectable family, would be greatly increased over the daughter of a "Private Edwards." Although she was a bright, well-educated woman, the identification with lower-class origins would have kept her from the post of governess in any household, much less in the king of Siam's.

In racial terms, it was a common practice for unmarried soldiers stationed in the far reaches of the British Empire to marry local women. Around 1862, a niece of Leonowens married an Anglo-Indian, a member of the class referred to as "Coloured Englishmen," and one child of that marriage, Anna's great-nephew, William, became the famous movie star Boris Karloff. No one knows whether or not Anna Leonowens' racial heritage was mixed, but a wish to avoid prejudice may well explain why she chose Wales rather than India as her place of birth.

The alteration of other details may have been an attempt to cover up her earlier sexual indiscretions. In terms of British social acceptability, traveling with George Badger as an unmarried woman was the height of folly, and although there is no hint of scandal in Leonowens' later life, her youthful indiscretions would have prevented her from being hired in any respectable capacity, and certainly as a teacher of the young. As a widow and sole support of her two children, remolding her life for the sake of obtaining work, even the change in her name, may have been a way of wiping the slate clean. Looked at from this perspective, the alterations of her history seem practical, sensible, and in a sense courageous.

In March 1862, Anna Leonowens sailed with her son, Louis, then about seven years old, from Singapore to Bangkok on the steamer *Chao Phya*. She was slated to take a position as the governess to the children of the king of Siam, particularly Crown Prince Chulalongkorn, who was nine years old, a good age to learn English. The new governess was also charged with introducing English culture to the mothers of the princes and princesses, and to other members of the king's harem.

Siam's King Mongkut had been born in 1804, and although Europe had so far had little effect on the culture of his country, he had a personal fascination with the West. In his childhood there had been no formal provision for his succession to the throne upon his father's death, and an elder half brother had become king while Mongkut entered the Buddhist priesthood, an experience that deeply affected his perception of the world. As a sincere student of Buddhist teaching, he followed the daily practice of Buddhist priests in begging for their food, an act of humility that brought him into close contact with his people and opened his eyes to a new world. Frequent pilgrimages taught him more about his country, and in 1837 the royal monk had become abbot of a Buddhist monastery, a position he held for 14 years, until he was made king in 1851.

While a monk, Mongkut had studied English with Christian missionaries. Since no Siamese-English dictionary existed, words had to be translated from Siamese into ancient Pali and then into English, a difficult and convoluted process that may account for the king's highly original English. He studied history, geography, physics, chemistry, mathematics and astronomy, and regularly read books and newspapers in Eng-

From the movie The King and I, *starring Deborah Kerr and Yul Brynner.*

lish; he even installed a printing press, the first of its kind in Siam outside the walls of a mission.

As king, Mongkut's intention was to modernize Siam while preventing its colonization by a European power, a goal which he would achieve during his reign (1851–68). The employment of Anna Leonowens was part of his plan: her duties were cultural and intellectual but not religious. She was to teach English to the members of his harem but not convert them to Christianity. Anna was not the first Western governess in the royal harem; she had been preceded by Mrs. Mattoon, Mrs. Jones, and Mrs. Bradley, all of whom lost their positions because of their attempts to proselytize for Christianity.

Leonowens and her son were installed in Nang Harm, a small walled city of about 9,000 people, which included an enormous harem. Inside this enclosure, Nang Harm had wide avenues, graceful houses, parks, flower gardens, shops, and apartments on small crowded streets. The inhabitants were members of the nobility as well as seamstresses, gardeners, cooks and other servants. Most women and children lived there in slavery, although it should be pointed out that as much as 75% of the entire Siamese population, male as well as female, were then considered to be slaves. In terms of their culture, slavery usually meant an obligation to another individual rather than harsh servitude, and while harems in the Mideast were guarded by eunuchs or castrated males, Siamese harems were guarded by women or Amazons. In Nang Harm, the standard of living was quite high, but the harem was a golden cage, restricting the lives of its inhabitants.

The king's harem was a unique world, inaccessible to Westerners and even to most Siamese, but it also acted as a kind of glue, holding the entire country together. The harem was so large that almost everyone had a relative residing with the king. Proximity to the throne was more a matter of perception than of reality, however, since some members of the harem rarely met the king, much less gave birth to his children.

Some aspects of Leonowens' position in the harem are open to speculation; clearly, she was more than just a governess to his children. At a time when Siam was entering into many new international business agreements, she describes part of her job as helping the king with his correspondence and serving as a sounding board. Mongkut corresponded with many Western leaders, including Queen *Victoria and President Abraham Lincoln, so it is likely that he consulted Leonowens about Western attitudes and customs. Certainly the king's proximity to the European woman was unusual, and his interest in the British no doubt ensured a unique relationship, but the two were never on especially intimate terms.

Called "Mem" by her pupils, Leonowens taught 20–25 princesses and princes of royal blood. Her schoolroom was in the Temple of the Mothers of the Free, a name that belied the actual circumstances, but underscored her purpose as governess. She was an excellent teacher, but her pupils had little concept of the world outside Siam, and she was sometimes faced with unusual obstacles, as when they simply refused to believe in snow, for example. Faced with such disbelief, "Mem" sometimes resorted to going to the king, who could enforce his word inside as well as outside the classroom as law. She also learned a great respect for her pupils. She describes one instance when a snake fell from the vaulted roof onto a chart across her table. While she screamed in horror, her pupils quietly watched until it had crawled away, then clustered around their teacher with shouts of joy that she had been favored by the gods, because a snake was considered a good omen.

There is some evidence that Leonowens' teaching greatly influenced the heir apparent, Prince Chulalongkorn, who abolished slavery during his reign and began other social reforms. When he met Leonowens in London 30 years later, he told her that he had kept his promise that he would rule over a free Siam.

Some of Leonowens' observations about life in the harem have been criticized as wild and fanciful. Others criticized her for relaying stories which had occurred in previous reigns as if they had happened in the 1860s. She was accused of being "on the fringes of reality, often escaping into make-believe." But Leonowens' objective in her later books and lectures was less to provide a detailed social history than to document an inhumane social custom which degraded women, a point many critics have overlooked. Women in the harem were slaves and playthings, a status she found intolerable. Although some of the atrocities she cites may have happened in earlier reigns, no one disputes that Siamese women suffered. Leonowens may not be an unimpeachable historical witness, but she is important as one of the few Europeans ever to experience life in a royal harem.

After Leonowens left Siam in 1867, she wrote *The Romance of the Harem* which appeared later as *Siamese Harem Life* and *The Romance of Siamese Harem Life*. She lectured widely, gaining a modest income to support herself, but her own accounts never had the renown that her life achieved after the appearance of *Anna and the King of Siam*, based on Leonowens' books, written by ***Margaret Landon** in 1944. Landon's book became the basis for the musical *The King and I*, written by the American composing team of Richard Rodgers and Oscar Hammerstein, which remained true to Leonowens' perspective on the treatment of women.

In her own life, Anna Leonowens was something of an adventurer, overcoming many limitations placed on her by her culture to become a highly articulate woman. She loved people, including the absolute monarch who employed her and the women under his domination, whom she praised for their grace and courage. In *The King and I*, Anna Leonowens becomes the king's friend and equal. Her audacity changes a kingdom. Although this may be the stuff of fiction, it sums up the spirit of the actual woman who educated a generation of royalty important to the evolution of their country into modern Thailand, and helped to free them from rigid traditional bonds.

SOURCES:

Audrig, John. *Siam. Kingdom of the Saffron Robe.* London: Robert Hale, 1969.

———. *Siam: Land of Temples.* London: Robert Hale, 1962.

Behrman, Cynthia F. "Governesses," in *Victorian Britain: An Encyclopedia.* Edited by Sally Mitchell. CT: Garland Publishing, 1988, pp. 337–338.

Howe, Bea. *A Galaxy of Governesses.* London: Derek Verschoyle, 1954.

Hughes, Kathryn. *The Victorian Governess.* London: Hambledon Press, 1993.

Leonowens, Anna. *The Romance of the Harem.* Edited by Susan Morgan. Charlottesville: University Press of Virginia, 1991.

Leonowens, Anna Harriette. *Siamese Harem Life.* NY: E.P. Dutton, 1953.

Moffat, Abbot Low. *Mongkut, the King of Siam.* Ithaca, NY: Cornell University Press, 1961.

Renton, Alice. *Tyrant or Victim? A History of the British Governess.* London: Weidenfeld and Nicolson, 1991.

Vicinus, Martha, ed. *Suffer and Be Still: Women in the Victorian Age.* Bloomington, IN: Indiana University Press, 1972.

RELATED MEDIA:

Anna and the King of Siam (128 min. film), starring ***Irene Dunne**, Rex Harrison, ***Linda Darnell**, Lee J. Cobb, and ***Gale Sondergaard**, directed by John

From the movie Anna and the King, *starring Jodie Foster and Chow Yun-Fat.*

Cromwell, screenplay by Talbot Jennings and *Sally Benson, based on the book by Margaret Landon, Fox, 1946.

Anna and the King, film starring **Jodie Foster** and Chow Yun-Fat, 20th Century-Fox, 1999.

The King and I, musical by Richard Rodgers and Oscar Hammerstein II, starring *Gertrude Lawrence and Yul Brynner, opened on Broadway at the St. James' Theater, New York, 1951.

The King and I (133 min. film), starring *Deborah Kerr, Yul Brynner, and *Rita Moreno, directed by Walter Lang, based on the Rodgers and Hammerstein musical which was based on the Landon book, costumes by *Irene Sharaff, Fox, 1956.

Karin Loewen Haag,
freelance writer, Athens, Georgia

Leontia (fl. 602–610)

Byzantine empress. Flourished between 602 and 610; married Phocas I (Phokas), Byzantine emperor (r. 602–610).

Leontia was married to Phocas I, a formidable tyrant who executed his predecessor, Emperor Maurice Tiberius, husband of ◄ᴥ **Constantina** (fl. 582–602), and all nine of their children, including her babe in arms. (The fate of Constantina is unknown.) Practically nothing is known of Phocas' wife Leontia, except that the public considered her "as bad as Phocas."

Leontias, Sappho (1832–1900)

Greek writer and educator. Born in Constantinople (now Istanbul), in 1832; died in 1900.

Well educated in her native Istanbul, Sappho Leontias spent many years as the headmistress of several girls' schools on the Greek islands. Considered one of the few enlightened women of her time, she viewed education as a means for women to improve their status within Greek society. Leontias fought hard for equal educational rights for women, lecturing on the subject and publishing the literary journal *Euridice*, which printed women's literary efforts and published works written in the Greek vernacular, or the common language. (At the time, there was controversy between those who advocated the strict use of *katharevousa* [pure Greek], and those who preferred the spoken language of the people.) Leontias believed strongly that the vernacular should be used in the schools and introduced the Greek classics in modern translation into the curriculum. She translated Aeschylus' *The Persians* into modern Greek, as well as Racine's *Esther* from the French. Well-spoken and pragmatic in her ap-

proach, Leontias participated in numerous open debates on the language controversy and wrote many works on the subject of education. She died in 1900.

Leontovich, Eugénie (1894–1993)

Russian-born actress, director, playwright, and drama coach. Name variations: Eugenie Leontovich. Born in Moscow, Russia, on March 21, 1894 (also seen as 1900); died on April 2, 1993; daughter of Konstantin Leontovich and Ann (Joukovsky) Leontovich; studied at the Imperial School of Dramatic Art, Moscow; married Paul A. Sokolov (divorced); married Gregory Ratoff (an actor-director), around 1923 (divorced 1949).

Selected theater: made New York debut in Revue Russe *(Booth Theater, October 1922); toured for several seasons as Bella Bruna in* Blossom Time; *appeared as Mrs. Pepys in* And So to Bed, **Sarah Bernhardt** *in* Fires of Spring, *and Maria in* Candle Light *(Chicago, 1929); appeared as Grusinskaya in* Grand Hotel *(National Theater, November 1930) and on subsequent tour (1931–32); appeared as Lilly Garland in* Twentieth Century *(Broadhurst Theater, December 1932); made London debut as the Grand Duchess Tatiana in* Tovarich *(Lyric Theater, April 1935) and played Tatiana on subsequent U.S. tour (1937–38); appeared as Natasha in* Dark Eyes, *which she wrote with* **Elena Miramova** *(Belasco Theater, New York, 1943); appeared as Nadya in* Obsession *(Plymouth Theater, New York, October 1946), and Gen. Tanya in* Caviar to the General, *which she wrote with George S. George (New Lindsey Theater, London, January 1947); founded The Stage Theater in Los Angeles, California (1948); directed and played Mrs. Esther Jock in* The Web and the Rock *(Las Palmas, CA, October 1952); founded the Leontovich Workshop in Los Angeles (1953); appeared as the Empress in* Anastasia *(Lyceum Theater, New York, December 1954), and on subsequent tour in U.S. and Australia; directed* A Month in the Country *(Studebaker Theater, Chicago, IL, November 1956); appeared as the Queen in* The Cave Dwellers *(Bijou Theater, New York, October 1957), and on subsequent tour; was artist-in-residence at the Chicago School of Drama (1963–64); wrote, directed and starred in* Anna K. *(Actors Playhouse, New York, May 1972); directed* Medea and Jason, *which she also adapted from the Robinson Jeffers' version of Medea and Euripides (Little Theater, New York, October 1974); founded the Eugénie Leontovich Workshop for actors in New York City (1973).*

Constantina (fl. 582–602). See Sophia (c. 525–after 600 CE) for sidebar.

Selected filmography: Four Sons *(1940);* The Men in her Life *(1941);* Anything Can Happen *(1952);* The World in His Arms *(1953);* Homicidal *(1961).*

Russian actress Eugénie Leontovich, a graduate of the Imperial School of Dramatic Art in Moscow, was a veteran of the Moscow Art Theater and Russian State Theater when she made her first appearance at the Booth Theater in New York in 1922 in *Revue Russe,* a Paris revue that was brought to America by the Shuberts. After learning English, Leontovich spent her early career performing on Broadway and touring the country in countless plays, including *And So to Bed* and *Twentieth Century.* In April 1935, she made her first appearance in London, at the Lyric Theater, playing the Archduchess Tatiana in *Tovarich.* In Hollywood in 1950, Leontovich both acted in and directed a production of *The Cherry Orchard,* and in 1952, she appeared in *The Web and the Rock,* staging the production as well.

In December 1954, back in New York, she won a Tony Award for her performance as the Dowager Empress in *Anastasia,* a play about a young girl who claims to be *Anastasia, the youngest daughter of Tsar Nicholas II of Russia and *Alexandra Feodorovna. *Viveca Lindfors, who played the title role, recalls that Leontovich was an invaluable source of background material for the play, having escaped the Russian Revolution herself. "She was not only a superb actress, but a superb human being," Lindfors writes in her autobiography *Viveka . . . Viveca.* "She would bring me some old remedy to treat my throat if it was sore, or some Russian delicacy to nourish me, or Russian fairy tales for my children that they came to love. She never stayed to chitchat or gossip. She knew about the need for space, for bareness. We came to love each other."

From 1940 on, Leontovich also appeared in films, and during the late 1940s she operated The Stage Theater in Los Angeles, where she acted and directed. In 1953, she founded the Leontovich Workshop in Los Angeles, where she directed and coached professional actors. Leontovich continued to act and direct throughout the 1960s and 1970s. In 1964, she joined the faculty of Chicago's Goodman School of Drama, where she also directed a number of productions, including *The Three Sisters* (1963). She also taught at Smith College in Northampton, Massachusetts, and at Columbia College in Chicago. In 1972, she directed *Anna K.,* her own conception of Tolstoy's *Anna Karenina,* in which she also portrayed two old

aristocrats, a performance called "riveting" by Clive Barnes of *The New York Times.* In 1973, the actress founded a second workshop for actors in New York City.

Petite in stature but dynamic in personality, Leontovich was married twice; her second husband was the Russian-born actor-director Gregory Ratoff, who had a successful career in Hollywood. "My husband was making very big money as a moving-picture director, and I spent it, to my pleasure," she said about her tumultuous years with Ratoff. The couple divorced in 1949, but they apparently remained friends, as Ratoff left her his house in Pacific Palisades, California, after he died in 1960.

Eugénie Leontovich

SOURCES:

Halliwell, Leslie. *The Filmgoer's Companion,* 4th ed. NY: Hill and Wang, 1974.

Lindfors, Viveca. *Viveka . . . Viveca.* NY: Everest House, 1981.

McGill, Raymond D., ed. *Notable Names in the American Theater.* Clifton, NJ: James T. White, 1976.

Barbara Morgan,
Melrose, Massachusetts

Leopoldina.

Variant of Leopoldine.

Leopoldina of Austria (1797–1826)

*Empress of Brazil. Name variations: Marie-Leopoldine; Marie Leopoldina; Leopoldine; Dona Maria Leopoldina; Leopoldina von Habsburg; Leopoldine Habsburg-Lotharingen. Born Marie Leopoldine on January 22, 1797; died of septicaemia after a miscarriage on December 11, 1826; daughter of Francis II, Holy Roman emperor (r. 1792–1806), emperor of Austria as Francis I (r. 1804–1835), and Maria Teresa of Naples (1772–1807); sister of Marie Louise of Austria (1791–1847, who married Napoleon); married Peter IV, king of Portugal (r. 1826), also known as Pedro I, emperor of Brazil (r. 1822–1831), on May 13, 1817; children: Maria II da Gloria (1819–1853), queen of Portugal (r. 1826–1828, 1834–1853); Miguel (1820–1820); João Carlos (1821–1822); *Januaria (1822–1901); Paula Mariana (1823–1833); *Francisca of Portugal (1824–1898); Pedro II (1825–1891), emperor of Brazil (r. 1831–1839).*

Leopoldina of Austria was born on January 22, 1797, in Vienna, the daughter of Habsburg Francis II, Holy Roman emperor, and *Maria Teresa of Naples. She received an excellent education, showing considerable ability as a painter and throughout her life displaying broad intellectual curiosity, especially for the natural sciences. Her parents initially thought to arrange her marriage to the king of Saxony but changed their minds when a Portuguese emissary proposed that she wed the crown prince, Pedro (I). Leopoldina approved, the parties signed the marriage contract on November 29, 1816, and she married Pedro by proxy on May 13 of the following year. A few weeks later, she left Vienna to join her husband, who had fled to Brazil with the Portuguese court when Napoleon's armies invaded in 1807.

Leopoldina arrived at Rio de Janeiro on November 5, 1817. She was delighted with her husband, whom she found handsome if impetuous and poorly educated. He reportedly was a little disappointed that she was not beautiful and that she took little care with her appearance. Nonetheless, he treated her respectfully and grew to love her, even temporarily giving up his carousing at taverns and womanizing. They enjoyed riding horses together, and, a good pianist herself, she encouraged his musical talents. Leopoldina was especially close to her father-in-law, John VI, whose interests and personality re-

sembled her own. In 1819, she had her first child, *Maria (II) da Gloria, who would later rule Portugal. Other pregnancies followed on an almost annual basis. Pedro (II), born in 1825, succeeded his father as ruler of Brazil.

The turmoil of Brazilian independence overshadowed most of Leopoldina's married life. By the time she arrived in South America, Portugal had long since been liberated from Napoleon's forces, and the Portuguese demanded that John VI and his family return to Europe. Fearful that if the court did so, Brazil would revert to a colonial status under Portuguese dominion, Brazilians insisted that the ruler remain in Rio de Janeiro. Finally, in 1821, Portuguese pressure forced John to sail for Portugal, but Brazilians obliged him to leave Pedro behind to govern Brazil. This displeased the Portuguese, who insisted that the prince and his family return also. With Leopoldina's strong support, Pedro responded in 1822 by declaring Brazilian independence and assuming the title of emperor. Leopoldina thus became the empress of Brazil.

Her four remaining years of life brought more children, frustration and exhilaration over the political drama that unfolded with the birth of the nation, and dismay at her husband's extramarital affairs. (To her anger and resignation, Pedro took a beautiful mistress from São Paulo, **Domitila de Castro**, in mid-1822.) Leopoldina encouraged Austrian immigration to Brazil, including the colony of São Leopoldo (1824) in Rio Grande do Sul. She died from a miscarriage on December 1, 1826. Rumors that Pedro had caused the miscarriage reflected her popularity and growing dissatisfaction with him. Buried first in the convent of Santo Antônio in Rio de Janeiro, her body was later transferred to the crypt in the monument of Ipiranga, where Pedro had declared independence.

SOURCES AND SUGGESTED READING:

Henderson, Linda Roddy, and James D. Henderson. *Ten Notable Women of Latin America.* Chicago, IL: Nelson-Hall, 1978.

Macaulay, Neill. *Dom Pedro: The Struggle for Liberty in Brazil and Portugal, 1798–1834.* Durham, NC: Duke University Press, 1986.

Oberacker Júnior, Carlos H. *A Imperatriz Leopoldina: Sua Vida e Sua Epoca.* Rio de Janeiro: Conselho Federal de Cultura, 1973.

Kendall W. Brown,
Professor of History, Brigham Young University, Provo, Utah

Leopoldine.

Variant of Leopoldina.

Leopoldine (1776–1848).

See Maria Leopoldina.

Leopoldine (1837–1903)

Princess of Hohenlohe-Langenburg. Born Leopoldine Wilhelmina Pauline Amelia Maximiliana on February 22, 1837; died on December 23, 1903; daughter of William, prince of Baden, and *Elizabeth of Wurttemberg (1802–1864); married Hermann, 6th prince of Hohenlohe-Langenburg, on September 24, 1862; children: Ernest, 7th prince of Hohenlohe-Langenburg (1863–1950); *Feodore of Hohenlohe-Langenburg (1866–1932).

Leopoldovna, Anna (1718–1746).

See Anna Ivanovna for sidebar.

Lepaute, Hortense (1723–1788)

French astronomer and mathematician. Name variations: Nicole Reine Lepaute; Nicole-Reine Lepaute. Born Nicole Hortense Reine in 1723; died in 1788; her father was attached to the court of the queen of Spain; married Jean André Lepaute (1709–1789, a machinist and royal clockmaker), in 1748.

Born Nicole Hortense Reine in 1723, Hortense Reine married the celebrated clockmaker, Jean André Lepaute, in 1748, and was the principal author of his *Traité d'horlogerie* (1755). In 1757, she assisted Alexis Clairaut and Joseph-Jérôme Lalande in work on planetary theory, calculating the attraction Jupiter and Saturn had on Halley's comet. Though Clairaut was impressed with her work, calling her *La savante calculatrice*, he was too envious to acknowledge it. Thus, he alone is usually given credit. Lalande, however, recognized her services in his *Théorie des Comètes*, and Jacques Babinet likewise spoke of her genius.

From 1760 to 1775, Hortense Lepaute helped Lalande edit *La Connaissance des Temps*, an astronomical annual of the Académie des Sciences. She rendered calculations for the eclipse of 1762 and for the annular eclipse of 1764, which included a table of parallactic angles published by the French government. In 1761, a monograph on the transit of Venus was also published. From 1774 to 1783, she worked on the seventh and eighth volumes of *Ephemeris*, containing future calculations for sun, moon, and planets. Though her eyesight degenerated with age, she also wrote other scientific works, and was regarded as one of the most learned women of her time. A Japanese rose, named *Lepautia* in her honor, was later renamed *Hortensia*.

Lepaute, Nicole Reine (1723–1788).

See Lepaute, Hortense.

Lepel or Lepell, Mary (1700–1768).

See Hervey, Mary.

Lepeshinskaya, Olga (1916—)

Soviet ballerina. Born in 1916; attended Bolshoi Ballet School.

In 1925, nine-year-old Olga Lepeshinskaya entered the Bolshoi Ballet School; one year later, she was dancing the part of Cupid in *Don Quixote*. Before graduating from the Bolshoi in 1933, she also danced the principal part of Masha in *The Nutcracker*. In 1935, Lepeshinskaya created the role of Suok the Circus Dancer for *Three Fat Men*, and played the title role in *Svetlana* in 1939. Known for her powerful presence, charm, and masterful technique, Lepeshinskaya appeared as Aurora in *The Sleeping Beauty*, Lise in *La Fille Mal Gardée*, Jeanne in *Flames of Paris*, Kitri in *Don Quixote*, and Tao Hoa in *The Red Poppy*. She graced the stages of Paris, Japan, China, Hungary, Czechoslovakia, and Mexico.

Leporin-Erxleben, Dorothea (1715–1762).

See Erxleben, Dorothea.

Lermontova, Julia (1846–1919)

Russian-German chemist. Name variations: Yulua Vsevolodovna Lermontova. Born in 1846; died in 1919; friend of Sophia Kovalevskaya (1850–1891).

In 1869, because Russian universities were closed to women, Julia Lermontova and *Sophia Kovalevskaya journeyed to Heidelberg to study for two years. Though the twosome could not register, they were allowed to attend lectures; the Germans were slightly less myopic when it came to women. Lermontova moved on to Berlin, published an article on her research on diphenene, and was awarded a degree from the University of Göttingen *in absentia* with her thesis, "The Study of Methylene Compounds."

She then returned to Russia to work in the Moscow University laboratory of V.V. Markownikov. From there, she went to St. Petersburg to work with A.M. Butlerov. Her findings, concerning the catalytic synthesis of the dimer and trimer of isobutylene and of 2-butyne, were published in 1881. Summoned back to Moscow because of family problems, Lermontova again worked with Markownikov, aiding in his research on petroleum. Five years later, Julia Lermontova had to retire as a chemist in order to take on family obligations.

Lermontova, Nadezhda Vladimirovna (1885–1921)

Russian painter who was influenced by Cubism. Born in St. Petersburg in 1885; died in 1921 in Petrograd (later Leningrad, now St. Petersburg).

Nadezhda Lermontova's premature death in the chaos of revolutionary Soviet Russia left a question that can never be answered: had she lived, would she have become a great painter? During her short life, Lermontova produced a number of impressive works, including what is probably her best-known painting, *On the Sofa: Self-Portrait* (1910s), a large (106.8 x 124.5) oil on canvas now displayed at the State Russian Museum. Born in St. Petersburg, she studied there at the Zvantseva School from 1907 to 1910. Starting in 1911, the painter participated in a number of exhibitions, including those of *Soyuz Molodezhi* (the Union of Youth) in 1912–13. With Petrov-Vodkin, she executed paintings in the church at Ovruch, Ukraine. Lermontova also designed sets for theater productions in St. Petersburg.

SOURCES:
The Twilight of the Tsars: Russian Art at the Turn of the Century. Hayward Gallery, London, 7 March–19 May 1991. London: South Bank Centre, London/All-Union Artistic Production Association, Moscow, 1991.

John Haag,
Athens, Georgia

Lerner, Gerda (1920—)

Influential American historian who is considered responsible for the establishment of women's history as a recognized academic field. Born Gerda Kronstein on April 30, 1920, in Vienna, Austria; daughter of Robert Kronstein and Ilona (Neumann) Kronstein; New School for Social Research, B.A., 1963; Columbia University, M.A., 1965, Ph.D., 1966; married Carl Lerner, in 1941 (died 1973); children: Stephanie Lerner; Daniel Lerner.

Arrived in the United States (1939); published first book (1955); created first women's history department in U.S. (1972); established first doctoral program in same field (c. 1980).

Selected writings: No Farewell *(1955);* The Grimké Sisters from South Carolina: Rebels Against Slavery *(1967);* The Woman in American History *(1971);* Black Women in White America: A Documentary History *(1972);* Women Are History: A Bibliography in the History of American Women *(1975, revised ed., 1986);* A Death of One's Own *(1978);* Women and History, *Volume 1:* The Creation of Patriarchy *(1986);* Women and History, *Volume 2:* The Creation of Feminist Consciousness: From the Middle Ages to 1870 *(Oxford University Press, 1993);* Why History Matters *(Oxford University Press, 1997).*

The name Gerda Lerner may not possess the recognition factor of *Gloria Steinem or *Barbara Tuchman, but her work as a feminist historian is both unparalleled and equally significant. Since the 1960s, she has been a trailblazer in establishing the field of women's history as an academic discipline; she may have taught the first postwar college class on women's history, and her books have become important texts that have provided her successors with contextual maps for uncharted territory.

Lerner was born Gerda Kronstein in 1920 in Vienna, Austria, into a prosperous and educated family. Her mother **Ilona Neumann Kronstein** was a painter, but her parents' marriage was less than happy; although they cohabitated, they remained emotionally distant from one another for years. They were of Jewish heritage, but Lerner herself was usually assumed to be gentile because of her fair looks. When Austria was annexed to Nazi Germany in 1938, her life changed dramatically, and she later recounted in her 1978 nonfiction work *A Death of One's Own* that a young man near her own age, whom she did not particularly like, simply disappeared one day just weeks after they had celebrated a Jewish holiday together with their families. His parents were sent a note that informed them they could pick up his ashes for a fee at a certain address.

Though her family managed to flee Austria itself just before the situation became pogrom-like in November of 1938, Lerner was the only one who obtained a visa for the United States. When she sailed in 1939, she knew that her mother, father, and sister would not be able to leave Europe, and she cried the entire six days of the sea voyage. She never saw her parents again, though they did survive the war, unlike some other members of their families. In 1941, Gerda married Carl Lerner and devoted herself to raising her children and doing writing and translation work. Early on, she developed an interest in women's lives, recalling her mother's plight and early death from multiple sclerosis. As Lerner later wrote in *A Death of One's Own*, her mother was an artistically gifted but temperamental person, who in another era might have flourished.

Lerner's first book, the novel *No Farewell*, was published in 1955. She returned to school and earned a B.A. from New York's New School for Social Research in 1963. She then went on to earn both an M.A. and a Ph.D in history from Columbia University in just three years. She embarked upon a career as an academic, and is considered to have taught the first women's history class in the postwar era. Teaching jobs included stints at the New School, Sarah Lawrence College, and Long Island University. In 1972, she created the first-ever women's history department in the United States at Sarah Lawrence College, where she taught until 1980. Lerner's next accomplishment was to create the first doctoral program in women's history at the progressive University of Wisconsin at Madison. She remained there as the school's Robinson-Edwards Professor of History, then was named professor emerita.

Lerner is the author of several significant works in her field. Her 1972 tome *Black Women in White America: A Documentary History* was groundbreaking for its academic exploration of what was at that time uncharted historical territory. One of its important contributions to multicultural feminist scholarship is its discussion of the lingering ramifications of slavery. In her other books, Lerner has sought to explain how and why "men's" history is different from women's history: the former has milestones and divisions that are not pertinent to the latter. In her precedent-setting two-volume work *Women and History*, Lerner delves into the prehistoric era in the first volume, *The Creation of Patriarchy* (1986), to question how male-dominated societies, where women had little legal or economic power, arose and maintained hegemony. In the second volume, *The Creation of Feminist Consciousness, From the Middle Ages to 1870* (1993), Lerner posits that women in history were virtually invisible for a very long period, and that the lack of a collective consciousness allowed patriarchy to flourish. In her works, however, Lerner gives equal access to the ideas that race and class also shape destiny, not just gender; this is the result of her experiences in a suddenly Nazi-occupied Austria, where she went from being a middle-class young woman to someone described as "vermin."

Her memoir, *A Death of One's Own*, actually chronicles the 1973 death of her husband Carl from a brain tumor. Lerner uses notes, poetry, diary entries, and memories of her childhood in

Gerda Lerner

Austria to connect events. She writes of her husband's courage, their children, the team of doctors, an indifferent medical system, the loss of friends, his chemotherapy, and simply the tough, daily difficulties of dealing with medication and a paralyzed husband whose illness is terminal.

Gerda Lerner was a founding member of the National Organization for Women (NOW) and in 1976 was instrumental in having March declared Women's History Month. She later served as the president of the Organization of American Historians and was named senior distinguished research professor by the University of Wisconsin Alumni Research Foundation in 1984. She is the recipient of numerous awards and honors, including fellowships from the National Endowment for the Humanities (1976) and the Ford Foundation (1978–79); in 1992, Gerda Lerner was honored with a scholarly distinction award from the American Historical Association.

SOURCES:

Contemporary Authors, New Revisions Series. Vol. 45. Detroit, MI: Gale Research, 1995.

Lerner, Gerda. *A Death of One's Own.* NY: Simon and Schuster, 1978.

Carol Brennan,
Grosse Pointe, Michigan

Lesbia.

See Erinna (fl. 7th c. BCE).
See Clodia (c. 94–post 45 BCE).

Lesczinska, Maria (1703–1768).

See Marie Leczinska.

Leslie, Eliza (1787–1858)

American writer who produced one of the earliest American cookbooks. Name variations: Betsey Leslie. Born Elizabeth Leslie on November 15, 1787, in Philadelphia, Pennsylvania; died on January 1 (some sources cite January 2), 1858, in Gloucester, New Jersey; buried in St. Peter's churchyard in Philadelphia; eldest of five children of Robert Leslie (a self-taught mathematician and a watchmaker) and Lydia (Baker) Leslie; educated at home; never married; no children.

The daughter of a watchmaker who was a friend of Thomas Jefferson and Benjamin Franklin, Eliza Leslie was born in 1787 in Philadelphia, and grew up there and in London, where the family resided for six and a half years when she was a child. Following their return to the United States and the death of Eliza's father in 1803, the family fell on hard times, and Eliza and her mother Lydia were forced to open a boardinghouse. In the mid-1820s, along with her mother, Eliza moved to West Point to live with her brother Thomas Jefferson Leslie, an army engineer who was serving as treasurer of the military academy.

Eliza, who was educated at home, began writing verse as a youngster, but her first published work was the cookbook *Seventy-five Receipts for Pastry, Cakes, and Sweetmeats.* It was followed by several collections of children's stories, the first of which was titled *The Mirror.* Her initial story for adult readers, "Mrs. Washington Potts," resulted in frequent contributions to the magazine *Godey and Graham.* Leslie's magazine articles were later collected in three volumes under the title *Pencil Sketches.* She also produced several more cookbooks and a manual on etiquette, *The Behavior Book,* which enjoyed several editions. Her only novel-length work was *Amelia; or A Young Lady's Vicissitudes.* Eliza Leslie died on January 1, 1858.

Leslie, Euphemia (d. after 1424)

*Countess of Ross. Name variations: Euphamia of Ross; Euphemia of Ross. Died after 1424; daughter of Alexander Leslie, 7th (some sources cite 9th) earl of Ross, and *Isabel Stewart (fl. 1390–1410).*

Euphemia Leslie renounced her inheritance and became a nun at North Berwick.

Leslie, Mrs. Frank (1836–1914).

See Leslie, Miriam Folline Squier.

Leslie, Lisa (1972—)

African-American basketball player and model, one of the most popular players in the world of sports. Born Lisa Deshaun Leslie on July 7, 1972, in Los Angeles, California; daughter of Walter Leslie (a semiprofessional basketball player) and Christine Leslie-Espinoza (a truck driver); graduated from Morningside High School in Inglewood, California; attended University of Southern California, 1990–94.

Won the Dial Award (1989); named Pacific-10 Freshman of the Year (1990); was a member of the World University Games team, winning a gold medal (1991); was a member of the Jones Cup team, winning a gold medal (1992); named National College Player of the Year (1993); was a member of the Goodwill Games team, winning a gold medal, and the World championship team, winning a bronze medal (1994); led University of Southern California in scoring and rebounding and the Pac-10 in blocked shots (1993–94); named All-Pac-10 all four years of her college career, the only player in Pac-10 history to do so; played one season for Sicilgesso in Italy (1994–95); was a member of the undefeated U.S. National team (1995–96); was an Olympic gold medalist with the U.S. National team at Atlanta, scoring 29 points in the gold-medal game against Brazil (1996); was a founding member of Los Angeles Sparks.

Known for her athletic prowess, grace, and style, Lisa Leslie helped to establish national respect for women's basketball. She was among the first to sign a contract with the Women's National Basketball Association (WNBA) at its inception in 1996, while also maintaining a high-profile career with Wilhelmina Models, one of the nation's top modeling agencies. Independent, determined, and highly successful, Leslie became a role model for many young women, advising them to pursue their dreams. "You can be whatever you want to be," she often said, echoing

what she had heard from an inspirational speaker when she was in the second grade.

Born on July 7, 1972, in Los Angeles, California, Lisa Deshaun Leslie was the daughter of Walter Leslie, a semi-professional basketball player who deserted the family early on, and Christine Leslie, who struggled to provide for the family, working as a mail carrier and on a General Motors assembly line before becoming a cross-country driver for North American Van Lines. While her mother was scaling the gender barrier to become a successful trucker, Lisa and her sister **Tiffany Leslie** stayed with an aunt in Carson, three miles from Compton. "Give me five years, and I'll give you a better life," Christine told her children. She would often be on the road for weeks at a time, returning to the family whenever she could. At Christmas and on school holidays, the girls would sometimes accompany their mother on her trucking route. The long separations were painful for Lisa, who was so attached to her mother she was nicknamed Shadow. As well, her classmates teased her about her height. By the time she was in the second grade, Leslie was 5'2"—taller than her teacher, and the tallest child ever to cross the threshold of the school. By age 12, she had passed the 6' mark, eventually reaching 6'5". However, under the guidance of her 6'3" mother, Lisa learned to carry her height with pride, sometimes walking with books balanced atop her head to correct her posture.

Initially, Leslie resisted expectations that she would be interested in basketball because of her height. She nonetheless agreed to play when some of her classmates asked her to join the middle-school team. During her freshman year of high school, Leslie began practicing with an older male cousin who assumed the role of private coach, instructing her in the discipline of push-ups, sit-ups, and shooting hoops. She played on all-male teams, excelling at the sport, as her skills developed and her interest grew. When her mother was assigned to a local truck route, and the family moved to Inglewood, California, Leslie joined the Morningside High School girls' basketball team, quickly becoming their premiere player. During one remarkable game in her senior year, Leslie scored 101 points in a 16-minute period. The national scoring record was 105 points, but that was for an entire game. The other team, wincing with mortification, forfeited the game at half-time. Had the game continued, Leslie most certainly would have broken the national record. That fact was not lost upon the scouts and national news teams present. She was identified as "the best high school player in the nation" by *Sports Illustrated*, without qualifying her by gender. Her high school record included an average of 27.3 points and 15 rebounds per game. A member of the U.S. Junior Olympic team, Leslie also received the Dial Award for being the outstanding female scholar-athlete of 1989.

Heavily recruited by colleges throughout the nation, Leslie decided to attend the University of Southern California in the fall of 1990. Voted Pacific-10 Freshman of the Year, she began to recognize her responsibilities as a role model for younger women and athletes. By the time she left the University of Southern California in 1994, she had been named All-American three times and was that year's National College Player of the Year. Now deeply committed to the game of basketball, Leslie wanted to play for the U.S. National team, but she was unable to gain the necessary professional experience in the United States. She therefore signed a contract with an Italian league, remaining for one season before gaining a slot on the U.S. team. She was the tallest player on the squad. Just as women's basketball was gaining popularity in the United States, the National team embarked upon a rigorous training program, which included a world tour, to prepare for the 1996 Olympics. They played against the top international and college women's teams, under the coaching of **Tara Van-Derveer**, and went undefeated throughout their tour, bringing prestige to the sport. The team went on to the Olympics to defeat Brazil in front of millions of television fans and claimed the coveted gold medal. In that highly charged game, Leslie scored 29 points.

During the pre-Olympic tours, Leslie averaged 17.3 points and seven rebounds per game, and became noted for her aggressive court style. Concurrently, she devoted more time to her modeling career. Seeing herself primarily as an entertainer, Leslie was impeccably groomed off the court and well-trained and prepared on the court. She became one of the most recognizable celebrities and had a lucrative contract with Nike shoes. Following the Olympic victory, Leslie took a brief break from basketball before signing on with the newly formed Women's National Basketball Association in December 1996. The formation of a professional women's league, financed and supported by the National Basketball Association, marked national acceptance of women's basketball in the United States. For Lisa Leslie, it meant remaining in her hometown, where she became a founding member of the Los Angeles Sparks. Following a successful modeling season, during which she appeared in such national publications as *Vogue*, *Women's Wear Daily*, and *Shape*, Leslie played in her first U.S. professional game in June 1997.

SOURCES:

Contemporary Black Biography. Vol. 16. Detroit, MI: Gale Research.
Sports Illustrated. Spring 1997.

SUGGESTED READING:

Corbett, Sara. *Venus to the Hoop* (biography). Doubleday, 1997.

Lolly Ockerstrom,
freelance writer, Washington, D.C.

Leslie, Mary (d. 1429)

*Countess of Ross. Name variations: sometimes seen as Margaret; Mary Macdonald. Died in 1429 (some sources say she died around 1435); sister of Alexander Leslie, 7th earl of Ross; daughter of Andrew Leslie and *Euphemia Ross (d. 1394), countess of Ross; married Donald Macdonald, 2nd lord of Isles (died 1420); children: Alexander Macdonald, 1st earl of Ross (d. 1449); Angus Macdonald, bishop of Isles.*

Leslie, Miriam Folline Squier

(1836–1914)

American editor, essayist, lecturer, socialite, and, ultimately, suffragist who legally took her husband's full name to save his business empire after his death, and whose celebrity in the U.S. and abroad grew out of both business triumphs and personal scandal. Name variations: Minnie Montez; Miriam Peacock; Miriam Squier; Frank Leslie; Florence M. Wilde; Baroness de Bazus; Florence de Bazus; Baroness Leslie de Bazus; used both "Miriam" and "Florence" as first name; "Folline" was later spelled "Follin"; legally changed name to Frank Leslie on June 4, 1881. Born Miriam Florence Folline on June 5, 1836, in New Orleans, Louisiana; died of a heart attack on September 18, 1914, in New York City; daughter of common-law marriage of Susan Danforth and Charles Folline (Follin, a businessman); married David Charles Peacock, on March 27, 1854 (annulled, March 24, 1856); married Ephraim George (E.G.) Squier, on October 22, 1857 (divorced, May 31, 1874); married Frank Leslie (born Henry Carter), on July 13, 1874 (died, January 10, 1880); married William Charles Kingsbury Wills Wilde, on October 4, 1891 (divorced, June 10, 1893); no children.

Began career as an editor (1863); published first book (1877); saved Leslie Publishing House from foreclosure (1881); made American lecture tour (1890); willed $2 million to the cause of women's suffrage (1914).

Editor of publications: Frank Leslie's Lady's Magazine (1863–82); Frank Leslie's Chimney Corner (1865–84); Frank Leslie's Lady's Journal which began as Once A Week: The Young Lady's Own Journal (1871–81); Frank Leslie's Illustrated Newspaper (1880–89); Frank Leslie's Popular Monthly (1880–95, 1898–1900); Frank Leslie's Budget of Fun (1880–95); Frank Leslie's Pleasant Hours (1880–95); Frank Leslie's Boy's & Girl's Weekly (1880–84); Frank Leslie's Sunday Magazine (1880–89); New York Illustrated Times (1880–81); Frank Leslie's Fact and Fic-

tion (1884–85); Frank Leslie's Afloat and Ashore (1888–90).

Books: California: A Pleasure Trip from Gotham to the Golden Gate (1877); Rents in Our Robes (1888); Beautiful Women of Twelve Epochs (1890); Are Men Gay Deceivers? And Other Sketches (1893); A Social Mirage (1899). Wrote more than two dozen articles for various Leslie publications (1865–89); also, articles for Harper's New Monthly Magazine (1866), The Ladies' Home Journal (1890–92), and several newspapers.

The woman who was best known as the wife of newspaper and magazine publisher Frank Leslie actually had many husbands and lovers, just as she had many identities—actress, translator, editor, travel writer, dispenser of domestic advice, publisher, lecturer, clubwoman, hostess, and champion of women's suffrage. In one sense, the story of her life, which spanned the Victorian era, is a Horatio Alger-like tale of gumption and determination rewarded by riches and fame. In another sense, her many successes were paradoxical: she edited conservative family magazines while living by her own unconventional moral and social standards; she took a man's name and made millions as a publisher while remaining a celebrated beauty in high society in America and abroad; she lectured alternately on women's business success and the art of flirtation. Once an actress, she never allowed herself to be typecast, and she frequently changed her identity to suit her circumstances and needs. Her most memorable role, however, was that of the strong-willed businesswoman who saved a publishing empire from bankruptcy, building an independent fortune of her own—which, in her final surprise move, she used to help other women succeed.

In her later years, Mrs. Frank Leslie would claim to have been born in the South "during the war" (implying the Civil War); she was actually born during the Mexican War, on June 5, 1836, in New Orleans. Her name at birth was Miriam Florence Folline, though soon afterward her father would change the spelling of his last name to Follin. Charles Follin held a variety of jobs during the family's years in New Orleans, Cincinnati, and New York; though he was not always a steady provider, he sent Miriam to finishing schools and encouraged her study of French, Spanish, Latin, and German. He also encouraged her interest in writing, which led to her successful submission of an essay (about a Venezuelan patriot) to the *New York Herald* in 1850. It was her mother **Susan Danforth**, however, who took an interest in the girl's social reputation—and who insisted on a marriage when she discovered that 18-year-old Miriam was sexually involved with a young jeweler's clerk named David Charles Peacock. The couple never lived together and the marriage was annulled two years later, but it marked Miriam's passage into adulthood.

Her next adventure was an indirect result of the accidental death of her half-brother Noel, who drowned while traveling as the companion of the stage actress *Lola Montez. When the grieving Montez met Noel's family, she became friendly with Miriam and invited the young woman to join her company. Billed as "Minnie Montez," Lola's "sister," Miriam toured the northeast in several plays during early 1857. Her beauty quickly drew admirers. In April, she became the mistress of the married William Churchwell, a banker and a former Tennessee congressional representative; by fall, that romance had ended but another had begun with Ephraim George ("E.G.") Squier, a 36-year-old

Miriam Folline Leslie

archaeologist and agent of the Honduras Interoceanic Railway.

On October 22, 1857, 21-year-old Miriam became Mrs. E.G. Squier. When E.G. established a Spanish-language newspaper company in South America, he turned to Miriam for help with the language. She also took on an editorial project of her own, a translation of *The Demi-Monde*, a play by the younger Alexandre Dumas. The couple's travels in Europe and South America enabled Miriam to keep her language skills sharp—and provided E.G.'s first opportunity to write travel pieces for his friend Frank Leslie.

Born Henry Carter to a family of glovemakers in England, Frank Leslie had taken a new name when he came to the United States in 1848 as an illustrator, and in only a decade he had revolutionized the American newspaper business with the introduction of *Frank Leslie's Illustrated Newspaper*, a New York-based weekly with a circulation of 164,000. In 1860, when Frank separated from his wife **Sarah Leslie**, he became a boarder in the Squier home on East 10th Street. At about the same time, he asked E.G., whose contributions to the newspaper had increased, to become its managing editor. In March 1864, after the Squiers' attendance at President Abraham Lincoln's first inaugural ball, a flattering illustration of Miriam and her dress appeared in *Frank Leslie's Illustrated Newspaper*.

The trio were together at home, in the social world of New York, and—after Miriam assumed the editorship of *Frank Leslie's Lady's Magazine* in 1863—at work. Miriam's fashion sense, combined with her editorial skills, turned the monthly into a huge money-maker for Frank Leslie. In 1865, she proposed the idea for a new monthly magazine for the whole family, *Frank Leslie's Chimney Corner*, and became its founding editor. Its circulation quickly grew to 80,000.

In early 1867, Frank Leslie was appointed a U.S. commissioner to the Paris Universal Exposition, and he took the Squiers along. They traveled first to England, disembarking at Liverpool, where—as only Miriam knew—E.G. had an unsettled business debt. Mysteriously, they were met at the docks by police responding to a complaint from E.G.'s creditor, and he was thrown in jail. Miriam and Frank (who, as it turned out, had cabled ahead to the creditor and set this plot in motion) traveled on together to London and Paris, while E.G. sat in jail for two weeks until payment could be arranged for his release.

When he was finally freed, E.G., amazingly, joined Miriam and Frank in Paris and acted as if nothing had happened. He remained unperturbed as the three of them summered at Saratoga in 1868 and made a second trip to Europe in 1870. His faith may have stemmed from Sarah Leslie's continuing refusal to give Frank a divorce, but when a large financial settlement removed that obstacle in 1872, E.G. found himself on the losing end of his own divorce. (For reasons too complicated to summarize, it was he who was proven the adulterer.)

On July 13, 1874, Miriam became Mrs. Frank Leslie. By then, she was also the editor of three magazines. In 1871, she had taken the helm of a new weekly fashion magazine, *Frank Leslie's Lady's Journal* (initially called *Once a Week: The Young Lady's Own Journal*), while continuing to edit the *Lady's Magazine* and *Chimney Corner*. At that point, the company had nearly 400 employees and was producing a dozen publications—a combination of weeklies and monthlies. Miriam studied all aspects of the business, including the technical production of the magazines and newspapers.

By the mid-1870s, though the circulation of Frank Leslie's flagship publication, *Frank Leslie's Illustrated Newspaper,* had dropped to 50,000, the company as a whole was thriving. Frank brought the same energy to his social life as to his business life, and he and Miriam lived in style. Miriam, always considered well-dressed, became known for her jewelry: at a reception for poet William Cullen Bryant at the mansion of New York Governor Samuel Tilden in 1875, she wore $70,000 worth of diamonds. That summer, the couple bought their own yacht, the *Frank Leslie,* to enjoy at Interlaken, their lakeside country estate in upstate New York where they entertained Cornelius Vanderbilt and Emperor Pedro II of Brazil.

In 1876, the year *Frank Leslie's Popular Monthly* magazine was launched, the Leslies served as official delegates to the United States Centennial Exposition in Philadelphia. The following year, they embarked, with an entourage of employees and friends, in a private railroad car on a two-month, cross-country journey, during which Miriam interviewed Mormon leader Brigham Young in Utah. Miriam was fascinated by the Western land and people, and her notes on them turned into her first book, *California: A Pleasure Trip from Gotham to the Golden Gate,* published later that year (and now considered valuable as an early record of the settled American west).

The couple's high living ground to a halt, however, when the depression of 1877 hit the Leslie Publishing House. Business losses—combined with a $15,000 bill for the cross-country trip, a new printing press that had cost $70,000, and some bad real-estate investments Frank had made—left them more than $300,000 in debt. During the next two years, Frank reduced the debt but developed inoperable throat cancer. When he died on January 10, 1880, leaving Miriam in charge of the company, he was still $50,000 in debt, and his creditors threatened to foreclose.

The old order is changing and the new coming. Woman . . . must free herself from her swaddling clothes and go out into the world with courage and self-reliance.

—Miriam Leslie

At the same time, Miriam faced a court battle against Frank's two sons from his first marriage, who were contesting his will. Frank had already been involved in legal struggles with his sons, who (though neither was named Frank) had tried to use the valuable name "Frank Leslie" in their own commercial ventures. After the will was upheld, Miriam legally changed her name to Frank Leslie to prevent future interference. In the meantime, she borrowed $50,000 from a wealthy New York widow, leaving her diamonds for security, and paid the company's debts.

The firm's coffers were soon replenished thanks to an extraordinary news event: on July 2, 1881, President James Garfield was shot. Miriam sent two artists on a train to Washington, where they got a full description of the event, made sketches, and returned the same night. In just three days, an edition of *Frank Leslie's Illustrated Newspaper* with full pictorial coverage of the assassination attempt was on the stands, followed by an "extra" edition a few days later. During the two months the president lingered, Leslie artists depicted his sick bed, the worried *Lucretia Garfield, the assassin in prison, and, finally, the president's death and funeral. When he died—two days before the paper was due on newsstands—Miriam Leslie literally stopped the presses, ordering her engravers to work around the clock to remake the front page and centerfold. During the Garfield drama, the circulation of the weekly *Illustrated Newspaper* jumped from 30,000 to 200,000. By its end, Miriam Leslie had repaid her debt and retrieved her diamonds.

Though the paper's circulation declined in the aftermath of the big news event, it remained about 50,000 above its previous level thanks to other changes Miriam Leslie made—hiring new writers, improving the quality of the printing of woodcuts, and switching to a heavier paper stock. Within a few years she would build another Leslie publication, *Frank Leslie's Popular Monthly* magazine, into an equally successful property, with a circulation reaching 125,000 at the end of the decade. In 1885, she pared the company's holdings down to two weeklies and four monthlies, so that she could focus on the money-making publications. The Leslie Publishing House was solidly back in the black, and, as "Frank Leslie," Miriam—who by then was taking home a salary of $100,000 a year—was hailed as "The Empress of Journalism" in the domestic and overseas press.

The crisis averted, Miriam again journeyed abroad. In London, she attended the Sunday-afternoon salons of Lady *Jane Wilde (mother of the writer Oscar), and their atmosphere inspired her to begin her own Thursday-evening salons when she returned to New York. She was especially drawn to European men with titles: in New York, she was briefly engaged to a French marquis, and a few years later she was courted by a Russian prince (though both men's claims to their titles were disputed). The publicity surrounding her relationships, along with her success as a publisher of popular periodicals, inspired her to write a series of essays on romance for her "dear sisters" across America. They were published in 1888 as *Rents in Our Robes,* a book that might now be called "self-help," with themes ranging from flirtation to marital happiness to keeping one's flesh firm through exercise.

By 1889, Miriam was 53 (though she told interviewers she was still in her 30s) and tired of the pace of producing weeklies. That year, she sold *Frank Leslie's Illustrated Newspaper* and another publication to W.J. Arkell and Russell B. Harrison, the publishers of *Judge,* for close to $400,000. In her new free time, she produced another book, *Beautiful Women of Twelve Epochs,* a history of feminine beauty, and wrote articles for a newspaper syndicate and a popular new women's magazine, *The Ladies' Home Journal.* A promoter persuaded her to go on a month-long lecture tour for which she was paid $200 a speech, an unprecedented rate for a woman speaker. In 20 cities across America, she declared her opinions on European royalty, American journalism, opportunities for women, and whatever else was on her mind—though her audiences were less interested in her topics than in seeing the famous "Frank Leslie" and her clothing and jewels.

Back in New York, Miriam devoted her attention to her remaining three monthlies and her activities in, among many organizations, the Professional Woman's League, the American Press Association, the Woman's Press Club of New York City, and the National American Women's Suffrage Association (for which she would host a suffrage debate at the Leslie Publishing House three years later). In October 1891, her personal life was again in the news when she abruptly married William ("Willie") Wilde, brother of Oscar, whom she had met eight years earlier at his mother's salons and who happened to be visiting America. Though Miriam briefly called herself "Mrs. Florence M. Wilde," she soon legally changed her name back to Frank Leslie.

The marriage was a mistake from the start. Willie, 16 years her junior, was fun but a freeloader and an alcoholic. In 1892, the couple sailed to Europe, but Miriam came back alone. Willie was doubtless the inspiration for her fourth book, *Are Men Gay Deceivers? And Other Sketches,* published in 1893, the year their divorce became final. The same year, Miriam tried her hand at playwriting with *The Froth of Society,* an adaptation of the Dumas work she had translated 35 years earlier; it opened in New York but met a quick demise after poor reviews.

In 1895, Miriam relinquished day-to-day control of the only remaining Leslie property, *Frank Leslie's Popular Monthly,* to another executive of the company. Three years later, distressed by a sharp drop in its circulation, she took over again and—in a feat much like her rescue of the *Illustrated Newspaper* 15 years earlier—made the magazine competitive with the several new monthlies on the market (such as *McClure's*). She improved its content, decreased its page size, and lowered its price from twenty-five cents to ten cents, and soon circulation soared to 200,000. "Frank Leslie" left the magazine for good in 1900 and sold her interest in it in 1903; two years later, it became *The American Magazine.*

In 1899, Miriam published her fifth and final book, *A Social Mirage,* which contained more essays on love. By then, however, she was in physical decline, suffering from a kidney condition and, after a minor stroke in 1901, mobility problems. No longer the toast of New York, she retained the interest and favors of society and club women by promising to remember them in her will. Upon her return from a European trip, she claimed to have traced her father's family to French nobility and took the title "Baroness de Bazus." Ironically, five years after she had created a title for herself, Miriam became engaged, at age 70, to an actual nobleman, a Spanish count

THE WAR IN PICTURES

AUG 2nd 1917

Leslie's

Illustrated Weekly Newspaper

Price 10 Cents
In Canada, 15 Cents

Notice to Reader

Three years after Miriam Leslie's death, her illustrated weekly was still in circulation.

with whom she had two happy years (though no marriage) before he died in 1907.

Seven years later, Miriam herself was dead, of a heart attack suffered on September 18, 1914, in New York City. But she had one more surprise for the American public. Despite her promises, Miriam left the bulk of her fortune—nearly $2 million—to "Mrs. *Carrie Chapman Catt . . . to the furtherance of the cause of Woman's Suffrage." Catt spent half the money fighting a two-year court battle against outraged "friends" and descendants of Frank Leslie who contested the will. Fittingly, the rest of the legacy was used to publish a suffrage newspaper, *The Woman Citizen,* issued by the National American Woman Suffrage Association (NAWSA) until the 19th Amendment was ratified in 1920, and then by the League of Women Voters until 1932.

SOURCES:

Mott, Frank Luther. *A History of American Magazines.* Vols. II, III, IV. Cambridge, MA: Harvard University Press, 1957.

Stern, Madeleine B. *Purple Passage: The Life of Mrs. Frank Leslie.* Norman, OK: University of Oklahoma Press, 1953.

Tebbel, John, and Mary Ellen Zuckerman. *The Magazine in America, 1741–1990.* NY: Oxford University Press, 1991.

Willard, Frances E., and Mary A. Livermore, eds. *American Women.* NY: Mast, Crowell, and Kirkpatrick, 1897.

SUGGESTED READING:

Frank Leslie's Illustrated Newspaper. December 1855–June 1889.

Frank Leslie's Popular Monthly. January 1876–May 1895; November 1898–October 1900.

Leslie, Miriam Florence Squier. *California: A Pleasure Trip from Gotham to the Golden Gate.* NY: Carleton, 1877.

Carolyn Kitch,
former editor for *Good Housekeeping* and *McCall's,*
and Assistant Professor at the Medill School of Journalism,
Northwestern University, Evanston, Illinois

Lespinasse or L'Espinasse, Julie de

(1732–1776).

See Salonnières.

Lessing, Doris (1919—)

Prominent English novelist who has combined a concern for such issues as Marxism, colonialism, and feminism with profound investigations of the nature, ailments, and potential of the human personality.

*Name variations: (pseudonym) Jane Somers. Born Doris May Tayler (sometimes given as Taylor), on October 22, 1919, in Kermanshah, Persia; daughter of Alfred Cook Tayler (a bank clerk) and Emily Maude (McVeagh) Tayler (a former nurse); attended convent school and Girls' High School, both in Salisbury, Southern Rhodesia, 1926–33; married Frank Charles Wisdom, on April 6, 1939 (divorced 1943); married Gottfried Anton Nicolai Lessing, in 1943 (divorced 1949); children (first marriage) John Wisdom; **Jean Wisdom;** (second marriage) Peter Lessing (b. 1946).*

Settled with family in Southern Rhodesia (1924); left family farm permanently for employment in Salisbury (1938); attended Communist Party cell in Salisbury (1942–44); left Southern Rhodesia for England (1949); joined British Communist Party (1951); visited Southern Rhodesia and then banned from returning by the white government, left Communist Party over invasion of Hungary (1956); began to study Sufism (1964); movie version of The Grass is Singing *appeared (1981); began to publish under pseudonym of Jane Somers (1983); received honorary doctorate from Princeton University (1989).*

Selected works: The Grass is Singing *(1950);* "Children of Violence" *series (1952–65), includes* Martha Quest *(1952),* A Proper Marriage *(1954),* Ripple from the Storm *(1958),* Landlocked *(1965), and* The Four-Gated City *(1965); (collection) The* Habit of Loving *(1957); The Golden Notebook (1962); Briefing for a Descent into Hell (1971); (as Jane Somers) "Canopus in Argos: Archives" series (1979–83), includes* The Diary of a Good Neighbor *(1983), and If the Old Could . . . (1984); The Good* Terrorist *(1985); The Fifth Child (1988); (as Jane Somers) The Diaries of Jane Somers; (nonfiction)* African Laughter: Four Visits to Zimbabwe *(1992);* Love, Again *(NY: HarperCollins, 1996); Under My Skin: Volume One of My Autobiography to 1949 (NY: HarperCollins, 1994); Walking in the Shade: Volume Two of My Autobiography, 1949–1962 (NY: HarperCollins, 1997).*

Starting with the publication of her first book, *The Grass is Singing,* in 1950, Doris Lessing has been both a critically acclaimed and popular author, one of the most distinguished and prolific English writers of the second half of the 20th century. Her body of writing includes 30 novels along with numerous short stories and several plays. Her style has ranged from realistic portrayals of modern life to science fiction and to experimental explorations of the individual psyche. Lessing's stature as a writer has made her a perennial candidate to receive the Nobel Prize in Literature.

Doris Lessing's work touches on some of the basic dilemmas of modern times, including colonialism in Africa, Marxism, and the status of women in Western society. She has taken up a number of such issues before they reached a wide public awareness, notably in her picture of a modern woman in *The Golden Notebook.* Lessing's inclination to shift her focus in prophetic fashion to new problems makes it difficult to pin her down to a specific ideological label, such as Marxist or feminist. Lessing herself, and the leading critics of her work, insist that her writing transcends such politically charged categories. Her unique voice and her depiction of unforgettable characters make her achievement essentially one of the exploration of the individual.

Doris Lessing was born in Kermanshah, Persia (called Iran since 1935), on October 22, 1919. Her parents, Alfred Cook Tayler and **Maude McVeagh Tayler,** had moved to that country following World War I in connection with Alfred's work as a bank clerk. Wounded while serving in the war, Lessing's father had had his mangled leg amputated. His stay in a military hospital brought him into contact with his future wife, who was working as a nurse.

In 1924, Alfred relocated his family to a farm in Southern Rhodesia. Doris spent the remainder of her childhood there except for the seven-year period she attended boarding schools in Salisbury, the country's capital and main city. Life in the isolated African countryside—on a family farm of 3,000 acres with a primitive dwelling—was to become a major source of material for much of Lessing's early writings.

The family's lack of financial luck in farming in Southern Rhodesia as well as the tension between Lessing's mother and father were dominant elements in her early years. Alfred Tayler's farm seldom made a profit, and the personality differences between the elder Lessings—he was content to spend his spare hours sitting outside the farmhouse meditating on the stars, she was frustrated at the lack of company in their isolated existence—made the marriage a fragile one. Critics like **Margaret Roan Moore** have noted the influence that psychological strains within Lessing's family had. Roan writes that in Lessing's fiction she "presents the father as dreamer, the mother as regulator."

Young Doris received the best education available at the time to a white girl in this part of Africa, attending convent school and high school—both as a boarding student—in Salisbury. She had no taste for formal education, however, and left secondary school when she was only 14. Her real education came through her prodigious reading. At the isolated family farmstead, she spent much of the rest of her teenage years absorbing the great European literature of the past century with emphasis on French authors like Stendhal and Balzac and Russians like Turgenev and Dostoevsky.

An initial period of living in Salisbury from 1934 to 1936 widened her horizons. Back on the family farm, Lessing wrote—and then destroyed—drafts of two early novels around 1937. But the aspiring author also completed and sold several short stories. She then left the family farm for good, moving to Salisbury when she was only 19 and taking a series of uninspiring jobs as a clerk and telephone operator. Lessing married and divorced twice in the decade between 1939 and 1949. Each marriage reflected the vastly different social circumstances in which she found herself. Initially, she plunged into the social life of Southern Rhodesia's white settler population. This led to her first marriage to a civil servant named Frank Wisdom. It lasted from 1939 to 1943 and produced two children, a boy and a girl. Thereafter, her social life centered on members of a Communist Party group that met in Salisbury. There, in 1943, she wed a German-Jewish émigré, Gottfried Lessing. That marriage, which

ended in divorce in 1949, was in part an outgrowth of her intensifying political involvement. The party group to which they belonged was comprised largely of rank-and-file members of the wartime Royal Air Force who were stationed in this remote colonial backwater as well as recent immigrants to Southern Rhodesia.

> *She has taken risks, changed and moved on in her life, and this change and growth is reflected in her novels.*
> —**Ruth Whittaker**

A key event in Lessing's life and literary development came in 1949, when she left Africa to settle in London. She took along her son Peter, the offspring of her marriage with Lessing, as well as the manuscript of her first novel. Published in London the following year under the title *The Grass is Singing*, it was a quick success and established her as a rising literary star. John Barkham, reviewing the novel in *The New York Times*, cited "the depth and maturity of this remarkable psychological study." The book, which was reprinted seven times within five months, tells the story of a white farm woman in Rhodesia who becomes involved with an African worker; in the end, he murders her. Like much of Lessing's work, it can be seen as a statement about a burning social or political issue, but, again like much of her work, it transcends these categories by its exploration of human psychology. Her heroine Mary Turner suffers a mental breakdown in a key development of the plot, and the process by which the mind disintegrates and leads to a greater awareness was to become a thread running through much of Lessing's fiction. Although African themes remained important in her later writing, *The Grass is Singing* is the only book centered in Africa that she wrote while she still lived there. In 1981, it was made into a popular film, starring **Karen Black** as the heroine, but its lurid tone departed sharply from Lessing's original book.

Over the three decades following publication of her first novel, Lessing produced two multi-volume works. The first of them, a five-volume series labeled the "Children of Violence," consisted of novels following the life of a fictional character named Martha Quest. Lessing's African background and her personal history provided a rich source of material for this work, since Martha's life and experiences were clearly modeled on those of the author. Beginning with Martha's youth, marriage, and attraction to Communism while living in British Africa, the series then saw the heroine transplanted into an English environment. *Martha Quest*, published in 1952, dealt with the earlier stages of the heroine's life, and the series ended with *The Four-Gated City*, which appeared in 1969. The latter work actually drove decades into the future, picturing a Britain devastated by a nuclear calamity at the close of the 20th century.

Lessing's ties to the political left led her to join the British Communist Party in the early 1950s. A record of her political views at this time can be found in her novel *Retreat to Innocence*, which appeared in 1956. **Ruth Whittaker** considers this work Lessing's "only piece that can be called propagandistic." In it, a well-connected young English woman, Julia Barr, becomes romantically linked to a Czech Communist refugee, Jan Brod. Their affair ends when, despite her help, he fails to gain British citizenship and is forced to return home. The book was completed before the dramatic events of 1956 such as Nikita Khrushchev's denunciation of Joseph Stalin and the subsequent repression of Hungarian independence, and it features a long passage in which Jan Brod paints an enthusiastic description of Stalin, even comparing him to the Messiah. Lessing abandoned her ties to the Communist Party following the actions of the Soviet Union in invading Hungary in 1956. Probably embarrassed by the book's message, or at least by its lack of psychological depth, Lessing has never let it be reprinted.

In 1962, in the midst of writing the "Children of Violence" series, Lessing produced what many critics consider her masterpiece, *The Golden Notebook*. Initially, it received a mixed reception with some reviewers finding it muddled, but the prevailing opinion was that it demonstrated her talents as one of the best English writers to emerge since World War II. The book focuses on what Whittaker calls "Politics, madness and the roles of women . . . now familiar Lessing themes." For **Jean Pickering**, it tells "the story of a woman's breakdown, fragmentation, and healing into unity." An exploration of the life of a woman living within the strictures of a male-dominated society, *The Golden Notebook* has been hailed as a pioneering literary exploration into modern feminism. It anticipates in striking fashion one of the major cultural trends of the ensuing decades. But it also introduced remarkably new techniques into the author's work.

Lessing's heroine, Anna Wulf, has become one of the most celebrated female characters in modern fiction. The author of a successful first novel, she has now become unable to break her writer's block. The novel consists of five notebooks, each one dealing with an aspect of her life and work. Writes Moore: "The obvious fragmentation of form invites separating Lessing from the nineteenth-century masters . . . away from the traditional realism that she championed in the 1950s." The fragmentation of the book in fact reflects the fragmentation in the personality and experience of the heroine.

A portion of *The Golden Notebook* is itself a separate novel entitled *Free Women*. It is the latest work by Anna Wulf. The remainder of *The Golden Notebook* consists of portions from the four notebooks Lessing's heroine keeps while practicing her craft as novelist. Each notebook views Anna's life from a different perspective, giving the reader what Whittaker describes as "the muddled, sometimes contradictory skein of events and feelings which may never amount to an adequate explanation of her." A powerful section comes from the blue notebook in which Anna records her activities on a single day, September 14, 1954. Here, some of the most notable passages deal in an unprecedentedly candid way with the everyday details of a woman's life, such as menstruation. Whittaker calls the description of the entire day "one of the most painful and claustrophobic passages in the novel," as it "forces the reader to realise how appalling was a fairly typical day in the life of a woman in the mid-twentieth century."

This book has been described as a watershed in Lessing's body of writing. The techniques that she developed in *The Golden Notebook* were incorporated into the final volumes of the "Children of Violence." *The Four-Gated City* placed Martha Quest in the home of a London family as a housekeeper, editor, and mistress for the owner, Mark Coldridge. It presents a picture of London social life in the Cold War years of the 1950s and 1960s, and, like many other novels by Lessing, it features a main character who descends into madness. The book ranges over a period of 50 years, and it leaves the present behind to speculate in gloomy fashion about the future. It ends with an appendix showing Britain in the aftermath of a cataclysmic experience, a nuclear accident or possibly a nuclear war. The heroine dies on an island off the coast of Scotland.

Lessing then launched herself on a second extended series entitled "Canopus in Argos: Archives." This was a set of five books which appeared from 1979 through 1983, and in them Lessing explored a world taken from science fiction. But in the years after she completed the "Children of Violence," she also produced a number of major individual works. These included *Briefing for a Descent into Hell*, published in 1971, and *The Good Terrorist*, which appeared in 1985. As a playful experiment, she offered the public two books, *The Diary of a Good Neighbor* (1983) and *If the Old Could . . .* (1984), under the pseudonym of Jane Somers.

The novels written as Jane Somers raise a number of new issues. Like several of Lessing's works of the 1980s, these books saw her style move back to a greater degree of realism. They may have reflected her response to the criticism she received for the "Canopus in Argos" series by showing that she was capable of continuing to write in a realistic vein. They also represented Lessing's attack on the shallowness and lack of perception of many literary editors and critics. She showed how quick those individuals were to reject meritorious work done by an unknown writer, and then how readily the same work was generally accepted when attached to the name of a famous author. Some critics responded, however, by accusing her of a publicity stunt designed to promote the books once her identity had been revealed.

The most striking element in the first of these two pseudonymous publications was its exploration of old age. Lessing's heroine in *The Diaries of Jane Somers* is a professionally successful middle-aged widow—an assistant editor of a London magazine—who takes on the task of caring for a 92-year-old woman dying of cancer. The emphasis of the book, notes Whittaker, is "ageing, slow deterioration, and death." As in *The Golden Notebook*, Lessing stresses the physical functions of the body, this time made even more vivid by their association with fatal illness. In the later portion of the book, the heroine herself is hospitalized and experiences the humiliating routine, to which she had recently been a witness, of being immobilized and nursed. In interviews given at the time, Lessing made it clear she was, once again, tapping her own experiences in dealing with the dying elderly and with the social services available to them.

Equally interesting in reflecting a new direction in Lessing's work was *The Good Terrorist*, which appeared in 1985. A sharply satiric novel that deals with left-wing radicals in contempo-

Doris
Lessing

rary London, it seemed to show a very different political viewpoint from the one Lessing had espoused since her days attending a Communist cell in Southern Rhodesia in the 1940s.

A society increasingly sinking into urban violence is also the backdrop for Lessing's *The Fifth Child*, published in 1988. A male child enters the quiet middle-class existence of a large English family only to show himself to be both mentally and physically abnormal. Violent toward animals and members of his family, "Ben" is confined in a mental institution in northern England but is taken back to his home by his mother, an action that leads to the breakdown of the entire family. The violent son, now a young man, comes to fit well into an English society characterized by gang violence, the collapse of middle-class norms, and the breakdown of urban life.

Lessing's versatility as a writer has been as remarkable as the themes of modern life that she has explored. Her own experience in psychoanalysis as well as her conversion to Sufism, a mystic form of Islam, have been incorporated into her writing. For example, the fourth volume of "Children of Violence," entitled *Landlocked* and published in 1965, reflects her involvement with Sufism by calling for an understanding of the world that goes beyond ordinary perception into the realm of telepathy and mental visions. The development of Martha Quest in the subsequent volume, *The Four-Gated City*, reflects what Jean Pickering calls "the Sufi belief in the evolutionary possibility of planned spiritual growth."

Lessing's success as a writer can be seen in her dual achievement of occasionally producing bestselling books while invariably attracting intense and serious attention from leading literary critics. *The Golden Notebook*, for example, has sold over 900,000 copies in hardbound editions alone. Serious examinations of her work began to appear in the mid-1960s with **Dorothy Brewster**'s *Doris Lessing*, and numerous additional book-length studies and journal articles have followed, along with a growing number of doctoral dissertations. The richness of Lessing's work can be seen in approaches students have used in assessing her achievement: her books and short stories have been examined from feminist, psychoanalytical, religious, and political perspectives. Some of the leading writers of the late 20th century have been called upon to review her work, including Gore Vidal, **Joan Didion**, Kingsley Amis, and **Margaret Drabble**.

In October 1956, the all-white government of Southern Rhodesia banned Lessing as a political undesirable. But in 1982, she returned to Africa to visit her childhood home in what was now the black majority nation of Zimbabwe. Several additional visits followed into the early part of the next decade. These trips led to her nonfiction book, *African Laughter: Four Visits to Zimbabwe*, which appeared in 1992. She also published *Under My Skin: Volume One of My Autobiography to 1949* (1994), followed by *Walking in the Shade: Volume Two of My Autobiography, 1949–1962* (1997).

SOURCES:

Brewster, Dorothy. *Doris Lessing*. NY: Twayne, 1965.

Draine, Betsy. *Substance under Pressure: Artistic Coherence and Evolving Form in the Novels of Doris Lessing*. Madison, WI: University of Wisconsin Press, 1983.

Fishburn, Katherine. *The Unexpected Universe of Doris Lessing: A Study in Narrative Technique*. Westport, CT: Greenwood Press, 1985.

Graham, Judith, ed. *Current Biography*. NY: H.W. Wilson, 1995.

Pickering, Jean. *Understanding Doris Lessing*. Columbia, SC: University of South Carolina Press, 1986.

Rowe, Margaret Moan. *Doris Lessing*. NY: St. Martin's Press, 1994.

Sprague, Claire, and Virginia Tiger. *Critical Essays on Doris Lessing*. Boston, MA: G.K. Hall, 1986.

Whittaker, Ruth. *Doris Lessing*. Houndsmills, Basinstoke, Hampshire, England: Macmillan, 1988.

SUGGESTED READING:

Ingersoll, Earl G. *Doris Lessing: Conversations*. Princeton, NJ: Ontario Review Press, 1994.

Kaplan, Carey, and Ellen Cronan Rose. *Doris Lessing: The Alchemy of Survival*. Athens, OH: Ohio University Press, 1988.

King, Jeannette. *Doris Lessing*. London: Edward Arnold, 1989.

Lessing, Doris. *Under My Skin: Volume One of My Autobiography to 1949*. NY: HarperCollins, 1994.

———. *Walking in the Shade: Volume Two of My Autobiography, 1949–1962*. NY: HarperCollins, 1997.

RELATED MEDIA:

The Grass is Singing (110 min. film), starring Karen Black, John Thaw, and John Kani, filmed by Bille August, Chibote-Swedish Film Institute, 1982.

Neil M. Heyman,
Professor of History, San Diego State University,
San Diego, California

Lestonac, Jeanne de (1556–1640).

See Jeanne de Lestonac.

Le Sueur, Meridel (1900–1996)

American writer who recorded the stories of Midwestern workers, farmers, women, and Native Americans, the subject matter of which delayed publication of much of her best work for 30 years because editors told her that the topics were not interesting. Pronunciation: L'-Sooer. Born Meridel Wharton on February 22, 1900, in Murray, Iowa; died in November 1996;

daughter of William Wharton (an itinerant preacher) and Marian (Lucy) Wharton (a feminist-socialist educator); gained a stepfather when Marian divorced William and in 1917 married Arthur Le Sueur (a socialist lawyer and educator); married Harry Rice ("Yasha," a Russian immigrant and Marxist labor organizer), in 1926 (divorced 1930); children: **Rachel Rice; Deborah Rice.**

Published first stories, "Persephone" and "Afternoon" (Dial, 1927); hailed as a promising and major writer after "Annunciation" (1935) and Salute to Spring *(1940); blacklisted during postwar McCarthy hearings (1940s and 1950s); rediscovered (1970s).*

Awards: "Annunciation" chosen for O'Brien's Best Short Stories *(1935); WPA Federal Writers Project (1939); Rockefeller Historical Research grant for* North Star Country *(1943); grant from the National Endowment for Humanities (NEH, 1980); Bush Artist Fellowship (1981); NEH grants for* I Hear Men Talking *(1984) and for reprinting of children's books (1987); Lumen Vitae Award, College of Saint Benedict (1987); founding of Meridel Le Sueur Center for Peace and Justice, Minneapolis, which also houses her personal collection of midwestern American literature (1987); American Book Award for* Harvest Song *(1991); NEH grant for* The Dread Road *(1990); Distinguished Minnesotan Award, "Voice of the Prairie," Bemidji State University (1991).*

Selected publications: Annunciation *(1935);* Worker Writers *(1939);* Salute to Spring *(1940);* North Star Country *(1945);* Little Brother of the Wilderness: The Story of Johnny Appleseed *(1947);* Nancy Hanks of Wilderness Road *(1949);* Sparrow Hawk *(1950);* Chanticleer of Wilderness Road: A Story of Davy Crockett *(1951);* The River Road: A Story of Abraham Lincoln *(1954);* Crusaders *(1955);* Corn Village *(1970);* Conquistadores *(1973);* The Mound Builders *(1974);* Rites of Ancient Ripening *(1977);* Harvest: Collected Stories *(1977);* Song for My Time *(1977);* The Girl *(1978);* Women on the Bread Lines *(1978);* I Hear Men Talking *(1984);* Ripening: Selected Work, 1927–80 *(1982);* Winter Prairie Woman *(1990);* Harvest Song *(*Harvest *and* Song for My Times, *1991);* The Dread Road *(1991);* I Speak from the Shuck *(1992).*

On April 20, 1914, two Colorado state militia companies met on Water Tank Hill above the Ludlow mining camp and attacked 1,000 miners, their wives and children. Advancing down the hill, the militia men kept up a murderous barrage from high-powered rifles and machine guns mounted on wheels, one of which was

nicknamed "The Death Special." Many women and children escaped into the hills or hid in pits dug under the campsite, but the militia men set fire to the tents. At the end of the day, two women and eleven children were found asphyxiated in a single cellar. Five more strikers and two boys were killed in the shooting, including Louis Tikas, an organizer for the United Mine Workers of America (UMWA), who was clubbed in the head and shot three times in the back.

The miners, who had been living in a tent colony during a strike against a Rockefeller-owned coal company, wanted better working conditions, hours, pay, and company compliance with state laws. Early in the strike, Governor Elias Ammons had sent state militia into the region to keep order, but complications arose when some militia joined the company men against the miners. The governor withdrew all but the two militia companies, one of which was made up of coal company men; these same companies launched the brutal massacre.

Partisans of the miners, unable to reach Ludlow in time to help, moved into other camps in the region. The Ludlow Massacre generated such bad publicity and rebellion that President Woodrow Wilson dispatched federal troops to settle the situation. Today a statue of a miner with his wife and child commemorates the scene. The plaque reads: "In memory of the men, women, and children who lost their lives in freedom's cause at Ludlow, Colorado, April 20, 1914. Erected by the United Mine Workers of America."

"This event changed me forever," said Meridel Le Sueur. Parades and memorials for the Ludlow victims took place across the country, including at People's College, a "labor school" to educate workers through correspondence, in Fort Scott, Kansas, where Marian and Arthur Le Sueur were teachers. Meridel Le Sueur was 14 years old when she marched with her mother in the parade commemorating the victims. The grieving miners, in Le Sueur's own words, "were starving. They were blacklisted. They had lost the strike. They marched down the street . . . silently. . . . The faculty of the People's College marched behind them. I held my mother's hand. We were weeping."

At age 14, Le Sueur reported on Ludlow for a labor journal, and at age 91, she published *The Dread Road,* a "communal creation of an image," juxtaposing the Ludlow massacre and 20th-century war with the story of a young mother traveling by bus to bury her dead child and excerpts from Edgar Allan Poe's stories. John

Crawford speculates that Le Sueur's narrative description in this story probably came from firsthand accounts: "I remember after the massacre there was a terrible passion to get the bodies. Don't let the dead children fall into their hands. Don't let the mothers, the women, the wives, fall into their murderous hands. To get the bodies out of there to Trinidad on that terrible night."

Words used to describe the landscape of Meridel Le Sueur's life are survival, ripening, harvest, song, community, and rebellion. Perhaps the key word is rebellion, rebellion against what Le Sueur sees as oppressors—federal and state governments, greedy capitalists, and plunderers of the earth's resources. "I Speak from the Shuck" (1992), which celebrates the power of "ancient corn" to redeem the "raped earth," ends with: "O corn of love/ O thunder of protein/ . . .The green corn/ The seed corn/ Rebellion."

My writing used to be described by the male hierarchy as lyrical and hysterical.

—Meridel Le Sueur

Rebellion for Le Sueur, the writer, was costly. Her resistance to the status quo, her refusal to compromise, her self-determination, and her openness to all types of people often made her an outsider. She was the communist who would not toe the party line (Whittaker Chambers, editor of *New Masses*, criticized her article "Women on the Breadlines" for her "defeatist" attitude and lack of "revolutionary spirit"); the feminist who celebrated motherhood and childbirth; the historian who told the untold stories of farmers, Native Americans, angry workers, hungry women (reviewers said her history was "eclectic" and "subjective"); the preacher-poet and the passionate biographer. "I'm probably the best known *un*published writer in the world," she wrote in a 1938 journal. "But I don't care."

During the McCarthy era of the 1940s and '50s, when unfair accusations and indiscriminate investigative methods were used against many actors, writers, and artists, her work was blacklisted in the name of fighting communism. Only her children's books, published by Alfred Knopf, generated a meager income to support her family in those lean years. The women's movement in the 1970s published many Le Sueur works for a new audience, making it seem as if feminists had discovered her, but she always had a small, committed audience in left-wing magazines.

Meridel Le Sueur was born in 1900 in Murray, Iowa, to William and **Marian Wharton**, just when the radical farmer and labor organiza-tions—the Non-Partisan League, the Farmer's Alliance, the Populists, the International Workers of the World—that would shape her thinking were forming. Her childhood and adolescence were spent in Midwest towns in Iowa, Texas, Oklahoma, and Kansas before she went to St. Paul, Minnesota, where she lived most of her adult life. She learned the inequalities of being a girl early. By 1910, her mother, unhappy in her marriage, left William and escaped to Oklahoma with her two small sons and ten-year-old Meridel. They lived with **Antoinette Lucy**, Marian's mother. "My mother had to kidnap her children out of Texas and take them over the border," writes Le Sueur, "because in Texas you were property of the husband; the children were property." Eventually, William Wharton applied for a divorce on the grounds that his wife read "dangerous literature."

Meridel made friends with Native American girls in Oklahoma, experiencing a sharp contrast between their culture and the strict, puritanical life of her grandmother. Le Sueur learned to record what she heard. "I've never considered myself so much a writer as a witness. . . . I began to write in order to bear witness to the struggle of women I saw around me." Hiding behind water troughs in the streets, near wagon wheels in Kansas, and under tables at home, she listened to the voices of struggling people. "I loved the farm women especially," she told **Patricia Hampl**. "I always thought they were the story-tellers, they were the poets."

Marian Wharton rode the Chautauqua circuit, giving a three-day course on "The Great Laws of Life." A confirmed socialist, she moved the family to Fort Scott, Kansas, in 1914. There she chaired the English department of People's College, met Arthur Le Sueur, president of the college and chair of the law department, and later married him. If Meridel experienced the Midwestern pattern of the "lost, silent" father in William Wharton, she found in her stepfather a man she could respect. A committed socialist and eloquent orator, he provided a firm base for the family.

Meridel's relationship to her mother was complex. "We were absolutely opposite," Le Sueur told **Amy Gage**. "She was a very beautiful, strong, and powerful woman. That kind of conflict—you either are destroyed, or you grow." Marian was aggressive and objective, whereas Meridel was subjective and dreamy. "But I probably would have gone to sleep and done nothing if she hadn't been goosing me." Le Sueur's life at People's College brought her into contact with *Helen Keller and with Eugene Debs, four-time

*Meridel
Le Sueur*

socialist candidate for president and chancellor of the college, as well as anarchists Alexander Berkman, ***Emma Goldman**, and ***Ella Reeve Bloor**.

When anti-socialist vigilantes destroyed People's College in 1915, the family moved to St.

Paul, Minnesota, where their Dayton Avenue house became a haven for workers, activists, and radicals. At 16, Meridel dropped out of high school, partly because "they concentrated on English writers, not American," but mostly because "I couldn't find my history there and so I quit." At 18, she told Gage, she weighed her options: "I could be a wife and mother, a nurse, a teacher; or a whore." Instead, she attended Bernarr McFadden's Physical Culture School in Chicago and spent a year at the American Academy of Dramatic Art in New York. There she lived with Goldman and Berkman, and landed a small part on Broadway in *Lady Windermere's Fan*, directed by David Belasco.

Soon, she was in Hollywood, doing stunts for *The Perils of Pauline* and portraying an Indian in *The Last of the Mohicans*. These jobs gave her enough money to live simply while she wrote for the *Daily Worker* and other publications. When Hollywood wanted to remake her "hooked" nose, she left, joining a traveling San Francisco theater group and meeting Harry Rice, a Marxist labor organizer, whom she married in 1926. By 1927, she was jailed for protesting the executions of Nicola Sacco and Bartolomeo Vanzetti, Italian anarchists accused of murder and theft and thought by many to be victims of political bias. Sitting in jail, Le Sueur decided to have a baby, her "gift to the world."

In 1928, she returned to St. Paul to live with Marian and Arthur Le Sueur and to have her baby, Rachel. A second daughter, Deborah, was born a year later. By this time her marriage with Rice was falling apart, and they were divorced. She then met Robert Aaron Brown, a painter, destined to become her lifelong friend and lover.

The Great Depression of the 1930s saw her trying to balance the life of a single mother and a writer. She supported herself by working various jobs as governess, bootlegger, factory worker, waitress, and washroom attendant. Her journals reflect her struggle. After waitressing all day, she returned home to two children and their needs. When she fell asleep over her writing, she stuck her head under the cold water faucet to wake herself up and to write her self-assigned two hours a day. When she was paid $200 for a story, she threw a party and invited her friends who were as poverty-stricken as she was. (The abandoned warehouse where poor women live together in *The Girl* is not fiction, but Le Sueur's reality at one time.)

She also frequented the Venice Cafe at Seven Corners where the bohemian crowd gathered: F. Scott Fitzgerald, Sinclair Lewis, *Wanda Gág, and others. Sam Darling reports Le Sueur's cryptic analysis of the St. Paul power groups: "They used to say that St. Paul was divided between Bishop Ireland at the Cathedral, Jim Hill at the Railroad, and **Nina Clifford** who had the great-

est whorehouses in America. They controlled not only St. Paul, but the whole Northwest."

In her 1933 journal, referring to *The Girl,* her classic novel about the survival of a young girl in St. Paul during the Depression, she noted: "I am going to write a great novel someday and feed people. This choice is my first choice. Choosing against indulgence." Nearly 40 years would pass before it would be published. One editor told her that her style was lyrical, but she should choose more interesting subject matter, as Hemingway did. "I can't write like Hemingway," she replied. "I don't have any of his experiences. Fishing, fighting, and fucking are not my major interests."

Harry Rice caught the essence of her poetry when he wrote to her in 1935: "Where do you acquire that sublime toughness, that real rare vitality that can weep and sing at the same time?" This lyrical quality informs *The Girl* and *Salute to Spring.* When *Salute to Spring* was published in 1940, containing her most frequently anthologized short story, "Annunciation," on the birth of her daughter, it was praised by Carl Sandburg, Sinclair Lewis, and Nelson Algren, who wrote to a friend: "Just finished Annunciation and an old belief has been confirmed: that Meridel Le Sueur is the finest mistress of prose in the land. No one remotely approaches her ability to weave the harshest reality with a high sense of beauty." Waldo Frank wrote to her: "Annunciation is a wonderful lovely poem: tender, true, large."

When Le Sueur joined the Teamsters' trucker strike in Minneapolis in 1934, she found it a riveting experience. In her classic essay, "I Was Marching," she reveals her discovery: the truckers were not competing with each other; they were acting together.

> I was marching with a million hands, movements, faces, and my own movement was repeating again and again, making a new movement from these many gestures, the walking, falling back, the open mouth crying, the nostrils stretched apart, the raised hand, the blow falling, and the outstretched hand drawing me in.

This breaking open of the self to reach out to others, this sense of community forged through suffering, this transforming the "I" to "we" are major themes in Le Sueur's work. Much later, when she was 90, she said: "When you age, you don't think so personally; you rot out the ego, the little thing that is you. I've been flying over my whole life and looking at it in a different way. That's probably what art is, an accumulation of experience."

The decade between 1930 and 1940 was productive for Le Sueur despite unsympathetic editors. She published 16 short stories and many articles for the *Daily Worker, American Mercury, Pagany, Partisan Review, The Nation, Scribner's*, the *Anvil, Dial, Poetry*, and *Woman's Home Companion*. She also joined the WPA (Works Progress Administration) Federal Writers' Project, "a wonderful motley crew." They were editors whose newspapers had folded, freelance writers, and writers of science fiction and ad copy. She taught creative writing classes at the College of Saint Catherine and at the University of Minnesota and spent countless hours at the Minnesota Historical Society to write *North Star Country*, a lyrical history of the Midwest.

Throughout her life, she wrote in her journals, over 170 of them. Her daybooks, she told Hampl, are like the thread that comes daily out of a spider. They come from a need to express herself, to make order out of chaos, and "the unknown into some kind of web. It seems to me, well, maybe in the journals I was catching food, I was catching butterflies, sustenance: I was starving." According to Jay Walljasper, she considers her journals her "master work because they show the progress of a writer and a person, as well as offering a comprehensive social history of the Twin Cities."

The years 1947 to the early 1960s were the "dark time" during the McCarthy era when she was blacklisted by the FBI and hounded everywhere she went. "You couldn't get a job. I couldn't teach a writing class; I couldn't even get a job as a waitress," she said. Once while she was walking to a political meeting, it began to rain. Le Sueur strolled up to the FBI agent following behind her in his car and asked for a ride "since we're both going to the same place." She survived on labor reporting and her children's books, though a *Milwaukee Journal* review called the stories "pink-tinged," designed to mislead young people.

She faced other misfortunes during this time as well. Harry Rice died in 1948, followed by her stepfather Arthur Le Sueur in 1950, and her companion Robert Brown and her mother Marian Le Sueur in 1954. Stunned though not defeated, Le Sueur traveled by bus, spending much time in Mexico and the American Southwest and tape recording stories of people. (Folksinger Pete Seeger gave Le Sueur her first tape recorder on her 50th birthday.) She also spent time with Native Americans in Northern Minnesota. Her money problems continued and, according to **Elaine Hedges**, the FBI even harassed Le Sueur's

boarders in the rooming house her mother had left her. To support herself before she qualified for Social Security and to supplement her income afterwards, she chauffeured a handicapped woman who commuted between Santa Fe and Iowa, worked in a factory for $1.00 an hour, was an attendant at the Minnesota State Asylum, and even lived in an abandoned bus in Santa Fe for a few years.

In the 1960s, Le Sueur visited college campuses, participated in the Poor People's March, protested the Vietnam War, and worked on rights for Native Americans. The women's movement in the early 1970s brought Le Sueur new life and her real audience: women. After 1977, a new generation of publishers worked with her to produce a poetry collection, *Rites of Ancient Ripening*; two novels, *The Girl* and *I Hear Men Talking*; and three story collections, *Harvest, Song for My Time* and *Ripening*. The earlier volumes *Salute To Spring, North Star Country*, and *Crusaders* were reissued during the same period. Enjoying the acclaim, yet always suspicious of it, she told Walljasper:

> I was buried for thirty years, but that's nothing new. Indian literature was buried. Black literature was buried. For years American literature meant white middle-class puritan male literature. I recently compiled a list of twenty women writers, twenty Midwestern women writers whose careers were trashed by critics and publishers. But when people get freed, their culture gets freed.

Another freeing event was her appearance, at age 85, at the 1985 Women's International Conference in Nairobi, Africa. Her poem, "Arise," celebrates strong women: "They came out of Nairobi. . . . We claim our earth. . . . We claim our bodies." Her 90th birthday was a community festival in the Twin Cities, beginning with a benefit concert by folksingers Pete Seeger and *Ronnie Gilbert for the Meridel Le Sueur Library (February 17, 1990) and ending the next day with an afternoon program of poems, songs, and readings honoring her at the College of Saint Catherine. The events were sponsored by a coalition of over 35 organizations from the Heart of the Beast Puppet Theatre to the Minnesota Peace & Justice Coalition. T-shirts reading "Songs for Our Time" and "Survival is a Form of Resistance" commemorated the event. A weekend of festivity, community, and solidarity, it illustrated what Le Sueur once wrote: "We must somehow find how to be committed to others, how to express that love which is an act of courage, not of fear, but of bravery and of seeing the liberation in each other, that makes us proud and human."

Early in her life, Le Sueur decided that goals and success are in the male world, in what she calls "the linear world, the world which goes toward the target." But she wanted to live in the circular world, the world of the seed, the flower, even the world of having a child. "I wanted to grow, and not to consume or not to become successful or to become a goal. I wanted to grow in the way the season grows. . . . I think I felt this very early and now I'm looking back on my life I feel I really wanted to ripen."

Common themes in her work are labor unrest, the Great Depression, poor people, human love, the natural beauty of the land, and regional history. Her earthy wisdom delighted and inspired her admirers. "A straight line goes toward a goal—ultimately to the bomb," she wrote. "It's called progress, but it leads to destruction. If you're thinking circularly, you know your shit's going to fall on you, because you know that you return again and again to the same place. Creation requires returning to the source of inspiration. That's what I'm still doing." Meridel Le Sueur, who died in November 1996, once told worker writers: "Don't tell yourself that it's not up to you to write the true history. Who is to write it if not you? You live it. You make it. You write it."

SOURCES:

Crawford, John, ed. "Note on the History of Ludlow," in *The Dread Road* by Meridel Le Sueur. Minneapolis: West End Press, 1991.

Darling, Sam. "A Witness to the People," in *The Community Reporter*. St. Paul, March 1987.

Gage, Amy. "The Insistent Voice," in *Minnesota Monthly*. March 1988, pp. 25–32.

Grossmann, Mary Ann. "Ninety Years of the Struggle," in *St. Paul Pioneer Press Dispatch*. February 11, 1990, pp. 1D, 3D.

Hampl, Patricia. "Meridel Le Sueur: Voice of the Prairie," in *Ms.* August 1963, pp. 62–66+.

Hedges, Elaine. "Introduction" in *Ripening: Selected Work, 1927–1980* by Meridel Le Sueur. Old Westbury, NY: Feminist Press, 1982.

Le Sueur, Meridel. Interview by Nancy Hynes, O.S.B. Hudson, WI: May 19, 1989.

———. Journals (1924–43). Unpublished. Minnesota Historical Society, St. Paul, MN.

Walljasper, Jay. "A Conversation with Meridel Le Sueur," in *Minnesota Daily*. Minneapolis: University of Minnesota, October 7, 1980.

SUGGESTED READING:

Barron, Ron. "Meridel Le Sueur." *A Guide to Minnesota Writers*. St. Paul, MN: Minnesota Council of Teachers of English, 1987.

Coiner, Constance. *Better Red: The Writing and Resistance of *Tillie Olsen* and Meridel Le Sueur*. Oxford University Press, 1995.

Pichaska, David R. "Meridel Le Sueur Reconsidered," in *Minnesota English Journal*. Winter–Spring 1985, pp. 11–26.

Pratt, Linda. "Afterword" in *I Hear Men Talking* by Meridel Le Sueur. Minneapolis, MN: West End Press, 1984.

Schleuning, Neala Yount. *America: Song We Sang Without Knowing*. Mankato, MN: Little Red Hen, 1983.

COLLECTIONS:

Journals of Meridel Le Sueur located in the Minnesota Historical Society, St. Paul, Minnesota.

RELATED MEDIA:

Hard Times Come Again No More, play adapted from Le Sueur's works by **Martha Boesing**, 1994.

My People Are My Home, a film by Meridel Le Sueur, 1977.

Ripenings, a one-woman play adapted by **Molly Culligan** and **Phyllis Paullette**, performed by Molly Culligan, 1979 (for over 15 years).

"The Voice of Meridel Le Sueur" (30 min.), first aired on Minnesota Public Radio, July 5, 1993.

Nancy Hynes, O.S.B.,
Professor of English, College of Saint Benedict,
St. Joseph, Minnesota

Leszczynska, Marie (1703–1768).

See Marie Leczinska.

Letitia.

Variant of Laetitia or Lettice.

Leuchtenburg, duchess of.

See Amalie Auguste (1788–1851).
See Maria Nikolaevna (1819–1876).

Leverson, Ada (1862–1933)

English novelist. Name variations: (pseudonym) Elaine. Born Ada Beddington on October 10, 1862, in London, England; died on August 30, 1933, in London, England; daughter of Samuel Beddington (a property investor) and Zillah Simon Beddington; educated at home; married Ernest Leverson (separated 1900); children: son (died in infancy); daughter, Violet Wyndham (a writer).

Selected writings: The Twelfth Hour (1907); Love's Shadow (1908); The Limit (1911); Tenterhooks (1912); The Bird of Paradise (1914); Love at Second Sight (1916); Letters to the Sphinx from Oscar Wilde with Reminiscences of the Author (1930).

A novelist of manners and marriage, Ada Leverson was part of a circle of late-Victorian and Edwardian authors and artists which included Oscar Wilde, Aubrey Beardsley, George Moore, *Edith Sitwell and her brother Osbert Sitwell, and Max Beerbohm. Born to a wealthy London family on October 10, 1862, Leverson was the daughter of Samuel Beddington, a property investor, and **Zillah Simon Beddington**, an amateur pianist of some talent. She was educated at home with the advantages of the upper middle class and married a gambler and speculator, Ernest Leverson, against her parents' wishes. The couple had two children, a son who died in infancy and a daughter, Violet. The marriage was never happy, but Ada Leverson was more a product of her class and times than she would allow, remaining in the marriage to avoid scandal until 1900, when her husband immigrated to Canada. He left behind a trail of bad debts and bankruptcy, and enough material for Leverson to begin her career as a novelist.

Ada Leverson first attracted the attention of Oscar Wilde in 1892, when she published "An Afternoon Party," a parody of his novel *The Picture of Dorian Gray*, in the periodical *Yellow Book*. Other early works, including sketches, articles, and parodies, were published in *Punch* and *Black and White*. She was dubbed "the Sphinx" after she wrote a parody of Wilde's work of the same name in 1894, and the nickname stuck. A strong supporter of Wilde throughout the time of his trial and incarceration for homosexual "offenses," she was present to greet him upon his release from prison in 1897.

Leverson published her first novel, *The Twelfth Hour*, in 1907. *Love's Shadow* followed in 1908, along with *Tenterhooks* in 1912 and *Love at Second Sight* in 1916; comedies of manners, the latter three formed a trilogy about a married couple, Edith and Bruce Ottley. (Bruce Ottley is thought to be based upon Ernest Leverson.) The novels were republished together in 1962 under the title *The Little Ottleys*. Highlighting Edwardian manners of the upper middle class, her work often depicts marital strife. Her characters are filled with jealousies and tension, evidenced most notably in her use of conversation which is thought to have been influenced by the techniques of Wilde and *Jane Austen. From 1903 to 1905, Leverson also wrote weekly columns for the periodical *Referee* under the pen name Elaine. She was noted for her ability to sum up her experience of her contemporaries using memorable phrasing, some of which is found in her memoir *Letters to the Sphinx from Oscar Wilde with Reminiscences of the Author*. Published in 1930, three years before her death, *Letters* offers a portrait of Wilde during the 1890s and a firsthand account of the opening night of his classic play *The Importance of Being Earnest*. As a writer and a personality, Leverson has been included in commentaries by Osbert Sitwell, V.S. Pritchett, and Charles Burkhardt. In 1963, her daughter, **Violet Wyndham**, published a biography entitled *The Sphinx and her Circle: A Biographical Sketch of Ada Leverson 1862–1933*.

SOURCES:
Drabble, Margaret, ed. *The Oxford Companion to English Literature*. 5th ed. Oxford: Oxford University Press, 1985.
Shattock, Joanne. *The Oxford Guide to British Women Writers*. Oxford University Press, 1993.

Lolly Ockerstrom,
freelance writer, Washington, D.C.

Levertov, Denise (1923–1997)

Major English-born poet, essayist, teacher and translator known for her attention to craft, sense of aesthetic ethics, weaving of a woman's private and public spheres of experience, and political activism. Pronunciation: Lev-er-TOFF. Born on October 24, 1923, in Ilford, Essex, a suburb outside London; died from complications of lymphoma in Seattle, Washington, on December 20, 1997; daughter of Phillip Paul Levertoff (an Anglican cleric) and Beatrice Adelaide (Spooner-Jones) Levertoff; educated at home, along with her sister Olga, by her mother, and by a library of her father's books; studied ballet formally; married Mitchell Goodman (an American novelist), on December 2, 1947 (divorced 1972); children: son, Nikolai (b. 1949).

Selected awards: Besshokin Prize from Poetry (1959), for poem "With Eyes at the Back of Our Heads"; Longview Award (1961); Guggenheim fellowship (1962); Harriet Monroe Memorial Prize (1964); American Academy and Institute of Arts and Letters grant (1965); D. Litt., Colby College (1970), University of Cincinnati (1973), Bates College (1984), Saint Lawrence University (1984); Lenore Marshall Poetry Prize (1976); Elmer Holmes Bobst Award in poetry (1983); Shelley Memorial Award from Poetry Society of America (1984).

During World War II served as a nurse; published first book of poems, The Double Image (1946); met and married American novelist Mitchell Goodman (1947); after brief hiatus in Europe, came to America (1948); naturalized U.S. citizen (1955); had teaching residencies at City College of the City University of New York (1965–66), Vassar College (1966–67), University of California, Berkeley (1969), Massachusetts Institute of Technology (1969–70), Kirkland College (1971), University of Cincinnati (1973), Tufts University (1973–79), Brandeis University (1981–83), and Stanford University (1981); co-founded Writers and Artists Protest against the War in Vietnam (1965); was active in anti-nuclear and human-rights movements.

Selected writings—poetry: The Double Image (Cresset, 1946); Here and Now (City Lights, 1957); Overland to the Islands (Jargon, 1958); Five Poems

(White Rabbit, 1958); With Eyes at the Back of Our Heads (New Directions, 1959); The Jacob's Ladder (New Directions, 1961); O Taste and See: New Poems (New Directions, 1964); The Sorrow Dance (New Directions, 1967); A Tree Telling Orpheus (Black Sparrow, 1968); Relearning the Alphabet (New Directions, 1970); To Stay Alive (New Directions, 1971); Footprints (New Directions, 1972); The Freeing of the Dust (New Directions, 1975); Life in the Forest (New Directions, 1978); Collected Earlier Poems, 1940–1960 (New Directions, 1979); Wanderer's Daysong (Copper Canyon, 1981); Candles in Babylon (New Directions, 1982); Poems, 1960–1967 (New Directions, 1983); Requiem and Invocation (William B. Ewert, 1984); Breathing the Water (New Directions, 1987); Poems, 1968–1972 (New Directions, 1987); Sands of the Well (New Directions, 1996).

Other: (translator and editor with Edward C. Dimock, Jr.) In Praise of Krishna; Songs from the Bengali (Doubleday, 1967); (translator from French) Eugene Guilevic, Selected Poems (New Directions, 1969); (essays) The Poet in the World (New Directions, 1973); (essays) Light Up the Cave (New Directions, 1981); (translator with others from Bulgarian) William Meredith, editor, Poets of Bulgaria (Unicorn, 1985); (translator from French) Jean Joubert (Black Iris, Copper Canyon, 1988); (memoirs) Tesserae (New Directions, 1995).

In Denise Levertov's book of prose memoirs, Tesserae (1995), she begins with a story about her father, as a little boy, who sees an old peddlar carrying a large sack through the streets of his Russian town. Levertov recalls that her father (a descendent of "The Rav of Northern White Russia" who understood the language of birds) "believed that he knew" what the sack contained: "wings, many wings, that would enable people to fly like birds." This very same peddlar was also depicted in Chagall's paintings, where he is seen "flying, though not with wings." The peddlar's constant burden of such a "concentration of wings" might have been "transmuted into his ability" to levitate himself. Such an ability is a prospect for both mystics and poets.

In Levertov's "A Poet's View" (in Religion and Intellectual Life 1, Summer 1984), she wrote that the core of her work lies in acknowledging "mystery" and celebrating it, and that mystery is "probably . . . the most consistent theme." Mystery forms the locus of the two metaphorical worlds the poet inhabits: the everyday realities of the "here-and-now" and the imaginative, unworldly realm of the dream and its secrets. Accordingly, Levertov accounted for two realms of

female experience. One is made of dailiness, domestic duties and physical pleasures, open and direct. The other is lit by moonlight, passions, a romantic spirit of dance and music. Together, they comprise the total woman, although they are often in conflict. Levertov attributed these complementary but opposing qualities to what she inherited from her mother (an educator) and her father (an Anglican priest). She remarked in her autobiographical account, "Denise Levertov Writes" (The Bloodaxe Book of Contemporary Women Poets), that her parents seemed to be "exotic birds . . . in the plain English coppice of Ilford, Essex." Her mother, **Beatrice Spooner-Jones**, a Welshwoman who had grown up in a mining town and later in a north Wales country town and subsequently had traveled widely, had a love for "seeking out and exploring" the small and commonplace nature around her. Her father Phillip Paul Levertoff, a Russian Jew who converted to Christianity. He was more mystical and theological than her mother, meditating on unearthly, spiritual worlds.

Levertov's ancestry was important to her because both of her parents were especially interested in language and books. Her father came from a learned family in Russia and studied the Talmud, and would have become a rabbi if he had not discovered the New Testament while studying at the university. (A story of the young boy finding and reading a fragment from the scriptures which he found on a scrap of paper is included in Tesserae.) He met her mother Beatrice in Constantinople, where the Welsh woman had gone to teach in a Scottish school for girls. They lived in Warsaw and Leipzig, coming to England after World War I. Her father then converted to Christianity and was ordained an Anglican priest. Educated at home, Levertov received religious training from her father, who was a prolific writer in Hebrew, Russian, German, and English, and from her mother, who read the great works of the 19th century, notably the poetry of Tennyson. The only formal lessons Levertov received were in ballet. She served as a nurse during World War II and wrote poems in the evenings, culminating in The Double Image (1946), a book that favors elaborate rhetorical adornments (with its extreme ellipses and literary allusions) that some critics have attributed to an academic style from which she never departed. Yet, this first volume also anticipates many of the themes Levertov would develop through a lifetime of writing. Although she said that she was, for a period, "embarrassed" by her first book, Levertov also came to accept it for its "intuitive signs" that linked it with her mature works. During the time of its publication, she met and married American novelist Mitchell Goodman, and, after traveling in Europe, they came to the United States, where their son Nikolai was born in 1949.

In 1950, the family returned to Europe and lived two years in Provence, France, where Levertov became acquainted with the American poet Robert Creeley. She began to read more American poets and was particularly impressed by the writings of William Carlos Williams. Harry Martin in *Understanding Denise Levertov* quotes her discussion of the influence of American voices and subjects on her poems. Marrying an American and coming to New York City as a young woman stimulated her writing for "it necessitated the finding of new rhythms in which to write" in accordance with her new surroundings and speech. Willams, Charles Olson's essay "Projectivist Verse," conversations with Robert Duncan, and a renewed interest in Hasidic ideas were other influences on her. Struck by Williams' simple, concrete imagery and language, and by the immediacy of his form, Levertov discovered her own distinctive American style. When her first American book, *Here and Now* (1957), was subsequently published, it found favor among critics who had complained about romantic excesses in Levertov's earlier poems. For example, Kenneth Rexroth wrote in his 1961 book, *Assays,* that "the *Schwarmerei* and lassitude" of her former book was gone and replaced by "a kind of wedding of form and content" that was fulfillment for the reader. Also, Ralph J. Mills, Jr. observes in *Poets in Progress* that Levertov's poems "revel in, [and carve] into lyric poems of precise beauty" the "quotidian reality" most people try to ignore. Mills' emphasis on Levertov's "persistent investigation of the events of her own life—inner and outer—in the language of her own time and place" provides a focus for thinking about the poet's developing social and political consciousness which became extremely significant in her works of the 1960s and 1970s.

While being influenced by American writers, Levertov became associated with the Black Mountain poets and published in *Origin* and *Black Mountain Review*. She advocated the poetics of projectivist verse, whereby the form manifests itself as the poet "projects" himself or herself into its field without any metrical constraints. In later years, Levertov continued to expound on the value of process, writing essays on craft, line breaks, and stanza forms, and presenting nonmetrical and organic poetry as an exploratory alternative to the certitudes of formal verse. *Eyes in the Back of Our Heads*, published in 1959, demonstrates her mastery of the open form and extends the theme of a double vision of commonplace and mystical experience. Here, a woman's sensual reality is set into meaningful balance with her deeper comprehension of spiritual forms. Revelations, self-disclosures, mythic awakenings are all part of the fabric of the poet's life as it is lived in the actual, and in the moment—fusing together inner and outer impressions. In the poem "Pleasures," Levertov invents her own poetics: "I like to find/ what's not found/ at once, but lies/ . . . within something of another nature,/ in repose, distinct." And in "The Goddess," an attending silence is to be filled by the poem's solitude: "the silence was answering my silence."

With the turbulent 1960s, Levertov composed the major works of her middle years, including *The Sorrow Dance, Jacob's Ladder, Relearning the Alphabet, O Taste and See,* as well as collections of her poetry, all of which, to some extent, address socio-political topics and themes. As

Denise
Levertov

a result of her commitment to pacifism and world peace, Levertov became involved in protest against the war in Vietnam, participating in several antiwar demonstrations, and was arrested and jailed at least once. Although she delved into a socio-political action and poetry, she never forfeited her artistic integrity, insisting that the poem be allowed to grow and develop on its own, and not be forced in any way that would prove to be too mechanistic or dogmatic. *Jacob's Ladder* extends Levertov's theme of the examined life, a theme that intertwines with her observations of natural process. According to Levertov, living authentically means having acute awareness of life's inextricability with death: "always/ a recognition, the known/ appearing fully itself." This strand of thinking also weaves itself into the "Olga Poems" of *The Sorrow Dance,* as an elegiac, lyrical thread. As a river flowing towards death, Olga is ultimately resurrected by the poems from the double death of a denied life and a painful dying.

In *Relearning the Alphabet*, language is relearned while hollowing itself out in the world with that which fills it up again; but it is also a culture-making language inclusive of political themes of resistance and protest. Levertov's overall insistence on the poem's vitality, as the seam that binds things together, allows the poet to collaborate with sensuous images that are spun into lines. With this end in mind, Levertov reaffirms the existence of an inner life to which she returns again and again, and to which she pays homage. And in writing the words that serve to edify the real, she must also acknowledge their direct influence on others, as in "Second Didactic Poem" from *Sorrow*:

> The honey of man is
> the task we're set to: to be
> "more ourselves"
> in the making. . . .

The poet goes on to assert that in our individuating process, likened to that of the flowers' honey-making, we become the "honey of the human" (*Sorrow* 82–83) which, in turn, is redolent of the spirit.

Throughout the 1970s and 1980s, Levertov continued to produce remarkable poetry, although some critics were not altogether receptive to the socio-political poems of *To Stay Alive, Footprints, Candles in Babylon,* and others. Resistant to the controversial topics of these poems, many readers complained that Levertov's political poetry had an agenda that was too ministerial and "confessional," exhibiting "presumptuousness" that swerved away from the pure directives of art-making. However, Levertov's admirers were equally strident. On the Vietnam poems, **Kathleen Spivack** remarked: "It is the disparity between the delicacy of Levertov's lines and the brute horror with which she—and we—must deal that is most poignant." John Martone, in *World Literature Today,* reviewed *Candles in Babylon* (1982) by praising Levertov's consciously "encyclopedic scope" and believed she remained "one of the most vitally innovative of contemporary poetry."

Levertov's life work paid close attention to a language that spoke to the poet's willingness to allow, and to rely upon, the music of verse to lift her into unanticipated realms of experience. The motive for any artist or writer is to visit a new "borderland" ("The Life of Art"), which is on the rim between the familiar and the unfamiliar and unworldly. In an essay in *Light Up the Cave,* for instance, she wrote that poetry is "a way of constructing autonomous existences out of words and silences." Poems (like the peddlar's sack of wings that enables people to fly) give form to words which stir and lift the life of those who experience them. The poems themselves are separate from their maker, not a reflection of the poet, because they have been nurtured by the poet's insights into the actual world.

Levertov's meditative essays and lyrics continually enunciated the importance of these inward experiences as a discipline for art and life. From the beginning of her career, she connected with the letters and poems of Rainer Maria Rilke. Edward Zlotkowski notes in a comparative analysis of the two poets how Levertov's passionate, "ecstatic" attention to things transported her beyond the world of objects into what Rilke calls "the center of the universe, something the angels serve that very day upon that matchless spot." It was to Rilke that Levertov looked in order to establish her own concept of the artist's task, a task of translating the visible into the invisible, "that glow from within" so that the tangible things of this world can find their correspondent "vibration and excitability" within our own natures.

During the 1970s and 1980s, Levertov continued to produce new volumes of writing. She addressed a wide range of subjects that encompassed her life as artist, woman, mother, and teacher. She wrote memoirs of her childhood and ancestral past, gave her female perspective on private and national events, charted the births and deaths of those people who touched her intimately, including her son Nikolai, her students, her sister Olga, and her poetic precursors. Levertov translated French and Bulgarian poetry and discussed her own process in numerous interviews. In *Contemporary Authors* (1988), Levertov recounted sending some of her poems to T.S. Eliot when she was just 12 years old. Eliot suggested that she learn to read poetry in a language other than her own, a piece of advice she valued and acted on. Although she traveled extensively, in the ordinary sense of the word, she also traversed the inner regions of memory and imagination. Levertov was a pilgrim of the creative process and a bearer of its fruits. Her importance was felt within the literary community for more than four decades and contributed to the registry and history of 20th-century women writers.

SOURCES:

Contemporary Authors: New Revision Series. Vol. 29. Detroit, MI: Gale Research.

Critical Survey of Poets. Vol. 2. Edited by Frank Magill. Englewood Cliffs, NJ: Salem Press, 1984.

Levertov, Denise. *Light Up the Cave.* NY: New Directions, 1981.

Martin, Harry. *Understanding Denise Levertov.* Columbia, SC: University of South Carolina Press, 1988.

Wagner, Linda Welshimer. *Denise Levertov.* NY: Twayne, 1967.

Zlotkowski, Edward. "Levertov and Rilke: A Sense of Aesthetic Ethics" in *Contemporary Literature.* Vol. 29, special edition on Denise Levertov.

SUGGESTED READING:

Jansen, Ronald, guest ed. *Twentieth Century Literature.* Vol. 38. Fall 1992, special issue on Denise Levertov.

Levertov, Denise. *Tesserae* (autobiographical prose pieces). NY: New Directions, 1995.

MacGowan, Christopher, ed. *The Letters of Denise Levertov and William Carlos Williams.* NY: New Directions, 1998.

Rodgers, Audrey T. *Denise Levertov: The Poetry of Engagement.* Teaneck, NJ: Fairleigh Dickinson University Press, 1993.

COLLECTIONS:

Levertov's manuscript collections are housed in the following locations: Humanities Research Center; University of Texas at Austin; Washington University; Indiana University; New York University; Yale University; Brown University; University of Connecticut; Columbia University; State University of New York at Stony Brook.

Judith Lynn Harris,
Assistant Professor of English,
George Washington University, Washington, D.C.

Leveson-Gower, Georgiana Charlotte

(1812–1885).

See Fullerton, Georgiana Charlotte.

Leveson-Gower, Harriet

(1785–1862)

Countess of Granville. Name variations: Lady Granville Leveson-Gower. Born Harriet Cavendish on August 28, 1785; died in 1862; daughter of *Georgiana Cavendish (1757–1806) and William Cavendish, *5th duke of Devonshire; married Lord Granville Leveson-Gower, 1st earl Granville, on December 24, 1809; children: five, including Lady *Georgiana Charlotte Fullerton (1812–1885), and Granville George Leveson-Gower, 2nd earl Granville (1815–1891, a liberal diplomat in charge of the foreign office under Gladstone).*

Leveson-Gower, Harriet Elizabeth Georgiana (1806–1868)

Duchess of Sutherland. Born Harriet Elizabeth Georgiana Howard in 1806; died in 1868; daughter of George Howard, 6th earl of Carlisle (1773–1848, a diplomat); married George Granville Leveson-Gower, 2nd duke of Sutherland, in 1823.

A close friend of Queen *Victoria, Harriet Elizabeth Georgiana Leveson-Gower was mistress of the robes under Liberal administrations, 1837–41, 1846–52, 1853–58, and 1859–61.

Levi, Natalia (1901–1972)

Soviet composer and actress whose best-known compositions were written during and about the Siege of Leningrad. Born Natalia Nikolayevna Smyslova in St. Petersburg, Russia, on September 10, 1901; died in Leningrad (present-day St. Petersburg) on January 3, 1972.

Natalia Levi was born in 1901 in St. Petersburg, grew up in Petrograd, and died in 1972 in Leningrad, all the same city. In 1991, her works were once again performed in St. Petersburg. The changing name of her birthplace indicates the tumultuous period Russians like Levi lived through in the 20th century. Long a cultural mecca, St. Petersburg produced many talented artists like Levi. She graduated from the Russian Drama School and then from the Leningrad Conservatory where she studied composition under P. Pyazanov. From 1924 to 1934, Levi was an actress who also headed the Mobile Theater. In 1936, she moved to Petrozavodsk and became involved in a project collecting the folk songs of the northern people in the Soviet Union. She returned to Leningrad during World War II, where she served as a translator. She survived the Siege of Leningrad, a period when many citizens of that city starved to death rather than surrender to the Nazis. During this time, Levi composed war songs and later was awarded two medals for works hailing the defense of Leningrad.

John Haag,
Athens, Georgia

Levi-Montalcini, Rita (b. 1909)

Italian-born medical doctor and neurobiologist who won the Nobel Prize for her discovery of Nerve Growth Factor. Name variations: Rita Levi Montalcini. Born Rita Levi in Turin, Italy, on April 22, 1909; youngest of four children of Adele (Montalcini) Levi (a painter) and Adamo Levi (an electrical engineer and mathematician); twin sister of Paola Levi-Montalcini (an artist); sister of Gino Levi (d. 1974), an architect and professor at the University of Turin; graduated Turin School of Medicine, summa cum laude degree in Medicine and Surgery, 1936, granted advanced degree in neurology and psychiatry, 1940; never married; no children; became a U.S. citizen in 1956.

Awards: William Thomson Wakeman Award of the National Paraplegic Foundation (1974); Lewis S. Rosenstiel Award for Distinguished Work in Basic Medical Research of Brandeis University (1982); Louisa Gross Horwitz Prize from Columbia University (1983); Albert Lasker Basic Medical Research Award (1986); Nobel Prize for Physiology or Medicine (1986); U.S. National Medal of Science (1987).

Her governess died (1929); admitted to the Turin School of Medicine (1930); her father Adamo Levi died (August 2, 1932); graduated from Turin School of Medicine (1936); fired from Institute of Anatomy (1938); fled to Belgium (1939); returned to Italy (1939); secretly resumed her research (1939); awarded degree in neurology and psychiatry, Turin School of Medicine (1940); read article by Viktor Hamburger (1940); Giuseppe Levi returned to Turin (1941); moved to the country (1942); hid from the Nazis in Florence (1943–44); worked in a refugee camp (1944–46); was reinstated by the Institute of Anatomy (1946); traveled to U.S. (1946); accepted position of research associate, Washington University (1947); promoted to associate professor (1951); undertook research at Institute of Biophysics, Rio de Janeiro (1952); Stanley Cohen joined research team (1953); discovered Nerve Growth Factor (1954); promoted to full professor (1958); death of Giuseppe Levi (1965); established research laboratory in Rome (1961); elected to U.S. National Academy of Sciences (1968); appointed head of the Cell Biology Laboratory of the Italian Council of National Research (1969); retired from Washington University (1977); retired from Italian Council of National Research (1979); jointly awarded the Nobel Prize for Physiology or Medicine with Stanley Cohen (October 13, 1986).

Selected publications: "Les Conséquence de la destruction d'un territoire d'innervation peripherique sur le développement des centre nerveuz correspondants dans L'embryon de poulet," in Archive de Biologie

(1942); "Selective Growth Stimulating effects of mouse sarcoma on the sensory and sympathetic nervous system of the chick embryo," in Journal of Experimental Zoology (1951); "A Diffusible agent of mouse sarcoma, producing hyperplasia of sympathetic ganglia and hyperneurotization of viscera in the chick embryo," in Journal of Experimental Zoology (1954); "In vitro experiments on the effects of mouse sarcomas 180 and 37 on the spinal and sympathetic ganglia of the chick embryo," in Cancer Research (1954); "NGF: An uncharted route," in Paths of Discovery (1975); "The nerve-growth factor," in Scientific America (1979).

On October 13, 1986, Rita Levi-Montalcini become only the fourth woman ever to be awarded the Nobel Prize for Physiology or Medicine. Her ground-breaking research during the 1950s has been crucial to our understanding of the factors that control the growth of cells, their development, and their maintenance. The Nobel committee jointly awarded the Prize to Levi-Montalcini and Stanley Cohen.

Rita Levi-Montalcini was born in Turin, Italy, on April 22, 1909, the daughter of **Adele Montalcini Levi** and Adamo Levi, an engineer and factory manager. It was not until the beginning of her medical career that Rita Levi added her mother's maiden name to her own surname. The Levis were of Jewish ancestry, although the family did not regularly attend synagogue. As Levi-Montalcini recalled: "Father could not be considered an atheist or intolerant of those of different ideas from his own in matters of religion. . . . But he was certainly secular in the deepest sense of the word." Such attitudes often caused friction with more devout relatives.

Adamo Levi's belief that the man was the head of the family and that a professional career would interfere with a woman's duties as wife and mother had a profound impact on his daughter.

> My experience in childhood and adolescence of the subordinate role played by the female in a society run entirely by men had convinced me that I was not cut out to be a wife. Babies did not attract me, and I was altogether without the maternal sense so highly developed in small adolescent girls.

Though Rita Levi-Montalcini displayed an aptitude for scholarship as a student, she received a typical Victorian education which did not prepare young women for university. "Our father decided that we should attend middle school and then the girl's high school—from which, in those days, there was still no possibility of going to university," she wrote. "The girl's high school differed from the boy's not so much in the teaching of languages and literature as in the training in mathematics and the so-called exact sciences."

In 1929, the death of Levi-Montalcini's governess Giovanna proved to be a turning point; she decided to study medicine. Her father was skeptical and expressed his belief that a professional career was unsuitable for a woman. He concluded, however, that "if this is really what you want, then I won't stand in your way, even if I'm very doubtful about your choice." After a summer of rigorous private tutoring in Latin, Greek, history, mathematics, and philosophy, Levi-Montalcini passed the entrance examination for the Turin School of Medicine and was admitted as a student in 1930.

Her mentor at the University of Turin was Dr. Giuseppe Levi, a well-known specialist in anatomy and histology. In describing "the extraordinary personality of the master," Levi-Montalcini wrote that he was "celebrated in Turin University for his reputation as a scientist, for the anti-Fascism he professed," and for his "terrible but short-lived fits of rage." She and Levi soon became friends, a friendship which would last until Giuseppe's death in 1965.

In 1928, Giuseppe Levi began research into the growth of nerve cells in vitro. His interest was sparked by the research of Ross Granville Harrison, who had pioneered the field in 1907. In the summer of 1936, Levi-Montalcini graduated from the Turin School of Medicine and began working as Giuseppe Levi's assistant in neurological research. Neurology became her chosen field of specialization, and in 1940 she obtained a degree in neurology and psychiatry. But the rise of Fascism under Benito Mussolini threatened her career. In 1938, when a government decree expelled all Jews from Italian universities and forbade them to practice medicine, Levi-Montalcini was fired from her position at the Institute of Anatomy. Following Giuseppe Levi's lead, she fled to Belgium in March 1939. There, she resumed her research at the Neurological Institute in Brussels. The imminent invasion of Belgium in 1939, however, forced her to return to Italy. In Turin, she began to practice medicine clandestinely, but soon found it impossible to secure prescriptions for her patients.

Instead, Levi-Montalcini secretly resumed the neuroembryological research she had begun in Brussels. With her family's consent, she assembled what she described as "a private laboratory à la Robinson Crusoe" in their small apart-ment. "The instruments necessary for the realization of this project were few," she wrote, "a small thermostat . . . a microtome . . . a stereomicroscope . . . and surgical instruments." Using chicken embryos, she studied the effects which the removal of peripheral nerve tissues had upon the development of motor cells in the spinal cord and the ganglia.

In 1940, Levi-Montalcini happened upon an article written by Viktor Hamburger of Washington University. In it, Hamburger argued that growing nerve fibers were guided to organs by the organs themselves. Hamburger's article became her "bible and inspiration." When Giuseppe Levi returned to Turin in 1941, after evading capture by the Nazis, he immediately began to assist Levi-Montalcini with her experiments.

With the systematic bombing of Turin increasing nightly, Levi-Montalcini and her family moved to a small farm in the fall of 1942. Giuseppe Levi was a frequent visitor. There, she continued her research and discovered that the cells of the central nervous system in the initial stage of differentiation moved "toward distant locations along rigidly programmed routes." The question, however, still remained. Why? In light of her discovery, she concluded that cell growth functioned in a substantially different way than the medical literature of the day suggested.

With the arrest of Mussolini on July 25, 1943, the tyranny of the Fascists seemed to be at an end. The Allied invasion of Italy, however, prompted Hitler to send in the German army. Levi-Montalcini made an attempt to escape to Switzerland, but the Germans sealed the border. The entire family traveled south in the hope of crossing Allied lines. Unforeseen circumstances led to a prolonged stay in Florence, where the family hid until the liberation of the city in 1944. Following the end of hostilities, Rita Levi-Montalcini worked as a doctor in the refugee camps. She described the episode as her "most intense, most exhausting, and final experience as a medical doctor." After the war, she returned to Turin and was reinstated at the Institute of Anatomy.

In 1946, the work of Levi-Montalcini came to the attention of Hamburger, who had read an article jointly written by Levi and Levi-Montalcini in 1942. Although Hamburger did not agree with her thesis that the programmed death of nerve cells influence the development of the central nervous system, he invited her to spend a semester in the United States. What began as a short stay turned into a sojourn of 30 years. Many years later, Levi-Montalcini still fondly recalled her first impression of St. Louis.

I marvelled for the first time at the splendid autumnal colours of the leaves in the setting sun, which have no parallel to the dull tones of the trees in the hills around Turin during the same season. . . . I still link that amazing spectacle with the recollection of my first contact with Washington University and the Midwest.

In 1947, Levi-Montalcini became a research associate in the department of zoology. She was plagued by doubts about her research, however, and soon after her arrival recalled being struck by the idea that "the discovery of migrator and degenerative processes affecting nerve cell populations at the early stages of their development might offer a tenuous yet valid path to follow into the fascinating and uncharted labyrinth of the nervous system."

One of her first tasks was to recreate an experiment performed by Elmer Bueker. It involved the transplantation of a cancerous mouse tumor into a chick embryo. The central nervous system of the embryo reacted by sending out masses of nerve fibers. Originally, Levi-Montalcini and Hamburger concluded that the nerve fibers had synchronized their growth rate to conform with that of the tumor. Soon, however, she hypothesized that the tumor itself was releasing a mysterious substance which was influencing the growth of the nerve fibers.

Embryological procedures of the day were slow and painstaking. In order to unravel the chemical composition of the mysterious compound, Levi-Montalcini turned to the developing science of tissue cultures. She traveled to the Institute of Biophysics in Rio de Janeiro to learn the technique in 1952. In Brazil, she worked with her old friend **Herta Meyer**. By the time Levi-Montalcini returned to the United States, the possibility of identifying the compound was within reach.

She teamed up with biochemist Stanley Cohen to conduct a new series of experiments. They extracted large quantities of what became known as "Nerve Growth Factor" from snake venom and mouse saliva. By experimenting on tissue cultures, Levi-Montalcini demonstrated that the substance manufactured by the tumor could induce nerve fiber growth. She presented her findings to a conference held by the New York Academy of Sciences in 1954. Nerve Growth Factor was the first growth factor to be isolated by science.

The experiments conducted by Levi-Montalcini and Cohen, between 1953 and 1959, formed the basis of Cohen's discovery of another growth agent, Epidermal Growth Factor. It was not until 1970, however, that Nerve Growth Factor was completely analyzed by Ralph Bradshaw, **Ruth Angeletti**, and William Frazier at Washington University.

In 1961, Levi-Montalcini returned to Italy and established a research facility in Rome with Pietro Angeletti. Their research was jointly funded by Washington University, where Levi-Montalcini was now a full professor. The project also offered her the opportunity to reunite with her family.

In 1968, Levi-Montalcini was elected to the U.S. National Academy of Sciences, only the tenth woman to be honored by this prestigious body. A year later, she established the Laboratory of Cell Biology for the Italian Council of National Research and became its director, dividing her time between the U.S. and Italy. In 1977, she retired from Washington University; she also retired from the Council of National Research in 1979, but retained the position of guest professor.

On September 22, 1986, she and her colleague Stanley Cohen were awarded the Albert Lasker Medical Research Award. A few weeks later, on October 13, the Kalolinska Institute for Medicine in Stockholm announced that Rita Levi-Montalcini and Stanley Cohen were that year's recipients of the Nobel Prize for physiology or medicine. By coincidence, the surprised Levi-Montalcini was in Sweden, attending a scientific conference. As she remembered: "I gave a talk at a neuroscience meeting in Stockholm and everyone was kind to me, but there was no mention of a Nobel Prize." The Nobel committee praised the discovery of Nerve Growth Factor: "As a direct consequence we may increase our understanding of many disease states such as developmental malformation, degenerative changes in senile dementia, delayed wound healing and tumour diseases."

The Nobel committee also noted that the discovery of Nerve Growth Factor was of decisive importance in furthering research into Parkinson's disease, Alzheimer's disease, Huntington's disease, and cancer. Nerve Growth Factor may hold important clues to the basic structure of cancer cells. As Harold M. Schmeck of *The New York Times* noted, Levi-Montalcini's work offers scientists a glimpse into one of the fundamental processes of human development:

Before her discovery, scientists had few clues to the complicated process by which embryonic nerve cells developed into a network of nerve fibers that pervade the entire body. Today it is known that nerve growth factor is central to this process. The substance exists in mammals, birds, reptiles, amphibians and fishes.

Rita
Levi-
Montalcini

The discovery of Nerve Growth Factor resulted in the identification of many other growth factors, including Colony Stimulating Factors, Platelet-Derived Growth Factor, Fibroblast Growth Factor, the Interleukins, and Cohen's Epidermal Growth Factor. It has been demonstrated that Nerve Growth Factor is a substance manufactured by various target tissues. Unlike Hamburger's original thesis, which postulated that organs guided nerve growth, Nerve Growth Factor is now recognized as an essential guide of nerves to their destination. Rita Levi-Montalcini's discovery has therefore shed important new light on the chemical processes of embryonic development.

In 1987, Levi-Montalcini was awarded the National Medal of Science, the United States' highest award for scientific excellence. As well, she is a member of the Belgian Royal Academy of Medicine, the National Academy of Sciences of Italy, the Pontifical Academy of Sciences, and the European Academy of Sciences, Arts, and Letters. Numerous institutions have granted her honorary degrees, including the Weizmann Institute of Science, the University of Uppsala, the Washington University School of Medicine, and St. Mary's College.

As she turned 90, Rita Levi-Montalcini made her home in Rome. Described by Tyler Wasson as "a vivacious, elegant woman who is warm and considerate in her associations with co-workers and friends," she shared an apartment with her twin sister, **Paola Levi-Montalcini**, a well-known artist.

SOURCES:

Kass-Simon, G. "Biology is Destiny," in *Women of Science: Righting the Record*. G. Kass-Simon and Patricia Farnes, eds. Bloomington: Indiana University Press, 1990.

Marx, Jean L. "The 1986 Nobel Prize for Physiology or Medicine," in *Science*. NY: American Association for the Advancement of Science, October 31, 1986.

Schmeck, Harold M. "Two Pioneers in Growth of Cells Win Nobel Prize," in *The New York Times*. October 14, 1986.

Wasson, Tyler. *Nobel Prize Winners: An H.W. Wilson Biographical Dictionary*. NY: H.W. Wilson, 1987.

Who's Who in the World. Wilmette, IL: Marquis, 1990.

SUGGESTED READING:

Levi-Montalcini, Rita. *In Praise of Imperfection: My Life and Work*. Translated by Luigi Attardi. NY: Basic Books, 1988.

Hugh A. Stewart, M.A.,
Guelph, Ontario, Canada

Levien, Sonya (1888–1960)

Russian-American screenwriter who won an Academy Award for Best Adapted Screenplay for Interrupted Melody. *Born near Moscow, Russia, on December 25, 1888; died on March 19, 1960, in Hollywood, California; graduated from New York University with a law degree; married Carl Hovey, in 1917; children: two, including daughter* **Tamara Gold Hovey** *(a screenwriter and biographer).*

Filmography as writer or co-writer: Who Will Marry Me? *(1919);* Cheated Love *(1921);* First Love *(1921);* The Top of New York *(1922);* Pink Gods *(1922);* The Snow Bride *(1923);* The Exciters *(1923);* Salome of the Tenements *(1926);* The Princess of Hoboken *(1927);* The Heart Thief *(1927);* A Harp in Hock *(1927);* A Ship Comes In *(1928);* The Power of the Press *(1928);* Behind That Curtain *(1928);* Lucky Star *(1928);* The Younger Generation *(1928);* Trial Marriage *(1928);* They Had to See Paris *(1928);* South Sea Rose *(1928);* Frozen Justice *(1928);* Song o' My Heart *(1930);* So This Is London *(1930);* The Brat *(1930);* Surrender *(1930);* She Wanted a Millionaire *(1932);* After Tomorrow *(1932);* State Fair *(1933);* Warrior's Husband *(1933);* Berkeley Square *(1933);* Mr. Skitch *(1933);* Change of Heart *(1934);* The White Parade *(1934);* Here's to Romance *(1935);* Navy Wife *(1935);* The Country Doctor *(1936);* Reunion *(1936);* In Old Chicago *(1938);* Kidnapped *(1938);* Four Men and a Prayer *(1938);* Drums Along the Mohawk *(1939);* The Hunchback of Notre Dame *(1939);* Ziegfeld Girl *(1941);* The Amazing Mrs. Holiday *(1941);* Rhapsody in Blue *(1941); (remake)* State Fair *(1943);* The Green Years *(1946);* The Valley of Decision *(1946);* Ziegfeld Follies *(1946);* Cass Timberlane *(1947);* Three Darling Daughters *(1948);* The Great Caruso *(1951);* The Merry Widow *(1952);* The Student Prince *(1954);* Hit the Deck *(1955);* Interrupted Melody *(1955);* Oklahoma! *(1955);* Bhowani Junction *(1955);* Jeanne Eagels *(1957);* Pepe *(1960).*

As co-writer with S.N. Behrman: Lightnin' *(1930);* Liliom *(1930);* Delicious *(1931);* Daddy Long Legs *(1931);* Rebecca of Sunnybrook Farm *(1932);* Tess of the Storm Country *(1932);* Cavalcade *(1933);* As Husbands Go *(1934);* Anna Karenina *(1935);* The Cowboy and the Lady *(1938);* Quo Vadis *(1951).*

Born in a small village outside Moscow in 1888, Sonya Levien immigrated to the United States with her parents when she was quite young. She received a law degree from New York University and practiced briefly before deciding on a career as a writer. Working as a journalist first, she was a staff writer for both *Woman's Journal* and *Metropolitan* magazines. In 1919, Levien's first screen credit appeared on the film *Who Will Marry Me?*

Levien worked as a journalist and as a free-lance screenwriter, but in 1929 she seems to have given up journalism when she joined the writing staff of 20th Century-Fox. During this time, often called Hollywood's "Golden Age," the studios cranked out hundreds of pictures every year, and it was not unusual for writers to work on several movies simultaneously. As is the case with Levien, it is difficult to determine her exact contribution to a film because she was given co-screenwriting credit or sometimes no credit at all. What is clear is that she was a well-respected writer. In an interview conducted by **Tina Daniell** in *Tender Comrades: A Backstory of the Hollywood Blacklist,* Levien's colleague *Marguerite Roberts said of Levien: "She was sweet, kind and simple and a damned good writer. She was also decent and not many people in the picture business were."

Levien left 20th Century-Fox in 1941 and joined the staff of Metro-Goldwyn-Mayer, where she worked until 1956. At both studios she was assigned to quality projects which allowed her to work with such notable directors as George Cukor, John Ford and Frank Capra. She won an Academy Award in 1955 for her work on *Interrupted Melody.* Starring *Eleanor Parker, also a nominee that year, the film was based on the life of Australian opera star *Marjorie Lawrence. In 1960, in a career that spanned 40 years, 72-year-old Levien received her final screen credit on the hit movie *Pepe.* She died that year on March 19 of cancer.

SOURCES:

Basinger, Jeanine. *American Screenwriters.* Edited by Robert E. Morsberger, Stephen O. Lesser, and Randall Clark. Detroit, MI: Gale Research, 1984.

Ceplair, Larry. *A Great Lady: A Life of the Screenwriter Sonya Levien.* Lanham, MD: Scarecrow Press, 1996.

McGilligan, Patrick, and Paul Buhle. *Tender Comrades: A Backstory of the Hollywood Blacklist.* NY: St. Martin's Press, 1997.

Variety: Obituaries, 1905–1986. Vol. 5. NY: Garland, 1988.

Deborah Jones,
Studio City, California

Levin, Rahel (1771–1833).

See Varnhagen, Rahel.

Levine, Lena (1903–1965)

American gynecologist and psychiatrist who was a pioneer in the field of marriage counseling and an activist in the birth-control movement. Born Lena Levine in Brooklyn, New York, on May 17, 1903; died in New York City on January 9, 1965; youngest of seven children of Morris H. Levine (a clothing man-ufacturer) and Sophie Levine; attended Girls High School in Brooklyn; graduated from Hunter College, A.B., 1923; University and Bellevue Hospital Medical College, M.D., 1927; married Louis Ferber (a physician), in 1929 (died 1943); children: Ellen Louise Ferber (b. 1939); Michael Allen Ferber (b. 1942).

Selected writings: The Doctor Talks with the Bride *(1936, 2nd ed., 1938); (with Beka Doherty)* The Menopause *(1952); (with Abraham Stone)* The Premarital Consultation *(1956);* The Modern Book of Marriage: A Practical Guide to Marital Happiness *(1957); (with David Loth)* The Frigid Wife: Her Way to Sexual Fulfillment *(1962);* The Emotional Sex: Why Women Are the Way They Are Today *(1964).*

Born on May 17, 1903, in Brooklyn, New York, Lena Levine was the youngest child of **Sophie Levine** and clothing manufacturer Morris H. Levine. In addition to Lena, the Levines, who had emigrated from the Vilno area of Russian Lithuania in the 1890s, had three other daughters and three sons. The family lived in the Brownsville neighborhood of Brooklyn and enjoyed a more financially comfortable lifestyle than most of their poor Jewish neighbors.

After graduating from Girls High School in Brooklyn, Levine commuted to Hunter College in Manhattan, obtaining an A.B. degree in 1923. She then pursued a medical degree at University and Bellevue Hospital Medical College, also located in Manhattan, receiving her M.D. degree in 1927. Two years later, she married fellow medical student Louis Ferber, keeping her maiden name, and served a residency with him at Brooklyn Jewish Hospital. When her residency was completed, Levine went into private practice as a gynecologist and obstetrician; her husband, with whom she shared an office in Brooklyn, was a general practitioner. Their first child, Ellen Louise, was born in 1939, followed three years later by a son, Michael Allen. While still an infant, Michael came down with an attack of viral encephalitis that left him profoundly retarded. Although Levine attempted to care for her son at home, employing the services of a nurse and an African-American housekeeper, **Pearl Harrison** (who would remain with her for over 20 years), Michael was put in an institution after five years. Levine would visit him there for the rest of her life.

Only a year after the birth of Michael, Louis Ferber suffered a massive heart attack and died. The loss of her husband caused Levine to confine herself to gynecology, dropping her obstetrics practice to avoid leaving her children when she had to perform unexpected deliveries. In time, she became more and more intrigued by psychiatry, underwent psychoanalysis at the Columbia Psychoanalytic Institute, and became a Freudian. Still practicing as a gynecologist, Levine made use of Freudian theory in counseling patients on matters of psychological and reproductive health. Eventually, she launched a small psychiatric practice at 30 Fifth Avenue in Manhattan, while continuing to maintain her gynecological practice in Brooklyn. After her daughter left for college, Levine moved to Greenwich Village in lower Manhattan, where she ran her medical practice from her home.

A strong proponent of birth control since the 1920s, Levine volunteered her services to the Birth Control Federation of America (later known as the Planned Parenthood Federation of America) in the 1930s. Arguably better known on the international birth-control scene than she was at home, she also served as the medical secretary of the International Planned Parenthood Federation, which was based in London. Although she continued her private practice, during the 1940s and 1950s she gradually became more involved with educational and organizational efforts in the areas of birth control and marriage counseling, all of which took an increasing amount of her time. With Abraham and **Hannah Stone**, she held marriage counseling sessions at the Community Church of New York. After the death of Hannah Stone in 1941, Levine teamed with Abraham Stone to pioneer a group-counseling program on sex and contraception, the first such undertaking of its kind in the United States. Starting as early as the 1930s, Levine worked at the *Margaret Sanger Research Bureau, one of the major birth-control clinics in New York City, and she later became its associate director. In that post, she served as an overseer of the clinic's medical services and conducted group therapy sessions for those with sexual problems. Levine also offered informational services for pregnant women, helping some to obtain illegal abortions (as with virtually all other birth-control advocates, she did not publicly support abortion for fear of jeopardizing the main goal of legalized contraception).

An enthusiastic supporter of liberal social thinking, Levine championed Franklin Delano Roosevelt's New Deal in the 1930s and favored an even greater degree of socialism as a remedy for some of the country's ills. In her later years, she devoted much of her energy to writings on women's medical and psychological problems, covering such sensitive topics as frigidity, menopause, virginity, sexual relations in marriage, and contraception. She also lectured throughout the United States and abroad on these topics and others, including the sexuality of youth, planned parenthood, sex education, marriage, and the family. Her greatest contribution to the mental and physical health of all Americans may have been her willingness to discuss openly subjects that had been largely considered taboo. She believed that marriage and family could only be strengthened by attacking some of the myths surrounding such matters as sexual arousal, technique, and the differences between the sexual needs of women and men. Lena Levine suffered a massive stroke and died on January 9, 1965, at the age of 61.

SOURCES:

Sicherman, Barbara, and Carol Hurd Green. *Notable American Women: The Modern Period.* Cambridge, MA: Belknap Press of Harvard University, 1980.

Don Amerman,
freelance writer, Saylorsburg, Pennsylvania

Leviska, Helvi Lemmiki
(1902–1982)

Finnish pianist, critic, and teacher, as well as her nation's most important woman composer. Born on May 25, 1902, in Helsinki, Finland; died on August 12, 1982, in Helsinki; graduated from the Sibelius Academy, 1927.

Helvi Lemmiki Leviska wrote almost 20 pieces for symphony orchestra, including four symphonies. She studied at the Sibelius Academy with Erkki Melartin, graduating in 1927. She then went to Vienna from 1928 to 1936 where she studied with L. Madetoja, L. Funtek, and A. Willner. In 1933, Leviska became librarian at the Sibelius Academy. From 1957 to 1961, she was music critic of *Ilta-Sanomat*, an evening newspaper. Throughout her varied career, Helvi Leviska continued to compose, and her works were widely performed in Finland.

John Haag,
Athens, Georgia

Levitt, Helen (1913—)

American photographer, best known for documenting New York street life. Born in Bensonhurst, an Italian-Jewish neighborhood in Brooklyn, New York, in 1913; only daughter and the middle of three children of Sam Levitt (a businessman) and May (Kane) Levitt; left high school at 17, one semester short of graduation; never married; no children.

Called a "photographer's photographer," Helen Levitt is best known for her documentary pictures of street life in New York, first in the Italian-Jewish neighborhood of Bensonhurst in Brooklyn, where she grew up, and later in the environs of the East Village, the garment district, and the Lower East Side. Her "theatre of life" images, particularly of women and children, are poignant and frequently wrenching in their message, but they have never attracted a mass audience. "[T]he pictures offer nothing sensational, overly stylish, or conventionally beautiful to the casual viewer," writes **Maria Morris Hambourg** in the biographical essay "A Life in Part," which she prepared in conjunction with the first full scale critical survey and catalogue of Levitt's work, prepared by the San Francisco Museum of Modern Art in 1991. "In addition, the artist is more interested in the pictures than in their reception, she has little faith in opinions or interpretations other than her own, and she wishes to live without the intrusions of publicity."

Levitt's family was Russian and Jewish on both sides, although nationality and religion were not crucial factors in her early development. From her father, who ran a wholesale knit goods business, she inherited her composure and sense of order, and from her mother, her wit, humor, and independent nature. The middle child, with a brother on either side, Levitt grew up loving music, dancing, and the Saturday afternoon movie matinees. Her early life was also defined by physical activity, the freedom of her own moving body. She roller-skated, jumped rope, bicycled on the street outside her house, and attended summer camp, where she swam, played tennis, and learned to ride and to love horses.

Formal education did not hold much charm for Levitt, although she was an avid reader from an early age. Books handed down from her brother—*The Swiss Family Robinson*, the "Frank Merriwell" series, and animal stories like *Black Beauty*—comprised her early library. High school was another half-hearted affair, although her reading list expanded to include the works of Somerset Maugham, H.G. Wells, F. Scott Fitzgerald, Ernest Hemingway, and John Galsworthy, authors who helped her define herself. "In the maze of ideas expressed," writes Hambourg, "Levitt followed a thread of her own sensitivity into realms of resistance and longing for which she had no handy map. She knew only that she was different and, vaguely, that others who were different in similar ways had become artists."

Levitt dropped out of school at 17, just one semester shy of graduation. Her self-conducted education, however, was just getting under way.

While living at home and working days as a sales clerk at Gimbel's department store, Levitt continued her voracious reading pattern, at one point selecting titles from a reading list she obtained from a friend who was taking a European literature course at Brooklyn College. She was most impressed by Alfred Doblin's *Berlin Alexanderplatz* and Thomas Mann's *Magic Mountain*. Levine also took advantage of the free performances of Shakespeare at the Davenport Theater, and chamber music concerts at the Metropolitan Museum and Hunter College. For socialization, Levitt attended the union hall dances which she found advertised in the "What's On" columns in *The Daily Worker*.

Though ideologically leftist in a time of social activism, Levitt was a half-hearted rabble rouser. "She recalls picketing D.W. Griffith's film *The Birth of a Nation* (1915) to protest its attitude toward Negroes," writes Hambourg. "While her colleagues resisted orders to disband, Levitt followed the officers' instructions: Handing over her picket to an incredulous friend, she went right home. Her sympathies have resisted organization ever since."

In 1931, at age 18, Levitt went to work for a photographer in the Bronx, a friend of her mother's who created standard portraits for confirmations, bar mitzvahs, graduations, and marriages. Although dark-room techniques were of little interest to her at the time, Levitt applied herself diligently, feeling that the craft held some artistic promise. Over the next four years, as she refined her skills, Levitt began to think of photography as a possible profession. By 1934, she had mastered the Voigtlander camera and the dark-room, and was taking pictures of her friends and joining her boss at monthly meetings of the Pictorial Photographers of America. At those gatherings, she encountered the work of commercial photographer Anton Breuhl and a "picture of a wave" by a Japanese photographer, which left indelible impressions.

Gradually, Levitt began to gravitate toward the Film Photo League, a group of young, socially conscious photographers and filmmakers whose influence moved her to begin to experiment with unposed shots. Although, characteristically, she did not formally join the League, she made some important connections from their ranks, including one with Sidney Meyers, a film editor who also wrote under the pseudonym Robert Stebbins as a critic for *New Theater Magazine*, and another with Willard Van Dyke, in whose studio she met the young French photographer Henri Cartier-Bresson, who was living in New York in 1935. Cartier-Bresson introduced Levitt to surrealism and, in Hambourg's words, "named her truth." "She saw that polish and polemics were tangential to the way of seeing she was seeking, and that her way also might lie in provinces of indirection and subtlety."

Inspired to turn the craft of photography into art, Levitt "consciously set about becoming the responsive instrument of her eye." She immersed herself in museum exhibitions, studying the compositions of such painters as van Gogh, Gauguin, Cézanne, Matisse, Daumier, and Toulouse-Lautrec. She ushered at *Eva Le Gallienne's Civic Repertory Theater, where she studied the plays of social protest, and she haunted the foreign movie houses where she was mesmerized by French and Russian films—particularly Aleksandr Dovzhenko's *Aerograd* (1935), a poetic film about the construction of an ideal Soviet city that she saw a half-dozen times.

The aesthetic is in reality itself.

—Helen Levitt

In 1936, marking the end of her apprenticeship, Levitt purchased a small, second-hand Leica camera and began to prowl the neighborhoods. The streets provided an endless cast of characters: a woman in galoshes and a strange hat hosing down her stoop, a down-and-out man sleeping on the sidewalk, a man in front of a factory smokestack. In her initial pictures, the canvas is broad, the people small and faraway, conveying the powerlessness of her subjects over the overwhelming urban background. In other photographs, Levitt captures pairs of people, related by place but not necessarily to each other: two women framing a blank window; two neighborhood boys playing in the street; two men seated near the El, one gesturing theatrically.

Emboldened, Levitt began to move closer to her subjects, attempting to describe "psychology through posture," to capture "the telling gesture." As she moved in tighter, she used a right-angle viewfinder that allowed her to catch her subjects unaware. She photographed children playing in East Harlem, where she briefly taught art under a Federal Arts Project program in 1937. "It is interesting that she did not choose to depict routine or organized play," writes Hambourg, "such as the hopscotch, jump rope, and stickball of her youth, but rather exclusively the play of the imagination. Levitt's kids mask, climb, mime, dance, and dream—all transitional activities creating temporary worlds existing solely for the players." Levitt remained fascinated by children at play throughout her early period.

Helen Levitt was selective about the elements of a scene, shunning "boring" streets and buildings for those more uniquely textured. Architectural details caught her eye, as did curtained widows, wash on the line, graffiti on the sidewalk, garbage ready for pick-up. "Her interest in the sites had nothing to do with documenting social conditions, and everything to do with expressive stage scenery," explains Hambourg.

From 1938 to 1939, Levitt shared a darkroom with Walker Evans, who worked in the streets much in the same manner as she did, and with whom she shared an artistic kinship. Levitt helped Evans with his exhibition "American Photographs" at the Museum of Modern Art in 1938, and through the experience learned the importance of cropping pictures carefully. Through Evans, Levitt also became close to author and film writer James Agee and **Janice Loeb**, a painter and art historian. Levitt blossomed during this period, gaining confidence as an artist from the praise and acceptance of those artists she respected. Having found personal techniques that worked, her photographs took on a new emotional shading and pathos. Hambourg remarks that in the pictures of this period, Levitt's moral and dramatic sense seemed to fuse. "She never took advantage of her subjects, neither ennobled nor belittled them, was not frightened or awed. Rather, standing on the same ground, she recognized them through a common language of expression."

In 1941, Levitt, who had traveled very little, went to Mexico with Agee's wife **Alma Neuman Agee**. Finding the culture too foreign, Levitt did little work there. She returned to New York and rarely left, having found in her familiar environment all that she needed in the way of subject matter. Soon after her return home, her friend Janice Loeb introduced Levitt to film director Luis Buñuel, who, upon seeing Levitt's photographs, hired her as an apprentice film cutter for some pro-American propaganda films he was making under the sponsorship of the Museum of Modern Art. Subsequently, Levitt received a commission from an independent firm to make a film about China using stock footage, and from 1944 to 1945 she worked as an assistant editor in the Film Division of the Office of War Information. During this time, Levitt and Loeb began to shoot scenes around New York with Loeb's old movie camera. After experimental outings, filming Gypsies (Roma) along a marsh river front and spectators viewing a parade in Yorkville, they joined with James Agee to create a cinematic version of Levitt's pictures. The idea was hatched while Agee was assembling Levitt's photographs into an essay on her way of seeing, an essay which later became the introduction to Levitt's book *A Way of Seeing* (1965). Filmed on the streets of East Harlem and titled *In the Street*, the documentary was released in 1952. Though not a "professional" presentation, the film, like Levitt's pictures, captures street life with, as Hambourg puts it, "understanding, humor, and dearness."

Another film, *The Quiet One*, about the psychological and social rehabilitation of a delinquent black boy at the Wiltwyck School, was shot in 1946–47 by Levitt, Loeb, and Sidney Meyers, with a commentary by Agee. Although the documentary won awards at the Edinburgh and Venice film festivals, Levitt never liked the film, feeling that the story limited the scope of her imagination. In truth, although she continued to work in films throughout the 1950s, Levitt took little pride in that part of her career.

Levitt returned to still photography in 1959, receiving a Guggenheim Fellowship to experiment with color. Unfortunately, many of her early color shots were stolen in the late 1960s. Her later pictures, in both black and white and color, echo her early period, although many of her old haunts had been altered, and she had to search for new locales. Levitt uses color only to extend the reality of the life around her, never in and for itself. This, according to Hambourg, may be why her color work is so extraordinary. "She is not distracted by a red shirt or seduced by an apricot wall; they are simply part of her experience of the world. "

During the mid-1970s, Levitt taught at Pratt Institute in Brooklyn, an experience that brought her in contact with the younger generation of photographers and caused her to re-evaluate her earlier work. While she had been accustomed to deciding the content of her pictures in the crop, she began using more of the negative, sometimes reprinting earlier pictures to expand the content of the scene. Her later work is larger, lighter, with less contrasts, reflecting her ongoing attempt to achieve completeness and clarity in the message she conveys.

Levitt's long career was dominated by personal and artistic modesty. She never advanced herself or her art, nor did she try to please an audience. "Levitt sought revelations—ordinary people becoming effectively mythic figures in moments of transport or trouble—that occur fleetingly in the course of things, usually seen from the corner of the eye when seen at all," writes Peter Schjeldahl in the *Village Voice*. "Her pictures need no analysis if you are familiar with them and beggar description if you aren't; they are so simple in impact while, in form and nuance, so complex."

SOURCES:

Brown, Chelsea. "New York Kids," in *USA Today*. Vol. 121, no. 2570. November 1992, pp. 72–78.

Phillips, Sandra S., and Maria Morris Hambourg. *Helen Levitt*. San Francisco, CA: San Francisco Museum of Modern Art, 1991.

Schjeldahl, Peter. *Village Voice*. Vol. 42, no. 25. June 24, 1997, p. 91.

Barbara Morgan,
Melrose, Massachusetts

Levy, Amy (1861–1889)

English poet and novelist of Jewish descent. Born at Clapham, London, England, on November 10, 1861; committed suicide on September 10, 1889; second daughter of Lewis Levin (an editor) and Isabelle Levin; educated at Newnham College, Cambridge (the first Jewish woman to matriculate there).

Called the forgotten poet, Amy Levy showed a precocious aptitude for writing verse of exceptional merit and, in 1884, published *A Minor Poet and Other Verse*. Some of the pieces had already been printed at Cambridge under the title *Xantippe* and contained strong feminist views. The high level of this first publication was continued in *A London Plane Tree and Other Poems*, a collection of lyrics published in 1889, in which Levy's despondency was apparent. In 1888, she had already tried her hand at prose fiction in *The Romance of a Shop*, which was followed by *Reuben Sachs*, a powerful novel and "bold delineation of Jewish life" that caused controversy in London.

Not much is known of Levy's last days. One writer maintains she worked in a loom factory; another has her living in a garret; the next depicts her as a teacher in London. What is known is that on September 10, 1889, a week after correcting proofs on *A London Plane Tree*, Amy Levy committed suicide at 7, Endsleigh Gardens, by suffocating herself with charcoal fumes. The coroner noted on the death certificate: "self destruction . . . cause unknown."

Richard Garnett speculated, however, that the cause might have been worries over a growing deafness, the fear of insanity, and grief over losses in her family. Whatever the reason, a writer of great potential and praiseworthy accomplishment has been passed over. At the time of her death, Thomas Bailey Aldrich wrote a poem in her honor; Oscar Wilde dubbed her "a genius." Her work, said the critics, held "prophetic notes" of future power.

Lewald, Fanny (1811–1889)

German novelist, essayist, and journalist who was one of the most popular writers in 19th-century Germany. Name variations: Fanny Markus; Fanny Lewald-Stahr; Fanny Stahr-Lewald. Born Fanny Markus in Königsberg, East Prussia (now Kaliningrad, Russia), on March 24, 1811; died in Dresden on August 5, 1889; daughter of David Markus, later David Lewald, and Rosa (Assing) Markus; had five sisters, two brothers; married Adolf Stahr (a historian), in 1854.

Fanny Lewald lived through a period in European, and particularly German, history that was marked by great change. In 1811, the year she was born, no united German state existed, and the many "Germanies" were suffering under the yoke of a still-triumphant France ruled by Napoleon Bonaparte. Lewald's Jewish family lived in a social regime that saw Jews as religious and cultural outsiders. But in many ways, the tide was turning. Romantic nationalism spread the ideal of a united German people and nation free of foreign control, and the assumptions of the Enlightenment continued to press for the full emancipation of formerly excluded elements in society, including the often-despised and sometimes feared Jews.

At the time of Fanny's birth in Königsberg, East Prussia, on March 24, 1811, her family's name was Markus but would later be changed to the more Germanic-sounding Lewald. The eldest of eight living children, Fanny grew up in solid middle-class comfort, as the daughter of parents from old, established Jewish families in Königsberg. Both her father David and mother Rosa were loving parents. David, a traditional patriarch who expected absolute obedience from both his wife and progeny, was kept busy with his wine business but also determined most details of the family's life. He sought out the best possible education for Fanny, who at age six was enrolled in Königsberg's Ulrich School (which was coeducational in some but not all of its classes). Many of the teachers there were Pietists (members of a Lutheran religious movement), and the school's standards were high. After the Ulrich School closed its doors when Fanny was 15, she was schooled at home, where her education included taking piano lessons which she did not care for. She met and fell in love with a young theology student named Leopold Bock who died before they could be married. In 1828, the entire family, now called Lewald, converted to Lutheranism. At first Fanny was enthusiastic about her new faith, but as she matured and

deepened her knowledge of theology and philosophy an inherently skeptical spirit won out. She came to sympathize with the ideas of Baruch Spinoza, who accepted the existence of a supreme deity while denying the superiority of any specific version of organized religious doctrine or practice.

Noting his daughter's discontent within the confining world of bourgeois domesticity, Fanny's father took her with him on an extended trip throughout Germany. In Baden-Baden, where her uncle Friedrich Jacob Lewald was a member of a circle of cutting-edge writers and artists, her intellectual horizons expanded after she met, among others, provocative figures like Ludwig Börne. While in Breslau (now Wroclaw, Poland), she met and quickly fell in love with her cousin, Heinrich Simon. Although her love was never reciprocated by Simon, who became a major figure in both German national politics and German-Jewish community life, over time their relationship evolved into a close friendship.

Lewald returned home to Königsberg to find her mother in ill health and took turns with her sisters in running the family household. Left with ample free time, she considered taking on a paid position as a governess or companion, but her father disapproved of this plan, feeling that it reflected poorly on his ability to maintain his family in comfort proper to their class. Although approaching the age when she would no longer be considered marriageable, Lewald was adamant on the issue of marrying only a man she loved, and thus she turned down the prospect of a marriage of convenience to a provincial lawyer and magistrate.

Rapidly sinking into the status of a hypochondriacal old maid, a fate not atypical of intelligent 19th-century women of leisure, Lewald was helped onto another path by her cousin August Lewald, editor of the Stuttgart periodical *Europa*. Encouraged by him, she published in *Europa* a long letter about a trial in Königsberg, and with this modest debut in print, she launched what would become a remarkable writing career. Starting in 1839, Lewald lived with relatives in Berlin, the city in which she would settle. There she entered the most influential intellectual circles, which included such social and literary luminaries as *Henriette Herz, *Therese von Bacheracht, and Heinrich Laube. While visiting Königsberg in 1840, Lewald was an eyewitness to the elaborate coronation ceremonies that marked the assumption of the Prussian throne by the new king Friedrich Wilhelm IV. August Lewald requested that she write a comprehensive report of this event for *Europa,* and Fanny's essay earned her an enthusiastic letter praising her talent and urging her to continue writing. Furthermore, the honorarium from *Europa* made it clear that writing might provide her with economic independence and thus a life free of her family's often suffocating embrace.

With the continuing support and encouragement of her cousin August, Lewald devoted herself to writing. Published by the Brockhaus publishing firm in Leipzig, her first novels *Clementine* (1842) and *Jenny* (1843) appeared in print anonymously because Lewald's father did not believe his daughter should pursue such a career. By 1845, when she published *Eine Lebensfrage* (A Vital Question), a novel in which she argued for divorce and the right of women to choose their own husbands, she had found a loyal audience of readers who were mostly but not exclusively female. Lewald's readers agreed with the liberal views she presented on the changing social position of bourgeois women, particularly in regard to their desire for much greater freedom in matters relating to marriage and divorce. Lewald's success as an author persuaded her father to relent on the issue of her continuing to publish anonymously, and henceforth her works appeared in print under her own name. With her (partial at first) economic independence, in 1843 she moved permanently to Berlin, where she had her own apartment conveniently located near her brother Otto. In 1845, she undertook the obligatory tour of Italy, meeting in Rome such established German writers as *Adele Schopenhauer, sister of the philosopher Arthur Schopenhauer, and **Ottilie von Goethe**, daughter-in-law of the literary giant Johann Wolfgang von Goethe. While in Italy, she also met and fell in love with Adolf Stahr, a historian of art and culture. Stahr, the father of five children, was trapped in a miserable marriage; he and Lewald would not marry until 1854, when he was finally able to secure a divorce.

Starting in the 1840s, Lewald's travels took her to many places not only in Italy but also in the British Isles, France, and Switzerland. Her acute observations of these places found their way into print in letters, essays, and book-length travel memoirs that showed her ability to both catch the flavor of various cultures and provide her readers with accurate insights into current political and cultural developments in several of Europe's most important regions.

Lewald's recollections of the 1848 revolution in Germany reflect her keen interest in political and social change while illustrating her ability to present a coherent view of contemporary events. Published in 1850 as *Erinnerungen aus dem Jahre 1848* (Memories of the Year 1848), her memoirs, written in an elegant style, provide information of great interest to posterity, thus ranking the volume among the most important eyewitness reports of this crucial period in modern European history. Lewald had visited Paris only weeks after the overthrow of the French monarchy, then followed the tide of revolution to Berlin in the spring of 1848. In the fall of that year, she was in Frankfurt am Main, where German democrats, at first optimistic about their chances of creating a modern constitutional state, eventually frittered away their initial advantages while reactionary forces regained the initiative. In the last two months of 1848, with the revolutionary impulses already fatally divided and weakened, Lewald went back to Berlin to witness the rapid return of conservative power in Prussia.

Fanny Lewald's portraits of individuals from these events remain valuable for historians, and her sympathetic depictions of the revolutionary masses in Berlin and Paris emphasize the people's courage, idealism, and selflessness. At the same time, she makes realistic assessments of revolutionary extremists like the poet Georg Herwegh, whose lack of political balance caused him to seriously misread the temper of the masses. Lewald's first-class reportage was owed not only to her own sharp eyes and ears, but also to her ability to move in the highest revolutionary circles, which enabled her to meet and interview such luminaries as Heinrich Heine, Heinrich von Gagern, Eduard Simson, and the ill-fated Robert Blum. Although her assessments are rationally grounded, Lewald's memoirs of 1848 are by no means a bland or neutral report of current events. She takes a strong advocacy position for the basic aspirations of the revolutionaries, calling for major reforms in the social and economic conditions of the working classes and impoverished peasantry, and she makes clear her demand for a radical extension of the political franchise. Lewald believed that only by initiating such sweeping changes would the propertied classes, of which she was a prosperous member, be able to prevent the almost inevitable eruption of a bloody revolution fueled by class hatred. She made additional comments on the failed revolution of 1848, many of them incisive, in her 1850 novella *Auf rother Erde* (On Red Earth).

Over the next four decades, Lewald solidified her reputation as Germany's most popular and successful woman writer. By the time of her death in 1889, she had published 27 novels and more than 30 novellas, as well as short stories, more than a dozen travel reports and memoirs, and countless essays in the leading journals of the day, which were then collected in book form. While creating this prodigious body of work, she also wrote a vast number of letters, many of them of literary merit, to family and friends. As she grew older, Fanny Lewald became more politically conservative, although it is more than likely that she would have defended her viewpoints as being based on rational rather than emotional underpinnings. Never a radical democrat or republican, in the 1870s she accepted the unification of Germany into a powerful Reich by Prussia's authoritarian chancellor Otto von Bismarck.

While advocating suffrage for women, Lewald did not believe that all women were qualified to vote. In her essays "Die Frauen und das allgemeine Wahlrecht" (Women and Universal Suffrage, 1870) and "Und was nun?" (And What Now?, 1871), she argued that only those women who could prove themselves to be politically knowledgeable—and thus be capable of voting differently from their husbands—deserved to be granted the ballot. Believing that such reforms were well within reach in her own time, she published articles in favor of the systematic education of women, including the influential "Osterbriefe für die Frauen" ("Easter Letters for Women," 1863).

In the last decades of her life, Lewald emerged as a powerful role model for women in the German-speaking world. Many of them read and were inspired by her three-volume autobiography *Meine Lebensgeschichte* (My Life History, 1861–1862). During these years, she often corresponded with young women who hoped that they too might one day live independent lives, earning a living by writing. Although her pen could be wielded in acidic fashion—as when in her 1847 novel *Diogena* Lewald presented a merciless parody of the artistic weaknesses of Countess *Ida von Hahn-Hahn*—more often than not she looked at the world with a balance of curiosity and compassion. As a 19th-century woman and intellectual, she believed in both the desirability and inevitability of the continued advancement of human reason and social progress. In addition to advocating a higher level of education for women and their right to choose their own marriage partners, she called for a continuing emancipation of Jews and a general lowering of social barriers. As a confident and successful member of the bourgeoisie, she regarded the ideals and lifestyles of the feudal nobility as outmoded and irrelevant to modern life, and she often satirized them in her books as being little better than social and intellectual fossils.

During her lifetime, Lewald was ranked by the Berlin journalist and novelist Karl Frenzel as a writer of the caliber of *George Sand and George Eliot (*Mary Anne Evans). As early as 1850, her literary "energy and virile perception" was highly praised by the eminent Swiss writer Gottfried Keller, even though he did not take to her personally. Among her contemporaries, the respected writers *Marie von Ebner-Eschenbach, Theodor Fontane, and Paul Heyse were all influenced by her stylistic and thematic innovations. Marie von Ebner-Eschenbach confessed to Lewald, "I have known and admired you from my youth; I have truly followed your bright paths. You have set an example for me, but one far above my reach." In the decades after Fanny Lewald's death in Dresden on August 5, 1889, her reputation declined significantly. The age in which she had lived and flourished came to be seen as the seedbed of the evils that would plague the 20th century, and a bourgeois writer like herself became associated with the failings of her class and epoch. During the Nazi dictatorship, her writings became part of the general ban on the works of Jewish authors. Since the 1960s, however, there has been a significant revival of interest in the life and work of Fanny Lewald in Germany and other Western nations.

SOURCES:

Bäumer, Konstanze. "Reisen als Moment der Erinnerung: Fanny Lewalds (1811–1889) 'Lehr- und Wanderjahre,'" in Ruth-Ellen Boetcher Joeres and Marianne Burkhard, eds. *Out of Line/ Ausgefallen: The Paradox of Marginality in the Writings of Nineteenth-Century German Women.* Amsterdam and Atlanta, GA: Rodopi, 1989, pp. 137–157.

Beaton, Kenneth Bruce. "Fontane's *Irrungen, Wirrungen* und Fanny Lewald," in *Jahrbuch der Raabe-Gesellschaft*, 1984, pp. 208–224.

Bruyn, Günter de, and Gerhard Wolf. *Freiheit des Herzens: Lebensgeschichte, Briefe, Erinnerungen.* Frankfurt am Main: Ullstein Verlag, 1992.

Fassmann, Irmgard Maya. *Jüdinnen in der deutschen Frauenbewegung 1865–1919.* Hildeshem and NY: Olms, 1996.

Goodman, Katherine R. *Dis/Closures: Women's Autobiography in Germany between 1790 and 1914.* NY: Peter Lang, 1986.

Helmer, Ulrike, ed. *Politische Schriften für und wider die Frauen.* 2nd rev. ed. Königstein-Taunus: Ulrike Helmer Verlag, 1998.

Holdenried, Michaela, ed. *Geschriebenes Leben von Frauen.* Berlin: Erich Schmidt Verlag, 1995.

Joeres, Ruth-Ellen Boetcher. "1848 from a Distance: German Women Writers on the Revolution," in *Modern Language Notes.* Vol. 97, no. 3. April 1982, pp. 590–614.

———. *Respectability and Deviance: Nineteenth-Century German Women Writers and the Ambiguity of Representation.* Chicago, IL: University of Chicago Press, 1998.

Krobb, Florian. "'Und setzten eine Triumph darin, abtrünnig zu werden . . .': Spiegelungen der Salonepoche in der deutschen Literatur des 19. Jahrhunderts," in *Menora*. Vol. 6, 1995, pp. 113–135.

Lewald, Fanny. *The Education of Fanny Lewald*. Edited, translated and annotated by Hanna Ballin Lewis. Albany: State University of New York Press, 1992.

———. *Italienisches Bilderbuch*. Frankfurt am Main: Ulrike Helmer Verlag, 1992.

———. *Jenny*. Edited by Ulrike Helmer. Frankfurt am Main: Ulrike Helmer Verlag, 1988.

———. *Meine Lebensgeschichte*. Edited by Ulrike Helmer. 3 vols. Königstein im Taunus: Ulrike Helmer Verlag, 1998.

———. *Prince Louis Ferdinand*. Translated by Linda Rogols-Siegel. NY: Edward Mellen Press, 1988.

———. *A Year of Revolutions: Fanny Lewald's Recollections of 1848*. Edited, translated and annotated by Hanna Ballin Lewis. Oxford: Berghahn Books, 1997.

Rogols-Siegel, Linda. "Fanny Lewald's *Prinz Louis Ferdinand* and Theodor Fontane's *Vor dem Sturm* and *Schach von Wuthenow*," in *The Modern Language Review*. Vol. 88, part 2. April 1993, pp. 363–374.

Schneider, Gabriele. "Fanny Lewald und Heine: Sein Einfluss und seine Bedeutung im Spiegel ihrer Schriften," in *Heine Jahrbuch*. Vol. 33, 1994, pp. 202–216.

Venske, Regula. "Discipline and Daydreaming in the Works of a Nineteenth-Century Woman Author: Fanny Lewald," in Ruth-Ellen Boetcher Joeres and Mary Jo Maynes, eds., *German Women in the Eighteenth and Nineteenth Centuries: A Social and Literary History*. Bloomington: Indiana University Press, 1986, pp. 175–192.

Watt, Helga Schutte. "Fanny Lewald und die Deutsche Misere nach 1848 im Hinblick auf England," in *German Life and Letters*. New series. Vol. 46, no. 3. July 1993, pp. 220–235.

John Haag,
Associate Professor of History,
University of Georgia, Athens, Georgia

Lewis, Agnes Smith (1843–1926)

Scottish Orientalist. Born Agnes Smith in Irvine, Ayr, Scotland, in 1843; died in 1926; daughter of John Smith (a Scottish jurist); sister of Margaret Dunlop Gibson; married Reverend Samuel Savage Lewis, in 1887 (divorced 1891).

Agnes Smith Lewis was born in Scotland in 1843, educated in private schools and by tutors, and became especially proficient in modern Greek, Arabic, and Syriac. Before her marriage in 1887 to Reverend S.S. Lewis, she wrote a number of novels and travel accounts. In 1892, with her twin sister, **Margaret Dunlop Gibson**, she journeyed to the Middle and Near East and discovered in the library of the convent of St. Catherine on Mt. Sinai a palimpsest (a manuscript on which the original writing has been erased and written over imperfectly enough that the original can still

be deciphered). It contained the Four Gospels in Syriac, representing the oldest text then known of any part of the New Testament.

Lewis, Augusta (c. 1848–1920).

See Troup, Augusta Lewis.

Lewis, Edmonia (c. 1845–c. 1909)

First African-American sculptor to receive international recognition. Name variations: Mary Edmonia Lewis; "Wildfire," the Indian name Lewis gave as her childhood name; "Edmonia," as she preferred to be called as an adult. Born probably in 1844 or 1845, of a West Indian father, and perhaps of a mother of mixed Mississauga Indian and African-American blood; date and place of death uncertain, last seen in Rome, Italy, in 1909; attended New York Central College, an abolitionist boarding school; enrolled at Oberlin College, 1859–63; left to study art in Boston.

Began professional career studying sculpture with Edward A. Brackett in Boston; sold first sculpted medallions of abolitionist John Brown; helped finance travel to Europe to study art with sale of 100 copies of bust of Robert Gould Shaw (1865); went first to Florence, later moved to Rome; became part of circle of American women sculptors living and working in Rome; became protégé of actress Charlotte Cushman who helped raise funds for Lewis' first marble statue, Wooing of Hiawatha *(1867); had first major public exhibition (of statue of* Hagar*) in U.S. at Farwell Hall in Chicago (August 1870); had public dedication at Boston of* Forever Free *(1871); had greatest triumph at Centennial Exposition in Philadelphia, where* Death of Cleopatra *became one of the most celebrated works on display (1876); traveled in America (early 1870s), and returned to Rome (1874); last seen there (1909); date and place of death unknown.*

Selected works: The Muse Urania *(Oberlin College Archives, 1862);* Colonel Robert Gould Shaw *(Museum of Afro-American History, Boston, Massachusetts, 1867);* Forever Free *(Howard University Art Gallery, 1867–68);* Hiawatha *(Private Collection, Washington, D.C., 1868);* Minnehaha *(Private Collection, Washington, D.C., 1868);* Marriage of Hiawatha *(Cincinnati Art Museum, 1871);* Henry Wadsworth Longfellow *(Harvard University Portrait Center, 1871);* The Old Arrowmaker and His Daughter *(National Museum of American Art, Washington, D.C., 1872);* Hagar *(National Museum of American Art, Washington, D.C., 1875);* Death of Cleopatra *(National Museum of American Art, Washington, D.C., 1876). Other famous works included* Asleep *and*

Awake, the former winning a gold medal at the Naples Exposition.

Bold, energetic, headstrong, and talented, Edmonia Lewis was the first African-American to garner international acclaim in the art world of the 19th century. Lewis' creative talent, evident in the body of sculpture she produced from age 19 on, also manifested itself in her efforts to overcome the twin handicaps of race and gender. By offering journalists, patrons, and friends multiple accounts of the details of her origins and early life, Lewis captured the imaginations of those who might otherwise have ignored or rejected her work. At times, Lewis claimed to have been born to a Chippewa Indian mother and to a freed-black father in 1845 in Greenbush, New York, a town across the river from Albany. In another account of her origins, Lewis said that she was born in Greenhigh, Ohio; and on yet another occasion, she swore that she had been born in 1854. Evidence unearthed by a scholar working on a children's biography suggests that Edmonia Lewis may have been born in Newark, New Jersey, in 1844 to middle-class immigrants from the West Indies.

The most commonly held belief is that Edmonia Lewis' father was a free black, most likely from the West Indies; he may have been the man described in an Indian Bureau agent's letter as a "colr. man named Lewis." Attempts to connect Lewis to the Indian background she claimed suggest that her mother may have been the child of a marriage between an Ojibway (Chippewa) Indian named Catherine and a free African-American named John Mike. John and **Catherine Mike** and their children lived on an Indian reservation in what is now Mississauga, Ontario, a town near Toronto.

The first recorded mention by Lewis of her Indian heritage was made in 1864 to **Lydia Maria Child,* the Boston abolitionist who became a friend and patron to Lewis in the early 1860s in Boston. Child's article about Lewis in the February 1864 *Liberator* aroused considerable interest in the artist and helped increase sales of her early sculptures. Lewis elaborated on her Indian heritage in a lengthy March 1866 interview published in the London *Atheneum,* in which she recounted her Indian upbringing to journalist Henry Wreford. She gave "Wildfire" as her Indian name, and described her mother as:

> a wild Indian . . . born in Albany . . . of copper color and with straight black hair . . . [who] often left her home, and wandered with her people, whose habits she could not forget, and thus we, her children, were brought up in the same wild manner. Until I was twelve years old, I led this wandering life, fishing, swimming, and making moccasins.

Orphaned as a young child, Lewis told her *Atheneum* interviewer that she spent the years following her mother's death living a nomadic life along the banks of the Niagara River, making moccasins and weaving baskets to sell to tourists.

This narrative of Edmonia Lewis' life following the death of her mother contrasts with the account of those years given by her older brother Samuel. Samuel W. Lewis, some 12 years older than Edmonia, had gone west at the time of the Gold Rush. He accumulated a small fortune as the result of shrewd real-estate investments, and by the 1860s had established himself as one of the leading citizens of Bozeman, Montana. According to Samuel Lewis, after the death of their parents, he assumed guardianship of his young sister. When he went west, he arranged to board Edmonia with a Captain Mills and paid her tuition at a local grammar school. Later, he sent her to boarding school at New York Central College, a Baptist abolitionist secondary school in McGrawville, New York.

The constraints of a small, strict Baptist school may have been too much for the high-spirited Edmonia, and by her own account, she was not there for very long. In her 1866 interview with Wreford, she ascribed her inability to settle in at boarding school to her Indian upbringing, saying, "I was declared to be wild—they could do nothing with me." Determined that his sister should have every possible advantage, Samuel Lewis arranged in 1859 to send Edmonia to Oberlin College in the state of Ohio.

Oberlin, founded in 1835 by abolitionists, had been a fully integrated facility from its inception; it was co-educational as well—the first of its kind in North America. Edmonia Lewis gained entrance to the Ladies Department, where she studied composition, rhetoric, algebra, botany, and the Bible. It is also likely that she received lessons in linear drawing, free to all first-year students in the Ladies Department. Lewis boarded at Oberlin with the family of John Keep, a retired theologian and the Oberlin trustee whose vote in 1835 had tipped the balance in favor of admitting women and blacks. Those fortunate enough to board at Keep's home enjoyed a standard of living far above that of ordinary college students. Although she was the only African-American boarding in the house, Lewis was well-liked and accepted in the family atmosphere created by the Keeps.

*E*dmonia
*L*ewis

If the Keep family had hoped that under their roof Edmonia Lewis would be saved the hardships endured by most African-Americans in the antebellum era, they did not wholly succeed. Ironically, it was during her years at Oberlin that Lewis fell victim to a beating so vicious that it left her bedridden for weeks. The attack followed the accusation by two fellow women boarders at the home of John Keep that Edmonia had poisoned them. Lewis denied the charge. The disputed incident had occurred in January 1862, on a particularly cold and snowy day. Hearing that the two women were about to go on a sleigh-riding excursion with their gentlemen friends, Edmonia had offered to prepare a warm drink for them in her room. She made three glasses of hot spiced wine; the two women drank theirs, while Lewis' own drink remained untouched.

During the sleigh ride, both women became violently sick, and for two weeks afterward remained gravely ill and under doctors' care for suspected poisoning. The young women were certain that Lewis had poisoned them. Before any criminal charge could be made, supporters of Lewis, who included the Keeps, retained a distinguished local attorney, John Mercer Langston, to defend her should the need arise. Langston was a prominent African-American lawyer, a graduate of Oberlin, and the first of his race to be admitted to the Ohio bar.

Some praise me because I am a colored girl, and I don't want that kind of praise. I had rather you would point out my defects, for that will teach me something.

—**Edmonia Lewis to Lydia Maria Child**

While Edmonia Lewis was awaiting word as to whether she would be charged, unknown persons seized and beat her severely. At her trial, Lewis was completely exonerated after Langston successfully argued that there was no proof that any poisoning had occurred, as the contents of the girls' stomachs had never been analyzed. Lewis was borne from the courtroom on the shoulders of jubilant friends and supporters, almost all of them white, and she was able to resume her college studies. She left Oberlin without completing her degree in early 1863, having decided to become a sculptor. With her brother's financial help, Lewis moved to Boston, Massachusetts, to pursue a professional apprenticeship under the master sculptor Edward A. Brackett.

Boston was the center of cultural and abolitionist activity, and John Keep had furnished Edmonia Lewis with a letter of introduction to the famed abolitionist William Lloyd Garrison. Through Garrison, she met many of the most wealthy and influential Boston abolitionists, among these the well-known woman of letters Lydia Maria Child, who befriended the young artist. Child was instrumental in bringing critical notice to Lewis' early work. It was in Boston too that Lewis met the celebrated actress *Charlotte Cushman, who would also take a personal and professional interest in Lewis' work.

Not yet out of her teens, Lewis was eager to establish herself as a professional artist. She quickly grew impatient with the laborious, lengthy apprenticeship prescribed by Edward Brackett. Instead, she ordered that a sign be hung outside the studio her brother Samuel had rented for her: it read, "Edmonia Lewis, Artist." Her first commercial attempt was a medallion of John Brown, the abolitionist martyr. The work met with modest success in the community of abolitionists. Lewis' next effort was a bust of Robert Gould Shaw, the Civil War hero who had perished while leading an all-black regiment in the battle of Fort Wagner. The Shaw bust, exhibited at the Soldiers' Relief Fair of 1864, was a great success; Lewis received orders for 100 plaster copies.

The profits from the Shaw sculpture and the generous support of her brother Samuel made it possible for Edmonia Lewis to pursue her dream of studying and working in Italy. She went first to Florence, where the noted American sculptor Hiram Powers welcomed her to his studio. After some months there, Lewis moved to Rome, then the center of American expatriate culture. Rome in 1866 was home to an international coterie of writers, poets, and artists. For wealthy American visitors, no Roman tour was complete without a visit to the studios of the well-known artists in residence there. Such visits often culminated in either a purchase or a commission.

Charlotte Cushman, Lewis' friend and patron, was at the center of the international artistic community in Rome. Known for her interest in the young women artists who had gathered to work in the Eternal City, Cushman offered advice and support to Lewis. At Cushman's celebrated social gatherings, the young African-American artist created a stir, and the older woman often directed her wealthy friends and acquaintances to the studio of Lewis. Soon all of Rome was talking about the marvelous young sensation. Lewis' Rome studio, formerly the studio of the great Italian sculptor Canova, became a required stop for wealthy art patrons on the grand tour.

There were a surprising number of American women sculptors at work in Rome when Lewis arrived in the 1860s—*Harriet Hosmer, *Louisa Lander, *Anne Whitney, *Margaret Foley, *Vinnie Ream, and *Emma Stebbins, among them. American novelist Henry James, in his *William Wetmore Story and His Friends,* referred to the women as "that strange sisterhood of American 'lady sculptors' who . . . descended upon the seven hills in a white, marmorean flock." Edmonia Lewis had come to Rome at a particularly propitious time, and she was readily accepted in the community of women sculptors. Both Harriet Hosmer and Anne Whitney took a special interest in her work.

Haunted by the fear that people would not believe that she, an African-American woman, was capable of doing her own work, Edmonia Lewis at first did all of her own carving. In this she was unlike her contemporaries, who modeled a conceptual sculpture and left the actual carving of the marble to Italian artisans. This struggle for authenticity added to the burdens of the young artist, and she welcomed the patronage of Charlotte Cushman. Marble was very expensive; thus Lewis was delighted when in the winter of 1866–67, Cushman financed the creation of Lewis' first full-scale marble work, *The Wooing of Hiawatha,* a statue inspired by Henry Wadsworth Longfellow's popular poem, *Song of Hiawatha.* Cushman purchased the completed sculpture and paid to ship it to Boston, where she donated it to the Boston YMCA in hopes of drawing wider stateside attention to Lewis' talents. The interview in which Lewis told of her nomadic Indian girlhood as "Wildfire" heightened interest in the Native American theme pieces, and Lewis followed the *Wooing* with a companion piece, *The Wedding of Hiawatha.*

Along with the two Hiawatha companion sculptures, Lewis created a third Longfellow-inspired work, *The Old Indian Arrowmaker and His Daughter.* One of Lewis' best sculptures, it blends neoclassicism with the naturalism that would come to infuse her later work. When Lewis learned in 1869 that Longfellow was visiting Rome, she studied his face on the street, then returned to her studio to work first on a sketch, and afterward on a bust that would later win her the praise and admiration of the poet's family, as well as securing her reputation among her fellow sculptors in Rome.

The following year, Lewis executed a sculpture to commemorate the Emancipation Proclamation. She carved *Forever Free* in 1868, afterward shipping it to the wealthy Boston abolitionist Samuel Sewall. That year, too, Lewis completed *Hagar,* begun the previous year in Rome and modeled on the Biblical Egyptian servant who had been cast out into the wilderness after bearing Abraham's child. While *Hagar was a popular subject for many 19th-century sculptors who saw her as a symbol of slavery, Lewis invested her *Hagar* with a deeper religious meaning as well. In 1868, Edmonia Lewis turned to Catholicism, and she later described her *Hagar* as symbolizing the moment when Hagar's despair is ended by an angel, linking it to her own moment of spiritual awakening.

When she did not immediately find a purchaser for *Hagar,* Lewis, with the help of a Chicago businessman, rented an exhibition room in Chicago's Farwell Hall. She placed an advertisement in the *Chicago Tribune* inviting patrons to see the statue for a fee of 25 cents. In the ad, she described herself as "the young and gifted colored sculptress from Rome." Viewers arrived by the hundreds, driven by curiosity. Eventually, Lewis would receive $6,000 for *Hagar.*

During her sojourn in America, Lewis met the noted woman physician *Harriot Kezia Hunt, who commissioned a life-size statue of Hygieia for her own grave in Mount Auburn Cemetery in Cambridge, Massachusetts. Lewis also created a *Portrait Medallion of Wendell Phillips,* a bust of Abraham Lincoln, and a pair of cherub figures that she titled *Asleep* and *Awake.* In 1873, she traveled to California, where her work won her praise in San Francisco, as well as in San Jose. She was able to sell almost all of the statues she had shipped across the country, the last, the bust of Lincoln, being bought by the Friends of San Jose Library.

Returning to Rome, Lewis found her contemporaries hard at work on entries for the upcoming Philadelphia Centennial Exposition. For the next year, Lewis would work on the piece that would prove her greatest triumph, *The Death of Cleopatra.* Strikingly original and the largest of Lewis' works, it went on to garner considerable critical acclaim at the Centennial. Unlike Lewis' smaller works, however, it did not sell, and in 1878, she shipped it to the Chicago Interstate Exposition, where it proved a major drawing card, but again did not sell. Only recently was the work discovered in a salvage yard. Restored at the National Museum of American Art, the work went on display in 1996, more than a century after its triumphant reception.

Although most of the American expatriate artists had left Rome by 1876, Lewis had come to regard Rome as her home. She returned to her studio in the Via Della Frezza, where she remained for the rest of her life. She continued to produce sculpture, concentrating more on religious works. Among these was an altarpiece that she sold to the Marquis of Bute for $2,000, and an 1883 commission from a Baltimore church for an *Adoration of the Magi.* The noted African-American leader Frederick Douglass visited Lewis in her studio in Rome in 1887 and described her as living in a very pleasant apartment with a splendid view. Lewis showed Frederick and his second wife, **Helen Pitts Douglass**, around the city, and they traveled together to Naples. On his return, Douglass described Edmonia Lewis as "cheerful and happy and successful."

Little is known of Lewis' career beyond the commentary by Douglass in 1887. The Philadelphia Centennial had marked the beginning of the decline of neoclassicism in sculpture. The blend of neoclassicism and naturalism that Edmonia Lewis had employed with such success was being replaced by a trend toward realism. It is believed that in her later years, Lewis concentrated on religious works, and indeed, the last known mention of Edmonia occurs in a February 1909 article in *The Rosary Magazine*. The article described her as "aging" but "still with us."

Where and when Edmonia Lewis died has not as yet been ascertained. What is known is that the legacy of Edmonia Lewis reaches beyond the body of work found in museums, galleries, and churches; in her struggle to define herself against a 19th-century wall of prejudice, Lewis has come to symbolize a triumph over race, gender, and cultural experience. Against incredible odds, Lewis left her mark on the international art world.

SOURCES:

Blodgett, Geoffrey. "John Mercer Langston and the Case of Edmonia Lewis: Oberlin, 1862" in *Journal of Negro History*. Vol. 53. July 1968, pp. 201–218.

Buick, Kirsten P. "The Ideal Works of Edmonia Lewis: Invoking and Inverting Autobiography" in *American Art*. Vol. 9. Summer 1995, pp. 5–19.

Burgard, Timothy Anglin. "Edmonia Lewis and Henry Wadsworth Longfellow: Images and Identities" in *American Art Review*. Vol. 7, no. 1, pp. 114–117.

"Edmonia Lewis," in *The Revolution*. Vol. 7. April 20, 1871, p. 8.

Langston, John Mercer. *From the Virginia Plantation to the National Capitol, or The First and Only Negro Representative in Congress from the Old Dominion*. Hartford, CT: American Publishing, 1894.

Lewis, Jo Ann. "An Afterlife for 'Cleopatra'" in *The Washington Post*. June 10, 1996, B1.

Richardson, Marilyn. "Edmonia Lewis" in *Harvard Magazine* Vol. 88. March–April 1986, pp. 40–41.

———. *Encyclopedia of African-American Culture and History*. Vol. 3, p. 607.

Wreford, Henry. "A Negro Sculptress," in *The Atheneum*. Vol. 39. March 3, 1866.

Andrea Moore Kerr, Ph.D.,
women's historian and author of *Lucy Stone: Speaking Out For Equality* (Rutgers University Press, 1992), Washington, D.C.

Lewis, Elma (1921—)

African-American arts administrator and educator.
Born in 1921 in Boston, Massachusetts; daughter of Edwardine Jordan Corbin Lewis (a maid) and Clair- mont Richard McDonald Lewis (a day laborer); educated in Boston public schools; Emerson College, B.A., Literature Interpretation, 1943; Boston University School of Education, M.A., 1944.

Founded Elma Lewis School of Fine Arts in Roxbury, Massachusetts (1950); founder and director, National Center of Afro-American Artists (1968).

A dancer, actress, teacher, director, choreographer, and speech therapist, Elma Lewis changed the artistic landscape in Boston when she opened the Elma Lewis School of Fine Arts in Roxbury, Massachusetts, in 1950. As the founder of the National Center of Afro-American Artists, Lewis promoted the work of black artists, attracting national attention throughout the 1990s. Her primary concern was to nurture the creative energies of the nation's black population, and to help develop what she called "good human beings" with pride in their black heritage; however, she also noted, "if in the process we develop good artists, that's all right, too."

The daughter of immigrants from Barbados, Elma Lewis was born in Boston, Massachusetts, in 1921. She was the only child of **Edwardine Lewis**, a maid, and Clairmont Lewis, a day laborer, and had two older half brothers from her mother's first marriage, which had ended when the boys' father died. Learning to read by the age of three with the help of one of these brothers, Lewis was evaluated that year by a group of white educators. She never forgot their report, which read in part: "This bright, precocious little Negro girl will, as is usual with members of her race, test at a much lower level as she gets older." Lewis had her stage debut the same year when she recited a poem at a meeting of the Marcus Garvey Universal Negro Improvement Association. Both her parents attended Sunday meetings of the association, which was aimed at fostering Garvey's goals of black pride, dignity, and self-sufficiency. Her mother was also a Black Cross nurse, and her father was a member of the African Legion. Both parents worked hard to provide an education for their children, and Elma studied dance, voice, and piano as a child, as well as taking elocution lessons. By the time she was 11, Lewis earned as much as $50 per week through dance and drama performances, an enormous sum in those early years of the Depression. She attended the prestigious Boston Latin School, graduating in 1939, and taught dance from 1935 to 1941 at the Doris W. Jones School of Dance in Boston. From 1942 to 1943, Lewis served as a speech therapist at Roxbury Memorial High School for Girls, also working as a student speech therapist for the Massachusetts Mental Health Habit Clinic in Boston to pay her way through Emerson College.

When Lewis graduated from Emerson with a B.A. in Literature Interpretation in 1943, she went on to take a Master of Arts degree at Boston University School of Education in 1944. With few opportunities for black actresses, she decided to turn her talents toward the education of exceptional children. She taught in the Boston public schools in 1945 and worked again at the Massachusetts Mental Health Habit Clinic from 1945 to 1949 before turning her attention to two social services agencies. At the *Harriet **Tubman** House in Boston's South End, she became a fine-arts worker; at the Robert Gould Shaw House, she directed and choreographed 21 operas and operettas for the Robert Gould Shaw House Chorus between 1946 and 1968. Dedicated to working in the arts in an urban setting with a large black community, Lewis opened the Elma Lewis School for Fine Arts in Boston's Roxbury section in 1950. Beginning in a six-room apartment, the school had a stated mission to "offer quality education in the arts to children in the neighborhood." She had $300—borrowed from her father—a few folding chairs, and a rented piano when she opened the doors to her first 25 students. Along with four teachers, she provided dance and drama instruction for local children.

In 1968, Lewis purchased a former synagogue and school for the price of one dollar. Formerly a predominantly Jewish neighborhood, the area had become inhabited by middle-class black families. Although her school had been popular, it had lacked a permanent home, and the changing demographics of the area presented an opportunity for her to buy property at a crucial time. Once she obtained property, fund-raising went beyond the bake sales of the school's earlier days. Lewis established an endowment and began rehabilitating the building. In January 1969, the school opened once again, this time with an enrollment of 250 students and courses including drama, various kinds of dance, African drumming, music, writing, and art. The school also began offering these programs to inmates at the Massachusetts Correctional Institute at Norfolk. The Technical Theater Training Program, started in 1970, helped to prepare inmates for such technical positions as stage managers, sound technicians, and electricians.

The Elma Lewis School of Fine Arts became a subsidiary of the National Center of Afro-American Artists, founded and directed by Lewis, in 1968. The center took on a range of projects, which included an experimental theater, jazz and classical orchestras, and a summer theater in Boston's Franklin Park. Lewis' ambitious range of arts projects began to attract attention in the larger Boston community. Her fund-raising efforts brought financial support from the Boston Globe, New England Telephone and other local companies and agencies, the same year the school re-opened. Grants also came from the Rockefeller Foundation, the Kresge Foundation, the National Endowment for the Arts, and the Ford Foundation. Keeping the school's tuition low, Lewis made it possible for anyone who wished to enroll to do so. While most students attended after primary and high school hours, evening adult programs were also established. Nationally acclaimed artists made appearances at the school, helping raise its profile and its fund-raising base. Harry Belafonte, Duke Ellington, *Odetta, Max Roach, Ossie Davis and *Ruby **Dee** all came to teach, perform, or help raise money. In 1981, Lewis was among the first recipients of the MacArthur Foundation Fellowships (the no-strings-attached "genius grants"). With a five-year grant of $280,000, she was able to have some necessary eye surgery and travel, while developing a curriculum on black culture.

In 1988, the school closed. Lewis was by then 67 years old but still endowed with the same vitality as when she began her school. The one project she continued to foster was the beloved annual production of Langston Hughes' Black Nativity, with a cast of 150, which she directed until she was nearly 80, suffering from kidney failure, and almost blind from diabetes.

Lewis has received more than 100 citations and awards, including the Mayor's Citation from the City of Boston in 1970 and on other occasions; the Henry O. Tanner Award from the Black Arts Council of California (1971); a resolution passed by both houses of the Massachusetts Legislature congratulating her for 25 years of contributions to the black community, the world, and Afro-American culture (1975); the Boston Chamber of Commerce arts award (1978); the Presidential Medal for the Arts (1983); and the Black History Achiever Award from Northeastern University (1988). More than 26 honorary degrees have been bestowed on her, including ones from Harvard University, Brown University, Colby College, the New England Conservatory of Music, Northeastern University, and the University of Massachusetts. She has been honored by many educational and arts societies, including the African Heritage Studies Association; the Black Big Brother Association;

the Black Educators Alliance of Massachusetts; the Governor's Committee on the Status of Women; the Museum of Afro-American History, Boston; the National Association of Dance, Health, and Recreation; the National Council of Teachers of English; and the United States Department of Health, Education, and Welfare. Throughout her life, Elma Lewis has been an illustration of the truthfulness of the message she delivered to her students: "Glory in yourself. Anything is possible."

SOURCES:
The New York Times. December 28, 1998, A-18.
Smith, Jessie Carney, ed. *Notable Black American Women.* Detroit, MI: Gale Research, 1992.

Lolly Ockerstrom,
freelance writer, Washington, D.C.

Lewis, Estelle Anna (1824–1880)

American dramatist and poet. Name variations: Stella. Born Estelle Anna Blanche Robinson near Baltimore, Maryland, in 1824; died in 1880; daughter of J.N. Robinson; attended the Female Seminary at Troy, New York; married S.D. Lewis (a Brooklyn lawyer), in 1841.

Estelle Lewis was born near Baltimore, at the country seat of her wealthy father J.N. Robinson, who died while she was an infant. Her mother was the daughter of an officer in the Revolutionary war. While a schoolgirl at *Emma Hart Willard's Female Seminary in Troy, New York, Lewis composed a verse rendering of the *Aeneid* into English and also published a series of stories in the *Family Magazine.* Leaving the seminary in 1841, she was married and lived in Brooklyn until she moved to Europe in 1858.

Her best dramatic work, the tragedy *Sappho in Lesbos* (1868), ran through seven editions, was translated into modern Greek, and played at Athens. Edgar Allan Poe said she was the rival of *Sappho, and Lamartine called her the "female Petrarch." Besides letters on travel, literature, and art published in American journals under the name of "Stella," Lewis wrote two other tragedies, *Helémah, or the Fall of Montezuma* and *The King's Strategem,* as well as several books of poems, a collection of which was illustrated in 1866.

Lewis, Ethelreda (1875–1946)

English-born novelist who wrote Trader Horn. *Name variations: (pseudonym) R. Hernekin Baptist; Mrs. Ethelreda Lewis. Born in 1875 in Matlock, England; died on August 1, 1946, probably in Johannesburg, South Africa.*

Selected writings: The Harp *(1924);* The Flying Emerald *(1925);* Mantis *(1926);* Four Handsome Negresses: The Record of a Voyage *(1931);* Love at the Mission *(1938);* A Cargo of Parrots *(1938); (edited)* The Life and Times of Trader Horn *(3 vols., 1927–1929).*

Born in Matlock, Derbyshire, England, in 1875, Ethelreda Lewis moved to South Africa in 1904. Her first three novels, *The Harp* (1924), *The Flying Emerald* (1925), and *Mantis* (1926), were all published under her married name of Lewis. Four others were published under the pseudonym R. Hernekin Baptist: *Four Handsome Negresses: The Record of a Voyage* (1931); *Wild Deer* (1933); *Love at the Mission* (1938); and *A Cargo of Parrots* (1938). In 1984, *Wild Deer* was reprinted under her own name. In addition, Lewis edited *The Life and Times of Trader Horn,* a three-volume text based on conversations and stories told to her by an itinerant trader named Alfred Aloysius Horn. Meeting him one day when he knocked at her back door trying to sell a gridiron, she spent that morning and a good portion of the following two years listening to him talk, convinced that he was a rich literary resource. She eventually edited his pencil-written manuscript and produced the first volume of the series, *The Ivory Coast in the Earlies,* in 1927. With an introduction by John Galsworthy, who had met both Horn and Lewis on a visit to South Africa, it became a choice selection for the Literary Guild of New York and was highly successful. Two other volumes, *Harold the Webbed* (1928) and *The Waters of Africa* (1929), followed, all from notes she took during conversations with Horn.

Lewis was described by *Vera Brittain in *Testament of Friendship* as having an "intense, serious mind," and was much preoccupied with the plight of black South African workers. They met when Lewis went to London to seek a publisher in 1923, with an introduction to Brittain's friend *Winifred Holtby. Lewis' novels address the exploitation of black South Africans at the hands of whites (not a popular subject even when *Doris Lessing first began to write about similar situations in Southern Rhodesia several decades later), and her concerns were thus sympathetic to the socially conscious Holtby. In 1926, Lewis organized a series of meetings at Workers' Hall in Johannesburg upon the occasion of Holtby's visit to South Africa, inviting white experts to discuss race relations. Although Lewis' fiction was intended to serve as an illustration of the horrors of imperialism, it has been criticized for being too facile, creating simple binary oppositions of the Western ideas of the civilized and the primitive, rather than showing the complications of imperialism. Ethelreda Lewis died in 1946, most likely in Johannesburg, South Africa, which had been her home since 1904.

Lolly Ockerstrom,
freelance writer, Washington, D.C.

Lewis, Graceanna (1821–1912)

American ornithologist and reformer. Born on August 3, 1821, in West Vincent Township, Chester County, Pennsylvania; died on February 25, 1912, in Media, Pennsylvania; third of four daughters and one son (who died in infancy) of John Lewis (a farmer) and Esther (Fussell) Lewis; schooled at home; attended Kimberton Boarding School for Girls; never married; no children.

Born into a Pennsylvania Quaker farm family, Graceanna Lewis was interested in science from as far back as she could remember. "I inherited from my mother a strong love of nature," she recalled, "she having guided our attention in this direction from our early youth." Lewis was three when her father died, leaving her and her three sisters in the care of her mother **Esther Fussell Lewis**, who endured a lengthy battle for control of the estate left to her by her husband. A teacher before her marriage, Esther began her children's education at home, then sent them to a Quaker Boarding School located two miles from the farm. Social awareness was also a strong trait in Lewis' family, and Graceanna grew up a staunch abolitionist, viewing slavery as "one of the greatest of crimes against humanity." The Lewis home, though small, was frequently a refuge for fugitive slaves.

Upon completing her education in 1842, Lewis was not yet ready to commit herself to science, and so she gravitated to teaching, one of the few professions open to a woman of her class and qualifications. Her first job was as a teacher of botany and astronomy at a small boarding school in York, Pennsylvania, run by her uncle Bartholomew Fussell, who, like the entire extended Lewis family, had one foot in social reform. The school lasted only two years, after which Lewis taught for a term in a similar school in Phoenixville. She was unhappy there, however, and in 1845 she moved back home, devoting herself to the farm and to abolition activities while pursuing her scientific studies independently Following her mother's death in 1848, Lewis took over more responsibility for the farm

and for the family's Underground Railroad activities. As the 1850s progressed, she became more active in the cause, organizing meetings and procuring speakers for local anti-slavery organizations. It was not until after the Civil War that she once again took up her scientific studies.

By then in her 30s, Lewis moved to Philadelphia, living within the close-knit community of Quakers active in science. Focusing her work in ornithology, in 1862 she met John Cassin, America's leading ornithologist and volunteer curator of birds at the Academy of Natural Sciences. In her words, he provided a "*sesame* to the scientific world." Over the next seven years, she read in the academy's library and studied the specimens in its museum. By 1865, she was giving parlor lessons in ornithology, and, as the years passed, her interest expanded to include the entire animal kingdom, and then the plant and mineral kingdoms as well. In 1874, and again in 1879, she lectured at Vassar, and in 1875 she presented a talk on frost crystals to the New England Women's Club in Boston. But freelancing was a difficult way to earn a living, so Lewis applied for numerous scientific positions both at the academy and in the private sector. However, her lack of formal education beyond high school

Graceanna Lewis

was a stumbling block, as was her gender. Twice she applied for a vacant professorship in natural history at Vassar, losing out both times to male applicants. Following her second interview in 1877, she was described as "unquestionably better acquainted with zoology as a science than any other person of her sex in the country." Despite her qualifications, the job went to Reverend William Buck Dwight. Unable to secure a college position, Lewis taught for several years at preparatory schools: first at the Friends' School in Philadelphia (1870–71), then at the Foster School for Girls in Clifton Springs, New York (1883–85).

During this period, Lewis also authored a number of scientific publications, the first of which, *Natural History of Birds* (Part 1 of a projected 10), was published in pamphlet form in 1868. Due to the high costs of publishing and a lack of public interest in her work, she never completed the remaining nine parts. Lewis also produced articles and drawings for the scientific journal *The American Naturalist* and contributed drawings for *Key to North American Birds* by Elliott Coues, although she was never credited.

In the summer of 1871, at age 50, Lewis suffered mental and physical problems, possibly caused by menopause, although she described it as "an affliction of the brain." Plans to develop some family land never materialized, and she eventually sold the property and used the profit to support her subsequent research, which focused on illustrating the relationships between members of the animal kingdom. Her plan was to produce a chart of the animal kingdom as well as phylogenic charts of plants, birds, fish, and geology, with special reference to paleontology. But she had difficulty keeping up with the rapid influx of new information, and refused to publish the charts in an incomplete form, so the project was never finished.

In 1885, Lewis returned to Media, Pennsylvania, and moved in with her widowed sister **Rebecca**. She remained there for the rest of her life, enjoying the activities of her extended family. She continued to write and produce illustrations of plants and animals, including a series of 50 large watercolors of the leaves of Pennsylvania trees, commission by the Pennsylvania Forestry Commission. They would be exhibited at the Columbian Exposition in Chicago in 1893, the Pan American Exhibition in Buffalo in 1901, and the Louisiana Purchase Exhibition in St. Louis in 1904. Lewis also became active in several community organizations, including the Media Women Suffrage Association, of which she served as secretary for a number of years. She was active in the Women's Christian Temperance Union and was a member of the Women's Club of Media, which she deemed "a very useful organization, taking hold of questions of real importance and giving courses of valuable lectures."

Graceanna Lewis died on February 25, 1912, following a stroke, and was buried in Media. On Memorial Day, 1915, the suffragists of Media held services at her gravesite to honor her work in both science and reform.

SOURCES:

Ogilvie, Marilyn Bailey. *Women in Science*. Cambridge, MA: MIT Press, 1986.

Warner, Deborah Jean. *Graceanna Lewis: Scientist and Humanitarian*. Washington, DC: Smithsonian Institution Press, 1979.

Barbara Morgan,
Melrose, Massachusetts

Lewis, Ida (1842–1911)

Nineteenth-century lighthouse keeper and hero, known as America's Grace Darling. Born Idawalley Zorada (also seen as Zoradia) Lewis in Newport, Rhode Island, on February 25, 1842; died in Lime Rock, Rhode Island, on October 24, 1911; second child and eldest daughter of Captain Hosea Lewis (keeper of Lime Rock Lighthouse in Newport Harbor); attended public school in Newport until the family moved to Lime Rock; married William H. Wilson (a fisherman), in October 1870 (separated and resumed her maiden name).

Born in 1842, the year of ***Grace Darling**'s death, Ida Lewis, like her courageous British counterpart, was also a lighthouse-keeper's daughter. In 1859, when her father became disabled from a stroke, she took over his duties at the Lime Rock Lighthouse in Newport Harbor, to which the family had moved in 1857. At age 16, she single-handedly saved four young men who had capsized their pleasure boat offshore. Unlike Darling, however, Lewis would perform 18 more rescues during her life.

She did not come to the public's attention until 1869, after she had rescued two soldiers from the nearby garrison at Fort Adams from the wreckage of a sailboat that had capsized in a sudden storm. The soldiers had managed to hang on to what was left of their boat until Lewis, with the help of her younger brother, rowed out to save them. They told the story of their rescue to the press, and, after an article appeared in the *New York Herald Tribune*, Lewis became known throughout the nation. She was the first woman awarded the Congressional Medal of Honor and was received by President Ulysses Grant when he visited Rhode Island. The Life Saving Benevolent Association of New York sent her a silver medal and a check for $100, and the secretary of state for Rhode Island sent a commendation passed by the Rhode Island General Assembly. At an Independence Day celebration in her honor, Lewis was presented with a skiff named *Rescue,* and the financier James Fisk later built her a boathouse. During the height of her fame, she received countless marriage proposals, and the lighthouse was inundated with visitors numbering around 100 a day. Except for a brief marriage in her 20s to a sea captain, Lewis spent all her days at the lighthouse at Lime Rock, although the federal government did not appoint her official keeper of the facility until 1879.

Even though she continued to perform daring feats during her 50 years at the lighthouse, Lewis' prominence was relatively short-lived. In 1906, at age 64, she rescued a woman vacationer from the icy waters. That same year, she was awarded a pension by the Carnegie Hero Fund and a gold medal from the American Cross of Honor Society. She died at Lime Rock on October 24, 1911.

Barbara Morgan,
Melrose, Massachusetts

Lewis, Mary Edmonia (c. 1845–c. 1909).
See Lewis, Edmonia.

Lewis, Mercy.
See Witchcraft Trials in Salem Village.

Lewis, Shari (1933–1998)

American puppeteer, ventriloquist, and entertainer. Born in New York City on January 17, 1933; died of complications from uterine cancer in Los Angeles, California, on August 2, 1998; daughter of Abraham Hurwitz (a college professor) and Ann Hurwitz (a school music coordinator); attended Herman Ritter Junior High School, New York; attended Music and Art High School, New York; married Stan Lewis (an advertising executive, divorced); married Jeremy Tarcher (a publisher), in 1958; children: (second marriage) one daughter, Mallory Tarcher.

Perhaps best remembered for her mischievous sock puppet Lamb Chop, the diminutive puppeteer and ventriloquist Shari Lewis was one of the most beloved and respected performers in children's television. The winner of 12 Emmys, five for her PBS series "Lamb Chop's Play-Along" (1992–97), Lewis had just launched a new show, "The Charlie Horse Music Pizza," when she died of complications from uterine cancer.

Born in 1933 and raised in New York, Lewis started playing the piano at age three and pulling rabbits out of hats at four. Her mother **Ann Hurwitz** was a music coordinator for the New York City Board of Education, and her father Abraham Hurwitz was a college professor and amateur magician. In addition to practicing her music, which included piano, violin, and accordion, Lewis excelled as a ventriloquist. She made her first appearance on a television variety show at age 13, and starred in NBC's "Facts 'n' Fun" at 18. In 1956, she and her sassy puppet Lamb Chop made their first television appearance on "Captain Kangaroo," and by 1960 the duo, who by this time had added pals Hush Puppy and Charlie Horse, premiered on their own NBC Saturday morning program, "The Shari Lewis Show." The program ran until 1963,

Shari Lewis

when television began producing animated shows for the younger set.

Except for a syndicated half-hour series, "The Shari Show" (1975–76), Lewis struggled for three decades before gaining another foothold in the television market. In the interim, she performed in Las Vegas, conducted symphony orchestras, and penned over 60 children's books. Lewis finally returned to television with "Lamb Chop's Play-Along," a PBS production premiering in 1992, which ran for five years. The show's easy format of music, comedy, riddles, and puns was always tempered by Lewis' goal to teach as well as entertain. Off-camera, she became an impassioned activist, hoping to expand the choices for children's television viewing. In 1993, she took Lamb Chop to Capitol Hill to plead with broadcasters to improve programming for children. "We need the best you grown-ups have to offer," she said through Lamb Chop. "If you give it to us, we will give you the good stuff back."

Lewis also tried to fill in the gaps herself. When she noticed that there was a lack of programming for Jewish children, she came up with the primetime specials "Lamb Chop's Special Chanukah" and "Shari's Passover Surprise." Sensing a need to foster music appreciation, she designed "The Charlie Horse Music Pizza." The show was but a year old when she was diagnosed with cancer in June 1998. Just hours after hearing the news, she was back rehearsing, hoping to shoot as many episodes as possible before starting chemotherapy.

Following the dissolution of an early marriage, Lewis wed publisher Jeremy Tarcher, with whom she had a daughter, **Mallory Tarcher**. A woman of boundless energy, Lewis filled her hours away from performing with family activities, including rafting trips with her husband. About all she didn't do was drive or keep house. "My mother told me not to learn anything that I didn't want to do," Lewis said in a 1992 interview with *People* magazine, "so I never learned to wash a floor or clean a toilet."

Ironically, Lewis' death on August 2, 1998, came just three days after the death of another beloved puppeteer, Robert E. Smith, Buffalo Bob of the "Howdy Doody Show." "She was a true advocate for kids," said **Peggy Charren**, founder of Actions for Children's Television. "Shari inherently understood what children need in order for them to grow up healthy, happy and wise. And she did it with laughs: Hers was a warm and fuzzy sense of humor. . . . Unlike a lot of people who operate in children's programming, Shari *cared* about children. She was in it for love."

SOURCES:

Aucoin, Don. "Appreciation," in *Boston Globe*. August 4, 1998.

Lewis, Shari. "Making the Difference: An interview with Shari Lewis," in *Music Educators Journal*. Vol. 78, no. 6. February 1992, pp. 56–59.

Logan, Michael. "The Voice of Childhood," in *TV Guide*. August 29, 1998.

Miller, Samantha, Monica Rizzo, and Eric Francis. "Sockcess Story," in *People Weekly*. Vol. 50, no. 5. August 17, 1998, pp. 82–84.

Tucker, Ken. "Legacy: The Puppet Masters," in *Entertainment Weekly*. No. 445. August 14, 1998, p. 15.

Barbara Morgan,
Melrose, Massachusetts

Lewisohn, Alice and Irene

American sisters who built the landmark Neighborhood Playhouse.

Lewisohn, Alice (1883–1972). Born in 1883; died in 1972; daughter of Leonard Lewisohn (a businessman) and Rosalie (Jacobs) Lewisohn; married Herbert E. Crowley, around 1925.

Lewisohn, Irene (1892–1944). Born on September 5, 1892, in New York City; died in April 1944 in New York; fifth daughter and youngest of ten children of Leonard Lewisohn (a businessman) and Rosalie (Jacobs) Lewisohn; attended the Finch School in New York; never married; no children.

Born into a wealthy and cultured Jewish family but orphaned when they were young, Irene Lewisohn and her older sister Alice inherited enough money to determine their own course in life. From an early age, Irene was drawn to the theater, particularly dance, and after finishing her formal education at the Finch School in New York, embarked on a course of independent study with various performing artists. With the encouragement of Alice, Irene also became involved in the Henry Street Settlement in New York City's Lower East Side, which had been one of her father's favorite charities. Together, the sisters taught acting and dancing, and organized amateur productions, among them a 1907 performance of the "Festival Dancers" in the settlement house gymnasium. In 1912, using both adults and children, the sisters formed the "Neighborhood Players," staging their first play for the public at a hall in the Bowery. The following year, to commemorate the settlement's 20th anniversary, the Lewisohns directed an elaborate pageant, showcasing the various ethnic music, dances, and costumes of their diverse neighborhood cast. Now thoroughly committed to all of the work being done at Henry Street, the sisters gave the settlement house an 80-acre farm, Echo Hill, located outside of the city, to be used as a holiday center for the children of the neighborhood.

In 1914, to further advance their theatrical visions, Irene and Alice purchased a lot on Grand Street and built the Neighborhood Theater, which they donated to the settlement. Opening in 1915, the theater slowly emerged as an independent entity and, by 1920, had replaced its amateur casts with a resident professional company. As one of the first "little theaters" in the country, it served as a center for experimental and avant-garde theater, producing plays by John Galsworthy, George Bernard Shaw, Eugene O'Neill, James Joyce, Sholem Asch, and Leonid Andreyev. Notable among the early productions was *The Little Clay Cart* (1924), a Hindu play, and *The Dybbuk* (1925), a classic Yiddish folk play which was greatly enhanced by the set designs of *Aline Bernstein. Beginning in 1923, the theater also produced the annual *Grand Street Follies*, a topical revue which was geared to the Lower East Side audience.

Irene and Alice Lewisohn remained a central financial and artistic force in the Playhouse. In addition to donating over a half-million dollars to the theater, they also directed productions, solicited new talent, and even performed (Alice taking acting roles, and Irene dancing). They were also pivotal in selecting some of the theater's more esoteric Asiatic and Middle Eastern productions, having become interested in these theater and dance forms during two world tours: one in 1910, and another in 1922–23.

Even while it flourished during the 1920s, the Playhouse experienced financial difficulties, the result of disappointing annual drives for subscribers and Alice's marriage to Herbert E. Crowley around 1925, after which she was less involved with the venture. The Playhouse closed in 1927, the building reverting back to the settlement house. Seeking other outlets for her creative energies, in 1928 Irene Lewisohn joined **Rita Morgenthau** in founding the Neighborhood Playhouse School of the Theater, of which she remained co-director for many years. In addition, she produced a series of "orchestral dramas" or "musical masques," dances or pantomimes performed to the accompaniment of a full symphony orchestra. The first of these performances was presented at the Manhattan Opera House in May 1928. Another, which Lewisohn directed in 1930, with dancer *Martha Graham, was performed in New York City and again at the dedication of Severance Hall in Cleveland. Yet another, commissioned by the *Elizabeth Sprague Coolidge Foundation, was performed in Washington, D.C., in 1931. With the onset of the Depression, however, Lewisohn's flights of artistic fancy seemed out of place, and she moved on to more practical endeavors.

In the course of her world travels, Irene Lewisohn had amassed an extensive collection of costumes, and in 1937, with Aline Bernstein, she founded the Museum of Costume Art (later the Costume Institute), in order to make the collection available to designers and to the public. After her death, the Costume Institute would become part of the Metropolitan Museum of Art. Apart from her personal artistic projects, Irene also gave freely of her time and money to outside causes. During the Spanish Civil War, she founded the Spanish Child Welfare Association and, during World War II, was active in the American Theater Group's Stage Door Canteen and the Club for Merchant Seamen. But her main love was always the theater, and those who knew her spoke of her dedication and artistic vision. Critic and playwright Stark Young said that "her response and friendship, asking nothing for itself, was of marvelous benefit to the artist." Irene Lewisohn died of lung cancer in 1944, at age 51. Her sister Alice survived her by 28 years and, in 1959, published a memoir, *The Neighborhood Theater.*

SOURCES:

James, Edward T., ed. *Notable American Women 1607–1950.* Cambridge, MA: The Belknap Press of Harvard University Press, 1971.

McHenry, Robert. *Famous American Women.* NY: Dover, 1983.

Wilmeth, Don B., and Tice L. Miller. *Cambridge Guide to American Theater.* NY: Cambridge University Press, 1993.

Barbara Morgan,
Melrose, Massachusetts

Lewson, Jane (c. 1700–1816)

English woman who inspired a famous Dickensian character. Name variations: Lady Lewson. Born Jane Vaughan around 1700 in England; died in 1816; married.

Jane Lewson became a recluse after the death of her husband in 1726. Her eccentricities are reputed to have been the basis for Miss Havisham in Charles Dickens' *Great Expectations.*

Leyburne, Elizabeth (d. 1567)

Duchess of Norfolk. Name variations: Lady Dacre of Gilsland; Elizabeth Howard. Died on September 4, 1567; daughter of Sir James Leyburne; married

Thomas Dacre, 4th lord Dacre of Gilsland (also seen as Gillesland); became third wife of Thomas Howard (1537–1572), 3rd duke of Norfolk (r. 1554–1572, also seen as 4th duke of Norfolk), in 1566; children: (first marriage) **Anne Dacre** *(who married Philip Howard, 17th earl of Arundel);* **Mary Dacre** *(1563–1578, who married Thomas Howard, 1st earl of Suffolk);* **Elizabeth Dacre** *(who married Lord William Howard); George Dacre, 5th lord Dacre of Gilsland. Thomas Howard was also married to* *Mar-garet Audley *(d. 1564) and* *Mary Fitzalan *(d. 1557).*

Leyster, Judith (1609–1660)

Dutch painter, mainly of genre scenes, who—due to the misattribution of her works for almost three cen-turies—reaped critical acclaim while remaining un-known. Name variations: JL. Pronunciation: Ly-ster. Born Judith Leyster in 1609 in Haarlem, Netherlands; died in Heemstede, Netherlands, in 1660; daughter of Jan Willemssen (a Haarlem brewery owner) and Trijn Jaspers; married Jan Miense Molenaer (a painter), in 1636; children: Joannes, Jacobus, Helena, Eva, Con-stantijn.

Painted first authenticated work, The Jester *(1625); joined the Haarlem Guild of St. Luke (1633); had three male pupils (1635); painted last known work,* Portrait of a Man *(1652).*

Paintings: Laughing Man with Wine Glass; The Jolly Toper *(1629);* The Jolly Companions *or* Carous-ing Couple *(misattributed to Frans Hals),* Musée du Louvre, Paris *(1630);* The Proposition *(1631);* Boy and Girl with Cat and Eel *or* Two Children and a Cat *(misattributed to Hals, National Gallery, London);* Still Life; Self-Portrait *(National Gallery of Art, Wash-ington, D.C., and another* Self-Portrait *is in the Frans Hals Museum, Haarlem);* Portrait of a Man *(1652). Signed work: JL attached to a star.*

The reappraisal of women's roles in art histo-ry has often uncovered a female influence in what was previously thought to be an indisputably male domain. The relatively recent inclusion of Judith Leyster in the canon of Dutch art marks a belated acknowledgement of the skills of a painter who, though highly respected in her own lifetime, suf-fered from misattribution to the extent that she became only a footnote in writings on the works of her husband or tutor. While the biographical details of her life remain scant, enough is known to appreciate the significance of her involvement as an artist in Holland's "Golden Age."

At the time of Leyster's birth in Haarlem in 1609, Holland was the major maritime nation of Europe. A growing middle class, made rich by the fruits of trade, eagerly adorned its pristine homes with material displays of wealth and taste. In this Protestant nation, the bourgeoisie, not the church, became the prime patrons of one of the most popular art markets ever seen, keep-ing prices affordable and encouraging artists to specialize to ensure a place within it.

Judith was the eighth of the nine children of Jan Willemssen and Trijn Jaspers. Their name "Leyster" was adopted, in a practice common to the time, from the family business, a brewery owned by her father, "De Leyster." It was this surname, translated as "leading" or "pole" or "lode" star, which formed the basis for the char-acteristic monogram on many of her paintings: a combined "J" and "L," with a star shooting out to the right.

By all accounts, she was born into a materi-ally and financially comfortable home: brewing was a lucrative and respected occupation. But for reasons unknown, the family suffered a major crisis with the bankruptcy of the business in 1625, leaving Willemssen with four depen-dent children. Art historians speculate that this reversal of fortune provided the catalyst for Leyster's career as a painter: when the family moved from Haarlem to a small town close to Utrecht, an opportunity was provided for her to study there. Many of her later works show the influence of the famous Utrecht Caravaggisti with their distinctive use of chiaroscuro.

By 1629, Leyster was back in Haarlem, her works of this period attesting to the fact that by now she was studying in the shop of Frans Hals. Like her tutor's, many of Leyster's works are, says the historian Simon Schama, "celebrations of unpretentious joys," and at first glance *The Jolly Toper,* one of her earliest known mono-grammed paintings, seems just that. With his jaunty beret, extravagant costume and toothy grin, the toper, lustily raising a tankard of beer, appears to be inviting us to join in his merri-ment. But a closer examination reveals the pipes, tobacco and other smoking paraphernalia on the table before him, adding a different perspective to the reading, an indication that this is a moral-ity painting. Smoking had become almost an ob-session in Holland both for those who craved it and those who denounced it as inducing a state of stupefaction known as "dry-drunkenness." (There is some evidence that the unwitting mer-chants were stoking up their pipes with cannabis.) Taken together with beer, the national drink, the tobacco in the painting prophesied an inevitable moral decay.

Many of Leyster's paintings include similar underlying messages, though her works encompass an unusually broad range of subjects—portraits, genre scenes, flower illustrations—unlike the specialization of other Dutch women artists of the time (such as *Clara Peeters, one of the vanguard of still-life painters, and *Maria van Oosterwyck who painted elaborate floral displays).

Training in an artist's studio necessitated the copying of and collaboration in the works of the master. Through this process, Leyster developed a style which, though similar enough to have been confused with Hals', perhaps made even more extreme use, notes Schama, of "the Caravaggist style of large and looming figures brought close to the picture edge in dramatic lighting and heroic posture" to represent everyday situations.

The Proposition, painted in 1631, demonstrates Leyster's mastery of the use of light. It relies upon a single flame to illuminate this scene of a sewing woman approached from the side by a man, hand outheld, offering coins. In this significantly unusual treatment of an oft-used

Self-Portrait *by Judith Leyster, c. 1630.*

theme of the time, Leyster painted a woman who meets the suggestion of such trade with embarrassment or shame, a far cry from the lusty maidens of her contemporaries' works depicted as willing purveyors of sexual exchange. This prototypical representation, argue feminist art historians, testifies to the sympathetic approach of the woman artist to her subject and was a direct influence on the more famous Vermeer and Metsu in their "interrupted moment" paintings.

The most remarkable case of a disappearing oeuvre (until the next one comes along) is probably that of Judith Leyster.

—Germaine Greer

In 1633, Leyster became the first woman to join the Haarlem Guild of St. Luke, allowing her to establish her own workshop and to take on students, which she did the following year. One of these, a Willem Woutersz, quickly became the subject of a dispute between Leyster and her former tutor, when, after only a few days in Leyster's shop, Woutersz decided to continue his studies with Hals. As a new member of the Guild with a keen sense of its rules (and apparently few qualms about challenging Hals), Leyster requested from Woutersz' mother a quarter of his tuition fees. When refused payment, she took this infraction to the dean of the Guild for judgment. His ruling forced a smaller payment from the mother, a fine for Hals, and the stipulation that Woutersz could no longer study in his shop. The fate of the young artist is not known.

This assertiveness in pleading her case was put to good use following her marriage to Jan Miense Molenaer in 1636. A painter mainly of low-life genre scenes with a penchant for fieldwork in taverns, Molenaer's life can be documented as a series of suits and countersuits within the highly established Dutch small court system. Even their marriage became a judicial subject when Molenaer reneged on his promise to pay family debts from Leyster's dowry. Soon after, the couple moved to Amsterdam, probably to evade the wrath of their creditors. And while Molenaer continued throughout their marriage to paint things such as his pastiches of the Five Senses, often using the pictures in lieu of money and even as part payment on a house, his wife's output drastically declined. In 1637, Leyster gave birth to her first child, who died only a few years later. Of their five children, only one, Helena, survived to marry and bear children of her own.

The difficulties of childbirth, the constant battles with her children's illnesses, and the un-

relenting legal disputes created by her husband evidently occupied most of the artist's time, yet in 1643 Leyster undertook a series of botanical illustrations for a catalogue produced by a tulip bulb merchant. In the previous decade, the incredible clamor for ownership of rare and exotic bulbs had given its name to a phenomena—"tulipomania." Bulb prices had soared as the rich burghers of Holland invested their life savings, their houses, or their belongings in these flowers. Then, inevitably, the market had crashed, leaving thousands of investors in financial ruin. Despite this, demand remained reasonably high, and the catalogues enabled purchasers to envisage the future glory of the bulb in addition to providing flower painters with selections for their representations of seasonally unlikely bouquets. For Leyster, this meant small-scale work which could more easily be combined with the role of mother and housewife, while also providing a source of family income. As the only extant examples of work of this type painted by her, the illustrations' delicate lines—in contrast to the bold, fast brushwork of many of her genre paintings—provide further proof of her skills.

Although the tulip illustrations are the latest signed works attributed to Leyster, a further painting, the *Portrait of a Man,* dating from 1652, is now known to be by her hand and stands as her final work: a simple, anachronistic portrait, it is believed to represent another Haarlem artist.

Leyster died in 1660, in Heemstede, where the family had lived for twelve years, not long after having completed her last will and testament in conjunction with her husband, both parties suffering from ill-health. Of their five children, only two—Helena and Constantijn—survived her, the latter to live only until eighteen. Despite his ailments, Molenaer lived on for eight more years.

The misattribution of Judith Leyster's work began during her lifetime with an engraving made after one of her paintings inscribed "Frans Hals pinxit." The piece, *Two Children and a Cat,* continued to be thought of as his for the next 300 years. During the 18th century, many more of her paintings were sold as work by Hals, Jan Molenaer, or other artists such as Gerard van Honthorst or Dirck Hals. Not until the end of the 19th century did the true identity of the painter come to light, in the appropriate setting of a courtroom. In 1892, the *Carousing Couple* (also known as *The Jolly Companions*), a Leyster painting now held at the Louvre, became the subject of a legal dispute when a purchaser sued the dealer for misrepresentation, having been assured the work was by Hals. The dealer, who had sold the painting for £4,500, claimed that it was not only a Hals but "one of the finest he ever painted," and Sir John Millars agreed with the dealer about the authenticity and value of the painting. When Leyster's evident and idiosyncratic monogram helped prove that Hals was not the painter, the plaintiffs agreed to keep the painting for £3,500 plus £500 costs. Writes Germaine Greer: "The gentlemen of the press made merry at the experts' expense." Delighted by the irony, they pointed out that all the litigation had succeeded in doing was to destroy the value of the painting. "At no time," notes Greer, "did anyone throw his cap in the air and rejoice that another painter, capable of equalling Hals at his best, had been discovered." In the following year, the famous art historian, Hofstede de Groot, undertook a study of Leyster's work, attributing seven paintings to her.

By the early 20th century, interest in Leyster had grown. The first major study of her works was published in 1926, following which her paintings became increasingly included in writings on the period, though not always to her advantage. "Women painters, as everyone knows, mostly imitate the work of some man" and "can occasionally contribute something pleasing of their own in their pastiches," writes R.H. Wilenski as his 1937 introduction to a passage on Leyster. For some art historians, her work merited far less interest than her imagined private life, in which Leyster, as the supposed mistress of Rembrandt, purportedly painted no less than 22 of his paintings. Though constantly repeated, these rumors are unfounded, history providing no evidence that they even knew each other, let alone shared the same easel. By the 1970s, the resurgence of interest in the work of Frans Hals had led to a rewriting of Judith Leyster's true status as a painter of importance, and her name was finally reclaimed.

The *Self-Portrait* of Leyster now hanging in the National Gallery of Art, Washington, D.C., presents an image of a lively woman at work. Turning away from her canvas, with a relaxed elbow resting on the back of a chair, the only known female artist in 1633 Haarlem represents herself as confident, assertive and undeterred by her difference.

SOURCES:

Greer, Germaine. *The Obstacle Race*. NY: Farrar, Straus, 1979.
Hofrichter, Frima Fox. *Judith Leyster: A Woman Painter in Holland's Golden Age*. Doornspijk: Davaco, 1989.
Petersen, Karen, and J.J. Wilson. *Women Artists*. NY: Harper Colophon Books, 1985.
Schama, Simon. *The Embarrassment of Riches*. London: Fontana Press, 1987.
Slatkin, Wendy. *Women Artists in History*. NY: Prentice-Hall, 1985.
Wilenski, R.H. *An Introduction to Dutch Art*. London: Faber, 1937.

SUGGESTED READING:

Harris, Ann Sutherland, and Linda Nochlin. *Women Painters 1550–1950*. Exhibition catalogue for the Los Angeles County Museum of Art, 1976.

Diane Moody,
freelance writer in London, with a B.A. in Art History,
Princeton, New Jersey

Lhevinne, Rosina (1880–1976)

Russian-born musician who spent much of her career playing dual-piano works with her husband and, after his death, went on to fame as a soloist and teacher of many of America's leading classical pianists. Name variations: Rosina Lhévinne. Pronunciation: Lay-VEEN. Born Rosina Bessie on March 29, 1880, in Kiev, Russia; died on November 9, 1976, in Glendale, California; daughter of Jacques Bessie (a Dutch merchant) and Maria (Katch) Bessie (a Russian); attended Imperial Russian Conservatory, 1889–98; married Josef Lhevinne, on June 20, 1898 (died 1944); children: Constantine (renamed Don) Lhevinne; Marianna Lhevinne.

Won gold medal upon graduation from Conservatory (1898); began career as dual pianist with husband (1899); moved to Tiflis (1899); interned in Germany during World War I (1914–18); settled in U.S. (1919); began teaching at Juilliard School in conjunction with her husband's appointment to Juilliard faculty (1924); appointed to faculty of Austro-American Conservatory in Mondsee, Austria (1930); with Josef, performed 40th anniversary concert as dual pianists at Carnegie Hall (1939); appointed to faculty of Juilliard School (1945); appointed to faculty of Los Angeles Conservatory (1946); underwent operation for breast cancer (1950); accepted Van Cliburn as her student at Juilliard (1951); joined faculty at Aspen Music Festival (1956); her student Van Cliburn won Tchaikovsky competition in Moscow (1958); became faculty member of University of California, Berkeley, and appeared with National Orchestral Association (1961); had second mastectomy and made debut with New York Philharmonic (1963); given 90th birthday party at Juilliard School (1970).

"She was quite simply one of the greatest teachers of this century," Peter Mennin, president of the Juilliard School, said of Rosina

Lhevinne. She was also one of the century's most notable female musicians. A brilliant pianist in her own right, she subordinated her playing career to that of her equally talented husband Josef Lhevinne for over 40 years. Her fiery and emotional personality was the perfect balance for his calm and moderation. In those years, she gave occasional solo concerts and more frequently played dual concerts with him. Following Josef's death in 1944, her career took a new direction. First, she replaced the late *Olga Samaroff as the most distinguished piano teacher in the United States, producing such eminent performers as Van Cliburn. Second, in her mid-70s, she reemerged as a noted soloist.

I accomplished what I wanted to: to give an example to the young people of what can be accomplished—even at my age—with work and dedication to music.

—Rosina Lhevinne

The future musical star was born Rosina Bessie in Kiev on March 29, 1880, the daughter of Jewish parents who were devoted to music. Her father Jacques Bessie had been born in Holland and worked in Russia as a merchant dealing in diamonds and wine. As a youngster, he had studied piano, and his education included a stay at the Sorbonne in Paris. Rosina's mother **Maria Katch Bessie** also came from a cultured and affluent background; like her husband, she had studied piano as a child. The family moved to Moscow in the early 1880s.

Rosina grew up under her mother's watchful—indeed, obsessive—eye. The child nearly died of diphtheria at age four; the dangerous episode made her naturally protective mother even more determined to safeguard Rosina against all perils. At age six, young Rosina began piano lessons. Three years later, having demonstrated exceptional talent, she was admitted to the Moscow Conservatory. A further testimony to her promise was the sharply limited number of places Jewish students were permitted to occupy at the distinguished school.

In attending the conservatory, Rosina remained under her mother's protective wing. She still received her basic education at home from private tutors and was permitted to attend the Conservatory only once a week as a student of the renowned Vasilly Safonov (1852–1918). Nonetheless, she soon made the acquaintance of Josef Lhevinne. Several years older than Rosina, he was already one of the Conservatory's outstanding students. Graduating in 1892 after

being awarded the gold medal, a prize given only to students who had attained the highest level of achievement, he soon attracted the attention of the composer Peter Tchaikovsky and the reigning piano virtuoso Arthur Rubinstein. Josef's reputation as a rising young performer was made in 1895 when he won the prestigious Rubinstein Prize Competition in Berlin. It quickly led to a triumphant concert tour throughout Western Europe.

By now, Josef was a frequent visitor at the Bessie house. He had prepared for his success in Berlin by using the pianos at the family's Moscow home while the Bessies were at their country cottage for the summer. As Rosina recalled, for a long time he still treated her as a young child. But when Josef had to interrupt his career for a year's service in the Russian army, he was stationed near Moscow, and their relationship became one of adult affection. Josef later divulged that he fell in love with her in May 1896 when he watched the 16-year-old play Chopin's E minor concerto with the Moscow Conservatory Orchestra.

Rosina graduated from the conservatory in June 1898. Like Josef, she was able to measure her success there by receiving the exceptional reward of a gold medal. On June 20, one week after her graduation, the two young pianists were married. During the following five-week honeymoon, which they spent at a resort town outside Moscow, they competed to see who could learn Mendelssohn's *Etude* in E minor more quickly. Rosina won the contest, but she was impressed by the superior performance he produced ten days later.

The honeymoon weeks led Rosina to a decision that marked the next four decades of her life. Writes their biographer Robert Wallace: "Buoyed by her first intimate exposure to her husband's pianistic craft, she decided to be content to be a wife." Friends who had speculated that the marriage between two such gifted and ambitious musicians could not survive now learned that Rosina had given up her potential for a career as a soloist. She would instead devote her energies to insuring Josef's success.

Within a year of their marriage, the Lhevinnes found themselves in the distant city of Tiflis in the Caucasus. Josef's army service had stopped the momentum of his concert career, and, in order to support himself and his wife, he accepted a position as professor at the Imperial Conservatory in the remote Georgian region of the Russian empire. After three years there, Rosina made the key decision that shaped their future. Josef had awed local audiences in his performances, and his salary at the conservatory was rising steadily. Nonetheless, Rosina convinced him to abandon this comfortable but isolated musical niche in order to return to the musical mainstream. "I thought about it for a long time," she said, "and finally decided that we should go to Berlin, then the musical capital of the world."

Success came quickly. Following warm-up concerts in Warsaw and Paris, Josef made a triumphal debut with the Berlin Philharmonic in March 1902. Later that year, with his musical reputation burgeoning, he was invited to take a position as professor at his alma mater, the Moscow Conservatory. When the Lhevinnes returned to their native city, Rosina briefly resumed her career as a soloist and also began teaching. A stint at a fashionable private school for the daughters of Russian noble families was disappointing due to her students' lack of interest, and she turned to teaching students privately at home. Meanwhile, her husband's career remained her paramount concern.

In the winter of 1905–06, Josef Lhevinne made his first journey to North America and created a sensation in his debut at Carnegie Hall on January 27. Rosina, pregnant with their first child, remained in Moscow. She gave birth to a son, whom they named Constantine, in Paris in July. Four months later, the entire family set sail for the United States.

Between 1907 and the outbreak of war in 1914, Josef Lhevinne toured the U.S. annually in addition to giving numerous concerts throughout Europe. Frequently, his concerts consisted of solo works broken up by duets with Rosina. From 1909 onward, they made their permanent home in Berlin, where both Josef and Rosina taught piano to advanced students. In a decision that brought future hardship to the family, Josef kept his substantial savings in banks in Moscow.

The Lhevinne family was trapped in Berlin when war broke out between Germany and Russia in the summer of 1914. As a reserve officer in the Russian army, Josef was not permitted to return home. The family shared the hardships of the German population during four years of food shortages, but they also suffered the special privations of being enemy aliens. Thus, the Lhevinnes were not permitted to give concerts or otherwise to earn money, and they were required to report regularly to the police. Nonetheless, Josef's status as a distinguished musician helped them through these years. Germany's monarch, Kaiser Wilhelm II, personally directed that Josef

and his family be interned in their villa outside Berlin rather than being placed in a prison camp. And government officials winked at the fact that Josef traveled regularly to Budapest to perform in public. Only by turning the gardens of the villa into farmland, however, were they able to feed themselves adequately. The Bolshevik Revolution in Russia in November 1917 added to their impoverishment when the new Communist government confiscated Josef's bank accounts. As the war moved toward its conclusion in 1918, the family had a rare piece of good news; Rosina gave birth to the couple's second child, a girl they named **Marianna Lhevinne**.

In the immediate postwar period, Josef was once again free to travel and perform. He now decided to make the United States the permanent home for the family, and, in September 1919, the Lhevinnes set sail from Copenhagen to New York. Within two days of their arrival, Josef was giving a recital in Connecticut.

In the following years, several times each season, Rosina sometimes joined Josef in concert performances as the couple formed a two-piano team. Josef disliked such duets, and these performances were his tribute to Rosina's talent and

Rosina
Lhevinne

desire to appear in public. Music for dual pianos was still a novelty for American critics as well as American audiences in general. They generally received favorable notices. One critic in Philadelphia noted that "they made two pianos speak with but a single thought." Nonetheless, Rosina refused to travel extensively where her children were young. Her style of parenting resembled that of her own mother; it was marked by extreme, even excessive, fears for their health and restrictions on their freedom. To the disappointment of both parents, neither Constantine (now renamed Don) nor Marianna showed any interest in the piano.

In 1924, Josef was appointed to the faculty of the newly established Juilliard School of Music. When he toured, Rosina filled in for him, and sometimes the two gave lessons together. On many occasions they gave various American students, who spoke only English, the disconcerting experience of sitting and listening to the Lhevinnes discuss his or her progress in Russian. Rosina soon acquired a reputation as the more severe teacher of the pair, with Josef's manner distinguished by its gentleness. In 1930, Rosina Lhevinne took on independent responsibilities as a teacher when she was appointed to the faculty of the newly created Austro-American Conservatory located in the Austrian village of Mondsee. She worked there for three summers.

As the children grew, Rosina became more comfortable about traveling substantial distances away from New York. Only a third of Josef's appearances from the late 1930s until his death in 1944 were solo concerts, and the Lhevinnes played together extensively. For small-town audiences in particular, the novelty of a two-piano performance, with husband and wife on the same stage, outweighed the great musical skills they displayed. Together, they also conducted summer master classes in Maine and then in Colorado. A reporter who interviewed the two in 1938 recorded a vivid picture of Rosina: "plumpish, black-haired, dark-eyed . . . she somehow reminds you of a dear mamma in a tin type of the Nineties."

A notable occasion for the Lhevinnes was a gala benefit concert marking the 40th anniversary of their first appearance as a two-piano team. The proceeds went to New York City's Greenwich Music Settlement House. Held at Carnegie Hall on January 14, 1939, the gala featured three concertos for dual pianos which they played to the accompaniment of the Juilliard Orchestra. At Josef's insistence, the program included a solo performance by Rosina. She chose to play the work that had induced Josef to fall in love with her so long ago in Moscow: Chopin's E minor concerto.

America's entry into the Second World War affected the Lhevinnes deeply. Their son went into the army, and many of their students from the Juilliard School likewise entered military service. Josef and Rosina gave concerts to support the government's bond program and to raise money for British children. In these charitable activities, they performed in numerous small towns where local organizations could not meet their regular fee. "To repay America for all it has done for us" was the explanation they gave for their efforts.

The duo's busy schedule of touring and concerts went on with no apparent threat to Josef's health. The onset of his final illness came in August 1944 while he was visiting their daughter in Los Angeles. He suffered a heart attack while swimming, and, after convalescing for several months in California, returned to New York on December 1. He died suddenly the next day. Rosina found herself with no insurance and a mass of debt, both attributable to Josef's lack of concern with finances.

Disoriented after her sudden loss, Rosina at first refused an offer from the president of Juilliard to take over Josef's position on the faculty. Nonetheless, in 1945 she took up teaching duties at the renowned music school and remained on the faculty even though she had technically reached the age for retirement. In the summer of 1946, she began a long career as a teacher at the Los Angeles Conservatory of Music. Students flocked to her studio, where she was the standard-bearer of the golden days of Imperial Russian Romanticism. John Browning, Daniel Pollack, Misha Dichter, Garrick Ohlsson, Tong i Han, Howard Aibel, and **Olegna Fuschi** were just a few, many of whom held posts at universities throughout the world.

At first she avoided performing; it raised painful memories of her years on stage with her husband. Nonetheless, in November 1947, she gave in to entreaties from Victor Babin, like Rosina a Russian-born pianist who had made a career in America, to play with the newly formed Little Orchestra Society in New York. This indicated, as Wallace described it, her "complete return to the vigorous musical life she had led while her husband was alive."

In the midst of her ongoing career, Rosina Lhevinne was struck by a new tragedy. In early 1950, she was diagnosed with breast cancer. The resulting operation involved removing part of her arm, but she made a rapid recovery. Rigorous exercises, which she performed with tears flowing freely, brought her body back to a condition in which she could once again play the piano with her old skill.

Her students at Juilliard invariably noted Rosina's Russian-accented English and her occasional errors in choosing the right English word. More important was her intense relationship with them in which she involved herself intimately in their personal as well as their professional lives. She claimed the need to get an intimate understanding of her students' ideas and emotions. Since this could not be achieved through weekly lessons, she would invite them for long walks. A regular part of training with Rosina Lhevinne for many students became walking with her and a group of fellow students at Jones Beach on Sundays. The success of her methods became evident in the years after 1950, when her students distinguished themselves in national competitions like the Piano Recording Festival put on by the National Guild of Piano Teachers. They did equally well in the annual competitions at the Juilliard School. Her teaching came to include master classes at Aspen, starting in 1956, and at the University of California at Berkeley in 1961.

Teachers of future concert performers rarely attain national fame, but Rosina Lhevinne proved an exception, largely due to the prominence of one student: Van Cliburn. She began teaching the 17-year-old Texan in 1951; in 1954, he won the prestigious Leventritt Competition. Four years later, at Rosina Lhevinne's urging, Cliburn entered the Tchaikovsky Competition in Moscow. Although it seemed unlikely, if not impossible, that an American could compete successfully in this contest given the ongoing tensions of the Cold War, she worked diligently to prepare Cliburn. His victory made him the most famous young musician in America, and his return to the United States featured a ticker-tape parade in Manhattan and a gala reception at the Waldorf-Astoria Hotel. In the words of one former student, **Jeaneane Dowis Lipman,** Cliburn's success made Rosina Lhevinne "the world's most famous piano teacher."

The renowned teacher moved in another new direction when, at age 75, she began to perform as a soloist. She was invited to teach at the Aspen Music School during the school's annual summer festival, and she accepted the accompanying obligation of giving concerts with the festival orchestra. Starting in 1956, she performed

there almost every summer until the mid-1960s, and she marked her 80th birthday with concerts in Indianapolis and New York. The capstone to her career as a performer came in January 1963 when she gave four concerts with the New York Philharmonic under the direction of Leonard Bernstein. One performance was broadcast over national radio, and she received tributes from listeners throughout the country.

The last years of Rosina Lhevinne's life combined illness and a determination to continue her work as long as possible. Her cancer recurred in 1963 and led to a second bout of surgery. Students continued to flock to her for lessons, many of them after encountering her at her summer sessions at Aspen and Berkeley. Others came at the behest of her former students, many of whom occupied teaching posts of their own.

At age 90, she received a tribute from her colleagues at the recently relocated Juilliard School. The birthday celebration, which brought together hundreds of her friends from the music world, marked the announcement of a scholarship at Juilliard in her name. A few months later, she gave her last series of lessons at Aspen, where she had been an instructor since 1956. Nonetheless, her zest for teaching remained. She taught at the University of Southern California from 1972 through 1974, and even a stroke in November 1974 did not prevent her from returning to the faculty in the fall of 1975.

Rosina Lhevinne expressed her awareness of increasing age by refusing to travel on streets that contained cemeteries. She likewise avoided presenting her students with the task of learning Chopin's B-flat minor sonata, which contains a funeral march. Remembering that she had been sickly as a child, the vibrant nonagenarian repeatedly noted that a healthy diet and lots of exercise had given her a more extended lifetime than anyone might have predicted.

Rosina Lhevinne died in Glendale, California, on November 9, 1976. She had helped train scores of distinguished performers, impressing on them both her musical sense and her distinctive personality. Her methods had combined a harsh insistence on superior technical skill with a deep respect for the individual talents of each student. All were impressed by her complex personality as they encountered both the facet that offered unlimited encouragement and the equally sharp facet that insisted on the standards she had learned as a youngster at the Moscow Conservatory. As Lipman put it, she combined "the merriness of a teddy bear with the majesty of a czarina."

SOURCES:

Lipman, Jeaneane Dowis. "Rosina: A Memoir," in *The American Scholar.* Summer 1996, pp. 359–378.

Wallace, Robert A. *A Century of Music-Making: The Lives of Josef and Rosina Lhevinne.* Bloomington, IN: Indiana University Press, 1976.

SUGGESTED READING:

Dubal, David. *Reflections from the Keyboard: The World of the Concert Pianist.* NY: Summit Books, 1984.

Ericson, Raymond. "Rosina Lhévinne, Pianist, Is Dead," in *The New York Times.* November 11, 1976, p. 44.

Kogan, Judith. *Nothing But the Best: The Struggle for Perfection at the Juilliard School.* NY: Random House, 1987.

Schonberg, Harold C. "Undoctrinaire Inspiration," in *The New York Times.* November 11, 1976, p. 44.

Neil M. Heyman,
Professor of History, San Diego State University,
San Diego, California

Lia.

See joint entry titled Rachel and Leah.

Liadan (fl. 7th c.)

Poet of Ireland. Flourished in the 7th century in Ireland.

Very little is certain about Liadan's life. Biographies of her written hundreds of years after her death tell that she was a noblewoman who rejected her lover, a handsome man called Cuirithir, and joined one of the convents of Christianized Ireland. She came to regret her haste and sought his love again, only to find that he had joined a monastery and refused to leave it. The only poem of hers to survive supports this story to some extent; it is a lament which names Cuirithir as a lost lover for whom Liadan is grieving.

Laura York,
Riverside, California

Liaquat Ali Khan, Begum (1905–1990).

See Khan, Begum Liaquat Ali.

Libbey, Laura Jean (1862–1925)

American author. Born on March 12, 1862, in Brooklyn, New York; died on October 25, 1925, in New York City; daughter of Thomas H. Libbey and Elizabeth (Nelson) Libbey; married Van Mater Stilwell, in 1898; no children.

Selected works: A Fatal Wooing (1883); All for Love of a Fair Face; or, A Broken Betrothal (1885); Madolin Rivers; or, The Little Beauty of Red Oak Seminary; A Love Story (1885); A Forbidden Marriage; or, In Love with a Handsome Spendthrift (1888); Miss Middleton's Lover; or, Parted on Their Bridal Tour (1889); Leonie Locke: The Romance of a Beautiful New York Working Girl (1889); Willful Gaynell; or, The Little Beauty of the Passaic Cotton Mills (1890); Little Leafy, the Cloakmaker's Beautiful Daughter: A Romantic Story of a Lovely Working Girl in the City of New York (1891); A Master Workman's Oath; or, Coralie the Unfortunate: A Love Story Portraying the Life, Romance, and Strange Fate of a Beautiful New York Working Girl (1892); Only a Mechanic's Daughter: A Charming Story of Love and Passion (1892); Parted at the Altar (1893); A Handsome Engineer's Flirtation; or, How He Won the Hearts of Girls (190?); Was She Sweetheart or Wife (190?); Wooden Wives: Is It a Story for Philandering Husbands? (1923).

Specializing in the so-called "working-girl" novel, author Laura Jean Libbey began contributing stories to the *New York Ledger* while still in her teens and in the course of her 30-year career produced over 80 romantic novels, most of which were printed serially and then reproduced in cheap paperbound editions that sold for between 15 and 25 cents.

Since Libbey meticulously guarded her privacy, the facts of her life are obscure. What is known is that she was a life-long resident of Brooklyn, New York, although she traveled from time to time to promote her work. The product of a strict upbringing, she was dominated by her mother who forbade her to marry. Only after her mother's death did Libbey wed, and she then stopped writing for close to a decade. Ironically, her stories about young women struggling in low-paying factory jobs provided her with a yearly salary in the vicinity of $50,000, more than many of her heroines (or her readers for that matter) would earn in a lifetime.

Libbey, whose work was described by critics as melodramatic and repetitious, used the same plot and characters over and over again, and preached a standard message: "Virtue is its own reward"; or, if a girl remains virginal, she will ultimately marry a respectable man and live a happy, prosperous life. In any given story, the heroine ("Leafy," "Guelda," or "Faynie") is forced to leave her idyllic rural home to find low-paying work in the harsh city. Enduring a hostile workplace and the unsolicited attentions of less-than-desirable men, she is eventually rescued by the hero, a virtuous and prosperous gentleman who marries her and saves her from further victimization. **Cathy N. Davidson**, in *American Women Writers*, compares Libbey's stories to those of Horatio Alger (1832–1899). "Alger's heroes worked hard, took advantage of every opportunity, and, against all odds, realized the American dream. L's [Libbey's] heroines worked hard too. But the 19th-century business world held few opportunities for women. So real success for L.'s heroines came through successful marriage." Davidson further points out that although Libbey's work did not stand the test of time, she provided a much-needed outlet for the millions of women who joined the labor force in America following the Civil War.

SOURCES:

Edgerly, Lois Stiles. *Give Her This Day.* Gardiner, ME: Tilbury House, 1990.

Mainiero, Lina, ed. *American Women Writers.* NY: Frederick Ungar, 1980.

Barbara Morgan,
Melrose, Massachusetts

Liberáki, Margaríta (1919—)

Greek novelist and dramatist. Name variations: Margarita Limberaki; Margaríta Karapanou. Born in Athens, Greece, on April 22, 1919; daughter of Themistuclis Liberáki and Sapho Fexi Liberáki; attended University of Athens; married Georges Karapanos, in 1941 (divorced); children: one daughter.

Born in Athens, Greece, in 1919, Margaríta Liberáki was raised by her maternal grandfather, a publisher, after her parents separated. She grew up in an environment bustling with intellectual and artistic energy and received an excellent education. Her major interests during these years were drawing (her passion for art would continue throughout her life, with painting remaining a strong avocation) and French. Liberáki enrolled at the University of Athens before World War II and continued to study for a law degree despite the privations she and other Greeks endured during the German occupation of her country, which began in April 1941. Although Liberáki was awarded her law degree in 1943, her interest in literature won out over a legal career. In 1947, after Greece was liberated from foreign rule and had descended into a bloody civil war, she published her first novel, *The Trees.*

This novel was an innovative work that relied on modern literary techniques being used in France. In her next two novels, *The Straw Hats* and *Three Summers,* both of which were published in 1950, the experimental approach of the earlier volume was further developed. After *The Straw Hats* achieved both critical and commercial success, Liberáki divorced her husband Georges Karapanos, with whom she had a daughter. She moved to Paris, henceforth dividing her time between Paris and Athens. Liberáki continued to write, and her work was broadened by her contacts with many of the leading writers and artists of the French capital. In her 1952 novel *The Other Alexander,* she used a single set of symbols to probe issues of both individual identity and the collective social and political identity of the ravaged modern Greek nation.

Many critics consider *The Mystery* (1976) to be Liberáki's most innovative and thoughtful novel. A symbolic political text which represents a synthesis of her novelistic and dramatic impulses, the work is set in Greece during the final phase of the brutal Greek military dictatorship. The title of the book refers to the Eleusinian mysteries of Classical Greek antiquity, with their myth of ritual destruction followed by rebirth. The novel's setting is the occupation of the Athens Polytechnic by students and its bloody repression by elements of the military regime in November 1973. The text's message is that the world needs to be turned on its head so that justice and true order can be restored to human affairs.

From 1952 until she wrote *The Mystery,* Liberáki wrote no novels, concentrating instead on the production of plays, most of which she wrote in both Greek and French versions. Her plays, which employ many of the same techniques found in her novels, include *Kandaules' Wife* (1955), *The Danaïds* (1956), *The Other Alexander* (1957), *Le saint prince* (1959), *La lune a faim* (1961), *Sparagmos* (1965), *Le bain de mer* (1967), *Erotica* (1970), and *Zoe* (1985). Most of her plays were collected and published in the 1980 volume *Mythical Theater,* and a number have been performed in France at the Festival d'Avignon and in Greece at the Festival of Athens. Liberáki also crafted several film scripts, including "Magic City" (1953) and "Phaedra" (1961), and dramatizations of her novels *The Straw Hats* and *Three Summers* were televised on European television channels in 1995 and 1996. For many decades she was an embodiment of multicultural modernism, as well as a significant literary presence in the intellectual life of both Athens and Paris.

SOURCES:

Buckley, Jerome Hamilton. *Season of Youth: The 'Bildungsroman' from Dickens to Golding.* Cambridge, MA: Harvard University Press, 1974.

Calotychos, Vangelis. "Kedros Modern Greek Writers Series," in *Journal of Modern Greek Studies.* Vol. 17, no. 1. May 1999, pp. 170–176.

Farinou-Malamatari, Georgia. "The Novel of Adolescence Written by a Woman: Margaríta Limberáki," in Roderick Beaton, ed., *The Greek Novel AD1–1985.* London and NY: Croom Helm, 1988, pp. 103–109.

Liberaki, Marguerite. *L'autre Alexander: Roman.* Translated by the author and Jacqueline Peltier. Paris: Gallimard, 1953.

———. *Trois étés.* Translated by Jacqueline Peltier. Paris: Gallimard, 1950.

Patsalidis, Savas. "Greek Women Dramatists: The Road to Emancipation," in *Journal of Modern Greek Studies.* Vol. 14, no. 1. May 1996, pp. 85–102.

Pynsent, Robert B., and Sonia I. Kanikova, eds. *Reader's Encyclopedia of Eastern European Literature.* NY: HarperCollins, 1993.

Spacks, Patricia Meyer. *The Female Imagination.* NY: Avon Books, 1976.

John Haag,
Associate Professor of History,
University of Georgia, Athens, Georgia

Libussa (c. 680–738)

Queen of Bohemia. Name variations: Libusa; Princess Libusa or Libuša. Born in Bohemia around 680; died in 738; daughter of Crocus, king of Bohemia; sister of Tetka and Kascha.

Very few sources remain that give evidence of this Bohemian queen and warrior. Her story is told by Aeneas Silvius in his *Historia Boëmii.* Libussa succeeded her father Crocus about 700 as his only heir; apparently, she was a great believer in both military conquest and women's rule. Her two sisters, **Tetka** and **Kascha**, became her closest advisors and held high offices in her reign, as did other women. Libussa spent much of her reign engaged in battles, with mostly female soldiers, against many neighboring regions in an effort to expand her realm. After about 40 years, Libussa was removed from office during a coup d'etat by *Valasca, one of her generals.

Laura York,
Riverside, California

Lichfield, countess of.

See Villiers, Barbara for sidebar on Charlotte Fitzroy (1664–1717).

Li Ch'ing-Chao (1083–c. 1151).

See Li Qingzhao.

Lichtenau, Countess von
(1753–1820)

*Mistress of the king of Prussia. Born Wilhelmine Enke in 1753; died in 1820; mistress of Frederick William II, king of Prussia (r. 1786–1797); children: (with Frederick William II) five sons. Frederick William II was first married to *Elizabeth of Brunswick (1746–1840), then *Frederica of Hesse (1751–1805).*

Licinia Eudoxia (422–before 490)

*Empress of Rome. Name variations: Eudocia; Eudoxia. Born in 422; died before 490; daughter of *Eudocia (c. 400–460) and Theodosius II, East Roman emperor; married Valentinian III (born 419), West Roman emperor, in 437 (died 455); daughter-in-law of Galla Placidia (c. 390–450); sister-in-law of *Honoria (c. 420–?); married against her will Petronius Maximus, around 456; children: (first marriage) two daughters: Eudocia (who married Huneric around 462) and Placidia.*

The daughter of Theodosius II, an Augustus (emperor) and *Eudocia, an Augusta (empress), Licinia Eudoxia never knew a life which was not overshadowed by the politics of the late Roman Empire. She was betrothed in 424 to Valentinian III, the third of his name to be acclaimed an emperor. Valentinian was the son of Constantius (a general who had been a dominant political force in the empire before being acclaimed an Augustus in 421, only to die a few months later) and *Galla Placidia (another Augusta, whose half-brother Honorius was also an Augustus). At the time there were, in theory, two Roman emperors, one ruling the East from Constantinople and another the West from one of several possible locals in Italy. The number of empresses was dependent upon how many mothers or wives of the emperors both existed and had the ability to maintain their political clout.

Licinia Eudoxia married Valentinian in 437 in Constantinople, the most important city in the empire, and was officially elevated to the rank of Augusta at Ravenna, in Italy, in 439, a status which she probably held until her death. This marriage produced two daughters, **Eudocia** and **Placidia**. Years before the consummation of this union (425), Theodosius II had elevated a six-year-old Valentinian III to the status of Augustus and established the seat of his authority in Rome. In reality, until around 440, Galla Placidia was the power behind her son as long as he was a minor, and she would remain a potent influence until her death in 450. Political rivalries during the period, however, ran deep, and one Flavius Aetius (with a power base in Gaul) effectively challenged the interests of both Galla Placidia and her son for as long as both lived.

For five years after the death of Galla Placidia, Licinia Eudoxia reigned as the most influential woman in the Western Roman Empire, but in 455 her husband was assassinated by Flavius Aetius personally, a deed which thrust the West into chaos. Aetius, however, did not benefit from his treachery, because a supporter of Valentinian assassinated Aetius shortly after Aetius murdered Valentinian. In the political fray which ensued, Licinia Eudoxia supported the imperial elevation of one Maiorianus, but her advocacy was not enough to enthrone her choice. Rather, one Petronius Maximus, who was only 22 at the time, was able to secure the Western throne and was even able to marry Licinia Eudoxia, albeit against her will. Tied to a usurper she did not care for, Licinia Eudoxia is rumored to have invited Geiseric, king of the Vandals (a powerful barbarian folk who had seen their seizure of Roman north Africa legitimized in return for technical pledges of allegiance to the Western Augustus), to invade Italy. Whether Licinia Eudoxia did so or not, Geiseric acted in his political interest by "rescuing" her and her daughters (one of whom, Eudocia, had previously been betrothed to Huneric, Geiseric's son) from the clutches of their abductor. In the process, Geiseric sacked Rome (455) before removing his imperial charges to Africa. There, Licinia Eudoxia languished for years before the diplomacy of the Eastern emperors, Marcian and Leo, finally won her return, and that of her daughter Placidia, to Constantinople. However, this was only accomplished after Huneric was allowed to wed Eudocia (about 462).

After her return to the East, Licinia Eudoxia apparently was satisfied to live on her estates near Constantinople, where religion replaced politics as her primary interest—although, at the time, it was often difficult to distinguish the two. She is known to have been a devotee of Daniel the Stylite, to whom she proffered an invitation, which he declined, to live on her land. It is not certain how long Licinia Eudoxia lived in retirement, but she seems to have died by 490.

William Greenwalt,
Associate Professor of Classical History, Santa Clara University,
Santa Clara, California

Liddell, Alice (1852–1934)

English woman who was the original Alice in Wonderland. Born Alice Pleasance Liddell on May 4, 1852; died in 1934 at Westerham, in Kent; one of four children of Dr. Henry Liddell (former head of Westminster School and dean of Christ Church, Oxford); her eldest sister was **Lorina Charlotte Liddell***; her younger sister was* **Edith Liddell***, known as Tillie, died in 1876 (age 22); married Captain Reginald Hargreaves, in 1880 (died 1928); children:* **Violet Hargreaves***;* **Norah Hargreaves***; Reginald Hargreaves.*

The inspiration for the *Alice in Wonderland* stories of Charles Lutwidge Dodgson (who

wrote under the pseudonym Lewis Carroll), Alice Liddell was one of four children of Dr. Henry Liddell, the dean of Christ Church College in Oxford, England, where Dodgson was a young lecturer in mathematics. According to Dodgson's diaries, which cover his life from 1855 to 1898, he first met Alice on September 4, 1855, while out sketching, and was promptly enchanted by her. Living in close proximity to the Deanery, Dodgson nearly became part of the Liddell family, and as such he accompanied Alice and her siblings on outings, instructed them in their studies, and used them as subjects for his photography. At one point a rumor circulated that Dodgson's interest in the children masked his crush on their pretty governess, Miss Prickett, but he denied it. (There has since been much speculation among Dodgson aficionados that he was in fact in love with the child Alice, albeit perhaps not sexually.)

During boating excursions on the River Isis, Dodgson began telling the children fairytales of Alice's adventures, which he extemporized but never wrote down. "[T]hey lived and died, like summer midges," he wrote in his diary, "each in its own golden afternoon until there came a day when, as it chanced, one of my little listeners [Alice] petitioned that the tale might be written out for her." Dodgson's first effort at putting the stories into writing was *Alice's Adventures Under Ground*, but the title was changed to *Alice's Adventures in Wonderland* so that it would not be mistaken for a book about mines. He presented Alice Liddell with a copy of the manuscript, including the original character illustrations, as a Christmas present in 1864. The book was published a year later with great success and was later adapted for the stage by Savile Clarke (first performed at the Prince of Wales' Theatre in London in 1886). A follow-up of Alice's adventures, *Through the Looking-Glass*, was published in 1872.

Alice Liddell, who, from a picture taken by Dodgson around 1865, looks to be an extraordinary creature, went on to marry Captain Reginald Hargreaves, who had also been a mathematics student of Dodgson's, and settled in Wraysbury, Berkshire, England. In *This England* (Winter 1985), there appears a letter from a 90-year-old woman by the name of **Blanche Webber**, recounting her childhood acquaintance with Alice and Reginald Hargreaves, whom she called marvelous people. She recalled that they attended the village church each Sunday with their three children and threw parties for the villagers at Christmas and in the summertime. Webber had revisited Wraysbury in 1980 and

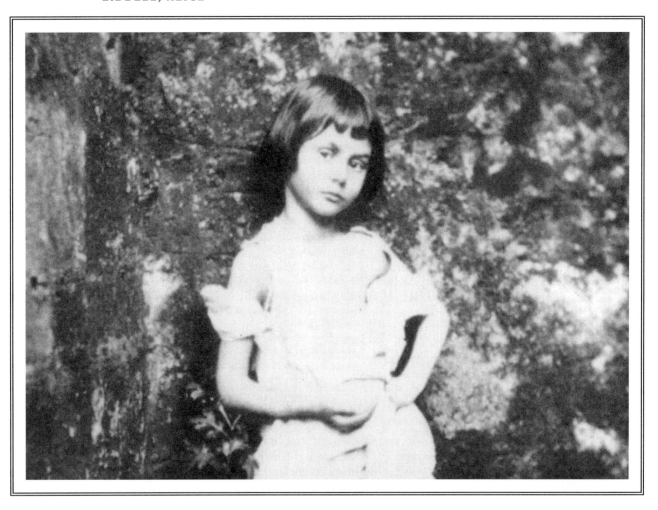

Alice
Liddell

found that the Hargreaves house ("Remen-ham") had been turned into apartments, and the family graves in the churchyard were untended and overgrown. "I felt very sad to see it so ne-glected," she wrote. "These people deserve something better, considering the 'Alice' stories are known all over the world."

SOURCES:

"Book Briefs," in *This England*. Winter 1985.

Commire, Anne, ed. *Yesterday's Authors of Books for Children.* Vol. 2. Detroit, MI: Gale Research.

"The Real Alice," in *This England*. Winter 1984.

Barbara Morgan,
Melrose, Massachusetts

Lidman, Sara (1923—)

Swedish novelist, dramatist and social commentator.
Born Sara Adela Lidman in Missenträsk, Sweden, on
December 30, 1923; daughter of Andreas Lidman and
Jenny (Lundman) Lidman; educated at the University
of Uppsala.

Sara Lidman was born in 1923 into a family of farmers in a remote village of the Västerbot-ten (West Bothnia) region in the far north (Nor-rland) of Sweden, an area that is regarded as part of southern Lapland. Later to describe her-self as "a pious child," she grew up in a land far removed from the sophistication of Stockholm, and her isolation from the modern world was re-inforced by the strict puritanical pietism of her conservative Lutheran parents and neighbors. A bout with tuberculosis in her early teens kept Lidman homebound for an extended period of time, and she became a voracious reader, im-mersing herself in works by Dostoyevsky and Kierkegaard as well as several Swedish regional novelists. At the same time, she began writing her own stories. Because of her fragile health, she continued her education through correspon-dence courses and completed her secondary edu-cation at a local private school. Moving to Stockholm in 1944, Lidman supported herself by working as a waitress, and she enrolled as a drama student at a local theater. In 1949, she completed her higher education at the University of Uppsala, having studied education, English and French.

After some years of searching for a style of her own, Lidman published her first novel, *Tjärdalen* (The Tar Well or Tar-Boiler), in 1953. Set in a poor village in her home region during the 1930s, it is the story of a malicious peasant known as The Fox who destroys an elaborate structure designed to extract barrels of tar, a valuable source of cash income for the entire community. Badly injured during his destructive act, the malefactor is allowed to die of gangrene as punishment for an action viewed by the village as not only vandalism but also a sin. In her premier book, Lidman raised moral questions about a community's "collective murder," presenting above all a strong critique of the Lutheran concept of a guilt-ridden humanity. The book also offers a strong critique of capitalist ethics, in that the only man in the village who speaks out against the murder of The Fox turns out to be under the thumb of a calculating neighbor for whom the entire tragedy is nothing more than an opportunity to make money.

After the critical and popular success of *Tjärdalen*, Lidman wrote three more novels set in the isolated village world of Sweden's Norrland. These were *Hjortronlandet* (Cloudberry Land, 1955), *Regnspiran* (The Rain Bird, 1958), and *Bära mistel* (Carrying the Mistletoe, 1960). In these books, she went beyond entering into the collective consciousness of a rural community as had been done so successfully in *Tjärdalen*. *Hjortronlandet* depicts a community even more desperately impoverished than that of her earlier novel and is the story of a talented young girl's desperate and ultimately tragic attempt to rise above her situation in life. Praised by reviewers for its characterization, *Hjortronlandet* became a bestseller and was chosen by a panel of critics as Sweden's best novel of the year.

The title of Lidman's third novel, *Regnspiran* or *The Rain Bird*, is a name which in her region of Sweden refers to the swallow, a bird regarded by local peasants as a magical creature in touch with the depths of the human psyche. The book's central character, a woman named Linda Stahl, has a magnetic personality that inflicts great harm on the people around her and ultimately on herself. One critic, Harold H. Borland, has remarked on this novel's power to unsettle and disturb readers, largely because of its subtle structure which creates an "obsessive, compulsive rhythm and pattern." In the last of her books set in her home region, *Bära mistel*, Lidman again probed the soul of Linda Stahl, who is more troubled than ever as she enters mid-life seeking ways to atone for her past sins.

By the early 1960s, Lidman had largely completed a spiritual odyssey begun in childhood. She had abandoned the Lutheran faith and what she saw as its culture of guilt but still struggled to move beyond its "negative attitude toward man." Radicalized by the injustices that she believed continued to exist in Sweden and elsewhere, she felt that the ideology of Marxism held at least some of the answers to these problems. Lidman had direct contact with gross social evils during her 1960 trip to South Africa. Her response to what she would later characterize as the "true colonial misery . . . the hopelessness, the despair, the disorganization" of the apartheid system in South Africa was visceral, and she was expelled from that bastion of state-sponsored racism. In response, Lidman wrote *Jag och min son* (I and My Son, 1961), a novel so brimming with anger that she could barely organize its message. Determined to discover more about Africa and the burdens of colonialism, Lidman lived in Kenya and Tanzania from 1962 through 1964. This experience became the basis for another novel, *Med fem diamanter* (With Five Diamonds, 1964). Set in Kenya during its final years as a British crown colony, *Med fem diamanter* relates the travails of a young Kenyan attempting to acquire the goats he is required to possess as a bride-price for the girl he loves. In the background, Lidman depicts the ugly reality of post-colonial Africa, where a handful of whites continue to hold power and the introduction of a money-based economy and modern technology has eroded the stabilizing aspects of traditional society and culture. Although some critics felt the white characters in the novel were little more than cardboard caricatures, for others, including **Ulla Folejewski**, Lidman deserved praise for having written a satisfying volume many readers would discover to be "absorbing—funny, sad, occasionally grotesque."

Changed by her years in Africa, in the mid-1960s Lidman repudiated her early novels set in Sweden, asserting that because they had only dealt "with the minds of people" they could not possibly contain a coherent conception of society. Abandoning fiction because she saw the world in a state of crisis, Lidman became a reporter. While she could never completely neglect the need to maintain a modicum of stylistic quality in her prose, she was drawn to participate in the immense upheavals that changed the face of the world in the 1960s. "I'll write stories if I have time," she said during an interview, "but my imagination really can't compete with today's reality. Why make up stories when life is so full of fanciful and powerful events?"

During the mid-1960s, no event was more powerful than the American war in Vietnam. Completely in sympathy with the cause of North Vietnam, Lidman visited that beleaguered nation in 1966 and wrote her impressions in a series of articles for Swedish newspapers, which appeared in book form as *Samtal i Hanoi* (Conversations in Hanoi, 1966). In North Vietnam she observed not only destruction and suffering, but also evidence of a society united in a common cause, a situation she regarded as profoundly different from a West in which she saw private acquisitiveness and personal neurosis resulting from a lack of moral direction and social purpose. No doubt idealizing what she had witnessed in North Vietnam, Lidman spoke of that country several years later as a society in which "[e]ven in the factories or the fields the atmosphere was very human: everybody worked with zeal and self-confidence. They were truly happy. At times you could sense their hilarious feeling—the youths at night, for instance, playing their musical instruments and singing all the time. They had a sort of ecstasy." Some critics and readers believed that they had discovered in Lidman's Vietnam reportage a sign of her lifelong search for absolute truth and reali-

Sara
Lidman

ty, possibly a secularized form of the religious fervor of her childhood.

Lidman returned from witnessing the horrors of foreign wars to the north of Sweden that was her home. In the nonfiction work *Gruva* (The Mine, 1968), she provided her readers with chilling details of inhuman working and living conditions among Lapland's hardrock iron miners. Although officials of the state-owned mines disagreed with her critique of the workers' situation, Lidman was vindicated two years after the publication of her book when the miners of Kiruna went out on strike for better conditions. Lidman remained angry at the indifference of Sweden—celebrated throughout the world as the model of social progress—to countless injustices. She called for a total revolution of state and society, but despaired of finding a precise blueprint or ideology that might point the way to the desired transformation. She also remained a literary artist, stating, "I'm not a Communist. I don't think I deserve a proud title like that."

By the end of the 1970s, Lidman had moved away from political activism and resumed writing fiction. Between 1977 and 1985, she published a five-novel suite which returned to the setting of the desolate and isolated far north of Sweden. In *Din tjänare hör* (Thy Obedient Servant, 1977), *Vredens barn* (Anger's Child, 1978), *Nabot's sten* (Naboth's Stone, 1981), *Den underbare mannen* (The Miracle Man, 1983), and *Järnkronan* (The Iron Crown, 1985), Lidman presents a panoramic chronicle of Lillvatnet, which corresponds to an inland area in the Swedish far north called Jörn. In this "railway suite," the rural parish is examined in pitiless detail over a period from the 1870s until shortly before the 1894 inauguration of the railroad that radically transformed the region's way of life starting. In her northland epic, Lidman presents characters both sympathetic and unsympathetic to the modern reader, all of them serving to deepen the reader's understanding not only of the past but also of our own modern dilemmas. In her own words, Lidman presented in these books a view of the world "in defense of people and forests." Following this prolific period, Lidman did not publish for some years. In 1996, her novel *Lifsens rot* (The Root of Life) was published to critical acclaim.

An author who has defined her role as one of sending uncomfortable messages to the complacent at the end of the 20th century, Lidman continued her lifelong struggle to find answers to perennial problems. It has been her hope that her labors as a writer and citizen might play a role in the emergence of a more just social order and a less destructive relationship between people and nature.

SOURCES:

Bäckström, Lars. "Eyvind Johnson, Per Olof Sundman, and Sara Lidman: An Introduction," in *Contemporary Literature*. Vol. 12, no. 3, 1971, pp. 242–251.

Bethke, Artur. "Regionales, Nationales, Internationales in der schwedischen Gegenwartsliteratur," in Ingeborg Imig, ed., *Nordeuropa: Wissenschaftliche Zeitschrift der Ernst-Moritz-Arndt Universität Greifswald*. Studien Nr. 19, 1985, pp. 5–11.

Borland, Harold. "Sara Lidman: Novelist and Moralist," in *Svensk Litteraturtidskrift*. Vol. 36, no. 1, 1973, pp. 27–34.

———. "Sara Lidman's Progress: A Critical Survey of Six Novels," in *Scandinavian Studies*. Vol. 39, no. 2. May 1967, pp. 97–114.

Forsas-Scott, Helena. "In Defense of People and Forests: Sara Lidman's Recent Novels," in *World Literature Today*. Vol. 58, no. 1. Winter 1984, pp. 4–9.

———. "Sara Lidman's *Järnkronan*—An Introduction," in *Swedish Book Review*. Vol. 1, 1990, pp. 34–36.

Grave, Rolf. *Biblicismer och liknande inslag i Sara Lidmans Tjärdalen*. Lund: Studentlitteratur, 1969.

Holm, Birgitta. *Sara Lidman: I liv och text*. Stockholm: Bonnier, 1998.

"An Interview with Sara Lidman," in *Contemporary Literature*. Vol. 12, no. 3, 1971, pp. 252–257.

Lide, Barbara. "Lidman, Sara," in Virpi Zuck et al., eds., *Dictionary of Scandinavian Literature*. Westport, CT: Greenwood Press, 1990, pp. 380–381.

Lidman, Sara. "The Heart of the World," in *They Have Been in North Viet Nam*. Hanoi: Foreign Languages Publishing House, 1968, pp. 9–13.

———. *Nabot's Stone*. Translated by Joan Tate. Norwich, U. K.: Norvik, 1989.

———. *The Rain Bird*. Translated by Elspeth Harley Schubert. NY: George Braziller, 1962.

Mawby, Janet. *Writers and Politics in Modern Scandinavia*. London: Hodder & Stoughton, 1978.

Scobbie, Irene, ed. *Essays on Swedish Literature*. Aberdeen, Scotland: Aberdeen University Press, 1978.

Tchesnokova, Tatiana. "Sara Lidman and the Art of Narration in *The Tar Valley*," in Paul Houe and Sven Hakon Rossel, eds., *Documentarism in Scandinavian Literature*. Amsterdam and Atlanta, GA: Rodopi, 1997, pp. 174–178.

Thygesen, Marianne. *Jan Myrdal og Sara Lidman: Rapportgenren i svensk 60-tals litteratur*. Grena: Forlaget GMT, Eksp.: Erik Bjorn Olsen, Lovenholm Kollegiet, 1971.

"The View from Left to Right," in *Newsweek*. Vol. 75, no. 12. March 23, 1970, pp. 41–42, 44.

RELATED MEDIA:

"Modern Swedish Writers, Part 7: Sara Lidman," Radio Sweden International/Swedish Broadcasting Company sound-reel tape, c. 1985.

John Haag,
Associate Professor of History,
University of Georgia, Athens, Georgia

Lidwina of Schiedam (1380–1433)

Dutch mystic and saint. Born in 1380; died in 1433.

The life of Lidwina of Schiedam has been re-counted in the writings of Thomas à Kempis and J.K. Huysmans. Her feast day is April 14.

Lieberman-Cline, Nancy (1958—)

American basketball player who holds the distinction of being the only athlete to have received the Wade Trophy twice. Name variations: Nancy Lieberman; Lady Magic. Born on July 1, 1958, in Brooklyn, New York; daughter and second child of Renee Lieberman and Jerome Lieberman; attended Old Dominion University, 1976–80; married Tim Cline (a basketball player and erstwhile teammate on the Washington Generals), on May 18, 1988; children: Timothy Joseph Cline.

Was a member of the Junior National team (1977); was a member of the Jones Cup team (1979); was a member of the Pan Am Games teams (1975 [gold medal], 1979 [silver medal]); was a member of the World championship teams (1975, 1979 [gold medal]); became the youngest basketball player in Olympic history to win a medal as a silver medalist on the Women's Olympic Basketball team in Montreal (1976); named once more to the Olympic squad (1980); named All-America (1978–1980); won the Broderick Cup (1979 and 1980); finished collegiate career with 2,430 points, 1,167 rebounds, 983 assists, and more than 700 steals in 134 games; led Old Dominion to two AIAW championships (1979 and 1980); began professional career as a member of the WBL's Dallas Diamonds (1980) and led the team in scoring during their successful championship series (1981); was leading scorer for the Diamonds (1984); played for the Dallas Diamonds of the WABA during its brief season (1984); became the first woman to ever play in a men's professional league (1986) by joining the USBL's Springfield Fame; played in the USBL for two years (1986 and 1987), second season as a member of the Long Island Knights; was a member of the Washington Generals (1987–88); inducted into the Naismith Memorial Basketball Hall of Fame (1996); was a basketball analyst for NBC (1988 and 1992); served as a broadcaster for ESPN, ABC, ESPN2, Fox Sports Network and NBC; signed on to play in the WNBA (1997) and was selected by the Phoenix Mercury in the second round draft; became coach of the Detroit Shock (1998).

When Nancy Lieberman-Cline started playing basketball as a freshman at Old Dominion, about 350 people showed up to watch the women's team. By her senior year, the audience averaged 10,000. Lieberman-Cline's basketball abilities had not been encouraged, especially by her mother who believed that sports were not for girls. Lieberman-Cline agreed it was an odd choice: "I guess a little Jewish girl who dressed in cutoffs and had a comb stuffed in her back pocket with a wad of gum in her cheek was not your typical basketball player." She spent most of her childhood shooting baskets anyway; neighborhood boys were always ready for a pickup game. Since the New York Public School Athletic League did not allow girls to play, Lieberman-Cline strolled over to the YMCA. She was so obsessed with the game, she said, she must have spent "a million hours" on the court. In high school, she played on the Far Rockaway basketball team. When school was out, she went to Harlem to play with the New York Chuckles, an AAU team. Lieberman-Cline made the U.S. Pan American team and, at age 17, in 1975, was the youngest player to make the U.S. National team, slated to play in the 1976 Olympics in Montreal. There, the team won a silver medal.

After many scholarship offers came her way, she chose Old Dominion in Norfolk, Virginia, where she would lead her team, the Lady Monarchs, to national titles in 1979 and 1980. A three-time All-America during her college career, Lieberman-Cline was also on the U.S. National team in 1979 which won the Women's World Basketball championship in Seoul, South Korea. But the boycott of the 1980 Summer Olympics by President Jimmy Carter over the Soviet invasion of Afghanistan, destroyed any hope that she could compete once again for gold.

In 1980, Lieberman-Cline signed a three-year $100,000 contract with the Dallas Diamonds in the Women's Professional Basketball League (WBL). Though she played for one season, the three-year contract did not pan out, as the league went bankrupt the following year. When the WABA was formed in 1984, Lieberman-Cline was Dallas' first draft pick and was signed for a $250,000 a year contact. The following year, however, this league also folded. In 1986, she joined a men's professional basketball league in Springfield, Massachusetts. In 1987, she played with another men's team, the Long Island Knights. In 1987–88, Lieberman-Cline played with the all-male Washington Generals against the all-male Harlem Globetrotters (except for *Lynette Woodard) on a yearlong European tour.

Because professional opportunities for women were then almost nonexistent in basketball, Lieberman-Cline was forced to use other

Nancy Lieberman-Cline

skills in order to survive economically. For a time, she was a sports commentator and columnist. From 1981 to 1983, using many of the fitness techniques she had acquired over the years, Lieberman-Cline trained, advised, and lived with *Martina Navratilova. With the help of

Nancy, coach **Renee Richards,** Dr. Robert Haas, and **Pam Derderian** (all known as Team Navratilova), Martina fought a premature career sag and went on to win the 1982 French Open and Wimbledon, and once again attained #1 rank.

Many honors came Lieberman-Cline's way. She won the Wade Trophy (named for legendary basketball coach **Margaret Wade** of Delta State University) twice, as well as the Broderick Cup, and her #10 college jersey hangs in the Naismith Memorial Basketball Hall of Fame. "As a result of Nancy Lieberman and her incredible abilities," wrote **Danielle Carver**, "the strategy and style of the women's game became comparable to the men's game." In 1996, Lieberman-Cline was elected to the Basketball Hall of Fame. In 1997, age 39, she was drafted by the Phoenix Mercury to play in the newly formed Women's National Basketball Association (WNBA). In 1998, she was named coach of the WNBA's Detroit Shock franchise.

SOURCES:

Guttman, Allen. *Women's Sports*. NY: Columbia University, 1991.

Jones, Betty Milsaps. *Nancy Lieberman: Basketball's Magic Lady*. NY: Harvey House, 1980.

Lieberman, Nancy. *Basketball My Way*. NY: Scribner, 1982.

Lieberman-Cline, Nancy, with Debby Jennings. *Lady Magic: The Autobiography of Nancy Lieberman-Cline*. Foreword by Martina Navratilova. NY: Sagamore Publishing, 1991.

Silverman, Buddy Robert S. *The Jewish Athletes Hall of Fame*. NY: Shapolsky Publishers, 1989.

Woolum, Janet. *Outstanding Women Athletes: Who They Are and How They Influenced Sports in America*. Phoenix, AZ: Oryx Press, 1992.

SUGGESTED READING:

Lieberman-Cline, Nancy, and Robin Roberts. *Basketball for Women: Becoming a Complete Player*, 1996.

Liebes, Dorothy (1897–1972)

American weaver, textile designer, and businesswoman, who was a major aesthetic influence in the textile industry's conversion to synthetic fibers and new technologies in dyeing after World War II. Born Dorothy Katherine Wright in Guerneville, California, on October 14, 1897 (she claimed 1899); died in New York City on September 20, 1972; daughter of Frederick Wright (an entrepreneur) and Elizabeth Calderwood Wright (a schoolteacher); attended public school in Santa Rosa, California, and San Jose Normal School; University of California at Berkeley, A.B., 1921; later studied weaving and design at Chicago's Hull House, Columbia University, and the California School of Fine Arts; married Leon Liebes (a businessman), in 1928 (divorced 1946); married Relman Morin (a Pulitzer Prize-winning journalist), in 1948.

The eldest child of Frederick L. Wright and **Elizabeth Calderwood Wright**, Dorothy Liebes was born Dorothy Katherine Wright in Guerneville, California, on October 14, 1897. Although her parents had both been teaching school when they met, her father later became clerk of Sonoma County, founder of a utility company, a rancher, and a land developer. Dorothy early showed a strong artistic interest and ability. While still a schoolgirl, she sold her first artistic creations, hand-painted flower pots. After her graduation from high school in Santa Rosa, she attended San Jose Normal School, after which she taught art for a year. In 1921, she graduated from the University of California at Berkeley with an A.B. degree. She then studied weaving and design at a series of institutions, including *Jane Addams' Hull House in Chicago, Columbia University in New York, and the California School of Fine Arts. Liebes sold some of her handicrafts, including handwoven items, to finance her first trips to Europe, where she made pilgrimages to see some of the world's greatest art and also visited weavers to see how they operated.

Dorothy married successful San Francisco retailer Leon Liebes in 1928. A prominent patron of the arts, Leon donated space to Dorothy to set up a studio in the same building that housed his store. This gave her the room and the freedom to begin experimenting with a variety of weaving techniques and designs. At first, she received commissions from friends to create custom weaves for their homes and businesses. In time, however, the interest in her work spread well beyond her circle of friends. At New York's Decorator's Club in 1933, she had her first group show. The following year, back home in San Francisco, she established Dorothy Liebes Design Inc. In 1935, she won two major commissions, from the San Francisco Stock Exchange Club and from the Ahwahnee Hotel near Yosemite National Park. Liebes served as director of the Decorative Arts Exhibition of the San Francisco World's Fair in 1939. The recipient of several design awards, she staged shows overseas as well as across the United States.

Liebes' innovative approach to color and design had already begun to revolutionize the American textiles industry by 1940. Before she appeared on the scene, the textile weaving business was a relatively straightforward and uninspired business, turning out the same basic fabrics—plain weaves, twills, and damasks—from cotton, silk, wool, and linen. She had strong feelings about the use of new colors: "There is no such thing as bad color, only bad color combinations." She was among the first American fabric designers to experiment with the use of such daring colors as fuchsia, tangerine, turquoise, chartreuse, and lacquer red. Liebes also introduced the use of other materials, including beads, bamboo strips, cellophane, and metallic threads, into the weaving process. Hired by Goodall Fabrics in 1940 to design 12 new fabrics, Liebes entered a whole new phase in her career. She felt strongly that the loss of beauty to mass production was too high a price to pay. Recognizing that power looms generally created less interesting weaves than could be crafted on a hand loom, she actively sought ways to overcome this drawback by introducing new colors, weaves, and yarns. Her uncanny ability to forecast what the public hungered for in terms of texture, color, and design created a strong demand for her services. She served as Dobeckmun's design and color consultant in the development of Lurex metallic yarns and provided similar services for DuPont in the development of acrylic, synthetic straw, and nylon rug yarns. She was able to bring to the public at large improved fabric selection and design as well as a much broader spectrum of color through her contract with Sears, Roebuck.

Constantly experimenting, Liebes adapted the hand loom to create dobby (figured fabric made with a dobby attachment) and leno (open mesh) weaves. Her production was not limited to fabrics but included colorful window blinds, rugs, draperies, and upholstery material. Employing some 20 weavers from all over the world, her San Francisco studio was famous for its creations, which included unique items commissioned for use in hotels, private homes, oceangoing ships, and theaters. For King Ibn Saud of Saudi Arabia, she produced stunning gold and silver fabrics.

Liebes' studio turned out designs for an amazingly broad array of products, including wallpaper, airplane upholstery, clothing, home furnishings, mattress ticking, and radio sound-filter screens. In the early 1950s, she began moving her base of operations from San Francisco to New York City, completing the move in 1952. By 1958, she had confined her business to designing for industry, creating as many as 2,500 swatches a year. Interviewed in the 1950s, she said of her work in design: "There is no more esthetic delight in the world than putting beautiful colors together in a loom, watching the juxtaposition of thread as it winds its way in and out, and the resulting vibration of tonal qualities." Liebes, often described as "the greatest weaver in the world," is widely credited with elevating the American textile industry to a level of excellence it had never previously enjoyed. Collections of her art are held by the Brooklyn Museum of Art, the Victoria and Albert Museum in London, the Detroit Institute of Art, and the Oakland Museum in Oakland, California.

Outside the world of textile design and production, Liebes served on the boards of a number of organizations, including the San Francisco Art Institute, the Museum of Modern Art Advisory Council, and Save the Redwoods. She was also the first woman named to the board of the United States Finishing Corporation. In 1946, she divorced her first husband. Two years later, Liebes married two-time Pulitzer Prize-winning journalist Relman Morin, who was also an author of some note. The New York apartment she shared with Morin boasted not only her own weavings and handicrafts but also works by modern artists Matisse, Calder, and Picasso, and she counted among her friends other artists, fashion designers, artisans, architects, and movie stars. Dorothy Liebes died in New York at the age of 74 after a heart attack.

SOURCES:

Current Biography. NY: H.W. Wilson, 1948.

Sicherman, Barbara, and Carol Hurd Green. *Notable American Women: The Modern Period*. Cambridge, MA: Belknap Press of Harvard University, 1980.

Don Amerman,
freelance writer, Saylorsburg, Pennsylvania

Liebling, Estelle (1880–1970).

See Sills, Beverly for sidebar.

Liencourt, Dame de (1573–1599).

See Estrées, Gabrielle d'.

Lieven, Princess de (1785–1857).

See Dorothea, Princess of Lieven.

Liggins, Ethel (1886–1970).

See Leginska, Ethel.

Lightfoot, Hannah (fl. 1768)

English Quaker. Flourished around 1768; daughter of a Wapping shoemaker; possibly married George III (1738–1820), king of England (r. 1760–1820), on April 17, 1759; children: (with George III) possibly three. Documents relating to the marriage have been impounded since 1866 and remain in the Royal Archives at Windsor.

Lightner, Candy (1946—)

American activist who founded Mothers Against Drunk Driving (MADD). Born Candy Doddridge on May 30, 1946, in Pasadena, California; daughter of Dykes C. Doddridge (a career serviceman) and Katherine (Karrib) Doddridge (a civilian employee of the U.S. Air Force); attended American River College,

*1966; married Steve Lightner (U.S. Air Force officer, divorced); children: (twins) **Cari Lightner** (died 1980) and **Serena Lightner**; Travis Lightner.*

Candy Lightner formed Mothers Against Drunk Driving (MADD) when her 13-year-old daughter, Cari, died after being hit by a car operated by a drunk driver on May 3, 1980. When a police officer told Lightner that the driver would probably never serve a jail sentence, she was enraged by judicial leniency toward drunk drivers. The driver who had killed her daughter had been arrested previously three times and convicted twice for driving while intoxicated, yet he retained a valid license. Lightner began to lobby for change in state and national legislatures, taking on the cause for victims of accidents caused by drunk driving. In a short time, local chapters of MADD sprang up throughout the United States, bringing the total number of members nationally to over 50,000 with an annual budget of $10 million. Largely as a result of Lightner's efforts, Congress passed a bill in June 1984 to establish a national legal drinking age of 21, overriding states' rights to establish a local drinking age.

From the movie M.A.D.D.: Mothers Against Drunk Drivers, starring Paula Prentiss and Mariette Hartley.

Born on May 30, 1946, in Pasadena, California, Candy Lightner was the daughter of Dykes C. Doddridge and **Katherine Karrib Doddridge**. Both parents were employed by the U.S. Air Force, her father as a career serviceman, and her mother as an exchange system employee. Lightner's husband Steve Lightner was an officer in the Air Force. The marriage produced twin daughters and a son before ending in divorce. Prior to her career as an activist, Lightner attended American River College in Sacramento, California, and worked as a dental assistant from 1964 to 1972. From 1979 to 1980, she worked as a real estate agent in Fair Oaks, California. Before the death of her daughter, Lightner had been so completely apolitical she had not even registered to vote, but Cari's death in 1980 energized her into a life of social action. Using her own savings and insurance money from Cari's death, Lightner financed nearly 60% of MADD's expenses during its first year of operation.

From its unlikely origins in a cocktail lounge (Lightner was waiting for a table in a restaurant the night prior to her daughter's funeral when she announced the formation of the organization), Mothers Against Drunk Driving (called Mothers Against Drunk Drivers until 1984) grew rapidly into a national presence. With a staff of three volunteers, including Lightner and her father, the organization focused on lobbying for mandatory sentencing for those convicted of drunk driving and on providing counseling for their victims. It also pressed for national reforms. Although initially denied access to Governor Jerry Brown of California to discuss setting up a state commission to study the problem of drunk driving, Lightner was deluged with calls from across the nation following the press conference she gave to publicize her concerns. The first out-of-state chapter was formed in Maryland by **Cindy Lamb**, whose five-month-old daughter, Laura, became a quadriplegic after a drunk driver hit the car in which they were traveling. By the fall of 1980, Governor Brown met with Lightner and agreed to establish a California task force on drunk driving, with Lightner as its first member. A year later, 25 chapters of MADD existed in five states. By July 1983, the organization claimed 184 chapters in 39 states. Its rapid growth and outspoken activists caught the attention of state and national lawmakers, who could not ignore the high-profile mothers. State and national attention focused on issues relating to drunk driving, as Lightner pointed out that more persons were killed yearly in drunk-driving accidents than by handgun incidents.

In 1982, President Ronald Reagan established a national commission on drunk driving, despite his own reluctance to interfere with states' rights. Lightner served on the 30-member commission, which coordinated efforts to draw public attention to the problem of drunk driving. While stricter laws against drunk-driving crimes passed in 27 states during 1982, Lightner began to focus her attention on alcohol-related accidents involving youth. An estimated 50,000 teenagers died in alcohol-related driving accidents between 1974 and 1984, making drunk driving the largest killer of Americans between the ages of 18 and 24 during those years. With these statistics in mind, Lightner founded the first chapter of Students Against Drunk Driving (SADD) in August 1980. Youth education became the focus for SADD and a main component of MADD's activities. An annual poster and essay contest was established to promote awareness of the problem of drunk driving.

In March 1983, NBC produced a television film about Lightner's life, *Mothers Against Drunk Drivers: The Candy Lightner Story*, starring **Mariette Hartley** and **Paula Prentiss**. Featured as the NBC "Movie of the Week," the story reached a large national audience, providing further publicity for Lightner's cause. After a relatively short period of lobbying, both houses of Congress passed bills establishing the legal drinking age as 21 (the Senate bill passed by a margin of 81 to 16). On July 17, 1984, President Reagan signed into law the National Minimum Drinking Age Act of 1984, thus overruling the many states which had lowered the legal drinking age in the 1970s. Within four years, Lightner had succeeded not only in raising the national consciousness about the dangers of drunk driving, but also in effecting state and national legislative changes; sentencing for drunk-driving offenses became mandatory throughout the country. The effects of Lightner's crusade against drunk driving reverberated throughout the legal system. In May 1984, for example, the U.S. Supreme Court upheld a California law declaring a .10 percent blood-alcohol content while driving a crime. A month later, the New Jersey Supreme Court ruled that if a guest left a social gathering intoxicated and caused an accident resulting in injury, the host could be sued. By the end of 1984, MADD boasted 325 chapters in 47 states. The national headquarters was relocated to Hurst, Texas.

By October 1985, however, public questions about finances and internal disputes within the organization resulted in administrative changes. At the request of her six-member executive committee, Lightner stepped down as head of Mothers Against Drunk Driving, although she retained the position of consultant. Named one of the California Jaycees' Five Outstanding Californians in 1982 (the first woman so honored), Candy Lightner received numerous awards and commendations, including the President's Volunteer Action Award and the Jefferson Award from the American Institute for Public Service (both 1983), an honorary doctorate from St. Francis College in Pennsylvania (1984), and the Human Dignity Award from the Kessler Institute of Rehabilitation (1985).

SOURCES:
Evory, Ann, and Peter M. Gareffa, eds. *Contemporary Newsmakers*. Detroit, MI: Gale Research, 1985.

Lolly Ockerstrom,
freelance writer, Washington, D.C.

Lihotzky, Margaret Schütte (1897–2000).
See Schütte-Lihotzky, Margarete.

Lilian.
Variant of Celia, Lillian, or Lily.

Liliane (b. 1916).
See Baels, Liliane.

Liliia.
Variant of Lidia or Lidiya.

Liliuokalani (1838–1917)

Queen of Hawaii and last sovereign of the Islands, whose monarchy, despite the support of her people, was illegally overthrown by white settlers prior to Hawaii's annexation by the United States. Name variations: Lili'uokalani or Lili'uokalani; Lili'uokalani Lydia Kamekaha; Mme. Aorena; named Liliu Loloku Walania Kamakaeha at birth, commonly called Liliu, later christened Lydia and known as Lydia Kamakaeha Paki or Lidia Kamakhaeha Paki; renamed Lili'uokalani by her brother Kalakaua; sometimes referred to as Lily of Kilarney by Americans who could not pronounce her name. Pronunciation: Lee-lee-ew-kah-lah-nee. Born on September 2, 1838, in Honolulu, Hawaii; died of a stroke in Honolulu on November 11, 1917; daughter of the high chief, Kapaakea, and the chiefess, Keohokalole, a councilor to King Kamehameha III; sister of Kalakaua (1836–1891), king of Hawaii (r. 1874–1891); according to the Hawaiian custom of hanai, she was adopted at birth by Abner Paki and his wife Konia, grand-

daughter of Kamehameha I; educated at the High Chiefs Children's School and Oahu College; married John Owen Dominis, in 1862; children: no natural children; was hanai *mother to Lydia, John Dominis Aimoku, and Joseph Kaipo Aea.*

Named Princess Liliuokalani when her brother was elected king (1874); named heir apparent (1877); served as regent while king was abroad (1881); adopted first of three children (1882); began Liliuokalani Educational Society for young girls (1886); attended Queen Victoria's jubilee (1887); succeeded brother as the queen of the Hawaiian Islands (1891); overthrown (1893); accused of treason, forced to sign an act of abdication and imprisoned for eight months (1895); protested annexation of Hawaiian Islands by the United States (1897); established the Liliuokalani Trust for the benefit of orphaned and destitute children of Hawaiian blood (early 1900s). Author of over 200 songs, including the Hawaiian National Anthem, "He Mele Lahui Hawaii," "The Queen's Prayer," and the romantic "Aloha Oe."

When Liliuokalani succeeded her brother to the throne in January 1891, Hawaii was already ripe for revolt by its *haole* (foreign) residents, whose visions for Hawaii's future differed dramatically from those of the Hawaiians. The first permanent American and European settlers had been in the islands for less than 75 years, but their influence had permeated nearly every facet of island life. Most historians agree that by the time Liliuokalani assumed the throne, there was little she could have done to change the direction in which her homeland was moving. On January 24, 1895, Queen Liliuokalani, under pressure from the provisional government, signed an act of abdication and formally ended the hereditary monarchy in Hawaii. She had been queen for two years.

I could not turn back the time for the political change, but there is still time to save our heritage. You must remember never to cease to act because you fear you may fail.

—Liliuokalani

Liliu grew up with strong Hawaiian sentiments that were in conflict with the lessons she received in school. Born in 1838 into the *alii* (chief class) and a chiefess in her own right, Liliu was elevated to an even higher status by her *hanai* (adoptive) parents, Abner and **Konia Paki**. The practice of *hanai*, in which a child is given to another family to raise as their own, was an old Hawaiian custom that grew out of the desire

to cement ties between clans and rulers and was considered a mark of high esteem, great trust and affection. The bond between a child and her or his *hanai* parents was often stronger than the child's ties to her or his natural parents.

At the age of four, Liliu began to attend the missionary school for children of the island chiefs. There she learned math and to read and write English, a language which was still new to the islands and not heard in most Hawaiian homes during the 1800s. Liliu was a capable student with an enquiring mind who expanded her knowledge to include music, becoming one of few Hawaiians who could read or write music at the time. This love of music stayed with her throughout her life and prompted her to produce over 200 pieces of music, including the Hawaiian national anthem and the romantic "Aloha Oe." Liliu's desire to learn never dimmed; in her late 20s, she used her considerable powers of persuasion to convince the Oahu College, which was restricted to males, to accept her as an informal student.

Liliu's early years in the missionary school, where she was taught strict, narrow views of morality and propriety that strongly contrasted with the warm easygoing ways of her own people, had a profound impact on her. She noted in later years that she grew up listening during the day to the missionaries stress the correctness of marrying a *haole* (European or American), and listening in the evening to her father, a staunch believer in Hawaii for Hawaiians, railing against the increasing influence of the *haoles*.

Both Abner and Konia Paki died during 1857, and Liliu was sent to live with her cousin, *Bernice Pauahi Bishop. Bernice, another *hanai* daughter of the Pakis, had strong ties to the reigning monarch Kamehameha IV and, through her, Liliu spent the next several years steeped in the life of the Hawaiian court. She experienced firsthand the king's power when Kamehameha IV shot and killed his private secretary over a breach in etiquette. Such summary executions were understood and accepted, but incidents like this reinforced the young girl's feelings about the responsibility vested in the Hawaiian monarch.

Although she was not then in the line of succession to the throne, Liliu's parentage, both natural and adoptive, made her an attractive prospective bride. She was courted by many young men, both Hawaiian and *haole*. Chief among these was Prince Lunalilo, a personable fun-lover who had been selected by Kamehameha IV to marry his sister, Princess **Victoria**. Victoria was strong-willed and, although very fond of Lunalilo, was determined to marry Liliu's brother, David Kalakaua. Victoria and David eventually became engaged, leaving Prince Lunalilo free to court Liliu. Victoria was unstable, however, and within a few months she called off her engagement to David and declared that she would marry Lunalilo after all. The following day, disregarding Victoria's pronouncement, Lunalilo asked Liliu to marry him, and they became publicly engaged. During Liliu's engagement to Lunalilo, Victoria's instability became more pronounced, and she turned to alcohol and sorcery. Liliu permanently replaced her at court.

Known for her compassion toward others, Liliu had an overriding and often misplaced sense of responsibility for their happiness. Contemporaries described her as one who took the blame for failure upon herself, whether or not it was rightly hers. Within weeks, she called off her engagement to Lunalilo, expecting him to return to Victoria. But the gesture was futile; neither Victoria nor Lunalilo ever married, and both lost their health to alcoholism.

In 1859, Liliu was reintroduced to John Owen Dominis, a good friend of the bishop's

Liliuokalani

and, as the son of a retired British sea captain, a former student with her at the missionary school. They became engaged in 1860 and were married in 1862, despite the objections of Dominis' mother, who so disapproved of her son marrying a Hawaiian that she refused to attend the ceremony. Unfortunately for Liliu, immediately after the wedding she and her husband moved into her mother-in-law's residence at Washington Place, Honolulu.

According to Liliu's friends, the marriage was far from ideal. Liliu felt that she was an interloper in her mother-in-law's home. Mrs. Dominis refused to allow any Hawaiian foods into her house, banishing Hawaiian delicacies, as well as poi and fish, in favor of baked beans. To avoid conflict with her mother-in-law, Liliu was reduced to receiving Hawaiian visitors in a small cottage on the grounds of the main house. The Dominises, mother and son, had strong ideas about most things that often conflicted with Liliu's opinions, and Dominis consistently took his mother's side against his wife. He criticized her handwriting, her use of English, and her Hawaiian-style generosity toward family and friends. Years later, when several of his infidelities became public, he accused Liliu of having absorbed too much of the missionaries' attitudes toward sexuality and pronounced her frigid.

In 1863, Prince Lot came to the Hawaiian throne as Kamehameha V, and—in a stunning challenge to the increasingly strong control of the *haoles*—he refused to take the oath to maintain the existing Hawaiian constitution, which had been drafted in 1852 under the supervision of the missionaries. Instead, he called a constitutional convention. The convention delegates, mired in conflicting interests, failed to produce anything useful. Disgusted with the process, Kamehameha V dissolved the convention, dismissed the delegates, and publicly abrogated the 1852 constitution, replacing it with one of his own that was to last for 23 years.

Liliu's personal life continued to deteriorate, due primarily to her failed relationship with her mother-in-law. Whatever private strife there was between Liliu and her husband, she never ceased to campaign for governmental roles for him. Kamehameha V was persuaded to appoint Dominis as his private secretary and, in later years, governor of the island of Oahu. The extent of their disaffection became obvious, however, in 1868, when Liliu inherited land containing two houses in Waikiki. It was the first property that Liliu had ever owned in her own right, and it meant freedom to do as she wished. She moved out of Washington Place and into the main house at Waikiki. Dominis elected to stay with his mother.

In December 1872, Kamehameha V died and was succeeded by Lunalilo, now a dissolute pawn of the *haoles*, who was reduced to receiving a living allowance from his guardian, an American banker. Lunalilo died of dissipation in 1874 without leaving an heir. The choice of the next Hawaiian monarch was left up to the legislature, which was split between those favoring David Kalakaua, Liliu's brother, and those favoring the widow of Kamehameha IV, Queen *Emma. Support for both factions was strong and divisive. The populace generally supported Queen Emma's claim, but the largely American legislature was afraid of her pro-British sympathies and backed Kalakaua. When Kalakaua was finally elected king, the populace rioted. Kalakaua responded by permitting troops to be landed from two American warships anchored in the harbor, as well as from the British man-of-war *Tenedos*. The dissention caused by both warring factions divided the Hawaiian people into two political camps and permanently weakened their ability to hold the *haole* interests at bay.

Upon David Kalakaua's accession to the throne, his sister Liliu's status changed from chiefess to princess. Along with the new title came a new name conferred by the king: Liliuokalani. In 1877, Prince Leleiiohoku, the heir apparent, died. In a bid for power, the boy's *hanai* mother, Princess Ruth (**Ruth Keelikolani**), declared that she was now next in line to the throne. Kalakaua countered Ruth's move by officially declaring Princess Liliuokalani the heir apparent.

In 1881, Kalakaua made a trip around the world. The original plans, put forward by what Liliuokalani referred to as "the missionary party" which controlled Kalakaua's Cabinet, were for her to remain behind as regent, supervised by a council of regency. Although she would be head of this council, she would be prohibited from taking any action without its approval. Interpreting this as an example of the party's efforts to undermine the constitutional rulers of the Hawaiian people, Liliuokalani argued the arrangement with Kalakaua, stating that if there was need for a council, then there was no need for a regent. Her arguments won Kalakaua over, and before he left Liliuokalani was named sole regent.

Her regency was a success, although it proved a precursor for future conflicts with Kalakaua's Cabinet ministers. While the king was gone, smallpox broke out in Honolulu. In direct opposition to the Cabinet (which feared loss of trade and damage to ongoing commerce), Liliuokalani stopped communication between the islands, prohibited vessels from taking passengers, and instituted a strict quarantine. The measures worked, and the disease remained confined to the city with reduced loss of life.

King Kalakaua had gone to the United States to formalize the lease of Pearl Harbor to the Americans in exchange for a reciprocity treaty which would give the islands trade benefits. Liliuokalani was strongly opposed to the lease, fearing it would be the first step toward annexation by the Americans. From the States, Kalakaua traveled to Japan, China, Siam (now Thailand), and India to negotiate for contract laborers for the sugar plantations. According to Liliuokalani, Kalakaua's solution to the problem of labor gave the sugar planters:

> the opportunity to raise sugar at an enormous profit; and he thus devoted the earlier part of his reign to the aggrandizement of the very persons who, as soon as they had become rich and powerful, forgot his generosity, and plotted a subversion of his authority and an overthrow of the constitution under which the kingdom had been happily governed for nearly a quarter of a century.

Liliuokalani remained childless and was thwarted in her attempts to become *hanai* to a child by both her husband and his mother, who disapproved of the practice. In 1882, however, she learned that her husband was the father of an illegitimate child born to a half-Hawaiian woman. With this information, Liliuokalani was able to break the resistance against her taking a child as *hanai*. The boy became known as John Dominis Aimoku. Shortly thereafter, Liliuokalani took in a little girl she named Lydia and another male child, Joseph Kaipo Aea. Always interested in the welfare of children, Liliuokalani organized an education society in 1886. This society was created to interest Hawaiian women in the proper training of young girls of their own race, whose parents were unable to prepare them for the duties of life. This was the beginning of the Liliuokalani Educational Society.

In 1887, Liliuokalani and her husband traveled to England with Queen **Kapiolani** for Queen *Victoria's grand jubilee. They first sailed to San Francisco and then traveled overland to Washington, D.C., where they dined with President Grover Cleveland before boarding a steamer for London. The power and the grandeur of the British court deeply impressed Liliuokalani,

as did the cordiality and respect they received from the British. Fresh from this triumph, they returned to Honolulu to find that the annexationist Reform Party had forced a new Cabinet on Kalakaua and prevailed upon him to sign a constitution of their own preparation. This document decreed that a foreigner, even without naturalization, was eligible to vote, but required all voters to be able to read and write in Hawaiian, English or some other European language, effectively disenfranchising 90% of the native population. The document became known as "The Bayonet Constitution." King Kalakaua maintained that he had signed the document because he feared for his life at the hands of his Cabinet ministers. The advent of the Bayonet Constitution brought a steady shift of power from the monarch to the hands of his ministers.

In 1889, Kalakaua traveled to the United States for a meeting with the Hawaiian minister to discuss the McKinley Bill, which placed a stiff tariff on imported sugar. Once again, he placed Liliuokalani in charge as regent. Kalakaua died

Liliuokalani

on the trip home, and official notification of his death was received in January 1891. Even before the funeral could be held, the ministers and councilors drew together, summoned Liliuokalani to appear before them and prevailed upon her to take the oath of office. They informed her, as they had Kalakaua, that she could make no changes in the Cabinet except by legislative approval. Immediately upon her assumption of the throne, Prime Minister John L. Stevens met with Liliuokalani and laid down the guidelines under which she would rule. In a complicated move which backfired, he urged her to give the Cabinet new commissions under her royal seal. Liliuokalani replied that before she could do so they would have to tender their resignations. Once the resignations were in her hand, she shrewdly appealed to Supreme Court Judge Samuel Dole, who upheld her right to dismiss the Cabinet. Liliuokalani quickly installed a new Cabinet made up of men whom she believed would support her monarchy.

Liliuokalani, described by Hawaiian and American newspapers as "well educated, tactful, a woman of state craft and even handsome," began her reign with the nation in debt and a financially crippling civil list. Kalakaua had reduced crown income by selling off large tracts of crown property to pay both his personal debts and some incurred by the country. In an attempt to economize, Liliuokalani reduced the allowances given to herself and the other royals. This move prompted angry rumors among the legislators that she also intended to reduce the monies paid to the ministers from $10,000 to $8,000.

During 1891, American businessmen in Hawaii were losing vast sums of money due to the McKinley Tariff and were, therefore, pushing for annexation. Prime Minister Stevens noted that Hawaii lost $12 million in revenue due to the tariff. He believed that annexation was necessary, if for no other reason than to protect the sugar interests, which were primarily owned by Americans. Recognizing the danger, Liliuokalani attempted to ameliorate the loss of trade due to the McKinley Tariff by instituting another reciprocity treaty. The U.S. angered her by refusing to respond, and her Cabinet began to fear that Liliuokalani, who was known to favor the English and had several part-British advisors, would put American interests aside in favor of the English. Following Kamehameha V's example, she sent emissaries to talk to her people and ascertain what they wanted from their monarch: the answer was a strong monarchy they could understand, a stronger place for themselves, and no annexation by a foreign power. All of this ran counter to the annexation spirations of the Reform Party.

In August 1891, John Dominis died. Although their personal life had been strained, Liliuokalani valued his judgment and had relied upon him for advice. His death left her alone to battle the opposition. Between May 1892 and January 1893, seven motions of no confidence in her Cabinet ministries were introduced; four succeeded. Liliuokalani turned to one of the few people she trusted, the British ambassador. He told her he believed she had the right to choose her Cabinet from her personal favorites. Liliuokalani compromised; she appointed one of her staunchest opponents, G.N. Wilcox, as premier and minister of interior and filled the rest of the Cabinet with her supporters. The House accepted the new Cabinet.

On January 4, 1893, the legislature passed two controversial bills. One was a lottery bill designed to generate funds that would be used to finance public works to benefit the Hawaiians. The other was a law regulating the traffic in opium, which they had given up trying to suppress. Liliuokalani signed the two bills on January 13, 1893, despite heavy opposition from the right. Prime Minister Stevens saw the queen's act as an affront, and the next day her Cabinet was subjected to another no-confidence vote. The queen retaliated by officially ending the session of the legislature.

Liliuokalani now believed that the only way to save her small country from "being given away by 'guests' was to change the form of government to a strong monarchy by promulgating a new constitution." Her proposed constitution contained three major changes: it increased the franchise to her people by restricting the vote to Hawaiian-born or naturalized citizens; it restricted the terms of justices of the supreme court to six years rather than life; and it increased the power of the queen by requiring Cabinet ministers to serve at the queen's pleasure, in addition to being subject to removal by legislative want of confidence. Additionally, Article 78 of the 1887 constitution, stating that "all official acts of the sovereign [are] to be performed with the advice and consent of the Cabinet," was to be removed. The ministers refused to sign it, and its contents were leaked to the press.

The local paper, which was decidedly in favor of annexation, declared that the queen had violated her oath by dissolving the legislature and putting forth a new constitution and, by violating her oath, "had absolved her subjects from allegiance; therefore the throne was vacant." This doctrine of self-abdication by violation of her oath became the official justification of the provisional government for overthrowing the monarchy. Sanford Dole, Hawaii's first president, said later, "The Queen was an insurgent. She had rebelled against her own government."

At 5 PM on January 16, 1893, 162 American troops marched fully armed through the streets of Honolulu and took control of the consulate, the legation, and the government building. The climax occurred the next day, January 17, when a lengthy proclamation deposing the queen was printed and broadcast. It called for absolute abolition of the monarchy, establishment of a provisional government until annexation by the United States, and details for the composition of a new government.

The queen's advisors cautioned her against any demonstration that would precipitate bloodshed, and, always mindful of the welfare of her people, she was persuaded to surrender under protest without a shot being fired.

Liliuokalani sent her protests to President Benjamin Harrison and his successor, Grover Cleveland (who was serving his second term, having skipped four years). Neither were really interested in annexing the islands. Cleveland believed that Stevens had plotted for overthrow and annexation for his own interests and requested an investigation. It concluded that the queen had been illegally overthrown with the aid of American naval forces and that John L. Stevens had been prominent in the overthrow.

In November, a new commissioner met with the queen and forwarded Cleveland's regret that she had been overthrown. He asked her to grant full amnesty of life and property to those instrumental in the overthrow, in return for her restoration to the throne. Liliuokalani replied that she would expect permanent banishment of all revolutionists and their families, but she later agreed to yield on the point of banishment. After Liliuokalani complied with Cleveland's requests, she expected the United States to reinstate the monarchy, but the strength of the provisional government surprised everyone. Hawaii's President Dole refused to abide by the decision of President Cleveland, stating that the provisional government did not recognize the right of the United States to interfere in its affairs.

Liliuokalani retired to private life, splitting her time between Honolulu and California, until, in January 1895, a band of Royalists tried unsuccessfully to overthrow the provisional government. Liliuokalani was arrested and confined at Iolani Palace. Her house at Washington Place was searched, and bombs, rifles and cartridge belts were found buried in her garden. Her private papers were confiscated along with those of her deceased husband, and the provisional government seized the house.

On the fourth day of her confinement, she was told that she and six others had been condemned to be shot for treason. On January 24, 1895, she was forced to sign an act of abdication. Once this document was signed, the charge of treason was changed to misprision (misconduct or neglect of duty), the death sentence was dropped, and she was fined $5,000 and sentenced to five years' hard labor. The sentence was never enforced, and she spent the following months confined to two rooms in the Iolani Palace.

Eight months after her arrest, Liliuokalani was paroled to her house. When a pardon followed in December, she sailed for San Francisco, Boston, and then Washington, D.C., where she met with President Cleveland and stayed for William McKinley's inauguration. When, in June 1897, McKinley sent the annexation treaty to the Senate, Liliuokalani protested the theft of her country to the Department of State. Her protests went unanswered, and in August 1898, in the midst of the Spanish-American War, the Hawaiian Islands were annexed by the U.S. as a territory. Liliuokalani continued to protest to the U.S. government through 1909 regarding the disposition of crown lands, some 911,888 acres valued at $22 each in 1908 that had been confiscated by the provisional government. In 1912, the Territorial government began to pay Liliuokalani approximately $12,000 a year, ostensibly in reparations for the crown properties.

Liliuokalani spent the remainder of her life traveling between California and Hawaii. In her later years, she used her lands to establish the Liliuokalani Trust for the benefit of orphaned and destitute children of Hawaiian blood. This trust was later challenged by her nephew, Kuhio Kalanianaole, who charged that she was mentally incompetent and that the lands should pass to him as her only surviving relative. The suit was decided in her favor, and the trust remains active.

While crowds of Hawaiians gathered in her Honolulu gardens to chant softly for their queen, Liliuokalani died of a stroke, at the age of 79, in 1917. She was honored and buried with the old customs of her people, her head crowned with the royal diadem she had not worn in 25 years.

SOURCES:

Allen, Helen G. *The Betrayal of Lili'uokalani Last Queen of Hawaii*. Glendale, CA: Arthur H. Clark, 1982.

Daws, Gavan. *Shoal of Time*. Honolulu, HI: University Press of Hawaii, 1968.

Irwin, Bernice Piilani. *I Knew Queen Liliuokalani*. Honolulu, HI: Distributed by South Sea Sales, 1960.

Liliuokalani. *Hawaii's Story by Hawaii's Queen*. Rutland, VT: C.E. Tuttle, 1964.

Russ, William Adam, Jr. *The Hawaiian Revolution (1893–94)*. Cranbury, NJ: Associated University Presses, 1959.

Paula Steib,
freelance writer, Kaneohe, Hawaii

Liliya.

Variant of Lidia or Lidiya.

Lillak, Tiina (1961—)

Finnish javelin thrower. Born Ilse Kristiina Lillak on April 15, 1961.

In 1982, Tiina Lillak broke the world record in the javelin with a throw of 72.40 meters, though **Sofia Sakorafa** of Greece topped that within weeks at a meet in Crete with a throw of 74.20. In 1983, Lillak regained the world record at the Helsinki World championships with a throw of 74.76. The following year, she won the Olympic silver medal in the javelin throw in Los Angeles, placing second to Britain's gold medalist **Tessa Sanderson**. Tiina Lillak was only the second Finnish woman to win an Olympic medal; the first was won by *Kaisa Parviainen who took the silver for the javelin in London in 1948.

Lillie, Beatrice (1894–1989)

Popular Canadian-born comedian of radio, stage and screen. Name variations: Lady Peel. Born Beatrice Gladys Lillie on May 29, 1894, in Toronto, Ontario, Canada; died on January 20, 1989, in Henley-on-Thames, England; daughter of John Lillie and Lucy Shaw Lillie; married Sir Robert Peel, in 1920 (died 1933); children: one son, Robert (died 1942).

Formed a singing trio at age 15 with her mother and sister Muriel (1909); made her debut on the London stage (1913) and on Broadway (1924); enjoyed a 50-year-long career as "the funniest woman in the world" on stage and on radio, while becoming known equally as well for her friendships with royalty and with such entertainment notables as Noel Coward and Charlie Chaplin; elevated by marriage to the British peerage (1920), becoming Lady Peel; published autobiography (1972) before retiring from show business (1977).

Films: Exit Smiling (1926); The Show of Shows (1929); Are You There? (1930); Dr. Rhythm (1938); On Approval (1944); Around the World in Eighty Days (1956); Thoroughly Modern Millie (1967).

One night in the late 1920s, an imposing vision swept into the lobby of the English Speaking Union in St. Louis, Missouri. It was a woman of aristocratic bearing, wearing a fashionable pillbox hat and a luxurious mink coat. She peered suspiciously at the lobby attendant who swept forward to inquire politely if Madam wished to check her coat. "Certainly not!" the woman retorted. "No one's seen it yet!" Lady Peel, known to most of the world as Beatrice Lillie, "the world's funniest woman," had arrived. The encounter was typical of Bea Lillie's delight in poking fun at society's pretensions and hypocrisies. Her marriage to a British peer gave her access to new and fertile ground for her material, but she had been examining human foibles to hilarious effect since childhood.

"I wasn't born, I was won on the playing fields of Eton," Lillie once declared in a bald attempt to divert attention from her birth into a middle-class family in Toronto, Ontario, on May 29, 1894. Her father John Lillie was an Irishman from County Cork who had settled in Canada after serving Her Majesty's government in India. He found work in Toronto as a guard at the city jail and was known for two traits which he would pass on to his youngest daughter Beatrice—a wry sense of humor and a jaundiced eye for the preening, ostentatious displays of the upper classes. His wife, the former **Lucy Shaw**, was ten years his junior and the daughter of a prosperous clothing retailer from Manchester, England, who had retired to a farm outside of Toronto. In contrast to her husband, Lucy had an outspoken, sometimes explosive temperament and considered herself a product of the upper classes which John ridiculed, much to her annoyance. John and Lucy had settled after their marriage in a section of Toronto then known as "Cabbage Town" because of its large Irish immigrant population. It was in a modest house on Dovercourt Road that their first daughter, Muriel, was born in 1893, followed the next year by Beatrice Gladys.

Lillie's earliest memories were of her mother's musical voice. Lucy, who entertained dreams of becoming a concert singer, trilled continually around the house and even sang her way through everyday conversation. "She used to run straight up the scale just saying hello," Bea once remembered. After John lost a good deal of money investing in a failed scheme involving an employment service for English and Irish immigrants, Lucy helped make ends meet by teaching singing and piano in the family parlor and was delighted to discover that her elder daughter Muriel had real talent as a pianist, while Bea seemed to have inherited her own predilection for singing. Lillie quickly turned her ability to good use, entertaining the local laundryman and greengrocer by singing for them until they handed over a few coins. At the George Street School, where the sisters attended classes, Bea's imitations of her mother's singing or Muriel's piano playing made her a popular student. When Lucie (who by now had decided to make her name more aristocratic by changing its spelling) was hired as the choir director at Cooke's Presbyterian Church, Muriel quickly became the choir's accompanist. Bea, much to Lucie's embarrassment, had to be removed from the choir after making the other children giggle.

Lillie's first formal education in the mimicry that would become the basis of her humor came from Harry Rich, an erstwhile music-hall entertainer who had set himself up in business as the Rich Concert and Entertainment Bureau. Although Bea disliked Rich intensely, it was from him that she first learned the art of the "character song," for which Rich himself had once been famous. Baldly trading in ethnic stereotypes and social stigmas, Lillie perfected her impersonations of everything from geisha girls to organ grinders to Irish clog dancers, trying them out on the audiences at her mother's Wednesday night *musicales* presented in the living room, and building the repertoire of gestures and facial expressions which would become her stock-in-trade. Rich was delighted with her progress. By the time Muriel and Bea had entered the Gladstone Avenue High School, Rich was sending the two girls out with their mother as The Lillie Trio. The act was such a success that Rich widened the territory, booking the women into a revue called *The Belles of New York*, which played mining camps and railroad towns in rural areas. Lucie, who felt such audiences were below the act's standards, changed its name for such bookings to The Francis Trio, while Bea appeared as "Gladys Montell," the name she intended to use for the film career she was sure lay ahead.

While the girls were in high school, the act was appearing across the border in New York State, playing to great response in such towns as Coburg, New York, a summer resort on Lake Ontario for Manhattan's upper crust. Bea had her own "window card" placed in storefronts and public spaces where the act was appearing,

identifying her as "Miss Beatrice Lillie, Character Costume Vocalist and Impersonator." She was already attracting attention in the press, with the *Toronto Globe* noting that "Miss Beatrice Lillie . . . is a remarkable and clever artist with a sweet, powerful voice," and the *Drayton Advocate* reporting that "her very appearance was a signal for applause, and she was repeatedly encored." When the girls graduated, the Lillie Trio was reluctantly disbanded. Muriel entered the Toronto Conservatory of Music and seemed headed for a distinguished concert career, while Lucie accepted an offer to direct Coburg's choir, leaving John to turn the family home in Toronto into a boarding house. Bea enrolled at St. Agnes' College in Belleville, Ontario, commuting to Coburg on school holidays to be with her mother.

Muriel's surprise announcement in 1912 that she had left the conservatory and married without her parents' consent threw Lucie into a fit of angry recrimination. Convinced that Muriel was throwing away a promising future, Lucie left her job in Coburg and hustled her eldest daughter onto a ship bound for Europe, determined to enroll Muriel at a German music academy. Bea, stranded at St. Agnes', soon learned that the ship had been diverted to England as the outbreak of war on the Continent seemed imminent. Later that year, after begging her father for the money, Bea made the first of scores of transatlantic crossings and arrived in London determined to find work in the theater.

I'm not making this up, you know!
—Beatrice Lillie

Lillie's first recorded appearance on the London stage came as an "extra turn" in a music-hall revue at the Camberwell Empire in 1913. Such semi-professional acts were often inserted between the main attractions as a way of filling out an otherwise skimpy program. Bea was given time for three numbers, for which Lucie wrapped her in three different layered costumes, the idea being that after each number, Lillie could quickly strip off one layer in the wings and run back onstage for the next. The public's response after the first number indicated that she needn't have hurried, with the audience chatter almost drowning her out. Desperate, Bea walked on for her third number, called for silence, summoned up the tears she had learned to produce copiously under Harry Rich's guidance, and chokingly announced that she would like to dedicate her next number to Irving Berlin who, as was well known to music-hall and vaudeville audiences on both sides of the Atlantic, had recently been left a widower by the death of his first wife. Bea's ploy, while it may not have made her a star, at least brought a respectful silence to the hall for her teary rendition of Berlin's "When I Lost You." The appearance was to be her last for some time. Bea made unproductive rounds to London agents, while Muriel earned money playing piano in silent movie houses and Lucie taught piano in the small flat the three shared in Chelsea.

Finally, in August 1914, on the day war was declared in Europe, Lillie was given her first contract by the man who would guide her career for the next 20 years. André Charlot had arrived in London from Paris some time earlier, had become famous for his "intimate revues" presented in London's smaller theaters, and would eventually become the English Flo Ziegfeld. Charlot offered Bea a three-year contract at £15 a week and put her in a show of his already running called *Not Likely*, into which a coy number, "I Want a Toy Soldier," had been inserted for her. Audiences noticed her low-cut, sleeveless costume more than anything else, and Lillie was promptly assigned to a number of touring productions in which Charlot hoped Bea would gain some experience. Since his roster of male performers was being greatly shortened by the demands of the military, Charlot began to cast Lillie in male roles, her slim figure and slight build being ideal for a male impersonator. Lucie was horrified but powerless to break Bea's contract.

It was during the next year, as Lillie stumped from one smoky, beer-laden music hall to another in a dreary round of gray industrial towns, that she refined the abilities Harry Rich had recognized back in Toronto. She learned to trust an audience's reaction as the only guide in developing an act, and loathed the vacuum of a rehearsal hall and the chore of learning lines, which she found especially difficult. Many of her bits of business, in fact, grew from genuine mistakes during a performance, brought about by her aversion to rehearsing. She learned how to deliver a double entendre with maximum effect in front of an audience of working men and women who were more interested in each other than what was happening on stage. By the end of 1914, Charlot decided Bea was ready for the London stage and cast her in a male role in his *5064 Gerard* (a reference to a telephone number which figured in the typically sparse plot). She appeared in formal evening suit and striped cravat, singing Berlin's "I Want to Go Back to Michigan" with such success that she was called back for several encores. Her next Charlot revue, *Now's the Time*, happened to open on the first night of bombing raids by German zep-

pelins, and it was a tribute to Lillie's skill that she managed to keep a decidedly edgy audience in their seats while the distant rumble of bombs punctuated her numbers. The experience inspired her to introduce a new song the next night, "Where Did That One Go, Herbert?," which became a favorite with wartime audiences who would supply their own bomb effects if the real thing happened to be lacking. Charlot was now sure he had a star on his hands.

Bea's life at home, however, was not as encouraging. Muriel's concert career, once so promising, was now moribund and a constant source of friction between mother and daughter. Lucie, for her part, seemed jealous of Bea's success and continually harped on the career lost by her marriage to John, still living in Toronto. Dreading the domestic atmosphere that awaited her after the gaiety and laughter of the theater, Bea would often bring friends home with her for the night. One of them was the understudy Charlot had hired for her, *Gertrude Lawrence, who would soon become Lillie's equal in popularity on the music-hall stage and her closest friend. Bea would often call in sick so that Gertrude could go on for her, although Charlot discovered the trick when he found himself sitting next to Lillie at another show during one of her "sick" nights. Through Lawrence, Lillie met Noel Coward, a young lyricist looking for his first break, and hobnobbed with royalty and the Bright Young Things of London society at parties given by composer Ivor Novello, who wrote the score for Charlot's 1918 revue, *Tabs* (which included the song that became a virtual second anthem for the British, "Keep the Home Fires Burning"). Lillie shocked proper London by appearing in *Oh, Joy* as a young actress who ends up in a man's bedroom wearing his pink pajamas—a risqué stage device that was the delight of audiences and critics. "Miss Lillie wears [the pajamas] with such grace and discretion that there is nothing outré about them," wrote one reviewer, who could not resist adding, "In fact, she is the very pink of piquant propriety." It was also during this period that Lillie began the first of her many affairs, embarking on a passionate *amour* with the dance director of a 1919 Charlot show in which she appeared.

By the end of the war, Lillie had assumed an assured place on the list of London music-hall stars, along with Gertie Lawrence, Jack Buchanan, George Robey, and *Gladys Cooper, in whose company she could be found most nights after the show at any number of choice London watering holes like the Ivy, Rules, or Simpson's. It was at Simpson's that Lillie met

Robert Peel, the youngest in a line of Peels named Robert stretching back to the 18th century which included the Robert who had established London's Metropolitan Police, ever after called "Bobbies." Bea's friend, **Phyllis Monkman**, who had been dating Peel before she introduced him to Bea, described him as "a sweet boy; very, very good looking [but] weak as water." It was no secret that the Peels of late had fallen on hard times, and that Robert had little else to offer besides the title of 5th baronet that he would inherit on the death of his father. He was, in fact, selling cars for a living when Lillie met him and the two began going about London together, Peel being smitten with theater types in general and fancying himself a playwright *manqué*. Not long after they began dating, Bea wandered into one of her costars' dressing rooms. "You know," she said, "I think I should marry Bobby Peel. He's an important man, a big name, and I should seriously do something about my life." It did not seem to occur to Lillie to wonder if she was actually in love with him. The engagement was announced in October 1919, the nuptials taking place in January 1920 in the chapel of Peel's ancestral home, Drayton Hall, not far from London. Muriel was bridesmaid, John traveled from Toronto to give his daughter away, and the pews were filled with London theater folk, the only ones missing being Peel's parents, who chose to remain at their alpine retreat in Switzerland but who sent several pieces of the family's jewelry for Bea's use.

The newlyweds honeymooned in Monte Carlo, where Peel promptly lost all their money at the gambling table. Peel's "champagne tastes," as Bea tactfully put it, would leave the couple entirely dependent on Lillie's income from the theater throughout their marriage. "He was known," she once wrote, "to buy a new dress shirt every morning for that evening's wearing and throw yesterday's away rather than bother sending it to the laundry. A fascinating concept, really." When Peel announced he had completed a screenplay which he was sure Hollywood would be eager to buy, the couple embarked with great fanfare for New York not long after their honeymoon. But Bea's reputation preceded her, helped by the thousands of American doughboys who had seen her in London after America had joined the war in 1917. She was besieged in New York with offers for appearances, especially from an eager Flo Ziegfeld, which she turned down to everyone's surprise by announcing she was pregnant. Returning to London, Lillie gave birth to a son—named, inevitably, Robert—in December 1920.

Although now the wife of a socially prominent man and the mother of a newborn son, Lillie longed to return to the sheltered world of the stage. John Gielgud, who as a struggling young actor appeared with Bea, once noted that her genius stemmed from an almost childlike view of a world from which the bright glare of footlights shielded her. The world in which Lillie now found herself, playing the real-life roles of mother and society wife, was not to her liking. "I was bored," she admitted many years later, "and every night at eight o'clock I became fidgety and nervous. Something important seemed to be missing from my life, so I went back to the stage determined never to leave it again." Placing her son's upbringing in her mother's care and accepting her relationship with Peel as a marriage in name only, Lillie returned to the stage in another Charlot revue, *Up in Mabel's Room,* and returned to her life of greasepaint, outrageous costumes, and after-show parties, where she traded cocktails and witticisms with the likes of her old friend Noel Coward, fresh from his first success as a playwright with *The Vortex*; Charlie Chaplin, already an international film star; and those two royal theater enthusiasts, the Prince of Wales (the future Edward VIII) and his brother (the future George VI).

Late in 1923, Lillie traveled once again to New York, having accepted an offer for her American debut in a Charlot revue imported to Broadway by the Selwyn Brothers, second only to Ziegfeld as purveyors of lavish vaudeville entertainment. Headlining with her were her old friends Gertie Lawrence and Jack Buchanan. Refusing the Selwyns' demands to Americanize the show by including songs written by American composers, Charlot gave Bea ten numbers written by Novello and Coward, including "March with Me," in which Lillie paraded around the stage dressed as Britannia, complete with shield, helmet, and sword. As usual, Lillie had paid only the slightest attention during rehearsals and consequently took a wrong turn, plowing into the line of chorus girls marching behind her and creating such total chaos that the exuberant audience was naturally convinced it had all been carefully choreographed beforehand. Despite the Selwyns' misgivings, the show was an instant hit with American audiences who were used to seeing hordes of anonymous chorines rather than three troupers who appeared in nearly every sketch. "In Charlot's revue," wrote one critic, "the stars do a great deal more and appear so often you feel that you know them very well at the end of the performance." Lillie attracted so much attention in the show that performers in other shows up and down Broadway began to imitate her. "There is no one in New York comparable to Beatrice Lillie," claimed *The New York Times*, which especially admired her willingness to sacrifice her aristocratic features and vocal talents in the interest of humor.

Just as she had in London, Lillie became the darling of New York's cultural and social elite. She was embraced by the Round Table, that infamous collection of wits and wags that gathered at the Algonquin Hotel each week. Playwright Marc Connelly, a member in good standing of the Round Table, found Bea and Gertie a duplex apartment on 54th Street that became the theater world's official party headquarters, and Bea herself began an affair with journalist Charles MacArthur that ended only when MacArthur, soon to become famous by co-writing *The Front Page*, announced his engagement to *Helen Hayes. As the Charlot revue's run was extended through the summer of that year, Lillie was swept into a round of weekend house parties in Southampton and invitations to visit her hosts in Palm Beach during the winter. Lucie brought young Robert to visit his mother in New York, to Bea's great delight, although their time together was cut short when the Charlot revue ended its run late in 1924 and Lillie set off on a tour with Gertie Lawrence.

Bea returned to London only briefly, in February 1925, after learning that Robert had officially become the 5th baronet on the death of his father, making her Lady Peel. She was delighted at the dramatic possibilities, played to the hilt when reporters swarmed around her as she boarded her ship in New York harbor. "I was playing it terribly grand, very Lady Peel all over the place," she once gleefully recalled, although trouble came along in the person of one of her fellow actors, also taking ship for the Old Country, who drunkenly teetered up the gangplank, yelled out a Cockney greeting, and slapped her on the back, sending the demure Lady Peel sprawling onto the deck. "I was livid," she remembered, not because of any disrespect to a peer of the realm, she said, but because her act had been spoiled. Bea's title, observed Kenneth Tynan at the time, "sits on her like a halo on an anarchist."

During the years between the wars, Lillie sailed back and forth across the Atlantic in a nearly continuous round of hybrid British-American shows. She quickly noted the difference between American and British audiences when a skit that had brought howls of laughter in New York fell flat during her first appearance at London's venerable Palladium, saved only when she changed into an outrageous costume and galumphed around the stage. "I don't know why it is," she complained, "but most Englishmen are from Missouri. They have to have their humor laid out on a table." Nonetheless, she was at the peak of her career, appearing regularly in André Charlot's yearly revues, touring on the Orpheum vaudeville circuit through the American Midwest and then traveling on to California to make her first film in 1926, *Exit Smiling*, during which she was sued for $100,000 by the wife of the film's writer, with whom Lillie was accused of having an affair.

(The suit was later dropped.) Bea never felt as comfortable in front of a camera as she did in front of a live audience and would appear in only a handful of pictures during her long career. It was during these heady years that she bobbed her hair, prompting one New York department store to offer its female patrons an "Eton Crop, as worn by Miss Beatrice Lillie in Charlot's Revue." She never failed to wear one of the growing collection of pillbox hats she ordered en masse each year from Bergdorf-Goodman, as much a part of her act as the ubiquitous silver cigarette holder she brandished with aplomb. She filled music halls in England and vaudeville houses in America with audiences who flocked to see her growing repertoire of misguided characters crashing, stumbling and warbling their way through songs like "It's Better with Your Shoes Off" and "Roses Always Remind Me of What a Girl Should Always Forget." In New York, she could be found most evenings after a show at Dinty Moore's on 46th Street or the old Reuben's further uptown, often

Bea Lillie in Ziegfeld Follies of 1957.

in the company of *Fanny Brice, with whom she became great friends, or with her latest lover; and in London, she hobnobbed with royalty and fellow peers when her marriage to Robert Peel required it, although the two saw little of each other outside of these social responsibilities. Lillie saw young Bobby as often as her schedule allowed, but continued to leave his upbringing in Lucie's hands. Her drinking grew to legendary proportions. Bea offered two explanations for her peculiar sensitivity to even small amounts of alcohol—either the metal plate she claimed had been inserted in her skull as the result of a shrapnel wound from World War I London bombings, or, in a second version, because of a skull fracture suffered in a fall from a horse in Hyde Park. Although few believed her, everyone loved to hear her recount such insults to her person, punctuated by her beloved cry of shocked outrage, "I could have eaten *parsnips*, darling!"

In April 1933, Sir Robert Peel died of peritonitis. Lillie mourned his passing as she would that of any good friend, but she frankly admitted to feeling no stronger emotion and told friends years later that she and "Big Bobby" would probably have been divorced if he had lived. She stayed in England for the remainder of that year, but returned to New York in the spring of 1934 to begin preparing for the premiere of her own radio program on NBC in January of 1935, on which she introduced such characters as The Honest Working Girl and Auntie Bea, a parody of New York Mayor Fiorello La Guardia's weekly radio reading of comic strips for children. The year 1935 also brought to Broadway Vincente Minnelli's production of *At Home Abroad*, billed as a "musical travelogue" in which Lillie appeared as a shopper attempting to order, with great difficulty, "one dozen double damask dinner napkins"; as a mountain-climbing golddigger whose lament for her lost lover, "Oh, Leo," turns into an unearthly yodel; and in a parody of *The Merry Widow*. "She is one of the greatest woman funmakers on the English-speaking stage," wrote one critic, while another noted that "no one else can hover so skillfully between beauty and burlesque."

Lillie returned to England just before Hitler's invasion of Poland in 1939 and remained there for much of World War II. Young Bobby, who was now the 6th baronet, enlisted and shipped out for Asia in 1942, bringing a more personal meaning to the appearances Bea made for the country's Entertainment National Service Association, the British counterpart of America's USO shows. She was a great favorite with wartime audiences. "It was as if she sensed our loneliness," an American GI who attended one of Lillie's shows recalled after the war. "I know I speak for every soldier in that large theater when I say she cheered our hearts for days, even weeks, afterwards." One of her more successful ENSA shows was *Big Top*, which opened in London not long after Bobby had sailed, and then toured throughout the country. It was during the show's run in Manchester that Bea was informed by the Defense Ministry that Bobby was missing in action in Ceylon (now Sri Lanka), where he had arrived just days earlier on the HMS *Tenedos*. The ship had received a direct hit during a Japanese bombing raid. *Big Top*'s producer offered to close the show, but Lillie insisted that she go on in that evening's performance. Even so, one cast member remembered that "the cold steel in her eyes was absolutely terrifying." Bobby's body was never found, and for months afterward Lillie clung to the belief that he was still alive, perhaps suffering from amnesia in some military hospital. She ran ads in newspapers and made sure to visit every hospital on the show's tour, despite the Ministry placing his name on the official deceased list and her own visit to the military cemetery in Ceylon containing a memorial to those lost in the disaster, on which she tearfully read her son's name. It wasn't until 1944 and the war's end that Lillie was forced to accept the truth when a shipmate of her son's, who had been onshore at the time of the attack, told her that Bobby's station had been only five feet from the site of the explosion that tore the ship apart.

Lillie's only solace lay in her work, but it was obvious to anyone close to her that she would never be the same. "The day Bobby died, Bea began her own death," one of them later wrote. The "futile waste," as she once described it, of her son's life drained away whatever happiness there had been in her own. Her drinking worsened, forcing stage managers and fellow performers to ply her with cups of black coffee in her dressing room before the curtain went up. She was as hilarious as ever onstage, appearing to great acclaim in 1948's *Inside U.S.A.* on Broadway and winning a Tony Award in 1953 for *An Evening With Beatrice Lillie*, which ran for 275 performances at the Booth Theater before going on a world tour that stretched over the next two years. Returning to England at the end of the tour, Lillie bought the small house in Henley-on-Thames in which she would settle after 50 years on the road. While she was rehearsing for her next show, *Milady Dines Alone*, Lucie died, leaving Bea to look after Muriel, who would spend the next 20 years suffering from various alcohol-related illnesses before passing away in 1973.

Although Lillie would not marry again, her constant companion was now John Philip, whom she had met in New York not long after the war. Philip had been hired during the run of *Inside U.S.A.* to carry Lillie to and from her dressing room for a number in which she was required to appear as a mermaid, and was thus immobilized. Philip had changed his name from the original John Huck after deciding to become an actor, although he spent most of his time offstage looking after Bea. By the early 1960s, it was increasingly apparent that Lillie needed someone like Philip. During the Broadway run of *High Spirits*—a musical version of Coward's *Blithe Spirit*, in which Bea took the role of the addled medium, Madame Arcati—Bea was often nearly late for her calls, missed her cues, and flubbed her lines, all of which the audience naturally took as more of Lillie's famous stage antics. "God bless Miss Lillie," effused one critic during the show's run, "the most durable and delightful comic of our era!" The situation worsened during the filming of what would be Lillie's last picture, the 1967 musical *Thoroughly Modern Millie*. Director George Roy Hill, along with Philip, had to gently coax her through take after take for the simplest of scenes, while Bea continually inquired "Who's that girl who keeps singing?," pointing to one of the film's female leads, **Julie Andrews**. Still, audiences made up of young people who had barely been born when Lillie was at the peak of her fame fell in love with her off-beat portrayal of a scheming 1920s landlady attempting to sell two of her flapper tenants (Andrews and **Mary Tyler Moore**) into white slavery. The less predictable atmosphere of a live television broadcast proved particularly troublesome. During a guest appearance with Johnny Carson on the "Tonight Show," Lillie seemed to have difficulty following the thread of conversation; and she forgot the expected formality of signing in when she was a mystery guest on *What's My Line?* Then, instead of walking offstage after her identity was discovered, Lillie wandered down into the audience and had to be escorted out of the studio. Restaurateur Vincent Sardi noted sadly in the early 1970s that while Bea was still a regular at his establishment, "she no longer knows it's Sardi's."

Two strokes suffered in the mid-1970s further reduced her abilities, and in 1977, Beatrice Lillie announced her retirement from show business, via a press release issued by Philip. One of the last to see her before she moved back to Eng-

land was Helen Hayes, who had lived next door to Lillie on Manhattan's East End Avenue for many years. Hayes later wrote that Bea was too weak to raise her head, "unable to lift that proud, cocky carriage . . . that had so distinguished her." Indeed, Bea didn't seem to know who Helen was until Hayes mentioned Charlie MacArthur, Lillie's one-time lover and Hayes' husband, who had died more than 20 years before. "Slowly, Bea stretched a hand toward mine, took my hand, and touched it to her lips," Hayes recalled. A few days afterward, Lillie was taken home to England in the company of Philip and three nurses, and lived on in near seclusion until her death on January 20, 1989, at 94 years of age.

Although she is often cited as the originator of "camp" and the inspiration for the work of such performers as **Carol Burnett**, **Bette Midler**, and *Carol Channing*, Bea Lillie's greatest legacy was the laughter she brought to a world torn apart by two world wars. "Bygone days. Halcyon days," she once wrote of the years between those tragic conflicts. "We were convinced that the future stretched endlessly ahead of us into ever sunnier, happier times." Whenever she stepped onto a stage, for however short a time, that conviction came true.

SOURCES:

Hayes, Helen, with Katherine Hatch. *My Life In Three Acts*. NY: Harcourt, Brace, Jovanovich, 1990.

Laffey, Bruce. *The Funniest Woman in the World*. NY: Winwood Press, 1989.

Lillie, Beatrice, with John Philip and James Brough. *Every Other Inch a Lady*. Garden City, NY: Doubleday, 1972.

Norman Powers,
writer-producer, Chelsea Lane Productions, New York

Lilly, Kristine (b. 1971).

See Soccer: Women's World Cup, 1999.

Lily of the Mohawks (1656–1680).

See Tekakwitha, Kateri.

Lilya.

Variant of Lidia or Lidiya.

Limerick, countess of (1897–1981).

See Pery, Angela Olivia.

Lin, Nora (b. 1910).

See Alonso, Dora.

Lincoln, Almira Hart (1793–1884).

See Phelps, Almira Lincoln.

Lincoln, countess of (1281–1348).

See Lacy, Alice.

Lincoln, Mary Johnson

(1844–1921)

American educator and cookbook writer. Born Mary Johnson Bailey in Attleboro, Massachusetts, on July 8, 1844; died in Boston, Massachusetts, on December 2, 1921; second daughter and one of three children of the Reverend John Milton Burnham Bailey (a Congregational minister) and Sarah Morgan (Johnson) Bailey; graduated from Wheaton Female Seminary, Norton, Massachusetts (later Wheaton College), in 1864; married David A. Lincoln (a clerk), on June 21, 1865 (died 1894); no children.

The daughter of a Congregational minister who died when she was just a child, Mary Johnson Bailey Lincoln was born in 1844 in Attleboro, Massachusetts, and grew up there and in Norton, Massachusetts, where she attended Wheaton Female Seminary. Upon graduating in 1864, she taught for one term in a Vermont country school before her marriage to David A. Lincoln, a clerk who was also from Norton. The couple moved to Boston, and, although Lincoln remained childless, she busied herself with homemaking, church activities, and a literary club. When her husband became ill in 1870, threatening the family income, she took in sewing and did housework in the neighborhood.

In December 1879, Lincoln took a job teaching at the Boston Cooking School, which had opened the previous March under the auspices of the Woman's Educational Association of Boston. For the next five years, Lincoln taught classes of homemakers, cooks, nurses, and other teachers. She also compiled her *Boston Cook Book*, written ostensibly as a textbook for her classes. Containing curriculum outlines and information on chemistry, physiology, and hygiene, as well as a collection of recipes, it was published in 1884. The book was extremely popular and went through several editions.

Lincoln resigned from the Boston Cooking School in January 1885, citing family responsibilities. From 1885 to 1899, she taught cooking at Lasell Seminary in Auburndale, Massachusetts, during which time she also prepared three new publications: *Peerless Cook Book* (1886), *Boston School Kitchen Text-Book* (1887), and *Carving and Serving* (1887). Afterward, she devoted herself to writing and lecturing, frequently traveling to speaking engagements across the country. For ten years beginning in 1894 (the year her husband died), she was associated with *American Kitchen Magazine*, of which she was also part owner. Her column, "From Day to Day," was widely read, as were her books, the last of which, *What to Have for Luncheon*, was published in 1904. During her final few years, Lincoln suffered ill health, and she died at the age of 77, following a cerebral hemorrhage.

SOURCES:

James, Edward T., ed. *Notable American Women 1607–1950*. Cambridge, MA: The Belknap Press of Harvard University Press, 1971.

McHenry, Robert, ed. *Famous American Women*. NY: Dover, 1983.

Barbara Morgan,
Melrose, Massachusetts

Lincoln, Mary Todd (1818–1882)

First lady, wife of President Abraham Lincoln, who served as a leading Washington hostess during the Civil War and endured the deaths of her husband, father, three half-brothers, and three sons over a 16-year span. Born Mary Ann Todd on December 13, 1818, in Lexington, Kentucky; died in Springfield, Illinois, on July 16, 1882, of a stroke; daughter of Robert Smith Todd (a banker, farmer, manufacturer, and state legislator) and Eliza Ann (Parker) Todd; attended Shelby Female Academy, 1827–32; enrolled in Madame Mentelle's boarding school, 1832–36; took classes from Dr. John Ward, 1837–39; married Abraham Lincoln (a lawyer and later president of the United States), on November 4, 1842; children: Robert Todd Lincoln (b. August 1, 1843); Edward Baker Lincoln (b. March 10, 1846); William Wallace Lincoln (b. December 21, 1850); Thomas Lincoln (b. April 4, 1853).

Mother Eliza Todd died (July 1825); father married Elizabeth Humphreys (November 1, 1826); moved from Lexington to Springfield, Illinois (1839); moved with family to Washington, D.C. (1847–48); father died (July 16, 1849); son Edward died (February 1, 1850); moved to Washington after Abraham Lincoln elected president (1861); son William died (February 20, 1862); Abraham Lincoln died (April 15, 1865); moved to Chicago (May 1865); lived in Europe (1868–71); son Thomas died (July 15, 1871); declared insane (May 19, 1875) and placed in mental institution in Batavia, Illinois; released (September 10, 1875) and declared sane (June 15, 1876); lived in Europe (1876–80); returned to Springfield.

If a first lady desired to be remembered in her own right, she would not choose Abraham Lincoln as her spouse. Any of her own accomplishments and contributions would be dwarfed by the giant who walked beside her. But Mary Todd's love for Abraham Lincoln was eternal; she seemed convinced to the end of her life that she had chosen the right man and was proud of the huge shadow that he cast. At the same time, she strove to be someone besides Mrs. Abraham Lincoln. In that, she was successful.

Mary Todd's family background contrasted sharply with that of her famous husband's. Whereas Abraham Lincoln's parents had little, Mary Ann Todd, born on December 13, 1818, in Lexington, Kentucky, was the daughter of rather well-to-do parents, Robert and **Eliza Todd**. Her father was a "solid and leading citizen," who was a prominent businessman as well as a Kentucky state senator and clerk of the Kentucky House of Representatives. The Todds were socialites who mingled with those at the top of Lexington's social ladder. As a young girl, Mary became acquainted with the venerable Henry Clay. According to family tradition, she once said to Clay, "My father says you will be the next President of the United States. I wish I could go to Washington and live in the White House."

Eliza Todd died in early July 1825, when Mary was six. **Elizabeth Humphreys**, whose mother had long "ruled Frankfort society," became Mary's stepmother when, on November 1, 1826, she married Robert Todd in Frankfort, Kentucky. Unlike most males of that era, Robert believed that women as well as men should be well educated. Thus, in the fall of 1827, Mary began her formal education when she entered the Shelby Female Academy, more popularly called Ward's Academy after its founder John Ward, an Episcopalian cleric. There she learned the three R's while also studying history, geography, natural science, French, religion, as well as poetry which she memorized and loved to recite. She also became so adept at sewing that, having finished her homework, she would complete "the ten rounds of a cotton sock required of the girls each evening" before a cousin had begun her needlework. At age 14, Mary moved on to Madame Mentelle's boarding school where she became fluent in French as well as "an inspired dancer" who was "featherlight on her feet." Here she evolved into a poised young lady who moved with ease among those in Lexington's polite society.

In the summer of 1837, Mary Todd graduated and soon thereafter moved to Springfield, Illinois, where she lived with her sister **Frances Todd Wallace**, who had married Dr. William S. Wallace. After three months, Mary returned to Lexington where she took more classes with John Ward. Two years passed before she decided that Springfield was indeed where she wished to live, and in 1839 she traveled back to that city where she made her home with her sister **Eliza-beth Todd Edwards**, who had married Ninian W. Edwards.

Shortly after her return, Mary met Abraham Lincoln, a young, aspiring Springfield lawyer, at a dance. Mary saw qualities in this man that drew her to him; Abraham in turn took notice of Mary whose brother-in-law once said of her demeanor, "Mary could make a bishop forget his prayers." In time, their friendship resulted in marriage on November 4, 1842, at the Edwardses' home. Inside the bride's gold wedding band, the words "Love Is Eternal" were inscribed. Rather ironically, one of Mary's unsuccessful suitors was Stephen A. Douglas, who later defeated Lincoln in a race for the U.S. Senate and then lost to Lincoln when both vied for the U.S. presidency in 1860.

Springfield, Illinois, was to be Mary's home until she went to the White House in 1861. Since her husband was a man of very modest means, the young couple's first residence was an eight-dollar-a-week room at the Globe Tavern on the corner of Adams and Third. During the first year of their marriage, Lincoln's work frequently kept him on the road and away from home. Apparently, Mary was willing to accept this and encouraged her husband; one biographer notes that Abraham "frequently came to rely on the careful study she made of books and reports on political affairs while he was traveling the circuit." Mary, who observed that her husband rather haphazardly collected fees due him, "applied her bright wits" to improve this situation, for the Lincolns needed every penny owed them, especially after their first son Robert arrived on August 1, 1843.

Partially because of complaints by boarders at the Globe Tavern over baby Robert's cries, the Lincolns in the autumn of 1843 moved to a small three-room cottage at 214 South Fourth Street. About six months later, the family moved once more, to the only home the Lincolns ever owned. It still stands on the corner of Eighth and Jackson in Springfield.

The Springfield years seem to have been relatively happy for Mary. The family grew with the birth of Edward on March 10, 1846, William or Willie on December 21, 1850, and Thomas or Tad on April 4, 1853. Since her husband was frequently on the circuit, Mary had to assume significant responsibilities in rearing their sons. At the same time, she continued to promote her husband. "He is to be President of the United States some day," she told Ward Hill Lamon; "if I had not thought so, I never would have married him, for you can see he is not pretty. But look at him: Doesn't he look as if he would make a magnificent President?" Another time, she said affectionately that "people are perhaps not aware that his heart is as large as his arms are long." Lincoln in turn rarely spoke harshly to her, even though at times Mary was known to be temperamental and tempestuous.

When Abraham won election to the U.S. House of Representatives, Mary moved to Washington for a short time. The Lincoln family lived temporarily at Brown's Hotel and then in Mrs. **Ann G. Sprigg**'s boardinghouse, now the site of the Library of Congress. Although her husband's term did not end until the spring of 1849, Mary in 1848 returned to Kentucky to live in more comfortable quarters near Lexington. Here the Lincoln boys, wrote one biographer, "went wild with joy as they frolicked at their grandfather's country place." Mary missed her husband, once writing, "How much I wish, instead of writing, we were together this evening. I feel very sad away from you." In 1949, Abraham returned home, but Mary's joy was somewhat tempered when on July 6, 1849, her father died of cholera; less than a year later, on February 1, 1850, her son Eddie, not yet four years old, died of diphtheria.

It was always music in my ears, both before and after our marriage, when my husband told me that I was the only one he ever thought of, or cared for.

—**Mary Todd Lincoln**

Lincoln's interest in politics never waned, and Mary encouraged him. Though she used her influence in convincing him to decline an appointment as Oregon's territorial governor, she continued to dream that he would one day be president. In 1855, much to her chagrin, Lincoln lost an election to the U.S. Senate after leading on the first ballot. (At that time, senators were elected by the state legislatures and not popularly elected as they are now.) Although Lincoln shook the hand of the victor, Lyman Trumbull, Mary could not. She believed that her erstwhile friend, **Julia Jayne Trumbull**, should have persuaded Lyman to back Lincoln, who was only a few votes shy of a majority on the first roll call. To Mary Lincoln, Julia Trumbull now was a "whited Sepulchre," "unsympathizing" and "cold."

Jean Baker, one of Mary's biographers, maintains that after Abraham's 1855 defeat, "Mary Lincoln's emerging sense of herself as a political counselor appeared in her explanations of his policies." She made sure that her husband

was not perceived to be an abolitionist, for then he might be thought to be a radical. "All he desires is that slavery shall not be extended, let it remain where it is," said she. "Like a toothache," wrote William Herndon, Abraham Lincoln's old law partner, Mary kept "her husband awake to politics day and night." When Lincoln reportedly stated that nobody knew him, Mary retorted, "They soon will."

In 1858, when Abraham Lincoln, now a Republican, gained that party's nomination for U.S. Senator, his Democratic opponent was Mary's old beau, Stephen A. Douglas. In that summer of 1858, Douglas and Lincoln engaged in a series of memorable debates. Mary remained in Springfield, rooting for her husband, saying that Stephen Douglas was "a very little giant" compared to "my tall Kentuckian." Despite her efforts and those of her husband, Stephen Douglas won the election. Mary did not agree with her husband when he said that he now would "sink out of view, and shall be forgotten." Although by the end of the campaign, Lincoln had barely enough money to pay for household expenses, Mary thought it all "worthwhile"; by spring, said biographer *Ishbel Ross, both she and Lincoln "were again full of hope—or ambition." In 1860, the Republicans nominated Lincoln for president. There's "a little woman at our house" who would "like to hear this," he said after being informed. "I'll go down and tell her."

In Abraham's successful campaign, Mary Todd Lincoln made certain that both she and her husband projected an image acceptable to the public. She set out to prove that Lincolns were not "uncivilized boors," and she appeared to be successful. Said one veteran observer, "She chats quite nicely and will be able to adapt herself to the White House without difficulty." During the campaign, a little girl named **Grace Bedell** suggested that Lincoln grow a beard which in Grace's opinion would make him a more attractive candidate. Mary apparently agreed. Writes one of her biographers: "He would never have made such a drastic change in his appearance without her approval."

When Abraham Lincoln won the election in 1860, the Civil War was imminent. In December, South Carolina seceded from the Union, and in February 1861 the Confederacy was born. By the time Lincoln assumed office, seven states had seceded. Four more states followed after his March inauguration. Mary Lincoln "had expected a proud entry by her husband's side," writes Ishbel Ross. Instead, because of a report-

Mary
Todd
Lincoln

ed assassination plot, Abraham had to steal into Washington.

As the first lady, Mary experienced other frustrations, disappointments, and heartaches during the time the Lincolns occupied the White House. Because some of Mary's relatives cast their lot with the Confederacy, rumors persisted that she was a traitor or spy, one not committed to the same cause as her husband, which was to preserve the Union. There was absolutely no evidence for the stories that kept circulating.

Notes one of her biographers, Mary "stood firm as a rock behind her husband where the secessionists were concerned." Said Mary, "Why should I sympathize with the rebels? They would hang my husband tomorrow if it was in their power, and perhaps gibbet me with him. How then can I sympathize with a people at war with me and mine?"

In February 1862, the Lincolns lost a second son when Willie died. "It is hard, hard to have him die," murmured Lincoln. An old friend of Mary's claimed that after Willie's death, "She could not bear to look upon his picture. And after his death she never crossed the threshold of the Guest's Room in which he died, or the Green Room in which he was embalmed."

Death visited the Todd family frequently during the Civil War. All three of Mary's half brothers were killed. Sam died at the Battle of Shiloh; David was mortally wounded at Vicksburg; and "everybody's favorite," Aleck, met death in a skirmish near Baton Rouge, Louisiana. General Ben Hardin Helm, husband of her half-sister **Emilie Todd Helm**, died fighting at Chattanooga.

Mary's desire to bring back her family may have led to her acceptance of spiritualism and the world of the occult. In seances held in the White House, she claimed to have heard and seen her sons. On one occasion, she exclaimed to her sister Emilie, "Willie lives. He comes to me every night and stands at the foot of the bed with the same adorable smile he always has had. He does not always come alone. Little Eddie is sometimes with him." When, shortly before his death, Lincoln confided to her that his dreams indicated that death for him was imminent, Mary was horrified. She believed her husband, too, would soon be taken from her.

Despite the heavy burdens borne by both the Lincolns, Mary left her mark as first lady. She refurbished the White House, transforming "the President's House into an appropriate setting for the leader of a great nation." She believed that the residence of America's chief executive should be a home of which all Americans could be proud. Such a dwelling would impress foreigners and citizens alike and prove that America was a great nation and its leader should be held in high esteem.

As first lady, Mary, like *Dolley Madison before her, was intent on becoming Washington's premier host. Thus, she made frequent public appearances at twice-a-week winter and spring receptions held in the East Room of the White House. Levees were planned for New Year's Day and other holidays where guests from the Congress, the judiciary, the diplomatic corps, and the armed forces were properly entertained. Despite criticisms that the Civil War required curtailment of such events, "Mary Lincoln demonstrated through these social affairs the political point that the Union government, no matter what the Confederate government threatened, would remain in Washington." At these receptions, Mary dressed like a queen, setting the pace as far as fashions were concerned. "Mrs. Lincoln's bonnets were as much discussed as the President's stovepipe hats," wrote one commentator.

Although Mary Lincoln has been perceived by some to have been a shrew, concerned only with herself and her own reputation, there was another side of this first lady of which many were unaware. For example, she took the time to visit hospitals where wounded Union soldiers were convalescing. At least on one occasion she was influential in saving the life of a young soldier who had been sentenced to die for falling asleep while on picket duty. After conferring with General George B. McClellan about the execution, President Lincoln commuted the death sentence "by request of the 'Lady President.'" In the White House, her closest friend was *Elizabeth Keckley, an ex-slave and a mulatto. During the Civil War, thousands of Virginia slaves had made their way to Washington where they were now free but lived under abysmal conditions. Elizabeth Keckley convinced Mary Lincoln to take up their cause. Wrote Mary about these unfortunates: "These immense number of Contrabands are suffering intensely, many without bed covering and having to use any bits of carpeting to cover themselves—many dying of want." Both Mary and Elizabeth raised money for the Contraband Relief Association. Although Mary may not have influenced Lincoln's decision to issue the Emancipation Proclamation, she certainly strongly supported it.

In 1864, President Lincoln won reelection, and in March 1865 he began his second term. On April 9, 1865, General Robert E. Lee surrendered to General Ulysses S. Grant at Appomattox. The war was effectively over, but Mary's elation would be short-lived. On April 14, President and Mary Lincoln, accompanied by Major Henry Rathbone and his fiancée **Clara Harris**, attended the Ford Theater to enjoy the production *Our American Cousin*. During the performance, Mary placed her hand in Lincoln's, asking him what Clara might think of this show of affection. "She won't think anything of it," he responded. Shortly thereafter, John Wilkes

Booth stole into the president's box and, at a distance of two feet, shot the president. Lincoln, who was carried across the street to William Petersen's house, lingered through the long night. He died at 7:22 the next morning. Although Mary initially insisted her husband be buried in Chicago, she finally agreed that Springfield, Illinois, would be his final resting place. There the president was buried beside his two sons, Willie and Eddie.

"The ten years between 1865 and 1875 were desperate for poor Mary Todd Lincoln," writes Carl Sandburg. She never fully recovered from that night of horror. On May 22, 1865, she left the White House for the last time. Financial matters would plague her remaining years. Initially, Congress agreed to compensate her $22,000. In 1870, Congress would grant her a lifetime pension of $3,000 per year and, in 1882, Congress would raise the pension to $5,000 plus granting her a lump sum of $15,000 to meet any financial obligations such as medical bills.

For a while, she lived in Chicago with her sons, Robert and Tad. After attending the marriage of her son Robert to **Mary Harlan** on September 25, 1868, Mary and Tad sailed for Europe on October 1. In an effort to find peace of mind, Mary traveled extensively, living for a time in Frankfurt, Germany, later in Nice, France, and then in London. In the autumn of 1869, word came that Mary had become a grandmother. The infant daughter of Robert and Mary was named Mary Todd Lincoln. Mary obviously was pleased. Probably reflecting on her own life, she wrote to her daughter-in-law, "Trouble comes soon enough, my dear child, and you must enjoy life, whenever you can."

In May 1871, Mary and Tad Lincoln sailed home from Liverpool, England, returning to Chicago where they lived in the Clinton House. While aboard ship, Tad had caught a cold, and, although at times he seemed on the road to recovery, he never fully recuperated from a respiratory infection. On the morning of July 15, 18-year-old Tad Lincoln died. His mother, who had now lost her father, husband, three half-brothers, and three sons, mourned, "I feel that there is no life for me, without my idolized Taddie. One by one, I have consigned to their resting place my idolized ones, and now, in this world there is nothing left for me but the deepest anguish and desolation."

Following his mother's return from a vacation in Florida, Robert Lincoln became acutely aware that Mary was mentally ill. He knew of her delusions and hallucinations, but when he heard her say that someone had tried to poison her in Jacksonville, and that a "wandering Jew" she met in Florida had taken her pocketbook, he feared the worst. Other irrational comments and actions followed. On April 1, 1875, when Robert sought to restrain his 57-year-old mother from appearing half-dressed in the hotel lobby where she lived, Mary accused her son of trying to murder her.

Genuinely concerned about his mother's health and safety, Robert sought to have her declared insane and confined. After hearings in the Cook County court, the jurors stated that "having heard the evidence in the case," we "are satisfied that the said Mrs. Lincoln is insane, and is a fit person to be sent to a State Hospital for the Insane." Thereupon, she was confined to the Bellevue Nursing and Rest Home in Batavia, Illinois, from May 20 until September 10, 1875.

The news that a former first lady, especially Mrs. Lincoln, had been declared insane and then confined gave rise to much comment and controversy. Mary Lincoln had supporters who believed that Robert had ulterior motives when he sought to have his mother declared mentally incompetent. After four months, on September 19, 1875, with the help of her friend, *Myra Bradwell**, Mary Lincoln was released and went to live with her sister Elizabeth in Springfield. She spent the next nine months in the Edwardses' house where she had married Abraham Lincoln many years before.

After the court ruled that Mary had regained her sanity, she was again free to move about. In 1879, she traveled to Europe for the second time. In the last years of her life, she seems to have been happier than she had been for a long time. Perhaps the reconciliation that she effected with Robert after a May 1881 visit gave her the most satisfaction. One writer claimed that if she had reservations about reconciling with her son, "she was won all over again by his small daughter" who bore Mary's name. A little more than a year later, Mary was back home in Springfield. She died there on July 16, 1882. "Her death was very sudden and unexpected to me," said Robert, "but it was a painless release from much mental and bodily distress. I have a great satisfaction that a year ago I broke down the personal barrier which her disturbed mind had caused her to raise between us, so that in the end her estrangement had ceased."

A controversial first lady, Mary Lincoln was often vilified because of her forceful, vivacious personality, a personality quite distinct from her husband's. She "was the first wife of a President to become a storm center while she was in the White House," wrote Paul Boller, although, as history has shown, she was by no means the last.

SOURCES:

Angle, Paul M., and Carl Sandburg. *Mary Lincoln, Wife and Widow.* Part I by Carl Sandburg. Part II by Paul Angle. NY: Harcourt, Brace, 1932.

Baker, Jean H. *Mary Todd Lincoln.* NY: W.W. Norton, 1987.

Boller, Paul. *Presidential Wives.* NY: Oxford University Press, 1988.

Randall, Ruth Painter. *Lincoln's Sons.* Boston, MA: Little, Brown, 1955.

———. *Mary Lincoln: Biography of a Marriage.* Boston, MA: Little, Brown, 1953.

Ross, Ishbel. *The President's Wife: Mary Todd Lincoln.* NY: Putnam, 1973.

Thomas, Benjamin P. *Abraham Lincoln.* NY: Alfred A. Knopf, 1952.

SUGGESTED READING:

Donald, David Herbert. *Lincoln.* NY: Simon and Schuster, 1995.

Evans, W.A. *Mrs. Abraham Lincoln: A Study of Her Personality and Her Influence on Lincoln.* NY: Alfred A. Knopf, 1932.

Helm, Katherine. *The True Story of Mary, Wife of Lincoln.* NY: Harper and Brothers, 1928.

Oates, Stephen B. *With Malice Toward None: The Life of Abraham Lincoln.* NY: Harper and Row, 1977.

Turner, Justin G., and Linda Levitt Turner. *Mary Todd Lincoln: Her Life and Letters.* NY: Alfred A. Knopf, 1972.

RELATED MEDIA:

*Julie Harris played Mary Todd Lincoln in James Prideaux's play *The Last of Mrs. Lincoln* (1972).

Robert Bolt,
Professor of History, Calvin College, Grand Rapids, Michigan

Lind, Jenny (1820–1887)

Swedish singer considered to be the greatest soprano of her day. Name variations: Madame Goldschmidt; Jenny Lind-Goldschmidt. Pronunciation: the i in Lind pronounced as in win. Born Johanna Maria Lind on October 6, 1820, in Stockholm, Sweden; died of cancer at home in Malvern Hills, Shropshire, England, on November 2, 1887; illegitimate daughter of Niclas Jonas Lind (a bookkeeper) and Anna Marie Fellborg Lind (a schoolmistress); instructed at her mother's private school for girls in Stockholm and the Swedish Royal Opera School, Stockholm; married Otto Goldschmidt (a pianist), on February 4, 1852; children: Walter Otto Goldschmidt; Jenny Goldschmidt Maude; Ernst Goldschmidt.

Made first stage appearance at age ten in The Polish Mine; *appeared in first operatic role as Alice in Meyerbeer's* Robert le diable *(1838); made formal operatic debut in Sweden as Agathe in Weber's* Der Freischutz *(1838); was a regular member of the Swedish Academy of Music (1840); made Berlin debut in title*

role of Norma *(1844); made Viennese debut as Norma (1846); made London debut as Alice (1847); retired as an opera singer (1849); toured U.S. as a concert singer (1850–52); moved to Dresden after her marriage (1852), then to London (1858); appeared in oratorio and concert performances throughout Europe (1852–83); was a professor of singing at the Royal College of Music (1883–87); lived in Malvern Hills, Shropshire (1883–87).*

A boisterous crowd converged on the area around the Canal Street pier in New York harbor on September 1, 1850. It was Sunday, and most New Yorkers were off from work. Between 30,000 and 40,000 people took advantage of their day of rest to await the S.S. *Atlantic*, arriving from Liverpool, England. Around 1 PM, the crowd heard a two-gun salute and the flag went up announcing the arrival of the ship. The excitement built as the *Atlantic* arrived at the dock and secured the gangway. As people surged forward to get a close look at the celebrity who had brought them to the pier, some onlookers were knocked into the water. Moments later, a gate gave way and dozens of bystanders were trampled, leading to some serous injuries. "Lindomania" had come to American shores, a fever that refused to relinquish its grip for 21 months.

During this period, Jenny Lind, the "Swedish Nightingale," embarked on the most spectacular concert tour in U.S. history, performing for 135 audiences. Countless items were named after the most beloved singer of the age, from pianos to sausages. Schools and streets still bear her name. During the 19th century, no visit by a prominent foreigner prompted more excitement, or had a more lasting effect, than the tour of the Swedish soprano. Even more so than in Europe, which had already experienced its share of "Jenny Lind Fever," America simply went mad over the extraordinary singer.

It is one of the inspiring stories of the 19th century how a rather unpretentious girl from the poor section of Stockholm became one of the most-loved figures of the age. Born Johanna Maria Lind on October 6, 1820, Jenny was the second daughter of **Anna Marie Fellborg**. Anna Marie had married a young army officer in 1810, Erik Johan Radberg, but secured a divorce on grounds of infidelity two years later. Under her maiden name, she opened a school for girls on the third floor of her house, and struggled to support herself and her first daughter **Amelia Radberg**. The discovery that she was pregnant with the child of Niclas Jonas Lind, the amiable though notably unambitious son of a lace manufacturer, was not a happy event. She gave birth secretly, then sent Jenny 15 miles away to the home of Carl Ferndal, a distant cousin in Ed-Sollentuna who served as the parish clerk and organist in the church.

By the time she was four, Jenny was back in her mother's home, though her maternal grandmother, **Fru Tengmark**, played a larger role in raising her. The grandmother also encouraged the girl's interest in music. When Jenny was nine, a dancer at the Royal Opera House heard her sing and helped secure an audition at the Swedish Royal Theater. The brilliance of Jenny's crystal-clear voice immediately won her a position in the Theater School, where she was the youngest ever admitted. Jenny received lessons in acting and dance while court singer Isak Berg helped with her early musical training. Assigned as her singing master in 1831, Berg sang duets with her at various informal and formal events, which helped introduce Jenny to Stockholm society.

Jenny Lind's first appearance on stage was in 1830, as the seven-year-old Angela in the Royal Theater production of the melodrama *The Polish Mine*. Over the next three years, she appeared in dozens of performances and received excellent reviews for her acting. Though her voice weakened a bit when she was 13, she remained at the Royal Theater School. By 1837, she had appeared on the stage 111 times. More important, her voice regained its strength.

During this period, troubles with her mother plagued the young artist. Anna Marie possessed a fierce temper and demanded perfection from those around her, especially young Jenny. When she was 14, Jenny left Anna Marie's home to live at the Opera House. After her parents finally married in May 1835, they sued the school for custody of their only daughter, a decision they won in court in the summer of 1836. Returning home against her will, Jenny found her mother prepared to make amends for some of the neglect and ill-treatment of the past. Older sister Amelia had died suddenly in 1835, shortly after being married. Jenny was the only daughter Anna Marie had left, and she seemed committed to treating Jenny with more kindness and respect. Though the relationship between mother and daughter remained better than before, disagreements often pushed the two apart. "Papa" Niclas was a decent man who tried to patch up differences, but the unassertive Swede was unable to exert much influence over his strong-willed wife.

Even before the ten years was up on her original contract, the Royal Theater placed Jenny on salary as an actress in January 1837. She appeared in 92 roles in that year, including as Daphne in Victor Hugo's *Angelo Malipieri* and as the Second Genius in Mozart's *Magic Flute*. When the Theater decided to present the fourth act of Giacomo Meyerbeer's opera, *Robert le diable,* Jenny was chosen to sing the part of Alice and received rave reviews from excited audiences. This led to her appearance as the lead soprano, Agathe, in Carl Maria von Weber's *Der Freischutz*, and a resulting meteoric rise to prima donna status in Sweden.

Between her first appearance as Agathe on March 7, 1838, and the summer of 1841, Jenny Lind became the new idol of Swedish opera. In addition to Alice and Agathe, she also sang the title role of Weber's *Euryanthe*, Julia in Spontini's *La Vestale*, Donna Anna in Mozart's *Don Giovanni*, and Lucia in Donizetti's *Lucia di Lammermoor*. The natural brilliance of the soprano's voice, particularly its spectacular top register, brought her fame. She was also hailed as a fine actress. But it would be Jenny's unpreten-

Jenny Lind

tious and unsophisticated personal style that made her a star—first in Sweden, and later outside her homeland. She stood a very thin 5'4", with rather plain, though very expressive, facial features. Emphasizing her youthfulness, she wore her ash-blonde hair parted in the middle, with tight curls on the sides of her forehead. She attended social events without cosmetics, attired in simple dresses. In conversation, she spoke honestly and directly, often revealing a natural timidness. Jenny Lind hardly proved to be the typical prima donna.

After a grueling schedule of performing, by 1841 Jenny Lind's voice began to deteriorate from fatigue. Her friend, the Italian baritone Giovanni Belletti, convinced her to seek the assistance of the great voice teacher Manuel Garcia. In July, Jenny went to Paris to meet with Garcia, who concluded that her voice was, indeed, badly damaged from overuse at a young age. After prescribed rest for three months, Jenny began an intensive ten-month period of training. She lived in a boarding house and paid for two lessons a week. Garcia believed that Jenny had never learned to breathe properly, a flaw that would destroy her voice if not corrected. As Jenny wrote to a friend: "I have to begin again, from the beginning; to sing scales, up and down, slowly, and with great care; then, to practice the shake—awfully slowly; and to try to get rid of the hoarseness, if possible. Moreover, he is very particular about the breathing."

It was not her wonderful execution, her pathos, varying expression, subtle flexibility, that surprised me, but the pure timbre which so vibrated and thrilled my very soul that tears came into my eyes.

—John Addington Symonds

Upon her return to Stockholm, she sang the title role in Bellini's *Norma* on October 10, 1842. Following the intense training with Garcia, her voice ranged two and three quarter octaves, from B below the stave to C on the fourth line above it. Both audiences and critics hailed the improvement. She added new roles, including Valentine in Meyerbeer's *Les Huguenots*, Susanna in Mozart's *Le nozze di Figaro*, and Amina in Bellini's *La sonnambula*. The latter role, first performed on March 1, 1843, would quickly become a favorite with audiences.

Though reluctant to sing outside of Sweden, Jenny performed at the Danish Royal Theater in 1843. While staying in Denmark, she spent a good deal of time with children's author Hans Christian Andersen, who fell in love with her. Though she rejected Andersen's frequent marriage proposals, the writer penned three stories inspired by his friendship with her: "The Angel," "The Emperor's Nightingale," and "The Ugly Duckling." Andersen helped introduce Jenny to the rest of Europe by suggesting to Giacomo Meyerbeer that Jenny Lind would be right for the part of Vielka in his new opera, *Ein Feldager in Schlesian*. Meyerbeer agreed—he had heard her sing while she studied in Paris with Garcia—and Jenny journeyed to Berlin and Dresden to prepare for the role, an effort which included perfecting her German. After a controversy involving a demand by her understudy to create the role of Vielka, the opera closed down in five days, before Jenny could sing the part. The Berlin public demanded to hear the Swedish soprano sing, however, and she made her triumphant debut on December 15 in *Norma*. Signed to a six-month engagement by the Prussian Royal Opera, she finally got to sing Vielka, and a wonderful performance of the part written for her revived Meyerbeer's composition. The rest of her German tour of 1844 was received with great excitement. By year's end, the simple Swedish girl from modest beginnings was Europe's new sensation.

During 1845 and 1846, Jenny forged a close friendship with the great composer and pianist Felix Mendelssohn. She sang to a frenzied crowd at one of his Gewandhaus concerts in Leipzig on December 4, 1845. Recognizing her genius, he subsequently provided guidance in important career decisions for the emerging star. It was Mendelssohn, for instance, who convinced Jenny to travel to London in the spring of 1847. It was no easy task to get her to Britain, however, as Jenny harbored a terrible fear of performing for English audiences. Finally, after rumors circulated that she would never sing again, she agreed to a date for her debut.

The resulting spectacle was a first for London's theatergoers. When the doors to Her Majesty's Theater opened on the evening of May 4, the crowd surged forward in a mad crush. Men were knocked into walls and the gowns of respectable ladies were crumpled, ripped, and, in some cases, torn off. In the presence of excited fans, as well as Queen *Victoria, Prince Albert, the Queen Dowager (*Adelaide of Saxe-Meiningen), and the Duchess of Kent (*Victoria of Coburg), Jenny performed Alice in *Robert le diable*. The audience continued to act wildly, barely letting the performance conclude. They were there to hear Jenny Lind, and seemed completely disinterested in anyone else singing. The queen wrote in her diary: "The great event of the

Jenny
Lind

evening was Jenny Lind's appearance and her complete triumph. She has a most exquisite, powerful and really quite peculiar voice, so round, soft, and flexible[,] and her acting is charming and touching and very natural." The *Illustrated London News* reviewed her performance in glowing terms and may have captured the essence of Jenny's natural appeal. "Were it even possible to detect a flaw in her voice," its critic noted, "her singing would still be resistless, for it reaches the heart, and touches the deepest chords of human feeling."

During the 1847 opera season in London, Jenny sang Amina, Norma, and Susanna. She also created the role of Amalia in Verdi's *I masnadieri*, which was well received. After the season, she toured Great Britain, including visits to Brighton, Manchester, Liverpool, Glasgow, Exeter, and Bath. As she arrived in each city for a concert, the church bells rang and an adoring public turned out to see the "Swedish Nightingale," as she was commonly known by this point. They loved her voice, but they also adored the simple, honest, pure woman who sang so beautifully.

After a triumphant year in England and Scotland, Jenny Lind returned home to Stockholm, welcomed as a national hero. What should have been a happy and restful time for the 27-year-old star turned tragic quickly, however. On November 4, her professional and personal guide, Felix Mendelssohn, died suddenly of a stroke at age 38. His death, coupled with her acceptance of a marriage proposal from her long-time friend, Julius Gunther, a German tenor of Swedish family background, accelerated Jenny's not-so-secret desire to leave the stage. Nonetheless, she would go to England for the 1848 season, where she sang Lucia in *Lucia di Lammermoor*, and Elvira in *I puritani*, among other roles. She also took another tour of the provinces at the end of the season, including a stop in Dublin. Many of her 1848 concerts were charity events for hospitals, scholarships, and similar causes. For a second year, Great Britain remained under the spell of Lindomania.

The public's fear that Jenny Lind would fulfill her wish to leave the stage came true the following year. The singer broke off her engagement to Gunther as their relationship soured, and accepted a new one from a 23-year-old captain in the British army, Claudius Harris. A deeply religious man, the puritanical Harris and his controlling mother condemned "the theater [as] a temple of Satan, and all the actors priests of the Devil," as Jenny herself described their views. Looking for reasons to reinforce her own desire to leave the rigors of the stage and live a more settled life, Lind consented. She agreed to give six farewell performances at Her Majesty's Theater in 1849. On May 10, Jenny Lind sang in *Robert le diable* as Alice. It was her 677th performance. The Swedish Nightingale had sung operas in her native tongue, German, Italian, French, and English for ten years, five as a star known throughout the world. After that evening, she never appeared again on the operatic stage.

Jenny Lind did not retire from public performances in 1849, of course, nor did she make the mistake of marrying Claudius Harris. For the rest of her career, she preferred to perform as a recitalist and oratorio singer. Near the end of 1849, she agreed reluctantly to meet with John Hall Wilton, sent by the American promoter Phineas Taylor Barnum to bring the Swedish Nightingale to the United States. Barnum had never heard Lind sing, but he wished to transform his own image from that of crass showman and promoter to a man who brought culture across the Atlantic. As he said in his memoirs, "Inasmuch as my name had long been associated with 'humbug' and the American public suspected my capabilities did not extend beyond the power to exhibit a stuffed monkey, I [committed to] bringing to this country, in the zenith of her life and celebrity, the greatest musical wonder in the world."

Lind shrewdly negotiated her own contract for $150,000 for at least 100 concerts, plus a salary for a secretary, accompanist, and male singer. She insisted the supporting artists be Jules Benedict and baritone Giovanni Belletti. The total payment of $187,000 was deposited in a London bank before Jenny set sail on the *Atlantic*. Barnum struggled mightily to promote his European celebrity to a somewhat uninformed, initially apathetic American public. The commotion on the docks when Jenny disembarked signaled that he had achieved some measure of success—and the excitement mounted rapidly.

Ten days after her arrival in New York, Jenny performed at Castle Garden, next to Battery Park. The doors opened three hours before the scheduled concert, 8 PM. Entrance to the event was orderly, and the program went off on time. After the preliminary musical program, Benedict led Jenny, dressed in white with a blue belt, to the stage. To the enthralled audience, she sang a number of her favorite operatic pieces, then some Scandinavian folk songs. The applause was thunderous as she left the stage. When Barnum announced to the crowd that Jenny was giving the proceeds of the concert to charity, her place in the heart of Americans was fixed. Lindomania hit great heights in the coming weeks.

Even more so than in England, all sorts of commodities came to bear the name "Jenny Lind" during her lengthy tour of the United States. Cakes, gloves, bonnets, chairs, cigars, tea kettles, chewing gum, and pianos were named after her. A clipper ship, *the Nightingale*, designed and built by Samuel Hanscomb, Jr., of Portsmouth, New Hampshire, was completed in 1851 in honor of the Swedish visitor. In San Francisco, which suffered from extreme "Lind fever" though she never considered a West-

Coast trek, a 65-ton bay steamboat was named in her honor. Unfortunately, this vessel suffered a terrible explosion in April 1853 that killed or severely injured nearly all on board.

On a more positive note, Lind received an avalanche of gifts from American admirers. She also spent an hour at the White House with President Millard Fillmore before her much anticipated first concert at the new—in fact, unfinished—National Theater on December 16, 1850. With most prominent national politicians in attendance, Jenny began the program with "Hail Columbia." When she reached the chorus, Secretary of State Daniel Webster rose to his feet and with his grand bass voice joined in. The crowd loved the unplanned duet. Jenny had wished to end the program in Washington with an American song, and Barnum suggested "Home, Sweet Home," by lyricist John Howard Payne and composer Henry R. Bishop. "Home, Sweet Home" was an old staple with wide international circulation that dated back to 1823. It had been written for a long forgotten opera, *Clari*, and Payne and Bishop had received little money and less recognition from the piece. But Payne sat in attendance that night in Washington, and when Jenny began singing she directed her voice toward the aging Bostonian. When she finished a spectacular rendition of his song, the patrons sat in awe, wiping tears from their eyes. No one clapped. Only when Payne stood and bowed did the audience stand to cheer wildly. "Home, Sweet Home" became the most popular song in America. Lind sang it at every subsequent concert, usually more than once.

After a series of triumphant appearances in New York, Boston, and Washington, Jenny Lind gave concerts throughout the South, including Richmond, Wilmington, Charleston, New Orleans, and in cities along the Mississippi. She went to Cincinnati, Pittsburgh, and Philadelphia, then back to New York in late spring 1851. Most of these engagements were sold out, and the excitement generated by her appearances proved unprecedented. All this would change, though, during the second half of the tour. Tired of the flamboyant publicity that often accompanied her concerts and concerned about the high price of tickets, Lind terminated her contract with Barnum on June 9 by paying a $7,000 forfeit fee. She continued to tour at a more leisured pace, visiting cities in New England, New York State, Ohio, and Canada during the rest of 1851 and early 1852. Without the work of the master publicist Barnum and his professional staff, Jenny rarely sold out her remaining concerts, about 40 in all.

After the break with Barnum, her orchestra director and accompanist, Jules Benedict, returned home for health reasons. Jenny needed to hire a new accompanist, and turned to Otto Goldschmidt, a young German who had worked with her in Europe on occasion. A Mendelssohn student at the Leipzig Conservatory who worshiped Lind from afar, Otto was hardly without talent. But he was prone to playing long classical piano solos and had a stiff, tepid stage presence which American audiences found dull. Jenny believed he was a great musician, and grew closer and closer personally to the 21-year-old pianist as they performed together. On February 4, 1852, Jenny and Otto were married in Boston at the home of businessman Samuel Gray Ward. The union caused quite a stir in the newspapers because the wedding was a shock to all, and because Otto was such an uncharismatic figure.

The Goldschmidts resided in Northampton, Massachusetts, during most of the time they remained in the United States. Lind gave a few concerts in New England and New York before her departure on May 29, making her final appearance at Castle Garden on May 24. The final concerts had not been received with the interest of two years before, and only 2,000 fans saw Jenny off at the docks as she left for England, again on the *Atlantic*. The tour had been a great success in many ways; other European performers began touring the United States regularly, American musical tastes were forever transformed, and Jenny Lind and P.T. Barnum each made a great deal of money. Lind's departure from the United States, however, proved somewhat anticlimactic. Lindomania had already run its course.

After the exhausting American tour, Jenny rested for a lengthy period in Dresden. Her mother had died while Jenny was in America, so she saw little reason to return to Sweden. She did not perform again for a year and a half, taking extra time away from singing during her first pregnancy and the subsequent birth of her son, Walter Otto, in September 1854. Two other children would follow: Jenny in 1857 and Ernst in 1861. For the rest of her life, Jenny lived with her family in Germany and England, the two places where she delivered most of her musical performances. Having amassed considerable wealth in the brief period of 1846 to 1852, she often dedicated performances to charity. Her tours were less frequent and usually limited in duration.

Though she continued to sing arias and duets from selected operas at some concerts, she increasingly limited performances to the famous oratorios of Hayden, Mendelssohn, and especially Handel. Most critics agreed that her voice was at its greatest between the mid-1840s and her return from America. But she still impressed listeners with her beautiful singing for many decades afterward. Her voice never lost the qualities that moved audiences to heights of emotion. As **Lady Frederick Cavendish** observed in 1863, "I suppose her high notes are a little gone, but the matchless expression and heart-feeling can never go out of her voice, and there is a ringing purity of tone unlike anything else." For years, people continued to remark that one of their life's most treasured moments was hearing Jenny Lind sing.

Jenny and Otto transplanted the family to London in 1858 and, after a few years moving from apartment to apartment, built a lavish home overlooking Wimbledon Park in 1864. Ten years later, they bought a large house in South Kensington, where they remained until 1883 when Otto and Jenny, the children grown, moved into a country cottage in Malvern Hills, Shropshire. That same year, Jenny gave her last public performance, at age 63, and "retired" to become professor of singing at the Royal College of Music in London. Her health remained relatively good until she was diagnosed with cancer and suffered a stroke in the fall of 1887. She died at home in Malvern Hills on November 2.

Over a hundred years after her death, the name "Jenny Lind" is still associated with singing greatness. Perhaps no performer of the 19th century had a more lasting impact on European and American society. Thousands of visitors to Westminster Abbey still pause at the site of her memorial in the Poet's Corner, beneath that of Handel. They gaze at the plaque that shows the head in profile of the simple and decent artist, wishing they were privileged to hear for themselves the awe-inspiring voice of the great "Swedish Nightingale."

SOURCES:

Shultz, Gladys Denny. *Jenny Lind, the Swedish Nightingale.* Philadelphia, PA: J.B. Lippincott, 1962.

Wagenknecht, Edward. *Jenny Lind.* Boston, MA: Houghton Mifflin, 1931.

Ware, W. Porter, and Thaddeus C. Lockard, Jr. *The Lost Letters of Jenny Lind.* London: Victor Gollancz, 1966.

SUGGESTED READING:

Barnum, Phineas Taylor. *Struggles and Triumphs, or Forty Years' Recollections of P.T. Barnum.* Buffalo, NY: The Courier Company, 1875.

Maude, Jenny. *The Life of Jenny Lind by Her Daughter.* London: Cassell, 1926.

John M. Craig,
Professor of History, Slippery Rock University, Slippery Rock, Pennsylvania, author of *Lucia Ames Mead and the American Peace Movement* and numerous articles on activist American women

Lindbergh, Anne Morrow (1906—)

*American poet, novelist, and aviator, particularly known for sensitive autobiographical observations and philosophical insights. Born Anne Spencer Morrow on June 22, 1906, in Englewood, New Jersey; daughter of Dwight Whitney Morrow (an investment banker and later ambassador to Mexico and U.S. Senator) and Elizabeth Cutter Morrow (later board chair and acting president, Smith College); Smith College, A.B., 1928; married Charles Augustus Lindbergh, Jr. (an aviation pioneer), on May 27, 1929 (died August 26, 1974); children: Charles Augustus Lindbergh, Jr. (1930–1932, killed in infancy); Jon Lindbergh (b. 1932); Land Lindbergh (b. 1937); **Anne Spencer Lindbergh** (1940–1993, who wrote 14 books for middle-graders and young adults as well as the novel* Nick of Time*); Scott Lindbergh (b. 1942);* **Reeve Lindbergh** *(b. 1945, who wrote the autobiographical novel,* The Names of the Mountains, *and the reminiscence of her youth in Darien, Connecticut,* Under a Wing).*

Selected writings: North to the Orient *(Harcourt, Brace, 1935);* Listen! the Wind *(Harcourt, Brace, 1938);* The Wave of the Future: A Confession of Faith *(Harcourt, Brace, 1940);* The Steel Ascent *(Harcourt, Brace, 1944);* Gift from the Sea *(Pantheon, 1955);* The Unicorn and Other Poems, 1935–1955 *(Pantheon, 1956);* Dearly Beloved: A Theme and Variations *(Harcourt, Brace, 1962);* Earth Shine *(Harcourt, Brace, 1969);* Bring Me a Unicorn: Diaries and Letters, 1922–1928 *(Harcourt Brace Jovanovich, 1972);* Hour of Gold, Hour of Lead: Diaries and Letters, 1929–1932 *(Harcourt Brace Jovanovich, 1973);* Locked Rooms and Open Doors: Diaries and Letters, 1933–1935 *(Harcourt Brace Jovanovich, 1974);* The Flower and the Nettle: Diaries and Letters, 1936–1939 *(Harcourt Brace Jovanovich, 1976);* War Within and Without: Diaries and Letters, 1939–1944 *(Harcourt Brace Jovanovich, 1980).*

On February 1, 1937, Charles and Anne Morrow Lindbergh, having left Reading, England, en route to Rome, were lost in the air. Their craft was a British-made Miles Mohawk, a monoplane. Suddenly in the midst of the hazardous Italian Alps, Charles looked at his map, shook his head, and reversed the plane's direction. Anne shouted, "This is a hell of a place to get lost!" Both knew there might be time to pull out. They also knew they might hook a wing on the side of a mountain. Finally, Charles put on his goggles and turned to his wife, asking as he began his blind descent, "Got your belt on?" Anne later wrote in her journal:

I nod. Yes, that means be prepared for anything. Very likely death. . . . We start turning. The flaps are out, a quiver of sensation as we go under. There is no turning back. We must go through it now. Nothing to do but wait. Down in the mist, darkly. . . . I do not mind dying. I am glad for our life.

The couple eventually spotted the coast of Genoa and landed safely in Pisa. Within a year, Anne Morrow Lindbergh was at work on a novella concerning the incident, one published in 1944 under the title *The Steep Ascent*. She communicated a curious sensation she felt through the persona of a leading character, Eve:

This then was life: not to be hurried, not to be afraid, not to be imprisoned in oneself. To be open, aware, vulnerable—even to fear, even to pain, even to death. Then only did one feel ecstasy filling one up to the brim.

On June 22, 1906, Anne Spencer Morrow was born in Englewood, New Jersey. Her mother ❧ **Elizabeth Cutter Morrow** was an extremely active writer and civic leader. Her father Dwight Whitney Morrow was a hard-driving, intensely ambitious banker, a partner in the firm of J.P. Morgan. Anne grew up serious, sensitive, and withdrawing, a girl who felt much overshadowed by her highly talented family. She

❧▶
See sidebar on the following page

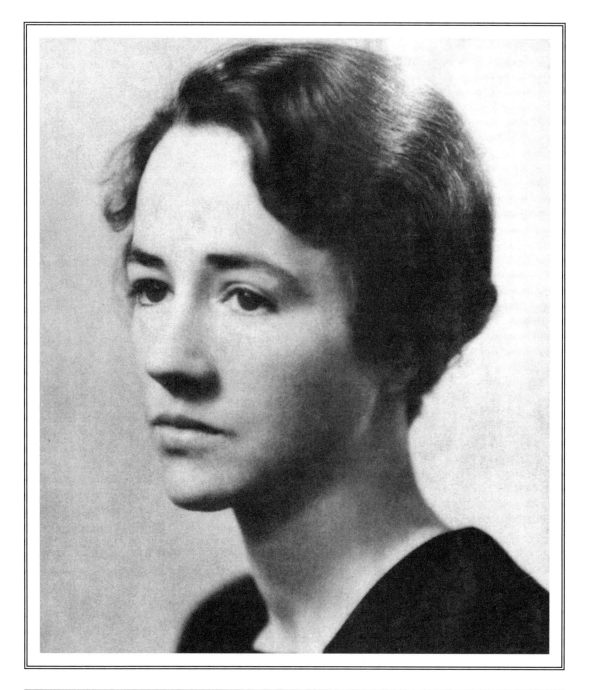

*A*nne
*M*orrow
*L*indbergh

❦▶ Morrow, Elizabeth Cutter (1873–1955)

American author and educator. Born Elizabeth Reeve Cutter in Cleveland, Ohio, on May 29, 1873; died on January 23, 1955; daughter of Charles Long and Annie E. (Spencer) Cutter; graduated from Smith College in 1896; further studied at the Sorbonne and in Florence, Italy; married Dwight W. Morrow (then a lawyer, later U.S. Senator and ambassador to Mexico), on June 16, 1903; children: *Anne Morrow Lindbergh (b. 1906); *Elisabeth Reeve Morgan (d. 1934); Constance Cutter Morrow; Dwight Morrow, Jr.

After her husband was appointed ambassador to Mexico, Elizabeth Cutter Morrow wrote many articles about the Mexican scene, including *The Painted Pig* (1930), a story for children; four other juvenile books followed. Made acting president of Smith in 1939, she became the first woman to head that college since its founding. Deeply opposed—though without naming names—to the isolationist views of her famous son-in-law, in 1940 she advocated repeal of the neutrality law and urged the government to send munitions and supplies to the Allies. "There are some things worse than war. There are some things supreme and noble that are worth fighting for." Active throughout the war years with War Fund drives, speechmaking, and the U.S.O., Morrow was also hopeful of the "Lasting Effects of Women's War Activities." Never before in history, she claimed, had women's potential been so recognized. On campuses, women were being trained in subjects seldom offered. Morrow urged that this continue in the postwar period, pleading for a "wider distribution of responsibility."

SUGGESTED READING:

Current Biography Yearbook. NY: H.W. Wilson, 1943.

❦▶

Houdetot,

Sophie d'. *See Épinay, Louise d' for sidebar.*

later wrote: "I was the youngest, shiest, most self-conscious adolescent that—I believe—ever lived." The slender brunette attended the Chapin School in New York City, but only began blossoming at Smith College, where she received distinction as a writer and poet. Essays on women in the time of Samuel Johnson and on Madame ◀❦ **Sophie d'Houdetot**, a woman who frequented the 18th-century French court, won two of the college's major literary prizes. In 1928, *Scribner's Magazine* published her poem "Height."

Never again would Anne's life be so tranquil. In late December 1928, her father—then U.S. ambassador to Mexico—sought to alleviate major tensions between the two nations by asking Charles Augustus Lindbergh, Jr. to fly his *Spirit of St. Louis* from New York to Mexico City. Because of his solo fight from New York to Paris in May 1927, the 26-year-old Charles had suddenly become the most famous person in the

world. During a visit to the Morrow residence, the retiring Charles took Anne on two flights, even giving her some basic instruction. It soon became known that the couple had fallen in love. Because of a natural desire for privacy at a time when Charles was literally besieged everywhere by admirers, the Morrow family arranged for a clandestine marriage at its Englewood residence on May 27, 1929.

Neither Anne nor Charles enjoyed being considered public property and hated the fact that crowds followed them everywhere. "I felt like an escaped convict," she later wrote. "This was not freedom." Indeed, "fame is a kind of death; it arrests life around you." Yet the couple were devoted to each other. Although for years Charles was definitely the dominant figure in the marriage, Anne felt liberated from the anxieties of adolescence. During a speech given in 1979, she said, "My husband always believed in me—believed in what I could do."

In the first year and a half of their marriage, the couple made eight transcontinental survey flights. Their planes were single-engine craft, poorly equipped for instrument flying and often dependent upon ground sighting. In September 1929, they flew from Florida to Central and South America with Pan American Airways president Juan Trippe. In April 1930, the Lindberghs set a transcontinental speed record by flying from Los Angeles to New York in under 15 hours. All this time, Anne was becoming an accomplished aviator. In January 1930, she became the first American woman to be awarded a first-class glider pilot's license. She later confessed that initial fears concerning her first takeoff gave way to "an ecstatic experience I have never forgotten or regretted." By May 1931, when Anne had received her private pilot's license, she had flown solo, and afterwards mastered high-frequency radio, navigation, and Morse code.

In July 1931, the Lindberghs began a round-the-world flight to see if the Great Circle route, close to the Arctic, was suitable for commercial flight. Beginning in Long Island, they made stops at Manitoba, the Northwest Territories, Alaska, Siberia, Japan, and China. During the trip, the plane was forced down three times. While in Nanjing (Nanking), the couple engaged in emergency flood relief. Near the walled city of Hinghwa, they were besieged by hundreds of starving Chinese about to sink their aircraft, who retreated only when Charles fired a pistol in the air. Another time, when the plane was beginning to turn over, the couple had to jump into rushing water. The trip was suddenly terminated in October while the Lindberghs were in Shanghai. Dwight Morrow, then U.S. senator from New Jersey and possible Republican presidential candidate, had unexpectedly died of a cerebral hemorrhage.

During these flights, Anne was co-pilot and navigator. At the outset of the Asian trip, when Charles was accused of needlessly exposing his wife to danger in Hudson Bay country, he replied, "You must remember that *she* is *crew*." Anne asked herself, "Have I then reached a stage where I am considered on equal footing with men?" While in the cockpit, she frequently wrote lyrical narrative accounts that, in some form, were often published.

The Lindberghs built an estate, "Highfields," near Hopewell, New Jersey, where in June 1930 Anne gave birth to her first child, Charles Junior. Tragedy struck the family when, at about 10 PM, on the bleak, windy evening of March 1, 1932, their infant son was found missing from the second-floor nursery. One of the most publicized crimes in American history, it generated 38,000 letters of advice and sympathy, led to massive federal police efforts, and involved continued efforts to contact the kidnappers. Charles sought, with some success, to mastermind the entire search, while Anne quietly and stoically lent support. One newspaper wrote, "Never in the history of motherhood has a more gallant fight been waged than is being waged by Anne Lindbergh." Biographer **Dorothy Herrmann** notes, "In Anne's case, the press was not resorting to hype. She was in fact handling the nightmarish situation with a dignity and courage that were awe-inspiring." At first, Anne believed that her son would be returned unharmed, but all hopes were shattered when, on May 1, the body of the dead infant, badly decomposed and half eaten by wild animals, was discovered near their home. Anne wrote in her diary:

> I feel strangely a sense of peace—not peace but an end to restlessness, a finality, as though I were sleeping in a grave. . . . To know anything definitely is a relief. If you can say "then he was living," "then he was dead," it is final and finalities can be accepted.

On July 30, however, she wrote to herself: "This is the hour of lead." Only in August, when her second son Jon was born, did she again find some happiness. She confided to her diary:

> I felt life given back to me—a door to life opened. I wanted to live, I felt power to live. I was not afraid of death or life; a spell had been broken, the spell over us that made me dread everything and feel that nothing would be perfect again. The spell was bro-

ken by this real, tangible, perfect baby, coming into an imperfect world and coming out of the teeth of sorrow—a miracle. My faith had been reborn.

Also therapeutic was a second major survey flight, begun in July 1933. Lasting five months, the trip involved 30,000 miles and four continents. Greenland, Iceland, Denmark, Sweden, the Soviet Union, Spain, Gambia, and Brazil were among the 20 countries visited. Charles claimed that this trip and the previous Asian one of 1931 were far more dangerous than his solo flight across the Atlantic. Scientifically and commercially, it was far more productive. Again Anne was co-pilot, radio operator, and navigator. This time, however, she was mentally fatigued and occasionally frightened, emotions she hoped to ward off by poetry. Fully aware of the frequency of air crashes in the early '30s, she confided to her log after one experience of dense fog and flying blind: "I . . . am in a panic the whole time, and every time we go through a day like that I think I cannot go on with that kind of life." She was, she continued, experiencing "a kind of uncontrolled physical terror, exaggerated by imagination." At this point, she held the world's record for ground-to-air radio transmissions. For her service during this flight, in March 1934 she was awarded the prestigious Hubbard Gold Medal of the National Geographic Society.

*L*ife is a gift, given in trust—like a child.

—Anne Morrow Lindbergh

Upon returning from China, the Lindberghs briefly rented an apartment in New York, then—seeking more privacy—lived on the Next Day Hill in Englewood. The latter move was a mixed blessing, for both Charles and Anne chafed under Elizabeth Morrow's dominant personality. Yet it was a Morrow houseguest who gave Anne the professional confidence she so sorely needed. British writer and diplomat Harold Nicolson had been commissioned to write the authorized life of Anne's father. Upon reading Anne's article "Flying Around the North Atlantic," published in the September 1934 issue of the *National Geographic,* Nicolson praised her writing, telling her it was worthy of far more than long letters to family and friends. Referring in October 1934 to Nicolson's appreciation of her latent talent, she wrote to herself:

> The Thing rose up inside of me and possessed me. For twenty-four hours I felt young and powerful. I felt life not long enough for all I wanted to do, and I lay awake at night, my mind racing and my heart pounding.

In the spring of 1935, Anne's first book, *North to the Orient,* was published. Based on her 1931 trip to China, it concentrated on her perception of such visual images as "the most beautiful pagoda." A second book, *Listen! the Wind* (1938), covered ten days of the 1933 flight, focusing on Santiago, an island in the Cape Verde group; Bathurst in Gambia, Africa; and flight across the Atlantic to Natal, Brazil. *North* is marked by exuberant innocence; *Listen!* is characterized by a contemplative caution. Although both books were bestsellers, Anne often lived under severe strain. Unlike Charles, who was working on a heart valve with Dr. Alexis Carrel of New York's Rockefeller Institute, Anne felt that she had no real vocation. A year after the kidnapping, she wrote: "I think about it all the time—it never stops—I never meet it. It happens every night—every night of my life." Such anxieties were reinforced by renewed kidnapping threats on her son Jon.

During this time, Anne had also felt deep anxiety for her ailing elder sister **Elisabeth Reeve Morgan**, who in December 1934 died of a defective heart at age 30. Pondering the transience of all life, Anne had written two years before: "I look at her and think, Life is captive here—now—soon it will go. Why can't we hold it, why can't we help it?" According to biographer Herrmann, by January 1933 Anne had been on the verge of a nervous breakdown. Sensing people courted her only to gain access to Charles, she wrote that September:

> Damn, damn, damn! I am sick of being this "handmaid to the Lord." They think they can wangle me, if they can't get at him, make up to me. . . . Where is my world and where will I ever find it?

The controversy over Bruno Richard Hauptmann merely capped the pressures to which Anne was subjected. "It is starting all over again!," she wrote. Arrested in September 1933 for the kidnapping of the Lindbergh baby, Hauptmann stood trial in the winter of 1934–1935. The press and the hordes of spectators soon turned the sleepy little town of Flemington, New Jersey, where the trial took place, into a circus. Anne had to relive publicly the agonizing last hours of her first son's life as she took the witness stand, though she never lost dignity and poise. From the start, she personally believed that Hauptmann, who was found guilty and executed, had been a party to the crime. The couple always retained absolute faith in the innocence of their own servants, although the perpetrators appeared to know sudden shifts in the Lindbergh family schedule, in fact the exact

hour on which to strike. (Hauptmann's conviction remains a source of controversy, however, and alternate theories abound.)

Finding no refuge from incessant public attention, in December 1935 the Lindberghs moved to England. At first, they rented Long Barn, a country house in Kent belonging to the Nicolsons, where they remained for two and a half years. When, in July 1936, Charles was invited to Nazi Germany to secure air intelligence for the U.S. military attache in Berlin, Anne accompanied him. In a letter to her mother that was published only in 1998, she referred to Hitler as "a mystic, a visionary who really wants the best for his country and *on the whole* has a rather broad view." She expressed admiration of Germany's sense of "a *directed* force," manifested in "hope, pride, and self-sacrifice," while opposing "their treatment of the Jews, their brute-force manner, their stupidity, their rudeness, their regimentation." Her diary entry for August 18, 1938, read: "The Nuremberg Madonnas in Nuremberg look down on a lot of un-Christian things." During this time, flights were made to such nations as France, Denmark, Ireland, Italy, and India.

In the summer of 1938, the couple moved to the beautiful if desolate island of Illiec, near St. Gildas, France, so as to be near Charles' scientific associate, Alexis Carrel. Anne was irritated by the primitive 19th-century house, which lacked heating, plumbing, and electricity. Moreover, she was apprehensive over the possible outbreak of another world war. When, in October 1938, at a stag dinner in the U.S. embassy in Berlin, Reich air minister Hermann Göring presented Charles with the Service Cross of the German Eagle, a high German air decoration for civilians, Anne was mortified. Knowing that a refusal by Charles, who had no foreknowledge of the event, would only embarrass the U.S. diplomatically, and realizing that he would be strongly attacked for accepting it, she privately called it "The Albatross."

Although the Lindberghs had decided to spend the winter of 1938–39 in Berlin, they balked upon hearing of the anti-Jewish atrocities of Kristallnacht. She asked, "How can we go there to live?" Charles and Anne lived instead in Paris, though both were by now being vilified as pro-Nazi. When in April 1939 a new world war became imminent, the family left for the U.S., living first at Next Day Hill, then at Lloyd Neck, Long Island, and Martha's Vineyard.

Having returned home just before the outbreak of the conflict, the Lindberghs opposed the interventionist measures of President Franklin D. Roosevelt, Anne because of her abhorrence of war and Charles on military and strategic grounds. She believed her outspoken husband was "criminally misunderstood, misquoted, and misused," claiming that only columnist Walter Lippmann debated Charles on fundamental issues. Because of their isolationism, many of their old friendships were broken, including those with the Carrells and the Nicolsons, and Anne suddenly entered into a strained relationship with her own mother, a strong interventionist. Anne's article, "A Prayer for Peace," was published in the January 1940 issue of *Reader's Digest.* Writing before the fall of France and the Battle of Britain, she called for a negotiated peace based on "mutual interests and mutual advantages." Otherwise, she feared, only Russia would emerge victorious and "other Hitlers will arise from the seeds of hate in another twenty years."

Anne's next effort, a 41-page book entitled *The Wave of the Future: A Confession of Faith* and published in September 1940, immediately became the nation's number one nonfiction bestseller. Fifty-thousand copies were published in

its first two months and *Reader's Digest* quickly offered a condensed version. In the book, she stressed that the U.S. must face the new world of dictatorships not by entering a destructive war, but by fostering domestic reform and spiritual renewal. Although the work is still misinterpreted as an apology for fascism, she specifically wrote, "I cannot pledge my personal allegiance to those systems I disapprove of, or those barbarisms I oppose from the bottom of my heart, even if they *are* on the wave of the future." The wave itself, she continued, involved new social and economic forces discovered—but often badly used—Germany, Italy, and Russia. Seeing how the term was misinterpreted after publication, she wrote: "Will I have to bear this lie throughout life?" Given her pacifist leanings, it was hardly surprising that she channeled all royalties to the American Friends Service Committee, the only group she found "living up to the reality of the word *mercy.*"

In a subsequent essay entitled "Reaffirmation," published in the June 1941 issue of the *Atlantic Monthly,* Anne defined the wave as "a

Charles and
Anne
Morrow
Lindbergh

movement of adjustment to a highly scientific, mechanized, and material era of civilization, with all its attendant complications." She opposed all dictatorial ways of meeting this adjustment "from the depths of my conviction."

In Anne's diaries, she called Hitler "that terrible scourge of humanity" and continually expressed horror over German atrocities. On September 11, 1941, Charles claimed that American Jews were in the forefront of interventionist agitation and spoke of "their greatest danger to their country" lying in what was later called the media. Anne was shaken. She had been unable to convince Charles to delete his attack, calling it "unconsciously a bit for anti-Semitism." Three days after Charles had given the speech, she wrote in her diary, "I would prefer to see this country at war than shaken by violent anti-Semitism." She wrote in 1976, "The degradation and horror that was uncovered at Auschwitz, Buchenwald, and Dachau was worse than war."

Once the U.S. entered the conflict, the Lindberghs moved to Bloomfield Hills, a suburb of Detroit, because Charles was involved in military aviation work at Henry Ford's Willow Run. Anne remained in Michigan when Charles worked for United Aircraft in Hartford; in 1944 he became a civilian test pilot in the Pacific, flying 50 combat missions for the U.S. navy and air corps.

In 1944, Anne produced a well-received novella, *The Steep Ascent*, the third of her trilogy of flight chronicles and her first attempt at fiction. Here she sought to translate the anxiety felt during her flight from England to Italy into a parable of universal experience felt by all women. In a letter to a friend, she wrote of the work:

> I have put everything in it—everything I learned from that life in the past. It is a flight over the Alps but it could be anything. Childbirth or getting married, or the mental and moral struggles one has. There are those same peaks ("Is this all there is to the Alps?") and those same abysses ("I am abandoned—they have abandoned me!") It is my whole life.

After the war, the Lindberghs lived primarily in Darien, Connecticut. In the summer of 1947, Anne traveled to Europe, there finding material for articles later published in *Reader's Digest, Life,* and *Harper's.* Commenting on Britain, France, and West Germany, she deplored the starvation, hopelessness, and Kafkalike bureaucracy. "The basic values of our civilization," she wrote, "are crumbling away like this rubble." By then, Anne had given birth to several more children, boys in 1937 and 1942 and girls in 1940 and 1945.

For the first time, tension existed in the Lindbergh marriage. Charles was frequently away as an aviation consultant, leaving Anne alone to fend with childrearing. Furthermore, according to Charles' biographer A. Scott Berg, "when he was at home, he monitored [her] so closely as to infantilize her." In the mid-1950s, she considered divorce, sought solace in psychiatry, and entered into an affair with her physician, Dana W. Atchley.

In one attempt to find her own identity, in the spring of 1955 Anne spent a week with her sister **Constance Cutter Morrow** at Captiva Island, Florida. Her meditations from that week, contained in eight essays published under the title *Gift from the Sea* (1955), again catapulted her into national prominence. The most popular of her works, the book remained at the top of the bestseller list for 51 weeks and so far has sold seven million copies. Finding symbols for such entities as aging, love, possession, and solitude in the shape of certain seashells found on the beach, she stressed the need for women to seek internal change through contemplation and self-renewal. She denied that complete sharing in marriage was ever possible and called upon partners to love "the distance between them which makes it possible for each to see the other whole and against a wide sky."

Anne's next book, *The Unicorn and Other Poems* (1956), contained 35 of her works. It too made the bestseller list, outselling by a wide margin all other poetry books published that year. Some critics, however, were negative. Poet John Ciardi, writing in the January 12, 1957, issue of the *Saturday Review of Literature,* called it "an offensively bad book—inept, jingling, slovenly, illiterate even." Ciardi received hundred of protest letters (one of which asked, "Why club a butterfly?") while *Review* editor Norman Cousins himself responded in Anne's defense, "There are few living authors who are using the English language more sensitively or with more genuine appeal."

Devastated by the review, Anne permanently abandoned poetry. Yet, she wrote another novel. Using a stream-of-consciousness technique, she produced *Dearly Beloved: A Theme and Variations* (1962), a work that focused on the deeply embedded ambiguities in modern marriage. Centering on a single incident, a wedding service, it conveys its message by exploring the psyches of the guests, both men and women.

By the late 1960s, the Lindberghs had focused their major attention on environmental issues. In 1966, Anne's *Earth Shine* was published. Consisting of two long essays that had previously been featured in *Life* magazine and her 1970 commencement address to Smith College, the book compared the tranquility of Cape Canaveral with the launching of Apollo 8, then described a family safari in East Africa. In addressing herself to the matter of the Vietnam War protests, she suggested that they were rooted in "a deep instinctive protest against the growing dehumanization of our world—against an industrialized, mechanized civilization in which the flame of life itself is sputtering."

Beginning in 1971, Anne Lindbergh started publishing five volumes of excerpts from her diary, which she had begun in 1922 and which she continued intermittently for much of her life. In 1979, she said publication was motivated by the "many false stories" about her and Charles, "so many rumors, and silly things said." Writes biographer Herrmann, "Few other writers have lived so documented a life." Indeed, literature scholar David Kirk Vaughn predicts that her published diaries and letters may be the most enduring of all her written works. Preferring to edit existing diaries rather than work on an autobiography, she prefaced the first volume by saying:

> Once started on the painful journey toward honesty, with the passage of time one has increasingly the desire not to gloss over, not to foster illusions or to create fixed images, inasmuch as this is humanly possible. One wants to be an honest witness to the life one has lived and the struggle one has made to find oneself and one's work, and to relate oneself to others and the world.

In the early 1970s, the Lindberghs built a simple house on Maui island, Hawaii, where Charles died of lymphatic cancer in August 1974. Since then, Anne Morrow Lindbergh has lived in seclusion at Scott's Cove, Darien. In 1991, she suffered her first stroke. Experiencing dementia and memory loss, she is nursed by trained caregivers.

SOURCES:

Herrmann, Dorothy. *A Gift for Life: Anne Morrow Lindbergh*. NY: Ticknor & Fields, 1993.

Mayer, Elsie F. *My Window on the World: The Works of Anne Morrow Lindbergh*. Hamden, CT: Archon Books, 1988.

Milton, Joyce. *Loss of Eden: A Biography of Charles and Anne Morrow Lindbergh*. NY: HarperCollins, 1993.

Vaughn, David Kirk. *Anne Morrow Lindbergh*. Boston: Twayne, 1988.

SUGGESTED READING:

Berg, A. Scott. *Lindbergh*. NY: Putnam, 1998.

Hertog, Susan. *Anne Morrow Lindbergh: A Life*. NY: Doubleday, 1999.

Lindbergh, Anne Morrow. *Bring Me a Unicorn: Diaries and Letters, 1922–1928*. NY: Harcourt Brace Jovanovich, 1972.

———. *The Flower and the Nettle: Diaries and Letters, 1936–1939*. NY: Harcourt Brace Jovanovich, 1976.

———. *Hour of Gold, Hour of Lead: Diaries and Letters, 1929–1932*. NY: Harcourt Brace Jovanovich, 1973.

———. *Locked Rooms and Open Doors: Diaries and Letters, 1933–1935*. NY: Harcourt Brace Jovanovich, 1974.

———. *War Within and Without: Diaries and Letters, 1939–1944*. NY: Harcourt Brace Jovanovich, 1980.

Lindbergh, Charles A. *Autobiography of Values*. NY: Harcourt Brace Jovanovich, 1978.

Lindbergh, Reeve. *The Names of the Mountains* (novel). NY: Simon and Schuster, 1993.

———. *Under a Wing: A Memoir*. NY: Simon and Schuster, 1998.

Sutherland, Gretchen Rolufs. "Of Winter Branches: The Literary Career of Anne Morrow Lindbergh." Ph.D. dissertation. University of Iowa, 1986.

Justus D. Doenecke,
Professor of History, New College,
University of South Florida, Sarasota, Florida

Lindfors, Viveca (1920–1995)

Swedish-born actress with an international reputation. Born Elsa Viveka Torstensdotter Lindfors on December 29, 1920, in Uppsala, Sweden; died on October 25, 1995, in Uppsala; one of three children, two girls and a boy, of Torsten Lindfors (a book publisher) and Karin (Dymling) Lindfors (a painter); graduated from the Lyceum School, Stockholm; attended the Royal Dramatic Theater School, Stockholm, 1937–40; married Harry Hasso (a cinematographer), in 1941 (divorced); married Folke Rogard (a lawyer), in 1946 (divorced 1949); married Don Siegel (a director), in 1949 (divorced 1953); married George Tabori (a novelist, playwright, and director), in 1954 (divorced 1972); children: (first marriage) John Hasso; (second marriage) **Lena Rogard**; *(third marriage) Kristoffer Tabori (an actor).*

Selected theater: made her stage debut in Anne Sophie Hedvig *(Royal Dramatic Theater School, 1937); at the Royal Dramatic Theater, Stockholm, appeared in* French Without Tears *(1940), as the Bride in* Blood Wedding *(1943), and Olivia in* Twelfth Night *(1945); made her Broadway debut as Inez Cabral in* I've Got Sixpence *(Ethel Barrymore Theater, December 1952); made her London debut as Sophia in* The White Countess *(Saville Theater, March 1954); appeared as Anna in* Anastasia *(Lyceum Theater, New York, December 1954, and subsequent tour), Cordelia in* King Lear *(New York City Center, January 1956), the title role in* Miss Julie *and Missy in* The Stronger *(Phoenix Theater, New York, February 1956); toured*

U.S. and South America as Catherine in Suddenly Last Summer *(1961); in Stockholm, played in* Brecht on Brecht *(1963); appeared as Portia in* The Merchant of Venice *(Berkshire, Massachusetts Theater Festival, July 1966), Alice in* Dance of Death *(Arena Stage, Washington, D.C., fall 1970); appeared in one-woman show* I Am a Woman *(1972–73, and tour).*

Filmography in Sweden: The Spinning Family *(1940);* If I Should Marry the Minister *(1941);* In Paradise *(1941);* The Yellow Ward *(1942);* Anna Lans *(1943);* Appassionata *(1944);* Black Roses *(1945);* Marie in the Windmill *(1945);* In the Waiting Room of Death *(Interlude, 1946). In the United States, unless otherwise noted:* To the Victor *(1948);* Adventures of Don Juan *(1948);* Night Unto Night *(1949);* Singoalla *(Sw./Fr., 1950);* Backfire *(1950);* No Sad Songs for Me *(1950);* This Side of the Law *(1950);* Dark City *(1950);* Die Vier im Jeep *(Four in a Jeep, Switz., 1951);* The Flying Missile *(1951);* Journey Into Light *(1951);* The Raiders *(1952);* No Time for Flowers *(1952);* Run for Cover *(1955);* Moonfleet *(1955);* The Halliday Brand *(1957);* I Accuse! *(UK, 1958);* La Tempesta *(The Tempest, It./Fr./Yug., 1958);* The Story of Ruth *(1960);* King of Kings *(1961);* The Damned *(These Are the Damned, UK, 1961);* Huis Clos *(No Exit, Arg./US, 1962);* An Affair of the Skin *(1963);* Sylvia *(1965);* Brainstorm *(1965);* Coming Apart *(1969);* Puzzle of a Downfall Child *(1971);* Cauldron of Blood *(US/Sp., 1971);* The Way We Were *(1973);* La Casa sin Fronteras *(Sp., 1972);* Welcome to L.A. *(1977);* Tabu *(Taboo, Sw., 1977);* Girlfriends *(1978);* A Wedding *(1978);* Voices *(1979);* Natural Enemies *(1979);* The Hand *(1981);* Creepshow *(1982);* Silent Madness *(1984);* The Sure Thing *(1985); (also directed)* Unfinished Business *(1987);* Rachel River *(1987);* Goin' to Chicago *(1990);* Luba *(Holl., 1990);* The Exorcist III *(1990);* Zandalee *(1991);* North of Pittsburgh *(1992);* The Linguine Incident *(1992);* Stargate *(1994);* Last Summer in the Hamptons *(1995).*

A tall brunette, often referred to as Garboesque, Swedish actress Viveka Lindfors (changed to Viveca when she was nine and first decided to be a performer) was born in Uppsala, Sweden, in 1920. She grew up in a traditional middle-class Swedish family and graduated from the Lyceum School for girls in Stockholm. At 16, having decided on an acting career, she passed the grueling three-day audition and was accepted at the Royal Dramatic Theater School, where she made her acting debut in *Anne Sophie Hedvig*, playing a young schoolgirl who witnesses a murder by her teacher and confronts her. After graduating in 1940, Lindfors continued with the Royal Dramatic Theater for two years, performing in classical and modern plays, while honing her craft. Though still with the theater, she took a five-line walk-on in the film *The Crazy Family*, which led to a starring role in *If I Should Marry the Minister* (1941), a movie that launched her career in cinema. A string of stage and film roles followed, including the movie *Appassionata* (1944), which caught the attention of the American agent *Kay Brown. Brown brought the stunning young actress to America in 1946, under contract to Warner Bros.

Leaving her two young children in Sweden (one with her first husband, cinematographer Harry Hasso), Lindfors arrived in Hollywood with her second husband, lawyer Folke Rogard, and spent close to six months without an assignment from Warner Bros. In her first American film, *Night Unto Night* (not released until 1949), she appeared opposite established star Ronald Reagan and was directed by Don Siegel, who would become Lindfors' third husband. After making four movies, none of which advanced her career, the actress became discouraged and expressed her bitterness in a layout in *Life* magazine. As a result, Warner Bros. dropped her option, after which she freelanced and spent part of her time in Europe. Just before leaving for Stockholm to make *Singoalla* (1950), the actress accepted a second lead in Columbia's *No Sad Songs for Me* (1950), a role that some called her finest effort in American films to date. Of her subsequent movies, the best were the multilingual Swiss film *Die Vier im Jeep* (*Four in a Jeep*, 1951) and *No Exit* (1962), both of which earned the actress acting honors at the Berlin Film Festival.

Many believe that Lindfors reached her high point as an actress on the stage rather than in films. She moved to New York in the early 1950s and made her Broadway debut in John Van Druten's *I've Got Sixpence* (1952). Her breakthrough performance, however, was in *Anastasia*, which opened in New York on her 33rd birthday, December 29, 1959. Co-starring with *Eugénie Leontovich, who was brilliant in the role of the Dowager Empress, Lindfors, as *Anastasia, the only supposed surviving member of the tsar's family, was remarkable in her transformation from a waif to a regal presence. Brooks Atkinson of *The New York Times* (December 30, 1954) praised the climactic recognition scene between Leontovich and Lindfors as "two pieces of acting that came out of the theater's treasure chest."

Lindfors went on to perform in classic plays by Shakespeare, Brecht, and Tennessee Williams, all the while keeping her film career on track. In 1966, following an idyllic summer of stock in the Berkshire mountains of Massachusetts, Lindfors and her fourth husband George Tabori founded the Berkshire Theater Festival in Stockbridge, where she served as the assistant artistic director. Following a successful first season, during which they presented *The Skin of Our Teeth* by Thornton Wilder, *The Cretan Woman* by Robinson Jeffers, *The Merchant of Venice* by Shakespeare, and *Waiting for Godot* by Samuel Beckett, Lindfors and Tabori fell victims to an unsavory scheme to unseat them and lost the festival project. Soon after, Lindfors organized her own company of five actors, The Strolling Players, which toured college campuses throughout the United States for three years.

Lindfors' personal life, which included four tumultuous marriages and numerous love affairs, was complicated by her inability to merge the traditional role of wife and mother with that of an independent actress who lived to work and wanted desperately to make a difference in the world. "Those two images, far apart in their goals, in a constant tug of war with each other, left me, the real woman, neglected, frustrated, ambivalent, and incapable of open and lasting intimacy," she wrote in the introduction to her autobiography, *Viveka . . . Viveca*. Born of this struggle to reconcile the various parts of her personality was her one-woman show *I Am a Woman* (1972–73), a compilation of works by, for, and about women, which she created over a six-month period in 1971 with her friend, director Paul Austin.

"Woman + Actress = Me," she wrote under the title in the published version of the play. "I was in a dilemma," she wrote. "A dilemma fabricated by society leading to a neurosis of my own. A dilemma I could no longer stomach. A dilemma that led to conflicts in my marriage as well as my work. And so the play came from many sources, many needs, spiritual, psychological, as well as realistic." The show, which contained such diverse material as a reading from the original diary of *Anne Frank and the introduction of *Lillian Hellman's *Pentimento*, opened at the Seattle Repertory Theater in 1972 to splendid reviews and played to full houses. In Washington, D.C., however, Lindfors was greeting with a particularly nasty review from a *Washington Post* critic who attacked the actress personally for her sagging breasts, her age, and her Swedish accent. Though unnerved by the review, Lindfors was heartened when subsequent audiences came to her defense, sending letters to the editor and

Viveca Lindfors

even organizing a picket line in front of the newspaper's offices. "In Washington, D.C., sisterhood became a practical reality to me," she wrote later. The show subsequently enjoyed a four-month run at Gene Frankel's Theater of Space in New York City, and toured theaters and college campuses across the country for years. Lindfors also performed the show abroad, including in her native Sweden.

Viveca Lindfors continued to act throughout the 1980s and early 1990s, and in 1987 both acted in and directed the film *Unfinished Business . . . .* She had just completed the movie *Last Summer in the Hamptons* (1995) and had returned to her home in Uppsala, Sweden, to tour in the play *In Search of Strindberg*, when she died of complications from rheumatoid arthritis. She was 74.

SOURCES:
Current Biography. NY: H.W. Wilson, 1955.
Katz, Ephraim. *The Film Encyclopedia.* NY: Harper-Collins, 1994.
Lindfors, Viveca. *Viveka . . . Viveca.* NY: Everest House, 1981.
Stout, David. "Obituary," in *The Day* [(New London, CT]. October 26, 1995.

Barbara Morgan,
Melrose, Massachusetts

Lindgren, Astrid (1907—)

Swedish writer who is especially famous for her "Pippi Longstocking" series. Born Astrid Ericsson in Vimmerby, Sweden, on November 14, 1907; daughter of Hanna (Jonsson) Ericsson and Samuel August Ericsson (both farmers); married Sture Lindgren, on April 4, 1931 (died 1952); children: (prior to her marriage) one son, Lars; **Karin Lindgren** *(b. 1934, who married Carl Olof Nyman).*

Awards: Nils Holgersson Medal (1950); Deutscher Jugendbuchpreis (1956); The Swedish State Award for Writers of High Literary Standard (1957); Hans Christian Andersen Medal; Boys' Club of America Junior Book Award (1958); New York Herald Tribune *Children's Spring Book Festival Award (1959); Golden Ship Award of the Swedish Society for the Promotion of Literature; Expressen's Heffaklumpa Award; Lewis Carroll Shelf Award (1970); Swedish Academy's Gold Medal (1971); The Dutch Silver Pen Award (1975); Adelaide-Risto Award; International Writer's Prize; honorary doctor of letters, Leicester University, England (1979); Mildred L. Batchelder Award to Viking Press; John Hansson Award (1984); Gold Medal awarded by the Swedish Government; Silver Bear Award, Berlin; French Children's Book Award; the Karen Blixen Award; Jovanovic Zmaj Award (1985); the Selma Lagerlof Award (1986); the Leo Tolstoy International Gold Medal (1987).*

Other prizes honoring her humanitarian activities: The Peace Prize of the German Booksellers' Association (1978); The Janusz Korczak Prize (1979); The Dag Hammarskjöld Award (1984); The Albert Schweitzer Medal (1989).

Selected works translated into English: Pippi Longstocking *(1945);* The Children of Noisy Village *(1947);* Bill Bergson Lives Dangerously *(1951);* Mio, Mio, My Son *(1954);* Karlsson-on-the-Roof *(1955);* Rasmus and the Vagabond *(1956);* Mischievous Meg *(1959);* Emil in the Soup Tureen *(1963);* The Brothers Lionheart *(1973);* Ronia, the Robber's Daughter *(1981).*

In 1941, at the beginning of the Second World War, Astrid Lindgren told stories at the bedside of her seven-year-old daughter Karin who was suffering from pneumonia. When, out of nowhere, Karin asked her mother to tell a tale about Pippi Longstocking (Pippi Laangstrump), Lindgren did not ask who Pippi was; she just supplied a story about the girl on request. Pippi, with her great name, turned out to be a most extraordinary girl who delighted Karin and her friends so much that she had to be kept alive in repeated and succeeding stories. Three years later, in the early spring of 1944, Lindgren slipped on the icy streets of Stockholm and sprained her ankle. To pass the time until she regained her mobility, she started writing down the stories of Pippi Longstocking. In the process, an author was born.

Lindgren has repeatedly stressed that she had a wondrous childhood. She grew up in a wooden house, old and red, which was surrounded by apple trees on a farm in Näs, outside the small town of Vimmerby, in Smaland, Sweden. With her three siblings, one brother and two sisters, she lived a life of both freedom and security, climbing trees and roaming the countryside. Their safety was undergirded by their parents' close relationship and the local traditions sustained by their culture and husbandry. The Ericsson children, however, did more than play, taking their turns at chores on the farm, where life was hard. Smaland's soil is stony, and, for many, hunger and starvation were steady companions. Astrid and her siblings grew up with people of all sorts and ages, from whom she learned "without their knowing it and without my knowing it—something about life's demands and how hard it can be to be a human being."

Lindgren's writing would tap into her early experiences which produced both a sense of belonging and a sensitivity to the beauty of nature around her: the "mounds of strawberries . . . meadows full of cowslips, bilberry patches, woods with the pink bells of linnea in the moss, the pastures round Näs, the water-lilies in the streams, ditches, slopes and trees." While she would grow up, like most children, to learn that people can be fickle, cruel and careless, nature never let her down. Her pastoral descriptions—persuasive to children who can relate to the notion that "stones and trees" can be "as close to [them] as living beings"—are among the most powerful passages in her books. Throughout her life, the natural world which "sheltered and nourished [the Ericsson children's] games and dreams," has provided Lindgren both with an escape from civilized life and all its vices, and with the impetus to support ecological and animal-rights issues. Lindgren has called herself a "little animal sucking in only that which was nature" who became a human being when she heard her first fairy tale. This event fueled her awareness of the power of words and the world of the imagination. An inveterate reader, she would become a storyteller (earning the nickname of "Vimmerby's *Selma Lagerlöf*"), whose tales reflect the rootedness of her own childhood. The care and trust in life established in her

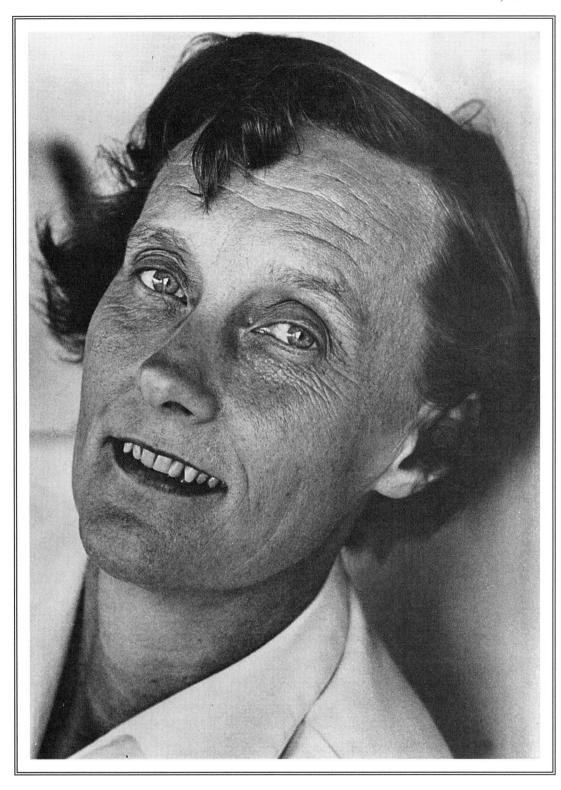

rural community lend to her stories an undercurrent of stability and confidence which makes even hazardous adventures and gnarly problems manageable. With an understanding of a child's attraction to chaos restored to order, and of the desire to encounter the scary and subdue it,

Lindgren addresses existential anxieties in her novels, such as loneliness and feelings of worthlessness, despite an emphasis on adventure and playfulness. *The Brothers Lionheart*, one of her last novels, deals with the inevitability of death and its occurrence even in childhood.

"A biography of Astrid Lindgren should end with the end of her childhood," writes her primary biographer, **Margareta Stromstedt,** who has been permitted a closer look at the writer than anyone else. Lindgren is known to treat journalists with kindness and interest in their affairs, but they often leave after a long and pleasant conversation only to realize they have been talking about themselves and have come away knowing nothing new about the author. She tells only what she wants to—and generally the same things.

A child, alone with his book, creates for himself, somewhere in the secret recesses of the soul, his own pictures which surpass all else. Such pictures are necessary for humanity.

—**Astrid Lindgren**

Lindgren has described her teens as a mere "state" without "tone or vitality." She succumbed to melancholy, thinking herself ugly and unable to fall in love despite a desire to do so. She developed a measure of independence during these years even in her relationship to her mother, the formidable Hanna. Astrid liked dancing, both folk dances and jazz, and she refused to stay home like a good farmer's daughter. Instead, she stayed out nights, later and more often than her mother sanctioned. At 17, when she called her father to say she had cut her hair, he suggested she not hurry home. On her eventual arrival there, she sat down on a chair in the kitchen, and no one said a word; they only walked about her in silence. Astrid endured it because, with her new bob, she felt less unattractive, and she caused quite a sensation in the little town of Vimmerby.

She graduated in 1923 from the local secondary school with good grades, especially in Swedish, at age 16. Astrid then took a job almost immediately at the local newspaper, *Vimmerby Tidningen,* where she did copy editing and wrote reviews and articles of local interest, including conferences, weddings and funerals. In 1926, when she was 19, she learned she was pregnant. In a small town like Vimmerby, such an event threatened to crush both her and her respected family. Astrid's determination to not marry the father of the expected child made matters even worse. "Never have so many gossiped about so little—at least not in Vimmerby," was her laconic comment. Wholly unwilling to stay at home, she left for Stockholm.

To make a living, she enrolled in a typing and short-hand course, but her advancing pregnancy forced her to seek help. The attorney **Eva Anden,** who belonged to a group of politically radical working women with a special interest in unwed mothers and women laborers, learned that Astrid had no one even to talk to because she was determined to deal with the predicament on her own. Anden arranged for her to go to Copenhagen, where she could deliver her baby at the state hospital, and found a place for her to stay until the time of delivery, which took place shortly before Christmas. Astrid was forced to give Lars, her son, up, but fortunate in that the family with whom she had stayed while awaiting his birth offered to take him in as a foster child. She subsequently returned to Stockholm and her studies. "Lars was fine during those years, but I was not," she would later recall. She missed him son terribly. The following year (1927), she finished her classes and landed a job as a private secretary. Without unions, office women, who had to pay for room and board on low wages, often went hungry in the 1920s. Astrid saved what she could for transportation to Copenhagen to see her son as often as possible, which was rarely.

In December 1929, she learned that Lars' foster mother was ill and could no longer care for him. Astrid brought him to Stockholm with her, and her landlady watched him while she was at work. His five-month stay there was a trying time, especially because he suffered from whooping cough which kept both son and mother awake at night. In May, Astrid finally brought him home to Näs where, as her mother put it, he really belonged.

Lars' life with his grandparents, aunts and uncle came to an end in 1931 when Astrid married her boss, Sture Lindgren. He was an executive with the royal Swedish Automobile Club where she worked writing travelogues and motoring guides. The three of them moved into an apartment in Stockholm, and when their daughter Karin was born in 1934, Astrid became a full-time mother. She also did occasional freelance work as a stenographer which earned her a little money; more significantly, however, it offered valuable information and insights. A job with Harry Soderman, professor in criminology at a Stockholm institute, not only taught her enough about the technicalities of crime to write a book about a master detective, but also gave her forewarnings about the rise of the National Socialist Party in Germany and Hitler's persecution of Jews. Prompted by increasing anxiety, she started a war diary on September 1, 1939, admitting that until that day she had avoided "hoarding" but now had bought such items as cocoa, tea and a little soap. Lindgren kept writing throughout the war years, and her loathing

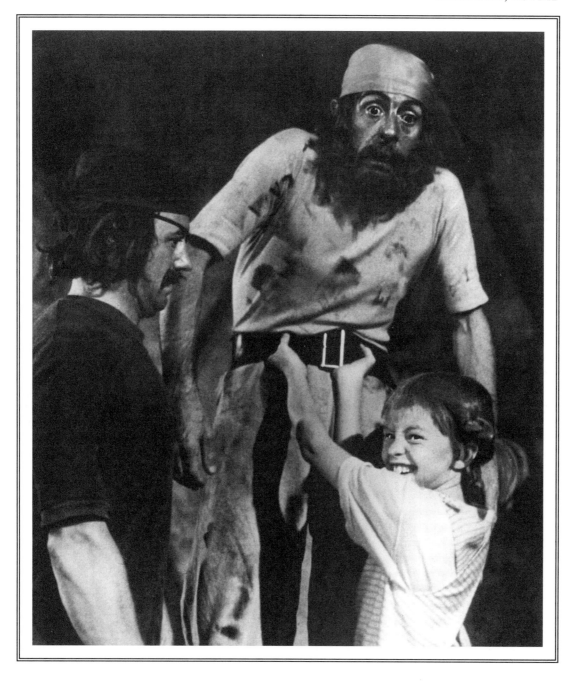

From the movie Pippi in the South Seas, *starring Inger Nilsson, based on the series by Astrid Lindgren.*

of Hitler and his regime runs like a red thread through her diary entries.

Early in the war, Soderman got her a job censoring letters in Sweden's Intelligence Service. Through the reading of these letters, she came to know war from individuals who reported losses in terms of family and friends. She both felt their anguish and recognized how fortunate was her family of four. In 1941, following Sture's promotion, the Lindgrens had moved to a larger apartment, and they, like numerous other Swedes, could spend summers in the Stockholm archipelago. Lindgren's conviction

that an individual's demonstration of care and responsibility must be commensurate with her power and good fortune prompted her to become an active participant in the efforts to rescue displaced Jews.

In May 1944, Lindgren presented her daughter Karin with the Pippi Longstocking manuscript as a birthday gift. She then sent a copy to Bonniers, the largest publishing house in Sweden, which rejected it. Lindgren entered *The Confidences of Britt-Mari*, a more traditional book, in a competition sponsored by a smaller publishing firm, Raben & Sjogren, and it took second prize. In 1945, a revised Pippi took first prize, and Raben & Sjogren published the manuscript, which set Lindgren on the road to fame and put the publishers in the black. *Pippi Goes on Board* followed in 1946, and 1948 saw the last of the series, *Pippi in the South Seas*. In 1946, Lindgren had become editor and head of the children's book department at Raben & Sjogren, a position she held until 1970. During her 24 years there, she wrote in the mornings at home, producing books, radio plays and film manuscripts (Pippi was broadcast on Swedish radio in 1946, the first feature film was made in 1949, and since then three more Swedish adaptations have appeared), as well as theater adaptations and lectures. Afternoons were spent at her editing job, and evenings with her family. From the late 1940s to the 1970s, she wrote at least one book a year, many of which have been translated into several languages. Lindgren's literary voice, which both entertains and encourages children to question and think for themselves, is unmistakable.

After a long illness, Sture Lindgren died in 1952. Astrid and her daughter stayed on together in their apartment until Karin married and left home. Lindgren, who did not remarry, was content in her privacy and quiet existence. After repeatedly voicing her desire to live in peace and away from publicity, to the surprise of many she launched a public protest in the 1970s. As an uncomplaining taxpayer who had sought no tax shelter abroad and invested in no foreign domiciles, she grew furious in March 1976 when a 102% tax was levied on her income. Realizing that such steep taxes likely affected others who were much less affluent, Lindgren wrote a scathing critique against the Social Democratic government in the guise of a satirical fairy tale. She attacked the bureaucratized, self-serving party apparatus whose leaders by this time ceased to resemble the activists of the early days of the social democratic movement in Sweden. Lindgren would have been proud to join them back when they had fought for the rights of the underprivileged; in their absence, she supported the party's demise. Her fairy tale, which tested her supposition that many others were equally dissatisfied with the government, found a wide readership and caused a debate which brought to an end the 40-year rule of the Social Democrats in Sweden.

In 1985, Lindgren took on the government again, this time with open letters to the minister of agriculture protesting the mistreatment of farm animals. In letter after letter, she spoke out against legalized and institutionalized cruelty towards domestic animals based on greed and shortsightedness. Objectifying such creatures by treating them as production units, she argued, would guarantee their continual suffering. She urged that a basic respect for life be maintained in large-scale operations as well as on individual farms. The major Stockholm newspapers printed her submissions, and three years of concerted efforts on her part resulted in Lex Lindgren, the Animal Protection Act, promulgated in June 1988.

Lindgren receives letters from all over the world where children have read her books. The Pippi books have been translated into 56 languages, and a total of 40 million are in circulation. Four million copies have been sold in Germany alone. Critics have noted that Pippi's initial popularity was partly owed to the fact that she was a symbol of freedom to the overly protected and strictly monitored middle-class children of the 1940s. (She is thus declared a prototype of the progressive and reformist school in pedagogy inspired by the writings of *Ellen Key, Alexander Sutherland Neill, and Bertrand Russell.) While that may be true, it is also true that child-rearing practices have since changed drastically, and Pippi has lost none of her popularity. "Her superhuman qualities," writes **Eva-Maria Metcalf**, "make her an ideal outlet for readers' compensatory fantasies." Lindgren herself reminds us that Pippi's will to power is invariably a will to do good. Even as she outsmarts teachers and professors, and ridicules narrow-mindedness and conceit, she is a caring and compassionate character.

Now in her 90s, Lindgren remains actively engaged despite impaired eyesight, which has left her virtually blind. Both her modest life and her work document her concern for the welfare of all life, and especially for those who are likely victims of the abuse of power because they cannot speak up for themselves.

SOURCES:

Lundqvist, Ulla. *Aarhundradets barn*. Stockholm: Raben & Sjogren, 1979.

Metcalf, Eva-Maria. *Astrid Lindgren*. NY: Twayne Publishers, 1995.

Stromstedt, Margareta. *Astrid Lindgren*. Stockholm: Raben & Sjogren, 1977.

RELATED MEDIA:

Pippi in the South Seas, film starring **Inger Nilsson**, GG Communications, 1974.

"Pippi Longstocking," 26-part animated series, 30 min. episodes, aired on Home Box Office in 1998, produced by Nelvana Limited.

Inga Wiehl,
a native of Denmark, teaches English at
Yakima Valley Community College, Yakima, Washington

Lindner, Herta (1920–1943)

German anti-Nazi activist, executed at Plötzensee Prison, who resisted fascism and was active in efforts to bring about German-Czech reconciliation. Name variations: Hertha Lindner. Born in Mariaschein, Czechoslovakia (now Bohosudov, Czech Republic), on November 3, 1920; executed at Plötzensee Prison, Berlin, on March 29, 1943; daughter of Heinrich Josef Lindner.

Herta Lindner was born in 1920 into a German-speaking working-class family in an ethnically mixed German-Czech region of Czechoslovakia. She received much of her political education from her father, a class-conscious and militant miner, and, at age nine, joined the Socialist youth organization Rote Falken (Red Falcons). Throughout the next years, she witnessed the rise of fascist terror and racial hatred in her town. As a member of the German minority in a Czechoslovak Republic in which the overwhelming majority of the population was Slavic, Lindner believed that only a socialist and multiethnic society would guarantee permanent peace in Central Europe.

She and a minority of Sudeten Germans in Czechoslovakia (ethnic Germans who had long lived in the area) supported the constitutional system and believed that the growing threat of Hitler's Germany could best be opposed by a strong alliance of German and Czech workers and intellectuals. Unlike many Germans who believed that their language and culture were superior to the Czechs', thus making themselves members of a "master race," Lindner thought neither group inferior. In keeping with her family's socialist and internationalist ideals, she attended both Czech and German schools and grew up speaking both languages.

As a militant anti-Nazi who opposed the pro-Hitler Sudeten German Party of Konrad Henlein, in 1937 Lindner joined the German Youth League (Deutscher Jugendbund), a successor to the banned Communist youth organization. She quickly emerged as the local leader of this entity, which carried on clandestine political work even before it was outlawed by the Prague government in 1938. In October 1938, the Sudetenland was annexed by Nazi Germany, and in March 1939 the remnant territory of Bohemia and Moravia was declared a "protectorate" by Berlin. Savage repressions of Jews, Marxists, and democrats now swept through the newly occupied regions, but Lindner and a small group of other German anti-Nazis refused to abandon their underground activities. Not yet 20, Lindner carried out her party assignments with courage and a cool head. In 1939, she moved to Dresden, where she found work as a salesclerk in the Müller grocery store and continued her dangerous political activities. As a cover for her underground cell, in 1940 she founded the Lindenbrüder Hohenstein Mountain Climbing Club in 1940, which permitted fellow anti-Nazis to meet on weekends and vacations for ostensibly innocent climbing trips while organizing future political work and carrying on ideological discussions.

While Lindner lived and worked in Dresden, her mother's health deteriorated. Lindner used much of her free time to travel to Mariaschein to be with her. It was on one of these trips, on November 27, 1941, that she was arrested by Nazi police who had uncovered details of her political activities. At the same time, her father was also arrested for his involvement in a subversive organization. For a full year, Lindner was jailed and interrogated in the town of Most. She was then taken to Berlin, where after a trial that bore little resemblance to a genuine judicial event she was found guilty of high treason and a sentence of death was announced in November 1942. Herta Lindner was executed in Plötzensee Prison, Berlin, on March 29, 1943.

German Democratic Republic stamp, honoring Herta Lindner, issued on February 6, 1961.

In the 1950s, after the establishment of the German Democratic Republic (GDR) in the former Soviet Occupation Zone of Germany, Herta Lindner became universally recognized as a martyr of the militant anti-Nazi working class. Several streets and schools were named in her honor. On February 6, 1961, the GDR postal service issued a postage stamp with her likeness to raise funds for the preservation of the national memorials at the sites of the Buchenwald, Ravensbrück and Sachsenhausen concentration camps.

SOURCES:

Gostomski, Victor von, and Walter Loch. *Der Tod von Plötzensee: Erinnerungen, Ereignisse, Dokumente 1942–1944.* Frankfurt am Main: bLoch Verlag, 1993.

Grünwald, Leopold. *Im Kampf für Frieden und Freiheit: Sudetendeutscher Widerstand gegen Hitler.* Munich: Fides-Verlagsgesellschaft, 1979.

Kraushaar, Luise. *Deutsche Widerstandskämpfer 1933–1945: Biographien und Briefe.* 2 vols. Berlin: Dietz Verlag, 1970.

Partington, Paul G. *Who's Who on the Postage Stamps of Eastern Europe.* Metuchen, NJ: Scarecrow Press, 1979.

John Haag,
Associate Professor of History,
University of Georgia, Athens, Georgia

Lindsay, Anne (1750–1825)

Scottish poet, author of the popular Scottish ballad "Auld Robin Gray," and diarist who wrote about colonial life on the Cape of Africa. Name variations: Lady Anne Lindsay; Lady Anne Barnard. Born Anne Lindsay at Balcarres House, Lindsay, in Fifeshire, Scotland, on December 12, 1750; died on May 6, 1825, in London; eldest daughter of James Lindsay, 5th earl of Balcarres, and Anne Dalrymple; educated at home; married Andrew Barnard (a son of the bishop of Limerick), in 1793; no children.

Work included in: (Dorothea Fairbridge, ed.) Lady Anne Barnard at the Cape of Good Hope, 1797–1802 (1924); (A.M. Lewin Robinson, ed.) The Letters of Lady Anne Barnard to Henry Dundas . . . together with her Journal of a Tour into the Interior (1973).

During a time of contention for the throne of England in the mid-1700s, prophecy held that the firstborn of Robert Lindsay, 5th earl of Balcarres, would return possession of the crown to the Stuart family. Lindsay, age 60, took a 22-year-old bride, **Anne Dalrymple**, and anxiously awaited the birth of a king. Hopes were quelled when, on December 12, 1750, a girl child, Anne, was born.

Thereafter, the Lindsays lived quietly in Edinburgh where ten more Lindsay children were born and educated at home with a governess and tutor. At age 19, Anne rewrote a popular but "lewd" Scottish ballad, publishing the work anonymously in 1783 as "Auld Robin Gray." Her creation became more popular than its predecessor and was set to music by the Reverend William Leeves (1748–1828).

In the company of her sister **Margaret Lindsay,** Anne left for London, where the two became the center of a circle of writers and were courted by several influential men. Anne chose the not so influential Andrew Barnard, 12 years her junior. She was 43 years old when they married in 1793.

After her marriage, Lady Anne Barnard obtained from Henry Dundas, 1st Viscount Melville, an appointment for her husband Andrew as colonial secretary at the Cape of Good Hope. In March 1797, the couple packed up and moved to South Africa, where they remained until January 1802 when the British Cape colony was returned to its previous Dutch ownership. Along with her journal, Lady Anne's remarkable letters to Lord Dundas, then secretary for war and the colonies, and Lord Macartney, governor of the Cape, were published in 1901, under the title *South Africa a Century Ago.*

In 1806, on the reconquest of the Cape by the British, Andrew Barnard was reappointed colonial secretary, but Lady Anne preferred to remain in England. She was not with him when he died in 1807. Resuming her salon life with her sister Margaret, who was also newly widowed, Anne spent the rest of her life in London, quietly pursuing her art and writing, until her death on May 6, 1825. In Scotland, she is known more for "Auld Robin Gray" then as a literary figure in South African history. Anne only acknowledged authorship of the lyrics two years before her death, in a letter to Sir Walter Scott. A century later, her voluminous personal writings were collected for the first time in *Lady Anne Barnard at the Cape of Good Hope, 1797–1802.*

SOURCES:

Blain, Virginia, Pat Clements, and Isobel Grundy, eds. *The Feminist Companion to Literature in English.* New Haven, CT: Yale University Press, 1990.

Buck, Claire, ed. *The Bloomsbury Guide to Women's Literature.* NY: Prentice Hall, 1992.

Powell, Anthony, ed. *Barnard Letters 1778–1824.* London: Duckworth, 1928.

Todd, Janet, ed. *British Women Writers.* NY: Continuum, 1989.

SUGGESTED READING:

Fairbridge, Dorothea, ed. *Lady Anne Barnard at the Cape of Good Hope, 1797–1802,* 1924.

Robinson, A.M. Lewin, ed. *The Letters of Lady Anne Barnard to Henry Dundas . . . together with her Journal of a Tour into the Interior,* 1973.

Crista Martin,
freelance writer, Boston, Massachusetts

Lindsay, Lilian (1871–1959).

See Murray, Lilian.

Line, Anne (d. 1601)

Catholic Englishwoman condemned as a heretic. Executed at Tyburn, England, in 1601.

During a period of Catholic persecution in England during the late 16th and early 17th centuries, Anne Line, a middle-aged woman, not only harbored Catholic priests, but allowed them to conduct masses in her home. She was eventually captured by authorities as she was helping a priest to escape and was condemned as a heretic. She was ordered to die on the gallows. Just before her execution at Tyburn in 1601, she angered onlookers by kissing the gallows and proclaiming: "Where I received one [priest], I would to God I had been able to receive a thousand."

Ling, Ding (1904–1985).

See Ding Ling.

Lingens-Reiner, Ella (1908—)

Austrian anti-Nazi activist and physician. Name variations: Ella Lingens. Born in Vienna, Austria, in 1908; became involved in underground Social Democratic activities starting in 1934 and was imprisoned by the Nazis at both the Dachau and Auschwitz concentration camps.

Ella Lingens-Reiner's social conscience took a practical turn during her university days, when she decided to study medicine. Despite the poor economic climate of the 1930s and strongly discriminatory pressures against female physicians, she never regretted her decision to devote her life to the art of healing. But the 1930s were a decade of turmoil and hatred, not healing or reconciliation. When the authoritarian Austrian regime of Engelbert Dollfuss crushed the Social Democratic party and its trade unions in a bloody uprising in February 1934, she determined to resist the "Austro-Nazi" system and its repression of the Austrian working class, in particular the impressive social achievements of "Red Vienna." She joined the resistance circle that formed around Otto and *Käthe Leichter, which remained in contact with the Social Democratic leadership which had fled to Czechoslovakia and France. A much harsher system of persecution was imposed on Austria in March 1938, when Hitler's Anschluss (connection) brought about the annexation of Austria by Nazi Germany.

Refusing to abandon her Social Democratic comrades, many of whom were Jewish, the "pure Aryan" Ella Lingens-Reiner was arrested by the Gestapo in 1942 for her unrepentant anti-Nazi attitudes and behavior. Imprisoned at the dreaded Auschwitz-Birkenau camp as well as at the Dachau concentration camp, as a skilled and compassionate physician she quickly became an indispensable member of the camp social system. Despite the inhuman living conditions and an almost total lack of medicines, on many occasions her intervention saved lives, or at least brought a glimmer of humanity into the final hours of dying prisoners. In one such case in 1944, Lingens-Reiner was able to arrange the transfer of the aged and deathly ill *Luise Kautsky to the Auschwitz hospital. After her 1945 liberation, Ella Lingens-Reiner resumed her medical practice, spending much of her leisure time informing the public, and particularly a younger generation that had not personally experienced the horrors of National Socialism, of her death camp experiences. She served for many years as president of the organization of former Auschwitz prisoners (Österreichische Lagergemeinschaft Auschwitz).

Ella Lingens-Reiner, newly liberated from Dachau, attends to a fellow inmate. Photo by Lee Miller, Dachau, 1945.

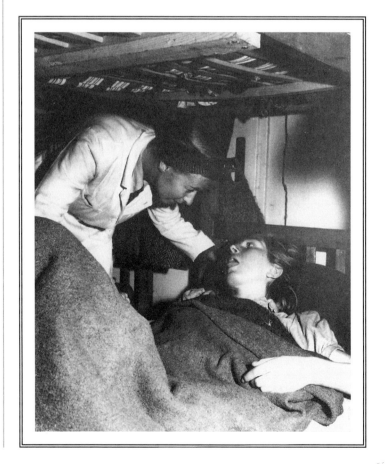

SOURCES:

Adler, H.G., Hermann Langbein, and Ella Lingens-Reiner, eds. *Auschwitz: Zeugnisse und Berichte.* 5th ed. Hamburg: Europäische Verlagsanstalt, 1994.

Biographical file, "Biografisches Lexikon der Üösterreichischen Frau," Institut für Wissenschaft und Kunst, Vienna.

Brauneis, Inge. "Widerstand von Frauen gegen den Nationalsozialismus 1938–1945." unpublished Ph.D. diss., University of Vienna, 1974.

Kubica, Helena. "The Crimes of Josef Mengele," in Yisrael Gutman and Michael Berenbaum, eds., *Anatomy of the Auschwitz Death Camp.* Bloomington and Washington, DC: Indiana University Press/ U.S. Holocaust Memorial Museum, 1994, pp. 317–337.

Leichter, Otto. *Zwischen zwei Diktaturen: Österreichs Revolutionäre Sozialisten 1934–1938.* Vienna: Europa Verlag, 1968.

Lifton, Robert Jay. *The Nazi Doctors: Medical Killing and the Psychology of Genocide.* NY: Basic Books, 1986.

Lingens-Reiner, Ella. *Prisoners of Fear.* London: Victor Gollancz, 1948.

"Miseries of War," in *The Times* [London] *Literary Supplement.* July 17, 1948, p. 396.

Naythons, Matthew, and Sherwin B. Nuland. *The Face of Mercy: A Photographic History of Medicine at War.* NY: Random House, 1993.

Posner, Gerald L., and John Ware. *Mengele: The Complete Story.* NY: McGraw-Hill, 1986.

Reiter, Andrea. "Die autobiographischen Berichte ehemaliger Konzentrationslagerhäftlinge im Englischen Exil: Bruno Heilig, Ella Lingens-Reiner, Kitty Hart," in *Zeitgeschichte* [Vienna]. Vol. 19, no. 5–6, May–June, 1992, pp. 172–186.

Sporrer, Maria, and Herbert Steiner, eds. *Rosa Jochmann: Zeitzeugin.* 3rd ed. Vienna: Europaverlag, 1987.

John Haag,
Associate Professor of History,
University of Georgia, Athens, Georgia

Ling Shuhua (1904–1990)

Chinese writer. Name variations: Ling Shu-hua; Su Hua Ling Chen. Born in 1904 in Kwantung, China; died in 1990; Cantonese father was an official; married writer and critic Chen Yuan (Ch'en Yüan), in 1920s; studied English literature, Yanjing (Yenching) University, early 1920s; studied painting in Paris and had several solo exhibitions of her works; professor of literature.

Wrote short stories, inspired by writer Katherine Mansfield; was a friend of writer Bing Xin; had stories published in weekly Contemporary Review *and in three collections.*

Selected works: The Temple of Flowers *(1928);* Women *(1930);* Little Brothers *(1935).*

Ling Shuhua was born in 1904 in Kwantung, moving to Beijing in the early 1920s to study English literature at Yanjing University. Her first stories were published in the early 1920s in the weekly *Contemporary Review* after she came to the attention of Chen Yuan, a professor of English at National Peking University and editor of the magazine. They married during the 1920s and became a celebrated literary couple in Beijing, Ling Shuhua writing short stories and working as a professor of literature, and Chen Yuan teaching and writing influential commentaries on politics and literature in the *Contemporary Review*, many of which were collected in his book *Causeries of Hsi-ying.*

Several women writers came to public attention in the 1920s, including **Huang Luyin, Feng Yuanjun** and **Bing Xin**, with whom Ling became friends at Yanjing University. None, however, are considered to have Ling's brilliance and originality. Ling's first book was *The Temple of Flowers*, published in 1928, collecting together a number of stories written between 1924 and 1926 with a foreword by Chen Yuan. Inspired by the deceptively light, ironic style and domestic subject matter of New Zealand short-story writer *Katherine Mansfield*, choosing similarly feminine titles like "The Tea Party" and "Embroidered Pillows," Ling's stories probe the nuances and quiet dramas of polite Chinese society during a turbulent and transitional era. Critic Don Holoch suggests that by "giving her fiction the feel and texture of everyday trivia and yet showing the enormity of the anguish they entail, Ling employs a 'realism' that endows every common object and cliché with a potentially explosive meaning and makes the matter-of-fact description of household life subversive."

Specializing in psychological portraits and telling details, Ling's work was never as popular as that of Bing Xin. But her deft touch and perceptive eye ensured that Ling found a dedicated and discriminating public. "Embroidered Pillows" is considered to be the first modern Chinese story sustained by the dramatic irony of a central symbol.

Ling published two further collections of stories, *Women* (1930) and *Little Brothers* (1935), the latter of which reflected both her new experiences as a mother and as a resident of Japan, where she lived during the early 1930s. Both she and her husband wrote less in the years leading up to World War II, partly because of her husband's withdrawal from public life in China. The couple moved to London in 1947 when Chen Yuan became a delegate to UNESCO, after which they split their time between London and Taipei. Ling also taught contemporary Chinese literature in Singapore, and later in Canada and the United Kingdom.

SOURCES:

Hoang, Dustin X. "Modern Chinese Women's Literature in the May Fourth Era," thesis, December 15, 1995.

Hsia, C.T. *A History of Modern Chinese Fiction, 1917–1957*. New Haven, CT: Yale University Press, 1961.

Paula Morris, D.Phil.,
Brooklyn, New York

Linley, Elizabeth (1754–1792)

*English soprano. Name variations: Eliza Ann Linley; Elizabeth Sheridan; Mrs. Richard Brinsley Sheridan. Born in Bath, England, in 1754; died in Bristol, England, in 1792; daughter of Thomas Linley, the Elder (1732–1795, a composer); sister of Maria Linley (1763–1784) and Mary Linley (1758–1787) who were also singers; married Richard Brinsley Sheridan (the playwright), in 1773 (died 1816); children: son Thomas Sheridan (1775–1817, a poet, who became colonial treasurer at Cape of Good Hope and married *Caroline Henrietta Sheridan nee Callander).*

Elizabeth Linley was born in 1754 in Bath, England, the daughter of the English musical composer Thomas Linley, who would eventually compose music for his son-in-law's comic opera, *The Duenna*. Her sisters *Mary Linley and *Maria Linley were also singers. Her granddaughters were *Caroline Norton, *Helen Selina Blackwood, and Lady *Jane Georgina Sheridan.

Elizabeth Linley sang in public as early as 12 years old, and was admired not only for her exceptional voice, but for her delicate beauty, which has been immortalized by the great painters Reynolds and Gainsborough. Linley had many suitors, but the brilliant playwright Richard Brinsley Sheridan gained her heart, and they were married in 1773, after eloping to France in 1772. Her life with the unpredictable genius of *The Rivals* and *School for Scandal* was not always happy, but she was a devoted wife until her death.

Elizabeth Linley was spoken of in glowing terms by those who knew her. A bishop declared her to be "the link between an angel and a woman," and the poet Thomas Moore wrote: "There has seldom perhaps existed a finer combination of all those qualities that attracted both eye and heart than this accomplished and lovely person exhibited."

Linley, Maria (1763–1784)

*English singer. Born in 1763; died in 1784; daughter of Thomas Linley, the Elder (1732–1795, a composer); sister of *Mary Linley (1758–1787) and *Elizabeth Linley (1754–1792).*

Maria Linley sang in oratorio and at the Bath concerts.

Linley, Mary (1758–1787)

*English singer. Name variations: Mrs. Tickell. Born in 1758; died in 1787; daughter of Thomas Linley, the Elder (1732–1795, a composer); sister of *Maria Linley (1763–1784) and *Elizabeth Linley (1754–1792); married Richard Tickell (a pamphleteer, dramatist, and commissioner of stamps), in 1780.*

Mary Linley made her singing debut in 1771.

Linsenhoff, Liselott (1927—)

West German equestrian who was the first woman to win the individual gold medal in dressage. Name variations: Linsenhoff-Schindling. Born on August 27, 1927; children: Ann-Kathrin Linsenhoff (b. August 1, 1960, also a dressage rider).

Won the Olympic individual bronze medal in dressage, as well as team silver, on Adular in Stockholm (1956); won the Aachen Grand Prix on Piaff (1955, 1956, and 1959); won the silver medal at two World championships; won Olympic team gold in dressage in Mexico City (1968); was European champion in dressage (1969, 1971); won the Olympic gold medal in individual dressage on Piaff (first woman to win individual gold medal in dressage) and team silver in Munich (1972).

In what is an unusual occurrence in a world championship sport, women in equestrian events compete directly against, and with, men. When Liselott Linsenhoff, **Hannelore Weygand**, and **Anneliese Küppers** won the team dressage silver medal for West Germany in 1956, it was the first Olympic equestrian event in which medals were won by a team comprised entirely of women. (In that same Australian Olympics, women participated with men in show jumping for the first time.) Australia had strict quarantine laws in 1956, so while the Summer Olympic Games were held in Melbourne, the equestrian events were held in Stockholm, Sweden. There, Linsenhoff also took the individual bronze medal in dressage on Adular behind gold medalist Henri Saint Cyr and silver medalist *Lis Hartel of Denmark. Linsenhoff was also awarded team gold in the summer Olympics in Mexico City in 1968.

In the 1972 Munich Olympics, 21 of the 33 riders in individual dressage were women. Linsenhoff topped her West German teammate, Dr.

Reiner Klimke, who had previously amassed eight Olympic medals, to win the individual gold medal in dressage. Again, she was the first woman to do so. That year, she also took team silver. Linsenhoff went on to coach later successful German teams, as well as her daughter; **Ann-Kathrin Linsenhoff** was a European Young Rider bronze medalist, a European individual silver and bronze medalist, and the recipient of a team gold in the Seoul Olympics in 1988.

SOURCES:

Watchen, Guy. *Great Horsemen of the World.* London: Trafalgar Square, 1991.

Linskill, Mary (1840–1891)

English novelist. Name variations: (pseudonym) Stephen Yorke. Born in Whitby, Yorkshire, on December 13, 1840; died in Whitby on April 9, 1891.

An English novelist, Mary Linskill wrote *Tales of the North Riding* which was published in *Good Words* in 1871. She also wrote short stories and four novels, including *Clevedale* (1876) and *The Haven under the Hill* (1886).

Linton, Eliza Lynn (1822–1898)

English novelist. Name variations: also wrote under name Eliza Lynn. Born Eliza Lynn at Keswick, England, on February 10, 1822; died in London on July 14, 1898; daughter of J. Lynn, vicar of Crosthwaite, in Cumberland; her mother (name unknown) died when she was an infant; granddaughter of Samuel Goodenough; married William James Linton (1812–1898, an engraver), in 1858.

Eliza Lynn Linton was born in 1822 in Keswick, England, the daughter of Reverend J. Lynn, vicar of Crosthwaite. Eliza revealed an independent nature early on and educated herself in her father's library. With a year's allowance and a large, eclectic supply of books, she arrived in London about 1845 to make her way as a journalist. By 1848, she had joined the staff of the *Morning Chronicle* and had already published her first novel, *Azeth the Egyptian* (1846). *Amymone,* a romance set in the days of Pericles, was published in 1848, and *Realities,* a tale of modern life, in 1851. But her first three "glaringly unreal and emotional" novels were not successful, and for several years she seems to have abandoned fiction.

Linton lived in Paris from 1851 to 1854, working as a correspondent for London papers. When, in 1865, she published *Grasp Your Nettle,* she had found a new writing style. Her well-constructed stories were exhilarating and retained tension throughout, although some felt they afforded little "to reflect upon and were entirely without feeling." *Lizzie Lorton of Greyrigg* (1866), *Patricia Kemball* (1874), and *The Atonement of Leam Dundas* (1877) are among the best examples of this more technical side of her talent. Notable exceptions included *Joshua Davidson* (1872), a bold but not irreverent adaptation of the story of Jesus of Nazareth to that of the French Commune, and *Christopher Kirkland,* a veiled autobiography (1885). Measured by their immediate success, her books gave Linton an honorable position among the writers of her day, and, having found her audience, she continued to write prolifically until her death.

Considered a kind-hearted and generous woman, Linton was also outspoken. Though her life provided an excellent example of the freedom that could be purchased by an economically independent woman, she was extremely anti-feminist. She was a polished writer whose articles often appeared in the journals of her day; her sketches on the "Girl of the Period" in the *Saturday Review* produced a sensation, and she was a frequent contributor to the *St. James's Gazette,* the *Daily News* and other leading newspapers. Many of her essays have been collected. In 1858, at the request of his dying wife, she married W.J. Linton, the engraver, but the union was soon ended by mutual consent. Eliza nevertheless brought up one of his daughters from his previous marriage. A few years before her death, Linton retired to Malvern. She died in London on July 14, 1898.

Eliza Linton's reminiscences appeared after her death under the title *My Literary Life* (1899) and a biography was written by G.S. Layard, *Eliza Lynn Linton: Her Life, Letters and Opinions* (1901).

SUGGESTED READING:

Anderson, Nancy Fix. *Woman Against Women in Victorian England: A Life of Eliza Lynn Linton,* 1996.

Lioba (700–779)

English saint and missionary. Name variations: Leoba; Leobgyth; Liobgetha; Truthgeba. Born Liobgetha in 700 in Wessex, England; died in 779 at Bischofscheim also seen as Bischofsheim abbey in Mainz, Germany; educated at the nunnery of Minster-in-Thanet and then at Wimborne in Dorset; never married; no children.

The English saint Lioba came from a noble family of Wessex who sent her to the convent at Thanet for her education. Some years later, she transferred to another nunnery, at Wimborne. Around 748, she developed a friendship through correspondence with the missionary St. Boniface, a distant relative also born in Wessex, who was working in Germany. Boniface recognized the high level of education and extreme piety of this nun, and asked her to join him in his work in Germany. She agreed and traveled there with some of her sister nuns, including *Walpurgis. Boniface and Lioba founded an abbey at Bischofscheim, and Lioba became its first abbess around 753. She was also put in indirect charge of several other Benedictine communities for women. In 754, her friend Boniface was murdered. From his letters, many still extant, we know how much he valued her. In one, he asked that she consent to be buried next to him "so that their bodies might await the day of resurrection together."

Lioba served as abbess for about 28 years. During this time, Bischofscheim became noted as a place of great learning and charity for the poor, and the abbess was often consulted by royal and noble German leaders on both religious and secular questions of government. Lioba's dedication to serving others led her to encourage her nuns and monks to pray in public for the benefit of the laity, and to develop and preside over the work of a large scriptorium. She died in 779, age 79, and was later canonized.

SOURCES:

Anderson, Bonnie S., and Judith P. Zinsser. *A History of Their Own.* Vol. I. NY: Harper & Row, 1988.

Uglow, Jennifer, ed. *International Dictionary of Women's Biography.* NY: Continuum, 1989.

Laura York,
Riverside, California

Liobgetha (700–779).

See Lioba.

Lioness of Lisabiland (1900–1978).

See Ransome-Kuti, Funmilayo.

Lipkowska, Lydia (1882–1958)

Russian soprano whose career took her to many of the world's great stages. Born Lydia Marschner on June 6, 1882, in Babino, Bessarabia, Russia; died in Beirut, Lebanon, on March 22, 1958; married Georgi Baklanoff.

After studying at the St. Petersburg Conservatory, Lydia Lipkowska made her debut at that city's Imperial Opera in 1908. An excellent actress who was graced with a pure, communicative voice, she became a favorite with audiences of the day. By 1909, she was singing in Paris,

and appeared that same year in the United States at New York's Metropolitan Opera as well as in Boston. She made her Covent Garden debut in 1911 and in the fateful year of 1914 appeared in Monte Carlo in the first performances of Ponchielli's *I Mori di Valenza*. Within the span of those three years, Lipkowska made 29 recordings, many of which remain highly rated by modern critics of vocal artistry. After the Bolshevik Revolution, she emigrated in 1919 to France and resumed her career with Russian emigré opera troupes throughout Western Europe. In 1928–1929, she made an emotionally difficult return tour of the Soviet Union, after which she lived, and taught singing, in Rumania. **Virginia Zeani** was among her students.

In 1945, Lipkowska returned to France, then settled some years later in Lebanon, living and teaching in Beirut, where she died on March 22, 1958. Her large repertory included Lakmé, Lucia, and the role of Marfa in Rimsky-Korsakov's *The Tsar's Bride*, as well as Tchaikovsky's Tatiana and Iolanta.

SOURCES:

Levik, Sergei Iurevich. *The Levik Memoirs: A Opera Singer's Notes.* Translated by Edward Morgan. London: Symposium Records, 1995.

John Haag,
Associate Professor of History,
University of Georgia, Athens, Georgia

Lipona, countess of.

See Bonaparte, Carolina (1782–1839).

Lippincott, Sara Clarke

(1823–1904)

American journalist and lecturer. Name variations: Sara Clarke Lippincott; Sara Jane Lippincott; wrote under Sara J. Clarke and Mrs. L.H. Lippincott; (pseudonym) Grace Greenwood. Born Sara Jane Clarke on September 23, 1823, in Pompey, New York; died on April 20, 1904, in New Rochelle, New York; youngest daughter and of one of 11 children of Thaddeus Clarke (a physician) and Deborah (Baker) Clarke; great-granddaughter of the Rev. Jonathan Edwards; attended school in Rochester, New York; married Leander K. Lippincott, in 1853; children: one daughter, Annie Lippincott.

Selected works: Greenwood Leaves (1850); History of My Pets (1851); Poems (1851); Greenwood Leaves, Second Series (1852); Recollections of My Childhood, and Other Stories (1852); Haps and Mishaps of a Tour in Europe (1854); Merrie England (1855); A Forest Tragedy (1856); Old Wonder-Eyes (1857); Stories and Legends of Travel and History

(1857); Stories from Famous Ballads (1859); Bonnie Scotland (1861); Nelly, the Gypsy Girl (1863); Records of Five Years (1867); Stories and Sights of France and Italy (1867); Stories of Many Lands (1867); New Life in New Lands (1873); Heads and Tails: Studies and Stories of My Pets (1874); Emma Abbott, Prima Donna (1878); (with R.W. Raymond) Treasures from Fairy Land (1879); Queen Victoria: Her Girlhood and Womanhood (1883); Some of My Pets (1884); Stories for Home-Folks, Young and Old (1884); Stories and Sketches (1892).

Sara Clarke Lippincott was born Sara Jane Clarke in 1823 in Pompey, New York, the youngest of 11 children of a physician. She attended school for eight years in Rochester, New York, and at 19 moved with her family to New Brighton, Pennsylvania. Lippincott had her first poetry published in several Rochester newspapers at the age of 13, and from 1844 she was a regular contributor to New Mirror and Home Journal. Adopting the pseudonym "Grace Greenwood," she later published prose and informal letters in Sartain's, Graham's, Union Magazine, and other journals of the day. A collection of her magazine pieces, Greenwood Leaves (1850), was a best-seller, as was its sequel two years later. Starting in

Sara Clarke Lippincott

1849, Lippincott also served on the staffs of Godey's Lady's Book, Graham's, Sartain's, the Saturday Evening Post, the abolitionist National Era, and The New York Times.

While making a solo tour of Europe in 1852–53, Lippincott sent back a series of travel pieces and interviews which appeared in National Era and the Saturday Evening Post and were later collected in a very popular book, Haps and Mishaps of a Tour of Europe (1854). Lively in style and frequently humorous, it records Lippincott's visits to historical sites and her meetings with notable literary, artistic, and political figures.

With her husband Leander Lippincott, whom she married in 1853, Lippincott coedited a popular children's magazine, The Little Pilgrim (1853–75). Her juvenile work includes historical sketches based on her early European travels (Merrie England [1855] and Bonnie Scotland [1861]), and stories or "tales," which, according to **Susan Sutton Smith** in American Woman Writers, are characterized by "heavy morality, sentimentality, and emphasis on sickbed and deathbed scenes." Lippincott's marriage was never happy. It ended in 1876, when Leander was indicted for embezzlement in connection with his job at the Department of the Interior and fled to Europe for good. Lippincott was left as the sole provider for their daughter.

Lippincott's accounts of her travels in Europe during the 1870s and 1880s, produced for the Independent, have stood the test of time. Her later letters from Washington, D.C., also reflect a more substantial journalistic style. Lippincott's "poetry, sentimental tales and sketches, and children's books merit obscurity," writes Smith, "but her strong-minded, firsthand reporting still deserves and rewards attention."

SOURCES:

Edgerly, Lois Stiles. Give Her This Day. Gardiner, ME: Tilbury House, 1990.
Mainiero, Lina, ed. American Women Writers. NY: Frederick Ungar, 1981.

Barbara Morgan,
Melrose, Massachusetts

Lipsius, Marie (1837–1927)

German writer. Name variations: (pseudonym) La Mara. Born in Leipzig, Germany, on December 30, 1837; died near Wurzen, Saxony, on March 2, 1927; sister of Richard Adelbert Lipsius (1830–1892, a German Protestant cleric and co-founder of the Evangelical Union) and Justus Hermann Lipsius (1834–1920, a classical scholar).

Marie Lipsius, who published under the pseudonym La Mara, was a noted writer on Liszt and Beethoven, and edited letters of Liszt, Berlioz, and others.

Li Qingzhao (1083–c. 1151)

China's greatest female poet, who lived during the Song dynasty and specialized in lyric ci (tz'u) verse, and who was praised for the originality of her poetic imagery, her emotional language, and the harmony of her verse. Name variations: Li Ch'ing-chao; Li Ch'ing Chao; Li Chiang-chao; Li Qing Zhao. Born Li Qingzhao in 1083; died around 1151; daughter of Li Gefei also seen as Li Ke-fei or Li Ko-fei (a scholar and minister at court) and a mother who was a poet (name unknown); educated at home; married Zhao Mingcheng (Chao Ming-ch'eng, a famous epigraphist who specialized in deciphering old inscriptions), around 1101 (died 1129); possibly married Zhang Ruzhou, in 1132 (divorced after 100 days); produced a body of work including six volumes of poetry and seven volumes of essays, most of which have been lost.

> The sky, the waves of clouds, the morning mist blended in one.
> The Milky Way was shimmering, a thousand sails were dancing.
> Methinks I was borne to the throne of God.
> "Whither are you going?" a celestial voice asked me.
> Sighing, I replied: "Long, long is the way, the day is dying."
> In vain, I compose astonishing verses.
> The roc-bird is soaring upon the wind for a ninety-thousand-mile journey.
> Stop not, O wind!
> Blow my boat to fairyland.
>
> —Translated by Hu Binqing

This poem was written nearly 900 years ago by Li Qingzhao, who is "universally accepted" as China's greatest woman poet, writes historian Hu Binqing (Hu Pin-ch'ing). Powerful and visionary, by turns heroic, playful, sensuous or imbued with despair, her poetry shows a woman confident in her art and ambitious enough to seek greatness in a society which, in the words of Hu Binqing, traditionally ascribed to women "no freedom of thought, no freedom of action, no freedom of love, and no freedom of expression." Her extant works, mostly in the ci (tz'u) style, a form of lyric verse written for musical accompaniment, display a vitality, energy, and emotional color that have remained vivid throughout the centuries.

Li Qingzhao (also written Li Ch'ing-Chao) was born in Shandong (Shantung) province, China, in 1083, during the reign of Emperor Shenzong (Shen-tsung) of the Song (Sung) dynasty. An interval of calm for the most part within centuries of war and upheavals, the Song dynasty (969–1278) was a fertile period for art and technology within China. It is considered the golden age of Chinese painting as well as a time of increasing sophistication in poetry, literature, porcelain and other arts; it also saw the invention of gunpowder and of moveable type. Li Qingzhao grew up in Chinan, called "The City of Fountains," where her childhood home is now a historical site. Both sides of her family were descended from scholars and notable officials: her father, Li Gefei (Li Ke-fei or Li Ko-fei), was a scholar at the Imperial Academy in the capital city of Gaifeng (Kai-feng) who later served the Song court as Minister of Rites, and her mother was a poet and a granddaughter of Wang Gongchen (Wang Kung-ch'en [1012–1085]), a poet and essayist. Because of her parents' appreciation of classical learning, Li Qingzhao received a good education. Although such an schooling for women was contrary to Chinese tradition, her father had discovered that she was more interested in scholarship than were her sisters or one of her brothers, Li Mang, and so he personally tutored her at home. She showed a talent early on for writing ci poetry, which was very popular during the Song dynasty, and her poetry, literary talent, and exquisite diction made her a well-known figure in her hometown.

Li Qingzhao first established herself as a poet when she wrote two shi (shih), or regular verse, poems to rhyme with a poem written by a friend of her father's, Zhang Lei (Chang Lei, also known as Zhang Wenqian [Chang Wen-ch'ian]). The initial poem was written upon the discovery of an 8th-century monument celebrating the restoration of royal authority after an uprising during the earlier Dang (Tang) dynasty; Li Qingzhao's responses were critical of Zhang Lei's shallowness and lack of understanding in the events commemorated on the monument. Far from being chastised for her audacity, Li Qingzhao found herself praised by her father and other scholars. In a society where such respect toward women was seldom granted, this may well have given her the confidence to develop her talents to the fullest.

At age 18, Li Qingzhao married Zhao Mingcheng, who at the time was a student of the Imperial Academy. The son of Zhao Tingzhi (Chao T'ing-chih), minister of the interior and later prime minister, he was also from Shandong province, and would later become well known for his explanations of inscriptions found on ancient bronzes and stone monuments. He encouraged Li Qingzhao in her poetry, and one of her early works, written to the tune of "Magnolia," speaks of her relationship with him:

I bought a spray of Spring in bloom
From a flower carrying pole.
It is covered with tiny teardrops
That still reflect the pink clouds of dawn
And traces of morning dew.
Lest my lover should think
The flowers are lovelier than my face
I pin it slanting in my thick black hair
And ask him to compare us.
  —Translated by Kenneth Rexroth and Ling
  Chung, from *Complete Poems*. (© 1979, by
  Kenneth Rexroth and Ling Chung. Reprinted by
  permission of New Directions Publishing Corp.)

One of Li Qingzhao's most famous poems, "Sorrow of Departure," was written to her husband on a silk handkerchief, to the tune of "Cutting a Flowering Plum Branch," while he was still a student and she longed for his return:

Red lotus incense fades on
The jeweled curtain. Autumn
Comes again. Gently I open
My silk dress and float alone
On the orchid boat. Who can
Take a letter beyond the clouds?
Only the wild geese come back
And write their ideograms
On the sky under the full
Moon that floods the West Chamber.
Flowers, after their kind, flutter
And scatter. Water after
Its nature, when spilt, at last
Gathers again in one place.
Creatures of the same species
Long for each other. But we
Are far apart and I have
Grown learned in sorrow.
Nothing can make it dissolve
And go away. One moment,
It is on my eyebrows.
The next, it weighs on my heart.
  —Translated by Kenneth Rexroth and Ling
  Chung, from *Complete Poems*. (© 1979 by Kenneth Rexroth and Ling Chung. Reprinted by
  permission of New Directions Publishing Corp.)

Two years after their marriage, Zhao Mingcheng graduated from the Imperial Academy and became a functionary at the royal court. They lived in Gaifeng, often entertaining the literati in their home and using their wealth to collect bronzes, calligraphy, paintings, pieces of jade, stone inscriptions and antiques of all types. Considered an ideal match, they wrote poems to each other expressing their intelligence and love, and enjoyed researching the histories of their treasures together, which they recorded in careful detail. At night, they often read and discussed books together. The poet frequently accompanied her husband on his official business and to social gatherings; when he went away alone, she would send him poems to maintain the strong link between them. It was during this time, using imagery including the chrysanthemum, Chinese flowering crabapple, wine, wind, moon and moonlight, birds, cold rain, and leaves, that Li Qingzhao founded a graceful and restrained school of ci poetry called the yi'an style. Some of her works, such as this, to the tune of "Red Lips," are nonetheless blatantly erotic:

Tired of swinging
indolent
I rise
with a slender hand
put right
my hair
the dew thick
on frail blossoms
sweat seeping through
my thin robe
and seeing
my friend come
stockings torn
gold hairpins askew
I walk over
blushing
lean against the door
turn my head
grasp the dark green plums
and smell them
  —Translated by James Cryer (copyright c 1984
  by Carolina Wren Press. Used by permission.)

A similar eroticism is found in a poem to the tune of "Picking Mulberries":

Come with evening
ranks of wind and rain
was away
the fires of sunset
I finish tuning the pipes
face the floral mirror
thinly dressed
crimson silken shift
translucent
over icelike flesh
lustrous
in snowpale cream
glistening scented oils
and laugh
to my sweet friend
tonight
you are within
my silken curtains
your pillow, your mat
will grow cold
  —Translated by James Cryer (copyright c 1984
  by Carolina Wren Press. Used by permission.)

Due to their involvement with the court, Li Qingzhao and her husband were subject to the power struggles there, where rival factions and intrigues were weakening the Song dynasty. In 1102, her father was exiled from the court. She wrote poems to her powerful father-in-law, then vice prime minister and one of the rivals of her father's faction, imploring him to reinstate her father. "Your fingers are burned," she wrote in one poem, "while your heart grows cold." In 1103, it was decreed that no further marriages could take place between the rival factions of her father and her father-in-law, placing Li Qingzhao in a politically precarious position. Two years later, however, her father was granted amnesty and returned to court. Her powerful father-in-law became the prime minister, but lost favor and was dismissed in 1107, and died soon thereafter. With their influence thus greatly reduced, the Zhao family members, including Li Qingzhao and her husband, suffered persecution. The couple left the capital for Qingzhou (Ch'ing Chou), in the south, where they remained in exile for at least ten years. Zhao Mingcheng served as magistrate, first in Laizhou (Laichow) and then Qingzhou. They continued their hobbies of deciphering stone tablets and bronze inscriptions and collecting antiques, paintings and precious jade, and reading from the classics, asking each other questions, and rewarding correct answers with sips of tea. They also began collaborating on an important book, *Jin Shi Lu* (*Chin Shih Lu* [The Study of Bronzes and Stone Inscriptions, also seen as Collection of Inscriptions on Ancient Bones and Stone Tablets]), explaining the ancient inscriptions that recorded history and told of the great accomplishments of Chinese leaders.

On the occasion of her 31st birthday, when Li Qingzhao had her portrait painted, her husband wrote the following poem in the top corner of the portrait:

> To Poetess I-an on the Occasion of Her
> Thirty-first Birthday Anniversary:
>
> Her poetry is pure and elegant,
> Her person modest and dignified,
> A real companion for me
> In my retirement

Soon after the couple went into exile, an invasion from the north occurred, led by the Jurchens, a Tartar tribe from Siberia. The Jurchens had recently overthrown the Khitan Tartars, founders of the Liao dynasty in Manchuria and parts of Northern China to which the Song dynasty had paid tribute, and were now continuing a slow push towards the Yangtze river. (The Jurchens shortly would found the Jin [Chin] dynasty.) In 1126, the capital of Gaifeng was laid seige by Jurchen horsemen who captured the emperor and several thousand of his retainers. The northern Song dynasty fell that year, and a boundary was established along the Huai River, dividing the area still controlled by the newly reconstituted government of the southern Song and the Jurchens' Jin dynasty. (The southern Song dynasty would last until the Mongol invasion in 1279.) In the resulting turmoil, Li Qingzhao and her husband were forced to flee, leaving behind most of their collected bronzes, antiques, and paintings. They remained on the run until 1128, when they settled in Jian Ning (modern Nanjing or Nanking). As the Jurchen invasion spread southward into the middle of China, the poet boldly satirized the Song emperor for behaving in a cowardly fashion and criticized the nobles and troops who crossed the Yangtze, fleeing southward:

> Alive we need heroes among the living
> Who when dead will be heroes among the ghosts.
> I cannot tell how much we miss Hsiang Yu
> Who preferred death to crossing to the East of
>   the River.

> The creative impulse makes me restless as a nocturnal bird
> Reluctant to perch after flying three rounds
> —Li Qingzhao

The same year, during the reign of Emperor Gaozong (Kao-tsung), Zhao Mingcheng resumed office in Nanjing as a magistrate. When he was appointed to Huchow in Zhejiang (Chekiang) province and made plans to establish his family in Jiangxi (Kiangsi), the couple took along their families' remains. In 1129, the poet's husband was en route to a new post in Jiankang when he died at age 48. As the Jurchen invaders attacked Jiankang, Li Qingzhao fled alone southward, to Yongzhai (Yung-chai), Shaoxing (Shao-hsing), and Chuxian (Ch'u-hsien). She arrived in Hangzhou (Hangchow) in 1132, where she wrote a poem, to the tune of "Andante," expressing her feelings as a bereaved widow:

> Search. Search. Seek. Seek.
> Cold. Cold. Clear. Clear.
> Sorrow. Sorrow. Pain. Pain.
> Hot flashes. Sudden chills.
> Stabbing pains. Slow agonies.
> I can find no peace.
> I drink two cups, then three bowls
> Of clear wine until I can't
> Stand up against a gust of wind.
> Wild geese fly overhead.
> They wrench my heart.
> They were our friends in the old days.
> Gold chrysanthemums litter
> The ground, pile up, faded, dead.
> This season I could not bear
> To pick them. All alone,
> Motionless at my window,
> I watch the gathering shadows.
> Fine rain sifts through the wu-t'ung trees.
> And drips, drop by drop, through the dusk.
> What can I ever do now?

How can I drive off this word—
Hopelessness?

—Translated by Kenneth Rexroth and Ling Chung,
from *Complete Poems.* (© 1979, by Kenneth
Rexroth and Ling Chung. Reprinted by permission of New Directions Publishing Corp.)

In Hangzhou she lived with her brother Jin-hua (Chin-hua). During the summer of that year, she was married to Zhang Ruzhou, possibly for protection during that period of turbulence (a minority of scholars dispute her second marriage). In September, after a union of only one hundred days, she divorced Zhang Ruzhou, who had mistreated her. Alone now, Li Qingzhao continued with the scholarly work she had begun with Zhao Mingcheng, completing their manuscript on ancient inscriptions. Her poems of this period took on a melancholy air of gloom and nostalgia, reinforced partly by the success of the invaders in weakening the Song dynasty; little of her work from this time is sublime or heroic, and information on the rest of her life is scarce.

According to the *History of the Sung Dynasty*, there existed six volumes of Li Qingzhao's poetry and seven volumes of her essays; most of these were lost during the Jurchen invasion. The date of her death is not recorded, although she is known to have lived to the age of 68. During her lifetime she was recognized, in the words of Hu Binqing, as an "epoch making poetess who was on an equal footing with her [male] contemporaries in prosody, rhetoric, and creation." Today her poetry is read partly for its commentary on the society of the Song dynasty, but also because of the eternal beauty of her compositions. One of her most important extant poems was written (to the tune of "Spring in Wuling") during the later part of her life, and speaks of the solitude of old age:

The gentle breeze has died down.
The perfumed dust has settled.
It is the end of the time
Of flowers. Evening falls
And all day I have been too
Lazy to comb my hair.

Our furniture is just the same.
He no longer exists.
All effort would be wasted.
Before I can speak,
My tears choke me.
I hear that Spring at Two Rivers
Is still beautiful.
I had hoped to take a boat there,
But I know so fragile a vessel
Won't bear such a weight of sorrow.

—Translated by Kenneth Rexroth and Ling Chung,
from *Complete Poems.* (© 1979, by Kenneth
Rexroth and Ling Chung. Reprinted by permission of New Directions Publishing Corp.)

SOURCES:

Cryer, James. *Plum Blossom: Poems of Li Ch'ing-Chao.* Chapel Hill, NC: Carolina Wren Press, 1984.

Hu Pin-ch'ing [Hu Binqing]. *Li Ch'ing-chao.* NY: Twayne Publishers, 1966.

Rexroth, Kenneth, and Ling Chung. *Li Ch'ing Chao: Collected Poems,* 1979.

Turner, John A. *A Golden Treasury of Chinese Poems.* Chinese University of Hong Kong (distributed by University of Washington Press, Seattle), 1976.

SUGGESTED READING:

Cheng jun-song, *et al. The Seventy-Two Great Figures of China's Nations.* Shanxi People's Publishing House, 1985.

Department of History Nanking University. *A Dictionary of the Famous Figures in the History of China.* Nanking: Jiangxi People's Publishing House, 1982.

Xu Gong Chi, *et al. The Heroes Before Our Time.* Beijing Press, 1986.

Xu Peijn. *Li Qing Zhao.* Shanghai Ancient Books, 1981.

Barbara Bennett Peterson,
Professor of History, University of Hawaii, author of *America in British Eyes* and editor of *Notable Women of Hawaii*

Lisa, Mary Manuel (1782–1869)

American wife of one of earliest Spanish fur-trading entrepeneurs. Born Mary Hempstead on October 25, 1782, in New London, Connecticut; died on September 3, 1869; daughter of Stephen Hempstead and Mary Lewis Hempstead; married John Keeny (a sea captain), on June 2, 1806 (died 1810); married Manuel Lisa, in 1818 (died, August 12, 1820); children: (first marriage) one son.

Born in New London, Connecticut, on October 25, 1782, Mary Manuel Lisa was the daughter of Stephen Hempstead and **Mary Lewis Hempstead**. She married a widowed sea captain, John Keeny, on June 2, 1806. He died four years later, and in 1811 she moved with her parents to St. Louis. There, on August 5, 1818, she married Manuel Lisa, explorer, fur trader and head of the Missouri Fur Company. She accompanied him on a trading expedition up the Missouri River as far as Council Bluffs, making her perhaps the first white woman to visit that region. Her husband died on August 12, 1820, widowing Mary once again. She received part of his estate, the remainder going to her stepchildren, and acted as executor of her late husband's business affairs. The partners in the Missouri Fur Company, however, pulled in different directions, and the business did not prosper. She sold part of her interest in 1822 and never received much income from Lisa's investment. Around 1860, she moved to Galena, Illinois, and spent the remainder of her life there. In both St. Louis and Galena, she was a leading figure in Protestant circles, and participated in the founding of the first Presbyterian congregation in Missouri. Mary Manuel Lisa died on September 3, 1869.

SOURCES:

Oglesby, Richard Edward. *Manuel Lisa and the Opening of the Missouri Fur Trade.* Norman, OK: University of Oklahoma Press, 1963.

Smith, Ambrose C. *Memorials of the Life and Character of Mary Manuel Lisa.* Philadelphia, PA: J.B. Lippincott, 1870.

Kendall W. Brown,
Professor of History, Brigham Young University, Provo, Utah

Lisa del Giocondo (1474–?).

See del Giocondo, Lisa.

Lisboa, Irene (1892–1958)

Portuguese educator and author. Name variations: Irene do Ceu Vieira Lisboa; (pseudonyms) João Falco and Manuel Soares. Born in Murzinheira, Arruda dos Vinhos, Portugal, on December 25, 1892; died in Lisbon on November 25, 1958.

Born on Christmas day, 1892, in the town of Murzinheira, Arruda dos Vinhos, Portugal, Irene do Céu Vieira Lisboa lived as an orphan from an early age. When her mother died (or possibly abandoned her), Irene's father showed no interest in raising the young girl. She consequently passed to her godmother's care. According to Ivone Leal, Irene's childhood "lacked the minimal conditions for the construction of her own identity: the kindness and security of a stable family." Irene studied for four years in a convent school (which she disliked) and then went to a "modern and cosmopolitan" English-style *colégio.* At 15, she entered the Liceu Maria Pia, where her academic abilities drew attention, and later to the Normal School, where she prepared to teach children. Restless and energetic, she founded *Educação Feminina,* a journal which the conservative faculty forced her to close after a few issues. Dissatisfied with the curriculum, she and colleagues gathered books on the psychology and education of young children, including works by Gabriel Compayré, Alfred Binet, Adolfo Coelho and Herbert Spencer.

Lisboa began teaching during the era of the First World War, which Portugal entered in 1917. Her first assignment was the Beato Parish school in Lisbon, where the students' great poverty made teaching them a challenge. She provided them with food, instructional materials and other necessities from her own salary, which she was able to do because she lived with her godfather and received free room and board. Devoted to the children, she perhaps created through them the emotional security missing in her own infancy. In 1920, she moved to the Tapada School, with the assignment of directing teachers engaged in pre-school education. The end of the war and the newness of Portugal's Republic (established in 1910) made it both an exhilarating time, full of hope and experimentation, and an era of political chaos. She joined with **Ilda Moreira,** a schoolhood friend, to lay the foundations of Portuguese pedagogy for young children. They studied the programs of Felix Klein, *Maria Montessori,** and Ovide Decroly, borrowing ideas but creating their own method for Portugal. This method emphasized interest centers, observation, group work, and considerable freedom for the students rather than structure.

The Portuguese government quickly recognized Lisboa and Moreira's pedagogical contributions. Upon the recommendation of Portugal's National Institute of Education, Irene spent the years from 1929 to 1931 on a fellowship at the University of Geneva's Institute of Educational Science, followed by a half year at the International Montessori Course in Rome. At her own expense, she then spent a year in Brussels studying Decroly's method (1931–32). She also brought back to Portugal an invaluable collection of books on educational theory. In 1933, she organized and directed an important conference on "The Methods and Ends of Early Childhood Education." Her official educational experimentation lasted for 18 years, part of which she served as director of Early Childhood Education (Inspectora Orientadora do Ensino Infantil) for the National Institute of Education. In 1938, the Antonio Salazar dictatorship forced her to retire as it had no interest in her endeavors.

Prior to that Irene Lisboa wrote and published prolifically, both in pedagogy and literature. Using the pseudonym João Falco, she published *13 Contarelos* in 1926, a series of children's stories. Under governmental auspices, she authored several official reports on early childhood education from 1933 to 1935. Her early unofficial works on pedagogy, however, appeared under the pseudonym Manuel Soares. Only in the early 1940s, after being forced to step down from her government post, did Irene Lisboa begin writing under her own name.

Lisboa's literary works, whether for children or adults, generally depict daily life in Lisbon. They focus on the mundane and contain virtually nothing linking them to the political climate of the time. Although widely studied by literary critics and scholars, her works, a precursor of Portuguese neo-Realism, failed to garner great public success. Lisboa's chief literary prose includes: *Começa uma Vida* (1940), *Esta Cidade!* (1943), *Uma Mão Cheia de Nada, Outra de Coisa Nenhuma* (1955), and the posthumous *Crônicas da Serra* (1961) and *Solidão II* (1974). *Um Dia e Outro Dia* (1936) and *Folhas Volantes* (1940) are two volumes of her poetry.

Physical ailments and unhappiness marked Lisboa's final years. She often complained of her loneliness, a sense of isolation that afflicted her during much of her life. Her insecurity made her shy, and her shyness sometimes made her seem arrogant to those who did not know her. In a letter to a friend, she remarked, "The sick person is infinitely alone, isolated, solitary, that's it!" She remained active in public life and was affiliated with the Movement for Democratic Union in the mid-1950s. Irene Lisboa died in Lisbon on November 25, 1958.

SOURCES:

Morão, Paula. *Irene Lisboa, Vida e Escrita*. Lisbon: Editorial Presença, 1989.

Portugal. Biblioteca Nacional. *Irene Lisboa: 1892–1958*. Lisbon: Instituto da Biblioteca Nacional e do Livro, 1992.

Kendall W. Brown,
Professor of History, Brigham Young University, Provo, Utah

Li Shuxian (1924–1997)

Chinese wife and widow of the last emperor of China. Born in 1924; died in Beijing on June 9, 1997; arranged marriage with Pu Yi, later known as Henry Puyi, in 1962 (died 1967).

In 1962, Li Shuxian, a nurse, was chosen by the prime minister of the People's Republic of China, Zhou Enlai, to be the wife of Pu Yi (Henry Puyi), who had been the last emperor of China. Born in 1906, Pu Yi was child-emperor of China for only three years before he was deposed and a republic proclaimed in 1911. With his forced abdication, the 268-year rule of the Qing Dynasty, and more than three millennia of imperial rule, ended in China. From 1931 to 1945, Pu Yi was first president and then emperor of the Japanese puppet state of Manchukuo (now China's province of Manchuria). Imprisoned soon after Communist China was created in 1949, Pu Yi was a captive for fully a decade until his release in 1959. The ex-emperor was then invited to dine with Mao Zedong at Mao's Zhongnanhai, Beijing's equivalent of the Moscow Kremlin. Soon after this, the Communist regime chose Li Shuxian as a bride for Pu Yi.

Their arranged marriage was never a love match, and Li Shuxian is said to have been dis-appointed that the impotent Pu Yi was unable to give her the child she had long desired. But being married to a celebrity of sorts did have advantages, and she went dancing and to the opera with her husband. The couple's last years together were often difficult, at least in part because the Cultural Revolution of the 1960s often disrupted the life of Pu Yi, who was ill with cancer and was moved from the private room to the public ward of a state hospital. On one occasion, Li Shuxian's house was ransacked by Red Guards who were determined to smash any reminder of the old, feudal China they hated. After her husband's death in 1967, Li Shuxian was rarely mentioned in the state-controlled media. She did emerge from obscurity on April 5, 1995, China's annual Tomb Sweeping Day, when Pu Yi's ashes were reburied on a hillside in Hebei province among the tombs of other Qing Dynasty emperors. Li Shuxian died in Beijing on June 9, 1997.

SOURCES:

"Li Shuxian," in *The Times* [London]. June 12, 1997, p. 25.

John Haag,
Associate Professor of History,
University of Georgia, Athens, Georgia

Lisiewska, Anna (1721–1782)

German artist. Name variations: Liscewska; Lisziewska; Anna Dorothea Lisiewska-Therbusch. Born Anna Dorothea Lisiewska in Berlin, Germany, on July 23, 1721; died in Berlin in 1782; daughter of George Lisiewski or Lisziewski, a Polish painter who may have been her first teacher; sister of Rosina Lisiewska (1716–1783); married Ernst Therbusch (an innkeeper and artist), in 1745; several children.

Born in 1721 in Berlin, Germany, into a Polish family of artists, Anna Lisiewska probably received her early instruction from her father and may have also studied with Antoine Pesne (1683–1757), whose rough impasto and loose brushwork is visible in her later style. Her early works, however, including a pair of canvases, *The Swing* and *A Game of Shuttlecock* (both located at the Neues Palais, Potsdam), are more indicative of the French Rococo style of Jean-Antoine Watteau (1684–1721) and his followers. In 1745, at age 24, Lisiewska married an innkeeper and painter, Ernst Therbusch, after which she gave up her professional career for some 15 years to raise a family. It is believed that she may not have avoided painting entirely during this hiatus, for when she returned to her public career in 1761, her work showed considerable improvement in drawing and composition. Between 1761 and 1764, Lisiewska was commissioned by the courts of Duke Charles Eugene in Stuttgart and Elector Karl Theodor in Mannheim.

In 1765, encouraged by her success with German royalty, Lisiewska moved to Paris, believing that she would be as warmly welcomed into the city's prestigious cultural circles as *Rosalba Carriera was in 1720. However, Lisiewska, now 40, possessed neither the beauty nor social grace of her predecessor, and she had difficulty ingratiating herself with the artistic community. The French philosopher and encyclopedist Denis Diderot (1713–1784), who befriended the artist and did his best to advance her career, later explained why:

> It was not charm that she lacked in order to create a great sensation in the country, for she had that in any case, it was youth, beauty, modesty, coquetry, one must go into ecstasies over the works of our great male artists, take lessons from them, have a good bosom and buttocks, and succumb entirely to one's teachers.

On the basis of her talent alone, Lisiewska was elected to the academy in 1767 and exhibited a number of paintings in that year's Salon. Her genre painting, *The Drinker* (located at the École des Beaux-Arts, Paris), depicting the figure of a man seen by candlelight, received good reviews. One critic thought it "excellent," while another noted its "lively effect, good chiaroscuro." Diderot, who like his fellow Parisians enjoyed more idealized treatments, found it "empty and dry, hard and red," and felt that the effect of candlelight lacked subtlety. He also found much of Lisiewska's subsequent work not to his liking, including her large mythological painting depicting *Jupiter and Antiope,* which the academy refused to hang. Although the official reason given was that it was indecent, there were also questions concerning its quality. Diderot thought it too realistic in style and objected to her plebeian models. "If I was Jupiter, I would have regretted going to the trouble of metamorphosing myself," he declared.

Diderot, who deeply admired Lisiewska's ambition and determination, if not always her work, continued to support her, finding her patrons and advising her on the politics of Parisian art. He bought her painting *Cleopatra* and even commissioned her to render his portrait. During the sitting, when he noticed she was having difficulty with his neck and nether regions, he obliged her by undressing. "I was nude, but completely nude," he wrote. "She painted me and we chatted with a simplicity and innocence worthy of earlier times." However, even Diderot eventually lost patience with Lisiewska, who blamed him for her failure to obtain commissions from the court of Louis XV and left him to pay off her creditors when she hastily departed to the Netherlands in 1768. By 1771, she was back in Berlin, where she remained for the rest of her life, mainly painting portraits. She later gained acceptance into the Bologna and Vienna academies, the latter of which granted her membership in 1776 on the strength of her portrayal of landscape painter Phillip Hackert (1737–1805).

Ann Harris and **Linda Nochlin** regard Lisiewska's work as uneven, but point to a few powerful portraits and genre pictures as outstanding. Among the latter is *An Evening Meal by Candlelight* (Puschkin-Museum, Moscow), depicting a young couple dining under the scrutiny of a young soldier, which Harris and Nochlin praise for capturing the intimacy of the scene without resorting to sentimentality. "The treatment of the light as it falls on the three figures and the various objects on the table is also wonderfully realized," they add. Many of Lisiewska's portraits are frank in their portrayals, some to the point of being unflattering. Her *Self-Portrait* (c. 1780) is a prime example, depicting Lisiewska as a plain woman in her late 50s. "The artist arouses our interest because she did not fit into the acceptable stereotype of the well-educated, well-spoken lady artist of beauty and charm," writes Harris and Nochlin, "and thus her career was not so easy as those of *Sofonisba Anguissola and *Elisabeth Vigée-Le Brun, for example."

Lisiewska's sister *Rosina Lisiewska was also a painter. Their brother's daughters, **Julie Lisiewska** (1767–1837) and **Frederica Julia Lisiewska** (b. 1772), also became artists.

SOURCES:
Greer, Germaine. *The Obstacle Race.* NY: Farrar, Straus and Giroux, 1979.
Harris, Ann Sutherland, and Linda Nochlin. *Woman Artists, 1550–1950.* LA County Museum of Art: Knopf, 1976.

Barbara Morgan,
Melrose, Massachusetts

Lisiewska, Rosina (1716–1783)

*German artist. Name variations: Anna Rosina Lisiewska, Liscewska or Lisziewska; Rosina Lisiewska-deGasc; Madame Matthieu. Born Anna Rosina Lisiewska in 1716 (some sources cite 1713); died in 1783; daughter of George Lisiewski or Lisziewski, a Polish painter who may have been her first teacher; sister of *Anna Lisiewska (1721–1782); married.*

Rosina Lisiewska had great success after 1755, following the death of her husband. As Madame Matthieu, she was invited to Brunswick to undertake royal commissions. She was also named to the Dresden Academy.

Liskiewicz, Krystyna Chojnowska

(b. 1937).

See Chojnowska-Liskiewicz, Krystyna.

Lisle, Alice (c. 1614–1685)

English sympathizer of religious dissenters. Name variations: Lady Alice Lisle; Alicia Lisle. Born Alicia Beckenshaw around 1614; executed in Winchester market-place on September 2, 1685; daughter of Sir White Beckenshaw, who was descended from an old Hampshire family; married John Lisle (1610?–1664), who had been one of the judges at the trial of Charles I and was subsequently a member of Cromwell's House of Lords—thus, his wife's courtesy title.

Lady Alice Lisle seems to have leaned toward Royalism but was sympathetic to religious dissent during a time of rebellion. The "Protestant duke," James, duke of Monmouth, an illegitimate son of Charles II, was leading an insurrection to claim the British throne. The rebellion ended on July 6, 1685, when his forces were decisively defeated by royal troops, led by the earl of Faversham, in the battle of Sedgemoor (the last ever fought on British soil). Two weeks later, on July 20, the 70-year-old Lisle agreed to shelter John Hickes, a well-known Nonconformist minister and fleeing member of Monmouth's army, at Moyles Court, her residence near Ringwood. Hickes brought with him Richard Nelthorpe, also a partisan of Monmouth who was under sentence for "outlawry." The two men passed the night at Moyles Court, and on the following morning were arrested. Their hostess, who had denied their presence in the house, was charged with harboring traitors.

When her case was tried by Judge George Jeffreys at the opening of the "Bloody Assizes" at Winchester, Lisle pleaded that she had no knowledge that Hickes' offense was anything more serious than illegal preaching, that she had known nothing previously of Nelthorpe (whose name had not been included in the indictment, but was, nevertheless, mentioned to strengthen the case for the Crown), and that she had no sympathy with the rebellion. The jury reluctantly found her guilty, and, since the law recognized no distinction between principals and acces-

sories in treason, she was sentenced to be burned. Jeffreys, notorious for his brutality (some 300 people were executed in connection with the failed rebellion and another 800 sold as slaves), ordered that the sentence be carried out that same afternoon. A few days' respite was subsequently granted, however, and James II allowed beheading to be substituted for burning.

Lady Lisle was executed in Winchester marketplace on September 2, 1685, and many critics termed her death a judicial murder. One of the first acts of the Parliament of William and *Mary II was to reverse the attainder (conviction of treason) on the grounds that the prosecution was irregular and the verdict injuriously extorted by "the menaces and violences and other illegal practices" of Jeffreys. It is, however, extremely doubtful whether Jeffreys, for all his cruelty, exceeded the strict letter of the existing law.

Lispector, Clarice (1925–1977)

Brazilian short-story writer, novelist, and journalist. Born in Chechelnick, Ukraine, in 1925; died in 1977; schooled in Recife, Brazil; studied law in Rio de Janeiro (1944); married to a diplomat.

Selected works: Close to the Savage Heart (1944); Family Ties (1960); The Foreign Legion (1964); The Passion According to G.H. (1964); An Apprenticeship or the Book of Delights (1969); The Hour of the Star (1977).

One of Brazil's leading writers of the postmodern period, Clarice Lispector was born in Chechelnick, Ukraine, in 1925, the daughter of Russian Jews who emigrated from the Ukraine to Recife, Brazil, when she was just two. As a teenager, Lispector moved to Rio de Janeiro, where she studied law and became a journalist. After her marriage to a diplomat, she lived in Europe and the United States, then returned to Rio in 1959. Her successful writing career, which began with her first novel, *Close to the Savage Heart,* published when she was 19, ended with her premature death at the age of 52.

Lispector's stories, written in the first person with bursts of stream-of-consciousness, frequently explore the inner lives of women through the trivialities of everyday life. Her later work, drafted during the nascent women's movement, takes a decidedly more feminist view, subtly denouncing women's subjugation in a patriarchal society. Her last novel, *The Hour of the Star,* which also became a successful film, traces the socioeconomic problems of a naive young working girl.

Lissiardi, Sibille (fl. 13th c.)

Parisian physician. Flourished in the 13th century in Paris; daughter of Lissiardus, a surgeon.

A townswoman of Paris, Sibille Lissiardi was a doctor credited with remarkable healing powers. She was the daughter of Lissiardus, a Parisian surgeon of considerable fame, and probably studied surgery, herbal healing, and other forms of medicine under him. Her medical skills were coupled with an intense devotion to God; the combination made some who witnessed her patients' recoveries believe she had the power to create miracles. One story recorded about Sibille tells of the cure of Geoffrey la Chapelle, a member of the royal household, who had suffered from hemorrhoids throughout his life until Sibille used her surgical skills and prayers to completely heal him.

Laura York,
Riverside, California

Lister, Anne (1791–1840)

English countrywoman, scholar and heir who kept a detailed account of her life in a 27-volume diary which includes coded passages recording her sexual and romantic relationships with women. Name variations: Jack. Pronunciation: LIS-ter. Born on April 3, 1791, in Halifax, England; died near K'ut'aisi, Russia, on September 22, 1840, after being bitten by a fever-carrying tick; daughter of Rebecca (Battle) Lister and Captain Jeremy Lister (a veteran of the American War of Independence); attended York's Manor School, age 14–15; for the majority of her life, engaged tutors to assist with a strict regimen of self-education in math, rhetoric, classical languages and literature; never married.

Began diary at age 15; at same age, met Eliza Raine, her first "wife"; met her second "wife," Marianna Belcombe (later Lawson, 1814); took up residence (as the heiress to the estate) in Shibden Hall at age 24 (1815); went to Paris for a sustained visit (1824–25); inherited Shibden Hall (1826); revisited Paris (1826–28); toured Europe (1827); returned to England (1828) and ended the relationship with Marianna Lawson; met her life-partner, Ann Walker (1832); Walker moved into Shibden Hall (1834); embarked on a journey with Walker to Russia, Persia and Turkey (1839), during which she died.

Anne Lister's exceptionally thorough diary (27 volumes) both serves as a witness to her unique life—blending scholarship, estate management, and a wealth of relationships with other women—and provides a rich portrayal of the life of landed gentry in early 19th-century England. She diligently writes about political issues, local gossip, prices paid for goods or services, and even exact times spent on each daily activity.

Fully one sixth of the diary was written in a code of her own devising. While Lister left no key to the code after her death, it is documented that one of her relatives, John Lister, cracked the cipher during the late 1800s. He found that the coded passages focused on a candid recounting of Anne's relationships, sexual as well as romantic, with women. In the words of his associate, Arthur Burrell, "The part written in cipher—turned out after examination to be entirely unpublishable. Mr. Lister was distressed but he refused to take my advice, which was to burn all 27 volumes." Although the code had been broken, each publication of her diary excerpts before 1988 deliberately omitted any of the more controversial coded passages. In 1988, **Helena Whitbread**'s translated excerpts of the diaries, including Lister's history of her same-sex relationships, were published in the book *I Know My Own Heart, The Diaries of Anne Lister 1791–1840*. Before this work, only a handful of scholars had any idea that Lister was what would now be called a lesbian, much less that her diaries provided a wealth of information on a historically overlooked and little-documented subject. The diaries, estimated by historian **Jill Liddington** to contain over four-million words, have presented their own obstacles to publication. According to David Ward of the *Halifax Guardian*, Lister has "one of the most illegible hands known to history." Notes Liddington, "Indeed, had Anne Lister written less, her journals would undoubtedly be better known." To date, it is estimated that all published transcriptions cover less than 10% of the total diary.

She was born in Halifax on April 3, 1791, one of two daughters and four sons of **Rebecca Lister** and Captain Jeremy Lister. Three of her brothers did not survive infancy. Although Anne began her first diary at age 15, little is yet known about her early life because this diary was lost for several years and thus not available to most of the scholars who transcribed other sections of her writings. She lived during the last years of the Napoleonic wars and the reign of King George III. Her family centered around Halifax, a busy town that was the focus of the West Riding worsted industry. Seen as a tomboy from an early age, Anne developed an eccentricity of dress and deportment that was to later earn her the nickname of "Jack" from the townspeople of Halifax. She enjoyed firing her father's pistols and later described several instances of using them to frighten off intruders at Shibden Hall, the family's estate. After attending a Manor boarding school for one year as a teenager, Anne began began what was to be a lifelong pursuit of education by engaging the Reverend Samuel Knight to tutor her in algebra, geometry, literature, Greek and Latin.

The first available journal documents Anne's relationship with another student at the Manor boarding school she had been attending. The student, **Eliza Raine**, was a wealthy daughter of an Indian surgeon. Lister's secret code is not used in the first diaries and is thought to have been developed with Eliza Raine around 1808. Anne initially wrote private passages in Greek but later modified the writing further until it became a full code, combining Greek letters, English letters and mathematical symbols. In one of the earliest coded passages, she talks of an evening spent with Eliza and Miss Alexander: "Drank tea at Mr A's and supped also—after tea at Eliza's instigat[ion] I had Miss A on my knee, kissed [her]." Lister had coded only the phrase "on my knee, kissed [her]." The coded writing becomes more prevalent, eventually recording her relationships with women, her menses, and anything else about which she felt the need to hide her actions or thoughts.

I might exclaim with Virgil, In tennui labor, but I am resolved not to let my life pass without some private memorial that I may hereafter read, perhaps with a smile, when Time has frozen up the channel of those sentiments which flow so fresh now.

—Anne Lister

In time, Eliza and Anne settled into a relationship that they equated with a marriage. After they fought, Eliza wrote in code of Anne: "my husband came to me and finally a happy reunion was accomplished." This was not to last long, however, as their relationship became more distant and in 1814 Eliza was pronounced insane. Thereafter, Anne would continue to call on her each time she visited York.

On Lister's first visit to York, the cultural and economic center of northern England, she got a glimpse of a more sophisticated social world than she had known in her hometown of Halifax. She developed an affinity for this society and spent much of the rest of her life in a calculated attempt to elevate her social position, often to the detriment of people who had previously been her close friends. Lister clearly distanced herself from her parents in the process, despairing of their vulgarity and spending time with her more respectable uncles, Joseph and James Lister.

At age 19, she became acquainted with the Norcliffe family, wealthy landowners who epitomized the level of society that Lister wanted to enter. She developed a close attachment with their eldest daughter **Isabella Norcliffe**, with whom she began a sexual affair that lasted over a decade. Although Norcliffe entertained thoughts of becoming Lister's life-partner, it was she herself who introduced Lister to the woman who would ultimately consume the largest part of Lister's romantic attentions, Marianna Belcombe (later **Marianna Lawton**). By 1814, a 23-year-old Lister had become Marianna's lover. Neither woman had an independent income, prohibiting them from even entertaining the unconventional idea of setting up a household together. Two years later, a wealthy landowner named Charles Lawton made an offer for Marianna's hand in marriage. Much to Lister's dismay, they were engaged immediately and married in 1816. As a result, Lister became very ill and wrote, "The time, the manner, of her marriage. . . . Oh how it broke the magic of my faith forever. How, [in] spite of love, it burst the spell that bound my very reason."

Lister's remaining brother Sam died in a boating accident during 1813 while serving in the army. It was agreed that, as the eldest remaining child, she should become the heir-presumptive to the family estate at Shibden Hall, into which she moved at the age of 24. Lister's unique appearance and (by the standards of the day) unladylike behavior apparently factored in this decision. She later commented about her uncle, "He had no high opinion of ladies—was not fond of leaving estates to females. Were I other than I am, would not leave his to me." Certain that the responsibility would one day fall to her, she became an apt student of the management of the estates.

Despite Marianna's marriage, Marianna and Anne continued their relationship, choosing to view the union with Charles as a temporary interruption that, since Charles was almost 50, would hopefully be solved by his early death. Even better, early widowhood would also leave Marianna with the economic resources needed to assure their independence. They continued to meet whenever possible over the next 12 years, during which time Lister's attitude towards their relationship ran from enthusiastic to despairing, eventually resolving itself into an understanding that Marianna was not to become the life-partner Lister so highly coveted.

In Lister's time, a romantic relationship between two women did not incur the social animosity with which same-sex relationships would later meet. In *Chloe Plus Olivia*, historian **Lillian Faderman** remarks of this earlier period: "Most men would not have felt threatened by such relationships because common wisdom had it, at various times, that well-brought-up middle- and upper-class women had no autonomous sexuality, that they were sexual only to fulfill connubial duties or for the sake of procreation, or that anything two women might do together was *faute de mieux* or insignificant, that without penetration by a penis nothing 'sexual' could take place." Because it was thought not to include any carnal involvement, the exalted romantic friendship between women was considered to be one of the most pure forms of love. The response to an incident which took place in 1811 involving two schoolteachers is representative of the public interpretation of such relationships. That year, the boarding house of **Marianne Woods** and **Jane Pirie** in Scotland was closed down because one student testified that they had climbed into bed with each other and made love. The mistresses sued for libel and won their suit (with a bit of circular reasoning) in part by proving their love for each other. According to Faderman's *Surpassing the Love of Men*, "They sought to establish that the women loved each other with great, unquestioning intensity, knowing that the judges would agree that such overwhelming love would not permit the demon of sex to wend its way in." Such was the belief that sexual congress between women could not even exist that one judge was heard to remark it more likely "that a person heard thunder playing the tune of 'God Save the King.'" These attitudes likely factored strongly in Lister's ability to fit her relationships within the context of acceptable behavior.

In 1822, Lister had occasion to pay a visit to the widely famed ***Ladies of Llangollen** (Eleanor Butler and Sarah Ponsonby), two upper-class Irishwomen who in 1778 had dressed in semi-masculine attire and eloped together to northern Wales. Their relationship, labeled one of the "romantic friendships" so common at the time, was exalted by local press as they settled in their idyllic little cottage, Plas Newydd. They were befriended by many a contemporary luminary, and Wordsworth said of them:

> Sisters in love, a love allowed to climb
> Ev'n on this earth, above the reach of time.

Anne
Lister

Lister was much struck by her visit to see Sarah (Eleanor was sick at the time). She writes, "'Tis the prettiest little spot I ever saw—a silken cord upon which the pears of taste are strung. . . . I cannot help but think that surely [their relationship] was not platonic. . . . I feel the infirmity of our nature & hesitate to pronounce such attachments uncemented by something more tender still than friendship."

Continuing her primary relationship with Marianna, Lister had occasional interludes with other women whom she met among her circle of friends. Halifax was growing quickly, with the existing landowning upper class gradually losing prominence to the newer wealthy industrialists. Lister despaired over this course of events, "the affairs of the town are now quite in the hands of second-rate people." In 1819, slowly resolving into the hardened Tory that she would become in her later years, she eagerly awaited all news of the growing unrest in the working classes (which would, in time, lead to the Reform Act of 1832). After reading a newspaper article decrying the need for reform, she writes, "'Rights of Women' is a curious list of authorities in support of the rights of women to take part in these reform meetings—to vote for Representatives in the house of commons &, in short, to be in every sense of the word, members of the body politic. What will not these demagogues advance, careless what absurdity or ruin they commit!" Interestingly, Lister would later record how she and a companion freely used their influence as voteless female landowners to sway the voting of their male tenants.

In 1824, Lister's life changed course in two ways. The health of her aunt and her Uncle James was failing, and she undertook more of the day-to-day management of the Shibden Hall estates. She also acted on her lifelong plan of extended foreign travel by embarking on a seven-month visit to Paris. At this point, her relationships with her two closest friends, Isabella Norcliffe and Marianna Lawton, were declining. Isabella's excessive snuff-taking and drinking alienated Lister, and Marianna's continued marriage was frustrating. Marianna had also expressed reservations at Lister's appearance and at disclosure of their unconventional relationship. Writes Lister: "It has taught me that, tho' she loves me, it is without that beautiful romance of sentiment that all my soul desires. But mine are not affections to be returned in this world." To complicate her relationships, she had previously contracted a venereal disease from Marianna (thought to be a result of her husband's adultery). Lister headed to Paris in 1824 troubled over Marianna but excited about the social opportunities her travel would provide and anxious to see if Parisian doctors could cure her permanently of her venereal complaint.

During her trip, she fostered a relationship with a 38-year-old English widow, **Maria Barrow**, that was to last into 1827. Prescribing such "medicines" as mercury rubbed directly on the skin, the French doctors could not cure her venereal disease. In March, she returned from Paris to her home in Shibden Hall. Dedicating herself to the successful management of the estate—which had a variety of interests, including tenant farmers, shares in the canal that carried goods to and from Halifax, and land leased for coal mining and quarrying—she drew up extensive plans of the improvements she hoped to make after her inheritance.

In January 1826, Lister's Uncle James died, leaving her the full Shibden Hall estate and all of its interests. She immediately took a firm hold on the business of running the estate, exerting stronger control than had her aging uncle. Simultaneously, she prepared for longer journeys abroad, which would make her, in effect, an absentee landlord. Over the coming years, she would realize many of her ambitions of improving Shibden Hall. Nonetheless, the income generated was barely enough to support Lister, her aunt, father, and sister, as well as her traveling and a moderate level of improvements on the estate. Lister managed the varied moneymaking interests diligently and stretched her income to its limits.

From 1826 to 1828, still maintaining relationships with both Marianna Lawton and Maria Barrow, she made an extended visit to Europe. In 1827, Lister cultivated a relationship with a Parisian widow, **Madame de Rosny**, eventually moving into her house as a lodger. She delighted in Madame de Rosny's acquaintance with the circle of aristocrats surrounding the king. At one point, it seems she was drawn into de Rosny's pursuit of smuggling contraband between England and France, but Lister appears to have been relieved when nothing came of it.

Returning to England in 1828, she finally severed the long relationship with Marianna, whose economic status had changed (not having provided an heir for her husband, she had no claim to his inheritance). Lister's increasing desire for social sophistication brought her to see Marianna as more provincial and a financial liability. She now wanted a life-partner who could bring money, sophistication, and preferably a title to the relationship.

Back in England, she met an increasing number of Scottish and British aristocrats through the auspices of her friend **Sibella MacLean**. As Lister's aspirations intensified, she was faced with the fact that her income was not generous enough to support a lifestyle comparable with that of the aristocracy. In 1832, she began to court a local young heiress named **Ann Walker**. Despite misgivings that they were not compatible, she encouraged Walker to move into Shibden Hall in September 1834. In 1836, Lister changed her will to leave the whole estate to Walker in the event of her death, with one caveat: if Walker were ever to marry, her claim to the estate "shall thenceforth cease . . . as if the said Ann Walker should have then departed this life." Walker had a history of neurotic behavior which continued into the new relationship; she was moody, sullen and prone to ailments. Lister persevered, taking Walker to doctors and encouraging her with rounds of social visits in York and beyond. Walker seemed inured to these efforts, however, and remained largely a convalescent.

Throughout Lister's life, her urge to travel had been crowned with the desire to visit the more exotic parts of the world. In 1839, despite significant reservations from Walker, the two women embarked on a trip to Russia, Turkey and Persia. They traveled for over a year, fulfilling Lister's dream. Unfortunately, the trip was not to be completed. In September 1840, in the foothills of the Caucasus Mountains in Imperial Russia, Lister was bitten by a fever-carrying tick and died. The diaries she left behind detail the life of a woman whom Whitbread has described as a "trail-blazer for the emancipation of women from the mores of her day." She had lived with the notion that she was unique. Faderman notes that while quoting in her diary from Rousseau's *Confessions*, Lister turned his self-description on herself: "I know my own heart and understand my fellow man. But I am made unlike anyone I have ever met. I dare to say that I am like no one in the whole world."

SOURCES:

Faderman, Lillian. *Surpassing the Love of Men: Romantic Friendship and Love Between Women from the Renaissance to the Present*. NY: William Morrow, 1981.

Liddington, Jill. "Anne Lister of Shibden Hall, Halifax (1791–1840): Her Diaries and the Historians," in *History Workshop: A Journal of Socialist and Feminist Historians*. Issue 35. Spring 1993, p. 45.

Whitbread, Helena, ed. *I Know My Own Heart: The Diaries of Anne Lister 1791–1840*. Washington Square, NY: New York University Press, 1992.

———, ed. *No Priest But Love: The Journals of Anne Lister from 1824–1826*. Washington Square, NY: New York University Press, 1992.

COLLECTIONS:

Diary, papers and memorabilia located in the Calderdale Library, England.

Scout,
freelance writer, Washington, D.C.

Lister, Moira (1923—)

South African-born actress. Born on August 6, 1923, in Cape Town, South Africa; daughter of Major James Martin and Margaret Winifred (Hogan) Lister; attended Parktown Convent, in Johannesburg; studied acting with Dr. Hulbert and Amy Coleridge; married Vicomte d'Orthez.

Selected theater: made stage debut at age six, as the Prince in *The Vikings of Helgeland (University Players, Johannesburg, 1929); made London debut as Jeeby Cashler in* Post Road *(Golders Green Hippodrome, April 1937); appeared as Diana in* Six Pairs of Shoes *(Playhouse Theater, London, April 1944), Margaret Heiss in* The Shop in Sly Street *("Q" Theater, London, June, 1944), Laurel Somerset in* Felicity Jasmine *(St. James's Theater, September 1944), Juliet in* Romeo and Juliet, *Desdemona in* Othello, *Olivia in*

Twelfth Night, Anne Bullen in King Henry VIII, *Charmian in* Antony and Cleopatra, *and Kate Hardcastle in* She Stoops to Conquer *(Stratford-on-Avon, Shakespeare Memorial Theater Company, 1946); appeared as Isabel Neville in* The Kingmaker *(St. James's Theater, London, May 1946), Palmyra in* Marriage à la Mode *(St. James's Theater, July 1946), Joanna Lyppiatt in* Present Laughter *(Haymarket Theater, April 1947); made New York debut as Madeleine in* Don't Listen Ladies *(Booth Theater, New York, December 1948); appeared as Diana Lake in* French Without Tears *(Vaudeville Theater, London, June 1949); appeared in the revue* Sauce Piquante *(Cambridge Theater, April 1950); appeared as the Princess in* The Love of Four Colonels *(Wyndham's Theater, May 1951), Monica Bestwood in* Birthday Honors *(Criterion Theater, October 1953); toured the Continent and the English provinces with the Shakespeare Memorial Theater Company (1955); appeared as Kate Waterhouse in* The Long Echo *(St. James's Theater, August 1956), Irene in* Paddle Your Own Canoe *(Criterion Theater, December 1957); toured Africa and Australia in one-woman show,* People in Love *(1958–59); appeared as Nell Nash in* The Gazebo *(Savoy Theater, London, March 1960), Virginia in* Devil May Care *(Strand Theater, March 1963), Sylvia in* The Uncertain Heroine *(Richmond Theater, May 1964), Sylvia Barr in* The First Fish *(Savoy Theater, July 1964); toured South Africa in* Bedtime Story *(December 1964–March 1965); appeared as Dorothy in* Any Wednesday *(Apollo Theater, London, August 1965), Lesbia Grantham in* Getting Married *(Strand Theater, April 1967), Connie in* The Snow Angel, *Woman in* Epiphany *(double bill), and Anne Preston in* A Woman Named Anne *(Lyceum Theater, Edinburgh, Summer 1969).*

Selected films: The Shipbuilders *(1943);* Love Story (A Lady Surrenders, *1944);* Wanted for Murder *(1946);* So Evil My Love *(1948);* Another Shore *(1948);* A Run for Your Money *(1949);* Pool of London *(1950);* White Corridors *(1951);* The Cruel Sea *(1952);* Trouble in Story *(1953);* The Deep Blue Sea *(1955);* Seven Waves Away (Abandon Ship!, *1957);* The Yellow Rolls-Royce *(1964);* The Double Man *(1967);* Stranger in the House (Cop-Out, *1967);* Not Now Darling *(1972);* Ten Little Indians *(1989).*

Born in 1923 in Cape Town, South Africa, and educated at a convent school in Johannesburg, actress Moira Lister made her stage debut with the Johannesburg University Players, at age six. In 1937, she first appeared on the London stage as Jeeby Cashler in *Post Road* at the Golders Green Hippodrome. From that time through the 1980s, Lister was never without work, acting on the British, South African, and American stages, as well as in British films and on television. Described as a "patrician" blue-eyed blonde, she frequently played sensuous aristocrats in films, although her stage roles were more varied. She appeared as Juliet and Desdemona with the Shakespeare Memorial Theater in 1945 and 1955, along with such roles as Olivia in *Twelfth Night*, Margaret in *Much Ado About Nothing*, and Regan in *King Lear*. In 1958–59, Lister toured Africa and Australia in the one-woman show *People in Love*, and in 1960, played Nell Nash in *The Gazebo*, a play that ran for over a year in London. Her film career, launched in 1943, included *The Deep Blue Sea* (1955), *The Yellow Rolls-Royce* (1964), and *The Double Man* (1967). On television, she played in the popular series "The Very Merry Widow," which inspired the title for her autobiography, *The Very Merry Moira*, published in 1969.

Liston, Melba (1926—)

American jazz trombonist and arranger. Name variations: Melba Doretta Liston. Born in Kansas City, Missouri, on January 13, 1926.

Selected recordings as sideman: D. Gordon's Mischievous Lady *(Dial 1018, 1947);* Lullaby in Rhythm *(Dial 1038, 1947); D. Gillespie's* Dizzy Gillespie at Newport *(Verve 8242, 1957).*

Selected arrangements, all recorded by Dizzy Gillespie: "Stella by Starlight," on World Statesman *(Norg. 1084, 1956); "My Reverie," and "Annie's Dance" (both 1956), on* Dizzy in Greece *(Verve 8017, 1956–57).*

One of only a handful of African-American female trombonists in history and a brilliant arranger, Melba Liston has been a leading force for women musicians the world over. In a career that has spanned over 40 years, Liston has worked with such music icons as William "Count" Basie, John Birks, Dizzy Gillespie, Albert "Budd" Johnson, Clark Terry, *Billie Holiday, and Quincy Jones, and no one has a bad word to say about her. "Melba is a woman of strength," said pianist, singer, and fan **Emme Kemp**. "A woman of integrity. A woman who is able to endure, and she is savvy."

Melba Liston was born in Kansas City, Missouri, in 1926, and moved to Los Angeles, California, with her family when she was 11. She studied trombone in high school and, in 1942, launched her career in a theater pit orchestra led

by Bardu Ali. In 1943, she joined Gerald Wilson's big band and was with him until 1948, when she joined up with Dizzy Gillespie. Around this time, however, the rigors of life on the road began to get to Liston, and, after a tour with Billie Holiday in 1949, she gave up playing and worked as a secretary and as a film extra before rejoining Gillespie in 1956. In 1958, she went out on her own, arranging on a free-lance basis and forming an all-woman quintet. During the 1960s, she worked with a series of band leaders, including Quincy Jones, Johnny Griffin, Milt Jackson, and Randy Weston. She also did arrangements for singers and television commercials.

On a trip with Weston to Jamaica in 1974, Liston decided to settle there. Over the next five years, she established a music program at the University of West Indies and headed up the African-American pop and jazz department at the Jamaica School of Music. Returning to New York in 1979, she formed her own septet, Melba Liston and Company.

Since 1985, when she suffered a serious stroke, Liston has been confined to a wheelchair. Although no longer able to play the trombone, she continues arranging with the help of specialized computer software. A cherished member of the jazz community, she has been supported by a contingent of friends who in 1997 helped her relocate to Harlem by raising money to pay her moving expenses and helping to renovate her apartment. Of particular note is her 40-year friendship and collaboration with Randy Weston, which has been compared to that of Billy Strayhorn and Duke Ellington.

SOURCES:
Andrews, Laura. "The Jazz Community Sponsors a Party for Beloved Melba Liston," in *New York Amsterdam News*. Vol. 88, no. 17. September 11, 1997, pp. 32–34.
Carr, Ian, Digby Fairweather, and Brian Priestley. *Jazz: The Rough Guide*. London: Rough Guides, 1995.

Barbara Morgan,
Melrose, Massachusetts

Lisziewska.

See Lisiewska.

Litchfield, Harriett (1777–1854)

English actress. Born Harriett Hay in 1777; died in 1854; married John Litchfield of the Privy Council Office, in 1794 (died 1858).

Known as Mrs. Litchfield, Harriet Litchfield made her stage debut in 1792. Five years later, she appeared at Covent Garden and remained there until her retirement in 1812. She is best known for her Emilia in *Othello*.

Litchfield, Jessie (1883–1956)

Australian writer. Born Jessie Phillips in Sydney, Australia, in 1883; died in Richmond, Australia, on March 12, 1956; second child of John Phillips (a contractor) and Jean (Sinclair) Phillips; attended Neutral Bay Public School, Sydney, Australia; married Valentine Augustus Litchfield (a miner), on January 21, 1908; children: four sons and three daughters.

Jessie Litchfield, the daughter of a contractor, was born in 1883 in Sydney, Australia, but spent her early years in various country towns until the family returned to Sydney in 1895. She was educated in public schools and, in 1908, married Valentine Litchfield, a handsome tin miner she had met on a ship. Over the next decade, Litchfield traveled with her husband from mine to mine across the Northern Territory, all the while raising seven children in crude and isolated conditions. She later recorded her adventures in the book *Far-North Memories* (1930).

In 1917, Valentine found employment at a meatworks in Darwin, while Litchfield took up writing. Prolific in her output, she completed five books and contributed numerous articles, short stories, and poems to a variety of magazines and newspapers. In 1930, she took a job as editor of the *Northern Territory Times*; her husband died the following year.

In 1942, during World War II, Litchfield and her children were evacuated to Sydney where she purchased and ran a small lending library, "The Roberta." Upon her return to Darwin after the war, she reopened the library there, serving as librarian and as local historian and expert on Territory affairs. She also conducted a letter campaign for Territory self-government. In 1951, Litchfield entered politics, contesting the Territory's federal parliamentary seat as an independent candidate. Her campaign, which was conducted by taxi cab, was ultimately unsuccessful.

In 1953, Litchfield was awarded the coronation medal for outstanding service to the Northern Territory. She remained active throughout her later years, helping to establish the *North Australian* monthly and serving as assistant editor. In 1955, she became the Territory's first woman justice of the peace. Jessie Litchfield died on March 12, 1956, while visiting Melbourne. Following her death, the Melbourne Bread and Cheese Club, recipients of her manuscripts, es-

tablished an annual literary award in her name. A biography of Litchfield, *Jesse Litchfield— Grand Old Lady of the Territory* (1982), was written by her granddaughter, **Janet Dickinson**.

SOURCES:

Radi, Heather, ed. *200 Australian Women*. NSW, Australia: Women's Redress Press, 1988.

Wilde, William H., Joy Hooton, and Barry Andrews, eds. *Oxford Companion to Australian Literature*. Melbourne: Oxford, 1985.

Litten, Irmgard (1879–1953)

German anti-Nazi activist and author of memoirs, Beyond Tears. *Born Irmgard Wüst in Halle/Saale, Germany, on August 30, 1879; died in East Berlin on June 30, 1953; married Fritz Julius Litten (1873–1939), a noted University of Königsberg law professor; children: Hans Achim Litten (1903–1938); Heinz Wolfgang Litten (1905–1955); Rainer Litten (1909–1972).*

Born in Halle/Saale, Germany, on August 30, 1879, into a respected academic family, Irmgard Wüst studied art history and married Fritz Julius Litten, a noted University of Königsberg law professor of Jewish origins who had converted to Lutheranism. Her son, Hans Achim Litten, became a well-known attorney who specialized in defending controversial Leftists in the often biased courts of Weimar Germany. As a consequence of her family being perceived by Nazis and nationalists as both racially and politically "un-German," even before 1933 Irmgard Litten began to feel the effects of xenophobia and ideological intolerance. The Nazi seizure of power was a catastrophe for the Littens: Fritz was dismissed from his academic post, and much worse, her son Hans was thrown into Dachau concentration camp as a "Marxist sympathizer." Litten used all the stratagems at her employ to secure her son's release. In the early years of the Nazi regime, world opinion was still deemed important, because the fragile German economy could be threatened by boycotts. As a consequence, Litten hoped for sufficient foreign pressure to effect her son's liberation from Dachau. For several years she worked to free him, using her contacts within Nazi Germany, as well as bringing the case to the attention of the foreign press. At times, it appeared that her son might indeed be released, but in February 1938 she and her husband received word that Hans had "committed suicide" while in Dachau.

Their struggle over, the Littens immigrated to Great Britain, where Irmgard wrote a book about her long battle. Appearing simultaneously in Paris, London, and New York, *Beyond Tears:*

A Mother Fights Hitler contained few revelations about the nature of Nazi rule, but impressed critics with its humanity and the tenacity of its author. A Spanish-language edition appeared in Mexico City in 1941. In England, where her husband died soon after their arrival, Litten received assistance from the Quakers and, despite her age, became active in the exile community's anti-Nazi work. She joined the German branch of the writers' club PEN, also becoming active in groups led by the author Kurt Hiller and in the Communist-dominated Free German Movement (FDB). She withdrew from the FDB in 1944, when the party line and her own viewpoints clashed over policy for postwar reconstruction of Germany. After the war, Litten returned to Germany, settling in East Berlin but eschewing a public life other than supervising the first German edition of her book in 1947. Her two surviving sons, Heinz and Rainer, both of whom had chosen careers in the theater, returned from exile to be with their mother in the German Democratic Republic. Irmgard Litten died in East Berlin on June 30, 1953.

Sally
Little

SOURCES:

Litten, Irmgard. *Beyond Tears*. NY: Alliance Book Co., 1940.

Röder, Werner, and Herbert A. Strauss, eds. *Biographisches Handbuch der deutschsprachigen Emigration nach 1933*. 4 vols. Munich: K.G. Saur, 1980.

John Haag,
Athens, Georgia

Little, Sally (1951—)

South African-born golfer. Born on October 12, 1951, in Cape Town, South Africa.

*Had 15 professional career wins, including the LPGA championship (1980), the *Dinah Shore (1982), and the du Maurier (1988); was LPGA Rookie of the Year (1971).*

Born in 1951 in Cape Town, South Africa, Sally Little started playing golf at the age of 12 and began winning titles almost immediately. In 1971, after stacking up victories in every tournament available to her at home, she joined the U.S. circuit and was named Rookie of the Year. Little reached a career high in 1976, when she won the Women's International, sinking a 75-foot sand shot on the last hole of the tournament to beat *Jan Stephenson. Little went on to win the LPGA championship in 1980, and the Women's International again in 1981. Slowed by abdominal and arthroscopic knee surgeries in 1983, she was out of the winner's circle for several years, although she was the tour's 12th million-dollar earner in 1985. After losing the U.S. Women's Open to **Jane Geddes** in 1986, Little came back strong to win the du Maurier Classic in 1988. *Nancy Lopez** felt that Little had everything one could want in a golfing competitor. "Like *JoAnne Carner, she's a long driver and a fighter, and that means you can't play lazy when Sally is around." Becoming a U.S. citizen in 1982, Little made her home in Palm Beach, Florida.

SOURCES:

Lopez, Nancy, with Peter Schwed. *The Education of a Woman Golfer*. NY: Simon and Schuster, 1979.

Markel, Robert, ed. *The Women's Sports Encyclopedia*. NY: Henry Holt, 1997.

Barbara Morgan,
Melrose, Massachusetts

Little Dove (c. 1491–1517).

See Willums, Sigbrit for sidebar on Dyveke.

Littlefield, Catharine (1755–1814).

See Greene, Catharine Littlefield.

Little Flower, The (1873–1897).

See Thérèse of Lisieux.

Littlewood, Joan (1914—)

English actor, dramaturg, founder and director of the Theater Workshop, who pioneered original methods of theater training and developed production styles which have had a profound influence on postwar theater and theater practitioners both in Great Britain and throughout the world. Born Joan Maudie Littlewood (known also as JL) on October 6, 1914, in Stockwell, South London; daughter of Kate Littlewood (not married); granddaughter of Robert Francis Littlewood and Caroline Emily Littlewood; attended la Retraite High School for Girls, S. London, and Royal Academy of Dramatic Art, London; married Jimmie Miller (later known as Ewan MacColl), in 1936 (marriage dissolved); married Gerry Raffles (died 1975); children: none.

Left school prematurely on winning scholarship to RADA; left RADA without completing course and moved to Manchester (1934); joined Theater of Action (agitprop street theater) and met Ewan MacColl (writer); founded Theater Union (1936); worked as freelance writer and broadcaster, though banned from the BBC for political outspokenness (1939–45); founded Theater Workshop with Gerry Raffles and others (1945); toured devised work and classical plays (mainly as "one-night stands") in England, Germany, Norway, Sweden and Czechoslovakia (1945–53); moved company to Theater Royal, Stratford-atte-Bowe, London, E.15 (1953); invited to Theater of Nations, Paris (1955), then annually, winning Best Production of the Year three times; with Mother Courage, offered first production of Bertolt Brecht in England (1955); ran workshops at Centre Culturel Hammamet, Tunisia (1965–67) and Image India, Calcutta (1968); created children's environments, bubble cities, learn and play areas around Theater Royal, E.15 (1968–75); left England to work in France (1975); Seminar Relais Culturel, Aix-en-Provence (1976).

Productions include: Ewan MacColl's Uranium 235 *(1949);* Operation Olive Branch, *a free adaptation of Aristophanes'* Lysistrata *(1953); Jaroslav Hasek's* The Good Soldier Schweik *(revival 1954); Ben Jonson's* Volpone *(1955); Brendan Behan's* The Quare Fellow *(1956); Shelagh Delaney's* A Taste of Honey *(1958); Behan's* The Hostage *(1958); Frank Norman's* Fings Ain't What They Used T'Be *(1959);* Sparrers Can't Sing *(1961), and film (1963);* Oh What a Lovely War *(1963); John Wells and Richard Ingrams'* Mrs. Wilson's Diary *(1967).*

*Awards include: Member of the French Academy of Writers (1964); Commandeur de l'Ordre des Arts et des Lettres (France, 1986); Society of West End The-*aters (SWET) Special Award (1983); Women of Achievement in the Arts Award (1993).

Selected publications: (editor) Milady Vine *(Cape, 1984); (autobiography)* Joan's Book *(Methuen, 1994).*

Among the many messages of congratulation Joan Littlewood received on her 80th birthday, in October 1994, was a greeting from Richard Eyre, artistic director of the Royal National Theater, London, England. Her reply, written on a postcard, was brief:

> Thank you for your card, Richard. I really don't know what you're up to. Whatever it is, you'd do better to bomb that building. I had to put up with an old slum in London. Yours need never have been.
>
> JL

The "old slum" to which she referred was the London home of her world-famous Theater Workshop, the Theater Royal, Stratford-atte-Bowe E.15 (an area which was still recovering from the impoverishing effects of World War II but known during its heyday in the 1950s and '60s as "the other Stratford"). The sentiment that 'JL' betrays in that terse message demonstrates that although the years may have saddened her they had withered neither her attitude nor her spirit.

Dilapidated it may have been, but that Victorian "Palace of Varieties" was the first real home her company had ever had and must have looked wonderful to the bedraggled but optimistic troupe of actors who arrived there in February 1953. What it came to represent was a revolution in British theater—part myth, part legend, and part history—with Joan Littlewood at the center, its vision and its inspiration.

Everyone set to work cleaning, repairing, replacing and rehearsing, living illegally in the dressing rooms, and cooking on a single gas ring in the gallery bar, until the proprietors of the tiny local cafe took pity and arranged to feed them on a weekly credit system. Their first local benefactor (a sanitary goods supplier) donated armfuls of toilet paper and disinfectant, as well as £250. The Theater Workshop Company had toured both nationally and internationally since 1946 and had won recognition and high praise abroad, but it was to be several years before they were financially supported from the public funding sector, the Arts Council of Great Britain.

Joan Littlewood was no stranger to hardship, poverty or deprivation. Her mother Kate, like her brother and sisters, had had to leave school at 12, go out to work and make a contribution to the family coffers. She had a post as a maid when she fell in love with an unreliable young man called Jack. By the time Kate could no longer conceal her pregnancy from her family, Jack was engaged to someone else and, though he agreed to pay a small sum towards the baby's welfare, Kate never saw him again.

It was 1914, Archduke Franz Ferdinand of Austria and his morganatic wife *Sophie Chotek had just been assassinated, Kaiser Wilhelm II was heading for Serbia, and Europe was in the throes of World War I. Littlewood's earliest memories are of the comings and goings of young men in uniform, home on leave from the Front, who were often rather drunk and singing irreverent words to traditional songs and hymns. She remembers a house full of people rejoicing at the end of the war and, although the family was never well off, "we were rich all right at Christmas" with games and conjuring tricks, singing, dancing and storytelling—all of which left an indelible impression.

> *I* do not believe in the supremacy of the director, designer, actor or even of the writer. It is through collaboration that this knockabout art of theater survives and kicks.
>
> —Joan Littlewood

Nearly half a century later, encouraged by Gerry Raffles, her partner in life and work, Littlewood and her Theater Workshop Company would set out to research this period of English history in great detail. The result would be their most well-known original collaborative production—*Oh What a Lovely War*—a richly entertaining and profoundly moving "Pierrot show" telling the story of what Littlewood calls this "grotesque catastrophe which should never have happened."

Littlewood's devoted but undemonstrative grandparents, Robert Francis Littlewood and **Caroline Emily Littlewood**, raised her as their youngest daughter. She appreciated their attempts to give her a stable home but her relationship with her pretty mother, a hot-tempered and unpredictable woman, was not easy. "I could never understand why Kate flew into a rage so easily, but I knew it had something to do with me. Sometimes she couldn't stand the sight of me." After Kate married, Littlewood continued to live with her grandparents and, after being taken on a school trip to see a matinee production of Shakespeare's *The Merchant of Venice*, often entertained them with vivid and

emotional renditions of Shylock's speeches. They were a mildly baffled but encouraging audience. At age 11, she won a scholarship to a convent school. Determined that she should take advantage of this opportunity, her grandparents dug deep into their pockets for the obligatory uniform, but there was no money left over for transport; Joan had to walk the three miles to and from school every day. She revelled, however, in the relaxed, orderly atmosphere, and there can be no doubt of the influence that the rituals and "theatricality" of Roman Catholicism had upon her development as a stage director.

Though she excelled at art and was a diligent student, she was seriously bitten by the theatrical bug during her early teenage years. She would regularly walk to and from the Waterloo Road (about one-and-half-hours each way) to attend *Lilian Baylis' productions at the Old Vic, and she was soon inspired to direct her first play, *Macbeth*—an interpretation so bloody that the visiting Mother Superior actually fainted.

As the decade referred to by the family as the "starving '20s" drew to a close, Littlewood found herself more and more at odds with her mother and less and less interested by the prospect of university. She quietly determined to "get the hell out of it" and applied for another scholarship, this time to the Royal Academy of Dramatic Art—skipping a chemistry exam in order to audition.

The young women that RADA attracted at that time were often the fashion-conscious daughters of the rich and famous who wanted to use the courses in "deportment and elocution" more as a finishing school than as training for a career as a dedicated artist. How surprised they must have been when Littlewood joined them in the waiting-room dressed in her school uniform. And how disappointed she was (the only scholarship student) both by her stuffy classmates and the dreary teaching at the Academy. Deeply disillusioned, she left after a year, noting that her only valuable experience had been occasional dance classes based on the work of Rudolph Laban, a European choreographer and theorist who had settled in England during the war. She retained her passion for everything this innovative man had written and taught. She had also made some useful contacts with radio drama producers, and decided to head north for Manchester—on foot once again—with the intention of finding work with the BBC before stowing away on a boat from Liverpool to a new life in the United States.

In terms of material prosperity, the gap between the North and South of England was at that time even wider than it is today. Culturally, however, Manchester was the Second City. In fact, the first Repertory Theater in Britain had been opened there in 1908 by *Annie Horniman ("why is it always the women who resurrect the theater in Britain?" Parisian theater director Jean Vilar asked years later when visiting the Theater Royal, E.15), and its influence on the cultural life of the city was still evident in the 1930s.

Littlewood was completely enthralled by the verve and unpretentiousness of Manchester: here was the life she had yearned for. It wasn't long before this talented, energetic young woman discovered that a local company, Theater of Action—a consciousness-raising form of street theater—was closer to everything she felt theater should and could be than anything she had encountered in London. Her enthusiasm led her to Ewan MacColl (real name, Jimmie Miller), a young writer, singer, and pacifist, deeply committed to working-class principles. He and Littlewood soon embarked on a long and fruitful professional collaboration, forming a company of similarly committed people and calling themselves Theater Union. They also married—briefly and against Littlewood's better judgment—and while supporting themselves by their work at the BBC embarked on a period of intensive training and study. Their published manifesto began:

> We live in times of great social upheaval; faced with an ever-increasing danger of war and fascism, the democratic people of the world have been forced into action. Their struggle for peace and progress manifests itself in many forms and not the least important of these is drama.

Heavily influenced by "agitprop" (agitation-propaganda) theater from abroad, they began to incorporate expressionist ideas of staging into their enterprises, experimenting with light, sound, and movement, and Littlewood's productions of little-known European classics already bore the hallmarks of her finest work. She set out to demonstrate support for the Republican cause in the Spanish Civil War and presented Lope de Vega's 17th-century piece *Fuente Oveuna*—renamed *The Sheepwell*—the story of a village's struggle for justice over a tyrannical landlord. As fascism raged through Europe, the company began work on an adaptation of a satirical Czech play, *The Good Soldier Schweik*; as the build-up to World War II began in earnest, they devised an original piece entitled *Last Edition*, which they advertised as "A Living Newspaper." *Last Edition* combined startling visual effects, humor, stylized movement, music, and burlesque with

what proved to be an unacceptable level of political comment. Since "anyone spreading alarm and despondency is liable for prosecution," a writ was issued; Littlewood and MacColl were taken to court and fined five guineas (about $12) each, and the show was forced to close. But they had made a tremendous impact. It was *Last Edition* that attracted Gerry Raffles to the company, and he remained with Littlewood and Theater Workshop (as it became known after the war) until his sudden death in 1975.

Nor was that the only time that Littlewood appeared in the dock. In 1957, she was accused of allowing indecent language to be used in *You Won't Always Be On Top* (her semi-improvised play featuring building and construction workers). Her victory in the courts was the first real blow leading to the demise of censorship in England.

During the remainder of the war, Littlewood continued with research into theatrical ideologies—popular theater both ancient and modern—so that when the nucleus of the company re-formed on a wave of postwar optimism, it was with a renewed determination that Theater Workshop should be a people's theater reaching as large an audience and drawn from as broad a social base as possible.

The period between 1945 and 1953 was richly creative and experimental, and Littlewood worked ceaselessly—chain-smoking, relying on others to remind her to eat and rest—her most effective work being productions of two scripts by Ewan MacColl: *Uranium 235*, a dynamic verse-play about the atom bomb, and *Operation Olive Branch*, a free adaptation of Aristophanes' *Lysistrata*. Although unsupported and largely unacknowledged by larger funding bodies, the company toured throughout England, Wales, and Scotland, where they initiated what has now become the Edinburgh Fringe Festival. They played in church halls, village halls, and mental hospitals as well as more conventional venues. Gerry Raffles' tireless work as promoter and booking manager brought connections with companies abroad who shared similar aspirations, and drew invitations to perform in West Germany, Scandinavia, and Czechoslovakia. Accolades were showered on them abroad: in Prague, an excited journalist reported: "Theater Workshop . . . captured the enthusiasm of the audience by its simple beauty and richness of ideas"; in Sweden, it was noted that "Theater Workshop is a very interesting experience, contrasting strongly with the other English theater which is rather stiff and dull"; and a leading Stockholm paper said of Littlewood: "Her name should be written in letters of fire until the blinkers are burned off the eyes of the English theater public."

The company's work reflected the ideas Littlewood was constantly developing. In addition to regular rehearsals for their various productions, the actors trained vigorously. Their days began with movement—a series of rigorous exercises based on Rudolph Laban's concept of the "human effort cube." This was followed by a period of vocal training and then by text and character work incorporating the theories Constantin Stanislavski set out in his book *An Actor Prepares* but adapted and extended into improvisation and theater games. From a later perspective, it is almost impossible to imagine how revolutionary Littlewood's teaching and directing methods seemed in England in the 1940s. Littlewood preferred to work with actors who were enthusiastic but previously untrained because they were largely unstructured, instinctive and highly individual, and not afraid to risk making fools of themselves. She ran weekend schools and summer workshops—most notably at Ormesby Hall, a grand mansion and garden in Yorkshire—from which she often garnered young recruits, molding them into the ensemble. She worked intensively and in great detail, believing that "the smallest contact between characters in a remote corner of the stage must become objectively true and relevant." One actor recalls, "She'd have all these ideas, more in an hour than I could think of in a lifetime." Said another, "We had intense emotional scenes very often . . . but I found Littlewood the most stimulating person to work with, the most co-operative person. She drew out whatever talent you had."

The work she produced—highly energetic, economic but powerful, often using a wide variety of theatrical forms, including vaudeville and circus—was a far cry from any kind of performance on view in commercial theaters in London's West End (or in the rest of the country), and the theatrical establishment was slow to recognize the dramatic richness Littlewood offered. Because her productions were so accessible, the greatest success she had in these early years was in taking them out into the community, reaching people whose enthusiasm was undimmed by value judgments or expectations. Consequently, not everyone in the company agreed with Littlewood and Raffles that the acquisition in 1953 of the Theater Royal, Stratford East, was a good idea. There was some anxiety that the ethos of creating theater "for the people" would be compromised by the need to create theater "for the London critics." But most members felt that it was high time London had a taste of the innovation, standards and

rapport that could be achieved with minimal resources and maximum imagination.

For a year or more, however, London seemed indifferent, as the company lurched from one financial crisis to another. They struggled along training, rehearsing, and mounting new productions every two or three weeks, gaining a local reputation but very little support from the West End critics. The company was on the brink of bankruptcy when Littlewood's production of *Volpone* was invited to play in the Paris Festival (with *Arden of Faversham*). Both shows were a resounding success and, with Paris at their feet, the company gained a tremendous boost of confidence.

At last the tide had begun to turn. The following year, *The Good Soldier Schweik* went to Paris and then transferred to Shaftsbury Avenue, London's equivalent to Broadway. Finally recognition came from the Arts Council in the shape of a very small grant. Perhaps more important, Littlewood had found and encouraged an extraordinary talent in the young, wild Irishman Brendan Behan. Then, in 1958, an 18-year-old named ❧▶ **Shelagh Delaney** submitted an unsolicited—and basically unworkable—script, the first draft of *A Taste of Honey*. Littlewood at once saw the freshness and originality in it. Using her skills as a dramaturg, she turned the play into Theater Workshop's first, unequivocal critical and box-office hit. The "House Full" boards were brought out again shortly afterwards for *The Hostage*, Brendan Behan's second play. *A Taste of Honey* was transferred to the West End in February 1959, while *The Hostage* was cheered at the Sarah Bernhardt Theater in Paris. Both plays eventually transferred to Broadway, but not before the sparkling musical *Fings Ain't What They Used T'Be* and *Sparrers Can't Sing* (two exuberant "cockney" shows) had broken more records for Theater Workshop.

For Littlewood, success had its price. Her precious ensemble, so carefully nurtured and maintained, was eroding as casts transferred with each new production. Needing a new play which would renew the Company spirit, reunite her loyal actors, and reinforce their commitment, she set her hopes on James Goldman's *They Might Be Giants*. Unfortunately, the critical response was cool, and Littlewood's frustration overwhelmed her. She left England suddenly, having made hasty arrangements to work in Nigeria, and there were no new Theater Workshop productions in London for two years. On her return, energy and hope restored, Littlewood threw herself into both the filming of *Sparrers Can't Sing* and researching and honing material for her inspired production of *Oh What a Lovely War*. Under Littlewood's direction, the tiny company she had assembled created a show that ran for a year in London and has since been seen throughout the world. Richard Eyre remembers it vividly: "This was political theater that unlike most of its genre, neither patronized its audience, nor did it try to reprimand or reform them. It sought to inform and to entertain, and it broke your heart in the process. It's one of the very few things I've seen in the theater that I'd call 'great.'" It is considered the zenith of Littlewood's achievement and the production that assured her a place in the annals of 20th-century theatrical history.

But Littlewood, always the pioneer and never content to rest on her laurels or embrace the establishment, had already begun to focus her attention on new horizons. In 1963, it seemed that rapid advances in technology heralded an age in which people would seek fulfillment through their increased leisure time—an incredible opportunity for theater. In partnership with architect Cedric Price (whom she nicknamed "the Arc"), and others who included Buckminster Fuller and Yehudi Menuhin, Littlewood came up with a plan to create a completely new type of environment in which theater could become art, science and technology all combined: "a 'Fun Palace'—a place of toys for adults, a place to waste time without guilt or discomfort, to develop unused talents, to discover the fund of joy and sadness within us." A visionary concept and far ahead of its time, it was to have such features as warm air curtains, optical barriers, and vapor zones.

During the following years, while spending an increasing amount of time abroad, especially in Hammamet, Tunisia, where she ran a summer school, Littlewood attempted to raise the money for her project. She still took an interest in Theater Workshop and the drama school which had opened there, and she even masterminded the transformation of the site next to the theater into a playground for local children, but her hopes for the future of European culture lay in the "Fun Palace." To her enormous disappointment, after ten years or more of working and reworking the designs, the project eventually collapsed, unsupported by colleagues and funding bodies alike. Joan Littlewood left for France in 1974, and, although she has received honors and awards acknowledging her legacy to the theater, she never worked in England again.

In 1975, Gerry Raffles died suddenly and prematurely. Semi-retired and still grief-stricken, Littlewood met Baron Philippe de Rothschild in

✤▶ Delaney, Shelagh (1939—)

English playwright. Born in Salford, Lancashire, England, on November 25, 1939; daughter of Joseph Delaney (a bus inspector) and Elsie Delaney; children: one daughter.

After leaving school at 16, Shelagh Delaney began to write while supporting herself with odd jobs: salesclerk, cinema usher, and assistant in a photo lab. At 18, she wrote *A Taste of Honey*. It was an explosive way to begin a career in theater. Following a successful production by *Joan Littlewood's Theater Workshop Company in 1958, the play moved to the West End, was awarded the Charles Henry Foyle New Play Award and an Arts Council Bursary, then moved to New York and won the New York Drama Critic's Circle Award. Adapting her play to film, Delaney then received a British Film Academy Award for her 1961 screenplay. The following year, her play *The Lion in Love* was produced at the Royal Court Theater. Delaney's later work has been primarily in television and film. She wrote the screenplay for the award-winning *Charlie Bubbles* (1968), directed by Albert Finney; she also wrote *Dance with a Stranger* (1985), the story of *Ruth Ellis, the last woman executed in England, which starred **Miranda Richardson** and Rupert Everett.

Vienne, France, in 1976. As a result of the unlikely friendship that sprang up between them, he invited her to help him write his autobiography. Living in a small outbuilding on his estate—the vineyards at Mouton—she produced *Milady Vine,* published in 1984. Ten years later, her 790-page autobiography *Joan's Book* was published. Her subtitle: *Joan Littlewood's Peculiar History as She Tells It.*

SOURCES:

Eyre, Richard. *Utopia and Other Places*. Vintage, 1994.
Goorney, Howard. *The Story of Theater Workshop*. London: Eyre Methuen, 1981.
Littlewood, Joan. *Joan's Book*. London: Metheun, 1994.
———. *Milady Vine*. Jonathan Cape, 1984.

SUGGESTED READING:

Barker, Clive. *Theater Games*. London: Eyre Metheun, 1977.

Bonnie Hurren,
freelance actor, director, and artistic director of the
Show of Strength Theater Company in Bristol, England

Litton, Marie (1847–1884)

English actress. Born Mary Lowe in Derbyshire, England, in 1847; died in London on April 1, 1884; married W. Robertson.

An English comedic actress respected for her portrayals of Lady Teazle and Lydia Languish, Marie Litton was also a theatrical manager, overseeing the Court Theater (1871–74), the Imperial Theater (1878), and the Theater Royal, Glasgow (1880). She first appeared as an actress at the Princess's Theater on March 23, 1868.

Litvyak, Lidiya (1921–1943)

Soviet fighter pilot during World War II, first woman to shoot down an enemy aircraft, and top woman ace in history. Name variations: Liliya or Lilya Litvyak; Liliia Litviak. Pronunciation: Lit-VYAHK. Born Lidiya Vladimirovna Litvyak on August 18, 1921, in Moscow, USSR; died on August 1, 1943, in Dmitreivka, Ukraine, as a result of air combat; daughter of Vladimir Leontovich Litvyak (a railway employee) and Anna Vasilevna Khmeleva Litvyak (a saleswoman); never married; no children.

Became a pilot (1937) and instructor pilot (1939–41); joined Soviet military (1941); was a fighter pilot with 586th Fighter Aviation Regiment (1942); transferred to 437th Fighter Aviation Regiment and achieved first kill (1942); transferred to 9th Guards Fighter Aviation Regiment (1942); transferred to 73rd Guards Fighter Aviation Regiment and achieved all subsequent kills (1943); disappeared in combat (August 1943).

Awards: Order of the Red Star; Order of the Red Banner; medal "For the Defense of Stalingrad"; Order of the Patriotic War, 1st degree; Hero of the Soviet Union (awarded posthumously in 1990).

Lidiya Litvyak was a rebel and something of a contradiction. She was the first woman in the world to shoot down an enemy aircraft—a fact that has gone completely unheralded—and she went on to become a double fighter ace before her untimely death a few weeks short of her 22nd birthday. Yet Litvyak would have seemed an unlikely choice for the demanding job of flying high-speed fighter aircraft. She was so short that she had to use extra seat cushions to see out of the cockpit; her feet could not reach the rudder pedals without the aid of wooden blocks to extend the pedal platforms. She was always doing the unexpected and the forbidden—and getting away with it.

Litvyak considered it more than coincidence that she was born on August 18—Air Force Day—in 1921. She lived with her parents and her younger brother Yuri in Moscow on Novoslobodskaia Street (Building 14, Apt. 88). A lively, cheerful girl, organizer of all the games, she had a happy childhood, and she and her

friends loved to stage impromptu performances of plays and music.

By the time she was 14, Litvyak knew that she wanted to fly. In the Soviet Union of the 1930s, flying instruction was free but only available for those 16 and older. Undeterred, Litvyak snuck into airclub training sessions without her parents' knowledge. Though she did not fool the instructor (her tiny stature made her look even younger than her actual age), she was permitted to remain unofficially after she proved that she had studied as well as the older students. When ground classes were over and flight training began, Litvyak hung around the airfield, assisting mechanics and cleaning airplanes. Eventually, a sympathetic instructor allowed her to begin flying.

It was not unusual for a Soviet girl to learn to fly in the late 1930s; about one out of every three or four student pilots was female. However, relatively few women were able to advance to higher levels of training to become instructor pilots. Fewer still became military pilots; although there were no legal barriers in the Soviet Union against women joining the service, there was strong social prejudice. Many women encountered opposition even in basic flight training.

In 1937, about the time Litvyak realized her dream of becoming a pilot, disaster struck. It was the height of the Stalinist purges, and her father was arrested as an "enemy of the people"; the family never heard from him again. Though specific charges against him are still unknown, the family was notified in 1956 that he had died of heart trouble in prison in 1943; a few months later, he was officially "rehabilitated."

It was difficult for Litvyak to carry on with her new career in flying after her father was arrested. Not only did she have to cope with the worry and stress of the event, she also had to endure the stigma of being the daughter of a "repressed" person. (After the war, her brother Yuri was fired from a succession of jobs whenever it was discovered that his father was an "enemy"; he eventually changed his last name when he married in 1951.)

At age 18, Litvyak set out to make aviation her career. She attended the Kherson Aviation School from January through May 1940, where she received training to be an instructor pilot. She then worked as an instructor pilot at the Kirov airclub in Moscow, where from 1940 to 1941 she trained 45 students to be pilots. After setting a record for 8 hours and 40 minutes of instruction in a single day, she was singled out as

one of the top instructor pilots in Moscow by *Samolyot* (Airplane) magazine on May 5, 1941.

After the Germans invaded the Soviet Union on June 22, 1941, thousands of Soviet women rushed to volunteer. Most were turned down, al-

though, as the war progressed, the Soviet military opened its ranks. Eventually, 800,000 women served. Litvyak made repeated requests for an assignment to military aviation, but was told she had to continue working as an instructor pilot and would be evacuated to the rear area with her airclub. But in early October 1941, the famous Soviet pilot ✤ **Marina Raskova** (a sort of Russian *Amelia Earhart) was authorized to form three aviation regiments to be staffed entirely by women. Litvyak was selected to join Raskova's training squad, Aviation Group No. 122.

The 122nd was sent to Engels, 500 miles southeast of Moscow, for intensive training. The students worked 12-to-14 hours a day, cramming what was normally three years of military flight training into six months. **Inna Pasportnikova**, a mechanic, remembers Litvyak from the first morning roll call. Raskova suddenly commanded Litvyak to step forward. As she did, the other girls began to laugh; instead of the usual brown fur collar that was part of the winter uniform, Litvyak was wearing a smart, fluffy white collar. She had cut the goatskin lining from her boots and sewn it on her jacket. "What's that on your shoulders?" Raskova demanded. "A goatskin collar. Why, doesn't it suit me?" Litvyak replied. She was ordered to replace the collar with the standard military issue. Pasportnikova was appalled; how could such a vain, frivolous girl become a combat pilot? Who could worry about their appearance at such a time, when soldiers were dying on the battlefield? She did not dream she would later become a member of Litvyak's crew and a witness to the fierce ability of that "vain, frivolous" combat pilot.

How rarely do we recall the names of the women fighter pilots! There weren't many of them, but their combat actions deserve the very highest appraisal. After all, they disproved the erroneous opinion that the profession of air combat is unacceptable for women. Katya Budanova and Lidiya Litvyak were, for us, dependable comrades-in-arms in the skies of the front.

—Vladimir Lavrinenkov

Litvyak quickly demonstrated her skill as a pilot and was selected for the 586th Fighter Aviation Regiment, the first of the three "women's" regiments to become operational. The 586th was assigned to the air defense forces, and rebased near Engels with the task of defending the city of Saratov against enemy attack. The missions of the 586th included performing combat air patrols to defend against enemy reconnaissance aircraft and bombers, and providing fighter escort to protect transport aircraft against enemy fighters. While stationed at Saratov, Litvyak completed 55 combat flights. The flying was fairly tame, however. Saratov was still a long way from the front lines.

On September 10, 1942, Litvyak finally got her wish to see "real" combat when she and seven other pilots from the 586th were transferred to Stalingrad. Soviet aviation regiments had endured heavy casualties in the Stalingrad region, and the eight women were divided between two regiments as replacement pilots. Litvyak, along with **Katya Budanova, Raisa Belyaeva**, and **Mariya Kuznetsova**, was sent to the 437th Fighter Aviation Regiment of the 8th Air Army; their female mechanics and armorers went with them. (At the time, Inna Pasportnikova was Belyaeva's mechanic.) The women were received with hostility. "This is combat, not a flying club!," they were told. "There are air battles every day. We're waiting for real pilots, and they sent us a bunch of girls." But the male commanders had to take what they could get.

The women acquitted themselves well. Within three days, Litvyak scored her first two kills, both during a single combat flight. She was flying as wingman in a standard combat formation, with her plane positioned behind and to the side of a male pilot's leading aircraft. Each succeeded in shooting down a Ju-88 bomber. Then she saw that Belyaeva, who had run out of ammunition, was being attacked by an Me-109 fighter. Litvyak attacked the German plane and shot it down; the pilot bailed out safely and was captured by Soviet forces. Eyewitnesses do not recall the German pilot's name, but they remember that he was a colonel who bore three Iron Crosses upon his chest. "He was a famous fascist ace, and considered himself unbeatable," says Pasportnikova. When his captors presented Litvyak to him as the pilot who had shot him down, he thought it was a joke to humiliate him. Then Litvyak recounted the details of their air battle, which no other pilot could have known.

For a pilot to achieve two kills in one flight on her third day of combat was a remarkable achievement. For that pilot also to be the first woman in history to shoot down an enemy deserves acknowledgement and credit, but Litvyak has gone unheralded. One of the women who remained with the 586th, ✤ **Valeriia Khomiakova**, shot down a German bomber ten days later and is often cited as the first woman with a kill, but records in the Soviet military archives make it quite clear that Litvyak was first. Her accomplishment probably went unnoticed in the heat of combat because she was a newly arrived woman in a male regiment which she and the other women soon left. Once Khomiakova was

✤▶

Raskova, Marina. See joint entry under Grizodubova, Valentina.

given credit, perhaps it became too troublesome for the Soviets to set the record straight.

Despite their dramatic success, Litvyak and the three other women pilots in her group were for some reason abruptly transferred three weeks later, on October 1, 1942, from the 437th to the 9th Guards Fighter Aviation Regiment. The 9th Guards was stationed at the time near the city of Zhitkur, where it was being reequipped with new aircraft. Some of the most famous Soviet fighter aces of the war were members of this renowned regiment. Though not in the hottest part of the fighting during this period, Litvyak and Budanova received excellent training from the seasoned pilots. One of the 9th's fighter pilots (later a Hero of the Soviet Union and a general), Vladimir Lavrinenkov, wrote about the women pilots in his memoirs. Litvyak and Budanova "served on an equal footing with the men," he notes, and he describes several air engagements in which the women acquitted themselves well. Their life was not easy; flying fighters required exceptional strength and endurance.

Budanova and Litvyak made an interesting pair. Both were excellent pilots, but they could hardly have been more different in character or physical appearance. Budanova was tall and mannish-looking with her short haircut. "The small, fair-haired Lidiya seemed like a little girl beside her," Lavrinenkov recalls. Many of the men were smitten with Litvyak, but Lavrinenkov writes that she "showed no preference for anyone" and acted with reserve. Somehow she managed to avoid emotional entanglements without alienating her fellow pilots; for Litvyak, personal relationships were strictly secondary to the job at hand. She was deadly determined to prove herself as a fighter pilot—not only from personal ambition and patriotism, but also in order to redeem her family name. She never stopped believing in her father's innocence, and believed that she could reclaim the family's honor by gaining fame in combat.

But if her father's status as an "enemy of the people" heightened her desire to fight, it was also the source of her deepest dread. More than anything else, Litvyak feared that she would end up missing in action. Any Soviet soldier whose body could not be found, who went "missing without a trace," was automatically suspected of desertion. Pilots often flew deep into enemy territory; they could be taken prisoner, or they might crash with their aircraft, leaving their bodies impossible to identify. Litvyak was determined not to die that way, but to land in friendly territory, even if it was with her dying breath.

Khomiakova, Valeriia (d. 1942)

Soviet fighter pilot during World War II. Name variations: *Valeria Ivanovna Khomyakova. Died in 1942.*

Wrongly credited as the first woman fighter pilot to shoot down an enemy bomber, Valeriia Khomiakova's kill occurred on September 24, 1942, ten days after *Lidiya Litvyak's first kill. Since Litvyak had been sent off to fill in at another regiment, nobody appeared to think her accomplishment was worth publicity. Most likely, no one back at Litvyak's assigned regiment even knew about it until later. On the other hand, Khomiakova's commissar was quick to publicize her achievements; she was sent to Moscow to receive an award and was written up in the newspapers. Khomiakova was killed two weeks later, due to the poor judgment of her commander.

On January 8, 1943, Litvyak found her true combat home when she and Budanova were transferred to the 296th Fighter Aviation Regiment. The 296th, part of the 8th Air Army, was a front-line regiment. Regimental commander Nikolai Ivanovich Baranov, who had been in the war since the first day, was known as "Batya" ("Father") to his pilots. It was Baranov who finally gave Litvyak and Budanova the opportunity to prove their skill. There were many well-known fighter pilots in the regiment, such as squadron commander Alexei Solomatin, who had participated in a famous air engagement a few months earlier, when seven Soviet fighters fought 29 enemy aircraft. Solomatin took Litvyak as his wingman, and Budanova was selected to fly with Baranov. In this way, the women were able to benefit from flying with highly experienced leaders.

On February 11, 1943, Litvyak was one of 4 fighters from the 73rd involved in an air battle with 29 enemy aircraft. Flying with Baranov, Solomatin, and a fourth pilot, Litvyak personally shot down a Ju-87 and shared a kill with Baranov against a Focke-Wulf 190 fighter. Later that month, she was selected to join the ranks of the elite, the "free hunters"—fighter pilots who, because of their skill, were sent out in pairs to find and destroy the enemy. She became a flight commander and was promoted from sergeant to junior lieutenant. On March 8, 1943, the 296th was renamed the 73rd Guards Fighter Aviation Regiment in recognition of its combat performance.

Early in her career, Litvyak adopted the showy, and strictly forbidden, habit of buzzing the airfield when she returned from a kill. Approaching the airfield after a successful mission,

Litvyak would break from formation and perform high-speed, low-altitude passes and victory rolls. "After her 'circus number' in the air," said Pasportnikova, Litvyak always asked her, "'Did Batya swear terribly?' And if I said, 'terribly!' she would hang her head and walk over to him with her post-mission report." In other words, Litvyak was careful to give the appearance of being appropriately contrite after breaking the rules.

Litvyak was badly wounded in air combat on March 22, 1943, while part of a group of six Yak fighters attacking a dozen Ju-88 bombers. After shooting down one of the bombers, she felt a sharp pain in her leg, and realized she was being attacked, from out of nowhere, by a pair of Messerschmitts. As she evaded the attack, four more enemy fighters joined in, and Litvyak found herself in a singlehanded dogfight against six Me-109 fighters. In an aerial game of "chicken," Litvyak employed a tactic often used by Soviet pilots possessed of especially steely nerves: she pushed the throttle forward and raced directly into a group of enemy fighters. At the last minute, they veered, and she was able to get into good firing position, shooting down a Messerschmitt before the fight ended. In severe pain and losing blood, Litvyak managed to return to her airfield and land her plane. She stopped on the runway, but lost consciousness before she could taxi to a parking spot.

After receiving field treatment, Litvyak was sent to a hospital in Moscow for surgery. Since hospital beds were in short supply, she received permission to recuperate at home, but she was restless and anxious to get back to the front. After a few days, Litvyak talked her way onto a transport and returned to her regiment.

Less than six weeks after her injury, Litvyak was back on the scoreboard. She shot down two aircraft in March; she would make three kills in May, and another four in July—all personal kills. Litvyak shot down Me-109 fighters on May 5th and 7th. Reportedly, she had not entirely regained her strength when she first returned to flying; she was so weak after her May 5th flight that Baranov refused to let her fly again that day. But the month of May brought tragedy as well as victory for Litvyak. On May 6, Nikolai Baranov died when he attempted to bail out of his burning aircraft; although his parachute opened, it was already on fire. His pilots saw him plummet to his death, with the burning parachute trailing in the air. On May 21st, Litvyak suffered an even deeper loss. Before the eyes of the entire regiment, while conducting training with a new pilot above the air-

Opposite page

Lidiya

Litvyak

field, Alexei Solomatin crashed and was killed. Only two weeks earlier, he had received the highest military decoration, the Hero of the Soviet Union medal.

A great deal has been written about the supposed romance between Litvyak and Alexei Solomatin, who flew together in the 73rd. But according to Litvyak's letters, she did not realize she loved Solomatin until after his death. She wrote a wrenching letter to her mother at the end of May, a few days after Solomatin's funeral:

> Fate has snatched away my best friend Lyosha Solomatin. . . . He was everyone's favorite and he loved me very much, but at that time he was not my ideal. Because of this there was a lot of unpleasantness. I transferred to another squadron and maybe that's why I was shot down over Rostov.

In the same letter, Litvyak described a dream she'd had:

> The river was seething, to swim across was impossible; [Solomatin] stood on the other bank and called me, he called so, simply to tears, and he said, "After all, Batya managed to get me for himself, he couldn't manage without me." And again Alyosha called me and asked: "Lilka, aren't you coming?" And I told him, "If they let me. . . ." But I know that I can't swim across this river anyway. And I woke up. And now it's terrible for me to endure, and I confide, mamochka, that I valued this friendship only in the moment of his death. If he had remained alive, then it seems this friendship would have become exceptionally beautiful and strong. You see, he was a fellow not to my taste, but his persistence and his love for me compelled me to love him, and now . . . it seems to me that I will never again meet such a person.

Litvyak seems to have become increasingly daring—some might say reckless—after the death of her friends. Her third May kill was the one for which she is most remembered by her comrades; and it was not an aircraft but a German artillery observation balloon near the village of Troitskoye, about ten miles behind the front lines. The balloon was tethered to the ground, and could be raised to permit artillery spotters to observe Soviet positions; they could then accurately direct German artillery fire. The balloon was protected by a heavy screen of anti-aircraft fire and could be quickly lowered. Several attempts had already been made by Soviet pilots to destroy the balloon, but all had been turned back by German defensive fire. Litvyak decided on a new tactic. First, she flew into friendly territory, far away from the front, before circling back and crossing the front lines. She then penetrated deep into enemy territory before turning to approach the balloon from the rear, behind its defenses. She destroyed it on the first pass.

On June 13, 1943, Litvyak was appointed flight commander in the 3rd Aviation Squadron of the 73rd Guards Fighter Aviation Regiment. A few days later, she was flying as wingman to the new regimental commander, I.V. Golyshev, when they set out to intercept an enemy reconnaissance aircraft and encountered four Me-109 fighters. Golyshev was wounded; Litvyak managed to cover his exit from the fight, but her aircraft was badly shot up in the process. Despite ten holes in her Yak-1, she was able to land the plane successfully.

Litvyak was wounded once more on July 16, 1943, when 6 Yak-1s battled against 30 Ju-88s escorted by 6 Me-109s. Though injured early in the battle, she stayed in the fight and shot down one bomber and one fighter. Forced to leave the area after receiving serious damage to her aircraft, she was attacked again during her return to base and wounded a second time. Litvyak received local medical attention for her shoulder and leg, but refused to be sent to a field hospital, claiming that the wounds were not serious.

On July 19, while escorting Il-2s, Litvyak shot down one Me-109. On the same day, Katya Budanova died. After shooting down two Me-109s (her fifth and sixth personal kills), Budanova was badly wounded and her aircraft severely damaged. She managed to land in a nearby field, but was already dying when local villagers pulled her from the plane. Pasportnikova recalls that Litvyak was stunned by Budanova's death; it must have seemed that she had lost all the fellow warriors who mattered most to her.

The next day, Litvyak barely survived a fierce air battle when she and Golyshev encountered ten enemy fighters. Litvyak bailed out of her burning aircraft; Golyshev was killed. Near the end of July, Litvyak wrote to her mother, "I am completely absorbed in combat life. I can't seem to think of anything but the fighting." Now, to add to her list of motivations, she had a very personal desire to avenge her fallen friends.

Litvyak's final flights took place on August 1, 1943. On her third flight of the day, she shared a kill against an Me-109. On her ill-fated fourth flight, she participated in a mass air battle involving 6 Yak-1s against 12 Me-109s and 30 Ju-88 bombers. Litvyak shot down an Me-109, then flew into the clouds, trailing smoke, as she attempted to evade two more attacking German fighters. She disappeared over enemy territory.

When Soviet forces recaptured the area a few days later, her regiment conducted extensive searches but could find no trace of Litvyak's aircraft. Her worst fear had been realized; her records were marked "missing without a trace." One of Litvyak's colleagues, pilot Ivan Borisenko, later wrote: "It is difficult to imagine our grief. Everyone without exception loved her. As a person and as a pilot she was wonderful."

During her brief life, Litvyak made her mark. She was the first woman in history to shoot down an enemy aircraft. She also holds the top rank for total number of kills among women fighter pilots; her tally of 12 personal kills is a respectable score for any fighter ace. Litvyak chose a thoroughly unfeminine profession, yet maintained an almost blatant femininity even in wartime. When the other pilots were having shark's teeth painted on their aircraft, Litvyak asked for flowers. She had her mechanic obtain peroxide so she could continue to bleach her hair the shade of blonde she preferred. Yet her skill as a fighter pilot is indisputable. She is remembered by her male colleagues as "a remarkable girl, smart, with the true character of a fighter pilot and a daredevil."

Litvyak was recommended for the Hero of the Soviet Union medal, but it was a military regulation that the medal could not be awarded to anyone who disappeared in combat. Inna Pasportnikova vowed that she would not rest until Litvyak's body had been found and her name cleared. She worked for many years with various groups that searched for and identified victims of the war. As it turned out, Litvyak had not gone down where she was thought to have landed. Apparently, she flew some distance before landing, in an attempt to return to friendly territory. In 1979, the searchers discovered that an unidentified woman pilot had been buried in the village of Dmitrievka. No personal identification was found, but the woman had been very short, had received a mortal head wound, and had been found dead in her aircraft. A search of military records revealed that Litvyak had been the only surviving woman pilot in the region at that time, and it was concluded that the body was hers. Finally, in 1988, Litvyak's records were amended; rather than being listed as missing, she was now officially "killed in action." The Hero of the Soviet Union nomination went forward at last. In May 1990, Soviet general secretary Mikhail Gorbachev signed the award, which was presented to Litvyak's brother Yuri Kunavin. Kunavin died soon after, but he had lived to see the names of both his father and his sister restored to honor.

Lidiya Litvyak completed 268 combat flights; her personal kills included 1 Ju-87 and 3 Ju-88 bombers, 7 Me-109 fighters, and 1 artillery observation balloon. Her shared kills included 1 FW-190 and 2 Me-109 fighters. All her kills were accomplished in less than one year of combat flying, between September 13, 1942, and August 1, 1943.

ARCHIVAL RECORDS, UNPUBLISHED DOCUMENTS AND PERSONAL INTERVIEWS:

Kanevskii, A. "Ia samaia schastlivaia . . ." ["I'm the Luckiest . . ."] *Aviatsiia i Kosmonavtika.* March 1990, pp. 36–38.

Lavrinenkov, Vladimir Dmitrievich. *Vozvrashchenie v nebo* (Return to the Sky). 2nd ed. Moscow: Voenizdat, 1983.

Pennington, Reina. "Wings, Women and War: Soviet Women's Military Aviation Regiments in the Great Patriotic War," Master's thesis, University of South Carolina, 1993.

Yeryomin, Boris Nikolaevich. *Vozdushnye boitsy* (Air Warriors). Moscow: Voenizdat, 1987.

SUGGESTED READING:

Cottam, K. Jean. *Soviet Airwomen in Combat in World War II.* Manhattan, KS: Sunflower University Press, 1983.

————, ed. and trans. *In the Sky Above the Front: A Collection of Memoirs of Soviet Air Women Participants in the Great Patriotic War.* Manhattan, KS: Sunflower University Press, 1984.

Noggle, Anne. *Dance with Death.* College Station: Texas A&M University Press, 1994.

Pennington, Reina. "Wings, Women and War," in *Smithsonian's Air & Space.* December–January 1993–94, pp. 74–85.

Reina Pennington,
Ph.D. candidate in military and women's history,
University of South Carolina, Columbia, South Carolina

Litwinde (fl. 850)

Bavarian princess. Flourished around 850; daughter of Count Ernest; married Carloman (c. 828–880), king of Bavaria (r. 876–880), around 850; children: Arnulf of Carinthia (b. around 863), king of Germany (r. 887–899), king of the East Franks (r. 896–899), and Holy Roman emperor (r. 896–899).

Liubatovich, Olga (1853–1917)

Russian revolutionary who was active in all phases of the Populist movement. Pronunciation: Lu-ba-TOE-vich. Born Olga Spiridonovna Liubatovich in 1853 in Moscow; committed suicide in Tbilisi, Georgia, on July 27, 1917; daughter of Spiridon Liubatovich (a wealthy factory owner); her mother was the daughter of a wealthy gold mine owner (name unknown); sister of Vera Liubatovich (1855–1907); attended Second Moscow Women's Gymnasium, c. 1866–71; Medical Faculty, University of Zurich, 1871–73; married I.S.

Dzhabadari; children: (with Nikolai Morozov) a daughter.

Was a member of the Fritschi Circle in Zurich and Bern (1872–74); was a Populist propagandist in the All-Russian Social-Revolutionary Organization (1875); arrested (1875), tried (1877), sentenced to exile in Siberia, and escaped (1878); was a member of Land and Liberty (1878–79); was a member of the Executive Committee of Narodnaia Volia (1879–81); arrested and exiled to Siberia (1882–1905?); returned to Georgia but was apparently inactive in further revolutionary activity.

Publication: "Dalekoe i nedavnee" (Distant and Recent), in Byloe *(Moscow, 1906, no. 5, pp. 208–241, no. 6, pp. 108–154).*

On July 27, 1878, Olga Liubatovich "committed suicide." She wrote a note to her sister *Vera Liubatovich saying she could no longer stand the life of an exiled revolutionary in Siberia, and she left some clothes scattered along the banks of the nearby rapidly flowing Tobol River. Suicide had been the fate of five well-bred young women of her generation who had gone abroad to get an education, been converted to socialism, and had returned to Russia to spread their message to the downtrodden masses. Inevitably, peasant apathy, police oppression, prison conditions and Siberian exile had produced disillusionment, resignation and despair. Olga was the exception. After leaving behind evidence of her "death," the 25-year-old woman spent a night wandering through a deserted forest where she realized she ran the risk of "meeting the beasts and brutalized vagrants of Siberia." Ultimately, a young peasant whom she had recruited to the socialist cause showed up, and with his help she managed to catch first a coach, then a boat, and finally a train to temporary freedom. "When I arrived in St. Petersburg," she recalled later, "I had the clothes on my back, a scant few kopecks in my pockets, and nowhere at all to go." In four days, she managed to re-establish contact with revolutionary colleagues in the Populist movement and soon was actively involved in the propaganda work of Land and Liberty. A year later, she joined the Executive Committee of Narodnaia Volia (The People's Will) and helped lay the groundwork for the assassination of Tsar Alexander II in March 1881. For a few months thereafter, this indefatigable woman was "the sole remaining representative of systematic terror" in the Russian capital. In November, the police finally caught up with her and sent her back to Siberia.

As a child Olga Liubatovich knew nothing of the hardships of the Moscow workers or Siberian peasants she later was to proselytize. She was born in 1853 into a life of luxury and privilege. Her father, Spiridon Liubatovich, held the title of Collegiate Assessor and owned a profitable brick factory outside of Moscow. Her mother was the well-educated daughter of a wealthy gold mine owner. Because of their "advanced" views—Spiridon Liubatovich had earlier fled Montenegro as a result of his own political activity— Olga and her four siblings received a good and a liberal education. After five years at the Second Moscow Women's Gymnasium, she left for Switzerland with her father's blessings to enter the Medical Faculty of the University of Zurich.

Olga Liubatovich

Study abroad was in fact the only option for women of her generation who wanted a university education. Many were attracted to Zurich because of its practice of admitting women on the same basis as men. They were drawn to the study of medicine not only by its social utility but also by the well-publicized example of ❧▶ **Nadezhda Suslova**, who had received a doctorate from the Faculty of Medicine in 1867—the first Russian woman to be awarded a

---

❧▶ **Suslova, Nadezhda** (1845–1916)

Russian doctor. Born in Russia in 1845; died in 1916; daughter of a serf; attended Medical Faculty, University of Zurich, qualifying in 1867.

A Russian medical pioneer, Nadezhda Suslova was the daughter of a serf and a remarkable example of social mobility in tsarist Russia. She studied medicine at the University of Zurich and became the first Russian woman physician.

SUGGESTED READING:

Bonner, Thomas Neville. "Rendezvous in Zurich: Seven Who Made a Revolution in Women's Medical Education, 1864–1974," in *Journal of the History of Medicine.* Vol. 44, no. 1. January 1989, pp. 7–27.

———. *To the Ends of the Earth: Women's Search for Education in Medicine.* Cambridge, MA: Harvard University Press, 1992.

degree by a continental university. Olga was 18 when she enrolled on October 14, 1871. Like many of her fellow Russians, she felt emancipated just being away from the conservative conventions of her autocratic homeland. A Swiss student has left a bemused picture of Liubatovich at this time:

> Behind the table was sitting an enigmatic being, whose biological character was at first all but clear to me: a roundish, boyish face, short-cut hair, parted askew, enormous blue glasses, a quite youthful, tender-colored face, a course jacket, a burning cigarette in its mouth—everything about it was boylike, and yet there was something which belied this desired impression. I looked stealthily under the table—and discovered a bright-coloured, somewhat faded cotton skirt. The being took no notice at all of my presence and remained absorbed in a large book, every now and then rolling a cigarette which was finished in a few droughts.

The focal point of emigré activity in Zurich was the Russian Library. Around it clustered numerous student circles devoted to self-education and to the discussion of social issues. One of these, to which Olga and later her younger sister Vera belonged, was the Fritschi Circle. Named after the owner of the rooming house where many of the young Russian women lived, the Fritschi provided companionship and an introduction to the radical ideas of the French utopian socialists and contemporary Russian revolutionary theorists. In time, the women decided that their own personal liberation and their future practice of medicine in Russia were less important than participating in the destruction of the political and economic order.

In late 1874, Olga, her sister, and ten other Fritschi returned to Russia to put their ideas into practice. They chose to work in and around Moscow, where police conditions were purportedly less stringent and where there was a concentration of large textile factories employing Russian workers. Unlike other Populists, who had gone out into the villages of Russia and Ukraine in the summer of 1874 to propagandize the peasantry directly, the Fritschi sought to convert more advanced factory workers who would then spread these ideas when they returned periodically to their native villages. To coordinate this activity, the women, several male Georgian revolutionaries they had met in Switzerland, and a few worker-recruits established the All-Russian Social-Revolutionary Organization in February 1875. This body—the first formal Populist organization in Russia—was based on ethical, egalitarian, and very democratic principles. Olga, who according to Sergei Kravchinskii "rejected marriage and love as unsuitable for a revolutionary," proposed that its members adopt a policy of celibacy. This was opposed by the men, who also objected to their female colleagues going into the factories and worker dormitories to read revolutionary tracts to illiterate proletarians. With reason, they pointed out that upper-class women, even if they dressed in old clothes, would attract attention in these strange surroundings and would put themselves and others at risk. Olga persisted, first in Moscow and then in Tula, but had to admit that her results were meager. Sometime in the summer of 1875 her apartment in Tula was raided, and she was arrested when the jealous girlfriend of a local worker she had recruited denounced her supposed rival to the police.

Olga Liubatovich and the other members of the All-Russian Social-Revolutionary Organization spent over a year and a half in jail, often isolated from one another, awaiting trial. To protest prison conditions and just to get needle and thread, Liubatovich—who was known among the Fritschi as "Shark" because of her ravenous appetite—went on a seven-day hunger strike. The "Trial of the Fifty," held in St. Petersburg during late February and early March 1877, was the first time that leading Populists had appeared in open court. As Liubatovich later recalled, many came to see the unrepentant "'Moscow Amazons,' who had grown up in baronial mansions, sampled all the charms of free intellectual work in the universities of Europe, and then, with such courageous simplicity, entered the filthy factories of Moscow as ordinary workers." She was found guilty and sentenced to nine years of hard labor, which was later reduced to exile in Ialutorovsk in western Siberia.

Exile did not agree with Liubatovich any more than prison. For a while, she used her medical training to help the local population and also to gain access to peasants and workers she might propagandize. On one occasion, she barricaded herself in her house, claimed to be armed, and refused to allow the local authorities to search it for four days. The police probably welcomed her "suicide" and escape in July 1878.

For the next three years, she lived intermittently and illegally in St. Petersburg as a member of increasingly more radical Populist organizations. Initially she belonged to Land and Liberty and was invited to help edit its newspaper. The conviction had been growing in her, however, that propaganda was no longer productive and that the time had come to punish the oppressive government by assassinating its key officials. In

1879, when Land and Liberty split over this issue, she joined Narodnaia Volia and supported its program of political terror. She was a member of its Executive Committee and once again helped to edit the group's underground newspaper. In February 1880, police pressure and ill health forced her to flee abroad with Nikolai Morozov—a poet, a fellow revolutionary, and the great love of her life.

Liubatovich says little about the year they spent in Geneva except to note that in late 1880 she gave birth to their child. Four months later, Morozov returned to Russia and was soon arrested. Olga, in despair, left their baby girl in the care of an emigré family and hastened back to St. Petersburg to try to arrange his escape. She was engaged in this hopeless task when Narodnaia Volia successfully assassinated the tsar on March 1, 1881. The police quickly arrested the perpetrators and broke the back of the terrorist movement. For the next six months, Liubatovich tried to coordinate the remnants of Narodnaia Volia and to provide a revolutionary presence in St. Petersburg. She also learned during this time of her infant daughter's death in southern France as a result of contracting meningitis. "I sat over Kravchinskii's telegram for hours on end before it fully registered on me that my daughter was dead," she wrote in her memoirs.

> I didn't cry; I was numb from grief. For some time thereafter, I suffered torments whenever I walked down the street or rode in a tram: the sweet, happy faces of small children tore at my heart, reminding me of my own child. Dulled by thoughts of her death, I temporarily lost my innate caution.

Liubatovich's personal loss was compounded by the failure of the cause to which she had devoted the last seven years of her life. "I agreed to go to Moscow," she wrote many years later, "without knowing what I would do there—almost certain, moreover, that there was nothing important that could be done. For me, there was no one and nothing to save my freedom for, anyway; the winning of Russia's freedom had been delayed, I felt, for a long, long time to come."

Discouraged and disillusioned, she almost welcomed her arrest on November 6, 1881. Without a trial, Liubatovich was banished to Irkutsk in eastern Siberia in November 1882 on the basis of her illegal flight four and half years earlier. Sometime in the next decade, she married Ivan Dzhabadari, a Georgian revolutionary she had met while studying in Switzerland and with whom she had served in the All-Russian Social-Revolutionary Organization. She was apparently freed by the general amnesty granted in 1905 and returned

with her husband to Tbilisi (Tiflis), where she died in 1917. Other than completing her memoirs in 1906, little is known about her activities during the last years of her life in Georgia.

SOURCES:

Engel, Barbara Alpern. *Mothers and Daughters: Women of the Intelligentsia in Nineteenth-Century Russia.* Cambridge: Cambridge University Press, 1983.

———, and Clifford N. Rosenthal, eds. and trans. *Five Sisters Against the Tsar.* NY: Alfred A. Knopf, 1975 (the quotations used above, most of which come from the translated excerpts of Liubatovich's memoirs, are found in this volume).

Knight, Amy. "The *Fritschi:* A Study of Female Radicals in the Russian Populist Movement," *Canadian-American Slavic Studies.* Vol. IX, no. 1. Spring 1975, pp. 1–17.

SUGGESTED READING:

Kravchinskii [Stepniak], Sergei. *A Female Nihilist.* Boston: B.R. Tucker, 1886.

Meijer, Jan Marinus. *The Russian Colony in Zuerich (1870–1873): A Contribution to the Study of Russian Populism.* Assen: Van Gorcum, 1955.

R.C. Elwood,
Professor of History, Carleton University, Ottawa, Canada

Liubatovich, Vera (1855–1907)

Revolutionary and founding member of the All-Russian Social-Revolutionary Organization, the first formal organization of Russian Populists. Pronunciation: Lu-ba-TOE-vich. Born Vera Spiridonovna Liubatovich on July 26, 1855 (o.s.) in Moscow; died in Moscow on December 19, 1907; daughter of Spiridon Liubatovich (a wealthy factory owner); her mother was the daughter of a wealthy gold mine owner (name unknown); sister of Olga Liubatovich (1853–1917); attended Second Moscow Women's Gymnasium, 1868–71; attended Medical Faculty, University of Zurich, 1873; married V.A. Ostashkin, in 1880; no children.

Was a member of the Fritschi circle in Zurich and Bern (1872–74); was a Populist propagandist and organizer for the All-Russian Social-Revolutionary Organization (1875); arrested (1875), tried (1877) and exiled to Siberia until 1890s; lived thereafter in Orel and Moscow but did not participate further in the revolutionary movement.

On April 9, 1873, Vera Liubatovich enrolled in the Medical Faculty of the University of Zurich. She was only 17 years old, but she had the opportunity to get a university education which was denied women in her native Russia. She had plenty of company in Switzerland. Over 100 Russian women were enrolled in the faculty along with scores of men attracted by the free and radical milieu of student life in Zurich. Together with her older sister *Olga Liubatovich,

Vera belonged to the Fritschi—a group of 14 young Russian women who shared humble apartments, supported each other and discussed social issues of the day. Many of their discussions centered on the competing views of Michael Bakunin and Peter Lavrov—Russian revolutionaries who frequented Zurich—concerning the appropriate way to change the autocratic tsarist system. In the fall of 1874, most of the Fritschi abandoned their studies and sought to put their radical theories into practice. Vera returned to Moscow, where she was a central figure in the formation of the All-Russian Social Revolutionary Organization. In August 1875, after less than eight months of trying to enlist the support of factory workers around Moscow and shortly after her 20th birthday, she was arrested. Her youth and moral fervor elicited great public support at the "Trial of the Fifty" in February 1877, but this could not save her from being banished to Siberia.

Vera Liubatovich, like most of the female Populists of the 1870s, came from a privileged background. She was born on July 26, 1855, in Moscow. Her father Spiridon Liubatovich, an engineer by training, was a political refugee from Montenegro who had prospered in Russia. After working in the Survey Office in Moscow, he had built a profitable brick factory and had been given the title of Collegiate Assessor. Her mother, the daughter of a wealthy gold mine owner, had at least five children. She had studied in the best French boarding school in Moscow and counted among her friends many of the leading literati of the day. Perhaps at her mother's insistence and certainly thanks to her father's wealth, Vera received a good and presumably liberal education for three years at the Second Women's Gymnasium in Moscow. In 1871, prior to graduation, she left the Gymnasium and shortly thereafter traveled abroad to join her older sister Olga at the University of Zurich. Despite her youth, Vera went abroad with her father's blessing and his financial support. A contributing factor in this decision may have been the death of her mother when Vera was

Vera Liubatovich

13 and her father's remarriage two years later to the family governess.

For a girl of 16, the personal, intellectual and political freedom of life in Zurich must have been invigorating. She lived with her sister in a local rooming house and spent her days discussing politics in coffee houses, reading in the Russian Library, and, not surprisingly, associating with the other Russian women at the university. For unexplained reasons—perhaps her youth, perhaps the need to prepare for newly instituted entrance examinations—she did not formally enroll in the Medical Faculty until April 1873. Far more important than the limited medical training she obtained was the companionship and political education she received through the Fritschi circle, named after **Madame Fritsch**, the owner of the boarding house where many of the young women lived. The formal discussions within the circle about utopian socialism and economic exploitation radicalized the political orientation of its participants. Vera, the youngest of the group, was known as "Wolfie" because of what *Vera Figner* called "her morose stare and her habit of swearing 'by the devil' and 'by the bourgeoisie.'" She took herself very seriously. When one of the group, **Sofia Bardina**, admitted to a liking for raspberries and Swiss cream, Vera labelled her "bourgeois" and reminded her of her "weakness" at every opportunity. Like the other members of the Fritschi, Vera attended meetings of the International Workingmen's Association, and she helped typeset Lavrov's revolutionary journal *Vpered* in Zurich.

In due course, the tsarist government became alarmed at the political activities of the Russian women in Zurich and in May 1873 issued an edict requiring that they leave the university by the end of the year or risk being denied employment when they returned home. Vera and her friends professed that, though they were concerned about the curtailment of their foreign education, they were more concerned about the false accusation that they were preaching that they had been "led astray by communist theories about free love" and were using their medical skills to perform abortions on each other. Indeed, since the edict mentioned only the University of Zurich, Vera and several of her friends simply moved to Bern and resumed their studies in the Swiss capital. Increasingly, however, they wanted to pass from thought to action; to be, in Vera Figner's words, "useful to society." Lavrov had said that the privileged minority to which they belonged owed "a debt to the people" and had a responsibility to help change Russian society. Together with some male radicals from Georgia living in Switzerland, the Fritschi discussed the formation of a revolutionary organization in Russia to coordinate their efforts to "go to the people." Rather than targeting the peasantry, as had most of the Populist students who had gone out into the countryside during the summer of 1874, the Fritschi decided to concentrate on preaching the gospel of socialism to the factory workers around Moscow.

Vera Liubatovich's involvement in the Populist movement was almost aborted before it began. On October 16, 1874, shortly after crossing the Russian frontier, she was arrested in Chernigov, having in her possession incriminating letters from friends abroad to compatriots in Russia. She was freed only when her father was allowed to post bail in December 1874. She then hastened to Moscow, where in February the All-Russian Social-Revolutionary Organization was constituted along lines discussed in Switzerland. This was the first formal organization set up by the Populists in Russia, and, not surprisingly, its young, well-born and foreign-educated members knew little about conditions in Russia or about conspiratorial techniques. At first Vera, like the 11 other Fritschi in the organization, put on old clothes and tried with limited success to propagandize textile workers in their factories and dormitories. When several members were arrested in April, she became part of a three-person headquarters group in Moscow that maintained communications with members in the provinces and with those already in jail. In August, when the police broke into their apartment, Vera unsuccessfully tried to resist arrest.

In February 1877, after a year and a half in jail and with much of that time spent in solitary confinement, Vera was one of 16 women to appear in the "Trial of the Fifty." Rather than plead for mercy, the defendants sought to explain the ethical basis for their actions and to use the occasion to propagandize their views. As **Barbara Engel** has noted, "by virtue of their 'high moral qualities, and boundless devotion and self-sacrifice', many felt they represented what was best in Russian womanhood." The judges, nevertheless, sentenced Vera Liubatovich to six years' hard labor, which on appeal was reduced to exile in Siberia.

She was sent to Tobolsk Province where in 1880 she married a fellow political prisoner, V.A. Ostashkin. The next year, because of their "harmful influence on the peasantry and insolent disobedience of local authority," they were banished farther east to Krasnoiarsk. Sometime in the 1890s, Vera was freed from exile and al-

lowed to return first to Orel and then to Moscow. She apparently played no further role in the revolutionary movement and died at the age of 52 in 1907.

SOURCES:

Deiateli revoliutsionnogo dvizheniia v Rossii: Bio-bibliograficheskii slovar' (Personalities in the Russian Revolutionary Movement: A Bio-bibliographic Dictionary). Vol. II, pt. 2, 1930, pp. 825–826.

Engel, Barbara Alpern. *Mothers and Daughters: Women of the Intelligentsia in Nineteenth-Century Russia.* Cambridge: Cambridge University Press, 1983.

———, and Clifford N. Rosenthal, eds. and trans. *Five Sisters Against the Tsar.* NY: Alfred A. Knopf, 1975.

Knight, Amy. "The *Fritschi*: A Study of Female Radicals in the Russian Populist Movement," in *Canadian-American Slavic Studies.* Vol. IX, no. 1. Spring 1975, pp. 1–17.

R.C. Elwood,
Professor of History, Carleton University, Ottawa, Canada

Liutgard.

Variant of Luitgard or Luitgarde.

Liutgard (d. 885)

Queen of the East Franks. *Died on January 25, 885; daughter of *Oda (806–913) and Liudolf (c. 806–866), count of Saxony; sister of *Gerberga (d. 896) and *Hathumoda (d. 874); married Louis the Young, king of the East Franks, around 876 or 877; children: Louise (b. around 877); Hildegard (d. after 895).*

Liutgard of Saxony (d. 953)

Duchess of Lorraine. *Name variations: Luitgarde. Born around 927; died on November 18, 953; daughter of *Edgitha (c. 912–946) and Otto I the Great (912–973), king of Germany (r. 936–973), Holy Roman emperor (r. 936–973); sister of Liudolf, duke of Swabia; married Konrad der Rote also known as Conrad the Red (d. 955), duke of Lorraine, in 947; children: Otto, duke of Carinthia.*

Liutgard married Conrad, duke of Lorraine, in 947. In 953, her husband joined with her brother Liudolf in a revolt against Otto I, Liutgard's and Liudolf's father. When Conrad was defeated and stricken of his duchy, he called in Magyars to aid him. Soon, however, he reconciled with his father-in-law Otto and took his side against the Magyars. Conrad was killed in battle at Lechfeld in 955. Liutgard and Conrad were ancestors to the Salian branch of Holy Roman Emperors.

Liutgarde.

Variant of Luitgard or Luitgarde.

Liuzzo, Viola (1925–1965)

American civil-rights activist, gunned down by the KKK, who was the only woman killed while participating in the civil-rights movement. Born Viola Gregg in Tennessee in 1925; murdered in Alabama, on March 25, 1965; married Anthony Liuzzo (a Teamster official); children: Penny Liuzzo; Mary Liuzzo; Thomas Liuzzo; Anthony Liuzzo, Jr.; Sally Liuzzo.

Many would argue that injustice against Viola Liuzzo, a white mother of five who was chased down by a car full of KKK members and murdered, did not end with her death. Following a brief moment of martyrdom, attacks against her character began to cloud the memory of this civil-rights activist who paid for a belief in equality with blood. In his review of **Mary Stanton**'s 1998 biography of Liuzzo, *From Selma to Sorrow*, Steve Watkins writes that the stories about her included accusations that the married Liuzzo was sexually involved with the black man who narrowly escaped being murdered at her side, "that she had abandoned her family, that she had a drug problem, that she had been institutionalized for emotional problems, that her husband had mob connections." In her biography, Stanton theorizes that accusations against Liuzzo were trumped up as a smoke screen to cover up a government conspiracy in the case. Although her hypothesis has yet to be proven, it has been regarded by some as more than plausible. Watkins comments: "Some of the stories came from the Klan, some from the local Alabama police. . . . But many of the stories, which had scant basis in fact, came from the Federal Bureau of Investigation, on orders from the FBI director, J. Edgar Hoover. The reason: an FBI informant had been riding with the Klansmen who murdered Liuzzo; he may even have been the one who shot her."

Among the irrefutable facts are Liuzzo's dedication as a civil-rights worker (she was one of the few whites of her time to join the NAACP); that she drove to Montgomery, Alabama, on the evening of March 24, 1965, and joined the last leg of the second Selma-Montgomery march organized by Martin Luther King, Jr.; and that she was gunned down by Klansmen while driving on March 25 with a black teenager, Leroy Moton, to pick up a group of marchers.

Born in Tennessee in 1925, Liuzzo was married with five children by the age of 36. Returning to school en route to becoming a lab technician, she graduated with top honors. Editor **Sara Bullard** notes that following a few months of work, Liuzzo protested the treatment of female secretaries by quitting her job.

Like the rest of the country, Liuzzo heard the reports of the brutal attack by Alabama state troopers against marchers for black voting rights outside Selma on March 7, 1965. Organized by Martin Luther King with the Southern Christian Leadership Conference (SCLC), the march had been scheduled to proceed down Route 80 from Selma to the Alabama capital of Montgomery. Governor George Wallace, who had banned the march, had the troopers stand shoulder to shoulder across the highway to block the route. The shouted command "troopers advance" sent them charging into the crowd, beating marchers with wooden billy clubs. Additional marchers who attempted to aid those who could not escape were sprayed with tear gas. A sheriff's posse on horseback joined in the attack, using rope, bullwhips, and rubber tubing wrapped with barbed wire. This display of violence on Highway 80, clearly showing peaceful black marchers being assaulted by the police, was captured on network television. Stunned Americans watched images of "Bloody Sunday."

"We have witnessed an eruption of the disease of racism which seeks to destroy all America," wrote King in telegrams to prominent clerics. "No American is without responsibility. The people of Selma will struggle on for the soul of the nation but it is fitting that all Americans help to bear the burden. I call therefore, on the clergy of all faiths, to join me in Selma." The court order which King and the SCLC won directed the state to protect those who would participate in the second scheduled march from Selma to Montgomery, beginning on March 21. The order specified that the march be limited to 300 people and be contained within a two-lane section of Highway 80. The White House was informed by Governor Wallace that Alabama did not have the money to cover the cost of mobilizing the National Guard. This gave President Lyndon B. Johnson the opportunity he needed to protect the march: Johnson authorized the use of 200 FBI agents and U.S. marshals in addition to 2,000 regular army troops, and he federalized 1,900 of Alabama's National Guard.

Liuzzo heeded King's call and traveled from her Michigan home to Selma, a three-day journey by car. In Selma, she spent the week before the march serving at the hospitality desk located in Brown Chapel. With her green Oldsmobile, she shuttled people to and from the Montgomery airport. The march began on March 21. Three days later, on March 24, the procession arrived in Montgomery. In his book *Selma 1965,* Charles E. Fager described the scene as the marchers neared Montgomery: "[T]he road widened, ending the 300 limitation and all through the afternoon cars and buses stopped along the line and discharged new marchers. There were thousands of them, exuberant and noisy, carrying banners and placards. . . . When they arrived at the final campsite, the march was like a tide coming in, inevitable and relentless, inundating everything." In addition to King, *Rosa Parks, John Lewis, Roy Wilkins, and Whitney Young were some of the important civil-rights leaders who attended.

On the evening of March 24, Liuzzo drove to Montgomery, where she assisted in the first-aid station. She said to Father Tim Deasy, with whom she had climbed a tower to watch the march: "Something is going to happen today, I feel it. Somebody is going to get killed," a premonition she also mentioned to others. When King made an attempt to take a petition for full voting rights to Governor Wallace, troopers prevented him from entering the Capitol building. Instead, the petition was received, outside, by Wallace's secretary.

The march's end left thousands in need of transportation out of the city. According to **Kay Houston** of *The Detroit News,* Liuzzo took a load of passengers in her car back to Selma. When her Oldsmobile, conspicuous with its Michigan plates, was bumped several times from behind by a car full of whites, she remarked to Leroy Moton, who'd helped her with the driving, that she thought these local whites "were crazy." After they delivered their group to Brown Chapel in Selma, the two were on their way back to Montgomery to pick up another load of passengers when they stopped at a traffic light. A car carrying four KKK members from the steel town of Bessemer, near Birmingham, pulled up beside them. In the car were Collie Leroy Wilkins, Eugene Thomas, William Orville Eaton, and Gary Thomas Rowe, whose identity as a paid FBI informant was not then known. Upon seeing the white woman and the black teenager together in the car, Wilkins reportedly remarked to Rowe, "I'll be damned. Look there." Driver Eugene Thomas replied, "Let's get them."

The light changed, and the Klan members chased the Oldsmobile at nearly 100 mph despite what Rowe later claimed were his pleas for his companions to call off the pursuit. As they closed in on Liuzzo and Moton, the four Klansmen each armed themselves. They pulled up to the Oldsmobile and, as Liuzzo looked at their car, fired, shooting her twice in the head and speeding away. Rowe would later claim that he had only pretended to fire his gun.

Liuzzo died instantly and fell against the wheel. Moton, bloodied, tried to take control of the car which finally stopped against an embankment. It was then that he discovered that Liuzzo was dead. He saw the Klan car approaching and feigned death while the killers shined a light into the car. When they were gone, Moton ran until he was picked up by a truck carrying marchers. He passed out after telling them what had happened. "Within 24 hours, President Johnson was on television," writes Houston, "personally announcing the arrest of the four assailants and vowing to exterminate the KKK." Said Johnson: "Mrs. Liuzzo went to Alabama to serve the struggle for justice. She was murdered by the enemies of justice who for decades have used the rope and the gun and the tar and the feather to terrorize their neighbors."

Bullard notes that after the murder Liuzzo's family was "besieged with hate mail and phone calls. The Klan circulated ugly lies about [Viola's] character, and these were repeated in FBI reports."

Viola Liuzzo

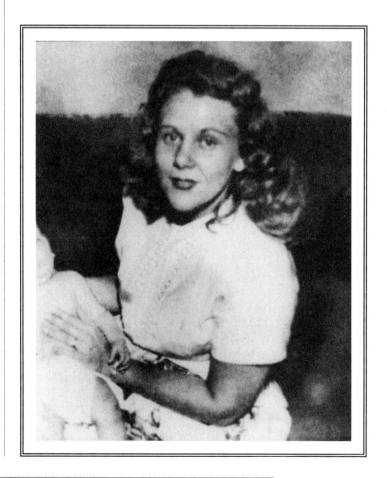

None of the assailants were convicted for murder in the Alabama court: Eugene Thomas was tried for murder (September 1966) and acquitted; Wilkins was tried twice for murder (May and October, 1965) and was twice acquitted; William Eaton died in 1966 of a heart attack; Gary Rowe was tried twice for murder, once resulting in a hung jury, then in an acquittal.

In federal courts, all except Rowe were charged with conspiring to deprive Liuzzo of her civil rights (December 1965). Called a traitor by a lawyer for the KKK, Rowe testified against the others who on December 3 were convicted. Each of the three received the maximum sentence, ten years in prison.

According to political columnist Jack Lessenberry of the *Detroit Metro Times,* it would be years before Liuzzo's children learned that two of the KKK members testified (and took lie-detector tests, with an expert declaring they were being truthful) that Rowe was actually the shooter who had murdered their mother. Lessenberry reports that although he denied those accusations, Rowe said on ABC-TV that he had beaten up other civil-rights demonstrators, bragging, "I was a hell of a man back then." In 1980, a Justice Department investigation admitted to the FBI's knowledge and cover-up of Rowe's involvement in non-deadly attacks on blacks. By his own admittance, in 1961 Rowe participated in the violent attack on Freedom Riders at a Birmingham bus station during which—in an arrangement made with Birmingham police—KKK members were allowed 15 minutes to beat up civil-rights activists with impunity. Also according to Rowe, in 1963 he was responsible for the shooting death of an unidentified black man during a Birmingham riot, a killing about which Rowe claimed he was instructed by federal authorities to remain silent.

Coming on the heels of Bloody Sunday, Liuzzo's death had an intense effect on public opinion, despite the character assassination which followed her murder. Many have regarded her death as the final provocation that resulted in Congress passing the Voting Rights Act of 1965, which gave hundreds of thousands of blacks the right to vote, five months later. "Within a few years," writes Lessenberry, "even George Wallace would be courting black votes."

Liuzzo is the only white woman named on the Civil Rights Memorial located three blocks from the Capitol in Montgomery, but she has been largely forgotten. It could be argued that this has been a result of the rumors, whatever their origins, which ascribed to her a question-able nature as a woman, as a wife, and as a mother. Writes Mary Stanton, "The media took only days to completely transform Viola Liuzzo from a murder victim to an outside agitator and a symbol of reckless female defiance." In a May 1999 interview with Times-Warner Bookmark, author **Octavia Butler** recalled reading letters in a women's magazine, subsequent to Liuzzo's murder, which declared that Liuzzo had no right to deprive her family by engaging in activities which led to her death. Butler recalled the way that the civil-rights worker, rather than her murderers, was condemned, particularly because of what was expected of her as a woman.

In 1966, Gary Rowe entered the federal witness protection program. He lived at least the last two decades of his life in Savannah, Georgia, and died in 1998. Although he used the alias Thomas Neil Moore, he did on occasion disclose his true identity. Writes Bob Sechler of the *Savannah Morning News:* "[D]espite the one-time high-profile, Rowe was buried June 2 with little notice from the Klan or anyone else. He was bankrupt at the time of his May 25 death from a heart attack—with debts totaling about $60,000—and only a handful of FBI agents, estranged family members and some friends, including Liakakis [his friend and employer], attended the funeral." Said Liakakis, who called Rowe by the alias despite his knowledge of his friend's true identity: "Tom was mostly a loner the last couple of years, but he was a really good guy."

In a civil claim filed by the Liuzzo family against the FBI in October 1977, it was charged that FBI employee Rowe had failed to prevent the death of Viola Liuzzo and that he may have taken part in her death. The suit was rejected in May 1983 by a judge who maintained that there was "no evidence the FBI was in any type of joint venture with Rowe or conspiracy against Mrs. Liuzzo. Rowe's presence in the car was the principal reason why the crime was solved so quickly."

To help ensure that Liuzzo's memory will be kept alive, her son Tony and his wife **Sue Liuzzo** established the Viola Gregg Liuzzo Institute for Human Rights/Assuring Human Dignity. Houston reports that after Liuzzo's death her husband Anthony spoke with President Johnson. "I don't think she died in vain because this is going to be a battle, all out as far as I'm concerned. . . . My wife died for a sacred battle, the rights of humanity. She had one concern and only one in mind. She took a quote from Abraham Lincoln that all men are created equal and that's the way she believed."

SOURCES:

Bullard, Sara, ed. *Free At Last—A History Of The Civil Rights Movement And Those Who Died In The Struggle*. Montgomery, 1989.

Fager, Charles E. *Selma, 1965: The March That Changed the South*. Beacon Press, 1985.

Houston, Kay. "The Detroit Housewife Who Moved a Nation toward Racial Justice," in *The Detroit News*. January 19, 1999.

Lessenberry, Jack. "A Liberated Woman Ahead of Her Time," in *Detroit Metro Times*. March 18, 1998.

———. "Lest We Forget," in *Detroit Metro Times*. March 24, 1999.

Publishers Weekly. September 7, 1998.

Sechler, Bob. "Hiding—in the Open," in *Savannah Morning News*. Wednesday, October 7, 1998.

Stanton, Mary. *From Selma to Sorrow: The Life and Death of Viola Liuzzo*. Athens, GA: University of Georgia Press, 1998.

Watkins, Steve. "From Selma to Sorrow: The Life and Death of Viola Liuzzo," in *World*. March–April 1999.

Williams, Monica. "Book Review: Viola Liuzzo Was a Woman Who Was Tragically ahead of Her Time," in *Detroit News*. February 24, 1999.

Livermore, Harriet (1788–1868)

American evangelist. Born on April 14, 1788, in Concord, New Hampshire; died on March 30, 1868, in Philadelphia, Pennsylvania; daughter of Edward St. Loe Livermore (an attorney, judge, and member of Congress) and Mehitable (Harris) Livermore; educated at Byfield Seminary and Atkinson Academy, New Hampshire; never married; no children.

Selected writings: Scriptural Evidence in Favor of Female Testimony in Meetings for the Worship of God *(1824);* A Narration of Religious Experience *(1826);* The Harp of Israel, to Meet the Loud Echo in the Wilds of America *(1835);* A Testimony for the Times *(1843);* Thoughts on Important Subjects *(1864).*

A self-described "Pilgrim Stranger," Harriet Livermore was an itinerant minister who in the mid-19th century traveled alone through Kansas, New England, and along the Eastern Seaboard to deliver her message. In "Snow-Bound," his poem about the people and places of New England, the Quaker poet John Greenleaf Whittier wrote of her as the "not unfeared, half-welcome guest." She wrote several religious tracts, beginning with *Scriptural Evidence in Favor of Female Testimony in Meetings for the Worship of God* in 1824. The book was reminiscent of *Margaret Fell's 1660 text, *Women's Speaking Justified*, and Livermore may have been influenced at the time by Fell's English Quakerism in her own search for religious self-definition.

Born on April 14, 1788, in Concord, New Hampshire, Harriet Livermore was the third of five children of Edward St. Loe Livermore and **Mehitable Harris Livermore**. Mehitable died when Harriet was five, and Edward remarried. A practicing attorney first in Concord, then in Portsmouth, New Hampshire, Edward Livermore served as a justice of the Supreme Court of New Hampshire from 1797 to 1799. Shortly after this, the family moved to Newburyport, Massachusetts. The Livermores were descendants of John Livermore (also known as Leathermore, Lithermore, and Lyuermore), an English potter who had immigrated to Watertown, Massachusetts, in 1635.

Harriet Livermore exhibited signs of a distinct personality from the time she was a very young child, alarming her mother with bursts of temper. Sent to a boarding school in Haverhill, Massachusetts, at the age of eight, Livermore later attended the Byfield Seminary and the Atkinson Academy in New Hampshire. At the age of 20, she spent a winter in Washington, D.C., when her father was elected to Congress. (Her paternal grandfather, Samuel Livermore, had served as U.S. senator from New Hampshire, from 1793 to 1801.) During the short time she spent in Washington, Livermore eagerly entered the social life of the city. A skilled conversationalist, she was also noted for her beauty. She became engaged around 1811 to Moses Elliott of East Haverhill, Massachusetts, who later became an army surgeon. However, Elliott's parents forced the dissolution of the engagement, concerned by Livermore's eccentricity and tempestuous outbursts. Convinced that the broken engagement was God's punishment for what she called her "wild and irregular" disposition, she turned to religion for comfort and empowerment.

Born an Episcopalian, Livermore explored Congregationalism and Quakerism before joining the Baptist church and undergoing adult immersion. She devoted much time to Bible study. In 1824, she experienced a mental breakdown, after which she identified herself as a "solitary eclectic" and a "Pilgrim Stranger." In May 1824, she left her parents' home, writing in her journal, "I took leave of my parents, and brothers, and sisters, with an aching heart, not knowing but our next meeting might be at the bar of a Holy God." Eschewing any further formal ties with a specific religious sect, Livermore embarked on a life of itinerant preaching, writing, and wandering. Using the proceeds from her first book to pay travel expenses, she went throughout New England by stage and by foot, passionately pursuing her ministry and often exhausting her frail constitution. In 1826, she published *A Narration of Religious Experience* and also extended her travels to New York and Philadelphia. In Washington, D.C., Livermore was invited to preach at a Sunday service in the House chamber of the U.S. Congress in January 1827. She returned several times throughout the 1830s.

In 1832, Livermore traveled alone through miles of wild country to Fort Leavenworth, Kansas, seeking Native Americans—whom she thought were the lost tribes of Israel—because her Bible studies had persuaded her that the millennium was at hand. Fort officials did not agree and refused to allow her to proselytize. Undaunted, Livermore turned the experience into *The Harp of Israel, to Meet the Loud Echo in the Wilds of America* (1835), and between 1837 and 1862 undertook ten Atlantic crossings to Jerusalem in anticipation of the second coming of Christ before poverty forced her permanent return to the United States. With a yearly income of $250 in a trust set up by her father, who had died in 1832, Livermore continued her solitary travels throughout the United States. She also published *A Testimony for the Times* in 1843, approaching John Quincy Adams, who had heard her preach before Congress, for contributions to help with expenses. He gave her five dollars out of kindness, writing in his diary that she insisted on spending what little money she had "to print books which nobody will purchase or read." In 1864, ever hopeful of returning to Jerusalem, she published *Thoughts on Important Subjects* to gain funds for travel.

Three years later, Livermore was committed to the Blockley Almshouse in Philadelphia by Thomas Haven, who was most likely her nephew. Impoverished and thought to be mad, Harriet Livermore died at the almshouse on March 30, 1868. She was saved from a pauper's burial by one of her few friends, **Margaret W. Worrel**, who donated her own burial plot in the Germantown Baptist Burial Ground in Germantown, Pennsylvania.

SOURCES:

Edgerly, Lois Stiles. *Give Her This Day*. Gardiner, ME: Tilbury House, 1990.

James, Edward T., ed. *Notable American Women 1607–1950*. Cambridge, MA: The Belknap Press of Harvard University Press, 1971.

Lolly Ockerstrom,
freelance writer, Washington, D.C.

Livermore, Mary A. (1820–1905)

Popular American reformer best known for her volunteer work during the Civil War and for her lectures and writing on behalf of women's social, political and educational rights throughout the late 19th century. Name variations: Mrs. D.P. Livermore. Born Mary Ashton Rice on December 19, 1820, in Boston, Massachusetts; died on May 23, 1905, in Melrose, Massachusetts; daughter of Timothy Rice (a laborer) and Zebiah Vose Glover (Ashton) Rice (a sea captain's daughter); attended Miss Martha Whiting's Female Seminary, Charlestown, Massachusetts (1836–38); married Daniel Parker Livermore, on May 6, 1845; children: Mary Livermore (1848–1852); Henrietta White Livermore (b. 1851); Marcia Elizabeth Livermore (b. 1854).

Was associate editor, New Covenant (1858–69); with Jane Hoge, directed Chicago Sanitary Commission (1862–65); convened first woman suffrage convention in Illinois (1868); was editor, Woman's Journal (1870–72); served as president, American Woman Suffrage Association (1875–78); was a professional lecturer (1870–95).

Publications: New Covenant (1858–1869); Pen Pictures (1863); Agitator (1869); Woman's Journal (1870–72); My Story of the War (1887); The Story of My Life (1897).

Mary A. Livermore, like many Anglo-American middle-class homemakers in both the North and the South, expanded her voluntary charitable and benevolent work during the Civil War in the United States (1861–65). In the process, she discovered that she had exceptional organizational capabilities, that she could endure the hardships and hazards of unprecedented geographic mobility, and that she could very effectively influence others through public speaking. Mary Livermore is, therefore, representative of the large numbers of married women who came away from their experiences in the war with new self-confidence and a determination to increase their participation in the public educational, social and political life of American society. She is particularly noteworthy for her popularity and for her persistence in campaigning for a broad range of reforms to equalize opportunities for women.

Mary, named for a maternal aunt, was born Mary Ashton Rice in 1820 on Salem Street in the North End of Boston, several doors from Old North Church. Her sister, **Rachel Rice**, was born three years later, and another sister, **Abbie Rice**, was born when Mary was seven or eight years old. Two brothers and a sister had died before Mary was born, making the three sisters the only children born to the Rices to survive infancy.

A serious child, Mary seems always to have been a voracious reader. Even before she began attending dame's school, she learned to read.

Sometimes, however, reading led her into trouble. On her eighth birthday, she received her first book, *Robinson Crusoe,* from her Aunt Mary; although reading was not allowed on Sunday, she could not resist devouring it immediately, and consequently the book was burned by her parents before the end of the day. While she was in grammar school at the Hancock School in Boston, her unusually mature ideas and writing style caused her English teacher to accuse her of plagiarism.

At age 14½, two years earlier than expected, she was awarded a Benjamin Franklin medal, a sign that she had successfully completed the highest level of public education offered for girls. During a four-month apprenticeship in dressmaking, she gained the satisfaction of acquiring a practical skill, but she was elated when her parents arranged for her to continue her formal education at Miss Whiting's Seminary, a Baptist school at Charlestown (1836–38). Following her first term, she became a teaching assistant, a position which not only assured that she would be able to pay her tuition at the school but also allowed her, much to her pride, to achieve her longstanding desire for economic independence from her parents. An eager student, she completed the four-year course of study in only two years and was offered a position to stay on as an instructor in French, Latin, and later Italian.

While Mary was at the seminary in Charlestown, her sister Rachel died. In her autobiography, *The Story of My Life* (1897), Mary described this crisis as a "pivotal point" in her life. It caused her to reject the severe exclusionary doctrines of Calvinism which she had been taught by her father's Baptist church and to look for a theology that better suited her belief in a loving and compassionate God. Her sister's death also encouraged her to leave her family and the familiar surroundings of New England in an effort to move on from the tragedy to a more hopeful future. After Mary left home, her parents adopted an orphaned two-year-old, Annie.

Mary then lived as a governess with the Henderson family on their Virginia plantation for three years (1839–42). Her lively account of this time is rich with fresh, balanced observation, humor and unconventional attitudes on both the education of her young charges and on life among whites and blacks involved in the system of slavery. "I learned while in Virginia, that ethical greatness and a high order of character are to be found among people of all sects, and of no sect, and thenceforth placed character higher than creed," she wrote in her autobiography.

Mary's religious tolerance, however, never prevented her from taking firm positions on issues of moral and social justice. When she returned to the North to become head of an academy (private high school) in Duxbury, Massachusetts (1842–45), she saw herself as "a pronounced abolitionist" who "attended every accessible anti-slavery meeting." In Duxbury, she also became active in organizing activities and writing pamphlets to recruit children for the "Cold Water Army" branch of the Washingtonian Total Abstinence Reform Society, founded in Baltimore in 1840.

In Duxbury, Mary not only adopted two lifelong social reform interests—the civil rights of disenfranchised groups and temperance—but also attended Christmas services for the first time in her life (1844). She fell in love both with the message of Universalism which she heard that night and with the "mild-mannered and refined" pastor, the Reverend Daniel Parker Livermore. They were married on May 7, 1845, and Mary Ashton Rice Livermore entered into the life of a housewife in small-town New England with the same determination which invigorated all the other causes she adopted during her lifetime. With the help of her sister Abbie who came to

Mary Livermore

live with them in Fall River, Massachusetts, for several months, she developed her abilities as a cook, "domestic business" manager, decorator, and hostess. She sometimes rebelled against the standard expectations and living conditions for a pastor and his family, but she managed to retain her integrity and, above all, her sense of humor.

> For nearly forty years I have been convinced that if the world is to be helped onward in its progress, or assisted towards a nobler civilization, it can only be accomplished by as complete a freedom and development of women, as is accorded to men.
>
> —Mary Livermore

Despite the demands of a growing family—Mary Eliza (1848–1853), Henrietta White (b. 1852), and Marcia Elizabeth (b. 1854)—she managed to write hymns, stories, poems, essays and sketches which were published both in local newspapers and in periodicals, including the popular *Putnam's Magazine* and *Ladies' Repository*. Favorite topics included abolitionism and temperance. She also edited *Lily of the Valley* for a few years. At first, the extra $200–300 her literary work brought into the family supplemented the modest salary of a cleric, but, as the family's circumstances changed, Livermore's economic contribution became more crucial.

While Mary and her husband were united in their views on abolitionism and temperance, not all members of the congregations they served agreed with them. In Stafford, Connecticut, where Daniel successfully campaigned for the passage of legislation to prohibit the sale of liquor in 1852, he was forced to resign his pastorate. At the time, the couple had two children. For the next six years, he was pastor of churches in Weymouth, where their daughter Mary Eliza died, and Malden, Massachusetts; but the couple felt uncomfortable expressing their anti-slavery views as the issue became more and more controversial and divided congregations and denominations. Daniel was considering withdrawing from the ministry when the opportunity came to join a 15-member group of abolitionists intent on establishing a farming community and helping to make Kansas a slave-free state. In 1857, the family started out for the frontier with the group, though not without misgivings; in the end, they settled in Chicago, where Mary could provide better care for Marcia Elizabeth who had become seriously ill.

In Chicago, Daniel purchased and took over as editor of *The New Covenant*, a Universalist monthly paper. In the struggle for financial sol-vency, Mary became manager and associate editor. Because her husband was frequently away for long periods of time, her duties expanded until she was entirely in charge of business and was writing for all departments except theology. Her work as a reporter took her to the Republican Convention in Chicago when Abraham Lincoln was nominated in 1860; she was the only woman among the more than 100 journalists there. A volume of the stories she wrote for the Universalist monthly, *Pen Pictures*, was published in 1863. Mary unabashedly used the paper to promote her favorite causes, such as the work of the Chicago Sanitary Commission which became her passion during the Civil War. The Livermores operated the paper from 1858 until 1869.

Mary Livermore was now in her 30s. By her own account, she was "endowed with an almost phenomenal capacity for work, and could work without friction" with those associated with her. Livermore's energies were consumed not only by running her household and *The New Covenant* but also by teaching a Sunday school class of 16 young men at the Second Universalist Church, where her husband was pastor, and by working on behalf of three newly established institutions for women and children: the Home for Aged Women (founded in 1861), the Hospital for Women and Children, and the Chicago Home for the Friendless, a refuge for destitute women and children founded in 1858.

It was through their work together on the board of the Chicago Home for the Friendless that she and *Jane Hoge, one of its founders and its president, originally became acquainted. When the Civil War broke out in 1861, the two women, eager to help the Union cause, began working for the Chicago (later Northwestern) Sanitary Commission, an organization of volunteers who supported the work of the government's medical bureau on the Western front. In December 1862, they were appointed co-directors of the commission and served in that capacity until October 1865. The two women were known for their creative, energetic and warmly personal administration of a monumental series of tasks which included writing letters for soldiers, recruiting nurses, organizing collection and distribution of hospital supplies and food to the field, visiting the front and hospitals to investigate needs, writing reports, founding 3,000 local aid societies (in Iowa, Wisconsin, Illinois, Michigan and Indiana), and raising thousands of dollars to support the work of the commission. In October 1863, their Sanitary Fair, which by Livermore's account raised $100,000, became the model for fairs in other cities. These activities and those of other women involved in the war effort appear in detailed form in Livermore's best-selling book, *My Story of the War* (1887).

After the war, Livermore turned her energies to the newly revived woman suffrage movement. Always concerned about attaining a broad range of equal opportunities for women, she had now come to view enfranchisement as the central issue. "Under a republican form of government," she wrote in her autobiography, "the possession of the ballot by woman can alone make her the legal equal of man, and without this legal equality, she is robbed of her natural rights." With characteristic resolution, she began lecturing in public on the subject, called a Woman Suffrage Convention (the first in Illinois) in Chicago in 1868, helped organize the resultant Illinois Woman Suffrage Association (and was elected its first president), and started a woman suffrage paper, *The Agitator,* in 1869. Her paper merged with the national *Woman's Journal* in 1870 when *Lucy Stone called her to Boston to become its first editor-in-chief, a position Livermore held until 1872. The family moved from Chicago to Melrose, Massachusetts, where they lived for the rest of their lives.

At the same time, encouraged by James Redpath of the Boston Lyceum Bureau, who served as agent in arranging the engagements, Livermore launched what was to become a very successful, 25-year career as a public lecturer. According to Livermore, Redpath, who was very influential in the whole lyceum movement for adult education, advised her that if she wanted to be popular and make money she would have to "ignore the two vexed questions, Woman Suffrage and Temperance." Instead, she chose to use these two topics as the centerpiece for nearly all her talks, and she never lacked for engagements. Her first lecture, and one of her most popular, was delivered over 800 times and became the title for a collection of her speeches, *What Shall We Do With Our Daughters?*, published in 1883. Her second lecture, "Superfluous Women," was "a plea that women should receive so complete a training, that, married or unmarried, they would have firmness and fibre, and be able to stand on their own feet, self-supporting, happy in themselves, and helpful to the world." Her speeches were full of the same truthful observation, color and humor which gave her writing style such flair. Her stature, voice and ability to speak extemporaneously without notes contributed to her effectiveness as a speaker.

Although Livermore gave up the formal lecture circuit in 1895, when she was 75, she continued to speak occasionally on behalf of her two lifelong causes, temperance and suffrage. From 1875 to 1885, she had served as president of the Massachusetts Women's Christian Temperance Union; in her autobiography, she says that while she held that position her "faith and patience were taxed to the utmost." By now, she also had new charities and institutions which demanded her attention, particularly the Boston Women's Educational and Industrial Union which she helped to found and of which she was a life member. The Union ran a Protective Bureau to help guard women's wages, a Women's Exchange where women could sell their products if they had no other market, a lunchroom for women of limited means, and an Employment Bureau for women skilled to do more than domestic work. In 1896, when Tufts College graduated its first class of women, Mary Livermore was awarded an honorary LL.D. degree.

In 1895, the Livermores celebrated their 50th wedding anniversary surrounded by their daughter Henrietta, granddaughters **Marion K. Livermore** and **Mary Livermore Norris**, and by Mary's sisters Abbie and **Annie Rice**. Four years later, Daniel Parker Livermore died. Mary Ashton Livermore lived until May 23, 1905.

SOURCES:

Brockett, L.P. *Woman's Work in the Civil War.* Philadelphia, PA: Ziegler, McCurdy, 1867.

Hoge, Mrs. A.H. [Jane Currie]. *The Boys in Blue.* NY: E.B. Treat, 1867.

Livermore, Mary A. *My Story of the War.* Hartford, CT: A.D. Worthington, 1889.

———. *The Story of My Life.* Hartford, CT: A.D. Worthington, 1897.

———. *What Shall We Do With Our Daughters?* Boston, MA: Lee and Shepard, 1883.

Riegel, Robert E. *Notable American Women, 1607–1950.* Edited by Edward T. James. Cambridge, MA: Belknap Press of Harvard University Press, 1971, pp. 410–413.

SUGGESTED READING:

Massey, Mary Elizabeth. *Bonnet Brigades.* NY: Alfred A. Knopf, 1966.

McCarthy, Kathleen D. *Noblesse Oblige: Charity & Cultural Philanthropy in Chicago, 1849–1929.* Chicago, IL: The University of Chicago Press, 1982.

COLLECTIONS:

Correspondence in Kate Field Collection, Boston Public Library; Sophia Smith Collection, Smith College; Women's Rights Collection, Schlesinger Library, Radcliffe College; Isabella Beecher Hooker Papers in Stowe-Day Library, Hartford, Connecticut; National American Woman Suffrage Association Records and Mary Ann (Ball) Bickerdyke Papers, Library of Congress, Manuscript Division.

Manuscripts in Mary A. Livermore Collection, Princeton University Library.

Margaret Dorsey Phelps,
Adjunct Assistant Professor, University of Iowa, Iowa City, Iowa

Livia (fl. 100 BCE)

Roman noblewoman. Flourished around 100 BCE; daughter of M. Livius Drusus (a consul in 112 BCE); sister M. Livius Drusus; married Q. Servilius Caepio (divorced); married M. Portius Cato; children: (first marriage) a son, Q. Servilius Caepio; *Servilia (who married L. Licinius Lucullus); *Servilia (who married M. Junius Brutus the Elder); (second marriage) Cato the Younger (whose daughter *Portia [c. 70–43 BCE] married M. Junius Brutus, one of the assassins of Julius Caesar); daughter, *Portia (fl. 80 BCE).

Livia (58 BCE–29 CE).

See Livia Drusilla.

Livia Drusilla (58 BCE–29 CE)

First empress of the Roman Empire, who was considered a model of womanly decorum and influence. Name variations: usually referred to simply as Livia; after Augustus died, Julia Augusta. Pronunciation: Liv-ee-ah. Born on January 30, 58 BCE; died in 29 CE; daughter of Marcus Livius Drusus Claudianus (a senator) and Alfidia; married Tiberius Claudius Nero, 43 or 44 BCE and divorced 39 BCE; married Octavian (future emperor Augustus), January 17, 38 BCE; children: (first marriage) Tiberius (42 BCE–37 CE), emperor of Rome; Drusus.

Granted tribunician protections and freed from legal guardianship (35 BCE); granted the rights of a mother of three children (9 BCE); adopted into the Julian family and renamed Julia Augusta at the death of Augustus; revered in conjunction with her son the new Emperor Tiberius; appointed priestess to the cult of Augustus (14 CE); deified by the emperor Claudius (42 CE).

Livia Drusilla enters the historical narrative only because of her marriage to Octavian (Augustus), first emperor of Rome, who reshaped all Roman political structures. But because of her honored position as his consort and her creative use of the attendant privileges, she became a revered model of correct feminine behavior in her own time and for centuries after her death.

Livia was a member of the Claudian clan which could trace its ancestry back to the beginnings of Rome. These family connections would enhance Octavian's prestige, since he could not personally claim such strong traditional roots, but there was clearly more to the marriage decision than political considerations. Velleius Paterculus, an ancient historian, tags Livia as "the most eminent of Roman women in birth, in sin-cerity, and in beauty." Ovid, the flattering love poet of Rome, claimed that she combined the beauty of Venus with the character of Juno—evidently an irresistible combination. Octavian fell in love with Livia, "the one woman whom he truly loved until his death," Suetonius, an ancient biographer, informs us.

It is surprising that Livia and Octavian ever met, and even more so that they married. Livia's first indirect contact with him was through her father, M. Livius Drusus Claudianus, a Roman senator who supported the losing side in the civil war and committed suicide rather than surrender to Octavian and Mark Antony. When these two commanders developed an open rivalry, Livia's husband Tiberius Claudius Nero chose loyalty to Mark Antony. As a result, he had to flee from Italy with Livia and their young child Tiberius. Not until a new accord was struck between Octavian and Mark Antony was the family able to return in safety. Cassius Dio, a historian writing in the third century CE, says: "This was one of the strangest whims of fate; for this Livia, who then fled from Caesar, later on was married to him, and this Tiberius, who then took flight with his parents, succeeded Caesar in the office of emperor."

When Livia met Octavian, he was one of the most powerful figures in Rome, still in contest for ultimate supremacy, and married. He divorced his wife *Scribonia on the day his child *Julia was born in 39 BCE, because, as he stated, "I could not bear the way she nagged at me"—and most likely because he had set his sights on Livia. Livia was not only married at the time but also pregnant with her second child. Octavian asked the Pontifical College whether he could marry her, given the circumstances. The college, perhaps prompted by the military power at Octavian's disposal, replied that if the conception was certain, marriage was permissible after a divorce. Tiberius Claudius Nero meekly gave Livia away at the wedding.

These unusual circumstances led to rumors. One popular epigram speculated: "How fortunate those parents are for whom their child is only three months in the womb!"—implying that Drusus, the child in question, was actually the son of Octavian. Octavian wrote in his diary, however, "Caesar returned to its father Nero the child borne by Livia, his wife." Given the fact that throughout their years of marriage Livia remained childless (apart from one premature birth), and that Octavian never formally acknowledged Drusus as his own, it is improbable that Drusus was his son. Nevertheless, both Livia's boys joined the household of Octavian at their own father's death in 33 BCE.

In 35 BCE, Octavian succeeded in passing a unique law granting Livia and *Octavia, his sister and the wife of Mark Antony, "the right of administering their own affairs without a guardian, and the same security and inviolability as the tribunes enjoyed." The "security and inviolability of the tribunes" was an honor designed to give Octavian a legal basis from which to declare war on Mark Antony should he offend Octavia in any way. But this honor was unprecedented and came uncomfortably close to associating women with high public office. The very idea of a woman in public office was anathema to Romans and, indeed, this honor was never again bestowed on any other woman.

Livia may have been particularly pleased with the freedom to manage her own affairs, however, for she owned many properties. Among others, she owned a house on the Palatine Hill in Rome, the "House of Livia," which is still open to visitors. The size of her involvements may be judged by the great burial monument on the Appian Way which Livia established for her extended household, with space for about 1,100 people. Most of those buried were slaves and freedmen attached to her family who were involved in the extensive administration of her various households.

Octavian overcame Mark Antony in 31 BCE and achieved sole rulership of the Roman Empire, later taking the inspired name Augustus, which implied divinely sanctioned authority. As he began to deemphasize raw force and to cultivate more subtlety in rule, Livia moved into the role of ideal wife and mother for the Roman Empire. She had to define this new role, and she seemed always to sense what was appropriate. Her exemplary behavior was legendary, as witnessed by the numerous statements which come down to us 2,000 years later: "Chastity stood beside her marriage bed"; "she guarded her good name jealously"; "her private life was of traditional purity." Her closest friends were women and there was never any suspicion of sexual wrongdoing on her part. She wove the material for the clothes that Augustus wore—a sure sign of chastity and virtue in the ancient mind. She managed her extensive households thriftily and effectively. In one telling incident, Augustus announced to the other senators that "you yourselves should guide and command your wives as you see fit—that is what I do with mine."

Livia is famous for her kindness to various people. For instance, in addition to generously helping to raise friends' children, she also contributed to dowries for them. In one incident,

when some naked men met her on the road and consequently were in danger of being put to death, she saved their lives by averring, according to Dio, that, "to chaste women such men are no whit different from statues." In later years, although she had previously been at odds with Augustus' granddaughter *Julia (c. 18 BCE–28 CE), who had been in a long exile, Livia showed mercy to her.

Livia was granted many honors throughout the reign of Augustus. Cities were named for her in Pontus and Judea. Inscriptions later discovered in outlying areas of the empire associated her with divinity. She was voted the privilege of sitting with the Vestal Virgins in a superior spot at the theater. When her younger son Drusus died in 9 BCE, statues were erected in her honor, and she was voted the legal privileges of a woman who had borne three children. With her many financial resources, Livia restored temples and shrines, particularly those associated with goddesses and women, including the temples of Fortuna Muliebris, Bona Dea Subsaxana, and Concordia. She was also involved in the construction of a provision market called the Macellum Liviae in Rome. All these honors and activities placed her in the public eye and went beyond the traditional norms of behavior associated with women.

Since power was now concentrated in the hands of one man, those who had personal access to him were in a position of unparalleled influence. Many stories confirm this. In one famous incident soon after their marriage, as Livia traveled to her house at Prima Porta, an eagle flew by and dropped a white pullet with a berried laurel branch in its beak. Interpreting this event as an omen, Livia kept the bird for breeding and planted the twig. The hen was so prolific that the house was nicknamed "The Poultry"; the twig took root and grew so luxuriantly that Caesars always plucked laurels from it to wear as they celebrated their triumphs. While we may suppose that Livia interpreted the omen positively, others believed that "Livia was destined to hold in her lap even Caesar's power and to dominate him in everything," as Cassius Dio records.

A dominating mother and an accommodating wife, [Livia] was a match for both her devious husband and her insincere son.

—Tacitus

According to Cassius Dio, when Livia was asked later in life "how she had obtained such a commanding influence over Augustus, she answered that it was by being scrupulously chaste herself, doing gladly whatever pleased him, not meddling with any of his affairs, and, in particular, by pretending neither to hear of nor to notice the favourites that were the objects of his passion." (Incidentally, Livia is said to have procured young virgins for Augustus to deflower—a charge which may be slander intended to undermine her moral reputation, or a truth that was meant to be hidden from public view.)

Livia's influence certainly went beyond public paradigmatic living. The ancient sources agree that she was Augustus' best confidant and counselor. According to Suetonius, who had access to imperial records, Augustus would jot down lists of items to be discussed with Livia, and then take careful notes of her replies to be consulted again later. In one famous example, Augustus met with Livia to discuss what should be done with Cinna, a grandson of the great Pompey, who had been involved in a conspiracy. Livia's advice was to pardon the fellow, suggesting that Augustus "follow the practice of physicians, who when the usual remedies do not work try just the opposite." After listening to her advice, Augustus canceled a meeting of counselors previously called to discuss the matter and later even appointed Cinna consul, a very great honor.

In Augustus' efforts to rejuvenate traditional morality, he held up his family as an embodiment of the ideal. Often Augustus would make public appearances at games with Livia and the children in his family. The famous Altar of Augustan Peace in Rome was dedicated on Livia's birthday and had carefully organized bas-relief sculptures glorifying his family and dynastic fecundity in general. In gratefulness for the new stability in the empire, the Roman people granted Augustus the title Pater Patriae (Father of the Country). Livia was correspondingly referred to as Mater Patriae (Mother of the Country), although her title was not official.

Livia was very much involved in influencing Augustus' dynastic plans, even though their own marriage remained childless. Originally Octavia's son Marcellus, husband of Augustus' daughter Julia, seemed to be the favored designate, with Livia's son Tiberius as a back-up candidate. Unfortunately for Octavia's hopes, Marcellus died young. It is said that Octavia hated Livia from then on, because Tiberius seemed to be the probable successor.

However, Livia's position as mother of the next emperor was far from secure. Augustus, we are told, did not care for Tiberius, viewing him as dutiful but dour and lacking in inspiration. Tiberius therefore remained only a marginal possibility, because Augustus next turned to Julia's new husband, his trusted commander Agrippa. When Agrippa died, however, Tiberius was forced to divorce his wife *Vipsania Agrippina*, whom he loved very much, and to marry Julia. By now Julia's moral laxity was proverbial, and Tiberius deeply resented the marriage, although it placed him closer to the succession. He was appointed general and, according to Roman lights, did a creditable job of increasing stability along the Balkan borders of the Roman empire. Livia is generally credited with influencing this sequence of events.

When in 7 BCE Tiberius celebrated a triumph for military achievements, he included his mother by dedicating a colonnade for her in an area near Naples which was named the "Precinct of Livia." He gave a banquet for the senate, and Livia gave a corresponding banquet for the prominent women of Rome. Augustus followed by granting Tiberius further authority, and we may assume that Livia felt Tiberius was not only next in line, but that also she would share in his future honors.

Again Livia's hopes were interrupted. Tiberius profoundly dismayed Livia by taking an action that nearly cut him off from everything she had worked for. He left his responsibilities in Rome and withdrew to the island of Rhodes, later saying he did it to step aside for Augustus' grandsons who would be more probable successors. His withdrawal was in stubborn opposition to his mother's wishes, and Augustus only reluctantly permitted it. When a few years later all his official powers lapsed, Tiberius asked permission to return to Rome. Augustus flatly refused, angry because Tiberius had disrespectfully abandoned him while needed. Livia, however, begged that Tiberius be at least granted the title of legate, a favor she succeeded in procuring. When a few years later Tiberius again asked Livia to intercede, he was allowed at last to return.

Because all the other hopeful candidates had died, in 4 CE the aging Augustus adopted Tiberius, facing the fact that Tiberius, least preferred of all possibilities, would likely be the next emperor of Rome. Augustus announced, "I do this for reasons of state," a statement which gave legal force to Tiberius' position. Final confirmation was added in 13 CE, when Augustus reinstated Tiberius' tribunician power and gave him equal military authority with himself over all the provinces and armies.

In August of 14 CE, Augustus lay dying. His famous last words were, "Goodbye, Livia: Never forget our marriage!" Always pragmatic, Livia took matters in hand, sending a letter recalling Tiberius from his armies in Illyricum (some versions of the story present Tiberius as having already returned); she then restricted access to the surrounding areas and continued to publish news about Augustus' state of health. In Tacitus' words, "Then two pieces of news became known simultaneously. Augustus was dead, and Tiberius was in control." Livia's long patience and determination had finally paid off.

For Livia, Augustus' death was a major turning point. He had bequeathed one third of his considerable property to her, a fortune so great that a legal exception had to be made to allow her to inherit it. Livia paid a considerable sum of money to the senator who had sworn to have seen Augustus' spirit ascending into the heavens, for, as a result, not only was Augustus deified by the senate, but Livia was also appointed priestess for the new cult to the Deified Augustus. In conjunction with this honor, she was granted a ceremonial *lictor,* an ancient symbol of authority, to precede her in public.

In Augustus' will, he adopted Livia into the Julian family and gave her the name Julia Augusta. The name "Julia" allowed her technically to claim she was the daughter of a god, but the title "Augusta" was enigmatic. Did her new name imply that Livia should be co-ruler with her son Tiberius, who was given the title "Augustus" in the same will? Cassius Dio says that for a time Livia's position was so prominent that letters to the emperor bore both her name

and that of Tiberius. Dio says, "She occupied a very exalted station, far above all women of former days, so that she could at any time receive the senate and such of the people as wished to greet her in her house; and this fact was entered in the public records."

In the first years of his rule, Tiberius actually sought Livia's advice on occasion in private. But the power struggle that they were to be involved in for the remainder of Livia's life was already apparent. Tiberius promptly blocked many honors which the senate tried to offer her: proposals to set up an Altar of Adoption in her honor; to name the month of October for her; and to formally bestow the title of Mater Patriae. He was deeply offended when the senate added "Son of Livia" to his own honorific titles. On one occasion, when there was a fire near the temple of Vesta and Livia "was directing the populace and soldiers in person, as though Augustus were still alive, and urging them to redouble their efforts," Tiberius warned her to stick to affairs becoming to a woman and to stop interfering with matters of state. Tacitus says that Tiberius "regarded this elevation of a woman as derogatory to his own person."

Eventually Tiberius ordered Livia to remove herself from all public affairs and stick to managing her own household. Effectively blocked from official avenues, Livia went after de facto power, attempting to force her points through lawsuits. In one case, a lawsuit was brought against her friend Urgulania who refused a summons to court because, according to Tacitus, her "friendship with the Augusta had placed her above the law." When the prosecutor tried to physically drag **Urgulania** from Livia's house, to which she had fled for protection, Livia used the language usually reserved for treason trials: she felt "violated and diminished." In the end, Tiberius was cajoled into agreeing to appear in court as Urgulania's counsel, which in effect determined the outcome. After Livia had won this battle with Tiberius, she simply paid the money for her friend, which resolved the dispute.

The next year Livia fell ill. Tiberius did return from Campania to be near her, and the senate proclaimed games in her honor. It was probably for this occasion that a coin was issued in her honor to the *salus augusta,* or health of Augusta, in 22 CE. Tiberius tempered the permission for these honors with a notice that prayers for her recovery should not go beyond the norm.

After Livia recovered, she attempted to force Tiberius into appointing a certain citizen to be a juror. Tiberius agreed on condition that the man's name be marked "forced on the emperor by his mother." In anger, Livia exhibited some letters by Augustus which complained of Tiberius' "sour and stubborn character." Soon after this, Tiberius left Rome, ending up on Capri in self-imposed exile. According to Tacitus, "he was driven away by his mother's bullying: to share control with her seemed intolerable, to dislodge her impracticable—since that control had been given him by her." When she fell ill again, he did not visit her.

Livia died in 29 CE. The funeral was postponed until Tiberius sent a letter from Capri saying that because of important business he was unable to attend. So Livia was given a belated and modest funeral at which Caligula, her grandson, delivered the eulogy, and she was buried in Augustus' mausoleum in Rome. Women were ordered to mourn for a year, and the senate proposed and voted for her deification, an honor which Tiberius refused on her behalf. The senate also voted an arch in her honor—a distinction conferred on no other woman—but since Tiberius was designated to pay for it, it was never built. Indeed, Tiberius ignored Livia's will, and it was not until Caligula was emperor that her will was honored. When Claudius, a grandson whom she had treated with scorn as a young boy, became emperor, she was declared a goddess of the state, sharing the honors with Divine Augustus. Claudius set up a statue to her in the temple of Augustus and ordered the Vestal Virgins to offer the proper sacrifices, commanding women to use her name in oaths as well. He also issued coins depicting Livia and Augustus on almost equal terms.

Livia's reputation remains basically positive, although there are also attempts from antiquity to invert the interpretation as well. Tacitus calls her "a real catastrophe to the nation as a mother, and to the house of the Caesars as a stepmother." He suggests, for instance (as do certain others), that Livia poisoned a number of potential candidates for emperorship. The very number of accusations (Marcellus, Lucius, Gaius, Agrippa Postumus, Germanicus, and Augustus himself) and the ambiguity associated with each instance make the theories suspect.

Several summations of her life come down to us. Velleius Paterculus calls her "a woman preeminent among women, and who in all things resembled the gods more than mankind, whose power no one felt except for the alleviation of trouble or the promotion of rank." And even Tacitus comments at last: "Her private life was of traditional strictness. But her gracious-

ness exceeded old-fashioned standards. She was a compliant wife, but an overbearing mother. Neither her husbands' diplomacy nor her son's insincerity could outmanoeuvre her."

Indeed, Tacitus divides Tiberius' rule by her death. "Now began a time of sheer crushing tyranny. While the Augusta lived there was still a moderating influence, for Tiberius had retained a deep-rooted deference for his mother. Now, however, the reins were thrown off." But that's another story.

SOURCES:

Balsdon, J.P.V.D. *Roman Women: Their History and Habits.* NY: John Day, 1962.

Bauman, Richard A. *Women and Politics in Ancient Rome.* NY: Routledge, 1992.

Dixon, Suzanne. *The Roman Mother.* Norman: University of Oklahoma Press, 1988.

Purcell, Nicholas. "Livia and the Womanhood of Rome," in *Proceedings of the Cambridge Philological Society.* Vol. 32, 1986, pp. 78–105.

Richardson, Geoffrey Walter and Theodore John Cadoux. "Livia Drusilla," in *Oxford Classical Dictionary.*

Rutland, Linda W. "Women as Makers of Kings in Tacitus' *Annals*," in *Classical World.* Vol. 72, 1978–79, pp. 15–29.

Treggiari, Susan. "Domestic Staff at Rome in the Julio-Claudian Period, 27 BC. to AD. 68," in *Histoire Sociale*, pp. 241–255.

———. "Jobs in the Household of Livia," in *Papers of the British School at Rome.* Vol. 43, 1975, pp. 48–77.

ANCIENT SOURCES:

Cassius Dio. *Roman History.* Translated by Earnest Cary. Vols V, VI. Loeb Classical Library. Cambridge, MA: Harvard University Press, 1917.

Suetonius. "Life of Augustus"; "Life of Tiberius"; "Life of Claudius," in *The Twelve Caesars.* Translated by Robert Graves, 1957. Revised by Michael Grant, 1979. NY: Viking Penguin, 1986.

Tacitus. *Annals of Imperial Rome.* Translated by Michael Grant. NY: Viking Penguin, 1987.

Velleius Paterculus. *Compendium of Roman History.* Translated by Frederick W. Shipley, 1924. Cambridge, MA: Harvard University Press, 1961.

Sylvia Gray Kaplan,
Adjunct Faculty, Humanities,
Marylhurst College, Marylhurst, Oregon

Livia Orestilla (fl. 32 CE)

*Roman noblewoman. Flourished around 32 CE; second wife of Caligula (12–41), Roman emperor (divorced). Caligula's first wife was *Junia Claudilla; his third was *Lollia Paulina; his fourth was *Milonia Caesonia.*

Livilla (c. 14/11 BCE–c. 31 CE)

Roman noblewoman. Name variations: Livia Julia. Born between 14 and 11 BCE; died around 31 CE; daughter of Antonia Minor (36 BCE–37 CE) and Drusus the Elder (also known as Nero Drusus, brother of the future emperor Tiberius); sister of Germanicus and Claudius (10 BCE–54 CE, future emperor); married Drusus the Younger (Drusus Julius Caesar, who died in 23 BCE); children: possibly a daughter Julia.

Livilla, daughter of *Antonia Minor and Drusus the Elder, was caught up in the conspiracy to overthrow Tiberius by her lover Sejanus, captain of the Praetorian Guard, who promised marriage. It was rumored that Livilla poisoned her husband Drusus the Younger, the adopted son of Tiberius, in 23 CE. Even though Tiberius spared Livilla "out of regard" for her mother Antonia, Antonia executed Livilla by starving her to death. Livilla had brought shame on the imperial family, reports Greco-Roman historian Cassius Dio, since Sejanus was not even of senatorial rank.

Livilla (c. 16 CE–after 38 CE).

See Julia Livilla.

Livingstone, Mary Moffatt
(1820–1862)

Daughter of missionaries and wife of missionary and explorer David Livingstone. Born on April 12, 1820, in Griqua Town, South Africa; died in 1862 on Zambesi delta, Africa; daughter of English missionaries Robert Moffat and Mary Smith Moffat (1795–1870); married David Livingstone (the explorer), in January 1845, in Kuruman, Cape Province, South Africa; children: six, one of whom died in infancy.

Born in 1820 and raised in a mission environment in South Africa, Mary Moffatt Livingstone was uniquely suited to life as a missionary wife. The daughter of English missionaries Robert and *Mary Smith Moffatt, she was educated at a Wesleyan school in Grahamstown. She married David Livingstone in January 1845. Livingstone was a Scottish missionary and explorer whose devotion to his calling often overshadowed concerns for the welfare of his own family.

Mary Moffatt Livingstone endured innumerable hardships during her marriage, typically without complaint. She accompanied her husband as he moved from place to place, establishing missions and exploring central Africa. Experiencing a recurrent partial paralysis following the birth of her fifth child, Mary sailed with her children for England in 1852. There they lived for four years in poverty while David Livingstone continued to explore Africa. He returned to England in 1856, to great acclaim. Leaving their children in Scotland, Mary accompanied her husband on another trip to Africa. A sixth pregnancy again brought on serious illness, so she soon returned to Scotland. A final journey to meet her husband on the Zambesi delta resulted in a bout with an infectious fever, and she died there in 1862, about six months after her arrival.

Livry, Emma (1842–1863)

French ballerina. Born in 1842; died in Neuilly, France, in 1863; studied with Maria Taglioni.

The illegitimate daughter of a 16-year-old dancer in the Paris Opera's corps de ballet, Emma Livry made her debut as La Sylphide at the age of 16, and was praised as a reincarnation of the great Romantic ballerina *Maria Taglioni, who had originated the role a generation earlier. Taglioni, who came out of retirement to see the young dancer perform, was so impressed that she took her on as a pupil. In 1859, Livry appeared as Erigone in a *divertissement* in the opera *Herculaneum*, and in 1860, Taglioni staged *Le Papillion* as a vehicle for her protégé, who triumphed in the ballet. Three years later, Livry was rehearsing for the ballet *La Muette de Portici* when a gas jet mounted on the scenery ignited her ballet skirt, and she was severely burned. She survived for eight months in great agony before succumbing to her injuries. In a portrait of the dancer, Théophile Gautier described her as passing through space "without an audible tremor of the air."

Lizzie.
Variant of Elizabeth.

Ljudmila or Ljudmilla.
Variant of Ludmila.

Llangollen, the Ladies of.
See Ladies of Llangollen.

Llanover, Lady (1802–1896).
See Hall, Augusta.

Llewelyn Davies, Margaret (1861–1944).
See Davies, Margaret Llewelyn.

Lloyd, Chris Evert (b. 1954).
See Evert, Chris.

Lloyd, Dorothy Jordan
(1889–1946)

English biochemist. Born in 1889; died in 1946.

An English biochemist, Dorothy Lloyd joined the British Leather Manufacturers' Research Association in 1920 and served as its director from 1927 to 1946. She also planned and contributed to all three volumes of *Progress in Leather Science, 1920–45*, published between 1946 and 1948.

Lloyd, Marie (1870–1922)

One of the most popular and highest paid stars of the late Victorian and Edwardian music halls of England, adored especially by the working classes. Name variations: Tillie, and stage names Bella Delmere and Miss Marie Lloyd; Matilda Wood. Pronunciation: LOYD. Born Matilda Victoria Wood in Hoxton, a suburb of London, England, on February 12, 1870; died in London on October 7, 1922; daughter of John Wood (a waiter and maker of artificial flowers) and Matilda (Archer) Wood; attended elementary school in London; married Percy Courtney, in 1887; married Alexander Hurley, in 1904; married Bernard Dillon, in 1914; children: (first marriage) Marie Courtney.

Began career at Grecian Saloon at age 15, and shortly changed stage name to Miss Marie Lloyd (1885); rose rapidly to stardom, earning £100 a week (1886); led strike for poorer members of her profession (1907); snubbed by exclusion from royal command performance of music-hall stars, rented a hall for the same night and drew an audience of 6,000 (1912); detained by U.S. immigration officials on Ellis Island at beginning of an American tour for traveling with a man out of wedlock (1913); died while attempting a musical comeback (1922).

Songs associated with Lloyd: "Oh, Mr. Porter," "Everything in the Garden's Lovely," "Twiddley Wink," "The Boy I Love Is Up in the Gallery," "Piccadilly Trot," "It's a Bit of a Ruin That Cromwell Knocked About a Bit," "A Little of What You Fancy Does You Good," "My Old Man Said Follow the Van (but I Dillied, I Dallied)," "Every Little Movement."

Beginning in the 1850s, the British music hall became the most popular form of public entertainment among England's working classes. At a sixpence apiece, they filled the large halls for a cheap evening, as performers reflected their problems, values and aspirations through patter and songs that were by turns raucous, funny, sentimental, and sad. Between 1890 and 1912, the broad, and often bawdy, comedy of the music halls reached its peak, commenting on class structure in the newly industrialized Britain. One woman, Marie Lloyd, became the best known of many female music-hall

stars, so personifying the attitudes of her audiences that she became the "Queen of the Music Halls." "No other comedian succeeded so well in giving expression to the life of [her] audience, in raising it to a kind of art," wrote the celebrated poet T.S. Eliot. He was only one of Lloyd's many admirers, who included George Bernard Shaw, Compton Mackenzie, James Agate, and Edmund Wilson. Max Beerbohm included her, along with *Florence Nightingale and Queen *Victoria, on his short list of the most memorable women of the age. "Above all others," writes D.F. Cheshire, Lloyd was "the epitome of the real spirit of British music hall of the pre-1914 period." When she died, thousands filled London's streets to mourn her.

The girl who became Marie Lloyd was born Matilda Victoria Wood in 1870 at 36 Plumber Street in Hoxton, a working-class suburb of London where the Marie Lloyd pub still perpetuates her memory. Her father was a waiter at the Eagle Tavern in City Road and made artificial flowers. The oldest of 11 children, Marie was known to her family as "Tillie." She was a happy but obstreperous child; she was hyperactive, hated school, resented authority, and dominated her siblings. In an era when children frequently went to work in factories, her mother got her daughter several factory jobs, but Tillie never lasted more than a week. A supervisor in a bead factory fired her after four days for dancing on the work tables.

Even as a child, Lloyd had a strong sense of drama and performed for her siblings in the attic and coal cellar. She and her sisters formed the Fairy Bell Minstrels and toured local missions, singing such temperance songs as "Throw Down the Bottle and Never Drink Again." Several sisters also became music-hall performers but never achieved her fame.

At age 14, Lloyd announced that she was going on the stage. A year later, with her father's help, she made her first appearance at the Grecian Saloon on May 9, 1885. By June, she had employed the stage name of Bella Delmere and was playing successfully in other halls. But Marie dated the beginning of her career from an appearance at the Falstaff Music Hall, where she was spotted by a manager and adopted the stage name she would carry to fame after seeing advertisements in the streets of London for *Lloyd's Weekly Newspaper*. On October 5, 1885, Lloyd made her first appearance at the famous Oxford Music Hall in the West End, remaining on the bill there for a year. The following October, she received her first newspaper review, which described her as "a pretty little soubrette who dances with great dash and energy." By the end of 1886, her income had risen to £100 per week. At her peak, she was the highest-paid female star, earning up to £800 per week when lesser "artistes" were paid £20–50.

Until her mid-30s, Marie played the coquettish but innocent girl who sang about love. Her theme song, "The Boy I Love Is Up in the Gallery," was "borrowed" from another performer, but it was her rendition that aroused the fantasies of every working-class lad in the gallery. After she took up "When You Wink the Other Eye," she adopted a wink that became a trademark. Caricaturists perpetually depicted her mid-wink.

Lloyd lived hard and did not age well. In her middle years, when she could no longer play youthful roles, she became famous—or infamous, in middle-class circles—for the sexual innuendo and vulgarity of such songs as "Oh, Mr. Porter," "Everything in the Garden's Lovely," "Every Little Movement," and "A Little Bit of What You Fancy Does You Good." Appearing onstage in high-fashion clothes, she rubbed her pearls provocatively across her teeth as she transformed such parlor songs as "Come Into the Garden Maude" (words by Alfred, Lord Tennyson) into suggestive come-ons with her body movements, tone of voice, and winks. "With her famous wink, timed to the fraction of a second," wrote one contemporary, "she could make an apparently simple remark very much more." Her working-class audiences loved her vulgarity, and even dirty jokes she did not tell began to be attributed to "our Marie." On the streets of East London off-color stories were often introduced with: "Hear Marie's latest?"

Provocative, sensual, suggestive but never lewd, Lloyd knew her audience and gave the people what they wanted. "They don't pay their sixpences and shillings at a Music Hall to hear the Salvation Army," she said. Even after she became a well-corseted carrier of considerable weight, her reputation as a sex symbol did not entirely disappear. Without abandoning her suggestiveness and double entendres, she began to include more character sketches in her stage turns, aping upper-class women to the delight of her fans. She also made a specialty of characterizing working-class women, with whom she had considerable empathy. She talked and sang about their problems, of alcohol, children, homelessness, crime, poverty, police, and wife-beating. The song "My Old Man Said Follow the Van" concerned the frequent moves of the poor, trying to keep one step ahead of the rent collector. In her later years, one of her

most popular songs was "It's a Bit of a Ruin That Cromwell Knocked About a Bit." While seeming on the surface to refer to English history, it was actually about the violence done to women at a pub called the Cromwell Arms, managed by a latter-day Oliver Cromwell, who actually knocked the singer "about a bit" on two occasions.

The naughtiness of Lloyd's performances inevitably got her into trouble with prudish members of the middle class who fought against the music hall as decadent, immoral, and corrupting of the lower classes. In 1896, she appeared before a committee of the London County Council which was reviewing the licenses of the music halls. Performing for the committee, she did her act straight and denied the provocativeness of her songs. "The people are looking for blue, and I can't help it . . . if they want to turn and twist my meanings," she told them. "I don't make them blue. It's the people." By promising the committee that she would "only sing songs like 'Home Sweet Home,' if you guarantee the audience will be as morally unimpeachable as the songs," Lloyd had the last word. The licenses were renewed, and her performance cannot be considered totally fudged, since she had a reputation for being far more risque than she actually was.

All right then, play "God Save the Queen" and tell 'em she's here.
—Marie Lloyd

A fighter, Lloyd led the successful Variety Artists' Federation's strike against unfair management practices in 1907. Plans for the strike were formulated at her pink house beside the underground station at Golders Green, and she was active on the picket lines, telling a reporter of the *Daily Telegraph*, "We are fighting . . . for the poorer members of the profession." When **Belle Elmore**, a third-rate actress later murdered by her American husband, crossed the picket line to perform, Marie observed that it was better to let her pass, for she would single-handedly empty the theater.

By 1912, Lloyd was overworked and possibly an alcoholic, doing two or more turns a night in different areas of London. She frequently sang "I Can't Forget the Days When I Was Young," which included the poignant lines, "It don't seem so very long ago/ When I sit for hours and stare; Oh, I can't forget the days when I was young." On July 1 of that year, she was snubbed by the royals when, despite her top billing in the music halls, she was not invited to appear at the Palace Theater as part of the first royal command performance of music-hall artistes. "Every performance by Marie Lloyd is a performance by Command of the British Public," said Lloyd. The night of the event at the Palace, she rented the Coliseum and put on her show, filling 6,000 seats. Told the curtain was going up, she said to the master of ceremonies, "All right, then, play 'God Save the Queen' and tell 'em she's here."

Lloyd's style was most suited to London, where she had her greatest popularity. She toured Australia and South Africa, and made three tours in the U.S., but her humor and material were too topical, too British, and too class-oriented to be understood outside Britain, and she did not develop a rapport with foreign audiences.

By modern standards, Lloyd was not especially attractive; one contemporary compared her front teeth to "those of a jovial horse." Another described her as "just a rather short, fair, pretty woman with a wide 'toothy' smile, and a voice which is most attractively hoarse." Even allowing for the crudeness of early recording techniques, her singing voice was shrill and nasal. Marie "never had what you could call a good voice," said her sister **Daisey Wood**. What the "Queen of the Halls" had was energy; she gave her all onstage. "When she sang a song, she was in it," said Daisey. "She got into her words. She was the character."

One key to her popularity was that she never lost touch with her working-class background. Music-hall audiences, who "gave the bird" to performers who got uppity and forgot their origins, could force a performer offstage. Lloyd embodied the soul of the working class and could develop a rapport with the rowdiest of audiences. In the tough industrial city of Sheffield when she was once "given the bird," she refused to leave the stage. "So, this is where you make your knives and forks," she said, looking out over the audience. "Well, you know what you can do with them, don't you. And your circular saws as well." Her listeners were won over.

Marie was 17 at the time of her first marriage, to Percy Courtney. They had one child, **Marie Courtney**, and divorced in 1905. By then, Marie had been living openly with Alexander Hurley, another music-hall performer who became famous for "the Lambeth Walk." Their marriage, begun in 1907, lasted only five years, and probably ended because of Hurley's professional jealousy. Her relationship with her third husband, Bernard Dillon, was also scandalous from the beginning, and the marriage was a disaster. Dillon was a successful jockey who won the Derby in 1910, and Lloyd was nearly twice his age. In violation of the mores of times, they lived openly together, out of wedlock, and paid dearly for their refusal to be bound by the standards of the day. Dillon lost his coveted position in the Jockey Club, and in 1913, when Lloyd was entering the U.S. for a tour, immigration officials charged the couple with moral turpitude and detained them on Ellis Island until they agreed to live separately during their visit. With the Statue of Liberty as background, Lloyd fumed: "What irony! The statue ought to be pulled down. It is a stinking lie." She and Dillon were married on February 21, 1914, in Portland, Oregon. Eventually, they lived apart.

Lloyd, who loved people, held open house every Sunday evening in her London home. Extravagant with her money, she was also famously generous with the less fortunate. "She had a heart had Marie," said a friend. "The size of Waterloo Station." Though she probably earned £500,000, she left an estate worth only £7,000. Marie was also known for her temper and allowed no one to get the best of her. "It's better out than in," she said, "and anyway it relieves my feelings." On one occasion, irritated by a shopkeeper, she paid her bill in bags filled with the large, heavy English pennies of the period.

In her last years, Lloyd was frequently ill, and her feistiness and rebellious spirit disappeared. "All my oof has gone," she told her friends. She continued to work but began drinking before performances and had trouble remembering lines. Regarded as unreliable, she was forced to work the smaller halls. In August 1922, when she tried to make a comeback, her singing voice was so feeble that a woman performer was positioned in the wings to sing along with her. On October 5, Lloyd was onstage at the Edmonton Empire, singing "It's a Bit of a Ruin That Cromwell Knocked About a Bit," when she staggered and collapsed, evoking shrieks of laughter from the audience who thought it was part of the act. Taken home to Golders Green, Marie Lloyd died of kidney failure two days later, age 52.

It is hard to separate fact from legend about "Our Marie." She was an institution in her time, a star and an individualist on and off stage. Like other female performers of her genre, she was an inspiration to working-class women who could hope that with luck and talent they too might escape their drab lives. She also had brilliant timing and magnetism. It was charisma that carried her to top billing and kept her there. Significantly, of the 50-odd songs associated with her performances, not one remained in the popular repertoire for long after her death.

In her obituary in *The Times,* H.H. Child described Marie Lloyd as having "a vivid personality whose range and extremely broad humour as a character actress were extraordinary." On October 13, 1922, *The Times* reported that the East End of London virtually closed down for her fu-

neral, pubs were draped in black crepe, and an estimated 50,000 followed her motor car behind the hearse through the streets to Hampstead. Titled people as well as costermongers sent floral tributes. Symbolically, her death also marked the end of the music hall. "It is not cruel to say that she died opportunely," wrote H.G. Hibbert. "The music hall is on the eve of a crisis."

SOURCES:

Cheshire, D.F. *Music Hall in Britain*. Teaneck, NJ: Fairleigh Dickinson University Press, 1934.

Farson, D.N. *Marie Lloyd and Music Hall*. London: Stacey, 1972.

Mander, R., and J. Mitchison. *British Music Hall*. London: Gentry Books, 1974.

Naomi, Jacob. *"Our Marie" [Marie Lloyd]: A Biography*. Bath: Cedric Chivers, 1936.

The Times. October 9, 1922 and October 13, 1922.

SUGGESTED READING:

Macqueen-Pope, W. *The Melodies Linger On: The Story of the Music Hall*. London, W.H. Allen, 1950.

Wilson J. Hoffman,
Thorn and Frances Pendleton
Professor of History, Hiram College, Hiram, Ohio

Lloyd, Marilyn Laird (1929—)

*American Democratic congressional representative, 94th–103rd Congresses. Name variations: Mrs. Mort Lloyd; Marilyn Lloyd Bouquard. Born Rachel Marilyn Laird on January 3, 1929, in Fort Smith, Arkansas; daughter of James Edgar Laird and Iva Mae (Higginbotham) Laird; attended Talco (Tex.) Elementary School, 1941; graduated from Western Kentucky College High School, Bowling Green, 1945; graduated from Shorter College, Rome, Georgia, 1963; married Mort Lloyd (a businessman); married Joseph P. Bouquard; children: (first marriage) **Nancy Lloyd Smithson**; Mort Lloyd II; **Deborah Lloyd Riley**.*

Owned and operated radio station WTTI, in Dalton, Georgia; owned and operated Executive Aviation, Winchester, Tennessee; elected as a Democrat representing Tennessee to the 94th and nine succeeding Congresses (1975–95).

Marilyn Lloyd

Born on January 3, 1929, in Fort Smith, Arkansas, Marilyn Laird Lloyd attended schools in Texas and Kentucky and studied at Shorter College in Rome, Georgia. She was the co-owner and manager, with her husband, of the radio station WTTI in Dalton, Georgia, before owning and operating Executive Aviation in Winchester, Tennessee.

In 1974, standing as a Democrat, Marilyn Lloyd was elected by Tennessee to the House of Representatives of the 94th Congress, defeating Republican incumbent Lamar Baker. She proceeded to win reelection to nine succeeding Congresses, holding political office until 1995 and maintaining the loyalty of a district that usually voted Republican in presidential contests.

During her first term in office, Lloyd won a place on the Committee on Science, Space and Technology, an important appointment because of the committee's jurisdiction over legislation related to the atomic energy facilities at Oak Ridge in Lloyd's district. She went on to chair its Subcommittee on Energy Research and Development, beginning with the 97th Congress. During her political career, Lloyd also served on the Committee on Public Works (later Public Works and Transportation), the Committee on Armed Services, and the House Select Committee on Aging. In 1990, Lloyd was appointed chair of the Subcommittee on Housing and Consumer Interests. In the 96th through 98th Congresses, Lloyd served under the name Marilyn Lloyd Bouquard. She did not stand as a candidate for re-election to the 104th Congress.

SOURCES:

Office of the Historian. *Women in Congress, 1917–1990*. Commission on the Bicentenary of the U.S. House of Representatives, 1991.

Paula Morris, D.Phil.,
Brooklyn, New York

Lloyd George, countess (1888–1972).

See Lloyd George, Frances Stevenson.

Lloyd George, Frances Stevenson (1888–1972)

Countess Lloyd George of Dwyfor. Name variations: Frances Louise Lloyd George. Born Frances Louise Stevenson in 1888; died in 1972; daughter of John Stevenson; educated at Clapham High School and Royal Holloway College, London; married David Lloyd George (1863–1945, a Liberal politician and prime minister), in 1943; children: (earlier marriage) Jennifer (b. 1929).

Frances Stevenson worked closely with David Lloyd George, as his personal secretary and mistress, throughout his political career, and she was involved in the research and writing of all six volumes of his *War Memoirs* (1933–36). After the death of his first wife *Margaret Lloyd George, Frances married David in 1943 and settled into the family estate at Criccieth in Wales. Following his death in 1945, because of numerous wrangles with his children, Frances moved to the family's English estate at Churt, Surrey, one that she had helped purchase with Lloyd George in 1921. Her diary from 1914 to 1944 was edited by A.J.P Taylor and published in 1971.

SUGGESTED READING:

Taylor, A.J.P., ed. *Lloyd George: A Diary by Frances Stevenson.* Harper, 1971.

Lloyd George, Margaret (d. 1941)

*England's "first lady" as wife of the prime minister of England. Name variations: Dame Margaret Lloyd George; Margaret Owen. Born Margaret Owen in Mynyddednyfed, Wales; died in January 1941; daughter of a prosperous Methodist farmer; became first wife of David Lloyd George (1863–1945, British prime minister, and one of the most dominant international figures of the early 20th century), on January 24, 1888; children: (two sons and three daughters) Richard, Mair Eiluned (died at age 17), Olwen, Gwilyn (later Viscount Tenby), *Megan Lloyd George (1902–1966, a Liberal and later a Labour member of Parliament).*

On January 24, 1888, Margaret Owen married David Lloyd George. Theirs was never a happy marriage because his affairs and infidelities were notorious throughout his life. One such was her daughter Megan's French and music teacher, *Frances Stevenson (Lloyd George).* By 1913, Stevenson was David's mistress and per-sonal secretary and would remain in that capacity for 30 years until Margaret's death in January 1941. In October 1943, David married Frances.

Lloyd George, Megan (1902–1966)

First woman member of the British Parliament from Wales. Name variations: Lady Megan Lloyd George. Born Megan Arvon Lloyd George at Criccieth, North Wales, in 1902; died in 1966; third daughter and youngest child of David Lloyd George (1863–1945, a Liberal politician and prime minister) and Margaret (Owen) Lloyd George (d. 1941); educated at Garratts' Hall, Banstead, and in Paris.

The third daughter and youngest child of Liberal politician and prime minister David Lloyd George, Megan Lloyd George grew up in Downing Street during her father's residence there from 1916 to 1922, first as chancellor of the exchequer and later as prime minister. However, her mother, Dame *Margaret Lloyd George, gave birth to all her children in Wales, to make sure that they were Welsh-born, and Welsh was always the language of the home.

From Downing Street, Megan had every opportunity to pursue her interest in radical politics, though she also studied modern history and politics at King's College, University of London. She accompanied her father to the Paris Peace Conference of 1919 and on other visits abroad, and was closely associated with his political activities, creating a precedent for ❧ **Mary Churchill**'s public participation in her father Winston's concerns during World War II.

In 1929, Megan Lloyd George campaigned successfully (in the Welsh language, as she always did) for the Liberal constituency of Anglesey (Ynys Mon), and joined her father and brother in the House of Commons. Twenty years later, she became deputy leader of the Parliamentary Liberal Party. She was, however, defeated at the General Election of 1951 after 22 years at Westminster. The following year, she became president of the Parliament for Wales campaign. In 1955, she resigned from the Liberal Party and joined Labour, for which she fought for the West Wales parliamentary seat of Carmarthen (Caerfyrddin) in 1959, and was returned to the Commons.

Her maiden speech in 1930 showed her to be a champion of women's causes, particularly of those working or unemployed. In that decade, she spoke against Fascist Spain and against the appeasement of Nazism. She also championed Welsh issues, focusing on equality for the lan-

Churchill, Mary. See Churchill, Clementine for sidebar.

guage in broadcasting and in the law courts, thus paving the way for the nationalist revival of the 1960s and 1970s when these matters came to a head and resulted in legislation. In a speech at a rally in 1950, she described Home Rule for Wales as "400 years overdue."

Lord Cledwyn of Penrhos, to whom she lost her seat in the 1951 election, describes her as possessing "charm, gaiety, enthusiasm and sparkle"; further, she was a "natural orator" who "would have been an imaginative and lively Minister . . . but she was not put to the test." To mark Megan Lloyd George's 20 years in Parliament, other women MP's presented her with a book in which she was described as a "true daughter of the Welsh wizard: she bewitches friend and foe alike."

SOURCES:

Europa Biographical Dictionary of British Women. London: Europa, 1983.

Price, Emyr. *Megan Lloyd George.* Gwynedd Archives Service, Caernarfon 1983.

Lobo, Rebecca (1973—)

American basketball player whose popularity helped propel women's sports to the next level. Born in Southwick, Massachusetts, on October 6, 1973; daughter of Dennis Lobo and RuthAnn Lobo (both school officials in Granby, Connecticut); sister of Rachel Lobo, *an assistant basketball coach at Salem State College; graduated University of Connecticut, B.A. in political science, 1995.*

Named pre-season All-American by the AP (1994); voted Big East player of the year (1993, 1994, 1995); earned first-team academic All-America honors (1994, 1995); was University of Connecticut's all-time career leader in rebounds (1,286) and blocks (396) at end of senior year (1995); named player of the year by the U.S. Basketball Writers Association, College Sports Magazine, and the Women's Basketball News Service; named to the 10-member Kodak Division I Women's Basketball All-America team (1995); won the Naismith award (1995); named national player of the year in women's basketball by the Associated Press (1995), the first time the AP awarded that honor to women; received the Wade Trophy (1995); was a member of the undefeated USA Basketball Women's National Team that played 52 games around the world (1996); won a gold medal with the U.S. Women's Olympic Team at the Atlanta Games (1996); signed by the New York Liberty of the WNBA (1997).

For anyone attempting to illustrate the success of Title IX, they need look no further than Rebecca Lobo. There is no doubt that the slow but steady movement in women's sports was brought about by the federal law passed in 1972 that forbade gender discrimination in educational programs or in activities that received federal funds. Sports bias had been so culturally entrenched, it could only be dislodged with a legislative wrecking ball. In 1972, there were no college athletic scholarships for women; women's programs received one-half of 1% of the college athletic budget; less than 300,000 girls in high school competed in competitive sports; 16,000 competed in colleges. In deference to their fragility, women played half-court basketball; they were able to pass the ball across the center line but not allowed to cross it. There was enormous resistance to Title IX. At the time the bill was ratified, the board of the National Collegiate Athletic Association (NCAA) warned: "This will mean the end of intercollegiate athletics as we know it."

Born in 1973, one year after Title IX went into effect, Rebecca Lobo honed her basketball skills playing two-on-one games against her sister Rachel and brother Jason in the backyard of their home in Southwick, Massachusetts. By fourth grade, for lack of a girls' squad, she was playing on a local boys' team. One teacher told her "to dress more like a girl and act more like a girl," said her mother **RuthAnn Lobo.** "I was incensed. I told her she could do whatever she wanted to. She was a very happy kid. I didn't need somebody to browbeat her." In her first game at Southwick-Tolland Regional High School, Lobo scored 32 points. While in high school, she amassed 2,710 points to become the all-time leading scorer, male or female, in Massachusetts state history. She was also class salutatorian, played the saxophone, and spent five summers working in tobacco fields.

Though offers poured in from over 100 colleges, Lobo agreed to attend the University of Connecticut at Storrs, only 90 minutes from home. UConn Coach Geno Auriemma told his staff: "For the next four years, we're going to be all right." They were. By her senior year, the 6'4" All-American center forward was averaging 17.1 points, 9.9 rebounds, and 3.6 blocked shots per game and was third in assists at 3.8. A political science major with a grade-point average of 3.63, Lobo had also made the dean's list every semester of her college career. If she had a flaw, it was being too unselfish, claimed Auriemma. Too often, she would pass the ball rather than shoot.

Throughout her four years at UConn, Lobo's parents had been hugely supportive, attending most of her games. In December 1993, Lobo

Rebecca
Lobo

learned of her mother's diagnosis of breast cancer while sitting in the bleachers, post-game. When Rebecca began to tear up, her mother said, "You take care of your thing on the court, I'll take care of this." After a mastectomy and chemotherapy, RuthAnn Lobo remains cancer free.

In Rebecca's final year, the 1994–95 season, she led the Huskies to a perfect 29–0 record, and the team won the Big East championship. But, as they headed into the NCAA championships, all those wins were considered a fluke by a large delegation of scoffers: the team lacked depth, it was said; their lopsided victories proved they played in a weak conference. The clear favorite was *Pat Summitt's Tennessee Lady Volunteers, who had ended their season with a record of 33–2 (one of those losses was to UConn). It was widely known that the Lady Vols were not at full strength during their first meeting; they were also suffering jet-lag, while Connecticut had the home-court advantage. Still, it was widely assumed that Tennessee, which had not been defeated by the same team in one season since 1986–87, would be impossible to beat twice. Even after Connecticut trounced Stanford 87–60 in the NCAA semifinal with the help of a 31-point performance by UConn's **Kara Wolters**, Stanford's coach **Tara VanDerveer** predicted, "Tennessee is going to win tomorrow, but I think it will be a good game."

On Sunday, April 2, at the Target Center in Minneapolis, the final game of the women's NCAA Final Four was played before a television audience that rose throughout the game to a concluding 7.3 Nielsen rating for CBS. This was almost triple the rating for Fox's National Hockey League games, which aired opposite, and 14% better than the ratings of NBC's pro-basketball games. During the first half, Lobo, Wolters, and *Jennifer Rizzotti, all key players for UConn, sat on the bench in foul trouble. Six-foot **Jamelle Elliott** was sent out with a group of what she called "non-All Americans" with instructions to hang on until half time. Elliott and her shorter crew managed to stay close to Tennessee, ending only six points under at the buzzer.

In the second half, "the Rebecca Lobo show was about to begin," wrote Austin Murphy. "In rapid succession Lobo scored a layup off a post-up move; posted up again, drove the lane and hit a reverse layup; pulled up and drained an 18-footer from the left wing; then nailed a 17-footer." In the flurry, she had scored eight of UConn's next ten points, bringing her team within three points of their opponents. "Lobo did what she had to do," said Summitt. "She made huge plays." Then, in the matchup between two of the nation's best point guards, Jennifer Rizzotti vs **Michelle Marciniak**, a Rizzotti steal and left-handed layup brought the Huskies within one, and Summitt called a quick timeout.

With 2:17 remaining, Jamelle Elliott's layup tied the score at 61. Then Rizzotti's mad dash down the length of the floor turned the game around. "Gathering in a long defensive rebound, she went coast to coast with Marciniak right with her," wrote Murphy. "An instant before she reached the basket, Rizzotti crossed over to her left and sank a sweet, left-handed layup with 1:51 remaining." It was the snapshot of that fast break that made the East coast cover of *Sports Illustrated*, which sold out within an hour after it hit newsstands. The Huskies led the rest of the game.

In that second half, the team had out-rebounded the Lady Vols 25–10, with five by Lobo. "We didn't deny her the ball," said Summitt. "She made herself hard to guard and got herself jumpers. She beat us one-on-one. We should have been able to defend her, but we did not." The Huskies had staged a 70–64 comeback to beat Tennessee's Lady Vols and win the NCAA championship. At 35–0, they had a perfect season. They were also the first women's team to go undefeated since the Lady Longhorns of Texas in 1986 went 34–0, and the first Division I team—men's or women's—to go 35–0. Lobo was named most valuable player of the tournament and, for the first time in history, four of the Huskies team were named to the All-Final Four team: Lobo, Rizzotti, Wolters, and Elliott. Tennessee's **Nicki McCray** took the fifth spot.

Thousands, including Connecticut's governor and a squad of elbowing news media, turned out at Bradley Airport in Hartford to greet the returning team; weeks later, tens of thousands stood curbside for a triumphant parade down the streets of Connecticut's capital, while public-address systems blared what had become the team's battle cry: **Aretha Franklin**'s "R-E-S-P-E-C-T." "I could never imagine this day would happen," said Lobo, "8,000 people singing *Respect*, even though most of them don't know the words." Lobo was on David Letterman; Lobo jogged with Bill Clinton; Lobo shot commercials for Reebok and Spalding.

The unassuming Lobo had given hundreds of interviews and had signed autographs for at least an hour after each game. Until it became overwhelming, she answered all her fan mail, most of which was from young girls. She had even retained her sense of humor when a male reporter asked UConn players at their NCAA championship press conference in Minneapolis: "It's a given that women love to shop. Have you been to the Mall of America yet?" Lobo never seemed to tire of answering the same questions. The most frequent one was, what did the future hold for her amazing talent? The answer: not a thing.

"Were she a man," wrote *Newsweek,* she "would be looking at a fat contract from the NBA." After college graduation, the woman then deemed by *Newsweek* as "the most-talked-about basketball player in America" would sign no seven-figure contract with the NBA. There were no professional women's leagues in the United States. There was nowhere to go with her talent unless she took it to Europe, where America's best women basketball players had been known to vanish from view, and possibly memory, while they took in six-figure incomes. "I don't know if it's necessarily unfair," said Lobo. "But it is a little frustrating." When she was offered $300,000 to play professionally in Italy, Lobo was resigned: "I'm thankful that I can get paid at all just to continue playing this game."

Years before the groundbreaking Tennessee-Connecticut game, the prevailing argument had been that there was not enough interest in women's sports. But from 1984 to 1995, total attendance for women's basketball had tripled, from 1.3 million to 3.6 million. Throughout UConn's 1994–95 season, the seats were sold out at Gampel Pavilion in Storrs, Connecticut; for the regular season game against Tennessee, $8 tickets were going for $100. Target Center in Minneapolis seats 18,000; tickets for the Final Four had been sold out months before.

Huskiemania was not an isolated incident. "I liken the game to a beautiful flower that is only now coming into bloom," wrote Mel Greenberg of the Philadelphia *Inquirer*. "Heck, when I first started covering the girls in 1976, 50 was a big crowd at UConn." **Marie Blais**, who spent a year following the Lady Hurricanes of Amherst Regional High School, wrote in her book *In These Girls, Hope Is Muscle*: "The Hurricanes' determination and talent demonstrated how women could be taken seriously in a male-dominated arena. Their compelling struggle won them a legion of fans—early in the season the gym would be nearly empty; in the end, people had to be turned away from stuffed stadiums." When she was growing up, writes Blais, physical activity was discouraged. Girls were steered toward synchronized swimming or marching in the St. Patrick's Day parade. She saw a complete change in attitudes around Amherst. "It's not that people don't like to watch or like to follow women's sports," said Amherst's co-captain, **Jen Pariseau**, "it's just that they are not exposed to it. In Amherst we had to get a successful team going. People started knowing us and coming to the games. Plus, everybody likes to pick up on a winner." As in any sport, when the team is unbeatable, seats are unobtainable.

"For years, I took a lot of ridicule for covering the women," wrote Greenberg. "But now my friends talk about Rebecca Lobo the way they did last year about Grant Hill. We're finally getting some respect here." *Sheryl Swoopes,

who did commentary for CBS during the NCAA championship game, felt it "really opened the public's eyes. . . . I didn't think ours was the big breakthrough. Nobody had heard of us before. But after I scored 47, **Charlotte Smith** last year and now UConn going undefeated, that just builds it up for everybody." (In the 1994 NCAA finals, North Carolina's Charlotte Smith made a 3-pointer with seven-tenths of a second to go to beat Louisiana Tech. In 1993, Swoopes scored 47 points to lead the Red Raiders of Texas Tech to an 84–82 victory over Ohio State.)

Lobo's heady season at U-Conn gave many columnists a forum for their own reflections. "Little League baseball excluded girls," wrote columnist **Maura Casey** in the New London *Day*, of growing up before Title IX. "There were no soccer leagues in my town that involved girls. My brothers competed in crew through a local rowing club, which also banned females. So during gym class, while my fellow classmates practiced chanting 'Tony! Tony! He's our man! If he can't do it, nobody can!' I worked off my anger, and my envy, by practicing foul-shots on the gym's basketball court." Twenty years after Title IX, 2.12 million high school girls were participating in competitive sports, as were 158,000 college women, representing 35% of college athletes worldwide, and they played a rugged full court. If not for Title IX, Rebecca Lobo would have been waiting on the sidelines for the men's game to finish so she could get her 20 minutes of practice time on the court.

Despite these gains, there was still not much of a basketball future at home for Rebecca Lobo. If she wanted to play in the United States, the best she could hope for was a token slot on a men's professional team. In April 1995, in the 8th and final round of the men's U.S. Basketball League draft, Lobo was the 77th overall pick, selected by the Jersey Turnpikes. Only two other women— *Cheryl Miller of Southern California in 1986 and Sheryl Swoopes of Texas Tech in 1993—were chosen in USBL drafts. In the NBA drafts, **Lusia Harris** of Delta State was selected by the then-New Orleans Jazz in the 7th round in 1977; *Ann Meyers tried out for the Indiana Pacers in 1979. The first woman to play on a men's team in one of the four major pro sports was hockey's *Manon Rheaume, who goaltended for the Tampa Bay Lightning in the National Hockey League (NHL) exhibition game in 1992. Rheaume went on to play for the Las Vegas Thunder in the International Hockey League (IHL).

"I'm just waiting for the timer to buzz and my 15 minutes [of fame] will be over," said

Lobo. Maybe not. Because of Pat Summitt, *C. Vivian Stringer, Cathy Rush, Carol Eckman, *Carol Blazejowski, Margaret Wade, *Lisa Leslie, *Lynette Woodard, *Nancy Lieberman-Cline, the *Edmonton Grads, and all the others who went before, women's basketball exploded. In 1996, ABC went from airing one women's game to several and ESPN signed a seven-year, $19 million deal to televise 31 women's NCAA tournament games. That year, Lobo was selected for the U.S. Women's National Team and won a gold medal at the Atlanta Olympics Games. In 1997, Rebecca Lobo signed with the New York Liberty in the newly formed Women's National Basketball Association (WNBA). She could earn a living, and she could stay in America.

SOURCES:

Casey, Maura. "Shooting for the Best," in *The* [New London] *Day.* April 9, 1995.

"The Enforcer," in *People Weekly.* March 20, 1995, pp. 61–62.

Grant, Traci. "These Girls Played Hoops for Keeps," in *The* [New London] *Day.* April 11, 1995, p. B1.

Murphy, Austin. "Storybook Ending," in *Sports Illustrated.* April 10, 1995, pp. 39–43.

"She Shoots . . . She Scores," in *Newsweek.* April 17, 1995, p. 69.

Wulf, Steve. "Call It March Maidness," in *Time.* March 27, 1995, p. 68–69.

SUGGESTED READING:

Lobo, RuthAnn, and Rebecca Lobo. *The Home Team: Of Mothers, Daughters, and American Champions.* Kodansha, 1997.

Lock, Jane Melinda (1954—)

Australian golfer. Born in Sydney, Australia, in 1954; received the MBE in 1974.

Born in 1954 in Sydney, Australia, but raised in Melbourne, Jane Lock took up golf at the age of 16 and, within a year, was playing with a single-figure handicap. While still a teenager, she won three successive Australian junior championships and, in 1975, won both the Australian junior and senior championships. She subsequently won three Australian championships and represented her country in 30 competitions, setting course records six times. In 1978, she won the Espinrito Santo World Amateur Golf championship for Australia for the first time. Lock turned professional in 1980 and went on to play on the American circuit. She returned to Australia in 1986, after fracturing her arm at the Glendale Open.

Locke, Sumner (1881–1917)

Australian playwright and novelist. Name variations: Sumner Locke Elliott. Born Helena Sumner Locke in Sandgate, Brisbane, Australia, in 1881; died in Sydney, Australia, on October 18, 1917; married Henry Logan Elliott (a journalist), in 1916 or 1917; children: Sumner Locke Elliott (an actor, novelist, and playwright).

Although Sumner Locke enjoyed some success as a playwright (her *The Vicissitudes of Vivienne* was produced in Melbourne in 1908), she was better known for her popular "Mum Dawson" books, *Mum Dawson, Boss* (1911) and *The Dawsons' Uncle George* (1912). In both novels, Mum presides over a family of provincials who are caught up in a humorous succession of misadventures. Locke's last novel, *Samaritan Mary* (1916), was set in America, where she lived for a period during World War I.

In 1916 or 1917, Locke married journalist Henry Logan Elliott, who went off to war ten days after their wedding. Sumner Locke died in childbirth nine months later. The couple's son, Sumner Locke Elliott, was raised by an impoverished aunt and uncle until a wealthy aunt from England appeared to claim him, provoking a six-year court battle. He later recalled the sad events of his childhood in his first novel, *Careful, He Might Hear You* (1963), which was adapted into an award-winning film by the same name in 1984.

SOURCES:

Contemporary Authors. New Revision Series. Volume 21. Detroit, MI: Gale Research.

RELATED MEDIA:

Careful, He Might Hear You (film), starring **Wendy Hughes**, Robyn Nevin, and Nicholas Gledhill, screenplay by Michael Jenkins, directed by Carl Schultz, produced by **Jill Robb**, Syme International Productions, 1984.

Lockwood, Annea F. (1939—)

*New Zealand-born composer. Born on July 29, 1939, in Christchurch, New Zealand; daughter of Gladys (Ferguson) Lockwood (a history and physical education teacher) and George Lockwood (a lawyer); B.Mus (hons); further study at the Royal College of Music, London, with Peter Racine Fricker (1961–63), at the Darmstadt Ferienkurs für Neue Musik (1962–63) and with Gottfried Michael Koenig at the Musikhochschule, Cologne, Germany, and in Holland (1963–64); lives with **Ruth Anderson** (a composer and flutist).*

Annea F. Lockwood was born in 1939 in Christchurch, New Zealand, where she received her early training as a composer. After completing a B.Mus., she went on to study composition

at the Royal College of Music, London, with Peter Racine Fricker (1961–63), at the Darmstadt Ferienkurs für Neue Musik (1962–63), and with Gottfried Michael Koenig at the Musikhochschule, Cologne, Germany, and in Holland (1963–64). Returning to London in 1964, she freelanced as a composer-performer in Britain and Europe until moving to the United States in 1973, where she continued to freelance and also taught, first at City University of New York (CUNY), Hunter College, then, from 1982 to 2001, on the faculty of Vassar College.

During the 1960s, she collaborated frequently with sound-poets, choreographers, and visual artists and created a number of works which she herself performed, such as *Glass Concert* (1967) later published in *Source: Music of the Avant-Garde* and recorded on Tangent Records, then on What Next CDs. In this work, a variety of complex sounds were drawn from industrial glass shards, and glass tubing and presented as an audio-visual theater piece. In homage to Christiaan Barnard's pioneering heart transplants, Lockwood created the *Piano Trans-*

plants (1969–72) in which old, defunct pianos were variously burned, "drowned" in a shallow pond in Amarillo, Texas, and partially buried in an English garden.

During the 1970s and 1980s, Lockwood turned her attention to performance works focused on environmental sounds, life-narratives and performance works using low-tech devices such as her Sound Ball (a foam-covered ball containing six small speakers and a radio receiver, originally designed to "put sound into the hands of dancers"). These included *World Rhythms* (1975), widely presented in the U.S., Europe, and New Zealand, as well as *Conversations with Ancestors* (1979), based on the life stories of four women over 80, *A Sound Map of the Hudson* (1982), *Delta Run* (1982), built around a conversation she recorded with the sculptor Walter Wincha, who was close to death, and the surreal *Three Short Stories and an Apotheosis* (1985), using the Sound Ball.

In the 1990s, Lockwood began writing for acoustic instruments and voices, sometimes incorporating electronics and visual elements, producing pieces for a variety of ensembles: *Thousand Year Dreaming* (1991) is scored for four didgeridus and other instruments and incorporates slides of the cave paintings at Lascaux; *Ear-Walking Woman* (1996), for pianist **Lois Svard**, invites the pianist to discover a range of sounds available inside the instrument; *Duende* (1997), a collaboration with baritone Thomas Buckner, carries the singer into a heightened state, similar to a shamanic journey, through the medium of his own voice. Much of Lockwood's music has been recorded on American, English, and New Zealand labels and published in the U.S. and in New Zealand.

Lockwood, Belva Ann (1830–1917)

American lawyer and women's rights advocate who was the first woman admitted to the bar of the Supreme Court and the U.S. Court of Claims, as well as the first woman to receive votes in a presidential election. Name variations: Belva McNall; Belva Bennett Lockwood. Born Belva Ann Bennett on October 24, 1830, in Royalton, New York; died on May 19, 1917; daughter of Lewis J. Bennett (a farmer) and Hannah (Green) Bennett; attended country schools, Royalton Academy (one year), Gasport (N.Y.) Academy, 1853–54, Genesee Wesleyan Seminary and Genesee College at Lima, N.Y. (later Syracuse University), 1854–57, National University Law School, 1871–73; married Uriah H. McNall, on November 8, 1848 (died 1853); married Ezekiel Lockwood, on March 11, 1868 (died 1877); children: (first marriage) Lura McNall (1848–1894, who married DeForest Ormes); (second marriage) Jessie Lockwood (1869–1871).

Awards: Hon. LL.D., Syracuse University (1909).

Taught in district schools (1844–48), and summers while attending college; appointed preceptor, Lockport (N.Y.) Union School (1857–61), and at seminaries in Gainesville, Hornellsville, and Oswego, N.Y. (1861–66); founded McNall's Ladies Seminary in Washington, D.C. (1867); lobbied to pass laws in Congress granting women equal pay for equal work (1872) and to permit women to be admitted to the bar of the U.S. Supreme Court (1879); became first woman admitted to practice before the Supreme Court; nominated as presidential candidate of the National Equal Rights Party (1884 and 1888); founded law firm of Belva A. Lockwood & Co. (1887–94); served as a delegate for the Universal Peace Union to International Peace Congresses (1889–1911); served on the nominating committee for the Nobel Peace Prize.

Belva Ann Lockwood was nearly 40 years old, but the law school of Columbia College (later George Washington University) rejected her application to study there because her presence might be "an injurious diversion of the attention of the [male] students." Georgetown University and Howard University also refused to admit her. Finally, in 1871, she and 14 other women were allowed to attend the newly established National University Law School. "I had to contend for every inch of ground that I gained," Lockwood observed. When she completed the course, she was not allowed to graduate with her male classmates; not until she wrote a stinging letter to President Ulysses S. Grant, who was also president of the university, did she receive her degree. The District of Columbia admitted women to the bar (though at the time she applied, one justice remarked, "Bring on as many women lawyers as you choose. I do not believe they will be a success"). However, when one of her cases was brought to the federal Court of Claims a few months later, she was refused admission, both to the Court of Claims, and later to the Supreme Court. Belva Lockwood petitioned Congress to pass a law to prohibit any woman "otherwise qualified" from being debarred from practice before any U.S. court. For more than five years, she lobbied; "Nothing was too daring for me to attempt," she later wrote. "I addressed Senators as though they were old familiar friends, and with an earnestness that carried with it conviction." Her relentlessness paid off, and the bill became law in February 1879. Lockwood claimed, plausibly, that "my bill was . . . an entering wedge for woman suffrage."

Belva Ann Bennett, the second of the five children of Lewis and **Hannah Bennett**, was descended from pioneer families in Royalton, New York. She was born in 1830 and grew up on the family's 100-acre farm in Niagara County, with its orchard of pear, peach, and plum trees. At age five, she and her older sister **Rachel Bennett** began to attend the summer sessions of country schools. As the schools were sometimes two miles away, winter sessions, because of bad weather and muddy roads, were not possible for young children who had to walk. Despite the hard benches in one-room schools and the effort it cost her to "toe the mark" (a white line painted on the floor where she recited her lessons), Belva later explained, "I always wanted an education, even when a girl."

When Belva was 14, Hannah somehow found the money to send her daughter to the Royalton Academy for one year. The private school, housed in a two-story brick building, offered "thorough English and classical education for admission to college, for study of a profession, or for business." Belva's father did not support her ambition, however, so the following year she had to stop studying and begin teaching in the summer sessions of district schools, for ten shillings a week and "boarding round." While still in her teens, she spoke before the Teachers' Association of the Town of Royalton; her remarks were later published in the Lockport Niagara Democrat.

Soon after her 18th birthday in 1848, Belva married Uriah McNall, the son of a tavernkeeper and farmer at McNall's Corners. The couple moved to a farm south of Gasport, New York, where Uriah operated a sawmill on Eighteen Mile Creek. Their daughter **Lura McNall** was born on July 31 of the following year. Belva occasionally wrote for the local newspapers, sometimes to console neighbors who had lost young children. Three years into their marriage, Uriah injured his foot in the mill while sawing logs, and died of complications from the wound about two years later, on May 11, 1853.

Left a widow with a four-year-old child, Belva knew that in order to support herself and her daughter she needed more education. She sold her farm and stock and, in the fall of 1853, enrolled in the Gasport Academy, along with her younger brother and sister and her brother-in-law, all of whom boarded with her. That year's study prepared her to enter the Genesee Seminary in the fall of 1854; later she transferred to Genesee College. While there, she had to leave Lura to the care of her mother. When the Bennetts moved to Illinois, it would be three long years before Belva could go west to see her daughter, which she considered "a very serious trial."

"After much mending and turning of a scanty wardrobe," wrote Belva, she packed her trunk and journeyed to the college in Lima, 18 miles from Rochester, connected by a "good plank road." Tuition was $8.50 a term, but students had to supply their own "lights, pails, wash-bowls, towels, and mirrors." The women had to pay an additional $1.25 per term "for sawing and carrying wood" to their rooms. The curriculum included the study of electricity, magnetism, electro-chemistry, geometry, and, significantly, the law of nations, political economy, and the Constitution of the United States. She later admitted she had:

> studied in season and out of season, and while fond of my room-mates and kind to them, I deliberately banished them from my room. . . . [T]he three years of my college life are to me a blank, so far as the political or fi-

nancial history of the country is concerned. . . . The only recreation allowed was a walk after the evening meal, and a reception at the president's once per quarter.

During the vacations she probably taught summer school, because her first job application cited "seven years teaching experience." Lockwood received her B.S. degree in June 1857.

Lockwood had become very indignant upon learning early in her career that male teachers were paid twice as much as women for the same work. She protested to the school trustees, but even the wife of the Methodist minister refused to take her part. "I can't help you; you cannot help yourself. . . . [I]t is the way of the world," she had told the young widow. While at Genesee, Belva heard *Susan B. Anthony speak at the teachers' institute. Anthony made a strong impression on her. "She was trying to gain for women teachers places with the men on the several committees. She would arise in the meetings amid cutting silence and move that such a woman be appointed on the ways and means committee. . . . I always seconded her motions."

> *My cause was the cause of thousands of women. I pushed forward when I could and retreated when I had to, but always returned to the attack.*
>
> —Belva Ann Lockwood

After graduation, Lockwood accepted a position as "preceptress" of the Lockport Union School, where her daughter was able to enroll as a student, as did a younger sister. In addition to teaching courses in higher mathematics, logic, rhetoric, and botany, she added skating, gymnastics, nature walks, and public speaking, to the amazement of the more conservative of her patrons. In 1860, she offered her ideas on "The Life School" before a convention of teachers in Niagara Falls.

During the Civil War, Lockwood served as president of the Lockport Ladies Aid, supervising the sewing of hickory blouses, cotton flannel shirts and other gear for the New York Volunteers. She stayed at Lockport Union four years, then moved on to other female seminaries in Gainesville, Hornellsville, and Oswego, New York. Finally, in 1866, she moved to Washington, D.C., where she opened her own school, one of the earliest private co-educational schools in the district, assisted by her daughter Lura. There she became involved in peace and suffrage meetings at the Union League Hall, where she conducted her school. On March 11, 1868, Belva, 37, married Dr. Ezekiel Lockwood, 65, a dentist who had served as chaplain of the 2nd D.C. Volunteer Infantry in the war, and who shared her liberal views. Their daughter Jessie was born the following year, but died at the age of 18 months.

Ezekiel encouraged his wife to pursue her interest in the study of law. After graduating from Genesee, she had taken a few classes in law, and had become increasingly interested in the issues being debated in the nation's capital while living there. In October 1869, she applied to Columbia, but it would be two years before she finally gained admission to a law school. Meanwhile, her husband had taken over the administration of the school, leaving her free for her next endeavor: support for a law to give female federal workers the same pay as men for the same work. In 1870, she attended the conventions of the National and the American Woman Suffrage Associations to collect signatures for a petition to pass such a bill. Belva Lockwood's relations with the mainstream suffrage movement were always fragile at best. "*Lucy Stone would not help me," she later recalled, "because the proposition did not come from Boston." Susan B. Anthony, *Elizabeth Cady Stanton, and other women in the National were more supportive, however, and Lockwood collected about 150 signatures there. With the assistance of Rep. S.M. Arnell of Tennessee, chair of the House Committee on Education, she saw the bill passed into law in 1872. In January 1871, she had also presented a testimonial to the U.S. Senate on the right of women to vote, but she came to believe that the best way to win woman suffrage was through a series of "practical" steps toward equality, such as her equal-pay bill. This attitude did not endear her to the suffrage leaders.

Of the 15 women admitted to the National University Law School, only two completed the course of study. During the last quarter, they were barred from attending lectures altogether. The men did not want women present at graduation, their names did not appear on the list of graduates, and it seemed that they were not going to receive their diplomas at all. On September 3, 1873, Belva Lockwood undertook to write to President Grant, who was by virtue of his office also president of the National University:

> You are, or you are not the President of the National University Law School. If you are its President I wish to say to you that I have been passed through the curriculum of study of that school, and am entitled to, and demand my Diploma. If you are not its President then I ask you to take your name from its papers and not hold out to the world to be what you are not.

Though she did not receive an answer, she soon received the diploma, duly signed by Grant and the faculty. On September 24, she was admitted to the District Bar, and five days later filed papers in her first case. In many ways it was typical of what was to come. She was bringing a bill of divorce for a woman who charged her husband with drunkenness, cruel treatment, and refusal to support. She won a divorce decree and alimony with costs. However, the husband refused to pay. "The judge told me there was no law to make him pay. . . . I told him there was and I showed him I could issue a *ne exeat*." Ahead lay a long career of fighting for oppressed women and challenging court decisions.

Lockwood made a specialty of claims. One of her earliest successes was to obtain a sailors' bonus bill from Congress. However, she had only been working a few short months when one of her cases was carried before the U.S. Court of Claims. She applied for admission to that Court. Her application was denied, first on the grounds that she was a woman, and then because she was a married woman "who might conceivably misapply the funds of a client, and under the common law her husband might be sued for the wrong she had committed as an attorney." (This argument had also been used to try to prevent *Myra Bradwell from practicing law.)

Lockwood petitioned Congress to prohibit qualified women from being debarred from federal courts, citing Queen *Victoria as a precedent, and stating that "the right to practice law" was "one of the privileges of citizenship." While her petition was being considered by the Senate Committee on the Judiciary, she also applied for admission to the Supreme Court in October 1876. Chief Justice Morrison I. Waite read their decision that "the Court does not feel called upon to make a change until such a change is required by statute." She then drafted such a statute, which became HR 1077, providing for the admission to practice before the Supreme Court of the United States any woman who had been admitted to the highest court in any state, territory, or the District of Columbia for three years.

Despite the death of her husband on April 23, 1877, Belva Lockwood continued to lobby Congress month after month. In February 1878, Rep. Bill Butler, a supporter of the rights of labor and women, reported favorably on HR 1077, and it passed comfortably. It was then referred to the Judiciary Committee of the Senate,

Belva Ann Lockwood

which determined that the Supreme Court was entitled to make its own rules admitting persons to practice, and recommended an indefinite postponement. However, Senator Aaron A. Sargent, a shrewd and energetic politician, asked that the bill be placed on the calendar. In April 1878, Lockwood presented her petition, signed by 155 D.C. lawyers. The bill was referred back to committee, and amended to state that "no person should be excluded from practicing as an attorney and counsellor at law from any court of the United States on account of sex."

After prolonged maneuvers, the bill was finally brought to debate on the floor in early February 1879. Sargent urged a vote: "In this land man has ceased to dominate over his fellow—let him cease to dominate over his sister." Senator George F. Hoar of Massachusetts, another defender of women's rights, used the argument not that it would benefit women, but that it was a bill to assure U.S. citizens the right to select their counsel. He even invoked Shakespeare: "If Portia herself were alive," he exclaimed, "she could not defend the opinion she had given before the Supreme Court of the United States." The bill passed February 7, and Belva Lockwood went to the White House in the evening to be congratulated by *Lucy Webb Hayes. On March 3, Lockwood was admitted to the bar of the U.S. Supreme Court, and on March 6 to the U.S. Court of Claims. A year later, on February 2, 1880, she once again appeared before Justice Waite, with a motion to admit to practice Mr. Samuel R. Lowery, the first Southern African-American to pass the bar of the Supreme Court.

Winning a landmark victory did not put an end to Lockwood's pioneering spirit. She bought a 20-room house at 619 F Street, N.W., in Washington where she would live for nearly 40 years. The office of Belva Ann Lockwood, Attorney and Solicitor, was on the ground floor. She took every type of case, from assault to murder, land and patent cases, divorce and probate; she worked to overturn English common law to win for widows property rights and guardianship of their children. She continued to specialize, however, in back pay claims and pension cases.

In 1880, she spoke to the platform committee of the Republican National Convention to urge them to adopt a woman suffrage plank. She lobbied to have matrons employed in D.C. jails and police stations. She made applications to be sent abroad as a U.S. consul, but despite her study of international law and the consular manual, she was refused. She rode a large English tricycle all over town, causing a sensation wherever she went.

Her most remarkable breakthrough, however, was her campaign as candidate for president of the United States. *Victoria Woodhull had run for the presidency in 1872 on the Equal Rights ticket with Frederick Douglass, the black abolitionist leader, but she was in jail on election day on a charge of sending obscene material through the mail. Lockwood had spoken for Woodhull at Cooper Union in New York, but later had campaigned in the south for Horace Greeley, the liberal Republican candidate.

In 1884, Lockwood failed once again to get the Resolutions committee at the Republican Convention to support woman suffrage, and was chagrined that Stanton and Anthony were advising women to support the Republican candidate, James G. Blaine. Lockwood wrote a letter to the *Woman's Herald of Industry,* published in California by **Marietta L.B. Snow**, who pioneered innovations in dress, diet, and the use of electricity to cure problems of mobility. Lockwood asked simply:

> Why not nominate women for important places? Is not Victoria Empress of India. . .If women in the States are not permitted to vote, there is no law against their being voted for. . . . We shall never have rights until we take them, nor respect until we command it. Reforms are slow, but they never go backward.

Lockwood was enthusiastically nominated at a meeting of the Equal Rights Party of the Pacific Slope in San Francisco, with Snow as her running-mate. Their platform supported equal opportunity for women to seek public office, uniform marriage and divorce laws, citizenship for Native Americans, temperance, and peace. Other "third-party" candidates that year included John P. St. John, representing the Prohibition Party, and General Benjamin F. Butler, representing Labor. The Democrats had nominated Grover Cleveland, whose embarrassment of the party over an illegitimate son caused some to support Lockwood as one who would "bring no blush or barnacles or youthful, or mature wild oats sowing."

Nevertheless, Lockwood's candidacy was subject to a certain amount of ridicule. Men, dressed in poke bonnets and Mother Hubbard dresses, formed "broom brigades." The suffrage leadership criticized her for subjecting the woman suffrage movement to "an abundance of odium and contempt at a time when it was commanding respect and enlisting help." Some accused her of seeking publicity to get more business. But Belva Ann Lockwood saw her opportunity to obtain even one vote in the electoral college as "the first practical movement in the history of woman suffrage."

Although women could not vote in national elections, she polled 4,149 votes in six states (less than one-tenth of one percent of the total). In a petition to Congress, she claimed that the electors of the state of Indiana, which had gone to Cleveland, had changed their minds and cast their votes for her. Supporters also claimed that substantial votes in Oregon and Pennsylvania had simply been rejected as false votes. In 1888, she was nominated again by the Equal Rights Party in Iowa, with pacifist Alfred H. Love as their vice-presidential candidate, but the novelty had worn off, and she received little attention. Her nominations, however, led to an increase in her speaking engagements, which she continued into her 80s, bringing in a substantial income not only from the lecture tours, but from new pension claims which she picked up along the way.

In 1887, Lockwood and her daughter, by then married to DeForest Ormes, formed the firm of Belva Ann Lockwood & Co., Attorneys at Law, which lasted until Lura's death in 1894. Lura's husband died soon after, and Lockwood reared her young grandson DeForest, Jr.

Although she continued to work for woman suffrage, especially by lobbying Congress to include woman suffrage in the statehood bills for new states after 1900, Lockwood's campaigns had alienated her somewhat from the mainstream suffrage movement. She continued, however, to attend meetings on women's rights, as well as temperance, labor reform, and, increasingly, world peace. A large room staffed by an attendant on the ground floor of 619 F Street was devoted to a library of books on the subject. An early member of the Universal Peace Union, Lockwood was their delegate to the International Peace Congress in Paris in 1889 and to subsequent ones in London, Milan, Antwerp, Berne, Budapest, and The Hague. She dictated the Sherman Resolution granting the president authority to mediate between two countries on the verge of war. She also served on the nominating committee for the Nobel Peace Prize.

Belva Ann Lockwood's most notable legal case was representing the Eastern Cherokee Indians in a claim against the United States, which had begun in 1835 with a treaty that called for the Cherokees to leave North Carolina, their land to be purchased by the U.S. government. In 1905, she argued before Judge Charles C. Nott, who agreed that the United States had "broken and evaded the letter and spirit of their agreement," but did not award the full amount of interest due, which, after so many years, amounted to several times more than the original purchase price. The case was appealed to the Supreme Court in the following year, where Lockwood, 75, felt she "rose to inspired heights." She won the case, although a disagreement about her fee led to a suit against her which was to leave her financially troubled at the end of her life.

Belva Lockwood never stopped being controversial. In a lengthy newspaper interview in the *New York World* in 1912, she said she had never "devoted much time" to working for suffrage, only for equal rights, "feeling that the ballot would naturally follow." She thought that along with equal rights, women should be given equal responsibility "to educate and support the family." She criticized the "professional woman suffragists" who, in her opinion, "talk too much." Nevertheless, in 1914 she stood with the leaders of *Alice Paul's Congressional Union on the Capitol steps to present to Congress a resolution calling for woman suffrage.

Belva Ann Lockwood died on May 19, 1917, from "a complication of diseases incident to old age," according to her obituary in the *Evening Star*, and was buried in the Congressional Cemetery in Washington, D.C. Her last public speech had been in 1916, to support President Woodrow Wilson, during whose administration the Equal Suffrage Amendment would finally be signed into law.

SOURCES:

Proctor, John Clagett. "Belva Ann Lockwood: The Only Woman Candidate for President of the United States," in *Records*. Vol XXXV–XXXVI. Columbia Historical Society of Washington, D.C., 1935, p. 192–204.

Stern, Madeleine B. *We, the Women: Career Firsts of 19th Century America*. NY: Schulte, 1963.

Winner, Julia Hull. "Belva A. Lockwood—That Extraordinary Woman," in *New York History*. October 1958, p. 321–339.

COLLECTIONS:

Papers are located in the Peace Collection at Swarthmore College, Swarthmore, Pennsylvania.

Kristie Miller,
author of *Ruth Hanna McCormick: A Life in Politics 1880–1944,*
University of New Mexico Press, 1992

Lockwood, Margaret (1916–1990)

British stage and film actress. Born on September 15, 1916, in Karachi, India (now Pakistan); died in 1990; only daughter and one of two children of Henry Lockwood (a British civil servant) and Margaret Evelyn (Waugh) Lockwood; attended Sydenham Girls' High School; studied acting at the Royal Academy of Dramatic Art; married Rupert W. Leon (a steel broker), around 1937 (divorced 1955): children: Julia Lockwood (b. 1941).

Selected theater: first appeared on stage as a fairy in A Midsummer Night's Dream *(Holborn Empire Theater, 1928); appeared in the pantomime* The Babes in the Wood *(Scala Theater, December 1929); appeared as Myrtle in* House on Fire *("Q" Theater, June 1934), Margaret Hamilton in* Family Affairs *(Ambassadors' Theater, August 1934), Helene Ferber in* Repayment *(Arts Theater, January 1936), Trixie Drew in*

Miss Smith *(Duke of York's Theater, July 1936), Ann Harlow in* Ann's Lapse *("Q" Theater, July 1937); toured as Amanda in* Private Lives *(April 1949); title role in* Peter Pan *(Scala Theater, December 1949 and December 1950); appeared as Eliza Doolittle in* Pygmalion *(Edinburgh Festival, 1951), Clarissa Hailsham-Browne in* Spider's Web *(Savoy Theater, London, December 1954), Dinah Holland in* Subway in the Sky *(Savoy Theater, February 1957); toured as Jane Palmer in* Murder on Arrival *(1958–59); appeared as Sally Seymour in* And Suddenly It's Spring *(Duke of York's Theater, November 1959); toured as Barbara Martin in* Milk and Honey *(February 1961); appeared as Sally Thomas in* Signpost to Murder *(Cambridge Theater, February 1962), Caroline in* Every Other Evening *(Phoenix Theater, November 1964), Mrs. Cheveley in* An Ideal Husband *(Garrick Theater, December 1966), Claire Williams in* The Others *(Strand Theater, September 1967), Diane in* On a Foggy Day *(St. Martin's Theater, July 1969), Lady Frederick Berelles in* Lady Frederick *(Vaudeville Theater June 1970); appeared in* Double Edge *(1975).*

Filmgraphy in England, unless otherwise noted: Lorna Doone *(1935);* The Case of Gabriel Perry *(1935);* Some Day *(1935);* Honours Easy *(1935);* Man of the Moment *(1935);* Midshipman Easy *(Men of the Sea, 1935);* Jury's Evidence *(1936);* The Amateur Gentleman *(1936);* The Beloved Vagabond *(1936);* Irish for Luck *(1936);* The Street Singer *(1937);* Who's Your Lady Friend? *(1937);* Dr. Syn *(1937);* Melody and Romance *(1937);* Owd Bob *(To the Victor, 1938);* Bank Holiday *(Three on a Weekend, 1938);* The Lady Vanishes *(1938);* A Girl Must Live *(1939);* Susannah of the Mounties *(US, 1939);* Rulers of the Sea *(US, 1939);* The Stars Look Down *(1940);* Night Train to Munich *(Night Train, 1940);* The Girl in the News *(1940);* Quiet Wedding *(1941);* Alibi *(1942);* The Man in Grey *(1943);* Dear Octopus *(The Randolph Family, 1943);* Give Us the Moon *(1944);* Love Story *(A Lady Surrenders, 1944);* A Place of One's Own *(1945);* I'll Be Your Sweetheart *(1945);* The Wicked Lady *(1945);* Bedelia *(1946);* Hungry Hill *(1946);* Jassy *(1947);* The White Unicorn *(Bad Sister, 1947);* Look Before You Love *(1948);* Cardboard Cavalier *(1949);* Madness of the Heart *(1949);* Highly Dangerous *(1950);* Trent's Last Case *(1953);* Laughing Anne *(1953);* Trouble in the Glen *(1954);* Cast a Dark Shadow *(1955);* The Slipper and the Rose *(1976).*

The daughter of **Margaret Evelyn Lockwood** and Henry Lockwood, a British civil servant serving in India, actress Margaret Lockwood was born in 1916 in Karachi, but spent most of her childhood in a London suburb where she lived with an aunt while attending school. At an early age, she decided on a career in the theater and was enrolled at the famous training school conducted by Italia Conti, who also taught Noel Coward, Brian Aherne, *****Gertrude Lawrence**, and other notable actors. She made her stage debut at 12, playing a fairy in *A Midsummer Night's Dream* at the Holborn Empire Theater in London. The next year, she played in the Christmas pantomime *Babes in the Wood* at the Scala. After high school, she enrolled at the Royal Academy of Dramatic Art.

Lockwood made a successful West End debut in *Family Affair* (1934), which led to her first film role in *Lorna Doone* (1935). Between 1934 and 1935, she made five more films and rose to "leading lady" status in *The Amateur Gentleman* (1936) and *The Beloved Vagabond* (1936). Notable among her films of the late-1930s was *The Lady Vanishes* (1938), made under the auspices of the British studios of Twentieth-Century Fox, which subsequently brought Lockwood to Hollywood, casting her with Randolph Scott and *****Shirley Temple (Black)** in *Susannah of the Mounties* (1939). "I didn't know what I was supposed to do," she later said of the shoot, in which she appeared to be miscast. Her second American film, *Rulers of the Sea* (1939), with Douglas Fairbanks, Jr., proved to be an equally dismal experience.

Returning to England, Lockwood's popularity soared during the 1940s. She was particularly successful in unsympathetic roles, especially those opposite actor James Mason in *Alibi* (1942) and *The Man in Grey* (1943). With her third picture with Mason, *The Wicked Lady*, the actress won the first of her three "Silver Star" awards as the most popular screen actress of the year. The award, which was established by the London *Daily Mail* in 1946 to commemorate the newspaper's jubilee year, was presented to Lockwood again in 1947 and 1948. With the success of her performance in *The Wicked Lady*, the actress went on to play a succession of malevolent femme fatale roles, until she finally declared she was "tired of being a wicked lady" and wanted to do something comic for a change.

Unfortunately, Lockwood was not as adept in lighter fare. *Look Before You Love* (1948), in which she played a blind girl whose husband's ex-fiancée keeps trying to murder her, has been ranked by at least one critic as the worst film of its year. As *****Nell Gwynn** in *Cardboard Cavalier* (1949), a role she strongly petitioned for, she was well meaning but unconvincing. With her film career waning, she dissolved her long-standing contract with J. Arthur Rank and signed a two-year contract with Herbert Wilcox, who had been producing successful vehicles for his wife *Anna Neagle. Wilcox, however, failed to ignite interest in Lockwood, and her final effort was a dreary independent film, *Cast a Dark Shadow* (1955).

Meanwhile, Lockwood was reclaiming her stage career, notably in a tour of *Private Lives* in 1949 and an appearance as Peter Pan that same year. Subsequently, she performed in a string of plays, including *Spider's Web* (1954), *Subway in the Sky* (1957), *And Suddenly It's Spring* (1959), *An Ideal Husband* (1966), and the suspense thriller *Double Edge* (1975). She was also seen as a barrister in the "Justice" television series and in her own successful series, "The Flying Swan." She returned to films briefly in 1976, playing the wicked stepmother in a musical version of Cinderella, *The Slipper and the Rose.*

In her heyday a petite raven-haired beauty, Lockwood was sometimes compared physically to *Joan Bennett. She was married to a London steel broker, Rupert Leon, with whom she had one daughter Margaret Julia Leon, known as "Toots," who made her screen debut with her mother in *Bad Sister* (1947) and went on to a successful film career of her own as **Julia Lockwood**. Divorced in 1955, Lockwood spent her later years living quietly in a small suburban house at Kingston-upon-Thames, Surrey. The actress died in 1990.

SOURCES:
Current Biography. NY: H.W. Wilson, 1948.
Katz, Ephraim. *The Film Encyclopedia.* NY: Harper-Collins, 1994.
Shipman, David. *The Great Movie Stars: The Golden Years.* Boston: Little, Brown, 1995.

SUGGESTED READING:
Lockwood, Margaret. *Lucky Star* (autobiography), 1955.

Barbara Morgan,
Melrose, Massachusetts

Locusta (fl. 54 CE)

Roman poisoner. Name variations: Lucusta. Flourished around 54 CE; executed in 68 or 69 CE; said to be of Gallic origin.

Locusta was a professional poisoner living in Rome around 54 CE. Juvenal speaks of her as the means for ridding wives of unwanted husbands, while Tacitus claims she was "long reckoned as among the instruments of government." Locusta was employed by *Agrippina the Younger to prepare poison for the emperor Claudius. For providing Nero with his own supply of poison in a golden casket and aiding in his schemes against Britannicus, Locusta was richly rewarded with estates. She was executed under orders of Galba in 68 or 69, during his reign.

Loden, Barbara (1934–1980)

American actress and film director. Name variations: Barbara Loden Kazan. Born Barbara Ann Loden in Asheville, North Carolina, in 1934; died of cancer in New York City on September 5, 1980; daughter of George T. Loden and Ruth (Nanney) Loden; attended local schools; married film producer Laurence Joachim (divorced); became second wife of Elia Kazan (the director), in 1967; children: (first marriage) Leo Alexander Joachim; Jon Marco Joachim.

Describing herself as a "hill-billy's daughter," Barbara Loden was born in 1934 in Asheville, North Carolina, and grew up in the poverty of the Appalachians. She later called her childhood "desperate," a time she spent fantasizing about the good things that might happen to her some day. A *Marilyn Monroe look-alike by age 16, Loden escaped to New York, where she took jobs modeling for detective stories and romance magazines, and danced in the chorus line at the Copacabana nightclub. Eventually, she started playing minor parts in the films of Elia Kazan, including *Wild River* (1960) and *Splendor in the Grass* (1961), and from 1960 to 1964 was a member the Lincoln Center Repertory. Her break came when Kazan, with whom she was having an affair, cast her as Maggie in Arthur Miller's *After the Fall* (1964), a character based on Miller's wife Marilyn Monroe. Loden won a Tony Award for her stunning performance and was, by all accounts, headed for stardom. She shunned opportunities, however, turning down script after script and distancing herself from the theater scene. "I didn't enjoy the fame and sort of became a recluse," she said. "I had two sons to raise, and acting just seemed rather unimportant compared with life."

In 1967, after divorcing her husband, film producer Laurence Joachim, Loden married Kazan, who had also been married at the time of their affair. (His first wife **Molly Day Thatcher** died in 1963.) In his autobiography, *Elia Kazan: A Life*, Kazan took most of the credit for Loden's success on the stage. "There was a naked truth in her acting that we rarely see," he wrote. "I knew I'd made this possible by giving her confidence in her talent, encouraging her boldness, bringing her to Miller and urging him to accept her. So I was pleased."

In 1971, Loden resurfaced from her self-imposed retirement as the producer, director, and star of *Wanda*, an extraordinary film about a woman from the Appalachian coal-country of her own childhood. In reviewing the film, critic Rex Reed described it as:

> a portrait of people for whom nothing ever happens, in which Miss Loden is simply brilliant as an ignorant [woman] from the coal mines of Appalachia who does nothing, thinks nothing, gives up her children to a judge because they'll be better off, and heads down the highway toward a depressing encounter with a bank robber and ends up with an empty life of greasy hamburgers eaten in lonely motel rooms and a future blank and gray as a mortuary slab.

Loden had originally asked Kazan to direct her in the film, but he had no interest in the project and encouraged her to direct it. Assisted by her friend Nicholas Proferes, who helped her craft the screenplay and encouraged her to direct it, Loden embarked on the project with a tiny budget of $100,000, a three-person crew, and only two professional actors. Shooting in 16mm (blown up to 35mm), she worked in a European cinema verité style. "I know *Wanda* is crude," she told Reed, "but I wanted to make an anti-movie, to present a story without manipulating the audience and telling them what their responses should be. To do that you have to take chances and you can't depend on anyone else."

The film not only won a number of awards, including the International Critics Prize at the 1970 Venice Film Festival, but sparked a storm of controversy as to whether it was profeminist or antifeminist in intent. Loden insisted that the film had nothing to do with the women's movement, which was just becoming a media obsession around the time she finished shooting. "It was really about the oppression of women, of people," she said in an attempt to clarify her theme. But debate only escalated, eventually diminishing Loden's image as a pioneering filmmaker. One misguided reviewer suggested that the only films worth viewing were those about women achieving and setting examples. "Those are the people who wouldn't want me to exist," Loden said, "and they would say that I was not valid or that I shouldn't be heard." Loden's debut film also served as her swan song. Although she was eager to tackle additional projects exploring the neglected side of American life, she was stricken with breast cancer and died at the age of 46.

SOURCES:
Acker, Ally. *Reel Women*. NY: Continuum, 1991.
Butterfield, Marni. "After A Long Silence, Barbara Loden Speaks on Film," in *Show*. July 1971, pp. 39–41.

Barbara Morgan,
Melrose, Massachusetts

Loeb, Sophie Irene (1876–1929)

Russian-born journalist and welfare worker. Born Sophie Irene Simon in Rovno, Russia, on July 4, 1876; died in New York City on January 18, 1929; oldest of three daughters and three sons of Samuel Simon (a jeweler) and Mary (Carey) Simon; graduated from McKeesport High School, McKeesport, Pennsylvania; married Anselm Loeb (a merchant), on March 10, 1896 (divorced 1910); no children.

Born in 1876, Sophie Loeb was one of six children of a Russian-Jewish family who immigrated to the United States in 1882 and settled in McKeesport, Pennsylvania. Sophie's father, a jeweler, died when she was 16, and it became necessary for her to hold a part-time job while finishing high school. She worked briefly as a grade-school teacher before her marriage in 1896 to Anselm Loeb, an older man who was also the proprietor of the store in which she had worked. Over the next 14 years, Sophie's interest in various social causes blossomed, and she began writing articles about the industrial unrest in McKeesport and sending them off to the New York *Evening World* and other newspapers.

In 1910, having grown apart from her husband, Sophie obtained a divorce and moved to New York City, where she became a reporter and feature writer for the *Evening World*. In the course of her reporting duties, she became particularly interested in the plight of impoverished widows who were forced to give up their children for adoption because they could no longer support them. Feeling strongly that families would benefit by remaining together, as her own had done after the death of her father, she used her column both to expose the problem and to promote the work of advocates like **Hannah Bachman Einstein,** who was seeking public support of mothers' pensions, which would help widows keep their families intact. In 1913, Sophie and Hannah Einstein were appointed to the newly created State Commission of Relief for Widowed Mothers. Under the auspices of the commission, Loeb traveled to England, Scotland, France, Switzerland, German, and Denmark to study their welfare laws, and, in the commission's report in 1914, she proposed a bill for a state-supported relief program for impoverished widows with children. Although originally defeated by one senatorial vote, the bill passed in 1915. The legislation authorized both a child welfare board in every county and the use of public money to support its work. The same year, Loeb was appointed to the child welfare board of New York. Shortly thereafter, she became the board's president, a position she held until 1923. The board not only increased the city's annual appropriations (from $100,000 to over $4,500,000 in a seven-year period) under her leadership, but kept its own administrative expenses in check. Loeb prevented any political influence in the board's grants by enlisting social workers as case investigators.

In 1920, Loeb served on the commission appointed by Governor Alfred E. Smith to codify the laws in the field of child welfare. Hoping to promote welfare legislation across the country, Loeb also published *Everyman's Child* (1920), and, in 1924, founded and became president of the Child Welfare Committee of America. In 1925, Loeb addressed the First International Congress on Child Welfare at Geneva, which later accepted her resolution in favor of keeping children with their families and out of institutions. In 1927, Loeb submitted a report on the care of blind children to the League of Nations.

Loeb's interests were by no means confined to child welfare. She spearheaded a probe into reports of corruption in the New York Public Service Commission in 1916, and worked for a broad spectrum of other reforms, including cheaper school lunches, lower gas rates in Brooklyn, cheaper and safer taxi cabs, health and safety regulations for movie theaters, and maternity care for indigent mothers. In 1917, Loeb settled a New York City taxi strike in a record seven hours.

Sophie Loeb refused compensation for her public service and earned only around $10,000 a year from her job at the newspaper and various outside writing and speaking engagements. In 1925, while on assignment covering the settlements in Palestine, she became a Zionist; she later donated the royalties of a resultant book, *Palestine Awake: The Rebirth of a Nation* (1926), to the Palestine Fund. Loeb succumbed to cancer at the age of 52. She was buried at Mount Hope Cemetery in Westchester Hills, New York, her gravestone carrying her favorite motto: "Not charity, but a chance for every child." A marble children's fountain in Central Park, donated by philanthropist August Heckscher in her memory, was dedicated in 1936.

SOURCES:

James, Edward T., *Notable American Women 1607–1950*. Cambridge, MA: The Belknap Press of Harvard University Press, 1971.

McHenry, Robert. *Famous American Women*. NY: Dover, 1983.

Barbara Morgan,
Melrose, Massachusetts

Loebinger, Lotte (1905—)

German actress who had a long and successful career on the stage and survived the great upheavals of the 20th century. Name variations: Charlotte Loebinger; Lotte Wehner-Loebinger (used in USSR and preferred by Loebinger even after her 1952 divorce); Lotte Loebinger-Wehner. Born on October 10, 1905, in Kattowitz, Upper Silesia, Germany (now Katowice, Poland); daughter of a physician; sister, Traute; married Herbert Wehner, in June 1927; children: one daughter.

In 1905, Lotte Loebinger was born, the daughter of a bourgeois physician, in Kattowitz, Upper Silesia. The privations of World War I and her father's death at the end of that conflict brought considerable changes to her family's circumstances. In 1920, Lotte moved with her mother and sister to Kiel, Schleswig-Holstein, where she began to work as a kindergarten teacher before switching to a job in retail sales. Secretly, she took lessons in elocution, hoping one day to become an actress. Lotte's older sister Traute, who had become an ardent member of the German Communist Party (KPD), persuaded her to join the *Rote Hilfe* organization, a KPD auxiliary which rendered assistance to political prisoners and other foes of the German capitalist state and society. Lotte's acting aspirations found at least a partial outlet when she began to participate in KPD agitprop (agitation and propaganda) activities, which included acting in impromptu plays and other forms of guerilla theater. In 1925, she set the basic direction of the remainder of her life when she joined the KPD, accepting its ideology and discipline. The same year, she began her acting career with a theater engagement in Breslau, Lower Silesia (now Wroclaw, Poland). Her performance was a success and soon brought her to Berlin.

There, she came to the attention of one of Germany's most innovative stage directors, Erwin Piscator. Working with him, Loebinger was an apprentice at the Volksbühne (People's Stage) where fellow apprentices were Heinrich Greif and **Steffie Spira**, actors who were also destined for distinguished careers. By 1929, Loebinger had become a highly regarded member of

Piscator's ensemble, and for several years she toured Germany and Switzerland in Carl Crede's play *Paragraph 218* (Women in Distress), a powerful attack on the German law that criminalized abortions. In 1931, Loebinger traveled to the Soviet Union, where she participated in Piscator's plan to make a motion picture based on the bestselling novel by *Anna Seghers, *Der Aufstand der Fischer von St. Barbara* (The Revolt of the Fishermen of St. Barbara). There, she experienced the energies of a society in rapid change, while also being struck by its poverty, inefficiency, and the growing tendency of the Stalin dictatorship to stifle artistic creativity. But for Loebinger and her contemporaries in the theater, the enemy in the early 1930s was not Stalinist repression but the growing Nazi movement in Germany.

Back in Berlin, Loebinger continued to act in various theaters, earning critical plaudits. In her spare hours, she engaged in lively political debates and worked to create a coalition of actors from various political backgrounds in order to more effectively combat fascism. During this period, she often appeared on stage as a member of a non-socialist actors' collective, the Spielgemeinschaft Berliner Schauspieler (Performance Collective of Berlin Actors). Due to her marriage in June 1927 to Herbert Wehner, a Dresden-born KPD functionary, she was close to the center of KPD politics on the eve of the Nazi takeover. Almost from the start of their marriage, however, Loebinger did not live with her husband whose Communist activities, centered in Dresden, took up virtually all of his time and energy. In 1929, Wehner began living with **Charlotte Treuber**, and his marriage to Loebinger became no more than a matter of document. In 1937, they would meet for a final time in Moscow's Club for Foreign Workers. Frightened by the purges then underway, Wehner tore up a picture of himself that Loebinger had continued to display. He also requested from her a gold brooch that she had been given by her mother, in order to use the gold to replace the Soviet nickel metal in his dental fillings, thus eliminating all evidence that he had lived in the Soviet Union before his return to the capitalist West. Their marriage would not officially end until its termination by a civil court in Hamburg during November 1952.

In December 1933, Loebinger fled Nazi Germany to Poland, from which she was soon expelled as an undesirable foreigner. After a brief time in Czechoslovakia, she immigrated to the Soviet Union, where she first found work as a member of Gustav von Wangenheim's German theater troupe "Kolonne Links" (Column Left), a Moscow-based ensemble composed of emigré agitprop performers. In 1936, she collaborated with von Wangenheim to produce the anti-fascist motion picture *Kämpfer* (Those Who Struggle). In Moscow, she met a German refugee physician with whom she had a daughter, but within a few years he was arrested in the purges and died in a Gulag camp. Loebinger supported herself and her daughter by working as a German-language announcer in the foreign branch of Radio Moscow, where along with Heinrich Greif and Maxim Vallentin she became one of the best known among the personalities personifying "the good Germans." Loebinger was also active as a reader of German literature at meetings, and she taught the German language to some of her Russian comrades. Occasionally, she performed as an actress on the radio, as in 1940 when she took a role in the Johann Strauss, Jr., operetta *Eine Nacht in Venedig* (A Night in Venice). Unlike many of her fellow German exiles, Loebinger was not imprisoned in the Gulag. Herbert Wehner too was fortunate. He was sent on a mission to wartime Sweden, where in 1942 he would be expelled from the KPD. Wehner was able to recreate a life in politics, becoming one of the most influential Social Democratic leaders in postwar West Germany.

In 1945, Loebinger was among the first of the Soviet-based German emigrés to return to a war-shattered Berlin. In 1945–1946, she appeared on stage at the Deutsches Theater in several plays and also was featured in the first post-Nazi films made in occupied Germany. From 1947 through 1950, she appeared at several different theaters in Soviet-controlled East Berlin. Starting in 1952, and continuing well into the 1970s, she was one of the featured actresses of East Berlin's Maxim Gorki Theater, which produced mostly Russian and Soviet plays. In these, Loebinger customarily took the roles of warm-hearted maternal personalities, and she became one of the favorite actresses of East Berlin theatergoers. By the end of her career at the Maxim Gorki Theater, Loebinger had more than 60 roles in her repertoire. She also served occasionally as a director, mainly producing the Soviet plays she had come to cherish during her years in Moscow. In 1975, she was honored with a commemorative article in the Socialist Unity Party (SED) newspaper *Neues Deutschland*, which congratulated her on several achievements that year, including her 70th birthday, the 50th anniversary of her having become a member of "the Party of the Working Class [KPD, later SED]," and her 50 years of work in the theater.

In her last years as an actress, Loebinger made appearances in two GDR television films, both directed by Thomas Langhoff, "Ich will nicht leise sterben" (I Will Not Die Quietly), and "Guten Morgen, du Schöne" (Good Morning, Beautiful Lady). On October 10, 1995, having survived governments, purges, wars, friends, and foes, she celebrated her 90th birthday in Berlin.

SOURCES:

Diezel, Peter. *Exiltheater in der Sowjetunion, 1932–1937.* Berlin: Henschelverlag Kunst und Gesellschaft, 1978.

Haarmann, Hermann *et al. Das "Engels" Projekt: Ein antifaschistisches Theater deutscher Emigranten in der UdSSR (1936–1941).* Worms: Georg Heintz, 1975.

Freudenhammer, A. and K. Vater. *Herbert Wehner: Ein Leben mit der Deutschen Frage.* Munich: C. Bertelsmann Verlag, 1978.

Loebinger, Lotte. "Ich war Wehners erste Frau," in *Bild am Sonntag.* June 24, 1990, pp. 4–5.

"Lotte Loebinger," in *Theater der Zeit,* Vol. 50, no. 6. November–December, 1995, p. 103.

Pike, David. *German Writers in Soviet Exile, 1933–1945.* Chapel Hill, NC: University of North Carolina Press, 1982.

Thompson, Wayne C. *The Political Odyssey of Herbert Wehner.* Boulder, CO: Westview Press, 1993.

John Haag,
Associate Professor of History,
University of Georgia, Athens, Georgia

Loewenstein, Helga Maria zu (b. 1910).

See Löwenstein, Helga Maria zu.

Loftus, Cissie (1876–1943)

Scottish actress and impersonator. Name variations: Marie Cecilia Loftus; Marie Cecilia McCarthy. Born Marie Cecilia Brown on October 22, 1876, in Glasgow, Scotland; died of a heart attack on July 12, 1943, in New York City; daughter of Marie Loftus (1857–1940, a Scottish music-hall singer) and Ben Brown (an actor in a minstrel show); educated at the Convent of the Holy Child in Blackpool, England; married Justin Huntly McCarthy (a writer), on August 29, 1894 (divorced 1899); married Alonzo Higbee Waterman (a physician), on June 9, 1909 (divorced); children (second marriage): Peter John Barrie Waterman.

Made stage debut in Belfast, Scotland (October 1892); most significant roles included Viola in Twelfth Night *(1900), Hero in* Much Ado About Nothing *(1900), Katherine in* If I Were King *(1901), Ophelia in* Hamlet, *and the mother in* Three-Cornered Moon *(1933). Films:* East Lynne *(1930s);* The Old Maid *(1930s).*

A gifted impersonator with a vocal range that enabled her to sing soprano, contralto, tenor, or bass, Cissie Loftus was known for her expert mimicry. The multitalented Loftus appeared in vaudeville as well as theater, doing comedy as well as Shakespeare and Ibsen, and she could reproduce the breathing and voice patterns of such 19th- and 20th-century stage personalities as *Sarah Bernhardt and *Ethel Barrymore with such precision that those who saw her were entirely convinced by her impersonations.

Born into a theatrical family in Glasgow, Scotland, on October 22, 1876, Marie Cecilia Brown was the daughter of the world-renowned Scottish music-hall singer *Marie Loftus. Her father, Ben Brown, was part of the minstrel act of Brown, Newland, and LeClerc, who performed for 45 years in a skit called "Black Justice." Cissie Loftus was educated at the Convent of the Holy Child in Blackpool, England. She also attended school at the age of six in Cambridge, Massachusetts, when her mother was on tour in the United States. Loftus took her mother's name when she began her stage career, debuting in Belfast, Scotland, in October 1892 to immediate acclaim for her superb mimicry. In July 1893, she appeared at the Oxford Music Hall in London.

On August 29, 1894, Loftus eloped to Edinburgh with the writer and ex-member of Parliament Justin Huntly McCarthy. McCarthy was the son of the Irish Nationalist party leader Justin McCarthy, who served in the House of Commons. Although both Loftus and McCarthy were Catholic, the marriage was performed in a civil ceremony. The couple divorced in 1899. Loftus was then married on June 9, 1909, to Chicago physician Alonzo Higbee Waterman; they had one son before the marriage ended in divorce.

Performing on the American stage for the first time on January 21, 1895, Loftus appeared in vaudeville at Koster and Bial's Music Hall in New York. From then on, she crossed the Atlantic many times, alternating appearances in England and America and switching from variety roles to traditional theatrical performances. She was often torn between her

Cissie Loftus

own ambition as a serious actress and the demands of her music-hall audience. As a member of *Helena Modjeska's company, she played her most memorable dramatic roles between 1900 and 1906. Her Shakespearean performances included Viola in *Twelfth Night*, Hero in *Much Ado About Nothing* (both in 1900), and Ophelia in *Hamlet*. In 1901, she appeared as Katherine in *If I Were King*, under the direction of Daniel Frohman, a part written for her by her first husband. In 1902, she appeared in London as Marguerite in *Faust*, and also in another of McCarthy's plays, *The Proud Prince*. One of her greatest triumphs was her Peter Pan in London, December 1905.

By 1905, the always frail Loftus began to show signs of ill health and stress and may have been in the early stages of narcotics addiction. She argued with managers and became unreliable, dropping out of productions, losing her voice, and withdrawing from bookings. Rumors circulated that she had drowned or had been involved in suicide attempts disguised as accidents. By 1915, her stage career was all but behind her. In 1922, she was indicted on a narcotics charge. Her attorneys argued that her addiction was the result of a nurse's carelessness in administering medication during Loftus' illness, and a number of loyal theater friends continued to support her. Many of the stage personalities she had at one time or another impersonated—*Nora Bayes, Laura Hope Crews, *Jeanne Eagels, and John McCormack—helped Loftus revive her sinking career. In 1923, she enjoyed a brief success in vaudeville at the prestigious Palace Theater in New York. Still in poor health, however, as she would be for the rest of her life, she was forced to end her engagement after a few weeks.

After a brief foray into film acting during the 1930s, including parts in the movies *East Lynne* and *The Old Maid*, Loftus made another comeback. Her performance in a Broadway comedy, *Three-Cornered Moon*, brought accolades in 1933. In 1938, she returned to New York for a final series of impersonations of contemporary Broadway performers and stage personalities from the past. The critic Alexander Woollcott called it one of the century's greatest theatrical performances, and so she left the theater world as she had entered it, widely acclaimed for her gift of mimicry. On July 12, 1943, Loftus died of a heart attack in New York at the Hotel Lincoln. She was buried at Kensico Cemetery in Valhalla, New York, following a funeral service at the Little Church around the Corner, an Episcopal church long popular with Broadway actors.

SOURCES:

James, Edward T., ed. *Notable American Women 1607–1950*. Cambridge, MA: The Belknap Press of Harvard University Press, 1971.

Lolly Ockerstrom,
freelance writer, Washington, D.C.

Loftus, Marie (1857–1940)

Scottish music-hall star. Born in Glasgow, Scotland, in 1857; died in 1940; married Ben Brown (an actor in a minstrel show); children: Marie Cecilia Brown (1876–1943, who performed as Cissie Loftus).

A music-hall luminary known as "the *Sarah Bernhardt of the Halls," Marie Loftus often appeared as a principal boy, always stunningly dressed. She made her debut in Glasgow in 1874, and her London debut in Oxford in 1877, then had a successful tour in South Africa and America. In 1892, Marie was involved with the Drury Lane all-star pantomime which included *Marie Lloyd, Ada Blanche, Dan Leno, Herbert Campbell, and **Mabel Love**. Marie Loftus was the mother of *Cissie Loftus.

Logan, Ella (1913–1969)

Scottish-born singer-actress. Born Ella Allan on March 6, 1913, in Glasgow, Scotland; died on May 1, 1969, in Burlingame, California; married Fred Finkelhoffe (a playwright and producer), in 1952 (divorced 1956); children: one daughter.

Ella Logan will forever be remembered as the charming Sharon McLonergan in the long-running Broadway show *Finian's Rainbow*, in which she introduced a number of songs that went on to become standards, including the lilting "How Are Things in Gloccamorra?," now always associated with her. Although Logan reached her zenith in *Finian's Rainbow*, her career began many years before on the stage of the Grand Theater in Paisley, Scotland, where, at age three, her rendering of "A Perfect Day" stopped the show.

Ella Logan was born in Glasgow, Scotland, in 1913, into a theatrical family. She toured European music halls during her early career, and in 1928 made her London debut in *Darling, I Love You*. In 1934, she arrived in the United States, appearing on Broadway in *Calling All Stars* with *Judy Canova and **Gertrude Niesen**. Logan went on to make a series of movies, including *Flying Hostess* (1936), *Top of the Town* (1937), *Woman Chases Man* (1937), *42nd Street* (1937), and *Goldwyn Follies* (1938). Concurrently, she also began a recording career, vocalizing with bandleader Abe Lyman, among others. In 1939, Logan returned to Broadway in *George White Scandals*, the last of that producer's famous shows. She later performed in *Sons O'Fun* (1941) and the vaudeville revue *Show Time* (1942).

After a stint entertaining the Allied troops during World War II, Logan returned to Broadway in *Finian's Rainbow*, which also introduced such hit songs as "Old Devil Moon," "If This Isn't Love," "Look to the Rainbow," and "When I'm Not Near the Girl I Love." While the show was a huge success, running for 725 performance, it turned out to be Logan's last Broadway appearance. She subsequently performed in nightclubs and on television, but the closest she ever came to Broadway again was in the ill-fated show *Kelly*; she left before it reached New York, and it closed after only a single performance. Logan was married for four years to playwright and producer Fred Finkelhoffe, with whom she had a daughter. They divorced in 1956. The singer-actress, who had homes in New York and Los Angeles, died of cancer in 1969, age 56.

SOURCES:

Clarke, Donald. *The Penguin Encyclopedia of Popular Music.* London: Viking, 1989.

Lamparski, Richard. *Whatever Became of . . . ?* 1st and 2nd ed. NY: Crown.

Barbara Morgan,
Melrose, Massachusetts

Lohman, Ann Trow (1812–1878)

American abortionist, dispenser of contraceptives, and operator of a clandestine maternity hospital and adoption agency. Name variations: Madame Restell. Born in 1812 in Painswick, Gloucestershire, England; committed suicide on April 1, 1878, in New York City; married tailor Henry Summers, in 1828 (died 1833); married newspaper compositor turned quack physician Charles R. Lohman, in 1836 (died 1876); children: (first marriage) stepdaughter Caroline Summers.

Ann Trow Lohman was born in 1812 to indigent parents in the village of Painswick, Gloucestershire, England. She married widowed tailor Henry Summers at age 16, gaining a stepdaughter Caroline. In 1831, the Summers family immigrated to New York City; however, Henry died in 1833 from various speculated causes, including typhoid fever, yellow fever, and alcoholism. Ann worked as a seamstress until 1836, when she married "Dr." Charles R. Lohman, a newspaper typesetter turned quack physician. Together, they began selling diverse medications alleged to prevent contraception and unwanted

fetuses. The medications were created by Joseph F. Trow, Ann's brother, who also worked in a pharmacy. Unbeknownst to Ann, the newspaper advertisements that stated her alias as "Madame Restell" would be the beginning of both a lucrative career and an infamous reputation.

Ann Trow Lohman faced several arrests, trials and convictions throughout her career. The year 1841 was Lohman's first documented altercation with the law. She was tried and convicted for performing an abortion on a woman who later died. However, a more publicized case took place in February 1846 when a 17-year-old Philadelphia woman gave birth to a baby girl at Madame Restell's Greenwich Street establishment. The woman complained to William F. Havemeyer, the newly appointed mayor of New York City, that the baby was given up for adoption against her will. Although Lohman was found innocent, public protest was intense. On February 22, an angry mob descended upon Madame Restell's house, fueled by a sensational editorial in the *National Police Gazette* the day before. The mob broke up only after the mayor promised to do everything in his power to send Lohman to prison. As a result of this public demonstration, a new law was enacted, declaring that the abortion of a quickened fetus was considered manslaughter. (In the 19th century, quickening was considered to occur when the pregnant woman could feel the fetus move, which might be at any time between four to six months into the pregnancy.) Lohman was arrested under the new manslaughter law in September 1847, charged with having completed an abortion upon **Marie Bodine**, the mistress of a Walden, New York, factory agent. Public indignation against Madame Restell increased further due to the full clinical details exposed at the trial. She was convicted, however, on a lesser misdemeanor charge after conflicting medical testimony, and served a year at Blackwell's Island prison. Lohman's preferential treatment during her incarceration was so conspicuous that the board of aldermen eventually dismissed the warden.

In 1848, the Lohmans' fortune grew even more after they relocated to a larger and newer establishment on Chambers Street. In 1864, they moved to fashion-conscious uptown, into a four-story brownstone at 52nd Street and Fifth Avenue. The Chambers Street location was renovated into a hospital and a mail-order contraceptive distribution center. New York politicos and the public largely ignored Lohman's business practices. Even William Tweed, better known as "Boss" Tweed, political leader of New York City from 1859 to 1873, ignored not only Lohman's business activities, but also her financial contributions and social invitations.

Charles Lohman died in 1878. That February, Madame Restell had her final brush with the law, which some newspapers defined as a moral entrapment. Anthony Comstock, secretary of the New York Society for the Suppression of Vice, acted as a customer for contraceptives and made a purchase. Afterwards, he obtained a search warrant and found enough proof to bring Madame Restell to trial under a new law that prohibited the possession of any materials used for any "immoral" purposes. Early in the morning of April 1—her set trial date—Ann Lohman committed suicide by slitting her throat with a carving knife in her bath. She received no funeral services and was buried in Sleepy Hollow Cemetery in Tarrytown, New York, next to Charles Lohman. Lohman's estate, estimated from $600,000 to $1 million, was awarded to her step-grandchildren; a $3,000 annuity was given to her stepdaughter. Comstock called Madame Restell's suicide "a bloody ending to a bloody life."

Madame Restell was both troubled and perplexed by the public's condemnation of her life. After her death, her attorney stated, "Everything that the papers published she read with intense interest. She was deeply affected by all that was said against her." Ann Trow Lohman played a key role in a paradoxical time of rigid moral standards yet increasingly relaxed social situations for men and women. Despite her dubious historical reputation, Lohman provided a clandestine means for women to gain control over their reproductive health.

SOURCES:

James, Edward T., ed. *Notable American Women 1607–1950.* Cambridge, MA: The Belknap Press of Harvard University Press, 1971.

Kim L. Messeri,
freelance writer, Austin, Texas

Löhr, Marie (1890–1975)

Australian-born actress. Name variations: Marie Lohr. Born on July 28, 1890, in Sydney, New South Wales; died in 1975; daughter of Lewis J. Löhr (at one time treasurer of the Melbourne Opera House) and Kate (Bishop) Löhr; married Anthony Leyland Val Prinsep (divorced).

Selected theater: made first stage appearance in The World Against Her *(Sydney, NSW, 1894); made London debut in* Shock-Headed Peter *and* The Man Who Stole the Castle *(Garrick Theater, 1901); toured with the Kendals (1902), as Barbara Trecarre in St.*

Martin's Summer; *appeared as The Princess in* White Magic *(St. James's Theater, 1905), Miss Petherton in* The Duffer *(Comedy Theater, 1905), Ernestine in* The Little Michus *(Daly's Theater, 1906); toured with the Kendals (1906), as Clara in* A Tight Corner; *appeared as Rosey Mackenzie in* Colonel Newcome *(His Majesty's Theater, 1906), Lillian Nugent in* The Adventurer *(Shakespeare Theater, 1906); with the Kendals (1907), as Joy Marable in* The Other Side; *appeared as Irene Forster in* Her Father *(Haymarket Theater, 1908), Mrs. Reginald Bridgenorth in* Getting Married *(Haymarket Theater, 1908), title role in* Smith *(Comedy Theater, 1909), Josepha Quarendon in* Preserving Mr. Panmure *(Playhouse Theater, 1911), Lily Paradell in* The "Mind-the-Paint" Girl *(Duke of York's Theater, February 1912), Lady Thomasin Belturbet in a revival of* The Amazons *(June 1912), Adèle Vernet in* The Grand Seigneur *(Savoy Theater, October 1913), Yo-San in* The Darling of the Gods *(His Majesty's Theater, January 1914), Lady Babbie in* The Little Minister *(Duke of York's Theater, September 1914), H.M. Queen Charlotte in* Kings and Queens *(St. James's Theater, January 1915), title role in* Marie-Odile *(His Majesty's Theater, June 1915), Lady Ware in* The Ware Case *(Wyndham's Theater, September 1915); appeared in Sir J.M. Barrie's skit* The Real Thing at Last *(Coliseum Theater, March 1916); appeared as Constance Luscombe in* Home on Leave *and title role in* Remnant *(Royalty Theater, October and March 1916), Joan Rochford in* The Mirror *(Haymarket Theater, June 1917), Francis in* L'Aiglon *(which she also produced in aid of a war charity, November 1918), Lena in* Victory *(March 1919), Lady Caryll in* The Voice from the Minaret *(August 1919), Constance in* Birds of a Feather *(April 1920), Dahlia Lavory in* Every Woman's Privilege *(September 1920), Lady Aline Draper in* The Hour and the Man *(February 1921); toured Canada in repertory (late 1921); made New York debut as Lady Caryll in* A Voice from the Minaret *(Hudson Theater, New York, January 1922); appeared as Colette Vandières in* The Return *(London's Globe Theater, September 1922), Lady Marjorie Colladine in* The Laughing Lady *(November 1922), the Hon. Margot Tatham in* Aren't We All? *(April 1923), Mrs. Darling in* Peter Pan *(Gaiety Theater, December 1927); toured as Lady Lancaster in* The Temptation of Eve *(January 1928); appeared as May Smythe in* These Pretty Things *(Garrick Theater, December 1928), Lady Patricia in* Beau Geste *(His Majesty's Theater, January 1929), The Duchess of Devonshire in* Berkeley Square *(Lyric Theater, March 1929), Mary Howard in* The Silent Witness *(Comedy Theater, April 1930), Margery Battle in* The Breadwinner *(Vaudeville Theater, September*

1930), Margaret Armstrong in The Love Game (Prince of Wales's Theater, July 1931), Margaret Westcott in Important People (Vaudeville Theater, London, February 1932), Empress Marie Thérèse of Austria in Casanova (Coliseum, May 1932), Lady L'Estrange in So Good! So Kind! (Playhouse Theater, October 1933), Mrs. Sydney Rankin in Chase the Ace (Daly's Theater, May 1935), Muriel Weston in Call It a Day (Globe Theater, October 1935); appeared in the revue And On We Go (Savoy Theater, April 1937); appeared as Duchess of Cheviot in Crest of the Wave (Drury Lane Theater, September 1937), Mary Jarrow in Quiet Wedding (Wyndham's Theater, October 1938), Pansy Bird in Somewhere in England (Lyric Theater, December 1939), Vera Sheldon in Other People's Houses (Ambassadors' Theater, October 1941), Mrs. Brown in National Velvet (Embassy Theater, April 1946), Mrs. Jennings in Sense and Sensibility (Embassy Theater, August 1946), Marquise de St. Maur in Caste (Duke of York's, January 1947), Gertrude Pardine in My Wives and I (Strand Theater, July 1947), Dame Maud Gosport in A Harlequinade (Phoenix Theater, September 1948), Consuelo Howard in Treasure Hunt (Apollo Theater, September 1949), Hester Bellboys in A Penny For a Song (Haymarket Theater, March 1951); toured as Philippa Bennington in Adam's Apple (April 1952); appeared as Mrs. Jevens in Sweet Peril (St. James's Theater, December 1952), the Countess of Lister in The Manor of Northstead (Duchess Theater, April 1954), Matilda "Hope" in The Devil Was Sick (Fortune Theater, November 1956), Lady Charlton in Silver Wedding (Cambridge, July 1957), Lady Bracknell in Half in Ernest (Belgrade, Coventry, March 1958), Winifred Wing in These People, Those Books (Grand, Leeds, September 1958), Lady Mortlake in The World of Paul Slickey (Palace Theater, May 1959), May Davenport in Waiting in the Wings (Duke of York's Theater, September 1960), Aunt Fluffy in The West Lodge (Ashcroft, Croydon, March 1963), Lady Julia Marcia in The Ides of March (Haymarket Theater, August, 1963), Mrs. Whitefield in Man and Superman (New Arts Theater, November 1965, transferred to the Garrick, February 1966).

Selected films: Aren't We All? (1932); Pygmalion (1938); Major Barbara (1940); The Winslow Boy (1948); A Town Like Alice (1956).

Born in Sydney, Australia, in 1890, actress Marie Löhr made her stage debut there at the age of four in the play The World Against Her. She first appeared in London in 1901, in Shock-Headed Peter and The Man Who Stole the Castle, at the Garrick Theater. During her early career, Löhr occasionally toured with the Kendals

(*Madge Kendal and her husband W.H. Kendal), and was engaged by actor-manager Beerbohm Tree in 1908 to play Margaret in Faust. For several years beginning in January 1918, she was employed by the management of the Globe Theater. For the most part, the actress confined herself to London and the provinces, making only two appearances in the United States: one at the Hudson Theater in January 1922, playing Lady Caryll in A Voice from the Minaret, and another at the Booth Theater in September 1931, playing Margery in The Breadwinner. She also toured briefly in Canada in conjunction with her first trip to the United States. In addition to her work on the stage, Löhr made countless films, including Aren't We All? (1932), Pygmalion (1938), Major Barbara (1940), and The Winslow Boy (1948). The actress made her home in London and was married and divorced from Anthony Prinsep. She died in 1975.

Barbara Morgan,
Melrose, Massachusetts

Lois.
Variant of Aloisia and Heloise.

Lois
Biblical woman. Mother of Eunice (who married a Greek); grandmother of Timothy.

A devout Jew living in Lystra, in Asia Minor, Lois instructed her daughter *Eunice and her grandson Timothy in the Old Testament. Both mother and daughter became Christians, and the apostle Paul later credited them for Timothy's spiritual education. Timothy became an ardent missionary.

Loise.
Variant of Louise.

Loisinger, Joanna (1865–1951)
Bulgarian royal. Born in 1865; died in 1951; married Alexander I, prince of Bulgaria (r. 1879–1886), on February 6, 1889.

Alexander of Battenberg was elected prince of Bulgaria as Alexander I on April 29, 1879, but he was soon embroiled in a conflict with the Bulgarian national assembly (Sobranye). He modified the constitution and appointed a Russian-led ministry. Under pressure, he revoked his modification. Eventually, Alexander was forced to abdicate in 1886. In 1883, his intended had been Princess *Victoria (1866–1929), granddaughter of the German emperor Wilhelm I, but the union was bitterly opposed by Bismarck. In 1889, he married Joanna Loisinger.

Lokhvitskaia, Mirra (1869–1905).

See Teffi, N.A. for sidebar.

Lokhvitskaia, Nadezhda (1872–1952).

See Teffi, N.A.

Lola Montez (1818–1861).

See Montez, Lola.

Lollia Paulina (fl. 38–39 CE)

Roman noblewoman and empress. Reigned as empress, 38–39 CE; daughter of M. Lollius (consul in 21 BCE); married Memmius Regulus; married Caligula (12–41), Roman emperor (divorced).

Known for her dazzling beauty, Lollia Paulina was taken from her husband Memmius Regulus by Caligula and briefly reigned as his third wife from 38 to 39 CE. (Caligula's first wife was *Junia Claudilla; his second was *Livia Orestilla; his fourth was *Milonia Caesonia.) Following the death of *Valeria Messalina in 48 CE, Callistus the freedman suggested that Lollia Paulina would be a suitable rival to *Agrippina the Younger for Emperor Claudius' hand. Agrippina disagreed; her jealousy led to Lollia Paulina's exile and eventual death.

Lollobrigida, Gina (1927—)

Italian actress and photographer. Name variations: modeled under the name Diana Loris. Born on July 4, 1927, in Subiaco, Italy; second of four daughters of Giovanni (a furniture manufacturer) and Giuseppina Lollobrigida; received private instruction in singing, dancing, drawing, and languages; attended the Academy of Fine Arts, Rome, Italy; married Drago Milko Skofic (a physician and her manager), in 1950 (divorced 1966); children: one son, Andrea Milko Skofic.

Selected filmography: Aquila Nera *(1946);* Elisir d'Amore *(1946);* Lucia di Lammermoor *(1946);* Il Delitto di Giovanni Episcopo *(1947);* Il Segreto di Don Giovanni *(1947);* Follie per l'Opera *(Mad About Opera, 1947);* I Pagliacci *(Love of a Clown, 1948);* Campane a Martello *(1949);* Cuori senza Frontiere *(The White Line, 1950);* Miss Italia *(Miss Italy, 1950);* Vita de Cani *(1950);* Alina *(1950);* A Tale of Five Cities *(A Tale of Five Women, UK/Fr./It./Ger., 1951);*

Achtung! Banditi! *(1951);* Enrico Caruso *(The Young Caruso, 1951);* La Città si difende *(1951);* Altri Tempi *(Times Gone By, 1951);* Fanfan la Tulipe *(Fanfan the Tulip, Fr./It., 1952);* Les Belles de Nuit *(Beauties of the Night, Fr./It., 1952);* Moglie per una Notee *(Wife for a Night, 1952);* Le Infedeli *(The Unfaithful, 1952);* La Provinciale *(The Wayward Wife, 1953);* Il Maestro di Don Giovanni *(Crossed Swords, It./Us, 1953);* Pane Amore e Fantasia *(Bread, Love and Dreams, 1953);* Beat the Devil *(UK/It., 1954);* Le Grand Jeu *(Fr./It., 1954);* La Romana *(Woman of Rome, 1954);* Pane Amore e Gelosia *(Frisky, 1954);* Bread, Love and Jealousy *(1954);* La Donna più Bella del Mondo *(Beautiful but Dangerous, 1955);* Trapeze *(US, 1956);* Notre Dame de Paris *(The Hunchback of Notre Dame, Fr./It., 1956);* Anna di Brooklyn *(Fast and Sexy, It./Fr., 1958);* La Loi *(Where the Hot Wind Blows, Fr./It., 1959);* Solomon and Sheba *(US, 1959);* Never So Few *(US, 1959);* Go Naked in the World *(US, 1961);* Come September *(US, 1961);* Vénus impériale *(Fr./It., 1962);* Mare Matto *(It./Fr., 1963);* Woman of Straw *(UK, 1964);* Le Bambole *(The Dolls, It./Fr., 1965);* Strange Bedfellows *(US, 1965);* Hotel Paradiso *(UK/US, 1966);* Cervantes *(The Young Rebel, Sp./It./Fr., 1968);* La Morte ha Fatto l'Uovo *(Plucked, It./Fr., 1968);* The Private Navy of Sgt. O'Farrell *(US, 1968);* Un Bellissimo Novembre *(That Splendid November, It./Fr., 1968);* Buona Sera, Mrs. Campbell *(US, 1969);* Bad Man's River *(Sp., 1971);* Herzbube *(King Queen Knave, Ger./US, 1972);* Roses rouges et Piments verts *(The Lonely Woman, Fr./It./Sp., 1975);* Widow's Nest *(1977);* Stelle Emigranti *(1983).*

Born in 1927 in Subiaco, Italy, a small mountain town outside of Rome, movie actress Gina Lollobrigida was the second of four daughters of a successful furniture manufacturer and, as a child, took private lessons in singing, dancing, drawing, and languages. During World War II, the family fled to Rome, where Lollobrigida, having developed into a voluptuous beauty, contributed to the family income by modeling for the *fumetti* (Italian comic strips that use photographs instead of cartoons). Following the liberation, she won a scholarship to the Academy of Fine Arts, where she studied painting and sculpture for three years.

In 1947, film director Mario Costa noticed Lollobrigida on the street and offered her a screen test. This led to small roles in several films and work as a stand-in for a star. (Lollobrigida later said the arrangement ended when the star became jealous of her good looks.) Her first major role was that of a beauty contestant in

Miss Italy (1950), a part she could personally relate to having won the title of "Miss Rome" two years earlier. That same year, the actress had her first American screen test under the auspices of RKO's Howard Hughes, who subsequently signed her to an exclusive seven-year contract. Although he never used her in a picture, he made it impossible for her to work for any other American studio for the duration of the agreement.

In 1949, Lollobrigida married a refugee Yugoslav doctor, Milko Skofic, who became her manager. With her growing importance in Ital-

ian films and her driving ambition, the actress launched herself in the international film arena. By the early 1950s, "La Lolla," as she was dubbed, was one of Continental Europe's most famous stars. Ephraim Katz notes that the French even coined the word "lollobrigidienne" to describe the curvaceous female form. Particularly notable during this period was her role in *The Wayward Wife* (1953), for which she was awarded the Grolla d'Oro (the Italian equivalent of the Oscar), and her portrayal of a peasant girl in the highly successful *Bread, Love and Dreams* (1953), which won the highest award of the Ital-

From the movie The Hunchback of Notre Dame, *starring Gina Lollobrigida.*

ian Journalists guild. A sequel to the latter, *Bread, Love and Jealousy* (1954), was also a major success.

Lollobrigida's first European-made film with an American cast was *Beat the Devil* (1954), with Humphrey Bogart and **Jennifer Jones*, after which she made her first picture for a major American studio, *Beautiful but Dangerous* (1955), a Fox bio-pic about the Italian soprano **Lina Cavalieri*. Her next effort, *Trapeze* (1956), with Burt Lancaster and Tony Curtis, opened with great fanfare, but received lukewarm reviews. Lollobrigida subsequently appeared in the French version of *The Hunchback of Notre Dame* (1956), co-starring Anthony Quinn, and *Solomon and Sheba* (1959), with Yul Brynner. A glossier Lollobrigida emerged in subsequent Hollywood-produced movies: *Go Naked in the World* (1961), *Come September* (1961), *Strange Bedfellows* (1965), *The Private Navy of Sgt. O'Farrell* (1968), and *Buona Sera, Mrs. Campbell* (1969).

Lollobrigida's temperament apparently grew in direct proportion to her popularity, and at one time she was involved in as many as ten simultaneous lawsuits. Always very much in control of her screen image, she frequently designed her own costumes and tended to her own make-up. "I am an expert on Gina," she was once quoted as saying (*This Week*, October 7, 1956). Lollobrigida even negotiated her own financial deals, sometimes pricing herself out of good roles. When she demanded half the profits for *Bread, Love and Nostalgia*, another sequel to *Bread, Love and Jealousy*, she lost the part to another comely Italian actress, **Sophia Loren*.

Throughout an extremely successful career, Lollobrigida retained her image of a glamour girl, but was never viewed as a great actress. "I am a painter and a sculptor, and by chance I did movies," she said many years after her heyday. Lollobrigida retired from films in the early 1970s, and since then has had a second career as a photographer, a talent she pursued after the birth of her son in 1957. Divorced from her husband in 1966, she has published five books of her photographs, the latest, *The Wonder of Innocence* (Abrams, 1994), containing over 150 photomontages of children and animals from around the world. Distinct from her previous books which were almost all single images, each photograph in this volume is a composite of many individual photos, sometimes incorporating as many as 15 images in one surrealistic montage. "Technically, the composites are virtually seamless," writes a reviewer for *Popular Photography*, "it's hard to detect any artifice. Subjects overlap, limbs entwine, and delicate strands of hair glow in the sunlight." Although Lollobrigida would not reveal her techniques, she claimed that the composites were done entirely in her home darkroom (no computers), using a method that took over two years to devise. "You can imagine what I went through is craziness!" She felt that her background as a painter was an enormous help in creating her composite images.

Over the years, the actress has also returned to films on a limited basis. She directed the acclaimed documentary *Rittrato di Fidel* (*Portrait of Fidel Castro*, 1975) and was lured back to acting in 1984, appearing in the American television series "Falcon Crest." In June 1999, she also joined a new wave of women entering the Italian political arena. Drafted by the splinter centrist Democrat party to run for a seat in the European Parliament, Lollobrigida, at age 71, was hoping "to be a voice for Italy's women," although she admitted that it was difficult for people to believe that she was not just in town to promote a movie or television series. "Politics isn't easy," she said.

SOURCES:

Appelo, Tim. "A Sex Symbol's Innocence," in *Entertainment Weekly*. No. 254. December 23, 1994, pp. 18–20.

Current Biography. NY: H.W. Wilson, 1960.

"Gina Lollobrigida: A Photographer?," in *Popular Photography*. Vol. 59, no. 5. May 1995, pp. 78–80.

Israely, Jeff. "In Italy, women's political star rises," in *The Boston Globe*. June 5, 1999.

Katz, Ephraim. *The Film Encyclopedia*. NY: HarperCollins, 1994.

Barbara Morgan,
Melrose, Massachusetts

Lombard, Carole (1908–1942)

American film actress and comedian who, before her untimely death, was the highest paid star in Hollywood. Born Jane Alice Peters on October 6, 1908, in Fort Wayne, Indiana; killed in a plane crash near Las Vegas, Nevada, on January 16, 1942, while returning to Los Angeles after a war bonds drive in her hometown; third child of Elizabeth Knight Peters and Frederic Peters; had two older brothers, Frederick, Jr., and Stuart; married William Powell (an actor), in 1931 (divorced 1933); married Clark Gable (an actor), in 1939; no children.

Filmography: A Perfect Crime (1921); Marriage in Transit (1925); Hearts and Spurs (1925); Gold and the Girl (1925); Durand of the Badlands (1925); Dick Turpin (1925); The Road to Glory (1926); Smith's

Pony *(1927)*; Hold That Pose *(1927)*; The Girl from Everywhere *(1927)*; The Swim Princess *(1928)*; Run Girl Run *(1928)*; The Divine Sinner *(1928)*; Power *(1928)*; Me Gangster *(1928)*; Show Folks *(1928)*; Ned McCobb's Daughter *(1928)*; His Unlucky Night *(1928)*; The Girl from Nowhere *(1928)*; The Campus Vamp *(1928)*; The Campus Carmen *(1928)*; The Bicycle Flirt *(1928)*; The Best Man *(1928)*; The Beach Club *(1928)*; High Voltage *(1929)*; Big News *(1929)*; The Racketeer *(1929)*; Matchmaking Mamas *(1929)*; Dynamite *(1929)*; Safety in Numbers *(1930)*; Fast and Loose *(1930)*; The Arizona Kid *(1930)*; Up Pops the Devil *(1931)*; Man of the World *(1931)*; Ladies' Man *(1931)*; It Pays to Advertise *(1931)*; I Take This Woman *(1931)*; Virtue *(1932)*; Sinners in the Sun *(1932)*; No One Man *(1932)*; No More Orchids *(1932)*; No Man of Her Own *(1932)*; White Woman *(1933)*; Supernatural *(1933)*; From Hell to Heaven *(1933)*; The Eagle and the Hawk *(1933)*; Brief Moment *(1933)*; We're Not Dressing *(1934)*; Twentieth Century *(1934)*; Now and Forever *(1934)*; Lady by Choice *(1934)*; The Gay Bride *(1934)*; Bolero *(1934)*; Rumba *(1935)*; Hands Across the Table *(1935)*; The Princess Comes Across *(1936)*; My Man Godfrey *(1936)*; Love Before Breakfast *(1936)*; True Confession *(1937)*; Swing High, Swing Low *(1937)*; Nothing Sacred *(1937)*; Fools for Scandal *(1938)*; Made for Each Other *(1939)*; In Name Only *(1939)*; Vigil in the Night *(1940)*; They Knew What They Wanted *(1940)*; Mr. and Mrs. Smith *(1941)*; To Be or Not to Be *(1942)*.

Divorce court in Lake Tahoe, Nevada, was crowded that August morning in 1933. Even the judge, normally a weary audience of one for the endless parade of attractive, recent Nevada residents seeking quick release from their husbands in the only state that then permitted it, seemed unusually alert as Mrs. William Powell stood to address the court. Her charges of "extreme cruelty" against her husband had been the source of much mirth in the show-business press, but outright laughter erupted when Mrs. Powell accused her husband of "using foul language" against her, her own salty vocabulary having been a Hollywood tradition for some years. Furthermore, her marriage to William Powell had been marked not by any unkindness from the always dapper and gentlemanly actor, but by sheer boredom. "It was a waste of time," she later described her three years with Powell, "his, and mine." Before she could complete her official tale of woe for the court, the judge cut her off, banged his gavel, and declared Hollywood's mistress of screwball comedy to be, once again, plain Carole Lombard.

The good grace and easy humor with which her first marriage ended was typical of her life in general. Carole Lombard was one of Hollywood's best-loved personalities, "filmdom's best pal and good-time girl," as one biographer wrote of her, "the one person in town whom everyone liked, the brightest and the best, and no mistake." She never took her stardom very seriously, never threw scenes on sound stages, and never demanded a separate dressing room, being perfectly happy with a table and chair in a corner of a soundstage. She was ready for a scene at least 20 minutes before anyone else, often did her own stand-in work on her pictures, and was known for showing up on the set even on days when she wasn't needed to trade jokes with the crew and watch the day's rushes. She managed to maintain her equilibrium even after she became Hollywood's highest paid star and married one of its most glamorous leading men. "Most people can't be flexible," she once told an interviewer who wondered why she seemed so unaffected by her success. "I can, so I am."

She had learned adaptability early on from her mother, **Bessie Knight Peters**, who had gone from being a society hostess to a movie mother without batting a carefully tended eyelash. Bessie Knight was one of the most eligible young women in Fort Wayne, Indiana, before she married Frederic Peters at the turn of the century, a union that raised not a few eyebrows in Fort Wayne society. Bessie's family was a wealthy and socially prominent one, while Frederic came from more modest roots. He would later prove himself, however, by building a small hardware store in Fort Wayne into a profitable statewide chain, providing a comfortable life for Bessie and their three children—two sons, Fred, Jr., and Stuart, and his youngest child, Jane Alice, born on October 6, 1908. Although Frederic suffered from ill health, particularly from crippling headaches that plagued him after a hunting accident, the Peters family seemed typical of the optimistic, progressive times of pre-World War I America. They clanked around town in a Tin Lizzie dubbed "The Weedburner," spent summers with relatives on verdant country estates, and hosted parties during the social season that were the delight of Fort Wayne's upper crust, Bessie being known as a superb host to her friends and as a consummate organizer and problem-solver to her family. The children especially remembered Bessie's heroics in turning their home into a refuge center for flood victims when the St. Mary's River disastrously overflowed its banks in 1913. Everyone noted that little Jane was growing up into a pretty young girl, much taken with the serials playing down at the "picture palace." Her roughhouse tendencies were remarked upon, especially by her older brothers, whom she browbeat into letting her play baseball and football with the other neighborhood boys.

> *O*f course there is a real me, but I don't value her so highly that I have to force her on people.
>
> —Carole Lombard

Bessie Peters once again caught her hometown by surprise by announcing in 1916 that she and her children would be traveling to California for a vacation, leaving her ailing husband behind. After the four-day train journey and a brief stop in San Francisco to visit relatives, the Peters family *sans père* arrived in Los Angeles, where Bessie promptly fell in love with the place and announced she would remain permanently. For propriety's sake, she took care to mention that Frederic would join them when his health improved; but the truth was that she and her husband had come to an amicable estrangement, although it would take more than ten years for a formal divorce to be announced.

Hollywood in 1916 was still mostly orange groves and farmhouses basking in the last moments of sunny isolation before the arrival en masse of "the picture people." D.W. Griffith had just begun production in nearby Santa Ana on his epic *Birth of a Nation* when Bessie and her children arrived. Thomas Ince was about to begin construction on the first permanent movie studio in Culver City, on the southern edge of the orange groves; while to the north, in the valley on the other side of the rugged hills thrusting east from the Pacific, Carl Laemmle was buying up acreage for a studio complex he would call Universal City. In between them was Hollywood, a semi-rural tract of land which a Midwestern dowager who had settled there in the 1880s had named after the estate she had left behind in colder climes. Bessie Peters bought a small bungalow with money sent to her by Frederic and set about acquainting herself with the locals, many of whom told her that her little Jane was pretty enough to be in the pictures. Their opinion seemed confirmed in 1921 when Allan Dwan, one of the most prolific and imaginative of early film directors, happened to be visiting a friend in the neighborhood and spotted Jane playing baseball (or boxing with one of her brothers, depending on which account is preferred). Bessie agreed to his suggestion that Jane take a part in his new film, *A Perfect Crime,* a melodrama in which Jane appeared in three scenes as the younger sister of the film's star. It was Dwan's opinion that Jane was clever enough to be an actress, prompting Bessie to take the child on a round of interviews which produced no results. It was the first of what would be three false starts to Lombard's hopes for a movie career.

The second came when Jane was named Queen of the May at Fairfax High School in the spring of 1924, an honor normally reserved for the girl deemed to be the school's prettiest and an event closely watched by talent scouts looking for fresh young faces. One of those scouts got her a test for Charlie Chaplin, then casting the ingenue role for *The Gold Rush*. The diminutive Chaplin felt that Jane's beauty, not to mention her height, would draw screen attention away from himself and declined to hire her, but the test found its way to Vitagraph Studios, which signed her to a one-year contract and asked her to choose a screen name for herself. Jane chose Carol Peters, taking as her inspiration a tennis star she particularly admired, **Carol Peterson**.

Once again, however, it appeared her film career was not to be, for Vitagraph declared bankruptcy soon after her signing. Jane reluctantly returned to high school in the fall, although she had decided by now that her life's desire was to be in pictures. Bessie's peripatetic social touring had produced a friendship with **Louella Parsons*, who had taken a liking to her friend's daughter and who suggested that an interview with William Fox might be arranged. Fox was just setting about building his new studio and a talent roster to go with it. Jane's third attempt in films came in October of 1924, when she left high school in her junior year to sign a one-year contract with Fox at $65 a week. Fox suggested that "Peters" sounded too weak for movie audiences to remember and encouraged Jane to come up with a new name. It was Bessie who suggested "Lombard," recalling friends back in Fort Wayne of whom she had been particularly fond. By Thanksgiving of 1924, Carole Lombard appeared in the first of a number of the cheap, two-reel Westerns Fox cranked out to build his audience and his bank account. She was little more than decoration in the pictures, with limited acting time. Her only notable achievement during this period was beating **Joan Crawford* in the annual Charleston contest at the Coconut Grove, a popular jazz-age hangout for young movie hopefuls with money to burn.

Fox began to take Lombard more seriously when the great John Barrymore asked to screen test her for an upcoming film. This prompted the studio to move her into the cast of one of its "A"

films just before misfortune once again threatened to derail Carole's career. Lombard was sitting in the front seat of a racy Bugatti driven by one of her Coconut Grove cronies when the car ahead of them slammed on its brakes. The resulting impact shattered the car's windshield and sprayed her face with shards of splintered glass, although there were no other injuries to herself or the driver. The resulting gash, running from her right cheekbone to her nose, was successfully repaired in a four-hour operation, leaving only a small scar that was barely noticeable—except,

Fox feared, to a movie audience seeing a closeup of her face. The studio canceled her contract, citing a clause that made an employee responsible for the results of any alteration in appearance or physical condition. Friends noted the change in Lombard's outlook as she lay motionless for the four weeks she spent at home after the operation. "Carole . . . became very self-critical, ashamed of herself for having been so shallow," one of them later said. "And while she became more jovial later on, you were aware of her depth." Everyone predicted it was the end of Lombard's short film career, especially when Sam Goldwyn called her an imposter after not noticing her scar during an interview. He found out about it later when he called William Fox to ask why such a beautiful creature had been fired. Lombard had other plans, however.

Mack Sennett had introduced himself to her at the Coconut Grove some months before the accident, and it was to Sennett that Carole committed the care of her future in films. Sennett was a Hollywood original, having established a beachhead early on with his Keystone Kops and a successful series of short films that amounted to little more than a genial ogling of young women in bathing suits. Sennett's "bathing beauty" films were long on feminine pulchritude but cheerfully short on artistic technique, including closeups. Sennett cared nothing for Lombard's nearly invisible scar, although he had some suggestions for her as he welcomed her into his "chorus," the members of which he preferred to be on the plump side. "We gotta get some meat on you," he told her the first morning she reported for work, and his prescription was simple. "Carole, honey, you go right home and eat some bananas, a lot of bananas," he said. "Just keep on eatin' 'em. That'll fatten you up, especially in the tits." Sennett may have had his quirks (he claimed to get all his ideas while sitting naked in a steaming hot tub in the middle of his office), but Lombard later said her two years with him taught her everything she knew about comedy. It was Sennett who pointed out to her that any situation could be funny or tragic, depending on the attitude of the actor. He advised her that the way to make a scene funny was to act as if she didn't believe any of it for a minute, a talent much in evidence in her later films. For the next two years, Sennett put her to work in a string of his shorts, as well as loaning her out to Pathé, which distributed his films, and to her old studio, Fox, which used her in many of its "programmers"—cheap, quickly produced films used as filler for movie audiences willing to spend an entire afternoon watching films.

Like most beautiful but inexperienced young actresses, Lombard was subjected to the usual pinchings and gropings from male actors and crew members; but unlike her peers, Carole decided to do something about it, asking her brothers to teach her every dirty word and sexually descriptive phrase they knew. "She memorized all the terms and our definitions like she was studying for a test," brother Fred remembered. "And from then on, if some guy made a pass at her or tried to, he'd hear such talk as he just wouldn't expect to come from such a beautiful girl." Thus was established Lombard's well-deserved reputation for exuberantly earthy language, to the shock of some and the delight of others, like writer and director Garson Kanin. "She used the full, juicy Anglo-Saxon vocabulary," he wrote of her, "yet it never shocked, never offended, because she was clearly using the language to express herself, and not to shock or offend." She put her homework to an early test during an interview with the famously vulgar predator Harry Cohn, founder of Columbia Pictures, to which Lombard was often loaned out by Pathé and, later, Paramount. Her stream of invective at his expected, and not particularly subtle, propositioning was sufficiently bombastic to impress even Cohn and establish a long-running relationship that became a strictly professional one from then on.

Lombard had landed at Paramount after Pathé went bankrupt, and it was for her new studio that she first came to wide public notice as an elegant, sophisticated "orchid lady," so-called because of her sensual adornment of such lightweight films as *Safety in Numbers, Fast and Loose,* and *It Pays to Advertise.* Paramount was sufficiently impressed with her to cast her opposite one of its most popular leading men, William Powell, in *Man of the World* and *Ladies' Man.* Powell, one of the few character actors from the silent era to have survived the transition to sound, was known around the business as a thorough professional. He responded to Carole's equally professional attitude, to say nothing of her physical attractions, while Lombard was smitten by Powell's aristocratic bearing and sophisticated manners. The two were married at Bessie's Rexford Drive house on June 26, 1931, Powell being 39 at the time and Lombard 23. Always fond of nicknames, Lombard tagged Powell as "Philo" (after Philo Vance, the detective character on which Powell had built his early career in a series of mystery films) and settled down to the sedate married life Powell preferred. "That's how I learned to put a house together," she later told Garson Kanin, "and have everything supplied, and how to take care of his clothes. I mean, I was the best fuckin' wife you ever saw. I mean a ladylike wife, because that's how Philo wanted it." But two years of quiet domesticity were enough for Lombard, while Powell was gentlemanly enough to realize that his talented young bride's future should include more than he could offer. Their 1933 divorce was a friendly one, despite the required performance Lombard gave in Lake Tahoe that August day (no-fault divorces would not become available anywhere in the U.S. until 1970). The two were often seen in public together for some years afterward, and it was Powell who, three years later, would insist on Carole playing opposite him in what would be one of her most successful films, *My Man Godfrey*. There were rumors that Lombard would marry a second time when her passionate affair with singer and bandleader Russ Columbo became public early in 1934. Columbo, a smooth baritone who was being groomed as a rival to Bing Crosby, had even taken Lombard to meet his family in Philadelphia before he was tragically killed at the age of 26 when an antique rifle accidentally discharged, sending a bullet into his brain. One of the few times the public saw Carole Lombard cry was at Columbo's funeral.

On screen, however, all was light and laughter. Lombard's breakthrough picture, 1934's *Twentieth Century,* was the first to make Paramount realize they had a major comedic actress on their hands. It was also John Barrymore's chance to make good on his earlier promise to put her in one of his pictures. Barrymore had specifically requested her for the role of Lily Garland, the renegade actress who is pursued by Barrymore's Oscar Jaffe, a theatrical producer. Barrymore's request was somewhat of a backhanded compliment, for his drinking was making the studio nervous, and better-known actresses who had been approached for the role refused to work with him. But it was Barrymore's histrionics as Oscar Jaffe that seemed to act as a catalyst for everything Mack Sennett had taught Lombard back in her bathing beauty days. Although Barrymore said she was the greatest actress he had ever worked with, Carole's brilliant portrayal of Lily surprised everyone else. "Miss Lombard . . . never seemed to be more than a passably fair performer," said one critic, "but she has now given a more than ordinarily good performance in which she holds the attention, even though she is opposite one of the finest actors in films, in one of his best roles." Lombard quickly followed her success with another widely admired performance as a gold-dig-

ging manicurist in 1935's *Hands Across the Table,* a script she had herself helped develop at Paramount and for which she had chosen her leading man, Fred MacMurray, in one of his first comedic roles. "[They] make an all-time copybook example of how to play a movie for all it's worth," wrote *Variety*'s reviewer, "with . . . the open, sustained kind of charm that can be projected through the shadows of a mile of celluloid." Her position at the top of Hollywood's roster of stars was secured with the release of *My Man Godfrey* in 1936, in which she played the wealthy, if not particularly bright, heiress Irene Bullock, who finds the homeless Godfrey on a bet and passes him off as her family's valet. Lombard landed the role after Powell, playing Gregory, refused to do the picture unless his ex-wife was given the role. The film was so successful that Carole became Hollywood's highest paid star when she renewed that year with Paramount, guaranteed $450,000 a year for the seven-year life of her contract.

Typically, Lombard (who had decided to change the spelling of her name from Carol to Carole) joked about her rising fortunes, telling Garson Kanin: "I think that *e* made the whole fuckin' difference"; but in more serious moments, she attributed a good deal of her success to playing opposite great actors, like Barrymore and Powell. "I'm really not a leader, but a follower," she said. "I respond to any pace, but I don't set one." That may have been true on a sound stage, but Lombard was definitely a pacesetter for Hollywood's social life. Like Bessie, she became known for her inventive, amusing, and sometimes raucous buffet suppers and parties, each of which was organized around a theme. Noticing that many of her friends seemed to be complaining of various aches, pains, and other physical indignities, for example, Lombard threw a "hospital party," in which everyone was required to attend wearing hospital gowns. When a dinner guest moaned that he was too tired to sit up at the table, she organized a Roman banquet during which guests sprawled out on sofas; and at the 1936 Mayfair Club Ball, which she had been asked to organize, she commanded everyone to wear white and was enraged when *Norma Shearer arrived in a brilliant, scarlet gown. Shearer was saved from a barrage of Lombard insults by a quick-thinking Clark Gable, who whisked Carole out of the room. It may have been at the Mayfair Ball that one of Hollywood's most famous love affairs was born, for many noted that it seemed an inordinately long time before Gable ushered Lombard back into the room.

The two had worked together only once, in 1932's *No Man of Her Own*, when Lombard was still married to Powell, and Gable had recently taken society belle **Rhea Langham** as his second wife. Gable had had his own false start in movies; after arriving in Hollywood in the '20s to work as an extra, he was forced to find work with touring theatrical companies before being discovered by MGM in 1930. Thirty-five at the time his relationship with Lombard began, Gable had become the heartthrob of millions of American women with his work opposite **Claudette Colbert** in *It Happened One Night* and **Jeanette MacDonald** in the sprawling *San Francisco*, and had already been dubbed "the King of the movies." Lombard relished the memories of the early days of their affair, in which Gable would rent a motel room in some obscure little town outside Los Angeles, making a copy of the room key and sending it to her; and she traced the beginning of his serious interest in her to a "nervous breakdown party" in which she arrived in an ambulance and had herself carried into the room on a stretcher, wearing a white operating room gown. By 1937, their affair had become such public knowledge that *Photoplay* included them in a feature story on "Hollywood's Unmarried Husbands and Wives."

While her love for Gable deepened, Lombard's career reached a new pinnacle in 1937. Finishing work on a Friday on that year's *Nothing Sacred*, she reported to the set on Monday to start *True Confessions*, both films being released simultaneously on Thanksgiving Day of that year and both remaining classics of the screwball comedies of the era. She played for a second time opposite Fred MacMurray in *True Confessions* as an otherwise normal young housewife whose only failing is an inability to tell the truth. John Barrymore, by then crippled by alcoholism, nevertheless turned in an hysterically funny performance as the eccentric con man who finds a cure for the young woman's malady. The next year, Lombard surprised her audience in her first picture for RKO, *Made for Each Other*, a light romantic comedy that emphasized her dramatic range rather than her by-now familiar genius for comedy. The picture was named one of the year's ten best by *The New York Times*.

But Lombard had more on her mind that year, for Gable had now divorced Rhea Langham. On March 29, 1938—the first day off Gable had from playing Rhett Butler in David Selznick's *Gone With The Wind*—Lombard became the third Mrs. Clark Gable in a private, closely guarded ceremony at a small church in tiny Kingman, California. "Carole was madly in love with him," a friend of theirs told an interviewer years later. "When she would zero in on something, that was it, and she wanted this relationship." Lombard's view was more prosaic. "I just think about that husband of mine all the time," she said. "I'm really stuck on the bastard. That's *something*, isn't it!" The pair set about renovating a 20-acre ranch which Gable had bought from director Raoul Walsh in Encino, then still a rural Valley enclave. They indulged in the kind of pastoral fantasy that their combined salaries allowed, keeping horses and chickens (which Carole tried to turn to good use by selling as "the King's eggs") and mowing an alfalfa field with the yellow tractor that was Gable's pride and joy. They even called each other Maw and Paw, and were much photographed together in Gable's favorite pastime, duck shooting.

The careers of Hollywood's reigning love birds seemed just as fantastically sublime. Gable, after screening the completed *Gone With The Wind*, was convinced his Rhett Butler would earn him the Oscar. The 1939 award went instead to Robert Donat for *Goodbye, Mr. Chips*, and Gable found little solace on the way home from the ceremonies when Carole predicted they'd bring an Oscar home the next year. She was thinking of her own work in *Vigil in the Night*, a hospital drama released in 1940 in which she played one of two nurses in love with the same doctor. It was one of a pair of dramatic roles she took on that year, the other being *They Knew What They Wanted*, a poignant story of a mail-order bride in California's Napa Valley (and the inspiration for the subsequent musical *The Most Happy Fella*). However, her work in *Vigil* impressed critics more than audiences, who found the story grim and depressing. Lombard took the hint and returned to comedy. Her next film was 1941's *Mr. and Mrs. Smith*, the only romantic farce directed by Alfred Hitchcock, in which Lombard and Robert Montgomery play a married couple who find out that an obscure legal technicality has left them decidedly un-married.

Meanwhile, her real-life marriage to Gable, it was said, was foundering. Lombard had discovered that while she and Gable would always remain close, the passion they had felt for each other had flickered out. "The romance had ended, but the marriage endured," as one close friend later put it. Gable's fumbling lovemaking had become almost a joke between them. A houseguest remembered when Gable, during a futile attempt to learn to play bridge, threw down his cards in exasperation and declared, "Dammit, I don't think I'll ever learn to finesse!" Lombard rose quickly to the occasion.

"Well, sweetie," she cooed, "every Metro script girl knows *that*." Carole tolerated Gable's frequent affairs, objecting loudly only at his attraction to his co-star in *Honky-Tonk*, *Lana Turner, and vigorously denied rumors of a separation that were circulating in 1941. "I ain't dying and I ain't divorcing Clark," she said. "I simply ain't any of the things they say."

The two of them remained as professionally committed as ever, Lombard turning in what some consider to be her finest work in Ernst Lubitsch's World War II comedy *To Be or Not to Be,* playing opposite Jack Benny as half of a Polish theatrical pair involved in espionage for the Allies who confront and outwit suspicious Nazis. While she was working on the picture, Lombard told *Hedda Hopper, "I want to keep working as long as I have my looks and my sanity."

With America now resolutely at war, Gable was named as the chair of the Hollywood Victory Committee and agreed to the suggestion that Lombard open a war-bonds drive for the Midwest in her hometown. Carole and Bessie, along with Carole's publicist, left by train for Indiana on January 12, 1942, and arrived in Fort Wayne in time for the public ceremonies on the 15th, at which Lombard was mobbed by thousands wanting to see the hometown girl who had married "the King." Anxious to complete pre-production on her next picture and to return to the Encino ranch, Lombard sent Gable a telegram the night of the 15th saying she had decided to fly back to Los Angeles, even though Bessie hated flying. Gable set about planning a homecoming party as Transcontinental and Western Airways Flight #3, a DC-3 with 21 passengers aboard, left Fort Wayne at four o'clock in the morning. Carole, along with her mother and PR agent, were the only civilians aboard, the rest of the passengers being military personnel bound for assignments at Army and Air Force bases in California. Many hours later, as the flight passed south of Las Vegas, the pilot casually radioed that he had decided to fly some 35 miles off his planned course in order to save time.

As he was about to leave for the airport to meet the flight, Gable learned that Lombard's plane had gone down. Frantic, he flew to the crash site to discover that the plane's collision with Table Rock Mountain had left no survivors. Except for the bodies of three military passengers thrown clear of the wreckage, all on board had been trapped in the cabin and burned nearly beyond recognition. Lombard, only 33 at her death, and her mother became the first American women to die in a war-related accident during World War II.

A shocked Hollywood felt as if it had lost its best friend. "Without her, this place changed permanently," said director Wesley Ruggles, who had worked on three pictures with Lombard. "She was irreplaceable, and we just kept on missing her." Garson Kanin, who had directed Lombard in *They Knew What They Wanted,* thought her one of the finest performers he had ever met and consoled himself by recalling Carole's brilliant combination of physical beauty, genial professionalism, and bawdy good humor. "If Carole did six takes," he said, "it was six *different* takes. Each one had some small development, some sense of growth. There was always something going on inside Carole." He especially missed her laugh. It had, he said, "the joyous sound of pealing bells."

Gable stumbled through the memorial service and received condolences, including a telegram from President Franklin Roosevelt, with hollow-eyed grief. He completed work on the picture he had begun before Carole's death, *Somewhere I'll Find You,* then enlisted in the Air Force and stayed away from Hollywood for the rest of the war. He returned to the empty Encino ranch when the war ended, starred in 27 more films, married twice more, and had a son before his own death in 1961 of a heart attack. During all that time, close friends knew he never really recovered from the loss of his greatest love; and the world at large realized it, too, when his last wife honored his dying wish and saw to it that he was buried at Forest Lawn Cemetery, next to Carole Lombard.

SOURCES:

"Clark Gable and Carole Lombard," in *People Weekly* (special section, "Great Love Stories of the Century"). Vol. 45, no. 6. February 12, 1996.

Kanin, Garson. *Hollywood*. NY: Viking Press, 1967.

Swindell, Larry. *Screwball: The Life of Carole Lombard*. NY: William Morrow, 1975.

Norman Powers,
writer-producer, Chelsea Lane Productions, New York

Lombarda (b. 1190)

Troubadour of Provence. Born in 1190 in Toulouse.

A poet of Provence in southern France, Lombarda came from Toulouse. Little is known about the details of her life; she married in her teens, and gained a reputation for writing beautiful love poetry. Her troubadour-lover was Bernart Arnaut, a petty noble who became count of Armagnac in 1217, with whom she composed at least one *tenson* (poem written as a dialogue) which still exists. Lombarda was also a noted proponent of Catharism (also known as Albigensianism), a heretical religious sect popular in southern France during the 12th century.

Laura York,
Riverside, California

Lombardi, Lella (1942—)

Internationally famous Italian racing-car driver, known as "the Tigress of Turin," who was the first woman to compete in the U.S. Grand Prix. Born in 1942 in Italy.

Women began competing as grand-prix racing drivers as early as 1958, when **Anna-Maria de Fillipis** competed in three Formula One events. Not until the early 1970s, however, did a woman racing driver become internationally famous. Credit for this achievement goes to the Italian driver Lella Lombardi, who came up through the ranks in European Formula car racing. She started in Formula Italia, the Italian single-seaters which use the Fiat 850 engine, and from there went into Formula Three and finally Formula 5000. Known to her fans and the media as "the Tigress of Turin," Lombardi quickly developed an international reputation for skill and daring. Her achievements served to inspire other women in racing, including Australia's **Sue Ransom**, who saw Lombardi race in Australia during 1973. In 1974, when Lombardi made her first Formula One outing at the wheel of a privately entered Brabham in the British Grand Prix, she just missed qualifying. In 1975, she finished sixth in the Spanish Grand Prix, and soon after became the first woman to score a point counting toward the world driving championship. At Watkins Glen, New York, in October 1975, Lombardi became the first woman to compete in the U.S. Grand Prix.

SOURCES:

Katz, Michael. "James Hunt and Lella Lombardi: Racing 'Odd Couple,'" in *The New York Times Biographical Service.* August 1974, pp. 1107–1108.

Pash, Phil. "Miss Lombardi Aims At Auto Sex Barrier," in *The New York Times Biographical Service.* October 1975, p. 1297.

Stell, Marion K. *Half the Race: A History of Australian Women in Sport.* North Ryde, New South Wales: Angus & Robertson, 1991.

John Haag,
Associate Professor of History,
University of Georgia, Athens, Georgia

Lombards, queen of the.

See Clotsinda.

See Theodelinda (568–628).
See Guntrud of Bavaria (fl. 715).

Lombardy, queen of.

See Adelaide of Burgundy (931–999).

London, Julie (1926–1992)

American singer and actress whose "Cry Me a River" stayed on top of the music charts for months. Born Julie Peck in Santa Rosa, California, on September 26, 1926; died in 1992; daughter of Jack and Josephine (Taylor) Peck (song-and-dance vaudeville performers who ran a photography studio on the side); attended Arrowview Junior High School, San Bernardino, California; married Jack Webb (an actor), in 1947 (divorced 1953); married Bobby Troup (a jazz musician and songwriter), on December 31, 1959; children: (first marriage) two daughters, Stacy Webb and Lisa Webb.

Filmography: Jungle Woman *(1944);* Nabonga *(1945);* On Stage Everybody! *(1945);* A Night in Paradise *(1946);* The Red House *(1947);* Tap Roots *(1948);* Task Force *(1949);* Return of the Frontiersman *(1950);* The Fat Man *(1951);* The Fighting Chance *(1955);* Crime Against Joe *(1956);* The Great Man *(1956);* The Girl Can't Help It *(1956);* Drango *(1957);* Saddle the Wind *(1958);* Voice in the Mirror *(1958);* Man of the West *(1958);* The Wonderful Country *(1959);* Night of the Quarter Moon *(1959);* A Question of Adultery *(1959);* The Third Voice *(1960);* The George Raft Story *(1961);* Sanctuary *(1961).*

Records: Cry Me a River/ 'S Wonderful *(Lib 55006),* Baby, Baby, All the Time/ Shadow Woman *(Lib 55008); LPs:* Julie Is Her Name, Vol. 1 *(Lib 3006),* Make Love to Me *(Lib 3060),* Julie Is Her Name, Vol. 2 *(Lib 3100),* Swing Me an Old Song *(Lib 3119),* Send for Me *(Lib 3171),* The Best of Julie *(Lib 5501),* All Through the Night *(Lib 7434),* Nice Girls Don't Stay *(Lib 7493),* With Body and Soul *(Lib 7514),* Easy Does It *(Lib 7546),* Yummy, Yummy, Yummy *(Lib 7609),* Soft and Sweet *(Sun 5161).*

A stunning woman with arguably one of the most sensual singing voices ever recorded, Julie London was well into a second-rate film career when jazz musician Bobby Troup put her in front of a microphone and encouraged her to sing. Her first album, *Julie is Her Name,* produced her most memorable song "Cry Me a River," which, when it was later released as a single, remained on the charts for months and led *Theme* magazine to vote her the "most exciting new vocalist" of 1956. On the heels of her breakthrough as a singer, London was cast as an alcoholic singer in the movie *The Great Man* (1956), a role which proved her merit as an actress as well as a singer and reignited her faltering career.

London was born in Santa Rosa, California, in 1926 to a song-and-dance vaudeville team who ran a photographic studio on the side. At the age of three, she made her radio debut, singing "Falling in Love Again." Never a great student, London quit school at 15 and took a job as an elevator operator in a department store on Hollywood Boulevard. It was there that **Sue Carol**, the actors' agent and wife of Alan Ladd, discovered her and suggested a screen test. On the strength of her looks alone, London won a movie contract and, over the next four years, appeared in secondary roles in low-budget films. Between films, she went back to her $19-a-week job at the department store.

In 1947, London married Jack Webb, who was a struggling radio performer at the time. In 1950, after Webb hit it big with the "Dragnet" television series, London virtually retired from show business. The couple had two daughters before they divorced in 1953. After suffering what she later called a failure of self-confidence, London resumed her career, aided in part by her relationship with Bobby Troup, whom she met in 1954. They would marry in 1959. Troup had heard her sing at a private party and tried for over a year to get her in front of a larger audience. After much cajoling, she agreed to a stint at John Walsh's 881 Club in Los Angeles. Originally booked for three weeks, she stayed for ten and, soon after, was signed by Liberty Records.

London's sound has been characterized as "a voice for a smoke-filled room," with a husky, breathy, intimate quality that lends itself perfectly to the blues and torch songs she preferred. "If I have to, I can belt songs out, but I don't like them that way," she once said. "That's not the natural me." After her role in *The Great Man* (1956), based on the Al Morgan novel of the same name and directed by José Ferrer, London made a string of mediocre movies. Concurrent with her movie and singing career, she was a frequent guest on television, including appearances on "The Bob Hope Show," "The Steve Allen Show," "The *Dinah Shore* Show," and "The Perry Como Show." In 1960, she starred as a nightclub owner in her own series, "Maggie Malone," and during the 1970s did a long stint as a nurse on the hospital drama "Emergency." Contrary to her image, London liked to hang around in blue jeans and slouchy sweaters, and was crazy about football.

SOURCES:
Current Biography. NY: H.W. Wilson, 1960.

Katz, Ephraim. *The Film Encyclopedia.* NY: Harper-Collins, 1994.

Barbara Morgan,
Melrose, Massachusetts

Julie
London

Long, Catherine Small (1924—)

American congressional representative, 99th Congress. Born on February 7, 1924, in Dayton, Ohio; married Gillis W. Long (1923–1985, a lawyer and politician); educated at Camp Hill, Pennsylvania; Louisiana State University, Baton Rouge, B.A., 1948.

Served as U.S. Navy pharmacist's mate; was staff assistant to Senator Wayne Morse of Oregon and Representative James G. Polk of Ohio; was a delegate to the Democratic National Conventions (1980 and 1984); was a member of the Louisiana State Democratic Financial Council and State central committee, and Democratic leadership council; served as Democrat member of the 99th Congress by special election (March 30, 1985–January 3, 1987).

Catherine Small Long, who was born in Dayton, Ohio, on February 7, 1924, and attended Camp Hill High School in Pennsylvania, is most closely associated with the state of

Louisiana, where she attended university in the 1940s. Her early career included working as a pharmacist's mate in the U.S. Navy, and subsequently becoming staff assistant to Senator Wayne Morse and Representative James G. Polk. Politics was to become the dominating force in her life after her marriage to lawyer Gillis Long, member of a formidable political dynasty of high-profile Louisiana Democrats. Among Gillis Long's close relatives were Representative George Shannon Long (1883–1958), Governor and Senator Huey Pierce Long (1893–1935), Senator **Rose McConnell Long** (1892–1970) and Senator Russell B. Long (b. 1918).

Catherine Long acquired substantial political experience during her marriage, serving as delegate to the Democratic National Conventions of 1980 and 1984; she was also a member of the Louisiana State Democratic Financial Council, the state party's central committee, and the Democratic leadership council. When Gillis Long died on January 20, 1985, after serving eight terms as representative from Louisiana's Eighth

Catherine
Small
Long

District, Long stood for his seat in a special election held on March 30. By defeating four other candidates, she became only the fourth woman to represent Louisiana in Congress, following in the footsteps of fellow Democrats Senator **Elaine Schwartzenburg Edwards**, Senator Rose McConnell Long, and Representative *Lindy Boggs.

During her two years as a congressional representative, Long was an advocate for Louisiana's economy, arguing the need for price supports for sugar. She was also the opponent of an amendment to the Mississippi River and Tributaries Project Bill which would have placed a large flood-control financial burden on local governments in the lower Mississippi Valley. Long co-sponsored the Economic Equity Act of 1985, which secured pension and health benefits for women and helped to restrict discrimination by race or gender in insurance practices. She supported economic sanctions against South Africa and was a proponent of aid for Nicaraguan refugees. Along with the other members of the Louisiana delegation, Long helped introduce legislation authorizing the Legal Services Corporation to make a grant to the Gillis W. Long Poverty Law Center at Loyola University in New Orleans. Long chose not to stand for reelection in 1986, but remains a resident of Washington, D.C.

SOURCES:

Office of the Historian. *Women in Congress, 1917–1990.* Commission on the Bicentenary of the U.S. House of Representatives, 1991.

Paula Morris, D.Phil.,
Brooklyn, New York

Long, Jill Lynette (1952—)

American congressional representative, 1989–95. Born on July 15, 1952, in Warsaw, Indiana; attended Columbia City Joint High School; Valparaiso University, B.S., 1974; Indiana University, M.B.A., 1978, and Ph.D., 1984.

Taught at Indiana University, Bloomington, Valparaiso University and Indiana University/Purdue University-Fort Wayne; served as Democratic member of Congress (1989–95); was a fellow at the Institute of Politics, John F. Kennedy School of Government, Harvard University; served as a member, board of directors, Commodity Credit Corporation; was under-secretary for rural, economic and community development, Department of Agriculture.

Jill Long was born in Warsaw in Kosciusko County, Indiana, on July 15, 1952. Raised on a farm, Long attended public schools in Whitley County, Indiana, graduating from Columbia

City Joint High School and, in 1974, from Valparaiso University. After receiving her M.B.A. in 1978 and Ph.D. in 1984 from Indiana University, Bloomington, Long embarked on an academic career. With experience teaching business at Indiana University during her years as a graduate student, Long became an assistant professor of business at Valparaiso University and an adjunct professor at Indiana University/Purdue University-Fort Wayne.

During the mid-1980s, while also acting as a management consultant to small businesses, Long became a member of the Valparaiso city council, serving from 1983 to 1986. Inspired by this political experience, in 1986 Long challenged Dan Quayle in his successful bid for a second Senate term. In 1988, she again lost to a Republican incumbent—this time Representative Dan Coats—in the election for the 101st Congress. When Dan Coats left the House after appointment to Dan Quayle's Senate seat the following year, Long stood for national political office for the third time in the special election for Indiana's Fourth District. Concentrating on local issues in a close-fought campaign which attracted national attention, Long scored a surprising victory over Republican Dan Heath and was elected as a Democrat to the 101st Congress on March 28, 1989.

Long took her oath of office on April 5, 1989, and served on the Veterans' Affairs Committee, the Committee on Agriculture and the Select Committee on Hunger. Unsuccessful in her attempt to be reelected to 104th Congress in 1994, Long became a fellow at the Institute of Politics at the John F. Kennedy School of Government, Harvard University, and a member of the board of directors of the Commodity Credit Corporation. In 1995, she became under-secretary for rural, economic and community development at the Department of Agriculture.

SOURCES:

Office of the Historian. *Women in Congress, 1917–1990.* Commission on the Bicentenary of the U.S. House of Representatives, 1991.

Paula Morris, D.Phil.,
Brooklyn, New York

Long, Kathleen (1896–1968)

English pianist, author of Nineteenth Century Piano Music, *who introduced the music of Gabriel Fauré to the British public. Born in Brentford, England, on July 7, 1896; died in Cambridge, England, on March 20, 1968.*

Kathleen Long began her studies at the Royal College of Music when she was 13, win-

ning the Hopkinson Gold Medal in 1915. After graduation, she received a faculty appointment at the Royal College. Long played with great distinction both as a solo performer and in chamber-music ensembles. Her performances of the music of Gabriel Fauré were unusual at the time and did much to familiarize the British musical public with the output of this subtle and profound composer. In 1957, she gave the world premiere performance of Gerald Finzi's *Eclogue* for Piano and String Orchestra. Her book *Nineteenth Century Piano Music* was well received.

SOURCES:

Dubal, David. *The Art of the Piano.* NY: Summit Books, 1989.

Lyle, Wilson. *A Dictionary of Pianists.* NY: Schirmer Books, 1985.

McVeagh, Diana. "Long, Kathleen," *New Grove Dictionary of Music and Musicians.* Vol. 11, p. 219.

John Haag,
Athens, Georgia

Long, Marguerite (1874–1966)

French pianist who was a noted interpreter of Ravel, Debussy and Fauré. Name variations: Marie-Charlotte Long; Marie Charlotte Long. Born on November 13, 1874, in Nimes, France; died on February 13,

Jill Lynette Long

1966, in Paris; studied piano at Nimes Conservatory (1880s); studied at Paris Conservatory under Tissot and Antoine Marmontel from 1887; married Joseph de Marliave (a musicologist who died in 1914).

Taught at Paris Conservatory (1906–40); was professor of piano from 1920; began own school (1920); ran École Marguerite Long-Jacques Thibaud with violinist Jacques Thibaud (from 1940); inaugurated Long-Thibaud international piano and violin competition (1943); was a favored performer; toured internationally performing classical, romantic and contemporary repertoire; noted interpreter of and authority on French music.

Books include: Le piano (The Piano, 1959); Au piano avec Claude Debussy (At the Piano with Claude Debussy, 1960); Au piano avec Gabriel Fauré (At the Piano with Gabriel Fauré, 1963); Au piano avec Maurice Ravel (At the Piano with Maurice Ravel, 1971).

Marguerite Long

Marguerite Long was born in the south of France, in the town of Nimes, in November 1874. After beginning her piano studies at home, she entered the Nimes Conservatory. In 1887, Long moved to Paris, attending the Paris Conservatory as a student of Tissot and Antoine Marmontel. Long won first prize for pianoforte playing in her first year in Paris, and made her public debut in 1893, although she did not perform in public again until 1903.

Regarded by her contemporaries as a virtuoso performer, Long was asked to join the staff of the Conservatory. In 1906, she took charge of the preparatory pianoforte classes, and in 1920 succeeded Louis Diémer as professor of piano, a position she would hold until 1940.

In addition to teaching, Long toured the major concert halls of Europe and South America performing solo recitals and concertos, sometimes under the direction of her friend Maurice Ravel, who dedicated his Concerto in G major to her. At a concert of his works conducted by the composer in 1932, Long gave the concerto its first performance; they would later record it together.

Long was married to musicologist Joseph de Marliave, who was killed in 1914. Ravel dedicated *Le tombeau de Couperin* to de Marliave, and

Long gave its first performance on April 11, 1919. At the heart of musical circles in Paris, Long was also a friend of Claude Debussy and a colleague of Gabriel Fauré. Like Ravel, these composers dedicated compositions to her, and she performed world premieres of many of their piano works, along with pieces by Satie, Poulenc and Deodat de Séverac. Towards the end of her life, Long wrote books on the works of Ravel, Debussy and Fauré, drawing on her intimate knowledge of their lives, working methods, and interpretive concerns.

In demand as a lecturer on French music, as a recording artist, and as a performer of the classical, romantic and contemporary repertoires, Long published the well-regarded book *Les Quatuors de Beethoven*, with an introduction by Fauré, in 1925. In 1920, she had founded her own school, and in 1940 was joined in this endeavor by violinist Jacques Thibaud. Long developed her own method of teaching, about which she would later publish a book, and the École Marguerite Long-Jacques Thibaud became a highly successful and well respected institution, with pupils including Jean Doyen and Jacques Février, *Jeanne-Marie Darré, Bernard Ringeissen, Peter Frankl, Ludwig Hoffman, *Nicole Henriot-Schweitzer, and Philippe Entremont. In 1943, she and Thibaud established the Long-Thibaud competition, an international piano and violin contest which quickly became one of the most prestigious in the world.

Regarded throughout her life as one of the most important French pianists of the 20th century, Marguerite Long died in Paris in February 1966.

SOURCES:
Dubal, David. *The Art of the Piano.* NY: Summit Books, 1989.

Lyle, Wilson. *A Dictionary of Pianists.* NY: Schirmer Books, 1985.

Millington, Barry. "Long, Marguerite (Marie Charlotte)," in *New Grove Dictionary of Music and Musicians.* Vol. 11. p. 219.

Timbrell, Charles. *French Pianism: An Historical Perspective.* White Plains, NY: Pro/Am Music Resources, 1992.

SUGGESTED READING:
Dunoyer, Cecilia. *Marguerite Long: A Life in French Music, 1874–1966.* Bloomington, IN: Indiana University Press, 1993.

Paula Morris, D.Phil.,
Brooklyn, New York

Long, Naomi (b. 1923).

See Madgett, Naomi.

Long, Tania (1913–1998)

German-born war correspondent. Born Tatiana Long on April 29, 1913, in Berlin, Germany; committed suicide on September 4, 1998, in Ottawa, Canada; daughter of Robert Crozier Long and Tatiana Mouraviev; graduated from Malvern Girls College in England (1930); did post-graduate work in history and economics at the Sorbonne, Paris (1930–31), and the Paris École des Sciences Politiques; married Raymond Daniell (London bureau chief, The New York Times), in 1941; children: (from a previous marriage) Robert M. Gray.

A trail-blazing female war correspondent, Tania Long was born in Berlin in 1913 to a Russian mother and a British father. She acquired an early familiarity with a variety of languages and got her first journalistic experiences at the side of her father, who was a *New York Times* financial columnist and Berlin correspondent to *The Economist* of London.

Long lived and studied in cities across Europe, but became an American citizen in 1935, beginning her career at New Jersey's *Network Ledger* the following year. By 1938, she had returned to Berlin to work for the *New York Herald Tribune*'s bureau there, where her sound writing skills soon earned her the job of assistant chief correspondent. Upon the outbreak of World War II in 1939, she transferred to Copenhagen, then on to Paris, and finally to London, where in 1941 she won an award for her reporting on the bombing of that city. One of these award-winning stories was an account of bombs falling on the Hotel Savoy—the hotel where she was living.

That same year, Long's future husband, Raymond Daniell, London bureau chief for *The New York Times*, called her a serious journalistic competitor in what he had, up until then, considered man's work, and said that "her calm and courage during the frightful days of the blitzkrieg helped us all to keep our nerves steady." Daniell and Long—"an attractive girl with . . . alert eyes and the most infectious smile"—married in November 1941. Long joined *The Times* as a reporter about three months later. She reported on war-torn London and covered the Allied advance through France from just behind the lines. She is thought to be the first female reporter to follow the Allies into Berlin.

After the war, Long returned to Germany as a *Times* correspondent, assisting Daniell in covering the Nuremberg trials. In 1946, she was awarded a campaign ribbon of service by the European theater secretary of war. From 1952 to 1964, she and Daniell headed *The Times*' bureau in Ottawa, Canada, where they became part of a distinguished journalistic and political society. Decades later, after suffering from a series of illnesses which, according to a friend, made life just too painful for her, Long committed suicide at age 85.

SOURCES:
Current Biography. NY: H.W. Wilson, 1946.

Jacquie Maurice,
Calgary, Alberta, Canada

Longabarba, Bona (fl. 15th c.)

Italian noblewoman and military leader. Flourished in 15th century in Lombardy; married.

An Italian military leader, Bona Longabarba fought with her husband in several battles. She was a Lombard noblewoman who became a respected leader of soldiers, known for her great strategic abilities and her skill at inspiring bravery even when a battle seemed lost. In one instance, Bona led troops to the castle of an enemy who had taken her husband prisoner; under her command, the troops stormed the castle, rescued her husband, and killed her enemy and his supporters.

Laura York,
Riverside, California

Longfellow, Frances Appleton
(1819–1861)

Frances Appleton Longfellow

Second wife of Henry Wadsworth Longfellow. Name variations: Fanny. Born Frances Elizabeth Appleton in Boston, Massachusetts, on October 6, 1819; died in Cambridge, Massachusetts, on July 10, 1861; one of two daughters of Nathan Appleton (a wealthy merchant); married Henry Wadsworth Longfellow (1807–1882, the poet), on July 13, 1843, in Boston; children: two sons and three daughters.

The second wife of American poet Henry Wadsworth Longfellow, Fanny Appleton was born in 1819 in Boston, Massachusetts, the daughter of a wealthy merchant. A well-educated and traveled young woman, she met Henry while they were both touring in Switzerland, and during their long courtship

she succeeded in assuaging his deep grief and loneliness after the loss of his first wife, **Mary Storer Potter**, who died in 1835. The couple married on July 13, 1843, while Henry was a professor at Harvard University, and settled into blissful life in a large house ("Craigie Castle") on Brattle Street, in Cambridge, Massachusetts. Fanny was deeply in love with her new husband. "How completely my life is bound up in his love," she wrote in her journal on May 27, 1844, just 12 days before the birth of her first son, "how broken and incomplete when he is absent a moment; what infinite peace and fullness when he is present. Can any child excite as strong a passion as this we feel for each other?"

The happy union produced two sons and three daughters before coming to a tragic end. On July 9, 1861, Fanny was heating sealing wax to close a packet containing a lock of one of her children's hair, when the sleeve of her light cotton dress caught fire. She was immediately engulfed in flames. She ran from the library into the front room, where Henry was working. Although he was able to save her face from the flames, she was severely burned and died the next day. Henry was so badly burned in his attempt to save his wife that he was unable to attend her funeral.

SOURCES:
Edgerly, Lois Stiles. *Give Her This Day.* Gardiner, ME: Tilbury House, 1990.
Thompson, Lawrence. *Young Longfellow (1807–1843).* NY: Macmillan, 1938.

COLLECTIONS:
Fanny Longfellow's journal is with her papers at the Longfellow House, Cambridge, Massachusetts.

Barbara Morgan,
Melrose, Massachusetts

Longford, Elizabeth (1906—)

*English historian. Name variations: Countess of Longford, formerly Lady Pakenham; Elizabeth Harman Pakenham. Born in London, England, on August 30, 1906; daughter of Nathaniel Bishop (an ophthalmologist) and Katherine (Chamberlain) Harman; received her degree in Literae Humaniores at Oxford; married Francis Aungier Pakenham, 7th earl of Longford (a writer and politician), in 1931; children: Thomas Pakenham; Patrick Pakenham; **Judith Kazantzis**; **Rachel Billington**; Michael Pakenham; Catherine Pakenham (died 1969); Kevin Pakenham; **Antonia Fraser** (b. 1932, a writer).*

A woman of numerous interests and achievements, Elizabeth Longford was twice a Labour candidate for Parliament, is a Trustee of the National Portrait Gallery and a Member of the Royal Society of Literature. She is also the author of the bestselling books, *Queen Victoria: Born to Succeed*; *Wellington: The Years of the Sword* and *Victoria, R.I.* Her 1986 autobiography is entitled *The Pebbled Shore: The Memoirs of Elizabeth Longford.*

Longhi, Lucia Lopresti (1895–1985)

Italian biographer, translator, novelist, founder and editor of Paragone, *who focused on women's place in Italian society. Name variations: (pseudonym) Anna Banti. Born Lucia Lopresti in 1895 in Florence, Italy; died in 1985 in Ronchi, Italy; educated at University of Rome; married art historian Robert Longhi (died 1970).*

Selected works: Itinerario di Paolina *(Guide to Paolina, 1937);* Il corraggio delle donne *(The Courage of Women, 1940);* Artemisia *(1947, translation by Shirley D'Ardia Caracciolo, University of Nebraska Press, 1995);* Il bastardo *(The Bastard, 1953);* Un grido lacerante *(A Piercing Cry, 1981);* Quando anche le donne si misero a dipingere *(When Women Too Began to Paint, 1982).*

Lucia Lopresti Longhi lived in some of Italy's greatest cities and found the inspiration for much of her literary work among its paintings. Raised in Rome and Bologna, she was educated primarily in art history, taking a degree at the University of Rome. There she met Robert Longhi, an art historian, whom she married. The couple later co-founded the journal *Paragone,* of which she was literary, and he artistic, editor.

Assuming the name of a childhood acquaintance, Anna Banti, for her pseudonym, Longhi began writing in her 30s and would produce more than 20 books, not all of her which were written in Italian. The first, *Itinerario di Paolina,* published in 1937, was a collection of short stories. Among her most famous novels was the recreation of 16th-century painter *Artemisia Gentileschi's life, *Artemisia,* published in 1947, an amazing feat in light of the fact that her original manuscript was lost during World War II and had to be entirely rewritten. She also translated William Makepeace Thackeray's *Vanity Fair* and *Virginia Woolf's *Jacob's Room.*

In 1940, the Longhis settled permanently in Florence. When Robert died in 1970, Lucia assumed his duties in addition to her own at *Paragone.* One of her last novels was the autobiographical work *Un grido lacerante* (*A Piercing Cry*), published when the author was 86. Of primary importance throughout her writing was

Longhi's belief that women were assigned to unfulfilling tasks in life.

Elizabeth Longford

SOURCES:

Bondanella, Peter, and Julia Conaway Bondanella, eds. *Dictionary of Italian Literature.* Westport, CT: Greenwood Press, 1979.

Buck, Claire, ed. *The Bloomsbury Guide to Women's Literature.* NY: Prentice Hall, 1992.

Russell, Rinalda. *Italian Women Writers.* Westport, CT: Greenwood Press, 1994.

Wilson, Katherina M., ed. *An Encyclopedia of Continental Women Writers.* NY: Garland Publishing, 1991.

Crista Martin,
freelance writer, Boston, Massachusetts

Longman, Evelyn Beatrice

(1874–1954)

American sculptor. Born Mary Evelyn Beatrice Longman in a log cabin on a farm near Winchester, Ohio, in 1874; died on Cape Cod at age 80 in March 1954; one of six children of a farmer; studied at the Art Institute, Chicago; married Nathaniel Horton Batchelder (headmaster of the Loomis School in Windsor, Connecticut), in 1920.

From age 14 to 20, Evelyn Longman supported herself by day working for a wholesaler while studying at night at the Chicago Art Institute; she eventually graduated with honors. From 1901, Longman worked in New York as assistant to the popular sculptor Daniel Chester French, who had sculpted the seated Lincoln in the Lincoln Memorial in Washington, D.C. Her first important piece was a male statue, *Victory*, shown in the Festival Hall at the St. Louis Exposition (1904), for which she was awarded a silver medal. (A replica now resides in New York's Metropolitan Museum of Art.) In 1906, she won the $20,000 competition to create the bronze doors of the U.S. Naval Academy Chapel of Annapolis. These doors, executed in low relief, are remarkable for their beauty of line and balance of composition. A second pair of doors was designed for Wellesley College. In addition to her Spanish War Memorial in Hartford, Connecticut, and other statues, Longman produced a number of fine portrait busts, including that of *Alice Freeman Palmer for the American Hall of Fame. She was the only sculptor that Thomas Edison posed for and the first woman sculptor to be elected a full member of the National Academy of Design.

Longshore, Hannah E. (1819–1901)

American physician. Born Hannah Myers on May 30, 1819, in Sandy Spring, Maryland; died in Philadelphia, Pennsylvania, on October 18, 1901; eldest child of five daughters and two sons of Samuel Myers (a teacher) and Paulina (Iden) Myers; attended Quaker schools in Washington, D.C., until the age of 13 or 14; attended New Lisbon Academy, New Lisbon, Ohio; awarded M.D. from the Female (later Woman's) Medical College of Pennsylvania, December 31, 1851; married Thomas Ellwood Longshore (a teacher), on March 26, 1841; children: son, Channing Longshore (b. 1842); daughter, Lucretia Longshore (b. 1845).

The eldest of seven children of a liberal Quaker family, Hannah Myers was born in 1819 in Sandy Spring, Maryland, but was raised and educated in Washington, D.C., and, from 1833, in Columbiana County, Ohio. Her early interest in academics, especially science, was encouraged by her father and at the Lisbon Academy, where she adopted a middle initial "E" in her name to distinguish herself from a classmate with the same name. Inspired by the family physician, whose prescriptions she administered to the family, Hannah wanted desperately to be a doctor and hoped to go on to study medicine at Oberlin College, but the family simply lacked the money to send her.

In March 1841, at age 22, Hannah married Thomas Ellwood Longshore, a philosopher of religion who was a teacher at Lisbon Academy. An enlightened man, Thomas was also a reformer who supported education and women's rights. His later writings would include works on peace, temperance, labor, and woman suffrage. For the next four years, the couple lived with Hannah's family while Thomas continued to teach and Hannah tended to their two children, Channing (b. 1842) and Lucretia (b. 1845). In 1845, after losing his job because of his anti-slavery views, Thomas moved his family to his hometown of Attleboro, Pennsylvania. Here, Hannah finally had an opportunity to study medicine, apprenticing under Thomas' brother Joseph Skelton Longshore, who was a practitioner of Eclectic medicine. Hannah's enthusiasm and ability may have inspired Joseph to assist in the establishment of the Female Medical College of Pennsylvania, which opened its doors in 1850. A member of the college's first class, Longshore was one of eight classmates (including her sister-in-law **Anna Longshore** and *Ann Preston, future dean of the college) who completed the first four-month session in 1851. During the second session, running from September to December 1851, Longshore both studied and served as a demonstrator, thus qualifying as the first woman faculty member of an American medical school. After completing a thesis on the treatment of neuralgia by water, she was awarded an M.D. degree on December 31, 1851. The graduation exercises were marked by a strong police presence, necessary to guard against the threat of violence from male medical students.

In the climate of prejudice against female physicians at the time, Longshore had difficulty building a private practice. She continued to teach, demonstrating anatomy at the New England Female Medical College in Boston, at the Female Medical College of Pennsylvania, and at the Penn Medical University. Her practice was helped immensely by a series of public lectures she initiated in the spring of 1852, a project that required her to overcome her intense shyness. The first, an address on medical education for women, supported by *Lucretia Mott as well as by prominent Quakers in the area, proved such a success that she followed up with a series on physiology and hygiene. Although Longshore's frank discussions of sexual matters shocked conservatives, they also drew patients into her practice, which within three years was so large that she was forced to give up her teaching and lecturing. Eventually, she was caring for 300 families in the area, a record that surpassed any of her colleagues, male or female. Her reputation was such that some of her male colleagues, while not openly supporting her, sent their own wives and daughters to her for treatment. Longshore continued to practice for 40 years, retiring in 1892. She died of uremia in 1901 and was buried in Philadelphia's Fair Hill Cemetery. Her remains and those of her husband were later removed to Chelten Hills Cemetery. Although Hannah Longshore may have inspired much hostility against women physicians in Philadelphia during the 1850s, she is also credited with the acceptance of women into the profession later in the century.

SOURCES:

James, Edward T., ed. *Notable American Women 1607–1950.* Cambridge, MA: The Belknap Press of Harvard University Press, 1971.

McHenry, Robert, ed. *Famous American Women.* NY: Dover, 1983.

Parton, James, ed. *Eminent Women of the Age.* Hartford, CT: S.M. Betts, 1872.

Barbara Morgan,
Melrose, Massachusetts

Longueville, Anne Geneviève, Duchesse de (1619–1679)

French princess who, after a life crowded with excitement, romance, and intrigue, turned her back on the ways of the world and lived the life of a penitent for 20 years before her death. Name variations: Anne de Bourbon; Anne Geneviève de Bourbon, Duchesse de Longueville; Anne Geneviève de Bourbon-Conde. Born Anne Geneviève de Bourbon-Condé or Conde on August 28, 1619, in the Bois de Vincennes; died on April 15, 1679, at the Convent of the Carmelites, Paris; daughter of Charlotte de Montmorency and Henry II de Bourbon, third Prince de Condé; sister of the Great Condé; married Henry, the Duc de Longueville, on June 2, 1642; children: daughter, name unknown (c. 1646–1650), and two sons, Jean-Louis-Charles, the Comte de Dunois, Abbé d'Orleans (c. 1647–1694) and Charles-Paris, the Comte de Saint-Paul (c. 1649–1672); stepdaughter ❦▸ Marie d'Orleans, Mlle. de Longueville, who became Duchesse de Nemours (c. 1625–1707).

Born during her father's imprisonment (1619), was attracted to the religious life as a young girl but, with her family's position restored, made a glittering debut into French society at age 14; a captivating beauty, made a politically advantageous marriage to a much older man (1642); had three children, saw an admirer killed in a duel defending her reputation, conducted a notorious affair, and became one of the major participants in the Fronde, a sporadic civil war against the court (1642–52); deserted and betrayed by

her lover, returned to her family and gradually resumed her earlier religious devotion; became an influential supporter of the nuns and theologians of Port Royal (1660s) and played a primary role in securing the Peace of the Church (1669); lived with the nuns of Port Royal and at the Carmelite house (1672–79).

A popular song of the 1640s portrayed the heartless beauty, the new duchesse de Longueville, peering from behind a curtain as the brave young champion of her honor was killed in a duel in the street below. A princess of the French royal house, born in a prison, a woman of incomparable beauty who deserted her husband and children to aid her lover in rebellion against the king but subsequently found peace among the strict, self-denying nuns of Port Royal, Anne Geneviève de Bourbon's life appears at first glance to be one of contrasts and contradictions.

She was descended from the most revered of the kings of France, the saintly Louis IX (d.

Anne Geneviève, Duchesse de Longueville

Marie d'Orleans. *See Nemours, Marie d'Orleans, duchesse de.*

1270), and her father Henry II de Bourbon, third Prince de Condé, was second cousin to the reigning monarch, Henry IV. Henry, a notorious philanderer, arranged the marriage of Anne's father to ❧▶ **Charlotte de Montmorency** and then attempted to seduce the beautiful Charlotte, causing the couple to flee to Belgium. After the assassination of Henry IV in 1610, the couple returned from exile, only to be arrested on suspicion of plotting against the new ruler, Louis XIII, and it was during their confinement in the Bois de Vincennes that their daughter Anne was born. A few months later, however, the family was released and their home, the Hôtel de Condé, became known as one of the most lavish and elegant houses in Paris.

Yet despite the social atmosphere in which she grew up, Anne's early influences were also spiritual ones. These were turbulent political times, and after her uncle had perished on the scaffold, her newly widowed aunt became a Carmelite nun. Anne's mother, no doubt under the influence of her sister, became a *dévote*, a lay woman who lived as spiritual a life as possible while remaining in the everyday world. Anne often accompanied her mother on visits to the convent where they had their own rooms. At the age of 13, the girl announced her desire to become a nun; while her mother might have been persuaded to allow it, her father was resolutely opposed, and Anne was told that she must prepare to make her entrance into society instead.

❧▶ **Charlotte de Montmorency** (fl. 1600–1621)

French aristocrat. Name variations: Charlotte of Montmorency; Princesse de Condé or Conde; Princess of Condé. Flourished between 1600 and 1621; married Henry II de Bourbon, third prince de Condé (1588–1646); children: Louis II de Bourbon, prince de Condé (1621–1686, known as The Great Condé); *Anne Geneviève, Duchesse de Longueville (1619–1679).

Charlotte of Montmorency, the princesse de Condé and an influential member of the French court, was involved with her good friends, her cousin *Anne of Austria and *Marie de Rohan-Montbazon, in the *Conspiration des Dames*. Their intent was to spoil a matchmaking scheme of Cardinal Richelieu's to better position Gaston, duke of Orléans, brother of Louis XIII, in line for the throne. The princesse preferred her husband Henry, who was next in line. When Henry headed a revolt against the regency during the minority of Louis XIII, he was imprisoned for three years at Vincennes; he then became a partisan of Richelieu. Charlotte's son, the Great Condé, was a celebrated French general.

According to one account, the 14-year-old Anne was wearing the hair shirt of a religious penitent when she made her public debut in February 1635, but spiritual thoughts were not to preoccupy her for much longer. Her radiant beauty made her the center of attention; her brilliant blue eyes, pearl-like complexion and silver blonde hair combined with her pleasing personality to inspire admiration and affection in all who met her. Anne soon became accustomed to the pleasures of society and seems to have forgotten her earlier plans to forsake it for the life of a nun.

In 1641, the elder of her two brothers, the Duc d' Enghien, later to become known as the Great Condé, made a loveless but politically advantageous marriage to **Clarie-Clémence de Maillé de Brézé**, niece of the powerful Cardinal Richelieu. The following year it was to be Anne's turn. At age 22, on June 2, 1642, she was married off to a widower with a 17-year-old daughter, a man 24 years older than herself. The Duc de Longueville, although not a man of intellectual distinction or wit, was the French noble closest in rank to the princes of the blood.

Almost from the first, the new Madame de Longueville found that she had left behind the charmed life of her girlhood; shortly after her marriage, she suffered an attack of smallpox, a dreaded disease in the 17th century. Deserted by almost all her friends, Anne survived, her beauty unmarred. An incident which occurred in the period following her recovery was to bring a different kind of danger.

The notorious and powerful *Marie de Rohan-Montbazon who, rumor had it, had been, and perhaps was still, the mistress of the Duc de Longueville, had developed an implacable dislike for her lover's new wife. It was Madame de Rohan-Montbazon who circulated a rumor concerning a letter Anne had supposedly written to a lover; her supporters insisted that Anne's honor be cleared but it was impossible, given the etiquette of the day, to confront the source of the allegation directly. Rather, Madame de Rohan-Montbazon's champion, the Duc de Guise, was challenged to a duel on Anne's behalf by the youthful Comte de Coligny. Rumors spread that the young duchess had witnessed the death of her brave champion from behind the windows of a house in the Place Royale and a popular song alleged that he had died in the attempt to become her lover.

While most of Madame de Longueville's biographers consider her to have been the innocent victim of a jealous rival in the incident which led to the tragic duel, even her staunchest defenders agree that, commencing in 1649, she began an affair with a man whom she loved so passionately as to rebel against her king and abandon her family.

Shortly after their marriage, the Duc de Longueville had been sent on a diplomatic mission to Magdeburg. It soon became obvious to Anne that he was a mere figurehead, and that he lacked the talent for either negotiation or administration. She quickly returned to her mother's house in Paris, and it was there that her eldest son was born. She was much in the company of her unmarried younger brother, the Prince de Conti, who greatly admired his beautiful sister, and it was probably through him that she came to know François, Prince de Marsillac, afterwards to become the Duc de la Rochfoucauld. A dashing, witty man of 36, he later coldly recorded in his *Mémoires* that he had seduced Madame de Longueville solely in order to win her, and through her, her brothers, to the cause of rebellion against the court.

The Fronde or slingshot wars, were a series of rebellions against the French government which broke out sporadically between 1648 and 1653. The ineffectual monarch Louis XIII had been succeeded, in 1643, by his son Louis XIV, but because the new king was still a boy, France was being governed by a regency consisting of his mother, *Anne of Austria, and her supposed lover, Cardinal Mazarin. Not only was there resentment against the Habsburg queen and her Italian advisor, but the costs of continuing warfare, several years of bad harvests, and the government's continuing attempts to curb local autonomy prompted aristocratic discontent. In what Ranke called the "burlesque war," the outbreaks of rebellion were generally small scale and sporadic, with most of the nobles involved concerned only with their own self-interest. Like many of his class, the Duc de la Rochfoucauld was convinced that he was being passed over for lucrative office and that rebellion would improve his fortunes.

Anne de Longueville's involvement in the rebellion has been ascribed to Rochfoucauld's "boundless influence" over her, but, deep as her attachment to him undoubtedly was, there were other reasons why this royal princess should have turned against the court which had generally treated her with kindness. Her impulsive husband was quick to join the rebels, and her brother, now called the Great Condé because of his brilliant success on the battlefield, shared the popular dislike for Cardinal Mazarin. But per-

haps just as important as her devotion to her lover was Anne's desire for greatness; she longed to be a leader and to play an active part in politics. As **Ethel Romanes** records, in later years she was to reveal to her confessor that "her great fault was pride, that she longed to be first, to be distinguished."

There were faults; who is without a blemish? She saw and lamented them; that is almost all which God demands of us.

—Pontchâteau

Both the Fronde and the love affair were soon over; a treaty of 1652 restored peace to Paris, but Rochfoucauld's interest in the rebellion and in Madame de Longueville had cooled the previous year. With his estates devastated by the conflict, he withdrew his soldiers from battle and his affections from his mistress. Anne, who had lost her only daughter in 1650 at the age of four, remained devoted to Rochfoucauld and stayed active with the malcontents, hopeful of his return and unwilling to rejoin her husband. The final break-up of the Fronde party in 1653 found her alone, deserted by her lover, separated from her husband and two young sons, her older brother proclaimed guilty of treason and the much-loved younger one, now allied with the court party, estranged from her. In despair, she reestablished contact with the Carmelites, visiting her widowed aunt, now superior of the convent of the Filles de la Visitation, and she subsequently wrote that she wished to end her days with them, since all her worldly attachments were now broken and severed.

During her visit to her aunt, she seems to have experienced a genuine religious conversion, for she recorded in a letter written June 11, 1653, to Mother Agnes of the Carmelites that:

> I found myself like a person who suddenly awakens from a long sleep in which she has dreamed she was great, happy, honoured, and esteemed, and discovers that she is loaded with chains, pierced with wounds, overcome with languor, and shut up in an obscure prison.

But great as was her desire to retreat from the world, Madame de Longueville still had responsibilities to fulfill. She reconciled with her husband, joining him in his post as governor of Normandy, and reunited with her children. As she observed in a letter to her Carmelite friends: "Having left God of my own free will it would not be right that I should find Him in the very first moments of seeking: if only at the end of my life I find I am not separated from Him, it would mean very much for me."

Her time of trial was not yet over; the Duc de la Rochfoucauld published his *Mémoires* in which the course of their affair was laid bare for the world and in which Anne was trivialized and ridiculed. Also, desperate to alleviate the ravages of the warfare which their rebellious intrigues had brought about, Madame de Longueville and her new sister-in-law, *Anne-Marie Martinozzi, the Princess de Conti, poured much of their remaining fortune into supporting the most damaged areas. But Anne was also able to find an increasingly important new source of support and a new cause to which she could devote herself; through her friendship with *Madeleine de Sablé she came to know the nuns and *solitaires* of Port Royal.

Some description of the controversies surrounding the religious house of Port Royal is essential to an understanding of the final phase of Anne de Longueville's stormy life. A religious center since medieval times, Port Royal was situated in an isolated spot some 20 miles west of Paris. In time, under the firm guidance of Mère ◄ Angélique Arnauld, the community was to abandon the somewhat lax and comfortable ways into which it had fallen and adopt habits of worship which were reminiscent of the vigorous devotion of its earliest times. Of the numerous Arnauld family, three of Angélique's sisters, two brothers, several nieces and even her mother, joined the Port Royal community and within a relatively short period it achieved a reputation for uncompromising piety. It was also an important center of intellectual activity, with its male recluses (*les solitaires*) in particular producing important theological and devotional works and establishing influential schools.

Madame de Longueville seems to have first become acquainted with the works of the Port Royal theologians in 1643 when she read Antoine Arnauld's *On Frequent Communion*. However, she had been too preoccupied with worldly matters to look any more deeply at that time. A decade later, she was more responsive to its spiritual message, and Port Royal was certainly in need of her friendship. Opposition to the so-called "Jansenist" theology of Port Royal was mounting, particularly from the Jesuits. To reduce a complex dispute to its barest essentials, the Jesuits were firm adherents to the doctrine of free will and strong supporters of papal authority, while the Port Royalists stressed the significance of original sin and were less enthusiastic about the prospect of unquestioning obedience to the pope of Rome.

As in so many centuries of European history, inevitably interwoven with theological matters were political considerations. Louis XIV might be said to have invented the notion of an absolute monarchy and within his theory of the state there was no room for plurality in matters of religion. His dictum was *un roi, un loi, un foi* (one king, one law, one faith) and within that faith it was the Jesuit approach he favored; Louis saw the stern intellectualism of Port Royal as a form of Calvinism and, early in his reign, he seems to have determined to exterminate it. The Jesuits began the persecution in 1649 when seven propositions, meant to represent erroneous trends in Jansenist thought, were submitted to the Sorbonne for investigation. In 1652, a tract entitled *Confusion of the Jansenists* was widely circulated in France. It listed five erroneous propositions, supposedly drawn from Jansen's work, *Augustinus*, and, in 1653, Innocent X declared the propositions to be heretical.

Arguing strenuously that the heretical principles were not in fact to be found in Jansen's work, refusing to agree that the pope's edict could establish fact, and insisting that his role be limited to defining matters of faith, the Port Royalists laid themselves open for the action which Louis had long been contemplating. In 1655 Antoine Arnauld, Mère Angélique's brother, leapt to the defense of Port Royal's theology and of the works of St. Augustine from which it was drawn, but he was forced to go into hiding after his letter was censured. Blaise Pascal distilled the debate into two words, *fait* (fact) and *droit* (right). While the popes were certainly infallible in matters of dogma and morals (*droit*), he argued, they might well be mistaken in asserting that the condemned propositions attributed to Jansen were contained in the *Augustinus* (*fait*). But despite the best efforts of their influential friends, Port Royal's *solitaires* were ordered dispersed in 1656, and, by 1660, the remaining schools were closed.

In 1661, a formula was drawn up by an assembly of the clergy which all priests and members of religious orders in France were required to sign. In April, the king, who had increasingly come to regard the Port Royalists, like the Frondeurs, as serious threats to his absolutist regime, ordered the expulsion from the Paris house of the female students and postulants and the replacement of the spiritual director. It was in this turbulent year that Madame de Longueville made her retreat at Port Royal.

Anne's friend, Madame de Sablé, had retired to Port Royal and for many months had

❧▶
Arnauld, Angélique. *See Arnauld, Jacqueline Marie in entry titled Port Royal des Champs, Abbesses of.*

urged Anne to visit. Her first audience with the dying Mère Angélique immediately convinced Madame de Longueville that here was a cause worthy of her devoted support. The same sense of sympathy for those who had been treated unfairly which had initially won her to the Fronde now drew her to this very different persecuted group. The attraction appears to have been mutual, for Mère Angélique wrote to Madame de Sablé that "all I have seen of this Princess in such a short time seems to me to be of finest gold."

Mère Angélique suggested that Anne place herself under the spiritual guidance of M. Singlin, her own confessor. Although the priest was in hiding because of the royal persecutions, he reluctantly accepted his new charge and visited her disguised as a physician, wearing a wig and a concealing cloak. On Singlin's recommendation Madame de Longueville wrote out her confession, a lengthy analysis of her own character, identifying her greatest sin as that of pride, a defect which had led her to the mistaken belief that she could conquer temptation and that her virtue was unassailable. With her pride in tatters, she was in danger of despair, but Singlin convinced her to devote herself to the good of others, her children, and the wider community of those in need. Port Royal was soon to clearly demonstrate its need.

The embattled Mère Angélique Arnauld died on August 6, 1661, at the age of 70. With great reluctance, her sister ❧➤ **Agnes** and her nuns signed a new formula which excluded the famous distinction between *fait* and *droit* in November 1661, but their signatures, which they almost instantly regretted giving, did not win them much respite.

In June 1664, the archbishop of Paris insisted that the sisters sign a new formula under which they would have to agree to the entire contents of the Papal Constitutions. Despite the most intense pressure from the authorities, which included suspension of the administration of the sacraments, 12 of the nuns, including Mère Agnes, refused to sign. Instead, they attempted to insert a dissenting clause. The compromise was rejected, and the long-anticipated expulsion took place in August 1664. The community was dispersed.

The sisters were separated and sent to various convents, frequently enduring conditions which resembled a form of house arrest. Two of *les solitaires*, Antoine Arnauld and his friend Pierre Nicole, a theologian and former teacher at Port Royal, went into hiding in the Hôtel de Longueville. Anne seems to have genuinely

mourned the death of her husband in 1663, for they had long been reconciled, but she was now free to devote all her resources to the support of her spiritual friends. For five long years, Madame de Longueville sheltered the dissidents, heedless of the dangers of incurring the king's displeasure. She was more mindful of the violations of etiquette which she had to endure on the occasions when Arnauld absent-mindedly removed his braces in her drawing room or Nicole abandoned his hat, gloves, cane and muff on her bed. It was under her roof that a new translation of the New Testament was composed, demonstrating, when it appeared in 1667, that the Port Royalists were doctrinally sound, despite the accusations still circulating against them.

Meanwhile, Madame de Longueville was far from resting content with the role of provider of refuge; in July 1667, she wrote an eloquent letter of appeal to Pope Clement IX, describing the Port Royal reformers as: "the greatest and smallest people in the world; the strongest and the most frail." She stressed that they were full of humility but that among this persecuted group were some of the most influential people in France. Her letter of support itself reaffirmed her submission; the plea of a royal princess on behalf of the embattled Port Royalists.

In 1669, the Peace of the Church was finally agreed; after delicate negotiations and vigorous efforts by Port Royal's friends, especially Madame de Longueville, a formulary was arrived at which allowed for a clear dissenting clause drawing a distinction between *droit* and *fait*. According to Sainte-Beuve's history of Port Royal, Anne's unremitting efforts to win over both the court and the papacy "contributed as much as any prelate to the Peace of the Church" and succeeded in securing peace for Port Royal for the remaining ten years of her life.

Despite Louis XIV's specific request that she not hold gatherings of Jansenists at her home, Madame de Longueville continued to offer shelter and support to the Port Royalists, making, as **Lilian Rea** remarks "no concession but that of greater discretion." As well as giving generously to the poor, she aided and ransomed many prisoners, perhaps identifying with their plight, for she had taken to calling her earlier years "my criminal life." In 1672, she moved into a house which she had built at Port Royal, from which a covered walkway led directly into the church, and she divided her time between this place and her rooms in the convent of the Carmelites, becoming ever more devoted in her prayer and penance.

Arnauld, Agnes.
See Arnauld,
Jeanne
Catherine in
entry titled Port
Royal des
Champs,
Abbesses of.

Anne had been at Port Royal only a short time when the news reached her that her youngest son, the Comte de Saint-Paul, had been killed in battle. The boy, although not a particularly dutiful son, had always been her favorite; indeed it may be that he was the child of her faithless lover. Her elder son, to whom she had never been close, had left for Rome in 1665 and been ordained a priest. Madame de Longueville's only consolation in her grief on the death of her child was that he had experienced a religious conversion and made his confession before departing for war. Prayer, penance, and works of charity dominated the remaining seven years of her life. Anne de Longueville died at the convent of the Carmelites on April 15, 1679, at the age of 59. Indication that the court had not forgiven her political intrigues nor her subsequent adoption of the cause of Port Royal is evident from the delivery of her funeral eulogy by a minor bishop a full year after her death. According to *Madame de Sévigné who heard the sermon, for it was not allowed to be printed, the bishop of Autun preached with dignity, "passing the delicate points, saying or not saying what should be said or not said."

In a manuscript discovered by Sainte-Beuve, an unidentified author, who may have been Pierre Nicole, praised Madame de Longueville's generosity, stressing that she was never known to speak badly of anyone. Sainte-Beuve observed that "she was not a learned or even a very clever woman, but she was an excellent judge of character; she was kind, affectionate, and loyal to her friends."

Just as all those who saw her in her radiant youth were captivated by her translucent beauty, all those who knew the mature Anne de Longueville admired her humility. M. de Pontchâteau, one of the most stern of the Port Royal *solitaires*, wrote admiringly of her unfailing regularity in her religious duties and her "absolute self-disregard . . . even in her dress." In an age which prized wealth, rank, and political influence, her uncompromising rejection of the material world had the power to move all who observed it. But her transformation was more than that of a beautiful great lady to a *dévote*; she was a woman of pride and ambition who subdued those instincts to live almost 20 years as a humble penitent, entering the public arena only to safeguard the interests of her family and her beloved spiritual friends, and spending the last seven years of her crowded life in religious seclusion. Anne de Longueville was a woman of great passion who eventually found the most complete fulfillment of that passion in spiritual devotion.

SOURCES:
Catel, Maurice, ed. *Les Écrivains de Port-Royal.* Mayenne: Mercure de France, 1962.
[Villefore]. *La Vie de Madame la Duchesse de Longueville.* N.p., 1738.

SUGGESTED READING:
Bibliographie Universelle, Nouvelle Édition. Vol 25. Graz, Austria: Akademische Druck, 1968, pp. 82–86.
Rea, Lilian. *The Enthusiasts of Port Royal.* London: Methuen, 1912.
Romanes, Ethel. *The Story of Port Royal.* London: John Murray, 1907.

(Dr.) Kathleen Garay,
Assistant Professor of History and Women's Studies,
McMaster University, Hamilton, Canada

Longueville, duchesse de.

See Mary of Guise (1515–1560).
See Longueville, Anne Geneviève, duchesse de (1619–1679).

Longworth, Alice Roosevelt
(1884–1980)

American socialite, daughter of President Theodore Roosevelt, who captivated American society throughout much of the 20th century with her iconoclasm and witticisms. Name variations: Alice Roosevelt. Born Alice Lee Roosevelt on February 12, 1884, in New York City; died in Washington, D.C., on February 20, 1980, from cardiac arrest and bronchial pneumonia; daughter of Theodore Roosevelt (1858–1919, a soldier and 26th president of the U.S.) and Alice Hathaway Lee Roosevelt (1861–1884); married Nicholas Longworth III (U.S. congressional representative), on February 17, 1906 (died, April 10, 1931); children: Paulina Longworth Sturm (1925–1957).

Mother died (February 14, 1884); father married Edith Kermit Carow (December 2, 1886); family moved from New York City to Washington, D.C. (1889); family moved from Washington, D.C. to New York City (1895); family moved from New York City to Washington, D.C. (1897); family moved from Washington, D.C. to Albany, New York (1898); father became president of U.S. (1901); made formal debut (January 3, 1903); father died (January 6, 1919); published Crowded Hours (1933); daughter Paulina married Alexander McCormick Sturm (August 26, 1944); grandchild Joanna Sturm born (1946); son-in-law Alexander Sturm died (November 13, 1951); daughter Paulina Sturm died (January 27, 1957).

After returning from her European honeymoon, Alice Roosevelt Longworth apparently had had her fill of royalty. "If I see one more king," she said, "I'll have him stuffed." Yet, Alice herself was called Princess Alice. As such, she had begun captivating the American public while still a teenager, as the daughter of one of America's most popular presidents. When she died in 1980, *The New York Times* referred to her as Washington's "dowager empress" who had continued to reign nearly 80 years after she went to live in the White House. Unlike monarchs who have become figureheads, America's princess through the years had "influential political connections." Alice once said that her father "always wants to be the corpse at every funeral, the bride at every wedding, and the baby at every christening." Whether she intended it or not, Alice, too, attracted constant attention, not only because she was a president's daughter who had an abiding interest in politics, but also because, as *The New York Times* put it, she was "renowned for her caustic wit" and "her happy iconoclasm." Her home was for many decades a gathering place for political luminaries of all stripes. "You have to have a bit of malice to be a good hostess," she once noted. "I'm afraid I'm rather malevolent about people." Of her 1935 visit to the capital, *Rebecca West wrote, "Physically, the city is dominated by the Washington Monument. . . . Intellectually, spiritually, the city is dominated by the last good thing said by Alice Roosevelt Longworth."

Alice Roosevelt was born in New York City in 1884 on Abraham Lincoln's birthday, the daughter of Theodore Roosevelt and *Alice Hathaway Lee Roosevelt. Two days later, on St. Valentine's Day, both her mother and her paternal grandmother, **Martha Bulloch Roosevelt,** passed away. Distraught, Theodore Roosevelt moved to the Dakota Territory to become a rancher and left Baby Lee, as he called Alice, in the care of his sister **Anna Roosevelt Cowles,** called Bamie or Auntie Bye. Over two years later, on December 2, 1886, Theodore Roosevelt married Edith Carow (*Edith Kermit Carow Roosevelt). In a letter, Anna offered to continue raising the baby, but Theodore responded, "I hardly know what to say about Baby Lee. Edith feels more strongly about her than I could have imagined possible." It finally was determined that the child would live with her father and stepmother. "It almost broke my heart to give her up," said Anna years later.

After his second marriage, Theodore Roosevelt saw his family grow rapidly with the birth of Theodore, Jr. (1887), Kermit (1889), **Ethel Carow Roosevelt** (1891), Archibald (1894), and Quentin (1897). Possibly because this expanding family required much of her stepmother's time

and energy, Alice never felt entirely wanted in her own home. While Edith was a rather strict disciplinarian, insisting that Alice call her "mother," Alice was a free spirit chafing under the code of conduct expected of her. (A friend of her father's later inquired as to why he did not "look after Alice more." Theodore Roosevelt responded, "I can be President of the United States—or—I can look after Alice!") Biographer **Carol Felsenthal** notes that "at the core of the mother-stepdaughter relationship was a profound difference" over religion. Whereas Edith took religion seriously, Alice considered Christian dogma "sheer voodoo," and, when her father dragged her to church, Alice would often read a book or practice her "one-sided nose wrinkle" during the service.

After returning from the Dakota Territory, Theodore became ever more involved in politics. In 1886, he ran unsuccessfully for mayor of New York City. In 1889, appointed Civil Service commissioner by President Benjamin Harrison, Theodore moved the family to Washington. When Mayor William Strong named Theodore chief police commissioner, they went back to New York. In 1897, the Roosevelts returned to Washington when President William McKinley appointed Theodore assistant secretary of the navy. After the Spanish-American War, during which Theodore won fame as a leader of the Rough Riders, the citizens of New York elected him governor which meant another move, this time to Albany. The stage was set for his nomination at the Republican national convention as McKinley's vice-presidential running mate. When McKinley won reelection, the Roosevelts again pulled up stakes and returned to the nation's capital.

During these early years, the relationship between Alice and her father was ambivalent. Felsenthal writes that Theodore "couldn't resist, after long days at the office, leading his children in games—or, as Alice characterized them, 'perfectly awful endurance tests masquerading as games.'" Theodore surely did not ignore his children, but certain physical activities led by her father "terrified Alice to the point of tears" for she wore ankle-to-knee braces for prevention of orthopedic problems from age 10 until she was 13. Alice also seemed envious of her first cousin, *Eleanor Roosevelt, because of the attention Theodore gave Eleanor, especially after the death of Eleanor's father.

Soon after William McKinley began his second term in 1901, he was assassinated by Leon Czolgosz. Alice later admitted that she danced "a little jig" upon hearing the news that her father was now president of the United States. The 17-year-old Alice was soon fascinating the nation with her antics. When her father said that she could no longer smoke *in* his house, she climbed on the roof and smoked *on* his house. At a time when few women took the wheel of the still newly invented automobile, she drove her car around Washington with such abandon that she was once stopped for speeding. She bet on the horses and boasted of her winnings. When one eccentric suitor persisted in his attempts to wed his daughter, Theodore responded, "Of course he's insane. He wants to marry Alice."

If you haven't got anything good to say about anyone, come and sit by me.

—Alice Roosevelt Longworth

Alice made her debut in the East Room on January 3, 1903, the first American president's daughter to have such an event staged in the White House. In planning the festivity, Alice and her stepmother disagreed as to whether champagne should be served. When Edith finally vetoed the idea, Alice complained, "I think my coming-out party was a hangover from the brownstone-front existence of my stepmother when they had little parties with a modicum of decorous dancing and an amusing fruit punch." Some 600 guests attended the gala, including Alice's fifth cousin Franklin Delano Roosevelt. "From start to finish it was glorious," he wrote. Franklin, then a student at Harvard, twice danced with Alice, and although he seemed taken with her, Alice did not respond in kind. Throughout her life, Alice held Franklin in rather low esteem; a Little Lord Fauntleroy, she called him, "a good little mother's boy" who was afraid to "rough it." When on March 17, 1905, Franklin married Eleanor Roosevelt, Alice's father gave away the bride while Alice was maid of honor.

In 1905, Alice traveled with a group of some 80 U.S. congressional representatives and their spouses to the Orient on what was billed an inspection tour. Although Alice had many interesting experiences, including a proposal of marriage from the sultan of Sulu, the most significant happening was the evolvement of a relationship with Nicholas Longworth III, a member of the U.S. House of Representatives from Ohio. Although Longworth was 14 years older and at one point Alice referred to him as "that old bald-headed man," by the time the tour ended she had fallen madly in love. In her diary, she wrote, "I love you with everything that is in me

Nick, Nick, my Nick." In December 1905, the engagement of Alice Roosevelt to Nicholas Longworth was formally announced despite some misgivings by Alice's stepmother.

In America, Alice's wedding seemed to transcend all other events as newspapers concocted front-page stories "out of the smallest detail." The time set for the social event of the year was Saturday, February 17, 1906; the place was the White House. Prior to the occasion, much to Alice's dismay, Theodore Roosevelt stymied an attempt by certain Americans to raise $800,000 as a wedding gift. Other gifts were received from monarchs around the world, including the kings of Italy, England, and Spain, the emperors of Japan and Austria-Hungary, the kaiser of Germany, and *Cixi, the empress-dowager of China. By eleven o'clock on the day of the wedding, the White House grounds were filled with many of the curious who were not among the fortunate invited to the festivities, and every florist's shop in the city had been emptied. At noon, the ceremony began. Alice chose to have no bridesmaids, for she intended to be the "star of the show." The Episcopal bishop of Washington, the Right Reverend Henry Yates Satterlee, officiated; Douglas MacArthur, who would become an American hero during World War II, was one of eight ushers; Theodore Roosevelt gave the bride away; and Cousin Franklin Roosevelt attended with his mother. Near the end of the reception, as the newlyweds prepared to leave, Alice thanked Edith for the memorable day. Her stepmother responded, "I want you to know that I'm glad to see you go. You've never been anything but trouble."

Alice's two-month European honeymoon was one befitting a princess, though Nick at times became exasperated when he heard himself called Mr. Alice Roosevelt. In London, Princess Alice and her consort stayed with *Elisabeth Mills Reid and Whitelaw Reid, the American ambassador to Britain. They dined with King Edward VII and *Alexandra of Denmark, along with Winston Churchill and Lord Curzon. The famous operatic tenor, Enrico Caruso, entertained. In France, the president of the Republic served as host at a function at which Georges Clemenceau, the famous World War I French leader, sat on Alice's right. In Germany, they visited Kaiser Wilhelm II aboard his royal yacht, the *Meteor*.

With a husband who served in the House of Representatives for many years and a father who became one of America's most popular presidents, it seemed inevitable that Alice would be-

come deeply immersed and interested in American politics. Some political analysts consider Theodore Roosevelt's 1904 pledge not to seek another term to be one of his greatest mistakes. (Alice thought so too.) In 1908, Alice Roosevelt Longworth demonstrated little enthusiasm for her father's handpicked successor, William H. Taft. "They called Taft great," she mocked. "Great in girth, perhaps, but great in nothing else." Some years later, when Taft became chief justice of the U.S. Supreme Court, he remarked that he enjoyed the position so much that he hardly remembered being president. Cracked Alice, "Neither can the country."

Despite Alice's advice that he not openly challenge Taft for renomination in 1912, Theodore Roosevelt did so anyway. Even so, Alice loyally stuck by him and worked steadfastly for his nomination. When the Republicans nominated Taft, the Bull Moose Party came into being, with Theodore Roosevelt as its presidential candidate. While her husband backed Taft, Alice openly supported her father, especially after a would-be assassin wounded him in Milwaukee.

Politically, the year 1912 was not a good one for the Republicans and the Roosevelt family. Woodrow Wilson became the first Democratic chief executive since Grover Cleveland while Alice's husband lost his seat in the House of Representatives. Not much love was ever lost between Wilson and Roosevelt, but relations worsened during World War I when Wilson refused Theodore's request to raise and lead a division of volunteers to fight in France. After Wilson denied permission, Theodore called the president an "infernal skunk," and Alice felt the same. After the war, she used her influence to prevent the realization of Wilson's dream which was ratification of the Treaty of Versailles and participation by the United States in the League of Nations. She stayed in constant touch with League opponents such as Senator William Borah of Idaho. When Senator Henry Cabot Lodge demonstrated any sign of compromise, she called him "Mr. Wobbly." She prayed for "a murrain" on President Wilson and celebrated victory when, for the third time, the Senate rejected the Treaty of Versailles in March 1920.

On the personal side, Alice had little to cheer about throughout the next decade. Although Nicholas recaptured his seat in the House of Representatives in 1914, he began to drink more and spent countless hours playing poker with the "boys." Their marriage began to unravel as he became "attracted to more than one pretty girl." Alice herself struck up a relationship that was more than political with Senator Borah of Idaho. She, who had seemed so in love with Nick, later commented on her marriage, "I didn't exactly revel in it." In addition, Alice's youngest brother Quentin died fighting in Europe towards the end of World War I. Theodore Roosevelt had little chance to win the Republican nomination in 1916 because he had bolted the party in 1912; it seemed that after more time had elapsed, he might have been the nominee in 1920. However, he died on January 6, 1919.

In 1920, the Republicans recaptured the White House when Warren G. Harding defeated James M. Cox. Franklin Roosevelt had been Cox's running mate. Although Alice referred to the 1920s, a period when the Republicans held sway, as a time when "the golden calf gave triple cream," no one, as far as Alice was concerned, could equal her father. Warren Harding, said Alice, "was not a bad man. He was only a slob," although she also commented that he resembled "a debauched Roman emperor." (This comment is particularly apropos in light of the infamous corruption, including the Teapot Dome scandal, of Harding's administration.) Harding, like Alice's husband, seemed taken with attractive women, poker parties, and alcoholic beverages. When Harding died in August 1923, he was succeeded by Calvin Coolidge who smiled little and to Alice seemed "as if he had been weaned on a pickle."

On December 7, 1925, Nicholas Longworth was elected Speaker of the House and served in that capacity until the Democrats gained control in 1930. In 1928, there was enough speculation about Nick being nominated for president to warrant this newspaper headline, "Will Princess Alice Return to the White House?" As it turned out, the Republicans chose Herbert Hoover, who won the nomination but lacked the charisma of both her father and cousin Franklin. Noted Alice, "The Hoover Vacuum Cleaner is more exciting than the President. But, of course, it's electric."

On February 14, 1925, Alice gave birth to her only child, daughter Paulina; the news was reported around the world. "I'm always glad to try anything once," said Alice to those who wondered whether, at 41, she really wanted a baby. On April 10, 1931, Nicholas Longworth died. Soon after the funeral, House Republicans urged Alice to run for her husband's seat. She refused, saying she wanted to spend as much time as possible raising her daughter. Despite her refusal, Alice Longworth was as involved in politics as she had ever been. In 1932, she became a member of the board of counsellors of the women's division of the Republican National Committee, and in 1936 served as delegate to the Republican national convention. For a time, she published the column "Capital Comment" which sometimes appeared side-by-side with Eleanor Roosevelt's "My Day." Longworth also published her memoirs, *Crowded Hours*. During the 1930s and early 1940s, years of Democratic hegemony, Alice staunchly opposed her cousin Franklin and his New Deal. She refused to call him "Mr. President," referring to him as a "feather duster." Eleanor, said Alice, was "a great dear but a very boring dear."

In 1932, Longworth campaigned for Republican nominee Herbert Hoover and in 1936 for Alf Landon, whom she knew lacked the appeal of her popular cousin Franklin. "Do you know J.P. Morgan won't allow the name of Franklin Roosevelt to be mentioned in his presence because it raises his blood pressure," said Alice. "I'm for Landon, but I do wish he'd stop lowering my blood pressure."

By the end of the 1930s, foreign policy became an important issue, especially after the start of World War II in 1939. Longworth proved to be a strict isolationist and entertained leaders of the America First Committee. An organization determined to keep America out of war and championed by Charles Lindbergh, America First was strongly right-wing and anti-Semitic. (There is little evidence that Alice, though a bit of a snob, was herself anti-Semitic or otherwise prejudiced. The following exchange took place some years later, when a car with Southern places cut in front of Alice's car, which was being driven by her African-American chauffeur: "'What do you think you're doin', you black bastard!' the other driver shouted. Without a pause, [she] rolled down her window [and answered] 'Driving me to my destination, you white son-of-a-bitch!'") She supported Senator Robert Taft for the Republican presidential nomination both in 1940 and 1944. When Wendell L. Willkie won the 1944 nomination, seemingly with much grass roots support, Alice quipped, "Willkie sprang from the grass roots of American country clubs." About Thomas E. Dewey, the Republican nominee in 1944, Longworth wondered how Republicans could expect Americans "to vote for a man who looks like a bridegroom on a wedding cake."

Within Alice's family, death continued to claim a sibling from time to time. On June 4, 1943, her brother Kermit committed suicide. The following year, her oldest brother, Theodore Jr., a brigadier general in the U.S. Army, died shortly after distinguishing himself when the Allies invaded France. On August 26, 1944, Alice's daughter, Paulina married Alexander McCormick Sturm. In 1946, Alice's only grandchild was born when Paulina gave birth to a daughter named **Joanna Sturm**. Alice's son-in-law died on November 13, 1951, and then a little more than five years later on January 27, 1957, Paulina died, leaving Joanna without parents. Alice took custody of her and became a doting grandpar-

ent, resulting in a close relationship between grandchild and grandmother.

After Franklin Roosevelt died in 1945, Alice seemed to become less partisan, less reactionary than she had been during the days that FDR occupied the White House. She continued to arrange dinner parties to which she invited both Republicans and Democrats. She took delight in inviting, to the same gathering, guests who had a decided dislike for each other. Said Alice, "I put people next to each other who are going to fight, who are disagreeable to one another." Alice kept a pillow in her sitting room upon which was embroidered her well-known quote, "If you haven't got anything good to say about anyone, come and sit by me." She retained her sense of humor after her second mastectomy at the age of 86. After the surgery, she referred to herself as Washington's only "topless octogenarian."

The Kennedys' style pleased Alice as well as the fact that they were "all for one and one for all . . . which is quite different from our family, who were completely individualistic." She had "an affection for them," she said, and the press often compared *Jacqueline Kennedy** to Alice in her heyday. (Later, upon hearing of the former first lady's impending marriage to Aristotle Onassis, she wondered, "Hasn't anyone ever warned [her] about Greeks bearing gifts?") Alice also liked Lyndon Johnson, whom she called "a lovely rogue elephant," despite his inclination to touch. Longworth's signature apparel, a wide-brimmed hat, made it impossible for him to kiss her, said LBJ. Retorted Alice, "That's why I wear it." When he took to lifting his shirt in front of all and sundry to display the scar from recent surgery to remove his gallbladder, she commented, "Thank god, it wasn't his prostate."

Although for a time she found Joseph McCarthy interesting, when the Wisconsin senator became too friendly with her during the HUAC days, Alice admonished, "My gardener may call me Alice, the trash man on my block may call me Alice, but you, Senator McCarthy, may call me Mrs. Longworth." She supported Richard Nixon because she thought him to be a fighter like her father. Her friendship began to cool with Watergate (which she later called "good unclean fun"), not because Nixon had broken the law, but because he seemed indecisive. She felt he should have destroyed the infamous tapes that incriminated him. "Dick is a weaker man than I thought him." Even she had little to say about President Gerald Ford. Informed of the election of his successor, Jimmy Carter, she asked, "Oh, the one who's always so happy and smiles so much?"

Alert to the last, Longworth, who once claimed that "the secret of eternal youth is arrested development," was cared for by her granddaughter Joanna as her life drew to a close. She died, age 96, on February 20, 1980.

SOURCES:

Bingham, June. "Before the Colors Fade," in *American Heritage*. Vol. 20, no. 2. February 1969, pp. 42–43, 73–77.

Brough, James. *Princess Alice: A Biography of Alice Roosevelt Longworth*. Boston, MA: Little, Brown, 1975.

Felsenthal, Carol. *Alice Roosevelt Longworth*. NY: Putnam, 1988.

Teichmann, Howard. *Alice: The Life and Times of Alice Roosevelt Longworth*. Englewood Cliffs, NJ: Prentice-Hall, 1979.

Vanden Heuvel, Jean. "The Sharpest Wit in Washington," in *Saturday Evening Post*. December 4, 1965, pp. 30–33.

SUGGESTED READING:

Hagedorn, Hermann. *The Roosevelt Family of Sagamore Hill*. NY: Macmillan, 1954.

Harbaugh, William Henry. *Power and Responsibility: The Life and Times of Theodore Roosevelt*. NY: Farrar, Straus, and Cudahy, 1961.

Longworth, Alice Roosevelt. *Crowded Hours: Reminiscences of Alice Roosevelt Longworth*. NY: Scribner, 1933.

Teague, Michael. *Mrs. L: Conversations with Alice Roosevelt Longworth*. Garden City, N.Y.: Doubleday, 1981.

COLLECTIONS:

Alice Roosevelt Longworth Collection and Nicholas Longworth Papers located in the Library of Congress.

Robert Bolt,
Professor of History, Calvin College,
Grand Rapids, Michigan

Longworth, Maria Theresa

(c. 1832–1881)

Irish writer best remembered as the plaintiff in a long-running British legal case. Born around 1832 in Ireland; died in 1881; married William Charles Yelverton, later 4th viscount Avonmore, in 1857 (marriage repudiated in 1858).

Selected writings: The Yelverton Correspondence *(1863).*

Born in Ireland around 1832, Maria Theresa Longworth achieved her greatest recognition as a key player in the Yelverton case. In 1857, she was married to William Charles Yelverton, later the 4th viscount Avonmore, by a priest in a Roman Catholic church in Rostrevor, Ireland. William Yelverton soon repudiated the marriage and in 1858 married the widow of a Professor Edward Forbes. Furious at her husband's renunciation of their marriage, Longworth turned to the courts to resolve the matter. In 1861, an Irish court upheld the validity of her marriage to Yelverton. Only a year later, however, a Scottish court granted her husband an annulment. The Scottish court's ruling was confirmed by the House of Lords two years later.

Longworth published a number of novels between the years of 1861 and 1875. She also recounted the legal battle surrounding the validity of her marriage in a book entitled *The Yelverton Correspondence,* published in 1863. She died in 1881.

Don Amerman,
freelance writer, Saylorsburg, Pennsylvania

Lonsbrough, Anita (1941—)

English swimmer. Born on August 10, 1941.

A clerk for the Huddersfield Corporation in Yorkshire, England, 19-year-old swimmer Anita Lonsbrough was docked in wages for the time she took away from her job to train for the 1960 Rome Olympics. Her gold medal win in the 200-meter breast-stroke was accomplished in the final 25 meters of the race, when she overcame Germany's **Wiltrud Urselmann** who was beginning to tire. **Barbara Göbel** of East Germany was third. Lonsbrough's time of 2.49.5 was lower than **Ursula Happe**'s record time of 2.53.1 in the 1956 Olympics because of the rule banning underwater stroking from breast-stroke competition, which was instituted in 1957.

Lonsdale, Kathleen (1903–1971)

Irish-born crystallographer and pacifist who was one of the first two women to be elected a fellow of the Royal Society, and first woman president of the British Association for the Advancement of Science. Born Kathleen Yardley on January 28, 1903, in Newbridge, County Kildare, Ireland; died in University College Hospital, London, England, on April 1, 1971; daughter of Harry Frederick Yardley (a postmaster) and Jessie (Cameron) Yardley; attended Ilford County High School for Girls; Bedford College for Women, London University; married Thomas Jackson Lonsdale, in 1927; children: Jane Lonsdale *(b. 1929);* Nancy Lonsdale *(b. 1931);* Stephen Lonsdale *(b. 1934).*

Had research appointments at University College, London and the Royal Institution (1922–27); was Amy Lady Tate Scholar at Leeds University (1927–29); became a Quaker (1935); was a Leverhulme Research Fellow (1935–37); was a Dewar Fellow at the Royal Institution (1944–46); elected fellow of the Royal Society (1945); was a special fellow of the U.S. Federal Health Service (1947); was a profes-

sor of chemistry and head of the department of crystallography, University College, London (1949–68); was a member of a Quaker delegation to the Soviet Union (1951); delivered Swarthmore Lecture, "Removing the Causes of War" (1953); was president of the British section of the Women's International League for Peace and Freedom; awarded DBE (1956); awarded the Royal Society's Davy medal (1957); was vice president (1960–66) and president (1966) of the International Union of Crystallography; served as president of the British Association for the Advancement of Science (1968).

Publications: Simplified Structure Factor and Electron Density Formulae for the 230 Space-Groups of Mathematical Crystallography *(1936);* Crystals and X-rays *(1949); (with N.F.M. Henry)* International Tables for X-ray Crystallography *(vol. I, 1952); ed.* Quakers visit Russia *(1952);* Prisons for Women *(1952);* Security and Responsibility *(1952);* Removing the Causes of War *(1953);* Is Peace Possible? *(1957); (with J. Kasper)* International Tables for X-ray Crystallography *(vol. II, 1959); (with C.H. MacGillavry and G.D. Rieck)* International Tables for X-ray Crystallography *(vol. III, 1962);* I Believe . . . *(1964). Also many articles on scientific, humanitarian and religious topics.*

As a young girl living in London during the Great War, Kathleen Lonsdale was witness to both the vast strides made by science since the beginning of the century, and its potential for devastation and death. Born, as she often remarked, in the year in which the Wright brothers built and flew the first airplane, in 1916 Lonsdale found herself the target of bombing raids by German Zeppelins, and was disturbed by the implications of war not only for its innocent victims but also for its perpetrators. "We sometimes watched them being shot down in flames," she recalled 40 years later in her pacifist manifesto, *Is Peace Possible?*, "and my mother cried, because she had read that some of the German crews were boys of 16. Somehow this seemed to have very little connection with the science I was learning, but it may have had something to do with my own growing feeling that war was utterly wrong." Later, as one of the leading British scientists of her generation, Lonsdale confronted science's potential for evil as well as good and, as a Quaker and a pacifist, sought to convince politicians and the public of the virtues of disarmament, of nonviolent resistance, and of the settlement of disputes on the basis of justice rather than by armed force.

Born in 1903 in the small Irish town of Newbridge, County Kildare, Kathleen Lonsdale was the youngest of ten children of **Jessie Cameron Yardley** and Harry Frederick Yardley. Her English father had been a postal worker and a soldier and, on leaving the army, became postmaster at Newbridge, close to the Curragh military camp. An intelligent and widely read man, he was also quarrelsome, miserly, and sometimes drank heavily. In later years, he lived apart from his family, retired early due to ill health, and died when his youngest daughter was 20. He was clearly a rather distant parent, and the adult Kathleen wrote somewhat wistfully of her relationship with him. "I think he was fond of us and did not know how to show it. I wish that I could have been fonder of him. I think that it was from him that I inherited my passion for facts." Jessie Yardley, however, played a much greater part in the lives of her children. A lively and strong-minded woman of Scottish descent, she had been brought up in London, where she had picked up many Italian and music-hall songs which in old age she sang to herself. She had worked as a waitress and as a cutter in a shirt factory, and was a devout Baptist who brought up her children in her own faith. The Yardleys were poor, at times extremely so, and of the six children who survived, all but the youngest, Kathleen, had to leave school as early as possible in order to supplement the family income. The eldest brother, Fred Yardley, seems to have shared his sister's scientific bent. Unable to continue his education because of poverty, he became one of the first wireless operators, and in 1912 picked up the last signals from the sinking *Titanic*.

Lonsdale received her first formal education in the local school at Newbridge, and, after the family moved back to England in 1908, in the elementary school at Seven Kings in Essex. She quickly showed herself to be an exceptionally able pupil, and in 1914 she was awarded a county minor scholarship to the County High School for Girls at Ilford. Because physics, chemistry, and higher mathematics were not included on the curriculum there, she attended classes in these subjects at the County High School for Boys, the only girl to do so at that time. In 1919, she won a further scholarship, as well as a medal awarded by the Royal Geographical Society for the highest marks in geography and physical geography in the Cambridge Senior Local Examination and, at the early age of 16, entered Bedford College for Women in London. Initially, she chose to read mathematics, but at the end of her first year changed to physics, reportedly because she feared that the only career open to her as a mathematics graduate would be teaching, and because she was attracted by the experimental aspects of physics. A brilliant student, she also involved herself in student social life, was secretary to the Music Society, and coxed the college eight. In 1922, she graduated first in her class in the B.Sc. examination with the college's highest marks in ten years, and was recruited by Sir William Bragg to join his research team working on the structure of organic crystals, first at University College, London, and later at the Royal Institution.

There is such a thing as moral strength and moral leadership which does not depend upon the possession of hideously destructive weapons.

—**Kathleen Lonsdale**

Winner with his son of the 1915 Nobel Prize for physics, Bragg was a leader in the field of radioactivity and founder of the modern science of crystallography. By using ionization and by studying glancing reflections at the face of the crystal, he had greatly improved on Max Von Laue's 1912 demonstration of the diffraction of X-rays by the atoms of a crystal. However, although X-ray diffraction methods had been used to determine the arrangement of atoms in the crystalline forms of a few chemical substances, considerable difficulties still remained in the process of determining crystal structures. As part of Bragg's team, Lonsdale was one of an international group of research students who collaborated on scientific work and spent their free time together, playing table tennis or discussing a wide range of contemporary issues. Years later, she described the exhilaration and optimism of that period which, politically as well as professionally, seemed so full of promise.

> When I became a research student, training under Sir William Bragg in the very place where Sir Humphry Davy, Michael Faraday, John Tyndall, Sir James Dewar, and other world-famous scientists had carried out their researches, the war was over and, as we thought, won. We genuinely hoped for a peace settlement that would end all war. . . . Meanwhile my work was fun. I often ran the last few yards to the laboratory.

She found Bragg an inspirational teacher, who left her completely free to follow her own line of research. Two years after joining his team, in 1924, she made her first major contribution to crystallography when, together with W.T. Astbury, she published "Tables for the Determination of Space Groups." In 1927, the same year in which she married Thomas Lonsdale, a fellow student at University College, Kathleen took up a research appointment at Leeds University, where she worked on what she herself regarded as the most fundamental of her researches. This was the discovery of the structure of the hexamethylbenzene molecule: by analyzing the structures of crystals of hexamethylbenzene and hexachlorobenzene, she found that the benzene ring consisted of a flat regular hexagon of the six carbon atoms with the other six carbon atoms of attached methyl groups coplanar with the ring.

According to her friend and colleague *Dorothy Hodgkin, Lonsdale did contemplate giving up scientific research at the time of her marriage "and settling down to become a good wife and mother." Her husband, however, dissuaded her. "He had not married, he said, to get a good housekeeper" and, indeed, throughout their life together Kathleen was to find in Thomas an invaluable emotional and practical support. Nevertheless, in the short term, marriage and particularly motherhood did pose their own problems: much of her work during her time at Leeds and following the Lonsdales' return to London in 1929 was carried out at home and even in the nursing homes where her children were born.

In 1931, Bragg, having obtained for her an allowance to pay for home help, invited her to return to the Royal Institution as his research assistant. She was to remain there for the next 15 years, until in 1946 she turned towards academic work with her appointment as reader in crystallography and, in 1949, professor of chemistry and head of the department of crystallography at University College. During her time at the Royal Institution, she was engaged in a range of researches: finding that there was no X-ray equipment that she could use, she instead took advantage of the offer of a big electromagnet, on which over the next ten years she made measurements of diamagnetic anisotropy, in the course of which she provided experimental verification of the postulated delocalization of electrons and the existence of molecular orbitals. She also investigated thermal diffuse reflections and was interested both in X-ray work at different temperatures and the thermal motion of atoms in crystals, and in ways of investigating the texture of crystals.

At University College, while maintaining and widening her research interests, she was also responsible for teaching and for the development both of new undergraduate and graduate courses and of her own research school. In 1946, she became general editor of the *International Tables for X-ray Crystallography,* a task which entailed a huge amount of work. Although this curtailed her research activities, she continued investigations into synthetic diamonds, writing a number of papers on the subject, and giving her name to the hexagonal diamond found in meteorites and now known as lonsdaleite. Further projects arose out of her desire to apply X-ray crystallography to the field of medical research. She initiated work on methonium compounds and on endemic bladder stones, this last prompted by a visit in 1962 from the chief medical officer of the Salvation Army, who had observed the incidence of stones among patients in certain underdeveloped countries, notably India. She was to continue this work even after her retirement in 1968, and was in fact still engaged on it at the time of her death.

As a scientist, Lonsdale found herself reacting against the strict fundamentalist Baptist faith of her mother. Her search for an alternative spiritual home ended when in 1935 she joined the Society of Friends (Quakers). With her husband, who also became a member of the Society, she became aware of relief efforts operated by the Quakers among the unemployed in South Wales, and later opened her home to refugees from Hitler's Germany sent to her by Friends' relief organizations. Combined with her existing concerns about international political developments and the responsibilities of science, Lonsdale's conversion to Quakerism served to confirm her loathing of militarism, a stand which on the outbreak of war in 1939 was to confront her with a dilemma. Compelled by law to register for employment and for civil-defense duties, she refused to do so as a conscientious objector, although she was in fact already doing voluntary work and would in any case have been exempted as the mother of young children. Declining to pay the small fine imposed for this offense, she was committed to jail for a month. In addition to doing normal prison work, she asked for, and was allowed to have in her cell scientific papers and instruments with which to continue her researches, and at the end of her term told the governor that she had managed to do "about seven hours each day of really concentrated scientific work." Lonsdale went on to suggest improvements in the treatment of prisoners and in prison conditions. She maintained her interest in this subject and in

Kathleen Lonsdale

1949 was appointed a prison visitor at a female institution, going on in 1961 to become deputy chair of the Board of Visitors of Bullwood Hall Borstal Institution for Girls. Visiting Russia in 1951, she toured a prison and impressed the governor, who did not know her past history, by her intensive knowledge of the penal system.

The early 1940s were a period of considerable change in Kathleen Lonsdale's life. Her term in Holloway Prison was described by her husband as the single most formative experience of her career, while the death in 1942 of her mentor, Sir William Bragg, coincided with a growing recognition of her own status in the field of crystallography. In 1943, the year of her imprisonment, she received the first of many invitations to participate in scientific meetings abroad, this one appropriately in her country of birth. Her lectures at the Institute of Advanced Studies Summer School in Dublin were attended not only by leading scientists such as Max Born, P.P. Ewald and Erwin Schrodinger, who chaired the conference, but also by the *taoiseach* (prime minister) of the now-independent Irish Free State, Eamon de Valera. In 1945, she became one of the first two women (with *Marjory Stephenson) to be elected fellow of the Royal Society. Other honors included her creation in 1956 as a Dame Commander of the Order of the British Empire and the award of the Royal Society's Davy Medal in 1957. In 1968, Dame Kathleen Lonsdale became first woman president of the British Association for the Advancement of Science, and in her presidential address to the association touched on a number of the issues which had preoccupied her throughout her career: these included the uses of science and technology, the arms trade, and the responsibility which scientists held for the uses to which their discoveries were put.

As a pacifist during the years of the Cold War, Lonsdale continued to campaign for disarmament and international co-operation, serving as president of the Women's International League for Peace and Freedom and as a member of the East-West Committee of the Society of Friends. In 1951, she visited Russia as part of a delegation of Friends which met representatives of the Soviet Peace Committee, leaders of the Baptist and Orthodox churches, and Jacob Malik, deputy foreign minister of the Soviet Union. In 1952, she edited the report of this delegation, and in 1957 produced her own justification of pacifism. *Is Peace Possible?*, aimed at a general audience, warned of the dangers of nuclear weapons and sought total disarmament and the establishment of "an impartial and objective World Court of Justice as a body to which all international disputes or grievances involving nations or governments can be referred." Citing Martin Luther King, Jr.'s civil-rights campaign, she demonstrated the power of nonviolent protest and the ability of individuals to resist community evil by such methods. She also identified population growth as a major threat to world peace as well as to health and living standards, while admitting the necessity of allowing countries such as China to develop their own response to this problem and pressing for increased aid from developed nations to disadvantaged areas in order to improve agricultural methods and to increase food supply.

The record of Kathleen Lonsdale's travels makes clear the extent to which her scientific, social, and religious concerns were interlinked: as **Judith Milledge** remarked, "she seldom . . . undertook a journey for one purpose without managing also to further the other." In 1954, for instance, she embarked on a two-month journey around the world, initially at the invitation of Australian Methodists and Friends, during which she delivered lectures "on crystallography, science and religion, pacifism and peacemaking, scientists' responsibilities, right use of science in general and atomic energy in particular, etc." Other travels during these years, both on scientific and humanitarian missions, included visits to the United States, Japan (where she received a particularly enthusiastic welcome for her own efforts on behalf of peace), Australia and New Zealand, India, the Far East, the People's Republic of China and in 1966 the Soviet Union again, for the meeting in Moscow of the Assembly of the International Union of Crystallography, which she chaired.

Lonsdale maintained her exceptionally heavy workload almost to the end of her life. A bad sleeper, she often woke at 4:30 and rose at 5:30 AM and, after moving with her husband to live on the coast in 1965, had a daily five-hour journey to and from her laboratory in London, although she said the inconvenience was worthwhile. Admitted to hospital in December 1970, she accepted with equanimity the news that she was suffering from cancer. She spent the final weeks of her life trying to complete a book on her work on stones; the nurses who came to call her in the morning frequently found her already awake and at work. She died in University College Hospital on April 1, 1971.

In a discussion on the shortage of women in science written towards the end of her career, Kathleen Lonsdale outlined her own recipe for success:

For a woman, and especially a married woman with children, to become a first-class scientist, she must first of all choose, or have chosen, the right husband. . . . Then she must be a good organiser and be pretty ruthless in keeping to her schedule, no matter if the heavens fall. She must be able to do with very little sleep, because her working week will be at least twice as long as the average trades unionist's. She must go against all her early training and not care if she is regarded as a little peculiar. She must be willing to accept additional responsibility, even if she feels that she has more than enough. But above all, she must learn to concentrate in any available moment and not require ideal conditions in which to do so.

Confounding the obstacles implied here, Kathleen Lonsdale became an acknowledged leader in her field: Dorothy Hodgkin recalled her first sight of Lonsdale's paper on the structure of hexamethylbenzene, published in 1929, and "the marvelling pleasure with which I read her very definite conclusions." Not the least of her achievements was the role which she played in the development of her subject. Although, according to Milledge, who was one of her postgraduate students, she was not really a good teacher to the majority who did not share her intellectual capacity, she took an active interest in the training of crystallographers and in popularizing science through many broadcasts, lectures, and articles aimed at non-specialist audiences. She helped to found the Young Scientists' section of the British Association, and was conscious of the need to stimulate interest in science among students at every level. "Never," she reminded herself, "refuse an opportunity to speak at schools," and her last public engagement was, in fact, at a prize giving at Hastings High School for Girls. But her true greatness lies in her insistence on the moral responsibility not only of the scientist but of every individual to seek new ways of dealing with conflict in an era of unparalleled technological advance. An idealist but not an innocent, she accepted the difficulties and dangers involved in the search for peace, freedom, and justice, while never losing confidence in the validity of her own creed that "a life of non-violence is essentially one of spiritual out-reach to the good in other men and of belief that, even if there is no response, even if we appear to fail, goodness will in the end prevail."

SOURCES:

Dictionary of National Biography 1971–1980. Oxford: Oxford University Press, 1986.

Hodgkin, D.M.C. "Kathleen Lonsdale," in *Biographical Memoirs of Fellows of the Royal Society, 1975.* Vol. 21. London: Royal Society, 1975, pp. 447–484.

Lonsdale, Kathleen. *Is Peace Possible?* London: Penguin, 1957.

Milledge, H.J. "Kathleen Lonsdale," in *Acta Crystallographica.* Vol. A31. Copenhagen: Munksgaard-International Union of Crystallography, 1975, pp. 705–708.

The Times obituaries, 1971–1975. Reading: Newspaper Archive Developments, 1978.

SUGGESTED READING:

Ewald, P.P., ed. *Fifty years of X-Ray diffraction.* 1963.

Rosemary Raughter,
freelance writer in women's history, Dublin, Ireland

Looney, Shelley (1972—).

See Team USA: Women's Ice Hockey at Nagano.

Loos, Anita (1893–1981)

American novelist, playwright and screenwriter who gave the world the unflappable Lorelei Lee in Gentleman Prefer Blondes. *Born Corinne Anita Loos on April 26, 1893, in Sisson, California; died on August 18, 1981, in New York City; daughter of Richard Beers Loos (a newspaper publisher) and Anita "Minnie" (Smith) Loos; married Frank Pallma (a composer), in 1915 (divorced 1920); married John Emerson (a film director), on June 21, 1920; no children.*

Briefly pursued a career on the stage until she sold her first "scenario" for a silent film and embarked on a career in the movie business; many of her early efforts were for pioneering director D. W. Griffith, for whom she wrote the subtitles for the director's landmark silent film, Intolerance *(1916); though her long and prolific career was closely tied to films, her talent for sharp social and sexual satire came to full prominence with novel* Gentlemen Prefer Blondes *(1925); by the time of her death, had written, alone or in collaboration, some 200 scripts for stage and film, as well as three novels and as many volumes of memoirs of her years in Hollywood.*

Selected writings: Gentlemen Prefer Blondes *(1925);* But Gentlemen Marry Brunettes; *(memoir)* A Girl Like I *(Viking, 1966); (with Helen Hayes)* Twice Over Lightly; *(memoir)* The Talmadge Girls; *(memoir)* Cast of Thousands *(1977).*

Filmography—as screenwriter, alone or in collaboration: The New York Hat *(1912);* The Telephone Girl and the Lady *(1913);* The Power of the Camera *(1913);* The Hicksville Epicure *(1913);* Highbrow Love *(1913);* A Narrow Escape *(1913);* The Widow's Kids *(1913);* The Lady in Black *(1913);* The Wedding Gown *(1913);* His Awful Vengeance *(1914);* Gentleman or Thief *(1914);* A Bunch of Flowers *(1914);* When a Woman Guides *(1914);* The Road to Plaindale *(1914);*

The Wall Flower *(1914)*; The Saving Presence *(1914)*; The Fatal Dress Suit *(1914)*; The Girl in the Shack *(1914)*; For Her Father's Sins *(1914)*; The Million-Dollar Bride *(1914)*; A Flurry in Art *(1914)*; Mixed Values *(1915)*; Symphony Sal *(1915)*; The Deacon's Whiskers *(1915)*; Pennington's Choice *(1915)*; His Picture in the Papers *(1916)*; A Corner in Cotton *(1916)*; *(titles only)* Macbeth *(1916)*; Wild Girl of the Sierras *(1916)*; The Little Liar *(1916)*; The Half-Breed *(1916)*; *(titles only)* Intolerance *(1916)*; The Social Secretary *(1916)*; Stranded *(1916)*; The Wharf Rat *(1916)*; Manhattan Madness *(1916)*; American Aristocracy *(1916)*; The Matrimaniac *(1916)*; The Americano *(1916)*; A Daughter of the Poor *(1917)*; In Again Out Again *(1917)*; Wild and Wooly *(1917)*; Reaching for the Moon *(1917)*; Let's Get a Divorce *(1917)*; Hit-the-Trail Holiday *(1918)*; Come on In *(1918)*; *(co-story, co-producer only)* Getting Mary Married *(1919)*; Oh You Women! *(1919)*; *(also co-producer)* A Temperamental Wife *(1919)*; The Isle of Conquest *(1919)*; *(also co-producer)* A Virtuous Vamp *(1919)*; Two Weeks *(1920)*; *(also co-producer)* In Search of a Sinner *(1920)*; The Love Expert *(1920)*; The Perfect Woman *(1920)*; The Branded Woman *(1920)*; Dangerous Business *(1920)*; Mama's Affair *(1921)*; Woman's Place *(1921)*; *(also co-producer)* Red Hot Romance *(1922)*; Polly of the Follies *(1922)*; Dulcy *(1923)*; Three Miles Out *(1924)*; Learning to Love *(1925)*; *(story only)* Stranded *(1927)*; *(story only)* Publicity Madness *(1927)*; *(co-adaptor from her novel and play)* Gentlemen Prefer Blondes *(1928)*; *(co-story only)* The Fall of Eve *(1929)*; The Struggle *(1931)*; Red-Headed Woman *(1932)*; *(dialogue only)* Blondie of the Follies *(1932)*; Hold Your Man *(1933)*; *(story only)* Midnight Mary *(1933)*; The Barbarian *(1933)*; The Girl from Missouri *(1934)*; The Biography of a Bachelor Girl *(1935)*; Riffraff *(1936)*; San Francisco *(1936)*; Mama Steps Out *(1937)*; Saratoga *(1937)*; The Women *(1939)*; Susan and God *(1940)*; Blossoms in the Dust *(1941)*; They Met in Bombay *(1941)*; When Ladies Meet *(1941)*; I Married an Angel *(1942)*; *(remake, co-play basis only)* Gentlemen Prefer Blondes *(1953)*.

Halfway through the 20th century, America rediscovered Anita Loos. Few were more surprised than Loos herself, then nearing 60 years of age. She had never felt as if she had been lost in the first place, especially since the occasion of her reconstituted fame was a musical based on a wildly popular book she had written 25 years before, and movie audiences had been watching films produced from her scripts since the days of silent pictures. She particularly scoffed at one critic's mention of her as "the last of the flap-pers." "Me? A flapper?," she hooted. "The only things I ever flapped were the pages of a yellow legal pad."

Loos had been scribbling on a long line of notepads since her childhood in a household boasting several memorable characters. To begin with, there was her father Richard Beers Loos, whom she described as "a first scale rogue." Richard, a raffish newspaper publisher from Ohio with an eye for women and a fondness for saloons, had come to rural northern California in the late 19th century to establish a new paper in mountainous Sissons, California (now Mount Shasta), *The Sissons Mascot*. He attracted the attention of Sissons' young women by appearing at a dance in blackface and performing a popular music-hall song of the day. "He was an overnight sensation," Loos wrote of her beloved "Pop" years later, "witty, outrageous and with the urbane type of good looks which foretells early baldness." Among the women who caught his eye was **Anita "Minnie" Smith**, a pretty brunette and the daughter of an adventurous Easterner who had made a fortune in California's mid-century gold rush. Minnie Smith defied her father's wishes and married Richard Loos in the early 1880s. "With her marriage," Loos said, "began the lifelong heartache of being in love with a scamp." Anita was the second of the couple's three children, born in April 1893.

Although it was the rollicking behavior of her father that ruled much of Anita's childhood and adolescence, Minnie's side of the family was not without color. There was, for instance, Minnie's sister **Nina Smith**, who had caused a scandal in her teens by running away from home and returning some years later as the wife of a wealthy confidence man. Loos would always remember Aunt Nina as the glamorous black sheep of the family, always well taken care of by a series of men friends after her divorce and periodically descending on the family, plumed and bejeweled, from her travels in Europe. Then there was Minnie's grandmother, the daunting **Cleopatra Fairbrother Smith**, who had come West as a young bride during the gold rush and who by the time Anita was born had become a virtual recluse. Cleopatra would consent only rarely to a visit by her grandchildren to her darkened bedroom filled with the scent of lavender and stories of survival in a man's world.

By the time Anita was four, *The Sissons Mascot* had prospered sufficiently for her father to sell the journal and move his family to San Francisco, where he was sure he would meet with similar success by buying a theatrical jour-

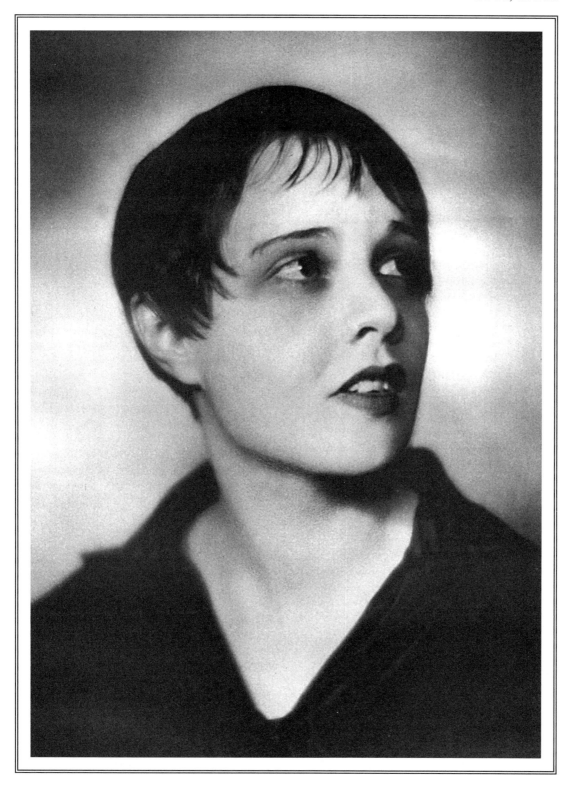

*A*nita
*L*oos

nal called *Music and Drama,* which he patrioti-
cally renamed *The Democratic Event.* The
show-business connections that came with the
purchase provided Richard Loos ample opportunity to indulge in brief affairs with young star-
lets and stage hopefuls, along with two other favorite activities, fishing and drinking. Over Minnie's protests, Richard would often bring Anita
along for a morning spent on San Francisco's
docks with a fishing rod, followed by a lengthy
visit to one or another of the city's wharfside saloons, where Anita dined on hard-boiled eggs

and pickled beets while her father downed beer with the locals. In those pre-earthquake years, San Francisco was one of America's most liberal-minded cities, looked down on by the more puritanical regions of the country as a sink of debauchery, especially for its "Barbary Coast" district lined with burlesque houses, brothels, and raucous taverns. "Its honky-tonks and sporting houses welcomed colored musicians at a time when they were barred from most white places," Loos once recalled, adding that several of the most famous stars of the American stage first learned their trade there. Many of her father's paramours, she said, were little better than street walkers from the red light district—one of whom had the courage to actually pay a visit to Minnie to demand a divorce. Loos, who claimed to have witnessed the confrontation, remembered her mother's calm response for the rest of her life. "She explained that she had suffered for years because of other women's infatuations [with her husband]," Loos recalled, "and that it would be best for the young lady to be assured of his feelings before trying to legalize her penchant for him." Thwarted in her expectations of a dramatic scene, the young beauty was left speechless and flounced out of the house, never to be seen again.

> $\mathcal{B}$eauty combined with a lack of brains is extremely deleterious to the health.
>
> —Anita Loos

Richard Loos' fondness for show business propelled Anita on the stage before long, again over Minnie's strenuous objections. At the suggestion of a producer friend of her father's, Anita and her younger sister **Gladys Loos** found themselves in a stock-company production of *Quo Vadis,* in which they were among a group of Christians about to be fed to the lions. Anita wailed in terror to such effect that she went on to appear in *East Lynne,* a popular melodrama of the day in which she played the heroine's young son and moved the audience to tears with her death scene, complete with harp music. Her reputation grew to such an extent that David Belasco, a San Francisco native who had become Broadway's leading producer, chose her for the title role of his first production in his hometown, *Frances Hodgson Burnett's Little Lord Fauntleroy.* Anita's income as an actress became more than a frivolous perk as Richard Loos' *Democratic Event* began to lose subscribers and income, so much so that by her early teens Anita was touring throughout northern California with a number of stock companies to provide much of the family's finances. The strains at home became

apparent to her when her sister Gladys died suddenly of appendicitis while Richard was off on a boozy, weeklong fishing jaunt with his cronies and female companions. Minnie arranged for her younger daughter's burial in her husband's absence, angrily revealing to Anita what "Pop" was up to while his child was dying.

By the time the 1906 earthquake rocked San Francisco, Richard had moved his family to San Diego to take a job managing a theater which combined live entertainment with one-reel silent films, which were then still a novelty. The business went well enough to lead to a partnership with a husband-and-wife vaudeville team to purchase the Lyceum Theater and, later, the Empire Theater, both of which had repertory companies in which Anita often appeared. When both companies had shows on the boards at the same time, Anita appeared at the Lyceum under her own name and borrowed her grandmother's for appearances at the Empire, appearing as Cleopatra Fairbrother in a blonde wig and high heels. Further income was provided when Anita cribbed articles from several East Coast newspapers and fashioned them into a New York City news sheet for wealthy Easterners vacationing at San Diego's elegant Del Coronado hotel. There were also the royalties from her first play, *The Soul Sinners,* which her father's business partners bought and took on the road. Nothing survives of this first effort except the name of its heroine, Fiamma LaFlamme, leaving the question of whether it was a melodrama or a comedy still in doubt. Despite all this extra-curricular activity, Loos managed to graduate in 1907 from San Diego High School, where she had often been criticized for not participating in school activities. "I was always standing on the sidelines, making impudent comments," she remembered, adding, "I was destined to be an outsider, too much the observer to ever be deeply involved in anything but my work."

All the while, Loos had been fascinated by the one-reel "flickers" shown at her father's theaters, noticing that the best of them were made by a New York company called Biograph. In a few days, she had produced a five-page scenario for *The Road to Plaindale,* about a young married couple who move to the country only to find the delights of city living more to their liking. Loos had also noticed that none of the writers credited on the films were women, so she merely signed her submission letter to Biograph "A. Loos." Biograph promptly bought her work for $25 and bought three more from her during 1912. Among them was *The New York Hat,* which was the first of the four to be produced.

Loos' story of a dying mother in a small Vermont town who persuades her minister to buy her daughter a fancy hat as a parting gift, causing much scandal, occupied a mere 12 minutes of screen time; but Biograph considered the story good enough to give the role of the daughter to one of its more promising actresses, a young *Mary Pickford, and that of the minister to the respected stage actor Lionel Barrymore. The film was directed by David Wark Griffith, about to become early Hollywood's most influential artist. With his aristocratic features and sophisticated demeanor, Griffith reminded Loos of "an Egyptian god" on their first meeting in 1913, when Biograph sent the director west to set up its first studio in Los Angeles. Griffith, surprised to find that "A. Loos" was a 20-year-old girl, was equally impressed and offered her a role in the film he was then shooting. But Minnie, who had made sure to accompany Anita to the meeting, was scandalized by Griffith's hold on Anita and quickly whisked her daughter back to San Diego.

During 1913, Loos sold 36 scenarios to Biograph and several other movie companies, relishing all the while the excitement of a business from which her mother was determined to keep her. Her method of escaping was to marry. She had already received two marriage proposals from eager young men who were among the inhabitants of San Diego's "Tent City," an off-season community of middle-class vacationers living on the Del Coronado's beach. Richard Loos had moved his family into a bungalow nearby by wangling a job as the editor of a Tent City community newspaper. Loos decided to accept the offer of marriage from a hopeful young composer named Frank Pallma because, as she frankly admitted later, it might lead to further contacts in show business free of Minnie's stern protection. Even her father was dismayed at her acceptance. "Look, Pop, it didn't count," Loos told him after the ceremony in 1915. "I kept my fingers crossed the whole time." It soon became painfully obvious that Pallma had no intention of promoting a career for his wife. After six months, Loos sent Pallma out one day to buy her some hat pins, packed her things and left for home as soon as he was out of sight. But the brief union was not without its benefits, for Minnie reluctantly accompanied her daughter back to Los Angeles and D.W. Griffith.

By now, Griffith had formed his own company, Triangle/Fine Arts, with two other pioneers of the film business, Thomas Ince and Mack Sennett. While Griffith handled the company's dramatic and comedy productions, Ince produced and directed its Westerns and Sennett its vaudeville-inspired slapstick material. Griffith was then in the midst of production on his epic *Intolerance* and offered Loos $75 a week to help reduce the film's sprawling plot to a series of title cards inserted in the action, providing the story advancement and dialogue that silent actors could not. Loos' first credited production for Triangle was an adaptation of *Macbeth,* the plot of which she condensed so effectively that the picture's title sequence lists "William Shakespeare and Anita Loos" as its authors. She quickly learned the mechanics of filmmaking from *Macbeth*'s director, John Emerson, and made friends with actresses *Mae Marsh and *Lillian Gish, who was impressed by Loos' habit of reading everything from popular novels to philosophical works for new story ideas. "I was positively in awe of her," Gish said. "We called her Mrs. Socrates."

Minnie was never far away, even when Griffith included Anita in his party traveling to New York for the premier of *Intolerance* in 1916, the first trip East for both women. Loos fell in love with the city that would be her home in later life, so much so that she stayed behind with Mae Marsh and, of course, Minnie, after Griffith returned to California. Loos was fascinated with the scruffy intellectuals and artists she met in Greenwich Village, thanks to Mae Marsh's friendship with poet Vachel Lindsay, and she made good use of her time by arranging a luncheon at Delmonico's with Frank Crowninshield, the editor of *Vanity Fair,* which had printed several of her short stories and essays.

Called back to Los Angeles, Loos found Triangle in turmoil over rumors that Griffith was threatening to leave the studio and take some of its top talent with him. Among the actors Triangle was struggling to keep was Douglas Fairbanks, a former stage actor who had built his reputation on good looks and athleticism. Although Fairbanks' pictures were immensely popular, especially with female audiences, Griffith considered his acting talent negligible and suitable only for lightweight comedies. He had always handed the direction of Fairbanks' films to Triangle's second-string directors, like John Emerson. It was to Emerson and Loos that Triangle's executives turned in their efforts to keep Fairbanks in their stable. Loos and Emerson quickly turned out *His Picture in the Papers,* which Anita adapted from one of Fairbanks' stage successes about a mild-mannered salesman who inadvertently becomes an overnight celebrity. It was the first of ten films that she would write for Fairbanks, and Emerson would direct, over the next year. All of them were great successes, especially Loos' Western spoof *Wild and Wooly*. The hardest part of writing for the agile Fairbanks, Loos said, was "finding a variety of spots from which Doug could jump."

When Fairbanks eventually left Triangle for Famous Players/Lasky (the forerunner of Paramount Pictures), he took his writer and director with him. He also provided Loos a front-row seat for his very public and scandalous romance with Famous Players' leading actress, Mary Pickford, who had, since the days of *The New York Hat,* become Hollywood's highest paid actress and would soon emerge as the industry's most powerful woman. Meanwhile, Loos' own relationship with John Emerson was becoming more than professional. Like Fairbanks and most of Hollywood's artists in those early days, Emerson had begun on Broadway as a director and actor before being hired by Triangle to direct adaptations of material written for the legitimate stage. Many of the couple's associates thought Loos and Emerson an odd match, especially since Emerson was her senior by 14 years. But Loos was attracted by Emerson's witty urbanity and gave him credit for refining her writing skills and, even more important, teaching her the value of self-promotion, at which Emerson was a master. Fairbanks, in fact, confided to friends that he was jealous of Loos for capitalizing on her association with him to such an extent that she had become the only writer for the screen known by name to movie audiences. Fairbanks' opinions probably were a factor in Famous Players' offer to move Loos and Emerson to its New York facilities at higher salaries while Fairbanks embarked on the series of swashbucklers for which he is most remembered.

In New York, while Loos cranked out adaptations of stage works for the likes of George M. Cohan and *Billie Burke, she and Emerson indulged enthusiastically in the city's fervid artistic life. Friends continued to speculate on the odd relationship between the two. "When Emerson wasn't around," one of them later noted, "she was mischievous, giddy, very funny. But once he walked on the set . . . she became very subdued, very ladylike. She deferred to him *completely*. It was obvious she worshiped him." Emerson had enjoyed early success at Triangle when few competent directors for the new medium were to be found, although by the time he relocated to New York the industry's artistic sensibilities were maturing beyond his capabilities. But such was Loos' infatuation with Emerson that she agreed to his suggestion of sharing writing credits for material to which he had contributed little or nothing, and even allowed his name to appear before hers on screen, Emerson airily explaining that a woman should naturally take second place to a man of his stature. The truth was that attention for Loos' work was fast superseding that given to his directorial skills. Some critics, in fact, accused Loos of overwriting, interrupting a picture's action with an overabundance of title cards. "I kept wondering," commented one reviewer after screening a Loos-decorated picture, "whether Miss Loos never suffered from writer's cramp."

By now, Loos' work had attracted the attention of William Randolph Hearst, the bombastic newspaper publisher who had been carrying on a well-known affair for years with actress *Marion Davies. Davies would become the first of a number of actresses whose careers would be resuscitated by Loos' imagination and skill. Hearst hired Anita to help him turn a frustrated Davies, who had been cast in a series of heavy melodramas to much critical disdain, from America's most famous mistress into a respected screen star. Loos' solution was *Getting Mary Married,* a domestic comedy that was the first film starring Davies to actually make money at the box office. Loos did the same for *Constance Talmadge, whom she had met at Triangle and who had appeared in one of Fairbanks' Loos-scripted films. Talmadge had failed to attract an audience at the box office but, as with Davies, Loos saw that it was a question of the proper material for Talmadge's talent. She was fascinated by Talmadge's odd combination of a sharp and sometimes earthy wit with an elegance of manner and speech. The result was a series of films, beginning with *A Temperamental Wife*, which played Talmadge's off-beat comedy against an elegant, upper-class background. Loos and Constance Talmadge, along with Connie's actress sister *Norma Talmadge, became fast friends in the process, being seen together around New York's shops and restaurants when not working at a makeshift studio that had been built especially to house the Talmadge sisters' films by Connie's husband, producer Joseph Schenck. So close was her relationship to the Talmadges that Loos' marriage to John Emerson, on June 21, 1920, took place at Schenck's Long Island estate.

The more cynical of Anita's friends saw the marriage as Emerson's way of ensuring an income, for Emerson's career as a director seemed over. He had long been complaining of various illnesses and discomforts and had been leaving much of the daily tasks of directing a film to an assistant; these same friends noted that the marriage followed swiftly on the heels of Loos' rumored affections for Emerson's replacement behind the camera. Publicly, however, Emerson continued to insist on taking center stage. Perhaps inspired by his influential role in organizing Actors' Equity during the actors' strike on Broadway in 1919, Emerson announced that he and Loos would henceforth devote their talents to the legitimate stage, about which Anita acknowledged her husband knew more than she. The first of their nine plays written for Broadway was *The Whole Town's Talking,* a romantic comedy which Emerson himself directed. Loos also gamely agreed to Emerson's suggestion, a popular one in New York society at the time, that their marriage would benefit by their taking one day a week off from each other. Loos thus found herself a member of the "Tuesday Widows" club, in the company of Connie Talmadge, Marion Davies, *Adele Astaire, *Tallulah Bankhead, and a number of other outspoken, sharp-tongued New York show-business women. Loos called their weekly meetings "cat parties," but she was surprised at how much the women shared in common. "They had an unusual kindness toward each other," she later wrote, "having been mauled by practically every man they met, who freely picked and dropped mistresses only as a way to call attention to themselves." On the other hand, she was equally surprised by how the most glittering of New York's male sophisticates and intellectuals were putty in the hands of a pretty, if not particularly bright, young lady.

This was especially evident to her in the person of H.L. Mencken. She had been reading Mencken's tart social observations for years and shared his disdain for his "booboisie," characterized by what Mencken saw as the middle class' vulgar imitations of upper-class manners and lifestyles. The two writers had met through Frank Crowninshield at *Vanity Fair,* and Loos made sure to lunch with Mencken whenever he traveled to New York on business from his beloved Baltimore. She observed firsthand his helpless infatuations with bubbly young women and, on a train trip to Los Angeles to work on a film with Connie Talmadge, began to sketch out the story of a cheerfully scheming female successful at bending any man, and particularly older ones, to her will. She cast her short story in the form of a diary written by an unnamed woman of incomplete education and imperfect grammar, given to such pronouncements as "Fate was just about to start happening" and such profound musings as "Bird life is the highest form of civilization." This anonymous heroine reveals that she has begun writing her memoirs because of a recent affair with a prominent U.S. senator who might be interested to know she is setting it all down on paper, and recounts past acquaintances with a well-known "Chicago button king" and a British novelist. Loos dashed off the story before her train crossed the Mississippi and stuffed it in the flap of her suitcase, thinking Mencken might find it amusing on her return to the East.

Mencken was, indeed, amused; so much so that he arranged for the story's publication in *Harper's.* It became so popular that the magazine's editor asked for a second installment, for which Loos came up with a name for her narrator, Lorelei Lee ("after the girl who became famous for sitting on a rock in Germany," Lorelei explains). The continuation of Lorelei's story details her adventures in Europe, where the button king has sent her to keep her away from the British novelist of the first installment, and the generosity of a Philadelphia millionaire she meets in Austria who agrees to bankroll her dream of a film career if she will only marry him. *Harper's* soaring circulation figures, and the fact that thousands of men were buying copies of what was a traditionally woman's magazine, convinced Mencken that Lorelei should see the light of day in book form. Loos arranged the material under the title *Gentlemen Prefer Blondes,* and the book appeared in November 1925. Six months later, it had gone through nine editions and the name Anita Loos had leaped off the movie screen and into homes across the country.

Blondes' popularity lay in Loos' skill at making fun of sex without ever resorting to crude language or salacious descriptions, at a time when America's social mores were beginning to loosen after the horrors of World War I. "Miss Loos' book is civilized, ironic, and never crude in its effect," said *The New York Times,* and some critics went so far as to locate Lorelei's ancestor in the character of Cunégonde in Voltaire's *Candide.* Although Loos had certainly read such exalted material, she variously attributed her creation to the blonde girlfriend of a prominent judge she had met on her train journey; to Lillian Gish, from whom Loos cheerfully admitted stealing the line about the nobility of avian civilization; and to Mary Pickford, whose much-publicized embrace of Christian Science was skewered in Lorelei's brief flirtation with that religion. No doubt other women ranging from Anita's Aunt Nina to Constance Talmadge were part of the mosaic, too, for Loos had invented a wholly new character, one that Irving Berlin called "the virtuous vamp."

Despite its success, however, *Blondes* marked the beginning of what Loos would later call her "wasted years," self-imposed when a doctor whom John Emerson had consulted suggested that the only way to help Emerson's hypochondria was for Loos to abandon her career. The doctor's opinion that Emerson's complaints were a desperate attempt to attract attention and overcome his wife's celebrity filled Loos with guilt. "My own experience is sex turned a strong-willed character I had adored into a sick man," she later wrote. "If only we'd remained sympathetic co-workers, without the complication of marriage, no stranger would have ever addressed [Emerson] as 'Mr. Loos.'" For the next few years, Anita attempted to follow the doctor's advice and produced little work. A Broadway adaptation of *Blondes* closed after only a few months, and a companion novel to *Gentlemen Prefer Blondes* which Loos called *But Gentlemen Marry Brunettes* was not well received, although it is considered the literary superior to the first book. As the years passed, the psychological component of Emerson's ailments became more apparent and his behavior more erratic, while Loos sought comfort in an affair with Wilson Mizner, the dashing younger brother of Palm Beach architect Addison Mizner. Wilson Mizner died of a drug overdose in 1933, and Anita would circle the date in black on her calendar each year for the rest of her life.

But even her husband's worsening condition could not overpower Loos' compulsion to write. When MGM offered her a permanent staff position at $1,000 a week, she went west while Emerson stayed behind in New York. "It's you they want," he told her. "I'm just an afterthought." Her arrival at MGM brought a fresh challenge to make over the stalled career of a promising young actress. In this case, the actress was *Jean Harlow and the film, 1932's *Red-Headed Woman*. The script was based on a lurid novel of mistresses and murder, but it was Loos' genius to turn the story on its head and make it into a sex comedy which jump-started Harlow's tragically brief career and marked the beginning of Loos' most successful relationship with a studio. Films which are now considered classics of 1930s Hollywood flowed from Loos' typewriter, either alone or in collaboration, including *Hold Your Man, San Francisco, Saratoga, The Cowboy and the Lady,* and Loos' best-known work of this period, the 1939 film adaptation of *Clare Boothe Luce's play *The Women*.

By 1938, however, John Emerson had been diagnosed with severe schizophrenia and was confined to the sanitarium where he would spend the rest of his life. It was the first time, Loos said, that she suffered from writer's cramp, with her right hand literally clenched uncontrollably on the train ride home from Emerson's confinement. Her output slowed after Emerson's hospitalization, and it was not until 1946 that she returned to Broadway, with *Happy Birthday*. *Helen Hayes played the prim schoolteacher Addie Beamis, who tries to rescue her alcoholic father from a bar but instead finds a way to liberate herself from her own inhibitions. In a year when such weighty plays as *Another Part of the Forest* and *The Iceman Cometh* were playing Broadway, Loos' comedy ran for more than 600 performances to full houses. She found a new, younger audience with the musical version of *Gentlemen Prefer Blondes,* which swept onto Broadway in 1949. Loos turned her story into a star vehicle for a young and still relatively unknown *Carol Channing, who was cast as Lorelei at Anita's insistence over the producers' and director's protests. "She can play Lorelei like a Great Dane under the delusion it's a Pekingese," Loos said of the gangly, wide-eyed Channing, and Broadway audiences proved her instincts correct. The show ran for almost two years at the Ziegfeld Theater and then went on an equally successful national tour. In 1953, *Blondes* appeared in a film version, this time with *Marilyn Monroe, whom Loos called the "most luscious" of all the Loreleis.

Loos' success on Broadway during the 1950s also included her adaptation of *Gigi*, *Colette's story of a 16-year-old Parisian girl trained to be a courtesan who outwits her family and marries the man to whom she is given. *Audrey Hepburn delighted audiences in the role for five months, with the show closing in May 1952 only because of the star's film commitments. But in 1956, with John Emerson's death, Loos once again withdrew from the public eye.

She returned nearly ten years later with the first of her memoirs, *A Girl Like I*. "It is perhaps the most remarkable Hollywood memoir ever written for its candor, its wit, and its intelligence," said one reviewer. Loos followed this success with *Twice over Lightly*, a survey of New York's lesser-known attractions written with Helen Hayes, and another memoir called *The Talmadge Girls,* about her days with Norma and Constance Talmadge. Yet a third memoir, *Cast of Thousands*, was published in 1977. But by the late 1970s, Loos' strength seemed to be leaving her. In an odd echo of her husband's fate, doctors were unable to find a specific ailment, although it was clear that she was seriously ill, weighing only 75 pounds by

Opposite page

$\mathcal{E}$ncarnación

$\mathcal{L}$opez

the time she was admitted to New York's Doctor's Hospital during the summer of 1981. She died there on August 18, at the age of 88.

Anita Loos' wry humor and deft sexual satire are still much admired even if the deeper sources of her talent are less well known. Her relationships with the opposite sex, starting with her father and culminating in her long and, in the end, tragic marriage to John Emerson, proved her as helpless as anyone else in dealing with the mysteries of human foibles. But her great gift was the ability to memorialize her experience with high spirits. Hidden by all the attention paid to Loos' sources for Lorelei Lee was the autobiographical basis for Lorelei's best friend, Dorothy Shaw. "Fun is fun," Loos says, through Dorothy, "but no girl wants to go on laughing all the time."

SOURCES:
Carey, Gary. *Anita Loos: A Biography*. NY: Knopf, 1988.
Loos, Anita. *A Girl Like I*. NY: Viking Press, 1966.

Norman Powers,
writer-producer, Chelsea Lane Productions, New York

Lopes de Almeida, Julia (1862–1934).

See Almeida, Julia Lopes de.

Lopez, Encarnación (1898–1945)

Argentinean dancer. Name variations: Encarnacion Lopez; known professionally as Argentinita. Born Encarnación Lopez on March 25, 1898, in Buenos Aires, Argentina; died on September 24, 1945, in New York City; daughter of Felix Lopez and Lominga Lopez; sister of Pilar Lopez (a dancer).

Regarded as one of the leading exponents of Spanish dance, Encarnación Lopez, professionally known as Argentinita, was one of the unique talents of her time. "Argentinita is no mere beater of heels and clicker of castanets," wrote dance critic John Martin in 1942, at the height of the dancer's popularity in America, "nor is she concerned with swinging a mean hip or tearing passion to tatters. She ranges easily over the wide area of a wonderfully spacious medium, dancing in the full sense of the word, making music with voice, heels, and castanets, acting with the flair of a true comedian."

Born in 1898 in Buenos Aires, Argentina, to Castilian parents, Lopez was raised in Madrid, Spain, where she studied dancing and acting from the age of seven. When she was a child, her schoolmates dubbed her Argentinita, "the little Argentinean," and she later adopted the nickname for the stage. She sometimes said that her

career began in a police station, where she and her brother once ended up after an impromptu dance recital in a local park, but by the time she was 15, Lopez was known throughout Spain as "Queen of the Dance." She was also a self-taught mime and singer, having spent some time with a popular Spanish acting company. At one point in her career, she had her own theatrical group which specialized in revivals of 19th-century plays.

After mastering Spanish dance, Lopez became interested in learning the Gypsy or "Flamenco" style of dance (from the province of Andalusia). To do so, she lived among Gypsies (Roma) until she had mastered the *bulerias, alegrias*, and tangos which comprise the Flamenco style. She also studied the *sevellanas*, or *cuadro Flamenco*—the individual variations of Flamenco that were performed in small cafes or in a cleared square of the town. Lopez once described Flamenco as utilizing all the elements of dance, "the feet, the head, the waist, static and dynamic rhythm." Although following well-defined rules, the dance is always open to individual interpretation. "The most difficult part of the bulerias and the alegrias is the *desplante*—a haughty gesture of defiance—and it is at the same time its principal attraction," she explained further. "The dancer gives warning of the coming *desplante* by tapping twice with her heel. Sometimes this tempo is only a *zapateado*—repeated stamp of the heel—or it may be shown by movements of the body. But the rhythm is always the same."

In 1927, Encarnación Lopez first introduced Flamenco to Madrid audiences, performed by her own troupe of *gitanos*. She subsequently toured in France, Mexico, Cuba, and Argentina, finally bringing the troupe to the United States in 1930, as part of the *International Revue*. Neither the dance, nor Lopez, who was often confused with the then-famous La Argentina (*Antonia Mercé), made much of an impression. According to *The New York Times*, the visit "resulted in unmerited disaster."

Returning to Spain, Lopez collaborated with poet-musician Federico Garcia Lorca to found the Madrid Ballet, for which she choreographed dances, utilizing original folk music that she and Lorca collected and recorded. The group had several successful years before the Civil War forced Lopez to leave Spain. She then embarked on a series of recitals, performing in Paris, Switzerland, Morocco, Algiers, and London, where she performed for Queen *Mary of Teck and gave four concerts at the Aldwych

Theater. In November 1938, she returned to the United States with a recital at the Majestic Theater in New York. On this occasion, she was greeted warmly by both audiences and critics. John Martin not only found her an extraordinary dancer, but a fine actress, particularly in her comic numbers. "With the economy of means which is characteristic of all she does, she is able by the slightest inflection, by the smallest flick of her hand or shrug of her shoulder, to establish a character or a mental attitude teeming with comment," he wrote. In a subsequent tour of the United States, Lopez won acclaim in every city she visited.

At the conclusion of the American tour, Lopez went to Paris, then on to Monte Carlo, where she collaborated with Léonide Massine and the Ballets Russes in the creation of *Capriccio Espagnol*, which had its American premiere in April 1940 at the Metropolitan Opera House. "It was an odd experience," wrote one critic, "to witness the lithe, spontaneous, improvisational quality of Argentinita's dancing surrounded by the academic virtuosity of the Russian group." Still, most of the reviews were favorable, and Argentinita's subsequent performances in the United States were extremely popular. Frequently appearing with her was her sister **Pilar Lopez**, who was première danseuse of the Madrid Ballet for four years, and was also noted for her comic sense.

Encarnación Lopez's last appearance in the United States was with the Ballet Theater in April 1945. She died on September 24 of that year, at age 47.

SOURCES:
Chujoy, Anatole, and P.W. Manchester, eds. *The Dance Encyclopedia*. NY: Simon & Schuster, 1967.
Current Biography. NY: H.W. Wilson, 1942.

Barbara Morgan,
Melrose, Massachusetts

López, Leonor (1362–1412).

See López de Córdoba, Leonor.

Lopez, Nancy (1957—)

Mexican-American golfer. Born Nancy Marie Lopez in Torrance, California, on January 6, 1957; daughter of Marina Lopez and Domingo Lopez (owned an auto-body repair shop); attended University of Tulsa on a golf scholarship; married Tim Melton (a television sportscaster), in 1979 (divorced); married Ray Knight (a professional baseball player), in 1982; children: Ashley Marie Knight (b. November 7, 1983); Erinn Shea Knight (b. May 26, 1986); Torri Heather Knight (b. October 30, 1991).

Awards: named All-American and University of Tulsa's female athlete of the year (1976); named LPGA Rookie of the Year (1978); won twin honors of LPGA Player of the Year and Vare Trophy (1978, 1979, and 1985); inducted into the LPGA Hall of Fame (1987).

Led otherwise all-male high school golf team to state championship; entered the U.S. Women's Open as a senior in high school, finishing in second place (1975); won the Association of Intercollegiate Athletics for Women (AIAW) golf championship (1976); in her first full season in the Ladies Professional Golf As-

sociation (LPGA), won eight tournaments—a record five in a row—to break the prize money record winning by more than $189,000 (with more than $3.2 million, was second in career earnings); only golfer, male or female, to be named both Rookie of the Year and Player of the Year in the same year (1978); won the LPGA championship (1978, 1985, and 1989); her last major LPGA win was the Mazda (1993).

Born in 1957 in Torrance, California, the daughter of avid golfers **Marina Lopez** and Domingo Lopez, Nancy Lopez followed her parents around the Roswell public golf course throughout her childhood. When she was eight, Domingo pulled a sawed-off 4-wood out of Marina's golf bag and told Nancy to hit the ball until she landed it in the hole. On that day, recalled Lopez, "apparently I never missed, but would just step up and swing and I kept knocking that one ball on the nose and down the fairway." A year later, she played in her first tournament, winning by 110 strokes.

With her father her only coach, she was New Mexico State Women's Amateur champion at age 12. By 16, the only girl on her high school team, she led her golfing teammates to a state championship. During her senior year, she competed in the U.S. Women's Open and finished second. By then, Lopez was the top-ranked amateur golfer in the world and was given an athletic scholarship to the University of Tulsa. She finished second in the U.S. Women's Open again in 1975. In 1976, she won the Association for Intercollegiate Athletics for Women (AIAW) national championship. In July 1977, Lopez joined the Ladies' Professional Golfer's Association (LPGA) tour.

All this had been achieved with monies earned from her father's auto-body repair shop. The Lopez family was far from rich, and Marina Lopez had given up her own golfing so that her greens' fees could go to her daughter. To Nancy Lopez's continuing sadness, Marina Lopez died during an appendix operation before Nancy had won her first professional tournament. "It is some consolation that she did have the joy of seeing me emerging as a star in my rookie year as a pro, and to know that I was likely to fulfill the promise she wanted so badly for me. . . . When I finally did go back on the tour, I won my first professional tournament." The following year, Lopez won a total of nine events. Her winnings were $189,000, breaking LPGA records. In 1979, Lopez won eight of the nineteen events she entered.

After her 1982 marriage to Ray Knight, a professional baseball player, Lopez cut back on her playing schedule and gave birth to Ashley Marie in 1983 and Erinn Shea in 1986. However, she won 12 tournaments between 1980 and 1984, topping the million dollar mark in career earnings in 1983 at the National *****Dinah Shore** Classic. Lopez was a media star. Her popularity guaranteed endorsements and increased earnings.

In 1985, Lopez returned to the tour full time, winning five tournaments, including a second LPGA championship. At the Henredon Classic, she set a record with her 20 under par score of 268 (66, 67, 69, 66) for 72 holes. Two years later, she was inducted into the LPGA Hall of Fame and in 1989 was inducted into the PGA/World Golf Hall of Fame. In 1991, Nancy Lopez once again cut back her playing schedule when her third daughter, Torri Heather, was born.

With such an incredible career, awards were numerous. The Associated Press named Lopez Female Athlete of the Year in 1978 and 1985. She was selected Golfer of the Decade by *Golf Magazine* from 1978 to 1987. Four times LPGA Player of the Year, Lopez held the title in 1978, 1979, 1985, and 1988. She won the Vare Trophy three times, in 1978, 1979, and 1985. In 1987, she won the LPGA's annual Powell Award.

With all her trophies, Lopez had never won a U.S. Women's Open. In July 1997, in a bid to win the only championship that had eluded her, Lopez was beaten by one stroke by England's **Alison Nicholas**. Lopez's 15-foot birdie putt on No. 18 slipped an inch off to the right. Despite the fact that she was the first golfer to shoot in the 60s in all four rounds, Lopez finished second for the fourth time in 21 Opens. Near tears, she promised to keep on trying. "I think this is the beginning of many more good U.S. Opens for me," she said.

Nancy Lopez became an athletic superstar despite two hindrances to success in American society: she was born a woman and a Mexican-American. "All of us Lopezes are definitely and unashamedly Mexican Americans in Roswell, a town where that surely wasn't a social asset." She was allowed to play on the poorly kept municipal course but not at the Roswell country club, where the greens could have challenged her developing game. "Mexican Americans like my parents would not have been welcome members." She readily admits that when she did play at the club in city tournaments, "There was a polite frostiness about the whole place that made me quite reconciled to going back and playing on the municipal course."

"I'd like to leave behind me a record that would kind of demand that golfers will think of it as 'The Age of Nancy Lopez,'" she wrote in 1979. In refutation of her addendum that "it may be too much to hope for," Nancy Lopez is one of the most successful women golfers of all time.

SOURCES:

Condon, Robert J. *Great Women Athletes of the 20th Century.* Jefferson, NC: McFarland, 1991.

Lopez, Nancy, with Peter Schwed. *The Education of a Woman Golfer.* NY: Simon & Schuster, 1979.

"Nicholas Denies Lopez at Open," in *The Day* [New London, CT]. July 14, 1997.

Woolum, Janet. *Outstanding Women Athletes: Who They Are and How They Influenced Sports in America.* Phoenix, AZ: Oryx Press, 1992.

Karin L. Haag,
Athens, Georgia

López de Córdoba, Leonor

(1362–1412)

Spanish noblewoman and author. Name variations: Leonor López Carrillo; Leonor Lopez of Cordoba. Born in 1362 in Córdoba; died in 1412; daughter of Martin López, Grand Master of Calatrava, and Sancha Carrillo of Córdoba; married Ruy Gutiérrez de Henestrosa (son of the high chamberlain to the king of Castile), in 1369; children: Juan Fernandez.

Leonor López de Córdoba, a Spanish noblewoman, composed an autobiography which is the primary source of her life. She was the daughter of Martin López de Córdoba and **Sancha Carrillo**, who was closely connected to the royal house of Castile. Her mother died when she was only a few years old; at age seven, Leonor was married to Ruy Gutiérrez de Henestrosa, son of the High Chamberlain to the king of Castile. Her dowry, as she herself records, was 20,000 gold coins, further enriching the already tremendously wealthy Ruy Gutiérrez.

Leonor's life reveals the unpredictable nature of politics in her time. She grew up in a highly privileged family and married well; yet, in 1370, when she was about eight, her father was executed by order of the new king Henry II Trastamara (Enriqué II), for supporting the late King Peter the Cruel (Pedro el Cruel), Henry II's brother and rival. Leonor, her husband, and numerous other family members were imprisoned for the same crime. All of their properties were confiscated by the crown; they remained in prison for nine years, suffering, as she records, great hunger as well as disease, for the plague took the lives of her older brother and several others during that time. When King Henry II

was on his deathbed in 1379, he agreed to release Leonor's family and restore them to their former estates.

Leonor's husband, however, was unable to reclaim his properties because he had lost his rank at court; according to Leonor, Ruy left her with an aunt for seven years while he tried to regain his fortune, but he was unsuccessful and eventually returned to her. They remained in Córdoba for many years, in which time Leonor eventually gained a high position at the royal court of King Henry III (Enriqué III), becoming lady-in-waiting to *Catherine of Lancaster (1372–1418), queen of Castile. Leonor stayed at court for many years, but around 1412, the political tide once more turned against the López and Henestrosa families; Leonor again found herself without allies, and this time she had to retire under pressure from the court of Henry III's son, King John II (Juan II). It was after her final days as a lady-in-waiting that she wrote down her life story.

Her autobiography is primarily narrative, but there are anecdotes included which reveal more personal thoughts and moments, such as the pain caused by the jealousy her aunt's children felt toward her, and the loneliness of being an orphan in her aunt's home in the years before Ruy returned. As an adult, Leonor López was very devout; she tells of rescuing an orphaned Jewish boy whose family was killed in a raid on the Jewish ghetto of Córdoba, and how she had him baptized and raised as one of her own children. Leonor's writing is also filled with the fear and danger caused by the recurrent epidemics of plague which struck Córdoba. She fled the city with her family many times but her son Juan Fernandez died of plague at age 12, an anguishing experience which she records touchingly. The autobiography of Leonor López is a rare example of a medieval woman's life story preserved in her own words, and is an important source of information on the daily life of 14th-century Spanish nobility.

SOURCES:

Amt, Emilie. *Women's Lives in Medieval Europe: A Sourcebook.* NY: Routledge, 1993.

Laura York,
Riverside, California

Lopokova, Lydia (c. 1892–1981)

Well-known Russian-born ballerina who performed mainly in the U.S., Britain, and Western Europe and married the noted English economist John Maynard Keynes. Name variations: Lopukhova or Lopoukhova; Loppy; Lady Keynes. Pronunciation: Lopokova:

LOW-poe-KOE-va; Keynes: KAYNES. Born Lydia Vasilievna Lopukhova in St. Petersburg, Russia, on October 21 in either 1891 or 1892; died at Tilton, Sussex, on June 8, 1981; daughter of Vasili Lopukhov (a St. Petersburg theater attendant) and Constanza Karlovna Douglas Lopukhova; sister of Evgenia Lopukhova (1884–1941); attended Imperial Ballet School, 1901–09; married Randolfo Barocchi, in 1916 (marriage annulled, 1925); married John Maynard Keynes, on August 4, 1925 (died 1946); no children.

Joined Maryinsky Theater (1909); joined Diaghilev company in Paris, left for America (1910); changed her name (1914); married Barocchi and returned to Europe (1916); met Keynes (1918); disappeared mysteriously (1919); married Keynes and made first trip back to Russia (1925); made final appearance with Diaghilev's ballet company (1927); started career as London actress (1928); visited her family in Leningrad (1932); gave last public performance as a ballerina (1933); made final visit to Russia (1937); made wartime trips to Canada and the U.S. (1941–45); death of Keynes (1946).

Major roles: (as a dancer) Harlequin, Le Carnaval (1916), Mariuccia, The Good-humored Ladies (1918), title role, The Firebird (1919), Lilac Fairy, The Sleeping Princess (1921), The Dancer, Petrushka (1925), Polovtsian girl, Prince Igor (1927), Swanhilda, Coppelia (1933); (as an actress) Olivia, Twelfth Night (1933), Nora Helmer, A Doll's House (1934), Hilda Wangel, The Master Builder (1935), Célimène, Le Misanthrope (1937).

During the first five decades of the 20th century, Lydia Lopokova participated in widely different but significant areas of European cultural life. As a prominent ballerina and a member of Sergei Diaghilev's dance troupe, she played an important role in bringing Russian ballet to Western Europe and the United States. As the lover, then the wife, of John Maynard Keynes, she linked the ballet world with the Bloomsbury group, an influential coterie of British intellectuals. From the close of the 1920s until the death of her husband in 1946, she served as personal protector, intellectual sounding board, and emotional companion to the most influential economist of the era.

The ballet world in which she flourished was in the midst of dramatic transition at the start of the 20th century. The static and unimaginative ballet scene in Western Europe, dominated by French and Italian dancers and choreographers, was shaken by the arrival of the Russians. Starting in 1909, the impresario Sergei Diaghilev brought a dazzling mixture of Russian music and choreography, energetic and charismatic ballet stars, and superlative costumes and set designs first to Paris, then to the other Western European capitals. His Ballets Russes was cut off from its homeland by World War I and the Bolshevik Revolution. Nonetheless, Diaghilev continued his spectacular dance innovations with an international company until his death in 1929.

The world of Bloomsbury, in which Lopokova also found a place, was far different. It consisted of a group of young men and women who both individually and collectively made an important mark on British intellectual and public life. Centered around a number of talented young men who had drawn together during their university years at Cambridge prior to World War I, it came to include brilliant women as well. Members of the group sought to challenge the intellectual conventions of the time. Sanctioning both heterosexual and homosexual liaisons, they also challenged social conventions. The Bloomsbury group included the economist John Maynard Keynes, the politically minded intellectual Leonard Woolf, and the painter *Vanessa Bell. It counted *Virginia Woolf, Lytton Strachey, and Roger Fry as its most influential writers and cultural critics.

John Maynard Keynes, who brought Lopokova from the world of ballet to the Bloomsbury circle, was the group's most significant contributor to the world of public affairs. A brilliant mathematician and economist, he served as a high-ranking figure in the British Treasury during World War I and emerged as a leading critic of the Versailles Peace Settlement that ended the conflict. In the interwar period, he wrote his *General Theory of Employment, Interest and Money*. The work was a response to the Depression of the 1930s, and it stands as one of the most influential pieces of economic writing to appear in the 20th century. During World War II, Keynes returned to the Treasury to play a leading role in directing the British government's financial operations. With Lopokova at his side, he attended crucial financial negotiations with the government of the United States from early 1941 to the close of the war.

Lydia Lopokova's exact birth date is uncertain, but she was probably born in St. Petersburg on October 21, 1892, although some authorities give her birth year as 1891. She was the product of a colorful ethnic mix. Her father was of Buriat-Mongol stock, with his origins in the Central Asian peoples under the control of the tsarist empire. Her mother was the descendant of a Scottish family that had settled in Sweden, and then moved to the Baltic provinces held by the Russian tsar.

Her father's position made it possible for Lydia, her sister, and two of her three brothers to enter the Imperial Ballet School and to receive a free education there. She later recalled that he had taken her to a ballet matinee as a child, and she reacted with "a heart-pulsing wish that I might be one of the beautiful angels I had seen at the theater." She put her dreams into action when she entered the ballet school, probably at the age of eight.

In the musical world in which she now found herself, Lydia associated with some of the great names in the Russian artistic community: the ballerina *Matilda Kshesinskaia, the opera singer Fedor Chaliapin, the ballet master Marius Petipa. A visitor to the ballet school in 1907 was the renowned American dancer *Isadora Duncan. Lopokova graduated in the spring of 1909.

The aspiring ballet star remained in her first post, as a member of the corps de ballet in the Maryinsky Theater in St. Petersburg, for only a year. In the spring of 1910, she left for Paris to

Lydia
Lopokova

join the touring company of Sergei Diaghilev. According to a fellow ballerina, Lopokova fainted from joy as soon as she descended from the train and set foot in the artistic capital of Europe.

Diaghilev promoted her immediately from the corps de ballet to fill in for the star ballerina *Tamara Karsavina, who was frequently absent from the Ballets Russes due to commitments in London. Not yet 18, Lopokova performed to critical acclaim in such ballets as *The Firebird* and *Le Carnaval*.

Always "a bit of a bolter," in the words of ballet critic Richard Buckle, she impulsively left Europe in 1910 and spent the next six years in the United States as a dancer and actress. She was a successful performer in vaudeville and operettas as well as in dance companies. From the middle of 1913 through the following winter, Lopokova temporarily dropped her career to prepare for a new artistic role: she spent these months improving her English and studying drama. In 1914, she toured the East Coast in *Just Herself*, a play that had been written for her. Despite a dance sequence that was inserted into the play for its Broadway debut, reviewers found the production mediocre at best, and it closed in less than a week. Nonetheless, the young Russian found other stage roles as well as places in touring dance companies. It was in America that she changed her name from Lopukhova (pronounced La-POOKH-ova) to the more pronounceable Lopokova.

$\mathcal{S}$ he was the darling of the twenties balletomane public.

—**Ninette de Valois**

Continuing her pattern of moving from one artistic environment to another with dramatic suddenness, Lopokova rejoined Diaghilev in 1916 when the great ballet director was leading his company in an American tour. While in Minneapolis, she married Randolfo Barocchi, Diaghilev's business manager. Milo Keynes has suggested that Diaghilev pushed the two into marriage, hoping to tie the notoriously restless ballerina to his company.

During the final year of World War I, Lopokova returned to Europe and began a long friendship with the artist Pablo Picasso, who designed sets for Diaghilev's company. She danced for the first time in London in 1918, where Keynes witnessed one of her performances. Unimpressed, he described Lopokova to a friend as he left the theater: "She is a rotten dancer—she has such a stiff bottom."

Indeed, Lopokova was short and lacked the other physical attributes of a traditional star ballerina. According to dancer-director Frederick Ashton, "She was not really a great ballerina, . . . but she had incredible charm and was always a strong and most interesting dancer to watch." As one of her contemporaries wrote, "Few dancers have performed with such assurance or flown through the air as she did." Her brother described her as "an elegant little doll," who danced "as if she was tripping on air." He added that she combined leaps of almost masculine power with a technique that "was delicate and typically feminine." Still another observer described her as "a tiny, happy blonde, with rounded arms and the cheeky manner of a London sparrow."

Lopokova and Keynes probably met for the first time sometime in early 1918. The economist had a longstanding interest in music, and the Bloomsbury group had numerous social contacts with Lopokova's ballet company throughout the year. Their friendship apparently began in earnest at a party held at the Adelphi Hotel in London on Armistice Day 1918, as all of Britain celebrated the end of World War I.

Lopokova made an abrupt departure from the Diaghilev company in the early summer of 1919, disappearing for a time in connection with the collapse of her marriage. She wrote Diaghilev that she had suffered a serious nervous breakdown. Rumors suggested that she was also romantically involved with a Russian officer. Keynes' biographer Robert Skidelsky believes that her romantic entanglement led her to follow her lover to the port of Batum on the Black Sea in Russian Georgia before their relationship crumbled. Her disappearance lasted until the early months of 1921, when she reappeared to dance in a musical play in New York. That same year, she rejoined Diaghilev's company, dancing for him sporadically during most of the 1920s.

By 1922, Keynes was openly attracted to the Russian ballerina, attending every one of her performances of *The Sleeping Beauty*, renamed by Diaghilev *The Sleeping Princess*. As he did for many of his close friends, the economist began to direct her financial affairs. She moved to Bloomsbury and confined most of her dance and stage appearances to England. Diaghilev's productions, such as *The Sleeping Princess*, were often financially unsuccessful, and, in June 1923, she wrote Keynes of her fading enthusiasm for life as a dancer.

Keynes' niece and nephew, **Polly Hill** and Richard Keynes, have eloquently described the firm basis for the relationship between the economist and the Russian ballerina. Keynes needed the companionship of an honest and lively personality, and his wide intellectual interests included a desire for contact with the world of the arts. His long series of homosexual affairs no longer provided him with the joy they once had. As early as World War I, he had begun to establish relationships with women. Although Lopokova was no economist, she lavishly praised his newspaper articles with an enthusiasm his Bloomsbury friends never showed.

Lydia was also at a turning point in her life. She faced an uncertain future after the failure of her marriage and in light of the continuing financial difficulties of Diaghilev's ballet company. She too was ready to settle into a conventional marriage with a stable and supportive figure.

Thus, the unlikely relationship between Lopokova and Keynes flourished. The two moved in together before they were legally wed. During their moments apart, for example when Keynes was busy at Cambridge, they carried on an extended correspondence starting in these early years. She wrote numerous letters to her "Maynardochka" or "Lank" (for lanky), and he responded to his "Lydochka." After Lopokova had formally ended her marriage to Barocchi, she wed Keynes in London in August 1925. Keynes' friends in the Bloomsbury set found the Russian woman an exotic and unappealing personality. She had no interest in the political and intellectual issues that dominated their conversations. Virginia Woolf wrote in June 1924: "You can't argue solidly when Lydia's there." She also noted that seeing Keynes with Lopokova on his knee made "a sublime but heartrending spectacle." Lytton Strachey dismissed her brutally as "a half-witted canary" and made fun of her thick Russian accent. In the Cambridge faculty, there were disparaging remarks that Keynes had "married a chorus girl."

Soon after the wedding, Lopokova and her new husband left for Russia. It was Lydia's first voyage back to her homeland since 1910. She introduced Keynes to her family, and he attended the festivities occasioned by the anniversary of the Academy of Sciences in Leningrad (as St. Petersburg was then called). Lydia's elder sister ❧▶ Evgenia Lopukhova had remained in Soviet Russia and become a leading ballerina. Her brother Fedor was achieving fame in the Russian dance world as a ballet master.

Back in Britain, the pair settled down in a farmhouse near the small village of Tilton in Sussex. Lydia was to live there with her husband until his death, and then until her own demise in 1981. She encouraged his interest in literature, and the two spent hours reading poetry to one

❧▶ **Lopukhova, Evgenia** (1884–1941)

*Russian prima ballerina. Name variations: Yevgenia Lopoukhova. Born in 1884; died in 1941; daughter of Vasili Lopukhov (a St. Petersburg theater attendant) and Constanza Karlovna Douglas Lopukhova; sister of Andrei Lopukhov (1898–1947, character dancer and teacher), Fedor Lopukhov (b. 1886, Soviet choreographer), and *Lydia Lopokova (c. 1892–1981).*

another. As he wrote and consulted with his colleagues in economics and the university community, she busied herself with long walks and domestic chores. She usually stayed in the countryside or in London during the stretches from Friday to Tuesday that Keynes spent at Cambridge, and they communicated with each other by mail each day. Meanwhile, Keynes entered a period of remarkable scholarly creativity, possibly due to the emotional security and the stimulation his wife provided.

From her earliest days as a ballerina, Lopokova had impressed people in the world of ballet and theater with her lively and uninhibited personality. She expressed herself with striking verbal frankness. Now friends in the Keynes circle also recorded her exuberant and whimsical characteristics. She sunbathed nude in front of the farmhouse at Tilton, unconcerned by the occasional passerby. On a trip with her husband to North America in 1944, she reacted to a severe heat wave one night by walking naked through the corridors of an Ottawa hotel and planting herself inside a large kitchen refrigerator. She purchased a sizable number of shoes and a larger number of hats. Her eccentric dress, which became even more colorful after her husband's death, made her instantly recognizable to acquaintances on the streets of London.

Lopokova continued to dance in Diaghilev's company immediately after her marriage, but she was now in her mid-30s and her enthusiasm for the dancer's life faded. She appeared in films, including *Dark Red Roses* in 1929, possibly the first English movie to use sound, and she continued to dance publicly with English companies in the early 1930s. As one friend noted years later, "She kept that wonderful elastic body fit doing high kicks over the bar in her room at Tilton." She reviewed ballet performances for a number of publications, and gave several radio broadcasts commenting on the ballet and reading Russian literature in English translation.

In the 1930s, Lopokova concentrated on an acting career. She remained hampered by her Russian accent, characteristically referring to her husband as "May-NAR," but nonetheless took on roles from Shakespeare to Ibsen. She continued to misuse English words in conversation, deliberately according to some acquaintances. Her witty repartee led most who knew her to conclude that she could speak without mistakes, and that her verbal oddities appeared because she wanted to give added spice to her speech. A typical remark was her comment on the beautiful country house with its exotic birds and their "beautiful ovaries."

During her acting career, critics lauded her charm and enthusiasm, and, perhaps in deference to her husband, tempered their reviews of her performances. Occasionally, however, the comments were harsh. The critic of London's *Evening Standard* wrote of one performance: "For those who like their Shakespeare with a very broken accent, this was a charming experience." *The Times'* critic in 1933 wrote of her performance in *Twelfth Night* that her Shakespearean English came "with so strong an Illyrian accent that much of its sense and all its music vanish." Lopokova reacted by giving up any further plans to perform Shakespeare; Ibsen became her playwright of choice.

Both husband and wife took up the cause of promoting the ballet in England in the 1930s and helped to found the Camargo Society. Named after *Marie-Anne Cupis de Camargo, a Parisian ballet star of the 18th century, the Society presented new English ballets with established dancers between 1930 and 1933. The work of the Society paved the way for the formation of the Royal Ballet. Lydia helped to attract guest artists; she herself danced in six ballets for the Society.

In 1932, along with an English friend, Lopokova visited Leningrad to see her family. She found them living in abject poverty in the midst of the Soviet Union's First Five Year Plan of rapid-fire industrial growth. Lydia also encountered the political repression of the time: she was told not to make negative comments about the Russian scene after her return to Britain lest her family suffer reprisals. Her efforts to get two of her brothers out of the Soviet Union had no success.

Keynes' most important contribution to the world of economics, his *General Theory*, appeared in 1936. By the start of 1937, he was showing clear signs of heart disease. Lydia, who had been concerned about her husband's health

problems throughout the 1930s, was probably not surprised when Keynes suffered a serious heart attack that May. Even though he never fully regained his health, he continued an active role as an economist and, during World War II, as an advisor to the British chancellor of the exchequer. In 1942, he was elevated to the nobility for his services to his country. John Maynard Keynes now became Lord Keynes; Lydia gained the title of Lady Keynes.

After 1937, Lopokova took on the role of nurse and protector for her husband. At confidential government meetings at which servants could not be present, she played the role of waitress. Even old associates from the Bloomsbury set, who had once been critical of her, now praised the energy and concern with which she cared for Keynes. She became famous for rationing his time and abruptly expelling visitors when she thought they were tiring her husband.

Wartime duties led Lord Keynes to take six trips to the United States, on which Lopokova accompanied him. Numerous choice anecdotes have survived in their friends' memories. For example, when her husband was negotiating with American secretary of the treasury Henry Morgenthau in 1944, Keynes expressed his frustration to Lopokova about the American position on a monetary issue. Lydia supposedly accosted Morgenthau in his office, demanded a more equitable settlement of the problem, and got the results she and Keynes wanted. During their return to England on the ocean liner *Nieuw Amsterdam,* now transformed into a troopship, Lopokova dealt with the vessel's captain in equally energetic fashion. She demanded that she and Maynard receive the unique privilege of meals in their cabin; otherwise, she would hold the captain responsible for Maynard's health when she rushed to report to Winston Churchill. Her assault on the ship's routine brought immediate success.

Lord Keynes died on Easter Sunday, 1946, at the age of 62. His last public appearance had been with Lopokova at the Royal Opera House, Covent Garden, for a performance of *The Sleeping Beauty*, the ballet in which his wife had danced a leading role while he was courting her in the early 1920s.

Lopokova felt that she would need a decade to recover from Maynard's death. In fact, she showed her devotion to her deceased husband by wearing his clothes for years. She continued an active involvement in the arts, serving as trustee of the Cambridge Arts Theater until 1960. A memorable moment in these years came in 1951, when Pablo Picasso visited England for the last time. Lopokova and Picasso danced together in front of her house in London.

Lopokova's careers as a dancer and actress have been overshadowed by her association with her husband. She, nonetheless, is particularly remembered for her vibrant personality. As one admirer, Dennis Arundell, put it, "Her chief quality was that she was always as straightforward as a child, and her eager enthusiasm for trying something new or challenging—no matter how different or difficult—was the enthusiasm of a child." Despite his public and professional image as a ferociously independent being, Keynes depended upon her for emotional support, especially during the stressful time when he was writing *General Theory*, his most important book. As one friend of the couple wrote Lopokova after Keynes' death: "I always thought it was through your will, devotion and care that Maynard was spared to do the great work that he did."

In her later years, Lopokova rotated among the three residences that she and Keynes had occupied: the farmhouse at Tilton and their apartments in London and at Cambridge. At Tilton, visitors noted, she was surrounded by a remarkable collection of paintings, including Cézannes and Picassos. Keynes' investments in the stock market had prospered in the 1930s, and he had put much of his profits into these great works of art. As the years continued, she gave up the apartments, ceased to attend the ballet in London, and spent her time at Tilton with long walks in the Sussex countryside. To her nephew Milo Keynes, she described her experience of aging in a vivid image: "Every day a little bit of me flies away, like a bird." By the mid-1970s, her mind wandered, but she could still regale visitors with vivid verbal portraits of the great dancers she had known. Lydia Lopokova spent her last years in a nursing home near Tilton, where she died on June 8, 1981. She was probably 88 years old.

SOURCES:

Hill, Polly, and Keynes, Richard. *Lydia and Maynard: The Letters of John Maynard Keynes and Lydia Lopokova*. NY: Scribner, 1989.

Keynes, Milo, ed. *Essays on John Maynard Keynes*. Cambridge, England: Cambridge University Press, 1975.

———, ed. *Lydia Lopokova*. London: Weidenfeld and Nicolson, 1983.

Skidelsky, Robert. *John Maynard Keynes: The Economist as Saviour, 1920–1937*. NY: Penguin, 1992.

Spencer, Charles. *The World of Diaghilev*. NY: Penguin, 1974.

SUGGESTED READING:

Au, Susan. *Ballet and Modern Dance*. London: Thames and Hudson, 1988.

Buckle, Richard. *Diaghilev*. London: Weidenfeld and Nicolson, 1979.

Edel, Leon. *Bloomsbury: A House of Lions*. Philadelphia, PA: J.B. Lippincott, 1979.

Hession, Charles H. *John Maynard Keynes: A Personal Biography of the Man Who Revolutionized Capitalism and the Way We Live*. NY: Macmillan, 1984.

Neil M. Heyman,
Professor of History, San Diego State University,
San Diego, California

Lopoukhova, Lydia (c. 1892–1981).

See Lopokova, Lydia.

Lopukhova, Evgenia (1884–1941).

See Lopokova, Lydia for sidebar.

Lopukhova, Lydia (c. 1892–1981).

See Lopokova, Lydia.

Lord, Mary Scott (1858–1948).

See Harrison, Mary Scott Dimmick.

Lord, Pauline (1890–1950)

American actress. Born in Hanford, California, on August 13, 1890; died in Alamagordo, New Mexico, on October 11, 1950; one of four children of Edward Lord (a tinsmith) and Sara (Foster) Lord; attended Holy Rosary Academy in Woodland, California; studied acting at the school of the Alcazar Theater, San Francisco, California; married Owen B. Winters (an advertising executive), on April 27, 1929 (divorced 1931).

Selected theater: made stage debut as the maid in Are You a Mason? *(Alcazar Theater, San Francisco, California, 1903); made New York debut as Ruth Lenox in* The Talker *(January 1912); appeared as Sadie in* The Deluge *(1917), Anna in* Anna Christie *(1921), Amy in* They Knew What They Wanted *(1924), Nina in the touring company of* Strange Interlude *(1928–29), Zenobia in* Ethan Frome *(January 1936), Amanda Wingfield in the touring company of* The Glass Menagerie *(1946).*

One of the leading actresses of the new realism during the first half of the 20th century, Pauline Lord made an important contribution to the development of the American theater. She did not have a particularly easy time of it, however. Slight of stature, with tawny hair and a face once described as "victoriously paying the price of intelligence," she was not a conventionally pretty woman and had difficulty finding roles to fit her physical characteristics. Furthermore, she was not always discriminating in her choice of scripts.

Born in Hanford, California, in 1890, Lord moved with her family to San Francisco when she was a child. While attending Holy Rosary Academy in Woodland, Lord spent her weekly 25-cent allowance attending Saturday matinees in the city. Eventually, she enrolled in the school of the Alcazar Theater to study acting, and it was there that she made her professional debut at the age of 13, playing a maid in a Belasco Stock Company production of *Are You a Mason?* She then endured years of touring until 1912, when she enjoyed her first New York success as Ruth Lenox in *The Talker.* For five year after that, Lord was not offered another good role, and filled in with vaudeville and tours. In 1917, she finally landed a role as Sadie, a streetwalker, in the short-lived production *The Deluge,* directed by Arthur Hopkins. Impressed with her talent, Hopkins promised to find another role for her, but it was a long time coming. Finally in 1921, at the age of 31, she was offered the title role in Eugene O'Neill's *Anna Christie,* which opened at the Vanderbilt Theater on November 2. It was the breakthrough role Lord had waited for, and, after a successful Broadway run,

Pauline Lord

she toured with the show in the United States and in England, where she received a full half-hour ovation at London's Strand Theater.

The floodgates had opened for the actress and throughout the decade of the 1920s, she was rarely without work. Notable among her roles were Amy in Sidney Howard's *They Knew What They Wanted* (1924) and Nina Leeds in the touring company of another O'Neill play, *Strange Interlude* (1928). On April 27, 1929, however, Lord's career was halted by her marriage to advertising executive Owen B. Winters. The union lasted until 1931, when Winters filed for divorce, charging incompatibility.

Lord returned to the theater in 1932. Following a successful run as Abby in Sidney Howard's *The Late Christopher Bean,* she made her first and only film, playing the title role in *Alice Hegan Rice's Mrs. Wiggs of the Cabbage Patch.* Lord found the process of movie-making boring, however, and returned to the stage. In 1936, she was cast as Zenobia in *Ethan Frome,* a dramatization of the *Edith Wharton novel, which turned out to be her last Broadway appearance and her only role of note for the next decade. It was not until 1946, when she was offered the role of Amanda Wingfield in the touring company of Tennessee Williams' *The Glass Menagerie,* that she found another character worthy of her talent. In the superbly crafted role of the mother, who desperately manipulates the lives of her crippled daughter and impractical son, Lord achieved what Arthur Hopkins described as "acting that was not acting, poignancy that came from deep wells."

In October 1950, Lord sustained rib and chest injuries in an automobile accident in Alamagordo, New Mexico. She died shortly thereafter, on October 11, 1950.

SOURCES:

James, Edward T., ed. *Notable American Women 1607–1950.* Cambridge, MA: The Belknap Press of Harvard University Press, 1971.

McHenry, Robert, ed. *Famous American Women.* NY: Dover, 1980.

Wilmeth, Don B., and Tice L. Miller, eds. *Cambridge Guide to American Theater.* Cambridge, England and NY: Cambridge University Press, 1993.

Barbara Morgan,
Melrose, Massachusetts

Lorde, Audre (1934–1992)

American poet, essayist, and activist now acknowledged as one of the foremost feminist voices of the 20th century, whose work confronts issues of identity, racism, sexism, and heterosexism. Name variations:

also published under the name Rey Domini, a Latinate version of Audre Lorde, and later, sometimes known by the African name, Gamba Adisa. Pronunciation: Aw-dree. Born Audrey Geraldine Lorde on February 18, 1934, in New York, New York; died of cancer in St. Croix, U.S. Virgin Islands, on November 17, 1992; daughter of Frederick Byron Lorde (a real estate broker) and Linda (Belmar) Lorde; attended National University of Mexico, 1954; Hunter College, B.A., in 1959; Columbia University. M.L.S., in 1961; married Edward Ashley Rollins (an attorney), on March 31, 1962 (divorced); life partner of Frances Clayton; children: **Elizabeth Rollins** and Jonathan Rollins (both born in the mid-1960s).

Worked at Mount Vernon Public Library (1960–62), and St. Claire's School of Nursing as a librarian (1965–66); was head librarian of the Towne School library (1966–68); invited to Tougaloo, a black college in Jackson, Mississippi, to teach her first poetry workshop (1967); met Frances Clayton who became her life partner; published The First Cities with Poet's Press (1967); joined the faculty of City College of the City University of New York as a lecturer in creative writing (1968); was a lecturer in the education department of Herbert H. Lehman College (1969–70); taught as associate professor of English at John Jay College of Criminal Justice (1970–80); read Love Poem at a public reading and published it in Ms. (1971); traveled to Dahomey, in South Africa with her children (1974); published The Black Unicorn (1977); delivered her essay, "The Translation of Silence into Action," at the MLA Convention (1977); diagnosed with breast cancer (1978); published The Cancer Journals (1980); became a founding member of The Kitchen Table Press (1980); began to teach as a professor of English at Hunter College of CUNY (1980); taught for a semester at the Free University in Berlin, Germany (1984) where she also pursued alternative responses to the cancer with which she was to struggle for the rest of her life; moved to St. Croix, the U.S. Virgin Islands (1987), saying that she needed to be where it was warmer and where being Black was not an anomaly; in the wake of Hurricane Hugo (1989), wrote a fierce response to U.S. handling of aid relief for the islands; wrote Today Could Be the Day in which she connects an unblinking acknowledgement of her own impending death with a deep love of the sensual, immediate world (April 22, 1992); died (November 17, 1992) and the poem was published in Ms. the following spring, an assertion in her own words of her continued presence among us.

Selected awards and honors: Walt Whitman Citation of Merit (1991, making Lorde the Poet Laureate of New York); The American Book Award for A Burst of Light (1989); The Manhattan Borough President's Award for Excellence in the Arts (1988); National Endowment for the Arts Writing Grant (1968, 1981); Woman of the Year Award, Staten Island Community College (1975); Honorary Commission, Governor of Louisiana (1973); and honorary doctorates from Hunter, Oberlin, and Haverford colleges, and the University of Osnabruck in Germany.

Poetry: The First Cities (introduction by Diane Di Prima, Poet's Press, 1968); Cables to Rage (Broadside Press, 1970); From a Land Where Other People Live (Broadside Press, 1973); The New York Head Shop and Museum (Broadside Press, 1974); Coal (Norton, 1976); Between Ourselves (Eidolon, 1976); The Black Unicorn (Norton, 1978); Chosen Poems Old and New (Norton, 1982); Our Dead Behind Us (Norton, 1986); Undersong: Chosen Poems Old and New (Norton, 1992); The Marvelous Arithmetics of Distance (Norton, 1993).

Prose: The Uses of the Erotic: The Erotic as Power (The Crossing Press, 1978); The Cancer Journals (Spinsters Ink, 1980); Zami: A New Spelling of My Name (Crossing Press, 1982); Sister Outsider (Crossing Press, 1984); I Am Your Sister: Black Women Organizing Across Sexualities (Women of Color Press, 1985); Turning the Beat Around: Lesbian Parenting (1986); Burst of Light (Firebrand Books, 1988); Need: A Chorale for Black Women's Voices (Women of Color Press, 1990).

"My words will be there," Lorde wrote in a characteristically courageous and understated promise. She was a child who didn't speak until she was four, and then began to speak, and think, in poetry. The Harlem of Lorde's childhood was ethnically diverse and racially oppressive. There was not a lot of room for a shy, passionate, black girl to figure out who she was. As she grew, Lorde says, she "looked around . . . and there was no one saying what I wanted and needed to hear." When she was 13 she began to write, and so began her lifelong pursuit both to speak to the truths she knew, and to stand as an agent for change. Even before she knew it consciously, Lorde was an individual who resisted categorization. Insisting upon the diversity and complexity of her own self, Lorde frequently introduced herself as a "Black, Lesbian, Feminist, warrior, poet, mother doing my work." Her different parts were not paradoxical fragments, but integrated parts of a whole individual.

In her autobiographical novel (or biomythography), Zami, Audre Lorde begins with an act of renaming. Born Audrey Geraldine Lorde in 1934, she re-wrote herself as Audre Lorde in first grade because she liked the symmetry. This is a poet's metaphor for her life's work: continuous and powerful acts of naming and re-naming both herself and the world as she saw it. In her lifetime she was many people: *Zami*, a Cariacou name for women who work together as friends and lovers; *Audre*, not Audrey; *Rey Domini*, a Latin version of Audre Lorde; *Gamba Adisa*, an African name; and *The Black Unicorn* —rare, beautiful, "impatient," and transformative. As a writer, she learned to take her feelings and experiences, her pain, anger, and love, and place them inside a language that seems charged with possibility and hope. That her words are here, that she was willing to acknowledge sisterhood with anyone who would genuinely enter the sphere of her conversation, is the gift she has left for future generations.

Linda Belmar Lorde and Frederick Byron Lorde came to the United States from Grenada in 1924. She was 27, he 26; they had been married just a year. They settled in Harlem, New York City, never intending to spend the rest of their lives in America. But theirs is a familiar story of immigrant aspiration, the Depression, and American racism. In the opening pages of *Zami*, Lorde describes the difficult work of their early years. The only jobs were menial, and the hiring practices were racist. Byron first got a job as a laborer in the old Waldorf Astoria Hotel, and Linda worked there as a chambermaid. When the hotel was closed for demolition, Linda eventually got a job as a scullery maid in a teashop because her skin coloring was "light" and the manager mistook her for "Spanish." She was fired in 1928 when her more darkly complected husband stopped to pick up her uniforms and the manager realized she was black.

Throughout her childhood, Lorde experienced life in two separate, nearly incompatible worlds. Her parents, who "spoke with one unfragmentable and unappealable voice," kept their dream of "home" alive through stories and food, ritual, and the "voice" of the West Indies. They made decisions in patois when they wanted to exclude their American-born daughters. Lorde remembers the sensuality and poetry of phrases like "raise your zandalee" (a massage), and foods like "bluegoe" and "sapadilla." At the same time, everyday reality was the gray concrete and high-rise tenements of urban New York.

All of Lorde's writing is highly metaphoric. Though she is a deeply personal writer for whom politics and moral choice can never be separated from private experience, she is not confessional, as the term is understood to refer to writers who use the intimate materials of their lives as subject. *Zami*, which chronicles Lorde's childhood through her early 20s (and which is the primary source for autobiographical data from that period) was written in 1982. It is a reflective, mature work—the poet's voice speaking through prose. It is this voice that shapes the conundrum of Lorde's experience of "home": the cold, urban landscape where she was often lonely and misunderstood on the one hand, and her imagined home island of Cariacou, where women lived and loved among other women, towards which Audre yearned though she could never find it on a map.

Audre's first sentence, at the age of four, was "I want to read." The youngest of three girls, she was a difficult child: legally blind, silent, moody, and awkward. The world that books opened to her was a revelation. Still, her early school experience was rocky. She was not expected to excel, so exceeding any assignment, or a teacher's expectations, brought swift punishment or humiliation. She was sent home in disgrace the first day of first grade because she wrote her entire name across two pages of her composition book, rather than sticking with the *A* her teacher required. And home brought little sympathy. For Lorde's mother who was trying to get by in an alien world, Audre's nonconformity was painful and troublesome. Even a shift to her sisters' more challenging Catholic school didn't erase the difficulties. The school world remained divided by race and class—or "brownies" (bad) and "fairies" (good). Lorde was generally a "brownie" with all the negative connotations it implied. Elections for class president in sixth grade put a cap on these experiences. The seat was to have gone to the best student in the class, and that was Audre, with the highest grade-point average. She was crushed when a favorite white girl won. But her pain and humiliation, her declaration that "it wasn't fair" elicited a beating from her mother, who daily had to face the fact that she could not protect her children from the effects of racism.

This helplessness in the face of institutionalized racism was made even more clear during a family trip to Washington, D.C., when Lorde was in eighth grade. Audre's older sisters were to have gone with their class until a teacher explained to them that they would not be "comfortable" on such a trip, a euphemism that put the blame for racism—exclusion from the hotel and restaurants the class would patronize— squarely on the shoulders of the victims. The Lorde family decided to go on their own. Lorde

Audre
Lorde

says of her parents, "American racism was a new and crushing reality that [they] had to deal with every day of their lives once they came to America. They handled it as a private woe, . . . and never once gave it a name." But though she describes her parents' silent struggle with some empathy, what Lorde remarked in the nation's capital was its metaphoric whiteness: the whiteness of the buildings, of the light, of the ice cream they were never served, and of those who were privileged who denied her family. She describes the trip as the "summer she left childhood."

Audre Lorde's relationship with her father (who would die when she was 18 and far from home) is described by Jerome Brooks as "a vital presence in her life." He is invoked over and over again in her work in "a spiritual effort to reach [him], to be transformed into him." Lorde's affinity and longing for her father is part metaphoric, in that she depicts him mythically as Africa, her homeland, in *The Black Unicorn.* This is the place, Brooks suggests, to which she must come if she is to be fully all her selves. Brooks also argues that Lorde's father represented the solid "intellectual and moral" vision that centered her sense of the world. In *Zami,* Lorde implies that her father, who shared his decision-making power with his wife when tradition dictated it was his alone, was profoundly moral. She also felt most identified with and supported by him as she writes in *Inheritance—His:* "I owe you my Dahomian jaw/ the free high school for gifted girls/ no one else thought I should attend/ and the darkness we share."

Lorde's relationship with her mother appears to have been more complicated. In *Zami,* she ties her love of the sensuous to her mother's body and language, and to the imagined homeland of Cariacou where strong women lived and worked together. But while Linda could "pass for white" in a racist world, her youngest, nonconformist daughter could not. This was to be a deeply troubling issue for Audre. In a world where "black" means "bad," what did this mean about her? It was a question her mother had no means to answer. Lorde recognizes in her mother a female sensuality and power that is central to her understanding of herself, and that she connects to her West Indian and African heritages. But at the same time she describes herself as the dark daughter her mother would not, or could not, love and accept.

> My mother had two faces and a frying pot
> Where she cooked up her daughters
> Into girls
> . . . two faces
> and a broken pot
> where she hid out a perfect daughter
> who was not me
> —*From the House of Yemenja*

As a little girl, Lorde remembers people spitting on her as she held her mother's hand and they walked down the street. Linda's response was to complain about stupid people "spitting into the wind." It was too painful to speak directly to the viciousness of everyday racism. But it was an issue that mother and daughter would struggle over, as Lorde grew into a writer who would say, "I'm not going to be more vulnerable by putting weapons of silence into my enemies' hands." West Indian daughters are expected to follow their mothers' examples as they prepare for their adult lives. But in *Zami,* Lorde remarks that what her mother knew didn't always fit with their American lives. The silence with which Linda handled the pain of racism could not be her daughter's way. In a later interview/conversation with *Adrienne Rich, Lorde would say, "I didn't deal all that well with how strong my mother was inside of me."

At Hunter High School ("the free high school for gifted girls"), Audre Lorde made friends with the other bright outcasts. They named themselves "The Branded"; they wrote stories and poetry, and they played at being on the fringes of society, though Lorde was the only black member. It was in this group that Lorde first experienced the full, intoxicating pleasures of female friendship. **Diane Di Prima**, who would later publish Lorde's first volume of poetry, *The First Cities,* was a member of that group. This was a time of personal growth and experimentation. Lorde was the editor of the school's literary magazine. She had a best friend, Genny. She also published her first poem in *Seventeen* magazine after her teachers had rejected it as sentimental (it was a love poem about her then boyfriend). But life at home had become a battle, or in Lorde's words, "a West Indian version of the Second World War." Audre's need for privacy and understanding clashed with her parents' open-door policies and strictness. Her best friend's suicide and her mother's apparent lack of empathy precipitated her leaving home as soon as she graduated from high school. The period immediately following was grueling and lonely. Lorde worked at two or three low-paying jobs while trying to go to school and to write. A brief affair ended in pregnancy and abortion. At that time, abortion was still illegal and cost 300 impossible dollars for none but the crudest of medical care. Lorde survived it, but the semester was a blur as she passed her classes, struggled to write, attended the Harlem Writers Guild, sold blood, sold her typewriter in an effort to continue. Of that time, she says, "I never re-read what I was writing." Finally, in 1952, Lorde abandoned school and moved to Connecticut to take a job in a factory.

Factory work earned Lorde 90 cents an hour. As a member of the union, she would have earned $1.15 (then the minimum wage), but black workers were fired before they were eligible to join. Perhaps ironically, Connecticut was for Lorde the site of two serious awakenings. The first was political. The white clerk in the newly renamed Crispus Attucks Center could not help her find a good job, but that paradox is multiplied by Lorde's later awareness that she did not even know that a black man, Crispus Attucks, had been the first man to die in the Revolutionary War. "I wondered what kind of history I had been taught," Lorde wondered, as irony piled upon irony. The only work she could find involved radiation and chemicals and no health regulations. Eventually the tips of her fingers darkened from exposure. Out of this misery, though, came her second awakening when she fell in love with a woman and began her first lesbian relationship.

During the difficulties of Connecticut, Lorde always promised herself Mexico. In 1954, she went. Suddenly, she says, she felt "visible," as she moved through streets filled with other people with brown faces. "I felt myself unfolding like some large flower." Mexico was also a time of awakening. Lorde registered at the university in Mexico City, rented a little apartment in Cuernevaca, and made friends with other women. Of her writing, she says, "For the first time I had an insight into what poetry could be. . . . my words could recreate feeling." This emphasis on the relationship between language and feeling is a connection that Lorde would later return to many times in interviews and essays. In Mexico, Lorde also met Eudora, an older woman who had lost a breast to cancer years before. Eudora became Lorde's mentor and lover, telling her "to write poems" and offering an intimacy and sexuality that was nurturing and new. Metaphorically, Lorde centers self-knowledge and self-love in this relationship of a younger woman loving and being loved by an older woman scarred by cancer. *Zami* was written when Lorde was already struggling with her own cancer; this section of the book seems healing, as if self were reaching out to self in love and acknowledgment.

Back in New York City, knowing she loved women, Lorde returned to college, continued writing, and joined the "gay-girl" scene in the Village. As always, though, she had to struggle with the needs of the different groups with which she was connected to deny one or more aspects of who she was. The "gay-girl" scene was predominantly white. The Harlem Writers Guild was predominantly male. There Lorde experienced the old dynamics of her family life: she was good, she was special, if only she'd clean up her act. After she finished her degree at Hunter College, Lorde attended Columbia University, earning her master's of library science in 1961.

Though she does not speak of it in any detail, Audre Lorde married Edward Rollins, a white attorney, in 1962. They had two children, Elizabeth and Jonathan. She remembers the early '60s as many working mothers might—a kind of blur of working (in her case as a librarian), child care, negotiation with a partner, writing, and, in her case, political activism. Out of this time, however, came the offer to teach a poetry workshop at Tougaloo, a black college in Mississippi, in 1967. The teaching was a revelation. Lorde and her students immersed themselves in poetry. She says she learned from them. *The First Cities* had just come out to good reviews, and her life was changing. At Tougaloo, Lorde also met and fell in love with **Frances Clayton**, the woman who would eventually become her life partner.

Silence has never brought us anything of worth.

—**Audre Lorde**, *The Cancer Journals*

After Tougaloo, Lorde recognized her need to teach. Students have described her tremendous warmth and openness, her fierce passion for language and honesty, and her willingness to really listen to their words. She was also willing to confront difficult subjects, for instance teaching courses in race relations in the late 1960s and '70s. As her teaching career developed, she was also writing and publishing regularly. In 1974, Audre Lorde traveled to Dahomey, Africa, with her children, noting that the year she was born was the year of the last three Dahomian Amazons—warrior women from a culture to which she drew in poetry lines of connection. (*See* Amazon Army of Dahomey.) *The Black Unicorn*, Lorde's seventh collection of poetry, met critical acclaim. In it, the lyric and mythic descriptions of Africa are integrated with poems of social and political protest, descrying the deaths of black children by white policeman, the loss of black men to racist violence, and the destructiveness of internalized forms of racism that can turn people against themselves. Friend and poet Adrienne Rich celebrates "the complexity of her vision, her moral courage, and the catalytic passion of her language."

In 1978, Audre Lorde was diagnosed with breast cancer and underwent a radical mastectomy. Despite so intimate a pain and loss, she chose not to be silent. *The Cancer Journals* are in fact partly an indictment of the medical and larger communities that demand the wounded be silent. Told that she ought to wear her (white) prosthesis for the morale of the doctor's office, Lorde tells us that she is a warrior, that her wound is honorable. *The Cancer Journals* is a courageous personal and political description of a battle. From it, Lorde emerges a survivor, still, as she would say, stronger for all her parts.

For the next 14 years, Lorde would continue to write, to love, and to respond fully and honestly to the needs of the world around her. In 1980, while she was still recovering from the initial cancer, Lorde was a founding member of The Kitchen Table Press, a publishing house in the service of the voices of women writers who were and are too often overlooked by mainstream publishers and publications. She also helped to establish the St. Croix Women's Coalition, an advocacy group concerned with domestic violence. When she traveled to Germany seeking alternative treatments for her cancer, Lorde also taught a course on African-American women poets at the Free University in Berlin and began the process of compiling *Farbe Bekennen,* an anthology of writings by black German women. After a second surgery for cancer, Audre Lorde moved to St. Croix, the U.S. Virgin Islands, in 1987, saying that she needed to be warmer. In interviews, she suggests that this is a form of re-integration with her mother's original island home that never was pictured on a map. In St. Croix, Lorde continued to be active socially, artistically, and politically. Until she died on November 17, 1992, Lorde never was silent, choosing instead always to find those parts of herself that were useful in the expression of what she saw and knew to be true.

For Audre Lorde, poetry, sexuality, moral vision, and the world we live in were all inseparable. Just before her first cancer, she described the realm of the erotic "as power, . . . something deeply spiritual and female, . . . the 'yes' within ourselves." Moving from that "yes" is her poetry, "the way we give name to the nameless so it can be thought." On the day her tiny obituary appeared in *The New York Times*, there were also stories of police brutality in Africa, genocide in Somalia, and an op-ed piece titled "The Bigotry Trade." These are just some of the issues Audre Lorde spoke to in her lifetime. It is to the good of all "that her voice was here." But it is a voice that asks for ours to join in. Lorde's "poetry is not a luxury"; it is a way of speaking a vision that is moral because it resists categorization to include all our parts.

SOURCES:

"Audre Lorde" in *Contemporary Literary Criticism.* Vol. 18. Detroit, MI: Gale Research.

"Audre Lorde: A Special Section," in *Callaloo.* Vol. 14, no. 1. Winter 1991.

Evans, Mari, ed. *Black Women Writers (1950–1980): A Critical Evaluation.* Garden City, NY: Anchor/Doubleday, 1984.

Homans, Margaret. "Audre Lorde," in *African American Writers.* Edited by Valerie Smith. NY: Scribner, 1990.

Lorde, Audre. *The Black Unicorn.* NY: W.W. Norton, 1978.

———. *The Cancer Journals.* Argyle, NY: Spinsters Ink, 1980.

———. *Sister Outsider.* Trumansburg, NY: Crossing Press, 1984.

———. *Zami: A New Spelling of My Name.* Freedom, CA: Crossing Press, 1982.

SUGGESTED READING:

Bell-Scott, Patricia. *Life Notes: Personal Writings by Contemporary Black Women.* NY: W.W. Norton, 1994.

Moraga, Cherrie, and Gloria Anzaldua. *This Bridge Called My Back: Writings by Radical Woman of Color.* NY: Kitchen Table, Women of Color Press, 1983.

Munt, Sally, ed. *New Lesbian Criticism: Literary and Cultural Readings.* NY: Columbia University Press, 1992.

Nelson, Emmanuel S. *Critical Essays: Gay and Lesbian Writers of Color.* NY: Haworth Press, 1993.

Singer, Bennett L. *Growing Up Gay/ Growing Up Lesbian: A Literary Anthology.* NY: New Press, 1994.

RELATED MEDIA:

Abod, Jennifer, and Angela Brown. *A Radio Profile of Audre Lorde* (audiotape), Cambridge, MA: Profile Productions, 1988.

Lorde, Audre. *To Be Young, Lesbian, and Black in the 50's* (1 cassette), interview with Helene Rosenbluth, Los Angeles, CA: Pacifica Tape Library, 1983.

National Women's Studies Association. *Reading Their Work: Audre Lorde and Adrienne Rich* (2 cassettes), College Park, Maryland, 1988.

Singer, Suzanne. *Gamba Adisa.* A Third World Newsreel Production, 1996.

Susan Perry Morehouse,
Associate Professor of English,
Alfred University, Alfred, New York

Loren, Sophia (1934—)

Internationally renowned Italian film actress who won an Oscar for her work in **Two Women**. *Born Sofia Scicolone in Rome, Italy, on September 20, 1934; daughter of Romilda Villani and Riccardo Scicolone; sister of* **Maria Scicolone**; *married Carlo Ponti (a film producer), in 1966; children: two sons, Carlo Jr. (b. December 29, 1968) and Eduardo (b. January 1973).*

Raised near Naples by her unmarried mother amid great poverty during World War II; appeared as an extra in her first film Quo Vadis? *(1949); film career began in earnest after meeting producer Carlo Ponti; was rivaled only by Gina Lollobrigida as Italy's best-known actress on both sides of the Atlantic (1950s); appeared in the first of many Hollywood-made films (1958), but her finest work is still considered to be her portrayal of a mother in war-ravaged Italy in Vittorio De Sica's La Ciociara (US title: Two*

Women, *1960), for which she won an Oscar; married Carlo Fortunato Pietro Ponti as a French citizen (1966), after a protracted legal battle with Italian authorities who refused to recognize Ponti's annulment of an earlier marriage.*

Films (featured roles only): La Favorita *(1952);* La Tratta delle Bianche *(1952);* Affica sotto I Mari *(1953);* Ci troviano in Galleria *(1953);* Carosello Neapolitano *(1953);* Tempi Nostro *(1953);* La Domenica delle Buono Gente *(1953);* Il Paese dei Campanelli *(1954);* Pellegrini d'Amore *(1954);* Miseria e Nobilita *(1954);* Due Notti con Cleopatra *(1954);* Atilla *(1954);* L'Oro de Napoli *(1954);* Un Giorno in Pretura *(1954);* La Donna del Fiume *(1955);* Peccato che sia una Canaglia *(1955);* Il Segno de Venere *(1955);* La Bella Mugnaia *(1955);* Pane Amore E . . . *(1955);* La Fortuna Essere Donna *(1956);* Boy on a Dolphin *(1957);* The Pride and the Passion *(1957);* Timbuctu *(1957);* Desire under the Elms *(1958);* The Key *(1958);* Houseboat *(1958);* The Black Orchid *(1959);* That Kind of Woman *(1959);* Heller in Pink Tights *(1960);* It Started in Naples *(1960);* A Breath of Scandal *(1960);* The Millionairess *(1960);* La Ciociara *(Two Women, 1960);* El Cid *(1961);* Madame Sans-Gène *(1961);* Boccacio '70 *(1962);* Le Couteau dans la Plaie *(1962);* I Sequestrati de Altona *(1962);* Ieri Oggi e Domani *(Yesterday, Today, and Tomorrow, 1963);* The Fall of the Roman Empire *(1964);* Matrimonio all'Italiana *(Marriage Italian Style, 1964);* Operation Crossbow *(1965);* Lady L *(1965);* Arabesque *(1966);* A Countess from Hong Kong *(1967);* C'era una Volta *(1967);* Questi Fantasmi *(1967);* I Girasoli *(1969);* La Moglia del Prete *(1970);* La Mortadella *(1971);* Man of La Mancha *(1972);* Bianco Rosso e . . . *(1973);* Il Viaggio *(1974);* Le Testament *(1975);* La Puppa del Gangster *(1975);* The Cassandra Crossing *(1977);* Una Giornata Speciale *(1977);* Angela *(1978);* Brass Target *(1978);* Shimmy Lugano e Tarantelle e Vino *(1978);* Fatto di Sangue *(1979);* Sabato *(1990);* Domenica e Lunedi *(1990);* Prêt-à-Porter *(1994);* Grumpier Old Men *(1995);* Messages *(1996);* Soleil *(1997).*

The Italian fishing village of Pozzuoli, eight miles west of Naples, is known for several curious features. One is the small but occasionally restless volcano, Solfatara, just outside the city limits, much smaller than its towering neighbor, Vesuvius, but no less moody. Another is the slow rising and falling of the ground on which the town sits, a result of the viscous earth deep below; and there are the steaming fumaroles of the famed Campi Flegrei, the Burning Fields said to have inspired Dante's *Inferno.* But to most Italians, Pozzuoli is known for only one thing. It is the hometown of Italy's most famous and most beautiful movie star, Sophia Loren, whose 50-year career continues to show more life than either of the peaks that loomed over her poverty-stricken childhood. "She has emerged as beautiful as Aphrodite rising from the Aegean," film critic Rex Reed once effused, while *Vogue* noted more laconically that "After Loren, bones are boring."

Her birth in Rome, however, on September 20, 1934, seemed only the beginning of the kind of bleak life facing many poor Italians between the two World Wars, with the added burden that Sophia was born illegitimate. Her mother **Romilda Villani** had come to Rome from Pozzuoli to study piano after her dreams of an acting career had been scotched by her family. Romilda was beautiful enough to have won a country-wide contest to find the Italian girl who looked most like *Greta Garbo, the first prize being a trip to Hollywood and a screen test; but the Villanis, suspicious of America in general and Hollywood in particular, forced her to refuse the prize. She had run away and been in Rome barely a year when she found herself pregnant by a married engineering student who had told her he worked in films. Riccardo Scicolone legally acknowledged paternity of the baby girl Romilda named Sofia and allowed the child to carry his surname, but he remained an aloof and somewhat mysterious presence, even when his daughter became known around the world as Sophia Loren. His visits to Pozzuoli were rare, but Sophia always remembered him as "tall, strong, distinguished-looking, with a nose hooked like the beak of a bird." His trips to Pozzuoli may have been infrequent, but Romilda claimed him as the father of her second daughter, Maria, born four years after Sofia. This time, Riccardo refused to admit paternity until many years later, when Loren had earned enough to pay him for Maria's right to use his last name.

The Villanis—Romilda, her two daughters, Romilda's parents, and an aunt—shared two bedrooms on an upper story of a house on Pozzuoli's Via Soltafara, with the volcano visible at the end of the street and its sulphurous fumes mixing with the smell of fish piled on the docks by local fishermen who harvested an already polluted Bay of Naples. Everyone worked—at local munitions factories, as day laborers or secretaries or piano teachers. There was usually food on the communal table until war broke out when Loren was barely six years old, bringing the devastation and suffering that she would later so poignantly depict in many of her films. "Suffering means maturity," Loren once said, "even when you're a baby. I've always been old." At times, the only water to drink was the few drops to be found in the radiators of abandoned cars. Hungry mothers and children would be killed while standing in breadlines, unwilling to give up their places even when the bombs began to fall, sometimes five times a night as Allied planes pounded away at Naples' strategic port and railway stations. Loren and her family spent much of the war living in a rat-infested railroad tunnel. "I saw death in the streets when I was six and eight years old," she recalled many years later. "That you live with all your life. But I don't understand people who hide from their past. Everything you live through helps to make you the person you are now."

My complexes have been good to me. They help to make people what they are. When you lose them, you might also lose yourself.

—Sophia Loren

With the German retreat and the Allied occupation of Naples, the Villanis got by as best they could by selling homemade beer to American GI's and scrambling desperately for the aid packages distributed by the troops. Loren would later, in several films, portray Neapolitan women who turned to prostitution to feed their families, but she has always been quick to point out that she herself was only nine years old at the time of the occupation. "I was a rather mature child," she once told a reporter, "but not *that* mature." She was, in fact, considered a rather plain child, tall, with a long neck, wide mouth, and so scrawny that she was tauntingly called *stuzzicadenta* ("toothpick") and *stecchetta* ("little stick"). But she had blossomed enough by the age of 13 to receive her first marriage proposal, Romilda angrily chasing away the gym teacher who was rash enough to offer his hand; and she was a runner-up at 14 in Naples' Queen of the Sea beauty contest, for which she was given a prize of about $40. Romilda was sufficiently encouraged to enroll her daughter in a few acting classes, at one of which Loren learned that the first major American picture to be shot in postwar Italy was looking for extras. So it was that in July 1949, Romilda and her daughter boarded a train for Rome and its fabled Cinecittà studios; and so it is that on close examination of one scene of *Quo Vadis?*, a thin, long-necked slave girl can be seen standing behind the regal Roman woman played by *Deborah Kerr, the girl peering intently toward us. "I was trying to see where the camera was," Loren explained later. Throughout her life, Sophia would credit

Romilda for the career that brought worldwide admiration. "I would have been happy being a teacher in Pozzuoli, marrying a good local fellow, raising a family," she claimed. "Without my mother's ambition . . . I doubt that on my own I would have pushed myself out of Pozzuoli."

She was paid $30 for her work in *Quo Vadis?* and would have been paid more for a small speaking part if she had been able to master English. The lesson was not lost on Loren, who sought out tutors in English, French, and Spanish and paid for the instruction with the few dollars she and Romilda earned from work as extras. There was money to be made, too, from modeling, especially for *fumetti*, rather like comic books in format but filled with photographically illustrated crime stories and true confessions. Sophia was paid $16 a day to pose as gun molls, hapless housewives or jilted mistresses, every cent of the proceeds going toward the rent for the small apartment on Via Consenza she and Romilda had taken. When several casting directors told her Scicolone was too hard to pronounce, Sophia, with tongue firmly in cheek, adopted Lazzaro, the Neapolitan slang for a layabout, as her first professional surname. Her film work was entirely forgettable, bit parts in films with such names as *I Am the Guerilla Chief* or another that starred the entire Neapolitan soccer team. About the only work to survive from this period is a scene from a shabby desert saga in which Loren played one of several bare-breasted harem girls. Stills from the shoot regularly popped up in cheap movie magazines during the peak of her career in the 1960s, much to the dismay of one of her co-stars, William Holden, who found such a publication on the set of *The Key* one day in London. "This is dreadful!" he complained, staring in horror at the magazine's display of Sophia's exposed attributes. "Why?" Sophia wanted to know. "They look pretty good to me."

There were also, in those early days, beauty contests as sources of income; Sophia made it all the way to the finals in Rome's Queen of the Adriatic Sirens festival in 1950. She had chosen not to compete, however, in 1951's Miss Rome contest, preferring instead to take a front-row seat with friends as a spectator, when one of the contest judges approached and coaxed her into entering at the last minute. The judge was Carlo Ponti, a rather dour and dowdy Milanese lawyer turned film producer who was 20 years Sophia's senior. By the time of their meeting that June night in the moonlight shadows of the Coliseum, Ponti had been in the film business for a dozen years, had been jailed by Mussolini during the war for an anti-Fascist picture he had produced, and had founded Lux Studios, Italy's first important post-war production company. He had most recently produced Roberto Rossellini's *Europa 51*, starring *Ingrid Bergman**, and Fellini's *La Strada*, starring *Giulietta Masina**, which would soon be awarded America's Oscar for best Foreign Film.

Ponti knew he had found someone special in the 17-year-old girl from Naples, even after she placed second and was passed over as Miss Rome. "I saw in Sophia all the best that is Italian," he explained many years later, "not just Neapolitan gaiety, but a vitality, sensitivity and sense of rhythm that no actor's studio can teach." Sophia, with two years' experience of Italian movie men, was initially suspicious of Ponti's suggestion that she come to his office for an interview, but eventually borrowed a dress with red polka dots and appeared as Ponti had asked. A screen test followed, during which the cinematographer complained to Ponti that Sophia was too tall, too heavy and big-boned. Her face was too short, he said, her mouth too wide and her nose too big. Still, Ponti persisted.

He sent Sophia to a speech teacher to erase her Neapolitan accent, to a film school to learn how films were made, and to a school of deportment to learn how to carry herself elegantly and self-confidently. He prevailed on Sophia to lose 20 pounds (although she angrily refused to have her nose bobbed) and carefully chose her wardrobe and her reading list, making sure she was familiar with the classics of Western literature. Ponti's associates soon took to calling him the "Pizza Pygmalion" to Sophia's earthy Galatea.

A year later, Ponti was casting Sophia in small parts in his films with the new name a friend had suggested, Sophia Loren, the surname close to that of a Swedish star of the day said to be the next Bergman, *Marta Toren**, and the new spelling of her first name thought to look more sophisticated. By the time of Ponti's 1953 potboiler *La Tratta della bianche* (*The White Slave Trade*), Sophia had been given a small featured part.

That same year, Loren stunned everyone by taking a leading role that no other actress want-

Sophia
Loren

ed and turning it into an international sensation. She agreed to play Aïda in a film version of Verdi's opera—not for Ponti, but for another studio to which he had loaned her. It was a potentially awkward and embarrassing exercise in lip-synching to soprano *Renata Tebaldi's soundtrack. But Sophia managed to create a full-fledged screen character that went far beyond a mere mouthpiece for Tebaldi, so much so that audiences were stunned to learn that this unfamiliar Aïda was neither an opera singer nor an Egyptian, but a *bella napolitana* in blackface. It was Loren's good fortune that the film was her first to be released in the United States, distributed by entrepreneur Sol Hurok, with equally enthusiastic praise from the Americans. "Around this girl you could really build something super-colossal!" Cecil B. De Mille was said to exclaim, while *The New York Times* film critic Bosley Crowther noted, "The advantage is that a fine voice is set to a stunning form and face, which is most gratifying (and unusual) in the operatic realm." For Loren, who impressed her co-workers during production for her conscientious attitude and patience, the experience taught her how much acting meant to her. "For me, acting is like lying on a couch at a psychiatrist's," she later said.

By 1955, the relationships that would mark Sophia's long and prolific career were in place. She and Ponti had become lovers (despite Ponti's ten-year marriage to **Giuliana Fiastri**); she had shot the first of many pictures directed by Vittorio De Sica (1954's *L'Oro di Napoli* [*The Gold of Naples*]); and she had appeared onscreen a year later in the first of 15 films with fellow Neapolitan Marcello Mastroianni in De Sica's *Peccato che sia una canaglia* (*Too Bad She's Bad*). Her roles made full use of her considerable physical attractions, often overshadowing the genuine acting talent that De Sica had called "a natural force." Indeed, by the time of 1955's *La Donna del Fiume* (*The Woman of the River*), in which she spent most of the picture wearing little more than a wet shirt, the press was already calling her "Sophia the Sizzler." Ponti, meanwhile, had begun actively promoting her in the United States, where the "Battle of the Bosoms" was waged in the American press between Loren and *Gina Lollobrigida. Admiring men and envious women carefully compared Loren's proportions of 38-24-38 to her rival's 36-22-35, and much was made of Lollobrigida's comment to *Hedda Hopper that "Sophia's may be bigger, but mine are better."

Under Ponti's guidance, Loren appeared on the front cover of *Life* in August 1955, while

Newsweek offered a four-page article entitled "Italy's Sophia Loren—a new star, a Mount Vesuvius." Ponti's work led to leading roles in three major American-produced pictures in 1957 alone—Jean Negulesco's *Boy on a Dolphin,* shot in Greece with Alan Ladd; the African adventure *Legend of the Lost,* with John Wayne; and Stanley Kramer's epic story of the Napoleonic Wars, *The Pride and the Passion,* with Frank Sinatra and Cary Grant. Reports of affairs with her leading men were more public relations fantasy than fact, although Cary Grant did propose marriage and was gently refused. "He had his own problems of insecurity," Loren later said, "and the mixture with my own would not have made for a lasting marriage."

Marriage was, however, very much on Sophia's mind, for she and Ponti had long wanted to formalize a relationship that was already a marriage in everything but name. "When we first met," Loren said, "he was just a kind producer who gave me a chance. But the more we were with each other, all kinds of bonds held us together. He was friend, counselor, lover, father, teacher, everything." But her increasing stature in American films was subjecting the couple's adulterous liaison to intense scrutiny, with rumblings of moral outrage from the American Catholic Church and its Legion of Decency. Since Ponti's marriage had been in trouble long before he met Loren, and since Giuliana Fiastri wanted a divorce as much as her husband, it would have been an easy thing to accomplish had it not been for Italy's strict laws of the time against divorce. Nor did the Church believe Ponti's grounds for annulment—that he had not believed in the sacrament of matrimony at the time of his marriage to Giuliana. Ponti thought he had hit on a solution while he and Sophia were in America. On September 17, 1957, a proxy divorce from Giuliana and a proxy marriage to Sophia took place in Mexico with lawyers as stand-ins, a perfectly legal technique under American law. But Italy's response was to promptly charge Ponti with bigamy and issue a warrant for his arrest as soon as he set foot in the country, even after Ponti had the proxy marriage annulled.

Catholic organizations, even in Loren's hometown, excoriated her in public and in one instance called for her public burning; while in America, the Italian Men's Catholic Action group called for a boycott of Sophia's films. "I give up!" Loren said to the press in exasperation. "I'm married, I'm not married. I'm this, I'm that! Enough! I *feel* married, and lots of married people don't!" Although Loren herself could not be charged with bigamy and the furor against her eventually faded, Ponti remained criminally liable under Italian law and was forced to remain outside Italy for nearly ten years. So implacable were the Italian authorities that the couple was finally obliged to become citizens of France, where more liberal domestic laws permitted Ponti's divorce from Fiastri in December of 1965 and his belated marriage to "Sofia Scicolone, artiste" in a civil ceremony outside Paris on April 9, 1966. "It's a little like reading the theater program long after you've seen the show," Loren sourly told reporters after the ceremony; and when she called Romilda to tell her she was finally married, the older woman remarked ruefully, "Yes, but not in white, and not in a church."

Loren might have permanently turned her back on her native country if it had not been for her old friend De Sica, who pleaded with her to return to Italy to shoot "an Italian story made in Italy by Italians," as he described his screen adaptation of Alberto Moravia's wrenching novel *La Ciociara*, about a widow and her 19-year-old daughter during the Allied bombings of Rome. In a testament to Sophia's maturing skills as an actress, De Sica wanted Sophia, now 28, to play the daughter and had cast *Anna Magnani as the mother. Magnani had become an international star at the end of World War II with her performance in Rossellini's *Open City* and had later won an Oscar for her work in the screen adaptation of Tennessee Williams' *The Rose Tattoo*. Loren, unfortunately, had publicly criticized Magnani's bombastic handling of Williams' Sicilian heroine by commenting that "no Italian woman should depict an Italian woman like that." Now, Magnani told De Sica she had no intention of playing the mother of "a Neapolitan giraffe"; and even though she was nearly 30 years older than Loren, Magnani went on to tell De Sica she was too young to play the mother. "Let her play the part herself," Magnani said, withdrawing from the picture at the last minute. De Sica took Magnani's advice, rewrote the script to make Sophia Loren the older of the two women, and cast newcomer **Eleanora Brown** as the daughter. "I had not the experience of being a mother, let alone the mother of a teenage daughter," Sophia later remembered. "But De Sica was one expert I trusted totally, so when he said I could do it, I went along with him." Her faith in De Sica proved wise, for her performance as Cesira won her Best Actress awards at the 1961 Cannes Festival, from the British Film Association, from the New York Film Critics Circle and, as her crowning glory, that year's Oscar as Best Actress. Loren was so sure that *Audrey Hepburn would capture the award for *Breakfast at Tiffany's* that she remained in Rome for the ceremonies and was telephoned with the news by Cary Grant. "Before I made *Two Women* I had been a performer," she later said. "Afterward, I was an actress."

By the time Sophia began work on 1964's *Ieri Oggi e Domani* (*Yesterday, Today, and Tomorrow*), playing three different women in De Sica's trio of romantic comedies, the thin little girl who had roamed the streets of Pozzuoli 25 years earlier was an international celebrity with homes in New York, Paris, and in Rome, where Ponti had restored the 16th-century Villa Sara in the Alban hills. But one of the crew members on the De Sica film noticed the way Loren gazed at the women, many of them pregnant, who were extras. "Here was the star of the world, the woman who had everything," he said, "watching them with the most envious look I've ever seen." Loren had, in fact, been pregnant when shooting had begun but had miscarried in her fourth month. It was the first of two such tragedies, the second occurring in 1967, both of which Sophia blamed on her doctors. Pregnant for the third time in 1968, Loren traveled in great secrecy to Geneva and to a hormone specialist recommended by a friend of Ponti's. Her whereabouts remained unknown to a frantic press until one of Romilda's maids leaked the story to an Italian newspaper. Fan mail immediately flooded Sophia's luxurious private suite in Switzerland, much of it from women around the world offering advice and encouragement. Finally, on December 29, 1968, Carlo Ponti, Jr., was born by Caesarean section, to Loren and Ponti's great joy; five years later, in January 1973, Sophia gave birth at the same clinic to the couple's second son, Eduardo.

During the 1990s, Sophia Loren projected the calm self-assurance brought by a full, productive life, having appeared in some 25 films since the birth of her sons and having done full justice to her reputation as one of the world's most beautiful women. A photographer for whom she sat in Paris on her 60th birthday, in 1994, wrote later that "a blind man could get great photographs of her. The lady is magnificent; sixty—yes, sixty!—has never looked better." Loren had just appeared in her 81st film, Robert Altman's *Prêt-à-Porter*, and was soon to leave for America to begin work with Jack Lemmon, **Ann Margaret**, and Walter Matthau on her 82nd, *Grumpier Old Men*. In an interview just a few days before her birthday with journalist **Heather Kirby**, Loren spoke tenderly of Romilda, who had died four years earlier; contentedly of her own two sons, both pursuing careers in the arts; and proudly of Ponti, then 82 and still, she said, her chief promoter and protector. And what, Kirby wanted to know, did it feel like to be sixty? The answer came quickly, accompanied by the brilliant Loren smile. "Fifty-nine," Sophia said.

SOURCES:

Bernstein, Gary. "Sophia Loren: Dream Session," in *Petersen's Photographic Magazine*. Vol. 23, no. 2. June 1994.

Hotchner, A.E. *Sophia: Living and Loving*. NY: William Morrow, 1979.

Kirby, Heather. "Sophia Loren at Sixty," in *Good Housekeeping*. Vol. 219, no. 2. August 1994.

Levy, Alan. *Forever, Sophia: An Intimate Portrait*. NY: Baronet Publishing, 1979.

SUGGESTED READING:

Harris, Warren G. *Sophia Loren*. NY: Simon and Schuster, 1998.

Norman Powers,
writer-producer, Chelsea Lane Productions, New York

Lorengar, Pilar (1928—)

Spanish soprano. Born Pilar Lorenza Garcia on January 16, 1928, in Saragossa, Spain; studied with Angeles Ottein, Carl Ebert, and Martha Klust.

Pilar Lorengar

Debuted in Madrid (1949), Covent Garden (1955), Glyndebourne (1956–60), Salzburg (1961–64), Metropolitan Opera (1966); named Austrian Kammersängerin (1963).

The Spanish soprano Pilar Lorengar had a long operatic career which led her from a youthful Cherubino in Mozart's *Le nozze di Figaro* (*Marriage of Figaro*) to a mature countess. Lorengar was successful in light opera and also sang in the *zarzuelas* (musical comedies) of her native land. As she performed in theaters throughout Europe, her reputation grew and finally in 1966 she appeared at the Metropolitan Opera, as she would for 12 seasons following. "Her once rather limited lyric soprano has grown surprisingly in volume and power," wrote one critic, "while still retaining its perfection of tonal beauty and resonance in the upper register."

John Haag,
Athens, Georgia

Lorentzen, Ingeborg (b. 1957)

Granddaughter of Olav V. Name variations: Ingeborg Ribeiro. Born on February 27, 1957, in Oslo, Norway; daughter of Erling Lorentzen and *Ragnhild Oldenburg (daughter of Olav V, king of Norway); married Paolo Ribeiro, on June 4, 1982.

Lorentzen, Ragnhild (b. 1930).

See Oldenburg, Ragnhild.

Lorentzen, Ragnhild (b. 1968)

Granddaughter of Olav V. Born on May 8, 1968, in Rio de Janeiro, Brazil; daughter of Erling Lorentzen and *Ragnhild Oldenburg (daughter of Olav V, king of Norway).

Lorenzo, Teresa (fl. 1358)

Mistress of Peter I. Name variations: Teresa Gille Lourenco. Flourished around 1358; mistress of Pedro I also known as Peter I (1320–1367), king of Portugal (r. 1357–1367); children: (with Peter I) John I the False also known as John I of Aviz (1357–1433), master of Aviz, king of Portugal (r. 1385–1433).

Loretta de Braose (d. 1266).

See Braose, Loretta de.

Loretta de Briouze (d. 1266).

See Braose, Loretta de.

Loretta of Leicester (d. 1266).

See Braose, Loretta de.

Loringhoven, Baroness von Freytag (1875–1927).

See Abbott, Berenice for sidebar.

Loriod, Yvonne (1924—)

French pianist and Ondes Martenot player, known for performing Messiaen's works. Born in Houilles, Seine-et-Oise, France, on January 20, 1924; married her teacher Olivier Messiaen (1908–1992).

Born in 1924 in Houilles, Seine-et-Oise, France, Yvonne Loriod was a student of Lazare-Lévy and Marcel Ciampi at the Paris Conservatoire. She married another one of her teachers, Olivier Messiaen, and was closely associated with his music, which she played with virtuosity and understanding. The solo piano part of Messiaen's *Turangalila* symphony was written with Loriod in mind, and she presented the work with the Boston Symphony Orchestra at its world premiere performance in December 1949. She also performed on the Ondes Martenot, an electrical keyboard named after its inventor which produces only one note at a time.

John Haag,
Athens, Georgia

Lorme, Marion de (c. 1613–1650).

See Delorme, Marion.

Lorn, Lady of (fl. 1300s).

See Isaac, Joan.

Lorraine, duchess of.

See Liutgard of Saxony (d. 953).
See Ida de Macon (d. 1224).
See Margaret of Bavaria (fl. 1390–1410).
See Yolande of Vaudemont (1428–1483).
See Jeanne de Laval (d. 1498).
See Mary of Guise for sidebar on Antoinette of Bourbon (1494–1583).
See Mary of Guise for sidebar on Renée of Montpensier (fl. 1500s).
See Christina of Denmark (1521–1590).
See Philippa of Guelders (d. 1547).
See Claude de France (1547–1575).
See Gonzaga, Margherita (1591–1632).
See Nicole of Lorraine (d. 1657).
See Elizabeth-Charlotte (1676–1744).

Lorraine, queen of.

See Waldrada (fl. 9th c.).

Lortel, Lucille (1902–1999)

American theatrical producer. Name variations: Lucille Schweitzer. Born in New York City in 1902 (sometimes seen as 1906 or 1910); died in New York City on April 4, 1999; daughter of Harry (a garment industry executive) and Anna (Mayo) Lortel; briefly attended Adelphi College (now Adelphi University), Garden City, New York; attended the American Academy of Dramatic Arts, 1920; studied in Germany with Arnold Korf and Max Reinhardt; married Louis Schweitzer (a chemical engineer and cigarette-paper manufacturer), on March 23, 1931 (died 1971); no children.

Affectionately dubbed the "Queen of Off-Broadway," producer and theater proprietor Lucille Lortel produced over 500 plays in her remarkable career, including several nominated for Tony Awards. As founder of the White Barn Theater in Westport, Connecticut, and the owner of the Theater de Lys in New York's Greenwich Village (rechristened the Lucille Lortel Theater in 1981), she provided countless playwrights and actors with an opportunity to showcase their talent away from the pressures of Broadway. "You must try new ideas and new faces," she said in an interview for *Fifty Plus* magazine in June 1980, "You can't do it on Broadway because it costs too much. The costs are lower Off Broadway, so you can afford to take a chance, and you must take a chance."

The daughter of a garment industry executive, Lortel was born in 1902 and raised in New York City. She attended Adelphi College briefly before beginning her theater education, which took her to the American Academy of Dramatic Art and to Berlin, Germany, where she studied with the expatriate American actor and teacher Arnold Korf and the director and producer Max Reinhardt. In 1924, she made her stage debut with a stock company in Albany, New York, and a year later made her first Broadway appearance, playing a small role in the ill-fated *Two by Two*. She continued in a series of supporting roles and even made a few short films for Warner Bros. before her marriage in 1931 to millionaire businessman Louis Schweitzer. Her new husband did not approve of her performing career, so Lortel gave up the stage until 1947, when her restlessness got the better of her. "Just going from party to party watching people outdo each other didn't mean much to me," she told Haskel Frankel of *The New York Times* (August 5, 1979). "It can't compare to the thrill of seeing a play or performance come to life."

Serendipitously, Lortel was approached by her friends, actor Canada Lee and playwright Philip Huston, who wanted to try out Huston's new play *The Painted Wagon*, written with **Elizabeth Goodyear**, in front of an audience. Grasping the opportunity, Lortel offered them the empty stable on her 18-acre Westport, Connecticut, estate. On July 27, 1947, outfitted with a platform and folding chairs and decorated with Japanese lanterns, the White Barn Theater became a reality. "I told my husband that I needed this," she told Frankel, "and he backed me up."

At first, Lortel presented only weekend dramatic readings, but in 1949, she had the barn remodeled to accommodate more elaborate stage productions. To initiate the new facility, Lortel presented a translation of Federico Garcia Lorca's *Amor de Don Perlimplin con Belisa en su jardin*, directed by the then unknown Sidney Lumet. The theater soon earned a reputation as the showcase for diverse performing groups, ranging from the Lemonade Opera Company and the Oxford University Players to Geoffrey Holder's Trinidad Dance Troupe. In 1951, Lortel hosted the Dublin Players Company in a series of productions. including the American premiere of *The Rising of the Moon*, a comedy by Lady *Augusta Gregory. In 1951, when the White Barn Theater was chartered as a non-profit foundation, Lortel expanded the theater's physical plant again and established the White Barn Theater Apprentice School, which offered seminars for advanced students and professional actors. To house the actors, she built a residence hall, Derwent House, named for playwright Clarence Derwent, then the president of Actors' Equity.

In 1954, Lortel expanded her scope with the acquisition of the Theater de Lys, a facility on Christopher Street in Greenwich Village that was a 24th wedding anniversary gift from her husband. Although Lortel had intended to use the theater as a New York venue for worthy White Barn productions, her first show, a revival of Marc Blitzstein's adaptation of the musical *The Threepenny Opera*, starring *Lotte Lenya, turned into a runaway hit that ran for a record seven years. In order to remain true to her goal of presenting experimental works, Lortel instituted her Matinee Series, which continued for 20 years and included experimental productions like *Anna Sokolow's dance drama *Metamorphosis*, and *Siobhan McKenna's *Hamlet*. The Matinee Series' production of Frank O'Connor's *Guests of the Nations* was awarded an Obie as the Best One-Act Play of 1958. In 1961, the series' production *Brecht on Brecht*, a "living anthology" of the playwright's work compiled by actor George Tabori and again starring Lenya, was such a success that Lortel finally closed *Threepenny Opera* in order to give the new play a wider audience.

The list of actors and playwrights who benefited from Lortel's largesse over the years reads like a who's who of theater. Actors Peter Falk, Vincent Gardenia, *Sada Thompson, George Peppard, and Lois Nettleton all got their first break at the White Barn Theater, which also hosted more established performers like *Mildred Dunnock, Zero Mostel, *Eva Le Gallienne, James Coco, *Kim Hunter, and *Peggy Wood. In a 1981 interview with *Avenue* magazine, Dunnock described the White Barn Theater as "a wonderful opportunity, a place to try out new things, with great freedom to live and work. And yet," she added, "as progressive as it was, no actor who ever worked there ever felt he was taking a chance with his career because he knew no production would be shoddy."

In addition to providing a venue for the early noncommercial works of American playwrights Tennessee Williams, Edward Albee, and William Inge, Lortel also produced the works of such contemporary writers as Adrienne Kennedy, Norman Rosten, and Anna Marie Barlow. A variety of new works were given their initial performances at the White Barn, including Murray Schisgal's *The Typist*, Paul Zindel's Pulitzer Prize-winning *The Effect of Gamma Rays on Man-in-the-Moon Marigolds*, and Terrence McNally's *Next*.

Although Lortel ended her Matinee Series in 1975, the Theater de Lys continued to stage worthy new plays. Lortel also produced shows in other off-Broadway theaters, notably the world premiere of Samuel Beckett's trilogy of one-act plays, *Ohio Impromptu*, *Catastrophe*, and *What Where*, at the Harold Clurman Theater in 1983, and another Beckett trio, *Enough*, *Footfalls*, and *Rockaby*, at the newly opened Samuel Beckett Theater in 1984. Lortel occasionally produced shows on Broadway, such as a production of O'Casey's *I Knock at the Door*, at the Belasco Theater in 1957, and a revival of Williams' *A Streetcar Named Desire*, at the St. James Theater in 1973. She also served on the board of directors of the national and New York chapters of ANTA, and of the Lincoln Center for the Performing Arts, and was a cofounder of the American Shakespeare Festival Theater and Academy in Stratford, Connecticut, which opened its doors in 1955.

In 1958, Lortel received a special citation from the *Village Voice* "for fostering and furthering the spirit of the theatrical experience." Through the years, awards followed one upon another. They included the State of Connecticut's Distinguished Award in the Arts, the Double Image Theater Award, and the Theater Hall of Fame Arnold Weissberger Award. Lortel was the first recipient of the ❧ **Margo Jones** Award (1952), for her dedication to producing new plays, and the Lee Strasberg Lifetime Achievement Award (1984), for furthering the theater in America, and she was inducted into the Theater Hall of Fame in 1990. Lortel was also generous in supporting projects outside her purview. In 1980, for example, she bailed out the debt-ridden New York Senior Concert Orchestra with a generous donation. "That's what money is for," she explained. She also established theater funds and fellowships at Yale and Brown universities.

A petite, elegant woman, with heavy-lidded dark eyes and dark hair, which she wore in a sophisticated chignon, Lortel was widowed in 1971 and had no family. "My theatres are my children," she once told *The New York Times*. Following her husband's death, Lortel resided in an elegant New York apartment until her own death on April 4, 1999, at the age of 98.

SOURCES:
Moritz, Charles, ed. *Current Biography 1985*. NY: H.W. Wilson, 1985.
"Obituary," in *The Boston Globe*, April 7, 1999.

Barbara Morgan,
Melrose, Massachusetts

Lo-Ruhamah

Biblical woman. Name variations: Not Pitied. The daughter of Gomer (a harlot) and the prophet Hosea.

Lorvano, abbess of.

See Sancha (c. 1178–1229).
See Branca (1259–1321).

Los Angeles, Victoria de (1923—)

Spanish soprano. Born Lopez Cima on November 1, 1923, in Barcelona, Spain; studied with Dolores Frau in the Barcelona Conservatory until 1944; married Enrique Magrina, in 1948; children: two sons.

Debuted as Mimi in Barcelona (1941); won Geneva International Singing Competition (1947); debuted as Marguerite in Paris (1949); made Covent Garden debut as Mimi (1950); made Metropolitan Opera debut as Marguerite (1951), appearing for more than 100 performances until 1961; widely known for her 22 recorded operas.

Lopez Cima, who would become known on stage as Victoria de Los Angeles, was born in Barcelona, Spain, on November 1, 1923. The Spanish Civil War shadowed her childhood but it did not interrupt her development. Since her family was musical, singing seemed a natural

part of growing up. At 18, she was asked to sing Mimi at the Teatro Victoria in Barcelona, but she refused, professing that she was too young and not yet ready. Four years later in 1941, after studying with **Dolores Frau** at the Barcelona Conservatory, Victoria de Los Angeles debuted as Mimi. After winning the Geneva Singing Competition in 1947, she gained international recognition. An opportunity to perform for the British Broadcasting Corporation in 1949 convinced her to master several languages and broaden her repertory in order to appeal to wider audiences outside Spain. Soon she appeared in international opera houses in London, Paris, and New York.

De Los Angeles had a sweet, vibrant voice with a rich lower register. Her upper soprano range was not easy for her and a hardness in some notes could be noticed. A modest, easygoing performer, she was widely popular, especially in Great Britain. Victoria de Los Angeles made many recordings, committing 22 operas to disc, and had an even larger number of recitals.

❧◀
Jones, Margo.
See Women of the Regional Theater Movement in America.

Victoria de Los Angeles

One of her most successful recordings was Bizet's *Carmen* made with Sir Thomas Beecham in 1960. By 1969, de Los Angeles no longer appeared on stage but continued her concert work and recordings.

SUGGESTED READING:

Roberts, P. *Victoria de Los Angeles*. London, 1982.

John Haag,
Athens, Georgia

Losch, Tilly (1901–1975)

Austrian dancer, actress, and choreographer. Name variations: often wrongly seen as Tillie Losch. Born Ottilia Ethel Leopoldine in Vienna, Austria, on November 15, 1907; died of cancer in a New York hospital on December 24, 1975; studied at the Vienna Opera Ballet School; married Edward James (a poet, architect, and arts patron), around 1928 (divorced); married and divorced once more.

A graduate of the Vienna Opera Ballet School, Tilly Losch made her debut with the Vienna Opera in 1924, dancing the role of Princess Teaflower in *Schlagobers*. Her initial dramatic role was in *Leonce and Lena* at the Vienna Burgtheater. Losch's first choreographic effort was for Max Reinhardt's production of *A Midsummer Night's Dream* (1927), in which she also played First Fairy. She choreographed and danced with Reinhardt for some time, traveling with him to the United States in 1928 and dancing the role of the Nun in his production of *The Miracle* (1932). While in America, she appeared in several films, including *The Garden of Allah* (1936), *The Good Earth* (1937), and *Duel in the Sun* (1945). She choreographed the dances for the latter film, as well as those for *Song of Schéhérazade* (1946). Losch, who was heralded as one of the great beauties of her day, was also noted for her "hand dances." She once filmed a piece that featured her hands sensuously intertwining to a Bach melody.

Losch was married to arts patron and British eccentric Edward James, who met the dancer when he was 24 and was besotted. They wed around 1928, although it was an odd partnership. She purportedly had numerous, highly visible, liaisons, including an affair with Randolph Churchill. When Losch finally left James, he tried to win her back by bankrolling George Balanchine's first dance company, Les Ballet (1933), and financing three ballets for Losch, including the notable Brecht-Weill collaboration *The Seven Deadly Sins*, in which she performed with *Lotte Lenya. However, James' philanthropy did nothing to reignite Losch's passion,

and they eventually parted. The divorce was a messy affair, with her accusing him of homosexuality, and James counter-charging with claims of adultery. After the dust settled, James moved to Europe where he fixated on Salvador Dali and joined the Surrealist movement. He evidently retained a soft spot for Losch, however, having her bare footprints woven into the stair carpet at one of his several houses. Losch later enjoyed some success as a painter. She died on Christmas Eve, 1975.

SOURCES:

Kernan, Michael. "One Man's Fantasy Stands Tall in a Jungle in Mexico," in *Smithsonian*. Vol. 25, no. 1. April 1994, pp. 60–69.

Phillips, Sue. "Diary of an Edwardian Garden," in *In Britain*. Vol. 6, no. 5. May 1996, pp. 46–50.

Barbara Morgan,
Melrose, Massachusetts

Lothrop, Alice (1870–1920)

American social worker. Born Alice Louise Higgins on March 28, 1870, in Boston, Massachusetts; died on September 2, 1920, in Newton, Massachusetts; only child of Albert Higgins (a merchant) and Adelaide (Everson) Higgins; attended local private schools; married William Howard Lothrop (a businessman), on May 17, 1913; no children.

Born in 1870 and raised in Boston, Massachusetts, Alice Lothrop began volunteering at an early age, working as a Sunday School superintendent and at the Boston Children's Aid Society. At 28, she joined the Associated Charities of Boston as an agent-in-training, and within two years had risen to district secretary. In September 1903, she became general secretary of the organization, succeeding *Zilpha Drew Smith. Over the next ten years, Lothrop made a significant contribution to the field of social work, both in method and ideology. Working hard to broaden the scope of social work, she sought to link the field case worker to a wider range of community issues, including social reform and public health, and to create a spirit of cooperation between agencies.

Possessing inordinate organizational skills, as well as a sharp mind, quick wit, and the ability to surround herself with capable people, Lothrop won acclaim for organizing disaster relief after the great San Francisco fire (1906), local fires in Chelsea (1908) and Salem, Massachusetts (1914), and the enormous explosion in Halifax, Nova Scotia (1917). She also helped organize the Massachusetts mothers' aid laws, and served variously with the Massachusetts Child Labor Committee, the Massachusetts Commission to Investigate Employment Agencies, and the Massachusetts Civic League.

Deeply concerned with public-health problems, Lothrop was particularly active in the fight against tuberculosis. After initially opposing Dr. Richard Cabot's plan for a social service department at Boston's Massachusetts General Hospital, Lothrop eventually saw an advantage in linking the work of the Associated Charities with Cabot's innovative project. In addition to in-hospital service, which began in 1905, Lothrop also sought to link the work of Associated Charities with other agencies, like the Boston Association for Relief and Control of Tuberculosis.

Alice Lothrop was also instrumental in developing new training programs for professional social workers. In 1904, she helped establish the Boston School for Social Workers, operated jointly by Harvard and Simmons College. In addition, she helped found the National Association of Societies for Organizing Charity (which later became the Family Service Association of America).

Lothrop married Boston merchant William Howard Lothrop in 1913, and since her husband believed that her "supreme achievement" should be her success as a "home maker," she resigned from the Associated Charities. However, she continued to lecture at the Boston School for Social Workers and served on the board of the Associated Charities. With the outbreak of World War I, she became active with the Red Cross, serving as director of civilian relief of the New England division. In 1920, she was stricken with encephalitis lethargica, a rare disease very much like sleeping sickness, and after weeks in a coma, died at the age of 50.

SOURCES:

James, Edward T., ed. *Notable American Women 1607–1950*. Cambridge, MA: The Belknap Press of Harvard University Press, 1971.

McHenry, Robert, ed. *Famous American Women*. NY: Dover, 1983.

Barbara Morgan,
Melrose, Massachusetts

Lothrop, Amy (1820–1915).

See Warner, Anna Bartlett.

Lothrop, Harriet (1844–1924)

American author of the popular "Five Little Peppers" series. Name variations: (pseudonym) Margaret Sidney. Born Harriet (also seen as Harriett) Mulford Stone on June 22, 1844, in New Haven, Connecticut; died on August 2, 1924, in San Francisco, California; elder of two daughters of Sidney Mason Stone (an architect)

and Harriett (Mulford) Stone; graduated from Grove Hall Seminary, New Haven, Connecticut; married Daniel Lothrop (a publisher), on October 4, 1881 (died 1892); children: one daughter, Margaret Lothrop.

Selected works: Five Little Peppers and How They Grew *(1881);* So As By Fire *(1881);* The Pettibone Name *(1882);* Hester, and Other New England Stories *(1886);* The Minute Man *(1886);* A New Departure for Girls *(1896);* Dilly and the Captain *(1887);* How Tom and Dorothy Made and Kept a Christian House *(1888);* Five Little Peppers Midway *(1889);* Rob: A Story for Boys *(1891);* Five Little Peppers Grown Up *(1892);* Old Concord, Her Highways and Byways *(1893);* Whittier with the Children *(1893);* The Old Town Pump *(1895);* The Gingham Bag *(1896);* Phronsie Pepper *(1897);* A Little Maid of Concord Town *(1898);* The Stories Polly Pepper Told *(1899);* An Adirondack Cabin *(1900);* The Adventures of Joel Pepper *(1900);* The Judges' Cave *(1900);* Five Little Peppers Abroad *(1902);* Ben Pepper *(1903);* Sally, Mrs Tubbs *(1903);* Five Little Peppers and Their Friends *(1904);* The Five Little Peppers at School *(1907);* Five Little Peppers in the Little Brown House *(1907);* A Little Maid from Boston Town *(1910);* Our Davie Pepper *(1916).*

Harriet Lothrop, recognized largely by her pseudonym Margaret Sidney, was best known for her fictional series detailing the adventures of the five Pepper children, the first of which, *Five Little Peppers and How They Grew*, always remained the most popular. Simplistic and didactic by modern-day standards, the books were enormously successful in their time, and five of the stories were adapted into films by Columbia Pictures between 1939 and 1940.

Born Harriet Mulford Stone in 1844 in New Haven, Connecticut, the eldest of two daughters, Lothrop grew up in a cultured and religious home. Her ancestors included John Howland of the *Mayflower* and several colonial governors. Lothrop's childhood memories involved a cadre of invented playmates with whom she enjoyed an imaginary outdoor life that her city environment did not offer. The little brown house that eventually became the fictional home of the Pepper family was also a childhood fantasy, complete with its large green door, and surrounded by an expanse of country fields. "Oh, how I longed for that to be my home," she recalled. "I could not understand how my father who was a most successful architect, ever had been so foolish as to live in a big city and not in this place, where I might have hens and chickens, and scratch the back of the pigs."

Lothrop attended private school in New Haven and also heavily sampled her father's extensive library. Although she longed to be a writer from an early age, her stories and poems did not find their way into print until the late 1870s. In 1877, Lothrop's story "Polly Pepper's Chicken Pit," written under the pseudonym Margaret Sidney, appeared in *Wide Awake*, a children's periodical published by the D. Lothrop Company of Boston. It was followed by "Phronsie Pepper's New Shoes" in 1878. These two stories provided the impetus for *Five Little Peppers and How They Grew*, which was serialized by the magazine in 1880 and published in book form the following year. It was followed by 11 additional "Pepper" adventures, concluding with *Our Davie Pepper* in 1916. The books, some of the most popular of their time, would sell over two million copies by 1924 and would still be in print four decades later.

In 1881, Harriet married the publisher of *Wide Awake*, Daniel Lothrop, a widower 30 years her senior. In 1883, to surprise his wife, Daniel purchased "The Wayside" in Concord,

Massachusetts, the childhood home of **Louisa May Alcott*. When Daniel died in 1892, Harriet became the sole support of their daughter **Margaret Lothrop**, who was born in 1885. Harriet took over the management of the publishing firm for several years while continuing to write.

Besides her "Pepper" series, Lothrop wrote 40 or so other books, including *Little Maid of Concord Town* (1898), a romance about her beloved Massachusetts home, and *The Judges' Cave* (1900), a novel set in her birthplace, New Haven, Connecticut. Though carefully researched, they have been criticized as somewhat lifeless. "Primarily written for an adult audience, they lack the spark and energy of the Pepper novel, while retaining their didactic overtones," writes **Christiane Bird**. Lothrop provided another historical view of Concord in *Old Concord: Her Highways and By-ways* (1888), a guidebook of sorts, dealing with the months and the years prior to 1775.

Throughout her career, Harriet Lothrop was extremely active in her community. She was

From the movie Out West with the Peppers, *based on the book by Margaret Sidney (Harriet Lothrop).*

a founding member of the Concord branch of the Daughters of the American Revolution and was instrumental in organizing the national society of Children of the American Revolution. She also held memberships in numerous other historical and writers' clubs. Her interest in historical preservation ran so deep that in 1902, when the Orchard House in Concord, made famous by the Alcotts, was to be torn down, she bought it and preserved it for ten years, after which it was taken over by the Louisa May Alcott Memorial Association. She was also a leading force in the preservation and restoration of several other historical homes in Concord.

In her later years, Lothrop devoted much of her time to travel, touring with her daughter in Egypt and Palestine as well as in England, Norway, and the Continent. Her last winters were spent in California, where the climate was more forgiving. "The breadth of the continent, however, did not separate her spirit from Concord and the home which was filled for her with associations," said her daughter. Lothrop was at work on an article about Edgar Allan Poe when she died at the age of 80. The author was buried in her beloved Concord, on Author's Ridge in Sleepy Hollow Cemetery.

SOURCES:

Commire, Anne, ed. *Something About the Author*. Vol. 20. Detroit, MI: Gale Research.

James, Edward T., ed. *Notable American Women 1607–1950*. Cambridge, MA: The Belknap Press of Harvard University Press, 1971.

Mainiero, Lina, ed. *American Women Writers*. NY: Frederick Ungar, 1981.

McHenry, Robert. *Famous American Women*. NY: Dover, 1983.

SUGGESTED READING:

Lothrop, Margaret. *The Wayside: Home of Authors*, 1940.

Barbara Morgan,
Melrose, Massachusetts

Lottie.

Variant of Charlotte.

Lotz, Irmgard Flügge (1903–1974).

See Flügge-Lotz, Irmgard.

Lou, Henri (1861–1937).

See Andreas-Salomé, Lou.

Louchheim, Aline B. (1914–1972).

See Saarinen, Aline B.

Loudon, Jane Webb (1807–1858)

British botanist and writer on horticulture. Born near Birmingham, England, in 1807; died in London, England, in 1858; daughter of Thomas Webb; married John Loudon (a landscape gardener and horticultural writer), in 1830.

Born in Birmingham, England, in 1807, Jane Webb Loudon originally turned to writing to support herself after the death of her father. Her first book, a science-fiction romance, *The Mummy, a Tale of the Twenty-Second Century* (1827), came to the attention of John Loudon, a landscape gardener and horticultural writer who gave it a favorable review in a journal he was then editing. Out of curiosity, Jane sought John out, and they married in 1830. From that time on, Loudon immersed herself in her husband's work, learning about plants and serving as his assistant. During a period of particular financial strain, she began to write books on popular botany, the most successful of which was *The Ladies' Companion to the Flower Garden* (1841). She also wrote *The Young Naturalist's Journey; or, the Travels of Agnes Merton and Her Mama* (1840) and *Modern Botany; or, a Popular Introduction to the Natural System of Plants, According to the Classification of de Candolle*, 2nd ed. (1851).

Loughlin, Anne (1894–1979)

British trade unionist. Name variations: Dame Anne Loughlin. Born on June 28, 1894, in Leeds, England; died in 1979; eldest of four daughters of a shoe-factory worker; attended elementary school in Leeds until the age of 12; never married; no children.

Born in 1894 in Leeds, England, Anne Loughlin was the eldest of four daughters of a shoe-factory worker. When Anne was 12, her mother died; her father died four years later. To support her sisters, Loughlin took a job as a machine worker in a local factory at ten shillings a week, out of which she had to pay a penny a week for hot water and was fined threepence for being even 15 minutes late. Quickly sensing a need to improve conditions, she joined the National Union of Tailors and Garment Workers, and shortly thereafter led 200 young women workers in a formal strike. It was then that she realized her natural gift for oratory and, even more important, her ability to negotiate after the speeches were over. Continuing her formal education at night school, Loughlin became an organizer for the 10,000-member union in 1914, a job that took her throughout the British Isles to negotiate, consult on factory conditions, and settle disputes.

In 1929, Loughlin was elected to the General Council of the powerful Trades Union Congress, of which she was selected chair in 1943, the same year she was made a Dame of the Order of the British Empire (DBE). In 1948, she was elected as the first woman general secretary of the National Union of Tailors and Garment Workers, an event that was hailed by the London *Times* as "an important victory for the Right wing." In December 1949, she was one of two women (the other being *Florence Hancock) on the British delegation sent to the Free World Labor Conference. That conference resulted in the new International Confederation of Free Trade Unions, organized in opposition to the Communist-dominated World Federation of Trade Unions.

*Anne
Loughlin*

Small of stature (barely 5' tall), Loughlin was described as bringing a "brisk and businesslike efficiency" to her work. Never married, she lived in the country, in Hertfordshire, commuting to and from work in London, and filling her weekends with speeches, conferences, or lectures, all work related. She retired as general secretary of the Union in 1953, due to ill health, and died in 1979.

SOURCES:
Current Biography. NY: H.W. Wilson, 1950.
Uglow, Jennifer. *The Continuum Dictionary of Women's Biography.* NY: Continuum, 1989.

Barbara Morgan,
Melrose, Massachusetts

Louisa.
Variant of Louise.

Louisa, grand duchess of Naples
(1773–1802).
See Louisa Amelia.

Louisa (1622–1709), Princess Palatine.
See Elizabeth of Bohemia (1596–1662) for sidebar.

Louisa Amelia (1773–1802)
Grand duchess of Tuscany. Name variations: Ludovica; Luisa of Naples; Luisa of Bourbon-Two Sicilies; Louise de Bourbon or Louise of Bourbon; Marie Louise of Naples and Sicily. Born on July 17, 1773, in

*Naples; died on September 19, 1802, in Vienna; daughter of *Maria Carolina (1752–1814), queen of the Two Sicilies, and Ferdinand I (or IV), king of the Two Sicilies; married Ferdinando or Ferdinand III (1769–1824), grand duke of Tuscany (r. 1790–1802, 1814–1824) and archduke of Austria, on September 19, 1790; children: *Caroline (1793–1812); Francis (1794–1800); Leopold II (1797–1870), grand duke of Tuscany (r. 1824–1859); *Maria Ludovica (1798–1857); *Maria Theresa of Tuscany (1801–1855). Ferdinand's second wife was *Maria Anna of Saxony (1795–1865).*

Louisa Anne (1749–1768)
*English royal. Name variations: Louise Anne Guelph. Born on March 8, 1749, in London, England; died on May 13, 1768, at Carlton House, Mayfair, London; buried in Westminster Abbey; daughter of *Augusta of Saxe-Gotha (1719–1772) and Frederick Louis, prince of Wales; sister of George III, king of England (r. 1760–1820), and *Caroline Matilda (1751–1775).*

Louisa Carlotta of Naples
(1804–1844)
*Neapolitan princess and duchess of Cadiz. Name variations: Luisa of Sicily. Born on October 24, 1804; died on January 29, 1844; daughter of Francis I, king of the Two Sicilies (r. 1825–1830), and *Marie Isabella of Spain (1789–1848); sister of *Maria Cristina I of Naples (1806–1878), queen of Spain; married Francisco de Paula (1794–1865), duke of Cadiz (brother of Ferdinand VII, king of Spain), on June 11, 1819; children: Francisco de Asís or Asíz (1822–1902, who married *Isabella II, queen of Spain); Amalia de Paula (b. 1834, who married Adalbert Wittelsbach on August 25, 1856); Marie Christine de Paula (1833–1902, who married Sebastian de Bourbon); Enrique or Henry, duke of Seville. Francisco de Paula's second wife was Therese Arredondo.*

Louisa Christina of Bavaria
(fl. 1726)
*Duchess of Savoy. Name variations: Louise Christine; Polyxena-Christina of Hesse. Born around 1700; daughter of Ernest-Leopold of Hesse Rheinfelt; married Charles Emmanuel III (1701–1773), duke of Savoy (r. 1730–1773) and king of Sardinia; children: Victor Amadeus III (1726–1796), duke of Savoy (r. 1773–1796). Charles Emmanuel was also married to *Elizabeth of Lorraine (1711–1741).*

Louisa Henrietta de Conti

(1726–1759)

*Duchess of Orleans. Name variations: Louise-Henrietta von Conty; Louise-Henriette. Born Louise-Henriette de Bourbon-Conti on June 20, 1726; died on February 9, 1759; daughter of Louis Armand II, prince of Conti or Conty; married Louis Philippe (1725–1785), 4th duke of Orléans (r. 1752–1785), on December 17, 1743; children: daughter (born on July 12, 1745; died on December 14, 1745); Louis Philippe "Egalité" (1747–1793), 5th duke of Orléans (r. 1785–1793), Montpensier (r. 1747–1752), and Chartres (r. 1752–1785); *Marie Louise d'Orleans (1750–1822), duchess of Bourbon. Louis Philippe's second wife was the *Marquise de Montesson (1737–1805).*

Louisa Henrietta of Orange

(1627–1667)

*Electress of Brandenburg. Name variations: Louise Orange-Nassau; Louise Henriette of Nassau-Orange; Louise Henriette of Orange; (Ger.) Luise Henriette. Born in 1627; died in 1667; daughter of Frederick Henry, prince of Orange (r. 1625–1647), and *Amelia of Solms (1602–1675); married Frederick William (1620–1688), the Great Elector of Brandenburg (r. 1640–1688), on December 7, 1646; children: Frederick III (1657–1713), elector of Brandenburg (r. 1688–1701), later Frederick I, king of Prussia (r. 1701–1713).*

Louisa Isabel (1709–1750).

> See Louise Elizabeth.

Louisa Juliana (1576–1644)

*Electress Palatine. Name variations: Louise-Juliana of Orange; Luise Juliane of Nassau. Born on March 31, 1576; died on March 15, 1644; daughter of William I the Silent (1533–1584), prince of Orange, and stadholder of Holland, Zealand, and Utrecht (r. 1572–1584), and *Charlotte of Bourbon (d. 1582); married Frederick IV the Upright (1574–1610), elector Palatine; children: Frederick V (1596–1632), king of Bohemia (The Winter King).*

Louisa of Hesse-Darmstadt (1751–1805).

> See Frederica of Hesse.

Louisa of Prussia (1776–1810).

> See Louise of Prussia.

Louisa Ulrica of Prussia

(1720–1782)

*Queen of Sweden. Name variations: Luisa Ulrika. Born in Berlin on July 24, 1720; died on July 16, 1782; daughter of Frederick William I (1688–1740), king of Prussia (r. 1713–1740), and *Sophia Dorothea of Brunswick-Lüneburg-Hanover (1687–1757, daughter of George I of England); sister of Frederick II the Great, king of Prussia (r. 1740–1786); married Adolphus Frederick (1710–1771), king of Sweden (r. 1751–1771), on August 29, 1744; children: Gustavus III (1746–1792), king of Sweden (r. 1771–1792, who married *Sophia of Denmark); Charles XIII (1748–1818), king of Sweden (r. 1809–1818); Frederick Adolf (b. 1750); Albertine (1753–1829).*

A friend of Linnaeus, Louisa Ulrica of Prussia was known as an intelligent and commanding presence in the Swedish court. She was a patron of art and science.

Louisa Wilhelmina of Bavaria

(1808–1892).

> See Ludovica.

Louise (1692–1712).

> See Mary of Modena for sidebar.

Louise (1776–1810).

> See Louise of Prussia.

Louise (1808–1870)

*Prussian princess. Name variations: Louisa of Prussia; Louise Hohenzollern; Louise Augusta Hohenzollern. Born Louise Augusta Wilhelmina Amelia on February 1, 1808; died on December 6, 1870; daughter of *Louise of Prussia (1776–1810) and Frederick William III, king of Prussia (r. 1797–1849); married Frederick Orange-Nassau (son of William I of the Netherlands); children: *Louise of the Netherlands (1828–1871, who married Charles XV, king of Sweden); Frederick William (1833–1834); William Frederick (1836–1846); *Marie of Nassau (1841–1910, who married William, 5th prince of Wied).*

Louise (1817–1898), **Queen of Denmark**.

> See Louise of Hesse-Cassel.

Louise (1848–1939)

English princess, sculptor, Duchess of Argyll, and daughter of Queen Victoria. Name variations: Princess Louise; Louise Saxe-Coburg. Born Louise

Caroline Alberta on March 18, 1848, in Buckingham Palace, London, England; died on December 3, 1939; fourth daughter and sixth child of Queen *Victoria (1819–1901) and Prince Albert Saxe-Coburg; sister of King Edward VII of England; married John Campbell, 9th duke of Argyll (governor-general of Canada and Marquis of Lorne), on March 21, 1871 (annulled 1900); children: none.

SUGGESTED READING:

Longford, Elizabeth. *Darling Loosy: Letters to Princess Louise, 1856–1939*. London: Weidenfeld & Nicolson.

Packard, Jerrold M. *Victoria's Daughters*. St. Martin's, 1998.

Louise-Adelaide (1698–1743)

Abbess of Chelles. Name variations: Marie-Adelaide d'Orléans. Born on August 13, 1698; died on February 19, 1743; daughter of *Françoise-Marie de Bourbon (1677–1749) and Philip Bourbon-Orléans (1674–1723), 2nd duke of Orléans (r. 1701–1723); sister of *Louise-Diana (1716–1736) and *Louise Elizabeth (1709–1750), queen of Spain. Louise-Adelaide became abbess in 1719.

Louise Adelaide de Bourbon (1757–1824)

Princesse de Condé. Name variations: Louise Adélaide de Bourbon; Princess of Conde. Born Louise Adélaide de Bourbon in Chantilly, France, on October 5, 1757; died in Paris on March 10, 1824; daughter of Louis Joseph de Bourbon (1736–1818, a French general).

Louise Adélaide de Bourbon, the princess of Condé, became abbess of Remiremont in 1786. She emigrated as soon as the French Revolution broke out, and her father fled to Turin, then to Worms, where he recruited an army to serve England, Austria, and Russia. In 1801, his army was disbanded, and he moved to England. In 1815, Louise returned to Paris where her father became grand master of the King's Household; she subsequently founded the religious order of "l'adoration perpetuelle."

Louise Augusta (1771–1843).

See Caroline Matilda for sidebar.

Louise Bernadotte (1851–1926).

See Louise of Sweden.

Louise Caroline (1875–1906)

Princess of Schaumburg-Lippe. Name variations: Louise Caroline Oldenburg. Born Louise Caroline Josephine on February 17, 1875; died on April 4, 1906; daughter of *Louise of Sweden (1851–1926) and Frederick VIII (1843–1912), king of Denmark (r. 1906–1912); married Frederick, prince of Schaumburg-Lippe, on May 5, 1896; children: **Marie Louise** (1897–1938, princess of Schaumburg-Lippe, who married Prince Frederick Sigismund Hohenzollern); Christian Nicholas (b. 1898); **Stephanie** (1899–1925, who married Victor Adolf, 5th prince of Bentheim).

Louise Charlotte of Mecklenburg-Schwerin (1779–1801)

Duchess of Saxe-Gotha. Born on November 19, 1779; died on January 4, 1801; daughter of *Louise of Saxe-Gotha (1756–1808) and Frederick Francis (1756–1837), duke of Mecklenburg-Schwerin (r. 1785–1837); married August, duke of Saxe-Gotha, on October 21, 1797; children: *Louise of Saxe-Gotha-Altenburg (1800–1831).

Louise de Brézé (fl. 1555)

Duchess of Aumale. Name variations: Louise of Breze. Flourished around 1555; married Claude II of Lorraine, marquis of Mayenne and duke of Aumale (1526–1573); children: Charles, duke of Aumale (c. 1555–1621 or 1631).

Louise de Coligny (1555–1620).

See Coligny, Louise de.

Louise de Guzman (1613–1666).

See Luisa de Guzman.

Louise de la Miséricorde, Soeur (1644–1710).

See La Vallière, Louise Françoise de.

Louise de Marillac (1591–1660).

See Marillac, Louise de.

Louise de Mercoeur (1554–1601).

See Louise of Lorraine.

Louise de Montmorency (fl. 1498–1525).

See Margaret of Angoulême for sidebar.

Louise de Savoie (1476–1531).

See Louise of Savoy.

Louise-Diana (1716–1736)

Princess of Conti. Name variations: Princess of Conty. Born on June 28, 1716; died on September 26, 1736; daughter of *Françoise-Marie de Bourbon

*(1677–1749) and Philip Bourbon-Orléans (1674–1723), 2nd duke of Orléans (r. 1701–1723); sister of *Louise-Adelaide (1698–1743) and *Louise Elizabeth (1709–1750, queen of Spain); married Louis Francis, prince of Conti, on January 22, 1732.*

Louise d'Orleans (1812–1850), Queen of the Belgians.

See Carlota (1840–1927) for sidebar.

Louise Dorothea of Brandenburg (1680–1705)

*Prussian princess. Born in 1680; died in 1705; daughter of *Elizabeth Henrietta of Hesse-Cassel (1661–1683) and Frederick III (1657–1713), elector of Brandenburg (r. 1688–1701), later Frederick I, king of Prussia (r. 1701–1713); married Frederick (1676–1751), landgrave of Hesse-Cassel (r. 1730–1751), who would later be Frederick I, king of Sweden (r. 1720–1751), upon his marriage to *Ulrica Eleanora (1688–1741).*

Louise Elizabeth (1709–1750)

*Queen of Spain. Name variations: Louise Elizabeth Bourbon-Orléans; (Span.) Louisa Isabel. Born on December 11, 1709; died on June 16, 1750 (some sources cite 1742); daughter of Philip Bourbon-Orléans (1674–1723), 2nd duke of Orléans (r. 1701–1723), and *Françoise-Marie de Bourbon (1677–1749); married Louis I (1707–1724), briefly king of Spain (r. 1724–1724), on August 18, 1723.*

Louise Elizabeth (1727–1759)

*Duchess of Parma. Name variations: Elizabeth de France or Elizabeth of France; Marie Louise of France; Marie Louise of Parma; (Span.) Louisa Isabel. Born on August 14, 1727; died on December 6, 1759; daughter of Louis XV, king of France (r. 1715–1774), and *Marie Leczinska (1703–1768); had twin sister *Henriette (1727–1752); also sister of *Louise Marie (1737–1787); *Adelaide (1732–1800); *Victoire (1733–1799), and *Sophie (1734–1782); married Philip de Bourbon (1720–1765), duke of Parma (r. 1748–1765, son of *Elizabeth Farnese), on October 25, 1739; children: *Maria Luisa Teresa of Parma (1751–1819); *Isabella of Parma (1741–1763); Ferdinand (b. 1751), duke of Parma.*

Louise-Henriette (1726–1759).

See Louisa Henrietta de Conti.

Louise Margaret of Prussia (1860–1917)

*Duchess of Connaught and duchess of Clarence. Name variations: Louise of Prussia. Born Louise Margaret Alexandra Victoria Agnes on June 25, 1860, in Potsdam, Brandenburg, Germany; died on March 14, 1917, at Clarence House, St. James's Palace, London, England; married Arthur Saxe-Coburg (1850–1942, son of Queen *Victoria), duke of Connaught, on March 13, 1879; children: *Margaret of Connaught (1882–1920, who married Gustavus VI, king of Sweden); Arthur Windsor (1883–1938); Lady *Patricia Ramsay (1886–1974).*

Louise Marie (1737–1787)

*French princess. Born in 1737; died in 1787; youngest daughter of Louis XV (1710–1774), king of France (r. 1715–1774), and Marie Leczinska (1703–1768); sister of *Louise Elizabeth (1727–1759), *Henriette (1727–1752), *Adelaide (1732–1800), *Victoire (1733–1799), and *Sophie (1734–1782).*

Louise Marie, the daughter of *Marie Leczinska and Louis XV, king of France, became a Carmelite nun.

Louise Marie (1752–1824).

See Louise of Stolberg-Gedern.

Louise-Marie Bourbon-Penthievre (1812–1850).

See Carlota (1840–1927) for sidebar on Louise d'Orleans.

Louise Marie de Gonzague (1611–1667)

Queen of Poland. Name variations: Louise Marie e Gonzague; Louise Marie Gonzaga; Marie-Louise Gonzaga or Gonzague; Marie Louise Gonzague-Cleves or Clèves; Princess de Nevers. Born on August 18, 1611; died on May 10, 1667; daughter of Charles I, duke of Mantua; married Wladyslaw also known as Ladislas IV (1595–1648), king of Poland (r. 1632–1648), king of Sweden (r. 1632–1648), tsar of Russia (r. 1610–1634), on March 10, 1646; married his half-brother John II Casimir (1609–1672), also known as Casimir V, king of Poland (r. 1648–1668), on May 29, 1649; children: (second marriage) Marie Theresa (1650–1651); and a son (b. 1652).

The princess Louise Marie de Gonzague became queen of Poland on her marriage in 1646 to Ladislas IV. After his death in 1648, she soon married his half-brother and successor John II Casimir. It was a rocky reign. One of the darkest periods in Polish history, the interval from 1648 until 1660 is traditionally known as the "Deluge." Poland was faced with internal strife and unrest among the nobility because of the inept rule of John Casimir. The nation was also invaded from without by Swedes, Cossacks, Muscovites, Tartars, Transylvanians, and Germans.

Decades earlier, during the Jagiellon rule, the Polish nobility had secured the right to elect their future sovereigns. First, the nobles of the *Sejm* (Parliament) had used their newly gained power to briefly elect the future king of France, Henry III, to the Polish throne. They next elected the Transylvanian Stephen Báthory. With the death of Báthory in 1586, the nobility turned to the Swedish Vasa (Waza) family for a king, Sigismund III Vasa, father of Ladislas IV. The emergence of the Swedes as kings of Poland ultimately led to the Swedish invasion of Poland in 1654 during John Casimir's reign.

Louise Marie de Gonzague

As the Swedish forces of King Charles X Gustavus swept across Poland, King John Casimir and Queen Louise Marie eluded capture and fled to Silesia. Charles Gustavus soon conquered the half-hearted Polish defenders and proclaimed himself ruler of Poland. In 1655, the occupation force of Charles Gustavus committed countless atrocities throughout the Polish countryside and attempted to cart everything of value back to Sweden. This series of endless offenses soon rallied the lethargic and splintered Polish populace to defend their country, and by mid-1656 the Poles were effectively resisting Swedish authority. Despite their fierce and costly nature, the Polish Wars continued until 1660. By the end of the carnage, Polish forces had regained their country by successfully expelling all occupation troops.

Louise Marie had enormous influence over her second husband, enough to convince him to name his successor in his lifetime in order to avoid the vote of the *Sejm* after his death. In agreement with Cardinal Jules Mazarin, Louise Marie chose the Duc d'Enghien, son of the Great Condé. When opposition rose up, led by George Lubomirski, the grand marshal of Poland, the queen resorted to court intrigue to silence him. After a second attempt at rebellion in 1666, Lubomirski asked pardon from the king. In return, John Casimir agreed to give up the idea of altering the law of free election. Casimir, the last Vasa, abdicated in September 1668, the year after Louise Marie's death.

Louise Marie of Bourbon
(1753–1821)

Duchess of Orleans, Montpensier, and Chartres. Name variations: Louise Marie Adelaide de Bourbon-Penthième; Louise-Adelaide de Penthièvre or Penthievre; duchesse d'Orléans; Madame d'Orleans. Born Louise Marie Adelaide de Bourbon Penthievre on March 13, 1753; died on June 23, 1821; buried in Dreaux, France; daughter of Johann, duke of Penthièvre; married Louis Philippe "Egalité" (1747–1793), 5th duke of Orléans (r. 1785–1793), Montpensier (r. 1747–1752), and Chartres (r. 1752–1785), on April 5, 1769 (divorced 1792); children: daughter who died at birth (1771–1771); Louis Philippe I (1773–1850), king of France (r. 1830–1848); Anton Philip (1775–1807); *Adelaide (1777–1847); Louis Charles (1779–1808).

Louise Mountbatten (1889–1965)

Queen of Sweden. Name variations: Queen Louise. Born Louise Alexandra Mary Irene on July 13, 1889, in Jugenheim, near Darmstadt, Hesse, Germany; died

on March 7, 1965, in Stockholm, Sweden; daughter of Louis of Battenberg, 1st marquess of Milford Haven, and *Victoria of Hesse-Darmstadt (1863–1950); became second wife of Gustavus VI Adolphus (1882–1973), king of Sweden (r. 1950–1973), on November 3, 1923; children: one daughter died in infancy. Gustavus' first wife was *Margaret of Connaught.

Louise of Baden (1779–1826).

See Elizabeth of Baden.

Louise of Baden (1811–1854)

Princess of Baden. Born Louise Amelia Stephanie on June 5, 1811; died on July 19, 1854; daughter of Karl Ludwig also known as Charles Ludwig, grand duke of Baden, and *Stephanie de Beauharnais (1789–1860); married Gustavus of Sweden, prince of Vasa, on November 9, 1830 (divorced 1844); children: *Caroline of Saxony (1833–1907); and a son born in 1832.

Louise of Baden (1838–1923)

Grand duchess of Baden. Name variations: Louise Hohenzollern. Born Louise Mary Elizabeth on December 3, 1838; died on April 23, 1923; daughter of William I also known as Wilhelm I (1797–1888), kaiser or king of Prussia (r. 1861–1871), emperor of Germany (r. 1871–1888), and *Augusta of Saxe-Weimar (1811–1890); married Frederick I, grand duke of Baden, on September 20, 1856; children: three, including *Victoria of Baden (1862–1930, who married Gustavus V, king of Sweden), and Frederick II, grand duke of Baden (b. 1857).

Louise of Belgium (1858–1924)

Belgian princess. Name variations: Louise of Saxe-Coburg-Gotha. Born on February 18, 1858; died on March 1, 1924; daughter of Leopold II, king of Belgium (r. 1865–1909), and *Maria Henrietta of Austria (1836–1902); married Prince Philip of Saxe-Coburg-Gotha, on February 4, 1875 (divorced 1906); children: Leopold of Saxe-Coburg-Gotha (b. 1878); Dorothy of Saxe-Coburg-Gotha (b. 1881), princess of Saxe-Coburg-Gotha.

Louise of Bourbon-Berry (1819–1864)

Duchess and regent of Parma and Piacenza. Name variations: Louise du Berry; Louise Marie Thérèse d'Artois; Louise of Artois; Luise-Marie. Born on September 21, 1819; died on February 1, 1864; daughter

of *Caroline of Naples (1798–1870) and Charles Ferdinand (1778–1820), duke of Berry (second son of Charles X, king of France); sister of Henry V (1820–1883), duke of Bordeaux and count of Chambord; married Charles III (1823–1854), duke of Parma (1849–1854), on November 10, 1845; children: *Margaret of Parma (1847–1893); Robert (b. 1848), duke of Bourbon-Parma; *Alicia of Parma (1849–1935); Henry (b. 1851), count of Bardi.

£ouise of ℬelgium

Louise of Brunswick-Wolfenbuttel (1722–1780)

Mother of the king of Prussia. Name variations: Louisa Amalia; Louise Amelia of Brunswick. Born in 1722; died on January 13, 1780; daughter of Antoinetta Amelia (1696–1762) and Ferdinand Albert II, duke of Brunswick-Wolfenbuttel; married Augustus William (1722–1758, brother of Frederick II the Great, king of Prussia), on January 6, 1742; children: Frederick William II (1744–1797), king of Prussia (r. 1786–1797); Frederick Henry (1747–1767); *Wilhelmina of Prussia (1751–1820); George Charles (1758–1759).

Louise of Denmark (1750–1831)

Duchess of Hesse-Cassel. Name variations: Louise Oldenburg. Born on January 30, 1750; died on January 12, 1831; daughter of Frederick V, king of Denmark and Norway, and *Louise of England (1724–1751); married Charles of Hesse-Cassel, regent of Schleswig-Holstein, on August 30, 1766; children: *Marie Sophie of Hesse-Cassel (1767–1852, who married Frederick VI, king of Denmark); Frederick (b. 1771), governor of Rendesburg; Julie Louise Amelia (1773–1861), abbess of Itzehoe; Christian (b. 1776); *Louise of Hesse-Cassel (1789–1867, mother of Christian IX, king of Denmark).

Louise of England (1724–1751)

Queen of Denmark and Norway. Name variations: Louisa or Louise Guelph; Louisa Hanover. Born on

December 7, 1724, at Leicester House, St. Martin's, London, England; died at age 27 on December 8, 1751, at Christiansborg Castle, Copenhagen, Denmark; daughter of George II (1683–1760), king of Great Britain and Ireland (r. 1727–1760), and *Caroline of Ansbach (1683–1737); became first wife of Frederick V, king of Denmark and Norway (r. 1746–1766), on December 11, 1743, in Altona, Hamburg, Germany; children: Christian VII (b. 1749), king of Denmark and Norway (r. 1766–1808, who married *Caroline Matilda [1751–1775]); *Louise of Denmark (1750–1831); *Sophia of Denmark (1746–1813, who married Gustavus III of Sweden); *Wilhelmine (1747–1820); and one other. Following the death of Louise of England, Frederick V married *Maria Juliana of Brunswick (1729–1796).

Louise of Hesse-Cassel (1688–1765)

Mother of the prince of Orange. Name variations: Louise of Orange-Nassau. Born Mary Louise on February 7, 1688; died on April 9, 1765; married John William Friso of Orange-Nassau (1686–1711), in 1709; children: **Anna Charlotte Amalia of Orange** (1710–1777, who married Friedrich of Baden-Durlach); William IV, prince of Orange (1711–1751), stadholder of United Provinces (r. 1748–1751).

Louise of Hesse-Cassel (1789–1867)

Duchess of Schleswig-Holstein-Sonderburg-Glucksberg. Name variations: Princess Louise Caroline von Hessen-Cassel. Born Louise Charlotte in Gottorp, Schleswig, Germany, on September 28, 1789; died in Ballenstadt on March 13, 1867; daughter of Charles of Hesse-Cassel, regent of Schleswig-Holstein, and *Louise of Denmark (1750–1831); married Frederick William, duke of Schleswig-Holstein-Sonderburg-Glucksberg, on January 26, 1810; children: Frederick, duke of Schleswig-Holstein-Sonderburg-Glucksberg; Christian IX (1818–1906), king of Denmark (r. 1863–1906).

Louise of Hesse-Cassel (1817–1898)

Queen of Denmark. Born Louise Wilhelmina on September 7, 1817, in Cassel; died on September 29, 1898, in Bernstorff; daughter of William, landgrave of Hesse-Cassel, and *Charlotte Oldenburg (1789–1864); married Christian IX (1818–1906), king of Denmark (r. 1863–1906), on May 26, 1842; children: Frederick VIII (1843–1912), king of Denmark (r. 1906–1912); Alexandra of Denmark (1844–1925); Dagmar (1847–1928, also known as Marie Feodorovna); Waldemar (b. 1858); Thyra Old-

enburg (1853–1933); William of Denmark, who was elected king of Hellenes as George I (r. 1863–1913).

When Princess Louise of Hesse-Cassel married Prince Christian (IX) of Denmark, it was not certain her husband would become king. Because the male line of Frederick III was to end with the death of Frederick VII, Christian was designated crown prince in 1852, and assumed the throne in 1863 at the time of Frederick's death. But the succession was contested. Soon the withdrawal of Schleswig and Holstein from Danish authority led to war with Prussia and Austria. In the end, after five and a half months of conflict, the duchies were lost, and Denmark became one of Europe's smallest nations.

The country soon recovered, however. At times, Fredensborg in North Zealand, the summer palace of the Danish Royal family, was the center of European court life. The children of Louise and Christian led remarkable careers: Frederick was Frederick VIII, king of Denmark; *Alexandra of Denmark married Edward VII and became queen of England; Dagmar married Alexander III and became empress of Russia as *Marie Feodorovna; Waldemar married *Marie d'Orleans, daughter of Robert duc de Chartres; and *Thyra Oldenburg married Ernest Augustus, duke of Cumberland. William of Denmark was elected king of Hellenes (Greece) as George I and reigned from 1863 until his assassination in Salonica in 1913.

Louise of Hesse-Darmstadt
(d. 1830)

Duchess of Saxe-Weimar. Died in 1830; daughter of Louis IX, landgrave of Hesse-Darmstadt; married Charles Augustus (b. 1757), duke of Saxe-Weimar and Eis, on October 3, 1775; children: **Louise Augusta Amelia of Saxe-Weimer** (1779–1784); Charles Frederick, grand duke of Saxe-Weimar (b. 1783); *Caroline Louise of Saxe-Weimar (1786–1816); Charles Bernard of Saxe-Weimar (b. 1792).

Louise of Hohenlohe-Langenburg (1763–1837)

Duchess of Saxe-Meiningen. Born Louise Eleanor on August 11, 1763; died on April 30, 1837; daughter of Prince Christian; married George I, duke of Saxe-Meiningen, on November 27, 1782; children: four, including *Adelaide of Saxe-Meiningen (1792–1849); *Ida of Saxe-Coburg-Meiningen (1794–1852); Bernard II, duke of Saxe-Meiningen (b. 1800).

Louise of Lorraine (1554–1601)

*Queen of France. Name variations: Louise de Lorraine; Louise de Mercoeur; Louise de Vaudemont; Louise of Vaudemont; the White Lady of Chenonceau. Born in 1554 (some sources cite 1553); died in 1601; daughter of Nicolas de Mercoeur also known as Nicolas of Lorraine, count of Vaudemont, and Marguerite d'Egmont; sister of *Marguerite of Lorraine (c. 1561–?) and Philippe-Emmanuel, duc de Mercoeur; married Henry III (1551–1589), king of France (r. 1574–1589), on February 15, 1575; daughter-in-law of Catherine de Medici (1519–1589); no children.*

Born into the French aristocracy, Louise of Lorraine was the eldest of the 14 children of Nicolas of Lorraine, count of Vaudemont and member of the noble house of Lorraine. Her mother was Nicolas' first wife, **Marguerite d'Egmont**, who died when Louise was a year old. Louise was brought up by her father's second wife, the beautiful and intellectual **Jeanne de Savoie-Nemours**. As a young woman, Louise was described as tall, blonde, and strikingly beautiful, with a modest and quiet personality. It was perhaps her physical attractiveness which caught the eye of the heir to the French throne, Henry of Valois, who met Louise while on a tour of the province of Lorraine in 1573. At the time it was widely known that he was in love with the princess **Marie of Cleves** (d. 1575), and hoped to marry her. When he succeeded to the throne as Henry III on the death of his brother, Charles IX, in 1574, he still planned to marry Marie. Her death a few months after his succession threw him into a deep depression. When he recovered, he surprised the court by announcing that his future queen had been chosen: he would marry Louise of Lorraine. As yet this decision was unknown to Louise.

The question of Henry's marriage was a pressing concern for the ruling class of France and was watched closely by foreign heads of state. Henry's mother, the former regent *Catherine de Medici, had been negotiating for the hands of various princesses for him since he was a baby. It was almost unheard of for a prince to choose a bride for himself; a royal marriage was an alliance and a contract between the families and their states for the political and economic benefit of both, and to ensure that healthy male offspring would result. For a young man, especially a young king, to decide on his future wife alone was unprecedented and widely thought to be dangerous. Although one of Henry's sisters, *Claude de France, had married

Charles II, duke of Lorraine, Louise's cousin, the house was not considered elevated enough to provide the future queen of France and the mother of its future king. Henry therefore met opposition to his plans from many of his advisors, not least from his mother Catherine, who was clearly displeased but attempted not to let the breach between mother and son be made public. But Henry refused to yield.

Louise's own reactions when two royal envoys arrived at her father's court to inform her that she was to marry King Henry were, naturally, surprise and disbelief. But she did not have any real choice, nor did her father, in agreeing to the marriage. Two weeks later, she left Lorraine for Rheims, where she became queen of France at the magnificent wedding, mass, and public festivities in February 1575. She was then settled at the French court in Paris to fulfill her new roles: as wife to a man she barely knew, queen to an entire state, and daughter-in-law to one of France's most powerful dowager queens.

As the months passed, the difficulty of fulfilling those roles became clear. Catherine de Medici refused to retire or yield to Louise her place as France's first lady, and she attempted to keep Louise and Henry separated in order to minimize Louise's influence over the king. These efforts were largely successful in pushing Louise into the background; even references to "the queen" in chronicles of the time mean the queen-mother, Catherine; Louise is called "the young queen." Louise's new kingdom was also suffering from great unrest. Throughout the 1570s and 1580s, France was in a state of almost constant civil strife as the Wars of Religion divided the state between Catholics and Protestants and threatened Henry's hold on the throne, a violent situation complicated by the intervention of foreign powers.

Louise's marital relationship, which had appeared to be a love match, soon disintegrated as well. It became well known to the court that the royal couple rarely spent time together. King Henry apparently tired of his new wife quickly, perhaps in part due to his mother's efforts to keep them apart; he openly preferred the company of his handsome young courtiers and ladies-in-waiting. He also sought his mother's counsel instead of his wife's on administrative affairs.

Thus Louise, childless, was denied her rightful place: neither a queen, nor a wife, nor a mother of royal heirs, she suffered from a sort of anonymity in the very court which she should have dominated. Yet there was little she could do except tolerate her awkward and humiliating situation, which, according to court chroniclers, she did with considerable grace and forbearance. She divided her days between seeking the leisured company of court ladies and retreating into her religion. Devoutly Catholic, Louise often left the refined atmosphere of the court palaces to perform works of charity among the less fortunate of Paris. She visited hospitals, cared for the sick, patronized charitable foundations, and spent much of her time in prayer.

January 1589 brought the death of Catherine de Medici. Perhaps Louise looked forward to finally taking her place as France's only queen at the center of court. But the death of her mother-in-law was followed only a few months later by the sudden death of her husband. Only 38 years old, Henry III was assassinated in August 1589 by a Catholic extremist angered by his attempts to negotiate a peaceful end to the religious wars. There were no royal heirs, so after a brief struggle with other contenders, Henry's brother-in-law, Henry of Navarre, seized the throne as Henry IV.

The widowed queen, according to witnesses, was devastated by Henry's death, despite their unhappy marriage, and could not be consoled. Although she was given permission by Henry IV and his queen, *Margaret of Valois (1553–1615), to remain in Paris, Louise decided to leave the court for good. She spent the remaining 11 years of her life traveling between convents and residing with relatives across France, continuing her charitable activities wherever she was staying. In December 1600, she became ill and died a month later, at age 47, in the town of Moulins. She was first buried in the Paris cemetery of Saint-Fauberg, but in 1610 she and Henry III were re-interred together in the royal necropolis in the church of Saint-Denis in Paris.

SOURCES:

Bertière, Simone. *Les reines de France au temps de Valois*, vol. 2. Paris: Editions de Fallois, 1994.

Brantôme, Pierre de. *Illustrious Dames of the Court of the Valois Kings*. Trans. by Katharine Prescott Wormeley. NY: Lamb, 1912.

Laura York,
Riverside, California

Louise of Mecklenburg-Gustrow
(1667–1721)

Queen of Denmark and Norway. Name variations: Louise of Mecklenburg-Güstrow. Born on August 28, 1667; died on March 15, 1721; daughter of *Magdalena Sybilla of Holstein-Gottorp (1631–1719) and Gustav Adolf, duke of Mecklenburg-Gustrow; married Frederick IV (1671–1730), king of Denmark and Norway (r. 1699–1730), on December 5, 1695; chil-

dren: Christian (b. 1697); Christian VI (1699–1746), king of Denmark and Norway (r. 1730–1746, who married *Sophia of Bayreuth); Frederick Charles (b. 1701); George (b. 1703); *Charlotte Amalie (1706–1782). Frederick IV had three wives: Louise of Mecklenburg-Gustrow, *Elizabeth Helene Vieregg, and *Anne Sophie Reventlow.

Louise of Mecklenburg-Strelitz
(1776–1810).
See Louise of Prussia.

Louise of Orange-Nassau.
See Louise of Hesse-Cassel (1688–1765).
See Louise of the Netherlands (1828–1871).

Louise of Orleans (1812–1850).
See Carlota (1840–1927) for sidebar on Louise d'Orleans.

Louise of Orleans (1882–1952)

Princess of Orléans. Name variations: Louise de Orléans. Born on February 24, 1882; died in 1952; daughter of *Maria Isabella (1848–1919) and Louis Philippe (1838–1894), count of Paris; married Carlos, prince of Bourbon-Sicily, also known as Charles (1870–1949), prince of the Two Sicilies, on November 16, 1907; children: Karl (b. 1908); Dolores of Bourbon-Sicily (b. 1909); *Maria de las Mercedes (b. 1910); *Maria de la Esperanza (b. 1914), princess of the Two Sicilies (who married Pedro de Alcantra, prince of Grao Para, and was the mother of *Maria da Gloria [1946—]).

Louise of Parma (1802–1857)

Duchess of Savoy. Name variations: Luisa. Born on October 2, 1802; died on March 18, 1857; daughter of *Maria Luisa of Etruria (1782–1824) and Louis de Bourbon, also known as Louis I (1773–1803), duke of Parma (r. 1801–1803); became second wife of Maximilian (1759–1838), duke of Saxony (r. 1830–1838), on November 7, 1825; married Franz, count of Rossi; married Johann von Vimercati, on February 19, 1855. Maximilian's first wife was *Caroline of Parma (1770–1804).

Louise of Prussia (1776–1810)

Queen of Prussia during a time of profound crisis brought on by Napoleonic expansionism, who emerged as a much-revered icon of patriotism, national unity, and steadfastness in adversity. Name variations: Louise of Mecklenburg-Strelitz; Louisa, Luise von Preussen. Pronunciation: Lou-EE-za. Born

*Princess Luise Auguste Wilhelmine Amalie von Mecklenburg-Strelitz on March 10, 1776, in Hanover, Lower Saxony, Germany; died on July 19, 1810, in Hohenzieritz (duchy of Mecklenburg, Germany); buried in Charlottenburg, Berlin, Germany; daughter of Charles II Louis Frederick, hereditary prince (later duke) of Mecklenburg-Strelitz (1741–1816), and Frederica of Hesse-Darmstadt (1752–1782, daughter of Landgrave George of Hesse-Darmstadt); her stepmother was Princess Charlotte of Hesse-Darmstadt (1755–1785); sister of Frederica of Mecklenburg-Strelitz (1778–1841); educated at home by a Swiss governess at her maternal grandmother's court in Darmstadt; married the Prussian crown prince, the future Frederick William III (1770–1840), king of Prussia (r. 1797–1840), on December 24, 1793; children: Frederick William IV (1795–1861), king of Prussia (r. 1840–1861, who married *Elizabeth of Bavaria [1801–1873]); William I also known as Wilhelm I (1797–1888), the future kaiser or emperor of Germany (r. 1871–1888, who married *Augusta of Saxe-Weimar); Frederica (1799–1800); *Charlotte of Prussia (1798–1860, who married Nicholas I, tsar of Russia); Charles (1801–1883, who married *Marie of Saxe-Weimar-Eisenach); ❧▶ Alexandrine of Prussia (1803–1892); Ferdinand (1804–1806); *Louise (1808–1870); Albert (1809–1872, who married *Marianne of the Netherlands); and one other who died in infancy. Frederick William III's second wife was Auguste von Harrach, princess of Leignitz (1800–1873).*

Became queen of Prussia (1797), when her husband succeeded to the throne at the death of his father, King Frederick William II; best known for her dramatic meeting with Napoleon at Tilsit (1807), where she naively attempted to gain milder terms for her country, which had suffered a crushing defeat at the hands of the French; immortalized in traditional German historiography as the royal paradigm of virtuous, devoted, and patriotic Prussian motherhood.

On a chilly November day in 1805, Frederick William III, king of Prussia, and his lovely wife Louise of Prussia met for a dramatic encounter with Tsar Alexander I of Russia. Napoleon had advanced across the Rhine and was marching down the Danube, crushing Austrian resistance along the way. Austria, Russia, and Prussia had just entered into an alliance designed to stop the French juggernaut, and the tsar wanted to pay homage to the memory of Frederick II the Great before returning to St. Petersburg. That evening, Frederick William and Louise met Alexander at Frederick's tomb in the garrison chapel at Potsdam, where they solemnized their

pact. The way lit by smoking candles, Alexander and Louise stepped into the dank crypt, holding hands, while Frederick William waited outside. The tsar then stooped to kiss the coffin of the famous warrior-king and swore never to desert his friends or Prussia. Five years later, deserted by the gallant tsar, Prussia lay prostrate at the feet of imperial France, and the beautiful queen lay dead in her cold marble tomb.

Louise of Prussia was born Princess Luise Auguste Wilhelmine Amalie von Mecklenburg-Strelitz on March 10, 1776, in Hanover, Germany, in the Palais an der Leinestrasse. Both her paternal and maternal family backgrounds were that of the middling German aristocracy. Her father, hereditary Prince Charles II Louis Frederick of Mecklenburg-Strelitz, was the son of Duke Charles of Mecklenburg-Strelitz (1708–1752) and *Elizabeth of Saxe-Hildburghausen. First serving as lieutenant-general in the Hanoverian army, and resident in Darmstadt from 1787 to 1794, in 1794 he succeeded his brother, who had died without male issue, as duke of Mecklenburg-Strelitz. The family had strong dynastic connections to England, for Charles Louis' sister, *Charlotte of Mecklenburg-Strelitz, was the wife of King George III. Louise's mother, ❧▶ Frederica of Hesse-Darmstadt (1752–1782), was the

---

❧▶ **Alexandrine of Prussia** (1803–1892)

Grand Duchess of Mecklenburg-Schwerin. Born on February 23, 1803; died on April 21, 1892; daughter of *Louise of Prussia (1776–1810) and Frederick William III (1770–1840), king of Prussia (r. 1797–1840); married Paul Frederick (b. 1800), grand duke of Mecklenburg-Schwerin; children: Frederick Francis II (b. 1823), grand duke of Mecklenburg; William, duke of Mecklenburg-Schwerin (b. 1827).

❧▶ **Frederica of Hesse-Darmstadt** (1752–1782)

Duchess of Mecklenburg-Strelitz. Name variations: Frederica of Hesse; Frederika of Hesse. Born Frederica Caroline on August 20, 1752; died after the premature birth of her 11th child on May 22, 1782; daughter of imperial lieutenant field marshal Prince George William, landgrave of Hesse-Darmstadt (1722–1782) and *Marie Louise Albertine of Leiningen-Heidesheim (1729–1818); married Charles II (b. 1741), grand duke of Mecklenburg-Strelitz, on September 18, 1768; sister of *Charlotte of Hesse-Darmstadt (1755–1785), who married Charles II after Frederica's death; children: *Charlotte (1769–1818); Theresa (1773–1839); *Louise of Prussia (1776–1810); *Frederica of Mecklenburg-Strelitz (1778–1841); George (1779–1860), grand duke of Mecklenburg-Strelitz); and six others.

daughter of imperial lieutenant field marshal Prince George William of Hesse-Darmstadt (1722–1782) and *Marie Louise Albertine of Leiningen-Heidesheim (1729–1818), frequently referred to by Louise as "Princess George." Frederica died when Louise was six, after the premature birth of her 11th child. Two years after Frederica's death, Louise's father married his first wife's younger sister, Princess **Charlotte of Hesse-Darmstadt** (1755–1785). That marriage was also of short duration, for Louise's stepmother died a week before Christmas, just one year later, and young Louise was sent off to Darmstadt to live with her maternal grandmother Princess George in the "Old Palace" of that Hessian town.

A warm family atmosphere reigned at Princess George's, and with grandmother's relatively modest financial situation, the household was simple by prevailing noble standards. By all accounts, Louise enjoyed a happy childhood after the deaths of her mother and stepmother. She was a cheerful and lively girl, which earned her the nickname *Jungfer Husch,* or "Little-Miss-in-a-Hurry." Louise had five siblings: two elder sisters, ◄ Charlotte (1769–1818) and Theresa (1773–1839); one younger sister, *Frederica of Mecklenburg-Strelitz (1778–1814); one younger brother, George (1779–1860); and one half-brother Charles (1785–1837), the son of her stepmother. Initially living in Darmstadt with her sisters, in 1787 Louise was joined by her brothers who arrived from Hanover.

Little emphasis was placed on Louise's education, and she and her sisters were given a Swiss governess, one Demoiselle **Suzanne de Gélieu** from Neuchâtel. While French—the universal language of the aristocracy and of diplomacy—was the language of instruction, and polite French manners were cultivated, as was common at all 18th-century European courts, private conversations were often held in the regional German dialect. Thus, much of Louise's correspondence is in rather old-fashioned French with frequent spelling errors, and she often mixed French and German. French language instruction aside, the curriculum also included some history, geography, and English. Louise was a quite average, perhaps not overly diligent student, whose sense of her own faults is revealed in at least one self-deprecating copybook entry: "Contents hastily scribbled on April, 22, age 13: Oh shame of shames! 1789." Other copybooks contain little drawings and doodles, and sometimes Louise was sent to bed without dessert, as punishment for not having studied hard enough.

Later, as queen, she was to realize her lack of formal education, especially in history, and make plans for a course of self-improvement. This included the establishment of an informal literary circle, and readings of Schiller, Goethe, Herder, Wieland, Jean Paul, Robertson, Gibbon, and Hume. Still, she never became anything close to "intellectual." Conversely, her education in the Protestant faith figured prominently, and early on she developed a deep, simple trust in God, as evident in her religion copybooks. Indeed, religion provided her with important moral support for the rest of her days.

Life in Darmstadt was pleasant, and punctuated by occasional excursions to noble relatives scattered about Germany, or a ten-day trip to the Netherlands in the summer of 1791—described by Louise in a 34-page diary kept in French—with her grandmother and sister Frederica. In July 1792, Louise and Frederica, properly accompanied by their governess, also traveled to Frankfurt to witness the coronation of Holy Roman Emperor Francis II. The formal ball was held at the residence of the Austrian ambassador, Prince Esterhazy, and Count Metternich—later the Austrian chancellor and master of congress diplomacy—chose none other than Louise, an attractive young lady and a fine waltz partner, for the opening dance. But in early October, soon after the battle of Valmy, in which the French revolutionary forces turned the tide against the First Coalition, Louise and her family fled Darmstadt in the face of advancing French troops. They moved to Hildburghausen, in Thuringia, to the home of her sister Charlotte, who, in 1785, had married Frederick, duke of Saxe-Hildburghausen. Charlotte patronized the arts and sang well—the family called her *Singe-Lotte*—and thus concerts, dances, and gay masquerades brightened Louise's stay at Hildburghausen. Soon joined by her father, Louise remained there for six months. In March 1793, she returned to Darmstadt.

Louise first met her future husband in Frankfurt on March 14, 1793. The Prussian

❧► **Charlotte** (1769–1818)

*Duchess of Saxe-Hildburghausen. Born in 1769; died in 1818; daughter of Charles II Louis Frederick, duke of Mecklenburg-Strelitz, and *Frederica of Hesse-Darmstadt; sister of *Louise of Prussia (1776–1810); married Frederick, duke of Saxe-Hildburghausen, in 1785; children: *Catherine Charlotte of Hildburghausen (1787–1847).*

king Frederick William II was seeking suitable wives for his two eldest sons, Crown Prince Frederick William and Prince Louis. On the 18th, Frederick William II formally requested the hands of Princess George's granddaughters for his sons. While the crown prince initially had difficulties choosing between Louise and her equally attractive younger sister, the couple was officially engaged on April 24. Prince Louis was matched with Frederica. True to aristocratic fashion, the formalities were left in the hands of an accomplished diplomat and confidant of the king, the marquis Girolamo Lucchesini. But Frederick William's service in the Prussian army, fighting in the coalition against revolutionary France, and court etiquette made it hard for the young couple to get to know each other, though the crown prince visited Louise in Darmstadt as often as he could. In fact, between betrothal and marriage, Louise had to let her grandmother read all letters addressed to her fiancé, to ensure their propriety. To circumvent this censorship, Louise slyly added candid postscripts.

Louise was certainly an attractive wife-to-be. She was soon renowned for her beauty, and her physical attributes were described in minute detail by the famous period painter, Madame *Elisabeth Vigée-Le Brun. Louise was often compared to a Greek statue, and *Germaine de Staël, who met her in Berlin in 1804, was also struck by her comeliness. Louise was, in fact, attentive to her personal appearance, used cosmetics to good effect, and knew how to clothe herself with elegance. Yet many contemporaries stressed that her beauty came from within. Frederick William's memoirs describe a sweet-voiced, cheerful, humorous, often playful personality. But she had her little faults. Not very imbued with the Prussian spirit of order in daily life, she often slept till noon, was unpunctual, and ate between meals—giving rise to occasional disputes with her husband. And she appears not to have been immune to handsome and dignified men, her own letters indicating that she could be impressed by flattery. Her most celebrated virtue, however—fortitude in adversity—was not to be tested for some years. Louise's own writings indicate that she saw herself primarily as wife, parent, and mother of her people.

She had charisma . . . and her life-story was marked by the characteristic elements of brilliance, gloom, tragedy, even sentimentality. Her early death, interpreted by the populace as a personal sacrifice for the fatherland, completed the creation of a legend.

—S. Fischer-Fabian

On December 13, 1793, the young bride-to-be departed for Berlin. With her pleasant demeanor, natural charm, and beauty, she virtually came, saw, and took her subjects' hearts by storm. Draped in the fashionable "Directoire-style" gowns inspired by Greek antiquity, both revealing and flattering her gracious figure, she frequently flaunted the stiff court etiquette, e.g. choosing her own partner at masked balls. Both she and her fiancé even used publicly the informal German form of address, the *Du*. One famous episode recounts her bending down to pick up a little girl, sent to declaim a poem in her honor, and kissing her. "From that moment on," Heinrich Hartmann asserts, "everyone knew that Louise would not only be the Queen, but also the Mother of her people and fatherland."

The official reception was held in Potsdam on the 21st, the wedding on Christmas Eve. The match was something of a contemporary sensation, since the spouses-to-be really did love each other, while, in their social caste, marriages were typically arranged purely for reasons of dynastic union. **Constance Wright** described Louise's husband as "intelligent in practical affairs, kind-hearted, conscientious, upright and hardworking. He detested luxury and prided himself on his reserve." True to his thrifty middle-class character, Frederick William had asked his father to donate to the poor the money previously earmarked for the illumination of Berlin in honor of the wedding. After the ceremonies, the young couple immediately moved into the relatively simple Kronprinzenpalais, as Louise's husband considered the Berlin Palace too ostentatious. With his reserve and her vivaciousness, most sources agree they complemented each other nicely.

Unfortunately, their six-week honeymoon was soon rudely interrupted by the call to duty. Frederick William had to join the Prussian troops intervening to preserve order in Poland after the Second Partition, and Louise followed his movements on a map she had hung in her room. His letters written during the campaign reveal a sensitive nature and sympathy for the plight of the common soldier, especially the wounded. Louise shared this empathy for the situation of the unfortunate, and was later known by her subjects for her caring attitude. The campaign, however, was not successful—her husband complained of a miserable war and insufficient logistics—and Prussia withdrew by September 1794.

Until the death of the king in 1797, Louise and her husband lived mostly in privacy. In 1794, their first child, a premature daughter, was delivered dead at birth, for Louise had previously fallen down the stairs. In 1795 and 1797, Frederick William (later the crown prince, known as "Fritz") and Wilhelm (the future kaiser) were born, and seven more pregnancies were to follow. Of ten children, three failed to survive infancy. Still, Frederick William noted that her pregnancies tended to be happy ones, and after each delivery she seemed to emerge physically fresh and rejuvenated. The children were, of course, largely brought up by a succession of governors and governesses, but both parents always took a keen interest in their education, monitoring the work of the tutors closely. Particular attention was paid to the education of the eldest son, as future successor, and Johan Peter Ancillon, noted historian and member of the Berlin Academy, was ultimately chosen by Louise to oversee his instruction. Just as Louise was a tender and loving mother, Frederick William was a caring and affectionate father, a genuine family man—quite a rarity among Hohenzollern monarchs. Louise loved to horse around with the children on the floor, showing them how to do somersaults, and on Christmas, which was always spent alone with the family, only Frederick William was permitted to light the tree. Indeed, with his thrift and her cheer, they soon became the model of a happy, middle-class family.

Frederick William was excluded from affairs of state, and after Prussia concluded peace with France, at Basel (April 5, 1795), his duties were of a routine military nature, involving regular spring troop maneuvers, the inspection of fortifications, and the like. The family's domestic routine was enlivened by occasional summer sojourns at the Oranienburg Palace, or visits with Louise's father and grandmother. One of their favorite residences was the modest country seat Frederick William had built in 1795 at Paretz, near Potsdam, on the Havel River. Here they could escape the ostentation of Berlin, go for picnics and boat-outings, and visit the summer house on Peacock Island. S. Fischer-Fabian painted an idyllic picture of a couple "seen strolling arm in arm at the zoo, riding through the biting dust of troop reviews, traveling in their coach on arduous excursions to the most distant of provinces, and on jaunts with the children. They became the ideal of harmonious family life. In fact, it became fashionable to emulate them." But such private bliss could not last forever, for on November 16, 1797, the king died, and Louise's husband mounted the throne of the Hohenzollerns as Frederick William III.

Soon after Frederick William's accession, it became clear that his reign would be marked by a dramatic departure from the domestic policies of his father. First, he announced that the king

Louise of Prussia visiting the poor.

would live on the income of the crown prince, and he and his wife would continue their residence in the modest Kronprinzenpalais. This was not just a simple reflection of Frederick William's thrifty middle-class character—as for example his short hair style and bourgeois trousers—but almost a fiscal necessity, given Prussia's deep debt, the financial legacy of both the last war and unsound budgetary policies. To get a better picture of the precise state of his realm, he embarked on an official five-week fact-finding mission through the provinces, accompanied by Louise, as she was to do frequently throughout his reign. Convinced on various counts that profound reforms were in order, Frederick William proceeded first to abolish serfdom on crown estates, reform tariffs and taxation, and promote religious toleration. In addition, several committees were set up to consider other social and military reforms.

In foreign affairs, Prussia remained largely on the sidelines of the coalition wars being fought by the monarchies against Napoleonic France. In the Treaty of Basel, his father had recognized the French occupation of the west bank of the Rhine and been promised compensation through the later secularization of ecclesiastical territory to the east of that river. Finally, Prussia had declared its neutrality in the conflict, a successful policy until 1805.

For Louise, these first years of her husband's reign were fairly uneventful. She traveled throughout the realm with Frederick William, sometimes reviewing troops at his side; periodically visited her father, or other friends and relatives; and went to Bad Pyrmont, a famous spa near Hanover, to take the waters. A high point of this period was Louise's meeting with Tsar Alexander I in Memel, in June 1802. Much impressed with his personality, which she considered very humane and kindhearted (during the meeting, she was ill for a time, and he often sat by her bedside), she began an enthusiastic correspondence that lasted for years. Indeed, during the later war with France, she was to put all her faith in his aid, calling him "Our saviour, our support, our hope." Yet by 1808, her rather naive image of Alexander as a staunch ally of Prussia was to be cruelly shattered.

The last five years of Louise's life were dominated by the deep crisis of the Prussian monarchy. On May 18, 1804, Napoleon, the "vomit from hell"—as she once called him—crowned himself emperor of the French and embarked on an aggressive foreign policy. While another Franco-Prussian treaty (June 1, 1804) recon-

firmed the neutrality of northern Germany, by September 1805, France had violated Ansbach, an important holding of the Hohenzollern family. From this point on, Louise began to take greater interest in politics and worked hard to boost her husband's fragile self-confidence during these trying times. She also increasingly took the side of the opposition in Berlin against foreign minister Christian von Haugwitz's francophile foreign policy—indeed, as Hans-Joachim Schoeps notes, she became the central figure among the dissatisfied patriots. But Prussia needed allies, and on November 3, 1805, signed the Treaty of Potsdam with Austria and Russia, pledging first to mediate with France on behalf of the Third Coalition, but also to enter the war with 180,000 troops if Napoleon refused its good offices. The treaty was soon a dead letter, however, for by December 2, Napoleon had occupied Vienna and defeated the combined Russo-Austrian armies at Austerlitz.

Meanwhile, French diplomatic pressure on Prussia was increasing. On December 15, 1805, Napoleon and Prussian envoy Haugwitz signed the Treaty of Schönbrunn: Prussia was to obtain the electorate of Hanover, affiliated with Britain, in exchange for Ansbach, Cleves, and Neuchâtel, and the two nations were to join in an offensive-defensive alliance mutually guaranteeing each other's territory. Louise pleaded with Frederick William not to ratify the treaty, and her popularity with the army soared. "It had become a cult," explains Wright, and "Louise had become the army's *alma dea,* as truly a patriotic symbol as the brazen Goddess of Victory riding in her chariot atop the Brandenburg Gate." By February 15, 1806, France had imposed on Prussia the so-called *Pariser Traktat,* forcing the country to join the Continental System, an economic embargo against Britain. Frederick William reluctantly signed, though Louise had tried to sway him not to, and Britain—already furious over the loss of Hanover—declared war on Prussia on June 11. Prussia's foreign policy had become deeply divided, for the francophobe minister, Karl August von Hardenberg, secretly began approaching Russia, while Haugwitz, again the dominant minister in Berlin, continued a pro-French policy.

On April 1, Prussia commenced with the annexation of Hanover. But Napoleon reversed himself on August 9, promising Hanover to England, and Hardenberg's policy thus gained the upper hand. Louise fully supported the resulting Prussian mobilization, becoming the symbol of national fortitude and resistance against Napoleonic aggression, especially given the weakness and vacillation of her husband. An imprudent Prussian ultimatum, delivered on September 26, insisted that France withdraw behind the Rhine in two weeks. Napoleon, hardly to be deterred by such a rash demand, and well aware of the disarray of the Prussian army, struck with lightning speed. In less than a week, the conflict was virtually decided at the battle of Jena-Auerstädt (October 14, 1806), in which 123,000 French inflicted 38,000 casualties on 116,500 Prussians, themselves only losing 12,000. Louise received news of the defeat on the 17th, in a famous dispatch written by the adjutant-general of the king, Colonel Joachim von Kleist: "The king lives—the battle is lost!" Frederick William offered peace, but Napoleon refused, wishing to march on Berlin, whereupon Frederick William decided to side with Russia and continue the struggle. But to no avail: on October 27, Napoleon entered Berlin, and by November 7, the last significant Prussian army had surrendered.

At the Convention of Charlottenburg (November 16, 1806), Napoleon proposed a harsh armistice: French forces would occupy Prussia between the Oder and the Vistula rivers, the Vistula fortresses would surrender and the remaining Prussian troops be disbanded. Frederick William refused ratification and decided to fight on, prompting Napoleon to continue his advance. The royal family was forced to flee ever eastward so as not to fall into French hands. By mid-December, Louise had been sick with typhus or typhoid for almost three weeks. Still weak and convalescing, she was forced to make the brutal winter trip from Königsberg to Memel—a small town of 6,000 in the northeast extremity of the realm—along the Nehrung, a narrow strip of land bordered by the sea and a large lake. And yet the playwright and author Heinrich von Kleist could write his half-sister **Ulrike von Kleist** from Königsberg, shortly before the royal family's flight:

> I cannot think of our Queen without being deeply moved. In this war . . . she has gained more than she could from a lifetime of peace and happiness. She has developed a truly royal character. She has grasped all the implications of this hour. She, who a short time ago had nothing better to do than to amuse herself with dancing or riding horseback, has gathered about her all the able men whom the King neglects and from whom our salvation must come. Yes, it is she who holds us together.

At Preussisch-Eylau on February 7–8, 1807, under savage winter conditions, Russo-Prussian forces finally demonstrated that the French

could be stopped, though all participants incurred heavy losses. After the battle, Louise was approached by French General Bertrand, who hoped she might persuade Frederick William to make peace. Louise instead urged Hardenberg—the new chief minister since April, to her great joy—to stand fast against Napoleon. Frederick William decided he would have to consult with Tsar Alexander first. Meanwhile, the Russian army commanded by General Bennigsen—whose dismissal Louise had already recommended after Preussisch-Eylau—was decisively defeated at the Battle of Friedland (near Königsberg, on June 14, 1807), and Memel was soon flooded with refugees and wounded Russian soldiers, whom Louise characteristically made it her duty to help care for. Alexander subsequently broke the Bartenstein Convention—a recent renewal of the Treaty of Potsdam—by signing a separate peace with France on June 21. This was clearly a betrayal of Prussia, which was now forced to beg for an armistice. Louise was directly involved in the negotiations that followed at Tilsit.

On June 25, 1807, Napoleon met Alexander alone for discussions on a raft in the Memel River, laying out his plan for the dismantling of Prussia and the division of the Continent into

ℒouise of
𝒫russia

French and Russian spheres of influence. All three monarchs met on June 26, and agreed to a Franco-Prussian cease-fire. Frederick William had written Louise of his first meeting with Napoleon, noting the emperor's disapproval of Prussian policy, specifically that of Hardenberg. On June 30, he sent a letter requesting her presence at Tilsit, with the hope she might have a moderating effect on Napoleon's demands.

Louise arrived on July 4. She was three months pregnant, still convalescing from another bout of typhoid, and worried about the health of an ill child she had left at home. Her only hope was that her beauty and personal charm might somehow sway the little Frenchman. According to Hartmann, the sole notion that the queen might be able to influence Napoleon favorably indicated the political bankruptcy of Frederick William's advisers. Indeed, most recent historians agree that Napoleon never intended any serious diplomatic discussion with Louise at Tilsit. The meeting on July 6 was in fact a stage-managed show of public gallantry designed to give the lie to the slanderous comments of the French bulletins that had been issued after Jena, in which Napoleon portrayed Louise as a meddlesome, war-mongering queen, whom he admonished to return to her proper sphere of home, family, and female toiletries. Napoleon said as much to Count Goltz, Prussian ambassador in St. Petersburg, on the morning of July 7.

> I just made polite small-talk with the queen, obliging me to nothing, for I am firmly decided to give the King of Prussia the Elbe as his western border. There will be no further negotiations, for I have already arranged everything with the Emperor Alexander. . . . The [Prussian] King owes his position exclusively to the chivalric devotion of that monarch, without whose intercession my brother Jérôme would be King of Prussia, and the current dynasty turned out.

Though Louise's impact on the actual conditions were nil, she came away impressed with Napoleon's personality—as he did of hers. After Tilsit, she no longer heaped him with epithets of hate, and he stopped his personal attacks on her.

The terms of the Treaty of Tilsit, signed on July 9, 1807, devastated Prussia. The nation lost over half its territory—everything west of the Elbe and virtually all of Prussian Poland—and some five million inhabitants; it was occupied, saddled with an indemnity and forced to adhere to the Continental System against Britain; its army was capped at 42,000. The Treaty of Königsberg, signed three days later, stipulated that France would withdraw its occupation force from Prussia once the war contribution (subsequently set at 120 million francs) was paid in full. Prussia had left the ranks of the great powers.

On July 10, Frederick William and Louise returned to Memel. Rumors were already going around Berlin that the king had abdicated. At this juncture, Freiherr Karl vom und zum Stein succeeded Hardenberg as chief minister. Stein's historical mandate was to be a thorough overhaul of the Prussian state (completed by Hardenberg), but his immediate attention was devoted to the task of dealing with the punitive French demands. James Sheehan contends that the appointment, on Louise's advice, of a man as difficult as Stein, provided strong evidence of Prussia's predicament. Yet another measure of Prussian desperation was Louise's suggestion, in November, that she seek an interview with Napoleon in Paris, in another attempt at obtaining a reduction of the stupendous indemnity. Frederick William rejected the idea, sending other emissaries on the fruitless mission.

By January 15, 1808, the royal family could finally return to Königsberg, the French troops having evacuated western and eastern Prussia to the Vistula, following the partial Prussian fulfillment of the peace terms. Louise somehow managed to resume her program of self-education, devoting particular attention to historical studies. In Memel, she had already begun reading manuscript copies of the patriotic historian Johann Wilhelm Süvern's lectures on Greek and Roman history, held at the University of Königsberg. Through him, she also heard of the pedagogue Johann Pestalozzi and later helped found a Pestalozzi school in Königsberg.

The remaining two and a half years of Louise's life were overshadowed by heroic Prussian efforts to meet the exorbitant French pecuniary demands; the beginnings of a second round of domestic reforms designed, ultimately, to enable Prussia to return to the fold of the major powers; and intermittent attempts at organizing resistance against France. Thus, she supported chief minister Stein in his policy—against the opposition of Frederick William—of covertly preparing an insurgency against France while outwardly trying to meet Napoleon's demands. But Stein's plans were revealed to Napoleon in a captured letter, and by November 24, the emperor had forced Frederick William to dismiss the minister.

So Louise repeatedly pinned her hopes on Alexander, who had stayed in Königsberg for a few days while en route to a French-sponsored congress of European powers. The tsar promised to intercede with Napoleon on behalf of Prussia. Yet at the Congress of Erfurt (September 27–October 14, 1808), he only succeeded at inducing Napoleon to reduce the Prussian contribution by a paltry 20 million francs—with a slightly extended payment deadline—while French troops were to evacuate Prussian territory by December 3. On his way home, Alexander again stayed with the Prussian royal family, explaining his tactic of lulling Napoleon into the belief that he, Alexander, desired a rapprochement with France, thus buying time to strengthen Russian forces. Finally, he extended to Louise and Frederick William a gracious invitation to St. Petersburg.

On December 27, the party departed from Königsberg, arriving at their destination on January 7, 1809. At St. Petersburg, they were lavishly fêted, as pageants succeeded balls in a seemingly never-ending series, and the ladies were presented with elegant new Russian costumes. At the betrothal ceremony of Alexander's sister *Catherine of Russia, a vast ice palace was even constructed on the Narva River. But amid all this pomp and splendor, Louise failed to get the aid she desperately wanted from Alexander, finally realizing that no real help was to be expected from that quarter. By January 20, Louise and her family were back in Königsberg.

Prussia was becoming increasingly hard-pressed to make the payments demanded by France. The national debt had virtually doubled since before Jena, rising from 55 million to 100 million talers. The cession of Silesia was even being considered, but Louise sided with Finance Minister Hardenberg against this option. Meanwhile, Napoleon let it be known that further negotiations with the Prussian king could only be considered if he returned to the capital, where he belonged. Thus, after three years of internal exile, in December 1809, Frederick William took his court back to Berlin. The festive entry took place on the 23rd, in the midst of throngs of subjects joyfully greeting the royal couple at the approaches to the town.

The years of crisis had clearly sapped Louise's physical and psychological strength, and she was not destined to enjoy the surroundings of the early years of her reign for long. In late 1809, she should have gone to Bad Pyrmont for a cure, yet the budget would not permit it. Events had long prevented her from even visiting her beloved father, but on June 25, 1810, she finally accepted his invitation and left Charlottenburg for Neustrelitz. On the 30th, a planned family excursion was called off because Louise felt ill. During the next days, she was plagued by headaches, fever, an unremitting cough, and chest pains that would not subside. At first, her doctors were not overly concerned, for she had been bled and the fever had come down somewhat. Not until July 16 was the illness really taken seriously, for severe chest cramps had set in, and Frederick William was sent for on the 18th. He immediately dashed off from Sans Souci palace, accompanied by his sons Fritz and Wilhelm. Louise died around nine o'clock on the morning of the 19th, surrounded by most of her family and a few intimate friends. While the autopsy appears to have indicated pneumonia, legend soon had it that Louise had died of a broken heart at the fate of her beloved Prussia. She was interred in a mausoleum at Charlottenburg on December 23, 1810, the anniversary of her arrival in Berlin as a bride and her return there from exile. The tomb is decorated with an elegant recumbent statue by Christian Daniel Rauch, a protégé whom she had sent to the Berlin Art Academy.

As a central figure in Prussian and German national historical tradition, Louise of Prussia was very much idealized by both contemporaries and historians until as late as 1945, and popular or conservative-nationalist biographies continue in that vein. When she appeared in public during the preparations for the disastrous campaign of 1806, Fischer-Fabian writes, her subjects "perceived that this woman was the only man within the upper echelons of Prussian government." The same author titled a chapter introducing Frederick William III, "The Husband of Queen Louise." Hartmut Boockmann tells us that many German children grew up with an image of Louise, with her sons Frederick William IV and Wilhelm I, hung up in the family home. In 1943, when Griewank published an otherwise professionally edited collection of her letters, he attempted to draw a historical parallel between Prussia under the Napoleonic threat and the beleaguered Third Reich, introducing Louise as the quintessentially German woman and evoking her fortitude in misfortune.

Much of the patriotic myth surrounding Louise in historical writing can be attributed to the uncritical reception of an ostensible letter to her father, supposedly dated Königsberg, April 1808, containing her so-called "political manifesto." Serious recent scholars such as Hartmann—whose work must rank as the standard biography of Louise—and Countess **Malve Rothkirch**, have demonstrated the spurious nature of this most famous letter. Thus, while Louise was largely forgotten after the defeat of Germany in 1945, recent scholarly biographers have all aimed at penetrating the myth to get to the real woman, to demystify while continuing to honor where honor is due, and to deepen the human dimension of a fascinating figure whose charm still reaches out over the centuries.

SOURCES:

Backs, Silvia. "Luise, Königin von Preussen." Historische Kommission bei der bayrischen Akademie der Wissenschaften (Hg.) *Neue Deutsche Biographie*. Vol. 15. Berlin: Duncker & Humblot, 1987.

Emsley, Clive. *The Longman Companion to Napoleonic Europe*. London: Longman, 1993.

Fischer-Fabian, S. *Preussens Krieg und Frieden. Der Weg ins Deutsche Reich*. München: Droemer Knaur, 1981.

Friedrich Wilhelm III. *Vom Leben und Sterben der Königin Luise. Eigenhändige Aufzeichnungen ihres Gemahls König Friedrich Wilhelms III*. ed. Heinrich Otto Meisner. Berlin and Leipzig: K.F. Koehler, 1926.

Hartmann, Heinrich. *Luise, Königin von Preussen*. Moers: Steiger, 1981.

———. *Luise, Preussen's grosse Königin*. 2nd ed. Berg: Türmer Verlag, 1985.

Koch, Hansjoachim W. *A History of Prussia*. NY: Longman, 1978.

Luise, Königin von Preussen. *Briefe und Aufzeichnungen 1786–1810. Mit einer Einleitung von Hartmut Boockmann*. Edited by Malve Gräfin Rothkirch. München: Deutscher Kunstverlag, 1985.

Schoeps, Hans-Joachim. *Preussen. Geschichte eines Staates*. 8th ed. Berlin: Propyläen Verlag, 1968.

Sheehan, James J. *German History, 1770–1866*. Oxford: Clarendon Press, 1989.

Taack, Merete van. *Königin Luise. Eine Biographie*. 2nd ed. Tübingen: Rainer Wunderlich Verlag, 1978.

Taddey, Gerhard, ed. *Lexikon der deutschen Geschichte*. 2nd ed. Stuttgart: Alfred Kröner Verlag, 1983.

Wright, Constance. *Louise, Queen of Prussia: A Biography*. London: Frederick Muller, 1969.

SUGGESTED READING:

Adami, Friedrich. *Luise, Königin von Preussen*. Berlin: Dümmler, 1876.

Aretz, Gertrude Kuntze-Dolton. *Queen Louise of Prussia, 1776–1810*. Translated from the German of Gertrude Aretz by Ruth Putman. New York, London: Putnam, 1929.

Bailleu, Paul. *Königin Luise: ein Lebensbild*. Berlin-Leipzig: Giesecke & Devrient, 1908.

Federmann, Hertha. *Königin Luise im Spiegel ihrer Briefe*. Berlin: Schlieffen-Verlag, 1939.

Flocken, Jan von. *Luise: Eine Königin in Preussen*. Berlin: Neues Leben, 1989.

Hartig, Paul (Hrg.). *Prinzessin Luise von Mecklenburg-Strelitz: Die Reise an den Niederrhein und nach Holland 1791*. München: Deutscher Kunstverlag, n.d.

Horn, Georg. *Das Buch von der Königin Luise*. Berlin: G. Grote, 1913.

Ladiges, Therese Monika von. *Königin Luise*. Lübeck: Coleman, 1934.

Luise, Königin von Preussen. *Briefwechsel der Königin Luise mit ihrem Gemahl Friedrich Wilhelm III: 1793–1810*. Leipzig: Koehler, 1929.

———. *Briefwechsel König Friedrich Wilhelm III und der Königin Luise mit Kaiser Alexander I. nebst ergänzenden fürstlichen Korrespondenzen*. Leipzig: Hirzel, 1900.

Ohff, Heinz. *Ein Stern in Wetterwolken. Königin Luise von Preussen*. Piper: München, Zürich, 1989.

Rautenberg, Carl Ludwig. *Das Leben der Königin von Preussen, Luise Auguste Wilhelmine Amalie*. Leer: Gerhard Rautenberg, 1977.

Scherer, Stephan P. "Alexander I, the Prussian Royal Couple, and European Politics: 1801–1807," in letter to his sister Ulrike, Heinrich [von] Kleist writes in *Michigan Academician*. Vol. 13, no. 1, 1980, pp. 37–44.

Schroeder, Paul. *The Transformation of European Politics, 1763–1848*. Oxford: Clarendon Press, 1994.

Seidel, Ina. *Luise, Königin von Preussen: ein Bericht über ihr Leben*. Königstein: Langewiese, 1934.

Stamm-Kuhlmann, Thomas. *König in Preussens grosser Zeit, Friedrich Wilhelm III, der Melancholiker auf dem Thron*. Berlin: Siedler, 1992.

Treue, Wilhelm. "Preussen im Spiegel neuer Biographien. Nachlese zum 'Preussen-Jahr' 1981," in *Jahrbuch für die Geschichte Mittel und Ostdeutschlands, 1984*. Vol. 33, pp. 139–157.

COLLECTIONS:

Main archival collections, in Germany, of papers relative to Louise of Prussia: Geheimes Staatsarchiv Berlin-Dahlem; Geheimes Staatsarchiv Preussischer Kulturbesitz, Abteilung Merseburg (previously Zentrales Staatsarchiv der DDR in Merseburg); Bundesarchiv in Koblenz; Hessisches Staatsarchiv in Darmstadt; Fürst Thurn und Taxis Zentralarchiv in Regensburg.

William L. Chew III,
Professor of History, Vesalius College,
Vrije Universiteit Brussel, Brussels, Belgium

Louise of Savoy (1476–1531)

Duchess of Angoulême, mother of King Francis I, and regent of France who negotiated, with Margaret of Austria, the Peace of Cambrai. Name variations: Louise de Savoie. Regent of France (1515–1516, 1525–1526); born September 11, 1476, in the Châteaux de Pont-d'Ain in Savoy, now southwest France; died on September 22, 1531, at Grez-sur-Loing, south of Fontainebleau, France; buried on October 19, 1531, at Saint-Denis, Paris, beside the kings and queens of France, following her funeral at Notre-Dame de Paris on October 13, 1531; daughter of Philip II, count of Bresse, later duke of Savoy (d. 1497) and Margaret of Bourbon (d. 1483); married Charles of Orleans (1460–1496), count of Angoulême, on February 16, 1488, in the Châtelet at Paris; children: Margaret of Angoulême (1492–1549), queen of Navarre (r. 1527–1549); Francis I (1494–1547), king of France (r. 1515–1547).

Regent of France (June 1515–January 1516, and February 1525–July 1526); negotiated, with Margaret of Austria, the Peace of Cambrai, known as the "Ladies Peace" (1529); after the king's return to France, continued to serve as his chief adviser until her death (1531).

Louise of Savoy was a resolute, hardheaded, practical woman who rightly deserves to be remembered as a successful regent of France. The completion of the Peace of Cambrai in 1529, after weeks of patient negotiation with *Margaret of Austria (1480–1530), provided a fitting end to her career. Throughout her life, she had sought to solve disputes by peaceful means, preferring to compromise and negotiate rather than to resort to arms and the weapons of war. Born in relative obscurity in her father's castle in Savoy, she became, via a marriage of convenience and a course of events that could not have been foreseen, the mother of a king of France who had such confidence in her ability and loyalty as to leave his country in her hands while he sought to increase his position and power by fighting in Italy. Even after his eventual return in 1526, she remained at his side as his chief adviser, her name still appeared on Letters Patent and State Acts, and she continued to treat on his behalf with the ambassadors of other European powers. Reports which survive from these courts bear witness to her success and reflect the respect she commanded and the high regard in which she was held. Her childhood experiences in the household of her aunt, the formidable *Anne of Beaujeu (c. 1460–1522), taught her to keep her own counsel and to be ever watchful. She learned to hide her true feelings with a docile expression and a smile. It was excellent training for a woman who was to become a major player on the diplomatic stage of the early 16th century. Anne's advice to "never waste force on what you can achieve by guile" was taken to heart. The new art of diplomacy developed in the 16th century was tailor-made for Louise.

Although a devoted mother to both her children, it was her son, Francis (I), who was the mainspring of her life. He was her obsession; all her efforts were for him. He was at one and the same time her child and her master. She wrote of him as "my king, my lord, my Caesar, my son." From his birth, she dedicated her life to him and to preparing him for kingship.

No one challenged Louise in her position as regent. Her influence over Francis was acknowledged, accepted by all, resented by many. However, all the evidence indicates that her ambition was selfless and that, as regent, she gained and retained the confidence of many of the prominent men in France. Her endeavors were always for Francis and for his rights as king. She never took any decision or implemented any action without first consulting him and obtaining his consent, even when he was imprisoned in Spain

and it meant a delay of several weeks. This was a ploy that could be used to effect if necessary, since he rarely contradicted her.

Louise of Savoy's critics have sought to denigrate her achievements with accusations of avarice and immorality. She was certainly careful with her income and practiced economy in her expenditure, but her money was always at the disposal of her son. At her death, the money for her funeral had to come from Francis as she herself had none. As for charges of immorality, the obsession that she had for her son was overwhelming and would have left little room for a lover; even her daughter *Margaret of Angoulême stood a very poor second in Louise's list of priorities. The letters of this same daughter, whose reputation for integrity was renowned, are a better guide to Louise's conduct during and after the regency years than are the carping writings of Louise's discontented male contemporaries.

It is true, however, that little is known of her private life. The demands of her role were such

Louise of Savoy

that there was little time for her to indulge in contemplation or to express her thoughts in anything other than letters of official business. Her journal and a small collection of poems are exceptions. The former is a curious document compiled and completed by herself in 1522 from jottings she had made during earlier years. It is in no way a diary but rather a record of those events which she regarded as important. Louise was, as were many of her contemporaries, very superstitious and stated that the journal was to be used for astrological prognostications. Thus it records not only the date but the hour and minute these events occurred. The journal is, for the same reason, arranged monthly rather than chronologically, recalling all the events that took place in a particular month irrespective of the year, for example, in January her husband died (1496) and her son succeeded to the throne of France (1515). The events selected for the journal relate to herself, to her family, or to prominent persons whose fortunes were pertinent to Francis' success. There is very little about herself, except for her illnesses, and nothing at all about her daughter. Since it ends in 1522, there is no record by Louise herself of her thoughts and feelings during her second regency, or of the much debated Bourbon scandal or of the Semblançay affair. It does, however, bear witness to the depth of her affection for Francis and her hopes and fears for him.

Louise was well-educated, with a particular interest in books and learning, and took as her motto *libris et liberis* (for books and for children). She was a pious woman with orthodox religious beliefs, who was offended by outrages against holy shrines and relics. She had some sympathy for those who looked for reforms within the church, but she could never support any changes that might have undermined her son's authority as the absolute monarch.

The strain of official duties took its toll on her health, for, if Francis was happy and all was well, then so was Louise, but if he was ill or in trouble, she fell ill, often seriously. Throughout her life, she suffered from gout and allied kidney disorders which were to cause her death at the age of 55 years, but she never let her illnesses prevent her from serving her king and country or caring for her son and his children.

Louise of Savoy was born on September 11, 1476, in a gloomy castle in Pont-d'Ain in Savoy. She recorded the event in her own words: "I am informed . . . that I was born at Pont-d'Ain on 11 September 1476 five hours and 24 minutes after noon." She was the first child born of Philip II, count of Bresse, and *Margaret of Bourbon. Philip was a younger son of the House of Savoy; his parents were Louis of Savoy and ❧▸ Anne of Lusignan. Although Savoy was a vast and splendid duchy, Philip had no lands of his own and had had to fend for himself. He had become a cruel, greedy, and often violent man. He was frequently away from home on business or, more probably, indulging himself in his favorite pastimes of women and sport. He succeeded to the dukedom of Savoy in 1496 and died a year later. Margaret of Bourbon, Louise's mother, was sister to Pierre de Beaujeu, who was married to Anne of Beaujeu, elder daughter of King Louis XI. Margaret of Bourbon was continually ailing and died of "ulceration of the lungs" when Louise was seven years old. Louise, therefore, had a lonely early childhood deprived of any real affection, with only her younger brother, Philibert (1478–1504), who later married Margaret of Austria, and her older half-brother, René, for company. But, although she may have been lonely and deprived, her kinship with the greater dynastic families of France ensured that she was not forgotten. At age two, she was betrothed by King Louis XI to Charles of Orleans, count of Angoulême, then aged 18 years, because Louis feared Charles was about to marry the heiress *Mary of Burgundy (1457–1482). An alliance of Orléans with Burgundy would have constituted a serious threat to the French monarchy.

When her mother died in 1483, Louise was sent by her father to live in the household of her aunt and uncle, Pierre and Anne of Beaujeu. This meant living at the French court since, upon the death of Louis XI, the Beaujeus had been appointed joint guardians and regents during the minority of the young king Charles VIII. Anne of Beaujeu was a cold, calculating woman having a character much in common with that of her father, known as the "Spider King" because of his political machinations. Though she was named as joint regent with her husband, it was well understood that it was Anne who governed. She was, however, a woman of principle and high moral standards who did her duty by Louise even if she did not show her any affection. Louise did not suffer therefore from lack of moral guidance or for material comforts, for Anne saw that she was well trained and that she was dressed according to her status. Her father, true to character, continually failed to pay for her upkeep. Unloved and, for the most part, ignored, Louise learned those lessons that would serve her so well in the future. It was here too that she first met Margaret of Austria, who would marry her brother, Philibert, and with whom she would negotiate the Peace of Cambrai in 1529.

Release from the oppressive regime of the household of Anne of Beaujeu came on February 16, 1488, when Louise's marriage to Charles of Orleans, count of Angoulême, was celebrated in the Châtelet in Paris. Louise brought very little by way of land or money to the marriage. Her father donated 35,000 livres, but only after she had renounced any claim to her parents' estates. The king gave the couple the small lordship of Melle-in-Poitou as security for a promised 20,000 livres. Louise acquired as dowry the income from lands and castles of Châteauneuf-sur-Charente and Romorantin, near Bourges, which became her favorite residence.

Despite the disparity in their ages, the marriage was a reasonably happy one. Charles, although cousin to Louis of Orleans, later Louis XII, had no political aspirations; he was an easygoing, relatively weak man who demanded little of Louise. They lived in the castle of Cognac in the center of Charles' domain, together with Charles' two mistresses, **Antoinette of Polignac** and **Jeanne Comte**, and their children by Charles. Showing a maturity beyond her years, Louise befriended the women, leaving Jeanne to carry on managing the household and later to become the guardian of her own children, and making Antoinette her companion. They were to remain in Louise's household for the rest of their lives, moving with her to Amboise in 1500, despite the overt disapproval of such an unorthodox arrangement by, among others, the pious ***Anne of Brittany** (c. 1477–1514), by that time the queen of France. The caring side of Louise's nature is demonstrated by the fact that she did so provide for her husband's mistresses and their illegitimate children, **Madeleine** and **Jeanne of Polignac** and **Souverain Comte**, and took pains to see that they were placed advantageously. Marriages were arranged for Jeanne with the lord of Aubin and for Souverain with the lord of Chailly; Madeleine became the abbess of Farmoutier.

The court at Cognac, though smaller then that at Paris, was just as glittering, and attracted many leading exponents of the arts. Charles was well known as a patron of painting and literature, and he had followed the example of his ancestors in building up a splendid library. Among those he encouraged was Robert Testard, a talented illuminator of manuscripts. Louise is depicted in some of his works, for example, in *Echecs Amoureux* which Testard illuminated for the count and his wife. In one particularly strik-

❧▶ Anne of Lusignan (b. before 1430)

Duchess of Savoy. Name variations: Anne de Lusignan; Anne of Cyprus. Born before 1430; possibly daughter of John II, king of Cyprus (r. 1432–1458); possibly half-sister of *Charlotte of Lusignan (1442–1487); married Louis I, duke of Savoy (r. 1440–1465); children: *Charlotte of Savoy (c. 1442–1483); *Bona of Savoy (c. 1450–c. 1505); Agnes of Savoy (who married Francis, duc de Longueville); Margaret of Savoy (d. 1483, who married Pierre II, count of Saint-Pol); Marie of Savoy (who married Louis, constable of Saint-Pol); Philip II of Bresse, later duke of Savoy (d. 1497, who married Margaret of Bourbon and was the father of *Louise of Savoy [1476–1531]); Amadée also known as Amadeus IX (d. 1472), duke of Savoy (r. 1465–1472); Jacques de Romont (d. 1486); Janus of Geneva (d. 1491), count of Geneva (r. 1441–1491); Louis of Geneva (d. 1482), count of Geneva.

ing miniature, entitled *La Musique*, Louise is seen seated on a double-headed swan, a potent mother-symbol. Although her husband was unfaithful to her, this was a time of relative peace and happiness for Louise. She amused herself with music and books far away from the intrigues and stresses of court life. She gave birth to two children, Margaret, on April 11, 1492, and Francis, two years later, on September 12, 1494. This idyllic lifestyle came to an end in January 1496 when Charles died of pneumonia after a month of patient and tender nursing by Louise.

In his will, Charles appointed Louise tutor and guardian to the children, with all his goods and chattels going to them. The appointment was immediately challenged by Charles' nearest male relatives on the grounds that Louise, at 19, was under the minimum legal age for guardianship, which was 25. Louise opposed them by invoking a local custom of the Angoumois which fixed the age of guardianship at 14. The dispute was submitted to the high court and a compromise was reached. Louise was allowed to retain custody of the children, while Louis, the duke of Orléans, was appointed their honorary guardian. In effect, this meant that although she had won her first victory in the battle to have sole responsibility for her son, Louise could not transact any business without the duke's consent. More important, if she were to remarry, she would lose the custody of the children and their property. Louise did not remarry. The rest of her life was dedicated to her son.

The succession to the French crown was governed by the Salic Law, which excluded females. Thus, if a monarch died without a male heir, the succession passed to his nearest male relative. In 1496, at the time of the death of Charles of Angoulême, the French monarch was Charles VIII, a sickly man whose only son had died of smallpox the previous month. His heir was Louis of Orleans, second cousin and now honorary guardian of Francis. Louis was married to ✦❧ **Jeanne de France** (c. 1464–1505), younger daughter of Louis XI. She was a poor creature, childless, and variously described as either deformed or extremely ugly. Francis was at this time second in the line of succession. In April 1498, Charles VIII died suddenly after banging his head on a low beam. Louis of Orleans became King Louis XII of France and Francis the heir presumptive. In January 1499, Louis divorced Jeanne de France, citing her inability to bear children, and married Anne, the young duchess of Brittany, who at the age of 22 could be expected to produce a son. For the next 15 years, Louise's life was punctuated by periods of acute anxiety during Anne of Brittany's frequent pregnancies relieved by short periods of joy when the expected child was a daughter or a stillborn son. Her journal records one such birth, "Anne, queen of France, gave birth to a son on 21 January but he was unable to prevent the exultation of my Caesar, for he was stillborn." In any event, Louis and Anne were to produce only two living children, both daughters, *Claude de France (born in 1499), and *Renée of France (born in 1510). From 1512, Francis, having already been created the duke of Valois, was designated *Monsieur le Dauphin.*

> *ℋ*umility has kept me company and Patience has never abandoned me.
>
> —Louise of Savoy

These years were not easy for Louise. Apart from the anxieties created by the queen's pregnancies, Louise had other battles to fight in her determination to have complete control of the upbringing of her son. In 1500, the king had ordered her to move her entire household to Amboise so that Francis would be nearer the royal court. At the same time, he had granted custody of Francis to Pierre de Rohan, seigneur of Gié, an appointment deeply resented by Louise, who had cause to distrust Gié. When Gié proposed a betrothal between Francis and the Princess Claude, Louise opposed him. Her opposition was soundly based, for, with Claude's pedigree, healthy sons could hardly be guaranteed and Louise desired only the best for Francis; and, moreover, if Anne of Brittany were to have a son, Francis, married to Claude, would not be in

Jeanne de France (c. 1464–1505).

See Anne of Beaujeu for sidebar.

a position to make a more advantageous marriage elsewhere. Anne of Brittany, mother of Claude and acknowledged rival and enemy of Louise, was equally opposed to the match, but for different reasons. She wanted to preserve the independence of Brittany and favored an alliance between her daughter and Charles, the young grandson of Maximilian I, the Holy Roman emperor. However, despite her overt dislike of Louise, on her death in 1514, Anne entrusted Louise with the guardianship of Claude and the administration of her lands; presumably she realized that Claude could not be in safer hands than those of Louise.

Despite Louise's disapproval, the marriage of Francis and Claude took place on May 18, 1514, at Saint-Germain-sur-Laye. With the court still in mourning for the queen, the marriage was a somber occasion with the bride and groom dressed in black cloth. Louise did not attend. Claude and Francis were to be as happy as any royal couple. Their marriage lasted for ten years, during which Claude gave birth to eight children. Louise's fears had been unfounded since these included three sons. Two daughters, Louise and Charlotte, died in childhood; the rest lived to adulthood. Louise grew fond of her good-natured daughter-in-law, they traveled together, and Louise and her daughter Margaret of Angoulême took care of Claude during her pregnancies and illnesses and looked after the grandchildren. Claude de France died in 1524, as quietly as she had lived, shortly after Francis had departed for Italy. Louise is said to have collapsed on hearing the news.

Anne of Brittany's death had appeared to leave the way open for Francis' accession to the French monarchy. Louis had declared in his grief that he would shortly follow his wife to the grave, but suddenly in August 1514 he announced his betrothal to *Mary Tudor (1496–1533), the younger sister of King Henry VIII of England. They were married in October but by the end of the year Louis was dead. Louise's son was now the king of France.

One of the first acts of the new king was to make his mother, now nearing 40 years of age, duchess of Angoulême and grant her the revenue from the duchies of Angoulême and Anjou, the counties of Maine and Beaufort-en-Vallée, and the barony of Amboise. Louise gave thanks to "Divine Mercy, by which I am amply compensated for all the adversities and annoyances which came to me in my early years and in the flower of my youth." Her hand can be detected in the first appointments made by the new king.

For the most part, he confirmed the positions of those in office under Louis XII, thus ensuring a continuity of government. The new appointments went to men who had proved their worth and whose loyalty could be relied upon. These men were to fulfill their promise and Louise's trust in them. She could be said to have chosen well with skill and foresight, for most of them were still in office at her death. The notable exception was Charles, duke of Bourbon, who was appointed constable of France. This important military appointment was for life, and its holder had the right to command the army in the absence of the king. The appointment was just and well deserved as he was noble, brave and a gallant leader, but his pride and ambition led him to betray his king and his country.

Already a man of means, Charles of Bourbon inherited the considerable wealth and lands of his wife, ❧▶ **Suzanne of Bourbon**, daughter of Anne of Beaujeu, on her death in 1521. These holdings were increased a few months later when Anne of Beaujeu herself died and also left all her wealth to him. His total holdings now constituted a dominion within France which threatened its sovereignty. As early as 1519, Louise and Francis had reason to question Bourbon's loyalty when it became known to them that Bourbon was in secret communication with Spain and even planned a marriage alliance with Charles V's sister, *Eleanor of Portugal (1498–1558). Francis and Louise took immediate action to curb Bourbon by confiscating part of his lands. Francis claimed the territory that should revert to the crown in appanage, and Louise claimed, as next of kin, that part that was due to her mother, Margaret of Bourbon. Unfortunately, Francis granted these lands to his mother before the matter was referred to the court, which gave rise to accusations of cupidity against the queen-mother. Bourbon's subsequent treasonable behavior can be said to have justified the actions taken by the king, but Bourbon's supporters believed his treason came as a result of his treatment by the king and his mother and they said so loud and clear.

Even before 1515, when Francis' reign began, France had been engaged in war against the Italian states. Gradually all Western Europe became embroiled in a bitter struggle that lasted until the Peace of Cambrai in 1529 brought a lull in the hostilities. Francis' eagerness to go to war meant a constant supply of money was essential, for war was expensive. The demands it made for money and resources occupied Louise for the rest of her official life. Although she hated war and all it entailed, she was powerless to stop Francis from continuing to fight or to

❧▶ **Suzanne of Bourbon** (1491–1521)

*Duchess of Bourbon. Name variations: Susanne of Bourbon, Susanne de Bourbonne. Reigned as duchess of Bourbon or Bourbonnais from 1503 to 1521; born on May 10, 1491; died on April 28, 1521; daughter of *Anne of Beaujeu (c. 1460–1522) and Pierre II de Bourbon, lord of Beaujeu; married Charles II, count of Montpensier and later duke of Bourbon (constable of France), on May 10, 1505; children: three sons who died young. A painting of Suzanne of Bourbon is in the Robert Lehman Collection, Metropolitan Museum of Art.*

convince him that compromise and negotiation could be equally effective. She raised the money needed, sent him off with a heavy heart, celebrated his victories and gave thanks for his safe return. For his part, Francis would only leave his country in his mother's hands. In 1524, when she was ill, he postponed his departure until she had recovered.

Money was needed too when Francis became a contender for the title of Holy Roman emperor after the death of Maximilian I in 1519. When the title went to the Habsburg Charles V, Maximilian's grandson, Europe became the battleground for a Habsburg-Valois struggle which culminated in France's defeat and Francis' capture by the Imperial forces at the battle of Pavia, in northern Italy, in February 1525.

Louise was now on her own. Distraught at the imprisonment of her son, she faced the challenges of her new role with determination and courage. She had three main tasks: to defend the monarch-less and demoralized France against invasion, to uphold the authority of the crown against the opposition posed by the Parlement of Paris, and to secure the release of her son. That she succeeded in all three is a measure of her skill and character.

The defense of France was her first priority. She set up her headquarters at Lyons, forming a council which included representatives from the parlements of Paris, Rouen, and Bordeaux, a move that diluted the opposition. By anticipating taxes and curbing the expenditure of the royal household, the economy of the country was improved. The Paris Parlement was persuaded to take responsibility for provisioning the northern garrison towns. A force was equipped at Louise's own expense and based at Lyons. Louise opened negotiations with England, through Cardinal Wolsey, and successfully mediated with him the Treaty of the More which broke the Spanish-English alliance and secured the safety of northern France. Realizing the need for bargaining power with Spain, she initiated negotiations with the Turks in hopes that a threat from the east would distract Charles V, while at the same time she encouraged dissent between Italy and Spain. Her aim was to isolate Spain from its allies in an effort to force the country to agree to terms for Francis' release.

The Parlement of Paris was already in dispute with the king before his capture at Pavia. The basis of their complaints was the Concordat of Bologna agreed in 1516 between Francis and Pope Leo X, whereby the king had sole responsibility for ecclesiastical appointments, so increasing his power over Parlement. Louise, showing more tact than her son, invited them to submit a list of their grievances or remonstrances. The list criticized many of the decisions taken by Francis, especially against heresy. Louise accepted the remonstrances, continued to govern as before, and they were never referred to again. A point had been made. She did take some action, however, against heresy, agreeing to the setting up of a special commission to try such cases.

Louise of Savoy never forgot her son in his captivity in Spain. She was in daily correspondence with Francis, keeping him informed, asking for his consent to the actions she was implementing, and reassuring herself as to his health. When he fell ill and his life was thought to be in danger, she despatched her daughter to Madrid in her stead to offer comfort and cures. At the same time, she continued the negotiations with his Spanish captors that led to the signing of the Treaty of Madrid and the release of the French king. The conditions were severe. Among other demands, France was to relinquish Burgundy, which it had no intention of doing, and Francis' two elder sons, aged eight and seven years, were to be held as hostages. Louise, now a chronically sick woman, accompanied the children on the six-week journey to Bayonne and witnessed the exchange of grandsons for son.

Francis' return made little difference to the role Louise played. She continued to advise and to negotiate with foreign dignitaries. As usual the main problem was a lack of finance. Louise was reported to have complained that they were always being cheated by the financiers. The truth was that the monarchy was in the power of the bankers. It was Francis' desire to break this stranglehold that led to further vilification of Louise, this time in connection with the Count of Semblançay, the treasury minister, a clever

man whose methods did not bear close investigation. Louise had relied on his expertise to raise the money needed for Francis' wars in Italy. In 1521, after the defeat at Milan, he had laid the blame for missing funds on Louise, though it seems highly unlikely that she would have appropriated money meant for her son. When, in 1527, Semblançay was arrested on Francis' orders and tried on charges of embezzlement and fraud, there was no mention of this missing money but the suspicion of greed stayed with Louise. The trial was in effect the first of many such trials and the beginning of a process designed to cleanse France's fiscal system.

Louise had continued to be on amicable terms with her sister-in-law, Margaret of Austria, despite the fact that they were effectively on opposite sides. Margaret, as aunt to Charles V and acting as his regent in the Netherlands, naturally took the Spanish side. She had, however, interceded with Charles on Louise's behalf and had been instrumental in securing the French king's release by persuading Charles to agree to the terms of the Madrid Treaty. Now both women saw the wisdom and advantage of a break in hostilities. Since the situation was a delicate one, the initial overtures were made in secret through envoys under the guise of agreeing on trade routes. The two women, both experienced in politics and business, finally met at Cambrai in July 1529. After nearly six weeks of intense talks, the treaty was signed on August 5. Francis and Charles accepted it as a *fait accompli,* but their allies, especially England, were far from pleased.

Under the terms of the treaty, France retained Burgundy, the chief source of contention between the two countries, the young princes were to be ransomed for two million gold *écus de soleil,* and the marriage of Francis and Charles' sister Eleanor of Portugal was to take place. Raising the ransom took much longer than expected and her grandchildren suffered considerably, causing Louise much anguish. She appealed once more to Margaret of Austria for help and so managed to get the conditions of their imprisonment improved. Francis appealed for money from the clergy, who responded, and the nobility, who did not. Margaret of Angoulême, Francis' sister, pawned her jewels, and Henry VIII sent Francis a magnificent jewel containing a relic of the True Cross as a contribution. At last in July 1530, nearly 12 months after the Peace of Cambrai, and three years after the start of their imprisonment, Francis set off for Bayonne to meet his sons and his bride. Louise, now much weaker, followed at a slower pace, finally stopping at Bordeaux when her infirmity overcame her.

The royal family was complete once more, but Louise's health forced her to retire from public life. She never recovered her former strength and died, after months of suffering, on September 22, 1531, at Grez-sur-Loing, having left Paris, where the plague was raging. When she lay dying, devotedly and tenderly nursed by her daughter, her son was conspicuous by his absence. Although he provided for a lavish funeral and wrote an emotional epitaph for her, he himself did not attend. He could not bear the idea and then the reality of his loss.

The break in hostilities brought about by the Treaty of Cambrai lasted for seven years, allowing France time to replenish and strengthen itself. The country became united and prosperous, and Francis' authority grew; Louise of Savoy's work had survived her, and her farsighted policies had borne fruit.

SOURCES:

Brewer, J.S., ed. *Letters and Papers of the Reign of Henry VIII.* P.R.O., 1867 (Kraus Reprint, 1965).

Freeman, J.F. "Louise of Savoy: a case of Maternal Opportunism," in *Sixteenth Century Journal.* Vol. 3, 1972, pp. 77–99.

Henri-Bordeaux, Paule. *Louise de Savoie: Régente et "Roi" de France.* Paris: PLON, 1954.

Knecht, R.J. *Francis I.* Cambridge University Press, 1982.

Mayer, D.M. *The Great Regent Louise of Savoy 1476–1531.* London, 1966.

SUGGESTED READING:

Griffiths, S. "Louise of Savoy and Reform of the Church," in *Sixteenth Century Journal.* Vol. 10. Fall 1979, pp. 29–36.

Hackett, F. *Francis I.* 1934.

Jacquart, J. *François Ier.* Fayard, 1981.

Jacqueton, G. *La Politique extérieure de Louise de Savoie.* Paris: 1892.

Maulde La Clavière, M.A.R. *Louise de Savoie et François 1er Trente Ans de Jeunesse 1485–1515.* Paris, 1895.

Paris, P. *Ètudes sur François 1er.* 2 vols. Paris, 1855.

FOR LOUISE'S JOURNAL:

Buchon, J.A.C., ed. *Choix de chroniques et mémoires sur l'histoire de France.* Vol. IX. Paris, 1836.

Guichenon, S., ed. "Journal de Louise de Savoie," in *Histoire de la Maison de Savoie.* Vol. II. Lyons, 1660, pp. 457–464.

Petitot, C., ed. *Collection complête des mémoires relatifs â l'histoire de France.* Vol. XVI. Paris, 1819–20.

PORTRAITS:

Louise de Savoie, Duchesse d'Angoulême from a miniature in a Book of Hours belonging to *Catherine de Medici.

"La Musique à Cognac" by Robert Testard in *Echecs Amoureux.*

BUST:

Terracotta bust in le département des sculptures du moyen âge, de la renaíssance et de temps modernes in the Louvre, Paris.

Margaret E. Lynch, M.A.,
Lancaster, England

Louise of Saxe-Gotha (1756–1808)

*Duchess of Mecklenburg-Schwerin. Born on March 9, 1756; died on January 1, 1808; daughter of John August of Saxe-Gotha, and Louise Ruess of Schleiz; married Frederick Francis (1756–1837), duke of Mecklenburg-Schwerin (r. 1785–1837); children: Frederick Louis (b. 1778); *Louise Charlotte of Mecklenburg-Schwerin (1779–1801); *Charlotte Frederica of Mecklenburg-Schwerin (1784–1840).*

Louise of Saxe-Gotha-Altenburg (1800–1831)

*Duchess of Saxe-Coburg-Gotha. Born Dorothea Louise Pauline Charlotte Fredericka Augusta on December 21, 1800, in Gotha, Thuringia, Germany; died on August 30, 1831, in Paris, France; daughter of *Louise Charlotte of Mecklenburg-Schwerin (1779–1801) and August, duke of Saxe-Gotha; married Ernest I (1784–1844), duke of Saxe-Coburg and Gotha, on July 31, 1817 (divorced 1826); children: Ernest II, duke of Saxe-Coburg and Gotha (1818–1893); Prince Albert Saxe-Coburg (1819–1861, who married Queen *Victoria). One year after the death of Louise of Saxe-Gotha-Altenburg, Ernest I married *Mary of Wurttemberg (1799–1860).*

Louise of Saxe-Hilburghausen (1726–1756)

*Danish princess. Name variations: Louise Oldenburg. Born on October 19, 1726; died on August 8, 1756; daughter of *Sophia of Bayreuth (1700–1770) and Christian VI, king of Denmark and Norway (r. 1730–1746); married Ernest Frederick III, duke of Saxe-Hilburghausen.*

Louise of Spain (1832–1897).

See Luisa Fernanda.

Louise of Stolberg-Gedern (1752–1824)

Countess of Albany, princess of Stolberg-Gedern, and wife of Bonnie Prince Charlie. Name variations: Louise Marie; Louise Maximilienne of Stolbergg-Gedern; Louisa of Stolberg. Born Louise Maximiliana Caroline Emmanuele on September 20, 1752, at Mons, Hainault, Flanders (Belgium); died on January 29, 1824, in Florence, Italy; daughter of Gustavus Adolphus, prince of Stolberg-Gedern, and Elizabeth Philippine Claudine (daughter of Maximilian Emanuel, prince of Hornes); married Charles Edward Stuart (d.

1788), also known as Bonnie Prince Charlie, the Young Pretender, or Charles III, on April 17, 1772; possibly married Vittorio (d. 1803), count Alfieri (a poet), in 1789; possibly married Francis Xavier Fabre.

Wife of the last of the Stuarts and celebrated for her association with the Italian poet Alfieri, Louise of Stolberg-Gedern, countess of Albany, was the daughter of Prince Gustavus Adolphus of Stolberg-Gedern. In 1772, she married Charles Edward Stuart, known as the count of Albany and Bonnie Prince Charlie, who was her senior by 33 years. Charles was a grandson of James II, king of England, and pretender to the British crown. The marriage was said to have been arranged with the hope of menacing the English sovereign with a legitimate heir to the rival Stuart dynasty. It proved most unhappy.

The countess was young, refined and intellectual; the count was old, coarse, and intemperate. They lived at Florence, where she became acquainted with the poet Alfieri, and it was under her guidance that he began to write his tragedies. About a year after her husband's death in 1788, Louise is said to have been secretly married to Alfieri, but they never appeared in public as husband and wife, though he was constantly in her society in Paris, London, and Florence, where she was received with distinction in the highest circles. After the death of Alfieri in 1803, the countess resided chiefly at Florence; her name was also linked with the French artist Fabre.

In his autobiography, Alfieri claimed that without her inspiring influence he would have achieved nothing. Louise of Stolberg-Gedern was buried in the church of Santa Croce at Florence, in the same tomb with Alfieri, which is adorned with a monument by Canova.

Louise of Sweden (1851–1926)

*Queen of Denmark. Name variations: Louisa of Sweden; Louise Bernadotte; Louise Josephine Eugenie Bernadotte. Born on October 31, 1851, in Stockholm, Sweden; died on March 20, 1926, in Amalienborg; daughter of *Louise of the Netherlands (1828–1878) and Charles XV (1826–1872), king of Sweden and Norway (r. 1859–1872); married Frederick VIII (1843–1912), duke of Schleswig-Holstein-Sonderburg-Augustenburg (r. 1869–1880), king of Denmark (r. 1906–1912); children: Christian X (1870–1947), king of Denmark (r. 1912–1947); Charles or Carl (1872–1957), became Haakon VII, king of Norway (r. 1905–1957); *Louise Caroline (1875–1906); Harald*

*(b. 1876); *Ingeborg of Denmark (1878–1958); *Thyra of Denmark (1880–1945); Dagmar Louise Elizabeth (1890–1961, who married Jörgen de Castenskiold, chamberlain at court).*

Louise of the Netherlands
(1828–1871)

*Queen of Sweden. Name variations: Louise of Orange-Nassau; Lovisa; Louise of Nassau or Louise von Nassau. Born on August 5, 1828, at The Hague, Netherlands; died on March 30, 1871, in Stockholm, Sweden; daughter of Frederick Orange-Nassau (1797–1881, son of William I of the Netherlands) and *Louise (1808–1870, daughter of *Louise of Prussia); married Karl XV also known as Charles XV (1826–1872), king of Sweden (r. 1859–1872), on June 19, 1850; children: *Louise of Sweden (1851–1926); Charles Oscar (b. 1852).*

Louise of Tuscany (1870–1947).
See Toselli, Louisa.

Louise of Vaudemont (1554–1601).
See Louise of Lorraine.

Louise Victoria (1867–1931).
See Alexandra of Denmark for sidebar.

Louise, Augusta (1906–1984).
See Gaynor, Janet.

Louise, Ruth Harriet (1906–1944)

American photographer who was the first woman to manage her own portrait gallery at Metro-Goldwyn-Mayer. Born Ruth Harriet Louise Sandrich in Brooklyn, New York, in 1906; died in 1944; married Leigh Jason (a film director), in 1930.

A photographer to the stars, Ruth Harriet Louise Sandrich opened a portrait studio in New York City at age 17, while simultaneously dropping her surname. In 1925, she moved her operation to Los Angeles, where she became a contract photographer at MGM. She headed her own portrait gallery at MGM until 1930, and was the exclusive photographer for *Greta Garbo through 1929. Known for her ability to bring out the best in her subjects, Louise photographed such notables as Lon Chaney, *Marion Davies, *Joan Crawford, Ramon Novarro, and *Anna May Wong. After leaving MGM, she continued to photograph performers on a freelance basis until her death in 1944, at age 38. The photographer was married to film director Leigh Jason.

Louize.

Variant of Louise.

Lourenco, Teresa (fl. 1358).

See Lorenzo, Teresa.

Louyse.

Variant of Louise.

Love, Bessie (1898–1986)

American actress. Born Juanita Horton on September 10, 1898, in Midland, Texas; died in 1986; daughter of John Cross Horton and Emma Jane (Savage) Horton; attended school in Los Angeles, California; married William Ballinger Hawks (a director), in 1929 (divorced 1935); children: one daughter, **Patricia Hawks.**

Selected theater: first appeared on the stage as Bonnie in Burlesque *(Santa Barbara, California, 1928); made New York debut (Palace Theater, 1931); made London debut as Julie in* Say It with Flowers, *and as the Actress in* Zenobia *(Granville Theater, Walham Green, October 1945); toured as Miss Dell in* Love in Idleness *(1945–46); appeared as Mrs. Hedges in* Born Yesterday *(Garrick Theater, London, January 1947), Myrtle Keller in* The Male Animal *(Arts Theater, May 1949), Laughing Woman in* Death of a Salesman *(Phoenix Theater, July 1949), Amanda Wingfield in* The Glass Menagerie *(Gaiety Theater, Dublin, 1951), Bessie Bockser in* The Wooden Dish *(Phoenix Theater, London, July 1954), Mrs. Prioleau in* South *(Arts Theater, March 1955), Mrs. Kirke in* A Girl Called Jo *(Piccadilly Theater, March 1955), Mrs. Lily Mortar in* The Children's Hour *(Arts Theater, December 1955), Babe in her own play* The Homecoming *(Perth Repertory Theater, April 1958), Nurse in* Orpheus Descending *(Royal Court Theater, London, May 1959), Reba Spelding in* Visit to a Small Planet *(Westminster Theater, February 1960), Mrs. Ella Spofford in* Gentlemen Prefer Blondes *(Princes Theater, August 1962 and Strand Theater, November 1962), Grace Kimborough in* Never Too Late *(Prince of Wales Theater, September 1963), a Worker in* Saint Joan of the Stockyards *(Queen's Theater, June 1964), the White Woman in* In White America *(New Arts Theater, November 1964), Marguerite Oswald in* The Silence of Lee Harvey Oswald *(Hampstead Theater Club, November 1966), Aunt Nonnie in* Sweet Bird of Youth *(Palace Theater, Watford, November 1968); appeared as Aunt Pittypat in* Gone With the Wind *(London, 1972).*

Selected filmography: The Flying Torpedo *(1916);* The Aryan *(1916);* The Good Bad Man *(1916);* Acquitted *(1916);* Reggie Mixes In *(1916);* Stranded *(1916);* Hell-to-Pay *(1916);* Austin *(1916);* Intolerance *(1916);* A Sister of Six *(1917);* Nina the Flower Girl *(1917);* A Daughter of the Poor *(1917);* The Sawdust Ring *(1917);* Wee Lady Betty *(1917);* Polly Ann *(1917);* Cheerful Givers *(1917);* The Great Adventure *(1918);* How Could You Caroline? *(1918);* The Little Sister of Everybody *(1918);* The Dawn of Understanding *(1918);* The Enchanted Barn *(1919);* The Yankee Princess *(1919);* The Little Boss *(1919);* Cupid Forecloses *(1919);* Carolyn of the Corners *(1919);* Pegeen *(1920);* Bonnie May *(1920);* Penny of Top Hill Trail *(1921);* The Swamp *(1921);* The Sea Lion *(1921);* The Vermilion Pencil *(1922);* Forget-Me-Not *(1922);* Bulldog Courage *(1922);* The Village Blacksmith *(1922);* Deserted at the Altar *(1922);* Human Wreckage *(1923);* The Eternal Three *(1923);* St. Elmo *(1923);* Slave of Desire *(1923);* Gentle Julia *(1923);* Torment *(1924);* Those Who Dance *(1924);* The Silent Watcher *(1924);* Sundown *(1924);* Tongues of Flame *(1924);* The Lost World *(1925);* Soul-Fire *(1925);* A Son of His Father *(1925);* The King on Main Street *(1925);* The Song and Dance Man *(1926);* Lovey Mary *(1926);* Young April *(1926);* Going Crooked *(1926);* Rubber Tires *(1927);* Dress Parade *(1927);* A Harp in Hock *(1927);* The Matinee Idol *(1928);* Sally of the Scandals *(1928);* Anybody Here Seen Kelly? *(1928);* The Broadway Melody *(1928);* The Hollywood Revue *(1929);* The Idle Rich *(1929);* The Girl in the Show *(1929);* Chasing Rainbows *(1930);* Conspiracy *(1930);* Good News *(1930);* See America Thirst *(1930);* Morals for Women *(1931);* Atlantic Ferry *(UK, 1941);* Journey Together *(UK, 1945);* The Barefoot Contessa *(1954);* Touch and Go *(UK, 1955);* The Story of Esther Costello *(UK, 1957);* Next to No Time *(UK, 1958);* The Greengage Summer *(Loss of Innocence, UK, 1961);* The Roman Spring of Mrs. Stone *(US/UK, 1961);* Children of the Damned *(UK, 1964);* The Wild Affair *(UK, 1965);* Promise Her Anything *(UK, 1966);* Battle Beneath the Earth *(UK/US, 1969);* The Loves of Isadora *(UK, 1969);* On Her Majesty's Secret Service *(UK, 1969);* Sunday Bloody Sunday *(UK, 1971);* Catlow *(UK/Sp., 1971);* Vampyres *(1975);* The Ritz *(1976);* L'Amant de lady Chatterley *(Lady Chatterley's Lover, Fr./UK, 1981);* Ragtime *(1981);* Reds *(1981);* The Hunger *(1983).*

Throughout her long career on stage, screen, radio, and television, actress Bessie Love always hovered on the brink of stardom, never finding just the right vehicle to push her over the top. She was one of the few silent actresses to make a smooth transition to talking pictures, however, and she also had remarkable longevity, continuing to appear on stage and in film cameos into her 70s and 80s.

Petite (under 5' tall) and pretty, Love was discovered in 1915 and began appearing in silents while she was still in high school in Los Angeles. She may have appeared as an extra in the 1915 film *The Birth of a Nation,* although her participation in that project is unconfirmed.

She was featured as the Bride of Cana in the Judean episode of D.W. Griffith's *Intolerance* (1916) and also played opposite Douglas Fairbanks in several films, including *Reggie Mixes In* (1916). Love continued to portray sweet young heroines until the early 1920s, when she graduated to leading lady roles in melodramas. In the late 1920s, she made a series of light films, including *The King of Main Street* (1925) in which she introduced the Charleston.

Bessie Love's breakthrough role was in MGM's first sound musical *The Broadway Melody* (1929), for which she was nominated for an Oscar as Best Actress. That same year, she married director William Hawks; they would later have a daughter, Patricia. Around this time, Love also began appearing on stage in a series of variety shows and made her New York debut at the Palace in 1931. In 1935, she divorced Hawks and moved to London, where she continued in films and on the radio. During the war, she worked for the American Red Cross and also did a stint as a film technician at Ealing Studios. Following the war, she returned to the British stage, appearing in minor roles in *Born Yesterday* (1947), *Death of a Salesman* (1949), *The Children's Hour* (1956), *The Glass Menagerie* (1966), and *The Homecoming* (1958), which she also wrote. She was also seen on television, playing mostly character roles.

In her later years, Love remained sprightly, attributing her vitality to staying active and to dance movement classes. Her later films included *Isadora* (1969), in which she played **Vanessa Redgrave**'s mother, and **Penelope Gilliat**'s *Sunday Bloody Sunday* (1971), in which she was cast as a busybody phone operator. In 1972, Love scored a hit as Aunt Pittypat in the London stage production of *Gone With the Wind*. Her last film, *The Hunger* (1983), was made only three years before she died at the age of 88. Love's autobiography, *From Hollywood with Love*, was published in 1977.

SOURCES:

Halliwell, Leslie. *The Filmgoer's Companion.* NY: Hill and Wang, 1974.

Katz, Ephraim. *The Film Encyclopedia.* NY: HarperCollins, 1994.

Ragan, David. *Who's Who in Hollywood, 1900–1976.* New Rochelle, NY: Arlington House, 1976.

SUGGESTED READING:

Love, Bessie. *From Hollywood with Love.* London: Elm Tree Books, 1977.

Barbara Morgan,
Melrose, Massachusetts

Love, Nancy (b. 1914).

See Cochran, Jacqueline for sidebar.

Lovejoy, Esther Pohl (1869–1967)

American physician, administrator, feminist, and author. Born Esther Clayson on November 16, 1869, in a logging camp near Seabeck, Washington Territory; died on August 17, 1967, in New York City; the third of six children of Edward Clayson and Annie (Quinton) Clayson; attended lumber-camp school for a few years; Medical School of the University of Oregon, M.D., 1894; attended the West Side Post-graduate School, Chicago, Illinois; married Emil Pohl (a surgeon), in 1894 (died 1911); married George A. Lovejoy (a businessman), in 1913 (divorced 1920); children: one son, Frederick Clayson Pohl (1901–1908).

The extraordinary life of Esther Pohl Lovejoy began in 1869 in a logging camp near Seabeck, Washington Territory, where her father Edward Clayson worked briefly as a lumber merchant. Edward was subsequently employed as a hotel manager, a newspaper editor, and a farmer, but failed in all attempts to support his wife **Annie Clayson** and their six children. Esther's early education included several years at a lumber-camp school and some lessons from a classics professor who lived in one of the hotels her father managed. She decided on a medical career after watching a doctor deliver her younger sister, but she had to pay for her own education.

In 1890, having saved $60 from a year's work in a department store, Esther began work on her M.D. degree at the University of Oregon, graduating in 1894, with a medal for academic achievement. She was the university's second woman graduate and the first to actually take up the practice of medicine. Shortly after graduation, she married a fellow student, Emil Pohl, and opened a practice with him in Portland.

In 1896, Lovejoy's brothers, who were employed selling supplies to gold prospectors, convinced the couple to move to Skagway, Alaska. The Pohls became the first doctors in the area, working out of a log cabin and visiting patients by dog sled. In 1899, however, when her brother Frederick Clayson was mysteriously murdered, Lovejoy returned to Portland. Her husband remained in Alaska and Esther visited him during the summer months. Personal tragedy struck again in 1908, when the couple's only son Frederick (born in 1901) died of septic peritonitis caused by drinking contaminated milk, and in 1911, when Emil Pohl died of encephalitis.

Esther, who was active in the woman suffrage movement as early as 1904, became adept at combining political activism with her medical practice, supporting not only suffrage but the prohibition movement as well. In 1913, she married Portland businessman George A. Lovejoy, but divorced him in 1920, after he used her name to promote projects of which she did not approve.

During World War I, as a member of the American Medical Women's Association (AMWA), Esther petitioned unsuccessfully for a woman physician's right to serve in the war. In 1917, she set a personal example by going to France, where she worked for the Red Cross as an investigator for claims. In addition, she volunteered in a charity hospital at night, often working until the wee hours of the morning. She later documented her experiences in a book, *The House of the Good Neighbor* (1919).

Returning to the United States early in 1918, Lovejoy worked under the auspices of the AMWA, raising money for its war relief agency, the American Women's Hospitals (AWH). In 1919, she returned to Europe to help relocate the organization's first hospital which later served as a model for similar hospitals in other parts of the world. Now director of AWH, a position she held for 42 years, Esther often shuttled back and

Ada Byron, Countess of Lovelace

forth from Europe to the United States, soliciting funds for the organization's other projects, which included outpatient clinics, orphanages, and public-health services. Following an unsuccessful run for Congress in 1920, Lovejoy gave up politics and concentrated her efforts solely on her work with AWH in Europe. She also served as president of the AMWA from 1932 to 1933. In her memoir, *Certain Samaritans*, Lovejoy detailed her work during the 1920s, and the effort to assist the uprooted and impoverished of Europe. The AWH also aided victims of the Tokyo earthquake of 1923, and the Florida hurricane of 1926, and continued to be active through World War II and the postwar period.

Lovejoy was the recipient of numerous honors during her lifetime, including the medal of the Legion of Honor (France), the Gold Cross of Saint Sava (Yugoslavia), the Gold Cross of the Holy Sepulcher (Jerusalem), and the Gold Cross of the Order of George I (Greece). She was also a two-time recipient of the *Elizabeth Blackwell Medal of the AMWA.

By her example alone, Lovejoy inspired a number of women to take up medicine, but she also provided more practical support in 1936, endowing the Pohl Scholarships for medical students at the University of Oregon in memory of her husband and son, and stipulating that a third of the awards go to women. In two later books, *Women Physicians and Surgeons* (1939) and *Women Doctors of the World* (1957), Lovejoy also documented the work of women physicians all over the world. Esther Pohl Lovejoy retired in 1967, age 97, and died of pneumonia just five months later.

SOURCES:

Sicherman, Barbara, and Carol Hurd Green, eds. *Notable American Women: The Modern Period*. Cambridge, MA: The Belknap Press of Harvard University Press, 1980.

COLLECTIONS:

Lovejoy's papers are held by the Schlesinger Library of Radcliffe College.

Barbara Morgan,
Melrose, Massachusetts

Lovelace, Ada Byron, Countess of (1815–1852)

English mathematician and inventor of computer programming. Name variations: Lady Lovelace; countess of Lovelace; Augusta Ada Byron. Born Augusta Ada Byron on December 10, 1815, at Piccadilly Terrace, London, England; died on November 27, 1852, in England; buried in the Byron vault at Hucknall Torkard church, near Newstead Abbey, the Byron ancestral home; daughter of Anne Isabella Milbanke (1792–1860) and George Gordon Byron, Lord Byron (the poet); educated by Lady Byron, governesses, tutors, and self-study; married Lord William Noel King, later earl of Lovelace, on July 8, 1835; children: Byron Noel (b. May 12, 1836); Anne Isabella Blunt (1837–1917); Ralph Gordon Noel King Milbanke, 2nd earl of Lovelace (July 2, 1839–1906).

Anne Isabella Milbanke and Lord Byron separated (January 15, 1816); Lord Byron left England (April 25, 1816); Charles Babbage invented the Difference Engine (1822); Lord Byron died at Missolonghi, Greece (April 19, 1824); Lady Byron and Ada undertook a grand tour of Europe (1826–28); Ada, unable to walk after a severe attack of the measles (May 1829), recovered only gradually over a period of four years; eloped briefly with her tutor (1832); met Charles Babbage (June 5, 1833); met Mary Somerville (1834); suffered a nervous breakdown (1835); Lord King elevated to the earldom of Lovelace (June 30, 1837); hired Augustus de Morgan as a tutor (June 1840); earl of Lovelace appointed Lord Lieutenant of Surrey (August 11, 1840); publication of Luigi Federigo Menabrea's memoir on the Analytical Engine (October 1842); publication of Ada's translation of Menabrea's memoir with annotations (August 13, 1843); led gambling confederacy and suffered financial losses (1851); after a series of haemorrhages, diagnosed with cervical cancer (1851).

Publications: "Sketch of the Analytical Engine Invented by Charles Babbage, Esq. by L.F. Menabrea, of Turin, Officer of the Military Engineers: With Copious Notes by the Translator," in Scientific Memoirs (R. Taylor, ed. London: R and J.E. Taylor, 1843).

George Gordon Byron, Lord Byron and ☙▶ **Anne Milbanke** had been married slightly over a year when, on December 10, 1815, their only child Augusta Ada was born. Named after Byron's infamous half-sister ☙▶ **Augusta Leigh**, the child was known within the family simply as Ada. From the outset, the marriage of Ada's parents had been a stormy one. Byron, the fiercely temperamental poet, was an unstable personality who adapted poorly to the constraints of married life. Conversely, Anne Milbanke was a woman of strict social convention, with a predilection for self-righteousness.

Byron's early dissatisfaction with the marriage manifested itself in the torrent of abuse which he unleashed upon his wife. A few months after Ada's birth, Lady Byron fled with her daughter to the home of her parents. The separation was a brave, if risky, remedy in a society

☙▶ **Milbanke, Anne** (1792–1860)

English philanthropist. Name variations: Annabella; Lady Noel Byron. Born Anne Isabella Milbanke at Elmore Hall, Durham, on May 17, 1792; died in 1860; only child of Sir Ralph and Lady Milbanke; niece of Lady *Elizabeth Melbourne; married George Gordon Byron, Lord Byron, on January 2, 1815 (separated 1816); children: *Ada Byron, countess of Lovelace (1815–1852).

Following her brief marriage to Lord Byron, Anne Milbanke founded a progressive industrial and agricultural school at Ealing Grove, based on the theories of Swiss agriculturist Philipp Fellenberg. She also subsidized other educational institutes, including *Mary Carpenter's Red House, a girls' reformatory, in 1854. A close associate of *Barbara Bodichon, Lady Byron backed American abolitionists and Italian Republicans. Her grandson, author Ralph Gordon Noel King Milbanke, 2nd earl of Lovelace (1839–1906), in an effort to raise the reputation of Lord Byron, vindicated Lady Byron from slurs cast on her following her marriage to Byron, in his privately published *Astarte* (1905).

SUGGESTED READING:
Mayne, E.C. *Life and Letters of Anne Isabella, Lady Noel Bryon*, 1929.
*Stowe, Harriet Beecher. *Lady Byron Vindicated*, 1870.

which rarely recognized the rights of wives. The custody of Ada remained an unsettled issue. The uncertainty of the situation was finally put to rest with the death of Lord Byron in 1824. Byron's dying words were reportedly addressed to his daughter. "Oh, my poor dear child!—my dear Ada! My God, could I have but seen her! Give her my blessing!"

Ada inherited her father's dark and fine features. Physical similarities aside, however, they could not have been more disparate personalities. While Byron was the embodiment of the romantic poet, his daughter grew into a rational scientist. Like her father, Ada became a popular romantic figure. Byron contributed to the phenomena by mythologizing their relationship in the third canto of *Childe Harold's Pilgrimage*. "Ada! Sole daughter of my house and heart." As well, Benjamin Disraeli used Ada Lovelace as a heroine in his novel *Venetia*.

Ada's education was somewhat unconventional for a young woman of the period. She was largely educated by Lady Byron, who designed a demanding instructional regime for her daughter, primarily based on reward and punishment. Punishments included solitary confinement, lying still, and written apologies. A governess,

◀☙
Leigh, Augusta.
See Lamb,
Caroline for
sidebar.

Miss Lamont, recorded that Ada's daily curriculum consisted of:

> Lessons in the morning in arithmetic, grammar, spelling, reading, music, each no more than a quarter of an hour long—after dinner geography, drawing, French, music reading, all performed with alacrity and docility.

Ada inherited her mathematical aptitude from her mother, whom Lord Byron once referred to as "the Princess of Parallelograms." A later influence was that of *Mary Fairfax Somerville, the famous mathematician, who became a lifelong friend, advisor, and confidant.

*O*h, my poor dear child!—my dear Ada! My God, could I have but seen her!

—Lord Byron's dying words

Ada Lovelace was plagued by a series of incapacitating illnesses throughout her life. After returning from a tour of continental Europe with her mother in 1829, Ada developed an illness which left her unable to walk for the next four years. Lady Byron blamed "the loss of the power to walk or stand . . . [on] the effects of the measles, and too rapid growth." Ada also began to chafe increasingly under her mother's autocratic regime. In 1832, Ada fell in love with her tutor, and the young couple eloped. In an age when virginity was considered an essential prerequisite for marriage, this teenage indiscretion threatened Ada's future prospects. "Ada [had] fled from her mother's house to the arms of her lover who was residing at no great distance with his relations, Lady B's humble friends," wrote Woronzow Greig, Mary Somerville's son. "They received her with dismay and took the earliest opportunity of returning her to her mother before the escapade was known. The matter was hushed up."

In 1833, at a party held during her first London season, Ada was invited by Charles Babbage to view his Difference Engine. Babbage had received a gold medal from the Astronomical Society for this forerunner of the modern computer, invented in 1822, as well as a grant of £1,500 to further his research. Ada Byron's reaction made a significant impression upon **Sophia de Morgan** who had witnessed the scene:

> While the rest of the party gaped at this beautiful instrument with the same sort of expression and feeling that savages are said to have shown on first seeing the looking glass, Miss Byron, young as she was, understood its workings and saw the great beauty of the invention.

In 1835, Ada Lovelace suffered a serious nervous breakdown of a type to which she was subject for the rest of her life. Her father had also been the victim of mental instability, which seems to have run in the family. In a letter to Mary Somerville, Lovelace described herself as being weak. "I am always so exceedingly terrified at nobody knows what, that I can hardly help having an agitated look and manner," she wrote.

Shortly after her illness, Ada met William King. Ten years her senior and a diplomat who had served on various missions in the Mediterranean and the Middle East, Lord King also spoke several languages, among them Greek, French, Italian, and Spanish. In the aftermath of his father's death, King was beginning to focus his energies increasingly on national politics. Wrote Woronzow Greig:

> During the spring of 1835 I suggested to my friend Lord Lovelace, then Lord King, that [Ada] would suit him as a wife. . . . He received my suggestion without remark and he did not mention the subject to me until 12 June 1835 when he wrote to ask me to dine with him. . . . At dinner he surprised me by announcing his engagement to Miss Byron, as I was not even aware that he had been paying his addresses to her.

Ada and Lord King had fallen in love. In addition to the emotional bond, there was the added financial benefit for King of Ada's large dowry and her future inheritance. As well, the connection of the Byron family with Lord Melbourne, then prime minister of Great Britain, provided King with a suitable outlet for his political ambitions.

The marriage took place on July 8, 1835, only a month after their engagement was announced. Upon the coronation of Queen *Victoria in 1837, Lord King was elevated to the earldom of Lovelace, and Ada thus became the countess of Lovelace. A year later, King was appointed to the post of lord lieutenant of Surrey. Although busy with his political career, he remained unfailingly supportive of his wife's scientific interests.

On May 12, 1836, Ada gave birth to the first of their three children. Her relationship with her children, including her daughter ❧➤ **Anne Blunt**, would be one of fond dispassion. Like most women of her class, Ada left the child rearing to servants. Nevertheless, in later years her children were to remember their mother with great affection.

The example of Charles Babbage's Difference Engine inspired Lovelace to undertake an intensive study of mathematics. In June 1840, she engaged Augustus de Morgan to tutor her in arithmetic and algebra. De Morgan, a distinguished professor of mathematics at the newly created University of London, was poorly paid and supplemented his income by tutoring and writing. Ada often read and critiqued his articles, illustrating the high esteem in which de Morgan held his enthusiastic and gifted student. Augustus wrote to Lady Byron that "Mrs. Somerville's mind will never lead her into other then the details of mathematical work; Lady [Lovelace] will take quite a different route." His prognosis soon came to fruition.

Working with Babbage was a goal which Lovelace long sought. Her opportunity came sooner rather than later, when in 1842 Luigi Federigo Menabrea, an Italian mathematician, ambassador to France, and future prime minister of Italy, wrote a paper on the subject of Babbage's Analytical Engine (designed in the 1830s) for the Bibliotheque Universelle de Genève. Lovelace decided to translate Menabrea's work from French into English. She went to considerable lengths to expand on Menabrea's paper and consulted Babbage extensively. He was suitably impressed by her work and wrote that "the more I read your notes the more surprised I am at them and regret not having earlier explored so rich a vein of the noblest metal." Her annotations to Menabrea's work produced a manuscript three times the original length. At Babbage's suggestion, Ada inserted several illustrations which outlined the computer programming of the machine, and proposed a program for the computation of Bernoulli numbers.

Lovelace contrasted the Difference Engine, which she characterized as an ingenious calculator which followed a straight computational path, with the Analytical Engine, which could be programmed with punch cards, was more flexible in its computational analysis, and possessed, in her opinion, a greatly increased computational potential. In one of her annotations, she predicted the advent of artificial intelligence and computer-generated music:

> Supposing, for instance, that the fundamental relations of pitched sounds in the science of harmony and of musical composition were susceptible of such expression and adaptations, the engine might compose elaborate and scientific pieces of any degree of complexity or extent.

Her annotations also departed from Menabrea's commentary on the mechanical aspects of the machine to delve into the metaphysical implications of machine computing. What is surprising is that Ada Byron Lovelace grasped the implications of the Analytical Engine even though it was never built. It was merely a set of drawings.

❧ Blunt, Anne (1837–1917)

British explorer. Name variations: Baroness Wentworth; Anne Blount. Born Anne Isabella King on September 22, 1837; died in Cairo, Egypt, in 1917; daughter of *Ada Byron, countess of Lovelace (1815–1852), and Lord William Noel King, 1st earl of Lovelace; married Wilfrid Scawen Blunt (1840–1922, a poet, traveler, and diplomat), in 1869; children: one daughter.

Lady Anne Isabella Blunt was an Arabic scholar, equestrian, musician, traveler, and writer, and the first Englishwoman to explore the Arabian peninsula. She and her husband, who both spoke Arabic, traveled in Turkey, Algiers, and Egypt. They also visited India in 1878 and 1883–84. Blunt describes their desert journey from Aleppo to Baghdad in *The Bedouin Tribes of the Euphrates* (1878). Other desert excursions, including their penetration of the unknown territory of Nedj, is described in *Pilgrimage to Nedj* (1881). In 1906, the Blunts settled in Egypt, trading and breeding Arabian horses. She was named Baroness Wentworth in 1917.

However, Ada cautioned against overrating the abilities of computers, as many futurists of the period did. Nevertheless, she intuitively understood the implications of technological change upon the nature of science:

> The Analytical Engine has no pretension whatever to originate anything . . . but it is likely to exert an indirect and reciprocal influence on science itself in another manner. For, in so distributing and combining truths and the formulae of analysis, that they may become more easily and rapidly amenable to the mechanical combinations of the engine, the relations and nature of science are necessarily thrown into new light, and more profoundly investigated. This is a decidedly indirect, and a somewhat speculative consequence of such an invention.

Babbage considered Ada Lovelace's work so superior to that of Menabrea's that he suggested it be published as an original piece of research, rather than a translation. Women, however, particularly aristocratic ones, did not write scientific papers. Therefore, it was decided that the manuscript would be signed A.A.L. Thus the true identity of the author remained a mystery for the next 30 years.

The translation of Menabrea's work proved that Ada Lovelace was Charles Babbage's intellectual equal. Babbage began to refer to her as the "Enchantress of Numbers." Lovelace sent a copy of her work to Mary Somerville, who praised the "proficiency you have made in the highest branches of mathematics and the clearness with which you have illustrated a very difficult subject."

After the publication of her notes on the Analytical Engine, Lovelace contemplated several other projects which illustrated the depth of her intellect. In July 1843, she wrote to Babbage suggesting that she might write a pamphlet "On galvanic series, mathematically determined," for the *Philosophical Magazine*. To her mother, she intimated that she was contemplating a follow-up article on Babbage's research, and to her husband she spoke of bequeathing to the world a "Calculus of the Nervous System." As well, Ada Lovelace was hoping to undertake further translations, including one of Eilhardt Mitscherlich's "Chemical Reactions Produced by Bodies which Act only by Contact."

By the mid-1840s, German science was beginning to supplant ideas emanating from France, and Lovelace became interested in crystallography. In 1844, she met John Crosse, who had recently returned from studying in Germany and was also interested in crystallography. Crosse's presence, she wrote to her husband, would be helpful for: "I can get from him and by means of him, what I could from no one else." The turn of phrase was indeed ironic.

How long the affair between Crosse and Ada Lovelace lasted is unknown. But it was certainly not her first flirtation with marital infidelity. A year earlier, London newspapers had been commenting on her relationship with a certain Frederick Knight. One newspaper noted that "the resemblance of Lady Lovelace to her renowned father, beyond some parental likeness, has as yet been confined to a certain amount of eccentricity." The full details of Ada's involvement with Crosse remain a mystery, but they were clearly scandalous enough for the earl of Lovelace to have the bulk of the correspondence between the two destroyed upon his wife's death.

In later years, the collaboration between Ada Lovelace and Charles Babbage was ill-fated. Together, they explored the realm of mathematical probability and devised an "infallible system" to predict gambling odds on horse racing, an abiding passion of the English upper classes. Lovelace was a particularly avid fan. Improbability, however, interfered with the mathematical prognostications of the two mathematicians, and Ada Lovelace found herself increasingly in debt. In fact, she lost so much money that she was forced to pawn the Lovelace family jewels. She involved her husband in the betting scheme and creditors assailed the couple for the rest of their lives.

In 1852, Ada Lovelace died of cancer at the young age of 36. On her deathbed, she confessed her infidelity to her husband and recited a line from her father's poem *Cain*. "Believe—and sink not! doubt and perish." The usually restrained earl of Lovelace wrote that "for the past week I have been prey to the utmost wretchedness of mind—Every cherished conviction of my married life has been unsettled." Ada's last request was that she be interred beside her father in Hucknall Torkard church, near the Byron family seat.

Five years later, Charles Babbage wrote to Ada Lovelace's son, Viscount Ockham, highlighting the significance of her scientific contribution:

> In the memoir of Mr. Menabrea and still more in the excellent Notes appended by your mother you will find the only comprehensive view of the powers of the Analytical Engine which the mathematicians of the world have yet expressed.

Ada Lovelace's contributions to the science of mathematics, cut short by ill-health, were quickly forgotten. However, as computers increasingly dominated modern science in the postwar period, scientists began to reexamine her role in the field of computing. Ada Lovelace had devised the first complex set of instructions for the Analytical Engine, which delineated the function of input, calculation, output, and printing. Beyond her definition of computer programming, her predictions concerning the future of computers were truly visionary. In 1980, when the U.S. Department of Defense sought a label for its new computer language, the name "Ada" was chosen.

SOURCES:

Bernstein, Jeremy. *The Analytic Engine*. NY: Random House, 1963.

Breaud, Sylvie. "Ada, Analyste et Metaphysicienne," in *Pénélope pour l'histoire des femmes*. Paris: Publication du Group d'Étude Feministes de l'Université de Paris, 1983.

Moore, Doris Langley. *Ada, Countess of Lovelace: Byron's Legitimate Daughter*. London: John Murray, 1977.

Moseley, Maboth. *Irascible Genius*. London: Hutchinson, 1964.

Nabokov, Vladimir. *Ada or Ardor: A Family Chronicle*. NY: McGraw-Hill, 1969.

Rosenberg, J. *The Computer Prophets*. NY: Macmillan, 1969.

Stein, Dorothy. *Ada: A Life and a Legacy*. Cambridge, MA: MIT Press, 1985.

SUGGESTED READING:

Baum, Joan. *The Calculating Passion of Ada Byron*. Hamden, CT: Archon Books, 1986.

Hugh A. Stewart, M.A.,
Guelph, Ontario, Canada

Lovelace, countess of (1815–1852).

See Lovelace, Ada Byron, Countess of.

Lovelace, Maud Hart (1892–1980)

American writer of novels and children's books, best known for her popular "Betsy-Tacy" series, published between 1940 and 1955. Born Maud Hart on April 25, 1892, in Mankato, Minnesota; died on March 11, 1980, in California; daughter of Thomas Walden Hart (a salesman) and Stella (Palmer) Hart; studied at University of Minnesota, 1911–12; married Delos Wheeler Lovelace (a journalist), in 1917 (died 1967); children: one daughter, Merian Lovelace Kirchner (b. 1931).

Selected adult novels: The Black Angels *(1926);* Early Candlelight *(1929);* Petticoat Court *(1930);* The Charming Sally *(1932); (with Delos Wheeler Lovelace)* One Stayed at Welcome *(1934); (with Delos Wheeler Lovelace)* Gentlemen from England *(1937).*

Selected juvenile novels: Betsy-Tacy *(1940);* Betsy-Tacy and Tib *(1941);* Over the Big Hill *(1942); (with Delos Wheeler Lovelace)* The Golden Wedge: Indian Legends of South America *(1942);* Down Town *(1943);* Heaven to Betsy *(1945);* Betsy in Spite of Herself *(1946);* Betsy Was a Junior *(1947);* Betsy and Joe *(1948);* Carney's House Party *(1949);* The Tune Is in the Tree *(1950);* Emily of Deep Valley *(1950);* The Trees Kneel at Christmas *(1951);* Betsy and the Great World *(1952);* Winona's Pony Cart *(1953);* Betsy's Wedding *(1955);* What Cabrillo Found *(1958);* The Valentine Box *(1966).*

Born Maud Hart on April 25, 1892, in Mankato, Minnesota, Maud Hart Lovelace was one of three daughters of Thomas Walden Hart, a shoe salesman and county treasurer, and **Stella Palmer Hart**. Maud developed a precocious talent for writing that was to serve her well in her adult career as a writer. "I cannot remember back to a year when I did not consider myself to be a writer," she later wrote. Best known for her popular "Betsy-Tacy" series for children, she was to rely extensively on the personal journals—and exploits—of her childhood when working on the books that made her name as a writer.

Maud Hart began writing stories before she started school, hiding her first efforts in a maple tree outside her family's home. At 10, she had her father print up a booklet of her poems; at 18, after many submissions, she published her first short story, sold to the *Los Angeles Times* for $10. Maud graduated from high school in Mankato in 1910, and when the family moved to Minneapolis she attended university there. In 1914, she sailed for Europe, spending the months leading up to World War I in England.

In 1917, towards the end of the war, she married journalist Delos Wheeler Lovelace, who was then serving as an officer in a machine-gun battalion. After the war, Delos Lovelace took up newspaper work; he would later become a popular writer of short stories. The couple lived in Garden City, Long Island, and later at Lake Minnetonka, Minnesota, eventually making their home in Claremont, California. Their only child, Merian, was born in 1931.

Maud Hart Lovelace published her first book, the historical novel *The Black Angels*, in 1926; she followed with five more historical novels, two of which she wrote with her husband in the years preceding World War II. In the bedtime stories Lovelace contrived for daughter Merian about her own childhood in Minnesota, she found inspiration for her "Betsy-Tacy" series and wrote the first book in 1940. Originally, the "Betsy-Tacy" books were not planned as a series; titles were added as the books grew in popularity and readers demanded more details about the childhood, adolescence and eventually college career and marriage of the characters Betsy and Tacy, two best friends who palled around so much that people thought of them as one person. Lovelace was to write ten "Betsy-Tacy" books in all, publishing the last, *Betsy's Wedding*, in 1955.

This popular series, with its heartwarming tales of a Midwestern childhood, has enjoyed enduring popularity. Lovelace recreated the peaceful, pleasant Mankato of the early 1900s, renaming it Deep Valley, complete with the yellow cottage in which she grew up and the shoe store owned by her father; both her sisters appeared in the books too, as the characters Julia and Margaret. Anchored by annual traditions, seasons and events, and informed by a fond nostalgia, the books center around the friendship of Betsy Ray, Tacy Kelly and Thelma "Tib" Mueller, with aspiring writer Betsy leading the gang in its adventures, pranks, mishaps and rites of passage.

Maud Hart Lovelace

Like Lovelace herself, Betsy Ray marries her true love and becomes a writer, an occupation that Lovelace regarded as her vocation. "Although I maintain that writing is the work I prefer," she once wrote, "I shall not even now pretend that it is easy. . . . I am, nevertheless, glad that I chose writing and, if I had to do it all over, I would choose the same way." Maud Hart Lovelace died on March 11, 1980, in California. In 1993, HarperTrophy paperbacks issued revamped editions of all ten books in the series, with cover art by **Diane Goode**; the original inside illustrations by *Lois Lenski, however, were not altered.

Paula Morris, D.Phil.,
Brooklyn, New York

Lovell, Maria Anne (1803–1877)

English actress and dramatist. Name variations: Mrs. Lovell. Born Maria Anne Lacy in 1803; died in 1877; married George William Lovell (1804–1878, a dramatist), in 1830.

Maria Anne Lovell made her stage debut in 1818 and appeared at Covent Garden in 1822. Following her retirement from the stage, she turned to playwriting. *Ingomar the Barbarian* was produced at the Drury Lane in 1851, a role that would bring success to *Mary Anderson (1859–1940) over 30 years later. Maria Lovell also wrote *The Beginning of the End* which was performed at the Haymarket in 1855.

Lovisa.

Variant of Louisa or Louise.

Low, Juliette Gordon (1860–1927)

Founder of the Girl Scouts of the United States of America. Name variations: Daisy Low. Born Juliette Magill Gordon on October 31, 1860, in Savannah, Georgia; died of cancer on January 17, 1927, in Savannah, Georgia; daughter of William Washington II (a cotton broker and second lieutenant in the Confederate army) and Eleanor Kinzie Gordon; attended private day and boarding schools, and Mesdemoiselles Charbonniers' School, New York City, diploma, 1880; aunt of Daisy Gordon Lawrence (a writer); married William Low, on December 21, 1886 (died 1905); no children.

Moved with her family (without her father) to her maternal grandparents' home in Chicago for the duration of the Civil War (1864); with reunited family, returned to Savannah (August 23, 1865); began attending day school in Savannah; went to Stuart Hall

boarding school in Virginia and that summer made first visit to Europe (1873); at 15, transferred to Edge Hill boarding school in Virginia (1875) where she stayed until she began attending a French finishing school in New York City; graduated and returned to Savannah to make her debut (1880); went to Europe (1882) where she met and fell in love with William Low; traveled for the next four years and returned to Europe (1884) and accepted William Low's offer of marriage; treated by a physician who injected silver nitrate into her ear, which greatly impaired her hearing (1885); removal of a piece of wedding rice from her good ear resulted in an infection that left her completely deaf on that side (1886); with husband, established homes in Savannah, Perthshire, Scotland, and (1889) in Warwickshire, England; marriage crumbled and William Low died (1905) before the intended divorce was finalized; traveled, studied art, and searched for purpose; met Robert Baden-Powell and under his tutelage established Girl Guide troops in Scotland and London (1910); created the first troop of the Girl Guides in the U.S. (March 12, 1912); elected president of Girl Scouts of America which was incorporated in New York City (1915); resigned as president (1920); devoted the rest of her life to increasing the membership of and international involvement in Girl Scouting.

On June 17, 1911, 51-year-old Juliette Gordon Low confided to her diary: "I told [Robert Baden-Powell] about my futile efforts to be of use, and the shame I feel when I think of how much I could do, yet how little I accomplish, and when thrown with a man who has made a success of everything, by contrast I feel that my life brings forth 'nothing but leaves.' A wasted life. He looked so kindly when he said, 'There are little stars that guide us on, although we do not realize it.'" Baden-Powell guided Low toward her happiest and most fulfilling endeavor: the creation of the Girl Scouts of America.

Juliette Gordon was born in Savannah, Georgia, in 1860, just before the Civil War split the United States into two warring factions. While her father William Gordon, a wealthy and prominent Southerner, fought in the Confederate army, her mother **Eleanor Kinzie Gordon**, who came from one of Chicago's founding families, was left alone in their Savannah mansion with three young daughters. When General Sherman and the Union army marched through the city in December 1864, Eleanor Gordon took her children north to the safety of her family home. In Chicago, Daisy and her sisters grew strong again after the deprivation they had undergone in the war-torn South, proudly singing

Juliette
Gordon
Low

Confederate marching songs and awaiting news from their father. Late in August 1865, the Gordon family was reunited in Savannah. In the wake of the South's defeat, the Gordons' marriage faltered briefly, and William Gordon's cotton-brokering business suffered. The next five years were financially troubled.

Daisy grew up hardly noticing their temporary poverty. One constant was a love of animals. Throughout her life, she surrounded herself with cats and dogs, birds and horses, and any sick or stray animal commanded her immediate love and attention. Her education began with Bible lessons conducted by her mother and continued with her favorite sister Eleanor at schools taught by local women. Daisy loved art, languages, and literature, but never did well in mathematics or spelling; her friends and family joked about her atrocious spelling and erratic logic. Although she was raised a Southern belle, with strict rules of behavior, she would often do and say things that confused people. Her mother referred to such behavior as "Daisy's stunts." Her brother later recalled: "Two and two by no means made four to her. They made anything she chose to imagine they made, and once she had an idea in her head facts could not change it. The idea remained as she visualized it, in defiance of all argument and demonstration to the contrary."

I've got something for the girls of Savannah, and all America, and all the world, and we're going to start it to-night.

—Juliette Gordon Low

At age 13, Daisy was sent to boarding school in Virginia, where her flair for dramatics and her sense of humor made her popular with the other students. She also founded her first club, The Helpful Hands, in an effort to teach younger girls to sew and then give their handmade clothing to the poor. (Their charitable efforts were not always successful; at times, the sleeves fell off the shirts.) As an adolescent, Daisy spent a great deal of time away from home. When not at boarding school she often summered in north Georgia with her many cousins, exploring the woods and streams around Etowah Falls. Her 16th Christmas was memorable for a visit to relatives in Washington, D.C., where she attended her first adult parties with young male students from West Point, Harvard, and Princeton.

The following year, she transferred to a finishing school in New York City run by the Mesdemoiselles Charbonnier, where the young women students wore uniforms, spoke only French, and were escorted everywhere. In addition to her studies in literature and languages, Daisy added classes in dancing and advanced art; she was recognized as having genuine artistic talent in both drawing and oil painting. She also greatly enjoyed attending theater and the opera. After graduating with the traditional diploma, she made her debut into Savannah society in 1880.

In accordance with the customs of her class and era, Daisy's time was filled with parties, balls, dinners, and similar entertainments; she would later tap her large network of friends in the U.S. and in Europe for assistance with her burgeoning Girl Scout movement. Travel had become an accepted routine in her life, as she spent some part of every year visiting extended cousins, aunts, uncles, and friends in Washington, New York, Boston, and Chicago. In 1882, she took her first trip to Europe. While in England, she became acquainted with some friends of her family's, including a handsome, charming, and reckless young man named William Mackay Low. The scion of a wealthy American, William lived in England. Daisy Gordon and Willy Low began their romance in 1882, and by 1884 had agreed to marry. The couple courted for another two years, because both their fathers initially disapproved of the match, before finally setting a wedding date for late 1886.

On January 18, 1885, suffering from an earache, Daisy sought out a physician in Savannah and persuaded him to treat her with an injection of silver nitrate, a new method she had read about in a New York paper. The treatment severely, and permanently, impaired her hearing in that ear. Despite the months that passed before she was physically well again, she continued to prepare for her wedding. On December 21, 1886, Daisy Gordon and Willy Low were married in a lavish ceremony in Savannah, and the guests showered them with rice. In a freakish accident, a piece of rice lodged painfully in her good ear. When the ensuing infection healed, she was totally deaf in that ear.

Low learned to live with her hearing impairment. She watched lips when people spoke, and tried to seat guests on the side of what had now become her good ear, in which she retained some measure of hearing. She also got in the habit of speaking first as a way of avoiding misunderstandings with others. When she was older, she occasionally used her deafness to her advantage by hearing what she wanted to hear whether it had actually been said to her or not. This method was often employed to gain "volunteers" for her Girl Scouts. None of Low's family or friends ever suggested that she was defeated by her deafness; she did not dwell on the difficulties that the loss of her hearing caused her.

Daisy Low and her new husband set up homes in Savannah and in England and Scotland, where Willy's financial and social status conferred upon his wife membership in the English upper class. The Lows entertained often, and Daisy was twice presented at court. They explored Egypt and Europe and attended balls, formal parties, masquerades, and the London theater and opera. Daisy continued to indulge her love of the outdoors with fox hunting, fishing, swimming, tennis, hiking, and horseback riding. She often visited her family in the States, and they came to stay with her in England.

As the years passed, the couple became increasingly distant. Willy was interested in horse racing, took long trips away to hunt big game, and spent many nights drinking with his male friends. To assuage her unhappiness and to fill her time alone, Low threw herself into her art. She painted in oils, carved wood, and sculpted. She also learned to forge metal; one winter, she took lessons from a blacksmith, made her own tools, and designed and created a pair of iron gates for her home in England, decorating them with hammered copper daisies. Ill health began to plague her, adding to her unhappiness. Eventually, she started to go her own way, taking more trips alone, and once visited Egypt with her younger sister. She became good friends with author Rudyard Kipling and his wife Carrie (**Caroline Starr Kipling** [1865–1939]), and with several British military heroes. She tended to the poor and the indigent in the local village near her English home, and she never turned away a stray animal. In 1898, Low returned to the U.S. to assist her mother in setting up a convalescent hospital for soldiers wounded in the Spanish-American War.

By 1901, her marriage was in tatters. Willy Low, whose alcoholism had worsened, had taken a mistress and asked for a divorce. Before it could be finalized, however, he died in 1905, leaving almost everything to his mistress. Daisy, who had to sue for what was rightfully hers, felt betrayed, embarrassed, and hurt by his actions, but nonetheless she mourned for Willy and the love they had once shared. Maintaining a brave front, she resisted suitors and comforted herself with her family and further travel. For the next five years, she moved between London society, Egypt, the United States, and India. She also

Juliette Gordon Low

took up the serious study of sculpting. Although she enjoyed her life, she was nagged by the conviction that it was neither useful nor rewarding. In 1910, she met Baden-Powell, the great British war hero. They became fast friends, sharing an infectious enthusiasm for living as well as a love of art and the outdoors. Together they discussed these topics and, always, Baden-Powell's preoccupation—the Boy Scouts. Soon she began to compare her life, unfavorably, with his.

A hero of the Boer War, General Sir Robert Baden-Powell was also the founder of the Boy Scouts. The initial idea for the Boy Scouts came from his military experiences in India and at the battle of Mafeking, South Africa. In Mafeking, the outnumbered British soldiers under his command were relieved of some of their mundane tasks by a corp of boys trained to be messengers and scouts. The boys so enjoyed their duties that Baden-Powell began a similar program for English boys. Much to his surprise, when he announced the formation of the Boy Scouts in England, 6,000 girls also eagerly registered. Baden-Powell charged his sister, ✒➤ **Agnes Baden-Powell**, with the care and training of the girls, and she formed them into Girl Guide troops. Although the girls went on hiking trips

Baden-Powell, Agnes. See Baden-Powell, Olave for sidebar.

and learned outdoor lore like the boys did, they were also educated in first aid, homemaking skills, arts, crafts, and drama.

In June 1911, Daisy Low wrote of Baden-Powell in her diary: "A sort of intuition comes over me that he believes I might make more out of life, and that he has ideas which, if I follow them, will open a more useful sphere of work before me in future." Gradually, she became interested in the Girl Guides. "I like girls and I like the organization and the rules and pastimes," she wrote her father, "so if you find that I get very deeply interested you must not be surprised." With Baden-Powell's blessing, Low tried her hand at organizing a Girl Guide troop in the Scottish Highlands. She called together girls who lived near her home, and with friends taught them about nursing the sick, cooking, knitting, knot-tying, signaling, and personal health. Low enabled the poorer Scottish girls to provide for themselves and their families by beginning a program of carding and spinning wool from the girls' own sheep, then found a market for the homespun yarn in London. She also showed them how to raise and sell chickens to the wealthy visitors who came periodically to the area's hunting lodges. Thus, rather than having to leave their homes to take arduous industrial jobs in the cities, members of the Scottish Girl Guides learned useful skills, made money to help support their families, and had fun doing so.

Because she lived for part of the year in London, Low next started two successful Girl Guide troops in a poor section of that city. When she had to leave for America, she looked about for someone who could lead those troops in her absence. She selected a woman who protested that she was too busy, had no experience with girls, and did not even live in London. Low's selective hearing paid off: "Then that is all settled," she replied. "I have already told my girls you will take the meeting next Thursday." She then left England to establish her new project with the girls of America.

Savannah was to become the home of the first American Girl Guide troop. Low's cousin, **Nina Anderson Pape**, suggested that they contact a group of local girls who were already meeting together under the tutelage of naturalist Walter J. Hoxie to take nature walks, explore the habits of wildlife, and occasionally cook outdoors over a campfire. Low invited the girls to her house and explained about the Girl Guide promise, the uniforms, and the fun they would have learning new things. The Savannah girls clamored to join. On March 12, 1912, 18 girls enrolled in two troops, the White Rose Patrol and the Carnation Patrol. The troops made their own uniforms, studied the English Girl Guide handbook, and met in a building Low renovated that became, according to its placard, the Girl Guide Headquarters. Unusual for a time when exercise was regarded as quite possibly deleterious to a growing girl's health, they also played in the vacant lot across the street, where Low had built basketball and tennis courts.

Interest in the Girl Guides was immediate and nationwide. Newspapers spread the word, and in Savannah alone, six Girl Guide troops soon sprang up. Low bought some land along a river near the city so the girls could make day excursions. Patterning her methods on Baden-Powell's, she led the first troop on a five-day camping trip. She learned of a few, scattered Girl Scout troops in America that had been started by people who had heard of the Boy Scout movement in England, and worked to merge these with her Girl Guides. Eventually, the Girl Scout troops became affiliated with hers through their adoption of the first American version of the English Girl Guide handbook (prepared by Hoxie and published in 1913), *How Girls Can Help Their Country*. Low compromised with the other troops by agreeing to take on their name, and all the early Girl Guides were renamed Girl Scouts.

Girl Scouting began in a new era for American women. Although firmly in the pattern of 19th-century women's clubs, Girl Scouting attempted both to shape girls' characters—by molding them into model citizens and educating them for their role as wives and mothers—and to expand their boundaries. The latter notion was undoubtedly affected by Juliette Gordon Low's own life; raised to be a Southern belle, she found when her marriage faltered that she needed social survival skills she did not possess, and therefore had to invent. With the Girl Scouts, she wanted to offer girls and young women possibilities that had not existed for her. Girl Scouting taught self-sufficiency through wilderness skills, farming techniques, first aid, rescue work, and outdoor food preparation. Although then as now there might be only a slim chance that any given Girl Scout would actually need to put, say, her wilderness survival skills to the test, it was the sense of self-esteem and capability instilled by these abilities that was of crucial importance. *How Girls Can Help Their Country* also contained a short chapter on careers for women. While Low emphasized the sciences—astronomy, geology, ecology, botany—she did not neglect the more traditional women's fields. Care of infants and children, art, music, cooking, sewing, and housekeeping skills were all topics included in the Girl Scout agenda. Membership in the Girl Scouts brought with it an opportunity to fill leadership positions, boost self-esteem, enjoy community service, work and play within a supportive group of women, advance talents and develop new ones, and become more resourceful, independent, and self-aware.

In 1913, Juliette Gordon Low established a national headquarters for her growing movement in Washington, D.C. She installed her friend **Edith D. Johnston** as the first National Secretary, and Johnston was soon joined by a board of directors and advisors comprised of wealthy and aristocratic women, including America's first lady *Ellen Axson Wilson (who would die one year later). Low spent most of her time traveling around the country giving speeches, meeting with reporters, and soliciting volunteers to lead the Girl Scouts on the state and local levels. Every new acquaintance she made led to another one, creating a network of dedicated Girl Scout leaders that stretched from Savannah to Washington, D.C., to New York, to Boston, to Chicago, to St. Louis. In June 1915, the Girl Scouts of America (GSA) was incorporated, the constitution and bylaws of the organization were adopted, and Low was elected president. That year, there were approximately 5,000 girls enrolled as Girl Scouts. In 1917, the Girl Scouts formed their first troop of physically challenged girls. Later, troops for the deaf and the blind would be started—the first of their kind in America.

Juliette Gordon Low was the impetus for the Girl Scout movement, and her energy kept the movement growing. So did her money. From 1912 to 1917, Low paid all the administrative and salary expenses, as well as rent on the national headquarters, handbooks and uniforms for the Girl Scouts, out of her own pocket. She once sold her pearls to keep the movement alive. She also often returned to England and Scotland to socialize with friends and to learn from the Baden-Powells of the activities of the Girl Guides.

When the First World War broke out, Low helped with the relief of Belgian orphans and set up housing and transportation for the visiting relatives of wounded soldiers. In 1917, when the U.S. entered World War I, the national board of the Girl Scouts of America sent a telegram to President Woodrow Wilson offering their assistance. Girl Scouts participated in the conservation programs of the National Food Administration headed by Herbert Hoover, hosted Liberty Bond drives to help fund the war effort, assisted Red Cross nurses and canteen workers, and sewed and rolled bandages. Girl Scouting grew tremendously during the war years; by 1920, membership stood at 50,000, and neighborhoods throughout America boasted Girl Scout troops.

Juliette Gordon Low had become a celebrity. Her name and her photograph were intimately connected with the Girl Scouts, and she reveled in every good work her girls accomplished. She convinced the new first lady, Wilson's second wife *Edith Bolling Wilson, to become the honorary president of the Girl Scouts. Other first ladies followed suit: *Grace Coolidge and particularly *Lou Henry Hoover, who was elected president of the GSA in 1922, were enthusiastic supporters. When she was honorary president as first lady in 1929, in an extension of her husband's philosophy of volunteerism, Lou Hoover oversaw the Girl Scouts' efforts to alleviate the effects of the Great Depression. (Although well meant, this project was largely unsuccessful.)

After World War I, the Girl Scouts of America underwent standardization and professionalization. In January 1920, Juliette Low resigned as president so that she could spend more time among the girls across the country. Her birthday was designated as Founder's Day, and continues to be celebrated annually by Girl Scout troops. **Anne Hyde Choate**, who became the new president in Low's stead, presided over the rewriting of the handbook, retitled *Scouting for Girls*; saw the magazine of the GSA modernized and renamed *The American Girl*; and laid plans for training camps for Girl Scout leaders. More important, the first International Conference of Girl Guides and Girl Scouts was held in England, with Low representing the GSA. She became vitally interested in worldwide Girl Scouting and hoped that the exchange of ideas between girls would promote the cause of international peace.

In the mid-1920s, Juliette Gordon Low began to experience symptoms of the cancer that would eventually kill her. She suffered great pain without complaint and continued to attend the annual national conferences and the many regional meetings of the GSA. Hosting the fourth International Conference at Camp **Edith Macy** in New York State turned out to be her swan song. In typical fashion, "Miss Daisy" had promised at the third International Conference in July 1924 that the world delegates would have a lovely time during the next conference at Camp Edith Macy. The camp was at the time a totally undeveloped piece of land along the Hudson River with no roads, no campsites, no running water, no electricity, and no buildings, but

Low wanted the first International Conference held outside England to be hosted by the United States. Disregarding the cries of the board of directors of the Girl Scouts of America, she coaxed them into creating a blueprint for the camp, raising the money, and building the necessary infrastructure. Although it was a close call, Camp Edith Macy opened in time for the 400 delegates of the International Conference.

Juliette Gordon Low died in her beloved Savannah on January 18, 1927. She was buried, at her request, in her Girl Scout uniform with a telegram from Anne Hyde Choate and the Girl Scout National Council tucked into her breast pocket. It read, "You are not only the first Girl Scout but the best Girl Scout of them all."

Encomiums for Juliette Gordon Low took many forms. The Juliette Low World Friendship Fund was established in 1927 to support foreign exchange between Girl Scouts of the U.S. and Girl Scouts, or Guides, from other countries. During World War II, an American-made battleship, the *Juliette Low*, was named for her. The Girl Scouts of America purchased Juliette Gordon Low's birthplace in Savannah in 1953. In 1979, she was inducted into the Women's Hall of Fame in Seneca Falls, New York. President Ronald Reagan, in 1983, named a federal building in Savannah for her—only the second federal building ever to be named for a woman. Among the memorials to Low is one she herself donated before her death: Gordonston Memorial Park in Savannah. There she installed the wrought-iron gates with the copper daisies she had made so long ago in England.

Low's greatest monument is the continuation of her cherished principles in the ongoing Girl Scouting movement. When she died, GSA membership stood at approximately 200,000. In 1962, when the Girl Scouts celebrated the 50-year anniversary of their founding, 3,500,000 American girls wore the distinctive uniforms of the Brownies, Juniors, Intermediates, and Seniors. The time they spend as Girl Scouts—the skills they learn, the insights they have, the helpful deeds they do, and the friendships they form—helps to ensure that those millions of girls avoid what Juliette Gordon Low feared most for herself: a wasted life.

SOURCES:

Choate, Anne Hyde, and Helen Ferris, eds. *Juliette Low and the Girl Scouts: The Story of an American Woman, 1860–1927.* Garden City, NY: Doubleday, Doran, 1928.

Lyon, Nancy. "Juliette Low: The Eccentric Who Founded the Girl Scouts," in *Ms. Magazine.* November 1981, pp. 101–105.

Parker, Charlotte, "Juliette Magill Gordon Low," in Kenneth Coleman and Charles Stephen Gurr, eds., *Dictionary of Georgia Biography.* Vol. 2. Athens: University of Georgia Press, 1983, pp. 638–640.

Shultz, Gladys Denny, and Daisy Gordon Lawrence. *Lady from Savannah: The Life of Juliette Low.* Philadelphia, PA: J.B. Lippincott, 1958.

SUGGESTED READING:

"Biographic Sketch: Juliette Gordon Low, Founder, Girl Scouts of the U.S.A.," unattributed article, Girl Scouts of the United States of America National Headquarters, New York, New York, n.d.

Highlights in Girl Scouting, 1912–1991. NY: Girl Scouts of the U.S.A., 1991.

Kerr, Rose. *The Story of a Million Girls: Guiding and Girl Scouting Round the World.* London: The Girl Guides Association, n.d.

The New York Times (obituary). January 19, 1927, p. 23.

Reynolds, Moira Davison. "Juliette Gordon Low, 1860–1927, Founder of Girl Scouts," in *Women Champions of Human Rights.* NY: McFarland, 1991, pp. 54–66.

Rhodes, Don. "Juliette Low, Girl Scouts founder, led rich life," in *Augusta Chronicle-Herald.* January 19, 1986.

"Seventy-five Years of Girl Scouting." NY: Girl Scouts of the U.S.A., 1986.

Strickland, Charles E. "Juliette Low, the Girl Scouts, and the Role of American Women," in Mary Kelley, ed., *Woman's Being, Woman's Place: Female Identity and Vocation in American History.* Boston, MA: G.K. Hall, 1979, pp. 252–264.

COLLECTIONS:

Correspondence, papers, and memorabilia on the Magill and Gordon families can be found in the Gordon Family Papers, Georgia Historical Society, Savannah, Georgia and the Gordon Family Papers, Southern Historical Collection, University of North Carolina at Chapel Hill. Documentary information on Juliette Gordon Low and the Girl Scout movement is located in the Juliette Gordon Low Girl Scout National Center, Savannah, Georgia, and the Juliette Gordon Low Collection, Girl Scouts of the U.S.A. National Headquarters, New York City.

Stacy A. Cordery,
Associate Professor of History,
Monmouth College, Monmouth, Illinois

Low, Mary Fairchild (1858–1946)

American painter. Name variations: Mary Louise Fairchild MacMonnies. Born Mary Louise Fairchild in New Haven, Connecticut, in 1858; died in 1946; descendant of Governor William Bradford of the Mayflower; attended St. Louis Art Academy; studied at France's Académie Julian and with Carolus-Duran; married Frederick MacMonnies (a sculptor), in 1888 (divorced); married Will Hicok Low (a mural painter and illustrator), in 1909; children: (first marriage) two daughters.

Mary Fairchild Low was born in 1858 in New Haven, Connecticut, and studied at the St.

Louis Art Academy, where she won a three-year scholarship. She then studied in Paris under Carolus-Duran. While there, she met and married sculptor Frederick MacMonnies. Both successful artists, they lived in an elegant apartment on the Rue de Sèvres, summered in their 14th-century monastery at Giverny, and frequently entertained. Their next door neighbors were Claude Monet and *Isadora Duncan. The 1893 Chicago Exposition was a joint showcase for the MacMonnies where their work was well received. Frederick's large sculpture *Barge of State* was the central fountain, while Mary Low's mural *Primitive Woman* was displayed opposite *Mary Cassatt's *Modern Woman.* Their marriage ended, however, when Frederick turned his attention to one of his art students.

Mary Low's works include groups of nudes or modern figures painted in the open air and sunlight, with delicate charm, as well as landscapes and portraits. Under the name Mary Louise Fairchild MacMonnies, she was awarded several gold medals in European exhibitions; in 1902, she won the **Julia Shaw** prize of the Society of American Artists. After her second marriage to Will Low, Mary moved to Bronxville, New York, and dispensed with the name MacMonnies, deleting all references to her former husband.

Low Countries, queen of.

See Mary of Burgundy (1457–1482).

Lowell, Amy (1874–1925)

American poet, critic, and woman of letters who became a powerful leader in the modernist poetry movement known as Imagism. Born Amy Lowell on February 9, 1874, at her family's Sevenels Estate in Brookline, Massachusetts; died in the same house on May 12, 1925; youngest of five children of Augustus Lowell (a businessman) and Katherine Bigelow (Lawrence) Lowell; sister of Abbott Lawrence Lowell, president of Harvard, and Percival Lowell, an astronomer; privately tutored at Sevenels by a governess; attended several local private schools in Boston; never married; lived with Ada Dwyer.

Awards: honorary degree from Baylor University (1920); Helen Haire Levinson prize from Poetry *magazine (1924); (awarded posthumously) Pulitzer Prize for* What's O'Clock *(1926).*

At age 17, completed formal education and returned home to help maintain family estate during mother's illness (1891); inherited Sevenels estate after death of her father (1900); bought a summer home in New Hampshire and became involved in Brookline

*community affairs (1901); was inspired by a performance of actress Eleonora Duse to become a poet (1902); wrote first serious poem (1910); met Ada Dwyer, who would become her lifelong companion (1912); discovered Imagist movement in poetry and met Ezra Pound for first time (1913); quarreled with Pound in London and published her own Imagist poetry anthology, effectively taking over the leadership of the Imagist movement in America (1914); for the next several years, engaged in public debates about the new form of poetry; suffered from a hernia (summer 1916); began work on Chinese poetry with *Florence Ayscough (1917); had an abdominal rupture and underwent the first of many operations for hernia (1918); was the first woman to deliver a lecture at Harvard (1919); underwent two more hernia surgeries and received an honorary degree from Baylor University (1920); began biography of Keats and had a fourth hernia operation (1921); continued tiring schedule of reading tours cross country; after publication of Keats biography, suffered a severe hernial attack (1925); several works published posthumously.*

Poetry: Dream Drops or Stories from Fairy Land by a Dreamer *(1887);* A Dome of Many-Colored Glass *(1912);* Sword Blades and Poppy Seeds *(1914);* Men, Women and Ghosts *(1916);* Can Grande's Castle *(1918);* Pictures of the Floating World *(1919); (translation of Chinese poetry with Florence Ayscough)* Fir-Flower Tablets *(1921);* Legends *(1921);* A Critical Fable *(1922); (published posthumously)* What's O'-Clock *(1925);* East Wind *(1926);* Ballads for Sale *(1927);* Selected Poems *(1928);* Complete Poetical Works of Amy Lowell *(1955);* A Shard of Silence: Selected Poems of Amy Lowell *(1957). Anthologies:* Some Imagist Poets *(3 vols., 1915–1917); (with Louis Untermeyer)* A Miscellany of American Poetry *(2 vols., 1917);* Six French Poets *(1915);* Tendencies in Modern American Poetry *(1917); (biography)* John Keats *(2 vols., 1925);* Poets and Poetry *(1930).*

Amy Lowell, through will and determination, became a major force in American poetry at the critical moment of the birth of modernism. Though lacking the advantages of a first-rate education, she was drawn to poetry as by an irresistible force. Her energy and passion for the genre were boundless, and she became the leading speaker for the modernist movement known as Imagism. Lowell was also widely respected for her own poetry, literary criticism, and a substantial biography of John Keats. At the center of a circle of modernist artists in the 1910s and 1920s, she played the role of patron as well as promoter and practitioner. She was both beloved and despised for her outspoken manner and her challenge to gender conventions, and she exercised an important influence on a generation of American poets.

Amy Lowell was born into a wealthy and prominent family. The Lowells were among the oldest and most well known of the Boston Brahmins. The first members of the Lowell clan had arrived in New England in the 1630s, and since then their descendants had been extraordinarily successful in business, education, and the arts. In the early 19th century, they had given Massachusetts the mill town of Lowell, ushering in the Industrial Revolution in America. Amy Lowell's grandfather, John Amory Lowell, served as sole trustee of the Lowell Institute, a gathering place for intellectuals founded by a cousin, John Lowell, Jr.

Amy was also born into a family with a literary tradition. Her cousin, James Russell Lowell, who was 55 when she was born, was an eminent journalist, diplomat, and poet. The Lowell literary tradition would be carried on after her death by a distant cousin, poet Robert Lowell.

Poetry is at once my trade and my religion.

—Amy Lowell

Amy's father Augustus Lowell, a business tycoon with large interests in the nation's banks and cotton mills, was, noted one chronicler, "wealthy beyond dreams." In 1854, he married the daughter of his father's business partner. **Katherine Lawrence (Lowell)** came from a New England family as prosperous and distinguished as the Lowells. The town of Lawrence, Massachusetts, well-known in history books as the site of several textile strikes, was named for her family. Her father went on to serve as a U.S. congressional representative and an ambassador to Great Britain. A well-educated woman, Katherine spoke seven languages and excelled in music.

Augustus and Katherine had four children before the arrival of Amy. Indeed, she was something of an afterthought; at the time of her birth on February 9, 1874, her four siblings ranged in age from 12 to 19. Amy received little attention from her parents. Her father was caught up with his business dealings and his passion for botany. Her mother contracted Bright's disease, which brought on bouts of extreme nervousness and heightened blood pressure.

Yet Amy did not suffer from material deprivation. She was raised at a Brookline, Massachusetts, estate the Lowells had named "Sevenels" since it housed seven Lowells (Ls). The estate, which included a full staff of servants, has been described as "thirty acres of sprawling emerald meadow, grove, garden, walks and walls." The house was equally well-appointed, with sterling silver doorknobs, numerous chandeliers, an extensive library, and fine furnishings. Her father's passion for plants meant that Amy spent her childhood wandering extensive gardens filled with rare and exotic flowers, and her future poetry placed a heavy emphasis on nature.

Amy's education began at Sevenels, where she was tutored by a governess. Between the ages of eight and twelve, she attended several private schools in the Boston area. Though popular among her classmates, Lowell terrorized the faculty. Her precocious intelligence and tomboy ways, combined with a desire to gain attention, made her a notorious class clown.

But Amy suffered from the gender prejudices of her time, despite her privileged upbringing. While she was encouraged to write from an early age, the formal education she received was a girl's education, which was decidedly inferior to that of boys. In the Lowell family, boys were packed off to Harvard by age 13. Amy's formal education could not compare with an education from Harvard, and she would long regret one deficiency in particular. Unlike her brothers, she was never taught Greek or Latin. Lowell felt that her ignorance of classical languages was a hindrance to her development as a poet.

Amy Lowell was troubled by more than an inferior education. She was afflicted, from age ten, with a glandular condition that made her obese. By age 20, she weighed 200 pounds, though she was barely 5' tall. This condition plagued her throughout her life, and she was acutely aware of what this did for her marriage prospects in Boston high society. "I am ugly, fat, conspicuous and dull," she wrote in her diary, "to say nothing of a very bad temper." Although she received instruction in dance, Amy disliked the whirl of the formal Boston social scene, and she attended social dances with neither success nor happiness.

Although Lowell's formal education ended in 1891 when she was 17, she spent the years between 1891 and 1895 reading extensively in her father's library at Sevenels. Early on, she read Leigh Hunt's *Imagination and Fancy, or, Selections from the English Poets.* Hunt's book, which would have a serious impact on Amy's intellectual development, was designed to teach the general reader how to distinguish excellent poetry from poor poetry. According to Lowell, the book's extended essay defining poetry "opened a door that otherwise might have re-

Amy
Lowell

mained shut. . . . I did not read it. I devoured it. I read it over and over and over, and then I turned to the works of the poets referred to." The most important of the poets she sought out was John Keats. Lowell was deeply moved by the way he reveled in emotion and the five senses. Keats re-

mained a powerful influence on Lowell's work, and she would devote the last few years of her life to a two-volume biography of the poet. Another great discovery was the work of Victor Hugo. "I believe Victor Hugo woke me up to the meaning of style," she later wrote.

Katherine Lowell died in 1895. During the last few years of her mother's illness, Amy had increasingly taken over the role of woman of the household. This experience served her well, for in 1900, when her father passed away, Lowell inherited a substantial sum and bought Sevenels, the mansion and its grounds. Wealth brought independence, and the freedom to pursue her own interests. She became involved in Brookline's public-school system and while attending meetings discovered that she had a talent for debate and oration. In this setting, she honed her skills as a public speaker. Her peers eventually elected her to the executive committee of the Brookline Educational Society, where she chaired the library committee. Her civic responsibilities also included membership in the Women's Municipal League.

In addition to local responsibilities, Lowell continued to read extensively. In 1902, at age 28, her general interest in art and literature finally coalesced into a desire to become a poet. The catalyst came from the world of theater. Lowell attended three plays in Boston which featured the great Italian actress *Eleonora Duse. So inspired was Lowell over Duse's performance that upon returning to Sevenels, she wrote her first poem. "The effect on me was tremendous," she later recalled. "What really happened was that it revealed me to myself. . . . I sat down and with infinite agitation wrote this poem . . . . [I]t loosed a bolt in my brain and I found where my true function lay." With this revelation came a determination to forge a successful literary career. Lowell located a summer retreat in New Hampshire where she could write without distraction. She also energetically added to her collection of books and immersed herself in the intellectual circles of Boston.

The poetry came slowly. In 1910, "A Fixed Idea," her first published poem, appeared in the *Atlantic Monthly*. Several followed in the same magazine which would become the core of her first published volume of poetical works, *A Dome of Many-Colored Glass*, released in 1912. Conventional in style and influenced by Keats, *Dome* was deemed perfectly acceptable poetry by the critics; it lacked only one element: the ability to inspire excitement, anger, or emotion of any kind. Lowell was so upset by the lukewarm reviews that she became physically ill with gastric neuralgia and took to her bed for weeks. This setback was only temporary, however, for it took more than a few unenthusiastic reviews to dampen Lowell's desire to become a successful poet. She began writing again and would soon find herself caught up in a new movement that would prove to have a remarkable impact on American poetry.

As Lowell was putting the finishing touches on the manuscript of *A Dome of Many-Colored Glass* in 1912, several important literary events occurred, notes biographer Jean Gould, that were central to the birth of a new movement in American poetry. First, the young poet Robert Frost began putting together his initial volume of poems. Second, *Edna St. Vincent Millay gained attention when her extraordinary poem "Renascence" failed to garner first prize in a contest; the ensuing controversy launched Millay's career. Finally, *Harriet Monroe, art critic for the *Chicago Tribune*, gained financial support for an enterprising venture periodical, *Poetry: A Magazine of Verse*. In a departure from previous poetry magazines, Monroe promised to pay her contributing poets for their published work. Lowell's work caught Monroe's eye; she wrote to Amy, soliciting not only some of her work but some of her money to back the fledgling journal. Lowell obliged in both requests.

At about this time, modernist poet Ezra Pound's *Ripostes* was published in London. *Ripostes* contained an important appendix: five poems of the poet T.E. Hulme, the founder of a movement in poetry called Imagism. Earlier, Monroe had named Pound foreign editor of *Poetry*, and in 1913 the Imagist movement would fully emerge when the journal published a poem signed by "H.D. Imagiste" (*Hilda Doolittle). A later article by Pound officially proclaimed Imagism a movement and laid out its parameters. One literary critic described the Imagists as poets who "called for precision, economy, definiteness, and direct treatment." Ezra Pound also called on poets to learn from the methods of the musician, particularly the musician's use of rhythm. In many ways the Imagist poets were part of a more broad-based international movement in art and literature known as Modernism. This movement, which emerged in the 1890s and reached its zenith in the 1920s, was a reaction and challenge to the realism that dominated art and literature at the time.

As the Imagist movement in poetry was beginning to form, Carl Engel, a musicologist, composer, and one of Lowell's closest friends, introduced Lowell to a new type of poetry: the work of the French symbolist poets and their successors. Now Lowell had discovered free verse, or cadenced verse, as she preferred to call it, and it would profoundly affect her work. The Imagists had also begun to experiment with free verse forms, and it was this aspect of the movement that would most captivate Lowell's imagination. From that point on, Amy Lowell became engrossed in the New Poetry.

She reached a turning point in her personal life as well. In March 1912, Lowell was introduced to ❧▶ **Ada Dwyer** at a meeting of The Lunch Club, a group of "accomplished women" to which Lowell belonged. Dwyer was a character actress who at the time was playing the lead in Paul Armstrong's drama *The Deep Purple*. In private life, she was Mrs. Harold Russell, though she and her husband had divorced some time ago, after the birth of their daughter **Lorna**. Dwyer utterly charmed the members of the Lunch Club, so much so that they changed their group's name to the Purple Lunch Club in honor of Dwyer's current theater production.

Amy Lowell was especially entranced with Ada Dwyer's charms. Notes Gould: "The affinity Amy and Ada felt for each other was apparent immediately." Dwyer was a sympathetic listener as well as an engaging storyteller, and her ability to put people at ease made her a natural complement to the often high-strung Lowell. Intellectually the two shared similar passions as well, for Dwyer had a deep appreciation for poetry while Lowell had always been captivated by the theater.

It was not long before Lowell was trying to convince Dwyer to make Sevenels her permanent home, which Dwyer did in 1914. Dwyer effortlessly took responsibility for daily domestic affairs at Sevenels, freeing Amy to pursue her writing without interruption. Several of Lowell's poems, such as "The Letter" and "Madonna of the Evening Flowers," both published in 1919, are testaments to her abiding affection for Dwyer. Biographers agree that without Dwyer's support, Lowell would not have been able to maintain her almost frenetic working pace until her death in 1925.

Having fully embraced the new movement in poetry, Lowell was determined to seek out its leaders. In the summer of 1913, with a letter of introduction from Harriet Monroe, she traveled to London to meet Ezra Pound and others on the cutting edge of modern poetry. The trip was a success, and she returned to Boston with a clear mission: to crusade for Imagism. Despite the fact that Lowell was almost a decade older than most of the other Imagists—she was 39 when she met Pound—she pursued her mission with zeal. What Lowell lacked in experience she made up for in enthusiasm and promotional skill. She was convinced that Imagism would be the catalyst for a renaissance in American poetry, and she was confident that she would serve as its most influential prophet.

Problems quickly developed between Lowell and Pound, however. On a second trip to England

---

❧▶ **Dwyer, Ada** (1863–1952)

American actress. Name variations: Ada Dwyer Russell. Born in 1863 in Salt Lake City, Utah; died on July 4, 1952; educated in Boston; married Harold Russell (divorced); lived with Amy Lowell (the poet), from 1914 to 1925; children: Lorna Russell.

Ada Dwyer made her stage debut in *Alone in London* and was a prominent actress on the New York stage for many years. She appeared as Doña Julia in *Don Juan* (1891), Mrs. Greenthorne in *Husband and Wife*, and Malka in *The Children of the Ghetto* (1892), reprising her performance as Malka for her London debut at the Adelphi in 1899. For the next seven or eight years, Dwyer toured as a supporting actress in productions starring *Eleanor Robson** (Belmont), playing Lady Capulet in *Romeo and Juliet*, Fanchette in *A Gentleman of France*, Mrs. Leadbetter in *Merely Mary Ann*, Lady Fancourt in *Agatha*, Mrs. Waring in *The Girl Who Has Everything*, and Lize Heath in *Salomy Jane*. Throughout 1908, she toured in Australia as Mrs. Wiggs in *Alice Hegan Rice's* Mrs. Wiggs of the Cabbage Patch*. In 1909, Dwyer returned to the Lyric in New York to play Bet in *The Dawn of a To-Morrow*, reprised at the Garrick in London in 1910. Returning to the Lyric, she appeared as Kate Fallon in *The Deep Purple* (1911) and as Grandma in *Blackbirds* (1912). After meeting poet *Amy Lowell*, Ada Dwyer took on only a few more roles between 1913 and 1914. She moved into Lowell's Sevenels in 1914 and retired from the stage.

---

in 1914, their differences on Imagism escalated into a heated battle. The crux of their disagreement concerned the definition of Imagism. Pound had coined the term, published the first anthology of Imagism (*Des Imagistes*), and considered himself the unparalleled leader of the movement. Yet he was also organizing a more radical offshoot of Imagism, called vorticism, and many Imagists were dissatisfied with his leadership. Amy Lowell was perhaps the most dissatisfied of the group. Although she viewed Pound as the founder of the Imagism, she felt that he had relinquished his right to be its leader; she wanted to fill that vacuum and bring Imagism to a wider audience than it had reached thus far.

On July 17, 1914, at a dinner party organized by Lowell at London's Dieudonne Restaurant, these two forceful personalities clashed. Pound and a few others mocked Lowell. Though she did not retaliate in kind that evening, she was soon using her powers of persuasion to convince other Imagists like H.D. and Richard Aldington that she, rather than Pound, should serve as their representative. Lowell soon turned the tide in her favor, in part because several Imagists considered Pound's methods dictatorial. Lowell oversaw the next three Imagist anthologies.

The feud between Lowell and Pound never ended. Pound made every effort to distance himself from the American Imagist poets and referred to them thereafter as the "Amygist" movement. For her part, Lowell continued to insist that Pound had done little for the Imagists. In a letter to the critic Louis Untermeyer, she assessed Pound's influence thus: "The Imagists during the year and a half in which he headed the movement were unknown and jeered at, when they were not absolutely ignored. It was not until I entered the arena and Ezra dropped out that Imagism had to be considered seriously."

Lowell's showdown with Pound revealed not only her intense commitment to the new poetry, but also her sometimes obstinate disposition. She thrived on controversy, particularly when the subject for debate was literary. She once called critics "yapping terriers."

Lowell demonstrated a defiance of tradition and free spirit that was legendary. Though raised in the Episcopalian Church, she became an atheist. As one of her biographers noted, she was "a believer in the transcendent power of literature and the sacred property of art." Lowell also flouted conventions in her daily demeanor. Once, during a drive in the country, Lowell's car broke down, and she had difficulty getting it repaired at a nearby garage because the mechanic feared that her check might not be good. In order to convince him, she told the mechanic to call her brother Abbott Lawrence Lowell, then the well-known president of Harvard University. Once on the phone, Abbott asked the mechanic, "What is she doing now?" The mechanic replied, "She is sitting on a stone wall across the way, smoking a cigar." Abbott promptly assured the mechanic that the customer relishing her cigar was indeed his sister. Besides enjoying cigars, Lowell was notorious for her huge pack of pedigreed Old English sheepdogs. She gave the animals free rein at Sevenels, much to the horror of some of her guests, who were provided with bath towels to spread in their laps as a shield against the dogs' abundant drool.

Lowell's eccentricity even extended to her work schedule. She maintained an extraordinary level of production throughout her career by adhering to a rigorous routine. She breakfasted in the mid-afternoon, entertained friends in the evening, often until midnight, and only then started her working day. While the rest of the world slept, Lowell wrote, throughout the night and into the early hours of dawn, when she would retire to bed. This schedule allowed her to achieve an extraordinary output during the last decade of her life, and she became well known as the major propagandist for Imagist movement. Besides writing, Lowell also went on many speaking and reading tours, some as far away as Utah, in an effort to give the New Poetry a national audience. Even the showdown with Ezra Pound, with its serious disruption of the Imagist family, did not dampen her professional output. In 1914, she published numerous poems, including eight in the April issue of *Poetry* magazine alone, as well as a number of critical reviews and essays.

During the late 1910s, in fact, Lowell produced two of her most impressive tomes. In September 1918, *Can Grande's Castle* was released. This work, which one biographer pronounced more unified and "epic in its reach" than any of her others, was written entirely in polyphonic prose. She also published a critical work, *Tendencies in Modern American Poetry*, which examined the impact of such poets as Edgar Lee Masters, Robert Frost, and Edwin Arlington Robinson. In tracing their influence, Lowell was also tracing the rise of the New Poetry; one of her peers called the book "the most important critical work produced in the United States for many years."

In the early 1920s, amid her hectic professional schedule and several painful relapses of a chronic hernia problem, Lowell turned her attention to writing a biography of Keats. Working at an exhausting pace throughout 1923 and 1924, she confided in a letter to a friend that "I eat, drink, sleep and talk that man, and pretty soon I shall be signing his name to my letters." The two-volume biography, released in 1925, was a critical and commercial success; a fourth printing was ordered only days after the first published copies reached the bookstores. Lowell even appeared on the March 2, 1925, cover of *Time* magazine.

Exhausted from her work on the Keats biography yet still planning a trip to England to promote the book, Lowell received an invitation from a large group of friends to attend a dinner in her honor. The several hundred who gathered for the evening on April 4, 1925, praised Amy for her poetry and her skills in promoting the Imagist movement and listened appreciatively as she recited one of her finest poems, "Lilacs." Sadly, this was the last time Lowell's admirers would hear her recite, for less than a week later she suffered the last of her many crippling hernia attacks. Soon, she succumbed to a stroke, and, on May 12, 1925, she died at Sevenels with Ada Dwyer at her side.

Lowell left behind numerous works-in-progress, which Dwyer saw through to publication. These posthumous collections included *What's O'Clock*, which received the Pulitzer Prize in 1926, *East Wind*, published in 1926, and *Ballads for Sale*, released in 1927.

Biographer Richard Benvenuto has suggested that one of the most noticeable facts about Amy Lowell's life is its division into two distinct phases. Until her late 30s, she did little to set her apart from other wealthy, respectable Boston women of her era. This changed dramatically in 1912. Until her death in 1925, Lowell's life was, according to Benvenuto, "filled with activity: publications, lecture tours, controversies and feuds." The well-born Boston daughter, through sheer determination, made herself a figure to be reckoned with in the movement that would change American poetry in the early 20th century.

Yet critics still disagree over her influence on American poetry. The *Dictionary of Literary Biography* claims that "Lowell will not be remembered for her poetry, but her contribution as poet-critic, biographer, reviewer, propagandist, and spokesman for modern poetry is without parallel." Other critics like Louis Untermeyer hailed her work as a "pioneering energy" that "helped establish the fresh and free-searching poetry of our day." Her most interesting work is arguably that which experiments with unrhymed cadence and the free-verse style known as polyphonic prose. There is little disagreement, however, that Lowell's formidable persona and dedication to poetry exercised a remarkable influence on the American literary scene. In championing the New Poetry in general, and the Imagists in particular, Lowell made an important contribution to the development of Modernism in American literature and culture.

SOURCES:

Benvenuto, Richard. *Amy Lowell.* Boston, MA: Twayne, 1985.

Gould, Jean. *Amy: The World of Amy Lowell and the Imagist Movement.* NY: Dodd, Mead, 1975.

Heymann, C. David. *American Aristocracy: The Lives and Times of James Russell, Amy, and Robert Lowell.* NY: Dodd, Mead, 1980.

Untermeyer, Louis. Introduction to *The Complete Poetical Works of Amy Lowell.* Boston, MA: Houghton Mifflin, 1955.

SUGGESTED READING:

Gregory, Horace. *Amy Lowell; Portrait of a Poet in Her Time.* NY: Thomas Nelson, 1958.

McNair, Harley F., ed. *Florence Ayscough and Amy Lowell: Correspondence of a Friendship.* Chicago, IL: University of Chicago Press, 1946.

Christine Stolba,
Ph.D. candidate in American history,
Emory University, Atlanta, Georgia

Lowell, Josephine Shaw

(1843–1905)

American philanthropist and social reformer. Born Josephine Shaw on December 16, 1843, in West Roxbury, Massachusetts; died of cancer on October 12, 1905; buried beside her husband at Mount Auburn Cemetery, Cambridge, Massachusetts; third daughter of five children of Francis George Shaw and Sarah Blake (Sturgis) Shaw; sister of Robert Gould Shaw; married Charles Russell Lowell (a colonel in the 2nd Massachusetts cavalry and nephew of James Russell Lowell), on October 31, 1863 (killed in the battle of Cedar Creek, Virginia, during the Civil War in 1864); children: one daughter, Carlotta Russell Lowell.

Josephine Shaw Lowell was born in 1843 in West Roxbury, Massachusetts, into a family of radical abolitionists. Her father organized the Freedmen's Bureau, while her brother Robert Gould Shaw led the first black regiment from the free states into battle and is memorialized by a statue across from Boston's State House and in the movie *Glory*, starring Matthew Broderick. Josephine and her sister **Anna Shaw (Curtis)** joined the New York Association of [War] Relief.

In October 1863, during the Civil War, Josephine married Charles Russell Lowell, a colonel in the 2nd Massachusetts cavalry and nephew of the poet James Russell Lowell. Wounded a year later at the battle of Cedar Creek, Charles died in 1864, six weeks before the birth of their daughter **Carlotta Russell Lowell**.

Following the death of her husband, 20-year-old Josephine Lowell immersed herself in philanthropic work for the next 40 years, first turning her energies to the National Freedman's Relief Association of New York. In 1876, because of her impressive state-commissioned studies of New York paupers, Governor Samuel J. Tilden appointed Lowell the first woman member of the New York State Board of Charities. Lowell was reappointed by several succeeding governors, her period of service extending from 1877 until 1889. She also founded the Charity Organization Society, becoming one of the most influential women in the charity movement.

The remainder of her life was passed in active philanthropic work, particularly prison reform. Joseph H. Choate said of her: "If you should ask me to sum up in one word the life and character of Mrs. Lowell, I should call it Consecration." Said Theodore Roosevelt: "She had a sweet, unworldly character; and never man or woman ever strove for loftier ideals."

SUGGESTED READING:

Stewart, William Rhinelander, comp. *Philanthropic Work of Josephine Shaw Lowell*, 1911.

Lowell, Maria White (1821–1853)

American poet. Born Anna Maria White in Watertown, Massachusetts, on July 8, 1821; died, possibly of tuberculosis, at Elmwood, the Lowell home in Cambridge, on October 27, 1853; buried at Mount Auburn Cemetery, Cambridge; second daughter of five children of Abijah White (a cattle trader in the West Indies) and Anna Maria (Howard) White; along with her sisters, educated by a governess; attended the Ursuline Convent School in Charlestown; married James Russell Lowell (the poet), on December 26, 1844; sister-in-law of *Mary Traill Spence Putnam*; children: Blanche Lowell (1845–1847); **Mabel Lowell** (b. 1847); Rose Lowell (1849–1849); Walter Lowell (1850–1852).

Maria White was born in Watertown, Massachusetts, in 1821, the second daughter of five children of Abijah White, who had made his fortune as a cattle trader in the West Indies, and **Anna Maria White**. Both were Unitarians. With three of her sisters, Maria attended the Ursuline Convent School in Charlestown, until a Know-Nothing mob burned it down, thus ending the 13-year-old's formal education. She then joined the circle of women who met at *Margaret Fuller*'s home. In 1839, Maria met a young law student, the future poet James Russell Lowell. They married in 1844.

Maria White Lowell was important in her own right as an author of poems, 20 of which were published in 1855, and a complete collection in 1907 and 1936. An ardent liberal, she steered her husband from his natural conservatism, stimulating his interests in both the abolition and Transcendental movements—so much so that James Russell Lowell eventually became an editor for the *National Anti-Slavery Standard*. Her poetry, with a few exceptions, is considered cultivated but derivative, and her greatest work is the abolitionist poem "Africa." Maria had rescued her husband from severe depression when they met, but the loss of two of her children in infancy and another son while traveling in Italy in 1852, plunged her into grief. After she died a year later at age 32, possibly of tuberculosis, James Lowell did not publish another book for 11 years.

SUGGESTED READING:

Vernon, Hope. *The Poems of Maria White Lowell with Unpublished Letters and Biography*, 1936.

Lowell, Mary Traill Spence (1810–1898).

See Putnam, Mary Traill Spence.

Löwenstein, Helga Maria zu (1910—)

Norwegian-born anti-Nazi activist, lecturer, and principal organizer of the German Academy of Arts and Sciences in Exile. Name variations: Princess Helga Maria of Loewenstein or Lowenstein; Princess Löwenstein. Born Helga Maria Schuylenburg in Norway on August 27, 1910; daughter of Dutch parents; married Prince Hubertus zu Löwenstein-Wertheim-Freudenberg (whose full name was Hubertus Maximilian Friedrich Leopold Ludwig Prinz zu Löwenstein-Wertheim-Freudenberg), in 1929; children: Elisabeth Maria (b. 1939); Konstanza Maria (b. 1942); Margareta Maria (b. 1948).

Although usually overshadowed by her husband, the anti-Nazi activist Prince Hubertus zu Löwenstein, Princess Helga Löwenstein was an effective propagandist in the cause of German freedom and a hard-as-nails enemy of the Hitler regime in her own right, on many occasions acting as an equal partner with her spouse in their common struggle against Fascism. Both members of this remarkable husband-wife team were born into the highest ranks of European nobility. Prince Hubertus, who was born in 1906 in a castle near Kufstein in the Austrian Tyrol, was part of a family from the Franconia region of Germany who had for many centuries played important roles in the history of the Holy Roman Empire, the Habsburg monarchy, and the German Reich. His mother **Constance Baroness de Worms** (1875–1962) was from a prominent family of British aristocrats being the daughter of Lord Henry Pirbright. Although his parents divorced in 1912, Hubertus remained strongly attached to his mother, an intelligent, strong-willed woman of markedly liberal ideas. It is more than likely that his easy acceptance of his wife's strongly held views harkened back to the example set by his mother, who feared no one when it came to expressing her ideas either in public or private. The Löwenstein family history, with connections throughout Europe, helps to explain at least in part his later defense of freedom and hatred of all forms of national chauvinism and racial intolerance. His grandmother, **Baroness Todesco**, was a Viennese aristocrat with Jewish family roots, and like most members of the highest circles of the pre–1914 European nobility, the young Prince Hubertus grew up in a sophisticated, cosmopolitan milieu free of racism and prejudice.

Helga Maria Schuylenburg grew up in an aristocratic environment similar to that of her future husband. She was born in Norway on August 27, 1910, during a visit to that country by her Dutch parents (her birth took place in a house that had once been occupied by the composer Edvard Grieg). The young princess grew up in Norway but from the start of her life considered herself to be a citizen of Europe, learning to speak flawless Dutch, Norwegian, German, French, and English as well as Danish and Swedish. Her family tree was at least as distinguished as that of her future husband, for she was a direct descendant of the duke of Alba, the harsh ruler of the Netherlands in the 1500s. Her parents were very forward-looking for their day, believing that their daughter deserved an education that would develop both her intellect and personality. Accordingly, young Helga Maria was sent to the Wickersdorf Academy, a famous school run along progressive lines in Thuringia, Germany. It was here that she met and fell in love with Hubertus Löwenstein, four years her senior and already involved in the political life of Weimar Germany. Helga and Hubertus were married in Palermo, Sicily, in 1929. At the time of her marriage she was still a Protestant, and one journalist described her as being "the first heathen princess of the Holy Roman Empire since the days of Widukind." In 1932, she converted to Roman Catholicism.

After Hubertus completed his doctoral degree in 1931, having written a dissertation dissecting fascist political theories, he became ever more engrossed in the turbulent political life of Germany in the depression-ridden 1930s. Helga helped with his correspondence, organized the research materials for his prolific newspaper articles, and entertained the many friends who stayed late into the night arguing over the best ways to save German democracy. Husband and wife were devout Catholics, but they did not share the views of many Catholics and Protestants who hated Marxism so much that they turned a blind eye to the violent and dictatorial nature of a Nazi movement that claimed that through "strong leadership" it alone would be able to save Western Christian civilization from Bolshevism and chaos. Although aristocratic and born to privilege, the Löwensteins were deeply committed to democratic ideals both politically and socially. A magazine article of 1936 described Princess Löwenstein as being "tolerant and democratic in the extreme." Their circle of friends extended from left-wing Socialists to monarchists, but all shared a belief in the necessity of democracy and the preservation of individual human rights. The busy couple put off having children in the early years of their marriage, the demands on their time being too great. By 1933, having a family presented a couple with grave responsibilities and burdens, for in that year the Nazis took over in Germany.

Prince Löwenstein's outspoken anti-Nazism since the late 1920s made him *persona non grata* in the nascent Third Reich, and Helga too suffered from the fury of the Nazis in April 1933 when a group of stormtroopers broke into their Berlin apartment, verbally assaulting her with threats. She took the next train to Austria, renting Neumatzen, an ancient castle built on Roman foundation stones near Brixlegg in Austria's Tyrol province. Here the Löwensteins continued their anti-Nazi activities despite growing hostility toward them by local Nazi militants who regarded them as "Jew-lovers" and "traitors to the New Germany." A number of incidents made clear that despite their living in a castle, the couple's views exposed them to considerable physical danger. Particularly in 1933, when the Austrian government had little success in preventing German Nazis from crossing over the mountain passes to assist their Austrian comrades in destabilizing the Vienna regime, the province of Tyrol was swarming with brown-shirted stormtroopers spoiling for violent confrontations. On one occasion when a unit of Nazis laid siege to Neumatzen castle, the prince told Helga to remain in a safe room with some trusted servants while he made an attempt to break out and seek assistance. This he did by running out of the castle, leaping into his American automobile, and flooring it out of the castle grounds past the startled Nazi besiegers. After what seemed like an eternity to Helga, who waited patiently in the darkened ramparts, she greeted Hubertus the next day at the head of a force of friendly police. The Nazis fled.

On another occasion, Princess Helga made newspaper headlines throughout Europe. Driving her Duesenberg through the streets of Innsbruck, she was surrounded by a squad of about 50 Nazi toughs, mostly students, for whom the Löwensteins were "dangerous Reds." They were particularly incensed by the fact that the car had attached to its radiator cap the black, red and gold colors of German republicanism, first flown in the revolution of 1848 and the official flag of the now hated (by the Nazis and their allies) Weimar Republic. A Nazi on a bicycle rode by and tore off the flag, but he had not reckoned with Helga Löwenstein, who whipped out a revolver and fired a number of warning shots into the air. The Nazi youths fled, the cyclist dropped his stolen banner, and Helga drove home with the feeling that if only diplomats behaved in a similar fashion, Nazi aggression could be nipped in the bud. Newspapers throughout Europe reported the incident, while in Germany the Nazi-controlled press shrieked that "the shooting princess, wife of an anti-national emigré, threatens patriotic pedestrians."

Despite infrequent moral victories, the next years were not easy for the Löwensteins. Their situation in tiny, weak Austria was precarious, given the fact that the impoverished Alpine republic was situated between the Mussolini and Hitler dictatorships and lacked a strong democratic tradition after the destruction of Vienna-centered Social Democracy in February 1934. Although family wealth insulated them from material worries, the psychological uncertainty of emigration sometimes weighed heavily on the couple. Hubertus had long been regarded as an outlaw by the Nazi state, and a bounty of 5,000 marks was offered to any German citizen who returned him to Germany. This situation became even more acute in November 1934 when the Nazis stripped the prince of his German citizenship, turning him into "a man without a country." The Löwensteins fought off depression by keeping intensely busy, he with lecture tours and the writing of books and newspaper and magazine articles, and she by reading, critiquing her husband's manuscripts, and organizing his busy schedule. Her contacts with an ever-growing circle of refugee artists, scholars and scientists made it clear that there was a pressing need to coordinate the cultural, educational and academic goals of the many thousands of anti-Nazis scattered throughout the world. Working with her husband, Helga founded the German Academy of Arts and Sciences in Exile. Since this organization received most of its funding from individuals and organizations in the United States, and since many of the refugees were in the U.S., another organization, the American Guild for German Cultural Freedom, became the de facto body to coordinate these efforts. With Thomas Mann and Sigmund Freud as honorary presiding officers, these bodies did much good by providing a forum for anti-Nazi discussions. More practically, they gave grants to refugee writers and artists and often assisted in the process of emigration and initial settlement in a new and strange cultural environment.

In April 1936, Princess Helga visited the United States to alert the American public to the Nazi threat and to raise funds for the work of the American Guild for German Cultural Freedom. Interviewed at the pier by *The New York Times,* she took advantage of the occasion to inform the citizens of New York of her scheduled appearance at Madison Square Garden on a program of the Committee for the Relief and Liberation of Victims of Persecution in Europe. Her 1936 tour, which raised sufficient funding to carry on the work of her organizations, also alerted many Americans to the Nazi danger.

In 1939, Helga Löwenstein gave birth to her first child, Elisabeth Maria, in the United States, where Hubertus had taken out his first citizenship papers in 1938. Two more daughters would be born: Konstanza Maria in the United States in 1942, and Margareta Maria in Germany in 1948. Despite the responsibilities of a young family, Helga spent the war years in the United States actively assisting her husband in his work and vigorously participating in German exile politics and culture in her own right. Until 1941, the Löwensteins lived in Manhattan's Greenwich Village, moving in January of that year to an 18th-century farmhouse Helga had discovered in the small village of Newfoundland, New Jersey, about 30 miles from the George Washington Bridge. She quickly turned the picturesque house into a home that was often filled with European refugees arguing into the night about various political and cultural controversies of the day. Newfoundland became a place of spiritual rejuvenation for the prince when he returned from lecture tours, and a small piece of Central Europe for refugees. For Helga and Hubertus, however, there were few doubts in their minds about the future. They returned to Germany in 1946 when that country was occupied by its victors and still in ruins. Over the next decades, they often traveled together to nations around the world as representatives of the new democracy that had arisen in the Federal Republic of Germany. Their partnership ended only with the prince's death in Bonn in November 1984.

Princess Helga continued their work of fostering European reconciliation by maintaining their old personal ties in Europe and the rest of the world, working with scholars studying the history of the anti-Nazi resistance in which both had played such an important role. She also appeared at conferences and ceremonies commemorating the struggles of the 1933–45 period when freedom in the West was menaced by several varieties of totalitarianism. Her old friends from these difficult years were delighted to see Princess Helga Löwenstein as guest of honor on many of these occasions, including the one that took place on May 15, 1994, at Port Bou for the unveiling of a monument to the German writer Walter Benjamin, who had committed suicide on the nearby French-Spanish border while fleeing the Nazis in July 1940. Had it not been for Helga and Hubertus Löwenstein, there would have been many more cases of suicide among the German refugee intellectuals of the 1930s.

SOURCES:

"Exiled Princess Here," in *The New York Times.* April 17, 1936, p. 13.

Gibson, Michael. "A Memorial to Walter Benjamin," in *International Herald Tribune.* May 21–22, 1994, p. 7.

Helmond, Toke van. "'Dem Gedächtnis der Namenslosen,'" in *Neues Deutschland.* June 11–12, 1994, p.13.

Löwenstein, Hubertus Prinz zu. *Abenteurer der Freiheit: Ein Lebensbericht.* Frankfurt am Main: Ullstein Verlag, 1983.

———. *Botschafter ohne Auftrag: Lebensbericht.* Düsseldorf: Droste Verlag, 1972.

Mammach, Klaus. "Deutsche Emigration in Österreich 1933–1938," in *Jahrbuch für Geschichte.* Vol. 38. Berlin: Akademie-Verlag, 1989, pp. 281–309.

Pace, Eric. "Prince Loewenstein, Hitler Foe, Dies in Bonn at 78," in *The New York Times Biographical Service.* December, 1984, p. 1653.

"Princess Unterrified by Nazi Spies," in *Literary Digest.* Vol. 121, no. 18, May 2, 1936, p. 21.

Röder, Werner, and Herbert A. Strauss, eds. *Biographisches Handbuch der deutschsprachigen Emigration nach 1933.* 4 vols. Munich: K.G. Saur, 1980.

John Haag,
Associate Professor of History,
University of Georgia, Athens, Georgia

Lower Bavaria, duchess of.

See Elizabeth of Hungary (fl. 1250s).

Lower Lorraine, duchess of.

See Clementia.
See Doda (fl. 1040).
See Margaret of Limburg (d. 1172).

Lowery, Ellin Prince (1849–1921).

See Speyer, Ellin Prince.

Lowndes, Mrs. Belloc (1868–1947).

See Belloc-Lowndes, Marie.

Lowney, Shannon (1969–1994)

American advocate for women's reproductive rights and prevention of child abuse until her murder by an anti-abortion-rights activist. Pronunciation: LAUW-nee. *Born Shannon Elizabeth Lowney on July 7, 1969, in Norwalk, Connecticut; murdered at Planned Parenthood Clinic in Brookline, Massachusetts, on December 30, 1994; daughter of Joan (Manning) Lowney (an elementary school music teacher) and William T. Lowney (a middle school history teacher); Boston College, B.A. in history (Magna Cum Laude), 1991; never married; no children.*

Studied in Madrid, Spain (1990); as youth counselor volunteer at the Cambridge Rindge and Latin High School, tutored immigrating Central American teenagers in English (1990–91); was a Spanish translator for English-speaking volunteer work project in Ecuador (January 1991); worked as the flow coordinator and phone counselor at the Planned Parenthood Clinic of Greater Boston (1992–93); served as a child abuse prevention educator at Advocates for Children in Androscoggin County, Maine (1993–94); returned to Boston (fall 1994) to pursue a master's degree in Social Work; worked as receptionist at Planned Parenthood Clinic.

On the morning of Friday, December 30, 1994, Shannon Lowney proceeded through anti-abortion-rights demonstrators outside the Planned Parenthood Clinic in Brookline, Massachusetts, to start her work day. For the next two hours, she welcomed clients and assisted Spanish-speaking women to help them obtain services. A young man approached her desk and asked, "Is this Planned Parenthood?" She smiled and told him that it was; he pulled out a rifle and shot her several times in the throat. The man continued to fire in her direction, shooting an employee who stood behind her, and then turned and fired at clients and visitors seated in the waiting room.

Responding to what sounded like firecrackers, clinic employees ran toward the front office. They saw Lowney stand up at her desk, turn and walk toward them. She motioned with her arms to a nurse but was unable to speak; then she fell to the floor, bleeding from her neck. When medical personnel could not stop the bleeding, the doctor and nurses moved on to help those whose lives might be saved. During the panic, the gunman fled to Preterm, another clinic a few blocks away which also performed abortion services. He entered and shot employees and clients there too, fatally wounding the receptionist, 38-year-old ✧▶ Lee Ann Nichols. Seven people in total were shot, and all but Lowney were rushed to the hospital. Shannon Lowney died where she had fallen.

✧▶ **Nichols, Lee Ann** (c. 1956–1994)
American social worker. Born in North Olmsted, Ohio, around 1956; murdered in Brookline, Massachusetts, on December 30, 1994; daughter of Ruth Nichols; engaged to Edward McDonough.

Shannon Lowney was only three years old in 1973 when the U.S. Supreme Court ruled that the "right of privacy . . . founded in the Fourteenth Amendment's concept of personal liberty . . . is broad enough to encompass a woman's decision whether or not to terminate a pregnancy." In her young adult years, she learned that before abortions became legal clergy members and women's advocates developed an underground system to connect women with practitioners who could terminate unwanted pregnancies. She learned that during these years many women died from unsafe, botched abortions in private homes and back alleys. Too, she learned that though women seeking abortions now had protection under the law, women's advocates still had to fight hard to ensure that any woman could exercise her right to a safe and legal abortion. In the 1990s, the shootings in Brookline whick took Lowney's life were evidence that the war being waged by determined groups against a woman's right to choose abortion had reached a new level of crisis and tragedy.

The middle of three children, Lowney was born on July 7, 1969, to William and **Joan Lowney**. She spoke in almost complete sentences before she could walk and early showed a love of reading. Shannon and her siblings, **Meghan** and Liam, were fifth-generation Irish Americans. The family camped for recreation, including summer vacations at Martha's Vineyard Island, Massachusetts. With the encouragement of her mother, an elementary-school music teacher, Lowney learned to play the french horn and piano. She was chosen to perform with statewide student groups and traveled to Europe twice with amateur orchestras. Through music and academic studies, she developed strong self-discipline. During high school (1983–87), she played sports, belonged to many school clubs, while consistently earning high academic honors.

She also became increasingly intrigued by history. Interested particularly in both women's historical and contemporary roles in society, she eventually identified herself as an advocate for women's rights and maintained a desire to develop ideas through discussion, examining the connection between history and current events. Lowney's understanding of the oppression of women in world history led her to also identify with the oppression of animals, and she became a vegetarian. She spoke eloquently about the ethical and philosophical issues of subjugation. Later in life, Lowney would credit her family with her "love of education," "reverence for learning," and "dedication to social justice."

In the fall of 1987, she enrolled at Boston College, in Chestnut Hill, Massachusetts, where she studied history and Spanish, focusing on South American history, anthropological and philosophical issues, and women's role in history. Friends knew her to be a frequent and passionate debater of philosophy and ethics, whose arguments were informed by the lessons of history and a strong sense of "what's right." Inspired by a class with the renowned feminist author **Mary Daly** during her junior year, Lowney organized a campus debate regarding abortion rights with professors of differing perspectives. Since *Roe* v. *Wade* in 1973, family planning clinics had been providing affordable, accessible and safe abortions despite increased attacks against individuals and clinics by anti-choice/ pro-life groups. Lowney believed that every woman had the right to make decisions about her own body and life. She also valued, however, each individual's right to their own opinion about the controversial issue.

For Lowney, change through action was equally as important as discussion. She took a class on the development of racism and wrote in her journal, "I am tired of people afraid to rock the boat, afraid to think that they too might have an element of prejudice about them." Aware that the history she was taught in school was limited to a white, European male perspective which excluded women and ethnic minorities, she wrote: "Half a history is no history at all." She also considered the role of violence in history:

> I cannot get over the futility of violence in any other context than direct self-defense. . . . What I do not understand is how violence can bring about change in the mind of someone on the other side of a . . . dispute. . . . Hate is a destructive force in and of itself. The "hater" is making a choice to deprive him or herself of love and understanding. S/he is choosing to remain in ignorance and darkness and it is HER/HIS CHOICE.

For a semester in January 1990, Lowney studied in Madrid, Spain, while living in the home of a Spanish family. In her journal, she admired "the beauty of the cities and country . . . the old traditional buildings, the friendliness of people . . . the culture. . . . Smiles are like breaths here—they come without thought." She was disturbed, though, by the attitude of men toward women in Madrid despite reminders to herself to "keep an open mind." Following a walk during which she was whistled and heckled by men, she wrote, "I was angry that the men here think that they have that power over our bodies."

The following year, in January 1991, Lowney traveled to Ecuador with a college group. She worked and lived for ten days in the barrio of Duran, across the Rio Guayas from Guayaquil, and spent time with children who thrived "regardless of their extreme poverty." She was shocked when they ate ant-infested candy the students had thrown away. Overwhelmed with sadness, Lowney was enraged by her own inability to make any lasting improvement in the quality of their lives:

> My trip to Ecuador over Christmas break shattered the idealized image I had about the poor. . . . Spending this time in the heat and the stench of the garbage dump that these desperate families call their home, I realized there is nothing beautiful or pure about poverty. . . . Their experience is disgusting and degrading and no human should have to spend their limited days here on earth in such hell.

Lowney graduated in the top of her class in 1991 and began to look for employment. She continued waitressing, as she had done through college, until she was hired by Planned Parenthood as a phone counselor. A bilingual resource for Spanish clients, she often translated agency and medical procedures for them. Concerned that poor women had few medical options, Lowney was proud to be part of a team working to make health services available to all women. She worked at Planned Parenthood for a year, experiencing firsthand the effect of the abortion-rights debate.

With the *Roe* v. *Wade* decision, the Catholic Church and other groups had begun to organize to try to eliminate legal abortion, employing legal strategies to change the law and influence legislators. Some groups also used aggressive tactics that threatened clinics and the lives of doctors who performed pregnancy terminations. Clinics became targets. Demonstrations outside clinics became a common practice for such groups as Operation Rescue whose members claimed to counsel women going into the clinics to decide against abortions. To reach the clinic doors, clinic staff and clients were forced to make their way through groups of confrontational protesters. Lowney regularly passed through shouting demonstrators, one of whom, in frequent attendance outside her clinic, screamed epithets at her such as "Public Enemy Number One." At first Lowney talked to the demonstrators, trying to engage them in discussion; eventually, however, she became frustrated by what she saw as a lack of willingness to respect her different beliefs. Meanwhile, there were increased threats to clinics nationwide. Then, in March 1993, Dr. David Gunn was killed outside a Florida clinic where he worked.

Shannon Lowney

The killing was condoned by a some in the anti-abortion movement. In August, Dr. Gunn's former co-worker, Dr. Wayne Patterson, was murdered. Dr. George Tiller was shot and wounded later that month. Aware of the risks, and cautious as a result of these shootings, Lowney was not afraid to return to work.

In 1993, she left Planned Parenthood temporarily to move with her boyfriend, David Keene, to Maine where he had become employed. There she worked as an educator at Advocates for Children, an agency which focused on child abuse prevention and youth empowerment. She instructed children and teens on conflict resolution techniques and taught them about their right to choose safety. Lowney's work in helping children to remove themselves from abusive situations led her to consider a degree in social work.

Upon her return to Boston in 1994, she rejoined the Planned Parenthood Clinic and submitted applications for schools of social work.

Clinic harassment had escalated in her absence; more clinics were being torched, bombed, and vandalized. Death threats to abortion providers had increased. President Bill Clinton signed the Freedom of Access to Clinic Entrances Act in May 1994, prohibiting the use of force, threats, or physical obstruction to interfere with a person trying to enter an abortion clinic. In July 1994, Dr. Bayard Britton and clinic escort James Barrett were killed.

That Christmas, Lowney spent the holidays with her family in Connecticut. On Friday morning, December 30, she returned to work to welcome those who needed Planned Parenthood, determined to provide a smile and assistance to the clients who made it past the shrill demonstrators outside. Just recovering from a cold, she wore a new dress, perhaps to help her feel better. By 11:00 AM, she was dead.

The man who murdered Lowney, John Salvi III, was apprehended within two days when he shot at the windows of a Virginia family-planning clinic. His religious beliefs, similar to those of the men who had previously murdered other clinic personnel, were the basis for his opposition to abortion. He had attended protest gatherings, including at least one outside the Brookline clinic where Lowney worked. In March 1996, he was tried and convicted for the murders of Shannon Lowney and Lee Ann Nichols, and for the assault on the lives of five others.

These murders and assaults were mourned nationally. Most anti-abortion rights groups did not condone Salvi's actions, but a few did. Clinics throughout the country braced for attacks and installed expensive equipment to protect clients and staff. The events caused discussion about the level of violence surrounding this issue of choice and prompted President Clinton to order U.S. Attorneys to create task forces to improve security for providers. Many pro-choice advocates called for an end to the violence and increased security through legislation. They also advocated for the Federal Drug Administration (FDA) approval of RU486, a medicine that non-surgically ends pregnancy. Available through private doctors, RU486 might help diffuse the focus and potential violence of anti-choice demonstrators away from clinics. Meanwhile, anti-choice activists advocated for their right to free speech.

The concept of freedom and choice resonated strongly with Lowney. She considered her responsibility to a larger community with every choice she made. She encouraged others to make important decisions for themselves, to exercise their basic human rights. At the age of 25, she died violently, in a way that opposed everything for which she had lived. "Doesn't anyone take responsibility for their choices anymore?" she had written. "Somebody make some decisions, some choices, some change."

SOURCES:

The Boston Women's Health Book Collective. *The New Our Bodies Ourselves*. NY: Simon & Schuster, 1992, pp. 353–385.

Colker, Ruth. *Abortion & Dialogue*. Bloomington, IN: Indiana University Press, 1992.

Monagle, Katie. "How We Got Here," in *Ms.* May–June, 1995, pp. 54–57.

Personal writings of Shannon Lowney, personal stories as related by family, friends, and author's own.

SUGGESTED READING:

Boston Globe. December 31, 1994, and January 1, 1995, p. 1.

Daly, Mary. *Beyond God the Father*. Boston: Beacon Press, 1973.

de Beauvoir, Simone. *The Second Sex*. NY: Vintage Books, 1989.

Dworkin, Andrea. *Right-Wing Women*. NY: Perigee Books, 1983.

"The Killing Field," in *People Weekly*. January 16, 1995, pp. 40–43.

RELATED MEDIA:

"Murder on Abortion Row," written and directed by John Zaritsky, produced by **Virginia Storring**, aired on PBS on February 6, 1996.

Meghan K. Lowney, M.S.W., and sister of Shannon Lowney, Branford, Connecticut

Lowry-Corry, Dorothy (1885–1967)

Irish historian, genealogist, and archaeologist. Born in Castlecooke, County Fermanagh, Ireland, in 1885; died in 1967.

Known particularly for her studies of the Early Christian period, Irish historian, genealogist, and archaeologist Dorothy Lowry-Corry was the vice-president of the Royal Society of Antiquaries and contributed numerous papers to the Royal Irish Academy, the most important of which was the recording of the Boa Island and Lustymore stone figures. She also studied the Monuments of County Fermanagh and discovered the megalithic tomb in County Leitrim. Lowry-Corry served as the representative of County Fermanagh on the Ancient Monuments advisory committee and was a frequent contributor to the *Ulster Journal of Archaeology*.

Loy, Mina (1882–1966)

English-born poet, artist, and designer, highly regarded and influential among her contemporaries in the New York avant-garde of the 1910s and 1920s, who

broke ground with her erotic love poetry, satires, plays, paintings, and Modernist manifestoes. Born Mina Gertrude Lowy on December 27, 1882, in London, England; died on September 25, 1966, in Aspen, Colorado; changed her surname to Loy in 1903; daughter of Julian (Bryan) Lowy and Sigmund Lowy (a tailor); attended school in England until 1899; went to study art at Kunstlerrinen Verein, Munich; returned to London (1901–02) to study art with Augustus John; studied art in Paris (1903); became a member of the Salon d'Automne in Paris (1906); married Stephen Haweis, on December 31, 1903 (divorced 1917); married Arthur Cravan, in January 1918; children: (first marriage) Oda (May 31, 1904–May 31, 1905); Joella Haweis (b. July 20, 1907); Giles Haweis (February 1, 1909–1923); (second marriage) Fabi Cravan (b. April 5, 1919).

Moved with husband to Florence (1906), where she produced some of her best poems and paintings; identified herself with Futurism, an experimental movement within the Modernist revolution; adopted Christian Science (1909); met influential artists, writers, and performers at salons in Florence, including Gordon Craig, Eleonora Duse, Artur Rubinstein, John Reed, Carl Van Vechten and others (1906–16); took Van Vechten as her literary agent (1913); exhibited paintings in London (1913); published first poems in Camera Work *and* Trend *(1914); remained in Florence after the August 3 declaration of war; became a nurse in a surgical hospital; new poems appeared in* Rogue *and* Others, *avant-garde magazines published in New York; wrote feminist satire of Futurism, with which she became disillusioned; left Florence for New York, where she was invited into the circles formed around both magazines (1915); began selling designs for dresses and lampshades, modelled, and was guest-editor of* Others; *exhibited a painting at the Society of Independent Artists Exhibition, Grand Central Palace, New York (1917); sailed to Buenos Aires ahead of second husband, who was never seen again (January 1918); son kidnapped (1921); settled in Berlin (1922); returned to Paris (1923), where she became part of the artistic and expatriate communities; son died; poems appeared in* The Little Review; *first book published (1923); design work appeared in Madison Avenue windows; paintings exhibited in a Connecticut gallery (1925); opened retail shop (1926); beset by tax problems (1930); became agent for Julien Levy Gallery (1931); exhibited paintings in Connecticut and Paris galleries (1933); left Paris (1936) and moved to New York; became a naturalized American citizen (1946); moved to the Bowery (1949) and began to create montage and collage works; poems occasionally appeared*

in little magazines and anthologies (1936–53); withdrew from public life; moved to Aspen, Colorado; second book published (1958); several poems appeared in Between Worlds *(1961–62); lived an increasingly reclusive existence until her death.*

Books and awards: Lunar Baedecker [sic] *(1923);* Lunar Baedeker and Time Tables: Selected Poems *(1958); Copley Foundation Award (1959);* The Lost Lunar Baedeker: The Poems of Mina Loy *(1982 and 1996). Poems and other work in anthologies:* The Contact Collection of Contemporary Writers *(1925);* The Voice that is Great Within Us *(1971);* The Women Poets in English *(1972);* The World Split Open *(1974);* Revolution of the Word *(1974). Contributor to magazines:* Dial, Others, Little Review, *and* Contact.

Only two collections of Mina Loy's poems were published in her lifetime, and both went out of print almost as soon as they were released. The first, *Lunar Baedeker* (1923), was published by Contact, an important press for expatriates in Paris. Contact committed itself to marketing books by writers who were unlikely to be published otherwise, "for commercial or legislative reasons." *Lunar Baedeker* made it to America in only very small numbers, held up by New York City customs officers who decided it included pornography. The second, *Lunar Baedeker and Time Tables* (1958), was issued in an edition of 500 copies. Editions of each book are now extremely rare.

Loy's work (and some work in progress) appeared in a handful of little magazines during the 1910s and 1920s, loudly praised and championed by a few editors and critics (especially Kenneth Rexroth), or was introduced by others as arresting and controversial, if nothing more. Until 1958, when Jonathan Williams brought out the second volume of Loy's work, there was little certainty on how many of her poems she had seen published, or where they had appeared, or whether the texts of those poems were true to Loy's originals. Williams said that his "1958 Mina Loy was an improvement on what had gone before but it suffered from a callow assumption that the texts were correct in the first place." Many of the errors that Williams feared were extant in his work were researched and corrected for *The Lost Lunar Baedeker* (1982), a centenary edition of Loy's work edited by Roger L. Conover for the Jargon Society.

For a time during the 1920s, a rumor making the rounds in Paris asserted that there was no such person as Mina Loy, that she was an invention. According to Conover's introduction to

The Lost Lunar Baedeker, legend has it that she responded by showing up at one of the city's best-known salons with the following explanation: "I am indeed a live being. But it is necessary to stay very unknown. . . . To maintain my incognito the hazard I chose was—poet." Support for the rumor was fragile and fragmentary, but what is significant is that Loy herself contributed evidence to the story, intentionally or otherwise. She was fond of using pseudonyms that both concealed her identity and drew attention to themselves as such (e.g., "Ducie," a name given to her by friends to reflect her difficulty in remembering when to use *du* and *Sie* in German), and she occasionally dated her own paintings incorrectly, confusing those who sought to establish a tidy chronology for her career.

Loy also held an extremely variable opinion of celebrity, at times apparently revelling in her position at the center of social and intellectual circles wherever she was, at others dropping almost entirely from sight, for months or even years at a time, keeping her work as well as her person out of the public eye. The story of the rumor, if accurate, is illuminating on several counts: it demonstrates how effective her own subterfuges were; it attests to the centrality of her position in other people's lives; and it establishes one important function poetry had for Loy, as a "hazard," i.e., an obstacle between the larger world and her private self.

Our wills are formed by curious disciplines.

—Mina Loy, from "Apology of Genius"

Much of what is known of Loy's biography confirms and amplifies what this perhaps apocryphal story reveals. She manifested considerable artistic talent and great physical beauty early in her life, and found that cultural expectations about her appearance often limited her sense of freedom to pursue her artistic interests. (Loy's beauty and the expectations generated by her appearance were always part of the effect she had on people. Even otherwise careful criticism of her writing sometimes stops to marvel at how lovely she was. It is likely that this accident of birth contributed to sadness as well as happiness in her life.)

She left home—where she felt supported by her father and thwarted by her mother—while still in her teens, "in a subconscious muddle of foreign languages," and went to Munich to study art. She had little formal education otherwise. Teachers in Germany, London, and Paris praised and encouraged Loy. Her work began appearing in student exhibitions almost immedi-

ately, and she was invited to join the Salon d'Automne—a Parisian circle with considerable influence on 20th-century art—while still in her early 20s. Even then, she clearly felt ambivalent about her growing fame. Shortly after achieving this milestone, she went to Florence with her husband Stephen Haweis: "When I was twenty-three I was elected a member of the Autumn Salon and then I stole away from civilization—to live on the Costa San Georgio."

Loy's marriage to Haweis began to unravel almost at once, a casualty of frequent separations, parenthood, illness, and the marital infidelity of both partners. But as her marriage failed, her careers in painting and poetry gathered strength and influence. Her work in each arena was characterized by an experimental spirit; while in Florence, Loy threw herself into Futurism, a radical movement in art that brought the speed, the machinery, and the intensity of modern life onto the canvas. Like Cubism and Abstract Expressionism, Futurism violated many of the conventions of representational art.

Loy's poetry also broke with tradition; the early poems established the radical nature of her vision. Even in the midst of all the Modernist revolutions taking place around her, Loy stood out. The poems required a new kind of reader, one who was not frightened off by the elliptical, often intentionally distorted quality of her work. "Lunar Baedeker" travels down "Delirious Avenues," past "the eye-white sky-light / white-light district," encountering carousels, cyclones, Necropolis, "Onyx-eyed Odalisques" and a NOCTURNAL CYCLOPS along the way.

The poetry uses elements borrowed from collage, a technique Loy always favored in her art; it also experiments with punctuation and the white space on the page, and is rich in alliteration. The poetry reflects on both abstract ideas and specific experiences and images. Lines are generally short, as are most of the poems themselves, but Loy often links together short poems or segments to create larger units. There is little if any metrical regularity in a typical Loy poem and traditional stanza forms are nonexistent. Rhyme, if it happens at all, seems accidental.

In both painting and poetry, Loy's aim was to break old boundaries between media and expand the possibilities within a particular genre. Conover's introduction to *The Lost Lunar Baedeker* summarizes her far-reaching influence:

> She introduced Stieglitz and his circle to the work of Apollinaire, imported Futurist techniques to American theater, applied methods borrowed from the revolution in the visual

arts to the new poetics, and exerted an influence on the leaders of New York Dada.

Roughly half a generation older than the Lost Generation of American poets and influenced by trends in painting as well as literature, Loy was a figure of considerable romance and influence for younger Modernist poets.

Professional success and fame notwithstanding, Loy became increasingly unhappy in the years leading up to the First World War. She began talking about divorce from Haweis in 1913, and her decision to stay in Italy after the declaration of war the following year may have reflected a need to find something other than her own misery on which to concentrate, as well as a desire to serve. In 1914, she began an affair with Filippo Tommaso Marinetti, the founder of Futurism, but "his interest in [her] only weathered two months of war fever." The Futurists' subsequent identification with fascism ended Loy's interest in the movement, and she devoted some of her intellectual energies to writing satires of Futurist ideas, especially to what she saw as misogynist elements of the cause.

In 1915, Loy became something of a *cause célèbre:* two of her "Love Songs" were printed in the first issue of *Others,* a little magazine published in New York that was intended to challenge the supremacy of **Harriet Monroe*'s more conservative and mainstream *Poetry,* published in Chicago. Song #1 begins with the memorable image of Pig Cupid, "His rosy snout / Rooting erotic garbage." In *Our Singing Strength,* Alfred Kreymborg explains the effect of Loy's poems on the magazine's readership and the press more generally; citing her "madly elliptical style" and "the nudity of emotion and thought," he recalls the uproar:

> [T]he utter nonchalance in revealing the secrets of sex was denounced as nothing less than lewd. . . . Had a man written these poems, the town might have viewed them with comparative comfort. But a woman wrote them, a woman who dressed like a lady.

A subsequent issue of *Others* printed the whole of Loy's poem cycle, more than 30 poems. Decades after the magazine had folded, people were still fighting about Loy, *Others,* and the

Mina Loy (left) with Djuna Barnes.

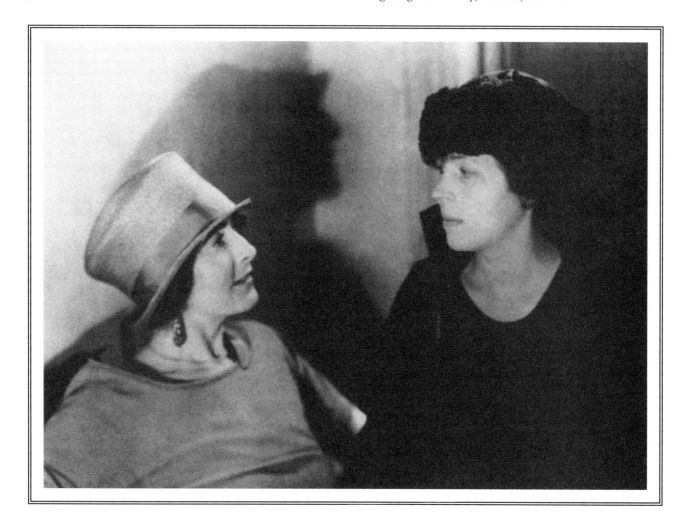

role each played in the Modernist era. Loy's influence far outstripped anything she or the editors of the magazine could have envisioned.

Loy's divorce from Haweis was final in 1917, shortly after her first meeting with Arthur Cravan, soon to become her second husband. Cravan, who identified himself as a poet-boxer, was a fugitive from conscription, a jack-of-all-trades, an Englishman originally christened Fabian Lloyd who was at home virtually anywhere in Europe. Conover calls him "the progenitor of all boxers who fight with their mouths": he typically sprang to his feet after the referee announced his name, to list all of the high points of his life on the road. He and Loy met in April 1917, one day before he created a scandal by undressing during his own lecture on "The Independent Artists in France and America."

Loy and Cravan married in Mexico City in January 1918 and then took off on a very low-budget wedding trip; they nearly starved to death. They decided to return to Europe separately, but Cravan disappeared shortly after Loy set off for Argentina on the first leg of her journey. As late as March 1920, Loy was still convinced Cravan was alive, and took a trip to New York to try to pick up his trail. The legends about his fate were various: he'd been murdered; he'd drowned; he was living a secret life. None of the stories were ever proven, one way or another. Although Loy did not give up writing and painting after this traumatic loss, she relinquished virtually all elements of a public life. The last 50 years of her life were spent in private work, with only limited contact with the world outside her immediate family.

Loy returned to Paris in 1923, still mourning for Cravan and newly grieved by the recent death of her son Giles, who had been kidnapped by his father in 1921. Although she once again found herself at the center of literary and artistic life in Paris, the pleasures of such an existence had palled for Loy. She continued to write: the first section of *Anglo-Mongrels and the Rose* came out in *The Little Review* in 1923, as did *Lunar Baedecker* [sic], her first book. Loy continued to be treated as radical and influential by poets and other readers throughout the 1920s; her work, publicly praised by both T.S. Eliot and Ezra Pound, appeared in *Others, Rogue, Trend, The Little Review,* and the issue of *The Dial* in which *The Waste Land* first appeared. Nevertheless, Loy's influence among her contemporaries did not translate into posterity with a larger, more popular readership. One of the most important factors in this phenomenon was Loy's own lack of interest in achieving fame, an element of her character that grew more pronounced over time.

This feature of her temperament fostered another of Loy's fundamental traits, a desire to devote herself to meticulous revision of any work she undertook. In 1926, in a common gesture of the period, Yvor Winters linked Loy's name with that of William Carlos Williams, treating the two as parts of a new foundation in American poetry for which "*Emily Dickinson will have been [the] only forerunner." He predicted that Williams stood a greater chance than did Loy of becoming "chief prophet" of their own and later generations; Winters was proved right, if for no other reason than that the two poets produced at vastly different rates. Williams wrote rapidly and with dazzling technique. Loy lingered over her own work much longer, sometimes taking years to complete single poems. And her poetry was often intentionally difficult as Williams' was not—full of alliteration and unfamiliar diction, rich in capital letters, cryptic fragments, and mysterious spaces.

Loy was also quite decided in her tastes and sometimes refused to contribute poems or lend her influence to new little magazines. Some editors, offended by what they saw as high-handedness, refused to back or publish her; waning interest in experimental writing and the financial failure of many little magazines also stunted the development of any larger popular interest in her work.

Loy continued to devote some attention to the politics as well as the aesthetic concerns of the Modernist era. Her political commitments, like her artistic endeavors, always bore an experimental, idiosyncratic edge. In the '20s, Loy created a political party she called Psycho-Democracy, a one-woman movement despite the fact that the party manifesto uses plural pronouns to establish Loy's tenets:

> Our purpose is the instatement of Actual Values to destroy the power—inimical to man—of those things he does not understand. . . . We fight with Brains for the substitution of Preference for Prejudice and the obviation of social crises by the Excavation of individual and group psychology.

But most of her time and energy went into her new enterprise, backed by two of her friends, a lampshade design business conceived as a source of steady income to support her writing. Her shop (and other design projects for fashion stores in New York) did support Loy for a time, but it eventually failed. Depressed, financially troubled, and convinced that others were stealing her ideas, Loy dissolved the business.

Loy found something of a new lease on life when Julien Levy, now married to her daughter **Joella Haweis**, hired her to act as a representative for his new gallery in New York. Between 1931 and 1936, Loy watched the Paris art scene, making recommendations about artists and properties and acting as Levy's agent in a variety of capacities. Some of her paintings were exhibited in the Julien Levy Gallery and the Wadsworth Atheneum in Hartford, Connecticut, in 1933, but most of her time went to developing her skills as a businesswoman. She left Paris in 1936 and returned to New York, where she lived for the next 17 years (part of the time with her daughter **Fabi Cravan**). These years in New York were intensely private ones, animated by "a metaphorical search to find Christ in the Bowery," writes Conover. She became very comfortable in the Bowery, moving there in 1949, and devoted herself to learning about the lives of the indigent. She wrote a series of poems about the people she met in her quest and constructed art works of garbage salvaged from streets and alleys. As ever, her work received admiring, even reverent attention.

Loy left New York in 1953 to visit her daughters, both now living in Aspen, Colorado. At some point, the visit turned into a permanent move. Her habits and interests became ever more eccentric, and she did little in the way of writing or other creation. She seemed unwilling to entertain others' interests in her work, past or present. She confronted Jonathan Williams (editor of the second book of her poems, published in 1958) about his project by saying: "But, why do you waste your time on these thoughts of mine? I was never a poet." William Carlos Williams was excited by the news of this forthcoming book and wrote an enthusiastic review, despite the fact that they had been out of touch for almost 30 years:

> Mina Loy was endowed from birth with a first-rate intelligence and a sensibility which has plagued her all her life facing a shoddy world. When she puts a word down on paper it is clean; that forces her fellows to shy away from it because they are not clean and will be contaminated by her cleanliness. Therefore she has not been a successful writer and couldn't care less. But it has hurt her chances of being known.

Aside from claiming that she hadn't realized Williams was still alive, Loy had nothing else to say about his reaction to the book. Books and exhibitions of her work went on without her;

she did not even appear when the Bodley Gallery mounted a show of her "Constructions." Mina Loy died in 1966, still going her own way, leaving no complete autobiographical memoirs to consult in reconstructing her remarkable, often hidden, life.

SOURCES:

Conover, Roger L., ed. *The Lost Lunar Baedeker*. Highlands, NC: The Jargon Society, 1982.

Winters, Yvor. *Uncollected Essays and Reviews*. NY: Swallow Press, 1973.

SUGGESTED READING:

Burke, Carolyn. *Becoming Modern: The Life of Mina Loy*. NY: Farrar, Straus and Giroux, 1996.

Dictionary of Literary Biography. Vol. 4. Detroit, MI: Gale Research.

Kouidis, Virginia. *Mina Loy: American Modernist Poet*. Baton Rouge: Louisiana State University Press, 1980.

Kreymborg, Alfred. *American Poetry: Our Singing Strength*. NY: Tudor, 1934.

Los Angeles Times Book Review. August 22, 1982.

The New York Times Book Review. November 16, 1980, May 16, 1982.

COLLECTIONS:

Joella Bayer Collection; Collection of American Literature, Beinecke Rare Book Room—Yale University; The Dial Collection; Julien Levy Collection, William N. Copley Collection; Bodley Gallery; private collections.

Mary M. Lacey,
Assistant Visiting Professor of English and Humanities,
Earlham College, Richmond, Indiana

Loy, Myrna (1905–1993)

American film actress who starred in the popular "Thin Man" series as the sophisticated, quick-witted Nora Charles. Born Myrna Adele Williams on August 2, 1905, in Radersburg, Montana; died on December 14, 1993, in New York City; daughter of Davis and Della Williams; had one younger brother, David; married Arthur Hornblow, Jr., in 1936 (divorced 1942); married John Hertz, Jr., in 1942 (divorced 1944); married Gene Markey, in 1946 (divorced 1950); married Howland Sargeant, in 1951 (divorced 1960); no children.

Moved to Los Angeles after her father's death (1918) and began getting bit parts in silent films, eventually working her way up to larger roles; though she successfully made the transition to sound films, seemed destined to a future of studio typecasting as an exotic and often murderous siren before being offered a comedy role in the first "Thin Man" film (1934), playing opposite William Powell's Nick Charles; her popularity increased during a series of "Thin Man" sequels to such an extent that she was eventually dubbed "Queen of the Movies"; devoted much of her time during World War II to charitable and fund-raising activities, but returned to the screen after the war to great acclaim in such films as The Best Years of Our Lives; *remained active in film and television through the 1980s; made Broadway debut (1973) and was awarded a special Academy Award for Lifetime Achievement (1991).*

Filmography: Sporting Life (1925); Pretty Ladies (1925); Ben-Hur (1926); The Cave Man (1926); The Gilded Highway (1926); Across the Pacific (1926); Why Girls Go Back Home (1926); Don Juan (1926); The Exquisite Sinner (1926); So This Is Paris (1926); Finger Prints (1927); Ham and Eggs at the Front (1927); Bitter Apples (1927); The Heart of Maryland (1927); The Jazz Singer (1927); If I Were Single (1927); The Climbers (1927); Simple Sis (1927); A Sailor's Sweetheart (1927); The Girl from Chicago (1927); What Price Beauty (1928); Beware of Married Men (1928); Turn Back the Hours (1928); The Crimson City (1928); Pay As You Enter (1928); State Street Sadie (1928); The Midnight Taxi (1928); Noah's Ark (1929); Fancy Baggage (1929); The Desert Song (1929); The Black Watch (1929); The Squall (1929); Hardboiled Rose (1929); Evidence (1929); The Show of Shows (1929); The Great Divide (1929); Cameo Kirby (1930); Isle of Escape (1930); Under a Texas Moon (1930); Renegades (1930); The Jazz Cinderella (1930); The Truth About Youth (1930); The Devil to Pay (1930); Rogue of the Rio Grande (1930); Body and Soul (1931); The Naughty Flirt (1931); A Connecticut Yankee (1931); Hush Money (1931); Transatlantic (1931); Rebound (1931); Skyline (1931); Consolation Marriage (1931); Arrowsmith (1931); Emma (1932); The Wet Parade (1932); Vanity Fair (1932); The Woman in Room Thirteen (1932); New Morals for Old (1932); Love Me Tonight (1932); Thirteen Women (1932); The Mask of Fu Manchu (1932); The Animal Kingdom (1932); Topaze (1933); The Barbarian (1933); When Ladies Meet (1933); Penthouse (1933); Night Flight (1933); The Prizefighter and the Lady (1933); Men In White (1934); Manhattan Melodrama (1934); The Thin Man (1934); Stamboul Quest (1934); Evelyn Prentice (1934); Broadway Bill (1934); Wings in the Dark (1935); Whipsaw (1935); Wife vs. Secretary (1936); Petticoat Fever (1936); The Great Ziegfeld (1936); To Mary with Love (1936); Libeled Lady (1936); After the Thin Man (1936); Parnell (1937); Double Wedding (1937); Man-Proof (1938); Test Pilot (1938); Too Hot to Handle (1938); Lucky Night (1939); The Rains Came (1939); Another Thin Man (1939); I Love You Again (1940); Third Finger Left Hand (1940); Love Crazy (1941); Shadow of the Thin Man (1941); The Thin Man Goes Home (1944); So Goes My Love (1946); The Best Years of Our Lives (1946); The Bachelor and the Bobby-Soxer (1947);

The Senator Was Indiscreet (1947); Song of the Thin Man (1947); Mr. Blandings Builds His Dream House (1948); The Red Pony (1949); That Dangerous Age (If This Be Sin, 1949); Cheaper by the Dozen (1950); Belles on Their Toes (1952); The Ambassador's Daughter (1956); Lonelyhearts (1959); From the Terrace (1960); Midnight Lace (1960); The April Fools (1969); Airport 1975 (1974); The End (1978); Just Tell Me What You Want (1980).

It is an odd tribute to Myrna Loy's film career that one of America's most notorious gangsters died because of her. John Dillinger had eluded federal agents for months, but one summer afternoon in 1934 he was unable to resist the temptation to see his favorite movie star in her new film playing at Chicago's Biograph. Dillinger was gunned down by waiting G-men as he left the theater. He shared his enthusiasm for Myrna Loy with a more exalted fan, Franklin Roosevelt, who always asked for private screenings of her films at the White House and made sure to take one of them with him overseas for comfort after a hard day of international diplomacy. In between these two extremes were millions of Americans who elected Myrna Loy "Queen of the Movies" in a 1936 Ed Sullivan newspaper poll and flocked to see her in pictures with her "King," Clark Gable. The press named her "the perfect wife" for her portrayal of Nora Charles, the wise-cracking mate of William Powell's Nick Charles in a wildly successful series of "Thin Man" films during the 1930s and 1940s. It all made Loy frankly uncomfortable. "Labels limit you, because they limit your possibilities," she once wrote.

Limits had been anathema to Myrna Loy since her childhood as a farm girl in Montana's "Big Sky" country, where she had grown up surrounded by the wide open spaces of Davis and **Della Williams'** cattle ranch, Crow Creek Valley, just outside tiny Radersburg. Davis had named his daughter, born in August 1905, after a town he had passed through during one of the many train trips he was required to take as a member of Montana's state legislature. After the birth of their second child, a son, Davis and Della left the ranch in the care of relatives and moved to Helena, the state capital. City life did nothing to erase young Myrna Williams' reputation as a scrappy, independent-minded roughneck with no time for sentimentality, not even toward a lovestruck neighborhood boy named Gary Cooper who had developed a crush on her. Her parents were not the doting kind. "Never once in the first few years of my life did anyone hug me or pat my head and say 'What a lovely . . . little girl,'" she once recalled with some satisfaction. "At least I escaped that." The seed of Loy's lifelong political liberalism may have been planted when Helena's first African-American family moved into the Williams' neighborhood. Unlike most of her neighbors, Della was quick to accept the newcomers. "My mother made no distinction at all," Loy remembered. "She welcomed them and encouraged us to play with their children." Her parents were ardent Democrats and supporters of Woodrow Wilson's pacifist policies, campaigning for Wilson's League of Nations after

World War I. "When I was growing up," she told an interviewer, "it was all Democrats. We wouldn't let a Republican in the back door."

Her first exposure to show business came in 1916, when doctors advised Della to recuperate in California after a nearly fatal bout with pneumonia. The warmer climate and gentle sunshine of Los Angeles and La Jolla proved the doctors right, leaving Della fit enough to take her children on a tour of the local movie studios. Myrna was fascinated and promptly convinced her parents to enroll her in a dance academy on their re-

Myrna
Loy

turn to Helena. By 1917, the Montana *Record-Herald* took note of Myrna's appearance in a class recital, in which she performed "The Bluebird Dance" at Helena's Marlow Theater. "Miss Williams, who is much admired for her grace and beauty, has received many compliments upon her interpretation of the dance," the newspaper politely told its readers.

Helena did not escape the disastrous influenza pandemic that swept the world in 1918. Among its victims was Davis Williams, who died just days after Myrna had recovered from the disease. Della decided to start her new life as a widow in California, moving with her two children to Culver City. Myrna attended Venice High School, continued her dance lessons, and posed for a sculpture called "Spiritual Man" which graced the school's entrance. The publicity surrounding the sculpture's installation led to her first job in show business, as a chorine at Grauman's Chinese Theater. Loy left high school in her senior year to appear at the theater in one of its famous "prologue" dances, elaborate stage numbers with a theme matching that of the silent film to follow. In Myrna's case, the film was Cecil B. De Mille's *The Ten Commandments*, requiring a farm girl from rural Montana to hoof it on the Grauman stage as an Egyptian courtesan.

> *If you live long enough and fight long enough, a sense of comforting continuity comes.*
>
> —Myrna Loy

Nonetheless, Loy's auburn hair and slightly oblique, green eyes seemed the perfect complement to the costume and attracted the attention of a photographer hired for publicity shots, who showed his work to friends Rudolph Valentino and Valentino's wife and manager, *Natacha Rambova. Valentino, an Italian immigrant who had become a silent film idol by playing seductive sheiks and desert princes in sand-strewn romantic potboilers, thought that Loy might be usable in his next film and told Rambova to arrange a screen test. Myrna's first experience in front of a camera was, by her own admission, a disaster, and Valentino quickly lost interest in her. Rambova, however, was convinced Myrna had a future in pictures and cast her in a film she was herself directing, *What Price Beauty*, an odd and awkward fantasy film set in a beauty parlor that failed to find a distributor until four years later, in 1928, when it predictably flopped at the box office. Loy appeared merely as window dressing in a red velvet tunic and black pants, but it was enough to whet her interest in film work. Quitting her job at Grauman's Chinese, she be-

came such a persistent inhabitant of various reception rooms at MGM that the studio finally gave her a bit part in the chorus line of its 1925 Ziegfeld Follies film *Pretty Ladies,* and used her as a living mannequin in a wardrobe test for its upcoming production of *Ben Hur,* which was to be an early experiment in color filmmaking. Makeup was unnecessary, but Loy appeared in full war paint anyway and attracted enough attention to land another bit part as one of the "hedonist handmaidens" to a Roman senator in the picture. By now, friends were suggesting that her chances might be better if she changed her name, there being too many actors called "Williams" in the business already. A writer friend much taken with the nonsensical sound poems of *Gertrude Stein came up with "Loy" as a suitable complement to her first name. The headshots Myrna sent to Warner Bros. were signed with the new name, which seemed to work its magic when the studio offered Myrna Loy a contract in 1925 at $75 a week.

Loy's fear of limiting labels was amply justified for the next six years. She was condemned to a dreary series of B pictures in which she was typecast as the sensuous, mysterious, and often treacherous foreign *femme fatale* of vague Asian extraction with such names as Yasmini, Nubi, and Fah Lo See. She was the "native girl" who ruins the career of an innocent young American sailor in *Across The Pacific;* a "Hindu princess" in *The Black Watch*, outfitted in silk pants, a halter top, and a strange black wig that one reviewer thought made her look like "a weird cross between Cleopatra and the goddess Kali"; and a Gypsy in *The Squall,* in which she arouses the passions of a group of naive farmers with whom she takes refuge during a storm. (Even the film's director, a young Alexander Korda, later remembered it as "that ghastly picture.") She murdered nine sorority girls in revenge for their racial taunts in *Thirteen Women,* killed her ex-lover with a bullet to the stomach in *Renegades,* and tortured young men with a whip in *The Mask of Fu Manchu* as the evil doctor's sadistic daughter. "Those roles were fun to play, despite their unreality," Loy remembered many years later. "The characters were always so nefarious that they had to die at the end." There were a few exceptions to the rule, notably her work as a Southern belle who saves her brother from an unjust murder charge in 1927's *The Girl From Chicago,* a starring role that led *The New York Times'* normally caustic film critic Mordaunt Hall to note that "an attractive actress named Myrna Loy officiates [in the film] as Mary Carleton." Loy had a small role in the industry's first talking picture, *The Jazz Singer,* and had successfully made the transition to all-sound pictures by the time film critic Creighton Peel speculated that Hollywood wasn't taking full advantage of Myrna Loy, whom he thought to be the only potential rival to *Greta Garbo. "Myrna Loy has intelligence, and it is high time somebody gave her a decent part. Give the girl a chance!" he suggested emphatically.

A few in Hollywood heeded Peel's suggestion. Rouben Mamoulian cast her as the Countess Valentine in *Love Me Tonight,* his frothy 1932 operetta with Maurice Chevalier and *Jeanette MacDonald. Mamoulian was sure enough of Loy's talent that he created the role of Valentine especially for her, over Paramount's objections, and handed Myrna her lines, scribbled on blue sheets of paper, when she arrived on the set each morning. That same year, MGM gave her the part of Joyce Lanyon in its film adaptation of Sinclair Lewis' *Arrowsmith,* directed by John Ford, bringing her to the attention of MGM's head of production, Irving Thalberg, who signed her to a contract. To

Thalberg's embarrassment, however, it was the two pictures Loy did for RKO, to which Thalberg had loaned her, that indicated her star potential. RKO's two dramatic films, *The Animal Kingdom* and *Topaze,* gave the first hint of a range far beyond Hollywood's idea of smoldering Oriental sexpots. This inspired Thalberg to cast Loy in MGM's *The Prizefighter and the Lady* as a gun moll who falls for a good-hearted boxer, played by real-life pugilist Max Baer in his first film role. The film was directed by W.S. (Woody) Van Dyke, who joined the ranks of Loy converts and cast her in 1933's *Penthouse,* Myrna's first role in a comedy.

By now, Thalberg was willing to move Loy on to the studio's A-list. She appeared in the first of a number of films with Clark Gable, 1933's *Night Flight,* and the following year with Gable and William Powell in *Manhattan Melodrama* (the film that had such disastrous consequences for John Dillinger, and the only film in which she appears with her two most popular leading men at the same time). Myrna plays a woman who reconciles two men, friends since childhood,

Myrna Loy with William Powell and Asta from "The Thin Man" series.

whose lives have taken drastically different paths—one having become an attorney (Powell) and the other a gangster (Gable). Loy, who confided many years later that she considered Gable "a terrible actor," found working with him challenging. "Clark was always trying to put me on the spot," she later said of their seven films together. "There was a constant one-upmanship. I had to play tough, independent women [opposite him]." But it was a different story with William Powell. "He was so naturally witty and outrageous that I stayed somewhat detached, always a little incredulous," she said. "We felt that particular magic between us." Woody Van Dyke, the film's director, noticed something, too. It was his next film that would make Myrna Loy a star.

A few years earlier, MGM had bought the rights to one of novelist Dashiell Hammett's mystery novels, *The Thin Man,* in which Hammett had first introduced his debonair if slightly dipsomaniacal sleuthing couple, Nick and Nora Charles, and their mischievous dog, Asta. Hammett had drawn on his own relationship with *Lillian Hellman to create the characters of Nick, with his working knowledge of thugs, cops, rackets and molls, and Nora, from a more socially impressive and wealthy background, but with an almost anthropological interest in her husband's former *milieu* and a talent for quick-witted riposte. Thalberg assigned Van Dyke to what he expected to be a typical and inexpensive B picture. Called "One-Shot Woody," Van Dyke was known for his rapid and usually under-budget shooting style. But it was precisely his efficient directing style and the film's short, 12-day shooting schedule that gave the final product the breezy, informal and amusing tone that would also mark six more such films over the next 13 years. Despite the fact that Loy had over 70 films to her credit by 1934, it was the part of Nora that made her career. "It put me right up there with the public and the studio, and it inspired the press," she recalled many years later. "They called me 'the perfect wife'. . . but at least this wife thing came closer to my own personality." Nora Charles was such a popular figure that "Men Must Marry Myrna Clubs" appeared throughout the country and thousands of women rushed to dress shops to have copies of Nora's wardrobe made for themselves. "She was a working, collaborative wife," film director Alan Pakula, a lifetime Loy fan, said of Nora. "Young guys today . . . want to marry . . . bright women with minds of their own, careers of their own, wit, sexuality. Myrna always had that."

The fame Loy achieved came with a price. Always careful to keep her private and professional lives separate, Myrna was dismayed at the publicity that surrounded her marriage to Arthur Hornblow, Jr., in 1936. Loy had met Hornblow some years earlier on the MGM lot, where he was an assistant producer, and their affair during her pre-Nora days had drawn little attention, even though Hornblow was still a married man. The couple's plan to marry quietly in Mexico when Hornblow's divorce from his first wife became final was disrupted by a trail of photographers and reporters, leading Loy to complain, "I can't see what [the marriage] has to do with my work. All I can say is, if you're successful at something, God help you!" The public scrutiny only increased with her performance in one of the best-loved of the "screwball" comedies of the 1930s, *Libeled Lady,* in which she again appeared with Powell and with *Jean Harlow. By the end of 1936, Loy was among MGM's highest-paid stars, earning as much as any of the studio's male stars, including Clark Gable, after waging a successful "equal pay for equal work" fight with Louis Mayer himself.

By the outbreak of World War II, Loy had amply justified her title of "Queen of the Movies" in such films as *I Love You Again* (once more paired with Powell, with whom she would make 13 films), *Third Finger, Left Hand,* and in three "Thin Man" sequels. But Loy's private life once again became tabloid news when her divorce from Arthur Hornblow in Mexico and, six days later, her marriage to millionaire John Hertz, Jr., were revealed. (Hertz was the heir to a vast business empire for which his father's rental-car company had been the catalyst.) Myrna's political activism was much reported on, too. She had spoken out publicly against Hitler as early as 1938, loudly enough that by the time of America's entry into the war, Hitler had banned from German movie screens any film in which Myrna Loy appeared. In 1941, Loy's public, to say nothing of MGM, was dismayed with her decision to quit film work altogether and devote herself to war work. "It's an astonishing thing to think that at the peak of her success, she quit acting," close friend Roddy McDowell once noted. "It was like she went into the service." Loy moved to New York and spent most of the war working full-time for the Red Cross, visiting wounded soldiers in hospitals, entertaining troops on leave, and appearing at war-bond rallies. She exchanged telegrams with Franklin Roosevelt and, in later life, regretted that she never actually met him, despite several trips to the White House and a close friendship with *Eleanor Roosevelt. In the midst of war, the president was usually otherwise engaged; on the one occasion when FDR was actually in residence, Myrna had to decline his invitation, citing ill health. What she did not reveal was that John Hertz, whose alcoholism and mental illness she had discovered too late, had thrown a heavy Rodin sculpture at her which left her face bruised and blackened for weeks. ("John always had great taste," she noted drily.) By the end of 1944, she and Hertz were divorced.

The only film in which Loy appeared in this period was released just at the end of the war. It was the fifth "Thin Man" film, *The Thin Man Goes Home*, after which Myrna decided to devote her energies to postwar recovery and declined to renew her contract with MGM. In April 1945, Roosevelt invited her to attend the San Francisco conference that formally ratified the creation of the United Nations. The following year, Roosevelt named her as the U.S. delegate to the UN's new cultural arm, UNESCO, for which Loy traveled extensively in Europe. But Hollywood wanted her back, and Myrna's marriage in June 1948 to screenwriter Gene Markey drew her back to the camera. Her return to the screen was a triumphant one, with her performance as Milly Stephenson in 1946's *The Best Years of Our Lives*, William Wyler's poignant story of three veterans adjusting to civilian life after wartime service. The film was awarded eight Oscars, including Best Picture, but the film's celebrity was not without political repercussions.

The anti-Communist fervor that began sweeping the nation in the late 1940s was rapidly gathering adherents, led by Senator Joseph McCarthy and solidified in Capitol Hill's House Un-American Activities Committee. By 1948, Wyler's film, with its frank portrayal of the difficulties faced by returning veterans, was listed in anti-Communist literature as unpatriotic, Communist-inspired propaganda. "You could feel this cold wind blow through Hollywood," Loy recalled. "A terror had seized the whole country, and in Hollywood the terror was that the Communists would take over." Myrna's liberal politics were by then well known, making her immediately suspect, but the daughter of two flinty Montana libertarians wasn't about to bow to pressure. She sued *The Hollywood Reporter* after an editorial accused her of Communist sympathies, forcing the magazine to print a retraction; and a telegram she sent to the House Un-American Activities Committee bluntly stated, "I dare you to call me to testify." The Committee declined her challenge.

Loy made her last appearance as Nora Charles in 1947's *Song of the Thin Man*. She then turned to more mature roles in what have since become classics of sophisticated comedy in which her performances, in the words of one biographer, were "as smooth as brandy-laced eggnog." She played the straight man to Cary Grant and *Shirley Temple (Black) in *The Bachelor and the Bobby-Soxer,* appearing as the judge who sentences Grant to date her teenaged sister. MGM paired her a second time with Grant in 1948's *Mr. Blandings Builds His Dream House*, and starred her in *Cheaper by the Dozen* and its sequel *Belles on Their Toes*, popular comedies that revolved around the lives of time-study experts Frank and *Lillian Gilbreth and their brood of 12 children.

The Ambassador's Daughter, in 1951, marked the first film in 20 years in which Loy did not take top billing. It was a deliberate decision on her part. "There's a big ego problem involved in making that transition," she said. "It was a matter of making up my mind to hang on and wait for star parts, and die of ennui or starvation, or play character roles and keep busy." She chose her roles carefully, however, refusing to take on what she called parts that "those horrible women *Bette Davis and *Joan Crawford accept." The result was a series of dramatically more interesting parts, including 1958's *Lonelyhearts* (from the Nathanael West novel "Miss Lonelyhearts"), with Robert Ryan and Montgomery Clift; and her moving portrayal of the bitter, alcoholic Martha Eaton in 1960's *From the Terrace*, adapted from the John O'Hara novel.

Although she was taking smaller roles on screen, Loy's off-screen life remained as active as ever. In the 1950s, she campaigned in California for equal housing opportunities for minorities, for Adlai Stevenson's presidential campaign against Dwight Eisenhower, and for funding for various social programs proposed during the Roosevelt years. Along the way, she amicably divorced Gene Markey and, in 1951, married Howland Sargeant, who had accompanied her UNESCO tour through Europe several years earlier and who had become an undersecretary in the State Department under Dean Acheson. They were divorced in 1960, both Loy and Sargeant finding their careers incompatible. During the mid-1960s, Myrna watched with dismay America's growing involvement in Vietnam; by 1972, she was actively campaigning for Eugene McCarthy's antiwar candidacy. Her beliefs only hardened during the Nixon and Reagan years, Ronald Reagan in particular being a frequent target in the later sections of her autobiography, *Being and Becoming*, published in 1987. "Can you imagine how all of us who worked for years with Mrs. Roosevelt and her socialist programs feel now, to see them wiped off the map?" she wrote. Early in the Reagan years, Loy pointedly walked out of a formal dinner with the president's daughter and son-in-law after the conversation turned disparagingly to Adlai Stevenson.

Her vow to continue working brought Loy her first theater role in 1966, as the addled mother in a Chicago production of Neil Simon's *Barefoot in the Park.* She made her Broadway debut in a 1971 revival of *The Women,* when she was 66 years old. She had already adapted her career to television, where she had appeared as early as 1955 on "General Electric Theater," had starred with Melvyn Douglas in an acclaimed version of "Death Takes a Holiday," and had even appeared in an episode of "Columbo" in 1971. Her final film appearance, in fact, was in a television movie, 1981's "Summer Solstice." Loy played opposite Henry Fonda (in one of his last roles before his death the following year) in a tender story of the relationship between an aging married couple.

There was no formal announcement of her retirement from films; Loy merely choose to spend more time in her modest, one-bedroom apartment on New York's Upper East Side, where she made a point of supporting Democratic causes and keeping up with current events. "It's not always pleasant," she said of her daily scrutiny of newspapers and periodicals, "but it's important." Now in her 80s and in weakening health, she gracefully accepted a special Carnegie Hall tribute in 1985 by the American Academy of Motion Picture Arts and Sciences, and the Kennedy Center Award in 1988 (following, ironically, a special ceremony at the White House hosted by Ronald Reagan). In 1991, Loy was given a Lifetime Achievement Award at that year's Oscar ceremonies. It was her last public appearance. On December 14, 1993, Myrna Loy died quietly at home. She was 88 years old.

The many retrospectives of Myrna Loy's work in the years since her death never fail to include her most famous role, and it was in describing Nora Charles that Loy may have unintentionally delivered her own eulogy. "She was courageous and interested in living and she enjoyed all the things she did," Myrna had said of Nora. "You understand, she had a good time, always."

SOURCES:

Brock, Pope. "Myrna Loy, So Perfect In Her Way," in *People Weekly.* Vol. 29, no. 13. April 4, 1988.

Kay, Karyn. *Myrna Loy.* NY: Pyramid Books, 1977.

Loy, Myrna, and James Kotsilibas-Davis. *Myrna Loy: Being and Becoming.* NY: Alfred A. Knopf, 1987.

Norman Powers,
writer-producer,
Chelsea Lane Productions, New York

Loyse.

Variant of Louise.

Lozier, Clemence S. (1813–1888)

American physician and reformer. Born Clemence Sophia Harned on December 11, 1813, in Plainfield, New Jersey; died on April 26, 1888, in New York City; youngest of 13 children of David Harned (a farmer) and Hannah (Walker) Harned; attended Plainfield Academy; attended Central Medical College of Rochester, New York; graduated with high honors from Syracuse (NY) Medical College; married Abraham Witton Lozier (a carpenter and builder), in 1829 or 1830 (died 1837); married John Baker, possibly in 1844 (divorced 1861); children: (first marriage) one son, Abraham Witton, Jr.

The youngest of 13 children, physician and reformer Clemence Lozier was born in 1813 in Plainfield, New Jersey, and received her early schooling at Plainfield Academy. Her interest in medicine may have been sparked by her mother **Hannah Walker Harned**, who had a natural predilection for healing and often attended to the sick in the neighborhood. Orphaned at age 11, Clemence was married in her teens to Abraham Lozier, a carpenter and builder. Not long into the marriage, her husband's health failed and Lozier opened a girls' school in her home which she ran for 11 years, supporting the family which now included a son. Enrolling 60 students a year, she offered an extremely progressive curriculum for the time, including such things as physiology, anatomy, and hygiene, along with the more standard subjects. As the years passed, Lozier's own interest in medicine began to develop, and, with the encouragement of her older brother, a doctor, she began to study medical books.

Following her husband's death in 1837, Lozier became active in the New York Female Moral Reform Society, an organization which attempted to prevent prostitution or rehabilitate the already fallen. Acting as one of the organization's "visitors," Lozier often encountered various diseases in the women she saw, and she became more and more interested in medicine. Sometime around 1844, Lozier moved to Albany, and married John Baker. Little is known about Baker, but the marriage was unhappy and ended in divorce in 1861. While continuing to lecture on physiology and hygiene, Lozier began to pursue the possibilities of formally studying medicine. In 1849, she entered Central Medical College of Rochester, one of the few medical schools at the time that would accept women. She completed her training at the Syracuse (NY) Medical College, graduating with highest honors in March 1853. Already separated from her husband, Lozier returned to New York City and set up a practice in obstetrics and general surgery. Eventually, she began to specialize in female disorders, particularly the removal of tumors.

In conjunction with her practice, Lozier held lectures in her home on anatomy, physiology, and hygiene, and organized a Medical Library Association to provide her patients with further reading. The popularity of her lectures gave rise to the idea of a medical college for women. After a difficult struggle, Lozier, with the support of *Elizabeth Cady Stanton who helped her lobby the legislature, obtained a state charter for the New York Medical College and Hospital for Women, the first women's school of medicine in the state. Opening its doors in November 1863, the homeopathic institution had seven students and eight faculty members, including Lozier who served as president and clinical professor of diseases of women and children. After a tour of European hospitals in 1867, Lozier reorganized the school, taking the title of professor of gynecology and obstetrics and serving as dean for the next 20 years. During her tenure, she also wrote a number of papers, notable among them *Child-Birth Made Easy* (1870), in which she condemned "tight-fitting heavy dresses."

Clemence Lozier was also a prominent woman suffragist, and was active in a number of reform and philanthropic movements. For 13 years, from 1873 to 1886, she was president of the New York City Woman Suffrage Society, and she also served one year (1877–78) as president of the National Woman Suffrage Association. In addition, she helped finance *Susan B. Anthony's suffrage weekly, the *Revolution*. Lozier also supported such causes as abolition, sanitary and prison reform, and Indian rights, frequently volunteering her own home as a command post, conference center, and storehouse. In her later years, she served as president of the Moral Education Society of New York and of the local women's Christian Temperance Union.

During the last decade of her life, Lozier experienced financial setbacks precipitated by the relocation of the college and hospital, against her wishes, to an expensive new site. In 1878, she was forced to declare bankruptcy. With the loss

in savings came the loss of her noted energy. Although she maintained her practice, she was limited by her own diminished strength and the number of competitors in her field of expertise. In her later years, she suffered from angina pectoris, and died of heart disease at the age of 74. At the time of her death in 1888, the medical college and hospital she founded had become nationally known and respected, with over 200 graduates. In 1918, it became part of the New York Medical College of the Flower and Fifth Avenue Hospitals.

Clemence S. Lozier

SOURCES:

James, Edward T., ed. *Notable American Women 1607–1950*. Cambridge, MA: The Belknap Press of Harvard University Press, 1971.

Parton, James, ed. *Eminent Women of the Age*. Hartford, CT: S.M. Betts, 1872.

Barbara Morgan,
Melrose, Massachusetts.

Lü, Empress (r. 195–180 BCE).

See Cixi for sidebar on Lü Hou.

Lubetkin, Zivia (1914–1978)

Polish-Jewish resistance leader in the Warsaw Ghetto Uprising and a founder of the Jewish Fighting Organization (ZOB). Name variations: Zivia Lubetkin-Zuckerman; Cywia Lubetkin; Ziviah Lubetkin; underground name: "Celina." Born in 1914 in Beten near Slonim, Polesie, Russian Poland; died in Israel in 1978; married Icchak Cukierman also seen as Yitzhak Zuckerman (1915–1981).

Active before World War II in the Jewish Socialist youth movement Dror-Hechaluts (Freedom-the Pioneer); along with husband, was one of the key leaders of both uprisings in the Warsaw Ghetto (January and April 1943); participated in the Warsaw Polish uprising during (summer 1944); immigrated to Palestine/Israel (1946); was a member of Kibbutz Lohamei ha-Getta'ot.

The lives of Jewish fighters like Zivia Lubetkin stand in defiance to the long-standing question about the Holocaust that asks, "Why did the Jews not resist?" Lubetkin, a key figure in the Warsaw Ghetto Uprising who organized armed retaliation by Jews against Nazis during one of history's most heroic struggles, left behind proof of resistance that answers simply, some did.

Born in eastern Poland in 1914, the first year of World War I, she grew up in a world marked by economic crisis, fear of war, and a pervasive spirit of anti-Semitism. Even after Poland achieved its independence from foreign rule in 1918, a majority of the new republic's Jewish population continued to live their lives in a traditional context grounded in conservative religious orthodoxy and long-tested social patterns. Long before Poland became the first nation to be conquered by Hitler's armed forces, Poland's Jews—many of whom spoke Yiddish rather than Polish and worked as poor artisans and peddlers—were regarded by the country's Roman Catholic majority as an alien element that could never be assimilated or modernized. Starting in the 1920s, a growing number of young Jewish women and men were attracted to Zionist youth movements emphasizing a secular world view which promoted training in artisan skills and agriculture to draw Jewish energies away from an undue emphasis on trade and commerce. The intent of these movements was to create a new generation of self-reliant Jewish leaders whose ultimate goal was emigration (*aliyah*) to the nascent Jewish state of Eretz Israel, at that time still the British Mandated Territory of Palestine.

Zivia Lubetkin

Zivia Lubetkin was one of the most talented and enthusiastic Zionist youth leaders in prewar Poland. Politically committed from an early age, by the late 1930s she had become a leading personality in the Dror-Hechaluts (Freedom-The Pioneer) movement, a group of young Socialist women and men with branches throughout Poland. Known for their dynamic political strategies, Dror-Hechaluts members were proud of the ties they maintained with other Jewish youth organizations, particularly to Po'alei Zion (Zionist Socialist Workers) and to Hakibbutz Hameuchad (the

United Kibbutz) in Palestine. As a Dror leader, Lubetkin was elected to represent that organization on the National Jewish Council of Poland. In 1939, on the eve of World War II, she was obviously a person to watch in the emerging leadership of the Polish Labor Zionist movement. Respected by her comrades in Jewish labor youth circles for the maturity of her judgment, she had married another up-and-coming young leader, Yitzhak Zuckerman. In the fateful summer of 1939, Lubetkin attended the World Zionist Congress in Basel, Switzerland. She returned home to find Poland invaded by Nazi Germany and conquered within a few weeks.

The inhumanity of the Nazi ideology became clear to all Poles within days of the start of the German occupation. Because they were Slavs and thus defined as "sub-humans" within the Nazis' pseudoscientific hierarchy of superior and inferior races, the Polish population found itself subjected to harsh measures designed to deprive them of their political, intellectual, and religious rights. Priests and intellectuals in particular were targeted for "special treatment," and thousands were executed or sent to concentration camps where many more would die over the next years. Polish Jews were deemed even more deserving of Nazi brutality. With a Jewish population of more than 375,000, about 30% of the total population, Warsaw had the largest number of Jews in any European city. In the entire world, only New York City was home to more Jews. The Nazi occupiers created a Jewish Council (Judenrat) to allow Warsaw's Jews a form of "self-government," but this was in most ways little more than a cruel deception, because from the outset the Judenrat struggled to serve two masters: the all-powerful Nazis, who regarded the body as an instrument for carrying out their commands, and the Jewish community of Warsaw whose ever-increasing desperation could never be adequately addressed. Conscripted as virtual slave laborers, Warsaw's Jews were forced to work long hours under harsh conditions for very low pay.

On November 16, 1940, with the official sealing off of the Warsaw Ghetto from the rest of the city, an even harsher phase of Nazi rule began. Living conditions in the already terribly overcrowded ghetto worsened dramatically as a policy of "clean violence"—death by starvation, disease, and exhaustion—went into effect. This policy caused immense suffering and loss of life for the Jews of the Warsaw Ghetto, which became an involuntary home to about 400,000 people. Although a large number of Jews under Nazi rule held the illusory belief that somehow they would be able to survive by offering no resistance and by making themselves economically useful to the German war effort, the Nazi ideology looked upon all Jews, even the young and healthy, as eternal and implacable racial enemies that had to be annihilated if Adolf Hitler's dream of an Aryan racial state was to be actualized. For many of Poland's Jews, intellectual acceptance of such a horrible reality was at first difficult to come to grips with, and their basic strategy, largely fueled by denial, was one of emphasizing the ideal of *Uberlebn*, of surviving the German occupation through total compliance with the conquerors' demands.

During 1941, at least 43,000 people in the Warsaw Ghetto, more than 10% of the total ghetto population, died. Even under these conditions, the majority of the ghetto's inhabitants continued to believe that they would be able to survive Nazi rule by not needlessly antagonizing the Germans. They concentrated instead on keeping life and limb intact by relying on trade and smuggling food and other items into the ghetto.

For a number of months during 1939 and 1940, Zivia Lubetkin had lived in her home region, at that time under Soviet rule as a result of the partition of Poland agreed upon in the Nazi-Soviet Pact of August 1939. In 1940, fully aware of the dangers, she made her way back to Warsaw to take part in the Zionist underground movement in the ghetto. Once there, she and her husband emerged as leaders in the small but growing Jewish resistance.

Designated by the leaders of the Nazi state as the Final Solution of the Jewish Question (Endlösung der Judenfrage), organized mass murder began in late June 1941, with Germany's invasion of the Soviet Union. Mobile killing units (Einsatzgruppen) carried out mass shootings of Jews, Gypsies (Roma), and others deemed undesirable, resulting in the deaths of many hundreds of thousands of men, women, and children. Seeking greater efficiency in killing, in December 1941 the Nazis began using mobile gas vans. This was also considered too slow and troublesome, so, starting in March 1942, the Nazis began operating stationary gas chambers at killing centers created on formerly Polish territory. To these death camps, located at Auschwitz-Birkenau, Belzec, Chelmno, Majdanek, Sobibór, and Treblinka, the victims were brought by rail and then killed in gas chambers using either carbon monoxide gas or the insecticide Zyklon B, which could take the lives of 2,000 people in less than 30 minutes. At the Wannsee Conference, held in the Berlin suburb of Wannsee on January 20, 1942, representatives of the top bureaucracies in the Nazi state agreed on the details of executing the genocidal Final Solution of the Jewish Question.

In early 1942, while the majority of Jews in the Warsaw Ghetto continued to live from day to day in the hope of surviving the horror of Nazi rule, it became clear to Zionist activists like Lubetkin and Zuckerman that the moment of mass murder had arrived. A signal of the impending disaster for Warsaw was the evacuation of the Jews of the Polish city of Lublin, which began in March 1942. Within two months, 30,000 Lublin Jews were sent to their deaths at Belzec. The underground press in Warsaw began warning readers that it was only a matter of time before they too would be annihilated. Although the Jewish resistance circles in the ghetto had access to few weapons and often lacked support from a population still largely in a state of denial, by April 1942 Lubetkin and other activists had agreed to the organization of a fighting unit. Created as a result of negotiations between Lubetkin's Dror organization, the Left Po'alei Zion, Hashomer Hatzair (the Young Guard), and the Communists, the unit was called the "Anti-Fascist Bloc," and it was hoped that this would become the nucleus of a full-fledged Jewish fighting force.

> *We* felt that the end had come for all our people and that we were the last to remain, the smoking and dying embers. . . . The heart wondered and asked, wondered and asked—but there was no answer.
>
> —Zivia Lubetkin

During the next few months, while the Anti-Fascist Bloc tried to acquire more weapons and debated their future strategy, the full extent of the horrors facing Jewish Warsaw became only too clear. In the summer of 1942, around 300,000 Jews were rounded up in the ghetto and marched to a central transit point (Umschlagplatz), from where about 265,000 of them were then transported 60 miles in cattle cars to the Treblinka extermination center. Sadly, much of the work of rounding up the ghetto population was carried out by its own Jewish police force, who were supervised and assisted by a 200-man force of German police and a unit of Latvian collaborators. Biding their time as the ghetto was rapidly being decimated, the members of the Anti-Fascist Bloc organized themselves into groups of five comprised mostly of members of the various youth movements, including Lubetkin's own Dror-Hechaluts organization.

On July 28, 1942, with the deportations from the Warsaw Ghetto in full swing, the youth movements, including the Dror-Hechaluts and Hashomer Hatzair, as well as the more religiously oriented Akiva, joined together to form a united military organization to offer armed resistance to the Nazi enemy. The result was the Zydowska Organizacja Bojowa (Jewish Fighting Organization or ZOB), and the group's first high command consisted of Shmuel Braslav, Josef Kaplan, Zivia Lubetkin, Mordechai Tenenbaum (Tamaroff), and Yitzhak Zuckerman. Soon after its birth, the organization called on the threatened population to resist deportation by standing up against both the Jewish police and their German overlords. Still hoping to survive by not defying the Nazis, the population ignored these appeals. Although unable to mount a significant campaign of resistance, ZOB gave a dramatic signal of its existence in August 1942, when one of its members shot and gravely wounded the hated ghetto police commandant, Joseph Szerynski. This victory, however, was soon followed by the loss of two members of the ZOB leadership executive, Shmuel Braslav and Josef Kaplan, who were captured and killed in early September. On the same day, September 3, 1942, a further catastrophe befell the struggling band of resisters when the entire ZOB arsenal—a pitiful collection consisting of no more than five pistols and eight hand grenades—fell into German hands.

Although the deportations from the Warsaw Ghetto would cease on September 12, the next weeks and months became a period of great psychological stress for all survivors of the ZOB leadership, including Lubetkin. Depressed and desperate at their inability to halt the deportations, they had difficulty resisting the impulse to fight the enemy with their bare hands, despite their knowledge of the utterly suicidal nature of such actions. In time, calmer heads prevailed, and the ZOB began a new stage of retrenchment and growth.

As winter approached, only 55,000 Jews remained in the Warsaw Ghetto. Of these, 35,000 were considered valuable to the German war effort since they worked in factories producing weapons, clothing, and other items of strategic value to the Reich. The other 20,000 were individuals who had been able to elude the Germans and their allies and had found places in which to hide. The new situation in the ghetto presented Lubetkin and her ZOB comrades with a very different psychological landscape from that of only a few months before. Now it was clear to virtually every Jew that the Nazis were in fact determined to kill all Jews in their domain, and that it

was likely only a matter of time before even those Jews who held jobs that appeared to be important to the war effort (*kriegswichtig*) would be deported to a death camp. Realizing that they were living on borrowed time, many of the ghetto's surviving population now held the ZOB in high regard, often voicing regret that they had not heeded its warnings during the summer, when the mass deportations were taking place.

In later years, Lubetkin would emphasize the importance of the educational and organizational activities that took place during the months before military resistance began in the ghetto, a period when she and her comrades worked tirelessly to halt the process of moral and spiritual disintegration which the German occupiers hoped would undermine the Jewish will to survive as a people long before the actual horrors of physical annihilation got underway. Thus she strove to consciously prevent the onset of the "spiritual Treblinka" that preceded the actual death camps.

On January 9, 1943, SS chief Heinrich Himmler visited the Warsaw Ghetto, ordering the deportation of an additional 8,000 Jews. Unlike the events of the previous summer, when the ghetto's inhabitants had reported for "resettlement," on January 18 few showed up. Although still possessing only a handful of weapons, the ZOB organization sprang to life, initiating attacks on the Germans and their allies in the streets, near the Umschlagplatz, and in various buildings. Many of the young Jewish fighters were killed in open battles with the enemy, invariably being outgunned. Use of partisan tactics, on the other hand, proved to be much more effective, and the Germans now refrained from entering dark, narrow hallways and cellars. Jewish women and men of the resistance learned to strike quickly, then successfully withdraw to hiding places by moving across the ghetto's rooftops. Within a few days, the frustrated Germans ended their January *Aktion*. Risking her life on numerous occasions, Lubetkin participated in the armed resistance of January 1943 and amazingly never received a scratch. She and her husband took on a legendary status, Lubetkin being known by her underground name of "Celina," and Zuckerman as "Antek."

When the Nazis began another sweep of the ghetto on April 19, 1943, they believed themselves to be well prepared to achieve a rapid and low-cost victory. But this would not prove to be a Blitzkrieg operation. The ZOB leadership had used the time between German assaults to prepare for a revolt that would serve to preempt a major blow by the enemy. Not only had weapons been procured, but the often shaky political coalition on which the ZOB was built had been strengthened considerably. Even so, one wing of the ghetto resistance movement, the Zydowski Zwiazek Wojskowy (Jewish Military Union or ZZW), comprised of militant Zionists of the Betar and Revisionist movements, always had monopolistic tendencies and proved difficult to bring into line as members of a united coalition. Lubetkin's diplomatic skills were crucial in the months leading up to the Warsaw Ghetto Uprising. As a member of the political arm of the ZOB, the Zydowski Komitet Narodowy, as well as of its Coordinating Committee, she was usually able to bridge the often considerable differences between the different groups comprising the overall organization, which by 1943 included the venerable Polish-Jewish labor organization, the Bund.

The signal for full-scale Jewish resistance in the Warsaw Ghetto was the total sealing off of the area early in the morning of April 19. Wishing to deliver the ruined ghetto and its captive population to Adolf Hitler on his 54th birthday (April 20), the German force of 2,000 men supported by tanks and flame-throwers was met by a disciplined Jewish army who had been able to turn many of the ghetto's cellars into fortresses. With its small arsenal of rifles, handguns, a few machine guns, and homemade Molotov cocktails, the ZOB used their weaponry effectively and routed German forces in less than two hours. Lubetkin later recalled:

> When the Germans came up to our posts and marched by and we threw those hand grenades and bombs and saw German blood pouring over the streets of Warsaw . . . there was much rejoicing. The tomorrow did not worry us. The rejoicing amongst the Jewish fighters was great and, see the wonder and the miracle, those German heroes retreated, afraid and terrorized from Jewish bombs and hand grenades, home-made.

Over the next few days, after fierce clashes including hand-to-hand combat, the Germans tightened their siege of the ghetto, cutting off its supply of water, electricity, and gas. They brought in police dogs to track down Jewish fighters in the buildings and cellars in which they hid. Within a few days, both sides changed tactics, going from using large groups to relying on small bands of soldiers. The Jewish resistance adapted quickly to the new situation, breaking up its larger units into smaller, more mobile squads. The future resistance leader Hermann Wygoda was located in an apartment directly across the street from the ghetto and later provided the following account:

> The rattling of different types of weapons coming from the ghetto was clearly audible as the Nazis attempted its complete destruction. That last handful of Jews knew their situation was hopeless, but there was no alternative left for them. They refused to submit voluntarily to the process of elimination that was requested and expected of them. In less than one year, the Nazis had managed to march to the gas chambers several million meek people and destroy them without as much as a protest. Those people had gone to their destruction terrorized and spiritless. Then, a few thousand desperadoes provided a rude awakening for the Nazis.

Throughout this time, Lubetkin and her husband were at the nerve center of the uprising, working day and night to maintain effective command and control of a rapidly changing situation.

A new German strategy was decreed by the frustrated German commander of the annihilation operation, General Jürgen Stroop, who ordered that the entire ghetto be systematically burned down. At its four corners, the ghetto was set on fire, first by German airplanes and then on the ground. Even under these nightmarish conditions, Warsaw's Jews died without contemplating surrender. Lubetkin wrote later that for the Germans this "was not the triumph they had planned."

> With their last vital energy the Jews found shelter behind every wall, among ruins that could no longer burn. The inhabitants of entire bunkers—men, women, and children—crawled out from their underground hiding places and wandered about, loaded with their last bits of food, blankets, pots. Babies were carried in their mothers' arms, older children trailed after their parents, in their eyes an abyss of suffering and a plea for help. . . . Many who could find no other shelter went down into the sewers to wait through the next day. For the time being, deep underground in bunkers and sewers, the pulse of Jewish life still beat on.

In the desperate battle, many women as well as men fought to defend Jewish honor. Even Nazi commander Stroop provided history with documentation on this theme when he noted in his personal report to Adolf Hitler:

> During the armed resistance, females belonging to fighting groups were armed just like the men. Some of them were members of the He-halutz movement. Not infrequently, these females fired pistols from both hands. Repeatedly, they concealed pistols or hand grenades (oval Polish hand grenades) in their underpants to use at the last minute

against the men of the Waffen-SS, Police, or Wehrmacht.

From the very start of their rebellion in the Warsaw Ghetto, Lubetkin and her comrades in arms knew that they could never beat the Germans. They sought a moral, not a military, triumph: "To live with honor and to die with honor." During the final days of the uprising, Lubetkin was in the ZOB command bunker located at 18 Mila Street, in an underground dugout she described as being "spacious and astonishingly well-equipped," with electric lights, a well, and such luxuries as a reading room and a game room. Until the start of the uprising, this luxury facility (by ghetto standards) had been part of the Warsaw Ghetto's underworld, the property of a gang of thieves and murderers led by a sinister Jewish criminal named Shmuel Asher. Despite his unsavory past, Asher now did not hesitate in sharing his supplies with the ghetto fighters and was in fact noted as "especially tender with the children." The criminals assisted the fighters, guiding them at night to spy out German positions. The densely crowded bunker could accommodate 120 ghetto fighters including the ZOB command. As days went by, more and more hiding places were discovered by the Germans. Sometimes, starving and demoralized Jews betrayed hiding places to the Nazis in return for a promise of immunity. The corpses of Lubetkin's comrades lay strewn everywhere, and she "dreaded walking at night for fear of stepping on them. Flocks of crows descended on the decaying bodies in the streets."

By the end of the first week in May, it became clear that the uprising in the Warsaw Ghetto had entered its last stage. Leaving the command post at 18 Mila Street, Lubetkin and a small group of colleagues crawled out of the bunker and proceeded along hidden pathways, meeting occasional survivors of the armed struggle. She found temporary refuge in another bunker, but soon the Germans pumped gas into it and some of the 120 fighters committed suicide so as not to surrender. Finding a hidden exit at the last minute before being asphyxiated, a small group including Lubetkin were able to escape. Of 120, only 21 had survived. Soon their flight from the Germans resumed, this time through the cold, filthy waters of the sewers. At first, Lubetkin felt that "nothing—not even freedom—was worth this." For 20 hours, she and her group half-walked, half-crawled through the sewers, "that terrible cavern," feeling their bodies weaken more and more from thirst and hunger. When members of the group fell down, begging to be left lying on the spot, their companions did not abandon them. Eventually, they reached Frosta Street on the Aryan side of the ghetto but had to remain in the sewer for many additional hours. Organized by three Jewish associates and a Polish Gentile who worked together in the resistance, a truck came to pick up the dirty, rag-wrapped ghetto survivors. During the last perilous stage of the escape, German sentries at the bridge which led out of Warsaw were distracted, and Lubetkin and her group were safely delivered in the truck to the Mlochini forest seven kilometers from Warsaw.

Lubetkin later wrote of their arrival in the forest:

> [We were] so dehumanized in our rags and filth, our dirty faces still unwashed, that we were hardly recognizable. They at once brought us warm milk, the first we had had in many days. Everything was strange. About us was the green forest and a beautiful spring day. It had been a long time since we had known a forest, spring, and the sun. All that had been buried and restrained in our frozen hearts for years now stirred. I burst into tears.

One of the group then died suddenly, his lungs destroyed by the gas attack in the ghetto.

> For hours we sat silent, till one comrade arose and began to dig a grave. That night we all sat about a campfire . . . and in our hearts we felt that we were the last survivors of a people that had been exterminated.

Physically restored and determined to continue the struggle, Lubetkin, her husband, and a small remnant of Warsaw Ghetto survivors participated in a Jewish unit that fought in the tragic Warsaw Polish uprising of August–September 1944. When bloody defeat ended in surrender to the Germans in early October, Lubetkin, Zuckerman, and several other Jewish survivors once again were at great risk of being captured. As it had in 1943, something akin to the miraculous occurred. A Polish Gentile physician, Dr. Stanislaw Switala, saved the lives of Lubetkin, her husband and several other Jews in November 1944, by taking them to the hospital he directed and hiding them from the Nazis.

In mid-January 1945, Warsaw was liberated by the Soviet Army and Lubetkin, Zuckerman and a handful of Jews could once more breathe freely. But for Poland's Jews, the end of fascism did not bring a new beginning in Poland but rather a realization that Jewish life in that country, with its glorious past, had no future. Nine out of ten of Poland's Jews had perished during the Nazi occupation. Anti-Semitic prejudices and fears remained deeply embedded among many in the Polish population, resulting in the infamous Kielce pogrom of 1946.

Determined to start a new life in Palestine, Lubetkin and her husband now concentrated on assisting Holocaust survivors in restoring their shattered lives. Much of their time at first went into restoration of the Hechaluts movement, and both quickly emerged as leaders of She'erit ha-Peleltah ("the saving remnant"), one of the most effective survivor-relief organizations. The couple played a key role in organizing Beriha, the mass exodus of Jews from Poland in 1946 and 1947. In 1946, Lubetkin settled in Palestine, which in May 1948 emerged as the State of Israel. Here she and her husband became founding members of Kibbutz Lohamei ha-Getta'ot, the Ghetto Fighters' Kibbutz. Unwilling to forget the past, and convinced that its lessons could and should never be forgotten, they founded Bet Lohamei ha-Getta'ot, the memorial center located at the same kibbutz. A committed Socialist as well as Zionist, over the next decades Lubetkin became a revered icon of the dwindling band of veteran ghetto fighters. She also emerged as a major speaker for the kibbutz movement, becoming one of the best-known representatives of its national organization, Hakibbutz Hameuchad. In the early 1960s, both Lubetkin and Zuckerman appeared in a Jerusalem courtroom as witnesses in the trial of Adolf Eichmann. Zivia Lubetkin died in 1978, and Yitzhak Zuckerman died three years later in 1981.

On April 23, 1943, in the early days of the Warsaw Ghetto Uprising, ZOB commander Mordecai Anielewicz wrote what has since become a much-quoted letter to Lubetkin's husband:

> What we have experienced cannot be described in words. We are aware of one thing only: what has happened has exceeded our dreams. The Germans ran twice from the ghetto. . . . I have the feeling that great things are happening, that what we have dared is of great importance. . . . Perhaps we shall meet again. But what really matters is that the dream of my life has become true. Jewish self-defense in the Warsaw ghetto has become a fact. Jewish armed resistance and retaliation have become a reality. I have been witness to the magnificent heroic struggle of the Jewish fighters.

SOURCES:

Dror, Zvika. *The Dream, the Revolt, and the Vow: The Biography of Zivia Lubetkin-Zuckerman (1914–1978)*. Translated by Bezalel Ianai. Israel: International Department, Diaspora Section, General Federation of Labor/ Lochamei Hagettaot Institute for "Remembrance of the Holocaust and Revolt," 1983.

Gutman, Israel. *Resistance: The Warsaw Ghetto Uprising*. Boston, MA: Houghton Mifflin, 1994.

The Jewish Quarter of Warsaw Is No More! The Stroop Report. Translated and annotated by Sybil Milton. NY: Pantheon Books, 1979.

Kurzman, Dan. *The Bravest Battle: The Twenty-Eight Days of the Warsaw Ghetto Uprising*. NY: Da Capo Press, 1993.

Lubetkin, Zivia. *Die letzten Tage des Warschauer Gettos*. Berlin-Potsdam: VVN-Verlag, 1949.

———. *In the Days of the Destruction and Revolt*. Translated by Ishai Tubbin. Tel Aviv: Beit Lohamei Haghettaot, Hakibuttz Hameuchad Publishing House/ Am Oved Publishing House, 1981.

Lubetkin, Ziviah. "The Last Days of the Warsaw Ghetto," in *Commentary*. Vol. 3, no. 5. May 1947, pp. 401–411.

Meed, Vladka Peltel. *On Both Sides of the Wall: Memoirs from the Warsaw Ghetto*. Israel: Beit Lohamei Haghettaot Ghetto Fighters' House and Hakibbutz Hameuchad Publishing House, 1973.

Nadelhaft, Erica. "Resistance through Education: Polish Zionist Youth Movements in Warsaw, 1939–1941," in *Polin: Studies in Polish Jewry*. Vol. 9, 1996, pp. 212–231.

Porat, Dina. "Zionist Pioneering Movements in Poland and the Attitude to Erets Israel during the Holocaust," in *Polin: Studies in Polish Jewry*. Vol. 9, 1996, pp. 195–211.

Switala, Stanislaw. "Siedmioro z ulicy Promyka," in *Biuletyn Zydowskiego Instytutu Historycznego*. No. 65–66, 1968, pp. 207–211.

Syrkin, Marie. "Zivia Lubetkin: A Last Stand at the Warsaw Ghetto," in *Ms.* Vol. 2, no. 3. September 1973, pp. 98–102.

———. "Zivia: The Passing of a Heroine," in *Midstream*. Vol. 24, no. 8. October 1978, pp. 56–59.

Toueg, Rebecca. *Zivia Lubetkin: Heroine of the Warsaw Ghetto*. Tel Aviv: Women's International Zionist Organisation, Education Department, 1988.

Wygoda, Hermann. *In the Shadow of the Swastika*. Urbana, IL: University of Illinois Press, 1998.

Zuckerman, Yitzhak. *A Surplus of Memory: Chronicle of the Warsaw Ghetto Uprising*. Translated and edited by Barbara Harshaw. Berkeley, CA: University of California Press, 1993.

SUGGESTED READING:

Hersey, John. *The Wall* (fictionalized account of the Warsaw Ghetto Uprising). NY: Alfred A. Knopf, 1950.

Uris, Leon. *Mila 18*. (fictionalized account of the Warsaw Ghetto Uprising). NY: Doubleday, 1961.

John Haag,
Associate Professor of History,
University of Georgia, Athens, Georgia

Lubin, Germaine (1890–1979)

French soprano who was well known for her Wagnerian roles. Born in Paris, France, on February 1, 1890; died in Paris on October 27, 1979; studied with F. Litvinne and *Lilli Lehmann as well as at the Paris Conservatory, 1909–12; married Paul Géraldy (a famous French poet).

Debuted at the Opéra-Comique (1912); made debut at Paris Opéra (1914), appearing there until

1944; made debut at Covent Garden (1937); was the first French singer to appear at Bayreuth (1938).

Born in Paris in 1890, Germaine Lubin was one of France's greatest sopranos of the 20th century, along with *Emma Calvé and **Régine Crespin**. Lubin transcended the French repertoire to perform many operatic works, including Wagner. Her beautiful, rounded tone and immediately recognizable timbre were her trademarks. Lauritz Melchoir sang *Parsifal* with Lubin in Paris in 1937 and was responsible for several of her appearances in Wagner's operas in Berlin. Numerous illustrious seasons followed at Bayreuth, and Lubin soon became the favorite of many high-ranking Nazis, including Adolf Hitler. Despite her abilities in Wagnerian roles, Lubin actually performed in many other operas, never restricting herself to Germanic repertoire. Lubin's voice has been most often compared with Dame *Eva Turner's. Both had voices which needed distance for the listener to hear to best effect. Perhaps recordings of Lubin's voice fail to do her justice in this respect. Lubin was reviled in her country for continuing to perform during the German occupation in World War II. For five years after the war, she was allowed neither to perform nor to leave the country.

John Haag,
Athens, Georgia

Lucas, Eliza (1722–1793).
See Pinckney, Eliza Lucas.

Lucas, Margaret Bright (1818–1890)

English reformer. Born in 1818; died in 1890; daughter of Jacob Bright (a bookkeeper and cotton spinner) and Martha (Wood) Bright (a tradesman's daughter); sister of John Bright (1811–1889, a reformer); married Samuel Lucas (1811–1865).

Along with her brother John Bright and her husband Samuel Lucas, Margaret Bright Lucas fought to benefit the industrial middle class by participating in the Anti-Corn Law League, a pressure group that agitated for the abolition of import tariffs on foreign foodstuffs as the preliminary to complete free trade in all commodities. The League and its representatives stood for what Tory politician Benjamin Disraeli called "the Manchester School," an economic doctrine that advocated a totally free market with only the minimum of government regulation, a political system favorable to middle-class business interests, and a social system in which middle-class values predominated. While on a visit to America, Lucas took an interest in temperance reform and women's suffrage; she returned to preside over the British Women's Temperance Association.

Lucas, Victoria.
See Plath, Sylvia.

Lucca, duchess of.
See Maria Luisa of Etruria (1782–1824).

Lucca, Elisa (1777–1820).
See Bonaparte, Elisa.

Lucca, princess of (1777–1820).
See Bonaparte, Elisa.

Lucca, Pauline (1841–1908)

Austrian soprano. Born on April 25, 1841, in Vienna, Austria; died on February 28, 1908, in Vienna.

Known more for her two-octave range and her dramatic flair than for the quality of her singing, Austrian soprano Pauline Lucca trained

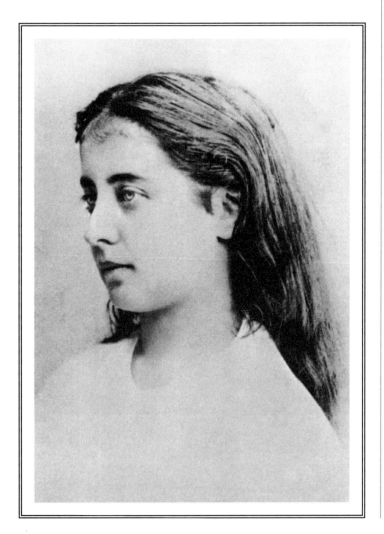

*P*auline
*L*ucca

in Vienna with Uffmann and Levy, and made her debut in Vienna in 1859, as the Second Boy in *Die Zauberflöte*. She appeared in Berlin, London, and Paris, and was in Russia between 1868 and 1869 and the United States between 1872 and 1874. Dubbed "the demon wild-cat," Lucca had a repertory that included the roles of Donna Anna, Zerlina, Valentine, Eva, Selika, Lenora (*Trovatore*) and Azucena, none of which were as celebrated as her Carmen. Off-stage, Lucca's purported relationship with Count Otto von Bismarck also created a stir. *****Cosima Wagner** wrote of their public familiarity: "Such things do no honour to the crown or to art."

Luce, Clare Boothe (1903–1987)

American editor, playwright, congresswoman, ambassador, and eminent convert to Catholicism. Born Clare Snyder Boothe in New York City on April 10, 1903; died on October 9, 1987; daughter of William F. Boothe (a theater violinist) and Anna Clara (Snyder) Boothe (a musical "chorus girl"); attended St. Mary's in Garden City, Long Island, New York, 1915–17; The Castle, Tarrytown, New York, 1917–19; Colby College, Fordham University, Litt.D., Creighton University, Georgetown University, and Temple University; married George Tuttle Brokaw (a garment-industry heir), on August 10, 1923 (divorced in Reno, 1929); married Henry R. Luce II (the Time magnate), on November 23, 1935 (died 1967); children: (first marriage) Ann Clare Brokaw (1924–1944).

Parents divorced and made first visit to Europe (1913); was associate editor of Vogue (1930); was associate editor of Vanity Fair (1931–32), and managing editor (1933–34); was a newspaper columnist (1934), and playwright (1935—); enjoyed success of The Women (1936); served as a war correspondent (1939–40); served as a member of 78th and 79th Congresses from 4th Connecticut district (1943–47); death of Ann Brokaw, her daughter, in a car accident (1944); served as U.S. ambassador to Italy (1953–57).

Selected writings: Stuffed Shirts (1933); Europe in the Spring (1940); Abide with Me (play, 1937); The Women (play, opened December 1936, ran for 657 performances); Kiss the Boys Goodbye (play, 1938); Margin for Error (play, 1939); Come to the Stable (movie based on a Luce story, 1949); Child of the Morning (play, 1951); Slam the Door Softly (1970).

Clare Boothe Luce was in many respects a pioneer among 20th-century American women, being one of the earliest supporters of a constitutional Equal Rights Amendment for women, first congresswoman from her home state, and first woman to represent the United States as ambassador in a major European capital. She has not been acclaimed by all, however, because she was a political conservative, single-mindedly ambitious, sexually profligate, a ruthless controversialist and infighter, and owed at least part of her success to the cultivation of rich and powerful men. Her legacy is ambiguous, but the life of this talented woman was unique in its combination of opportunities offered, accepted, and mastered.

Her father was a theater violinist and her mother a Broadway actress and ex-chorus girl who blended a lofty romanticism with a sharp-eyed ambition for her children. The couple was rarely together, and Clare's father played little part in her upbringing; her parents were officially divorced in 1913. In his place, her mother had a succession of men friends, including a Jewish tire-merchant, Joseph Jacobs, who took care of **Anna Boothe** and her two children, but whom she refused to marry. Anna tried to prepare Clare for social success by sending her to private schools in New York (though she never got a high school diploma), and scraped together the money to take her on a cultural tour of Europe when she was ten, and another when she was sixteen. Despite her patchy schooling, Clare was intellectually ambitious, read George Bernard Shaw, Oswald Spengler, and the Victorian novelists, and dreamed of becoming a writer, while penning reams of adolescent poetry.

Her mother's remarriage to a prosperous surgeon, Dr. Albert E. Austin, in 1919 alleviated the family's long era of financial worries, and Anna Boothe now turned to finding a good match for Clare. She worked at it assiduously, even trying to bag the heir to the British throne when he visited America. She made a valuable friend of *****Eleanor Robson Belmont**, one of the wealthy patrons of the women's suffrage movement, and, from the early 1920s right into the late 1970s, Clare was a supporter of the Equal Rights Amendment to the Constitution (finally withdrawing her support when ERA was linked to the pro-choice abortion position, which she opposed). With Belmont's encouragement Clare learned to fly, and on one occasion dropped women's suffrage leaflets over Syracuse, New York.

One promising romance, during their European travels, turned sour. A British Guards officer, Julian Simpson, courted her in London when she was just 17, and they declared their love for each other before she sailed home. When Simpson pursued her, however, he realized for the first time, on seeing the house she lived in, that she was not a rich heiress and turned away coldly from her declarations of love. Her mother's efforts succeeded in 1923 when Clare, aged 20, married a 43-year-old clothing industry heir and millionaire, George Brokaw. They lived in a mansion at Newport, Rhode Island, but Brokaw's status as a *nouveau-riche* made them unwelcome among the snobbish grandees who had made their own fortunes a generation or two earlier. Clare expressed later her resentment at social snubs during this period in a collection of short stories, *Stuffed Shirts* (1930), the title of which says it all. In his informal biography of her, Wilfrid Sheed writes:

> Clare's infuriating poise had obviously not been perfected yet, and certain insecurities peeped out, even while she toughed it out in her lonely salon. Perhaps this explains how someone as willful as Clare could have stood still for an arranged marriage with a dodo.

Brokaw showed a growing fondness for heavy drinking, which made him dangerously violent, and the marriage broke up in 1929 when she went to Reno to get a divorce. From the settlement, she received $26,000 per year for life and joint custody of their daughter Ann. She was now 26 and hardened by the experiences of this painful marriage.

[Henry Luce] did not put her on a pedestal: She built her own. She had made herself into an international celebrity, carved out her own careers in theater, magazines, and politics, and she raised herself up to be one of the most admired women in the world. Her life was a glittering Christmas tree, but in her own final summation, she admitted that she never fulfilled the dream of her life; she was never *really* a writer.

—Ralph G. Martin

Far from relaxing on what was then an ample income, Clare began to work, first for *Vogue* and then for *Vanity Fair*, beginning as a caption writer but climbing to the position of managing editor in 1933. There, among a long succession of celebrities and lovers, she met Bernard Baruch, the wealthy and influential advisor to a succession of presidents. Baruch fell in love with her (though they did not marry because, in his own way, he was devoted to his wife, **Annie Griffen Baruch**), introduced her to Franklin Roosevelt, and helped her to become established at the fringes of Democratic Party politics and to widen her already immense circle of acquaintances. Despite Clare's skills as an editor, a frivolous and costly magazine like *Vanity Fair* could not survive the long hard grind of the Great Depression, and it was merged back into its parent magazine *Vogue* in 1936 by owner Condé Nast. By that time, however, its editor had new and grander prospects.

In 1935, Clare Boothe had met Henry Luce, the editor of *Time* magazine and chief of a growing press empire. Son of American missionaries to China, he was already married to **Lila Hotz Luce** (1899–1999), was the father of two sons, and was possessed of an active Presbyterian conscience. Nevertheless, he proposed marriage to her, she accepted, and he divorced his first wife. Clare had had the idea for a new, mass-circulation illustrated magazine to take the place of *Vanity Fair*. When it began in 1936, *Life* bore many of the hallmarks of her idea. Henry Luce did not want his new wife editing one of his journals, however, though a subsequent court case proved that she was right to have claimed that the idea had been hers first. Her exclusion from the editorship of the successful new magazine annoyed her, and from that time on she always insulted or ignored the executives of Time, Inc., who had spoken against her appointment. Denied an editorship and unable for medical reasons to have more children, Clare Boothe Luce turned to writing a new play,

She had written several earlier plays and one, *Abide with Me*, had been performed, though without much acclaim—she even modified the *Time* review of it in a disillusioned mood and wrote that it was "stinking and lousy." But the debut of *The Women* was a roaring success and at once made her a literary "lion." Some reviewers thought it was so artful that its director, George Kaufman, must have written it—one of many occasions on which her own work was treated as though a "man under the bed" must really be responsible for it. Based on her experiences getting a divorce in Reno a few years before, the play featured only women on stage, many of them spiteful, but each with her own tale of marital woe, making for a hilarious sequence of coincidences and double entendres, and enriched with a bitingly satirical script. She followed this Broadway success with two more, *Kiss the Boys Goodbye* (1938) and the anti-Nazi drama *Margin for Error* (1939). By then, she was a fully established figure on Broadway and could probably have continued to get her work on stage, but the outbreak of the Second World War (along with her sense that Henry did not much care for her show-business friends) led her to take up another new career, this time as a war correspondent.

The European war began in September 1939—more than two years before Pearl Harbor—and during those years Clare Luce traveled extensively through the European and Far Eastern theaters of conflict. Because of her husband's eminence, she gained access to all the important politicians in Britain and France, and was accorded VIP treatment by most of the generals she met, so hers was far from the slow, slogging experience of an ordinary war journalist. The outcome of this work was a book, *Europe in the Spring,* which described the "Phoney War"—the period between late 1939 and mid-1940, when Britain and France calmly awaited German moves rather than pressing an attack into Western Germany while the Wehrmacht was engaged in Poland. Satirical in tone, *Europe in the Spring* proved prophetic when the German army turned on France and the Low Countries with annihilating power later that year. The book also demonstrated that she could become an accomplished political journalist if she stayed with it, though *Dorothy Parker headlined her review "All Clare on the Western Front."

Back in America in the summer of 1940, Luce found that her husband was backing Wen-

Clare Boothe Luce

dell Willkie as Republican presidential candidate for the forthcoming election. Although her earlier political dabbling had been with the Democrats, she now swung behind the Willkie candidacy too, and made a series of speeches on his behalf, showing yet another talent never previously exploited. Willkie lost to Roosevelt who won an unprecedented third term with the slogan "You don't change horses in mid-stream" (meaning don't give up an experienced president for an inexperienced one at the height of a world war). During the campaign, Clare Boothe Luce had developed a taste for the cut and thrust of electioneering. Two years later, she acted on this new obsession and ran successfully for Congress in the Connecticut district her stepfather, Dr. Austin, had held from 1938 to 1940. She won re-election in 1944, despite being the first woman to represent any Connecticut district in Congress.

In 1944, her reputation for hard-hitting speeches and her personal magnetism also led the Republican Party to offer her the keynote speech at the convention which nominated Thomas Dewey as their presidential candidate. In this speech, she broke a taboo by declaring (quite accurately, but in a way which enraged Democrats) that Franklin Roosevelt was so sick his death was imminent. She also said that Roosevelt was responsible for the death of "GI Jim," the soldier who did not return from the war to the hero's welcome reserved for "GI Joe." Roosevelt, she added, had "lied us into the war" (a line she later regretted, admitting that "lying was clearly the only way to get us there"). Her Democratic Party opponent in the Congressional election of 1944 was another attractive woman, **Margaret Connors**, who almost managed an upset; President Roosevelt had encouraged Connors to "continue the fight until the Congress is rid of that untamed shrew." Luce's hair-breadth victory was rumored to have been achieved by covert bribery on the part of her friend Bernard Baruch.

Her main political interest in 1942 and 1944, as it had been in 1940, was winning the war; her domestic policy proposals were uncontroversial, if anything quite liberal, and she was careful to mollify the trade unionists in her district. In an augury of things to come, she also avoided praising the Soviet Union, at the time America's ally—her constituency was full of anti-Communist Catholics, with whose views she was in ready sympathy. In a succession of speeches as the war ended, she urged presidents Roosevelt and Truman not to let the nations of Eastern Europe fall uncontested into the Soviet sphere of influence.

Luce as Congresswoman was in a bind. Already famous as a glamorous woman, she was treated by much of the media more as a fashion statement than as a politician, but if she tried to work hard on genuine policy questions, she was suspected of plotting on behalf of Henry Luce's sinister ambitions. There were many critics whom she was destined not to please whatever she did. On the other hand, her prior fame and notoriety meant that she never had to endure the years of obscurity suffered by most incoming congressional representatives. Her interest in a cause or issue would win for it instant publicity, and knowledge of this fact made her influential in the House from the start. Her political style was highly combative; she was willing to get into ugly political feuds and to make long-lasting enemies. The events of 1944 were typical. She hacked away mercilessly against Roosevelt in preelection speeches, making some analysts think she was doing more harm than good to the Republican cause. But she held her own seat, and then set off on a tour of the European theater of war, winning press plaudits at every stop, receiving royal treatment from generals Patton, Eisenhower, and Mark Clark, and keeping her fellow congressional delegation members completely in the shade.

Despite her successes in Congress, Clare Boothe Luce left Washington in 1946 and did not run for re-election. She had soured on politicians and the "fishbowl" life of a congresswoman, and was trying to come to terms with new difficulties in her life. Her daughter Ann Brokaw, aged only 19, had been killed in a car accident. In addition, Clare Luce realized that her magnetic hold over her husband was beginning to fade, and that he was having a love affair with ***Jean Dalrymple**, a theatrical agent, and flings with several other women. Luce herself was widely reported to be, at various times, the lover of Bernard Baruch, Joseph Kennedy (the future president's father), Buckminster Fuller, Irwin Shaw, George Kaufman, and others, so that a vigorous gossip mill in New York and Washington found plenty of material to keep the allegations flying. When Henry Luce asked her for a divorce so that he could marry Dalrymple, she would agree to it only if he gave her, as part of the settlement, 51% of *Time,* and to this surrender of his business he could not consent. Uneasily, they remained together.

Between 1946 and 1952, Clare Luce was out of the limelight for a time, during which she converted to Roman Catholicism, despite having shown no interest in religion during the earlier part of her life. Monsignor Fulton Sheen, the Catholic radio and television celebrity, was given the credit for bringing her into the Catholic Church; Sheen and New York's Cardinal Spellman both seemed willing to accept this convert's divorce and remarriage as a *fait accompli,* despite the strict Church teaching against divorce. In 1952, she tried to resume her political career by running for a U.S. Senate seat in Connecticut, but did not even get as far as the Republican nomination. As a consolation prize, President Eisenhower, that election year's big winner, appointed her American ambassador to Italy, making her the first woman to hold such a senior diplomatic post. Much of the Italian press considered the appointment a slight to their country's dignity, an indication that America now saw Italy as a third-rate power, though Luce proved to be a skillful diplomat and quieted their indignation. Luce was in Italy from 1953 to 1957 and quite actively supported Alcide de Gasperi's Christian Democratic Party against the strong Italian Communists, while trying to aid Italy in its claim on the port city of Trieste against Marshal Tito's Yugoslavia. Henry Luce spent half of each year with her in Rome (he had a makeshift office there so that he could carry on running the *Time* empire) and half back in New York. They apparently still enjoyed being a powerful public couple.

Her service in Italy finally proved satisfactory to the population and to the American government, but it ended in an odd way. Her hair began falling out, and she lost some teeth. An investigation by CIA men showed that poisonous lead and arsenic dust from the paint on her sitting room's ceiling was falling on her when she slept on the couch, causing a disorienting effect. She parried malicious reports of being drunk in public with an explanation that she was suffering a mild form of poisoning. But as Sheed notes, "Since she and Harry had long since been dubbed 'Arsenic and old Luce' the poison on the ceiling provided, so to speak, the icing on the cake." Back in America before the 1956 election, it seemed possible for a time that she might displace Richard Nixon and become Eisenhower's running mate for his second bid at the presidency, but the "Dump Nixon" mood soon passed, and Luce carried on for a few more months in Rome.

Eisenhower was sufficiently impressed by her work in Italy that he nominated her as his envoy first to the funeral of Pope Pius XII and then to the coronation of Pope John XXIII in 1958. Next, he offered her the post of ambassador to Brazil. This time, however, her reputation as a Republican firebrand led her into trouble during her Senate confirmation hearing. Senator Wayne Morse of Oregon, an enemy of

Henry Luce for *Time*'s rough handling of his own career, led the charge, and tried to veto her appointment by announcing that in the 1920s she had undergone psychiatric treatment (following her divorce). The allegation was true, but the combative Luce answered that Morse had been kicked in the head by a horse, on the right side, and that he had been "thinking left" ever since. She won the Senate confirmation 79–11 but the furor over this acid remark aroused Brazilian as well as American tempers and finally she decided to withdraw from the position altogether.

After that, she held no more public appointments. In the 1960s, she began to write frequently for *National Review,* the conservative magazine which William F. Buckley, Jr., had founded in 1955. She was an early and ardent defender of the American cause in Vietnam, treating the war in part as a defense of Catholic South Vietnam against "Godless Communism." With Henry Luce, she now moved to Phoenix, Arizona, where the two of them experimented with LSD in the days before it became a notorious and illegal "hippie" drug. Henry Luce died in 1967, having resisted the temptation, a few years before, to leave Clare and marry his girlfriend **Jean Campbell**, who was the granddaughter of the British press baron Lord Beaverbrook. Though she was upset about his affair, Clare quipped: "If Harry marries Jean and I marry Lord Beaverbrook, then I'll be Harry's grandmother."

In the 1970s, Luce became an ardent champion of the anti-abortion movement, and was dismayed by the Supreme Court's liberalization of the abortion laws in *Roe* v. *Wade* (1973). She became a regular contributor to the *Human Life Review,* a journal of the pro-life movement, and appeared frequently on Buckley's television show "Firing Line" where he treated her with amiable deference as the Grand Old Woman of American conservatism. She now spent long periods of time in Hawaii, but died back in New York in 1987 at the age of 84. Her life had witnessed a transformation of America's role in the world, and of the role of women in American public life. Her rare blend of beauty, charm, social grace, ambition, literary talent, and political acumen had made her one of the most visible women of the century, but certainly not one who could ever win universal esteem.

SOURCES:

Baughman, James L. *Henry R. Luce.* Boston: Twayne, 1987.

Hatch, Alden. *Ambassador Extraordinary: Clare Boothe Luce.* NY: Holt, Reinhart, and Winston, 1956.

Martin, Ralph G. *Henry and Clare: An Intimate Portrait of the Luces.* NY: Putnam, 1991.

Shadegg, Stephen. *Clare Boothe Luce: A Biography*. NY: Simon and Schuster, 1970.

Sheed, Wilfrid. *Clare Boothe Luce*. NY: E.P. Dutton, 1982.

SUGGESTED READING:

Morris, Sylvia Jukes. *Rage for Fame: The Ascent of Clare Boothe Luce*. NY: Random House, 1997.

Patrick Allitt,
Professor of History, Emory University, Atlanta, Georgia

Lu Chen (b. 1976).

See Chen Lu.

Lucia.

Variant of Lucy.

Lucia (r. 1288–1289)

Countess of Tripoli. Name variations: Lucy of Antioch; princess of Antioch. Ruled from 1288 to 1289; daughter of Bohemund VI, prince of Antioch and count of Tripoli (r. 1252–1275), and Sibylla of Armenia; younger sister of Bohemund VII (d. 1287), count of Tripoli (r. 1275–1287); married Narjot of Toucy (a grand admiral).

The daughter of Bohemund VI and *Sibylla of Armenia, Lucia married Narjot of Toucy, the former grand admiral under Sicily's king Charles of Anjou, and went to live in Apula. When her brother Bohemund VII died childless in 1287, Lucia was named heir, but the succession was bitterly opposed by her mother. In the interim, a Commune was established as the sovereign authority, but with maneuvering, Lucia won over the nobles of Tripoli as well as the Commune and came into power. Meanwhile her rivals had enlisted the sultan Qalawun from Cairo to intervene, and in 1289, he launched an assault on Tripoli. Lucia was deposed and escaped to Cyprus, while her subjects were either massacred or captured as slaves.

Lucia (1908—)

*Duchess of Ancona. Name variations: Lucia de Bourbon. Born on July 9, 1908; daughter of Ferdinand, duke of Calabria, and *Maria of Bavaria (b. 1872); married Eugene of Savoy, duke of Ancona, in 1938.*

Lucia, Saint (d. 303).

See Lucy.

Lucia of Narni (1476–1544)

Dominican nun and political adviser to Ercole I of Este, duke of Ferrara. Name variations: Lucia Broc-

cadelli; Lucia from Narni. Born Lucia Broccadelli on December 13, 1476, in Narni, a town in South Umbria; daughter of Bartolomeo Broccadelli and Gentilina (Cassio) Broccadelli; married Pietro di Alessio, count of Milan.

Following her husband's death, entered the Third Order of Penance of St. Dominic, and was received into a nunnery in Viterbo; received stigmata and was considered deserving of the name of saint (1501); served as political and spiritual advisor of Duke Ercole I of Este in Ferrara; following his death, fell into disgrace and spent her last years in the cloister, devoting herself to contemplation.

Pursuing a religious life during the final years of the 15th century, as the winds of the Reformation were beginning to stir, Lucia of Narni was caught in the religious complexity of her times and paid dearly for her radical choices.

Born in 1476, Lucia Broccadelli was the daughter of Bartolomeo and **Gentilina Cassio Broccadelli** of Narni, an ancient village in the Umbria of the Tiber River. She received an education typical of her family's status and at the appropriate age was given in marriage to Pietro Alessio, the count of Milan. Bound by their deep religious convictions, the couple lived a chaste life until Pietro's death. In 1494, the young widow decided to take the veil of St. Dominic's Third Order of Penance. As a novice, Lucia was greatly influenced by St. *Catherine of Siena (1347–1380), the devoted Dominican nun who administered to both religious and secular followers, and whose influence extended beyond spirituality to church politics and public affairs. Although a tertiary and able to live a secular life, Lucia chose to enter the Dominican convent in Viterbo, where a halo of fame soon surrounded her, kindled by the holiness of her life and her charismatic personality.

From Viterbo, Lucia contacted *Columba of Rieti, whom she considered to be the living embodiment of Catherine's goals and ideals. Columba kindly and discreetly responded to Lucia. Until her death in 1501, Columba was her spiritual guide. This was especially crucial to Lucia, particularly when she was approached by emissaries of Ercole I of Este (1431–1505), duke of Ferrara, Modena, and Reggio, who had succeeded his brother Borso in 1471. Ercole offered to grant Lucia the authority to found a religious community if she left the convent in Viterbo and took on the role of spiritual advisor for the duke and his family. (Ercole I was married to *Leonora of Aragon [1450–1493], and their eldest son

Alfonso I d'Este would later marry *Lucrezia Borgia, the daughter of Pope Alexander VI). Lucia was attracted by Ercole's offer, which she viewed as an opportunity to further emulate her ideal, Catherine.

Ercole's rule coincided with great upheaval within the Roman Catholic Church which preached social welfare and priestly vows, but failed to practice these ideals. The effort to reform the church brought with it criticism aimed at government policies which favored the rich and powerful and ignored the poor and suffering. Ercole's invitation to Lucia corresponded with a sincere attempt to ethicize court life, and the Dominican nun enjoyed a brief period of fame and prestige as the duke's advisor, particularly after 1501, when the stigmata—signs of her manifest holiness—appeared on her hands. Lucia collaborated with Ercole on matters of religion and also on strictly political issues, which embittered those factions already against the duke.

Following Ercole's death in 1505, the animosity against Lucia grew, and her religious authority was furthered called into question when her stigmata suddenly vanished. Forsaken by everyone and forced into seclusion, Lucia lived the rest of her life in isolation and misery, relieved only by her growing spirituality. Her autobiography, finished eight months before her death in 1544, was published in 1879.

SOURCES:

Granello, M. *la b. Lucia da Narni*. Ferrara, 1879.

Tozzi, I. "La religiosità femminile tra Umbria e Lazio dal Medioevo alla prima età moderna," in *Atlante Rieti*. Terni, Rieti, 1993.

SUGGESTED READING:

Zarri, G. *Le sante vive: Per una tripologia della santità femminile*. Trento 1980.

Ileana Tozzi, D. Litt.,
and member of Società Italiana delle Storiche
and Deputazione di Storia Patria, Rieti, Italy

Lucia of Rugia (fl. 1220)

Queen of Poland. Flourished around 1220; married Ladislas III Laskonogi (Spindleshanks) of Wielkopolska, king of Poland (r. 1228–1231).

Lucid, Shannon (1943—)

American biochemist and astronaut who set the American record in space, spending 188 days aboard the Russian space station Mir *in 1996. Born Shannon Wells in Shanghai, China, on January 14, 1943; daughter of Joseph Oscar Wells (a Baptist preacher) and Myrtle Wells (a missionary nurse); settled in Bethany, Oklahoma in 1949; graduated from Bethany*

(Oklahoma) High School, 1960; University of Oklahoma, B.S. in chemistry, 1963, Ph.D. in biochemistry, 1973; a member of NASA's first class of female astronauts, 1978; married Michael Lucid (a chemist), in 1968; children: two daughters, Kawai Dawn Lucid and Shandara Lucid, and one son, Michael Lucid.

On March 22, 1996, 53-year-old Shannon Lucid, a member of NASA's original class of women astronauts and a veteran of four previous space missions, lifted off from Kennedy Space Center aboard the space shuttle *Atlantis,* which transported her to the ten-year-old Russian space station *Mir.* There, she joined Russian astronauts Yuri Onufrienko and Yuri Usachev for what was to be a five-month research mission, but which turned into a record-breaking 188-day stay in space, the longest ever by an American. Lucid would circle the Earth more than 3,000 times, covering 75 million miles, before returning home on September 26, 1996. A down-to-earth mother of three, Lucid likened day-to-day life on *Mir* to "living in a camper in the back of your pickup with your kids . . . when it's raining and no one can get out."

The daughter of a Baptist minister and a missionary nurse, J. Oscar Wells and **Myrtle Wells,** Lucid was born in war-torn China in 1943. When she was just six months old, she and her parents were interned in a Japanese prison camp for a year. Oscar and Myrtle kept their daughter alive by feeding her their daily ration of rice, but almost starved to death themselves. The family was eventually turned over to U.S. officials in exchange for Japanese POWs, and remained in the United States until the end of the war, when they returned to China. When the Communists took over in 1949, however, they again returned to the United States, settling permanently in Bethany, Oklahoma, where Oscar embarked on a career as a tent evangelist.

As a youngster, Lucid was fascinated with American frontier history and its pioneering spirit. A biography of rocket pioneer Robert Goddard inspired her to be a space explorer. "People thought I was crazy, because that was long before America had a space program," she said. After graduating as salutatorian of her high school, Lucid earned a B.S. in chemistry from the University of Oklahoma. She also earned her pilot's license and purchased an old Piper Clipper, in which she occasionally flew her father to revival meetings. "The Baptists wouldn't let women preach," she has said, "so I had to become an astronaut to get closer to God than my father."

Seddon, Rhea.
See "Astronauts:
Women in
Space" for
sidebar.

**Kathryn
Sullivan, Judith
Resnik, and
Sally Ride.** See
"Astronauts:
Women in
Space."

Lucid was thwarted in her efforts to be part of America's burgeoning space program. The first seven Mercury astronauts were all men, which continues to rankle Lucid. She also faced discrimination in the commercial realm. When she could not get a job as a commercial pilot, she hired on as a chemist at Kerr-McGee Corporation. Her boss was Michael Lucid. Shannon married Michael in 1968 and returned to the University of Oklahoma to pursue a Ph.D. In 1978, when NASA began recruiting women for the astronaut corps, Lucid was ready. Now the mother of two, she was among NASA's first class of female astronauts, which included ◄ Rhea Seddon, ◄ Kathryn D. Sullivan, ◄ Judith Resnik (who would die in the 1986 *Challenger* disaster), ◄ Sally Ride, and **Anna Fisher**. After the rigorous training program, which included being dragged along dusty roads behind motorcycles to simulate what it would be like to be bounced along the ground tethered to a parachute, and spending hours in the stomach-churning centrifuge, Lucid emerged intact. Her first space mission was aboard the shuttle *Discovery* in 1985, and was followed by three subsequent journeys into space before her record-breaking mission aboard *Mir*.

*Shannon
Lucid*

In addition to maintenance and organizational duties aboard the Russian space station, Lucid carried out scientific experiments which involved documenting how a candle burns in space, how protein crystals grow, and how quail embryos developed in zero gravity. To counteract the muscle and bone loss encountered during long periods in space, she also spent two hours a day on the stationary bicycle and treadmill aboard the space station. Although outfitted with a phone-booth-sized sleeping compartment, Lucid preferred to bed down on the floor of her equipment-laden laboratory, which offered a bit more room. When the first shuttle scheduled to bring her home was plagued with safety problems and a second was stalled by Hurricane Fran, Lucid was unflappable, although she did issue an urgent request for a fresh stock of M&Ms and more books. An avid reader, she read close to 50 books while in orbit.

Lucid's arrival home aboard *Atlantis* on September 26, 1996, was greeted with a collective sigh of relief from NASA and the world at large. No one was happier to see her back on earth than her husband and three children, who had kept in touch through television conferences and daily e-mail. "Who has to write their wife a letter every day?," queried Lucid's husband Mike, who also admitted to not quite understanding why his wife enjoys "running around in circles up there." Upon landing at the Kennedy Space Center in Florida, Lucid surprised everyone by walking off the aircraft. Admitting to feeling a bit "wobbly and woozy," she nonetheless made it the 25 feet to the transporter, where the crew presented her with a 10-pound box of red, white, and blue M&Ms from President Bill Clinton, who later called the astronaut to congratulate her. "I couldn't believe you walked off the shuttle," he said.

From the moment of her touchdown, Lucid became the most valuable medical guinea pig that NASA has ever had, supplying invaluable data as to the effects of space travel. Poked and prodded every day for two weeks after her homecoming, Lucid continued to be monitored intermittently for three years after her space flight. Because only one other woman, Russian cosmonaut *Yelena Kondakova, has come close to Lucid's record time in space (169 days as compared to Lucid's 188), it is yet to be seen what long-term effects the prolonged mission might have on the astronaut. Of major concern is bone loss which could result in osteoporosis, and space radiation, which could cause cancer down the road. "That's the sort of thing that 10, 20 years from now maybe we'll have an answer

to," said Roger Billica, chief of medical operations at Johnson Space Center.

After initial debriefing, Lucid continued her recuperation at home in Houston, Texas. Although NASA predicted months of readjustment and lethargy, Lucid was browsing bookstores, riding her bike around town, and even skating with her two daughters within record time. In December 1996, a robust and beaming Shannon Lucid was presented the Congressional Space Medal of Honor by President Clinton at a White House ceremony. Said Colonel Richard Mullane, a veteran of three shuttle missions, "The 'Right Stuff' nowadays is being able to thrive in situations a lot of us couldn't have imagined—like six months on a space station with two Russians."

SOURCES:

Begley, Sharon. "Lucid's Long Road Home," in *Newsweek*. September 30, 1996.

Broad, William J. "Six Months in Russian space outpost, her longing for home nears fulfillment," in *The Day* [New London, CT]. September 19, 1996.

Carroll, Ginny, Peter Katel, Catharine Skipp, and Peter Annin. "Down to Earth," in *Newsweek*. October 7, 1996, pp. 31–36.

Dunn, Marcia. "After record space romp, Lucid looks forward to normalcy," in *The Day* [New London, CT]. November 25, 1996.

———. "Astronaut should feel lousy after space stay," in *The Day* [New London, CT]. September 25, 1996.

———. "Lucid surprises Earthlings by walking off the shuttle," in *The Day* [New London, CT]. September 27, 1996.

———. "U.S. woman putting in her time in space," in *The Day* [New London, CT]. July 16, 1996.

Jerome, Richard and Laurel Brubaker Calkins. "Above and Beyond," in *People Weekly*. Vol. 46, no. 4. July 22, 1996, pp. 36–40.

"Lucid honored," in *The Day* [New London, CT]. December 3, 1996.

Barbara Morgan,
Melrose, Massachusetts

Lucienne of Segni

(r. around 1252–1258)

Princess and regent of Tripoli and Antioch. Reigned around 1252 to 1258; great-niece of Pope Innocent III; cousin of Pope Gregory IX; second wife of Bohemund V, prince of Antioch and count of Tripoli (r. 1233–1252); children: Bohemund VI, prince of Antioch (r. 1251–1268), count of Tripoli (r. 1251–1275); Plaisance of Antioch (who married Henry I, king of Cyprus [r. 1218–1253]).

Chosen by her cousin Pope Gregory IX to become the second wife of Prince Bohemund V, ruler of Antioch and Tripoli, Lucienne of Segni provided her new husband with close ties to the papacy. Bohemund, however, was less delighted by the frequent visits of her relatives and friends from Rome. The couple, who held court in Tripoli and virtually ignored Antioch, had two children: a daughter *Plaisance of Antioch, who married King Henry I of Cyprus, and a son Bohemund VI, who was 15 when his father died in 1252. Lucienne assumed the regency for her underage son, remaining in Tripoli and leaving the governing of Antioch to her Roman relatives. When Tripoli came under the control of the Embriaco family in 1258, Lucienne was deposed, although many of her Roman relatives remained in positions of authority. The local barons, objecting to interference by foreigners, marched upon Tripoli to rid it of Lucienne's relatives, wounding Bohemund in the process. Later, Bohemund retaliated by arranging the murder of Bertrand, a young member of the Embriaco family. Although the rebels withdrew, the murder precipitated a long period of unrest between the houses of Antioch and Embriaco.

Lucilla (b. 150 CE).
See Faustina II for sidebar.

Lucille (1862–1935).
See Duff Gordon, Lucy.

Luckner, Gertrud (1900–1995)

British-born rescuer of Jews during the Holocaust, who was arrested by the Nazis, survived two years in the Ravensbrück concentration camp, and worked to increase understanding between Christians and Jews in postwar Germany. Born of German parents in Liverpool, England, on September 26, 1900; died in Freiburg im Breisgau, Germany, on August 31, 1995; undergraduate degree in political science, 1920; attended University of Frankfurt am Main; University of Freiburg im Breisgau, Ph.D.

Gertrud Luckner, described by **Gay Block** and **Malka Drucker** in *Rescuers* as a hunchbacked and profoundly deaf old woman who "might be mistaken for a gnome rather than the respected philosopher she is," may have looked like an unlikely hero, but she risked her life in assisting Jews during the Holocaust and would later be remembered for her unerring courage. She was born in England in 1900, the only child of German parents. The family relocated to Germany when she was seven, and Luckner grew up in Berlin and nearby Potsdam. It was not long before she became aware of the inequities of the

world, particularly during World War I, when the privations of the working classes brought Germany to the brink of social revolution even before the termination of hostilities (November 1918). As did many many young Germans of the day, Luckner became a pacifist and anti-militarist.

Soon after the war, her parents died and she was on her own. In 1920, she was awarded her undergraduate degree in political science from the recently founded University of Frankfurt am Main, probably the most progressive college in the country at the time. Years later, she received a Ph.D. degree from the University of Freiburg im Breisgau with a dissertation on self-help measures taken by the unemployed in England and Wales. During these years, Luckner was an active Quaker, being particularly impressed by the theological simplicity of that Christian denomination, as well as by its traditions of generously responding to those in need, including poor and impoverished women and children during and after World War I.

As a believer in international peace and reconciliation, Luckner made every attempt to link her thoughts and actions in a pragmatic fashion. In 1926, she went to Poland to study social and economic conditions there as well as to find practical means of rendering assistance to those most in need. She also worked to overcome national stereotypes and resentments, which had long poisoned relations between the Polish and German peoples. Upon her return to Germany, she continued her career in applied social work. With a command of the English language, she spent a year in the United Kingdom in 1930, studying slum conditions. In 1931, she moved to the charming university town of Freiburg im Breisgau, but by that year there was little charm to be found either in Freiburg or in the rest of Germany. The world depression had led to intense social distress due to mass unemployment, and many of Freiburg's students, long known for their extreme nationalism and anti-Semitism, were now adherents of the National Socialist Party of Adolf Hitler. Although many Germans, particularly conservatives, failed to recognize the danger to democracy and civilized values posed by Nazism, Luckner was not among them. Long before the Hitler regime was established, she recognized that this movement, based on racism and violence, posed great peril to civilization.

In 1933, soon after the Nazis established their dictatorship, Luckner established a small but vibrant study and discussion circle in Freiburg in order to better understand events as they developed. Most of the members of the group were young women and men of the upper classes. Luckner was convinced that by regularly bringing this future elite together and providing them with literature to enlighten them about the inhumane nature of the Nazis, she would be able to immunize them against the growing evils of the day. The same year, Luckner visited one of her Jewish friends, the much-respected Berlin rabbi Dr. Leo Baeck. From Rabbi Baeck, she got a master list of the names and addresses of all the Jewish organizations in Germany.

In 1934, she took a major step by becoming a convert to the Roman Catholic Church. For Luckner, Christian belief had to be experienced in the real world, with real, imperfect people, both sinned and sinned against. In the Nazi Germany of 1934, such thinking could easily place one in danger. With each passing day, Luckner watched the results of the Nazi ideology for Germany as a nation and for millions of individual Germans: thousands of Germans were suffering in concentration camps because of their political views, thousands more for having been born Jewish. On her own initiative, Luckner visited the Jewish organizations on her list to warn them of the dangers ahead as well as to bring those in peril some words of encouragement from a sympathetic German woman of Christian faith. She maintained these contacts over the next years, even as the Nazi terror against the Jews increased. Luckner assisted in the activities of the Raphaelsverein, a Catholic organization that helped Jews and others who were homeless due to Nazi persecution. By 1938, she was working in Freiburg for another Catholic group, the charity organization Caritasverband.

On the night of November 9–10, 1938, Luckner was an eyewitness to the most terrifying event yet in German public life, Kristallnacht, a carefully orchestrated attack on the synagogues and businesses of the Jews still remaining in the Reich. In Freiburg, a synagogue was directly across the street from the main offices of the Caritasverband. As a result, Luckner was able to witness the deliberate destruction of the Jewish house of worship by local storm troopers. Shaken but determined to do something, she got on her bicycle to alert her Jewish friends of the imminent threat and to provide them with the names and addresses of Christians who were willing to give them shelter. While on her mission of mercy, Luckner found her bicycle tires slashed, no doubt by local Nazis who already knew of her "un-German" assistance to Jews. Unfazed, she abandoned her bicycle and continued on foot to spread the warning that terrible night.

Now that Hitler and his millions of followers had seized the institutions of an advanced state, their ability to do harm was greatly enhanced. National Socialism ruled through terror, setting up a vast network of concentration camps. It had succeeded in forging a national consensus of mass support, largely because the regime had virtually eliminated unemployment. Most Germans also approved of the fact that through rearmament the Nazis had transformed the German Reich into a nation that was once again strong, proud and even feared. As a Catholic who believed that her faith must determine her actions in daily life, Luckner differed from many of her fellow Germans, both Catholic and Protestant, who identified themselves as Christians but did little to oppose the evils of the dictatorship or take the risk of rendering assistance to Jews and other victims of the Nazis. Fearless but also practical in her defiance of National Socialism, Luckner worked against Hitler's system by providing aid and encouragement to those most threatened by its arbitrary power.

Luckner continued her activities with the Caritasverband, helping Jews to flee Germany and rendering as much material and psychological support as possible. Trips to Switzerland, where she had friends sympathetic to her efforts, enabled her to remain in contact with the outside world and to send letters to other countries, thus keeping other Christian groups and individuals informed of the deteriorating situation in Germany. She continued to travel throughout Germany, visiting members of increasingly threatened and isolated Jewish communities. Although Luckner moved mostly in Catholic and Jewish circles, she retained many of her old contacts with Quakers, many of whom were also active in assisting Jews and others. Terrified—and with few if any of their former Christian friends and neighbors willing to engage in contact with them—these Jews were deeply grateful for even an hour's conversation with Luckner. "No one else visited them but me," she later recalled. "They never forgot it."

By now a well-known and much-respected personality in Germany's dwindling Jewish communities, Luckner was particularly welcome on her visits to Berlin and Munich. Living in the capital of what was now boastfully called the Greater German Reich, Berlin's Jews were at the mercy of Heinrich Himmler's SS and the vast propaganda machine of Joseph Goebbels. On her numerous visits to Berlin, Luckner invariably spent time with Leo Baeck, who had persuaded his daughter to emigrate to London but had determined that he must remain in Germany with his flock. While in Berlin, Luckner also visited and exchanged information and ideas with the Catholic priest Bernhard Lichtenberg, a man who shared with Luckner a deep hatred for the essence of Nazism.

In the Bavarian capital of Munich, which played a crucial role in the history of National Socialism and where the local Jewish community was at great risk from its anti-Semitic gauleiter, Luckner worked closely with one of that city's most determined anti-Nazis, the Jesuit priest Alfred Delp. Together, the two searched for ways to lessen the destruction caused by the dictatorship. During these trips, Luckner visited Jewish homes, sometimes spending the night with families whose lives were now dominated by fear. The diminutive Luckner, who weighed less than 100 pounds, was sometimes attacked and beaten by local Nazi toughs, but she continued her visits to families including those who were defined as Jews by the Nuremberg Laws although they had converted to Catholicism. By the end of 1940, with most of the European continent under German control, German Jews had few if any places to which to escape. Luckner's home in Freiburg im Breisgau was only a few miles from the German-Swiss border, enabling her to assist a small, fortunate number of Jews across the frontier. These rescues included the challenging task of procuring Swiss visas, but Luckner and her small circle of sympathizers accomplished such remarkable feats virtually on a routine basis.

By the summer of 1941, Nazi policy toward the Jews had radicalized to the point of systematic mass murder. Beginning with the German invasion of the Soviet Union in June of that year, special mobile killing squads (Einsatzgruppen) killed hundreds of thousands of Jewish men, women, and children in the recently occupied areas of the east. Although these activities were kept secret, rumors worked their way back to Germany through various channels. Luckner and a number of other Catholic welfare officials, including **Margarete Sommer** in Berlin, already knew about the murderous conditions in the Jewish ghettos of Warsaw, Lodz, and other cities of Nazi-occupied Poland. They sent as many packages of food and clothing as they could to German Jews whom they knew had been sent to these ghettos, fully realizing that their efforts could do little to relieve the immensity of suffering there. Many Germans had heard stories about terrible things taking place in the east, but made no attempt to discover more information for fear that such curiosity might bring a visit

from the Gestapo to their homes. Luckner was among the few to consider it imperative to find out more.

One family to whom Luckner sent packages and letters was that of **Gertrud Meyer**. The family had been "resettled" to the Maidanek camp, and, when in 1942 Luckner's offerings were returned to her unopened, she suspected that the Meyers had perished. She now redoubled her efforts to save as many Jewish lives as possible. In one case, that of the Rosenberg family of Freiburg, Luckner helped save the one Rosenberg child who had been defined as a "full-blooded Jewess" (both parents being Jewish). The girl's two brothers had been born during their father's first marriage, to a woman who was not Jewish, and they were thus defined as half-Jewish hybrids, *Mischlinge*. The brothers had even served in the German Wehrmacht in the early stages of the war. When their sister was scheduled to be evacuated to the east, Luckner took advantage of the boys' previous military service, coaching them to emphasize this fact when they pled on behalf of their sister. The stratagem was used on one of Adolf Eichmann's adjutants whom Luckner knew to be partial to the military, and was successful. The girl was sent to the "model" ghetto at Theresienstadt/Terezin, where by good fortune she was able to survive the war.

By early 1943, Nazi Germany had been decisively defeated in the battle of Stalingrad and it became clear that the war had been lost, but the Nazi death machine destroyed more lives than ever. The fiction of "normality" for Jews in the Reich was abandoned, one sign of this in Berlin being the arrest and deportation to Theresienstadt of Leo Baeck on January 24, 1943. Using her work for the Caritasverband as a cover, Luckner traveled around the country organizing rescue efforts. She made several risky attempts to gather information on the actual mechanisms of murder, crossing the border of the Reich to investigate the conditions in the German-occupied Polish territory known as the Generalgouvernement. Early in 1943, she got as far as the city of Kattowitz, which was located in the immediate vicinity of the Auschwitz camps.

The Gestapo had long viewed Luckner's travels throughout Germany with suspicion. On March 24, 1943, she was arrested while traveling on a train en route to Berlin. Her captors found on her person the sum of 5,000 reichsmarks, entrusted to her by Archbishop Gröber of Freiburg to take to the Jews of Berlin. Her interrogation began on the train and continued on a daily basis for the next nine weeks. Although she was not physically tortured, at times her interrogators' anger dominated the sessions, and on one occasion she was scolded for "riding trains for Jews" while, because of severe fuel rationing, most other Germans were forced to "ride their bikes for victory." For three of the nine weeks, Luckner was grilled every night from six in the evening to eight in the morning. Although she provided her interrogators with little information of substance, they concluded that her activities on behalf of Jews constituted sufficient evidence of *Reichsfeindlichkeit*, of being "an enemy of the Reich." Her case was deemed important enough for Ernst Kaltenbrunner, chief of the RSHA (Reichssicherheitshauptamt, the Reich Security Main Office), to personally sign papers condemning her to a permanent term of imprisonment given the fact that if released it was clear that she would again work "against the Reich" on the behalf of Jews. Upon learning that she would be sent to the women's concentration camp Ravensbrück, and not Auschwitz, Luckner felt "somewhat relieved."

Located about an hour's drive from Berlin, Ravensbrück began operation in 1939. Although it was supposed to accommodate 7,000 women, almost from the start it held more women than its maximum capacity. By the time Luckner arrived in early November 1943, the camp had several thousand more women than could be accommodated with even a minimum maintenance of decent health and living conditions. Immediately after arrival, she and her group had to undress and stand naked for hours outdoors in the bitter cold. Eventually, they were issued uniforms to replace their own clothing. Hers was not only filthy but blood-stained. Once during a daily roll call Luckner struck up a conversation with a woman in the line behind her. The woman turned out to be Gertrud Meyer, to whose family Luckner had sent letters and food parcels several years earlier. Meyer's husband, Luckner now learned, had been gassed and cremated at the Maidanek camp.

Ravensbrück concentration camp had never been intended to serve as an extermination facility by the Nazis, but the life of its inmates was precarious at best. From 1939 to 1945, an estimated 90,000 women from many nationalities lost their lives there, the weak and ill customarily being "selected" for gassing and cremation. Malnutrition and disease killed women every day. Survival in Ravensbrück depended not only on luck and robust good health but also on the human institution of solidarity. Possibly by chance, Luckner was assigned to barrack number 6, which was designated for Communist prison-

ers. Although there were deep ideological and philosophical differences between Luckner and her barrack mates, they accepted her, and in time a strong friendship and mutual respect grew to unite them in a common desire to survive their ordeal. On more than one occasion, her Communist cell mates saved Luckner's life by putting her on work details that allowed her to escape death, and several times she narrowly missed being killed in Ravensbrück's gas chambers. In July 1944, her Communist friends were able to prevent her from being sent on a death transport to Bergen-Belsen, where she would have been gassed. Occasional food parcels from her Catholic colleagues in Freiburg enabled Luckner to maintain sufficient strength not to die of disease. Even so, she barely survived a bout with severe intestinal influenza and almost died after being sent to the barracks for the sick and dying, where she lay for days in lice and filth, literally between dead and dying women. Although weak and ill, Luckner somehow smuggled food and a nightgown to her Jewish friend Gertrud Meyer; both women would survive Ravensbrück.

Luckner, who was liberated by Soviet soldiers in May 1945, was determined to restore not only her own life but those of her fellow Germans whose country was in chaos. A letter she gave to a British soldier addressed to Leo Baeck in London got through, and she was overjoyed to learn that he had survived more than two years in Theresienstadt. Amidst the immense suffering that Luckner had witnessed, she had also seen a nobler side of human nature, which included the courage and solidarity of Ravensbrück prisoners, as well as the dignity shown by victims facing inevitable deaths. Luckner regarded the Jews as a people of profound spiritual depth, noting "with what composure they met the horror."

Although her health had been shattered in Ravensbrück, Luckner was soon back in Freiburg at her Caritasverband office. Her official duties were mainly linked to assisting those Catholics of Jewish ancestry who had survived the Holocaust, but as far as she was concerned it was the duty of all Catholics to concern themselves with helping Jews restore their lives. Luckner believed that a new relationship between Catholics—indeed, all Christians—and Jews needed to be created. For this to take place, the animosities, theological and otherwise, that had poisoned Jewish-Christian relationships for almost two millennia would have to be abandoned if a better world were to emerge from the smoldering ruins of the Holocaust. Regarding a permanent forum as essential for the start of a productive Christian-Jewish dialogue, Luckner began to think of publishing a journal to advance such a purpose. With no funds and no church authorization, in August 1948 she began publishing the *Freiburger Rundbrief* (Freiburg Circular), the purposes of which were several. These included fostering interreligious dialogue, publishing reviews of events and books of interest to both Christians and Jews, providing catechists and priests with educational materials, exposing new manifestations of anti-Semitism, and preserving the memory of the Holocaust. Although it exerted considerable influence from the start, her *Freiburger Rundbrief* had only a small circulation in the 1950s, averaging 3,000 to 4,000 copies annually; by the late 1980s, it had risen to about 13,000.

Some priests and Catholic laity supported the *Freiburger Rundbrief* project, but many German Catholics after World War II were indifferent, with some arguing defensively, "We Germans also suffered in the war." Undismayed, Luckner wrote a letter to the Vatican in which she asked for support from Robert Leiber, the German Jesuit who was a personal secretary and confidant to Pope Pius XII. Instead of giving the *Freiburger Rundbrief* its support, the Vatican's response to Luckner's letter was to issue a monitum, an official warning, against the philosemitic work she was doing. Rome's justification was that Luckner's crusade against anti-Semitism was leading Catholics toward a dangerous attitude of religious indifferentism, the notion that one religion is as good as the next. Another sign of the hostility of the Catholic Church hierarchy toward Luckner's activities was its miserly allotment of funds for assistance to German Jews, which grew from 8,858 deutschmarks in 1950 to only 23,743 deutschmarks in 1958.

The serious signs of disapproval from the Vatican did little to stop Luckner. Her vigilance discovered age-old prejudices embedded in Catholic devotional traditions, including an annual procession in a south German city that continued to commemorate an alleged Jewish defilement of the sacred host in the Middle Ages. She also discovered and publicized the fact that of the actors in the world-famous Oberammergau Passion Play, all with the exception of one were former members of the Nazi Party. Most important, as time went by the ideas found in the *Freiburger Rundbrief* began to influence both Christian and Jewish writers and theologians. In his book *Jesus and Israel*, Holocaust survivor Jules Isaac challenged Christians to abandon their prejudices. In 1950, Luckner joined with other Catholics and Protestants to formalize

Isaac's challenge into ten assertions which came to be known as the Seelisberg Theses. By adopting this statement, the group around Luckner created an atmosphere for dialogue that was acceptable for both Jews and Christians.

At the start of the 1960s, the trial in Israel of Nazi war criminal Adolf Eichmann created a radically new intellectual and moral atmosphere in West Germany. Whereas most ordinary Catholics as well as their clergy had previously ignored the questions raised by the crimes of the Nazi regime, now these issues had become almost unavoidable. Two Catholic bishops, Julius Döpfner and Franz Hengsbach, told their flocks that the time had come to face the fact that "all of us have a share in the sin [of all atrocities]." Both Döpfner and Hengsbach had responded positively for years to Luckner's crusade for better understanding between Christians and Jews, and in May 1960 Bishop Hengsbach wrote a letter to Luckner encouraging her to continue her important work. Bishop Döpfner, who in 1948 had become the youngest Catholic bishop in Europe, was a lifelong supporter of Luckner and her Freiburg circle.

In 1965, the almost two decades of effort by Gertrud Luckner on behalf of Christian-Jewish dialogue came to fruition. In that year, the Second Vatican Council passed its important decree on Jewish-Christian relations, *Nostra Aetate*. No longer to be seen as the foes of Christendom, the Jews were now defined as a crucial part of a shared moral heritage. Written by Cardinal Bea, a German Jesuit who was in contact with Luckner and her circle, the statement met with enthusiasm from West Germany's Catholic bishops who recognized that it was time for German Christians to come to terms with their moral failings during the Holocaust, an era when one of the most advanced nations of Western civilization kept silent and allowed its Jewish minority, as well others deemed racially, morally and politically unacceptable, to be annihilated.

In the last decades of her life, Luckner continued her work and could look with pride upon the continuing positive impact of the *Freiburger Rundbrief*. Her many friends in Germany and elsewhere, including Israel (which she visited over 30 times), mourned her death in Freiburg im Breisgau on August 31, 1995. The assembly room of Freiburg's new synagogue was named in her honor. In Israel, Luckner's name is held in the highest regard. There is a Gertrud Luckner Home for the Aged in Nahariyya, and in 1960, on her 60th birthday, the Jewish National Fund honored her by planting a grove in Israel named after her. In 1966, she was designated a Righteous Gentile by Yad Vashem, Israel's Holocaust memorial and research center in Jerusalem.

SOURCES:

Adler, H.G. *Der verwaltete Mensch: Studien zur Deportation der Juden aus Deutschland.* Tübingen: J.C.B. Mohr (Paul Siebeck), 1974.

Behrend-Rosenfeld, Else, and Gertrud Luckner, eds. *Lebenszeichen aus Piaski: Briefe Deportierter aus dem Distrikt Lublin, 1940–1943.* Munich: Deutscher Taschenbuch Verlag, 1970.

Bergman, Samuel Hugo. *Tagebücher & Briefe, Band 2: 1948–1975.* Edited by Miriam Sambursky. Königstein/Taunus: Jüdischer Verlag bei Athenäum, 1985.

Block, Gay, and Malka Drucker. *Rescuers: Portraits of Moral Courage in the Holocaust.* New York and London: Holmes & Meier Publishers, 1992.

"Dr. Gertrud Luckner 75," in *AJR Information* [London]. Vol. 30, no. 9. September 1975, p. 12.

Ehrlich, Ernst Ludwig. "Gertrud Luckner (1900–1995)," in *Orientierung.* Vol. 59, no. 18. September 30, 1995, pp. 193–195.

Fogelman, Eva. *Conscience and Courage: Rescuers of Jews During the Holocaust.* NY: Doubleday Anchor Books, 1994.

Grossmann, Kurt R. "Gertrud Luckner," in *Rheinischer Merkur.* No. 46. November 13, 1970, p. 4.

Keim, Anton Maria, ed. *Yad Vashem: Die Judenretter aus Deutschland.* Mainz: Grünewald Kaiser, 1983.

Lamm, Hans. "Portrait of Three Germans," in *Chicago Jewish Forum.* Winter 1952–53, pp. 119–123.

Norden, Günther van. "Opposition by Churches and Christians," in Wolfgang Benz and Walter H. Pehle, eds., *Encyclopedia of German Resistance to the Nazi Movement.* Translated by Lance W. Garmer. NY: Continuum, 1997, pp. 45–56.

Paldiel, Mordecai. *The Path of the Righteous: Gentile Rescuers of Jews During the Holocaust.* Hoboken, NJ and NY: KTAV Publishing House, Inc./The Jewish Foundation for Christian Rescuers/ADL, 1993.

Phayer, Michael. "The German Catholic Church After the Holocaust," in *Holocaust and Genocide Studies.* Vol. 10, no. 2. Fall 1996, pp. 151–167.

——, and Eva Fleischner. *Cries in the Night: Women Who Challenged the Holocaust.* Kansas City, MO: Sheed & Ward, 1997.

John Haag,
Associate Professor of History,
University of Georgia, Athens, Georgia

Lucrece.

Variant of Lucretia.

Lucretia (?–510 BCE)

Roman matron of historic and legendary fame whose rape, plea for vengeance, and consequent suicide led to the overthrow of kings in Rome and the establishment of the Roman Republic. Name variations: Lucrece. Pronunciation: Loo-cree-sh(ee)-ah. Born in Rome; date of birth unknown; died in either Collatia or Rome, c. 510 BCE; daughter of Spurius Lucretius Tricipitinus, a prefect of Rome; married Lucius Tarquinius Collatinus, a first consul of Rome.

Raped by Sextus Tarquinius, the king's son; was a catalyst for the Roman overthrow of Etruscan kings and has been the subject of elaborate legend throughout Western history; considered a fictional figure by some.

Lucretia appears in the ancient narratives as a paradigm of womanly virtue and as a catalyst for one of the most dramatic events in early Roman history: the expulsion of Etruscan kings and founding of the Roman Republic. There are several versions of her story from antiquity, varying in details, but all agree that Lucretia was raped by Sextus Tarquinius, the king's eldest son, and that her consequent plea for vengeance precipitated the revolt which followed.

The stage for this story is set during a siege of a neighboring town, Ardea, led by Rome's Etruscan king, Tarquinius Superbus. Legend has it that several young nobles, bored with the lack of military action, turned to comparing their wives. Each claimed that his own was the most virtuous. The Roman poet Ovid recounts that the men further questioned, "What of the loyalty of the marriage bed? And are we as dear to our wives as they to us?" Lucretia's husband, Lucius Tarquinius Collatinus, finally offered a challenge: "No need of words! Trust deeds! The night is young. Let us mount our horses and ride for the city!"

On reaching Rome, they surprised many of the wives who were banqueting in luxury. Lucretia, however, in the neighboring village of Collatia, was spinning wool late into the evening and supervising her maidservants in the same activity. Industriously occupied at this traditional womanly task, she was a perfect model of virtue. She greeted her husband warmly, and he, pleased that his wife had vindicated him, extended hospitality to all his companions. Livy, an ancient Roman historian, states: "It was at that fatal supper that Lucretia's beauty and proven chastity kindled in Sextus Tarquinius the flame of lust, and determined him to debauch her." Ovid elaborates: "The royal youth caught fire and fury and, transported by blind love, he raved. Her figure pleased him, and that snowy hue, that yellow hair, and artless grace; pleasing, too, her words and voice and virtue incorruptible; and the less hope he had, the hotter his desire."

Sextus Tarquinius (Tarquin), the eldest son of King Tarquinius Superbus, was next in line to inherit the crown in Rome. He was also distantly related to Lucretia's husband, so that when he came back a few days later on a pretext, Lucretia offered him customary hospitality: dinner and a place to spend the night. After the household was asleep, sneaking past the slaves at Lucretia's door, Tarquin entered her room and attempted to seduce her. Dionysius of Halicarnassus, an ancient Greek historian, suggests that Tarquin offered her marriage and future joint rule over Rome. Livy, more simply, says he "pleaded, threatened, used every weapon that might conquer a woman's heart," including a drawn sword. She refused.

> *B*y this girl's blood—none more chaste till a tyrant wronged her—and by the gods, I swear that . . . never again will I let . . . any other man be King in Rome.
> —Junius Brutus, as quoted by Livy

When Tarquin saw that Lucretia valued chastity over life, he added to the threat: he would not only kill her but also a household slave, claiming to have discovered them engaged in illicit relations. As Ovid tells it, he menaced: "Resistance is vain; I'll rob you of honor and of life. I, the adulterer, will bear false witness to your adultery." Livy remarks, "Even the most resolute chastity could not have stood against this dreadful threat," for a liaison of this nature with a slave would have implied, by ancient Roman lights, that the offenders merited death. Motivated, therefore, by a sense of honor, Lucretia submitted to Tarquin's demands as the lesser of two evils.

The next day, according to Livy, Lucretia wrote to the men most important in her life: her father, Spurius Lucretius Tricipitinus, prefect of Rome, and her husband, Lucius Tarquinius Collatinus, who was still engaged in the siege of Ardea. When they arrived, they found her mourning and in great distress. She related the story of her violation, asking for vengeance: "Give me your solemn promise that the adulterer shall be punished—he is Sextus Tarquinius. He it is who last night came as my enemy disguised as my guest and took his pleasure of me. That pleasure will be my death—and his, too, if you are men."

They promised to avenge her and assured her that as a coerced victim she was innocent of wrongdoing. Lucretia, however, stated: "What is due to him is for you to decide. As for me, I am innocent of fault, but I will take my punishment. Never shall Lucretia provide a precedent for unchaste women to escape what they deserve." Or as Ovid records her response, "The pardon that

you give I do refuse myself." These were her last words. She drew a knife from her robe and plunged it into her heart. Lucretia died in her father's arms as he ineffectively attempted to minister to her in her last moments.

Inevitably there are some variations between Livy's version and that of Dionysius of Halicarnassus. Dionysius reports that instead of sending letters, Lucretia rode in mourning from Collatia to her father in Rome, asking him to call together friends and kin to hear her story. In this version, her husband Collatinus, delayed at the siege of Ardea, received the news only after Lucretia had taken her life.

Both narrators agree that Brutus, a companion of Collatinus, now seized the initiative offered by Lucretia's tragic death. Brutus had personal grievances against Tarquinius Superbus and perceived that the opportune moment to overthrow the Tarquin kings was at hand. He held the bloody knife before him, says Livy, vowing:

> By this girl's blood—none more chaste till a tyrant wronged her—and by the gods, I swear that with sword and fire, and whatever else can lend strength to my arm, I will pursue Lucius Tarquinius the Proud [Superbus], his wicked wife, and all his children, and never again will I let them or any other man be King in Rome.

The emotions of all turned from grief to anger. Lucretia's body, laid out on a black cloth and unprepared for burial, was carried to the public square and placed in a conspicuous position in front of the Senate house, her gaping wound exposed to the crowds. Brutus addressed the populace, relating the pathetic story of Lucretia and enumerating other common grievances under Tarquin rule: how all had been heavily taxed; how commoners were forced to labor on ditches and sewers underground; how Roman men who had formerly battled and conquered neighboring peoples had been robbed of swords and turned into stonecutters and artisans; and how laws had been revoked, assemblies abolished, and the performance of religious rites and sacrifices curtailed.

Brutus compared Lucretia's honor and chastity to the lifestyle of *Tullia, wife of Tarquinius Superbus the king. Tullia was infamous for having engineered the murders of her own and her husband's previous spouses. She had then inspired her husband to bid for kingship in Rome, which meant replacing her own father, whose body, after he had been killed, she ran over in a carriage. (This nefarious deed lived on in Roman memory for generations. Nearly 500

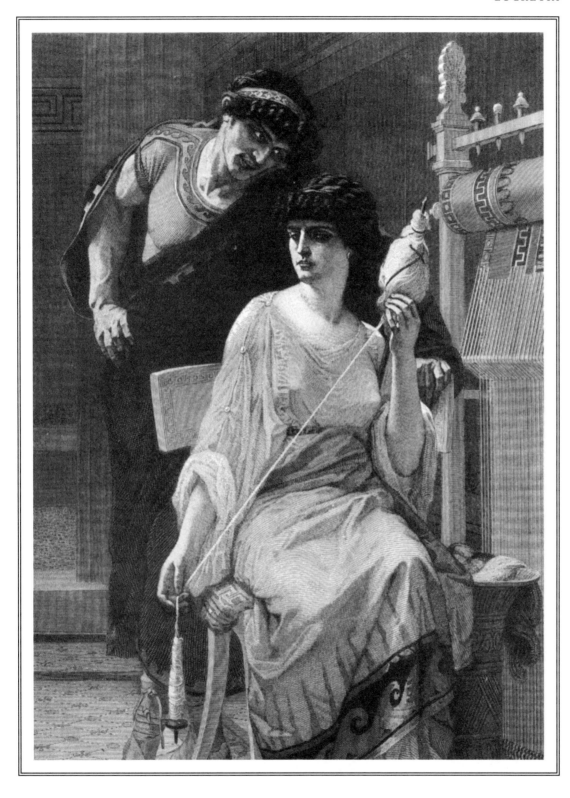

years later, Livy mentioned that there still existed a street in Rome called "The Street of the Crime" in reference to her lack of filial piety. There was no crime greater, in the Roman mind, than that of parricide.) Tullia epitomized the moral degeneracy of the current regime, a regime over which she still wielded womanly influence, while virtuous Lucretia was dead as a result of that very family's wickedness.

Brutus turned to Lucretia's inert body and addressed her:

O admirable woman and worthy of great praise for your noble resolution! You are gone, you are dead, being unable to bear the tyrant's insolence and despising all the pleasures of life in order to avoid suffering any such indignity again. After this example, Lucretia, when you, who were given a woman's nature, have shown the resolution of a brave man, shall we, who were born men, show ourselves inferior to women in courage?

Crying out that tears must give way to deeds, Brutus called for all to take up arms against the tyrants who had dared to treat them as a vanquished enemy. But Brutus went beyond the dramatic in his appeal. He pointed out pragmatic considerations: the revolution was being headed by the most prominent citizens of Rome; the king was out of the city at war; they had access to men, money, arms, generals, and equipment for warfare; and the army, with its own grievances, would be likely to support the revolution. (He also pointed out that if any man declined to participate in the revolt, his wife and children could be held hostage in the city.)

In short, Brutus' charismatic presentation of the wrongs done to the Romans, coupled with his reasonable expectation of success in the venture, incited the populace to revolt against the king. Lucretia's father was left in control of Rome. To enlist support of the army, Brutus led the way to the camp where they were still besieging Ardea, and was welcomed by the troops. The townspeople called down curses on Tullia, and when Tarquinius Superbus returned to Rome, having caught wind of the revolt, he was shut out of the city. He left for exile with Tullia in an Etruscan town, and Sextus Tarquinius, whose violence against Lucretia had precipitated the downfall of his family, fled to a different town, where he was later assassinated.

Not only did the Romans oust the Tarquin family, but they also changed their form of government from a monarchy to a republic. Following Brutus' example, all citizens took a solemn oath never again to allow any man to be king in Rome. After a transition period where Lucretia's father ruled Rome in anticipation of an election, her husband Lucius Tarquinius Collatinus was elected as one of the first two consuls (rulers who shared the power between them and were elected for terms of only one year). Unfortunately, his name made him suspect in the eyes of the Roman people, who had had their fill of Tarquins. In fact, his name held such disgust for the Romans that before his year as consul was completed he was asked to leave Rome. Having participated in the expulsion of the Tarquin king, he was aston-

ished by this, but when even Spurius Lucretius, his father-in-law, joined in the entreaties, he yielded to unanimous sentiment and left Rome with all his belongings. Future Etruscan attempts to retake rule in Rome were unsuccessful.

The historicity of this dramatic tale has often been questioned by scholars. In Livy's narrative, for instance, Lucretia's story follows hard on that of Tullia's, and he makes Lucretia the paradigm of the virtuous Roman woman (simple, industrious, and chaste), contrasted with a wonderfully debauched woman (avaricious, ambitious, and cruel). Both women inspired the men in their lives to act, one for good, the other for evil. Both epitomized, in the Roman mind, the characters of their respective cultures: upright Roman versus decadent Etruscan. Because the stories fit these patterns so nicely, among other considerations, some scholars relegate them to status of pure legend.

Others, however, believe that the evidence for the antiquity of these stories give them credence, at least in their bare outlines. For instance, R.M. Ogilvie, authoritative commentator on the work of Livy, argues that because Lucretia's story was mentioned by the very earliest Roman writers, and because it was so strongly entrenched in the Roman culture, the story should be considered historically based in its core form despite legendary elements.

Some aspects of the story can be confirmed by historical sources apart from literary and historical narratives. They are: that Lucretius is a traditional Roman name, and, since Roman women of that time customarily took the feminine form of the family name as their own, without doubt there were many undocumented women named Lucretia; that Tarquinius is a documented ancient Etruscan name; that the Etruscans did have a predominance in Rome in the late 500s BCE; that Etruscan culture valued celebratory living and urban culture, while Romans praised simple living and rural virtues; that kings in Rome were ousted around 510 BCE; that a new republican form of government was instituted in Rome about that time; and that the word *rex* (king) held such negative connotations for the Romans that even as late as the 1st century BCE powerful leaders such as Julius Caesar and Augustus made efforts to distance themselves from that appellation.

Lucretia's story was attached to these historical phenomena for the Roman people. Ovid, for instance, relates Lucretia's story in the context of a festival the Romans called *Regifugium* (Flight of the King) which was celebrated on

February 24. While scholars reject Ovid's connection of this particular festival in its earliest origins to the events surrounding Lucretia's tragedy, it is clear that the Roman mind had made its own link.

If the story is accepted as basically valid, the question arises as to why Lucretia committed suicide when she was innocent of wrongdoing. One theory is that in her era she might have expected a trial before a family council and foreseen condemnation despite her victimization. Even if she had been allowed to live, the idea that any subsequent offspring might be tainted by the violation would have been difficult to face, and perhaps she was unwilling to live life as what would have been seen as a marred woman. She certainly believed, accurately, that she would ensure a vendetta against the House of Tarquin by her death.

Lucretia is a stark figure on the white canvas of early Roman history, appearing only long enough to demonstrate industry and chastity as cardinal womanly virtues and then to motivate men to throw off political oppression. But her story has served moral purposes for writers ever since. Among the Roman authors who refer to her in extant writings, always in a laudatory vein, are Cicero, Varro, Valerius Maximus, and Seneca. St. Augustine, on the other hand, castigates Lucretia for her suicide. He argues from a Christian viewpoint, 900 years after the event, that her suicide was immoral and only added another sin to the chain of crimes already committed. Shakespeare, over 1,000 years after St. Augustine, retold her story in "The Rape of Lucrece," a long narrative poem describing her chastity, her dilemma, and her courage. Her suicide, a tragedy to the modern mind, was glorified for thousands of years.

SOURCES:

Cambridge Ancient History.

Dionysius of Halicarnassus. *The Roman Antiquities.* Translated by Earnest Cary. Loeb Classical Library. Cambridge, MA: Harvard University Press, 1937.

Hallett, Judith. *Fathers and Daughters in Roman Society: Women and the Elite Family.* Princeton, NJ: Princeton University Press, 1984.

Livy. *The Early History of Rome.* Translated by Aubrey de Sélincourt. London: Penguin, 1971.

Ogilvie, R.M. *A Commentary on Livy Books 1–5.* Oxford: Oxford University Press, 1965.

Ovid. *The Fasti.* Translated by Sir James George Frazer. Loeb Classical Library. Cambridge, MA: Harvard University Press, 1951.

Treves, Piero. "Lucretia," in *Oxford Classical Dictionary,* 1970.

Sylvia Gray Kaplan,
Adjunct Faculty, Humanities,
Marylhurst College, Marylhurst, Oregon

Lucretia Borgia (1480–1519).

See Borgia, Lucrezia.

Lucrezia.

Variant of Lucretia.

Lucrezia Borgia (1480–1519).

See Borgia, Lucrezia.

Lucrezia de Medici.

See Medici, Lucrezia de.

Lucusta (fl. 54 CE).

See Locusta.

Lucy.

Variant of Lucille, Lucina, Lucinda, Lucretia, or Lucrezia.

Lucy (d. 303)

Saint. Name variations: Lucia. Martyred in year 303.

A martyr from Syracuse, Saint Lucy perished during the reign of Diocletian, who, in an attempt to wipe out Christianity, had decreed in 303 that churches be torn down, sacred writings be destroyed, Christians be removed from public office, and all Christians be subject to torture. According to legend, Lucy rejected a pagan suitor whom her mother desired her to marry, and he denounced her as a Christian. She was condemned to a house of ill-repute. Though she escaped this fate, she was burned to death at the pyre, remaining alive in the midst of the flames until an executioner pierced her throat with a dagger. Lucy is the patron saint of the blind. Her feast day is December 13.

Lucy of Scotland (d. 1090)

Saint. Died in 1090; daughter of a king of Scotland.

Descended from Scottish royalty, Lucy of Scotland left the licentious court of her father and went to Lorraine, France, where she became a shepherd for a man by the name of Thiébaut. Upon his death, she inherited his fortune which she used to build a church and a hermitage on the mountain which still bears her name. *Anne of Austria made a pilgrimage to her shrine before the birth of Louis XIV, since it is believed that Lucy can help sterile women to conceive. Her feast day is September 19.

Lucy, Autherine Juanita (1930—)

African-American civil-rights activist. Born in 1930.

A nearly forgotten name in the modern civil-rights movement is that of Autherine Juanita Lucy, who was the first African-American to attempt to integrate the University of Alabama. A 1952 graduate of Miles College in Fairfield, Alabama, Lucy hoped to pursue a graduate degree in library science at the University of Alabama. Assisted by the NAACP, she eventually won a federal lawsuit that required the university to admit her. On February 3, 1956, as she was riding to class with the dean of women, rioters, numbering close to 1,000, stormed her car and later threatened the campus home of the president. Three days later, the university suspended her, citing her safety as the reason. Undaunted, Lucy went back to court and with the help of NAACP lawyer Thurgood Marshall, who later became the first African-American justice of the U.S. Supreme Court, she succeeded in having her enrollment upheld. In March, however, the university trumped up a technical violation of school rules and expelled her. Neither the NAACP nor Marshall pursued the case further, but Lucy would not be deterred. She returned to the University of Alabama in 1989 and earned a master's degree in education in 1992.

SOURCES:
"This Week in Black History," in *Jet*. February 8, 1999.

Lucy, Elizabeth (fl. 1460s)

Mistress of Edward IV. Born of humble origins in the Southampton area of London; mistress of Edward IV (1442–1483), king of England (r. 1461–1483); children: (with Edward) Arthur (d. 1541), Viscount L'Isle; Elizabeth Plantagenet; Grace Plantagenet.

Elizabeth Lucy was the mistress of Edward IV, king of England. "He loved her well," wrote Sir George Buck, a 17th-century historian, "and she was his witty concubine."

Lucy de Blois (d. 1120)

*French princess. Name variations: sometimes referred to as Agnes; Lucy of Blois. Died with her sister in the wreck of the White Ship on November 25, 1120, in Barfleur, Normandy, France; daughter of Stephen of Blois, count of Blois, and *Adela of Blois (1062–c. 1137); sister of *Matilda de Blois (d. 1120).*

Ludgarda (fl. 1200s)

Polish noblewoman. Flourished in the 1200s; daughter of Henry I, duke of Mecklenburg; first wife of Przemysl or Przemyslav II, king of Poland (1257–1296, r. 1290–1296).

Luding, Christa Rothenburger.

See Rothenburger-Luding, Christa.

Ludington, Sybil (1761–1839)

Hero of the American Revolution who rode 40 miles to warn New York militiamen of a British raid in nearby Connecticut. Pronunciation: LUD-ington. Born Sybil Ludington on April 5, 1761, in Fredericksburg, New York; died in New York in 1839; daughter of Henry Ludington (1738–1817, a mill owner and colonel in the New York militia) and Abigail (Ludington) Ludington (1745–1825); married Edward Ogden, in 1784; children: four sons and two daughters.

Very little is known about the life of Sybil Ludington. Except for a single courageous act, she would have escaped the notice of American history. On the night of April 26, 1777, Sybil Ludington, then 16, volunteered to ride 40 miles through the dark countryside of New York State, warning the local militia about a British raid at Danbury, Connecticut. This one extraordinary event, usually compared to the more well-known ride of Paul Revere, is the only historically important act of Ludington's life. Afterward, she once again faded from the view of history texts and her ordinary life merged with the rest of the forgotten women of her era.

Sybil Ludington was born in 1761 to Henry and **Abigail Ludington** in Fredericksburg, New York. Her father had worked his way up from private in the colonial New York militia to the rank of captain before the American Revolution. In 1760, he married his young cousin Abigail and the couple moved to the small village of Fredericksburg where he leased 200 acres. The mills he built there were the basis for the prosperity of the growing community; Fredericksburg was later re-named Ludington in recognition of his pivotal role in the foundation of the town. During the Revolution, Henry Ludington attained the rank of colonel of the 7th Regiment of the New York militia. He was elected member of the state legislature from 1778 to 1781 and again in 1786. He was a staunch Patriot, and was active during the war in the local committee of safety which prepared the defenses of the area and monitored the loyalty of the members of the community.

Sybil's mother Abigail was only 16 when Sybil, her first child, was born. By 1777, the year of her famous ride, Sybil was the eldest of eight children (her mother eventually gave birth to twelve—six girls, six boys). Abigail's life has also been obscured by the passage of time. As the wife of an important man, and the mother of a large and growing family, she undoubtedly relied heavily upon the assistance of her eldest daughter Sybil to help with cooking, cleaning, and raising the younger children.

In 1775, the American Revolution began when Americans in the colonies, resisting British imperial restrictions, fought British troops at Lexington and Concord. These battles in Massachusetts soon touched the lives of the Ludington family in Fredericksburg, New York, for New York saw some of the fiercest fighting of the Revolution. The former colony was strategically important for both the British and the Americans. The British calculated that if they controlled New York, they could cut New England off from the rest of the American colonies and cripple the budding rebellion. In 1776, British forces overwhelmed the Patriots on Long Island and reasserted British authority in New York City, the capital of the rebellious colony. While the British controlled this strategically important port city, the rest of the colony was engulfed in a civil war where the Patriot forces continued to resist British rule. The backcountry particularly was riven by skirmishes between Patriots and Tories, and community ties were shattered by accusations of treason, espionage, and disloyalty.

Fredericksburg and the sparsely populated surrounding countryside (less than 50 miles north of New York City) experienced all the terrors of the internecine conflict. There was so much contention in the area between Tory and Patriot supporters that in 1777 Colonel Ludington, along with John Jay and others, were appointed commissioners in charge of subduing the insurrections in the neighboring Dutchess and Westchester counties. One traveler on his way to Danbury, Connecticut, stopped at the house of Colonel Ludington and described some of the dangers of living in the middle of the conflict. A member of the First Continental Congress and a signatory of the Declaration of Independence, William Ellery arrived at the Ludington household at night and found Abigail and her young children home alone. Abigail described the horse stealers and Tory spies who terrorized the roads at night, and she reported that a guard patrolling the roads had been shot six miles from her home, while another man had also been murdered three miles away. Remembering Abigail's warnings, even Ellery and his two male traveling companions spent a nervous night at the Ludington farm. With Colonel Lud-

ington away much of the time, Abigail had only her elder daughters and two guns (only one of which worked) to help protect her young family from the nightly terrors of the war.

Patriot women like Abigail and Sybil Ludington did not just survive the war behind bolted doors, however. They found many ways actively to support the war effort. For instance, Colonel Ludington and his family were often targets of Tory sympathizers because of his activism on behalf of the Patriot cause. As a result, Sybil and **Rebecca**, the next eldest Ludington child, protected their family by acting as sentinels during the night to announce any Tory movements near the Ludington farm. Women during the Revolution bolstered their fighting male relatives with words of encouragement, and they provided shelter for Patriot sympathizers. They could even flex their consumer power by refusing to purchase imported English goods. Instead, they made their own clothes and even refused to drink tea. Few had the opportunity to show their support for the cause as dramatically or visibly as Sybil Ludington did on the night of April 26, 1777.

In late April 1777, the British, led by former governor of New York and British general William Tryon, raided the town of Danbury, Connecticut. Danbury was an important regional munitions and supply depot. The 150 militiamen stationed in the town were no match for the 2,000 British and Tory troops who proceeded to set fire to the storehouses; legend has it that "molasses and baconfat ran down the gutters like water." A lone messenger from Danbury reached Colonel Ludington's house 25 miles to the north later that night exhausted but filled with the news of the British raid. The colonel's regiment was sorely needed to assist the few remaining defenders of Danbury. Colonel Ludington's task of raising the 400 militiamen under his command was complicated by the fact that they were scattered throughout the surrounding countryside, each at home to prepare for the spring planting.

With no able man available for the task, the colonel enlisted the aid of his 16-year-old daughter to make the rounds of the countryside to rouse his militiamen. Sybil knew that it was unsafe to go out on the dark roads and ox-cart paths alone at night, but she swallowed any misgivings she may have had and bravely accepted her assignment. Her route was a 40-mile circuit of the neighboring farms and hamlets. Alone on her horse, Star, and equipped only with a stick to bang on the doors of the sleeping militiamen, Sybil traveled down through the hamlets of Carmel, Mahopac, Kent

Cliffs, Farmers Mills, and Peekskill. She then passed through parts of two New York counties before heading home through Stormville, reaching her own house at daybreak.

Roused by Sybil, the militiamen gathered at the Ludington farm, and they marched toward Danbury early that morning. They were too late to save that town, but they marched to Ridgefield to meet up with other Patriot forces. Colonel Ludington and his men arrived in time to engage General William Tryon's British and Tory forces. In the ensuing battle, the British suffered 27 fatalities, 120 wounded, and 29 missing men. The Americans lost over 100 men, and 250 men were wounded, while 50 were captured by the British. The burning of Danbury and the subsequent battle at Ridgefield were minor skirmishes in a brutal and extended struggle to control the interior of the former colony of New York. New York City remained occupied by British and Tory forces throughout the rest of the war; however, their control was continually contested by rural Patriots like the Ludington family.

Even though Sybil Ludington's ride did not save the town of Danbury, Connecticut, it was a dramatic and courageous example of the many, less obvious ways in which women were called upon to support the American war effort. Some women surprised their neighbors and friends by surpassing the limits of their traditional gender roles. While Sybil's ride was not as extraordinary as the exploits of a few women who became camp followers or actually disguised themselves as male soldiers in order to participate in the fighting, it did merit the comment of her contemporaries. General George Washington, who knew Colonel Ludington and had visited him in his home, acknowledged the event by sending his congratulations. Alexander Hamilton did the same. Women during the American Revolution were not expected to take such an active and visible role in the conflict. However, with the fighting going on in their own backyard, women like Abigail and Sybil Ludington bravely confronted the terrors of the war on a daily basis.

After the war and her bold ride, Sybil's life once again fades from view. In 1784, at the relatively late age of 23, she married Edward Ogden, a lawyer from Catskill, New York. She later moved with her husband to Unadill, New York, where they had four sons and two daughters. In 1839, Sybil Ludington died at the age of 78.

Sybil Ludington's remarkable ride through the night was commemorated by a statue erected by the town of Carmel, Connecticut, in 1961. A smaller replica of the statue is also on view in Washington, D.C. In 1974, the U.S. Postal Service remembered Sybil's ride by issuing an 8-cent stamp in her honor.

SOURCES:

Pelletreau, William S. *History of Putnam County, New York*. Philadelphia: W.W. Preston, 1886.

Somerville, Mollie. *Women and the American Revolution*. The National Society, Daughters of the American Revolution, 1974.

Townsend, Louise P. "Sybil Ludington: Bronze statue by *Anna Hyatt Huntington* Honors Teen-age Heroine," in *Daughters of the American Revolution Magazine*, pp. 580, 622.

SUGGESTED READING:

DePauw, Linda Grant. *Four Traditions: Women of New York During the American Revolution*. Albany, NY: New York State American Revolution Bicentennial Commission, 1974.

Johnson, Willis Fletcher. *Colonel Henry Ludington, A Memoir*. NY: n.p., 1907.

Jones, Mary Elizabeth. *The Midnight Ride of Sybil Ludington*. Wilton, CT: Pimpewaug Press, 1976.

Ludington, Ethel Saltus, and Louis Effingham de Forest. *Ludington-Saltus Records*. n.p.: The Tuttle, Morehouse & Taylor, 1926.

Christine Lambert,
Ph.D. candidate, Emory University, Atlanta, Georgia

Ludmila.

Variant of Ludmilla.

Ludmila (859–920)

Duchess of Bohemia, grandmother of Saint Wenceslas, and Christian saint of Bohemia. Name variations: Saint Ludmila, Ludmilla, Ljudmila. Born at Psov, a place also known as Melnik, about 859 CE; murdered on September 16, 920; daughter of a Lusatian Serb prince named Slavibor; married Borojov or Borivoj I, count of Bohemia (r. 871–894), in 873; children: three sons and three daughters, including Spithnjew also known as Spytihnev I (d. 915), king of Bohemia, and Ratislav also known as Vratislav I (887–920), duke of Bohemia (r. 912–920). Became a saint of Bohemia.

In the early 10th century, two women entered the center stage of a high drama which would determine who would be king of Bohemia, one of the most important regions of Central Europe. Legend portrayed their struggle in heroic terms: Ludmila championed Christianity and became a saint, while ❧➤ **Drahomira of Bohemia** defended paganism and ended her life in exile, branded a murderer.

Historical sources reveal little about the land of Bohemia before the 10th century. The earliest inhabitants of the area were a Celtic tribe, the Boii, from which the name "Bohemia" is derived. By 100 BCE, these Celts had been displaced by Germanic tribes who were themselves pushed from the region by the Slavic peoples who arrived in the 400s CE.

The Slavs entered Central Europe as the Roman Empire steadily crumbled under the onslaught of the Germanic invasions. The fall of Rome ushered in a chaotic period known as the Dark Ages; for nearly 300 years, little history was recorded. At the end of the 6th century, nomadic Avar tribes from the east invaded Central Europe and conquered most of the Slavs. After years of subjugation, the Slavs revolted and briefly maintained a precarious independence. Then, at the end of the 8th century, a new political power arose to the west under the leadership of Charlemagne, king of the Franks. The Roman Catholic Church crowned Charlemagne emperor, and acknowledged his domain as the heir of the Roman Empire.

Charlemagne's successors, known as the Carolingian Dynasty, began sending Roman Catholic missionaries to the pagan Slavs throughout the 9th century in order to convert them to Christianity. Simultaneously, the Eastern Roman or Byzantine Empire sent Eastern Orthodox missionaries. However, the spread of Christianity among the Slavs was slow and checkered, for many still clung to their pagan ways. More concretely, the Byzantine mission gave the Slavs their first written language. Further, Eastern Orthodox and Roman Catholic missionaries began to record some of the history of this tribal people.

The 9th century introduced new political challenges into the land of Bohemia. Moravia, a newly risen Slavic state, temporarily dominated the region. The Carolingian Empire to the west gradually fragmented under the press of the Vikings and internecine war. Nevertheless, the eastern part of the once mighty empire, comprised of Germans and consisting of a land area roughly corresponding to modern Germany, began making political inroads against Bohemia. Then a new invasion of eastern nomads, the Magyars, destroyed Moravian power in 894 CE and menaced Central Europe. Bohemia was caught between the German advance and the threat of the Magyars.

Before the Moravian collapse, Borivoj I, prince of Prague in western Bohemia and leading member of the Premyslid family, traveled to Moravia and accepted Christianity, allegedly from the hands of St. Methodius of the Eastern Orthodox Church. Borivoj had been born around 855 CE and married Ludmila in 873.

❧ Drahomira of Bohemia (d. after 932)

Duchess and regent of Bohemia. Name variations: Drahomire von Stoder; Dragomir or Dragomira (from the Slavic language, drah meaning "dear" or "precious" and mir meaning "world" or "peace"). Born in Germany (birthdate unknown); died after 932 in Bohemia; born into the Stodoran family; daughter of a chief of the Havolané tribe which lived north of Bohemia in Brandenburg; married Ratislav also known as Vratislav I (887–920), duke of Bohemia (r. 912–920); children: four daughters, of whom only the name of one (Pribyslava) is known; and three sons, Saint Wenceslas (b. around 907), Boleslav I (d. 972), and Spytihnev (who seems to have died while young). Fled to the tribe of White Croatians north of Prague.

Little is known of Drahomira's family or childhood, except that she was born into one of Germany's noble houses. She married Vratislav I, duke of Bohemia, and had three sons, (Saint) Wenceslas, Boleslav I, and Spytihnev (who seems to have died while young), and four daughters, of whom only the name of one (**Pribyslava**) is known. Drahomira was a staunch advocate of the pagan religion of Germany, but her husband was a Christian at a time when missionaries were bringing Christianity to Germany. Drahomira raised her son Boleslav in the pagan religion, although her elder son Wenceslas was brought up in the Christian church by his paternal grandmother, *Ludmila, whom Drahomira despised. Vratislav died in 920, and Wenceslas succeeded him as duke, although he was only 13. Ludmila was named regent for the boy, an event which increased the tension between Bohemia's pagan believers and its Christians. Drahomira quickly became the leader of the pagans and schemed to get rid of Ludmila. Ludmila was murdered on Drahomira's orders in 920, and Drahomira assumed the regency for her son.

The civil strife of the previous years evolved into civil war as pagans and Christians fought over the course of Bohemian worship and government. Drahomira and her pagans were outnumbered, and her Christian son Wenceslas dismissed his mother from the government when he came of age at 18. She continued to plot against the Christian faction, however, and was in the general vicinity when her son Boleslav murdered Wenceslas in 929. Wenceslas' deep piety and benevolence, as well as his death at the hands of his pagan brother, led the Bohemians to canonize him and worship him as Bohemia's patron saint. It is not known whether Drahomira lived to see the effects of Wenceslas' martyrdom in galvanizing the Christians to eliminate the remaining pagans of Bohemia, for she fled north shortly after his murder. Boleslav succeeded his brother and remained duke of Bohemia until his death in 972.

SOURCES:
Echols, Anne, and Marty Williams. *An Annotated Index of Medieval Women.* NY: Markus Wiener, 1992.
Jackson, Guida. *Women Who Ruled.* Santa Barbara, CA: ABC-Clio, 1985.

Laura York,
Riverside, California

Ludmila herself accepted Christianity shortly after Borivoj's conversion in 874.

Ludmila was the daughter of a Lusatian Serb prince named Slavibor. She seems to have been born at Psov, a place also known as Melnik, after the name of the regional castle. Psov, or Melnik, was located in Upper Lusatia, an area which bordered Bohemia. Various records refer to this general area as Milsko or the land of the Milcane.

Throughout his reign, Borivoj struggled against the Slavic pagans who resented his challenge to their traditional ways. He died at age 36 in 894. Ludmila received the castle of Tetín near the modern city of Beroun on the Mze River as a "widow's grant." Borivoj and Ludmila had had three sons and three daughters: the eldest son Spytihnev I became the new prince of western Bohemia.

Bohemia began to be recognized as a national state when Spytihnev and an eastern Bohemian prince called Viteslav journeyed to Regensburg, Bavaria, in 895 and placed their lands under the protection of the slowly rising German Frankish Empire to the west. By this move, the princes undoubtedly sought to maintain their independence from the Magyars.

Then [Drahomira] began to plot evil against [Ludmila] and sought every way to destroy her. Realizing this, Ludmila left for another town, one called Tetín. But [Drahomira] conspired with two boyars and sent them to Tetín.

—Prologue, *The Life of Saint Ludmila*

Although this submission may have been the only viable choice for the princes, this action opened the way to additional Roman Catholic influence from the west and thereby increased competition between the two mainstream variants of the Christian religion in Bohemia. Gradually, Roman Catholicism began to replace Eastern Orthodox. Association with the empire also embroiled the princes in future power struggles between Saxony and Bavaria, two regions which vied with each other for the imperial crown and sought political power in Bohemia.

According to the *Legenda Christiani*, Ludmila's conversion to Christianity had been sincere:

She was generous with alms, persevering in nocturnal devotions, devout in prayers, and perfect in charity and humble among the unknowing. She was so willing in her care for God's servants that to those to whom she

was unable to offer help during the light of day, she would send urgent help through her servants during the dark of night. . . . This mother to orphans, consoler to widows, and indefatigable visitor of the fettered and imprisoned was perfect in all good deeds.

Undoubtedly, she had a large hand in influencing her eldest son. Spytihnev fostered Christianity in Bohemia by building the churches of saints Peter and Paul at Budec and the Church of *Mary the Virgin at Prague Castle. Spytihnev was succeeded by his brother Vratislav I upon his death at age 40 in 915.

Little is known of Vratislav except that he built the Church of St. George in Prague and died at 33 years of age in 920, supposedly while fighting the Magyars. He had married Drahomira of the Stodoran family, whose father was a chief of the Havolané tribe which lived north of Bohemia in Brandenburg. Her tribe was part of the Veletians, a Baltic-Slavic tribal confederation who were sometimes known as the "Lutici" (meaning "Wild or Fierce Men") because of their warlike qualities and refusal to accept Christianity. Still, some sources suggest Drahomira had converted to Christianity herself. Ironically, Drahomira's name in Slavic meant dear or precious (*drah*) and world or peace (*mir*). Vratislav and Drahomira had seven children: three sons, (Saint) Wenceslas, Boleslav I, and Spytihnev (who seems to have died while young), and four daughters, of whom only the name of one (**Pribyslava**) is known.

Vratislav's untimely death left Bohemia with an heir, Wenceslas, who was only about 13 years of age, or five years short of the majority or legal age he would need to attain before he could assume the throne. Therefore, Drahomira was selected through the consensus of the Bohemian elites to rule as regent until Wenceslas came of age. Ludmila was placed in charge of the young noble's education.

Certainly, the stage had been set for potential political conflict, internally, and perhaps internationally. While Wenceslas' grandmother Ludmila was conspicuously Christian, his mother Drahomira came from a tribe steadfastly pagan. Most records indicate that pagan factions within Bohemia looked to Drahomira for an alternative answer to the new ways. Arnulf, duke of Bavaria, was sufficiently anxious about the Bohemian-Bavarian alliance to visit Wenceslas. The young future king assured Arnulf their relations would remain unchanged.

Wenceslas had been born in 907 CE near the town of Lubusin at Stochov. The Slavic priest

Paul of Prague Castle, who was Ludmila's confessor, baptized him and taught him his native language. He received formal instruction in Latin at school at Budec under the priest Ucen. Although he was an exemplary student, his studies were interrupted by internal strife involving the nobility of Bohemia who supported either his mother or his grandmother.

Historically, power elites within a country which has a young future ruler have been restless and have sought to press their own agenda, and 10th-century Bohemia was no exception. In addition to religion, the nobles who supported Drahomira seem to have been concerned about matters of state. Wenceslas was an exceptionally pious young man and may have ignored the necessary martial aspects of being a ruler in turbulent times. Historian A.P. Vlasto has suggested that the nobility of Bohemia feared Wenceslas would make a better monk than a warrior, and that Christianity, which espoused nonviolence, might not provide the philosophical strength needed to fend off outside aggression. Thus, some nobles believed Ludmila's influence on Wenceslas was negative.

Naturally, this faction encouraged Drahomira to take greater power upon herself. They pinned their hopes on the eventual succession of Wenceslas' younger brother, Boleslav, who enjoyed hunting and martial sport. According to the *Legenda Christiani*, this prospect may well have been consistent with Drahomira's own desires:

> Drahomira was no ordinary woman. She was energetic, ambitious and loved power. Her fiery character had been only imperfectly suppressed by the adoption of Christianity. Boundless ambition and jealousy drove her to crime.

Negotiations between Ludmila and Drahomira at this time were not cordial. Ludmila retired to her castle at Tetín and attempted to placate Drahomira by assuring her she did not desire undue power in Bohemia. Unfortunately, Drahomira determined to eliminate her rival and dispatched a party to Tetín led by two men, Gommon and Tunna. On September 16, 920, the marauders forced the castle gate and took Ludmila prisoner.

Seeing she was about to be killed, Ludmila asked to be beheaded so that her blood could flow in emulation of other martyrs. Instead, the two men strangled her with a rope. Tetín and the surrounding lands were seized by Drahomira's faction, and Ludmila's followers were hunted down or forced to flee.

But Drahomira's troubles were not over. Gommon and Tunna subsequently became powerful lords and too independent for Drahomira's taste. Therefore, her faction destroyed Gommon and his family. Tunna barely managed to escape with his life. Meanwhile, the people of Bohemia, deeply moved by the circumstances of Ludmila's death, visited her tomb where they testified miracles were occurring. Recognizing the danger of public reaction to her own rule, Drahomira built the Church of St. Michael over Ludmila's tomb so that she could claim the miracles were due to the archangel rather than to the grandmother of Wenceslas.

Despite this continuing turmoil, Wenceslas ascended the throne in 925 at the age of 18. He banished Drahomira to Budec, transferred Ludmila's remains to Prague, and recalled many of the priests who had been put to flight.

The rise of the young ruler and his aggressive attempts to Christianize Bohemia did not sit well with those who supported Drahomira and Boleslav. Although Wenceslas invited Drahomira back into society after her temporary banishment, she never enjoyed such power as she had previously. Consequently, her followers increasingly turned to her son and Wenceslas' brother, Boleslav. When Wenceslas had a son in 929, Boleslav saw his own path to the throne blocked in perpetuity.

International relations only deepened the divide between Wenceslas and Boleslav. Wenceslas favored an alliance with Saxony while Boleslav favored Bavaria. Saxony had become the leading political power in Central Europe under King Henry I the Fowler and had concluded a temporary peace with the Magyars. As Bohemia still had reason to fear a Magyar invasion, Wenceslas may have sought closer relations with Saxony in order to keep the Magyar threat at bay. In addition, since Bohemia could not have stood against the might of Saxony, Wenceslas may have preferred a closer relationship to possible subjugation.

Despite this rapprochement, Henry the Fowler invaded Bohemia in 929. While many Bohemian nobles favored resistance to Henry, Wenceslas submitted and accepted the Saxon king as his own overlord. Legend says Henry recognized Wenceslas as king of Bohemia in return. This was one more slap in the face of the nobles who favored Boleslav and an alliance with Bavaria.

Consequently, Boleslav decided to seize the throne. Determined not to assassinate Wenceslas in Prague where he was most popular, Boleslav lured his brother to a holiday feast at his own castle at Stará Boleslav. There, the two brothers met for the final time with Drahomira probably in attendance. As Wenceslas walked to church the following morning on September 28, 929, he was ambushed and killed by Boleslav and his henchmen.

Immediately, a reaction set in against the priests of Bohemia, and they and many of those loyal to Wenceslas were taken prisoner, killed, or forced into exile. Even Drahomira did not feel safe. Once more, she sought protection in flight, this time to the tribe of White Croatians living north of Prague. History records no more of her.

Boleslav, whom some called "the Cruel," at least proved to be an able ruler. During his reign, he extended the borders of Bohemia to include much of Moravia, Slovakia, Silesia, and Cracow. Ironically, Christianity, from its nucleus at Prague, continued to spread throughout Bohemia. In 932, Boleslav moved his brother's remains to the Church of St. Vitus in Prague. Wenceslas became the national hero, the national saint and the protector of the armies of Bohemia and subsequently of the Czech Republic. He primarily is known to the English-speaking world through the Victorian Christmas carol written by John Mason Neale "Good King Wenceslas."

Because of the importance of Wenceslas to the Bohemian-Czech nation, the lives of both Ludmila and Drahomira would have been significant even if they simply had remained in the roles of grandmother and mother. As the hand of fate dictated, however, both became key players and diametric opposites in a national and even international game.

In the end, the verdict of history judged each woman differently, polarizing them. The Roman Catholic Church elevated Ludmila to the sainthood between the 10th and 12th centuries and declared September 16 as her feast day on the Christian calendar. Drahomira became the proverbial evil woman.

SOURCES:

Dittrich, Zdenek R. *Christianity in Greater Moravia.* Groningen: J.B. Wolters, 1962.

Dvorník, Francis. *The Life of Saint Wenceslas.* Prague: Prague Archdiocese, 1929.

Farmer, David Hugh. *The Oxford Dictionary of the Saints.* 3rd ed. Oxford: Oxford University Press, 1992.

Holmes, George, ed. *The Oxford History of Medieval Europe.* Oxford: Oxford University Press, 1992.

Ingham, Norman W. "The Lost Church Slavonic Life of Saint Ludmila," in *Studia Slavica Mediaevalia et Humanistica.* Vol. 1, pp. 349–359.

———. "Sources on St. Ludmila, II: the Translation of Her Relics," in *International Journal of Slavic Linguistics and Poetics.* Vols. 31–32, pp. 197–206.

Jakobson, Roman. "Minor Native Sources for the Early History of the Slavic Church," in *Harvard Slavic Studies.* Vol. 2, 1954, pp. 39–73.

Kantor, Marvin. *Medieval Slavic Lives of Saints and Princes.* Ann Arbor, MI: University of Michigan Press, 1983.

———. *The Origins of Christianity in Bohemia: Sources and Commentary.* Evanston, IL: Northwestern University Press, 1990.

Seton-Watson, R.W. *A History of the Czechs and Slovaks.* London: Hutchinson, 1943.

Vlasto, A.P. *The Entry of the Slavs into Christendom.* Cambridge: Cambridge University Press, 1970.

SUGGESTED READING:

Englebert, Omer. *The Lives of the Saints.* NY: Barnes and Noble Books, 1994.

David L. Bullock, Ph.D.,
author of *Allenby's War: the Palestine-Arabian Campaigns, 1916–1918* (London: the Blandford Press, 1988)

Ludmilla.

Variant of Ludmila.

Ludmilla of Bohemia (fl. 1100s)

Duchess of Bavaria. Flourished in the 1100s; married Ludwig also known as Louis I (d. 1231), duke of Bavaria (r. 1183–1231); children: Otto II the Illustrious (1206–1253), count Palatine (r. 1231–1253, who married *Agnes of Saxony).

Ludovica.

Variant of Louisa or Luisa.

Ludovica (1808–1892)

Electress and queen of Bavaria. Name variations: Louisa Wilhelmina of Bavaria. Born in 1808; died in 1892; daughter of Maximilian I Joseph of Bavaria (b. 1756), elector of Bavaria (r. 1799–1805) and king of Bavaria (r. 1805–1825), and *Caroline of Baden (1776–1841); married Maximilian Joseph (1808–1888), duke of Bavaria; children: Louis also known as Ludwig (1831–1920); Charles Theodore also known as Karl Theodor "Gackl" (1839–1909, who married *Maria Josepha of Portugal); *Helene of Bavaria (1834–1890); *Elizabeth of Bavaria (1837–1898); *Maria Sophia Amalia (1841–1925, who married Francis II of Naples); *Mathilde of Bavaria (1843–1925); *Sophie of Bayern (1847–1897); Maximilian (1849–1893).

Ludwig, Christa (1924—)

German mezzo-soprano. Born in Berlin, Germany, on March 16, 1924; daughter of Eugenia Besalla and Anton Ludwig (both opera singers); studied with her mother and Hüni-Mihacek in Frankfurt; married Walter Berry, in 1957 (divorced 1970); married Paul-Emile Deiber (an actor and stage director), in 1972; children: (first marriage) one son.

Made debut in Frankfurt (1946), and Salzburg (1954); was a member of the Vienna Staatsoper (from 1954); made Metropolitan Opera debut (1959), appearing there for ten seasons; debuted at Bayreuth (1966–67), Covent Garden (1969); was an honorary member of the Vienna Staatsoper (1980).

Christa Ludwig's voice ranked with that of *Kirsten Flagstad and *Rosa Ponselle. Hers was the happy alliance of a beautiful instrument with fastidious training. Her parents **Eugenia Besalla** and Anton Ludwig both sang at the Vienna Volksoper. Her mother was her main teacher and for a long period "built" her voice note by note on the foundations of proper breath support. This strong training allowed Ludwig to perform a broad repertoire. She performed in Frankfurt, Darmstadt, and Hanover in the 1950s, moving on to the Vienna Staatsoper where she sang regularly from 1957. For several years, Ludwig focused on soprano roles before deciding to return to the mezzo-soprano repertoire. Although this choice was probably a good one, the higher voice seemed completely comfortable for her. As a soprano, she was probably the greatest Leonore of her time. Whether she performed Octavian in Strauss' *Der Rosenkavalier* or Fricka and Waltraute in Wagner's *Der Ring des Nibelungen*, Ludwig was equally impressive. When singing Wagner, her reserves seemed to be bottomless. A memorable performer, she continued to concertize into her 60s.

John Haag,
Athens, Georgia

Lugard, Lady (1852–1929).

See Shaw, Flora.

Lugo, duchess of.

See Elena (b. 1963).

Luhan, Mabel Dodge (1879–1962)

Early 20th-century American benefactor of the arts and of the Pueblo Indians of New Mexico, first through her salons in Florence and New York, later through her friendship and support of many artists and intellectuals at her home in Taos. Name variations: Mabel Dodge. Born Mabel Ganson on February 26, 1879, in Buffalo, New York; died in Taos, New Mexico, on August 13, 1962; daughter of Charles Ganson (a banker) and Sara McKay (Cook) Ganson;

married Karl Evans, in 1900 (killed in 1902); married Edwin Dodge (an architect), in 1905 (divorced 1914); married Maurice Sterne (an artist), in 1916 (divorced); married Antonio (Tony) Luhan (Lujan), in 1923 (died 1963); children: (first marriage) John Ganson Evans (a writer).

Ran a Florence salon (1905–12); ran her New York salon (1912–16); published her autobiographies (1933, 1935, 1936, 1937).

Selected writings: Lorenzo in Taos *(1932);* Intimate Memories: Background *(1933);* European Experiences *(1935);* Winter in Taos *(1935);* Movers and Shakers *(1936);* Edge of the Taos Desert *(1937);* Taos and Its Artists *(1948).*

Although she is now mentioned perhaps most often as a "friend of" or "patron to" many of the literary and artistic giants of the early 20th century (and not infrequently saddled with the adjective "eccentric"), Mabel Dodge Luhan was an intriguing and productive figure in her own right. She established influential intellectual salons, published eight books, and was a benefactor of the arts and of the Pueblo Indians over the course of a long and varied life that took her from a constricted household in upper-class Buffalo, New York, to the freedom of sunbaked Taos, New Mexico. Throughout it all, one senses, she remained intermittently frustrated.

Mabel Luhan was born in 1879 to Charles and **Sara Ganson** of Buffalo, New York. Her childhood was spent in the comfortable confines of the affluent in Buffalo, New York City, and the Berkshires, where material advantages were no shelter from loneliness. Her father was an angry and unhappy man who paid little attention to his daughter except when she was in his way, and her mother was kept busy managing the household in accordance with the long and detailed letters she received every day from her own mother, to which she also replied. In effect, Mabel's maternal grandmother ruled the roost from afar. In her autobiography, Mabel remembers that in her vain search for affection she would press her mouth to the Mother Goose figures on her wallpaper.

She had few memories of her early schooling at St. Margaret's Episcopal School for Girls, directly across the street from her parents' house. Then, her grandmother arranged for 16-year-old Mabel to attend Miss Graham's school in New York City. There she found a soul mate in **Mary Shillito**, another girl as isolated as she. Although her parents were American, Mary had spent most of her young life in Paris, and spoke little English; at Miss Graham's, she was almost overwhelmed by the loneliness of being in a strange country, far from home. Mary spoke to Mabel of her sister Violet, whom she idolized. Listening to her friend describe her sophisticated and cosmopolitan sister, Mabel fell under the spell of the remarkable **Violet Shillito** well before the two met.

Biographer **Winifred Frazer** notes that this friendship with Mary forecasts Mabel's later role as friend and facilitator to the smart set. The first summer after she entered Miss Graham's, Mabel traveled to Paris where she visited Mary and met the exceptional Violet. To read Dante and Plato, Violet had learned Italian and Greek; she was also studying higher mathematics and could perform Beethoven. Mabel, Mary and Violet spent the summer on long walks through the streets of Paris discussing philosophy, literature, and life, and by summer's end, Mabel, too, was in love with Violet.

After another year of school, Mabel made her New York debut at the Twentieth Century Club, which she had decorated for the occasion as a baronial hall with banners of coats of arms and reproductions of Rembrandt and Velázquez. Following her formal coming out, she spent her time in the idle ways then expected of young women of her class and entertained herself with the affections of men she had no desire to marry. When she became involved with the fun-loving and irresponsible Karl Evans, she wrote in her autobiography, it was because he was rumored to be engaged to another woman and thus could not marry Mabel. In July 1900, he tricked her into a secret marriage. For him, she said, "the world was a rabbit to hunt." A year and a half later, they had a son named John; several months after that, around the time that Mabel's father died, Karl was killed in a hunting accident.

In 1904, the young widow left Buffalo on a trip to Paris. En route she met Edwin Dodge, an architect who pursued her relentlessly in Paris. They were married in 1905 and, after a winter on the Riviera, settled in Florence. Seeing the great Italian city as indifferent to her upon her arrival, Mabel proclaimed: "I will make you mine!" It was in Florence that she began her career as a salon hostess and influential socialite.

She began with the renovation of a villa in the hills above Florence that had belonged to the Medici. With the Villa Curonia in which to entertain, Mabel courted Florentine expatriate society. Among the first figures she drew about her were Pen Browning, the son of Robert Browning and *Elizabeth Barrett Browning; Lady *Muriel Paget, who was considered the de facto head of English society in Florence; and Lord and **Lady Acton**, leaders of the local international set. Soon she was entertaining writers, actors, sculptors, singers, painters and other expatriate "characters." Mabel held grand house parties and banquets in Medicean style. Thinking of people in terms of the types of paintings they best represented, she began to cast herself as a Renaissance woman.

In the spring of 1911, in what proved to be a turning point, Mabel met *Gertrude Stein and her brother, American art connoisseur Leo Stein. Leo Stein was well known for his aesthetic philosophy, which involved enjoyment of and emotional reaction to art in addition to appreciation of technique and style; through him, Mabel learned to appreciate art, particularly modern art, in a new way. Turning from her absorption with the Renaissance, she began to embrace the 20th century. Through Gertrude Stein, with whom she had a close and creative relationship, she came to a clearer understanding of how language works, and of how to write. Mabel greatly

Mabel
Dodge
Luhan

admired her friend's use of language, and she was convinced that Stein's writing was important. Both sister and brother encouraged Mabel to pursue her own writing, and to follow her intuition, an influence which may have helped her to pursue a writing career later. Through this friendship, she also realized that she was tiring of her Florentine existence. The window to a new world that the Steins had opened provided the impetus Mabel needed to leave Florence, the Renaissance, and her husband behind. She moved to New York City.

In 1912, Mabel took up residence at 23 Fifth Avenue, just north of Washington Square, where she established her New York salon. Here she entertained journalists, socialists and psychiatrists as well as her usual collection of artists, writers and performers. Soon she had met Max Eastman, Alfred Stieglitz, ◄❧ **Neith Boyce** and Hutchins Hapgood, *Emma Goldman and *Margaret Sanger, all political and social radicals of Greenwich Village. Mabel later wrote: "Looking back upon it now, it seems as though everywhere, in that year of 1913, barriers went down and people reached each other who had never been in touch before; there were all sorts of new ways to communicate, as well as new communications."

❧▶
Boyce, Neith.
See Glaspell,
Susan for
sidebar.

I will make you mine!
—Mabel Dodge Luhan, to the city of Florence

The signal event of this new era was the International Exhibition of Modern Art, held at the 69th Regiment Armory on Park Avenue (and thus popularly known as the Armory Show). Everything about this exhibition—the location, the art, the artists—was being touted as new and different. Equally radical in a way was the organizers' intention of allowing the public to see, and to decide about for themselves, the new art of Europe free of the academic and other influences then controlling the art market. Although plans for the Armory Show were well under way when Mabel became involved, the exhibition might never have opened if not for her management of fund raising and publicity. Approximately 4,000 visitors crowded in on opening night; when the show closed a month later, 100,000 people had attended.

In the summer of 1913, Mabel became involved with John Reed, whom she met while they were both on the organizing committee for a pageant at Madison Square Garden. Representing the violent struggle of silk workers on strike in Paterson, New Jersey, the pageant drew a crowd of 15,000 and gained the strikers considerable publicity. Then newly graduated from Harvard and trying to establish himself as a writer, Reed would later become famous for his books about the Mexican and Russian Revolutions, and for his relationship with *Louise Bryant. Mabel was nine years older than Reed, and when they began living together without benefit of marriage their affair became an open scandal. Before the stormy relationship ended, she followed Reed as far as El Paso, Texas, when he was reporting on the Mexican Revolution.

After her breakup with Reed, Mabel moved to Finney Farm, in the Hudson River Valley, where she led a quieter life. She helped dancer *Isadora Duncan and her sister **Elizabeth Duncan** open a school on land she had given them, then became involved with the painter Maurice Sterne, whom she believed should be a sculptor. In 1917, despite the objections of friends, she married him. While continuing to live on the farm, she sent her husband on a trip to discover the American West, never realizing the change it would bring to her own life. His letters intrigued Mabel with their descriptions of the West, and particularly of the Native Americans living near Santa Fe, New Mexico. Finally she agreed to his pleas for her to join him, and with her son John traveled to Santa Fe, where Sterne had rented a house.

Mabel's love affair with the landscape of New Mexico and its people was immediate and long-lasting. During a day trip to Taos, she decided she wanted to stay there. On a visit to the nearby Taos Pueblo, she and her family were invited into a Pueblo Indian home, where their host, **Candalaria Luhan**, served them tea. When the guests were introduced to Candalaria's husband Tony Luhan, Mabel recognized him as a man she had seen in a dream. She began going to the pueblo daily to teach knitting to the local women. Despite the teasing of both her husband and her son, Mabel soon came to believe that her destiny was tied to Taos and to Tony Luhan. She sent Sterne back to New York, eventually obtaining a divorce. In 1923, at age 44, Mabel married Tony Luhan.

Although she had for some time been writing magazine articles and columns, it was only in Taos that she began writing books. And while her urban-style salon evenings were now a thing of the past, she provided the same creative stimulus on a quieter scale to a parade of houseguests. What began as a correspondence and later friendship with *Georgia O'Keeffe, who visited Mabel and her husband frequently, turned into an affair. (While Mabel was out of state, O'Keeffe also had a brief affair with Tony, about which she told Mabel in detail.) On a quest for a writer capable of bringing the wonders of Taos to the world's attention, Mabel sought, perhaps subconsciously, for someone who would accept her as his muse; English novelist D.H. Lawrence was the first writer on whom she pinned her hopes. In letters to both Lawrence and his wife *Frieda Lawrence, Mabel implored them to cease their wanderings and come to New Mexico. Lawrence, who had never been outside Europe, was skeptical about traveling to the American Southwest, but finally agreed to come to the U.S. by way of Asia. The couple's relationship to their self-appointed mentor became difficult as soon as they reached Taos. Mabel planned horseback expeditions to give Lawrence a feel for the New Mexico landscape and the local Native American culture, and gave the Lawrences a ranch to encourage them to stay; D.H. steadfastly resisted her efforts to control his work. He and Frieda spent some months in Mexico, and upon their return he wrote a story ostensibly about Mexico that used Taos as the background and Mabel as the main character. Believing that it should have been placed in its real setting of Taos (she had, after all, invited him to Taos solely to write about the place), Mabel viewed the story as a betrayal.

After the Lawrences departed for Europe, she turned to the poet Robinson Jeffers. Through correspondence, she developed a friendly relationship with Jeffers and his wife **Una Kuster Jeffers**, and wrote the first of her books, *Lorenzo in Taos*, to explain to him her disappointment with Lawrence. Portraying herself as a character in Jeffers' best-known poem, *Tamar*, she hinted that she had been transformed from a she-wolf to a dove through a marriage of peace with pain, an idea flattering to the poet since it was very close to his poetic outlook. *Lorenzo in Taos* succeeded in luring the poet and his wife to Taos, but Jeffers also failed to write about her beloved land in the way Mabel had hoped. The Jefferses did become regular guests, however, returning to visit Mabel every year.

Around this time, she had also become concerned about the welfare of the Pueblo Indians, and anxious to assist them in preserving their culture. In the 1920s, she had befriended John Collier, who was later appointed commissioner of the Bureau of Indian Affairs (BIA) and charged with the responsibility of implementing New Deal policies on the reservations. While Tony Luhan traveled throughout the Southwest as a liaison between the BIA and Native Americans, Mabel spent her time challenging Collier. Unhappy at first with some of his job appointments in the Taos area, she grew increasingly unhappy with Collier himself. Attuned mostly to the local needs of the Pueblo Indians, she rarely took into account the wider concerns of the BIA, or acknowledged that Collier himself was subject to the slow workings of government bureaucracy (she was not, however, alone in her criticism of him).

In the early 1930s, Mabel began her memoirs. These eventually spanned four volumes, and became, according to **Lois Rudnick**, "the most radical public act of her life." Originally undertaken as a form of therapy, and actively encouraged both by her analyst and by Lawrence, the memoirs eventually came to be seen by Mabel as serving a broader therapeutic purpose. She intended this portrayal of her own life to illuminate all that was wrong with Anglo-American society. Considering herself a product of society, she hoped to inspire others to change, or destroy, that very society. With the exception of her first volume, *Background*, the books were not well received. By the time of the Great Depression, an age of realism had set in that made the romanticism of the century's early years seem misguided and shallow, and the memoirs were criticized as confirmation of everything that had been wrong with the leftist movement prior to World War I.

By the end of World War II, Mabel was in her 60s, and confined herself to local interests. In 1948, *Taos and Its Artists* became her last published book, although she continued to write. After several years of serious illness, Mabel Dodge Luhan died in Taos in 1962.

SOURCES:

Frazer, Winifred. *Mabel Dodge Luhan.* Boston, MA: Twayne, 1984.

Luhan, Mabel Dodge. *Edge of the Taos Desert: An Escape to Reality.* Albuquerque, NM: University of New Mexico Press, 1987.

———. *Movers and Shakers.* Albuquerque, NM: University of New Mexico Press, 1985.

Morrill, Claire. *A Taos Mosaic: Portrait of a New Mexico Village.* Albuquerque, NM: 1973.

Nelson, Jane. *Mabel Dodge Luhan.* Western Writers Series, Boise: Boise State University Press, 1982.

Rudnick, Lois Palken. *Mabel Dodge Luhan: New Woman, New Worlds.* Albuquerque, NM: University of New Mexico Press, 1984.

SUGGESTED READING:

Gibson, Arrell Morgan. *Santa Fe and Taos Colonies: Age of the Muses, 1900–1942.* Norman, OK: University of Oklahoma Press, 1983.

Sarah Hunt,
freelance writer and historian, Las Cruces, New Mexico

Lü Hou (r. 195–180 BCE).
See Cixi for sidebar.

Luisa.
Variant of Louisa.

Luisa (1782–1824), **duchess of Lucca.**
See Maria Luisa of Etruria.

Luísa de Gusmão (1613–1666).
See Luisa de Guzman.

Luisa de Guzman (1613–1666)

Duchess of Braganza who played a decisive role in the restoration of Portuguese independence in 1640 and became queen of Portugal as a result. Name variations: Louise de Guzman; Luísa de Gusmão, Luisa de Gusmao, Luisa Maria de Guzmán. Born Luisa Francisca de Guzman on October 13, 1613, in San Lúcar de Barremeda in southern Spain; died on November 27, 1666, in Lisbon, Portugal; daughter of Juan Manuel Pérez de Guzman, duke of Medina Sidonia, and Juana de Sandoval; married João or John (1604–1656), 8th duke of Braganza or Bragança, later John IV the Fortunate, king of Portugal (r. 1640–1656), on January 12, 1634; children: Joanna of Portugal (1636–1653); Catherine of Braganza (1638–1705); Afonso or Alphonso VI (1643–1683), king of Portugal (r. 1656–1667); Teodósio or Teodosio (1645–1653), 9th duke of Braganza; Pedro or Peter II (1648–1706), king of Portugal (r. 1667–1706).

Born on October 13, 1613, in San Lúcar de Barremeda in southern Spain, Luisa Francisca de Guzman was the daughter of Juan Manuel Pérez de Guzman, duke of Medina Sidonia, and **Juana de Sandoval**. A close relative was the Count-Duke of Olivares, the chief minister of Philip IV, king of Spain. In 1633, Olivares saw an opportunity to advance family and state interests through Luisa's marriage to John, duke of Braganza (later John IV the Fortunate, king of Portugal). Since 1580, Spain had ruled Portugal, which nonetheless rebelliously sought an opportunity to reclaim its independence. Many Portuguese nationalists saw John as the legitimate claimant to their throne. Olivares believed that as a loyal Spaniard and John's wife, Luisa would help control Braganza's political activities. Thus, he helped arrange their marriage, which was celebrated on January 12, 1634, in Vila Viçosa, Portugal.

[John IV] might not have risked his vast possessions in a long and arduous struggle for the throne had it not been for the resolution of his Spanish wife, Luisa de Guzman.

—H.V. Livermore, *A New History of Portugal*

Luisa de Guzman proved to be more ambitious and independent-minded than Olivares had imagined. Her husband was the largest landholder in Portugal and the nationalists' prime candidate to head a revolt against Spain. Yet he proceeded cautiously, refusing to commit himself to the rebels' conspiracy. He was still temporizing in 1640 when crisis enveloped Spain and provided the opportunity for Portugal to seize its freedom. Olivares ordered John to raise troops to help put down a revolt in Catalonia. The conspirators selected nine o'clock on the morning of December 1 for their uprising, and Luisa pressed her husband to grab the chance. Her influence proved critical. The nationalists of Lisbon rose on the agreed day, and shortly thereafter John proclaimed himself king. Early in 1641, the Portuguese *cortes* (parliament) officially acclaimed him monarch. Luisa's ambition had helped make her queen of Portugal.

Of course, the new monarchy had to create an effective government and resist Spanish retaliation. When Olivares learned of the Portuguese rebellion, he refused to believe that the duke of Braganza, whom the Count-Duke called "stupid and drunk, without a glimmer of intelligence," could have carried out the coup d'état of December 1, 1640. Olivares found Luisa's behavior outrageous and ordered her name erased from their family genealogy.

Earlier, Luisa had given birth to two children. ***Joanna of Portugal** was born in 1636. Her sister ***Catherine of Braganza** arrived in 1638. Three other children were born after 1640: Alphonso (VI), heir to the throne (1643), Teodósio (1645), and Peter (1648, later Peter II). Sickness claimed Prince Teodósio in 1653.

On November 6, 1656, John IV died. Incapacitated by gout and lethargy, he had increasingly allowed Luisa and her confessor, Father Daniel O'Daly, to establish royal policy and negotiate an alliance with France to protect Portugal from Spanish revenge. Luisa governed as regent because Alphonso VI was only ten when the king died. Furthermore, illness had left the boy physically crippled and "mentally incapable" (in the words of a Portuguese historian), and the queen would have preferred Peter to inherit the throne. Nonetheless, the Braganzas had only recently gained the crown, and many advisers thought it important to proclaim Alphonso VI king. To guarantee France's help against Spanish aggression, Luisa hoped to marry her daughter Catherine to Louis XIV. When Spain and France signed the Peace of the Pyrenees in 1659, however, Louis decided to marry a Spanish princess, ***Marie Teresa of Spain** (1638–1683), thereby blocking Luisa's plans.

By 1661, a group of ambitious courtiers had won Alphonso VI's confidence, and they pressed him to govern personally. Unruly and poorly educated, Alphonso lacked the qualities to govern effectively, but he and his coterie insisted that

Luisa end the regency and declare him of age to rule. Luisa turned power over to him on June 23, 1662.

Before doing so, however, she had laid the necessary foundations for Portugal's survival as an independent nation with her descendants on its throne. From 1657 to 1661, Luisa and Alphonso's ministers had reorganized and strengthened Portugal's armed forces to resist Spanish aggression. In the spring prior to Alphonso VI taking the throne, she had completed negotiations for an alliance with the English, including the marriage of her daughter Catherine to Charles II, king of England. British forces helped repel several Spanish invasions of Portugal between 1662 and 1665, when Philip IV of Spain died, leaving his crown to Charles II, a disfigured and retarded four-year-old. This forced Spain to focus inward, and thus Portugal's security was increased.

Luisa de Guzman remained in the palace until March 1663, when she retired to the relative serenity of the Discalced Carmelite convent in Xabregas. She died there on November 27, 1666, leaving her adopted nation in her debt. Portugal owed "her the conditions for survival of the New Dynasty," writes Portuguese historian Joaquim Veríssimo Serrão, who continues, "no one can deny to the widow of [John IV] the merit of having defended vigorously the Restoration, of which she became one of the symbols."

SOURCES:
Elliott, J.H. *The Count-Duke of Olivares: The Statesman in an Age of Decline.* New Haven, CT: Yale University Press, 1986.

Livermore, H.V. *A New History of Portugal.* Cambridge: Cambridge University Press, 1966.

Raposo, Hippólito. *Dona Luisa de Gusmão; Duquesa e Rainha, 1613–1666.* Lisbon: Empresa Nacional de Publicidade, 1947.

Serrão, Joaquim Veríssimo. *História de Portugal.* 5 vols. Lisbon: Editorial Verbo, 1979.

Kendall Brown,
Professor of History, Brigham Young University, Provo, Utah

Luisa Fernanda (1832–1897)

*Spanish princess and duchess of Galliera and Montpensier. Name variations: Louisa Fernanda; Louise Bourbon; Louise of Spain. Born on January 30, 1832; died on February 2, 1897; daughter of Ferdinand VII, king of Spain (r. 1813–1833), and his fourth wife, *Maria Cristina I of Naples (1806–1878); sister of *Isabella II (1830–1904), queen of Spain; married Anton or Antoine (1824–1890), duke of Montpensier, on October 10, 1846; children: Amalie (1851–1870); Christine (1852–1879); Marie de Regla (1856–1861); Ferdinand (1859–1873); Anthony or Antoine Bour-*

*bon, 4th duke of Galliera and duke of Montpensier; *Maria Isabella (1848–1919); *Maria de las Mercedes (1860–1878, who married Alphonso XII, king of Spain); Philipp (1862–1864); Louis (1867–1874).*

Luisa of Baden (1779–1826).
See Elizabeth of Baden.

Luisa of Etruria (1782–1824).
See Maria Luisa of Etruria.

Luisa of Sicily (1804–1844).
See Louisa Carlotta of Naples.

Luise.
Variant of Louise.

Luise von Preussen (1776–1810).
See Louise of Prussia.

Luitgarde.
Variant of Liutgard.

Luitgarde (d. 800)

Queen of the Franks. Name variations: Liutgard; Luitgard. Died in 800; became fifth wife of Charles I also known as Charlemagne (742–814), king of the Franks (r. 768–814), and Holy Roman emperor (r. 800–814), in 794.

Luke, Jemima (1813–1906)

English hymn writer. Born Jemima Thompson on August 19, 1813, in London, England; died in 1906; married Samuel Luke (a Congregational minister), in 1843; no children.

Born Jemima Thompson in London in 1813, poet and hymn writer Jemima Luke was raised in a deeply religious family. Her father helped found the Sunday School Union, the Sailors' Society, the first Sailors' Home, and the Home Missionary Society, which was organized to send ministers out to isolated villages. In her autobiography *Early Years of My Life* (1900), Jemima recalled that the turning point in her life came at age ten; after

being punished for telling a lie, she attended a particularly moving church service that inspired her to live a truly Christian life.

Jemima also aspired to become a poet and by age 13 had some work published in a magazine called *The Juvenile Friend*. She then studied with **Caroline Fry**, a writer and editor of another magazine, *The Assistant to Education*. In her late teens, Jemima decided to become a missionary to India, in order to help young Hindu girls escape early marriages to men they had never met. Her father had agreed to sponsor her and pay her way to India when she was stricken with a virus and forced to cancel her plans. Following her recovery, she began to visit local schools to teach children to sing hymns, many of which she wrote herself.

Luke's most famous hymn, *The Child's Desire*, better known by its first line, "I think, when I read that sweet story of old," was written in 1841, while she was riding in a stagecoach on an errand for her father. "I'm quite certain God was there, whispering that song to me," she said later. She set the words to the tune of an old marching song she had once heard sung by school children. The work so impressed her father that he sent a copy to the *Sunday School Teachers' Magazine*, and it was also published anonymously in the *Leeds Hymn Book* of 1853.

Jemima Luke spent her later years editing missionary magazines for children and writing Sunday School curriculums to teach about missionary work. Following her marriage to Congregational minister Samuel Luke in 1843, she continued as a missionaries' advocate, encouraging single young women to travel to India to save young Hindu women.

SOURCES:
Parr, Lynn. "The Child's Desire," in *This England.* Autumn 1995.

Barbara Morgan,
Melrose, Massachusetts

Lukens, Rebecca (1794–1854)

American industrialist and iron manufacturer. Name variations: Rebecca Pennock Lukens; Rebecca Webb Lukens. Born Rebecca Webb Pennock in Chester County, Pennsylvania, on January 6, 1794; died near Coatesville, Pennsylvania, on December 10, 1854; eldest surviving child of six daughters and three sons (an older sister having died in infancy) of Isaac Pennock (an ironmaster) and Martha (Webb) Pennock; attended the Hilles Boarding School for Young Ladies, Wilmington, Delaware; married Dr. Charles Lloyd Lukens (a physician who later became an ironmaster), in 1813 *(died 1825); children: six, only three of whom, Martha, Isabella and Charlesanna, reached maturity.*

The eldest surviving child of nine, Rebecca Lukens was born in 1794 in Chester County, Pennsylvania, where her father's Quaker family had lived for several generations. Her father Isaac Pennock had given up farming in 1792 to start the Federal Slitting Mill, an ironworks on Bucks Run in Chester County. In 1810, he expanded the business, buying the Brandywine Mill at Coatesville. Although burdened by household chores at an early age, Rebecca later recalled her childhood "as wild, happy and joyous as youth could make me." At the Hilles Boarding School for Young Ladies in Wilmington, the second of two schools she attended, she excelled in French and chemistry and was popular with her teachers and classmates.

During a visit to Philadelphia with her father, Rebecca met Dr. Charles Lukens, a fellow Quaker who had a medical practice in Abington, Pennsylvania. The two fell in love and married in 1813, after which Rebecca busied herself with child rearing. She had six children, of whom only three survived to adulthood. In the meantime, Charles gave up medicine to join Isaac Pennock's iron business. After several years, he moved his family to the Brandywine operation, leasing the ironworks from his father-in-law. With the arrival of steam power, the Brandywine Iron Works began producing rolled iron and steel, much of which went to steamboat manufacturers. In 1825, the mill received a large commission from York, Pennsylvania, for plates to build an iron-hulled steamboat, the *Codorus*. Charles died that year, and Rebecca, fulfilling her husband's last wish, took over the mill, which was now almost bankrupt from the expenses of expansion. Further complicating matters was the fact that Charles died intestate, and the will of Rebecca's father, who had died a year earlier, was ambiguous. Because of litigation and several lawsuits brought by the Pennock heirs, Rebecca would not become the legal owner of the Brandywine Iron Works until 1853.

Rising to the challenge, Rebecca went to work with a newborn baby on her hip, putting to use much of what she had learned by observing her father and husband. While her brother-in-law, Solomon Lukens, handled day-to-day operations, she controlled the management of the mill, which included obtaining raw material for production and securing new contracts. Although plagued by seemingly insurmountable problems, including the Panic of 1837 (during which time she was forced to pay her workers with produce from her farm), and the tariff reductions of the 1840s, Rebecca managed to make a success of the business.

Under her direction, the mill manufactured iron for the new steam locomotives, producing such high quality plate that it was shipped to Boston and New Orleans, and was even exported to England. By 1849, Lukens had settled all her husband's debts and was able to retire, turning the business over to her two sons-in-law, Abraham Gibbons, Jr. and Charles Huston. She died at her residence near Coatesville in 1854, leaving an estate of over $100,000. In 1859, the mill was renamed Lukens Iron Works in her memory, and in 1890 was incorporated as Lukens Steel, a company that still flourishes. Rebecca Lukens, a pioneering CEO and perhaps the first woman in the United States to engage in heavy industry, was inducted into the National Business Hall of Fame in 1994.

SOURCES:

Gustaitis, Joseph. "Woman of Iron," in *American History*. April 1995.

James, Edward T., ed. *Notable American Women 1607–1950*. Cambridge, MA: The Belknap Press of Harvard University Press, 1971.

McHenry, Robert, ed. *Famous American Women*. NY: Dover, 1983.

Barbara Morgan,
Melrose, Massachusetts

Lukkarinen, Marjut

Finnish cross-country skier who won a gold medal at the 1992 Winter Olympics in Albertville-Les Saisies, France.

At the 1992 Winter Olympics in Albertville-Les Saisies, France, Finnish athlete Marjut Lukkarinen brought the obscure sport of cross-country skiing into sharp focus. Lukkarinen, who only took up racing seriously after receiving her nursing degree, and continued to work part-time at a hospital in her home town while training for the Olympics, won her gold medal in one of the fastest and closest cross-country skiing events in Olympic history. Her victory also involved some unusual tactics. Skiing in a snowstorm, Lukkarinen found herself trailing close on the heels of Czechoslovakian *Katerina Neumann. When she yelled "Track," as is customary in cross-country skiing to get someone to move over, Neumann did not provide clearance. Lukkarinen yelled again with no response, and finally resorted to tapping Neumann on the legs with her ski poles, which brought results. Italian **Manuela Di Centa** came in second in the race,

and Lukkarinen's teammate **Marja-Liisa Kirvesniemi** took third place. Neumann came in eighth.

SOURCES:

Wallechinsky, David. *The Complete Book of the Winter Olympics*. Woodstock, NY: The Overlook Press, 1998.

Lummis, Elizabeth (c. 1812–1877).

See Ellet, Elizabeth.

Lundeberg, Helen (1908–1999)

American artist. Name variations: Helen Feitelson. Born in Chicago, Illinois, on June 24, 1908; died in Los Angeles, California, on April 19, 1999; studied at the Stickney Memorial School of Art, Pasadena, California, 1930–33; married Lorser Feitelson (an artist).

A cofounder of California's Post-surrealist movement, an independent avant-garde trend of the 1930s, painter Helen Lundeberg evolved over six decades as one of America's foremost painters.

Rebecca Lukens

Born in Chicago in 1908, she grew up in California from the age of four and attended the Stickney Memorial School of Art in Pasadena, where she was greatly influenced by Lorser Feitelson, an early modernist whom she eventually married. The couple would work together for 50 years in the same studio. While still a student, Lundeberg had her work accepted in the Southern California Annual Exhibition at the San Diego Fine Arts Gallery, and also won honorable mention for her *Landscape with Figure* at the annual exhibition of the Los Angeles County Museum.

The California Post-surrealist movement that Lundeberg and Feitelson founded was an outgrowth of the European Surrealist movement of the late 1920s, which had its roots in the discoveries of Sigmund Freud. Drawing from the subconscious mind, the Surrealists, simply stated, expressed themselves through automatic intuitive imagery (automatism) and dreams, avoiding the consideration of rational thought. Lundeberg and Feitelson added another step to the process, however, attempting to reconcile subjective, introspective material with the logical and rational conscious mind. Lundeberg's painting *The Red Planet* (1939), discussed by Charlotte Rubinstein in *American Women Artists*, is characteristic of the Post-surrealist approach. "A red doorknob on a door suddenly reverses itself and can also be read as Mars, the red planet, moving in deep space. Unlike the surrealists, however, her lyrical shapes, colors, and forms, have an ordered classicism totally different from the chaos of the dream, and her themes are clearly readable." The same approach is found in *Double Portrait in Time* (1935), which appeared at a California Post-surrealist exhibit at the Brooklyn Museum in New York in 1936. The painting depicts a seated child, a little girl, with a flower and a clock set at two fifteen. The child is casting a shadow of an adult whose upper torso also forms a portrait on the back wall. The adult is studying the form of a flower intensely. Edward Alden Jewell, in a *New York Times* review of this painting, described Lundeberg as "handling a brush with cosmic authority."

Between 1933 and 1941, Lundeberg worked for the Southern California Federal Art Project, and her mosaic wall for Centinela Park in Inglewood is perhaps one of the largest works ever commissioned under the New Deal. Titled *The History of Transportation* (1940), the painting covers a 245-foot curved outdoor wall and is executed in an inexpensive mosaic made of colored cement and marble chips. Lundeberg also collaborated on other mural projects for the Federal Art Project, which she praised for providing artists with work during the Depression. On a more personal note, she praised it for allowing her to execute projects (such as the mosaic wall) that otherwise might not have been feasible.

Throughout the 1940s, Lundeberg continued in the Post-surrealist mode. In the late 1950s, she began to experiment in "hard-edge," a term coined by Jules Langsner to describe the work of a California group of avant-garde painters (John McLaughlin, Karl Benjamin, Frederick Hammersley, and Lorser Feitelson) who produced flat abstract works, using shapes of unmodulated color. Rubinstein suggests that although Lundeberg embraced the style, she never completely sacrificed subject matter or three-dimensional space. "The artist set herself the complex task of suggesting a landscape, interior, or still life, and at the same time reducing it to a satisfying hard-edge abstraction. Although she has never painted a landscape from nature, the Southern California ambiance of sea, sky, and desert is strongly felt in works like *Desert Coast* (1963) and *Waterways* (1962)."

Lundeberg had a retrospective at the La Jolla Museum of Modern Art in 1971, and another in 1979, at the Los Angeles Municipal Art Gallery. In 1980, following the death of Lorser Feitelson, a double retrospective was held at the San Francisco Museum of Modern Art. In 1996, Lundeberg's painting *Double View* was part of an exhibition, "City of Vapor: Capturing the Transitory Reality of Los Angeles," at the Tatistcheff/Rogers gallery in Santa Monica. Lundeberg died in April 1999.

In January 2000, another show opened at the Los Angeles County Museum titled "Four Abstract Classicists Plus One." It served as an echo of its original, 1959's "Four Abstract Classicists," curated by Langsner. The sponsors added a postscript:

> After World War II, Los Angeles proceeded to strengthen the foundation of Modernism begun the decade earlier. Art centers were expanded, prominent private collections were formed, young and mature artists examined, explored, experimented with techniques and expressions. Quietly, thoughtfully and independently, Feitelson, McLaughlin, Hammersley, Benjamin—and Feitelson's wife Helen Lundeberg worked at their easels. During the '50s, through the observations of Jules Langsner—writer, curator and *Los Angeles Times* art critic—and Peter Selz, then professor at the Claremont Colleges, a thread connecting these artists was noted. They all gathered in the Feitelsons' home with the goal of creating an exhibition; however, the climate for including Helen—a woman!—

was not prevailing. Helen Lundeberg is now included.

SOURCES:

Rogers, Terrence. "City of Vapor," in *American Artist.* Vol. 62, no. 672. July 1998, pp. 28–38.

Rubinstein, Charlotte Streifer. *American Women Artists.* Boston, MA: G.K. Hall, 1982.

Barbara Morgan, Melrose, Massachusetts

Lundequist, Gerda (1871–1959)

Swedish actress. Born in Stockholm, Sweden, in 1871; died in 1959; graduate of the Stockholm Academy of Music.

Called the "Swedish Bernhardt," actress Gerda Lundequist studied drama at the Stockholm Academy of Music and made her debut in 1889, in Strindberg's *Mäster Olof.* Spending most of the 1890s in Göteborg, she returned to Stockholm in 1896, and thereafter distinguished herself in such works as Leo Tolstoy's *Resurrection* and Maurice Maeterlinck's *Monna Vanna.* By 1906, she was considered one of the country's leading tragic actresses, with a range that included Antigone and Lady Macbeth (***Gruoch**), as well as more modern characters such as Mrs. Alving in Henrik Ibsen's *Ghosts.* Known for her sensuality and expressive voice, Lundequist appeared on stage until 1940. She also made several films, including the Mauritz Stiller classic *The Gösta Berling Saga,* which also marked the second screen appearance of ***Greta Garbo.** Lindequist's last film was *Giflas* (1955).

Luneburg, duchess of.

See Sophia of Mecklenburg (1508–1541).
See Dorothy of Denmark (1546–1617).

Lunjevica-Mashin, Draga (1867–1903).

See Draga.

Lunyevitza-Mashin, Draga (1867–1903).

See Draga.

Lupescu, Elena (c. 1896–1977)

Mistress and later wife of the ruler of Rumania, widely thought to be the power behind the throne, who heightened political tensions in her country throughout the 1930s. Name variations: Helena; Elenutza; Magda; Madame Lupescu; (nickname) Duduia. Pronunciation: Loo-PES-que. Born on September 15, possibly in 1896, in Hertza, Moldavia, Rumania; died on June 28, 1977, at the resort town of Estorial outside Lisbon, Portugal; daughter of a small-town Jewish druggist named Nicolas Grünberg Wolff, who changed his name to the Rumanian equivalent, Lupescu, and Elizei Falk Wolff, later Elizei Lupescu; attended Pitar Mos convent school, 1907–13; married Ion Tampeanu or Timpeanu, a lieutenant in the Rumanian army, in 1916 (divorced 1920); became third wife of the exiled Carol II (1893–1953), king of Rumania (r. 1930–1940), on July 5 (some sources cite June 3), 1947; no children.

Moved with her family to Jassy (1912); began love affair with Prince Carol (1923); during Carol's trip to England, started open relationship with him, which forced him to renounce his right to the Rumanian throne (1925); Carol's son Michael became heir to throne (1926); on death of King Ferdinand of Rumania, Michael named king, regency established (1927); returned with Carol to Rumania where he became king, also founding of the Iron Guard (1930); Carol established a royal dictatorship (1938); German-Soviet alliance, start of World War II (1939); loss of Rumanian territory; under German and Russian pressure, Elena and Carol forced into exile (1940); death of Carol (1953).

Elena Lupescu was one of the most colorful and politically influential figures in Rumania during the first half of the 20th century. Her personal tie to Prince (later king) Carol II of Rumania gave her enormous power, but it also provided Carol's political enemies with a potent weapon to use against him.

The kingdom of Rumania went through decades of political and economic turmoil following its creation in the mid-19th century. Ruled by kings drawn from the Hohenzollern family of Germany, it was endowed with rich resources, such as oil and fertile land. Nonetheless, the predominantly peasant population remained impoverished. Rumania's peasantry showed its temper by striking out at the country's Jewish minority in 1899 and rising up in a massive rebellion in 1907.

The political scene was traditionally dominated by venal leaders, both in Parliament and within the royal court. During World War I, Rumania was invaded by Germany and Austria and temporarily forced out of the conflict in 1917. Nonetheless, the country ended up on the winning side. As a reward for its efforts, it obtained the vast province of Transylvania, a traditional goal of Rumanian nationalists. A postwar land reform took place, stimulated by fear that the Russian Revolution might promote a new peasant uprising in Rumania, but the economic status of the peasantry remained pitiable. Opening the country up to foreign investors and rapid industrialization brought no widespread benefits, but it did heighten the opportunities for the legendary corruption at the top of the system.

The woman who dramatically shook Rumanian affairs was born in the small town of Hertza located in the northern province of Moldavia. Her various statements about her age make her date of birth uncertain, but it seems likely she was born in 1896. Her father Nicolas Grünberg Wolff was a Jewish druggist. Her mother **Elizei Falk Wolff** was from Vienna and was also Jewish. In the face of Eastern European anti-Semitism, first her mother, then her father converted to Christianity. In a further effort to assimilate into a hostile society, Elena's father changed Wolff into its Rumanian equivalent, becoming Mr. Lupescu. She herself became known in her family by the nickname Elenutza.

The young woman grew up in the port city of Sulina on the Black Sea and then in Bucharest,

Elena Lupescu

where in 1907 she was sent to a convent school, Pitar Mos, run by German nuns. Her six years of study there gave her a fluent command of German. Even before she had finished her school years, she had become a conspicuously beautiful young woman, with reddish hair, an alabaster complexion, and green eyes. Traveling with her family to the resort city of Sinaia or their new home in Jassy, she easily attracted the attention of young men.

In 1916, in the midst of World War I, Lupescu was married to an army lieutenant named Ion Tampeanu, though she continued to see other men, notably army officers. Her complaints about her husband's lack of funds—he was not considered a particularly promising or successful officer—led to violent quarrels. In 1920, the marriage ended in divorce. Sources disagree over which member of the couple initiated the proceedings.

Over the next several years, Elena Lupescu became a prominent member of Bucharest's café society. Her name was linked with a number of men who had become wealthy during the war and the immediate postwar period. Dissatisfied with the prospect of a permanent liaison with an individual from this circle, Lupescu deliberately set out to become the mistress of the crown prince.

Prince Carol had already gained a reputation as an attractive but irresponsible member of the royal family. In 1918, he had abandoned his duties as an army officer and eloped with ❧▶ **Jeanne (Zizi) Lambrino**, the daughter of a general. The marriage, to a woman his parents deemed unsuitable, ended formally with an annulment in early 1919, but Carol kept seeing Zizi for another year. A more acceptable marriage to Princess ❧▶ **Helen of Greece** in 1921 quickly produced a child, Michael, but all of Rumania knew that their relationship broke down soon after.

Elena approached the task of meeting Carol with energy and zeal. Through her contacts in Bucharest society, she was able to attend events put on by charities of which Carol was the honorary head. These efforts apparently succeeded, and Carol began to ask about the attractive redhead. A dashing sea captain named Tautu emerged as the link between the two. A frequent party-giver, he was both a friend of the crown prince and a friend, possibly even a former lover, of Elena. At one of Tautu's parties in 1923, the two finally met formally, and Carol quickly became infatuated.

Tautu inadvertently played a role in solidifying the burgeoning love affair. Alarmed at Carol's growing affection for Elena, Tautu staged a dramatic scene in front of her and the crown prince in the midst of a party. Throwing Elena's nightgown in her face, he made it clear that she had been his lover. Elena defused the situation with a remarkable display of coolheadedness. She asked dramatically if there was a gentleman present who would "protect the honor of a helpless woman." Carol took her arm in a display of support.

At first, they were discreet about their meetings, but, in time, King Ferdinand I of Rumania confronted his son with knowledge of the love affair. Carol gave an insincere pledge that he would give up Elena. When the king learned that the romance was continuing, it was Elena who responded by temporarily dropping out of sight. By now, Bucharest society whispered incessantly about "Duduia," Carol's affectionate name for Elena. The term meant "young lady" in the dialect of her native Moldavia.

Events took a dramatic turn in 1925 as Carol's relationship with Elena became entangled with Rumanian politics. Sent to Britain for the funeral of Queen *Alexandra of Denmark, Carol was supposed, according to his mother Queen *Marie of Rumania (1875–1938), to get a lesson in royal responsibilities. In fact, Elena secretly also left Rumania, met him in Paris, and carried their love affair to a new level of passion. Carol thereupon informed King Ferdinand and Queen Marie that he was renouncing his right to succeed to the throne. The queen, particularly outraged, proclaimed to her son, "One doesn't give up a throne for a Madame Lupescu." (During these dramatic events, a newspaper reporter misstated her first name, making her into "Magda Lupescu." As her biographer notes, "Magda was somehow such a suitable name for the girl friend of a Balkan prince" that the press continued to use it for the rest of her life.)

The political dimension of the scandal reflected the hostility of national leaders like Ion Bratianu to Carol as a future king. They apparently encouraged Lupescu to meet Carol in Western Europe, in order to widen the gap between Carol and his family. They also convinced the king to dispatch an army general with orders to Carol to return to Rumania, knowing that Carol was likely to refuse such a tactless overture. They were not disappointed. On December 28, 1925, Carol renounced his right ever to return to Rumanian soil along with his right to the throne. His young son Michael now became next in line.

Carol may well have been shocked by the speed with which his renunciation of the right to succeed his father was accepted and absorbed by

Lambrino, Jeanne (1898–1953)
Rumanian royal. Name variations: Joanna Labrina; (nickname) Zizi. Born Joanna Mary Valentina Lambrino on October 3, 1898, in Roman, Rumania; died on March 11, 1953, in Paris, France; daughter of Constantin Lambrino and Euphrosine (Alcaz) Lambrino; married Carol II (1893–1953), crown prince, then king of Rumania (r. 1930–1940), on August 31, 1918 (marriage annulled 1919); children: son, Mircea Carol Hohenzollern (b. January 8, 1920).

Helen of Greece (1896–1982)
Princess of Greece. Name variations: Helen Oldenburg; Helen of Greece; Helen of Romania; Helen of Rumania. Born on May 2 or 3, 1896, in Athens, Greece; died on November 28, 1982, in Lausanne, Switzerland; eldest daughter of Constantine I, king of Greece (r. 1913–1917, 1920–1922), and *Sophie of Prussia (1870–1932); sister of George II, king of the Hellenes; married Carol II (1893–1953), crown prince, then king of Rumania (r. 1930–1940), on March 10, 1921 (divorced, June 21, 1928); children: Michael (b. October 25, 1921), king of Rumania (r. 1927–1930, 1940–1947).

the Rumanian political system. He had perhaps hoped that a wave of public sympathy in Rumania would let him keep both Lupescu and his rights to the throne. The scandalous semi-royal couple now found themselves wandering in Western Europe, and they settled in Paris in the spring of 1926. The French newspapers lavished attention on the two of them.

The relationship between the exiled prince and his glamorous mistress reflected their respective personalities. Carol's weak and indecisive nature could not stand up to Elena's firmness. Fearful of her temper, he became increasingly dominated by her will. For example, when she reinvented and glamorized the story of her past life for visitors, he beamed with delight. Meanwhile, Princess Helen of Greece, the mother of his child, obtained a formal divorce from her straying husband in 1928.

The tug of politics remained strong, and a stream of visitors appeared in Paris to urge Carol to return home. The death of King Ferdinand in the summer of 1927 made Carol's five-year-old son Michael the king, although real power rested in the hands of a council of regents. Carol was outraged during these events by the government's refusal to let him return to Rumania to attend Ferdinand's funeral. With Elena spurring him on, the lackadaisical Carol grew increasingly committed to regaining the throne. The death of

Carol's political enemy Ion Bratianu in late 1927 increased his chances for success.

As she became a public figure, Elena made a substantial effort to avoid the limelight. Though she dodged newspaper interviews, the very lack of information about her relationship to Carol fed a wave of rumors. In 1927, she had an autobiography ghostwritten and published in the London *Sunday News*. With Carol thinking about a return to his country, the document was designed to ease the negative memories of his abdication. Among other points, in a concession to the prevalent anti-Semitism of Rumania, Elena's ghostwriter took great pains to stress that she was not Jewish. The account likewise made her several years younger.

> $\mathcal{S}$he kept Rumania in a constant state of turmoil for nearly fifteen years.
>
> —Alice-Leone Moats

A comic opera plot to bring Carol back, supported largely by military officers, failed dismally in 1928. But Carol's effort two years later succeeded. It was facilitated, in part, by the ineptitude of the council of regents. The growing economic crisis within Rumania brought on by the worldwide Depression heightened the instability of the political situation. Finally, the leader of the Peasant Party and Prime Minister Iuliu Maniu thought Carol's presence as constitutional monarch would shore up Maniu's government. Maniu insisted, however, that Carol return alone; his mistress Elena Lupescu was not to join him in Rumania.

When Carol flew alone to Bucharest in early June 1930, reporters immediately surrounded Elena, who had been left behind in France. She announced she had pleaded with Carol to return home. Moreover, she stressed how she had "renounced my perfect love." With these words barely out of her mouth, she made her way to Switzerland and then went on to Rumania. In short order, Carol deposed his son Michael and became King Carol II.

Within a few weeks of his return, Carol summoned Maniu to the royal palace to inform the prime minister that Lupescu would return to Rumania. Despite Carol's earlier pledges, he now insisted that he could not and would not live without her. By this time, Lupescu had already returned and was living in seclusion in Sinaia. By the fall, Carol permitted her to appear in public in the country's capital.

Word of her reemergence spread like wildfire even though newspapers, fearful of the king's re-action, refused to put the event into print. The political repercussions were immediate, as Maniu, considered by many the most capable leader in the country, was forced out of office. He had been hopelessly compromised by his actions in bringing Carol back to Rumania with the latter's false promise that Lupescu would remain in the West.

The political scene in Rumania remained troubled. Carol set out to weaken all of the existing political parties in order to strengthen his own position. These political maneuvers took place against the background of continuing poverty and misery for the country's peasant majority. Moreover, Carol's reign was compromised by the popular view that Elena was the true decision-maker for the couple. Rumania's fragmented political system allowed the king, or perhaps Elena, enormous scope in manipulating individual leaders and parties. Meanwhile, a fascist movement led by the charismatic figure Corneliu Codreanu emerged to offer a radical alternative to the existing system. Codreanu's Legion of the Archangel Michael (later known as the Iron Guard) offered a program of anti-Semitism, attacks on the existing form of government, and support for the hard-pressed peasantry.

Elena was ostracized by much of the country's aristocracy despite Carol's persistent efforts to get them to accept her. Her power remained visible, however, in the stream of petitioners who appeared at her home to ask for favors from the government. In a continuing effort to cover her Jewish origins in a country noted for its hostility to Jews, she encouraged the circulation of a wild rumor that claimed she was the illegitimate daughter of Carol's great-uncle, King Carol I of Rumania, who had ruled the country from 1866 to his death in 1914.

The traditional corruption of both the royal court and the government descended to new depths in the 1930s, with a corresponding fall in Carol's popularity. Rumanian authorities had long been notorious for enriching themselves in office, but the new regime seemed particularly open to such corruption. One former Cabinet minister described the king's motives succinctly: "The second Carol had even more reason than the [other members of the royal family] to want money; after all, he was forced to satisfy Elena's demands." Elena added directly to the atmosphere of scandal by selling her influence; so too did her father, her brother, and more distant relatives. The renovation of the royal palace created an especially lucrative opportunity for corrupt architects and contractors with Lupescu connections.

The unmarried couple maintained a semblance of propriety, although it fooled no one. Elena kept her own residence and rarely visited the royal palace. On the other hand, they played the role of man and wife, host and hostess, king and queen, at private gatherings at the king's villa in Sinaia.

The rising strength of the Iron Guard in the face of government ineptitude and the hardships brought on by the worldwide economic crisis led to flashes of violence. Carol had no steady policy *vis-à-vis* the Iron Guard. Sometimes he seemed willing to cooperate with it, but, in early December 1933, he sanctioned a brutal crackdown on the organization during which thousands of its members were arrested. In response, Prime Minister Ion Duca was killed by Iron Guard assassins later that month.

In early 1938, Carol ended the pretense of parliamentary government and established a royal dictatorship. The party he founded to match the new system, the National Rebirth Front, was modeled on the Fascist and Nazi parties of Benito Mussolini's Italy and Adolf Hitler's Germany. Lupescu's position in a system that smacked of official anti-Semitism now seemed threatened; these events showed a rare example of the king acting without her direction. In contacts with official German emissaries, she learned that Hitler wanted to cooperate with Carol; the German dictator insisted, however, that she must go into exile in Switzerland. She heatedly refused to consider such a step, and her personal hold on Carol remained secure.

By the close of 1938, both Rumania's international and domestic situations had become critical. The Munich Agreement, which had given Hitler control over Czechoslovakia, brought German power closer than ever to Carol's kingdom. The Rumanian monarch visited Britain, then Germany, hoping to find friends in the international community. At home, Carol's officials, possibly without his knowledge, cracked down once again on the Iron Guard. This time Codreanu and the top officials of the organization were murdered. Hitler was outraged and promised to destroy Carol.

A new spasm of violence followed the outbreak of World War II in September 1939. Members of the Iron Guard assassinated Rumania's prime minister; the government responded by killing Iron Guard members in every province. In a ghastly spectacle attributed by the public to Elena Lupescu, their bodies were placed on display in city squares throughout the nation.

The era of Carol and Lupescu came to a brutal end in 1940. Caught between Nazi Germany and the Soviet Union, Carol found himself helpless as these powerful neighbors tore away at Rumanian territory. Soviet forces occupied the northern regions of Bessarabia and Bukovina. Backed by Hitler and Mussolini, Hungary retook the western region of Transylvania, arousing a violent public reaction among Rumanian nationalists.

In early September 1940, an uprising of the Iron Guard seized key government centers in Bucharest while unorganized mobs took control of the streets. Carol hoped in vain to find a solution to the crisis; Elena was more realistic and began packing. She knew that the anger of the crowds was directed in a personal way at her. At the height of the unrest, Iron Guard forces approached the royal palace where Elena had taken refuge. Using the pejorative nickname by which she had become known, they called out: "Give us the She Wolf."

In these tumultuous circumstances, the key figure was the army strongman, General Ion Antonescu. He was determined to take power, and Carol's unpopularity, heightened by the king's connection with Lupescu, convinced the general that Carol could not remain in Rumania even as a figurehead. Without signing a formal statement of abdication, Carol nonetheless awarded the crown to his son Michael.

Along with their longtime courtier Ernesto Urdareanu, various servants, five dogs, and tons of paraphernalia, Carol and Elena fled by train to Hungary. As they approached the border, they learned that Iron Guard bands were waiting to attack the train. Lupescu was their main target, and she had a nervous collapse due to the strain. The train, moving at full speed, crossed the frontier as bullets peppered the passenger wagons. Elena lay in the train's bathtub to shield her from danger, while Carol shielded her with his body.

The fugitives went on to Switzerland, France, and Spain before settling in Mexico in 1941. Urdareanu remained their constant companion in the role of chief royal servitor, and Elena busied herself with the Red Cross. She and Carol were pleasantly surprised to discover that British and American expatriates in Mexico welcomed them into local society. They also found an unexpectedly warm welcome from the Soviet ambassador to Mexico. In 1944, this intermediary for Joseph Stalin hinted to Carol that the Soviet government might aid him to regain the Rumanian throne. With this in mind, Carol and Elena moved to Brazil. Located farther from the eyes of the American government, Brazil seemed a more comfortable spot from which to launch Carol's return. The couple soon discovered, however, that the Soviets had no serious interest in promoting their return to Bucharest.

One dramatic event took place during their Brazilian exile. In the summer of 1947, Lupescu seemed near death from pernicious anemia. Carol responded to the crisis by finally marrying her. The Brazilian government removed all legal obstacles to an immediate ceremony, and the longtime lovers were formally linked in marriage on July 5. A few days later, aided by a series of blood transfusions, Lupescu made a spectacular recovery. Following their marriage, and at the insistence of the courts in Brazil, she was known as "Her Royal Highness Princess Elena of Rumania."

Searching for a permanent refuge in a cooler climate, the two used their connections in the Brazilian government to get permission to take up residence in Portugal. They settled in Estoril, a fashionable seaside resort near Lisbon, set up a small but formal royal household with Urdareanu as royal chamberlain, and entered Lisbon society, although their welcome turned out to be a tempered one. The women of the Portuguese aristocracy in particular rejected instructions that they were required to curtsy to "Princess Elena." Carol and his wife found themselves entertaining noblemen who conspicuously left their wives at home.

Elena spent her last years with Carol playing an increasingly dominant role in his life. The former king had little to do besides writing his memoirs, and he found himself constantly in her company and under her supervision. A signal event in their routine was a formal ceremony in 1949 in which they were married by the authorities of the Rumanian Orthodox Church.

When Carol died suddenly on April 3, 1953, most of his family refused to attend the funeral. Thus, Elena was the central figure at the final ceremony, calling out that she too wished to die, and collapsing in the arms of the other mourners. Afterwards, she also found herself at the center of an ugly family dispute over Carol's financial resources. Legal records indicated that he had died leaving only a modest bank account, but Elena continued to live in considerable luxury. She had to fend off lawyers representing Carol's blood relatives who were convinced she had squirreled away a fortune in Rumanian assets.

Following Carol's death, in a basically meaningless gesture, Elena announced that his son Michael should not inherit the throne. With Rumania now under Communist control, it was a matter of no practical importance that Carol had not formally abdicated in 1940. Nonetheless, for her own reasons, Elena felt the claim to the crown should go to a more distant member of the Hohenzollern family.

Elena Lupescu remained in Portugal after becoming a widow. She lived in seclusion for almost a quarter of a century, and died at Estoril on July 28, 1977.

The story of the Jewish outsider who rose to power alongside the ruler of Rumania remains one of the most unlikely but fascinating tales of the 20th century. John Gunther has called her "one of the most remarkable women of the time." For **Alice-Leone Moats**, "Lupescu's life is a striking example of just how much stranger truth can be than fiction."

SOURCES:

Gunther, John. *Inside Europe*. Rev. ed. NY: Harper & Brothers, 1938.

Moats, Alice-Leone. *Lupescu*. NY: Henry Holt, 1955.

Pakula, Hannah. *The Last Queen: A Biography of Queen Marie of Roumania*. NY: Simon and Schuster, 1984.

Seton-Watson, Hugh. *Eastern Europe between the Wars, 1918–1941*. 3rd ed. Hamden, CT: Archon Books, 1962.

Stavrianos, Leften. *The Balkans since 1453*. NY: Holt, Rinehart and Winston, 1958.

SUGGESTED READING:

Elsberry, Terence. *Marie of Roumania: The Intimate Life of a Twentieth-Century Queen*. NY: St. Martin's, 1972.

Polonsky, Antony. *The Little Dictators: The History of Eastern Europe since 1918*. London and Boston: Routledge & Kegan Paul, 1975.

Neil M. Heyman, Professor of History, San Diego State University, San Diego, California

Lupescu, Magda (c. 1896–1977).

See Lupescu, Elena.

Lupicinia-Euphemia (d. 523).

See Theodora (c. 500–548) for sidebar.

Lupino, Ida (1914–1995)

American film and television actress, writer, director, and producer, who was one of the few female directors in Hollywood during the 1950s and 1960s. Born on February 4, 1914, in London, England; died on August 3, 1995, in Burbank, California; daughter of Stanley Lupino (a British film comedian) and Constance O'Shay (a British actress); sister of Rita Lupino (an actress); educated at private schools and at the Royal Academy of Dramatic Arts; married Louis Hayward (an actor), in 1938 (divorced 1945); married Collier Young, in 1948 (divorced 1950); married

*Howard Duff (an actor), in 1951 (divorced 1983); children: (third marriage) one daughter, **Bridget Duff.***

Made her film acting debut at 14 in England before emigrating to Hollywood (1933); appeared in more than 60 films (1933–1982); directed her first film (1949), becoming one of the few female directors in Hollywood (1950s–1960s); also wrote, directed and produced for television, as well as acting in several of her own productions.

Filmography: Her First Affaire *(UK, 1933);* Money for Speed *(UK, 1933);* High Finance *(UK, 1933);* Prince of Arcadia *(UK, 1933);* The Ghost Camera *(1933);* I Lived With You *(UK, 1933);* Search for Beauty *(1934);* Come on Marines *(1934);* Ready for Love *(1934);* Paris in Spring *(1935);* Smart Girl *(1935);* Peter Ibbetson *(1935);* Anything Goes *(1936);* One Rainy Afternoon *(1936);* Yours for the Asking *(1936);* The Gay Desperado *(1936);* Sea Devils *(1937);* Let's Get Married *(1937);* Artists and Models *(1937);* Fight for Your Lady *(1937);* The Lone Wolf Spy Hunt *(1939);* The Lady and the Mob *(1939);* The Adventures of Sherlock Holmes *(1939);* The Light That Failed *(1940);* They Drive By Night *(1940);* High Sierra *(1941);* The Sea Wolf *(1941);* Out of the Fog *(1941);* Ladies in Retirement *(1941);* Moontide *(1942);* Life Begins at Eight-Thirty *(1942);* The Hard Way *(1943);* Forever and a Day *(1943);* Thank Your Lucky Stars *(1943);* In Our Time *(1944);* Hollywood Canteen *(1944);* Pillow to Post *(1945);* Devotion *(1946);* The Man I Love *(1947);* Deep Valley *(1947);* Escape Me Never *(1947);* Road House *(1948);* Lust for Gold *(1949); (also co-producer, co-director, co-screenwriter)* Not Wanted *(1949);* Woman In Hiding *(1950); (as director, co-producer, co-writer)* Never Fear (The Young Lovers, *1950); (as director, co-writer)* Outrage *(1950); (director)* Hard, Fast and Beautiful *(1950);* On Dangerous Ground *(1952);* Beware My Lovely *(1952);* Jennifer *(1953); (director, co-writer)* The Hitch-Hiker *(1953); (as actress and director)* The Bigamist *(1953); (also co-writer)* Private Hell 36 *(1954);* Women's Prison *(1955);* The Big Knife *(1955);* While the City Sleeps *(1956);* Strange Intruder *(1956); (as director)* The Trouble With Angels *(1966);* Backtrack *(1969);* Junior Bonner *(1972);* The Devil's Rain *(1975);* The Food of the Gods *(1976);* My Boys Are Good Boys *(1978);* Deadhead Miles *(1982).*

He had been shot in the stomach and lay on the ground, senseless. But it wasn't enough. The director stopped the scene, strolled over to the prone, handsome young actor and cooed, "Lovey bird, you've been shot in the belly. You must suffer, darling." The cameras rolled again

on another episode of the television western "Have Gun, Will Travel," and soon Ida Lupino—the director everyone called "Mother"—had her scene.

The nickname was bestowed with great respect. Actors loved working with her, for she brought 30 years of her own acting experience to the job. "Ida stimulates me as an actor because she knows acting," Richard Boone, the weekly star of "Have Gun, Will Travel," once said. "In a weekly show you get into habit patterns. Ida gets you out of them." More important, Lupino was one of the pioneering women—like director *Lois Weber in the early 1900s and writer *Frances Marion in the 1920s—who staked out their own territory in a distinctly male world. Lupino was virtually the only female director working in Hollywood throughout the 1950s and early 1960s, and the first to work steadily at it since *Dorothy Arzner in the 1940s. Her secret, she once confessed, was in deception. "Men hate bossy women," she said. "Sometimes I pretend to know less than I do."

Few of her male contemporaries would argue with Ida Lupino's credentials. She had been born in London into a venerable English acting family on February 4, 1914. Her father Stanley Lupino was a popular music-hall and silent-film comedian; her mother Constance O'Shay enjoyed an equally successful career under the stage name ❧▶ **Connie Emerald**. Two of Ida's uncles managed the Drury Lane Theater, while another was a dramatic actor of some note. Two of her cousins acted in films (one of them, Lupino Lane, enjoyed early success in America in silent two-reelers), and her younger sister, **Rita Lupino**, would also become an actress. The Lupinos, in fact, could proudly trace their heritage back to Renaissance Italy, where their ancestors strolled the Neapolitan streets as musicians, acrobats, and players before being banished to

---

❧▶ **Emerald, Connie** (1891–1959)

*English actress. Name variations: Constance Lupino. Born Constance O'Shay in 1891; died on December 26, 1959; married Stanley Lupino; children: *Ida Lupino (1914–1995, an actress, director); Rita Lupino (an actress).*

Connie Emerald began her acting career as a child, appearing at the Shaftesbury Theater in 1904 in *The Prince of Pilsen.* A few years later, still in her teens, she toured the United States for 18 months, followed with a tour of Australia. Her last appearance was as Jane Howard in *Hold My Hand* in London in 1931.

England in the 17th century for political reasons. Although Ida would one day claim that she had never wanted to be an actress, any other career in the Lupino family was hardly imaginable.

Nonetheless, her parents were determined that Ida would have a conventional public-school education, although they were hardly surprised when Ida wrote and produced a play for her classmates when she was only seven years old. Three years later, Stanley even built Ida her own child-sized theater, complete with an orchestra pit and electrical fixtures, where his daughter presented scenes from Shakespeare. At 12, Lupino was appearing at London's Tom Thumb Theater, which specialized in children's programs; at 13, she had enrolled in the Royal Academy of Dramatic Arts; and at 14, she was touring the countryside with RADA's repertory company, although she modestly insisted on using the name "Ida Ray" to avoid trading on her family's fame.

It seemed inevitable that Lupino would be offered a film role sooner or later, although it turned out to be one for which her mother had auditioned. Prolific Hollywood director Allen Dwan came to London in 1932 to cast his first British film, *Her First Affaire,* a melodrama about a budding young girl who falls in love with an older man. Connie, 41 at the time, read for the part. It was painfully obvious to Dwan and everyone else (except, perhaps, Emerald herself) that she was much too old to play an ingenue; equally obvious to Dwan was that Connie's daughter was perfect for the part. It was Dwan who gave Ida the look for which she would be known in her first six pictures, as "the English *Jean Harlow." He insisted she bob her long, dark brown hair and dye it platinum blonde, as well as pluck and shape her eyebrows into more fetching arches. Although the film fared poorly with critics, Lupino's performance was more kindly reviewed. In her next film— *Money for Speed,* a lurid tale of motorcycle racing and mobsters— Lupino first created the "tough broad" character she would portray so often in her career. Her first dramatically challenging role was in the Ivor Novello melodrama *I Lived With You,* about an innocent career girl who falls under the sway of a worldly emigré Russian prince. "It was generally believed that the parts she secured in the past were because of her looks," noted *Variety,* "but in this she shows herself to be an emotional actress of no mean quality."

While Lupino was busy building her British film career, Paramount in Hollywood was looking for an ingenue to play the lead in its upcoming, lavish production of *Alice In Wonderland.* On the strength of one scene studio executives screened from *Money for Speed,* the part was offered to Ida Lupino. So it was that on August 19, 1933, Ida and her mother left for California. Paramount executives were surprised to welcome, not a shy, innocent young girl, but an experienced, intelligent, and ambitious 19-year-old actress. Although Lupino dutifully screen-tested for Alice, she suggested Paramount look at the rest of *Money for Speed,* especially the later reels when her character has been corrupted and turned into a gun-toting mob moll. "I could never, no matter how hard I tried, *feel* Alice," she said, "because I have never really been Alice's age." Paramount decided that she was, after all, not their Alice, but agreed to put her on salary at $600 a week while they looked for a part for her. It took six months, but Lupino eventually appeared in her first American picture, 1934's *Search for Beauty,* an unsuccessful spoof of the health and exercise industry, along with two more features that went mercifully unnoticed. She spent the rest of that year on the sidelines, felled by a polio epidemic that swept Los Angeles—although hers was a mild case, and she recovered fully.

By now, Lupino was restless and let Paramount know it. The studio's response was to cast her in a small role in its big-budget film version of Cole Porter's *Anything Goes,* in which she was sung to by Bing Crosby, and to lend her out to *Mary Pickford's United Artists to play another sweet young thing who becomes an older man's mistress. Once again, the critics spared her from their otherwise scathing reviews of *One Rainy Afternoon. The New York Times* told its readers that Ida Lupino "impressed us as having her tongue in her cheek, even while registering love's sweet surrender." Paramount began to realize they might have a legitimate leading lady on their hands, and agreed to Lupino's demands that she lose the blonde hair and stop being a sex kitten. "I don't care a fig about looking pretty-pretty on screen," she firmly told them. Her determination to be taken as a serious actress led her to leave Paramount when her contract expired in 1937, embarking on a series of forgettable melodramas for RKO, Columbia, and United Artists and, along the way, marrying actor Louis Hayward in 1938. But it was back at Paramount that she landed the role of the Cockney street girl Bessie Broke in 1939's *The Light That Failed,* based on the Rudyard Kipling novel. Sensing it could be her breakthrough part, Lupino assailed the film's director, William Wellman, until he agreed to give her an audition and, eventually, the job. Although she was billed fourth, behind Ronald

Colman, Walter Huston, and a now-forgotten actress named ☙➤ **Muriel Angelus**, critics and the public generally agreed that Lupino stole the picture from them all. Graham Greene thought that Ronald Colman was "acted right off the set" by Ida Lupino, and adjectives such as "splendid" and "superb" were not uncommon in describing her performance. An Oscar nomination seemed possible, but the competition that year was stiff, with pictures like *Gone With the Wind* and *Dark Victory* getting most of the Academy's attention and nominations. (*GWTW* and its starring actress, *Vivien Leigh*, won Best Picture and Best Actress that year.)

But *The Light That Failed* did manage to accomplish what Lupino had set out to do. Hollywood now regarded her as a serious and, even better, money-making actress. In 1940, she signed with Warner Bros., where she would spend the next seven years and appear in what she considered to be some of her best films, even though she was well aware that Warner's had hired her as a foil to *Bette Davis. Davis, the "queen of Warner's," was becoming notoriously difficult to please, and it was the studio's hope that an eager young actress waiting in the wings would make Davis more flexible. After Lupino's first picture for Warner's—1940's *They Drive By Night*—it seemed the strategy might be working. Ida's portrayal of Lana Carson, a bored wife who falls for a boozy truck driver but is driven insane by his infidelities, prompted *Newsweek* to point out to its readers: "Every so often, Hollywood discovers Ida Lupino. This time, she will undoubtedly stay discovered. [Warner Bros.] is convinced they have another Bette Davis and are hurriedly searching for screen stories to prove it." There followed in rapid succession over the next seven years many of Lupino's best-known roles in such films as *High Sierra, The Sea Wolf, Ladies in Retirement* (her favorite role), and *The Hard Way,* which won her a Best Actress award from the New York Film Critics. She played hard women, sympathetic women, scatter-brained women, and murderous women for Warner's, but all along she knew she was, as she described herself, "a poor man's Bette Davis." In between pictures, she decided to do something about it. "I used to go and sit on the set when I was on suspension," she once recalled, "which was a great deal of the time. I used to ask if I could sit in the cutting room, and I'd see how a film was put together. And . . . you learn why a director asked you to do such and such." By 1945, she was telling a fan magazine that she saw her future in "directing or producing, or both"; and when her Warner's contract came up

☙➤ **Angelus, Muriel** (b. 1909)

British actress-singer. Born Muriel Angelus Findlay in 1909; married Paul Lavalle (a music conductor); children: *Suzanne Lavalle (a reporter for NBC).*

Following a long stage career in England, Muriel Angelus was discovered by Hollywood when she starred on Broadway in *The Boys from Syracuse,* introducing the song "Falling in Love with Love." Her U.S. career included only four movies—*The Light That Failed* (1939), *The Way of All Flesh* (1940), *Safari* (1940), and *The Great McGinty* (1940)—"but few who ever saw her," wrote David Ragan, "and heard her melodious speaking voice—ever forgot this classic-featured blonde." Her British films include *The Ringer* (1930) and *Hindle Wakes* (1931).

SOURCES:
Ragan, David. *Who's Who in Hollywood: 1900–1976.* New Rochelle, NY: Arlington House, 1976.

for renewal in 1948, she decided to put her education to the test and declined the studio's offer, telling Jack Warner, "I don't want to be told someday that I'll be replaced by some starlet, as I was told I would replace Bette Davis."

Lupino made her decision to explore other areas of the business at a fortuitous time. Hollywood was just then entering a period of nervous conservatism, partly due to impending government anti-trust investigations and partly due to Senator Joseph McCarthy's House Un-American Activities Committee, which would produce the infamous "black list" of writers, directors, and actors suspected of Communist sympathies. Many of them would be forced to either retire from the business or seek work overseas. As a result of all the scrutiny, the major Hollywood studios were wary of anything that might appear to be outside what a later age would term "American family values," and it would be up to a growing number of independent filmmakers to handle serious social issues on the screen.

The decision to leave Warner's was just the first of several major events in Lupino's personal and professional life. She became a naturalized American citizen in June 1948, and later that year married Collier Young, an executive at Columbia Pictures (her earlier marriage to Louis Hayward had ended in divorce in 1945). Like Lupino, Young wanted to expand his professional horizons and thought he had the script with which to do it—a gritty social melodrama written by Marvin Wald (*The Naked City*) called *Not Wanted,* the story of a young woman who has a child out of wedlock, gives it up for adoption, then tries to regain her baby through a kidnap plot. Young tried to interest Columbia in the script, but given the controversial subject matter, the studio refused. Almost at the same time, Lupino met Anson Bond, the wealthy heir to a chain of men's clothing stores, who agreed to finance the picture. The four partners—Lupino, Young, writer Wald, and Bond—formed Emerald Productions and hired Elmer Clifton, a seasoned "B-film" director, to helm it for them. Only days into the shoot, however, Clifton suffered a heart attack, and, because there was no money to hire a new director, Lupino stepped in and put her Warner Bros. education to work—although she refused to take official credit for the job and insisted that the release prints carry Clifton's name.

*A*ny ladies who want to take over men's jobs . . . had better have strong stomachs.

—Ida Lupino

Not Wanted was shot in black-and-white, almost entirely on location, for under $100,000. The film featured two unknown actors, **Sally Forrest** and Keefe Brasselle, and, because Emerald Productions lacked a distribution deal with a large studio, played in a limited number of theaters. Nonetheless, it was noticed. "Much of the picture's force," said *The New York Times,* "comes from its flat insistence on telling the story straight. Its dirty children, dilapidated porches, and stuffy hall bedrooms are authentically grimy; its dialogue often catches the nagging overtones of everyday frustration and defeat." It was, in short, an example of the American cinema's social realism of the 1950s, a counterpoint to the big-budget melodramas and musicals churned out by an otherwise cautious Hollywood. On the strength of *Not Wanted,* RKO's Howard Hughes offered Lupino and her partners a three-picture distribution deal, each of the three films to be budgeted at $250,000. Emerald Productions was renamed The Filmakers, with Young as president, Lupino as vice-president, and Wald as treasurer (Bond had dropped out of the partnership after its first film).

Never Fear was the company's next production, and the first picture to bear Lupino's name as director. She and Young wrote the script, about a nightclub performer who is stricken with polio, and Ida once again cast Forrest and Brasselle as her two leads. The new arrangement with RKO wasn't yet in effect, however, and the film suffered from an erratic release pattern, even after it was more sympathetically renamed *The Young Lovers* and re-released. It went virtually unnoticed. Next came The Filmakers' most controversial picture, 1950's *Outrage,* which tackled the taboo subject of rape. This time, Lupino made sure she was working with a bigger budget, and hired **Mala Powers**—who was just making a name for herself—as her heroine. Lupino would later identify *Outrage* as the film in which she matured as a director, both technically and stylistically. "I just felt it was a good thing to do at that time, without being too preachy," she once said. "I just thought that so many times, the effect rape can have on a girl isn't easily brought out." She took great pains to handle her topic responsibly (the word "rape," in fact, is used only once in the picture—and is not spoken, but seen in a newspaper article) and spent several days screening the film for the Motion Picture Production Code office, incorporating all their suggestions, before the film was released. The critics were respectful, if not enthusiastic. "Miss Lupino and company," said one of them, "are pointing, in good taste, to a social blight. But," he added, "they are merely doing just that, and nothing more." Lupino's next film, *Hard, Fast and Beautiful,* fared no better.

Late in 1950, Lupino and Collier Young were divorced, although they would maintain a close professional relationship for many years to come, with Collier remaining as producer on her pictures. The next year, she married actor Howard Duff, with whom she had worked as an actress during her Warner years. The couple had a daughter, Bridget, in 1952.

Throughout these upheavals in her personal life, however, Lupino kept working. Early in her pregnancy, she acted for the first time in one of her own films—released in 1952 as *Beware, My Lovely,* a two-character thriller in which she is terrorized by a psychopathic handyman, played by Robert Ryan. The picture was conveniently shot in Lupino's home. The next year brought The Filmakers' most successful film, *The Hitch-Hiker,* a taut little drama about two men on a fishing vacation who are kidnapped by an escaped convict. Lupino would consider it her best directing effort; audiences and critics agreed. *The Hitch-Hiker* is still considered a classic of 1950's Hollywood *film noir.* Almost as successful was *The Bigamist,* in which Lupino again doubled as director and actress, playing opposite **Joan Fontaine* (who had become the second Mrs. Collier Young). By now, however, The Filmakers' distribution deal with RKO had expired, and the box office was sparse at the few theaters in which *The Bigamist* played. The same was true of what would be The Filmakers' last production, *Private Hell 36.*

But the company's demise didn't stop Lupino from working, and it was television that provided the opportunities. In 1953, she began appearing in the CBS series "Four Star Playhouse," which rotated through a quartet of actors and actresses with each week's episode.

Over several years, Lupino played everything from wronged wives to vicious movie queens to *femmes fatales,* in an echo of her years under contract at Warner's. (She was nominated for an Emmy award for her work, but lost to *Loretta Young,* who had her own weekly series.) In

1956, Lupino and Howard Duff starred in the sitcom "Mr. Adams and Eve" in which they played, not surprisingly, a Hollywood husband-and-wife acting team, the characters having been created by none other than Collier Young. The series ran for two seasons, went into a profitable syndication run, and earned both actors Emmy nominations.

Starting in 1958, Lupino took up directing for television, working on episodes of such well-known series as "The Twilight Zone," "Bewitched," "The Untouchables," and "Gilligan's Island." She was the only female director then working in TV, and she was admired as much for always bringing in a show on time and on budget as for her demonstrative directing style. "There are two kinds [of directors]," she said, "standers and sitters. The sitters are calm and can take anything. I'm a stander myself. I tried sitting once, and my mind went completely blank." Not always content behind the camera, Lupino also acted in several series and sitcoms—among them, "Mod Squad," "Family Affair," and "Batman"—and took small parts in feature films,

Ida Lupino (right) on the set of Never Fear *with Sally Forrest.*

being particularly praised for her performance as Steve McQueen's mother in Sam Peckinpah's *Junior Bonner.* In 1965, she directed Walt Disney's *The Trouble With Angels,* whose star, *****Rosalind Russell**, noted that Lupino came "to the job each morning thoroughly prepared. She knows what she wants and she knows how to do it."

Lupino's last film appearance was in 1982, when she was 64. The next year, she divorced Howard Duff, although the two had been separated for the past 11 years. (Asked what took her so long, Ida quipped, "I finally got off my duff, darling.") She continued to direct for television until being diagnosed with colon cancer in the early 1990s. The disease claimed her life on August 3, 1995, at the age of 77.

Sadly, the importance of Ida Lupino's work is often overlooked. Not only did she control her own career with a firm hand in an industry not known for its liberality toward women, but she managed to lay the groundwork for a growing number of contemporary women who have pursued independent film careers, from directors like

Martha Coolidge and Penny Marshall to producers such as *Dawn Steel and Kathleen Kennedy. Her films reflect a pragmatic, unsentimental approach to life's challenges rather than the escapist fantasies with which Hollywood is often associated, capturing, in the words of one commentator, "a realistic portrait of ordinary people confronting life. It is the everyday world we all share."

SOURCES:

Locayo, Richard. "Women in Hollywood: Talk about Dances with Wolves!" in *People Weekly*. Vol. 35. Spring 1991.

Stewart, Lucy Ann Liggett. *Ida Lupino as Film Director, 1949–1953: An Auteur Approach*. NY: Arno Press, 1980 (originally presented as the author's thesis, University of Michigan, 1979).

Vermilye, Jerry. *Ida Lupino*. NY: Pyramid Publications, 1977.

SUGGESTED READING:

Donati, William. *Ida Lupino: A Biography*. Lexington, KY: University of Kentucky Press, 1996.

Norman Powers,
writer-producer, Chelsea Lane Productions,
New York, New York

Lusk, Georgia Lee (1893–1971)

American educator and politician who was the first woman elected to Congress from New Mexico. Born Georgia Lee Witt on May 12, 1893, in Carlsbad, New Mexico; died on January 5, 1971, in Albuquerque, New Mexico; interred in Sunset Gardens Memorial Park, Carlsbad, New Mexico; eldest of four children, three daughters and a son, of George Witt (a surveyor and rancher) and Mary Isabel (Gilreath) Witt; graduated from Carlsbad High School, 1912; attended Highlands University, in Las Vegas, New Mexico, and Colorado State Teachers College, in Greeley, Colorado; graduated from New Mexico State Teachers College (later Western New Mexico University), in 1914; married Dolph Lusk (a rancher and banker), in August 1915 (died 1919); children: three sons, including Eugene Lusk who served in the New Mexico state senate.

Often referred to as "the first lady of New Mexico politics," Georgia Lee Lusk had a political career that spanned 35 years and included several terms in state education posts and a term as the first congresswoman elected by the voters in her state.

Lusk was born in 1893 and grew up on a ranch near Carlsbad, New Mexico. After high school, she attended Highlands University and Colorado State Teachers College, in Greeley. After graduating from the New Mexico State Teachers College in Silver City in 1914, she began a teaching career in Eddy County. One

year later, she married cattleman and banker Dolph Lusk and gave up teaching to begin a family. When her husband died suddenly in 1919, she was left with two small sons and was pregnant with a third.

The next few years were challenging for Lusk. In addition to managing the ranch, she returned to her teaching career, often taking her small sons to school with her. In 1924, she was elected school superintendent of Lea County, a post she held until 1929. After losing an initial bid for state superintendent, in 1930 she won the first of two successive terms and served from 1931 to 1935. Unable by law to succeed herself immediately following her second term, she served again as state superintendent from 1943 to 1947. (In the interim, she was a rural school supervisor in Guadalupe County.) During her tenure as state superintendent, Lusk succeeded in securing free textbooks for the public school and expanded the curriculum to include physical education and arts-and-crafts programs. She was also successful in establishing higher salaries and a teacher-retirement program.

In October 1944, Lusk took part in the White House Conference on Rural Education,

Georgia Lee Lusk

and in 1946 entered the campaign for the Democratic nomination for one of her state's two at-large congressional seats. She beat out six opponents in the primary and campaigned for election on a platform stressing improved educational facilities. "It's just as important for the Government to look over the business of education as it is to look over farming or railroading or anything else," she told an interviewer at the time. As it turned out, she was the leading vote-getter in the general election. True to her campaign promises, Lusk supported federal aid to education and worked for the improvement of school programs and the creation of a Cabinet-level department of education. Her congressional tenure was additionally marked by service as a member of the Committee on Veterans' Affairs. She supported many of the Truman administration's domestic programs, but voted to override Harry Truman's veto of the Taft-Hartley Act. She also backed the administration's foreign policy proposals and endorsed universal military training.

Lusk lost her bid for reelection to Congress in the June 1948 primary, and at the end of her term left public life for a short time. She was appointed to the War Claims Commission by President Truman in September 1949, and served until her dismissal by President Dwight Eisenhower in 1953. Returning to New Mexico, she served as superintendent of public instruction for another four years before retiring in 1959. Her later political activity was limited to advising her son Eugene Lusk, who served in the New Mexico state senate for four years and made an unsuccessful run for governor in 1966. (He committed suicide in 1969.) Georgia Lusk died of thyroid cancer in 1971.

SOURCES:

Current Biography. NY: H.W. Wilson, 1947.

Office of the Historian. Women in Congress, 1917–1990. Commission on the Bicentenary of the U.S. House of Representatives, 1991.

Sicherman, Barbara, and Carol Hurd Green. *Notable American Women: The Modern Period.* Cambridge, MA: The Belknap Press of Harvard University Press, 1980.

Barbara Morgan,
Melrose, Massachusetts

Lutgard (1182–1246)

Flemish Cistercian mystic, stigmatic, and saint. Name variations: Saint Lutgard; Saint Lutgardis. Born in Tongres (Belgium) in 1182; died in Aywières (near Brussels), on June 16, 1246.

Born of bourgeois parents, Lutgard joined the Benedictines of Saint-Trond in 1194 and be-

came prioress of the convent in 1205. Finding the observance of the Benedictines too lax, she transferred to the Cistercian convent of Aywières in 1208. There, she engaged in three seven-year fasts in reparation for the heresy of the Albigensians (Catharists of Albi in southern France) then in full sway. Originally, the lower classes of the Albigensians and the Waldensians rebelled against clerical corruption in the Catholic Church. But when their nobles, who saw a chance to confiscate church land, became involved, Pope Innocent III proclaimed a crusade against them, called the Albigensian Crusade. The Passion (the Crucifixion of Jesus Christ) was the center of Lutgard's religious life. When she was 29, she received the stigmata, a spear wound, and carried the scar to her death; she also frequently experienced the sweat of blood and in 1235 became totally blind. Lutgard predicted the day of her death, which was June 16, 1246.

Lutgardis (fl. 1139)

Duchess of Brabant. Flourished around 1139; daughter of Berengar of Sulzbach; married Godfrey II, duke of Brabant (r. 1139–1142), around 1139 (died 1142).

Luther, Katherine (1499–1550).

See Bora, Katharina von.

Luttrell, Anne (1743–1808).

See Ann Horton.

Lutyens, Elisabeth (1906–1983)

Pioneer in 20th-century music who was recognized in her later years as one of Britain's most important modern composers. Name variations: Mrs. Edward Clarke; Dame Elisabeth Lutyens. Born Agnes Elisabeth Lutyens in London, England, on July 9, 1906; died in London on April 14, 1983; daughter of Edwin Lutyens (a preeminent British architect) and Mary (Galway) Lutyens; studied with governesses, at Worcester Park School at Westgate-on-Sea, at the Paris Conservatoire, and the Royal College of Music; married Ian Herbert Campbell Glennie, in 1933 (divorced 1940); married Edward Clarke (the conductor), in 1942; children: (first marriage) a son and twin daughters; (second marriage) a son Conrad.

Major symphonic works: Fantasy for strings *(1937);* Five pieces *(1939);* Three pieces, op. 7 *(1939);* Wild Decembers *(1939);* Chamber concerto No. 2, op. 8 *(1941);* Three symphonic preludes *(1942);* Three salutes *(1942);* Bustle for the W.A.A.F. *(1942);* Divertissement *(1944);* Suite galoise *(1944);* Proud city

(1945); Petite suite (1946); Concerto, op. 15 (1947); Chamber concerto No. 4, op. 8 (1947); Chamber concerto No. 5, op. 8 (1947); Lyric piece (1951); The English Seaside Suite (1951); The English Theater Suite (1951); Music for orchestra, op. 31 (1955); Chorale, op. 36 (Homage to Stravinsky, 1956); Symphonies, op. 46 (1961); Music for orchestra, op. 48 (1962); Music for orchestra, op. 56 (1963); Music for piano and orchestra, op. 59 (1964); Novenaria (1967); The Winter of the World, op. 98 (1974); Eos (1975); Rondel (1978); Suite I and II (1978); Six Bagatelles (1978); Echoi (1980). Wrote hundreds of others.

While in her 70s, Elisabeth Lutyens danced in a Greek taverna on the island of Corfu, wearing butterfly specs, patterned tights, and an electric-blue fake fur. Dressing up had long been her passion. In the 1920s, she had shocked her boarding-school teachers by appearing at a non-costume ball at term's end dressed as Peter Pan—neither the first, nor the last, time she would be reprimanded for "unladylike behavior." In the practice of her art, as well, eccentricity was the norm for this preeminent British composer.

She was born the fourth daughter in a family of five children. Her mother **Mary Galway Lutyens,** the fifth of seven children of the earl of Lytton, gave the following account of her daughter's memorable first day:

> Agnes Elisabeth Lutyens born July 9th 1906 at 8:30 a.m. She weighed 9 lbs 6 oz. She was so fat—with bracelets round her wrists and such a fat face. She had masses of black soft hair—like a gollywog—about 2½ inches long and such long eyelashes. She is the image of [her father]. . . . Last night there were burglars in the house and [the infant] frightened them away by screaming so when she came in to me for food at 2 [o'clock]. They were next door in Father's room and must have made off when they heard baby cry. But for her we should have lost all our silver.

Elisabeth's father was Edwin Landseer Lutyens (the 11th of 14 children of Charles and **Mary Lutyens**). During Elisabeth's childhood, Edwin Lutyens became the foremost architect of the late Victorian and Edwardian eras. Now considered as important in British architecture as Christopher Wren, he designed some public buildings but was particularly known for his country houses.

Called Betty, Elisabeth Lutyens received the upbringing typical of a British upperclass family. With her oldest siblings, **Barbara** and Robert, away at school, Betty, **Ursula,** and **Mary** inhabited the nursery ruled over by Nannie Sleath,

while their parents, whom Betty adored, were often kept preoccupied by other duties. Her father's architecture had by then achieved some recognition, and her mother was immersed in the study of the then-fashionable Theosophy. (The children grew accustomed to the scent of incense wafting through the house, along with the chant, "I am a link in a golden chain of love which stretches round the world.") In the nursery, the children learned their lessons from governesses, and family holidays were spent at Knebworth House, in Herfortshire, with a large extended family of cousins, uncles and aunts.

Elisabeth's favorite relative was her "Aunt Con," *Constance Lytton, a suffragist active in British demonstrations. After her arrest for breaking windows, Constance Lytton went on a hunger strike and was force-fed, enduring rough treatment that resulted in her suffering a heart attack and stroke. Elisabeth idolized her and was determined, eventually, to be as radical in music as her aunt had been in politics. In Herfortshire, the two formed a special bond; Aunt Con seemed to understand her better than anyone else. Of her four-year-old niece, Constance Lytton wrote:

> Now I'm coming to my special lady. I'm so in love with her I'm really bad with it at times. Sister Agnes of course, I mean. And she flirts back with me quite rewardfully. I do think her such a tremendous personality.

Early in life, Elisabeth became aware of the differences between herself and her siblings and cousins. Her eccentricities, however, were generally cherished among the family members, allowing her to develop in her own way.

The Lutyenses were not a musical family, but Elisabeth began to compose pieces as soon as she started taking music lessons. Constance in particular encouraged her to continue to compose. At age nine, Elisabeth was sent to Worcester Park School at Westgate-on-Sea. Popular and well liked, she excelled in sports, especially hockey. Vacations at home were happy, and she would later remember the construction of the famous Queen Mary's Dolls' House, a miniature designed and executed by her father, during this time, according to Her Majesty's explicit instructions. Elisabeth never forgot the visits Queen *Mary of Teck made to their home to see this marvel under construction.

Lutyens' absorption with music increased when she began to study the violin. "Oh, Mummy darling I'm so happy in my music," she wrote her mother. "I feel that at last I've found happiness in myself, that whether I live here or there with this person or that I shall be happy." At 16, she was determined to study in Paris ("the beginning of my own life in my own world") and attended the Paris Conservatoire, where her talent for composition became increasingly evident.

In 1924, Lutyens traveled with her family to India to see, among other things, the monumental Viceroy's House in New Delhi, which had been designed by her father and was then under construction. Talk with her father during the trip about creative work led her to see that the two shared much in common, and it was from him that Lutyens learned how to dedicate herself entirely to her work.

At 21, she was back in London, attending the Royal College of Music where she studied with Harold Darke. *Elizabeth Maconchy, who would also become well known as a composer, was a fellow student. Immersed in London's musical world, Lutyens met Dame *Ethel Smyth, the legendary British composer, who had all but lost her hearing at the time, and they became friends. In 1931, Lutyens and her friends, Maconchy, Anne Macnaghten, the violinist, and Iris Lemare founded the Macnaghten-Lemare concerts at the Mercury Theater, Notting Hill Gate, for the performance of works by modern composers.

Although she had decided that music was incompatible with marriage, Lutyens fell in love several times. Eventually she changed her position on the subject and married Ian Herbert Campbell Glennie, a fellow student at the Royal College of Music, on February 11, 1933. Despite the fact that she became a wife, then a mother, she remained adamant about continuing her work. A son was born first, followed in quick succession by twin daughters, during whose birth Lutyens screamed at the midwife, "But I still want to compose!"

In the 1930s, the profound economic effects of a worldwide depression were being deeply felt in Great Britain, at the same time that Adolf Hitler's Third Reich was growing stronger and the clouds of war were beginning to loom over Europe. Lutyens, caught up in a whirlwind of composing and living a bohemian lifestyle among her family and friends, allowed much of these events to go unnoticed. During this time, she met Edward Clarke, an influential conductor in modern British musical circles. At one of the gatherings where they frequently met, Clarke suggested, "Let's go out and get drunk!," an occasion which commenced a new chapter in Lutyens' life. She fell increasingly in love with Clarke, who was 18

years her senior, and the discovery that he had few if any financial resources did not cool her passion. In 1940, Lutyens divorced Ian and, two years later, married Edward, with whom she had a son, Conrad.

Rarely a lucrative enterprise, music composition was even less lucrative for modernists like Lutyens. By 1944, acknowledging her husband's lack of earning power and the need to support her family, she began composing for film. Through the years, despite her commitment to composing modern, atonal music, she would compose over 200 orchestrations for films and documentaries. This work required great professionalism, but Lutyens learned the tricks of the trade. As soon as a score was commissioned, she booked a music copyist because the good ones were rare; then she immediately found a band so as to know exactly which instruments she could compose for. Because film music often requires writing timed specifically for a series of scenes, the composer has to keep set time-frames constantly in mind. Lutyens wrote for many film genres but became particularly adept at producing film scores for horror movies. Although it was not the kind of classical composing she preferred, she was proud of her ability to compose scores, a talent which eventually enabled her to earn a good living.

Throughout two marriages, the birth of four children, the bombing of London, and the intervention of the World War II, Lutyens continued to compose, sharing with her husband a devotion to the composition and performance of modern music. Through occasional jobs with Britain's famous broadcasting arm, the BBC, Edward Clarke introduced the listening public to the music of some of the greatest modern composers, including Bartók, Berg, Webern, and Kodály. Meanwhile, Lutyens continued to struggle against the musical establishment's general rejection of 12-tone music, which, with her husband's support, she refused to abandon.

Lutyens' life, while intense and exciting, was not always stable. From the beginning, alcohol had formed an important part of her second marriage, and by the mid-1940s she was a functioning alcoholic. In 1946, at age 40, she discovered she was pregnant with a fifth child, a situation which presented her with a dilemma. "Now I was faced with the necessity of committing an act of life-destroying blasphemy—to me—or coming up with an economic solution," she wrote. "I had no choice." The main family breadwinner, Lutyens had an abortion, which caused her great grief.

Elisabeth
Lutyens

Her family was sometimes critical of her lifestyle, and Lutyens realized that she was a less than perfect parent. She lashed out uncharacteristically when writing to her mother in the mid-1940s: "For years you've all given me the pit and pendulum—your children *or* your music— It's been a nightmare and even my strong shoulders are not carrying this burden longer." Eventually the years of drinking, efforts at being a good parent, and unprofitable work took their toll, and Lutyens had a nervous breakdown. Her mother, ever supportive, sent her for a psychiatric rest cure which seemed to help. During her stay in the hospital, Elisabeth continued to compose. When she emerged, she resisted family pressure to leave her husband in order to escape his alcoholic influence. Refusing to address the problem, she became friends with the poet Dylan Thomas and his wife, *Caitlin Thomas, whose drinking and marital problems were legendary. She often stayed with the Thomases in Wales where alcohol was as plentiful as funds were deficient. Eventually Lutyens decided she had to stop drinking and separated temporarily from Edward. Dylan Thomas meanwhile proceeded to drink himself to death, a loss she felt keenly. His death inspired her piece *Valediction (Dylan Thomas 1953)*.

> *If one can see a world in a grain of sand, that grain of sand for me is music.*
>
> —Elisabeth Lutyens

Edward Clarke remained the love of Lutyens' life, and in time the two reconciled. No sooner had she finally won her battle with alcohol than did the tuberculosis she had fought off in the 1930s return. To recover, she went on a regimen which included three pints of milk a day, antibiotics, and bed rest—while continuing to compose. Acceptance of her work was growing. When Lutyens was 56, Edward died suddenly of a stroke. Although he was almost two decades older than she, his death came as a shock, and she missed him greatly.

Lutyens, however, was a survivor. She continued to write 12-tone music, though it never became greatly loved by the public at large, and she increasingly became a respected figure in the musical world. Her total work eventually comprised some 2,000 pieces, a fact the public could no longer ignore. In 1969, she was honored with the title of Commander of the British Empire (CBE) for her contribution to music. That same year, she wrote a lyric drama, *Isis and Osiris*, which was followed in 1972 by an opera *Time Off? Not the Ghost of a Chance*. Growing acceptance did not change her outspoken and individualistic behavior. Once before an interview on England's Radio Four, she warned Russell Harty that if he "so much as mouthed the phrase 'lady composer'" she would call him a "homosexual interviewer." In their ensuing dialogue, the gender issue was not broached.

When Lutyens died in 1983, the musical public realized her importance. Willing to finance her creative work with the skillful crafting of commercial scores, she laid new groundwork for future serious composers and led music lovers worldwide into hitherto unknown territories of sound.

SOURCES:

Barron, Janet. "Shocking Talents," in *New Statesman and Society*. Vol. 2, no. 81. December 22–29, 1989, p. 45.

Craig, Robert M. "Lutyens, Edwin" in *International Dictionary of Architects and Architecture*. Vol. 1. Ed. by Randall J. van Vynckt. London: St. James Press, 1993, pp. 536–539.

"Elisabeth Lutyens," in *Sunday Times* [London]. April 17, 1983, p. 41.

Harries, Meirion, and Susie Harries. *A Pilgrim Soul: The Life and Work of Elisabeth Lutyens*. London: Michael Joseph, 1989.

Kemp, Jeffery. "Write What the Film Needs: An Interview with Elisabeth Lutyens," in *Sight and Sound*. Vol. 43, no. 4. Autumn 1974, pp. 203–205, 248.

Lutyens, Dame Elisabeth. *A Goldfish Bowl*. London: Cassell, 1972.

"Miss Elisabeth Lutyens," in *The Times* [London]. April 15, 1983, p. 12.

John Haag,
Associate Professor of History,
University of Georgia, Athens, Georgia

Lutz, Berta (1894–1976)

Brazilian feminist, writer, and activist committed to the enfranchisement of women. Pronunciation: BEAR-ta LOOHTS. *Born Berta María Júlia Lutz on August 2, 1894, in Sâo Paulo, Brazil; died on September 16, 1976, in Rio de Janeiro, Brazil; daughter of Adolfo Lutz (a pioneer of tropical medicine in Brazil) and Amy (Fowler) Lutz (a volunteer nurse among lepers in Hawaii); attended primary school in Rio de Janeiro, secondary and advanced study in France; earned a Licenciée dès Sciences at the University of Paris (Sorbonne), 1911–18; earned a bachelor's degree in law from the University of Rio de Janeiro in 1933.*

Founded many feminist organizations, including the influential Federaçao Brasileira pelo Progresso Feminino (Brazilian Federation for the Advancement of Women), of which she was president (1922–42), and led the battle for female enfranchisement.

"Miss Bertha Lutz, a beautiful young woman, is the 'propulsive force' at present," wrote American feminist *Carrie Chapman Catt in 1922. She was referring to the central and guiding role played by Berta Lutz in the creation of the Federaçao Brasileira pelo Progresso Feminino (Brazilian Federation for the Advancement of Women), an organization that pushed for the education of women, protective legislation for women and children, and, first and foremost, the right of women in Brazil to vote.

Lutz was well positioned for such a role. Born into an upper-middle class family, she enjoyed their support and was given the education and the freedom to advance her feminist agenda. Her father Adolfo Lutz, a renowned doctor and scientist, had been born in 1855 to Swiss parents who had immigrated to Brazil in 1849. Educated in Europe, he reputedly met Joseph Lister in London in 1880 and Louis Pasteur in Paris. Upon his return to Brazil, he engaged in biological research and published widely. His work won him international fame, and he was invited to visit the Molukai leprosarium in Hawaii, where he met and married an English nurse, **Amy Fowler** (**Lutz**). They returned to Brazil in 1893 and Adolfo was named interim vice-director of the Bacteriological Institute in Sâo Paulo. The following year, Amy Lutz gave birth to Berta María Júlia Lutz.

Berta had, from the outset, the advantages of the best possible education in Brazil and traveled to France, in 1911, for secondary and advanced study. At the Sciences Faculty of the University of Paris at the Sorbonne, she enrolled in courses in botany, natural sciences, zoology, embryology, chemistry and biology. A degree, the Licenciée dès Sciences, was awarded to her in 1918. She traveled to England the same year and observed firsthand the struggle of that country's suffragists. It was a cause which had piqued her interest while she studied in Paris. Some of Britain's women won the right to vote in 1918, but it had been a drawn-out campaign which embraced, from 1910, radical and occasionally violent tactics. Arson, smashing windows, destroying postal boxes, and hunger strikes marked the movement.

Intent on organizing women in Brazil to battle for equal access to education, public office, and the right to vote, Lutz, upon her return in 1918, initiated a public campaign with a letter to the *Revista da semana*, a weekly news magazine. "Surely most of the responsibility for this unfortunate state of affairs falls to men," she wrote, for men controlled "legislation, politics, and all public institutions." But women "are also a bit to blame." Lutz was witness to the progress of women in Europe who assumed tasks during the war that would have been unthinkable in other circumstances. While Brazilian women were not called "to the same level of sacrifice . . . even so we feel that we are worthy of occupying the same position." The empowerment of women would come through education, not only of women, but also of men, who "must become aware that women are not toys created for their amusement." Lutz was convinced that the violent approach of England's suffragists would not succeed in Brazil. She counseled instead "practical demonstrations" and the creation of a League of Brazilian Women who would lobby for their rights rather than "break windows along the street."

Employment with her father at the famous Instituto Osvaldo Cruz in Rio de Janeiro afforded Berta the means to pursue her campaign for women's rights. Because she was fluent in four languages, she was hired as a translator in the zoology section. This same facility with languages would determine, in part, that much of her career as a fighter for women's rights involved her with the international movement. Also instrumental in her international connections was the fact that in 1919 she was named secretary to the National Museum, a high civil-service post not usually held by a woman. In **June Hahner**'s words, "Lutz's position in government service provided her with opportunities to establish international ties as well as facilitate organizational activities within Brazil."

In that same year, 1919, Lutz and another woman represented Brazil at a conference sponsored by the International Labor Organization. Its focus was on the conditions endured by working women and possible remedies. In Brazil, the indefatigable Lutz also served as an officer in the Legiâo da Mulher Brasileira (League of Brazilian Women), a social-service organization established in Rio de Janeiro in 1919 with the motto "Aid and Elevate Women." The organization believed that self-help and good organization was the best way to represent women's interests and rights. The seed for another organization, the Liga para a Emancipaçâo Intelectual da Mulher (The League for the Intellectual Emancipation of Women), was planted in 1919 and would come to fruition in 1920.

Lutz, together with **María Lacerda de Moura**, a schoolteacher and writer from the state of Minas Gerais, led that nascent organization, which broke new ground in that its focus was neither religious nor philanthropic. It had both a political agenda and an educational mission. The Liga supported the campaign of Senator Justo Leite Chermont, a legislator in favor of the right of women to vote. It also wanted to emancipate women intellectually through rational and scientific education. Hahner feels that the Liga was actually little more than a "study group" that sought to promote women's intellectual freedom through public meetings and the printed media. A strong personality, Lutz served as president and enforced her will on the Liga.

One result was the gradual alienation of Lacerda de Moura, whose views did not coincide with those of Lutz.

Interested in pursuing her goals within the existing political system and social milieu, Lutz was not a radical. She pushed for legislation to enhance the political and legal rights of women which, in turn, would enhance their economic opportunities. In 1921, the Liga shortened its name to the Liga para a Emancipação de Mulher (League for the Emancipation of Women). No longer especially interested in "intellectual" or "sexual" freedom, Lutz pushed harder for political and legal rights as well as economic and educational issues. The right to vote would serve a twofold purpose: it would enable women to transform their position within Brazilian society, and it would be an important symbol of the equality of citizenship of women and men.

Lutz publicized her program through newspaper interviews in three Rio de Janeiro newspapers, *Boa Noite, A Noite,* and *O Imperial.* The unequal treatment of women in the workforce was a key target. Equal pay for equal work and equal educational opportunities could only be realized through the power of the ballot box. Critics charged that the tough world of politics was no place for women, whose chief role in society should be confined to the home and family. Others felt that feminists like Lutz had become masculinized, a characterization designed to humiliate women and remind them of their "true station" in life. To the chorus of dissent was added the powerful voice of the Roman Catholic Church which preached that motherhood, family, and religion should not be linked to the oppression of women. Lutz answered the critics in an interview. She said, in Hahner's translation, that "it is neither accurate nor logical to assert that when women acquire electoral rights they will abandon the place conferred on them by nature. . . . Woman's domain, all feminists agree, is the home. But . . . nowadays the home no longer is the space encompassed within four walls." The home, in a progressive Brazilian society, was in the factory and the legislature.

Because of her stature in the feminist movement, the Brazilian government chose Lutz to represent the nation at the Pan American Conference of Women, held in Baltimore, Maryland, in April 1922. It was a learning experience for the Brazilian delegate who now became even more convinced that her strategy of working within the system was the best way to realize women's political and legal rights. Her model was similar to that of women in the United States. Respect and restraint, not the violence of some European feminists, would produce results.

Upon her return to Brazil in August, Lutz dismantled the League and replaced it with the Federação Brasileira pelo Progresso Feminino (Brazilian Federation for the Advancement of Women, or FBPF). The birth of the new organization was celebrated by the visit of the famous U.S. feminist Carrie Chapman Catt, president of both the International Woman's Suffrage Alliance and the Pan American Association of Women. Catt wrote that Lutz had "organized a Brazilian Congress of Women to receive us . . . . Education, organization methods, child-welfare, laws for women, Pan Americanism and woman suffrage were subjects on the program." Catt was particularly impressed by the support afforded the Brazilian women by male lawyers and politicians.

Quickly, affiliates of the FBPF were established in 13 Brazilian states. The new organization was not designed for the poor women of Brazil, which would eventually turn some feminists away from Lutz. There was little doubt that the FBPF targeted and was supported by middle- and upper-class women in urban areas. Morris Blachman notes that the most insistent demand of the FBPF, the vote, was "in an immediate sense totally irrelevant to the majority of Brazilian women, who were illiterate and therefore not eligible to vote."

But the Federation helped lower-class women in other ways. Lutz in 1922 worked with the Union of Commercial Employees in Rio de Janeiro to shorten the work day for shop clerks; she also succeeded in gaining the entrance of girls to the prestigious Colégio (School) Dom Pedro II. Historian **Francesca Miller** notes that Lutz used her high-level contacts and appealed directly to the minister of education to lower the barrier that denied women high-quality secondary instruction. A diploma from the Colégio allowed women to prepare for university entrance examinations and, ultimately, to be competitive with men in the search for paid employment.

The Federation did not ignore poor or rural women. On the contrary, it developed extension programs in the states of São Paulo and Rio de Janeiro that concentrated on health issues and income-generating activities for rural women. Another program attempted to address the growing problem of abandoned children.

In 1925, Lutz was elected president of the Inter-American Union of Women at the Inter-American Congress held that year in Washington, D.C. Frequent foreign travel, even though it brought a measure of prestige to the Brazilian feminist movement in general, and enhanced the personal leadership of Berta Lutz, gradually separated her from other Brazilian feminists.

When in Brazil, she campaigned tirelessly for women's suffrage and in 1928 flew over Rio de Janeiro and dropped leaflets that called upon the Senate, the press and the people in general to support votes for women. Despite the novelty of the delivery and the importance of the message, the Senate remained unresponsive, and legislation with respect to female suffrage was allowed to die. Undaunted, Lutz threw the support of the Federation behind a gubernatorial candidate in the state of Rio Grande do Norte who was in favor of women's suffrage. He won the election and the right of women to vote became law in the state in 1928.

Lutz's international schedule remained full. In 1929, she was named to a leadership position at the 11th Congress of the International Woman Suffrage Alliance, which met in Berlin. Shortly after her return, she established yet another organization, the Uniâo Universitária Feminina (Feminist University Union).

The prospects for female suffrage in Brazil brightened considerably in 1930 with the collapse of the Old Republic and the emergence as president of Getulio Vargas, a reform-minded leader. By August 1931, legislation was passed which provided for a restricted franchise, i.e., single women, widows with their own income, and married women with their husband's approval were allowed the vote. Naturally, the Federation was displeased and immediately launched a publicity campaign to remove the offending restrictions. Lutz and other women leaders met personally with the Brazilian president, who left them with the impression that he was in agreement with an unrestricted franchise for women. True to his word, he supported a new civil code, issued by decree on February 24, 1932, that gave women the same right to vote as men. Illiterates of both sexes were excluded by law. The next battle for Lutz and the Federation was to incorporate the decree into Brazil's new constitution.

Vargas invited Lutz to serve on the drafting committee for the constitution, and she used her position not only to fight for the franchise, but also to incorporate constitutional guarantees with regard to the total equality of the sexes. In 1933, she published two studies, *13 principios basicos: sugestoes as anteprojecto da constituicâo* (*13 Basic Principles: Preliminary Sketches for the Constitution*) and *A nacionalidade da mulher casada* (*Nationality and the Married Woman*), which dealt with a host of issues of interest to Brazilian women. Included were Lutz's thoughts on equality before the law, equal pay for equal work, paid maternity leaves, the right of all women to hold public office regardless of their married state, child care, and homemaking.

With the support of other women's groups, Lutz and the Federation won their main battle. The right of women to vote was enshrined in the new constitution, which was adopted in July 1934. Additionally, Lutz's *13 Principles* also found a place in the document. She now turned her attention to using the vote to place women and men who had supported feminist issues in office. In a celebratory mood, Lutz represented Brazil at the VII Pan American Conference for Women, held in Montevideo. She also found the time to establish two more women's organizations, the Uniâo Professional Femenini (Professional Women's Union) and the Uniâo das Funcionárias Públicas (Union of Public Employees), and earn a bachelor's degree at the Law Faculty of the University of Rio de Janeiro.

> One of the greatest forces for emancipation and progress lies within our power: the education of women and men. We must educate women so that they can be intellectually equal and be self-disciplined. We must educate men so that they become aware that women are not toys for their amusement.
>
> —Berta Lutz (1918)

With the promulgation of the constitution, the women's movement hesitated and then began to fragment. The fissures masked by years of common struggle burst open. Factions quarreled and personality conflicts moved to center stage. Some women found Lutz "too authoritarian, brusque, and impatient" and abandoned the Federation for other organizations. More could have been accomplished, others complained, if Lutz had been less "difficult" and more "amiable."

With the elections of 1934, Lutz ran as a candidate of the Partido Autonomista (Autonomous Party) for the Federal District for the Chamber of Deputies (Lower House). The party was affiliated with the Liga Eleitoral Independente (Independent Electoral League) which in turn was linked to the feminist movement in Brazil. Lutz was elected as an alternate. In 1936, however, the incumbent died in office, and Lutz entered the Chamber of Deputies. She immediately set to work, and during her year in office helped to create the Commission for the Code for Women. As chair of the commission, she pushed for the enactment of a comprehensive law with regard to the legal status and social rights of women. Specific measures for women in the workplace were envisaged and were similar to those she had outlined in her publications in 1933. Also discussed was the creation of a government department charged with the supervision of services with regard to the protection of children and of women in the workplace and at home.

All the high hopes entertained by Brazil's women were dashed in 1937 with the forced closure of Congress. Vargas' declaration of the Estado Novo (New State) terminated all political activity, including that of women. Pending legislation on women's rights was lost. Vargas, who had been so conciliatory to Lutz and others in the early 1930s, abandoned women: they would play no significant role in the new order. Indeed, from the perspective of Vargas, social harmony demanded order and discipline which included the legal subordination of wives to husbands.

Forcibly retired from politics, Lutz became the interim director of the botanical section of the National Museum, and assumed the directorship in February 1938. It was a position she would hold until her compulsory retirement in 1964.

In 1940, Lutz penned a frustrated letter to Carrie Chapman Catt in which she noted that Brazil's women "had been unable to maintain what they had won." Indeed, it was as if the rug had been yanked from beneath their feet. Much damage was done to the women's movement by Vargas; it lost its momentum and, even with the collapse of the New State in 1945, the movement failed to recover.

Lutz maintained her high international profile, however. In October 1945 in San Francisco, she represented Brazil at the Inter-American Commission of Women, a group that offered advice with regard to the framing of the United Nations Charter. It was Lutz, together with representatives from the Dominican Republic and Mexico, who insisted, successfully, that the opening paragraph of the Charter include the phrase "the equal rights of men and women." In 1952, Lutz's input was important with regard to the formation of the United Nations Commission on the Status of Women, a body for which she served as an officer. In 1975, a year before she died, the tireless Lutz attended the International Women's Year conference in Mexico City. Death came to her in Rio de Janeiro on September 16, 1976.

A later generation of feminists in Brazil recognized the pioneering work of Berta Lutz and in 1982 gave her name to the Berta Lutz Tribunal, an interesting combination of mock trial and public forum that had as its focus the continuing discrimination in Brazil against working women.

SOURCES:

Blachman, Morris J. "Selective Omission and Theoretical Distortion in Studying the Political Activity of Women in Brazil," in June Nash and Helen Safa, eds., *Sex and Class in Latin America.* NY: Praeger, 1976, pp. 254–264.

Fundação Getúlio Vargas. *Dicionário Histórico-Biográfico Brasileiro, 1930–1983.* Vol. 3. Rio de Janeiro: 1984.

Hahner, June. *Emancipating the Female Sex: The Struggle for Women's Rights in Brazil, 1850–1940.* Durham: Duke University Press, 1990.

——, ed. *Women in Latin American History: Their Lives and Views.* Los Angeles: UCLA Latin American Center Publications, rev. ed., 1980.

Miller, Francesca. "Latin American Feminism and the Transnational Arena," in Seminar on Feminism and Culture in Latin America, *Women, Culture, and Politics in Latin America.* Berkeley: University of California Press, 1990, pp. 10–26.

——. *Latin American Women and the Search for Social Justice.* Hanover, NH: University Press of New England, 1991.

SUGGESTED READING:

Burns, E. Bradford. *A History of Brazil.* 3rd ed. NY: Columbia University Press, 1993.

Paul B. Goodwin, Jr.,
Professor of History, University of Connecticut, Storrs

Luxembourg, duchess of.

See Luxemburg, duchess of.

Luxemburg, countess of.

See Ermesind of Luxemburg (d. 1247).

Luxemburg, duchess of.

See Elizabeth of Gorlitz (c. 1380–c. 1444).
See Mary of Burgundy (1457–1482).
See Boufflers, Madeleine-Angelique, Duchesse de (1707–1787).

Luxemburg, grand duchess of.

See Charlotte (1896–1985).
See Charlotte (1896–1985) for sidebar on Marie Adelaide of Luxemburg (1894–1924).
See Josephine-Charlotte of Belgium (b. 1927).

Luxemburg, Madeleine-Angelique de Neufville-Villeroi, Duchesse de (1707–1787).

See Boufflers, Madeleine-Angelique, Duchess de.

Luxemburg, Rosa (1870–1919)

Polish-German economist and socialist political theoretician whose work contributed significantly to Marxist thought. Name variations: Rozalia or Róża

Luxsenburg. Pronunciation: Ro-za LOOKS-em-boorg. Born Rozalia Luxsenburg on March 5, 1870, at Zamosc, Russian Poland; murdered on January 15, 1919, in Berlin, Germany; fifth child of Line (Loewenstein) Luxsenburg and Elias (or Eduard) Luxsenburg (a timber merchant); attended the Second Women's Gymnasium, Warsaw, Russian Poland and the University of Zurich, Switzerland; graduated Doctor of Philosophy in economics, 1897; married Gustav Lübeck, in 1898 (divorced); no children.

Selected publications: Social Reform or Revolution *(1900);* Organizational Questions of Russian Social Democracy *(1904);* The Mass Strike, the Political Parties and Trade Unions *(1906);* The Accumulation of Capital *(1913);* The Crisis of Social-Democracy *(1916);* What Does the Spartacus League Want? *(1919);* The Russian Revolution *(1921).*

When the Bolshevik revolution broke out in Russia in October 1917, many socialists hoped that this event was the forerunner of a more extensive revolutionary upheaval throughout Europe. Nowhere were the hopes and expectations of such an event more eagerly anticipated than in Germany. Prior to the outbreak of the Great War, the German Social-Democratic Party (SPD) constituted the largest socialist party anywhere in the world and was the home of some of the most important revolutionary theoreticians of the era. Among them, one in particular stood out for the depth of her intellectual vision and radical commitment—Rosa Luxemburg.

She was born Rosa Luxsenburg in 1870, into a middle-class Jewish family in Zamosc, Poland, which was then part of the Russian Empire. Her father Eduard Luxsenburg was a timber merchant whose business fortunes fluctuated with the ups and downs of the local economy. Although he took no interest in political questions, Eduard was actively involved in a variety of local cultural and, in particular, educational issues.

Rosa's mother **Line Luxsenburg** was a reserved woman whose principal passion was classical Polish and German literature (a trait which she would pass on to her daughter). Both parents' interest in cultural matters was indicative of their refusal to identify closely with the narrow parochial interests of the Jewish community in Zamosc. Both Eduard and Line made a conscious attempt to assimilate themselves and their children into the broader, more cosmopolitan environment of Polish society.

There is little to suggest that the Luxsenburgs were a particularly close family. Later in life, Rosa would regret the lack of intimacy between her parents and their children. However, she herself would make little effort to regularly correspond with her family and, as she often complained to her friends, found her infrequent visits home tiresome.

For business reasons, Eduard moved his family to Warsaw in 1873. Shortly afterwards, the three-year-old Rosa was discovered to have a disease of the hip which was then wrongly diagnosed as tuberculosis. Her doctor recommended that the leg be placed in a cast and that she be confined to bed. After 12 months, Luxemburg was released from the cast only to discover that normal growth in the affected leg had been retarded. She was left with a permanent and pronounced limp which would continue to cause periodic pain throughout her life.

In 1884, Luxemburg was enrolled in the Second Women's Gymnasium, one of the top schools for girls in Warsaw. Entry into this institution was not easy for Rosa. First, she had to

Rosa Luxemburg

demonstrate a knowledge of what was for her a foreign language, Russian (the medium of instruction). Moreover, due to a government restriction on the number of Jewish students who could attend the gymnasium, she was required to attain a higher score than other students on the entrance exam. Despite these obstructions, Luxemburg was admitted and proved an able pupil, excelling particularly in mathematics and languages. She perfected her Russian and became fluent in Latin and French (later in life she also acquired a reading command of Italian, English, and Dutch).

While still at school, Luxemburg began to associate with the political organization Proletariat II, one of the first quasi-Marxist groups in the Russian Empire. By 1887, she was actively involved in underground discussion meetings and the illegal distribution of socialist propaganda. Although these activities were largely harmless, they proved a constant source of annoyance to the authorities. As a result, when Luxemburg came to graduate later that same year, she was denied the gold medal of achievement to which her high grades entitled her.

She was the sharp sword, the living flame of the revolution.

—Clara Zetkin

Following graduation, Luxemburg worked for a short time as a governess, but her real desire was to continue her academic studies. At that time, however, women were not accepted as students at any institute of higher learning in Poland. Consequently, Luxemburg matriculated at Zurich University in Switzerland, a school well known for its liberal policies regarding women students as well as for being an important political center for Eastern European radicals. When Rosa first registered at Zurich in 1890, she decided to adopt a more Germanized version of her name "Luxsenburg" and signed herself as "Luxemburg." She spent her initial two years at university studying natural science and mathematics before transferring her interests to economics, philosophy and law.

Shortly after arriving in Switzerland, Luxemburg met Leo Jogiches, a professed Marxist three years her senior who came from Vilna (now Vilnius in Lithuania). Jogiches' revolutionary activities as a journalist and strike organizer had been well known in Vilna, particularly to the tsar's secret police, the Okhrana. When the latter issued a warrant for his arrest (ostensibly on the grounds that he had evaded his military service), Jogiches had escaped to Zurich. There, he and Luxemburg became lovers.

In 1892, Luxemburg and Jogiches were among the co-founders of the Polish Socialist Party (PPS). Much to their disgust, however, the PPS was soon taken over by a faction which advocated the cause of Polish national independence. This was unacceptable to the couple, because they believed that the political struggle for national independence only served to distract the working class from its principal goal, the revolutionary overthrow of the capitalist system. Accordingly, in 1893, Rosa, Leo and several other leading Marxists made plans to found a genuinely radical party which would have as its goal the creation of a socialist society in Poland. After numerous difficulties and false starts, the Social-Democratic Party of the Kingdom of Poland and Lithuania (SDKPiL) was founded in 1898. This organization survived until 1918, when it merged with other left-wing groups to form the Polish Communist Party.

During the years leading up to the creation of the SDKPiL, Luxemburg became increasingly active as a socialist theoretician and served as the editor of the influential journal *Sprawa Robotnicza* (The Workers' Cause). She also worked on her doctoral thesis (an account of the emergence and development of Polish industry) and spent some time in Paris gathering research material. In addition, Luxemburg became increasingly involved in the activities of the German Social-Democratic Party (SPD), becoming a regular contributor to such party newspapers as *Die Neue Zeit*.

By the time her doctoral dissertation was accepted in 1897, Luxemburg had decided to move to Germany, then the leading center of radical political activity. There was, however, an important obstacle in the path of such a move. As a Russian citizen, she stood in constant danger of being expelled from Germany if her political activities proved unacceptable to the authorities. What she required was German citizenship. To this end (and with Leo's full approval), in 1898 Luxemburg entered a marriage of convenience with Gustav Lübeck, the son of a close friend. She and Lübeck parted immediately after the ceremony and, following some delay in receiving the necessary citizenship papers, were eventually divorced.

Initially, Luxemburg faced another, potentially more serious, obstacle once she arrived in Germany. As a young female Polish immigrant, she was not taken seriously by the senior, male-dominated echelons of the SPD leadership. Soon, however, her keen intelligence as a theoretician and her evident abilities as a public speaker brought Luxemburg to the attention of such key party leaders as August Bebel and Karl Kautsky.

In 1898, Luxemburg scored her first major success at the SPD congress held at Stuttgart. It was there that she launched her famous attack on the "reformist" faction within the party and, in particular, on its leading delegate, Eduard Bernstein. The latter had argued that recent social and economic improvements in the status of workers in Germany had now dispensed with the need for a class struggle to bring about a revolutionary overthrow of the capitalist system. Rather, Bernstein suggested, socialist aims could be fully attained through a series of gradual, legislative reforms in the national Parliament. For her part, Luxemburg denounced this tactic as playing into the hands of the ruling class and stridently reaffirmed the necessity of the revolutionary struggle.

Over the next few years, Luxemburg was deeply involved in propaganda work on behalf of the SPD. She embarked on an exhaustive series of speaking tours which were concentrated mainly in the eastern areas of the German empire and included large numbers of workers of Polish origin. This demanding schedule was augmented by her extensive journalistic activities on behalf of the SPD press and her editorship of a variety of Polish journals, such as the *Gazeta Ludowa* (People's Gazette), *Przeglad Socjaldemokratyczny* (Social-Democratic Review), and *Czerwony Sztandar* (Red Flag).

In 1904, Luxemburg attended an international socialist congress in Amsterdam at which she gave a speech attacking the autocratic German emperor, Wilhelm II. As a result, on her return to Germany, she was arrested by the authorities and sentenced to three months in the Zwickau prison in Berlin. Her time in jail, however, could not be considered onerous. She was permitted generous access to newspapers and books, and her friends could even supply her with meals from a local restaurant.

More significantly, it was during this period of imprisonment that Luxemburg wrote the *Organizational Questions of Russian Social-Democ-*

Rosa Luxemburg addressing the Congress of the Second International, Stuttgart, 1907.

racy. This text (along with the slightly later *The Mass Strike, the Political Parties and Trade Unions*) is highly significant because it is here that she launched her most telling criticisms of the centralizing and authoritarian tendencies of V.I. Lenin and the Bolshevik Party. Throughout her life, Luxemburg consistently rejected the Leninist strategy which viewed a minority "vanguard" party as the inaugurator and leader of the revolutionary process. Rather, she believed that, if socialism were to be achieved, it could only be the result of a spontaneous movement on the part of the vast majority of the working class itself.

Following the outbreak of revolution in Russia in 1905, Luxemburg and Jogiches traveled to Warsaw in order to participate in events firsthand. There, they engaged in a variety of agitational activities but were soon arrested and charged with conspiring to overthrow the Russian empire. Before the trial could take place, however, Luxemburg fell ill and was released from prison. Immediately on her return to Berlin, she was arrested by the German authorities (this time on a charge of incitement) and imprisoned for two months.

In 1907, Luxemburg's position as one of the SPD's leading theoreticians was further recognized by her appointment in economics at the party's recently founded institute of further education. Although initially hesitant about accepting this position, she quickly recognized the important opening this appointment offered. Not only did it afford her a level of financial security which she had previously lacked but, moreover, it granted her an opportunity to work in a dynamic intellectual environment in which she could hope to develop her own theoretical interests.

Despite her growing public stature within the ranks of the socialist movement, Luxemburg found herself becoming increasingly isolated in her private life. Her intimate relationship with Leo Jogiches ended, although they continued as friends and intellectual collaborators. She then embarked on a number of affairs, invariably with younger men, none of which provided the personal warmth and assurance she so ardently desired. The most passionate of these affairs (with Costa Zetkin, the son of her close friend and fellow socialist, *Clara Zetkin) ended when Luxemburg realized that she was acting more like a mother figure than a lover.

In 1913, Luxemburg published what is widely regarded as her most important theoretical work, *The Accumulation of Capital*. This difficult and demanding book contained one of the first sustained analyses of the role of capital

in the Third World. It carefully scrutinized the function of imperialist and colonialist policies in maintaining the capitalist system in the industrial heartlands of Western Europe and North America. The subject of much contemporary debate and criticism, *The Accumulation of Capital* remains one of the most notable and profound works in the Marxist canon.

Like many other socialists of this period, Luxemburg became increasingly concerned about the looming threat of war in Europe. Her speaking tours were almost entirely devoted to denouncing militarism and war as "barbaric, deeply immoral, [and] reactionary." As a result of these speeches, Luxemburg was arrested in February 1914. She was tried on a charge of sedition and sentenced to one year in prison, although she was subsequently released pending an appeal.

The SPD's decision, in July 1914, to support the German war effort came as a great disappointment to both Luxemburg and others on the radical left. She immediately threw herself into the pacifist movement but this engagement was cut short when her pending appeal was denied. Luxemburg served her sentence in the Barnimstrasse Women's Prison in Berlin where, once again, conditions were relatively pleasant. She resumed her study of botany (an interest ever since university) and was allowed to continue to write. She issued several replies to critics of *The Accumulation of Capital* and in *The Crisis of Social-Democracy* (1916) launched a forceful attack on the SPD leadership for its capitulation to militarism. She prophetically warned that the current conflict was laying the conditions not only for the defeat of socialism in Germany, but for future wars in Europe which would herald the beginning of a new era of "barbarism."

By the time of her release in February 1916, radical opposition to the SPD had gathered around the newly established International Group (also known as the Spartacus League, in reference to the 1st century BCE Greek slave and hero who led a rebellion against the Romans). Co-founded by Luxemburg and Karl Liebknecht, son of the SPD party chief Wilhelm Liebknecht, the League hoped to end the world war by fomenting revolution in Germany. Due to the strong feelings of German nationalism and patriotism engendered by the war, however, Luxemburg and Liebknecht found far fewer supporters than they had anticipated. On the first of May, this group organized a large antiwar demonstration in Berlin which was closely monitored by the police. Shortly afterwards, Luxemburg was designated a "danger to the safety of the Reich" and placed in "protective custody." In effect, this meant that she was to be held in prison indefinitely without charge. She was initially placed in solitary confinement in a darkened cell (during which time, it is said, her hair turned completely gray), although later her conditions were improved. Nevertheless, she suffered from severe depression and her friends were worried that she might attempt suicide.

The one bright moment of her imprisonment came with the news of the outbreak of revolution in Russia in February 1917. By the end of the year, however, her hopes were largely dashed when it became clear that the second Bolshevik revolution in October had failed to follow through with its socialist intentions. Although Luxemburg had known Lenin personally for many years, she bitterly denounced the lack of political democracy and personal freedom which was countenanced by the Bolshevik Party. These criticisms did not become widely known until the posthumous publication of her book *The Russian Revolution* in 1921. By that time, however, all organized opposition to the Bolsheviks had been suppressed, and her warnings about the future course of the revolution were all but ignored.

Following Germany's military defeat at the end of 1918, the revolutionary momentum in the country gathered pace. When Wilhelm II abdicated early in November, a new government under SPD control came to power. Much to the alarm of the SPD leadership, however, many workers and demobilized soldiers were not satisfied with the reformist stance adopted by the new regime. Instead, they loudly demanded the creation of workers' and soldiers' *soviets* as a first step towards the revolutionary reconstitution of society as a whole.

When Luxemburg returned to Berlin on November 10, 1918, the situation in the streets was fluid and uncertain. She immediately assumed editorship of *Die Rote Fahne* (The Red Flag) which, in the next few weeks, roundly denounced the new government and called for the satisfaction of the workers' and soldiers' demands. At the end of December, a special congress was held during which the Spartacus

From the movie Rosa Luxemburg, directed by Margarethe von Trotta, starring Barbara Sukowa.

League founded the German Communist Party (KPD). Luxemburg delivered the keynote address at this congress (known as *What Does the Spartacus League Want?*) in which she laid out the new party's revolutionary manifesto. This was to be her last public appearance.

Luxemburg was more aware than were many of her communist colleagues of the powerful position enjoyed by the SPD (and their new right-wing allies). Nonetheless, the KPD leadership decided to initiate an armed uprising in the hope that this action would spark a widespread working-class revolt. On January 10, 1919, their woefully ill-organized revolution began in Berlin. The final outcome was never seriously in doubt and, after three days of street fighting, was completely crushed by army units and assorted right-wing militias.

In the days that followed, the SPD government offered a substantial reward for the capture of "Red Rosa" whom it had now come to perceive as its most dangerous enemy. When she was apprehended on January 15, she was taken to the Hotel Eden in Berlin and subjected to a brutal interrogation. After several hours, Luxemburg was led from the hotel and, just outside the main door, knocked unconscious by a blow from a rifle butt. She was then placed in a car and taken away. The car had only traveled a few yards, however, before the officer in command, Lieutenant Vogel, drew his pistol and shot Rosa Luxemburg in the head.

"Luxemburg's causes failed; her vision was faulty," wrote Lamar Cecil. "But her intelligence, her forcefulness, her absorption in the cause of improving the world, her insistence that socialism have a human face give her today a reputation, and a relevance, that her socialist rivals, more famous and more successful in their own time, no longer enjoy."

SOURCES:

Abraham, Richard. *Rosa Luxemburg: A Life for the International.* NY: Berg, 1989.

Cecil, Lamar. "Rosa Luxemburg," in *Historic World Leaders.* Edited by Anne Commire. Detroit, MI: Gale Research Co., 1994.

Ettinger, Elzbieta. *Rosa Luxemburg: A Life.* Boston, MA: Beacon Press, 1986.

Luxemburg, Rosa. *Comrade and Lover: Rosa Luxemburg's Letters to Leo Jogiches.* Edited by Elzbieta Ettinger. Cambridge MA: MIT Press, 1981.

———. *Selected Political Writings.* Edited by Dick Howard. NY: Monthly Review Press, 1971.

Nettl, J.P. *Rosa Luxemburg.* 2 vols. Oxford: Oxford University Press, 1966.

SUGGESTED READING:

Bronner, Stephen E. *Rosa Luxemburg: Revolutionary for Our Times.* 1987.

———, ed. *The Letters of Rosa Luxemburg,* 1979.

Flechtheim, Ossip K., ed. *Rosa Luxemburg: Politische Schriften.* 3 vols. 1966–68.

Frolich, Paul. *Rosa Luxemburg, Her Life and Work,* 1940.

Shorske, Carl. *German Social Democracy.* NY: John Wiley and Sons, 1955.

RELATED MEDIA:

Rosa Luxemburg (film), directed by **Margarethe Von Trotta**, starring **Barbara Sukowa**, Artificial Eye, 1987.

Dave Baxter,
Department of Philosophy,
Wilfrid Laurier University, Waterloo, Ontario, Canada

Luynes, duchess de.

See Rohan-Montbazon, Marie de (1600–1679).

Lyall, Edna (1857–1903).

See Bayly, Ada Ellen.

Lydia (fl. 53 CE)

Biblical woman who was the first Christian convert in Europe. Name variations: Lydia of Thyatira. Born in Thyatira on the border of Lydia in Asia Minor.

A prosperous businesswoman from the city of Thyatira (she sold purple-dyed cloth, for which the city was known), Lydia was converted to Christianity by the apostle Paul and is considered the first Christian convert in Europe. Her story is recorded in Acts.

Around the year 55, Paul was making a voyage to Macedonia and stopped in the Roman colony of Philippi, where he stayed for several days. On the Sabbath, he ventured outside the city gates to preach to a group of women who had assembled near the river to pray. Lydia, identified as a proselyte, a worshipper of the true God, was among the group that had gathered. Opening her heart to Paul's message, she was baptized that very day along with her entire household. Afterwards, eager to hear more about the Messiah, she issued an invitation to Paul and his companions to lodge at her home, which he accepted.

After Paul left Philippi, he continued to communicate with Lydia through letters, which she treasured and memorized. After her conversion, she lost interest in her successful business, and used her money to spread the new faith.

Lyell, Lottie (1890–1925)

Australia's first female star, screenwriter, and director, whose films are considered classics of the silent-film era. Born Charlotte Edith Cox in Sydney, Aus-

tralia, on February 23, 1890; died on December 21, 1925; daughter of Charlotte Louise (Hancock) Cox and Edward Cox (a real estate agent); married Raymond Longford, in 1925; no children.

Filmography—as writer: Australia Calls *(1913);* The Sentimental Bloke *(1919);* Ginger Mick *(1920);* Rudd's New Selection *(1921); (also director)* The Blue Mountains Mystery *(1921).*

Selected filmography—as an actress: The Fatal Wedding *(1911);* The Romantic Story of Margaret Catchpole *(1911);* The Tide of Death *(1912);* The Midnight Wedding *(1912);* 'Neath Australian Skies *(1913);* Australia Calls *(1913);* The Silence of Dean Maitland *(1914);* Taking His Chance *(1914);* Mutiny on the Bounty *(1916);* A Maori Maid's Love *(1916);* The Church and the Woman *(1917);* The Woman Suffers *(1918);* The Sentimental Bloke *(1919);* Ginger Mick *(1920);* Rudd's New Selection *(1921).*

Lottie Lyell was a major pioneer in Australia's nascent motion-picture industry. She began her film career at age 21 and, by the time she died 14 years later, she had become Australia's first female box-office attraction, having starred in over 20 films. She had also become Australia's first woman screenwriter and had directed, or co-directed, films that are considered classics of the silent-film era.

Lyell was born Charlotte Edith Cox in 1890 in Sydney and grew up in Balmain. Having studied elocution as a child, she made her stage debut in 1907, taking the name Lyell. She then joined the Edwin Geach Popular Dramatic Organization and toured Australia and New Zealand, establishing her reputation as a dynamic actress. Raymond Longford was a fellow thespian on the tours. Though he was already married, he and Lyell began a professional and personal relationship which would last until Lyell's death.

In 1911, Lyell and Longford began working for Spencer's Pictures. With Longford as director and Lyell as the star, they had their first commercial successes as filmmakers with the release of *The Fatal Wedding*, followed by *The Romantic Story of *Margaret Catchpole* (both 1911). An expert equestrian, Lyell pioneered the image of the independent "bush woman," a swashbuckling film heroine who saved the lives of her hapless male co-stars.

Lyell was the first Australian woman to work behind and in front of the cameras. Her signature film, *The Woman Suffers* (1918), concerns two young pregnant women who have been abandoned by their lovers. One commits suicide; the other, played by Lyell, decides to raise the child as a single mother, after an unsuccessful abortion attempt. Ultimately, her lover returns, and the two marry. Depicting the "fallen" woman as a survivor who ultimately finds happiness was a clear departure from other films that addressed similar themes, most notably *Lois Weber*'s *Where Are My Children?*

In 1919, Lyell and Longford became internationally recognized with the release of *The Sentimental Bloke*, based on a popular novel written by C.J. Dennis. Lyell starred in the film, co-wrote it with Longford, and, though she most likely co-directed it as well, received only an on-screen acting credit. Far removed from her earlier heroines, the role she played was that of Doreen, a young city woman who works in a factory. The tale of seduction and revenge was hailed for its "naturalistic" performances, briefly banned by the New South Wales chief secretary, and is still considered one of Australia's best silent films. A reviewer for *Triad*, a journal of the arts, wrote in November 1919:

> Doreen in the book charms us so little that we feel like throwing things at her; but the little Australian girl who plays Doreen on the

Lottie Lyell

film is so sprightly and honest, so womanly and sweet, so unaffectedly Australian and human, that we find ourselves really believing in Doreen . . . and that is a great miracle.

Lyell also scripted and co-directed *The Blue Mountains Mystery* (1921) and *The Dinkum Bloke* (1923); the latter was the first Longford film for which she was officially credited as co-director. **Andrée Wright** maintains in *Brilliant Careers* that Longford was fearful of scandal, since back then "women's role was supposed to be confined largely to child-bearing and child-rearing."

Lyell's brilliant career was cut short when she contracted tuberculosis. Though she and Longford had carried on a 17-year affair, he would neither divorce his wife nor publicly acknowledge their relationship until it was clear that Lyell was dying. They were married just a few weeks prior to Lyell's death, at age 35, on December 21, 1925. Raymond Longford's career was never the same without Lottie Lyell.

SOURCES:

Foster, Gwendolyn. *Women Film Directors: An International Bio-critical Dictionary.* Westport, CT: Greenwood Press, 1995.

Long, Joan, and Martin Long. *The Pictures that Moved.* Hutchinson of Australia, 1982.

McFarlane, Brian. *Australian Cinema.* NY: Columbia University Press, 1988.

Porter, Hal. *Stars of Australian Stage and Screen.* Sydney: Halstead Press, 1965.

Wright, Andrée. *Brilliant Careers.* Sydney: Pan Books, 1986.

Deborah Jones,
Studio City, California

Lyell, Mary Horner (1808–1873)

British geologist and conchologist. Born Mary Horner in 1808, probably in London, England; died in 1873; eldest of six daughters of Leonard Horner (a geologist); married Charles Lyell (1797–1875, a geologist), in 1832.

Mary Lyell was born in 1808, the daughter of geologist Leonard Horner. In 1832, she married British geologist Charles Lyell, author of the well-known *Principles of Geology* (1830–33), a work that was used by Charles Darwin (1809–1882) in the formulation of his theory of evolution. Mary Lyell accompanied her husband on expeditions in Europe and North America, and, being fluent in German and French, she frequently translated scientific papers for him. When his eyesight failed, she read to him and handled his correspondence. Serving as an assistant to her husband over the years, Lyell became an accomplished geologist and conchologist in

her own right, although, like the wives of so many prominent men, she never received the credit due that fact.

Lympany, Moura (1916—)

English pianist who established an international career and whose many recordings from the 1950s were re-released as classic performances in the 1990s. Born Mary Johnstone in Saltash, England, on August 18, 1916.

Mary Johnstone, who changed her name to Moura Lympany for artistic reasons, first studied piano in Belgium and Vienna, before returning to London to work with Tobias Matthay and *Mathilde Verne. In 1938, she made her debut at age 12 with the Mendelssohn G minor Concerto, winning second prize in the Ysaye Competition in Brussels. After World War II, Lympany developed an impressive international career. Many of the recordings she made in the early 1950s were enthusiastically reviewed and quickly became modern classics; some of these were reissued in the 1990s in the new compact disc format. Her American debut took place in 1948. Long a champion of contemporary British music, in 1969 Lympany performed Cyril Scott's Piano Concerto, with the composer in attendance, on the occasion of his 90th birthday. **Margaret Anderson** noted that the pianist's playing represents "a rare responsiveness to great lyrical music." In 1979, she was made a Commander of the Order of the British Empire. When Lympany returned to Carnegie Hall in November 1981, after a long absence, her reputation was still so strong that a large audience turned out to hear her.

John Haag,
Athens, Georgia

Lynch, Anne Charlotte (1815–1891).

See Botta, Anne C.L.

Lynch, Caroline (1819–1884).

See Dexter, Caroline.

Lynch, Eliza (1835–1886)

Irish-born mistress of the dictator Francisco Solano López, who was a major figure in the cultural and political development of Paraguay. Name variations: Elisa; Ella; Eliza Lynch López. Pronunciation: Linch. Born Eliza Alicia Lynch, possibly in County Cork, Ireland, in 1835; died in Paris, France, in 1886; youngest daughter of John Lynch (a medical doctor) and Adelaide (Schnock) Lynch; married Xavier Quatrefages (a

French army surgeon), in 1850, but separated from him shortly before beginning a 17-year liaison with Francisco Solano López, in 1853; children: (with López) six sons and three daughters, most of whom survived to adulthood, including Juan Francisco (b. 1855); Enrique Venancio (b. 1858); Federico Noel (b. 1860); Carlos Honorio (b. 1861); Leopoldo Antonio (b. 1862); and Miguel Marcial (b. 1866); the daughters' names are not recorded.

Family barely survived the Irish famine of 1845; married French army doctor (1850); husband deserted her in Paris (1853), and she took a succession of lovers before meeting Francisco Solano López several months later; returned with him to Paraguay (1854) to live openly with him as his mistress; though never accepted by elite society in Asunción, as the lover of the son of the Paraguayan president, was nonetheless very influential: introduced the first pianos and sewing machines to Paraguayan society, was the leading force behind the construction of many public buildings, and helped improve the educational establishment of the country, especially after López assumed the presidency (1862); as de facto first lady, became the dominant force in Paraguayan cultural matters; as Paraguay entered a disastrous war against Argentina, Brazil, and Uruguay, joined López at the front (1864), and, according to some sources, actually commanded troops; five years later, accompanied what remained of the Paraguayan army as it retreated into the northern jungles; witnessed López's death in battle and buried him and their first-born son herself on the banks of the Aquidaban River (1870); at end of war, was deported, losing most of her wealth; spent the rest of her life unsuccessfully trying to reclaim her lost properties in Paraguay.

On the surface, the cold, windswept, and impoverished areas around County Cork, in Ireland, would seem to have little in common with tropical South America. But such are the ironies of history that it was precisely this locale that gave birth to Madame Lynch, a poor girl turned ingenue turned uncrowned queen of Paraguay. So many unpredictable twists and turns characterized her life that even from the distance of over a century her tale still has the ring of a romantic novel. And in such terms it is still recalled by schoolchildren in Asunción. But Eliza Alicia Lynch was far more than a romantic figure in an exotic country; she acted as a major cultural conduit, recreating a Parisian literary salon in the most rustic country in Latin America and overseeing, in some crucial ways, the modernization of Paraguay.

We know very little of Lynch's childhood. One commentator has gone so far as to suggest that she systematically destroyed the public records dealing with her birth and early life. She later claimed to have affluent antecedents. Her father John, she said, was the highest-placed physician in the district, with a practice that took him far and wide in Ireland. Her family mixed socially with members of the Anglo-Irish elite, and in all things her childhood was a happy one.

The reality was almost certainly different. Although clearly not a product of the lowest rung of Irish society, Lynch probably led a far more precarious existence in her early days than she would care to admit later. She was only ten years old when the famine of 1845 hit the island and left most of its inhabitants dead or in the greatest desperation. Lynch's burning ambitions, which expressed themselves in many ways great and small throughout her life, doubtless had their origin in this time of uncertainty and fear.

If, as a young person, Eliza Lynch worried deeply about her personal fate and even her day-to-day survival, by the time she reached her 15th year she knew what to do about it. When a French army surgeon, Xavier Quatrefages, offered his hand in marriage, she did not hesitate to accept. Soon, she was on her way to Paris.

Quatrefages was the scion of a respectable middle-class family. He was a career army officer with many years of experience behind him and was, to emphasize a point, old enough to be Eliza Lynch's father. That he should become entranced with her was understandable: the one picture we have of Lynch at this age reveals a young woman of surpassing beauty, with gray eyes, a fine figure, and a look of maturity far beyond her years. She displayed, moreover, a charm and a passion that might attract any man of substance and position.

These same qualities that led her so easily into marriage quickly led her out of it. A contretemps evidently took place involving Quatrefages' commanding officer in Algeria; the details of this affair remain hidden even today, but the inevitable result was that Lynch soon found herself cut free from her husband. She might return to genteel poverty in Ireland or England or she might take her chances in Paris. She chose the latter course.

Madame Lynch, as she was now called, became a full-time courtesan. Her flair for languages, her choice of fine furnishings and the best of wines, and a talent for gracefully flattering the most boring of gentlemen callers—all these attributes held her in good stead in the salons of the Second Empire. She knew Russian nobles, Parisian furriers, and the most exciting of military men of all nationalities. But she was constantly looking for a permanent protector, and finally, in 1853, she found him in the person of Francisco Solano López.

López in many ways fit the average Parisian's idea of a savage. Son of the Paraguayan president, he had come to Europe to "show the flag," to purchase armaments for his fledgling military, and to obtain modern machinery for public projects. To French eyes, though, he looked every bit the country bumpkin. Short and inclined to corpulence, with very bad teeth, he dressed grotesquely, yet his uniforms were always expensive and elaborately finished. He not only spent money but spent it carelessly and on people who could mean nothing to him. His behavior at court was extravagant if indelicate. He spoke of himself as being one with Napoleon III, and seemed absolutely heedless of the sneers and snubs that his presumption engendered. Finally, he found himself without any clear allies at court. This left him in a volatile mood. It was at this point that he met Madame Lynch.

The first encounter between the two has entered the history books in the most romanticized guise possible. Some commentators have said that she prostituted herself to him without delay. Whatever the exact circumstances of their first meeting, in short order Lynch joined López for the remainder of his European tour. Together they visited Spain and Italy (and one report even has it that they went to the battlegrounds in Crimea). Finally, at the end of 1854, they set sail for Paraguay. By then, she had become not only López's lover but his confidant, his chief adviser, and the only individual not afraid to forcefully disagree with him.

No record exists of Madame Lynch's feelings when, having crossed the Atlantic and made the 1,000-mile journey upstream to the center of the southern continent, she at last reached the tropical river port of Asunción. We do, however, know that the local Paraguayans were dazzled by her beauty and her Parisian finery. As one Briton who came on the scene a few years later noted:

> I could well believe the story that when she landed in Asunción the simple natives thought her charms were of more than earthly brilliancy, and her dress so sumptuous that they had no words to express the admiration that they both excited. She had received a showy education, spoke English, French, and Spanish with equal facility, gave capital dinner parties, and could drink more champagne without being affected by it than anyone I had ever met with.

Whereas the average Paraguayan might have been deeply impressed with Lynch, the López family proved less than ecstatic over their son's choice of partner. The bishop of Asunción was Francisco Solano López's uncle, and he could hardly be expected to approve the relationship (Lynch, after all, was still married). Carlos Antonio López, the president, refused to receive her in his home, and forbade his eldest son from living outright with her. It was understood within the family, therefore, that Lynch would act only as semi-official consort, never as wife. And so she was legally regarded throughout her years in Paraguay. There was one fact, however, that no one could deny: when she arrived in Asunción, Lynch was pregnant. With the subsequent birth of their first son, Panchito, no one could doubt that the names Lynch and López would thereafter be forever linked.

López's European tour made a deep impression on him. More than anything else, it showed him how very backward his country was. An inland republic, Paraguay had managed to avoid the civil wars and petty squabbles that had characterized South America since independence—but at a price. Earlier regimes had imposed a shroud of isolation on the nation by closing the borders. This had to some extent protected Paraguay, but it had also taken it out of the mainstream of Latin American economic development. Primitive agricultural conditions, barter, and an archaic mercantilism were all still very much a part of Paraguayan economic life when López returned from Europe. Now he set out to change everything in as short a time as possible, and Lynch was there beside him.

Given carte blanche by his father, López began a quick-paced program for the modernization of Paraguay. He hired British engineers and machinists to construct a wide array of public works, including an iron foundry, an arsenal, a merchant fleet, and a railroad. He saved his greatest energies, however, for the expansion of the military. He imported cannon, shot, and the latest weaponry. His engineers constructed a massive fortress, Humaitá, overlooking a bluff at the confluence of the Paraná and Paraguay rivers. This redoubt, often compared to that of Sebastopol, was designed to withstand any force that any foreign power might send against Paraguay by river. Its garrison amounted to tens of thousands of native recruits, all ready to die for López and for Paraguay. Within a few years, López had forged a formidable army, perhaps the largest in South America. Now even Napoleon III would hesitate to scoff at the man whom many had called savage.

Lynch, for her part, attempted to crash into the elite society of Asunción like a thunderbolt. López had showered her with money, properties, and luxuries of all kinds. Soon, she was demonstrably the richest woman in Paraguay. But it was not enough, for she craved the recognition and acceptance that the conservative society women of Asunción withheld from her. She might be good enough to bear López's "bastards," but she was not good enough for those women to dine with. Their snubs she would later repay. Meanwhile, she busied herself with her children, and with promoting education in the country. She had the government hire instructors and cultural advisers from Europe. She sponsored literary contests and advised journalists. She created a salon in Asunción that included many, though not all, of the members of the foreign community.

Eliza Lynch influenced Paraguayan culture in some basic ways. She introduced jewelled coiffures, straw hats decorated with flowers, imported perfumes, tulles and belts. Her dress broke away from traditional lines. The open way she flaunted her differences made the younger generation aware that they might express their prosperity in ways undreamt of by their parents. Members of the Paraguayan elite began to see themselves almost as Europeans— and they began to have European ambitions.

These ambitions sometimes went beyond the drinking of champagne and the wearing of Parisian fashions. In the case of López, they included making a major political impact within South America. In 1862, he succeeded to the presidency after the death of his father and soon thereafter began to flex his muscle.

Brazil had constantly encroached upon Paraguayan territory, and in 1864 López decided to retaliate by occupying the Brazilian province of Mato Grosso. In the following year, he rashly sent an expeditionary force across Argentine territory to attack southern Brazil, thereby bringing into existence against him a triple alliance of Argentina, Brazil, and Uruguay (at that time a Brazilian dependency). The bloody war that followed lasted until 1870.

Critics of Eliza Lynch have argued that she encouraged López to provoke the war in the expectation that Paraguay would emerge from it as an acknowledged Great Power, with her lover as emperor and their children—she had nine— assured of princely futures. There seems to be little to this tale. And, in any case, things did not turn out so well for Paraguay and its army. After a short offensive phase, López's troops were forced to retreat to Humaitá where they spent nearly four years under constant siege by the allies.

The campaign was the worst ever seen in South America. The sufferings of the uncomplaining Paraguayans assumed terrible proportions. Food was always scarce and became more so as time went on. Women were mobilized for agriculture and to weave the native cotton, a craft that just before the war had been almost given up because of the cheapness of English cotton goods. The carpets from the railway station in Asunción were cut up into ponchos for the soldiers. Supplies of iron were obtained by melting down church bells and quantities of Brazilian shell fired into the earthworks at Humaitá. Battles around the fortress exacerbated the losses still further. As at Fredericksburg during the American Civil War, thousands of men died in single engagements. Then, in 1867, epidemic disease—smallpox, cholera, and measles— struck both the Paraguayan and Brazilian lines simultaneously. The pestilence was soon communicated to the civilian population, with horrendous results. Almost half of the Paraguayan population of 500,000 died.

It is enough to see her ride by, gracefully and easily, firmly seated and handling her spirited horse with all the coolness of a woman who has overcome fear, to realize that she is like the women riders of gay background who ride daily in Regents Park and the Bois de Boulogne.

—Hector Varela

As these events unfolded, López began to lose his grip on reality. Constantly suspicious of treachery, he ordered the torture and execution of many of his key collaborators. Anyone who seemed to doubt the wisdom of continuing the hopeless struggle against the allies was liable for the harshest treatment. Only Madame Lynch was able to calm his rage. For the most part, she had been with him at Humaitá during the fighting. She ministered to the sick and gave encouragement to the troops. Some have maintained that she operated an espionage organization among the soldiery and that she herself directed torture against suspected opponents. No evidence supports this calumny, though it is clear enough that Lynch remained a strong partisan of the Paraguayan cause long after it was obvious that López could neither win nor long continue the fight. She several times volunteered to command female troops, and though the offer was rejected, she still wore a uniform of sorts, complete with riding crop as symbol of authority.

More and more, the Paraguayan scene came to resemble a Greek tragedy. Asunción fell in January 1869 at about the same time the starving remnants of the garrison at Humaitá finally gave up. Lynch and López fled to the interior and watched from a distance while the Brazilians installed a provisional government in the Paraguayan capital. Though López now commanded only a tiny army of children and old men, he used these to effectively harass the allies over the next months. Eventually they grew tired of these raids and mounted a new and well-provisioned expeditionary force against López.

This sparked the final diaspora. Lynch and López, accompanied by a few faithful associates, continued to fall back into the jungles of northeastern Paraguay. During these months on the run, López, his fury grown uncontrollable, shot many of his remaining cohorts, including some of his own relatives. Even Lynch and the children, who were now malnourished, failed to calm his wrath.

Finally, at the beginning of March 1870, the Brazilians caught up with López near the bank of the Aquidaban river at Cerro Cora. Called upon to surrender by his pursuers, he defiantly shouted back at them: "I die with my country!" A cavalryman then lanced him, and he fell back into the shallow water to die. At this moment, Lynch was on a nearby trail escaping in a carriage together with Panchito, now at 15 a colonel in the Paraguayan army. The Brazilians approached, Panchito fired his pistol, and then, like his father before him, he was lanced to death. His mother, covered in his blood, was permitted to dig out a grave with her hands for both her first-born son and for López.

Lynch was treated with deference once she was delivered as a prisoner to officers of the Brazilian navy. But there was never any doubt as to what would be done with her. Crowds had gathered at Asunción to jeer her, and to demand that the allies force her to hand over to them the jewels and other properties that López had bestowed upon her. She denied that she had anything, aside from some minor pieces of luggage. She demanded, moreover, to face her accusers, among whom she knew were many who had once called her friend. The Brazilians refused. They did, however, permit her to return to Paris with her children.

Still a relatively young woman, Eliza Lynch might have resumed the life of a courtesan. She chose, instead, to spend the rest of her life trying to clear her name and that of López. Her children, she argued, should still gain their inheritances from their father, no matter what he had done. She even returned once to South America in 1875 with this mission in mind. She made little headway in reclaiming the vast lands that López had transferred to her name during the war. In the end, tired and depressed, she returned to Europe and left her remaining Paraguayan matters to her lawyers. She went for a time to Jerusalem on a pilgrimage but in the end came back to Paris, where, alone and largely forgotten, she died in 1886.

The story of Eliza Alicia Lynch might appear to outsiders as a minor ripple along the stream of history. But for Paraguayans, her historical role has been central. She came to their country at a crucial juncture, helped them gain a more modern understanding of the world and their place in it, and went loyally with them through the maelstrom of total war. This more than qualified her as a national heroine, and on that basis her remains were brought back to Paraguay in the 1960s. Even there, however, she still remains a controversial figure.

SOURCES:

Brodsky, Alyn. *Madame Lynch and Friend*. NY: Harper and Row, 1975.

Pendle, George. "Eliza Lynch and the English in Paraguay, 1853–1875," in *History Today*. May 1954, pp. 346–353.

Pla, Josefina. *The British in Paraguay, 1850–1870*. Richmond: Richmond Publishing, 1976.

SUGGESTED READING:

Barrett, William E. *Woman on Horseback*. NY: Modern Library, 1952.

Kolinski, Charles J. *Independence or Death!: The Story of the Paraguayan War*. Gainesville, FL: University of Florida Press, 1965.

Warren, Harris G. *Paraguay: An Informal History*. Norman: University of Oklahoma Press, 1949.

Thomas Whigham,
Professor of Latin American History,
University of Georgia, Athens, Georgia

Lynch, Madame (1835–1886).

See Lynch, Eliza.

Lyngstad, Frida (b. 1945).

See ABBA.

Lynn, Diana (1926–1971)

American actress and pianist. Name variations: performed briefly as Dolly Loehr. Born Delores Loehr on October 7, 1926, in Los Angeles, California; died in a Los Angeles hospital after suffering a stroke and brain hemorrhage on December 18, 1971; only daughter of

Louis Loehr (an executive in an oil company); educated on the lot of Paramount Studio; married John C. Lindsay (an architect), on January 5, 1948 (divorced 1953); married Mortimer Hall; children: four.

Filmography: They Shall Have Music *(1939);* There's Magic in Music *(The Hard-Boiled Canary, 1941);* Star-Spangled Rhythm *(1942);* The Major and the Minor *(1942);* Henry Aldrich Gets Glamour *(1943);* The Miracle of Morgan's Creek *(1944);* And the Angels Sing *(1944);* Henry Aldrich Plays Cupid *(1944);* Our Hearts Were Young and Gay *(1944);* Out of This World *(1945);* Duffy's Tavern *(1945);* Our Hearts Were Growing Up *(1946);* The Bride Wore Boots *(1946);* Easy Come, Easy Go *(1947);* Variety Girl *(1947);* Ruthless *(1948);* Texas Brooklyn and Heaven *(1948);* Every Girl Should Be Married *(1948);* My Friend Irma *(1949);* Paid in Full *(1950);* My Friend Irma Goes West *(1950);* Rogues of Sherwood Forest *(1950);* Peggy *(1950);* Bedtime for Bonzo *(1951);* The People Against O'Hara *(1951);* Meet Me at the Fair *(1953);* Plunder of the Sun *(1953);* Track of the Cat *(1954);* An Annapolis Story *(1955);* You're Never Too Young *(1955);* The Kentuckian *(1955);* Company of Killer *(The Protectors, originally made for television, 1970).*

Diana Lynn was born in Los Angeles, California, in 1926. A musical prodigy, she began playing the piano professionally at age 10 and was taken to the Paramount lot at age 13 to accompany a child violinist who was auditioning. Lynn stayed on to play the piano in two films, *They Shall Have Music* (1939) and *There's Magic in Music* (1941), though she was given little in the way of dialogue. In 1941, she signed a long-term contract with the studio, and after some intense dramatic coaching, she made her acting debut as **Ginger Rogers'* bratty roommate in *The Major and the Minor* (1942), directed by Billy Wilder. Her next effort, *The Miracle of Morgan's Creek* (1944), in which she played the kid sister of *Betty Hutton, brought favorable notices from the critics and led to a string of "kid sister" and young adult roles, the best of which was Emily in *Our Hearts Were Young And Gay* (1944), based on the book by **Cornelia Otis Skinner* and **Emily Kimbrough**. "The ever-breathless, slightly madcap Miss Lynn is capital in everything she does," enthused *Variety* of her performance. The success of the picture inspired the mediocre sequel, *Our Hearts Were Growing Up* (1946).

While her star was rising, Lynn was more concerned with her approaching 18th birthday. "I won't have to have a teacher following every-

where in the studio, even into make-up and hair-dressing," she told **Eileen Creelman** in an interview for the *New York Sun*. "I was fond of my teacher. But it's not a pleasant feeling not to be allowed to be alone. That's the law. They have to watch you every minute. But I'll be eighteen next month."

As she matured into a leading lady, Lynn's assignments were typical ingenue roles in a variety of films, notably the young friend of **Marie Wilson** in *My Friend Irma* (1949) and its sequel, *My Friend Irma Goes West* (1950). During the 1950s, Lynn's film career began to wane, and she turned more and more to the stage, performing in stock and with the La Jolla (California) Players. In 1952, she appeared opposite Maurice Evans in the New York City Center's production of Ibsen's *The Wild Duck*, and in 1953 played opposite Sir Cedric Hardwicke in *Horses in Midstream*. Lynn also made regular appearances on the emerging medium of television. In addition to guest appearances with variety show hosts Jack Carter, Ken Murray, Milton Berle,

Diana Lynn

and Ed Wynn, she signed an exclusive contract with the Schlitz Playhouse. "In TV she has not only had a happy variety of romantic and comedy parts," noted *Life*, "but has played an entire concerto composed for her." Lynn had a more practical view of her television success. "More cab drivers recognize me now that I'm in TV than they ever did when I was only in movies," she observed. The actress was attempting a film comeback when she died of a stroke in 1971.

SOURCES:
Current Biography. NY: H.W. Wilson, 1953.
Katz, Ephraim. *The Film Encyclopedia.* NY: Harper-Collins, 1994.

Barbara Morgan,
Melrose, Massachusetts

Lynn, Eliza (1822–1898).

See Linton, Eliza Lynn.

Lynn, Janet (1953—)

American figure skater who won five national championships. Born Janet Lynn Nowicki on April 6, 1953, in Chicago, Illinois; daughter of Florian Walter Nowicki and Ethelyne (Gehrke) Nowicki; attended Rockford College, 1972.

Made the U.S. Olympic team at age 14 (1968); won the U.S. national championship (1969, 1970, 1971, 1972, 1973); won a bronze medal at the Sapporo Olympics (1972); was a silver medalist at the World figure-skating championships (1973); obtained a three-year contract for $1.4 million with Shipstad and Johnson Ice Follies, becoming the highest paid woman athlete at that time.

Janet Lynn was one of the first women to become an athletic superstar; her $1.4 million three-year contract with Shipstad and Johnson Ice Follies was the most lucrative deal signed by any woman athlete up to that time.

Born Janet Lynn Nowicki in Chicago in 1953, Lynn began to skate at age two-and-a-half on a southwest Chicago pond; by the end of her first afternoon, she could skate backwards. Before long, her parents switched her from dreaded dancing lessons to longed-for skating lessons. By age four, when she had learned all her teacher could offer, her parents moved to Rockford, Illinois, so that she could study with skating pro **Slavka Kohout** at the Wagon Wheel resort. It was Kohout who suggested that Lynn use her first and second names professionally.

Lynn began to win competitions and captured the national junior title when she was 12.

At 14, she made the U.S. Olympic team, but did not place. The next year, she won her first U.S. national championship; she would place first in 1969, 1970, 1971, 1972, and 1973. In 1972, Lynn competed in her second Olympics in Sapporo, Japan. Aware that she was weak in the compulsory school figures, she had stuck with a grueling five-hour-a-day practice schedule before the games, but it was not enough. She was seriously behind in points after the compulsories. Though Lynn seemed nervous during her the free-skating program, she enchanted on-lookers with her talent and dazzling smile and won the bronze medal. (**Beatrix Schuba** walked off with the gold medal.)

In 1973, Lynn was second in the World championships. The following year, at age 21, she decided she had had enough of the pressure of competition and left competitive skating to star in the Ice Follies.

SOURCES:
Hollander, Phyllis. *100 Greatest Women in Sports.* NY: Grosset & Dunlap, 1976.
Moran, Malcolm. "Life Is Returning Janet Lynn's Smile," in *The New York Times Biographical Service.* November 1982, p. 1498.

Karin L. Haag,
Athens, Georgia

Lynn, Kathleen (1874–1955)

Irish doctor and political activist. Born Kathleen Florence Lynn in Mullafany, County Mayo, Ireland, on January 28, 1874; died in Dublin, Ireland, on September 14, 1955; daughter of Reverend Robert Young Lynn and Catherine (Wynne) Lynn; educated at Alexandra College, Dublin; studied medicine at Royal University of Ireland and Royal College of Surgeons of Ireland, 1894–99; Fellow, Royal College of Surgeons of Ireland, 1909; co-founder of St. Ultan's Children's Hospital, 1919.

Kathleen Florence Lynn's father was a cleric in the Church of Ireland; on her mother's side, she was descended from the aristocratic Maxwell family. She grew up in one of the most beautiful, as well as one of the poorest, parts of Ireland which still bore the scars of the Great Famine (1845–48). Lynn was educated at Alexandra College in Dublin where she won a number of prizes and scholarships. Despite the obstacles faced by women who wished to study medicine, she was thus encouraged to pursue her ambition to become a doctor. She studied at the Royal University of Ireland and at the Royal College of Surgeons and was the most brilliant student in her class, winning in 1896 the first prize and medal in both practical anatomy and histology. Lynn graduated in 1899 but when looking for positions encountered the widespread prejudice against women doctors. At the Adelaide Hospital, the staff opposed her appointment, and she took up other short-term appointments in Dublin at the Eye and Ear Hospital, Sir Patrick Dun's, and the Rotunda maternity hospital, before commencing private practice.

Like other women of her generation—notably *Helen Chevenix, *Louie Bennett, and *Dorothy Macardle who were all, not coincidentally, educated at Alexandra—Lynn was drawn into politics through the suffrage movement and her concern for poverty. In 1913, during the employers' lock-out of Dublin workers which brought great hardship, she helped the Irish Citizen Army which had been set up to defend the workers. At the invitation of James Connolly, the Irish Marxist labor leader who took over command of the ICA, she became involved in the women's section of the ICA and in Cumann na mBan, the women's auxiliary of the Irish Volunteers, and gave lectures in first aid and ambulance work. She subsequently became chief medical officer of the ICA and was aware of the preparations being made for a rebellion in Dublin. Connolly promoted her to captain just before the rebellion started.

On Easter Monday, 1916, Lynn reported to the outpost based at her old alma mater, the College of Surgeons. It was commanded by Michael Mallin and Countess *Constance Markievicz, who was a distant relation of hers. However, the most immediate fighting took place at Dublin Castle, and Lynn tended the wounded there until the small garrison surrendered. She was taken to Kilmainham Jail and then to Mountjoy Jail before being released. Dorothy Stopford-Price, who was studying medicine in Trinity College and would later work at St. Ultan's with Lynn, was inclined to discount the stories she had heard about Lynn's involvement in the Rising: "I don't think anything was proved against her more than doctoring and bandaging Sinn Feiners. She is a very charming lady of an old fashioned type." Stopford-Price soon realized how much she had underestimated Kathleen Lynn.

In October 1917, Lynn was elected to the executive of the Sinn Fein, the political party dedicated to achieving a united Irish Republic. She spoke out strongly on the subject of equality, a message many men in Sinn Fein were reluctant to hear. In 1918, she took part in the campaign opposing the imposition of conscription in Ireland, and later that year she canvassed for Constance Markievicz, who was then in prison, when Markievicz stood as a Sinn Fein candidate in the general election. In 1920, Lynn was Sinn Fein candidate in the local elections and was elected to her local council in Dublin. When the war of independence was at its height, she sheltered people who were on the run and tended the wounded, often at great risk. She was also involved with the White Cross relief organization. In 1921, she opposed as inadequate the terms of the treaty which gave independence to Ireland and took the republican side in the civil war which broke out in June 1922. In 1923, she was elected Sinn Fein member for Dublin County in the new Irish Parliament but did not take her seat and lost it in the June 1927 election. This marked the effective end of her active political career, and after this she devoted her energies to medicine.

In 1918–19, Dublin, which already had some of the worst slums and child mortality rates in Europe, was hit by the influenza pandemic. The hospitals and dispensaries were unable to cope and Lynn, with the help of Madeleine Ffrench-Mullen whom she had known from the ICA, acquired a house in Charlemont Street, in south inner city Dublin, to look after flu victims. Lynn was overburdened at the time, but this did not inhibit her work at the new hospital. When the flu epidemic passed, it was decided to concentrate the hospital's work on children, and it was named St. Ultan's (after an Irish saint who was reputed to take special care of children). Lynn had a formidable team of doctors to help her, notably Ella Webb, Alice Barry, and Dorothy Stopford-Price.

The staff at St. Ultan's were particularly intent on teaching poor mothers the importance of hygiene and regular feeding. Tuberculosis was also a particular scourge in Ireland and thanks to the work of Dorothy Stopford-Price, St. Ultan's was the first hospital in Ireland to use the B.C.G. vaccine, in 1937–38. St. Ultan's was also the first hospital to have a Montessori ward. Kathleen Lynn had met *Maria Montessori in 1934 and took a great interest in her educational methods for children.

At the end of the Second World War, Lynn and her friend Dorothy Macardle were concerned at the plight of German children, and Lynn founded the "Save the German Children" Society which worked closely with other charitable groups in England and America. She died in September 1955 and as a mark of her abiding interest in young people left the cottage in County Wicklow, given to her by Constance Markievicz, to the Irish Youth Hostel Association, An Oige.

SOURCES:

Alexandra College Magazine.

O Broin, Leon. *Protestant Nationalists in Revolutionary Ireland: The Stopford Connection.*

Smyth, Hazel P. "Kathleen Lynn," in *Dublin Historical Record.* 1976–77.

Deirdre McMahon,
lecturer in history at Mary Immaculate College,
University of Limerick, Limerick, Ireland

Lynn, Loretta (1935—)

American country-music entertainer who was once the most popular female country star in America with a string of hits that appealed to working-class women. Born Loretta Webb on April 14, 1935, in Butcher Hollow, a poor coal mining district of rural Kentucky; daughter of Melvin Webb and Clara (Ramey) Webb; sister of Crystal Gayle (b. 1951, a singer); married Oliver Vanetta "Mooney" Lynn, on January 10, 1948 (died 1996); children: six, including (twins) **Patsy Lynn** and **Peggy Lynn**, who released their debut album *The Lynns* in 1998.

Married at 13, had four children by age 17, and was a grandmother at age 31; encouraged to sing by her husband as a way to earn money, began performing in small clubs and at agricultural fairs; recorded her first song (1960), driving cross-country from radio station to radio station with her husband to promote it; was eventually signed by Decca Records, for which she recorded her first hit song (1962); became the first woman to receive the Country Music Association's Entertainer of the Year Award (1972); was a familiar personality on network television and published a bestselling autobiography (1980), helping to make country music a mass-market phenomenon.

Highway 23 is an unremarkable stretch of state road meandering its way through the coal-mining country of northeastern Kentucky, hiding amid its strip malls and barbecue joints a natural resource that has, in its way, influenced America as much as the chunks of black anthracite that once fueled the nation. It was called "hillbilly music" back when Loretta Lynn sat barefoot in a schoolhouse in Butcher Hollow, before she took her place at the head of a parade of entertainers from coal country that turned hillbilly music into today's country music industry. The Kentucky group's more recent members include **Patty Loveless** (a distant cousin of Lynn's), **Crystal Gayle** (Lynn's youngest sister), **Naomi** and **Wynonna Judd**, Ricky Skaggs, and Dwight Yoakam; but it was Lynn who led the way almost 50 years earlier, teaching a nation just getting used to rock 'n' roll that country was cool.

Music was part of everyday life in the rural Kentucky of her childhood, far away from cities, telephones and nine-to-five jobs. It was a way to share troubles of the Depression and keep a sense of community. "Most of our songs were learned from friends and family," Lynn once noted, recalling that both her parents, as well as assorted uncles, aunts, and in-laws, chewed over the old traditional songs as easily as they did the latest gossip; and almost everyone could pick out a tune on a homemade banjo or guitar or mandolin. Her father Melvin Webb played the banjo, while her mother **Clara Ramey Webb** would often dance her "hillbilly hoedown" in front of the radio, tuned to the Grand Ol' Opry up in Nashville. Among Lynn's earliest memories were the songs she would sing to the six brothers and sisters who followed her own arrival in the Webb household on April 14, 1935. While she rocked the babies to sleep on the front porch of a mountain cabin that has become a country-music shrine, singing came as naturally to her as to anyone else in Butcher Hollow.

"I never rode in an automobile until I was twelve," Lynn proudly wrote in her first autobiography, an indication of the rural isolation in which she grew up. The "big city" to young Loretta was Van Lear, some 15 miles distant, a coal town built by the Consolidated Coal Company to house its miners and their families. It was the same company her father worked the mines for, but while Van Lear children attended school in a fine brick building, Loretta went to a one-room wooden shack down the valley from Butcher Hollow, where her attendance was infrequent enough that the written section of her test for a driver's license was a worry to her in later years. She slept on a pallet on the floor of her parents' cabin, wore shoes only during the winter, and consumed a diet that consisted of so much bread that eating a sandwich was difficult for her as an adult. Her first contact with a larger world came at 11 years of age, when her father installed a radio in the cabin. Saturday nights were spent listening to the Opry. "It was another world to me," Lynn later said, especially remembering the first time she heard *Kitty Wells, the singer after whom she would model herself.

Loretta's marriage at 13, just after her father's death from black lung disease, has since become the stuff of country-music legend, not only because of her age but because the marriage lasted nearly 50 remarkable years. Loretta had known Oliver "Mooney" Lynn—or "Doolittle," as everyone in Butcher Hollow called him—since early childhood. Mooney was some 15 years older than Loretta and had just returned from World War II when he began courting her, even though she was still in what would today be thought of as junior high school. "Doo," as Loretta took to calling him, walked her home one night after a school social and gave her her first kiss. "The truth is I fell in love right there," she later said. "I can't explain it, but it felt so nice to be kissed by this boy that I fell in love." In later years, Mooney would claim that Loretta's mature figure had fooled him into thinking she was older and it wasn't until later in their courtship that he learned her true age. "But it didn't change my mind," he said. "When you're in love, it don't make no difference."

After a month of dating, and despite Clara Webb's warnings about her beau's reputation, Loretta and Doolittle were married on January 10, 1948. Four months later, Loretta was pregnant with the first of her six children. The marriage did not seem destined for success when, while she was two months pregnant, Mooney left her for another woman, although Loretta saw to it that her husband came back to her. "Sure, I've heard people say men are bound to run around a little bit," she once scoffed. "Well, shoot, I don't believe in double standards, where men can get away with things that women can't." Her attitude toward philandering husbands is summed up in the title of one of her most popular songs, "Fist City."

Her baby was born, not in Kentucky, but in Washington State, where Mooney had moved to take a job as the manager of a ranch. It was the first time Loretta had left the mountains of her childhood. By the time she was 17, she had given birth to three more children and joked that "now I keep my knees crossed instead of my fingers." It was no wonder that 20 years later, she saw the easy availability of birth-control pills as a blessing—an opinion she expressed in her 1975 hit "The Pill," with such lyrics as, "This incubator is over-used/ because you kept it filled." The record was controversial enough in those days that many radio stations refused to play it—radio stations, as Lynn pointed out, that were programmed by men. "I love my kids," Loretta told one journalist, "but I didn't get a chance to enjoy the first four kids, I had 'em so fast."

During much of her time in Washington State during the 1950s, Lynn settled into the life of a housewife. Although her eldest daughter recalls Loretta trying to imitate Kitty Wells songs heard on the radio, Lynn's dreams in those days were the modest hopes of millions of other American women in her situation. She wanted to own her own house, rather than the rented one

Mooney had been given by his ranch bosses, and have enough money to order from the Sears and Roebuck catalogue.

It was Mooney who started her singing as a way to augment the family income, buying her a guitar and encouraging her to write her own songs. Early in 1960, Mooney arranged an audition for her at one of the local clubs, ignoring Loretta's protests that she was terrified of performing in public. To her surprise, the club's owners offered her a slot on the program for the following Saturday night, five dollars for her appearance, and a promise to record her performance and see that it was played on the local radio station. Although before her performance she spilled a cup of coffee on an audience member who turned out to be the state's governor, and tripped and fell during her entrance for her set, she was invited back for the next weekend. Before long, she was touring other local clubs with her first band, The Coalminers, although she was sure that her kind of music would never reach a wider audience. "People were kind of ashamed of country," she said of those days. "You had more fans for Perry Como and *Doris Day** than for Ernest Tubb and Kitty Wells." But audiences at small bars, at state fairs, at military bases, seemed to like what she sang—cover versions of current hits, along with some of the old songs from the Kentucky mountains. Such was the purity and honesty of her style that, at one state-fair performance, even a horse-pulling contest in a field next to the stage failed to draw her audience of farmers away. When Loretta won first prize and $25 at a singing contest, Mooney began to think it was time to head for Nashville.

Lacking a demo recording, Mooney managed to get Lynn a guest spot on a local television program in Tacoma, Washington, then being hosted by a young Buck Owens. The program was seen as far north as Vancouver, where a wealthy lumber baron named Norman Burley decided that Loretta Lynn was the artist who could help him launch the recording label that was his favorite hobby. Burley offered to pay the recording studio bill for Loretta's demo, called "Honky-Tonk Girl." Lynn had written the tune after noticing a tearful woman who appeared night after night in one of the bars her band had played. "Ever since you left me," she wrote,

> I've done nothin' but wrong. . .
> Now I'm a honky-tonk girl.

Burley also agreed to finance a trip to Los Angeles to promote the record, and he provided them with a list of country radio stations between the West Coast and Nashville. By the time Loretta and Mooney had driven nearly non-stop from Washington to California and then east to Tennessee, stopping at every country station they could find with copies of Loretta's record, "Honky-Tonk Girl" had reached #14 on Billboard's national charts. It was her time on the road with Mooney that laid the base on which Loretta still says her astonishing success rests. "I wouldn't have nothing if it wasn't for my fans," she once said, and it was the hundreds of people she met on her way to Nashville that spread the word about her, that traveled miles to see her perform and who offered their homes as rest stops. Four sisters in Colorado were so enamored of her music that they formed her first national fan club and became close friends. Arriving in Nashville in July 1960, Mooney arranged three or four dates a week in small clubs, while Loretta began using what she saw of the rough and tumble world of bar brawls and all-night gigs to write new material with titles like "You Ain't Woman Enough to Take My Man" and "Don't Come Home A-Drinkin (With Lovin' on Your Mind)."

They put your records on the jukebox

at the Truck Stop Inn

And I spend a dollar on you every

night, Loretta Lynn.

—From "I Love You, Loretta Lynn," by Johnny Durham, 1964.

On October 15, 1960, Lynn made her first appearance at the Grand Ol' Opry, the venerable radio show she had listened to with her parents back in Butcher Hollow. By the end of the year, after several more invitations to perform for the Opry, she was named one of its Promising Young Female Singers, had signed a management contract with the Wilburn Brothers, a popular country act on the Opry which also ran its own talent agency, and under their guidance had recorded her second song, "Fool Number One," for Decca Records. (Norm Burley had graciously torn up the contract Lynn had signed with him back in Vancouver.) Decca promoted Lynn as "The Decca Doll from Kentucky" and assigned her to the producer who would bring her to national fame, Owen Bradley. "Just pronounce the words the way you want, Loretta," Bradley told her, realizing that it was Lynn's natural, unsophisticated style and her plain-talking lyrics that might appeal to listeners outside the traditional country market. By the fall of 1961, Loretta and Mooney had become permanent residents of Nashville, a decision confirmed a year later when Lynn's Decca title "Success" became her first #1 hit.

Her meteoric rise to stardom attracted critics, not a few of whom were other female country singers still looking for their first invitation to step onto the Opry stage. Loretta denied the inevitable rumors about favors, attributing her success to a combination of the right material, the right producer, the right manager, and plain old hard work. On tour in 1962, for example, she played 42 dates in just 25 days, all of them at agricultural fairs, and she went to the best talent in the business to learn her craft. One of her mentors was the great *Patsy Cline who, just before her death in a plane crash in 1963, accurately predicted that Loretta would be named the top female country performer in the nation. "I had some sorry times before I got things right," Lynn once admitted, from her difficulty in learning to smile even when she was terrified to the time her first pair of panty hose proved too large and fell down around her ankles in the middle of a set. From then on, she took care to appear on stage in jeans and a cowboy hat, although it was not lost on her that her misfortunes only made her audiences more fond of her. "I'm proud and I've got my own ideas," she said, "but I ain't no better than anyone else. I think I reach people because I'm with 'em, not apart from 'em."

In 1964, as Patsy Cline had foreseen, Lynn was named Billboard's Top Female Vocalist after her first album, *Loretta Lynn Sings*, reached #1 on the magazine's country charts. She had by then played 17 straight shows at the Opry and had been formally inducted into that grand old group of performers. But even bigger things were in store, for Loretta and Mooney sensed that changes were afoot in what had been until then a relatively insular category of American music. "It was time for country music to get bigger," she once said of the late 1960s, and claimed that the artist who made it possible was not a country performer but soul master Ray Charles. Both country music and soul music, she said, were "about people letting their feelings out," and Charles' hit of that time, "I Can't Stop Loving You," subtly appropriated country-inspired backup vocals and instrumentation and led an entirely new audience toward country music. It was an audience ready for Loretta Lynn.

With songs like "Blue Kentucky Girl," "Somebody, Somewhere" and her signature, "Coal Miner's Daughter," Loretta Lynn's horizons expanded far beyond the confines of country music; and by picking up on social trends of the late 1960s and early 1970s with numbers like "The Pill" and "We've Come a Long Way Baby," she became an unlikely heroine of the feminist

Loretta
Lynn

movement. Such was her ability to bring country home to America, and particularly American women, that in 1972 she became the first woman named as the Country Music Association's Entertainer of the Year. The following year, Billboard named her a second time as its Top Female Vo-

calist; and in 1975, Lynn won the Academy of Country Music's prestigious Entertainer of the Year award. Her personal life seemed blessed, too, beginning with the birth of twin girls in 1964 and followed by the purchase of an old farm house and nearly 1,500 acres of land southwest of Nashville. The house also came with an entire town—Hurricane Mills, an old coal town that was then on the verge of crumbling into the Tennessee dust. Best of all, her marriage to Mooney survived intact. "Really, we're so entirely different," Loretta marveled at the time. "It's a wonder we've stayed together."

But inevitably, the pressures began to mount. An ominous sign was Lynn's ill-fated concern for the widows of 38 coal miners who had died in an explosion in Hyden, Kentucky, early in 1971. Although she raised nearly $100,000 through a grueling series of benefit concerts during the rest of that year, her insistence that the money be put in a trust fund for the education of the miners' children brought a protracted lawsuit from the widows, who accused her of purposefully withholding the funds. Lynn was forced to relent and agree to a plan to divide the money evenly. Then came her painful breakup with the Wilburns, who had represented her for ten years. The separation and legal acrimony that resulted was so severe that Lynn stopped eating for days at a time, developed

severe migraine headaches, and passed out so frequently on stage that rumors began to spread she had become an alcoholic. Even worse, two tumors were discovered in her right breast in 1972. She was hospitalized nine times that year, including once for an allergic reaction to a migraine medication so severe she nearly died. It was two years before her life returned to normal, helped by Mooney's purchase of a home in Mexico where Loretta was safe from the pressures of her career and found the rest she so badly needed.

By the late 1970s, Lynn was back on the road, appearing on national television and, with the publication of her autobiography *Coal Miner's Daughter* in 1976, finding herself drawn to Hollywood to serve as co-writer of the feature film of the same name which appeared in 1980, starring **Sissy Spacek**. Loretta and Mooney formed several satellite businesses based on her fame—a music publishing company, a chain of stores selling western clothing, not to mention the Loretta Lynn Museum, the Loretta Lynn Dude Ranch and touring rodeo show, and the talent management firm she created in partnership with Conway Twitty.

But the death of her eldest son Jack, who fell from his horse into a rain-swollen river in 1984, at age 34, marked the beginning of another decline. Mooney had developed severe diabetes coupled with heart disease, and by 1990 Loretta was spending most of her time at Hurricane Mills, tending to him until his death in 1996. The death of her husband of nearly 50 years was followed by the passing of Owen Bradley, several of her relatives from Butcher Hollow, and the death of *Tammy Wynette, who had been a close friend. Any hopes of reviving her career after these losses seemed dashed when doctors discovered that a breast implant she had undergone 20 years earlier had broken and leaked silicone over much of the right side of her torso, requiring surgery on her rib cage and right arm.

So it was with some surprise that Nashville learned in late 1998 that Loretta Lynn, at 64, was going back on the road and had written enough songs to record a new album. "We're still honky-tonking," the original Honky-Tonk Girl told a sold-out crowd at New York's Town Hall in the spring of 1999. "When love and honky-tonk and the Bible go out of style, it's over." It seems that Loretta Lynn intends to keep all three going for quite some time yet.

SOURCES:

Lynn, Loretta, with George Vecsey. *Coal Miner's Daughter*. Chicago, IL: Henry Regnery, 1976.

From the movie Coal Miner's Daughter, *based on the life of Loretta Lynn, starring Sissy Spacek.*

Pareles, Jon. "When Country Sang to Just Plain Folks," in *The New York Times*. May 15, 1999.

RELATED MEDIA:

Coal Miner's Daughter, starring Sissy Spacek and Tommy Lee Jones; directed by Michael Apted. Universal Pictures, 1980.

Norman Powers,
writer-producer, Chelsea Lane Productions, New York

Lynn, Vera (1917—)

English popular singer who became both famous and beloved entertaining English troops during WWII, when she was hailed as the "Sweetheart of the Forces." Name variations: Dame Vera Lynn; Mrs. Harry Lewis; hailed during WWII as Radio's "Sweet Singer of Sweet Songs," "The Wonder Voice of the Air," and "The Sweetheart of the Forces." Born Vera Margaret Welch on March 20, 1917; daughter of Bertram Samuel Welch (a plumber) and Annie Welch (a dressmaker); had one brother Roger (b. 1914); attended Brampton Road School, East Ham; married Harry Lewis, in 1941; children: one daughter, Virginia Lewis (b. 1946).

Awards: voted most popular singer in Britain in a Daily Express competition (1939); named "Sweetheart of the Forces" (1941); awarded the Order of the British Empire (OBE, 1969); made honorary citizen of Winnipeg, Canada (1974); received Music Publishers' Award, Show Business Personality of the Year, Grand Order of Water Rats, Ivor Novello Award, and Dame of the British Empire (all 1975); made honorary citizen of Nashville, Tennessee (1977); Freedom of the City of London (1978); granted honorary Doctor of Letters from the University of Newfoundland, Canada, where she established the Lynn Musical Scholarship (1978); was president of the Printers' Charitable Corporation (1980); awarded Commander of the Order of Orange-Nassau (1985); named International Ambassador of Variety Club International (1985); awarded Burma Star (1985); fellow of the University of East London (1990); also had 14 gold records; received seven invitations to give command performances before the British royal family.

Age seven, gave first performance at a workingmen's club (1924); appeared at various clubs on the workingmen's club circuit (1924–28); joined juvenile troupe (1928); opened own dancing school (1932); gave first radio broadcast with Joe Loss Band (1935); joined Charlie Kunz's Casani Club Band (1935); made first recording, anonymously (1935); signed with Crown Records (1935) which was purchased by Decca (1938); joined the Ambrose Orchestra (1937–40); went solo (1940); had own radio program "Sincerely Yours" (1941–47); starred in Applesauce at *the London Palladium (1941); became own manager (1941); filmed* We'll Meet Again *(1942),* Rhythm Serenade *(1943), and* One Exciting Night *(1944); entertained British troops in Burma and elsewhere (1944–45); was a regular cast member on Tallulah Bankhead's radio program* The Big Show *(USA, 1951); appeared at the Flamingo Hotel-Casino, Las Vegas (1951); appeared in* London Laughs; *was first British singer to top the American Hit parade (1952); appeared on various television programs in America and Britain; toured Holland, Denmark, Sweden, Norway, Germany, Canada, New Zealand, and South Africa (1956—); made frequent appearances in Canada and Scandinavia.*

A plain girl from dreary East Ham in the seedy East End of London, Vera Lynn is a striking example of how England, though a notoriously class-conscious society, nonetheless can be the land of opportunity for someone from even the humblest background. By age 7, she was a performer; by 20, she was a successful singer; by 25, she was one of the most beloved figures in England, and, by the time she was 50, she had become a veritable British institution, giving command performances for royalty and receiving the highest decorations awarded by her queen and country.

The daughter of **Annie Welch**, a dressmaker, and Bertram Welch, a Cockney plumber, Vera Lynn was born Vera Margaret Welch on March 20, 1917. As a child, she showed such gifts for singing that a friend of the family, a small time entertainer and tap dancer named Pat Barry, got her a chance to perform at the Midway Club, a workingmen's club in Newington Green, when she was only seven. These clubs, no longer functioning, were of great significance in the working-class neighborhoods from the later decades of the 19th century, designed, as they were, to provide places for rest, relaxation, and wholesome entertainment for working men and their families. Each club had its talent secretary, who served as a sort of booking agent and whose job it was to secure suitable performers for evening and weekend entertainments. Typically, a child performer was expected to sing three songs, usually of the sentimental "daddy's-gone-to-heaven" type, for six shillings and seven pence (then about $1.60), with an additional one and six (then 36 cents) for each encore demanded by the audience. Once little Vera had shown that she was capable of delighting an audience (an audience, one might add, that did not hesitate to assert its displeasure), she became a regular on the workingmen's-club circuit throughout the inner

London districts. In the course of her work, she got to know most of the music publishers, then largely located in Denmark Street (the London equivalent of "Tin Pan Alley"), who in those days depended on performers to popularize their songs with people who might subsequently purchase their sheet music or recordings, and for whom a child performer offered as good an avenue for public exposure as any other. In these early years, Annie Welch looked after her daughter's interests while Vera's easy-going and affable father somewhat bemusedly looked on. Having decided that singing was to be her career, she adopted her grandmother's maiden name and began to perform as Vera Lynn.

I happened to be singing the right songs in the right kind of voice to fit the mood of British servicemen during the war.

—Vera Lynn

In 1928, at age 11, Lynn joined an East Ham troupe of local amateurs styled "Madame Harris' Kracker Cabaret Kids," in which she remained for the next four years, still appearing almost entirely in the workingmen's clubs of east and north London, and learning to sew her own costumes. Soon, however, she was getting solo "gigs," as one-night stands were known in England, working various Masonic dinners, cabarets, and charity benefits. Never much of a student, Lynn took the fullest advantage of the lax compulsory education laws in the Britain of her day and dropped out of school at 14, the earliest age that she could. She was, however, anything but ignorant, and, like many British performers of her day and earlier, she knew the professional and social value of dropping her local speech patterns and learning to speak "the king's English." (The days of rock 'n' roll artists speaking proudly in "Liverpuddlian" brogues lay in the future.) That same year, young Vera's voice broke during a bout of laryngitis and turned somewhat deeper, enabling her to appear as a kind of teenage torch singer.

In 1932, at age 15, Lynn opened her own small dance school but continued to sing, first with Howard Baker, who invited her to sing with one of his several "Howard Baker" bands much in demand in the new era of swing and jive, then with Joe Loss, then with Charlie Kunz and his Casani Club Band. Kunz gave Lynn a surprisingly free hand. He let her select her own songs, subject to his approval, and she used her long acquaintance with the music publishers in Denmark Street to obtain the best of the latest material.

In 1935, while still only 18, Lynn cut her first record at a private studio on the Teledisk label, singing "Home" with Howard Baker's band. Although this was never released commercially, she soon made a second recording with the Casani Club Band: *Dorothy Fields' and Jimmy McHugh's now classic "I'm in the Mood for Love." That same year, she began cutting records on a regular basis with the Crown label, anonymously at first but soon under the citation "Vocal by Vera Lynn." In 1938, Crown Records would be purchased by Decca, which would remain Lynn's label for the next 22 years. The year 1935 also saw Lynn's first appearance in a motion picture, as an extra in a crowd scene in *A Fire Has Been Arranged,* for which she received the handsome sum of £1 per day. Later that year, she appeared as vocalist with the Joe Loss Band in one of a series of film shorts.

Vera Lynn's break as a singer came when, scarcely 20, she was invited to sing with the Ambrose Orchestra, the most popular "big band" in 1937 Britain. Of all the British bandleaders who undertook to replicate the American big-band sound, Bert Ambrose was the most successful, doing both radio and club work, and his band regularly played the best Mayfair venues. Lynn, however, was still unpolished and most decidedly from the "wrong side of the tracks." Though her lack of sophistication in manner and dress had been hidden on radio, and the audiences for the Baker and Kunz bands had not been particularly demanding, Ambrose was reluctant to take her on, even though he wanted a second, British, singer to complement his American find, **Evelyn Dall.** After some indecision, Ambrose took Lynn on as a sort of back-up to Dall.

Through all the years of one-night stands, there seems to have been little in the way of struggle for Lynn up the rickety ladder to success. Her career developed with a precision that took each rung one at a time, and she attributed all this to astonishing good luck, never vaunting herself as either a singer or an entertainer of any great talent. "I was at the right place at the right time" was her standard explanation for her success. By now, however, it was clear to Lynn that her life was entering a new phase. She was, in fact, growing up and making a successful career out of her singing voice. Her name was appearing in the press as well as on posters, her photograph was printed in *The Daily Sketch,* and music publishers began to seek her out to sing their songs. She bought a fur coat, then a car, and finally, in 1938, a nine-room house, complete with indoor bath, in which her widowed mother was still living nearly 40 years later. She was also becoming exposed to new experiences. In 1938, she appeared in an hour-long dance-band show in Dublin, her first trip abroad, and made a full tour of the Netherlands with the Ambrose Orchestra. She also appeared on one of the early prewar television programs broadcast live from the Alexandra Palace. That same year, Bert Ambrose reconfigured his large band first as a sextet, then as an octet, playing in variety theaters and music halls at the top of the bill. Vera Lynn appeared with both groups and also sang with the full band when it was occasionally reassembled. She seems to have enjoyed her

three years with Ambrose, even though Dall, feeling threatened, resented her, and nothing Vera did seemed to smooth their relations. Eventually, fed up with Dall, Lynn announced that she was quitting the band. To her surprise, Ambrose rushed to London from an engagement in Scotland and offered to double her salary from £20 to £40 (c. $100-$200) per week if she would stay on. For the first time in her career, Lynn came to realize that there was big money to be made through her singing voice. After due consideration, she accepted the offer and remained with Ambrose until 1940. In this way,

Vera
Lynn

through her recordings and her tours, Lynn had become a well-known and quite popular singer in Britain by the time of the outbreak of World War II on September 1, 1939.

In 1941, Lynn met and married Harry Lewis, a clarinetist and tenor saxophonist, who served in the Royal Air Force (RAF) during the war and then became her manager. A new phase of her professional life thus began in the winter of 1941–42, when, together with her husband, she became her own producer, arranging all her concerts and other appearances—songs, costumes, lighting—and accepting the financial risks on her own.

Vera Lynn's radio career began early in the war, when, after leaving Ambrose, she appeared on "Ack-Ack, Beer-Beer," a radio series for the men and women of the anti-aircraft and barrage balloon units, but her real contribution came about when the BBC gave her her own program, "Sincerely Yours," in November 1941. A musical request show produced by Howard Thomas, the program brought her some 1,000 letters per week with song requests. On the air, Lynn not only played records but sang songs of her own, including "It's a Lovely Day Tomorrow," "Room 504," "Lovely Weekend," "Wish Me Luck," and, above all, "Yours," "Smilin' Through," "When They Sound the Last All Clear" (her three greatest selling records), "We'll Meet Again" (the most popular song in Britain in 1941), and the American-written favorite "The White Cliffs of Dover." In addition, she transmitted messages from selected soldiers and sailors to their families and vice-versa. Soon, she was visiting hospitals where babies had just been born, offering congratulations from their servicemen fathers, and sending messages to the fathers from their wives at home. Sincerity was Lynn's stock in trade, and she insisted on personally signing each of the thousands of photographs that were sent out with her signature. In time, she was receiving thousands of letters each week and not all of them from military personnel. Until that time, Lynn's greatest rival for popularity in Britain had been the beloved musical-hall entertainer *Gracie Fields, but the latter's marriage to an Italian (now Britain's wartime enemy) had damaged her popularity, and she had taken herself to America early in the war. By the time of the entry of the United States into World War II at the end of 1941, Lynn was unchallenged as Britain's most popular singer and—just 22 when the war began and only 27 when it ended—the uncontested "Sweetheart of the Forces." Together with *Deanna Durbin, Bing Crosby, and *Judy Garland—all three

Americans—Lynn was one of the four most popular singers of the war years on both sides of the Atlantic, her records outselling those of her first two rivals in Britain. "I suppose that I'm the girl in the street singing to the man in the street" was Lynn's explanation for her popularity.

In its early days the BBC served as an arbiter and guardian of the taste of the common people—not for nothing was it known as "Auntie BBC"—and carried this so far as to concern itself with the edification and cultural uplift of the British soldier. In February 1942, B.E. Nicholls, controller of programs, while agreeing that there was a need for lighter programming to enable war-stressed citizens to relax and ease their tensions, especially after a day of extended working hours, nonetheless declared that both domestic and military broadcasting should be aimed less at frivolity and more towards cheerful and uplifting themes. To this end, for example, he rejected jazz in favor of "waltzes, marches and cheerful music of every kind." He then set up a committee the purpose of which was to encourage better and more virile lyrics and specifically the "elimination of crooning, sentimental numbers, drivelling words, slush, innuendo and so on." Included in this was a call for the banning of "insincere and over-sentimental performances by women singers." Concern was further expressed by Cecil Graves, then joint director of the BBC, that current songs that were overly sentimental or too cloying in their themes might send the lads off into battle in a demoralized or debilitated state unsuited to the valiant tasks that lay before them. Vera Lynn was caught in the middle of this and actually found herself criticized for the very thing that the soldiers and their families loved the most about her. Fortunately, as always in Britain, the mere emergence of such nonsense produced an immediate reaction and the salubriousness of Lynn's influence was successfully defended.

Though the press remained divided on the issue, even those that did not care for "Sincerely Yours" as a program recognized that the forces certainly did, and that this was what was important in a time of war. Not surprisingly, the difference in attitude was one between generations; the younger generation—the soldiers and their sweethearts—loved Vera Lynn, while the older generation—parents, veterans of the First World War and miscellaneous "Col. Blimps" of the upper class—deplored her as too saccharine. Eventually, Colonel Stafford, defense director of the BBC, admitted: "The British soldier was more likely to be brought to fighting pitch after hearing sentimental songs than by martial music" while the BBC board of governors equivocated, stating simply, "'Sincerely Yours' deplored, popularity noted." While it may have been true that the quality of the lyrics of Vera Lynn's most popular hits, "We'll Meet Again" and "The White Cliffs of Dover," were less than those of "art songs" or German *Lieder,* there is no question that they touched a chord in the hearts of the British soldier, expressing perfectly what he felt as he went off to do a dirty job on foreign shores far from home and loved ones. Though one member of Parliament might denounce her voice as the "caterwauling of an inebriated cockatoo," to the boys she could do no wrong, and it is probably a fact that her very ordinariness endeared her to the troops. Lynn's picture hung in many an army mess, and her appearances were warmly appreciated by the soldiers whenever and wherever she went to entertain them. To the English "Tommy," Vera Lynn was the "girl down the street" in a way that an American film star of the day could never have been.

By 1942, Lynn's popularity had reached such heights that it was felt that audiences might well respond to her image on the silver screen, and a British company presented her in three films in as many years. In the rather predictably titled *We'll Meet Again,* released by Columbia (1942), the story was set during the London Blitz, with Lynn as a girl who, while attempting to advance the career of her composer boyfriend, is discovered to have a singing voice and who then becomes a radio star—a sort of "The Vera Lynn Story." Her second film, *Rhythm Serenade* (1943), displayed her as a factory worker in wartime Britain, who sings in the canteen concerts produced in her plant. Finally, in *One Exciting Night* (1944), she is a singer involved in a strained and slightly ridiculous kidnapping plot. Lynn was justifiably dissatisfied by these pieces of froth, in which she was obliged to play Vera Lynn under successive pseudonyms. Although she acquitted herself respectably as an actress and her singing appeal transferred nicely to the screen, she was never allowed to get around her own character and truly play a part. Her films were, in effect, little more than another humble contribution to the war effort and, wisely perhaps, she never made another motion picture once the war was over.

But Lynn did more than merely entertain the troops from radio. In 1944, she joined the official British entertainment troupe and decided to go to Burma after learning that this, one of the most dangerous of the war zones, was where entertainers were the least often sent. Thirty years later, she would be given the Burma Star for her

efforts. While in Burma, successful attempts were made by her associates to dissuade her from going too close to the front, though their concerns were more for their own safety than hers.

After the war ended in 1945, Lynn, like most Britishers, at last was able to set aside time for personal concerns and, taking leave of her career the following year, gave birth to her only child, a daughter, named Virginia. When she attempted to resume her career 18 months later, there was some question raised in the press as to whether or not she could reclaim her place in British popular music. She could, and did. In February 1947, she was given a six-week radio series on Sunday evenings and, in May, was given another program for eight weeks. In June, when 9,000 veterans of the Burma campaign held a reunion in the Royal Albert Hall, they waited for Lynn to join them after her appearance at the Brixton Variety Theater (where she was playing to standing-room-only audiences), chanting "We want Vera." In May 1948, her recording of "You Can't Be True, Dear" was on the American hit parade and the following year, "Again" achieved the same success.

By 1951, television, which had become widely available for the first time immediately after the war, had begun to make serious inroads into the radio audience, and NBC radio decided to put together a program so spectacular that no American could afford to miss it. The result was "The Big Show," a radio program hosted by *Tallulah Bankhead, featuring a full orchestra, a live audience, and a dazzling galaxy of stars of stage and screen. Vera Lynn was engaged as a regular, singing her most popular songs and trading quips with Bankhead and other guests. However, "The Big Show" proved little threat to the challenge of television and went off the air.

Lynn gave some thought to the possibility of remaining in the United States. NBC offered her an attractive four-year contract, and Tutti Camarata, the well-known arranger and conductor, tried to get her to come to work for the Disney Studios. Ultimately, she declined these offers; she did not want to be parted from her family, and a certain feeling of loyalty to her country, played a role. Before returning to Britain, however, she appeared on the famed Sid Caesar-*Imogene Coca "Your Show of Shows," and then accepted a two-week engagement at the Flamingo Hotel-Casino in Las Vegas. Returning to England in 1952, Lynn recorded the ballad "Aufwiederseh'n," which became her greatest hit, selling over 12 million copies and making her the first British artist ever to top the American hit parade. She was then given a 16-week contract by Independent Television (ITV) to do a series of live shows. This was followed in 1956 by a two-year contract with BBC television with terms quite extraordinary for the time, allowing her to do other TV and radio shows and to have a separate program as a disk jockey.

In the last half of the 1950s, Lynn kept herself busy both on radio and television. She survived the coming of rock 'n' roll, gradually emerging as a sort of British *Doris Day or *Rosemary Clooney, not exactly up on the latest singing vogue but with a definite and reliable following of her own. Her status as a national institution, moreover, was guaranteed when on October 14, 1957, BBC television featured her on its adaptation of the successful American program "This Is Your Life."

In 1960, Lynn terminated her recording career with Decca. This was not by choice but because of the increasing difficulty Decca was having in finding suitable songs for her to record. Times had changed, she realized, and, rather than attempt rock 'n' roll, which she knew was wrong for her, she moved to the EMI label where there was a more concerted effort to come up with her kind of songs.

In 1963, Lynn undertook her first trip to New Zealand and Australia. Traveling with Eddie Calvert and a small band for accompaniment, she gave 48 concerts in 40 days, exhausting herself to the point that she collapsed in Sydney toward the end of the tour. In the mid-'60s, she also toured South Africa, appearing not only in Johannesburg but also in such provincial cities as Durban and Pretoria, giving separate concerts for white and black audiences and concluding that the latter were a more exuberant and enthusiastic crowd to perform before. Over the years, she gave regular performances in Scandinavia and made frequent trips to appear in Canada.

As a singer, Lynn was gifted with a strong, natural voice that some critics felt was more appropriate to music hall than to radio. Her approach to singing was based on an unaffected sincerity and was characterized by perfect diction, unexpected in a school drop-out from London's Cockney East End, and by a catch in her throat that became her hallmark. Light-hearted, up-beat and a genuinely pleasant personality, she brought the same warmth and sincerity to all of her appearances on television that she had to those on radio. The "boys," of course, never forgot their old "sweetheart," and wherever she toured she was always feted by service organiza-

tions and surrounded by steadily aging but always devoted fans from the war years. One of her last professional appearances was on the 1989 ITV program "Highway," as one of the guests in a production arranged to commemorate the 50th anniversary of the beginning of the Second World War, but she was still making occasional public appearances as recently as 1995.

In her no-nonsense and slightly slangy memoirs, Lynn comes across as a forthright, down-to-earth woman, with no affectations and a genuine sense of irony. In her private life, she remained married to the same man and passed up some enticing career opportunities rather than neglect her daughter. Her father, to whom she was devoted, was proud of her accomplishments, and this gave her the greatest satisfaction. Even when working, she did most of her own housework at her home in Regents Park; when not working, she enjoyed needlework, painting, gardening, preserving fruits, swimming, and writing. She was also the author of three books: *Vocal Refrain* (her autobiography, 1975), *We'll Meet Again* (co-author, 1989), and *Unsung Heroines* (1990), a tribute to the role of women in Britain in World War II. A royalist from a royalist family, her sincere patriotism could not encompass an England without its monarchy, and there is no doubt that she was honored to be invited to present herself at command performances. Though Vera Lynn would probably have scoffed at the notion, she represented all that was best in the ordinary English women of her generation.

SOURCES:
Hickens, Tom. *What Did You Do in the War, Auntie? The BBC at War, 1939–1945.* London, 1995.
Lynn, Vera. *Vocal Refrain.* London, 1975.
The Music Library Collection, Victoria Library, London.

SUGGESTED READING:
Black, Peter. *The Biggest Aspidistra in the World: A Personal Celebration of 50 Years of the BBC.* London, 1972.
"British Sweetheart," in *Newsweek.* June 16, 1947, p. 87.
"Straight-faced Kid," in *Time.* March 16, 1949, p. 76.

Robert Hewsen,
Professor of History, Rowan University, Glassboro, New Jersey

Lyon, Elizabeth Bowes- (b. 1900).

See Elizabeth Bowes-Lyon.

Lyon, Mary (1797–1849)

American founder of Mt. Holyoke Seminary, an innovation in higher education for women because of its commitment to educating women from all economic circumstances. Born in Buckland, Massachusetts, on

February 28, 1797; died on March 5, 1849; buried on the campus of Mt. Holyoke College; fourth daughter and sixth child of Aaron Lyon (a Revolutionary War veteran) and Jemima (Shepard) Lyon; attended Sanderson Academy, Amherst Academy, and Byfield Female Seminary; never married; no children.

Born into a family who came to America in the 1630s; attended one-room schoolhouses; father died (1802); mother remarried and moved away; started teaching in summer schools (1814); attended academies and Emerson's Ladies Seminary interspersed with continued teaching primarily at Sanderson Academy; opened a girls' school in Buckland (1824); taught summers at Ipswich Female Seminary; attended lectures by Amos Eaton at Amherst College; circulated a plan for a female seminary (1834); raised money; obtained a charter for Mt. Holyoke Seminary (1836); opened Mt. Holyoke Seminary (November 1837).

Selected publications: A Missionary Offering.

There is a revealing quote carved on Mary Lyon's tomb in the center of the campus of Mt. Holyoke College: "There is nothing in the universe that I fear, but that I shall not know all my duty or fail to do it." Descended from a long line of Puritans, Mary Lyon brought evangelical fervor to the task of creating an educational institution for women who were not wealthy, and she believed, with all her heart, that that was where her duty to God lay. Of the early American pioneers of women's higher education, who included *Emma Willard and *Catharine Beecher, Mary Lyon was the most imbued with intense religious convictions and her successful labors on behalf of women's education were virtually a religious crusade.

Mary Lyon's maternal ancestry consisted of ministers from the great Puritan migrations of the 17th century; her father was a Revolutionary War veteran. Born on February 28, 1797, Mary was the sixth of eight children of Aaron Lyon and **Jemima Shepard Lyon**, of Buckland, Massachusetts. Widowed in 1802, when Mary was not yet six, Jemima Lyon eked out an existence for the family until she remarried when Mary was 13. With three older daughters already married, Jemima took two younger daughters with her to her new home in Ashfield, Massachusetts. Mary remained behind to do the household chores at the Buckland Farm for her older brother until his marriage two years later. She saved the dollar a week her brother paid her and, by boarding with relatives and friends whom she assisted with domestic chores, continued her schooling at Ashfield and Buckland. These experiences undoubt-

edly contributed to her later sense that all women, no matter what their education or social station, should master domesticity for "independence."

At age 17, she began teaching in nearby communities, was paid 75 cents a week, and boarded and did domestic chores at pupils' homes. Thus, she was able to save enough money to attend Sanderson Academy in the town of Ashfield for several scattered terms. Her teachers, by this time, were remarking that Mary Lyon was "all intellect." It was at Sanderson that she became friends with **Amanda White** and her father Squire Thomas White, a leading citizen of Ashfield. Lyon boarded with the White family and both daughter and father became lifelong friends and supporters. Sanderson Academy offered an equal education to men and women and developed a spiritual rationale for the training of teachers. Pupils such as Mary Lyon were exhorted, in the words of historian **Kathryn Kish Sklar**, to "exercise spiritual authority and leadership in their schools, transforming their task of instilling 'virtue' in their pupils from a nominal to a vital responsibility, and [to view their calling] as female teachers as a sacred as well as a secular undertaking."

> *Take all the circumstances and weight [sic] them candidly. . . . You may see but one step where you can place your foot, but take that, and another will then be discovered.*
>
> —Mary Lyon

In the fall of 1818, Lyon studied at Amherst Academy (later Amherst College) and became friends with a young teacher named **Orra White** who would marry Edward Hitchcock, the future president of Amherst College. The couple remained staunch friends of Lyon's and were ardent supporters of her later seminary. After Mary Lyon's death, Edward Hitchcock would compile the first biography of her life. This pattern of friendship with women who were connected to powerful and well-educated men enabled Lyon to elicit support for her later educational efforts.

In 1821, after contributing to her expenses by weaving heavy blue-and-white coverlets, Mary Lyon, at the age of 24, left western Massachusetts in the carriage of Squire White and his daughter, Amanda. After a harrowing three-day journey, they arrived at Emerson's Ladies Seminary in Byfield, near Boston. Owned and operated by the Reverend Joseph Emerson, brother of Ralph Waldo Emerson, the school trained female teachers in much the same way "normal schools" would later in the 19th century.

In an 1822 *Discourse on Female Education,* Joseph Emerson called for improvements in female education commensurate with female responsibilities. He pointed out that women should engage in "the business of teaching [because] their instructions are at once more excellent and less expensive" and said that teachers could "do more to enlighten and reform the world and introduce the millennium than persons of any other profession except the ministers of Christ." Emerson concluded by pointing to two portents of positive change: fund-raising for good causes by women ("The numerous and noble institutions that so distinguish and bless the present day have been . . . urged forward by female hands, by female tongues, by female prayers") and the desire of women for improved education ("[M]any females are making vigorous efforts to enjoy and improve the means of their education"). Emerson's brilliant mind and magnetic zeal encouraged and inflamed Mary Lyon's desire for improved educational opportunities for her sex in order to enhance women's social usefulness. Lyon also learned to espouse Joseph Emerson's notion that "the station of woman is designed by Providence to be subordinate and dependent, to a degree far exceeding the difference in native talents."

While at Byfield Academy, Mary Lyon formed a deep friendship with Emerson's young assistant ◄ Zilpah Grant, whose religious convictions provided a system for monitoring the "conversion process" of students. This process had two stages: recognizing the obstacles within

one's own heart to the "Savior" and transcending those obstacles through "trust in God." Lyon was especially grateful to Grant who spoke at religious meetings. As historian Sklar points out, "Peer solidarity developed in a context removed from normal family influences. . . . Religion was the basis of a 'community of feeling' among students." Grant later recalled, "We learned to consider each other as sisters and this feeling did not cease with our connection with the school." This was particularly true for Grant and Lyon.

In 1824, Zilpah Grant was asked to organize the newly chartered Adams Female Academy in Londonderry, New Hampshire, and she invited Lyon to join her. With Mary Lyon as teacher and Zilpah Grant as director, the new school flourished. A graded three-year course with examinations required for promotion, culminating in the awarding of a diploma, led to prestige and endowment for the institution. Grant's evangelical aspirations for the seminary were shattered, however, in 1827, when the male trustees, who disapproved of her heavy emphasis on Calvinistic religious instruction, announced the introduction into the curriculum of instrumental music and dancing along with more liberal religious instruction.

Shortly thereafter, Grant, along with Lyon and several pupils, left Adams Seminary to organize a seminary in Ipswich, Massachusetts. Ipswich Female Seminary was successful and, in 1831, principal Grant and assistant-principal Lyon tried to secure a rent-free "boarding-home." However, lack of funds and Grant's illnesses—she had suffered from the suicide of her mother, a damaged Achilles' tendon, and typhoid fever—led her to depart for the South for a year and a half. Upon her return, in 1833, she learned that Lyon had decided upon an independent effort to found a seminary which would be permanent.

In 1834, a dozen gentlemen gathered in Mary Lyon's parlor to listen to her outline for a school, as she had become convinced that "the whole business must, in name, devolve on benevolent gentlemen." Aided by a committee of clerics and others, Lyon embarked on the task of soliciting funds for the new seminary.

Other events in Lyon's life had also increased her belief that God intended her to found an institution for women. In 1825, she studied with Professor Thomas Eaton of Troy, New York, and probably met Emma Willard who founded the successful Troy Seminary in 1821. In 1833, just before issuing her circular calling for a female seminary, Lyon met with Willard. Through Joseph Emerson and Zilpah Grant, she also had

---

⊱▸ Grant, Zilpah (1794–1874)

American educator. Born Zilpah Polly Grant on May 30, 1794, in Norfolk, Connecticut; died in Newburyport, Massachusetts, on December 3, 1874; attended local schools; attended the Female Academy of Byfield, Massachusetts; married William B. Banister (a lawyer and politician), in September 1841 (died 1853).

Zilpah Grant was born in Norfolk, Connecticut, in 1794. Always of frail health, she grew up under intense pressure, having to aid her widowed mother in holding on to the family farm. Before her work with *Mary Lyon, Grant taught at the Female Seminary in Byfield, Massachusetts, at a girls' school in Winsted, Connecticut, and was a preceptor at Adams Female Academy in East Derry, New Hampshire.

Mary
Lyon

contact with the Beecher family and probably knew Catharine Beecher who had started a seminary in Hartford, Connecticut, in 1824.

Lyon's plan for a new school was modeled upon Ipswich in its academic program but included a strategy whereby students would share in the household work, thus reducing the expenses. A committee was formed, a charter secured, and the women of Ipswich Female Academy contributed the first $1,000. Ipswich pupils made an additional offering of $200. According to Grant's biographer Sydney MacLean, "In 1835 Miss Lyon left Ipswich to devote herself to

Mount Holyoke Seminary, which opened in South Hadley, Massachusetts, two years later. Four of Miss Grant's teachers and many of her pupils transferred to the new institution." In 1839, Grant left Ipswich "never again to teach." MacLean points out that Grant "expressed no bitterness . . . and after Mary Lyon's death she helped to gather material for [Lyon's] biography suppressing her conviction that many of Miss Lyon's educational ideas had originally been hers." Sklar holds that "Zilpah Grant's preference for a life-style that transcended her own social origins prevented her from joining Lyon," and, indeed, in 1841, Grant married a former state senator, William Bostwick Banister, and, as his third wife, presided over his large house in Newburyport, Massachusetts.

By January 1837, Mary Lyon and her male supporters had raised $27,000 from 1,800 individuals in 90 towns. When criticized for aggressive fund-raising unseemly for a woman, Lyon wrote, "My heart is sick, my soul is pained with this empty gentility. . . . I am doing a great work. I cannot come down." Later, when accused that "her persevering eloquence" manipulated the women who donated, she replied, "Get the money; the money will do good."

The times were unfavorable for fund-raising, which makes Mary Lyon's accomplishment all the more impressive. By 1835, the country was in a severe economic depression. Cotton prices dropped; the price of flour rose. The Seminoles in Florida were resisting federal forces, U.S. expansion in the southwest disturbed the Mexican frontier, and war with Britain threatened because of problems with Canada.

On October 3, 1836, the cornerstone was laid for Mt. Holyoke Seminary in South Hadley, Massachusetts, which opened on November 8, 1837, and quickly enrolled more than 80 students. By 1841, a new wing had been added to the original building, more than $50,000 had been raised and expended, and 200-plus students were enrolled.

One of the reasons for the instant success of the enterprise was its accessibility to young women of moderate means. For the first 16 years, tuition and boarding fees remained around $60 per year, made possible by the domestic system designed by Lyon. Students were expected to work approximately an hour and a half a day, primarily cooking meals and cleaning up. There were no classes on Mondays (later Wednesdays) while the students cleaned the building and washed and mended clothes. Lyon further believed that her domestic system, in which she always fully participated, had other benefits: that it broke down social differences; developed a family feeling; and served as a means of physical training. An unanticipated consequence of the domestic system was that, early on, students expressed a sense of ownership in the school by forming a "society of inquiry" which aimed at self-improvement and discussed the seminary's needs.

Care was given that academics not be neglected and, at the end of the first year, two days of public examinations were held and three graduates received certificates of completion. Lyon designed the course of study and advised stu-

dents in course placement. She also taught chemistry to the second-year class until her death in 1849, thereby setting Mt. Holyoke on a path that would culminate in, according to **Carole Shmurak** and **Bonnie Handler,** "a citadel for women in science." Mt. Holyoke became the college that produced more women who went on for doctorates in the physical sciences from 1910 to 1969, more women who obtained doctorates in chemistry from 1920 to 1980, and more women listed in the 1938 *American Men of Science* than any other undergraduate institution in the United States. Influenced by her work with Edward Hitchcock, teacher of science and future president of Amherst College, and her observations of Amos Eaton's laboratory method of teaching at Amherst and at Troy, New York, Lyon employed the same textbooks used by most men's colleges of the time and insisted that conducting experiments was more important for females than for males. She endeavored to reveal chemistry's value in "enlarging and elevating the mind."

The study of science was always inextricably linked to the study of religion for Lyon, and she always maintained, "If the Bible [would] only take the lead in our schools, I care not how closely the science follow." Here again, as in the finances, the domestic system, and the curriculum, Lyon took charge. She conducted the daily devotional exercises for the entire school and urged students who were professed Christians to encourage "conversion" of their fellow students as she had learned to do under the tutelage of Joseph Emerson and Zilpah Grant.

Lyon and the Mt. Holyoke students became actively involved in the work of foreign missions through fund-raising, promoting missionary work, and encouraging marriages to missionaries. In addition, Lyon continued to see teaching as a form of religious calling for women, and at least three-quarters of the students during the seminary's first 50 years became teachers for some period of time.

By 1849, a successful Mt. Holyoke Seminary had 224 pupils and 16 teachers. But Mary Lyon was not well. The long years of extraordinary effort had taken their toll, and, from 1841 until 1849, she suffered from a series of debilitating illnesses. Recovering from an attack of erysipelas contracted from a student, she became distraught when she heard the news of a nephew's suicide. On March 5, 1849, at age 53, Mary Lyon died. She was buried on the Mt. Holyoke campus, close to the school's original building (which would be destroyed by fire in 1896), in a grave enclosed by a wrought-iron fence.

But Mary Lyon, unlike some of her predecessors in the building of seminaries, had provided, through her herculean efforts, sufficient endowment to ensure the continuity of the enterprise. In addition, her continued devotion to and cultivation of a circle of influential ministers and friends guaranteed their continued interest and support for the school. Led by President Hitchcock of Amherst, they compiled Lyon's first biography and took the administrative steps necessary as the school floundered in the first few years after Mary Lyon's death. In building an institution dedicated to God, science, and women of average means, Mary Lyon contributed a unique seminary for the higher education of women which served as a bridge to the successful women's colleges of the late 19th century.

SOURCES:

Allmendinger, David F., Jr. "Mount Holyoke Students Encounter the Need for Life Planning, 1837–1850," in *History of Education Quarterly*. Vol. 19, 1979, pp. 27–46.

Cole, Arthur C. *A Hundred Years of Mount Holyoke College: The Evolution of an Educational Ideal*. New Haven, CT: Yale University Press, 1940.

Edmonds, Anne Carey. *A Memory Book: Mount Holyoke College, 1837–1987*. South Hadley, MA: Mount Holyoke College, 1988.

Goodsell, Willystine. *Pioneers of Women's Education in the United States*. NY: AMS Press, 1931 (reprinted 1970).

Green, Elizabeth Alden. *Mary Lyon and Mount Holyoke: Opening the Gates*. Hanover, NH: University Press of New England, 1979.

Hitchcock, Edward. *The Power of Christian Benevolence Illustrated in the Life and Labors of Mary Lyon*. Northampton, MA: Hopkins, Bridgman, 1851.

MacLean, Sydney B. "Zilpah Grant" and "Mary Lyon" in *Notable American Women: Biographical Dictionary*. Volume II, Cambridge, MA: Belknap Press, 1971, pp. 73–75, 443–447.

Shmurak, Carole B., and Bonnie S. Handler. "'Castle of Science': Mount Holyoke College and the Preparation of Women in Chemistry, 1837–1941," in *History of Education Quarterly*. Vol. 32. Fall 1992, pp. 315–342.

Sklar, Kathryn Kish. "The Founding of Mount Holyoke College," in *Women and Power in American History: A Reader, Vol. 1 to 1880*. Edited by Kathryn Kish Sklar and Thomas Dublin. Englewood Cliffs, NJ: Prentice Hall, 1991, pp. 199–215.

Stow, Sarah D. Locke. *History of Mount Holyoke Seminary, South Hadley, Mass., During its First Half Century, 1837–1887*. Springfield, MA: Springfield Printing, 1887.

SUGGESTED READING:

Cott, Nancy. *The Bonds of Womanhood*. New Haven, CT: Yale University Press, 1976.

Horowitz, Helen Lefkowitz. *Alma Mater: Design and Experience in the Women's Colleges from Their Nineteenth-Century Beginnings to the 1930s*. NY: Knopf, 1984.

Rossiter, Margaret W. *Women Scientists in America: Struggles and Strategies to 1940*. Baltimore, MD: Johns Hopkins University Press, 1982.

Solomon, Barbara Miller. *In the Company of Educated Women: A History of Women and Higher Education in America*. New Haven, CT: Yale University Press, 1985.

COLLECTIONS:

Mary Lyon's extant letters, papers, and circulars are located in the archives at Mount Holyoke College, South Hadley, Massachusetts.

Anne J. Russ,
Professor of Sociology, Wells College, Aurora, New York

Lyons, Enid (1897–1981)

Australian politician and newspaper columnist. Name variations: Dame Enid Lyons. Born Enid Muriel Burnell on July 9, 1897, in Tasmania; died on September 2, 1981; daughter of William Burnell (a sawyer) and Eliza (Tagget) Burnell; attended Stowport and Burnie State Schools and Hobart Teachers' College; married Joseph Aloysius Lyons (1879–1939, a politician and prime minister of Australia, 1932–39); children: 12 (one of whom died in infancy).

Enid Lyons was just 17 and newly graduated from the Hobart Teachers' College when she married Joseph Aloysius Lyons, the 36-year-old minister for education and railways and Tasmanian treasurer who would later become prime minister of Australia. Over the course of her 24-year marriage, Lyons would have 12 children (one of whom died in infancy) and would become her husband's valued political partner. Between confinements, she accompanied him to state and federal Labor conferences and even ran for a contested seat in the 1925 election, losing by only 60 votes. Between 1932 and 1939, when her husband was prime minister, Lyons was invaluable in securing support among women constituents. A women's rights advocate and a skilled speaker, she addressed women's associations and conferences around Australia, encouraging women to fulfill their public responsibilities as citizens.

When Joseph Lyons suffered a heart attack and died in 1939, Lyons was overwhelmed with shock and grief. Adding to her sorrow was the fact that many objected to an annuity the government proposed for her and her family. She retired to her home in Davenport until 1943, when she returned to politics, running for the Tasmanian seat of Darwin which had been vacated by a retirement. Winning the election, she became the first woman member of the federal Parliament, and later the first woman to hold ministerial office. Dubbed "the mother figure in Parliament," Lyons continued to champion women's issues and humanitarian concerns.

Enid Lyons retired from politics in 1951 for health reasons; she had suffered a pelvic fracture during the delivery of her first child that went unchecked for 40 years. Although her condition required several surgeries, she managed to keep up with her public work, chairing the Jubilee Women's Convention (1951) and serving as a member of the Australian Broadcasting Commission from 1951 to 1962. She worked as a columnist for the *Sun* (1951–54) and *Woman's Day* (1951–52), and wrote three books: an autobiography, *So We Take Comfort* (1965); a volume of political reminiscences, *Among the Carrion Crows* (1972); and a book of short essays and sketches, *The Old Haggis* (1969). Lyons was awarded the Order of Australia in 1980, a year before her death.

SOURCES:

Radi, Heather, ed. *200 Australian Women*. NSW, Australia: Women's Redress Press, 1988.

Wilde, William H., Joy Horton, and Barry Andrews, eds. *Oxford Companion to Australian Literature*. Melbourne: Oxford University Press, 1994.

Barbara Morgan,
Melrose, Massachusetts

Lyons, Sophie (1848–1924)

American swindler and society columnist. Born Sophie Levy on December 24, 1848, in New York City; died of a brain hemorrhage on May 8, 1924, after being beaten by thieves in Detroit, Michigan; daughter of Sam Levy and Sophie Elkins (alias); married Maury Harris (a pickpocket), in 1865; married Ned Lyons (a bank robber, separated and reunited); married Billy Burke (a thief); children: (second marriage) George Lyons (b. 1870); Florence Lyons; Esther Lyons; and one other son.

Was first arrested (1859); sent to Sing Sing prison for five years (1871); escaped and fled to Canada with Ned Lyons (1872); caught pickpocketing and returned to Sing Sing (1876); became first American society columnist, for the New York World *(1897); published booklets on criminal reform; established a home for children with imprisoned parents in Detroit, Michigan; donated to various prisons a piano and money for libraries.*

Dubbed "the Queen of Crime" by the New York City chief of police in the 1880s, Sophie Lyons lived an outrageous life that encompassed both sides of the law. Born and raised a brazen con artist, she made her fortune through all manner of crimes before renouncing the underworld and becoming a paradigm of reform.

She was born Sophie Levy in December 1848 in New York City to a shoplifter mother and a father who was usually incarcerated, a result of his predilection for breaking into homes. Sophie never attended school; instead, she was taught the arts of shoplifting and pickpocketing at an early age. Surrounded by crooks, she knew no other life. In a brief stand on principles brought on by a conversation with some other girls, Sophie once refused to shoplift, but a hot poker wielded by her father prodded her dutifully back to criminal behavior.

At 16, she married Maury Harris, who had dazzled her with his claims of pickpocketing artistry. But when Harris was caught and imprisoned, Sophie, unimpressed, left him. Soon after, she fell in love with Ned Lyons, an underground idol both in America and England. Criminal society of the era had its own class system, and pride in the "craft"; in that society, Ned Lyons was considered a very eligible bachelor. When he and Sophie married, he promised her that she would no longer have to steal, for he would provide everything. He was true to his word, and Sophie lived like any wealthy woman, surrounded by servants, expensive furniture, and fine china. When Ned came home each night, she was there waiting, but he soon discovered that she was leaving their Long Island home daily to pickpocket and shoplift in Manhattan. After the birth of their son George, Lyons gave up her activities, albeit for only six months. When caught and arrested for pickpocketing at a large New Hampshire fair, she put on such a convincing act, with trembling, tears, and declarations that it was all a terrible mistake, that she was released.

In 1871, Lyons' compulsive stealing landed her a six-month jail term. Ned's luck ran out shortly thereafter, and he faced seven years at Sing Sing. Weeks after Lyons was released, she was arrested for grand larceny and sentenced to five years' imprisonment, also at Sing Sing. Having planned her own incarceration as part of a scheme to be near, and eventually to liberate, her husband, Lyons quickly set to work securing a position as personal servant to the prison's head matron. Soon, she was frequently allowed to walk the matron's children outside the prison walls.

On one of these strolls, she connected with a member of her husband's old gang, and together they executed a plan that allowed Ned Lyons to simply walk out of prison only days later. Ned returned the favor by springing Sophie on December 19, 1872, the result of a maneuver involving a piece of wax with which Sophie made an impression of a prison door key. They fled to

Canada, where, while still surviving on loot from robbed safes and vaults, Sophie tried in vain to convince her husband to forsake the criminal life. After a few years of constant arguing, they returned to the United States and promptly separated.

By 1876, they were reunited by their shared need to steal, but were quickly arrested picking pockets at the Long Island Fair and sent back to Sing Sing. This time, however, Lyons was determined to leave her husband behind and began hatching a plan to move herself up in the criminal world by turning to blackmail, con jobs, and well-executed bank heists. Having worked with some of the cleverest crooks of the time, the future Queen of Crime was more than prepared to begin her reign.

Fresh out of prison, Lyons found a new accomplice in Billy Burke. Although they would later marry, in business Sophie was the mastermind and Burke the assistant. Having a distaste for violence, Lyons instructed Burke that all their work would be accomplished through planning and guile. Together they carried out many clever heists, and Lyons began to get rich. Her reputation spread as her successes piled up, and Lyons took her craft to Europe. Using aliases such as Kate Wilson and Fannie Owens, she robbed banks and ran stolen jewels in virtually every major European capital.

By the 1880s, she had earned the title "the Queen of Crime" and, like legitimate royalty, enjoyed wealth and properties from the French Riviera to the American West. Lyons, never having learned to read or write, hired tutors to educate her in languages, art, and literature. With her new education and social graces, she began hobnobbing with moneyed Americans in Europe. Even the Vanderbilts accepted her as Mary Wilson, the daughter of a rich gold prospector. When Lyons was caught pickpocketing in Paris, her wealthy friends and even the American ambassador came to her aid, insisting that the arresting gendarme had surely made a mistake. Unruffled by the close call, Lyons soon pulled off another jewel heist in Paris which left her $250,000 richer.

Expensive living quickly depleted her riches, however, and Lyons found it necessary to return to the United States where she used her good looks to blackmail wealthy businessmen and public officials. At the same time, she reunited with Ned Lyons long enough to have three more children before finally leaving him for good. She later sent her two daughters to Canada to be raised in a convent; one daughter, **Esther Lyons**,

was so ashamed of her mother's reputation she asked her to never visit there, and the two were estranged for the rest of Sophie's life.

By the 1890s, after many arrests and prison terms, Lyons' stellar criminal career was fading, and she retired. When she was swindled by an associate during her last crime, Lyons took it as a sign that it was time to reform, saying later, "I want something more than property. I want the respect of good people." She made several successful and legitimate real estate investments, and by 1897 had become America's first society columnist, writing for the *New York World*. Her intercontinental travels and social contacts provided her with a steady supply of high-society news. Lyons also published pamphlets advising criminals to change their ways, established a home for children with imprisoned parents, and donated money to help build prison libraries throughout America.

Lyons married her former accomplice Billy Burke, whom she also reformed, and they stayed together in Detroit until his death in 1919. Then one May evening in 1924, three men whom Lyons had been trying to reform came to visit the wealthy 76-year-old woman in her Detroit home. Provoked by rumors that Lyons' riches were hidden somewhere in her home, they viciously attacked her, shattering her skull. She was found in a coma by neighbors and died in a hospital that night. Lyons' estate was later estimated to be worth approximately $1 million. Her will was generous to all her children except Esther. To her, Sophie Lyons left only $100 and a purse to keep it in.

SOURCES:

Nash, Jay R. *Look For The Woman: A Narrative Encyclopedia of Female Prisoners, Kidnappers, Thieves, Terrorists, Swindlers and Spies from Elizabethan Times to the Present*. NY: M. Evans, 1981.

Jacquie Maurice,
Calgary, Alberta, Canada

Lysandra (fl. 300 BCE).

See Arsinoe II Philadelphus for sidebar.

Lytton, Constance (1869–1923)

English militant suffragist. Name variations: Lady Constance Lytton. Born Constance Georgina Lytton in Vienna, Austria, on February 12, 1869; died on May 22, 1923; third child of (Edward) Robert Bulwer Lytton, 1st earl of Lytton (1831–1891, author and viceroy of India, as well as son of Edward George Earle Lytton Bulwer-Lytton) and Lady Edith Villiers Lytton; sister of Betty Balfour; granddaughter of Rosi-

*na Bulwer-Lytton; aunt of *Elisabeth Lutyens (1906–1983); never married.*

Until 1906, when a small inheritance from her godmother **Lady Bloomfield** afforded independence, Lady Constance Lytton had lived a quiet life with her mother Lady **Edith Villiers Lytton** in Vienna, Paris, Lisbon, New Delhi, and the family home at Knebworth, Hertfordshire. Constance's father Robert Bulwer Lytton, viceroy of India, had died in 1891.

While aiding working girls after receiving her inheritance, Lady Constance Lytton became interested in the suffrage movement. Her sister **Betty Balfour** had married Gerald Balfour, long a supporter of the movement, as was Betty's sister-in-law *Frances Balfour. Shaking off her disapproval of militancy, Constance joined the Women's Social and Political Union (WSPU). Though arrested numerous times and imprisoned, Lady Lytton was always released because of her health, her family's illustrious history, and because, as she wrote, "people whose relatives might make a fuss effectively are considered awkward customers." Lady Lytton came from fighting stock (her grandmother was *Rosina Bulwer-Lytton); thus, in 1911, in an effort to thwart her preferred treatment, she disguised herself as a seamstress and named herself Jane Wharton.

"I had noticed several times while I was in prison," she wrote, "that prisoners of unprepossessing appearance obtained least favour, so I was determined to put ugliness to the test." She donned pince-nez glasses, a cheap cloth coat, and had her hair clipped short "with resentful bristles." She then set out with others to protest forced feeding at a prison in Liverpool. Intent on being arrested, she picked up some stones, "not throwing them, but limply dropping them over the hedge into the Governor's garden," and was immediately arrested for inciting people to throw stones at the house of the governor of Walton jail in Liverpool. Treated with contempt and forcibly fed seven times while in prison, she became so ill that she eventually had a stroke and was partially paralyzed on the right side of her body, becoming a permanent invalid. Nursed at home by her mother, Constance turned her rebellion to writing, offering *Prisons and Prisoners: Some Personal Experiences by C. Lytton and Jane Wharton, Spinster* (1914). Her letters, edited by B. Balfour, were published as *Letters of Constance Lytton* (1925).

Lytton, Lady Rosina Bulwer- (1802–1882).

See Bulwer-Lytton, Rosina.

Lyudmilla.

Variant of Ludmila.

ACKNOWLEDGMENTS

Photographs and illustrations appearing in *Women in World History, Volume 9*, were received from the following sources:

Photo by Godfrey Argent, **p. 691**; Photo by Cecil Beaton, **p. 89**; Engraving by Benoist, after a drawing by Swebach, **p. 693**; Photo by Miriam Berkley, **p. 419**; Courtesy of the Bishop Museum, **p. 481**; Photo by Doug Boult, **p. 193**; Courtesy of British Airways, **p. 247**; Courtesy of British Information Service, **p. 678**; Photo by Eric Carpenter, **p. 63**; © Columbia, 1940, **p. 676**; From a painting by Antoine Coypel, **p. 267**; Painting by Jacques Louis David, **p. 211**; Photo by Charles Dodgson (Lewis Carroll), **p. 470**; © G.G. Communications, Inc., 1974, **p. 519**; Painting by Hugo Händler, **p. 691**; From the Rose Wilder Lane Papers collection in the Herbert Hoover Presidential Library-Museum, **p. 109**; From the portrait by Hoppner-Jackson, **p. 77**; © The Imogen Cunningham Trust, 1978, 1996, **p. 121**; Photo by Lotte Jacobi, 1929, **p. 385**; Photo by Bob Langrish, **p. 366**; Painting by Carl Larsson, 1908, **p. 49**; Courtesy of the Library of Congress, **pp. 101, 195** (photo by Carl Van Vechten), **591, 631, 757, 801, 841**; Courtesy of Meghan K. Lowney, **p. 733**; Courtesy of Lukens, Inc., **p. 789**; © Metro-Goldwyn-Mayer, **pp. 111, 341** (1939); Courtesy of MCA Home Video, **p. 478**; Photo by Rollie McKenna, **p. 429**; From an engraving by Henry Meyer, **p. 71**; From an engraving after the portrait by Mignard, **p. 623**; Courtesy of the Minnesota Historical Society, **p. 423**; Courtesy of National Aeronautics and Space Administration, **p. 762**; Reprinted by permission of the Board of Trustees, National Gallery of Art (Washington, D.C.), **p. 459**; Courtesy of the National Portrait Gallery, photo by Mayotte Magnus, **p. 807**; Courtesy of the National Portrait Gallery (London), photo by Paul Tanqueray, **p. 229**; Courtesy of the Nebraska State Historical Society, **p. 41**; Courtesy of New Yorker Films, **p. 817**; Courtesy of the Archives, Northwestern State University of Louisiana (Natchitoches), **p. 217**; Courtesy of the Dorothea Lange Collection, Oakland Museum, City of Oakland, gift of Paul Taylor, **119**; Courtesy of Inna Vladimirovna Pasportnikova and Reina Pennington, **pp. 551, 555**; Courtesy of the Schlesinger Library, Radcliffe Institute, Harvard University, **pp. 129, 171**; Photo by Man Ray, **p. 737**; Photo by Eugene Robert Richee, **p. 53**; Photo by A.L. Schafer for Paramount, **p. 85**; Photo by Dixie Sheridan, **p. 587**; Courtesy of Sophia Smith Collection, Smith College (Northampton, Massachusetts), photo by Moffett, **p. 723**; Photo by Paul Taylor, **p. 117**; Courtesy of Theodor W. Adorno Archive (Frankfurt), **p. 13**; © Twentieth Century-Fox, 1956, **p. 399**; Photo by Andrew Cooper for Twentieth Century-Fox, **p. 401**; Courtesy of the U.S. House of Representatives. **pp. 138, 580, 616, 617, 803**; © Universal, 1935, **p. 93**; © Universal Pictures, **pp. 289, 615, 832** (1980); Photo by Carl Van Vechten, **p. 165**; Courtesy of Virago Press, **p. 329**; Courtesy of W.W. Norton, photo by Dagmar Schultz, **p. 661**; © Warner Bros., **pp. 283** (1962), **343**; Courtesy of Wide World Photos, **p. 511**; Photo by Laszlo Willinger, **p. 337**; Courtesy of Women's International Bowling Congress, **p. 26**; © WNBA Enterprises, **pp. 409** (photo by Andrew D. Bernstein), **475** (photo by Barry Gossage), **583** (photo by Nathaniel S. Butler).